Readings in Organizational Behavior

This Reader covers all the topics that are essential for courses in Organizational Behavior. It complements the textbook *Organizational Behavior: Securing Competitive Advantage*, also authored by John Wagner and John Hollenbeck. However, it is a worthwhile addition to any course in Organizational Behavior.

John A. Wagner III is Professor of Management at the Eli Broad Graduate School of Business Administration at Michigan State University.

John R. Hollenbeck is the Eli Broad Professor of Management at the Eli Broad Graduate School of Business Administration at Michigan State University.

Readings in Organizational Behavior

Edited by

John A. Wagner III
Michigan State University

John R. Hollenbeck
Michigan State University

Routledge
Taylor & Francis Group

NEW YORK AND LONDON

First published 2010
by Routledge
270 Madison Avenue, New York, NY 10016

Simultaneously published in the UK
by Routledge
2 Park Square, Milton Park, Abingdon, Oxon, OX14 4RN

Routledge is an imprint of the Taylor & Francis Group, an informa business

© 2010 Taylor & Francis

Typeset in Baskerville by
RefineCatch Limited, Bungay, Suffolk
Printed and bound by CPI Antony Rowe, Chippenham, Wiltshire

Library of Congress Cataloging-in-Publication Data
Readings in organizational behavior / edited by John A. Wagner III,
John R. Hollenbeck.
    p. cm.
  Includes bibliographical references and index.
  1. Organizational behavior.   I. Wagner, John A., 1952–   II. Hollenbeck,
John R.
  HD58.7.R394 2009
  658.3—dc22   2009014788

ISBN 10: 0–415–99848–4 (hbk)
ISBN 10: 0–415–99850–6 (pbk)

ISBN 13: 978–0–415–99848–2 (hbk)
ISBN 13: 978–0–415–99850–5 (pbk)

Contents

* Practitioner article (unmarked articles are research articles)

Acknowledgments

Chapter 1

1.1 Michael Harvey and M. Ronald Buckley, "Assessing the 'Conventional Wisdoms' of Management for the 21st Century Organization." Reprinted from *Organizational Dynamics*, 30(4), 2002, 368–378, with permission from Elsevier. Reprinted from the *Lancet*, 30 (4), Michael Harvey and M. Ronald Buckley, "Assessing the 'Conventional Wisdoms' of Management for the 21st Century Organization," 368–378, with permission from Elsevier.

Chapter 2

2.1 Danny Miller, Jon Hartwick, and Isabelle Le Breton-Miller, "How to Detect a Management Fad—and Distinguish It From a Classic." Reprinted from *Business Horizons*, 47(4), 2004, 7–16, with permission from Elsevier. Reprinted from the *Lancet*, 47 (4) 2004, Danny Miller, Jon Hartwick, and Isabelle Le Breton-Miller, "How to Detect a Management Fad—and Distinguish It from a Classic," 7–16, with permission from Elsevier.

Chapter 3

3.1 L. Roberson and C.T. Kulik, "Stereotype Threat at Work." *Academy of Management Perspectives* 21 (2007), 24–40. Copyright 2007 by *Academy of Management Perspectives* (NY). Reproduced with permission of *Academy of Management Perspectives* (NY) in the format textbook via Copyright Clearance Center.

3.2 H. Le, I.S. Oh, J. Shaffer, and F. Schmidt, "Implications of Methodological Advances for the Practice of Personnel Selection: How Practitioners Benefit From Meta-Analysis." *Academy of Management Perspectives* 21 (2007), 6–15. Copyright 2007 by *Academy of Management Perspectives* (NY). Reproduced with permission of *Academy of Management Perspectives* (NY) in the format textbook via Copyright Clearance Center.

Chapter 4

4.1 B. Zhao and F. Olivera, "Error Reporting in Organizations." *Academy of Management Review* 31 (2006), 1012–1030. Copyright 2006 by *Academy of Management Review*. Reproduced with permission of *Academy of Management Review* in the format textbook via Copyright Clearance Center.

4.2 C.E. Shalley, J. Zhou, and G.R. Oldham, "The Effects of Personal and Contextual Characteristics on Creativity: Where Should We Go From Here?" *Journal of Management*, 30(6), 933–958, copyright ©2004 by *Journal of Management*. Reprinted by permission of SAGE Publications.

Chapter 5

5.1   A.M. Grant, "Relational Job Design and the Motivation to Make a Prosocial Difference." *Academy of Management Review* 32 (2007), 393–417. Copyright 2007 by *Academy of
Management Review*. Reproduced with permission of *Academy of Management Review* in the
format textbook via Copyright Clearance Center.

5.2   P. Steel and C.J. König, "Integrating Theories of Motivation." *Academy of Management
Review* 31 (2006), 889–913. Copyright 2006 by *Academy of Management Review*. Repro-
duced with permission of *Academy of Management Review* in the format textbook via
Copyright Clearance Center.

Chapter 6

6.1   S.G. Barsade and D.E. Gibson, "Why Does Affect Matter in Organizations?" *Academy
of Management Perspectives*, 21 (2007), 36–59. Copyright 2007 by *Academy of Management
Perspectives* (NY). Reproduced with permission of *Academy of Management Perspectives* (NY)
in the format textbook via Copyright Clearance Center.

6.2   M. Macik-Frey, J.C. Quick, D.L. Nelson, "Advances in Occupational Health: From a
Stressful Beginning to a Positive Future." *Journal of Management*, 33(6), 809–840, copyright ©2007 by *Journal of Management*. Reprinted by permission of SAGE Publications.

Chapter 7

7.1   A.S. Evangelista and Lisa A. Burk, "Work Redesign and Performance Management in
Times of Downsizing." Reprinted from *Business Horizons*, 46(2), 2003, 71–76, with
permission from Elsevier. Reprinted from the *Lancet*, 46(2) 2003, Evangelista, A.S. and
Lisa A. Burk, "Work Redesign and Performance Management in Times of Downsizing," 71–76, with permission from Elsevier.

7.2   Richard J. Torraco, "Work Design Theory: A Review and Critique with Implications
for Human Resource Development." *Human Resource Development Quarterly*, 16(1), Spring
2005, pp. 85–109. Copyright © 2005 Wiley Periodicals, Inc. Reprinted with
permission.

Chapter 8

8.1   R. Rico, M. Sánchez-Manzanares, F. Gil, and C. Gibson, "Team Implicit Coordination Processes: A Team Knowledge-Based Approach." *Academy of Management Review*,
33 (2008), 163–184. Copyright 2008 by *Academy of Management Review*. Reproduced
with permission of *Academy of Management Review* in the format textbook via Copyright
Clearance Center.

8.2   R. Cropanzano, D.E. Bowen, and S.W. Gilliland, "The Management of Organiza-
tional Justice." *Academy of Management Perspectives*, 21 (2007), 34–48. Copyright 2007 by
Academy of Management Perspectives (NY). Reproduced with permission of *Academy of
Management Perspectives* (NY) in the format textbook via Copyright Clearance Center.

Chapter 9

9.1   J.M. Wilson, P.S. Goodman, and M.A. Cronin, "Group Learning." *Academy of Management Review*, 32 (2007), 1041–1059. Copyright 2007 by *Academy of Management
Review*. Reproduced with permission of *Academy of Management Review* in the format
textbook via Copyright Clearance Center.

9.2   J. Mathieu, M.T. Maynard, T. Rapp and L. Gilson, "Team Effectiveness 1997–2007:
A Review of Recent Advancements and a Glimpse into the Future." *Journal of*

Management, 34(3), 410–476, copyright ©2007 by Journal of Management. Reprinted by permission of SAGE Publications.

Chapter 10

10.1 M. London, "Leadership and Advocacy: Dual Roles for Corporate Social Responsibility and Social Entrepreneurship." Reprinted from *Organizational Dynamics*, 37(4), 2008, 313–326, with permission from Elsevier. Reprinted from the *Lancet*, 37(4), 313–326 with permission from Elsevier.

10.2 G.A. Ballinger and F.D. Schoorman, "Individual Reactions to Leadership Succession in Groups." *Academy of Management Review*, 32 (2007), 118–136. Copyright 2006 by *Academy of Management Review*. Reproduced with permission of *Academy of Management Review* in the format textbook via Copyright Clearance Center.

Chapter 11

11.1 Jeff Weiss and Jonathan Hughes, "Want Collaboration? Accept—and Actively Manage—Conflict." *Harvard Business Review*, 83(3), 2005, 92–101. Reprinted with permission.

11.2 Jeffrey Pfeffer and Christina T. Fong, "Building Organization Theory from First Principles: The Self-Enhancement Motive and Understanding Power and Influence." *Organization Science*, 16(4), 372–388. Reprinted with permission.

Chapter 12

12.1 N. Anand and Richard L. Daft, "What is the Right Organization Design?" Reprinted from *Organizational Dynamics*, 36(4), 2007, 329–344, with permission from Elsevier. Reprinted from the *Lancet*, 36(4) 2007, N. Anand and Richard L. Daft, "What is the Right Organization Design?" 329–344, with permission from Elsevier.

12.2 Hettie A. Richardson, Robert J. Vandenberg, Terry C. Blum, and Paul M. Roman, "Does Decentralization Make a Difference for the Organization? An Examination of the Boundary Conditions Circumscribing Decentralized Decision-Making and Organizational Financial Performance." *Journal of Management*, 28(2), 217–244, copyright ©2002 by *Journal of Management*. Reprinted by permission of SAGE Publications.

Chapter 13

13.1 David Lei and John W. Slocum, Jr., "Organization Designs to Renew Competitive Advantage." Reprinted from *Organizational Dynamics*, 31(1), 2002, 1–18, with permission from Elsevier. Reprinted from the *Lancet*, 31(1) 2002, David Lei and John W. Slocum, Jr., "Organization Designs to Renew Competitive Advantage," 1–18, with permission from Elsevier.

13.2 Cynthia A. Lengnick-Hall and Tammy E. Beck, "Adaptive Fit Versus Robust Transformation: How Organizations Respond to Environmental Change." *Journal of Management*, 31(5), 738–757, copyright ©2005 by Journal of Management. Reprinted by permission of SAGE Publications.

Chapter 14

14.1 David W. Young, "The Six Levers for Managing Organizational Culture." Reprinted from *Business Horizons*, 43(5), 2000, 19–28, with permission from Elsevier. Reprinted from the *Lancet*, 43(5) 2000, David W. Young, "The Six Levers for Managing Organizational Culture," 19–28, with permission from Elsevier.

14.2 Jeana Wirtenberg, Lilian Abrams, and Carolyn Ott, "Assessing the Field of Organization Development." Jeana Wirtenberg, Lilian Abrams, and Carolyn Ott, *Journal of Applied Behavioral Science*, 40(4), 465–479, copyright ©2004 by Journal of Applied Behavioral Science. Reprinted by permission of SAGE Publications.

Chapter 15

15.1 Luciara Nardon and Richard M. Steers, "The New Global Manager: Learning Cultures on the Fly." Reprinted from *Organizational Dynamics*, January, 2008, 37(1), 47–59. Copyright 2008 with permission from Elsevier. "Reprinted from The Lancet, 37(1), Luciara Nardon and Richard M. Steers, "The New Global Manager: Learning Cultures on the Fly," 47–59. Copyright (2008) with permission from Elsevier.

Chapter 16

16.1 D.M. Rousseau, "Is There Such a Thing as Evidence-Based Management?" *Academy of Management Review*, 31 (2005), 256–269. Copyright 2005 by *Academy of Management Review*. Reproduced with permission of *Academy of Management Review* in the format textbook via Copyright Clearance Center.

1 Organizational Behavior

1.1 ASSESSING THE "CONVENTIONAL WISDOMS" OF MANAGEMENT FOR THE 21ST CENTURY ORGANIZATION

Michael Harvey and M. Ronald Buckley

It has become quite easy to bemoan the triviality of many of the new management tech-niques and theories that have come and gone in the past several decades. Many have opined that such theories have done little to assist managers in their day-to-day decision-making. At the same time, managers are concerned that the field of management has become significantly "cluttered" with outdated and useless concepts, given the continuous array of "new" being introduced into the field. We would argue that we must delete some of the basic wisdom of the 20th century and, at the same time, update the foundation concepts in management, as we enter the 21st century.

What has occurred? We believe that we are witnessing what Thomas Kuhn, in *The Structure of Scientific Revolutions*, referred to as a paradigm shift—a situation in which older ways of thinking no longer apply. This shift has not occurred overnight, nor is it directly attributable to the efforts of one person, idea, or group. In order to keep up with manage-ment practice, we need to reconstruct prior theory and reevaluate that which we consider to be historical management wisdom. This prevailing paradigm shift is why techniques and consulting "recipes" are quick to arise and just as quickly discarded by many managers. In spite of this rapidity, or perhaps due to it, those who chronicle events in our field have failed to discover the most efficient way to delete these "new approaches" as well as the basic foundation principles that have limited application today. This is due, in part, because paradigm shifts are both seamless and not easily discernable by those living through them. One need only look at our best-selling management textbooks to find this idea illustrated. A perusal of these textbooks gives one the impression that current management practice is an unbroken progression from the early contributions of Frederick Taylor to agency theory (it is not), and that current organizations still are concerned with old concepts, e.g., span-of-control, line/staff differentiation, and chain-of-command (many are not).

How Did We Land Here?

Products and services are continuously introduced by organizations into the marketplace; they come and go quickly. In management, new concepts and theories are frequently added but less frequently deleted from the "product line" of management knowledge. Recently, terms have been coined to capture the onslaught of new management fads, such as: "flavor-of-the-month management," "recipe management," and "airplane magazine syndrome." Over the past two decades, a significant number of new business concepts have been generated with dubious results. Yet, practicing managers continue to explore many of these new seemingly untested techniques.

The introduction of these new techniques has come from a number of different sources including: management consulting firms (the Boston Consulting Group, McKinnsey & Company), management consulting gurus (Tom Peters, Peter Senge), business press organizations (The Harvard Business Press, Oxford Business Press), business schools (Chicago, Carnegie Mellon Schools of Thought), prominent business faculty members (Michael Porter, Michael Hammer, Gary Hamel), and from successful high profile practicing "hero" managers (Jack Welch, Bill Gates, Steve Jobs, Michael Dell). There are some new management principles that have been derived through collaborative efforts of a number of sources. New business concepts have also been disseminated through a number of venues, including in-house executive education, contract development programs, consulting gurus, and the business press, as well as through management self-help tomes.

In spite of the increasingly available assistance smart companies occasionally do dumb things (i.e., Dell Computer Corp., Microsoft Corp., eBay Inc.) and not-so-smart companies (i.e., Montgomery Wards, TWA, KIA and myriad dot.coms) continue to make sub-optimal decisions. The supply of new management techniques and theories has not quelled the growing need for innovative approaches to today's complex management dilemmas. This may be due to the quality of the techniques being advanced, the process used to disseminate the ideas among managers, or the resulting confusion that is created by the on-going "flavor-of-the-month" approach to managing companies in the 21st century.

One explanation may be the huge volume of new information and techniques being generated by experts. Keeping abreast of the voluminous amount of new information is a daunting task for managers. One outcome of this information overload is that managers are beginning to question the standard techniques and rules-of-thumb that they have used to assist them in making decisions. Due to the paradigm shift, have the "conventional wisdoms" or foundations of management principles developed in the 20th century become obsolete? What changes in the environment are reducing the usefulness of the fundamental management decision-making template? While changes in the business environment continue to be dramatic, we anticipate that the future environment for decision-makers will increase in complexity, necessitating new standard operating procedures (SOPs). As General Electric Co.'s charismatic retiring Chief Executive Officer (CEO), Jack Welch, is fond of saying, "If the outside environment is changing faster than the inside environment, the company is doomed." It would appear that there are a large number of doomed 20th century companies in the 21st century.

The 21st Century Environment: The Need to Rethink Past "Wisdom"

Managers of the 20th century were trained as rational decision-makers. They were encouraged to utilize the left side of the brain to analyze information and to make management decisions. Managers were expected to develop high levels of functional expertise. To be successful they needed to learn the rigors of the domestic market in order to build a sustainable competitive advantage over rivals. These same managers were supported in their decisions by their positional/legitimate authority in hierarchical organizations. SOPs were clearly explicated for managers, due to the history of other managers making similar decisions over an extended time period. Managers were accustomed to making decisions within an industry that had well-defined boundaries and a cast of competitors that remained fairly constant (frequently referred to as "knowing" organizations).

By contrast, managers in the 21st century must be improvizational, creative, and innovative (i.e., to utilize the creative and innovative right side of the brain) in planning, making decisions, and developing appropriate management processes. Many of the decisions that they must make have not been previously made by them or by any other manager in the organization. For example, Motorola Inc.'s decision to build plants in China or GroceryWorks.com's decision to have customers order groceries over e-mail and then delivered to their homes are innovative. The marketplace has also become one with ill-defined industry boundaries and an almost free flow of competitors entering and exiting any particular industry. Organization structures have been flattened, as employees have become empowered. The virtual, or at least, a shared organizational structure (i.e., strategic alliance, joint venture) has blurred traditional lines of authority between buyer and supplier, customer and manufacturer. In short, an argument can be made that the fundamental knowledge needed to be a successful manager has been radically changed due to the paradigm shift we are experiencing early in the 21st century.

It would be disingenuous of us to propose that change in the environment has been absent until now. There has always been environmental change that has had both direct and indirect impact upon managers engaged in the conduct of business. The difference today is that the rate of change has steadily increased, and the cumulative effect of change has effectively rendered past experience and training to be of significantly less value than was previously the case.

Some Revolutionary Changes Taking Place in the Global Environment

Changing Concept of Time to Managers

It would appear that even a deceptively simple concept like time is being altered in today's business environment. This seemingly mathematically continuous variable has become a multidimensional construct. There are a number of dimensions of time that appear to be changing: (1) time frame—a particular time horizon that may be an expected length of time (i.e., days, months, or years) as well as a socially constructed time horizon (i.e., planning cycles, product life cycle); (2) tempo of time—the speed and intensity of the impact of change (i.e., the "quickening" of decision-making); (3) dependency of management decisions on time—the level of commitment and investment in decisions over time, making them difficult to abandon (i.e., the past investment of time and resources compels management to continue the strategy); (4) the level of asynchronization of events—the impact of virtual workforces to accomplish organizational goals is tied to different personal time schedules; and (5) modification of sequence of events due to time compression—standard operating processes are modified due to having less time to accomplish the given task (i.e., shortening the new product development process at Procter & Gamble is due to increased pressures to innovate and modify product offerings to be competitive globally against Nestlé). Therefore, time can no longer be regarded as a measure, but rather has to be translated into a key component of strategic decision-making by managers competing in the global marketplace.

Increasing Rate of Globalization

Globalization is frequently considered an opportunity for future sales and profit growth. It is not uncommon to find managers who do not have any international, much less global experience. The absence of experience renders managers unable to effectively assess the decision-making environment or those factors that should be taken into consideration in order to make good decisions. This ignorance is compounded by the absence of existing decision-making processes based upon the past experience of others. For example, when Larry Henderson, plant manager, and John Lichthental, manager of human resources, were assigned by Celanese Chemical to build a new chemical plant in Singapore, they encountered a unique problem. The $125 million plant was completed in July, but according to local custom, a plant should only be christened on "lucky" days. The next "lucky" day was September 3. Henderson and Lichthental had to convince executives at Celanese's Dallas headquarters to delay the plant opening. After many heated telephone conversations and flaming e-mails, the president agreed to open the new plant on September 3.

Lack of Protection for Intellectual and Physical Property Rights in the Global Marketplace

With the rapid diffusion of technology/knowledge, the ability of countries and regulatory agencies to control the intellectual property rights of organizations has diminished dramatically. This has complicated the marketing and distribution strategies of many globally oriented companies such as IBM Corp., Eastman Kodak Co., and Microsoft. Without the legal projection provided in the past by a sovereign state, managers must make decisions knowing that their property rights will be invaded. The software industry is replete with examples of product piracy (for example, Microsoft Windows software sales in China). Given this lack of logo/patent/copyright or even physical product protection, the decision to compete globally has become considerably riskier and more complex.

Additional Revolutionary Changes Taking Place within Global Organizations

At the same time that the external environment of business has dramatically changed, the ways organizations manage employees have experienced myriad radical changes. Many of these internal changes have as dramatic an impact on managerial procedures as changes that occur outside of organizations.

Virtual Work Groups and Organizations

The first signs of the "walls" of the organization coming down were experienced in the post-transformational organizations of the 1990s. Managers at IBM, Cisco Systems Inc., and McKinsey & Company, among others, are now expected to manage employees who do not physically "come to work." Employees may have limited interaction with the organization or other personnel. This virtualness is compounded by the geographic scope of employees being dispersed throughout the world. The lack of face-to-face interaction between management and employees has myriad potentially negative consequences for an organization. They include: limiting employee commitment, reducing the synergistic effects of team work, focusing on outcomes and not processes, limiting direct supervision, and loosening contact with key stakeholders like customers, suppliers, and channel-of-distribution members.

Penetration of Technology into Management Decision-Making

The incorporation of technology into decision-making processes has enabled managers to make better and more timely decisions. But at the same time, managers have become dependent on technology to support the complexity of the decisions that they are making. Therefore, any disruption in the fabric of technology exponentially reduces the managers' capacity to make decisions. In hyper-competitive markets, time delays are more value damaging than budget overruns. To maintain a seamless flow of new products and technology to customers, 3M maintains a stock of its flexible and adaptive technologies to supply new products on short notice to its relational partners (Motorola, Hewlett-Packard Co., AT&T Corp.). The success of this strategy is based on empowerment of front-line decision-makers, cross-functional team sharing of best practices and modular integration of available technologies, product succession planning, and an enterprise-wide integration of learning.

The need for technology also tends to minimize the value of tacit knowledge that allows managers to act more intuitively in making decisions. The accumulated "street smarts" of global managers may be one of the elements of greatest value when addressing complex problems in global markets. Therefore, if technology can trump the intuitive insights of experienced global managers, technology may become a filter that serves to systematize unstructured decisions where intuition is most needed.

Increased Dependence on Interorganizational Relationships

Management principles were developed in the 20th century for managers to plan, organize, direct, and control. In the 21st century, many of the key management issues/opportunities will be based on how to effectively manage relationships between organizations. These new cross-cultural relationships violate traditional management principles, such as span-of-control, and fads, like line-of-sight-management. Global business and the need to expand operations on multiple fronts have necessitated organizations that are able to develop cooperative arrangements with foreign suppliers, channel-of-distribution members, customers, and even competitors. Wal-Mart Stores encountered this problem when they attempted to enter Mexico, Brazil, Peru and several select European countries without having the same partners they had in the United States. It quickly became apparent that they needed to develop efficient relationships or encourage their suppliers to enter these foreign markets as well.

It is difficult to understand how any set of conventional wisdoms could be valid, given the magnitude of changes taking place in the external/internal environments of 21st century organizations. To paraphrase a popular television commercial of the 1990s: "This isn't your father's organization anymore." If new concepts and techniques have been added over the decades, why is there a problem? In many ways, what has transpired in the proliferation of management "theories" is similar to a new product development process that generates new products without a commensurate deletion process.

Cases in Point: Outdated Conventional Wisdoms

In an effort to illustrate the need to reexamine the conventional wisdoms of management, the authors undertook a content analysis of current basic management textbooks. It was anticipated that these leading management texts would illustrate the basic knowledge educators considered to be the foundation concepts for managers in the 21st century. It should not be construed that this analysis can be used as a proxy for management knowledge/wisdom, but rather as the basic principles that current managers were taught as cornerstones of management thought during their college education.

All of the books discuss numerous terms that seem to be inapplicable to many 21st century organizations. There are a number of concepts that would appear to illustrate the obsolescence in management terminology (e.g., span-of-control, line/staff, organization life cycle, chain of command, authority = responsibility, domestic vs. global strategy). As an example, look at the discussion in textbooks about the line/staff differentiation. Many of these distinctions have disappeared in virtual, business-to-business organizations. In fact, in some organizations, individuals serve as their own line and staff function. Furthermore, the ability to monitor and direct work behavior through technology makes the notion of limiting span of control to no more than 12 people need to undergo considerable revision. The notion of unity of command (i.e., an employee should have only one boss) must similarly be rethought.

Many management wisdoms were developed at the turn of the 20th century, when the basic orientation of business was one of "bricks and mortar" and higher production was achieved through ever increasing production/manpower improvements. For example, Frederick Taylor's work at Bethlehem Steel in the early 20th century yielded two guiding management principles. First, there was "one best way" to undertake a task. Second, people should be paid according to output (i.e., pay per output to stimulate/motivate workers to work more efficiently).

It would be hard to find many management "gurus" today who would support that there is one way to accomplish any management task. Contrarily, the concept of equal finality contends that finding new and different ways to accomplish management tasks provides an organization with a potential relative competitive advantage. As for pay, there are an increasing number of positions that do not have direct measurable output attached to them. In the service industry of today it would be difficult for managers to relate to the arbitrary production orientation. This is particularly true in companies that emphasize the importance of self-managed teams, such as Texas Instruments Inc. and Whole Foods Market Inc. Compensation of team members is based on the overall performance of the team.

Max Weber's groundbreaking work in the last century discussed the need for a well-defined hierarchy of authority and a clear delineation of work. Both of these principles are being violated, as organizations are becoming more virtual. Another of Weber's hallmarks was maintaining impersonal relationships in the work environment. In contrast, at the heart of many new business-to-business organizations today is the development of informal, casual, and personal relationships between employees and managers. Managers are coaches and facilitators. The resulting high level of *esprit de corps* has become one of the distinguishing characteristics of many successful companies in the latter half of the 20th century, including Southwest Airlines Co. and The Container Store.

Another stalwart of management thought was Henri Fayol. He contributed such wisdoms as unity of command, unit of direction, scalar chain of authority, and authority must equal responsibility. These all seemed to be appropriate in a more stable environment. But, in today's world of virtual, e-commerce and service-oriented companies, these guiding principles seem to have lost a lot of their managerial applicability. The concepts are still being taught in colleges across the country, and students do not recognize the limitation of this oversimplification of the complex task of management.

These terms continue to be presented as basic issues in modern management, and they continue to be used as the baseline of what we know about organizations. They have, in our opinion, become lost in the paradigm shift that is occurring. While this is not an exhaustive list, it does represent a number of concepts that are considered "conventional wisdoms" of management. The question is: "Are these fundamental principles of management pertinent in a hypercompetitive global management environment?" If they are not, two issues need to be confronted: (1) What can be done to revitalize the core concepts of management thought? and (2) What can be done to get rid of those wisdoms that no longer apply?

How to Address Obsolescence in Conventional Wisdoms

If the conventional wisdom of the past does not reflect how organizations function under the current paradigm, something must be done. What can we suggest in order to reduce the perpetuation of the conventional wisdoms of the past? How can the foundation concepts of management be updated to reflect the needs of managers competing in the hypercompetitive global marketplace? The following suggestions are offered as a number of actions that could possibly be taken by academics as well as practicing managers to evaluate the future of our past conventional wisdoms.

Encouraging and Developing Organizational Cultures that Learn as Well as Unlearn

There has been a great deal of attention paid to the concept of encouraging organizations to learn. What better way to address the chaos in the marketplace and the complex changes taking place relative to managing in the 21st century? But one has to recognize, given the rate of change and the influx of information, that managers can only process so much data. Therefore, we suggest that managers be encouraged and rewarded for discarding information that no longer is applicable in today's business context. This involves a systematic removal of information that is outdated or no longer useful to management decision-making. Koch Industries of Wichita, Kansas espouses the use of market-based management, which has as its basic foundation principle the idea of pushing decision-making as close to the consumer as possible. Frequently this entails the least experienced managers in the plants making sales calls. Through communicating with customers, they learn what is taking place in the market, as well as the unique demands of each customer. Koch managers learn and are rewarded for this learning. They are encouraged to share their new knowledge with others in the Koch family of operating units.

Developing a systematic process and training managers to undertake tasks which are unfamiliar to them is difficult, because frequently Koch managers will be required to relinquish information/data that was successfully used in the past. This was the case when Koch transferred a group of existing managers into their newly formed international division. It is difficult to give up information that was helpful to the manager/organization. Due to the dramatic shift in the environment of business, this data may be a handicap to managers making successful decisions in the future.

Recalibration of the Strategic Management Process That is Attuned to the Future and Not Tied to the Past

Many strategic management processes/practices (i.e., strategic planning, competitive analysis, industry analysis) are based upon a historic perspective of the environment. These techniques encourage managers to extrapolate the future from the past. If the past is sufficiently different from the future, however, these techniques can lead to underestimating the degree of change that has taken place. New techniques are needed that address the limited contribution of past strategies used by the organization—in other words, unlearning at the organization level. What was successful in the past more than likely will not meet the needs of the 21st century. Scenario planning is used by SmithKline Beecham, a global pharmaceutical company, to develop its strategic intent. In this approach, managers are expected to develop four or five scenarios for their product lines in light of the rapidly changing competitive context. British Petroleum, Barclays PLC and Reuters are also examples of companies that anticipate the future rather than building a plan based on the past.

Integrate the Abrogation of Organizational and Employee Commitment into the Philosophy of Management

Many of the principles of modern management were predicated on reciprocal commitment between employee and organization. Given the recent and continuing downsizing undertaken by companies like Daimler-Chrysler, AT&T, J.C. Penney Company Inc., The Associates, Dell Computer and Amazon.com, the era of free agency for employees has arrived. What role does commitment have in the management of the 21st century? Commitment has played a central role in training/development, compensation and benefits package of the last 50 years. If neither the organization nor the employee is willing to commit to one another, will entire human-resource management strategies be rethought? What do employees have to be given to offset their lack of commitment? If one of the key organizational resources is management and employees, how will organizations build effective competitive strategies with "transitory" management and employees?

Developing a Means to Incorporate the Implicit/Intangible Assets of a Company into Their Management Philosophy

As organizations move into the 21st century, the focus of many businesses is moving from bricks and mortar, or tangible assets, to an economy of "atoms and air," or intangible assets. According to Herb Kelleher, chairman and recently retired CEO of Southwest Airlines, an organization's distinctive competency is its corporate culture—because competitors can copy everything else.

The increased importance of intangible assets necessitates incorporating these resources into the responsibility of management. New managerial metrics are needed to measure and monitor intangible assets (e.g., activity-based accounting). At the same time, managers should be held accountable for maintaining and building the value of these assets. Intangible assets may be the means to effectively compete in the global marketplace and one of the strategic alternatives to differentiate one organization from another.

Historically, little attention has been given to intangible assets. As their importance grows, however, management responsibility must be aligned to match. For example, a recent market valuation of Coca-Cola Co. estimated the market value of the company at $39 billion, but the hard asset value of the company at less than $20 billion. The remaining $19 billion in value was in the value of the brand, trade secrets, logos, and trademarks. The recent action against Napster, the company that allows consumers to share music free of charge, illustrates the nexus of the argument over the value of intangible assets. Intellectual property issues are becoming salient for companies like Microsoft, Oracle and Sun Microsystems Inc. as they become more heavily involved in the global competitive arena. These organizations are becoming much more aware of the need for developing security systems to protect the "hidden" value in their companies.

Development of a "Reverse" Mentoring System

Mentoring has been a frequently debated aid to improving the quality of management in organizations. But due to the radical change taking place and the need to "unlearn," organizations may need to develop a reverse mentoring system—one where new employees assist in transforming 20th century managers into successful managers for the future. Nowhere is this more obvious than in the technology domain. New employees frequently have technical skills and knowledge that are absent in the senior management of the company. How to transfer this knowledge becomes an intricate communication problem that reverse mentoring might help to alleviate. At Dell Computer, the newest college recruits are given positions of much responsibility within certain market segments, due to their knowledge of the market segment. In addition, these same high potential recruits are told not to stay with the company for over 4 years, because their tacit/social knowledge will be obsolete.

Reexamining the Concept/Process of Control in the Organization

The "metrics" of management must be modified to reflect what is important in the 21st century. A classic article sums up the concern with formal control systems (the folly of rewarding "A" while hoping for "B"). If management is going through transformational change, it will stand to reason that what needs to be measured also will have to be dramatically altered. The increased importance of intangible assets would be a clear example of new resources that need to be monitored and rewarded by management. Economic value-added analysis used by Ikea, a Swedish furniture retailer, illustrates the shift to measures of intangible asset analysis. The company's annual report has nine levels of analysis, moving from traditional GAP analysis to very abstract accounting for intangible assets of the firm. There are few measures of these off-balance sheet types of assets. The roles of managers and what they are being held accountable for may also need to be reconsidered.

It should be noted that not one nor all of these potential "remedies" for reassessing the existing stock of management conventional wisdom is the sole means to determine what needs to be discarded from the current body of knowledge. The issue becomes: What is going to be done to delete those concepts/theories that are no longer applicable in a global hypercompetitive marketplace?

What's in Store in the Future?

Given the rate of change and the growing complexity of global hypercompetitive business, it could be beneficial to the field of management if the foundation concepts of the discipline were reexamined to more accurately reflect the business environment. Many of the conventional wisdoms in management that we have addressed in this paper were developed at the start of the 20th century, when the overwhelming majority of businesses were manufacturing, domestic, and labor-intensive. Management was conducted in a face-to-face manner; managers and employees had a similar frame of reference relative to the goals of the organization. In addition, many new concepts and theories have accumulated over the past 100 years, leaving the student of management with a bewildering collage of applicable/ not applicable material to master. We would suggest that it would be helpful to clarify the domain of management thought by eliminating those concepts that are no longer applicable.

The most difficult aspect of revising the conventional wisdoms of the field is determining who, among the many interested stakeholders, should undertake this daunting task. We imagine that what is deemed expendable by one stakeholder may be considered of critical importance to another stakeholder (managers/researchers). The task is daunting and must begin immediately. Let's get started.

Selected Bibliography

For the seminal work when speaking about paradigm shifts and the development of management as a science see Thomas Kuhn, *The Structure of Scientific Revolutions* (Chicago: University of Chicago Press, 1962). This book presents an outline of what occurs when science is confronted with radically transformed boundary conditions—where the old ways of thinking fail to fit into new ways of thinking. This is the situation we believe we now find many management truisms. The pages of most interest are 4–7 and 137–141.

There have been a number of recent articles on the fads/fashions in management, for example, see: Eric Abrahamson, "Managerial Fads and Fashion: The Diffusion and Rejection of Innovations," *Academy of Management Review*, 1991, 16, 586–612; Eric Abrahamson, "Management Fashion," *Academy of Management Review*, 1996, 21(1), 254–285; S. Bikhchandani, D. Hirshleirfer and I. Welch, "A Theory of Fads, Fashion, Custom, and Cultural Change as Informational Cascades," *Journal of Political Economy*, 1992, 100(5), 92–126; G. Rifkin, "When is a Fad not a Fad?" *Harvard Business Review*, 1994, 73(5), 11–15. See also Chester Spell, "Where Do Management Fashions Come From and How Long Do They Stay?" *Journal of Management History*, 1996, 5(6), 334–348; M. A. M. Worren, "Management Fashion," *Academy of Management Review*, 1996, 21(3), 613–614; Paula Carson, Patricia Lanier, Kerry Carson and Betty Birkenmeier, "A Historic Perspective on Fad Adoption and Abandonment," *Journal of Management History*, 5(6), 320–333; Paula Carson, Patricia Lanier, Kerry Carson and B. Guidry, "Clearing a Path through the Management Fashion Jungle: Some Preliminary Trailblazing," *The Academy of Management Journal*, 2000, 43(6), 1143–1158. This last article has reinforced our contention that we are in a paradigm shift. The authors have reported that fads are broader-based but shorter-lived—indicating to us a period of rapid change, where new paradigms are replacing old paradigms.

In addition, there appears to be ample evidence of organizations making management and/or strategic mistakes due to the use of outdated management concepts or theories. For example, see: Tom Peters, "We Hold These Truths to be Self-Evident (More or Less)," *Organizational Dynamics*, Summer 1996, 27–32; Jeffery Pfeffer, "Why Do Smart Organizations Occasionally Do Dumb Things?" *Organization Dynamics*, Summer 1996, 33–44; and Martin Bowles, "The Myth of Management: Direction and Failure in Contemporary Organizations," *Human Relations*, 50(7), 779–803.

Additional evidence that managers have increasing difficulty making decisions, given their background and training, see: Christopher Bartlett and Sumantra Ghoshal, "The Myth of the Generic Manager," *California Management Review*, 1998, 40(1) 92–116; Martin Bowles, "The Myth of Management: Direction and Failure in Contemporary Organizations," *Human Relations*, 50(7), 779–803; Joseph Foegen, "Are Managers Losing Control?" *Business*

Horizons, March–April 1998, 2–5; and David Garvin, "The Processes of Organizational Management," *Sloan Management Review*, Summer 1998, 33–47.

Acknowledgments

The authors would like to acknowledge the constructive suggestions offered by Professors John Slocum and Ramon Alonso.

2 Management and Managers

2.1 HOW TO DETECT A MANAGEMENT FAD—AND DISTINGUISH IT FROM A CLASSIC

Danny Miller, Jon Hartwick (1951–2002), and Isabelle Le Breton-Miller

From MBO to Theory Z, from TQM to reengineering, management thought over the past five decades has been altered profoundly by a few administrative fads that have shaped the vocabularies of managers but seem to have had no lasting influence on business practice. Eight properties distinguish between such fads and the more enduring classics: simplicity, over-promise, universality, step-down capability, zeitgeist resonance, exaggerated novelty, celebratory role models, and evocative prose. In helping firms spot a fad and determine the appropriateness of an approach, these properties also uncover a paradox: The very factors that make fads so attractive and cause their widespread adoption also cause their quick demise.

Many popular administrative ideas are epitomized by a search for the quick fix—a simple solution that all organizations can embrace to make employees more productive, customers happier, or profits greater. Although some companies are profoundly transformed by these ideas, many are merely grazed by them. The notions do not serve the core business, or are embraced ritualistically without having any profound effect on performance or any other desired outcomes. Before long, the fad is forgotten and the firm is left with the human costs of disappointment and the financial costs of fruitless implementation. Frequently, fads can have a lasting destructive influence as a practice is embraced that alienates employees or triggers an abortive reorganization. Downsizing and reengineering, for example, have often demoralized the workforce and robbed firms of vital talent.

To help managers identify such potentially dangerous trends, we undertook to compare fads to more durable practices and techniques—the "classics"—in an attempt to tell the two apart. Our research identified eight characteristics that reliably distinguish between fads and classics, which managers can use to avoid the former and capture the latter. Paradoxically, these characteristics accounted not only for the initial popularity and rapid spread of fads, *but for their quick demise* as well.

We define fads as ideas that (1) become very popular quickly, (2) stay popular for only a few years, and (3) experience a steep decline in interest and attention, leaving little trace. To avoid ambiguity, we have first *defined fads by their life cycles, not any common properties or outcomes they exhibit*. Although people can argue about things like utility or originality, the life cycle of an idea can be measured objectively, albeit approximately, through surrogates such as citations.

Having said that, we expect that many administrative fads—ideas with short life cycles—*will* have a lot in common. For example, they will typically have more impact on the superficial style and jargon of managers than on substantive behavior or fundamental practices. And even positive effects will often be quite temporary. As we will also see, most fads exhibit common traits in their content, scope, and presentation. We define classics as approaches or practices with an enduring life that can sustain positive interest for many years.

The Life Cycles of Some Prominent Fads—and Classics

Our objectives in this study were twofold: (1) to identify some prominent fads and classics by evaluating their life cycles; and, more important, (2) to identify key characteristics—warning signs for managers—that distinguish fads from classics. The first task was simple. We selected a set of *potential* fads and verified their status according to a quick rise and fall in the amount of journal and press coverage they received, as well as an increasingly negative tone of the coverage. Then we selected a set of potential classics and assessed their ability to sustain positive coverage over many years—coverage that would suggest their long-run utility.

In compiling our list of potential fads, we chose ideas that had elicited great excitement among American managers and a good deal of discussion in the professional media. We avoided techniques that were narrow in scope, such as quality circles, zero-defects, or management by walking around, because they tended to be component elements of the more general ideas and programs we researched. Moreover, because our interest was organizations, we ignored ideas that focused on personal rather than organizational improvement, such as t-groups, skunk camps, and personal motivation seminars. Our list of fads—incomplete, of course—is shown in Table 2.1.1.

Again, these fads were not necessarily without merit. Fad auteurs frequently made insightful and sensible observations. The rapid decline in interest, however, suggests that their ideas were quickly abandoned, were only fleeting sources of advantage, or were rapidly transformed into something different by vulgarization or sexy packaging. Following others who have studied fads, we used the 2002 global edition of the ABI/Inform database to count the number of articles written about the potential fads. ABI is a comprehensive computerized bibliographical index containing abstracts of articles from more than 1,700 academic, professional, and trade magazines and journals. It allowed us to document the rise and fall of

Table 2.1.1 Some Examples of Administrative Fads and Their Gurus

Management by objectives (MBO)	Drucker, Odiorne
Theories X and Y	McGregor; Likert
Orthodox job enrichment	Herzberg
Japanese management (Theory Z)	Ouchi; Pascale & Athos
Corporate culture*	Deal & Kennedy
Excellence*	Peters & Waterman
Total quality management (TQM)	Juran, Deming
Downsizing	(various sources)
Business process reengineering (BPR)	Hammer & Champy

It was impossible to obtain data for the corporate culture and excellence fads because of the many different uses of the keywords.

interest in administrative phenomena, but only since 1985. Accordingly, we identified three recent fads:

- *Business Process Reengineering* (keyword: "reengineering")
- *Total Quality Management* (keywords: "total quality," "TQM")
- *Downsizing*

Four older fads were included for comparison:

- *Japanese Management* (keywords: "Japanese management," "Theory Z")
- *Job Enrichment* (keyword: "job enrichment")
- *Management by Objectives* (keywords: "management by objectives," "MBO")
- *Theories X and Y* (keywords: "Theory X," "Theory Y")

We counted references to these fads for each year from 1985 to 2001. We would have liked to obtain data for the Excellence and Corporate Culture fads as well, but there were too many different uses of the keywords "excellence" and "culture."

In order to say anything meaningful about the life cycles and characteristics of fads, we had to compare them to their less fleeting counterparts—those we call "classics." Otherwise, we risked identifying properties that hold not just for fads but all administrative phenomena. Examples of enduring classics include the intensive use of *management information systems (MIS)*, *diversification*, and *decentralization*. There are also the more recent potential classics, or "risers": *globalization*, *outsourcing*, and *supply chain management (SCM)*.

The results of our research are shown in Figures 2.1.1 and 2.1.2 and Table 2.1.2. Clearly, TQM had relatively few references prior to 1989, then a dramatic growth in interest, peaking in 1993, followed by a sharp decline. As interest in TQM waned, references to reengi-

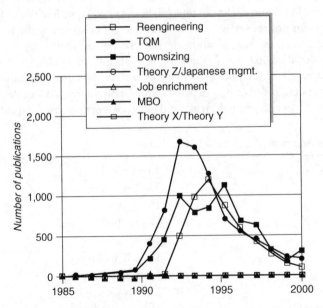

Figure 2.1.1 Publication Counts of Administrative Fads—Dead and Alive (1985–2001).

Source: ABI / Inform—Global edition

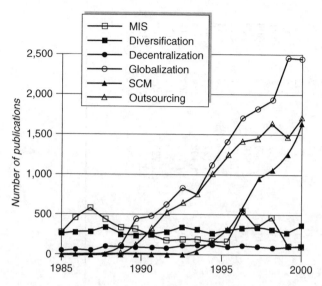

Figure 2.1.2 Publication Counts of Administrative Classics and Risers (1985–2001).

Source: ABI/Inform—Global edition

neering soared, cresting in 1995; downsizing peaked a year later. References to reengineering began to decline in 1996 and continue to do so.

References to the earlier fads—Theories X and Y, job enrichment, MBO, and Theory Z/Japanese management—were minimal. It seems that once a fad passes from popular interest it is, for the most part, forgotten. And this does not take long to happen. Interest in Theory Z, for instance, would have peaked in the early to mid-1980s. However, as we see from Figure 2.1.1, references to it had declined to a level similar to that of other past fads as early as 1987.

Figure 2.1.2 plots the citations of the more established classics—flat curves—as well as the long-term risers. All curves are well above those of our dead fads, and are flatter and more gradual than the recent fads of Figure 2.1.1. We can conclude that the life cycles of our fads and classics are indeed quite different.

Some might argue that TQM is not a fad, since it made real contributions to business practice by helping to foster six-sigma, the ISO certification system, and the enhancement of statistical quality control. But as Tables 2.1.2 and 2.1.3 show, TQM as a movement spawned many disappointments. There was the typical rapid surge and then sharp decline in interest, and many later articles discuss why it has so often failed. Indeed, it appears that the technical aspects of quality assurance have advanced, but the fad-like aspects—quality committees, quality circles, quality seminars, and so on—led to ritualistic behaviors that resulted in very little improvement and were quickly abandoned. For a while, many firms adopted the ritual without truly boosting their quality.

We should add that the content of the articles seemed to change over the lifetime of the fad. Table 2.1.3 presents a sampling of the changes, which progressed from enthusiasm and promise to instruction and doubt to disappointment and debunking. Indeed, after the thematic progression of Table 2.1.3 there is often a postmortem on the fad.

Table 2.1.2 Article Counts for Fads and Classics

	BPR	TQM	Down-sizing	Japanese mgmt.	Job enrichment	MBO	Theory X/Y	MIS	Diversification	Decentralization	Globalization	SCM	Out-sourcing
1985	0	5	6	15	15	17	3	275	289	61	3	2	0
1986	0	5	11	13	18	13	5	461	295	75	8	0	1
1987	0	8	18	5	25	20	5	594	294	64	14	2	3
1988	0	10	26	14	17	21	4	450	367	110	17	2	5
1989	0	34	40	15	31	21	6	350	267	104	115	0	19
1990	3	93	67	13	19	19	2	330	249	105	457	1	121
1991	13	403	227	14	3	15	3	256	263	100	486	2	309
1992	31	835	462	11	8	11	0	182	294	95	618	1	529
1993	517	1,670	1,002	11	14	23	3	208	352	128	835	7	642
1994	990	1,597	790	14	12	15	1	206	330	124	754	53	744
1995	1,190	1,266	844	14	3	15	1	168	289	137	1,127	174	1,006
1996	880	715	1,126	4	9	12	0	176	320	111	1,402	316	1,234
1997	581	540	692	7	7	4	0	546	350	119	1,703	567	1,414
1998	435	465	635	7	8	6	2	358	352	112	1,819	947	1,431
1999	287	337	335	5	5	4	1	470	331	97	1,925	1,052	1,632
2000	151	253	194	4	4	4	1	121	281	115	2,452	1,242	1,456
2001	114	218	311	1	6	4	0	110	368	129	2,438	1,622	1,690
	RECENT FADS			**DEAD FADS**		**CLASSICS**		**RISERS**					

Table 2.1.3 Fads over Time: A Sampling of Articles on TQM and Reengineering

STAGE 1: ASCENDANCY
- *Something new and revolutionary is here.* "Total Quality: Wave of the Future," *Canadian Business Review*, Spring 1990; "Reengineering: It's Totally Radical," *Journal of Business Strategy*, November–December 1993; "Welcome to the Revolution," *Fortune*, December 13, 1993.
- *Out with the old, in with the new.* "From Total Chaos to Total Quality," *Industrial Engineering*, September 1990; "Reengineering: Out of the Rubble," *Personnel Journal*, December 1993.
- *Descriptions and how-to's.* "TQM: Understanding the Basics of Total Quality Management," *Manage*, May 1991; "A Six-Step Guide to Process Reengineering," *Planning Review*, March–April 1993; "How to Make Reengineering Really Work," *Harvard Business Review*, November–December 1993.
- *Great praise and high promise.* "Total Quality Management: Giving Companies a Way to Enhance Position in Global Market," *Industrial Engineering*, April 1989; "The Promise of Reengineering," *Fortune*, May 3, 1993; "How to Work Wonders, Completely," *Management Today*, July 1993.

STAGE 2: MATURITY
- *Exhortations to jump on the bandwagon.* "Industry to B Schools: Smarten Up on TQM or Else," *Electronic Business*, October 1992; "Reengineering: The Hot New Managing Tool," *Fortune*, August 23, 1993; "The Reengineering Rage," *Industry Week*, February 7, 1994.
- *Initial questions of whether or not the technique is a fad.* "Warning: This Good Idea May Become a Fad," *Journal for Quality and Participation*, March 1991; "Quality: A Watchword for the 1990s or the Same Old Song?" *Health Care Supervisor*, June 1992; "Is Reengineering More Than a Fad?" *Personnel Journal*, December 1993.
- *Pleas to look beyond the superficial.* "Managing for Quality: High Priests and Hucksters," *Business Week*, October 25, 1991; "How to Stop Talking About, and Begin Progress Toward, Total Quality Management," *Business Horizons*, May–June 1993; "Reengineering: Beyond the Buzzword," *Business Week*, May 1993.

STAGE 3: DECLINE
- *Problems, pitfalls, and failures.* "Ten Reasons Why TQM Doesn't Work," *Management Review*, January 1993; "Management Fashion," *Administrative Science Quarterly*, December 1999; "TQM: The Mystique, the Mistakes," *Canadian Business Review*, June 1993; "Reengineering Isn't Enough," *Industry Week*, January 17, 1994; "The Hocus-Pocus of Reengineering," *Across the Board*, June 1994.
- *Questions of whether anything is worth saving.* "TQM: More Than a Dying Fad?" *Fortune*, October 18, 1993; "Why TQM Fails and What to Do About It," *Small Business Reports*, July 1994.

Warning Signs for Managers

Having identified some fads and classics on the basis of their life cycles, we explored which properties distinguished the two. The list we came up with (see Table 2.1.4) is incomplete and imperfect, but it does identify eight common characteristics or warning signs that virtually all our fads do have and most of our classics do *not*. Compare properties in Table 2.1.5, where fads scored positive on 76 percent of the warning signs and our classics on only 27 percent. These signs or properties should put managers on their guard. *It is not that any one of these qualities makes a practice suspect.* But when many appear together, we are most apt to be in the presence of a fad. Although some fads may have utility for certain companies, most on our list have led to lots of disappointments (the evolution shown in Table 2.1.3 was typical of our fads).

Before beginning to describe these properties, we must again point out one very central paradox that underlies all our fad warning signs: The *very same* properties explain (1) the initial attraction and appeal of the fad, (2) its contagion and spread, *and* (3) its quick demise. Easy come, it seems, leads to easy go.

Table 2.1.4 Eight Common Properties of Administrative Fads

Simple, straightforward	A fad's ideas are easy to communicate, comprehend, and reduce to a small number of factors, dimensions, or characteristics. Clear-cut distinctions, perfect contrasts, and ideal types are proposed. Simple solutions are suggested.
Promising results	Fad auteurs are confidently didactic. There is no false humility or hedging. Fads promise results such as greater control and efficiency, more motivated and productive workers, more satisfied customers, or some other valued result.
Universal	Fads propose solutions for everyone. Imparted truths are said to apply to almost all organizations, functions, tasks, individuals, or cultures. Fads claim enormous generality and universal relevance.
Step-down capability	Fads have the capacity to be implemented in ritualistic and superficial ways. Recommendations can be implemented quickly and easily, often without having much effect on organizational practices. Recommendations involving large expenditures of resources or substantial redistributions of power can be avoided.
In tune with zeitgeist	Fads resonate with the major trends or business problems of the day. They respond to challenges that are broadly felt and openly discussed. These might result from deficiencies in current administrative practices, technology changes, or shifts in economic or social conditions. Solutions are in tune with prevailing values.
Novel, not radical	Fads are novel, not radical. They question existing assumptions, criticize widespread practices, and point to fresh new ways of doing things. However, this novelty is not so much a new discovery as a rediscovery and repackaging of older ideas, values, and approaches.
Legitimacy via gurus and star examples	Fads are supported by tales of excellent companies and the status and prestige of gurus, not by solid empirical evidence. Stories of corporate heroes and organizational successes provide role models and suggest prestigious adherents, lending an aura of legitimacy to the ideas being espoused.
Lively, entertaining	Fads are almost always presented in a way that can be described as concrete, articulate, bold, memorable, and upbeat. They are filled with labels and buzzwords, lists and acronyms. Interesting anecdotes and corporate war stories abound. Descriptions are vivid and extreme, making fads fun to read about and listen to.

1. Fads Consist of Simple, Straightforward Ideas

The ideas behind fads are easy to communicate and comprehend. Typically, a small number of essential points or distinctions are used to convey some fundamental message. The eso-teric is eschewed in favor of the basic, shades of gray in favor of bold colors. Indeed, some of these ideas are staggering in their simplicity. Some fads simplify by pointing to clear-cut distinctions, archetypes, or perfect contrasts. McGregor (1960) contrasts Theory X with Theory Y. Other fads reduce complex ideas, tasks, or situations to a very small number of factors, dimensions, or characteristics. Herzberg's (1968) two-factor theory proposes two essential types of motivators, one intrinsic and one extrinsic. TQM has been said to rest on five key pillars. The one-minute manager (Blanchard and Johnson 1981) succeeds mostly by

Table 2.1.5 Paradoxical Properties of Fads and Classics

FADS	MBO	Theory X/Y	Enrichment	Theory Z	Culture	Excellence	Down-sizing	TQM	BPR
Simple	Y		Y					Y	
Promising			Y	Y	Y	Y	Y	Y	Y
Universal	Y	Y	Y	Y	Y	Y	Y	Y	Y
Step-down		Y	Y	Y	Y	Y	Y	Y	Y
Zeitgeist		Y	Y	Y	Y	Y	Y	Y	Y
Novel	Y	Y	Y	Y	Y	Y	Y		Y
Examples/gurus	Y	Y	Y	Y	Y	Y		Y	Y
Lively			Y		Y	Y	Y		

CLASSICS	MIS	Diversification	Decentralization	Globalization	Outsourcing	SCM
Simple						
Promising					Y	
Universal	C					C
Step-down	Y	Y		Y		Y
Zeitgeist		Y	Y	Y	Y	
Novel					Y	
Examples/gurus		Y	Y		Y	
Lively						

Y *indicates that the fad or classic possesses the quality in question;* **C** *indicates that the technique or approach is said to apply universally, but its application is expected to vary according to the circumstances of a business.*

paying attention to quick reward and punishment. Fads propose short lists of key factors that, if acknowledged and acted upon, hold the promise of economic or emotional salvation. In the forum of fads, very much can be based on very little.

Simple ideas appeal because they reduce cognitive demands, take relatively little time to absorb and master, and are easily communicated. Businessmen no doubt feel confident sharing straightforward ideas because there is little chance of error or confusion. The simple is far more memorable than the subtle or complex, so those who hear the ideas are able to impart them for quite some time. And simple ideas are especially convenient for consultants to pick up and spread because they appeal to such a broad audience.

Of course, the simplicity inherent in most fads may also cause them to be short-lived. Once everyone knows the secret, there is no more cachet, no more market for consultants or proselytizers, no room for any more "piggy-back" books. Perhaps more important, the simplicity of fads makes them appropriate for a simple world. But most administrators are not lucky enough to confront such a world. And because simple ideas ignore key realities, their usefulness is often limited.

LESSON 1: *Watch out for the really simple scheme: the one or two golden rules, the 2 × 2 matrix, the Theory A vs. Theory B. Think about the logic of the scheme and the complicating factors, perhaps critical to your firm, that are being left out. Consider the obstacles or exceptions to the scheme. Are there enough details to evaluate the approach being advocated?*

2. Fads Over-promise

Fad auteurs write about the spectacular successes that result from adopting the practices they advocate. Confidently didactic, they have little false humility or hedging. Their fads promise outcomes such as greater control and efficiency (MBO, BPR), more motivated and product-ive workers (human relations, Theory Y, job enrichment), more satisfied customers (TQM), perpetual renewal (excellence), or some other valued bottom-line result.

Indeed, hope and promise are what many fads are best at delivering. Their animated sagas suggest a cornucopia of rewards—rewards often attained by managerial "heroes." They give managers an incentive to read, listen, and tell others the news. Although their promises attract attention and enthusiasm, they also set up managers for a fall. Actual achievements could pale quickly in comparison to those promised. And high expectations are those most likely to produce disappointment and abandonment of the fad.

LESSON 2: *Caveat emptor. Watch for promises that seem excessive, for reported fad results that are unrepresentative, that appear more due to chance, manipulation, or inimitable brilliance than any technique that is being recommended or that your firm can effectively embrace. Can you realistically assess the costs and benefits of the new approach?*

3. Fads Propose Solutions for Everyone

Claiming enormous generality and universal relevance, fads appeal to a vast audience. They succeed in part because they propose practices that are believed to apply to almost *all* industries, organizations, or cultures. Theory Y, TQM, and reengineering are said to benefit all kinds of organizations—from General Motors to government bureaucracies, from giant utilities to mom-and-pop groceries. One size fits all.

This presumed general applicability makes fads that much easier to embrace. Managers do not have to worry about if, when, or where to use them. They are given the confidence to proceed without having to concern themselves with complications that may arise from their unique circumstances. The proposed universality of ideas broadens their perceived rele-vance. Indeed, many fad auteurs have a "This means you" subtext throughout their writings.

Moreover, the generality of their recommendations allows managers from different firms and departments to share in the new ideas, thereby enhancing the contagion. It also makes fads appealing to many consulting firms that can very efficiently use the same technique on a wide variety of clients.

Again, however, generality has a downside. Managers end up trying to implement notions that in many specific situations do more harm than good. Theory Y may be counterproduc-tive in highly routinized bureaucracies; Japanese management practices may not be accepted in other cultures; TQM may be superfluous to cost leaders or producers of basic goods; and in some cases, BPR has been shown to devastate a firm's human resources and divest it of core competencies in the name of efficiency. In a complex world, it is likely that fad followers will be doing the wrong things at the wrong time.

LESSON 3: *Ask whether the practice applies to your own company. Why would it be relevant in your particular business model? For your own strategy and market? Is there evidence that it works in your industry? Does it augment capabilities that are central to your business? Does it take into account the particular resources available to your firm?*

4. Fads have a "Step-down" Capability, Allowing Superficial Implementation

It follows from their simple and universalistic nature that fads cannot be overly explicit or exhaustive in their recommendations or implementation criteria. Many fad auteurs make vague, global suggestions about what to do, thereby encouraging ritualistic and superficial adoption. Indeed, cynics might claim that fads are *designed* to be implemented that way. Fads have what may be called a "step-down" capability—an ability to allow for primitive or partial implementation. Recommendations that involve considerable expenditures or redistributions of power are notoriously unpalatable, so most fads avoid them. Instead, they talk about new "attitudes," quality circles, job rotation, goal-setting exercises, training programs, and so on. Such changes can be implemented quickly and easily without having much effect on the firm or its principal power-holders.

A vagueness in expected outcomes may provide cover for this superficiality. Fads generally do not specify clear-cut success or failure criteria that could reveal whether or not the implemented techniques have been successful. And where specified, criteria may focus on whether the techniques have been implemented, or whether they were *perceived* as being important or useful. With such criteria, one could "successfully" implement, say, quality circles simply by having a prescribed number of members attend regular meetings. There is nothing to indicate that people will take away the right attitudes, overcome pet political concerns, or have enough power to alter the status quo. In the words of Oscar Wilde, "The play was a great success. The audience was a failure."

Superficial changes also allow managers to believe they are being modern and progressive while avoiding the need for politically risky upheavals. Ritualistic changes are "grafted onto" a firm. They do not run very deep, are localized in only one or two departments, or fail to alter how the firm performs its basic tasks. There are meetings, new titles, a few committees, and some novel buzzwords. But it is "business as usual." The superficiality of the changes makes them that much more palatable. Those in power can continue to do things in the old and comfortable ways while claiming to be using the latest management techniques. Workers know that things won't really change, not for long anyway. Given the limited scope and impact of the changes and their sporadic assimilation, substantive results are unlikely. Before long, managers realize that the fads have real costs but few benefits, and things revert back to the way they were.

In some companies, fads *have* triggered major changes. Reengineering has had a profound impact on the middle management tier of many companies; sometimes firms have benefited and become spry and efficient; sometimes too they have alienated their people and eroded core capabilities. TQM has also positively transformed some firms, but elsewhere has succeeded mainly in introducing unproductive rituals. The rapid decline of both these fads may be due partly to their unintended consequences and the fact that their broad application has rendered them less useful as sources of competitive advantage.

LESSON 4: *Ask if the firm will be doing enough to make a meaningful change, or just adding window dressing. Is real commitment being demanded for a new approach? Or is this another initiative without the staff, clout, or relevance to have any impact? Are specific, actionable recommendations being made that will change in a real and foreseeable way how the firm conducts its business?*

5. Fads are in Tune with the Zeitgeist

Fads resonate with acknowledged business problems of the day, responding to challenges being broadly felt and openly discussed. Such challenges may relate to deficiencies in current administrative practices, changes in technology, or shifts in economic or social conditions. MBO became popular with the advent of diversified businesses that demanded coordination and control from generalist managers. Ideas of corporate excellence, Japanese management, and TQM became popular when the US began losing market share to Japanese and European companies, often because quality was lacking. These fads provided solutions to problems that were on everyone's mind. The solutions also were in tune with evolving values. But they focused on one core issue rather than the soundness of overall business practices. Thus, they could respond more to concerns of the moment than fundamental weaknesses, and tended to vanish with the next issue of the day.

LESSON 5: *Sometimes there is a good reason for the broad popularity of an idea. But ask if that reason is germane to your own business. Although the problem being addressed may be on everyone's mind, that does not make the proposed solution appropriate. The very popularity of an issue creates a lucrative market for advisors and should trigger suspicions about any proffered resolution.*

6. Most Fads are Novel, not Radical

In some sense, fads have to create the "shock of the new," grabbing attention with freshness and unconventionality. However, they are novel, not radical. They question existing assumptions, criticize widespread practices, and point to new ways of doing things. But frequently the novelty is rhetorical. Many fads turn out to be not so much a new discovery or invention as a rediscovery and repackaging of ideas, values, and approaches—"old wine in new bottles."

For centuries, thinkers like Marx have worried about the quality of working life. The motivational distinctions made today by human relations psychologists were well understood in ancient Rome by the philosopher Marcus Aurelius and historian Titus Livius. Moreover, concern with efficiency *and* quality was very much in evidence in the writings of Adam Smith. Thus, the fad auteurs have taken old ideas and reformulated them to have greater appeal, perhaps by using simplification, memorable examples, and new vocabularies (satisfier vs. motivator; Theory X, Y, and Z). Another rhetorical device that dramatizes novelty is to contrast the old with the new. The old is supposed to refer to conventional practices, whose archaism may be exaggerated to highlight the benefits of the new approach. (How many managers *really* didn't know about quality or "one-minute manager" accountability, or embraced the prehistoric assumptions of Theory X?) But the novelty is rarely so radical as to challenge basic managerial values.

Fads are built mostly on credos that managers have long embraced: high motivation, fulfillment, success, efficiency, opportunity. And they rarely challenge the status quo in a way that would require significant redistribution of power or resources (see Point 4). In the domain of results, such constraints on radicalism may themselves be radically constraining. The superficiality of the novelty soon becomes apparent. Again, some fads, such as reengineering, did challenge basic approaches and power centers; most, however, did not. And even with reengineering, many firms opted for superficial implementation (see the reengineering titles in Table 2.1.3).

LESSON 6: *Ask whether there is any real substance to the ideas being proffered. How exactly will they* translate into concrete changes and new ways of doing things that will improve the business? Will the changes advocated go deep enough to have a lasting effect?

7. Fads Attain Legitimacy Via Gurus and Stellar Case Examples

Fads attain legitimacy through the status and prestige of their proponents, *not by solid empirical evidence.* Often, a fad is espoused by an individual who has achieved "guru" status. Testimonials from other experts are used to lend additional support. And stories of corporate heroes and organizational successes provide role models and suggest prestigious adherents. The latter may show legendarily successful companies thriving by following the fad. Peter Drucker showed how MBO was used in the 1950s by a burgeoning General Motors. Peters and Waterman celebrated a host of enterprises that embraced their pillars of excellence. In fact, such role model companies are often deemed heroes by a fawning business press. Recently, Amazon.com, AOL, and Yahoo! have served as poster firms for the e-commerce revolution. Central to that revolution, according to Hagel and Singer (1999), is a potential "disaggregation" fad-in-the-making that advocates extreme specialization in a core competency while partnering with others for "bricks and mortar" and other services.

Just as fashion designers acquire prestige via their rich and famous customers, fad auteurs are helped along by stories of high-flying firms or star executives who have embraced the new approach, however unintentionally or incidentally. Of course, such tales of success often involve post hoc rationalizations that attribute good results to fads that had no impact. This again leads to disappointment. Miller (1990) reports that more than half of Peters and Waterman's companies lost their luster and ran into significant problems a few short years after the book was published. And so many of the great Internet disaggregators have yet to turn a real profit. The problem is with the method of drawing inferences: Given an endless supply of potential cases, all highly multifaceted, one can illustrate any thesis or proposition, regardless of its merits.

LESSON 7: *Look for hard evidence of the efficacy of an approach. It is easy to be swayed by the words of gurus and stories of brilliant companies. But so often those gurus and companies fall from grace. And the stories may be of brilliant performance that has little to do with the approach being recommended. Ask too if the success stories apply to firms with resources and challenges similar to your own.*

8. Fads are Born of Lively, Entertaining Prose

Framed with labels and buzzwords, lists and acronyms, fads are often presented in a way that is articulate, memorable, and upbeat. Interesting anecdotes, sagas of success and failure, and corporate war stories abound. Descriptions are vivid, even extreme (recall Tom Peters's gripping accounts in *In Search of Excellence*). Problems are catastrophic, solutions near-perfect. Indeed, fads are very often made popular by interesting writing, usually in book form. The writer may be a consultant or an academic with a practical bent, almost never a practicing manager. And often the fad auteur writes in trenchant prose, adorning sometimes mundane notions with the sparkle of incisive phraseology. Although the expert status of a writer can confer some legitimacy, that is hardly enough to create a fad. Sober prose usually will not do the trick. To be influential, works must be at least bracing—more often lively and eloquent, with memorable tales, neat typologies, and an active and personal voice. Books or people that create fads are great fun to read and listen to; that is a major part of their appeal. Indeed, as in the realm of intended fiction, entertainment value is a major selling point.

In fact, fad auteurs write the way managers speak, or at least would like to speak. Tom Peters is perhaps the master of the medium. His adeptness at both oral and written communication no doubt accounts a good deal for the popularity of his ideas. He avoids jargon, except where he introduces it for purposes of panache.

Needless to say, ideas chosen for their ability to entertain usually do little to address organizational needs. And there may be a backlash from charismatic presentations that build up unrealistic expectations. Didactic tones also encourage quick acceptance, rather than reflective and selective usage; this also causes problems down the road.

LESSON 8: *We all pay more attention to an entertaining presentation. But in the long run, content rather than style must carry the day. Again, make sure there is substance in a recommendation, that it is relevant to your firm, and that it is specific enough to be implemented in a practical way.*

Paradox Revisited

If there is a central thread running through these eight aspects that makes a fad attractive and popular, it is that they *also contribute to its short life.* Because simple concepts are easy to grasp, they often fail to do justice to the challenges they address. Similarly, universal recommendations are too coarse to apply or inappropriate in important situations. Over-promising results and dramatic examples seduce people into action, but they also make it clear early on that reality does not match the wonderful stories. Step-down capability also renders it easy to get on board—and to get away with doing very little. Superficial novelty can contribute to this "cop-out" because there is always the possibility of pointing to existing successes and attributing them to the fad. Finally, attunement to the zeitgeist attracts widespread interest, but may be of no relevance to a particular firm, or may fasten onto a problem for which there is no solution. In short, our fad drivers giveth and soon taketh away.

These fad properties seem to be far rarer among classics, as Table 2.1.5 shows. Classics demand real changes in organizations and have lasting effects. They typically arise not from the writings of academics or experts but out of practitioner responses to economic and competitive challenges. They are complex, multifaceted, and applied in different ways in different businesses. There are no generally accepted primers of how to make such changes, nor are there any promised results or simple rules for all to follow. Globalization and outsourcing, for example, represent multifaceted responses to pressing business needs and opportunities. They elicit research into a multitude of strategic, corporate, and functional issues that, over time, change the way a large number of companies do business. Of course, such trends take longer to become widespread because of their significant costs and great impact on the firms that choose to adopt them. Moreover, though not always on the tip of everyone's tongue, they take much longer to go out of fashion.

As in all walks of life, if it looks too good to be true, it probably is. Executives would do well to bear in mind the relatively short life cycles of fads and the fact that many incur significant costs while producing few positive results. The constant shifting of bandwagons may cause distractions from important business, confuse and alienate people, and engender cynicism. Today's Dilbert-reading employees are all too aware of the fad-surfing going on in the corporate world.

Thus, when examining proposed changes relating to potential fads, managers should be constructively skeptical. They might do well to recognize the eight warning signs we have uncovered here and ask themselves some key questions. To recap, these are:

- What evidence is there that the new approach can produce positive results? Are arguments based on anecdote or on solid evidence from lots of companies followed over time?
- Has the approach worked in firms similar to our own that face similar challenges?
- Is the approach relevant to the priorities and strategies of our company?
- Is the advice specific enough to be implemented? Do we have enough information about implementation challenges and how to meet them?
- Is the advice practical for our company given our capabilities and resources?
- Can we reasonably assess the costs and the prospective rewards?

If encouraging answers are forthcoming, executives may be on the trail of a "classic." It will be especially useful to get inputs from different levels and functions of the firm in addressing these questions and to keep pushing for evidence of efficacy and relevance before embarking on any costly initiative. In dealing with management approaches, skepticism is a useful point of departure. We caution, however, that managers must not reject fads or potential fads out of hand, as these may have a positive impact on what the company is trying to do. Fads signal issues, problems, and techniques that managers really care about and may suggest approaches of value to specific contexts and enterprises. The trick for managers will be to evaluate them in light of the situations in their own firms.

Acknowledgments

The authors wish to thank The Social Sciences and Humanities Research Council of Canada and Fonds pour la Formation et l'Aide à la Recherche for providing funding for this project. Thanks also goes to Henri Barki for his useful comments.

References and Selected Bibliography

Abrahamson, Eric. 1996. Management fashion. *Academy of Management Review* 21/1 (January): 254–285.

——, and Gregory Fairchild. 1999. Management fashion: Life-cycles, triggers, and collective learning processes. *Administrative Science Quarterly* 44/4 (December): 708–740.

Aguirre, Benigno E., Enrico Quarantelli, and Jorge Mendoza. 1988. The collective behavior of fads: The characteristics, effects, and career of streaking. *American Sociological Review* 53 (August): 569–584.

Blanchard, Kenneth, and Spencer Johnson. 1981. *The one-minute manager*. New York: Berkeley Books.

Business fads: What's in and out. 1986. *Business Week* (12 July): 52–56.

Drucker, Peter F. 1954. *The practice of management*. New York: Harper.

Hagel, John, and Marc Singer. 1999. *Net worth*. Boston: Harvard.

Heenan, David. 1989. The downside of downsizing. *Journal of Business Strategy* 10/6 (November): 18–23.

Herzberg, Frederick. 1968. One more time: How do you motivate employees? *Harvard Business Review* 46/1 (January–February): 53–62.

Huselid, Mark. 1995. The impact of HRM practices on turnover, productivity and corporate financial performance. *Academy of Management Journal* 39/4 (August): 635–670.

McGregor, Douglas. 1960. *The human side of enterprise*. New York: Macmillan.

Miller, Danny. 1990. *The Icarus paradox*. New York: HarperBusiness.

Ouchi, William. 1981. *Theory Z: How American business can meet the Japanese challenge*. Reading, MA: Addison-Wesley.

Peters, Tom, and Robert Waterman. 1982. *In search of excellence*. New York: Harper & Row.

Shapiro, Eileen. 1995. *Fad surfing in the boardroom*. Reading, MA: Addison-Wesley.

Staw, Barry, and Lisa Epstein. 2000. What bandwagons bring: Effects of popular management techniques on corporate performance, reputation and CEO pay. *Administrative Science Quarterly* 45/3 (September): 523–556.

Worren, Nicolay. 1996. Management fashion. *Academy of Management Review* 21/3: 613–614.

3 Managing Diversity and Individual Differences

3.1 STEREOTYPE THREAT AT WORK

Loriann Roberson and Carol T. Kulik

Executive Overview

Managing diversity in organizations requires creating an environment where all employees can succeed. This paper explains how understanding "stereotype threat"—the fear of being judged according to a negative stereotype—can help managers create positive environments for diverse employees. While stereotype threat has received a great deal of academic research attention, the issue is usually framed in the organizational literature as a problem affecting performance on tests used for admission and selection decisions. Further, articles discussing stereotype threat usually report the results of experimental studies and are targeted to an academic audience. We summarize 12 years of research findings on stereotype threat, address its commonplace occurrence in the workplace, and consider how interventions effective in laboratory settings for reducing stereotype threat might be implemented by managers in organizational contexts. We end the paper with a discussion of how attention to stereotype threat can improve the management of diversity in organizations.

Ongoing demographic trends (increasing percentages of African Americans, Hispanics, and Asians in the American workforce, an aging population, expanding female labor force participation) have made diversity a fact of organizational life. When these trends were first identified in the mid-1980s, they were heralded as an opportunity for organizations to become more creative, to reach previously untapped markets, and in general to achieve and maintain a competitive advantage (Cox, 1994; Robinson & Dechant, 1997; Thomas & Ely, 1996).

However, employee diversity does not *necessarily* boost creativity, market share, or competitive advantage. In fact, research suggests that left unmanaged, employee diversity is more likely to damage morale, increase turnover, and cause significant communication problems and conflict within the organization (Jackson et al., 1991; Jehn, Neale, & Northcraft, 1999; Tsui, Egan, & O'Reilly, 1992; Zenger & Lawrence, 1989). Thus, "managing diversity" has become a sought-after managerial skill, and concerns about effective diversity management have spawned an industry of diversity training programs, diversity videos, and diversity consultants. But despite several decades of effort and millions of dollars invested, the evidence suggests that organizations continue to do a poor job of managing diversity. A recent comprehensive report concluded that organizations rarely are able to leverage diversity and capitalize on its potential benefits (Hansen, 2003; Kochan et al., 2003). What's the problem? Are we missing a key piece of the diversity management puzzle?

Most of the attention in the diversity management literature has been focused on the organizational decision maker—the manager who is prejudiced against certain groups and who allows these prejudices to influence how he or she treats employees. These individual-level prejudices become institutionalized—meaning, they become embodied in organizational policies and practices that systematically disadvantage some employees. In their efforts to reduce discrimination, organizations are increasingly concerned about hiring non-prejudiced managers, redesigning biased selection, appraisal, and promotion procedures, and generally eradicating stereotypes from managerial decision making (Greengard, 2003; Rice, 1996). If we eliminate stereotypes from organizational decision making, the logic goes, we'll create an organization where all employees can flourish and advance.

Unfortunately, even if an organization were successful in hiring only non-prejudiced managers and eliminating stereotypes from its formal decision making, stereotypes would still exist in broader society. As a result, every employee walking through the door of the organization knows the stereotypes that *might* be applied to him or her and wonders whether organizational decision makers and co-workers will endorse those stereotypes. Here, we discuss the effects of these stereotypes, and highlight an important aspect of diversity management that has not received much attention by diversity or management scholars: stereotype threat, the fear of being judged and treated according to a negative stereotype about members of your group (Steele, Spencer, & Aronson, 2002). Research on stereotype threat has shown that societal stereotypes can have a negative effect on employee feelings and behavior, making it difficult for an employee to perform to his or her true potential. Research has also indicated that stereotype threat can result in employees working harder, but not better. When stereotype threat is present, performance declines. Therefore, a non-prejudiced manager who uses objective performance indicators as a basis for decision making risks underestimating the employee's true ability. When an organizational context contains the conditions that create stereotype threat, nontraditional employees experience additional barriers to success despite the good intentions of everyone involved. Therefore, stereotype threat places certain demands on the manager of diverse employees—demands to create conditions that minimize the occurrence of stereotype threat, so that all employees can perform effectively.

Stereotype threat has been discussed almost exclusively as an issue for high stakes testing, particularly in educational arenas. For example, we're all familiar with the opportunities that hang on scores from tests such as the Scholastic Aptitude Test (SAT), the Graduate Record Examination (GRE) and the Graduate Management Achievement Test (GMAT): without the "right" scores, a student won't be able to get into the best college for his or her chosen field. In 1999, PBS aired a documentary concluding that stereotype threat was suppressing the standardized test performance of African American students (Chandler, 1999). These effects on high stakes tests are important, but stereotype threat is not limited to African-American students taking large-scale standardized academic tests. It is also present in the everyday, routine situations that are a part of all jobs. Thus, knowledge of stereotype threat and its corrosive effects on performance is needed to understand the work experience of members of stereotyped groups and to manage diversity more effectively in the organization. In this article, we answer the following questions: What is stereotype threat and what are its effects? How can stereotype threat be reduced?

We begin with a short review of the concept and the research evidence. We then describe the conditions that increase the risk of stereotype threat. Because these conditions regularly occur in the workplace, stereotype threat is also likely to be a common part of many people's work experience. Finally, we present strategies for reducing stereotype threat from the academic research literature, and consider if and how those strategies might be applied in organizations. We also discuss how attention to stereotype threat adds value to current organizational approaches to managing diversity.

Stereotype Threat at Work

Every job involves being judged by other people, whether you are giving a sales presentation to clients, representing your work team at a meeting, or showing your boss your work for some informal feedback. Being evaluated can raise anxieties for anyone. Apprehension in these kinds of situations is a common phenomenon, and in fact, a little anxiety can even boost performance (Cocchiara & Quick, 2004; Reio & Callahan, 2004; Yerkes & Dodson, 1908). But anxieties can be heightened for those employees who are members of a negatively stereotyped group, especially when they are performing a kind of task on which, according to the stereotype, members of their group do poorly. Consider these statements by people who are members of stereotyped groups:

> From a marketing manager: "You can see in someone's eyes when you are first introduced that you're dead in the water just because you're seen as old." Many older workers refer to "the look" on someone's face as they are introduced. A 57 year old accounts supervisor recounted that on meeting someone face to face for the first time, she was told with a tone of disappointment, "Oh, you have such a young voice on the phone" (Blank & Shipp, 1994).
>
> From a White loan officer (concerned about being perceived as racist or sexist): "I'm always worried about how I was heard. How will I be interpreted? Did I say the wrong thing?" (Blank & Shipp, 1994).
>
> From a Black manager: "I felt Whites had a lot of negative ideas about Blacks. I felt evaluated when I asked questions. Asking questions became painful for me" (Dickins & Dickins, 1991).
>
> From an overweight worker: ". . . I work extra hard because I know the stereotype, and I feel I need to prove myself. I work harder than most of my coworkers who do the same job. Yet my (skinny, size-10) boss continually talks about me behind my back to my coworkers—she says that I'm lazy and that I don't take any initiative, and who knows what else. She sees me for maybe half an hour out of the work week, which is hardly enough time to judge me on my work . . . It doesn't matter that I know the job inside-out, or that my customer-service skills are topnotch. It doesn't matter that I'm on time and do any stupid little task that I'm asked. All that matters is the width of my ass" (Personal blog, 2005).

The individuals quoted here are members of different identity groups, but they all voice a common concern: the fear of being seen and judged according to a negative stereotype about their group, and the concern that they might do something that would inadvertently confirm the negative stereotype (Steele, 1997; Steele et al., 2002). These individuals are experiencing "stereotype threat."

Stereotype threat describes the psychological experience of a person who, while engaged in a task, is aware of a stereotype about his or her identity group suggesting that he or she will not perform well on that task. For example, a woman taking a math test is familiar with the common stereotype that "girls aren't good at math." Or a Black faculty member preparing his case for promotion is aware that some people believe that Blacks are intellectually inferior. This awareness can have a disruptive effect on performance—ironically resulting in the individual confirming the very stereotype he or she wanted to *dis*confirm (Kray, Thompson, & Galinsky, 2001). Anyone can experience anxiety while performing a task with important implications (a test to get into graduate school or a presentation to a big client), but stereotype threat places an *additional* burden on members of stereotyped groups. They feel "in the spotlight," where their failure would reflect negatively not only on themselves as individuals, but on the larger group to which they belong. As singer and actress Beyoncé Knowles said in an interview with *Newsweek* in 2003: "It's like you have something to prove, and you don't want to mess it up and be a negative reflection on black women" (quoted in Smith, 2004, p. 198).

In the first (and now classic) study on stereotype threat, Claude Steele and Joshua Aronson (1995) asked Black and White students to take a very difficult test. The test was composed of items from the verbal section of the Graduate Record Examination, and it was deliberately designed to tax students' ability. For some students, this test was described simply as a laboratory problem-solving task. However, for other students, the test was described as a "genuine test of your verbal abilities and limitations." The important difference between these two descriptions was that race stereotypes were irrelevant in the "laboratory task" version—there was no reason for a Black participant to expect race to impact his or her performance, or to think that other people might expect race to have an impact. However, in the scenario where the test was described as a genuine test of abilities and limitations (the stereotype threat condition), the racial stereotype (that Blacks lack intellectual ability) *was* relevant, and the researchers predicted that Black participants would be both aware of the stereotype and want to avoid confirming it.

When Steele and Aronson examined the results, they found that White students' performance was largely unaffected by the test instructions—the White students performed about equally well whether the test had been described as an ability test or as a laboratory problem-solving task. However, the instructions made a big difference in the performance of Black students. They performed less well in the ability test condition than in the problem-solving condition—even though the test was equally difficult in both conditions. In fact, after Steele and Aronson controlled for pre-study differences in ability (measured by the students' SAT scores), they found that Black and White students in the laboratory problem-solving condition performed about the same—but Black students underperformed relative to Whites in the ability test condition (Steele & Aronson, 1995).

This basic experimental design, in which researchers compare the performance of two groups (one group is negatively stereotyped, the other is not) in two task conditions (one condition presents the task as stereotype-relevant, the other does not), has been replicated many times over the last twelve years with consistent results. The negatively stereotyped group underperforms when the stereotype is seen as relevant to the task. This research is summarized in Table 3.1.1.

As the table shows, the stereotype threat phenomenon has been documented in a large number of groups, across a wide range of diversity dimensions, and in many different performance domains. In the top (unshaded) part of the table, the "Who was affected?" column includes the people we generally think of as disadvantaged in the workplace due to negative stereotypes—racial and ethnic minorities, members of lower socio-economic classes, women, older people, gay and bisexual men, and people with disabilities. The academic literature sometimes describes members of these groups as "stigma conscious" (Aronson et al., 1999). That means that members of these groups can be very aware of the

Table 3.1.1 Examples of Stereotype Threat[1]

Who was affected?	How did the researchers create stereotype threat?	What stereotype was activated?	What happened?
Black students	Told the students that they were about to take a very difficult test that was a "genuine test of your verbal abilities and limitations"	"Blacks lack intellectual ability"	The students performed less well on the test
Latino students	Told the students that they were about to take a very difficult mathematical and spatial ability test that would provide a "genuine test of your actual abilities and limitations"	"Latinos lack intellectual ability"	The students performed less well on the test
Low socioeconomic status (SES) students	Asked the students to provide background information including their parents' occupation and education, then told them they were about to take a difficult test that would "assess your intellectual ability for solving verbal problems"	"Low SES students lack intellectual ability"	The students attempted to solve fewer problems and had fewer correct answers on the test
Women	Reminded the women that "previous research has sometimes shown gender differences" in math ability, then asked them to take a test that "had shown gender differences in the past"	"Women have weak math ability"	The women performed more poorly on the math test
Older individuals (60 years and older)	Gave the older people a series of memory tests and presented them with a list of "senile" behaviors ("can't recall birthdate") too quickly for conscious awareness. Then researchers gave the older people the memory tests a second time	"Older people have bad memory"	The older people had a significant decline in memory performance from pretest to posttest
Gay and bisexual men	Asked the men to indicate their sexual orientation on a demographic survey, then videotaped the participants while they engaged in a "free play" activity with children	"Gay men are dangerous to young children"	Judges rated the men as more anxious and less suitable for a job at a daycare center
People with a head injury history	Told participants that a "growing number" of neuropsychological studies find that individuals with head injuries "show cognitive deficits on neuro-psychological tests," then gave participants a series of tests assessing memory and attention	"Persons with a head injury history experience a loss of cognitive performance"	The participants performed worse on tests of general intellect, immediate memory, and delayed memory

(Continued Overleaf) |

Table 3.1.1 Continued

Who was affected?	How did the researchers create stereotype threat?	What stereotype was activated?	What happened?
Whites	Told participants that a "high proportion of Whites show a preference for White people" before asking them to complete the IAT (implicit attitude test) that would measure their "unconscious racial attitudes toward Blacks and Whites"	"Whites are racist"	The participants had a larger IAT effect (the difference in response time between incompatible and compatible trials), suggesting a preference for White faces
White students	Gave the students a packet of newspaper articles emphasizing a "growing gap in academic performance between Asian and White students" before asking them to take a very challenging math test	"White students have less mathematical ability than Asian students"	The students solved fewer problems on the math test
Men	Reminded participants that "it is a well-known fact that men are not as apt as women to deal with affect . . . and to process affective information as effectively" then asked them to indicate whether a series of words were "affective" or not	"Men are less capable than women in dealing with affective (emotional) information"	The men made more errors on the task
White men	Told the men that they would be engaged in a golf task that measured their "natural athletic ability." The men completed a demographic survey that included a question about their racial identity, then took the test	"White men have less athletic prowess than Black men"	The men made more strokes (performed worse) on the golf task

1 The research summarized in this table includes the following articles: Steele, C. M., & Aronson, J. (1995). Stereotype threat and the intellectual test performance of African Americans. *Journal of Personality and Social Psychology, 69*, 797–811; Gonzales, P. M., Blanton, H., & Williams, K. J. (2002). The effects of stereotype threat and double-minority status on the test performance of Latino women. *Personality and Social Psychology Bulletin, 28*, 659–670; Croize, J., & Claire, T. (1998). Extending the concept of stereotype threat to social class: The intellectual underperformance of students from low socioeconomic backgrounds. *Personality and Social Psychology Bulletin, 24*, 588–594; Spencer, S. J., Steele, C. M., & Quinn, D. M. (1999). Stereotype threat and women's math performance. *Journal of Experimental Social Psychology, 35*, 4–28; Bosson, J. K., Haymovitz, E. L., & Pinel, E. C. (2004). When saying and doing diverge: The effects of stereotype threat and self-reported versus non-verbal ability. *Journal of Experimental Social Psychology, 40*, 247–255; Suhr, J. A., & Gunstad, J. (2002). "Diagnosis threat": The effect of negative expectations on cognitive performance in head injury. *Journal of Clinical and Experimental Neuropsychology, 24*, 448–457; Frantz, C. M., Cuddy, A. J. C., Burnett, M., Ray, H., & Hart, A. (2004). A threat in the computer: The race implicit association test as a stereotype threat experience. *Personality and Social Psychology Bulletin, 30*, 1611–1624; Aronson, J., Lustina, M. J., Good, C., Keough, K., Steele, C. M., & Brown, J. (1999). When White men can't do math: Necessary and sufficient factors in stereotype threat. *Journal of Experimental Social Psychology, 35*, 29–46; Leyens, J., Desert, M., Croizet, J., & Darcis, C. (2000). Stereotype threat: Are lower status and history of stigmatization preconditions of stereotype threat? *Personality and Social Psychology Bulletin, 26*, 1189–1199; Stone, J., Lynch, C. I., Sjomeling, M., & Darley, J. M. (1999). Stereotype threat effects on Black and White athletic performance. *Journal of Personality and Social Psychology, 77*, 1213–1227.

social stereotypes other people associate with their group. Since the relevant stereotype is very likely to come to mind, concerns about stereotype confirmation are easily aroused. As a result, very subtle contextual variations (a slight wording difference in the way a test is described, for example) may be enough to make the stereotype salient and disrupt performance.

But research has shown that this phenomenon does not apply only to people in disadvantaged groups. In fact, the bottom (shaded) part of Table 3.1.1 shows that even members of high status groups can experience stereotype threat. For example, we don't normally think of White men as being disadvantaged in the workplace. White men generally enjoy more hiring opportunities, higher salaries, and more organizational status than women or members of racial minority groups with comparable education and ability (Hite, 2004; Parks-Yancy, 2006). However, even high status groups have some negative stereotypes associated with them, and one of the stereotypes most strongly associated with the White group is the belief that Whites are racist (Frantz et al., 2004). The research suggests that many Whites are chronically concerned with not appearing racist (and inadvertently confirming the stereotype). Therefore, task situations that are described as dependent on racial attitudes can trigger stereotype threat in Whites (and result in participants looking more prejudiced than they might actually be) (Frantz et al., 2004).

Further, members of any group may experience stereotype threat when their identity group is negatively compared with another group. For example, comparative stereotypes suggest that Whites have less mathematical ability than Asians, men are less effective in processing affective (emotional) information than women, and White men have less athletic prowess than Black men. These negative comparisons can induce stereotype threat, and members of the target group demonstrate the short-term performance detriments associated with stereotype threat, as the studies listed in the table have found. One conclusion that can be drawn from looking at the table is that stereotype threat can affect all of us because each of us is a member of at least one group about which stereotypes exist. If you think about the stereotypes that could be applied to your own social group, you might recall situations where you personally experienced stereotype threat. If you think about the stereotypes that could apply to your employees, you can also identify the situations where they might be vulnerable to stereotype threat.

The research referred to in the table has decisively shown that stereotype threat has a negative impact on short term performance. But an unresolved question is *why* does stereotype threat have this negative impact? Researchers have suggested several different answers to this question (the literature calls these answers "mediating" explanations), but there is no consensus on which is the "right" answer. The dominant explanation has to do with anxiety (Aronson, Quinn, & Spencer, 1998), but there is still some disagreement over how anxiety affects performance. One argument suggests that anxiety increases a person's motivation and effort. Stereotype threatened participants are very motivated to perform well, and sometimes they try *too* hard or are too cautious in performing (Cadinu et al., 2003). For example, Steele and Aronson (1995) found that the Black participants in their research spent too much time trying to answer a small number of problems. They worked too hard on getting the right answer, and they disadvantaged themselves by not answering enough questions. Another argument proposes the opposite—that anxiety decreases a person's motivation and effort (Cadinu et al., 2003). The explanation is that stereotype threatened participants lose confidence that they can perform well, and in a self-fulfilling way this undermines performance. Given that the evidence thus far is still mixed and unclear, we will have to wait for further research to provide a more definitive answer to the *why* question.

However, research has clearly identified the conditions under which stereotype threat is more and less likely to occur. This brings us to the next section of our paper.

Conditions for Stereotype Threat

We've seen that the content of stereotypes about groups includes beliefs about the abilities of group members to perform certain kinds of tasks. Stereotype threat will only occur for those tasks associated with the stereotype. But simply being *asked* to perform a stereotype-relevant task is not enough to create stereotype threat. Research has identified two additional conditions needed for stereotype threat to emerge: task difficulty and personal task investment. In addition, the context can influence the perceived relevance of the stereotype for performance of the task or job. We have diagrammed these conditions, and the stereotype threat process, in Figure 3.1.1.

Stereotype Relevance of the Task: What Does it Take to Perform Well?

Stereotype threat is situation specific, felt in situations where one can be "judged by, treated and seen in terms of, or self-fulfill a negative stereotype about one's group" (Spencer, Steele, & Quinn, 1999, p. 6). These situations occur when doing well on the task requires an ability on which, according to the stereotype, the person performing the task has a deficit. In the studies we have reviewed, the stereotype relevance of the task has often been created by telling participants that the task is a direct "test" of the stereotyped ability. So, for example, math tests have been used to create a stereotype relevant task for women and verbal or cognitive ability tests used to create stereotype relevant tasks for African Americans and Hispanics. But stereotype relevance isn't limited to standardized tests. Laura Kray and her colleagues surveyed participants to show that negotiation tasks are stereotype relevant for women. The researchers found that people believed that good negotiators were "assertive and concerned with personal gain" *and* that "men are more likely to be assertive than women" (Kray, Galinsky, & Thompson, 2002). Therefore, it logically follows that "men are better negotiators than women."

Research has shown that in our society many people believe successful managers have attributes more similar to those of men and Whites than to those of women, Hispanics, or African Americans (Chung-Herrera & Lankau, 2005; Heilman, Block, Martell, & Simon, 1989; Tomkiewicz, Brenner, & Adeyemi-Bello, 1998). But beliefs about the traits necessary for jobs can also be organization specific. The potential for stereotype threat exists any time employees' beliefs about the particular traits needed for good job performance are linked to stereotypes about groups.

Task Difficulty: Why is this so Hard?

Stereotype threat is most likely to influence performance on very difficult tasks—those that are at the limits of a person's abilities (Steele et al., 2002). On easier tasks, stereotype threat doesn't have much negative effect. According to psychologist Claude Steele, experiencing frustration with task accomplishment is an important trigger for stereotype threat (Steele et al., 2002). On a simple task there is little frustration—the person is doing well and knows it. But with a difficult task, progress is not so smooth. People who experience frustration with a task try to explain their difficulty to themselves: "Why is this so hard? Is this job just

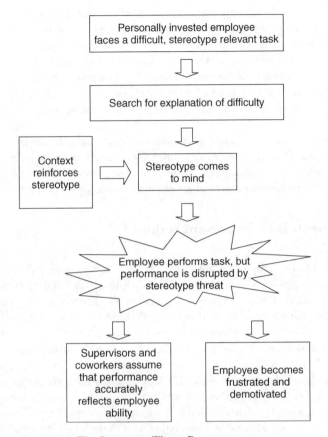

Figure 3.1.1 The Stereotype Threat Process.

impossible? Am I not working hard enough? Am I having a bad day?" They also think about how others (co-workers, supervisors) will explain their difficulty: "Will they think I'm not working hard enough?" But when the person is a member of a stereotyped group, the stereotype is also likely to come to mind as a potential explanation that others might use: "Will they think the stereotype is true? It's going to look like the stereotype *is* true."

A negative dynamic operates between task difficulty and stereotype threat. When a task is difficult, stereotype threat evokes concern over performance. But this concern also has a greater *impact* on the performance of difficult tasks. Difficult jobs require concentration and focus; all of one's cognitive/mental resources must be directed toward accomplishing the work. If some of those resources are diverted towards worrying about one's skills and how one will be viewed by others, performance decrements occur (Beilock & Carr, 2005; Verbeke & Bagozzi, 2000). Thus, difficult tasks trigger stereotype threat, and also are most affected by it.

In work settings then, difficult, complex, and challenging tasks are where stereotype threat is most likely to occur. This creates a dilemma for managers. Task difficulty is not just a fact in many (especially professional) jobs, it is a desired condition. For years, job design experts have recommended that every job contain some challenging aspects to increase job involvement and avoid boredom and skill atrophy (Greenberg, 1996; Hackman & Oldham, 1980). In fact, giving demanding assignments to new hires is sometimes recommended as a good way to develop employees. Early demanding experiences predict later career success (Habermas & Bluck, 2000). In many organizations, "stretch" assignments (assignments for which an employee is not yet fully qualified, "stretching" the employee's skills and abilities) (McCauley, Eastman, & Ohlott, 1995) are used as developmental tools throughout a person's tenure (Noe, 1999). Stretch assignments are needed for skill development, but managers must be aware of the extra potential for stereotype threat these assignments might involve for stereotyped employees, and counteract this risk. (We discuss how managers might do this later in the paper.)

In addition, tasks that are new and unfamiliar to the person performing them may be more at risk for stereotype threat than routine, familiar ones. New employees in particular are likely to find task accomplishment challenging as they learn their responsibilities. Thus, managers also must be aware of the higher potential for stereotype threat for their new hires.

Personal Task Investment: How Important is this to Who I Am?

Personal task investment refers to how important doing well on the task is to the individual's self-esteem and identity. Some employees strongly identify with a particular skill or competency as a part of who they are. We often hear people say, "I'm good with people," or "I'm a techie." For these people, the skill is a part of how they define themselves. For such invested people, doing well in that task domain is important for their self-esteem and for feeling good about themselves. Researchers have argued that people who are personally invested in the task would be most influenced by stereotype threat because they are the ones who really care about their performance (Steele, 1997; Steele et al., 2002). If you want your work performance to say something about you personally, then the prospect of being viewed in terms of a negative stereotype is most disturbing. Studies have consistently confirmed this. Those invested in the task are more negatively affected by stereotype threat than those without such personal task investment.

What does this mean, practically? People tend to be invested in tasks they are good at (Steele, 1997). So the heavy impact of stereotype threat on the personally invested means that "the most capable members of stereotyped groups tend to be the most adversely affected in their performance by stereotype threat" (Kray et al., 2002, p. 388). This carries an important reminder for managers: the employees who care about their work and really want to do well are generally the ones that a manager is least likely to worry about since they are the ones he or she thinks will succeed on their own, and thus don't need coaxing, coaching, or extra attention. Yet, these are the people *most* likely to be affected by stereotype threat, and therefore, most in need of a manager's efforts to address and reduce it. For example, a manager might think that because the talented Hispanic salesperson graduated at the top of his class, he's already proven that stereotypes don't apply to him and isn't bothered by them. Or that the efficient accountant who earned her CPA despite caring for four children no longer worries about not being taken seriously by male managers. But it's exactly these employees, the ones who have made a big investment in their work, who might be most likely to suffer the effects of stereotype threat.

The Context: Is this a Place Where Stereotypes Operate?

We've seen that the most important condition for stereotype threat is stereotype relevance: stereotype threat only occurs when the stereotype seems relevant to performing the task (Steele et al., 2002). In the academic research described earlier, stereotype relevance was created by the way the researchers described the tasks in a laboratory setting. In work settings, the relevance of the stereotype for performance can also be signaled and reinforced by the diversity (or the lack of diversity) of people who are currently performing the job. Rosabeth Moss Kanter used the term "token" to describe individuals who are different from others on a salient demographic dimension—race, sex, or age (Kanter, 1977). Kanter and others have shown that tokens feel very "visible"—that they stand out from the rest of the group. In addition, those in the majority are more likely to view tokens in terms of their distinguishing characteristic: as *the* woman or *the* Asian. Because everyone (the tokens and the tokens' colleagues) is more aware of group memberships under these conditions, associated stereotypes are more likely to come to mind (Niemann & Dovidio, 1998). In addition, the numerical differences reinforce the relevance of the stereotype for performance in the setting. Consider the solitary woman in a team of software engineers. Being the "only one" suggests that the stereotype about women lacking quantitative skills is true, and therefore sex is relevant to job performance. After all, the reasoning goes, if "those people" were good at this kind of job, wouldn't we see more of them performing it? Two studies have provided evidence of the link between token status and stereotype threat. In one, laboratory experimenters found that token women showed lower performance than non-tokens only on a math task (a stereotyped domain) and not on a verbal task (a non-stereotyped domain) (Inzlicht & BenZeev, 2003). In the other, field researchers found that Black managers who were tokens in their work group reported higher levels of stereotype threat than non-tokens (Roberson, Deitch, Brief, & Block, 2003).

Thus, group representation can raise the relevance of the stereotype for performance. Work situations involving lone members of a social or demographic group are common. For example, in the field research described above, 18% of the Black managers were tokens in their work group (Roberson et al., 2003). Managers need to be aware of this effect of the environment and find ways to neutralize it.

In summary, these conditions make stereotype threat more likely for members of negatively stereotyped groups:

- The employee is invested in doing well, on:
- a difficult, stereotype relevant task, where:
- the context reinforces the stereotype.

When stereotype threat occurs, performance is disrupted. But the effects of stereotype threat go beyond short-term performance decrements. The Black managers who experienced stereotype threat in the field research said that they spent more time monitoring their performance (for example, by comparing themselves to peers) and were more likely to discount performance feedback that they received from the organization (Roberson et al., 2003). So, for example, a Black employee who is regularly exposed to stereotype threat about his intellectual ability might dismiss performance feedback from his White manager that would have helped him to meet organizational performance expectations and get on the promotion "fast track."

But maybe these responses are functional. If your manager holds a negative stereotype about you, maybe you *should* discount feedback from that person (or at least, take it with a large grain of salt). If you can't trust your manager, monitoring the performance of your peers might yield more credible information with which to assess your performance. And if stereotype threat causes people to work harder, couldn't that be a positive benefit? Earlier, we quoted Beyoncé Knowles as feeling like she had "something to prove." Beyoncé has clearly been able to channel those feelings in a positive way in order to become a successful performer. Maybe a strong motivation to disprove a negative stereotype about your group can increase persistence and determination to succeed. Research on achievement goals has shown that a desire to prove one's ability can be a powerful form of motivation (Elliott & Harackiewicz, 1996), most effective in improving performance and persistence on simple tasks that are familiar to the performer (Steele-Johnson, Beauregard, Hoover, & Schmidt, 2000; Vandewalle, 2001). If you know *how* to perform a task, this kind of motivation can help you to perform better. But remember the Black students in Steele and Aronson's research—the ones who spent a lot of time answering very few questions? Those students were very motivated, but they were working on very complex, challenging problems and their efforts did not pay off. This kind of motivation often works for you, but it can work against you.

Questions about whether employee responses to stereotype threat can be functional or potentially beneficial indicate that we need to know a lot more about the long-term consequences of repeated exposure to stereotype threat. To answer these questions, research has to study stereotype threat over time in real-world organizational settings. So far, the research suggests that repeated exposure to stereotype threat may have serious, and primarily negative, side effects. Stereotype threat is accompanied by physiological reactions such as an increase in blood pressure, leading researchers to speculate that long-term exposure to stereotype threat conditions might contribute to chronic health problems such as hypertension (Blascovich, Spencer, Quinn, & Steele, 2001). Stereotype threat is also associated with lower job satisfaction (Niemann & Dovidio, 1998; Roberson et al., 2003). Researchers have further suggested that repeated, regular exposure to stereotype threat may lead a person to disengage (or "disidentify") with the performance domain (Steele, 1997). That solo female in your engineering group may begin to think that an alternative career path might be preferable. This leads one to wonder whether long-term exposure to stereotype threat could be one cause of turnover for women and racial/ethnic minorities in professional and managerial jobs. Indeed, some studies have found that members of these groups leave jobs at a higher rate than White men (Hom, Roberson, & Ellis, 2007).

Fortunately, research on the conditions under which stereotype threat is most likely to occur also provides information about reducing the risk of stereotype threat. Recent studies have directly examined ways to reduce or eliminate stereotype threat by changing the conditions that produce the effect—in essence, interrupting the process. These studies are important because they point to some steps that can be taken by managers to lessen the possibility that stereotype threat operates for their employees. We now turn to specific strategies for reducing the likelihood of stereotype threat.

Interrupting the Stereotype Threat Process

Strategies for Reducing Stereotype Threat

We have mentioned that stereotype threat effects are strongest for people who are highly identified with the task domain. Researchers fear that over time, stereotyped people may find one way to reduce stereotype threat themselves—by disidentifying with the affected task domain. In other words, they break the psychological connection between their performance and their self-esteem so that doing well on that kind of task is less important. This is the only solution under the individual's control, but it is also perhaps the worst solution, costly for both the individual who gives up a valued part of the self, and for the organization that loses an engaged and motivated employee. Here we describe some alternatives to this worst case scenario—other strategies for reducing stereotype threat. These strategies, demonstrated to be effective in laboratory studies, all involve changing the conditions for stereotype threat. The strategies, and the points in the process at which they intervene, are shown in Figure 3.1.2.

Provide a Successful Task Strategy

We know that stereotype threat influences people only on very difficult tasks—those at the outer limits of ability and skill. Evidence suggests that stereotype threatened people seek to distance themselves from the stereotype by acting opposite to it (Aronson, 2002). They often put their noses to the grindstone, work harder and longer to prove the stereotype wrong—to show it does not apply to them. In the original study by Steele and Aronson, stereotype threatened Black students worked harder and more diligently at the task, expending more effort than the unthreatened. Unfortunately, working harder and more carefully didn't increase performance. The task they were working on was extremely difficult, right at the outer limit of their abilities. Effort *alone* couldn't boost performance—what the students needed was an effective strategy for solving the problems.

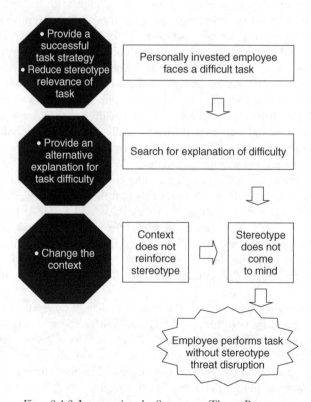

Figure 3.1.2 Interrupting the Stereotype Threat Process.

A recent study provided stereotype threatened participants with a strategy to successfully counteract the stereotype. In a negotiation task, women were explicitly told about gender stereotypes suggesting that women are less assertive than men and tend not to act in their own self-interest; these characteristics reduce their effectiveness in negotiations. The women in the study were able to counteract the stereotype by acting particularly assertively when making opening offers to their partners, and this strategy improved their performance in the negotiation. However, the women acted this way only when they were *explicitly* told about gender's effect on negotiation. The women already knew how to act assertively—all they needed to perform successfully was a cue that this context was one in which acting assertively was a good strategy (Kray et al., 2001).

This research suggests that one way to reduce stereotype threat is to teach affected employees behavioral strategies for improving performance and counteracting negative stereotypes. This intervention addresses task difficulty—one of the conditions for stereotype threat. Having good strategies available to cope with challenges makes the task seem less difficult and less frustrating. This research suggests that when using stretch assignments, managers should set goals, and also help employees develop strategies towards attaining them. The "sink or swim" attitude toward stretch assignments common in many organizations can be particularly detrimental for stereotype threatened individuals. If managers discuss and suggest task strategies to employees, stereotype threat should be reduced.

Reduce the Stereotype Relevance of the Task

We also know that stereotype threat happens when the stereotype is relevant to the task; when performance on a task is believed to reflect an ability or trait that differentiates stereotyped and non-stereotyped groups (e.g., women and men; Blacks and Whites). Several studies have eliminated stereotype threat effects by refuting or diminishing the stereotype relevance of the task. In one study, researchers asked men and women to take a difficult math test composed of items from the GRE exam. All participants were told that they were taking the math test as part of an effort to develop new testing procedures for the university. Half of the participants were also informed that this particular test had been shown not to produce gender differences—that men and women performed equally well. The other half were not given any information about gender differences. The researchers predicted that stereotype threat would operate when there was no information given about gender differences, because when labeled simply as a "math test," the gender stereotype that "women can't do math" would be relevant. However, being told explicitly that there were no gender differences would reduce the relevance of the stereotype to the task, and hence reduce stereotype threat. By presenting the test as one with no gender differences, the stereotype would be irrelevant to interpreting performance on the test. These results were confirmed: women underperformed relative to men in the "no information" (stereotype relevant) condition, but performed equally to men in the "no gender difference" (stereotype irrelevant) condition (Spencer et al., 1999).

Another study reduced the stereotype relevance of the task in a slightly different way, by emphasizing characteristics shared by both groups. Male and female college students participated in a negotiation exercise. For half of the participants, researchers made gender stereotypes relevant by saying that the most effective negotiators are "rational and assertive" rather than "emotional and passive" (cueing gender stereotypes). For the other half, researchers eliminated the relevance of the gender stereotype for performance. They told this half of the participants that "rational and assertive" people do better than "emotional and passive" individuals. But then they added, "people who are in competitive academic environments, like you, do exceptionally well in the negotiation. This is true for men and women alike." This description highlighted characteristics important for performance that are shared by both men and women, diminishing the stereotype relevance of the task. This strategy was also successful in decreasing stereotype threat and gender differences in performance (Kray et al., 2001).

These studies show that reducing the stereotype relevance of the task—one of the conditions for stereotype threat—is effective in removing stereotype threat. But is this a realistic strategy in organizations? In the laboratory, it is possible to label an unfamiliar task as one showing group differences or not. It is easy to manipulate participants' beliefs about whether a task reflects group differences when those participants have no prior experience with the task. The situation is different with real world tasks or jobs where employees and co-workers may have strong opinions about the types of people who do well in various jobs or roles. Consider technical or mathematical tasks. Belief in gender differences on such tasks is widespread (Brown & Josephs, 1999), so when faced with a technical or mathematical task, a woman may not believe a manager who says it does not reflect gender differences. It might be more effective for managers instead to use the strategy in the second experiment. For example, rather than try to discredit gender differences, one could make gender differences irrelevant by stressing *common* characteristics of employees that are relevant for performing the task. This could be done by identifying characteristics important for task success that are unlinked to group stereotypes. Perhaps a manager could inform all employees that they were hired precisely because they have the skills needed to do well. For example, "We have such good hiring procedures—the people who we bring in, both men and women, have the skills to perform well."

Provide an Alternative Explanation for Task Difficulty

Task difficulty is a trigger for stereotype threat because people try to explain their difficulty to themselves: on a stereotype relevant task, where the context reinforces the stereotype, they are more likely to think of the stereotype as a potential explanation. The resulting anxiety and distress then disrupts performance. Several studies have shown that by giving an explanation for task difficulty *besides* the stereotype, stereotype threat can be reduced.

In one study, men and women students who came to the laboratory were told they would take a math test being developed by the psychology department for placement purposes. Immediately after this general description, half of the students were asked to begin the test, and were given 20 minutes to complete 20 problems. The other half were told that there would be a practice session before the test, administered on a computer. The experimenter explained that this would help them to "warm up," allowing a better assessment of their true ability level on the actual test. However, when the experimenter turned on the computer, the screen was unreadable (the computer had been rigged). After fiddling with the knobs and controls to no avail, the experimenter then announced that the students would have to take the test without the benefit of warming up, and this extenuating circumstance would be noted on their answer sheets. The researchers designed this study because they reasoned that being denied the "warm up" opportunity would provide a viable alternative to the gender stereotype as an explanation for any experienced task difficulty, reducing stereotype threat effects for women. Results confirmed this: men's performance was not affected by the test conditions. However, the performance of women was greatly affected. Women performed better on the math test when they were denied their "warm up" opportunity (Brown & Josephs, 1999).

In another study, researchers induced stereotype threat for White men by heightening the salience of the stereotype that Whites have less natural athletic ability than Blacks. The researchers then informed half of these participants that the lab space where they would perform athletic tasks had recently been renovated, and that the lab administration wanted "to know if the new changes made research participants feel tense or uneasy." Because of this concern, the participants would be asked to rate the lab space and its effects on their emotions after the experiment (Stone, Lynch, Sjomeling, & Darley, 1999). This information provided participants with another explanation (the renovated lab space) for any anxiety they experienced during the task. White men who received this alternative explanation for poor performance performed better than those who did not.

Again, however effective these manipulations are in the laboratory, their feasibility for the work setting may be limited. Managers certainly shouldn't lie to their employees (as in the first study) to give them an excuse for task difficulty and poor performance. But managers could remind employees about real-life factors that might be constraining their performance (e.g., a difficult client, limited resources, or a tight deadline). Another feasible strategy for providing an alternative explanation comes from a third study. The experimenters induced stereotype threat for women using the usual setup—telling participants that they would be completing a standardized math test for a study of gender differences. One group received just these instructions. With another group, in addition to these instructions, the experimenters described the phenomenon of stereotype threat and said, ". . . if you are feeling anxious while taking this test, this anxiety could be the result of these negative [gender] stereotypes that are widely known in society and have nothing to do with your actual ability to do well" (Johns, Schmader, & Martens, 2005: 176). These instructions had a positive effect on test performance. Women underperformed on the math test relative to men when given only the "math test" description. When stereotype threat was explained and offered as a possible cause of their anxiety, the performance of men and women was similar.

Telling people who might be affected by stereotype threat about the phenomenon has some advantages. Stereotype threat is real, and its effects on performance are well-documented. You might think that explicitly raising the issue of stereotype threat with a potentially affected employee might make matters worse by drawing attention to the stereotype—better to keep quiet and act like it doesn't exist. But instead the opposite appears to be true. Telling employees that you know stereotype threat can happen, and that they should be aware of it, gives them a different attribution for their difficulty and anxiety (it's not the stereotype, it's the stereotype *threat*).

Change the Context

The context is another condition that can affect the likelihood of stereotype threat. We discussed how one aspect of the context—the diversity of people performing the job—can reinforce or diminish the relevance of stereotypes. The research showing that tokens are more likely to experience stereotype threat also suggests a way to reduce stereotype threat: change the context by removing people from token situations.

This strategy may work in the laboratory, but how can managers realistically achieve this goal? In organizations, the composition of work groups is already constrained by employee skills, task interdependence, and other factors. Managers can't shuffle employees around based on their demographics to avoid token situations. However, several studies have changed the context using another strategy that does not involve changing the demographic make-up of the work group: presenting a role model who contradicts the stereotype. In one study, participants were administered a difficult math test by either a male or female experimenter. The experimenters gave identical instructions designed to accomplish two goals: 1) induce stereotype threat in the women by presenting the test as diagnostic of ability; and 2) create perceptions of the experimenter's competence in math. Scores on the math test showed that women underperformed relative to men only when the test was administered by a male experimenter. A follow-up study revealed that it was not the physical presence of the female experimenter, but rather her perceived competence that protected the women from stereotype threat. Seeing a woman who was competent in the math domain boosted women's beliefs in their own mathematical abilities and maintained their performance (Marx & Roman, 2002).

Other researchers found similar results when role models were presented in a different way. One study asked participants to read and critique four biographical essays. Half of the participants read essays concerning successful women in a variety of fields such as medicine and law. The other half read essays concerning successful corporations. Then all the participants completed a math test administered by a male experimenter. Results indicated that the role model manipulation reduced stereotype threat: Women scored worse than men on the test when they had read about successful corporations, but women scored at the same level as men when they had read about successful women (McIntyre, Paulson, & Lord, 2003).

These studies suggest that managers may be able to change the context for stereotyped employees by boosting the salience and visibility of role models. Note that in the "essay" study, the physical presence of a role model was not necessary—what was important was that the competence of the role model was salient. This strategy could be feasibly implemented in organizations. Managers can increase access to role models by encouraging employee participation in mentoring programs, professional associations, and employee network groups (Friedman & Holtom, 2002; Friedman, Kane, & Cornfield, 1998). If managers maintain a diverse network of associates themselves, they can be more aware of potential role models for all of their employees, and attempt to connect people.

Implications for Diversity Management

Would a greater focus on reducing stereotype threat add anything new to diversity management? We think it would. Existing diversity management programs tend to have two major objectives (Kellough & Naff, 2004): One goal is to change managers' *attitudes*—to reduce negative attitudes, stereotypes, and prejudice against members of different groups. Much diversity training is geared toward this goal. A second related goal is to change managers' *behaviors*—how they select, appraise, and develop employees (Brief & Barsky, 2000). For example, managers are encouraged, and often required, to specify explicit behavioral and performance standards for promotion or advancement, and to adhere to these in making decisions. These are important objectives. However, these objectives ignore two realities. First, changing attitudes and reducing stereotypes is a long term endeavor. Stereotypes are embedded in the culture, and reinforced outside of the work setting (Brief, 1998). Until society changes, stereotypes about different groups will remain. Even if a particular manager is unprejudiced, others in the workgroup may not be, and employees may still feel stereotype threat. While we need to try to reduce stereotypes, in the foreseeable future we have to deal with existing attitudes, and try to reduce the *impact* of stereotypes on affected employees. Second, while increasing the objectivity of measurement and decisions is necessary, the presence of stereotype threat means that performance *itself* may convey biased information about a person's true ability. So the well-intentioned manager who relies on objective performance data without understanding the impact of stereotype threat will still unfairly underestimate performance. Focusing on stereotype threat takes these realities into account, and highlights two principles that are currently downplayed in most diversity management efforts:

1. **Acknowledge stereotypes and address them directly.** Unfortunately, the goal of eliminating stereotypes from organizational decision making sometimes leads organizational members to deny their existence. People sometimes confuse stereotype awareness with stereotype endorsement (Adler, 2002). Yet research has shown that even unprejudiced people are familiar with the content of common stereotypes and can easily describe what prejudiced people believe about members of certain groups (Devine, 1989). Putting our strategies into action means that a manager has to honestly acknowledge the stereotypes that exist. The manager who acknowledges the existence and potential impact of stereotypes does not have to endorse or support those stereotypes. Only a manager who acknowledges stereotypes can acknowledge the opportunity for stereotype threat and take corrective action.

The strategies for reducing stereotype threat further imply that managers should talk explicitly about stereotypes with their potentially threatened employees (Kray et al., 2001). Rarely are stereotypes directly named and described—particularly to the affected parties. Although many people (managers and subordinates alike) might see this as a risky step, explicit discussion about stereotypes can be useful in reducing their impact. If supervisors and subordinates trust one another, it can be a good strategy. David Thomas' comparison of successful and plateaued non-White executives demonstrated that successful executives found mentors early in their careers who were able to talk directly about race and the challenges it presented (Thomas, 2001; Thomas & Gabarro, 1999). Such openness about the existence of stereotypes and stereotype threat provides employees with alternative explanations for task difficulty and also may decrease concerns that they will be judged in light of the stereotype. Many managers would shy away from such a frank discussion, but the evidence says that evasion is not always helpful. Honest engagement of the problem and an exploration of action strategies to counteract perceptions can increase trust, reduce stereotype threat, and improve performance. How can managers be encouraged to take these risks? Perhaps diversity training should focus on providing managers with the skills and confidence to talk about stereotypes with their employees.

2. **Shift the focus from the manager to the environment.** Diversity management programs tend to focus on the manager as the target of change. Diversity training programs, for example, are designed to change managerial attitudes and behavior (Bendick, Egan, & Lofhjelm, 2001). In contrast, the strategies for reducing stereotype threat focus on the *environment* as the target of change. In other words, changing the conditions that lead to stereotype threat. Managers need to attend to managing the environment and reducing the cues that signal to employees that stereotypes are operating.

Effective diversity management has always meant creating an environment where all can succeed (Cox, 1994; Thomas, 1991). Knowledge of stereotype threat increases our understanding of what that really means. It is more than being personally nonprejudiced and unbiased. It means actively reducing cues that limit the contributions of *all* employees. Only in this way can the benefits of diversity be realized.

Acknowledgments

We wish to thank Caryn Block and Benjamin Galvin for their helpful comments on an earlier draft of this paper, and Jeanne Tao for her assistance with the figures.

References

Adler, N. J. (2002). *International dimensions of organizational behavior*, Fourth Edition. Cincinnati OH: South-Western Publishing.

Aronson, J. (2002). Stereotype threat: Contending and coping with unnerving expectations. In J. Aronson (Ed.) *Improving academic achievement: Impact of psychological factors on education* (pp. 279–301). San Francisco: Elsevier.

Aronson, J., Lustina, M. J., Good, C., Keough, K., Steele, C. M., & Brown, J. (1999). When White men can't do math: Necessary and sufficient factors in stereotype threat. *Journal of Experimental Social Psychology, 35*, 29–46.

Aronson, J., Quinn, D. M., & Spencer, S. J. (1998). Stereotype threat and the academic underperformance of minorities and women. In Swim, J. K. & Stangor, C. (Eds.) *Prejudice: The target's perspective* (pp. 83–103). New York: Academic Press.

Beilock, S. L., & Carr, T. H. (2005). When high-powered people fail: Working memory and "choking under pressure" in math. *Psychological Science, 16*, 101–105.

Bendick, M., Egan, M. L., & Lofhjelm, S. M. (2001). Workforce diversity training: From anti-discrimination compliance to organizational development. *Human Resource Planning, 24*, 10–36.

Blank, R., & Shipp, S. (1994). *Voices of diversity: Real people talk about problems and solutions in a workplace where everyone is not alike.* New York: AMACOM.

Blascovich, J., Spencer, S. J., Quinn, D., & Steele, C. (2001). African Americans and high blood pressure: The role of stereotype threat. *Psychological Science, 12*, 225–229.

Brief, A. P. (1998). *Attitudes in and around organizations.* Thousand Oaks, CA: Sage.

Brief, A. P., & Barsky, A. (2000). Establishing a climate for diversity: The inhibition of prejudiced reactions in the workplace. *Research in Personnel and Human Resources Management, 19*, 91–129.

Brown, R. P., & Josephs, R. A. (1999). A burden of proof: Stereotype relevance and gender differences in math performance. *Journal of Personality and Social Psychology, 76*, 246–257.

Cadinu, M., Maass, A., Frigerio, S., Impagliazzo, L., & Latinotti, S. (2003). Stereotype threat: The effect of expectancy on performance. *European Journal of Social Psychology, 33*, 267–285.

Chandler, M. (1999, October 4). *Secrets of the SAT* (FRONTLINE, #1802). New York and Washington, DC: Public Broadcasting Service.

Chung-Herrera, B. G., & Lankau, M. J. (2005). Are we there yet? An assessment of fit between stereotypes of minority managers and the successful-manager prototype. *Journal of Applied Social Psychology, 35*, 2029–2056.

Cocchiara, F. K., & Quick, J. C. (2004). The negative effects of positive stereotypes: Ethnicity-related stressors and implications on organizational health. *Journal of Organizational Behavior, 25*, 781–785.

Cox, T. H. Jr. (1994). *Cultural diversity in organizations: Theory, research, and practice.* San Francisco, CA: Berrett-Koehler.

Devine, P. G. (1989). Stereotypes and prejudice: Their automatic and controlled components. *Journal of Personality and Social Psychology, 56*, 5–18.

Dickins, F., & Dickens, J. B. (1991). *The Black manager: Making it in the corporate world.* New York: AMACOM.

Elliott, A. J., & Harackiewicz, J. M. (1996). Approach and avoidance achievement goals and intrinsic motivation: A mediational analysis. *Journal of Personality and Social Psychology, 70*, 461–475.

Frantz, C. M., Cuddy, A. J. C., Burnett, M., Ray, H., & Hart, A. (2004). A threat in the computer: The race implicit association test as a stereotype threat experience. *Personality and Social Psychology Bulletin, 30*, 1611–1614.

Friedman, R. A., & Holtom, B. (2002). The effects of network groups on minority employee turnover intentions. *Human Resource Management, 41,* 405–421.

Friedman, R. A., Kane, M., & Cornfield, D. B. (1998). Social support and career optimism: Examining the effectiveness of network groups among Black managers. *Human Relations, 51,* 1155–1177.

Greenberg, J. (1996). *Managing behavior in organizations: Science in service to practice.* Upper Saddle River, NJ: Prentice Hall.

Greengard, S. (2003). Gimme attitude. *Workforce, 82,* 56–60.

Habermas, T., & Bluck, S. (2000). Getting a life: The emergence of the life story in adolescence. *Psychological Bulletin, 12,* 748–769.

Hackman, J. R., & Oldham, G. R. (1980). *Work redesign.* Reading, MA: Addison-Wesley.

Hansen, F. (2003). Diversity's business case doesn't add up. *Workforce, 82,* 28–32.

Heilman, M. E., Block, C. J., Martell, R. F., & Simon, M. C. (1989). Has anything changed? Current characterizations of men, women, and managers. *Journal of Applied Psychology, 74,* 935–942.

Hite, L. M. (2004). Black and White women managers: Access to opportunity. *Human Resource Development Quarterly, 15,* 131–146.

Hom, P. W., Roberson, L., & Ellis, A. D. (2007). *Challenging conventional wisdom about who quits: Revelations from corporate America.* Manuscript submitted for publication, Arizona State University.

Inzlicht, M., & Ben Zeev, T. (2003). Do high-achieving female students underperform in private? The implications of threatening environments on intellectual processing. *Journal of Educational Psychology, 95,* 796–805.

Jackson, S. E., Brett, J. F., Sessa, V. I., Cooper, D. M., Julin, J. A., & Peyronnin, K. (1991). Some differences make a difference: Individual dissimilarity and group heterogeneity as correlates of recruitment, promotions, and turnover. *Journal of Applied Psychology, 76,* 675–689.

Jehn, K. A., Neale, M., & Northcraft, G. (1999). Why differences make a difference: A field study of diversity, conflict, and performance in workgroups. *Administrative Science Quarterly, 44,* 741–763.

Johns, M., Schmader, T., & Martens, A. (2005). Knowing is half the battle: Teaching stereotype threat as a means of improving women's math performance. *Psychological Science, 16,* 175–179.

Kanter, R. (1977). *Men and women of the organization.* New York: Basic Books.

Kellough, J. E., & Naff, K. C. (2004). Responding to a wake up call: An examination of Federal Agency Diversity Management Programs. *Administration & Society, 36,* 62–91.

Kochan, T., Bezrukova, K., Ely, R., Jackson, S., Joshi, A., Jehn, K., Leonare, J., Levine, D., & Thomas, D. (2003). The effects of diversity on business performance: Report of the diversity research network. *Human Resource Management, 42,* 3–21.

Kray, L. J., Galinsky, A. D., & Thompson, L. (2002). Reversing the gender gap in negotiations: An exploration of stereotype regeneration. *Organizational Behavior and Human Decision Processes, 87,* 386–409.

Kray, L. J., Thompson, L., & Galinsky, A. (2001). Battle of the sexes: Gender stereotype confirmation and reactance in negotiations. *Journal of Personality and Social Psychology, 80,* 942–958.

Marx, D. M., & Roman, J. S. (2002). Female role models: Protecting women's math test performance. *Personality and Social Psychology Bulletin, 28,* 1183–1193.

McCauley, C., Eastman, L., & Ohlott, P. (1995). Linking management selection and development through stretch assignments. *Human Resource Management, 34,* 93–115.

McIntyre, R. B., Paulson, R. M., & Lord, C. G. (2003). Alleviating women's mathematics stereotype threat through salience of group achievements. *Journal of Experimental Social Psychology, 39,* 83–90.

Niemann, Y. F., & Dovidio, J. F. (1998). Relationship of solo status, academic rank, and perceived distinctiveness to job satisfaction of racial/ethnic minorities. *Journal of Applied Psychology, 83,* 55–71.

Noe, R. A. (1999). *Employee training and development.* Boston, MA: Irwin McGraw-Hill.

Parks-Yancy, R. (2006). The effects of social group membership and social capital resources on career. *Journal of Black Studies, 36,* 515–545.

Personal blog. (2005, June 3). Available at: http://www.big fatblog.com/archives/001607.php.

Reio, T. G. Jr., & Callahan, J. L. (2004). Affect, curiosity, and socialization-related learning: A path analysis of antecedents to job performance. *Journal of Business and Psychology, 19,* 3–22.

Rice, F. (1996). Denny's changes its spots. *Fortune, 133,* 133–138.

Roberson, L., Deitch, E., Brief, A. P., & Block, C. J. (2003). Stereotype threat and feedback seeking in the workplace. *Journal of Vocational Behavior, 62,* 176–188.

Robinson, G., & Dechant, K. (1997). Building a business case for diversity. *Academy of Management Executive, 11,* 21–31.

Smith, J. L. (2004). Understanding the process of stereotype threat: A review of mediational variables and new performance goal directions. *Educational Psychology Review, 16,* 177–206.

Spencer, S. J., Steele, C. M., & Quinn, D. M. (1999). Stereotype threat and women's math performance. *Journal of Experimental Social Psychology, 35,* 4–28.

Steele, C. M. (1997). A threat in the air: How stereotypes shape intellectual identity and performance. *American Psychologist, 52,* 613–629.

Steele, C. M., & Aronson, J. (1995). Stereotype threat and the intellectual test performance of African Americans. *Journal of Personality and Social Psychology, 85,* 440–452.

Steele, C. M., Spencer, S. J., & Aronson, J. (2002). Contending with group image: The psychology of stereotype and social identity threat. *Advances in Experimental Social Psychology, 34,* 379–440.

Steele-Johnson, D., Beauregard, R. S., Hoover, P. B., & Schmidt, A. M. (2000). Goal orientation and task demand effects on motivation, affect, and performance. *Journal of Applied Psychology, 85,* 724–738.

Stone, J., Lynch, C. L., Sjomeling, M., & Darley, J. M. (1999). Stereotype threat effects on Black and White athletic performance. *Journal of Personality and Social Psychology, 77,* 1213–1227.

Thomas, D. A. (2001). The truth about mentoring minorities: Race matters. *Harvard Business Review, 79,* 98–107.

Thomas, D. A., & Ely, R. J. (1996). Making differences matter: A new paradigm for managing diversity. *Harvard Business Review, 74,* 79–91.

Thomas, D. A., & Gabarro, J. J. (1999). *Breaking through: The making of minority executives in corporate America.* Boston, MA: Harvard Business School Press.

Thomas, R. R. Jr. (1991). *Beyond race and gender: Unleashing the power of your total work force by managing diversity.* New York: AMACOM.

Tomkiewicz, J., Brenner, O. C., & Adeyemi-Bello, T. (1998). The impact of perceptions and stereotypes on the managerial mobility of African Americans. *Journal of Social Psychology, 138,* 88–92.

Tsui, A., Egan, T., & O'Reilly, C. (1992). Being different: Relational demography and organizational attachment. *Administrative Science Quarterly, 37,* 549–579.

Verbeke, W., & Bagozzi, R. (2000). Sales call anxiety: Exploring what it means when fear rules a sales encounter. *Journal of Marketing, 64,* 88–102.

Vandewalle, D. (2001). Goal orientation: Why wanting to look successful doesn't always lead to success. *Organizational Dynamics, 30,* 162–171.

Yerkes, R. M., & Dodson, J. D. (1908). The relation of strength of stimulus to rapidity of habit formation. *Journal of Comparative Neurology, 18,* 459–482.

Zenger, T., & Lawrence, B. (1989). Organizational demography: The differential effects of age and tenure distributions on technical communications. *Academy of Management Journal, 32,* 353–376.

3.2   IMPLICATIONS OF METHODOLOGICAL ADVANCES FOR THE PRACTICE OF PERSONNEL SELECTION

How Practitioners Benefit From Meta-Analysis

Huy Le, In-Sue Oh, Jonathan Shaffer, and Frank Schmidt

Executive Overview

We discuss how meta-analysis, a method for synthesizing research findings, can meaningfully impact personnel selection practices. Specifically, we review important changes in professional and legal practices from the past 30 years resulting from meta-analytic findings. The implications of using meta-analysis methods for evaluating utilities of selection procedures and for assessing relative predictive capabilities of three popular selection tools (general mental ability tests, personality tests, and structured interviews) are further discussed. Based on these implications, we propose that meta-analysis can play an important role in bridging the gap between academic research and organizational practices.

It is well-known that there is a gap between knowledge accumulated from academic research findings and the applications of human resources practices (Anderson, Herriot, & Hodgkinson, 2001; Rousseau, 2006; Rynes, Colbert, & Brown, 2002). Practitioners are often reluctant to adopt solutions informed by organizational and psychological research in their practices. Several recent investigations (Rynes et al., 2002; Schmidt, 2006) indicate that the gap is especially large in the area of personnel selection, where human resource managers tend to favor discredited selection approaches that have little validity (e.g., years of education, values and interests; Schmidt & Hunter, 1998), while failing to apply scientifically established valid employment selection tools (e.g., cognitive ability tests,[1] integrity tests; Schmidt & Hunter, 1998).

Researchers have offered many explanations for the existence of this troubling gap. Some have "blamed" the consumers of research for lacking adequate training or the fact that HR practitioners have such tremendous workloads and do not have the time to read academic journals (Klehe, 2004). Others have found problems within the nature of academic research, arguing that research articles are needlessly complicated and difficult to understand, that the topics of academic interest are not directly relevant to problems faced by organizations, and that seemingly inconsistent, non-replicable results reduce the credibility of research findings. Also contributing to the gap between researchers and practitioners has been the belief that practices and problems associated with an organization are specific and unique to that organization and cannot be properly addressed by general research findings (Rousseau, 2006; Schmidt & Hunter, 1998). While practitioners and researchers will need to work together to bridge the research-practice gap, recent research developments may eventually help in this area (Rousseau, 2006; Rynes et al. 2002). Ironically, the developments that hold the most promise for making research findings more comprehensible and convincing to practitioners are likely to be those involving methodological advancements, especially those occurring in the area of meta-analysis, a method for quantitatively combining and summarizing research results (Rynes et al., 2002). This is rather paradoxical because such methodological advancements are often deemed inaccessible to outsiders.

Historically, the most common method for summarizing research findings has been qualitative review. To perform a qualitative review, a researcher gathers all available studies for a particular topic and inspects them in an attempt to identify common themes among the results. More often than not, the only common theme found among individual studies is that their results are highly conflicting. Often, qualitative reviews end with the suggestion that additional studies be conducted so that conclusions may be drawn in the future. The inability of qualitative reviews to answer broad research questions has been one of the major factors making academic research confusing to practitioners and researchers alike.

Meta-analysis addresses the impression of inconsistency in research findings by providing unequivocal answers to the questions that traditionally have been marred by conflicting research outcomes. Thus, as surprising as it might sound, meta-analysis can facilitate communication between researchers and practitioners. This is because meta-analysis allows general conclusions and principles to be drawn from a previously overwhelming body of organizational and psychological research. In this paper, we describe the development of meta-analysis and discuss its implications for organizational practices. We start by briefly reviewing the evolution of meta-analysis methods in industrial and organizational psychology.

How Has Meta-Analysis Changed the Landscape of Personnel Selection Practices? Past Practices

The basic purpose of an employment test is to predict the future job performance of job applicants. Beginning in the 1920s, when employment tests were first introduced, researchers often found that the same test had different predictive power for identical or similar jobs across organizations (Ghiselli, 1966). That is, a particular test seemed to predict job performance in some organizations, but not in other organizations. Typically, researchers found that a given selection test was useful for predicting performance in about 50% of situations, and not useful in the other 50% of situations. The same pattern of variation in predictive capability was often found from one job to another even within the same organization. As a result of the inconsistent study results, researchers at that time concluded the following: (a) Employment testing is organization-specific—a test may predict performance for a job in one organization but not for the same job in another organization, and (b) employment testing is job-specific—a test may predict performance for one job, but not for another job even within the same organization (Schmidt & Hunter, 1981).

Researchers sought an explanation for the vast differences between studies and eventually developed the "situational specificity hypothesis." According to this hypothesis, each individual work situation includes subtle yet significantly different characteristics in terms of the nature of job performance which cause the predictive capability of a given employment test to fluctuate from very low in one situation to very high in another situation (McDaniel, 2007; Schmidt & Hunter, 1981; Schmidt & Hunter, 1998). The differences in situations across organizations and/or jobs were believed to be so subtle as to be undetectable through traditional job analysis techniques. Therefore, researchers concluded that organizations needed to conduct separate prediction studies for virtually all jobs in their organization in order to determine what type of selection method was the most predictive of job performance for each job (Ghiselli, 1966; Schmidt & Hunter, 1981). By the 1970s, the situational specificity hypothesis was accepted by many researchers and practitioners as a well-established fact even though there was no empirical evidence to support the position (McDaniel, 2007; Schmidt & Hunter, 2003).

Belief in the situational specificity hypothesis led many organizations to hire industrial and organizational psychologists to perform prediction studies for their organizations. If an organization was large and had multiple offices or factories in various locations, each local study could yield a different set of "optimal" employment tests. Both practitioners and researchers alike were understandably confused and frustrated by the inability of research to find conclusive answers about the predictive capabilities of employment tests. The situational specificity hypothesis was seen by some, and rightly so, as an example of the failure of research to address broad organizational needs. This conception has helped to alienate academic research from real-world human resources practices.

The Meta-Analytic Approach

The situational specificity hypothesis was first attacked in 1976. Schmidt, Hunter, and Urry (1976) showed that most employment test studies lacked large enough sample sizes to yield reliable results. They went on to show that holding the predictive capability of a given employment test constant across all studies and altering only the sample size of the studies caused the results to change. Their calculations showed that sampling error had led to erroneous performance predictions in about 50% of the jobs in their analysis. Inspired by this finding, Schmidt and Hunter (1977) developed analytic methods which are now generally known as meta-analysis. Using meta-analysis, they tested their hypothesis that the variation in performance predictions across situations for the same job could be largely accounted for by study imperfections such as sampling error, and variations in measurement errors and degrees of range restriction. Meta-analytic methods thus would enable researchers to "correct" for most major imperfections, disentangling their effects from the real effects underlying variations across studies, thereby providing more accurate estimates of predictive power.

Early meta-analytic prediction studies focused on tests of general mental ability (GMA) (Pearlman, Schmidt, & Hunter, 1980; Schmidt, Gast-Rosenberg, & Hunter, 1980; Schmidt & Hunter, 1977; Schmidt, Hunter, Pearlman, & Shane, 1979). Schmidt, Hunter, and colleagues demonstrated a number of things: (a) that GMA tests are excellent predictors of performance on the job and in training for all jobs in all settings, (b) that GMA tests predict equally and fairly for minority and majority applicants, and (c) that the situational specificity hypothesis was completely false. Though it initially met with some objections and doubts, those doubts were soon dispelled (Schmidt, Hunter, Pearlman, & Hirsh et al., 1985). Meta-analysis has since been applied to a wide variety of selection procedures, including work sample tests, assessment centers, evaluations of education and experience, integrity tests, employment interviews, job knowledge tests, bio-data measures, personality tests, and college grade point average.

The proven utility of meta-analysis has influenced policy makers. In the early 1980s, the US Department of Labor launched the most large-scale and ambitious meta-analysis to date, revisiting an immense amount of data from the US Employment Service's General Aptitude Test Battery (GATB) (Hunter, 1983). After reducing the 12 GATB subtests into three broad abilities and classifying all jobs into five complexity levels in terms of information processing demands, Hunter found that the higher the complexity level of a job, the greater was the predictive power of GMA for that job. In short, Hunter empirically proved that job complexity levels caused variation in the predictive capability of GMA tests and that GMA is a robust predictor of job performance across all job complexity levels (cf. Hunter, 1986; Schmidt, 2002). This finding has now been well accepted. Wilk and Cappelli (2003), in a study examining employers' decisions based on national probability data from over 3,000 firms, found that "as complexity of work increases, firms use more selection methods and use selection methods that capture the applicant's capability to do the work" (p. 199), suggesting that managers understand that the importance of measuring ability in hiring increases as job complexity increases.

Findings obtained using meta-analysis have increasingly gained acceptance in the courts (Schmidt, 2002). There are two noteworthy cases from the 1980s—Bernard v. Gulf Oil Corp. (1980) and Taylor v. James River Corp. (1989)—in which the court gave deference to meta-analytically derived evidence (McDaniel, 2007). One recent and significant case is US Department of Justice v. City of Torrance, CA (1996; Schmidt & Hunter, 2003). The court's rejection of the Department of Justice's challenge to the Torrance police and firefighter tests appears to be based mostly on the court's acceptance of the meta-analytic findings regarding the predictive capability of these employment tests. In addition to US court cases, the use of meta-analysis as the basis for selection systems was upheld in Canada in 1987 (e.g., Maloley v. Canadian Civil Service Commission; Schmidt & Hunter, 2003). A recent review of the relative frequency of litigation associated with nine selection procedures (Terpstra, Mohamed, & Kethley, 1999) found that procedures backed by meta-analytic evidence are less likely to be challenged and are more likely to prevail in US Federal courts.

Applications of meta-analysis have expanded to other research areas beyond personnel selection. For example, researchers have used meta-analysis to examine the relationships between job satisfaction and job performance (Judge, Thoresen, Bono, & Patton, 2001), job performance and turnover (McEvoy & Cascio, 1987), and the traits that help make a person a successful leader (Judge, Bono, Ilies, & Gerhardt, 2002). Meta-analysis has radically changed how researchers understand, analyze, and interpret their research findings. By means of meta-analysis, researchers are able to provide more conclusive answers to organizational issues and phenomena, which, in turn, make research findings more understandable to research consumers. Though there are still lags between research findings and the adoption of such findings by practitioners, meta-analysis has played, and will continue to play, an important role in connecting research and practice. Already the method has contributed significantly to improving the image of academic research among organizational practitioners.

The Economic Implications of Meta-Analytic Findings

Is meta-analysis simply the brainchild of disconnected statisticians, or does the technique offer real and measurable value to organizations? To answer this question, we discuss the role that meta-analysis plays in ascertaining the economic impact of employee selection. First, we explain how to calculate the tangible, economic value—the *utility*—of a selection method, and then we compare the relative values of several widely accepted selection tests.

Calculating the Utility of a Selection Method

Predicting the future performance of job applicants has important implications for any organization, since the difference between the economic value of the work output of high

Table 3.2.1 Per Hire Utility Estimates Under Two Selection Ratio Conditions

Job Complexity	Annual Salary	SD of Job Performance	r_{xy}[a]	Utility of Selection Method .70 Selection Ratio	.30 Selection Ratio
High	$120,000	$48,000	.73	$17,520	$40,997
Medium	50,000	20,000	.66	6,600	15,444
Low	16,000	6,400	.39	1,248	2,920

[a] Estimates taken from Hunter, Schmidt, and Le (2006).

performers and that of low performers is significant. When job performance is measured as the dollar value of work output, the practical value of a selection method can be estimated by using Brogden's basic utility equation (Brogden, 1949):

$$SD_y \, \bar{Z}_x \, r_{xy} = \bar{U}$$

In order to calculate the utility of a selection method ($\bar{U}$), three pieces of information are needed—the dollar value of the standard deviation of job performance (SD_y), the average standardized score on the selection method of applicants that are hired ($\bar{Z}_x$), and the predictive power of the selection method in question (r_{xy}).[2] Previous research has shown that there is considerable variance in work output among employees across all jobs and has indicated that a conservative estimate for that variance, labeled here as the standard deviation of job performance, is 40% of the average salary of the job in question (Schmidt, Hunter, Outerbridge, & Trattner, 1979). Therefore, if the average salary of a job is $50,000, SD_y is at least $20,000. $\bar{Z}_x$ is dependent on selection ratio, which is the ratio of the number of selected applicants to the total number of applicants. As the selection ratio decreases, $\bar{Z}_x$ increases. Selection ratios reported in real world settings typically range from .30 to .70 (Schmidt & Hunter, 1998). If an organization's selection ratio is .70 (the top seven of every ten applicants are hired), then $\bar{Z}_x$ = .50. If applicants that score at the 70th percentile or higher on the selection method are hired (a selection ratio of .30), then $\bar{Z}_x$ = 1.17. The final component of the utility equation, the predictive power of the selection method, is usually found in the research literature or from the publishers' manuals for a particular selection test. It is important to note that the utility equation is a product of three variables and that a change in any one of the three variables results in a change in the overall dollar value of the selection process. One should also note that the relationship between the three components of the equation and the final utility estimate is linear. Thus, a change in one of the components of the equation results in a commensurate change in utility. For example, if, holding other factors constant, the predictive power of a personnel selection method were to increase by 25%, then the utility of the selection process for that job would also increase by 25%.

In order to illustrate the practical implications of meta-analysis, consider the findings of Hunter and his colleagues (Hunter, Schmidt, & Le, 2006) in terms of their effects on utility estimates. Using the US Employment Service database, they analyzed the predictive power (r_{xy}) of tests of GMA by applying the most accurate meta-analysis methods currently available. Based on their findings, Table 3.2.1 shows the utility of GMA for two different selection ratios at three different levels of job complexity, using hypothetical annual salaries for each job complexity level.

As seen in Table 3.2.1, if the organization in this example has a selection ratio of .70, then the estimated utility of using GMA tests to select employees (as opposed to using no selection tests at all) for high complexity jobs such as a vice president of manufacturing is $17,520; the utility for medium complexity jobs such as a first-line supervisor is $6,600; and the utility for low complexity jobs such as a janitor is $1,248. If the organization instead adopts a selection ratio of .30, then the utility of using GMA tests to select employees more than doubles for all job complexity levels. For high complexity jobs the utility increases to $40,997, for medium complexity jobs it increases to $15,444, and for low complexity jobs it increases to $2,920.

Precisely speaking, the reader should note that the utility estimates presented to this point are actually incomplete. The results that we have presented thus far consider the hiring of a single employee for one year. To determine the overall utility of the GMA tests, one must take into account the total number of workers hired, the number of years that each worker stays with the organization, and the cost of administering GMA tests to job applicants (Schmidt, Mack, & Hunter, 1984). The final utility equation then becomes:

$$\bar{T} N_s\, r_{xy}\, SD_y\, \bar{Z}_x - C = \bar{U}$$

In this new equation, $\bar{T}$ is the average number of years that new hires remain on the job, N_s is the number of people hired each year. Thus, if an organization hires a large number of employees on a regular basis, the predictive power of the organization's selection methods becomes absolutely crucial. C is the total cost of administering GMA tests to the job applicants. Because the overall cost of administering selection tests is usually relatively small, for the sake of clarity we assume that C is zero in each of our hypothetical examples.

The above example is not intended to highlight the importance of GMA as a predictor of job performance. This is already well established in industrial and organizational psychology (Hunter and Hunter, 1984; Hunter, 1986; Schmidt, 2002; Schmidt & Hunter, 2004). Instead, here we wish to draw attention to the fact that the economic value of a selection method can be quickly and accurately calculated by applying meta-analytic estimates of its predictive power to the utility equation.

Comparing the Relative Predictive Power and Utility of Three Popular Selection Methods

The development of meta-analysis has enabled researchers in the field of personnel selection to quantitatively combine research findings from a broad range of selection methods, thereby allowing them to put side by side the predictive capabilities and economic values of the most widely used selection tools to determine which are the most effective. To follow, we will compare the predictive capability of GMA to two other popular selection tools: employment interviews and personality assessments.

Employment interviews are among the most frequently used personnel selection methods (Dipboye, 1994; 1997). The predictive capability of employment interviews has been established through a number of meta-analyses (Huffcut & Arthur, 1994; McDaniel, Whetzel, Schmidt, & Maurer, 1994). According to these meta-analyses, the two major types of interviews, job-related structured versus job-related unstructured, have different validities for predicting future job performance. It is generally accepted that structured interviews predict job performance better than do unstructured interviews (McDaniel et al., 1994).

Another popular selection tool is the personality assessment. Barrick and Mount (1991) showed that certain personality traits, specifically Conscientiousness, predict job performance across all types of jobs. Measures of Conscientiousness capture, in part, an individual's tendency to be dependable, hard working, and to strive for achievement. Many practitioners believe that the predictive capability of personality is superior to that of GMA (Rynes et al., 2002). This belief is very intuitively appealing—almost everyone can recall an example of a highly intelligent but lazy employee, or an employee of average intelligence who excels in their profession through hard work and determination—but has no empirical basis.

Meta-analysis allows us to compare the relative predictive power of these selection tools and calculate the economic values of each tool. Figure 3.2.1 shows the most current estimates of the predictive capabilities of assessments of Conscientiousness, structured interviews, GMA tests, and the combination of all three methods used simultaneously. Note that although most practitioners believe that Conscientiousness is a better predictor than is GMA, Conscientiousness is actually much less effective than employment interviews or

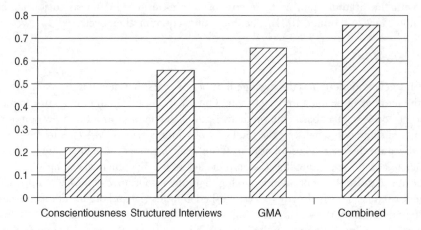

Figure 3.2.1 Meta-analytically derived correlations between selection methods and job performance.

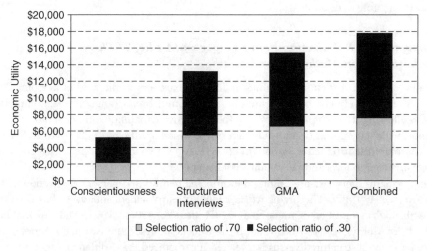

Figure 3.2.2 Per Hire Utility of Selection Methods under the Conditions of Two Different Selection Ratios.

GMA tests. To be precise, employment interviews and GMA tests are 2.55 and 3 times more effective than assessments of Conscientiousness for predicting job performance, respectively. Combining all three selection methods yields the highest estimates of predictive capability. The predictive power of the combination of the three selection methods is 1.15 times higher than that of GMA tests, 1.36 times higher than that of employment interviews, and 3.45 times higher than that of Conscientiousness assessments.

Using the meta-analytic estimates of r_{xy} presented in Figure 3.2.1, the utility equation can be applied to each selection method. For the sake of simplicity, in this example we consider only medium complexity jobs, which constitute approximately 60% of the jobs in the US economy (Hunter & Hunter, 1984), and we assume the same $50,000 salary that was used in our earlier example. Figure 3.2.2 shows the utility estimates for Conscientiousness, structured employment interviews, GMA tests, and the combination of all three selection methods.

In this hypothetical example, for an organization whose selection ratio is .70, the average annual increase in work output per employee is $2,200 when assessments of Conscientiousness alone are used to make hiring decisions, $5,600 when employment interviews alone are used, and $6,600 when GMA tests alone are used. If all three selection tools are used, the average annual increase in work output is $7,600. As explained earlier, when the selection ratio of an organization decreases (the organization becomes *more* selective), the utility of its selection tools increases. If the selection ratio in this example is .30, the average annual increase in work output per employee reaches $5,148 when assessments of Conscientiousness are used to make selection decisions, $13,104 when employment interviews are used, and $15,444 when GMA tests are used. If all three selection tools are combined, the average annual increase in work output is an impressive $17,784.

At this point, the reader may have noted that the pattern of the results in Figures 3.2.1 and 3.2.2 seem extremely similar. In fact, they are identical. Recall that the utility equation is linear, and therefore any change in any one component of the equation will cause a directly proportional change in the final utility estimates. In Table 3.2.1 we showed that employment interviews and GMA tests are 2.55 and 3 times more effective, respectively, than Conscientiousness for predicting job performance and that the predictive power of the combination of the three selection methods is 1.15 times that of GMA tests, 1.36 times that of structured interviews, and 3.45 times that of Conscientiousness. For the organization with a selection ratio of .30 the annual utility of employment interviews per employee, $13,104, is exactly 2.55 times $5,148, which is the annual utility of assessments of Conscientiousness for that same organization. The utility of the combination of the three methods is $17,784–1.15 times the $15,444 of value provided by GMA tests, 1.36 times the $13,104 of value realized from employment interviews, and 3.45 times the $5,148 of value gained from using assessments of Conscientiousness.

The utility estimates presented in this paper represent only a single year's worth of increased work output for only a single employee. If the $17,784 gain in utility realized from using the combination of all three selection methods was applied to 1,000 employees over the course of five years of job performance, the total economic value of using the selection methods would be $88,920,000 of additional work output. Because this paper presents only a hypothetical example of utility, it is tempting to doubt that such enormous gains in work output can be achieved in the real world. However, studies of actual organizations supply ample empirical evidence that prove the legitimacy of utility estimation (Hunter & Schmidt, 1982; Schmidt & Hunter, 1983; Schmidt, Hunter, McKenzie, & Muldrow, 1979).

Measuring utility as the dollar value of work output is only one of several options. Utility can also be calculated as a percentage increase in total output of the average new employee resulting from using more effective selection methods. Perhaps an organization does not wish to increase its total output. Instead, the organization wants to decrease payroll costs while maintaining the same level of work output. Utility equations can be applied to determine the percentage reduction in new hiring that is possible without any reduction in output.

No matter how utility is estimated, as a dollar value, as a percentage increase in hiring, or as a percentage decrease in new hiring, it cannot be calculated without accurate estimates of the predictive power of the selection methods in question. Before the development of meta-analysis no such credible estimates were available. Two of the three components of the basic utility equation—the standard deviation of job performance and the selection ratio of the organization under examination—have been readily available for decades. Historically, the most elusive component of the utility equation has been an accurate estimate of the predictive capabilities of selection tools. The situational specificity hypothesis made it impossible for researchers and practitioners to estimate with confidence the economic benefits of selection methods because, as previously explained, the predictive power of selection tools seemed to vary from organization to organization and from job to job. With the debunking of the situational specificity hypothesis and the successful application of meta-analysis to employee selection research, accurate estimates of the final component of the utility equation have become easily obtainable to researchers and practitioners. In this context, the importance of meta-analysis to practitioners is apparent.

Conclusions

While quantitative methodology is undoubtedly a critical element in most research, it is hardly an easy and interesting topic for practitioners. Nevertheless, developments of research methods can have important implications for the improvement of organizational science and practices. Meta-analysis, the state-of-the-art quantitative methods for synthesizing research findings, is especially relevant to both organizational researchers and practitioners. We explained that meta-analysis is not an esoteric product of distant academics living in inhospitable ivory towers, but is an important tool that researchers can employ to translate conflicting results from single studies into conclusive and credible answers to their research questions, thereby making their research more relevant to practitioners. We then reviewed how meta-analysis methods have contributed meaningfully to organizational practices in the past, and discussed how meta-analytic findings can greatly impact personnel selection practices. Certainly, the implications of these methods for organizations are not limited to applications of personnel selection practices but can be seen in many areas of relevance to organizations.

Because the potential benefits that may be gained from the wealth of knowledge accumulated from research findings are enormous, it would be a great loss for any competent researcher or practitioner to overlook the importance and developments of meta-analysis. In a recent move toward bridging the research-practice gap, Rousseau (2006) promotes evidence-based management collaboration with the goal of informing managerial decisions by the best available scientific evidence. Meta-analysis is the tool that delivers such evidence and holds the most promise for bridging the gap between academic and organizational practices thanks to its ability to provide research conclusions that are generalizable, unambiguous, and more easily acceptable to organizations.

Notes

1 Cognitive ability is only one term for the construct that psychologists have identified as general intelligence. We use the term "general mental ability," or "GMA" in this article. GMA is most commonly measured in job candidates by assessments such as the Wonderlic Personnel Test, the Wesman Personnel Classification Test, or the Watson-Glaser Critical Thinking Appraisal Form.
2 r_{xy} denotes the correlation between an independent variable (x) and a dependent variable (y). In this case, r_{xy} is the correlation between scores on a selection method and job performance corrected for study imperfections. The higher the correlation between the predictor and the criterion, the greater the predictive power of the predictor.

References

Anderson, N., Herriot, P., & Hodgkinson, G. P. (2001). The practitioner-researcher divide in industrial, work and organizational (IWO) psychology: Where are we now, and where do we go from here? *Journal of Occupational and Organizational Psychology, 74,* 391–411.

Barrick, M. R., & Mount, M. K. (1991). The Big Five personality dimensions and job performance: A meta-analysis. *Personnel Psychology, 44*, 1–26.

Brogden, H. E. (1949). When testing pays off. *Personnel Psychology, 2*, 171–183.

Dipboye, R. L. (1994). Structured and unstructured selection interviews: Beyond the job-fit model. In G. Ferris (Ed.), *Research in personnel and human resources management* (Vol 12, pp. 79–123). Greenwich, CT: JAI Press.

Dipboye, R. L. (1997). Structured interviews: Why do they work? Why are they underutilized? In N. Anderson & P. Herriott (Eds.), *International handbook of selection and assessment* (pp. 455–473). New York: Wiley.

Ghiselli, E. E. (1966). *The validity of occupational aptitude tests.* New York: Wiley.

Hough, L. M. (1992). The Big Five Personality variables—Construct confusion: Description versus prediction. *Human Performance, 5*, 139–155.

Huffcutt, A. I., & Arthur, W. (1994). Hunter and Hunter (1984) revisited: Interview validity for entry-level jobs. *Journal of Applied Psychology, 79*, 184–190.

Hunter, J. E. (1983). *Test validation for 12,000 jobs: An application of job classification and validity generalization analysis to the General Aptitude Test Battery.* Washington, DC: US Employment Service, USDOL. USES Test Research Report No. 45.

Hunter, J. E. (1986). Cognitive ability: Cognitive aptitude, job knowledge, and job performance. *Journal of Vocational Behavior, 29*, 340–362.

Hunter, J. E., & Hunter, R. F. (1984). Validity and utility of alternate predictors of performance. *Psychological Bulletin, 96*, 72–98.

Hunter, J. E., & Schmidt, F. L. (2004). *Methods of meta-analysis: Correcting error and bias in research findings* (2nd ed.). Beverly Hills, CA: Sage.

Hunter, J. E., Schmidt, F. L., & Le, H. (2006). Implications of direct and indirect range restriction for meta-analysis methods and findings. *Journal of Applied Psychology, 91*, 594–612.

Hurtz, G. M., & Donovan, J. J. (2000). Personality and job performance: The Big Five revisited. *Journal of Applied Psychology, 85*, 869–879.

Jackson, S. E., & Schuler, R. S. (1985). A meta-analysis and conceptual critique on research on role ambiguity and role conflict in work settings. *Organizational Behavioral and Human Decision Processes, 36*, 16–78.

Judge, T. A., Bono, J. E., Ilies, R., & Gerhardt, M. (2002). Personality and leadership: A qualitative and quantitative review. *Journal of Applied Psychology, 87*, 765–780.

Judge, T. A., Thoresen, C. J., Bono, J. E., & Patton, G. K. (2001). The job satisfaction–job performance relationship: A qualitative and quantitative review. *Psychological Bulletin, 127*, 376–407.

Klehe, U. (2004). Choosing how to choose: Institutional pressures affecting the adoption of personnel selection procedures. *International Journal of Selection and Assessment, 12*, 327–342.

McDaniel, M. A. (2007). Validity generalization as a test validation approach. In S. M. McPhail (Ed.), *Alternative Validation Strategies* (pp. 159–180). San Francisco: Jossey Bass.

McDaniel, M. A., Whetzel, D. L., Schmidt, F. L., & Maurer, S. D. (1994). The validity of employment interviews: A comprehensive review and meta-analysis. *Journal of Applied Psychology, 79*, 599–616.

McEvoy, G. M., & Cascio, W. F. (1987). Do poor performers leave? A meta-analysis of the relation between performance and turnover. *Academy of Management Journal, 30*, 744–762.

Mount, M. K., Barrick, M. R., & Strauss, J. (1994). Validity of observer ratings of the Big Five personality factors. *Journal of Applied Psychology, 79*, 272–280.

Ones, D. S., Viswesvaran, C., & Schmidt, F. L. (1993). Comprehensive meta-analysis of integrity test validities: Findings and implications for personnel selection and theories of job performance. *Journal of Applied Psychology, 78*, 679–703.

Pearlman, K., Schmidt, F. L., & Hunter, J. E. (1980). Validity generalization results for tests used to predict job proficiency and training success in clerical occupations. *Journal of Applied Psychology, 65*, 373–406.

Rousseau, D. M. (2006). Is there such a thing as "evidence-based management"? *Academy of Management Review, 31*, 256–269.

Rynes, S. L., Colbert, A. E., & Brown, K. G. (2002). HR professionals' beliefs about effective human resource practices: Correspondence between research and practices. *Human Resource Management, 41,* 149–174.

Salgado, J. F. (1998). Big Five personality dimensions and job performance in army and civil occupations. A European perspective. *Human Performance, 11,* 271–288.

Salgado, J. F. (2003). Predicting job performance using FFM and non-FFM personality measures. *Journal of Occupational and Organizational Psychology, 76,* 323–346.

Schmidt, F. L. (2002). The role of general cognitive ability in job performance: Why there cannot be a debate. *Human Performance, 15,* 187–210.

Schmidt, F. L. (2006). The orphan area for meta-analysis: Personnel selection. *The Industrial and Organizational Psychologist, 44,* 25–28.

Schmidt, F. L., & Hunter, J. E. (1977). Development of a general solution to the problem of validity generalization. *Journal of Applied Psychology, 62,* 529–540.

Schmidt, F. L., & Hunter, J. E. (1981). Employment testing: Old theories and new research findings. *American Psychologist, 36,* 1128–1137.

Schmidt, F. L. & Hunter, J. E. (1998). The validity and utility of selection methods in personnel psychology: Practical and theoretical implications of 85 years of research findings. *Psychological Bulletin, 124,* 262–274.

Schmidt, F. L., & Hunter, J. E. (2003). History, development, evolution, and impact of validity generalization and meta-analysis methods, 1975–2002. In K. R. Murphy (Ed.), *Validity generalization: A critical review* (pp. 31–66). Hillsdale, NJ: Erlbaum.

Schmidt, F. L., & Hunter, J. E. (2004). General mental ability in the world of work: Occupational attainment and job performance. *Journal of Personality and Social Psychology, 86,* 162–174.

Schmidt, F. L., Gast-Rosenberg, I. F., & Hunter, J. E. (1980). Validity generalization results for computer programmers. *Journal of Applied Psychology, 65,* 643–661.

Schmidt, F. L., Hunter, J. E., & Pearlman, K. (1981). Task difference and validity of aptitude tests in selection: A red herring. *Journal of Applied Psychology, 66,* 166–185.

Schmidt, F. L., Hunter, J. E., & Urry, V. W. (1976). Statistical power in criterion-related validity studies. *Journal of Applied Psychology, 61,* 473–485.

Schmidt, F. L., Hunter, J. E., Outerbridge, A. N., & Trattner, M. H. (1986). The economic impact of job selection methods on size, productivity, and payroll costs of the federal work force: An empirically based demonstration. *Personnel Psychology, 39,* 1–29.

Schmidt, F. L., Hunter, J. E., Pearlman, K., & Hirsh, H. R. (1985). Forty questions about validity generalization and meta-analysis (with commentary by P. R. Sackett, M. L. Tenopyr, N. Schmitt, J. Kehoe, & S. Zedeck). *Personnel Psychology, 38,* 697–798.

Schmidt, F. L., Hunter, J. E., Pearlman, K., & Shane, G. S. (1979). Further tests of the Schmidt-Hunter Bayesian Validity Generalization Model. *Personnel Psychology, 32,* 257–281.

Terpstra, D. E., Mohamed, A. A., & Kethley, R. B. (1999). An analysis of federal court cases involving nine selection devices. *International Journal of Selection and Assessment, 7,* 26–34.

Wilk, S. L., & Cappelli, P. (2003). Understanding the determinants of employer use of selection methods. *Personnel Psychology, 56,* 103–124.

Williamson, L. G., Campion, J. E., Malos, S. B., Roehling, M. V., & Campion, M. A. (1997). Employment interview on trial: Linking interview structure with litigation outcomes. *Journal of Applied Psychology, 82,* 900–912.

4 Perception, Decision Making, and Creativity

4.1 ERROR REPORTING IN ORGANIZATIONS

Bin Zhao and Fernando Olivera

We develop a framework of individual error reporting that draws from research on human error, learning, discretionary behaviors, and high-reliability organizations. The framework describes three phases that underlie error reporting: error detection, situation assessment, and choice of behavioral response. We discuss theoretical implications of the framework and directions for future research.

Many problems in organizations are related to human error. For instance, from a study of the causes of airplane crashes in the 1970s, the National Aeronautics and Space Administration (NASA) concluded that 70 percent involved human error as opposed to irremediable mechanical failure (Helmreich, 1997). A recent report of the Institute of Medicine (quoting statistics from publications using pre-1993 data) states that medical errors cause between 44,000 and 98,000 deaths annually in U.S. hospitals (reported in Chiang, 2001). Errors of less severe but also important consequences are part of the day-to-day life of most organizations. Errors occur in activities ranging from service encounters to accounting and product development. For organizations, errors increase economic costs, create negative publicity, damage reputations, and decrease customer satisfaction. Errors can also increase employees' psychological stress and job dissatisfaction and can lead to turnover (Frese, 1987). In extreme situations, errors cause injury and loss of human life.

Despite the negative consequences of errors, organizations benefit when errors stimulate learning (Argyris, 1993; Edmondson, 1996, 1999; Sitkin, 1992). Organizations can learn from errors by understanding their causes and implementing changes that will prevent future errors or reduce the negative consequences when errors reoccur (Reason, 2000). However, research suggests that learning from errors is difficult for most organizations (Argyris, 1993; Carroll, Rudolph, & Hatakenaka, 2002; Edmondson, 1996; Sitkin, 1992). One important reason for this is that employees often do not disclose their own errors (Edmondson, 1996; Tax & Brown, 1998; Tucker & Edmondson, 2003; Uribe, Schweikhart, Pathak, & Marsh, 2002), creating a barrier to learning at the group or organizational level.

Error reporting is often the only means by which organizations become aware of errors and of the circumstances leading to them. Customers are often reluctant to complain about problems that occur in service delivery (e.g., Tax & Brown, 1998), leaving frontline employees as the only source of firsthand knowledge about what went wrong (Tucker, Edmondson, & Spear, 2002). Although researchers have recognized the importance of error reporting for organizational learning, there has been limited theorizing about why individuals choose to report or not report their errors. Our research is aimed at addressing this gap.

The focus of this paper is on understanding error reporting in organizations. We use the term error reporting to describe the act of individuals communicating their errors to their managers or supervisors, either verbally or through formal error reporting systems. We address the following two questions. Why do individuals report—or not report—the errors they make at work? How do individuals reach decisions about error reporting? We develop a conceptual framework elaborating on the decision processes underlying error reporting. A central premise of this framework is that the error reporting decision involves careful and purposeful assessment of the potential costs of reporting (including effort, fear of reprisal, damaged reputations, and financial costs) against potential benefits (such as learning, maintaining one's self-concept, and preventing negative consequences). Further, we assume that error reporting cognitions are affected by the negative emotions (such as fear and guilt) that individuals typically feel when they make an error. Finally, we consider a range of reporting and nonreporting behaviors, including rationalized reporting, blaming others, and covering up the error. Our objective is to provide a theoretical framework that integrates insights from various disciplines concerned with error reporting and that will stimulate further research and theory.

We delineate the scope of our discussion in a number of areas. First, we focus on errors made by individuals. Errors at the group or organization level may stem in part from individual-level errors, but they are also likely to involve a variety of structural factors, such as intraorganizational linkages (Goodman, 2000) and enabling conditions (Vaughan, 1999). These factors are beyond the scope of our framework. Second, our concern is with situations in which individuals have discretion in error reporting. Hence, the proposed framework does not apply to situations where individuals have little or no discretion in error reporting. Third, we focus on self-made errors. We recognize that the locus of an error (self, a colleague, one's workgroup, or one's organization) has theoretical implications in terms of individuals' cognitions, emotions, and behaviors. It is thus pertinent to specify whose errors we think about when studying individuals' error reporting.

In the following section we provide a definition of error. We then review the types of errors identified in the literature and briefly discuss how errors differ from other constructs, such as suboptimal results, failures, and violations. We next describe a framework for error reporting that is constituted by three phases: error detection, situation assessment, and behavioral response. We conclude by discussing theoretical implications and directions for future research.

Definition and Types of Errors

To effectively discuss error reporting, we must first clarify the meaning of *error*. Zapf and Reason (1994) observe that most current theories on errors assume that human behavior is goal oriented and conceptualize error as the nonattainment of a goal. Theorists also agree that errors should be potentially avoidable (e.g., Brodbeck, Zapf, Prumper, & Frese, 1993; Norman, 1981; Reason, 1990).

Building on these arguments, we define errors as individuals' decisions and behaviors that (1) result in an undesirable gap between an expected and real state and (2) may lead to actual or potential negative consequences for organizational functioning that could have been avoided.

Consider the following examples of errors in a variety of work environments: a pharmacist filling a prescription incorrectly, a software programmer typing an erroneous code, a stockbroker quoting an incorrect price, or an engineer using incorrect specifications in designing a product. In each of these examples, individuals' decisions or behaviors result in a state that is neither ideal nor desired and is likely to have negative consequences for the individuals, their organizations, or those affected by the action or service. These consequences could have been avoided had the activities been carried out correctly.

Distinction Among Errors, Suboptimal Results, Failures, and Violations

Errors are different from decisions and actions that lead to suboptimal results. Decisions or acts that, in hindsight, turn out to be suboptimal means of fulfilling a plan are not errors. We say that people who execute their jobs in an optimal way are top performers or innovators, but we do not say that they err if their work is suboptimal. That is, an error is considered in relation to the success of action in fulfilling a goal, rather than optimization (Rizzo, Bagnara, & Visciola, 1987).

Failure refers to a negative or undesired outcome. Failure is a possible consequence of error—the decision or behavior that caused the undesired outcome. However, failure need not involve human error (such as when caused by factors external to the individual), and error may not result in failure (such as when actions are corrected before they have negative consequences). In some cases, failure may be an expected outcome. Such is the case with experimentation, where it is assumed that some trials will result in success while others will fail (Lee, Edmondson, Thomke, & Worline, 2004; Sitkin, 1992). Failure in the context of experimentation is unavoidable and therefore does not constitute error.

Reason distinguished between errors and violations, although he conceded that "the boundaries between errors and violations are by no means hard and fast" (1990: 195). Violations refer to situations where the act performed is a *deliberate* deviation from organizational practices. The key distinction is that violations imply a prior intention (which may or may not be malicious), whereas errors are unintended.

Error Types

The literature on human error distinguishes among three different types of errors: slips, rule-based mistakes, and knowledge-based mistakes (Reason, 1987, 1990). This classification is concerned primarily with the cognitive origins of errors. *Slips* are actions that are not carried out as planned, even though the intentions are appropriate for accomplishing a desired goal (Norman, 1981; Reason, 1987). Slips are often caused by internal or external distractions that disrupt task execution (Rizzo et al., 1987; Stewart & Chase, 1999). For example, a server at a restaurant may accurately hear an order from a customer but write it down incorrectly. A cashier at a supermarket may inadvertently scan an item twice or type the incorrect code for a produce item. In these cases the individual knows how to carry out the task but does not carry it out appropriately.

Rule-based mistakes happen when well-known rules or procedures are wrongly applied in familiar, or so presumed, situations (Reason, 1987; Rizzo et al., 1987). The actions are carried out as planned, but the plan is inappropriate for the desired goals. People make rule-based mistakes, in both identifying the situation and adopting a plan of action, when they are biased in rule selection or when they let more familiar rules override the proper ones. For example, a technical support specialist may mistake a hardware malfunction for a software virus when assisting a computer user. A surgeon may competently perform an inappropriate surgical procedure on a patient.

Knowledge-based mistakes, however, occur when people are not able to properly analyze a problem or recognize the relations among its elements. Incomplete mental models and/or faulty causal thinking lead to knowledge-based mistakes (Rizzo et al., 1987). For instance, a server may incorrectly inform a customer that a menu item does not contain peanuts because the server does not know that the oil used in preparing that item contains peanuts. A travel agent may mistakenly make travel arrangements for the wrong destination (e.g., Portland, Oregon) because he or she is unfamiliar with the intended destination (Portland, Maine).

Organizations may benefit when individuals report any of the error types described above. Consider an environment where slips occur regularly. Careful diagnosis upon reporting may reveal that slips occur because of flaws in procedures or system design. For example, servers may write down incorrect items in their orders because the names of menu items are too similar. In the case of rule-based mistakes, managers may realize that mistakes occur because employees do not have enough time to carefully analyze the situation and to determine the appropriate rule for action. Or managers may learn that organizational procedures and rewards discourage employees from using some rules and bias them toward others. Reports of knowledge-based mistakes may lead managers to introduce more appropriate training. In all these scenarios, error reporting provides information that the organization can use to make changes to structures, practices, and procedures so as to reduce error occurrence or minimize the negative effects of errors.

The distinction between error types is important in at least two ways. First, error detection rates vary by error type. For example, research suggests that slips are more likely to be detected than rule- and knowledge-based mistakes (Rizzo et al., 1987; Sellen, 1994; Zapf, Maier, Rappensperger, & Irmer, 1994). In presenting our framework below, we elaborate on the role of error detection in the error reporting process. Second, work environments differ in the frequency and distribution of error types that are likely to occur. Jobs in services, for example, have been found to generate a larger proportion of slips and rule-based mistakes than knowledge-based mistakes (Stewart & Chase, 1999). In our discussion we present arguments about how the distribution and types of errors may affect error reporting.

A Framework of Error Reporting

Theoretical and Empirical Bases

There is no single theory specifying the elements that make up a framework of error reporting. Rather, we derived the framework using insights from various research domains. Specifically, we drew from research on discretionary and risky behaviors (e.g., Ashford, Rothbard, Piderit, & Dutton, 1998; Morrison & Phelps, 1999), human error (e.g., Reason, 1990), medical errors (e.g., Bosk, 1979; Uribe et al., 2002), psychological safety (Edmondson, 1999), high-reliability organizations (e.g., Roberts, 1990; Weick & Sutcliffe, 2001), emotions (Forgas, 1995; Loewenstein, Weber, Hsee, & Welch, 2001; Zajonc, 1998), and attributions (e.g., Weiner, 1985).

Of particular importance to our understanding of how individuals experience and decide to report errors were qualitative studies on errors in medical settings (Bosk, 1979; Edmondson, 1996; Paget, 1988). Bosk's (1979) eighteen-month ethnography of a university teaching hospital contributed to our understanding of how an organization's culture about errors affected error reporting by medical interns. Paget's (1988) in-depth interviews revealed the psychological turmoil that physicians go through when confronting their errors. Edmondson's qualitative study of nursing teams (1996), as well as her multimethod field study of teams in a manufacturing company (1999), highlighted the psychological barriers that deter individuals from talking about their own errors and prevent groups and organizations from learning from errors.

Risky and discretionary behavior. Our conceptual point of departure is recognizing that error reporting is a discretionary and potentially risky behavior. Studies of learning from mistakes (Cannon & Edmondson, 2001; Edmondson, 1996, 1999) and safety in medicine (Baker & Norton, 2001; Barach & Small, 2000; Chiang, 2001; Uribe et al., 2002) show that employees are often reluctant to admit and talk about their errors, even when doing so will benefit their teams or organizations. This reluctance is due, in part, to concerns about impression management and job security, particularly in "blaming cultures" where errors are punished (Pearn, Mulrooney, & Payne, 1998). Afraid of being seen as incompetent, these employees "may incur more tangible costs if their actions create unfavorable impressions on people who influence decisions about promotions, raises, or project assignments" (Edmondson, 1999: 351). People working in several fields (e.g., food industry, chemical manufacturers, hospitals) also have real concerns that their errors will result in punitive legal action (Barach & Small, 2000; Uribe et al., 2002).

Morrison and Phelps (1999) suggest that there are two important factors to consider when thinking about employees' risky and discretionary activities. The first is that effortful, discretionary behavior involves a calculated and deliberate decision process. This perspective has been applied to a number of other voluntary and risky behaviors, such as taking charge (Morrison & Phelps, 1999), issue selling (Ashford et al., 1998), whistle-blowing (Dozier & Miceli, 1985; Gundlach, Douglas, & Martinko, 2003), and feedback seeking (Ashford & Cummings, 1983). Our framework applies this perspective to error reporting and focuses explicitly on the cost-benefit evaluations that individuals make when deciding whether to report an error.

The second consideration is that both individual- and contextual-level factors affect the decision process. With respect to individual-level factors, our framework is concerned primarily with the individual cognitions and emotions that errors generate. With respect to contextual factors, there is evidence that culture and norms are important determinants of error reporting (Bosk, 1979; Edmondson, 1996, 1999; Weick & Sutcliffe, 2001). For example, Edmondson (1999) found that the psychological safety of work teams influences team members' intention to report errors. Team psychological safety refers to a shared belief among team members that "the team is safe for interpersonal risk taking" (Edmondson, 1999: 354). Teams with high levels of psychological safety are likely to alleviate individuals' concerns about others' reactions to disclosing and discussing errors. In teams with low levels of psychological safety, however, team members are more preoccupied with impression management and fear of punishment and, thus, are unwilling to disclose their errors (Edmondson, 1999). Our framework considers contextual factors primarily in terms of their effects on individual cognitions about error reporting. Our approach is aimed at understanding how contextual factors affect individuals' perceptions, rather than identifying contextual determinants of reporting.

Negative emotions. Research on human error indicates that experiencing errors is unpleasant and can cause negative feelings, including fear, guilt, and shame (Rybowiak, Garst, Frese, & Batinic, 1999). Psychological research suggests that facing errors, which can be seen as an unpleasant form of accurate feedback, can dampen people's perceived self-efficacy and, thus, their performance (Cannon & Edmondson, 2001; Heimbeck, Frese,

Sonnentag, & Keith, 2003). Research on emotions and decision making suggests that negative feelings can influence the decision-making process in important ways (Forgas, 1995; Loewenstein et al., 2001; Raghunathan & Pham, 1999). We elaborate on the role of negative emotions in error reporting.

Error recognition. We derived other theoretical considerations from the literature on cognition and human error (Rizzo et al., 1987; Sellen, 1994; Zapf et al., 1994). An important observation from this literature is that individuals often do not detect their own errors (Sellen, 1994; Zapf et al., 1994). A theory of error reporting must therefore account for the possibility that individuals do not report their errors simply because they are unaware of them (e.g., Uribe et al., 2002). As we explain below, error detection is critical for initiating the error reporting process. This approach is similar to Dozier and Miceli's (1985) model of whistle-blowing, where recognizing a wrongdoing is the first step in the whistle-blowing process.

Nonbinary responses. Finally, prior research on how individuals react to their errors reveals that the behavioral response is not binary—to report or not report. Rather, there is a range of possible responses. For example, Rizzo and colleagues (1987) found that reported errors were often a rational reconstruction of the events, rather than a real account of what happened. Pearn et al. (1998) argue that people tend to blame others for their errors as a way of reducing negative emotions. Tucker and Edmondson (2003) note that, in medical settings, nurses and other health care professionals often handle errors by themselves, without reporting them. Rybowiak and colleagues (1999) found that employees sometimes cover up their own errors. Given this insight, the framework presents a more differentiated picture of error reporting than a *report/not report* behavioral response; it incorporates the range of behavioral responses that have been described in the literature.

The framework presented in Table 4.1.1 reflects the above theoretical considerations. We conceptualize error reporting as constituted by three sequential phases: error detection, situation assessment, and behavioral response. The situation assessment is composed of cost-benefit evaluations as well as emotional reactions to the error.

The following sections describe each of the phases in the error reporting decision process.

Error Detection

Error detection refers to individuals' realization that an error has occurred, whether or not they understand its cause and nature (Zapf & Reason, 1994). Error detection plays a critical role in the decision-making process: a person who fails to recognize his or her own error will not engage in the situation assessment that precedes error reporting.

An error may be detected in several ways. Sellen (1994) proposes three modes of error detection, based on action, outcome, and external limiting function. *Action-based detection* refers to catching errors as they occur, typically by perceiving some aspect of the erroneous action itself (e.g., from visual or auditory signals). For example, individuals using computers often realize they are making errors as they press incorrect keys (Rizzo et al., 1987; Sellen, 1994). A cashier who scans an item twice may become aware of the erroneous action from the repeated sound produced by the price scanner.

Outcome-based detection is based on some aspect of the consequences of the erroneous action, not on perception of the action itself. In this mode, individuals become aware of errors when their actions do not produce the results they intended. For example, a computer support specialist may realize that a problem was diagnosed incorrectly because the problem's symptoms do not disappear.

Table 4.1.1 A Framework of Error Reporting

Phase	Description	Key Elements
Error detection	The realization that an error has occurred	Error types • Slips • Rule-based mistakes • Knowledge-based mistakes Error detection modes • Action based • Outcome based • Limiting function
Situation assessment	Cognitions and emotions about error reporting	Cost-benefit evaluations • For self • For group or organization • For potential victims Influenced by negative emotions • Fear • Shame • Embarrassment • Guilt
Behavioral response	Choice of behavior, following the situation assessment	Reporting behaviors • Reporting as it is • Rationalized reporting • Blaming someone else Nonreporting behaviors • Covering up • Handling on one's own • Ignoring

Detection by external limiting function occurs when the error is detected because constraints in the outside world prevent further action. In this mode, it is the external environment that signals to the individual that an error was made. A person who schedules an appointment incorrectly will discover the error when the other party does not show up at the presumed specified time and place.

Sellen (1994) identifies factors that contribute to error detection in each of these three modes. For action-based detection to occur, individuals need to sufficiently monitor their own behavior, and the discrepancies between actual and intended actions need to be noticeable (see also Reason, 1990; Rizzo et al., 1987; Zapf et al., 1994). Outcome-based detection also requires that the error have observable consequences. Both outcome-based detection and detection by limiting function require that individuals have accurate expectations of the outcomes of their actions and that they understand how any observed discrepancies relate to their own actions.

Building on these findings and applying them to organizational settings, we elaborate below on three factors that are relevant for understanding error detection in organizations: the visibility of the error, the individual's level of error anticipation, and the individual's understanding of organizational goals. We relate these factors to the error detection modes described above (see Figure 4.1.1).

Visibility of error. Visibility refers to how noticeable or observable the occurrence(s) or consequence(s) of an error is (are) to an individual (e.g., Sellen, 1994). An error's visibility

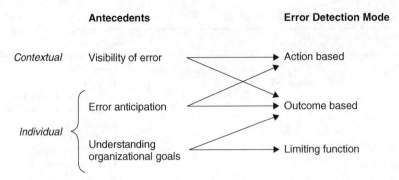

Figure 4.1.1 Antecedents of Error Detection.

depends on the timing and frequency of its occurrence and the magnitude of its negative outcomes. Thus, the visibility of an error is likely to enhance both action-based and outcome-based error detection. As noted above, research on error detection has shown that slips are more easily detected than mistakes (Reason, 1990; Zapf et al., 1994). Slips have higher rates of detection partly because their consequences tend to be immediate and observable.

We note that error visibility is likely to be primarily a function of the task environment. That is, the technology and activities that constitute the task are key determinants of whether errors will be observable. Chase and Stewart (1995), for instance, describe how introducing technological devices that either create or amplify error cues can increase error detection rates. They offer as an example automated teller machines (ATMs), which produce a beeping sound that alerts users to remove their cards after completing their transaction. Researchers have also noted the possibility of *latent errors*, which have no obvious, immediate manifestations or effects (Reason, 1990). The consequences of latent errors may go undiscovered within the system for a long time, usually until their effects are compounded by other errors or specific environmental conditions (Goodman, 2000; Reason, 1990). Latency of errors is, in part, a function of the context or system in which the errors are made (Stewart & Chase, 1999). Given the right circumstances, both slips and mistakes (rule or knowledge based) may remain latent (Stewart & Chase, 1999).

Error anticipation. Error anticipation refers to a general and realistic expectation that errors will happen (Rybowiak et al., 1999). Attentional monitoring of work progress is critical for action-based and outcome-based error detection (Rizzo et al., 1987; Sellen, 1994). People have limited attentional resources, and these resources will be allocated according to the priority of each task at hand. The higher the individual's level of error anticipation, the more the individual will allocate attentional resources to monitor his or her own work performance and, thus, the more likely the individual will detect an error. In Sellen's empirical study, "subjects reported checking for errors in situations where they knew they tended to be error-prone" (1994: 488). Gawande (2002) describes research on human error in medicine showing that errors led to incidents in the middle of anesthesia, when vigilance waned. This was because anesthesiologists generally believed that the start of anesthesia was the most dangerous phase.

Research on vigilance provides further evidence that anticipation increases error detection. Vigilance refers to individuals' ability to pay attention to stimuli for prolonged periods of time (See, Howe, Warm, & Dember, 1995). Vigilance is a critical determinant of performance in certain job contexts, such as airport security, industrial quality control, police surveillance, and nursing (Hollenbeck, Ilgen, Tuttle, & Sego, 1995). Research suggests that expectations that target stimuli will occur are positively related to target detection (See et al., 1995). Expectations increase detection because individuals focus their attention on identifying critical cues that signal that the target stimuli will occur (e.g., Hollenbeck et al., 1995).

Understanding organizational goals. Detection by outcomes and external limiting function requires that individuals understand how their actions relate to the objectives they want to achieve (Sellen, 1994). If individuals do not see the relationship between their actions and undesired outcomes, they will not detect errors. In the context of organizations, individual objectives need to relate to organizational goals. Goals help employees understand how their actions relate to the broader organizational objectives. When employees clearly understand organizational goals, they are more likely to notice when they stray from the goalward path and are more likely to detect their own errors.

Scholars have recognized the importance of understanding goals in error detection. Zapf and colleagues (1994) suggest that error detection depends on one's knowledge about one's goal. Roberts and Bea (2001) argue that a high-reliability organization consistently and widely communicates the big picture—what the organization seeks to do—so that employees can detect anomalies and errors. Similarly, in their study on learning from mistakes in teams, Cannon and Edmondson (2001) argue that a lack of understanding about group goals deters group members from identifying errors. When confusion and ambiguity around what needs to be accomplished exist, members simply do not know when an error can be called an error. In summary, clearly understanding organizational goals is positively associated with error detection.

Situation Assessment

We propose that a situation assessment phase will follow error detection. In the following sections we describe the two main elements of the situation assessment phase: cost-benefit evaluations and emotional reactions.

Cost-benefit evaluations. Morrison and Phelps (1999) argue that individuals consider potential risks and benefits when making decisions to engage in effortful and discretionary behaviors, such as taking charge. Following this theoretical perspective, we argue that error reporting also involves carefully evaluating costs and benefits (e.g., Uribe et al., 2002). Through this evaluation, individuals attempt to resolve the tension between the reasons to report and not to report, and to decide on a specific path of action that is consistent with this assessment. Consideration of costs and benefits is central in other theories of discretionary and potentially risky behaviors, such as seeking feedback (Ashford & Cummings, 1983) and whistle-blowing (Dozier & Miceli, 1985; Gundlach et al., 2003).

A second theoretical consideration in this evaluation is that individuals assess costs and benefits in relation to multiple referents: self, the workgroup or organization, and potential victims. The notion that individuals can differentiate among multiple referents in their cognitions is consistent with theories of commitment that recognize that individuals may be differentially attached to their supervisor, workgroup, or organization (Meyer & Herscovitch, 2001). Research on whistle-blowing also recognizes that individuals make cost-benefit calculations in relation to various targets, including themselves, colleagues, and the organization (Dozier & Miceli, 1985).

Other research suggests that individuals consider both individual and organizational factors as barriers to reporting (Barach & Small, 2000; Edmondson, 1999; Uribe et al.,

2002). Consider the following two barriers to medical error reporting identified by Uribe and colleagues (2002): fear of being blamed and thinking that reporting will not improve quality of care. The first—fear of being blamed—reflects consideration of costs to self, whereas the second reflects consideration of (limited) benefits to the organization. Barach and Small (2000) also differentiate between barriers to reporting that relate to the individual (such as damage to reputation) and those that relate to the organization (such as bad publicity).

Research suggests that individuals may also consider the effects of error reporting on potential victims (Bosk, 1979; Paget, 1988). Victims are people, groups, or organizations that are subject to the harm caused by the error. They may be part of the individual's workgroup or organization, or they may be customers or members of the general public.

Our framework includes all key components in the individual's cost-benefit evaluations, but we do not suggest that all components will be considered in any given error situation. In fact, even if all three parties (self, workgroup, or potential victims) should be considered, an individual may estimate the cost-benefit trade-offs of the error with only one party in mind, especially if the individual identifies strongly with that party. Similarly, an individual may make a composite cost-benefit trade-off estimate that considers two of the three parties without giving serious thought to the third. Borrowing insights from research on helping behaviors (Bendapudi, Singh, & Bendapudi, 1996), we argue that the motivation for error reporting may be egoistic, altruistic, or a mix of both. We assume that the presence and importance of each element in the cost-benefit evaluation are likely to vary by decision maker and decision situation. In the discussion section we elaborate on how individual differences and error types may influence the extent to which different elements of the cost-benefit evaluations will be salient to each individual.

Different factors affect individuals' estimation of costs and benefits when considering each of the three parties. That is, estimating costs with respect to self involves thinking about elements that are distinct from those involved in estimating benefits to self, as well as from those related to the organization or a potential victim. We elaborate below on the elements that are involved in cost-benefit considerations with respect to self, the group or organization, and potential victims.

The costs of reporting. There are several reasons individuals may not want to report their errors: material costs, potential damage to their image, and the effort costs associated with reporting. In addition to these personal costs, individuals may also consider the potential economic costs or reputation damage to their workgroup or organization. Below we elaborate on each of these potential costs of error reporting.

Material costs. Individuals may be reluctant to report errors because they fear concrete, material costs to themselves, such as monetary penalties, suspension, or job loss. In some organizations individuals may have to pay the monetary costs of their errors—for example, servers may have the costs of meals ordered by mistake deducted from their wages. In a questionnaire survey among health care staff, over 60 percent of respondents reported that fear of reprisal and concerns about job security made it difficult for them to acknowledge or discuss errors (Sexton, Thomas, & Helmreich, 2000). In some professions there may also be a fear of legal action or "decertification"—for example, being disbarred or losing license to practice (Barach & Small, 2000; Uribe et al., 2002). Fear of reprisal has been recognized as one of the top psychological barriers to error reporting by several researchers (Barach & Small, 2000; Bosk, 1979; Edmondson, 1999; Pearn et al., 1998; Reason, 1997). Researchers have found that anonymity increases the use of reporting systems in part, because individuals do not risk reprisal from reporting (Barach & Small, 2000).

Damage to personal image. Individuals may also be reluctant to report errors because they fear the potential damage it will do to their image—that is, the extent to which an individual believes that disclosing an error may harm perceptions about his or her competence and professionalism (e.g., Baker & Norton, 2001; Barach & Small; 2000; Bosk, 1979; Edmondson, 1999; Weick & Sutcliffe, 2001). Individuals have a general need to establish and protect a positive self-image (Rosenberg, 1979) and to present themselves favorably to others (Baumeister, 1998). Error reporting can be perceived as detrimental to one's image because it makes public one's shortcomings. Individuals, thus, may fear that reporting their errors will damage their reputation and even future career opportunities. Individuals may also be concerned about damage to interpersonal relationships, including being rejected by coworkers or losing the support of the group or organization (Edmondson, 1999).

Edmondson and colleagues (Cannon & Edmondson, 2001; Edmondson, 1996, 1999) provide evidence that concern for one's image can inhibit error reporting. They have shown that work environments that are high in psychological safety promote individual error reporting. As noted earlier, psychological safety refers to a shared belief among group members that the group is safe for interpersonal risk taking. In environments that are high in psychological safety, individuals do not fear that error disclosure will bring rejection, embarrassment, or punishment.

Effort costs. Reporting an error takes time, as well as cognitive and physical effort. When individuals believe that the effort costs of reporting an error are high, they may choose not to report it because they do not want to increase their workload (Chiang, 2001; Tucker et al., 2002; Uribe et al., 2002). In an exploratory study on perceived barriers to medical error reporting, Uribe and colleagues (2002) found that the time needed to document an error and the extra work involved in reporting it were the top two barriers to error reporting for physicians and nurses at a large academic medical center. Similarly, Tucker and colleagues (2002) found that lack of time and difficulty accessing key people prevented nurses from reporting errors and problems.

In addition to the above personal costs, individuals may be concerned about potential costs to their workgroup or organization (Barach & Small, 2000).

Economic costs. Individuals may be concerned about the economic costs to the group or organization if an error is disclosed. For example, individuals with a group-based incentive compensation plan may fear that the entire workgroup will be penalized for their error. They may also fear that fixing the error will impose time and effort costs on other group members. In some cases, such as medical errors, the organization may be obliged to disclose the error to potential or actual victims, possibly incurring the financial costs of compensation or litigation (Barach & Small, 2000). Error disclosure may also lead to costly product recalls.

Reputation costs. Individuals may also fear that their errors will reflect negatively on their workgroup or organization, thus damaging its reputation. An individual's error may be perceived as representative of the professionalism or skills of the group or organization as a whole, particularly in the eyes of customers (Barach & Small, 2000). Research on service failures, for example, suggests that customers who experience a negative service interaction can develop negative impressions of the entire organization (Tax & Brown, 1998). A recent study on organizational accountability by Naquin and Kurtzberg (2004) suggests that individuals hold organizations more accountable for human errors than for technical errors. Their study shows that individuals judged an organization more accountable for injuries caused by an operator's negligence than for injuries caused by computer malfunction. Individuals within organizations may thus perceive that the organization will be held responsible for their errors.

The benefits of reporting. There are several reasons individuals may be motivated to report their errors: maintaining their self-concept, attaining learning or stimulating learning at the group or organizational level, and reducing harm to potential victims.

Self-concept benefits. Individuals may be motivated to report an error when doing so will help maintain their self-concept. Self-concept is the composite of attributes individuals use to describe themselves (Pinder, 1998). The desire to preserve and maintain one's self-concept is central to individuals' motivational systems (Rosenberg, 1979; Swann, 1985). One's concept of self serves as a frame of reference for evaluating one's actions and decisions. To maintain their self-concept, individuals will actively strive to seek self-confirmatory feedback (Swann, 1983).

Although research has not explored which specific personal attributes are reinforced through error reporting, we anticipate that honesty and altruism are likely to play an important role. For example, some individuals may report errors because doing so reconfirms their view of themselves as honest. Other individuals, who view themselves as altruistic, may see error reporting as a self-sacrifice for the benefit of their peers, the organization, or potential victims. It is worth noting that, in some situations, individuals maintain their self-concept by removing themselves from situations they believe reflect negatively on their self-concept (Lecky, 1945; Swann & Hill, 1982). An example of this phenomenon is guilt dissipation. As we elaborate below in the section on emotions, individuals may be motivated to report errors in order to reduce their feelings of guilt and, thus, to reassert their positive self-concept (e.g., Tangney, Miller, Flicker, & Barlow, 1996; Tangney, Wagner, Fletcher, & Gramzow, 1992).

Learning benefits. Individuals may consider the learning benefits of error reporting in their cost-benefit evaluation. Research on the use of error reporting systems suggests that individuals are motivated to report errors when they perceive learning benefits to themselves (Barach & Small, 2000). Discussing errors with others can help individuals understand and interpret the causes of their errors, which leads to the development of task knowledge (Rybowiak et al., 1999).

Studies of errors in medical settings (Bosk, 1979; Paget, 1988) have shown that individuals often recognize the learning benefits of errors. Paget notes that participants in her study believed that "making mistakes is not an issue; recognizing mistakes, understanding them, correcting them, and avoiding their repetition is" (1988: 98). Learning from errors in this context often requires the involvement of others. Paget describes the case of a psychiatrist trying to learn from mistakes in a patient's treatment: "I re-examine it again, I guess, trying to understand it. I spent a lot of time with the supervisors, too, going over it because it's a hard experience to go through—I've gone over it with people in a group, gone over the whole, you know, case, and the hours and the, you know—and the clues" (Paget, 1988: 82).

Group or organizational learning. Individuals may also perceive that reporting their own errors will stimulate group or organizational learning and prevent error recurrence (Edmondson, 1996, 1999; Weick & Sutcliffe, 2001). Bosk, for example, notes that the benefits of reporting errors can outweigh the costs when "legions of patients yet unseen have the lessons gleaned from this error passed on to them" (1979: 41). The empirical studies of Edmondson and colleagues (Cannon & Edmondson, 2001; Edmondson, 1996, 1999) show that, given psychological safety, group members are willing to share information about their own errors for the benefit of group learning. In a study of errors in navigation, Seifert and Hutchins (1992) found that errors served as opportunities to identify the training needs of novices but also promoted learning at the group level. To be motivated, an employee must believe that reporting will trigger organizational processes that investigate the root causes of the error and lead to appropriate changes in the work environment. A person who does not believe the group or organization will engage in such learning processes will not be motivated to report the error.

Victim benefits. Finally, individuals may feel motivated to report errors because they recognize the effects of their errors on potential victims. By potential victim, we mean not only the victims affected by the error (direct victims) but also those who may be affected by similar errors made by other organizational members in the future (indirect victims). The benefits of error reporting to potential victims include avoiding negative consequences and launching a timely response to undo the error's negative effects (Reason, 2000). We anticipate that this benefit of error reporting will be particularly salient when the individual identifies with the potential victim (Barach & Small, 2000). Identifying with the victim should increase empathy and appreciation of undoing potential or actual harm caused by the error.

Emotions. Errors can generate strong negative emotions (Bosk, 1979; Paget, 1988; Pearn et al., 1998; Rybowiak et al., 1999). Rybowiak and colleagues (1999) have observed that errors can cause guilt, shame, and fear in employees. In studies of errors in medical settings, individuals often describe feelings of guilt, embarrassment, and fear associated with their errors (e.g., Edmondson, 1996; Paget, 1988). Such strong emotional responses can influence judgment and decision making (e.g., Anderson, 2003; Forgas, 1995; Lerner & Keltner, 2001; Loewenstein et al., 2001; Zajonc, 1998). In extreme circumstances, such as panic reactions, emotions may directly affect behavior, circumventing decision-making processes altogether (Loewenstein et al., 2001). More often, emotions affect behaviors indirectly, through their effects on cognitions (e.g., Anderson, 2003; Forgas, 1995; Loewenstein et al., 2001).

Researchers have not yet explored the effects of emotions on error reporting cognitions. However, based on recent research on the effects of emotions on judgment, we anticipate that emotions will play an important role in error reporting. Specifically, we expect that emotions will indirectly influence error reporting through their effect on individuals' cognitions about the costs and benefits of reporting. This argument is consistent with Forgas's (1995) affect infusion model, which suggests that emotions will affect behaviors through cognitions in cases where the judgment or decision is of high personal relevance.

In general terms, we anticipate that individuals who feel strong, negative emotions upon detecting an error are more likely to attend to the perceived costs than to the perceived benefits of reporting it. Research has shown that negative emotions are likely to cause individuals to attend to threats and become risk averse (Lerner & Keltner, 2001; Loewenstein et al., 2001). Also, individuals may use negative emotions as a simplifying heuristic to infer their judgment (Forgas, 1995), preventing them from considering the benefits of reporting and predisposing them to inaction (Anderson, 2003). Schwarz (1990) has argued that affective states may be consulted as relevant information when individuals make evaluative judgments. Individuals may simplify the difficult task of cost-benefit evaluation by asking themselves, "How do I feel about it?"—thus using emotions as heuristically relevant information. Individuals may believe, for example, that their feelings of fear carry information about risk. Therefore, individuals who feel fearful may conclude that the situation they are evaluating is indeed risk bearing and threatening to their well-being.

An important theoretical consideration is that not all negative emotions are likely to operate in the same manner. Although research on this topic is still in an early stage, there is evidence that different negative emotions have different effects on judgment (e.g., Lee & Allen, 2002; Roseman, Wiest, & Swartz, 1994; Smith & Ellsworth, 1985). Lerner and Keltner (2001), for example, found, in a series of studies, that although fear makes individuals risk averse, anger makes individuals risk seeking. Below we elaborate on the likely effects of four negative emotions that have been associated with errors: fear, shame, embarrassment, and guilt.

Fear is experienced in situations where individuals perceive obstacles and do not know whether they can escape or avoid an unpleasant or harmful outcome (Ellsworth & Smith, 1988; Smith & Ellsworth, 1985). Feelings of fear have been found to be associated with the experience of errors (Bosk, 1979; Edmondson, 1996; Paget, 1988; Pearn et al., 1998; Rybowiak et al., 1999). As we noted in the previous section, individuals may fear that reporting will result in significant costs to themselves, their workgroup, or organization. Given that fearful individuals tend to be pessimistic (Lerner & Keltner, 2001), we expect they will be more likely to attend to the costs than to the benefits of error reporting.

Shame is a strong emotion involving negative evaluations of the self. Shame arises from a discrepancy between a desired and a perceived self (Lazarus, 1991) and has been argued to be "the product of a complex set of cognitive activities: the evaluation of an individual's actions in regard to her standards, rules, and goals and her global evaluation of the self" (Lewis, 1992: 75). Research suggests that individuals will try to rid themselves of this negative emotion by hiding, or escaping, from the situation (Lazarus, 1991; Lewis, 2000; Tangney et al., 1992, 1996). Researchers have also found that shame is positively associated with the tendency to externalize blame (Tangney, 1990; Tangney et al., 1992). Detecting one's errors may result in shame in situations where the error is interpreted to have significant implications for one's sense of self in terms of, for example, competence and professionalism. Consequently, we expect that shame will influence error reporting cognitions by making salient the perceived costs to self in terms of image damage.

Embarrassment is a less intense and more transient emotion than shame (Smith, Webster, Parrott, & Eyre, 2002; Tangney et al., 1996). Compared to shame, embarrassment involves fewer or no negative evaluations of the self. Rather, public exposure may be the key cause of embarrassment (Lewis, 2000; Tangney et al., 1996). We anticipate that, in many situations, individuals will experience embarrassment, rather than shame, from their errors, and this has two implications for error reporting. First, embarrassed people are less motivated to hide from others or to take reparative actions than those who feel shame (Tangney et al., 1996). Research suggests that, when embarrassed, people tend to respond in a socially desirable, conciliatory way to the embarrassing situation (Tangney et al., 1996). Thus, if individuals engage in situation assessment while embarrassed, the benefits of reporting may be salient, particularly in environments where reporting is perceived to be socially desirable. Second, embarrassment also tends to be a transient emotion. If individuals postpone assessing the situation to a time when they can carefully consider their options, embarrassment may not affect error reporting cognitions at all.

Embarrassment may also affect error reporting cognitions as an anticipated, rather than experienced, emotion. Researchers have distinguished between emotions that are experienced during decision making and emotions that are not experienced but that individuals anticipate they will experience in the future if they choose some course of action (Anderson, 2003; Loewenstein et al., 2001). Anderson (2003), for example, argues that individuals avoid making decisions because of the regret they anticipate they will feel if they make the wrong decision. In the case of error reporting, individuals may anticipate feeling embarrassed when talking about their errors with a manager or supervisor. The effect of this anticipated emotion will be to make salient the costs of reporting.

Guilt is experienced "when individuals evaluate their behavior as failure but focus on the specific features or actions of the self that led to the failure" (Lewis, 2000: 629). In contrast to shame, "guilt involves a negative evaluation of specific behaviors somewhat apart from the global self" (Tangney et al., 1992: 674). Research shows that guilt motivates reparative action in the form of "confession, apologies, and attempts to undo the harm done" (Tangney et al., 1996: 1257). Therefore, we theorize that guilt may enhance the salience of perceived benefits of error reporting in terms of maintaining one's self-concept. A study by Tangney (1991) also suggests a positive association between guilt and empathy, which suggests that individuals who feel guilt may be likely to perceive the benefits to victims to be salient in reporting.

Behavioral Responses

As a result of the composite cost-benefit trade-offs, an individual may perceive that the benefits of error reporting are substantial and, thus, may be inclined to report the error. Alternatively, an individual may perceive that the costs of error reporting are substantial and, thus, may be inclined to not report the error. As we noted above, however, the potential behavioral response is not binary. Rather, we propose that an individual's decision about error reporting may fall within a range of possible behavioral responses.

We specify six possible behavioral responses—three classified as *reporting* and three as *not reporting*. We derived this typology of responses primarily from research on how individuals react to their errors (Pearn et al., 1998; Rizzo et al., 1987; Rybowiak et al., 1999; Tucker & Edmondson, 2003). Research on error reporting often assumes that individuals provide accurate and truthful accounts of the errors and the conditions that led to the errors. Although such truthful reporting has been observed (Rybowiak et al., 1999), there is also evidence that individuals provide rationalized versions of what happened (Rizzo et al., 1987). In some cases, individuals blame others for their errors (Pearn et al., 1998). Some take actions to correct their errors (Tucker & Edmondson, 2003), whereas others cover them up (Rybowiak et al., 1999). This differentiation of behavioral responses has not been acknowledged in the literature to our knowledge, yet, as we argue below, it is important for understanding error reporting behaviors.

Reporting behaviors. The three behavioral responses in the reporting category are (1) reporting as it is, (2) rationalized reporting, and (3) blaming someone else. *Reporting as it is* describes situations where an individual reports an error truthfully, without trying to hide or disguise any facts about the error's occurrence. *Rationalized reporting* occurs when an individual decides to report an error but considers that truthful reporting may harm all or any of the three parties involved in the error. Therefore, the individual chooses to report the error with a rationally reconstructed story in order to protect the vulnerable parties (including self, the workgroup or organization, or potential victims). *Blaming someone else* is reporting one's own error as someone else's error. This response can be thought of as a form of rationalized reporting, but we note that it is distinct in that, while rationalized reporting attempts to make one's own error sound more acceptable, blaming attempts to deny any part in the error and place the responsibility on someone else.

Nonreporting behaviors. The three behavioral responses in the nonreporting scenario are (1) covering up, (2) handling on one's own, and (3) ignoring the error. *Covering up* is the individual's decision not to report an error and to purposefully hide it from other organizational members without attempting to fix the error or its effects. *Handling on one's own* refers to the situation where an individual chooses not to report the error but takes actions to fix it. This response is available only in cases where the individual has the necessary resources and the ability to correct the error alone. We note that handling an error on one's own does not imply that the individual intends to cover up the error—the individual may believe that it is his or her responsibility to handle the error without involving others. Finally, when an individual chooses to take no action in relation to an identified error, we say that this individual decides to *ignore it*.

Each behavioral response entails a distinct set of considerations in the preceding situation assessment step. For example, a person who chooses to blame someone else for an error may believe that reporting will have a negative effect on his or her career but will benefit the victim. Someone who decides to ignore an error may believe that reporting will entail high effort costs with no benefits to him/herself, the organization, or potential victims. Clearly, there are multiple possible configurations of situation assessment elements that result in identical behavioral responses. Table 4.1.2 illustrates some possible configurations of perceived costs and benefits leading to each of the six behavioral responses. Our objective here is not to provide a predictive model of each behavioral response but, rather, to stimulate new thought and theory on the decision processes that underlie error reporting behaviors. As we discuss in the next section, the framework is useful for developing propositions about predictors that have not yet been explored in the literature but deserve attention.

Discussion

In the sections above we developed a framework for understanding the decision process that underlies error reporting. We now turn to additional theoretical considerations and future research directions for error reporting, focusing on the potential role of individual differences, attributions, error types, and time pressure.

Table 4.1.2 Examples of Configurations of Cost-Benefit Perceptions Leading to Behavioral Responses

Perceived Costs		Perceived Benefits			
To Self	*To the Group or Organization*	*To Self*	*To the Group or Organization*	*To Potential Victims*	*Likely Response*
Low	Low	High	High	High	Reporting as it is
Low	Low	Low	Low	High	Rationalized reporting
High	Low	Low	Low	High	Blaming someone else
High	Low	Low	Low	Low	Covering up
High	High	Low	Low	High	Handling on one's own
High	High	Low	Low	Low	Ignoring it

Individual Differences

We currently know little about whether and how individual differences affect error reporting, although there is evidence that individuals differ in their attitudes and reactions to errors. Rybowiak and colleagues (1999) have developed a scale that measures individuals' error orientation along several dimensions. These dimensions include the extent to which individuals believe errors can contribute to their own learning, experience negative emotions from errors, anticipate errors in their work, feel capable of correcting their errors, and are willing to talk about their errors with others. Responses to this scale have been found to correlate with measures of several individual differences, including self-efficacy, need for achievement, optimism, and negative affectivity (Rybowiak et al., 1999). Researchers have not yet explored why there is an association between attitudes toward errors and individual differences or whether these attitudes relate to cognitions and behaviors in response to actual errors. The framework presented here, however, can serve to delineate the theoretical links between individual differences and error reporting.

Consider the potential role of self-efficacy—one's belief in one's ability to perform a specific task (Bandura, 1977)—on the error reporting process. Kirkpatrick and Locke (1991) suggest that self-confident leaders are more likely to admit their mistakes and use them as learning opportunities than to cover them up. Self-efficacy also has been found to alleviate individuals' image concerns when they are taking part in risky and discretionary "taking charge" activities at work (Morrison & Phelps, 1999). To our knowledge, the effects of self-efficacy on error reporting behaviors have not been studied. Given the framework proposed, we expect that individuals who are high in self-efficacy will tend to experience fewer negative emotions about errors and will be less likely to consider the negative effects of reporting an error on their self-image than individuals with low self-efficacy. This is because individuals with high self-efficacy tend to be confident about success in their work. We also predict that self-efficacy will affect individuals' perceptions of the learning benefits of error reporting such that individuals with high self-efficacy will perceive high learning benefits because they are confident that they can apply their learning to positive effect.

Similar arguments can be drawn to relate other important individual differences, such as optimism and conscientiousness, to elements of the error reporting process. For example, conscientiousness is likely to be associated with error detection, because individuals who are highly conscientious may be more alert to discrepancies between expected and actual states (e.g., because they both anticipate errors and closely monitor their work and because they make a greater effort to understand organizational goals). Given the early state of research in this field, these arguments are clearly speculative. As we noted earlier, our goal is not to generate a comprehensive list of independent variables that may be associated with error reporting but, rather, to provide a framework that can be used to develop meaningful theoretical arguments relating predictors to error reporting through their effects on mediating mechanisms (i.e., error detection, cognitions about the costs and benefits of reporting, and emotions).

We now turn to two theoretical considerations that merit attention and have not yet been discussed in detail in the literature or this framework: the roles of attributions and error types on error reporting.

Attributions

Attribution theory suggests that individuals may cope with negative feedback, such as that experienced because of errors, by attributing their behavior to uncontrollable, external causes (Ilgen & Davis, 2000; Weiner, 1985). An individual's tendency to make external attributions is likely to influence error detection. Errors are, by definition, avoidable. Behaviors that are attributed to uncontrollable causes may not be recognized as errors. Consequently, errors may not be detected because they are "defined away" through attributions (Sellen, 1994). If the behavior is not perceived as an error, the error reporting process will not be initiated.

Attributions are also likely to affect the situation assessment phase as the individual attempts to further understand the causes of the error ("Why did I make this error?") and to assess the potential costs and benefits of reporting ("Will I be blamed and punished for this error? Will the organization or victim benefit from learning about this error?"). Although individuals make errors, the *root* causes of the error may, in fact, not reside in the individuals themselves (e.g., carelessness) but in structural elements, such as faulty procedures or inadequate training (Reason, 2000). Errors can also originate in the actions and decisions of others, including customers, coworkers, and top management. For example, a call center customer service representative may attribute his or her mishandling of a call to unusually high inbound call volume or to being distracted by a coworker.

Determining the causes of errors is likely to entail ambiguities, since multiple factors may contribute to the errors. This is an important theoretical property of errors; ambiguity means that individuals may have difficulty determining the origin of errors they have made. To our knowledge, research has not examined the attributions that individuals develop about their own errors. We anticipate that in situations where the causes of errors are ambiguous, individuals will be likely to attribute the errors externally.

The effects of external attributions on error reporting are likely to be complex and determined by individual dispositions (such as self-efficacy), as well as by organizational factors (such as quality of training, the nature of the task environment, and organizational norms about errors). A likely effect of external attributions on error reporting is that individuals will perceive little cost to self in terms of reprisal or image damage, because they can point to the external causes of their behavior. External attributions may increase perceived benefits to the organization if individuals believe that reporting will result in changes to the external conditions that contributed to the error. However, external attributions may also discourage reporting when they diffuse responsibility ("Why should I be the one to report the error?"; Latané & Darley, 1970). External attributions may also contribute to the development of rationalized accounts of what happened and to a desire to blame others for the error.

Further research and theorizing are needed to understand how attributions affect individuals' cognitions about errors. The framework presented here provides a useful point of departure for thinking about how attributions relate to error reporting.

Error Types

We noted earlier that error detection rates have been found to vary by error type (Rizzo et al., 1987; Sellen, 1994; Zapf et al., 1994). Specifically, research suggests that slips are more likely to be detected than rule- or knowledge-based mistakes. Therefore, we expect that slips will be more likely to be reported than mistakes, simply because they are more likely to be detected. However, there has been, to our knowledge, no research exploring whether individuals react differently to detecting a slip versus a mistake.

We anticipate that reactions to different types of errors are likely to be context dependent. For example, in environments where slips are common (such as service organizations), knowledge-based mistakes may seem more threatening to an individual's image, particularly if the tasks are of low complexity. In contrast, in environments that require vigilance and where errors can result in injury or loss of human life (such as hospitals and airport security), slips may be perceived as highly threatening in terms of potential reprisal.

It is also conceivable that different types of errors result in different emotional reactions. For example, knowledge-based mistakes may generate feelings of shame and may seem particularly threatening to one's self-image because they demonstrate incompetence. We believe that the type and distribution of errors within task environments will have an impact on the error reporting process and that this is an important topic for further research.

Time Pressure

Situational factors, such as time pressure or other stress-eliciting conditions, are likely to affect error reporting cognitions (Svenson, 1996). Research examining the effect of time pressure on judgment and decision making suggests that, as time pressure increases, people use information-processing strategies that demand less cognitive resources. For example, Ford, Schmitt, Scheitman, Hults, and Doherty (1989) found that, when time constraints are introduced, people quickly reject alternatives when they fail to meet a minimum acceptable level on any attribute, rather than evaluate all attributes of each alternative under consideration. In addition, people may adjust to time pressure by filtering or neglecting information that is perceived to be of low priority (Wright, 1974). Hence, we expect that individuals under time pressure will simplify the decision process by considering few rather than multiple elements in the situation assessment.

We note, however, that individuals may also postpone their situation assessment until a time when they are able to carefully contemplate the costs and benefits of reporting. Also, some behavioral responses, such as handling the error on one's own, may not be possible choices under time pressure. Although a comprehensive discussion of contextual factors like time pressure is beyond the scope of this paper, we note that the framework offers opportunities for researchers to elaborate on their potential effects.

Conclusion

Reason (1990) argued that studies of human error should go beyond cognitive theories to include the interaction of individual tendencies with situational factors inherent in groups or organizations. We see our proposed framework as a first step in this direction. First, we have focused on an important and understudied aspect of human errors in work settings—why and how do individuals report their own errors? Second, we have considered cognitive as well as emotional and motivational elements in the error reporting process. Third, by integrating research from various disciplines (human error, learning, discretionary behaviors, and high-reliability organizations), we have developed a framework that helps us understand individuals' error reporting in various organizational settings.

To err is human. Human behavior is subject to cognitive biases, and human beings are predisposed to err in a variety of situations (Norman, 1981; Rasmussen, 1987; Reason, 1990). While some errors can be reduced through training, most errors are intrinsic to mental functioning and cannot be eliminated entirely by training programs (Frese, 1991; Reason, 1990). In fact, the nature of many tasks is such that knowledge and expertise can be gained only through trial-and-error learning. Individuals' error reporting is a critical antecedent to the detection, study, and analysis of errors and, thus, to learning.

Acknowledgments

We are grateful for the valuable feedback provided by Natalie Allen, Brian Golden, Amy Hillman, John Meyer, and Christine Pearson on earlier drafts of this paper and to Elizabeth Mannix and three anonymous reviewers for their insightful and constructive guidance in the review process. This research was supported by a grant from the Social Sciences and Humanities Research Council of Canada.

References

Anderson, C. J. 2003. The psychology of doing nothing: Forms of decision avoidance result from reason and emotion. *Psychological Bulletin*, 129: 139–167.

Argyris, C. 1993. *Knowledge for action: A guide to overcoming barriers to organizational change*. San Francisco: Jossey-Bass.

Ashford, S. J., & Cummings, L. L. 1983. Feedback as an individual resource: Personal strategies of creating information. *Organizational Behavior and Human Performance*, 32: 379–398.

Ashford, S. J., Rothbard N. P., Piderit, S. K., & Dutton, J. E. 1998. Out on a limb: The role of context and impression management in selling gender-equity issues. *Administrative Science Quarterly*, 43: 23–57.

Baker, G. R., & Norton, P. 2001. Making patients safer! Reducing error in Canadian healthcare. *Healthcare Papers*, 2(1): 10–31.

Bandura, A. 1977. *Social learning theory*. Englewood Cliffs, NJ: Prentice-Hall.

Barach, P., & Small, S. D. 2000. Reporting and preventing medical mishaps: Lessons from non-medical near miss reporting systems. *British Medical Journal*, 320: 759–763.

Baumeister, R. 1998. The self. In D. T. Gilbert, S. T. Fiske, & G. Lindzey (Eds.), *The handbook of social psychology*, vol. 1: 680–740. Boston: McGraw-Hill.

Bendapudi, N., Singh, S. N., & Bendapudi, V. 1996. Enhancing helping behavior: An integrative framework for promotion planning. *Journal of Marketing*, 60(3): 33–49.

Bosk, C. L. 1979. *Forgive and remember: Managing medical failure*. Chicago: University of Chicago Press.

Brodbeck, F. C., Zapf, D., Prumper, J., & Frese, M. 1993. Error handling in office work with computers: A field study. *Journal of Occupational and Organizational Psychology*, 66: 303–317.

Cannon, M. D., & Edmondson, A. C. 2001. Confronting failure: Antecedents and consequences of shared beliefs about failure in organizational work groups. *Journal of Organizational Behavior*, 22: 161–177.

Carroll, J. S., Rudolph, J. W., & Hatakenaka, S. 2002. Learning from experience in high-hazard organizations. *Research in Organizational Behavior*, 24: 87–137.

Chase, R. B., & Stewart, D. M. 1995. *Mistake-proofing: Designing errors out*. Portland, OR: Productivity Press.

Chiang, M. 2001. Promoting patient safety: Creating a workable reporting system. *Yale Journal on Regulation*, 18: 383–407.

Dozier, J. B., & Miceli, M. P. 1985. Potential predictors of whistle-blowing: A prosocial behavior perspective. *Academy of Management Review*, 10: 823–836.

Edmondson, A. C. 1996. Learning from mistakes is easier said than done: Group and organizational influences on the detection and correction of human error. *Journal of Applied Behavioral Science*, 32: 5–32.

Edmondson, A. C. 1999. Psychological safety and learning behavior in work teams. *Administrative Science Quarterly*, 44: 350–383.

Ellsworth, P. C., & Smith, C. 1988. From appraisal to emotion: Differences among unpleasant feelings. *Motivation and Emotion*, 12: 271–302.

Ford, J. K., Schmitt, N., Scheitman, S. L., Hults, B. M., & Doherty, M. L. 1989. Process tracing methods: Contributions, problems, and neglected research questions. *Organizational Behavior and Human Decision Processes*, 43: 75–117.

Forgas, J. P. 1995. Mood and judgment: The affect infusion model (AIM). *Psychological Bulletin*, 117: 39–66.

Frese, M. 1987. The industrial and organizational psychology of human-computer interaction in the office. In C. L. Cooper & I. T. Robertson (Eds.), *International review of industrial and organizational psychology:* 117–166. Chichester, UK: Wiley.

Frese, M. 1991. Error management or error prevention: Two strategies to deal with errors in software design. In H. J. Bullinger (Ed.), *Human aspects in computing: Design and use of interactive systems and work with terminals:* 776–782. New York: Elsevier Science.

Gawande, A. 2002. *Complications: A surgeon's notes on an imperfect science.* New York: Henry Holt.

Goodman, P. S. 2000. *Missing organizational linkages: Tools for cross-level research.* Thousand Oaks, CA: Sage.

Gundlach, M. J., Douglas, S. C., & Martinko, M. J. 2003. The decision to blow the whistle: A social information processing framework. *Academy of Management Review*, 28: 107–123.

Heimbeck, D., Frese, M., Sonnentang, S., & Keith, N. 2003. Integrating errors into the training process: The function of error management instructions and the role of goal orientation. *Personnel Psychology*, 56: 333–361.

Helmreich, R. L. 1997. Managing human error in aviation. *Scientific American*, May: 62–67.

Hollenbeck, J. R., Ilgen, D. R., Tuttle, D. B., & Sego, D. J. 1995. Team performance on monitoring task: An examination of decision errors in contexts requiring sustained attention. *Journal of Applied Psychology*, 80: 685–696.

Ilgen, D. R., & Davis, C. A. 2000. Bearing bad news: Reactions to negative performance feedback. *Applied Psychology: An International Review*, 49: 550–565.

Kirkpatrick, S. A., & Locke, E. A. 1991. Leadership: Do traits matter? *Academy of Management Executive*, 5(2): 48–60.

Latané, B., & Darley, J. M. 1970. *The unresponsive bystander: Why doesn't he help?* New York: Appleton-Century-Crofts.

Lazarus, R. S. 1991. *Emotion and adaptation.* New York: Oxford University Press.

Lecky, P. 1945. *Self-consistency: A theory of personality.* New York: Island Press.

Lee, F., Edmondson, A. C., Thomke, S., & Worline, M. 2004. The mixed effects of inconsistency on experimentation in organizations. *Organization Science*, 15: 310–326.

Lee, K., & Allen, N. J. 2002. Organizational citizenship behavior and workplace deviance: The role of affect and cognitions. *Journal of Applied Psychology*, 87: 131–142.

Lerner, J. S., & Keltner, D. 2001. Fear, anger, and risk. *Journal of Personality and Social Psychology*, 81: 146–159.

Lewis, M. 1992. *Shame: The exposed self.* New York: Free Press.

Lewis, M. 2000. Self-conscious emotions: Embarrassment, pride, shame, and guilt. In M. Lewis & J. M. Haviland-Jones (Eds.), *Handbook of emotions* (2nd ed.): 623–636. New York: Guilford Press.

Loewenstein, G. F., Weber, E. U., Hsee, C. K., & Welch, N. 2001. Risk as feelings. *Psychological Bulletin*, 127: 267–286.

Meyer, J. P., & Herscovitch, L. 2001. Commitment in the workplace: Toward a general model. *Human Resource Management Review*, 11: 299–326.

Morrison, E. W., & Phelps, C. C. 1999. Taking charge at work: Extrarole efforts to initiate workplace change. *Academy of Management Journal*, 42: 403–419.

Naquin, C. E., & Kurtzberg, T. R. 2004. Human reactions to technological failure: How accidents rooted in technology vs. human error influence judgments of organizational accountability. *Organizational Behavior and Human Decision Processes*, 93: 129–141.

Norman, D. A. 1981. Categorization of action slips. *Psychological Review*, 88: 1–15.

Paget, M. A. 1988. *The unity of mistakes.* Philadelphia: Temple University Press.

Pearn, M., Mulrooney, C., & Payne, T. 1998. *Ending the blame culture.* Brookfield, VT: Gower.

Pinder, C. C. 1998. *Work motivation in organizational behavior.* Upper Saddle River, NJ: Prentice-Hall.

Raghunathan, R., & Pham, M. T. 1999. All negative moods are not equal: Motivational influences of anxiety and sadness on decision making. *Organizational Behavior and Human Decision Processes*, 79: 56–77.

Rasmussen, J. 1987. Cognitive control and human error mechanisms. In J. Rasmussen, K. Duncan, & J. Leplat (Eds.), *New technology and human error:* 53–62. New York: Wiley.

Reason, J. T. 1987. Generic error-modeling system (GEMS): A cognitive framework for locating common human error form. In J. Rasmussen, K. Duncan, & J. Leplat (Eds.), *New technology and human error:* 63–86. New York: Wiley.

Reason, J. T. 1990. *Human error.* New York: Cambridge University Press.

Reason, J. T. 1997. *Managing the risks of organizational accidents.* Brookfield, VT: Ashgate.

Reason, J. T. 2000. Human error: Models and management. *British Medical Journal*, 320: 768–770.

Rizzo, A., Bagnara, S., & Visciola, M. 1987. Human error detection processes. *International Journal of Man-Machine Studies*, 27: 555–570.

Roberts, K. H. 1990. Some characteristics of high reliability organizations. *Organization Science*, 1: 160–177.

Roberts, K. H., & Bea, R. 2001. Must accidents happen? Lessons from high-reliability organizations. *Academy of Management Executive*, 15(3): 70–78.

Roseman, I. J., Wiest, C., & Swartz, T. S. 1994. Phenomenology, behaviors, and goals differentiate discrete emotions. *Journal of Personality and Social Psychology*, 67: 206–221.

Rosenberg, M. 1979. *Conceiving the self.* New York: Basic Books.

Rybowiak, V., Garst, H., Frese, M., & Batinic, B. 1999. Error Orientation Questionnaire (EOQ): Reliability, validity, and different language equivalence. *Journal of Organizational Behavior*, 20: 527–547.

Schwarz, N. 1990. Feelings as information: Informational and motivational functions of affective states. In E. T. Higgins & R. M. Sorrentino (Eds.), *Handbook of motivation and cognition: Foundations of social behavior*, vol. 2: 527–561. New York: Guilford Press.

See, J. E., Howe, S. R., Warm, J. S., & Dember, W. N. 1995. Meta-analysis of the sensitivity decrement in vigilance. *Psychological Bulletin*, 117: 230–249.

Seifert, C., & Hutchins, E. 1992. Errors as opportunity: Learning in a cooperative task. *Human Computer Interaction*, 7: 409–435.

Sellen, A. J. 1994. Detection of everyday errors. *Applied Psychology: An International Review*, 43: 475–498.

Sexton, J. B., Thomas, E. J., & Helmreich, R. L. 2000. Error, stress, and teamwork in medicine and aviation: Cross sectional surveys. *British Medical Journal*, 320: 745–749.

Sitkin, S. B. 1992. Learning through failure: The strategy of small losses. *Research in Organizational Behavior*, 14: 231–266.

Smith, C. A., & Ellsworth, P. C. 1985. Patterns of cognitive appraisal in emotion. *Journal of Personality and Social Psychology*, 48: 813–838.

Smith, R. H., Webster, J. M., Parrott, W. G., & Eyre, H. L. 2002. The role of public exposure in moral and nonmoral shame and guilt. *Journal of Personality and Social Psychology*, 83: 138–159.

Stewart, D. M., & Chase, R. B. 1999. The impact of human error on delivering service quality. *Production and Operations Management*, 8: 240–263.

Svenson, O. 1996. Decision making and the search for fundamental psychological regularities: What can be learned from a process perspective? *Organizational Behavior and Human Decision Processes*, 65: 252–267.

Swann, W. B. 1983. Self-verification: Bringing social reality into harmony with the self. In J. Suls & A.

G. Greenwald (Eds.), *Psychological perspectives on the self*, vol. 2: 33–66. Hillsdale, NJ: Lawrence Erlbaum Associates.

Swann, W. B. 1985. The self as architect of social reality. In B. R. Schlenker (Ed.), *The self and social life:* 100–125. New York: McGraw-Hill.

Swann, W. B., & Hill, C. A. 1982. When our identities are mistaken: Reaffirming self-conception through social interaction. *Journal of Personality and Social Psychology*, 43: 59–66.

Tangney, J. P. 1990. Assessing individual differences in proneness to shame and guilt: Development of the Self-Conscious Affect and Attribution Inventory. *Journal of Personality and Social Psychology*, 59: 102–111.

Tangney, J. P. 1991. Moral affect: The good, the bad, and the ugly. *Journal of Personality and Social Psychology*, 61: 598–607.

Tangney, J. P., Miller, R. S., Flicker, L., & Barlow, D. H. 1996. Are shame, guilt, and embarrassment distinct emotions? *Journal of Personality and Social Psychology*, 70: 1256–1269.

Tangney, J. P., Wagner, P., Fletcher, C., & Gramzow, R. 1992. Shamed into anger? The relation of shame and guilt to anger and self-reported aggression. *Journal of Personality and Social Psychology*, 62: 669–675.

Tax, S. S., & Brown, S. W. 1998. Recovering and learning from service failure. *Sloan Management Review*, 40(1): 75–88.

Tucker, A. L., & Edmondson, A. 2003. Why hospitals don't learn from failures: Organizational and psychological dynamics that inhibit system change. *California Management Review*, 45(2): 55–72.

Tucker, A. L., Edmondson, A., & Spear, S. 2002. When problem solving prevents organizational learning. *Journal of Organizational Change Management*, 15(2): 122–137.

Uribe, C. L., Schweikhart, S. B., Pathak, D. S., & Marsh, G. B. 2002. Perceived barriers to medical-error reporting: An exploratory investigation. *Journal of Healthcare Management*, 47(4): 264–279.

Vaughan, D. 1999. The dark side of organizations: Mistake, misconduct, and disaster. *Annual Review of Sociology*, 25: 271–305.

Weick, K. E., & Sutcliffe, K. M. 2001. *Managing the unexpected: Assuring high performance in an age of complexity.* San Francisco: Jossey-Bass.

Weiner, B. 1985. An attributional theory of achievement motivation and emotion. *Psychological Review*, 4: 548–573.

Wright, P. L. 1974. The harassed decision maker: Time pressures, distractions and the use of evidence. *Journal of Applied Psychology*, 59: 555–561.

Zajonc, R. B. 1998. Emotions. In D. T. Gilbert, S. T. Fiske, & G. Lindzey (Eds.), *The handbook of social psychology*, vol. 2: 591–632. Boston: McGraw-Hill.

Zapf, D., Maier, G. W., Rappensperger, G., & Irmer, C. 1994. Error detection, task characteristics, and some consequences for software design. *Applied Psychology: An International Review*, 43: 499–520.

Zapf, D., & Reason, J. T. 1994. Human errors and error handling. *Applied Psychology: An International Review*, 43: 427–432.

4.2   THE EFFECTS OF PERSONAL AND CONTEXTUAL CHARACTERISTICS ON CREATIVITY

Where Should We Go From Here?

Christina E. Shalley, Jing Zhou, and Greg R. Oldham

This article systematically reviews and integrates empirical research that has examined the personal and contextual characteristics that enhance or stifle employee creativity in the workplace. Based on our review, we discuss possible determinants of employee creativity that have received little research attention, describe several areas where substantial challenges and unanswered questions remain, present a number of new research directions for theory building, and identify methodological improvements needed in future studies of creativity in organizations.

Considerable evidence now suggests that employee creativity can substantially contribute to organizational innovation, effectiveness, and survival (Amabile, 1996; Nonaka, 1991). When employees exhibit creativity at work, they produce novel, potentially useful ideas about organizational products, practices, services or procedures (Shalley & Gilson, 2004). The presence of these creative ideas increases the likelihood that other employees will apply the ideas in their own work, further develop the ideas, and then transfer them to other individuals in the organization for their own use and development. It is the use and development of creative ideas that allows the organization to adjust to shifting market conditions, respond to opportunities, and thereby, to adapt, grow and compete (Nonaka, 1991; Oldham, 2002).

Given the potential significance of employee creativity, it is not surprising that a number of recent empirical studies have examined the personal and contextual factors that enhance or restrict it (e.g., Amabile, Schatzel, Moneta & Kramer, 2004; Rodan & Galunic, 2004; Tierney & Farmer, 2002; Zhou, 2003). The purpose of this article is to review and integrate the results of this literature. Since most of the earlier research has addressed the determinants of creativity exhibited by individual employees, this will be the emphasis of our review. We provide a synthesis of what we currently know about creativity, and then suggest a number of new directions for creativity research.

Background

Over the past two decades, most theorists have defined creativity as the development of ideas about products, practices, services or procedures that are (a) novel and (b) potentially useful to the organization (see Amabile, 1996; Zhou & Shalley, 2003). Ideas are considered novel if they are unique relative to other ideas currently available in the organization. Ideas are considered useful if they have the potential for direct or indirect value to the organization, in either the short- or long-term. Given this definition, creativity could range from suggestions for incremental adaptations in procedures to radical, major breakthroughs in the development of new products (Mumford & Gustafson, 1988). The definition makes no assumptions about the relative value of incremental vs. radical ideas, and it may be that in some circumstances management might consider incremental ideas desirable, whereas in other circumstances more radical ideas might be valued. Finally, our definition assumes that creative ideas may be generated by employees in any job and at any level of the organization (Madjar, Oldham & Pratt, 2002; Shalley, Gilson & Blum, 2000).

Most studies have measured creativity using ratings by individuals who are believed to have advanced knowledge within the domain of interest. Specifically, laboratory studies have generally used expert judges to rate the creativity of ideas produced by research participants (e.g., Shalley, 1995; Zhou, 1998). By contrast, most field studies have relied upon supervisors to judge an employee's creativity (e.g., George & Zhou, 2001; Tierney & Farmer, 2002). Additionally, some field studies have included objective measures that may reflect creativity, such as, patent disclosures, technical reports, and ideas submitted to suggestion programs (e.g., Frese, Teng & Wijnen, 1999; Oldham & Cummings, 1996; Tierney, Farmer & Graen, 1999).

It is important to distinguish creativity from innovation. Creativity refers to the development of novel, potentially useful ideas. Although employees might share these ideas with others, only when the ideas are successfully implemented at the organization or unit level would they be considered innovation (Amabile, 1996; Mumford & Gustafson, 1988). Therefore, creativity might best be conceptualized as a first step that is necessary for subsequent innovation (West & Farr, 1990). In this article, we focus exclusively on creativity.

Finally, we limit our review to published studies that (a) have included measures of creativity that match our definition (novel, potentially useful ideas), (b) have used samples from normal, adult populations, and (c) assessed variables that have clear implications for organizations. Personal or contextual factors are included in our review if they have been examined in a minimum of three published research investigations. In conducting our review, in order to be comprehensive in our coverage of the creativity literature, we searched PsychInfo and major journals in the field (e.g., *Academy of Management Journal, Journal of Applied Psychology, Journal of Management, Organizational Behavior and Human Decision Processes,* and *Personnel Psychology*).

Employee Creativity: An Organizing Framework

Our framework argues that creativity is a function of the employee's personal characteristics, the characteristics of the context in which he or she works, and also the interactions among these characteristics. The argument that personal and contextual characteristics interact with one another essentially asserts that certain contexts "match" individuals' personal characteristics and that this match results in high levels of employee creativity. This framework is derived from earlier theory on creativity that has emphasized the importance of person-context interactions (e.g., Amabile, 1996; Woodman, Sawyer & Griffin, 1993), and from the broader literature on person-environment fit (e.g., Kristof, 1996; Schneider, 1987).

The personal characteristics described in our review include personality and cognitive style dimensions that have received substantial attention in the creativity literature. Both sets of characteristics are expected to affect individuals' creativity by influencing the extent to which they apply various strategies that may facilitate creative idea production. For example, individuals with certain personality characteristics may be especially effective at recognizing problems or at combining new information, which may enable them to produce more creative work. Thus, our review includes the studies that have examined the direct effects of personality and cognitive style variables on the creativity individuals exhibit at work.

We broadly define contextual characteristics as dimensions of the work environment that potentially influence an employee's creativity but that are not part of the individual. As such, characteristics of the job, work setting, and relationships with coworkers and supervisors would all be considered contextual factors. Drawing on early theory and research (e.g., Amabile, 1996; Deci & Ryan, 1985), we posit that each contextual characteristic affects creativity via its effects on employees' "intrinsic motivation" to perform a work assignment.

Intrinsic motivation refers to the extent to which an individual is excited about a work activity and engages in it for the sake of the activity itself (Utman, 1997). Scholars have long argued that individuals are likely to be most creative when they experience high levels of intrinsic motivation (see Amabile, 1996) since such motivation increases their tendency to be curious, cognitively flexible, risk taking, and persistent in the face of barriers (Utman, 1997; Zhou & Shalley, 2003) all of which should facilitate the development of creative ideas.

The expected effects of contextual characteristics on intrinsic motivation can be explained using Cognitive Evaluation Theory (Deci & Ryan, 1985). This theory posits that all contextual factors have two aspects: informational and controlling. The relative salience of these aspects determines whether a contextual factor has positive or negative effects on intrinsic motivation. When the controlling aspect is more salient, individuals perceive that their thoughts, feelings, or actions are being constrained by the contextual factor itself and feel that they are no longer the origin of their own thoughts or actions. As a result, intrinsic motivation should diminish, and individuals would be expected to exhibit low levels of creativity. By contrast, when the informational aspect of a contextual factor is more salient, individuals perceive that the factor exerts little external pressure to achieve things in prescribed ways and provides relevant information about their personal competence. In this situation, individuals should feel supported and encouraged, resulting in enhanced intrinsic motivation and subsequent creativity.

Finally, our framework argues that to more fully understand creativity it is necessary to consider both interactions between personal and contextual characteristics and interactions among different contextual characteristics. Thus, in addition to reviewing studies that have examined the direct effects of contextual and personal characteristics on creativity, we also review those that have examined the possibility that these contextual characteristics interact with one another to affect individuals' creative accomplishments. The argument for addressing person-context interactions is that individuals with certain personal characteristics are most likely to value the rewards and opportunities provided by particular contextual factors and, as a result, exhibit higher creativity when they are present. Further, the argument that contextual characteristics might interact with one another is that employees may be more likely to attend to or appreciate the qualities of one contextual variable when another contextual factor is simultaneously present.

The Impact of Personal Characteristics on Creativity

A large body of literature has examined the possibility that creativity is affected by a variety of individual difference characteristics (e.g., demographic and biographic variables) (Rodan & Galunic, 2004; Schaefer, 1969; Tierney & Farmer, 2002). Our review focuses on those characteristics that have received the most research attention—namely, individuals' personalities and cognitive styles.

Personality

Much of the early work examining the effects of personality used either Gough's (1979) Creative Personality Scale (CPS) or measures of one or more dimensions associated with the Five Factor Model of personality (FFM; Costa & McCrae, 1992). The CPS measure is intended to provide an index of an individual's overall creative potential. Those who score high on the measure are expected to approach problems with broad interests that enable them to recognize divergent information and opinions (Barron & Harrington, 1981).

In addition, these individuals are thought to possess the self-confidence and tolerance for ambiguity to be patient with competing views, and to persist in developing their own original ideas.

Results of previous studies provide some support for the expected positive relation between CPS and creativity (Feist, 1998, 1999; Oldham & Cummings, 1996; Zhou & Oldham, 2001). For example, Gough (1979) found positive, significant correlations between the CPS and creativity ratings for 10 of 12 groups of individuals (e.g., architects and scientists).

All of the FFM dimensions (i.e., neuroticism, agreeableness, conscientiousness, extraversion, and openness to experience) have several components but research has found that they hang together as five relatively stable factors (see Feist, 1998). Studies that have examined the FFM dimensions have demonstrated that each is connected to individuals' creativity. However, the FFM dimension that has been most consistently related to creativity is openness to experience (Feist, 1998, 1999). Individuals high on the openness dimension are those who are broad minded, curious, and untraditional. By contrast, those low on openness tend to be conventional, unartistic, and unanalytical. Moreover, McCrae and Costa (1997) argue that open individuals are both more flexible in absorbing information and combining new and unrelated information, and also have a higher need to seek out unfamiliar situations that allow for greater access to new experiences and perspectives.

As indicated above, results of earlier studies show that openness to experience generally relates positively to creativity across a variety of domains (Feist, 1998). For example, a recent study of creativity in organizations showed a positive, significant correlation between openness to experience and creativity as rated by managers (Scratchley & Hakstian, 2000). Research has also shown that measures of openness correlate positively with CPS (McCrae, 1987; Piedmont, McCrae & Costa, 1991).

Cognitive Style

Early theory suggests that individuals' cognitive style might have a direct effect on their creativity (Amabile, 1996; Woodman et al., 1993). The approach to understanding and measuring cognitive style that has received the most attention in the literature is based on Kirton's (1976, 1994) Adaption-Innovation Theory. This theory posits that individuals have a natural orientation or a preferred means of creative problem solving. Specifically, Kirton proposes a bipolar continuum of cognitive styles with adaptors and innovators being located at opposite ends. Individuals with an adaptive cognitive style (adaptors) tend to operate within given paradigms and procedures without questioning their validity, whereas those with an innovative style (innovators) tend to be more willing to take the risk of violating the agreed-upon way of doing things in order to develop problem solutions that are qualitatively different from previous ones.

A number of investigations have examined the relation between individuals' cognitive style and creative outcomes (see Kirton, 1994; Masten & Caldwell-Colbert, 1987). Results suggest that individuals with an innovative style tend to be more creative than those with an adaptive style (e.g., Keller, 1986; Lowe & Taylor, 1986). For example, Tierney et al. (1999) showed that an innovative cognitive style was predictive of two indicators of employee creativity (supervisory ratings and number of research reports).

Although a few previous studies have shown significant relations among measures of cognitive style and personality (see Kirton, 1994; Kwang & Rodrigues, 2002), previous research has not examined whether cognitive style and personality make independent contributions to creativity or whether they interact with one another to affect individuals' creative responses. This is a potentially fruitful topic for future research that would allow us to determine if individuals with particular personality profiles are most creative if they also possess a certain cognitive style.

The Impact of Contextual Characteristics on Creativity

Next, we review those contextual characteristics that have received attention in the literature, and explain how each characteristic might affect creativity based on the intrinsic motivation perspective described earlier. The characteristics we examine here are (a) job complexity; (b) relationship with supervisors; (c) relationship with coworkers; (d) rewards; (e) evaluation; (f) time deadlines and goals; and (g) spatial configurations of work settings.

Job Complexity

The design of jobs has long been considered an important contributor to employee creativity (West & Farr, 1990). When individuals work on complex jobs (i.e., those characterized by high levels of autonomy, feedback, significance, identity and variety) (Hackman & Oldham, 1980) they are likely to experience high levels of intrinsic motivation and to respond to this motivation by developing creative ideas. Specifically, complex jobs should enhance individuals' excitement about their work activities and their interest in completing these activities, and this excitement should foster creativity.

Previous studies provide results that are generally consistent with these arguments (e.g., Amabile & Gryskiewicz, 1989; Farmer, Tierney & Kung-McIntyre, 2003; Oldham & Cummings, 1996). For example, Tierney and Farmer (2002, 2004) showed positive, significant relations between supervisory ratings of creativity and objective measures of employees' job complexity derived from the Dictionary of Occupational Titles (Roos & Treiman, 1980). Also, Hatcher, Ross and Collins (1989) found significant relations between employee self-reports of job complexity and the number of creative ideas they submitted to an organization suggestion program.

Relationship with Supervisors

Numerous studies have examined relations between a supervisor's leadership style and employee creativity. Following the intrinsic motivation perspective, supportive leadership styles are expected to boost intrinsic motivation, whereas those that are controlling in nature are expected to diminish intrinsic motivation and creativity (Deci & Ryan, 1985). When supervisors are supportive they show concern for employees' feelings, provide non-judgmental, informational feedback about their work, and encourage them to voice their own concerns (Deci, Connell & Ryan, 1989). By contrast, controlling supervisors closely monitor employee behavior, make decisions without involving employees, and generally demand that employees follow strict rules and guidelines (Deci et al., 1989).

Although a few studies have failed to show significant relations between supervisory support and employee creativity (e.g., George & Zhou, 2001; Zhou, 2003), the vast majority of earlier studies provide substantial support for the expected relations between supportive and controlling leadership styles and creativity (e.g., Amabile & Conti, 1999; Amabile et al.,

1996, 2004; Amabile & Gryskiewicz, 1989; Andrews & Farris, 1967; Madjar et al., 2002; Oldham & Cummings, 1996; Shalley & Gilson, 2004; Tierney & Farmer, 2002, 2004; Zhou & George, 2003). For example, Frese et al. (1999) demonstrated that the more supervisors encouraged employees, the more creative ideas they submitted to the organization's suggestion program. Shin and Zhou (2003) found positive relations between "transformational" leadership (i.e., providing intellectual stimulation, individualized consideration, and inspirational motivation) and creativity measures. Stahl and Koser (1978) found negative relations between supervisors' controlling behavior and R&D scientists' creative output. Similarly, George and Zhou (2001) and Zhou (2003) showed that controlling behavior (i.e., close monitoring) on the part of supervisors was negatively related to employee creativity.

Relationship with Coworkers

Just as supportive, noncontrolling supervisory behavior is expected to boost employees' intrinsic motivation and creativity, analogous behaviors on the part of employees' coworkers are expected to have similar effects. That is, employees are expected to exhibit high levels of creativity when their coworkers are nurturing and supportive, since such behavior enhances intrinsic motivation. Conversely, nonsupportive, competitive coworkers should undermine intrinsic motivation and lower creativity.

Previous research provides only mixed support for these arguments (Amabile & Gryskiewicz, 1989; Cummings & Oldham, 1997; Madjar et al., 2002; McGlynn, Gibbs & Roberts, 1982; Torrance, 1965). For example, Amabile et al. (1996) found that individuals in work teams were more creative when their coworkers were supportive and encouraging. Similarly, Zhou and George (2001) showed positive, significant relations between employee creativity and coworker support and informational feedback. However, other studies failed to support these arguments. George and Zhou (2001) found nonsignificant relations between employee creativity and the extent to which coworkers provided constructive "helping" at work or inaccurate communication. Van Dyne, Jehn and Cummings (2002) found a nonsignificant relation between creativity and "work strain" (i.e., the extent to which the employee argued with members of his or her work group and experienced conflict with them). Finally, Shalley and Oldham (1997) showed that individuals in competition with others generated ideas higher in overall creativity than those who were not in competition.

Rewards

Although the effect of contingent rewards (e.g., monetary incentives and recognition) on individuals' creativity has received much research attention (Amabile, 1996; Eisenberger, 1992), there is little agreement among scholars concerning the likely direction of the effects of such rewards. That is, some authors argue that contingent rewards serve to control individuals' behavior, thereby resulting in diminished intrinsic motivation and creativity (Amabile, 1996). Others argue that such rewards boost creativity because rewards have informational value and recognize individuals' personal competencies (Eisenberger, 1992; Eisenberger & Armeli, 1997).

Early empirical research has done little to sort out which of these positions is valid, and support has been found for both positions (e.g., Amabile, Hennessey & Grossman, 1986; George & Zhou, 2002). For example, Eisenberger and Rhoades (2001) showed that story titles produced by college students who were promised money were significantly more creative than the titles of students not promised rewards. Conversely, Kruglanski, Friedman and

Zeevi (1971) showed that college students not promised a reward exhibited higher creativity on two tasks than those who were promised rewards.

Evaluation

A number of early studies examined the effects of anticipated evaluation of an individual's work on the creativity of that work (Zhou & Shalley, 2003). Most of this earlier work focused on the effects of an anticipated judgmental evaluation, that is, an evaluation that critically assessed the creativity of an individual's work and contrasted it to some standard (Oldham, 2002). A smaller set of studies examined the effects of an anticipated developmental evaluation (i.e., an evaluation that is nonjudgmental and intended to facilitate the development of an individual's skills) (Shalley, 1995). Following the intrinsic motivation perspective, it is expected that individuals would experience judgmental evaluations as controlling. Consequently, they should focus their attentions on the evaluation rather than on their work activities; this would result in lowered intrinsic motivation and subsequently lower creativity. Conversely, individuals should experience developmental evaluations as supportive and informational, and therefore exhibit higher creativity.

Previous studies provide results that are generally consistent with the argument that creativity is lower when individuals expect their work to be critically judged. Moreover, these effects tend to emerge regardless of the source that is expected to conduct the evaluation (e.g., experimenters, experts, computers, or the individual him/herself) (Bartis, Szymanski & Harkins, 1988; Cheek & Stahl, 1986; Szymanski & Harkins, 1992). For example, Amabile (1979) showed that individuals who expected their artwork to be critically evaluated by experts submitted less creative work than individuals in no-evaluation conditions. Likewise, Amabile, Goldfarb and Brackfield (1990) showed that the creativity of poems and collages was significantly lower among individuals expecting a judgmental evaluation of their work than of those expecting no critical evaluation.

Studies that focused on the effects of developmental evaluation typically produced results showing its positive effect on creativity (Shalley, 1995; Zhou & Oldham, 2001). For example, Shalley and Perry-Smith (2001) demonstrated that the creativity of individuals who anticipated a judgmental evaluation was significantly lower than those expecting a developmental evaluation (i.e., experts would review individuals' work and provide suggestions for alternative approaches to be considered in the future). In addition, Zhou (1998) demonstrated that evaluative feedback on a preliminary task that was delivered in a developmental, informational style (i.e., "You did very well. Congratulations! Keep up the good work.") yielded higher creativity on a subsequent task than early task feedback provided in a controlling fashion (i.e., "You did very well, just as you should. But remember, you must keep your creativity at this level so that we can use your data.").

Time Deadlines and Goals

The presence of time deadlines or production goals has often been mentioned as a possible constraint on creativity (see Amabile, 1996). When tight deadlines or production goals are present, individuals are expected to feel pressured to meet these deadlines or goals, resulting in lowered intrinsic motivation and creativity (Amabile, Hadley & Kramer, 2002).

Previous studies provide only mixed results for these expected effects (e.g., Amabile et al., 1996; Amabile & Gryskiewicz, 1989; Carson & Carson, 1993; Shalley, 1995; Soriano de Alencar & Bruno-Faria, 1997). For example, Shalley (1991) found that creativity was low when individuals were given either a "do-your-best" or difficult productivity goal. Andrews and Smith (1996) showed a negative relation between experienced time pressure and the creativity of ideas produced by marketing professionals. However, Andrews and Farris (1972) found positive, significant relations between scientists' experienced time pressure and their creativity. Finally, Kelly and McGrath (1985) found that products generated by individuals working under a 10-minute time limit were less creative than those working under a 20-minute limit.

There is some evidence that the presence of a different type of goal, a creativity goal (e.g., 90% of the ideas you generate should be creative) might have positive effects on employee creativity and mitigate the effects of production goals (Carson & Carson, 1993; Shalley, 1995). For example, Shalley (1991) showed that individuals assigned to both "do-your-best" and difficult productivity goal conditions exhibited higher creativity if either a do-your-best or difficult creativity goal also was assigned. It may be that a creativity goal causes individuals to focus their attention on the task itself, and allows them to disregard the pressure from a production goal or deadline.

Spatial Configuration of Work Settings

A few studies have examined the possibility that dimensions of a setting's spatial configuration (e.g., number of physical boundaries present in the setting, distance between individuals in the setting, and the overall density of the setting [i.e., number of individuals per unit of space]) might have a substantial impact on individuals' creativity (Aiello, DeRisi, Epstein & Karlin, 1977; Shalley & Oldham, 1997). Early work established that individuals who worked in dense settings with few boundaries experienced more unwanted or unexpected interpersonal intrusions, which then affected their attitudes and behaviors (Oldham, Cummings & Zhou, 1995; Sundstrom, 1986). It may also be that the unexpected interruptions present in dense settings distract individuals' attention from the work itself, lowering their intrinsic motivation and thereby diminishing creativity.

Results of earlier research provide some support for this position. For example, Aiello et al. (1977) showed that individuals working in low spatial density areas exhibited higher performance on a creativity task than individuals in higher density areas. An interview study by Soriano de Alencar and Bruno-Faria (1997) found that employees mentioned "inadequate physical environment" (i.e., lack of space and presence of noise) as a factor that inhibited their creativity. Finally, Shalley and Oldham (1997) showed that when competitors were present, individuals who worked in a room without physical boundaries exhibited lower creativity than those who worked in a room with boundaries.

Conclusions: Contexts and Creativity

Our review suggests that several contextual characteristics have consistent, significant effects on individuals' creativity and that the direction of these effects is in line with the intrinsic motivation perspective. Specifically, individuals tend to exhibit high creativity when: their jobs are complex, their supervisors engage in supportive, noncontrolling behaviors, their work is evaluated in a developmental, nonjudgmental fashion, and their setting's configuration restricts unwanted intrusions. However, the picture is less clear with regard to the effects on creativity of other characteristics reviewed. Although some studies suggest that individuals exhibit high creativity when coworkers are supportive, contingent financial rewards are absent, and few time deadlines or production goals are present, other studies show that these characteristics have either nonsignificant effects or significant effects that are opposite in direction of those expected by the intrinsic motivation perspective.

There are several possible explanations for these inconsistent results. First, it is possible that contextual characteristics differ in the extent to which they provide clear and salient informational or controlling cues to individuals. That is, it may be that contextual character-istics shown to have generally consistent effects on creativity (e.g., job complexity) provide less ambiguous cues about an individual's personal competencies than do those shown to have inconsistent effects (e.g., contingent rewards). Second, based on the person-context interaction perspective discussed earlier, it may be that the effect of a given contextual characteristic on creativity is a function of the employee's personal characteristics (e.g., personality). For example, individuals with certain personalities may respond negatively to contingent rewards, whereas individuals with different personality profiles might respond quite positively, thereby explaining the inconsistent effects of this contextual dimension described earlier. Finally, it may be that the mixed results are a function of the presence (or absence) of multiple, competing contextual conditions. For example, it may be that the controlling aspect of time deadlines is highly salient when a second contextual factor is present, resulting in lowered creativity. However, when this second factor is absent, the controlling aspect might be less salient and time deadlines have weaker effects.

The latter two explanations for the inconsistent results involving contextual characteristics and creativity essentially argue that contextual characteristics may interact with individuals' personal characteristics or with other contextual characteristics to affect creativity. Both of these possibilities are examined in the section below. Specifically, in this section we examine the literature that has investigated the extent to which personal and contextual character-istics interact with one another to affect employee creativity. In addition, we review the few studies that have examined the effects of interactions involving two or more contextual characteristics.

Interactions Among Personal and Contextual Characteristics

A few studies have examined the possibility that contextual factors interact with either an individual's personality or with their cognitive styles. Most of the work addressing employee personality has focused on the CPS or on openness to experience (George & Zhou, 2001; Oldham & Cummings, 1996). The authors of these studies argued that those who score high on CPS or openness value contextual conditions that support creativity (e.g., supportive supervision) and respond to these conditions by exhibiting high creativity. Conversely, those who score lower on openness or CPS tend to devalue these conditions and respond less positively to them.

Results provide mixed support for these arguments. For example, Oldham and Cummings (1996) found that high CPS employees, who worked on complex jobs, and were supervised in a supportive, noncontrolling fashion, had the highest numbers of patent disclosures and high creativity ratings. Similarly, Zhou and Oldham (2001) showed that individuals who were high on CPS and expected a developmental assessment of their work had the highest creativity. George and Zhou (2001) showed that individuals who were open to experience responded positively when they received positive supervisor feedback and had flexibility in their work roles. However, two studies showed that CPS had moderating effects different than expected. Zhou (2003) found that employees with low CPS exhibited higher creativity when creative coworkers were present and supervisory behavior was noncontrolling than when creative coworkers were present and supervisors engaged in controlling behavior. Madjar et al. (2002) found that CPS did not moderate the relation between supervisor/coworker support and creativity, but that it did influence relations involving support from family/friends. Those with low CPS responded most positively to this support.

Only two studies have examined interactions between cognitive style and contextual conditions and both showed that style had significant moderating effects. Tierney et al. (1999) found that employees with an adaptive cognitive style produced the greatest number of invention disclosure forms when they had supportive, high-quality relationships with their supervisors. Baer, Oldham and Cummings (2003) found a positive relation between contingent rewards and creativity for employees with an adaptive style who worked on simple jobs. Those with an innovative style in complex jobs were generally unaffected by extrinsic rewards. Finally, those in the adaptive style/complex job or innovative style/simple job conditions exhibited lower creativity as extrinsic rewards increased.

In addition to studies that have examined interactions among personal and contextual characteristics, a few studies have examined interactions between one or more of the contextual characteristics reviewed (e.g., Baer et al., 2003; Shalley, 1991; Van Dyne et al., 2002). For example, Shalley and Oldham (1997) argued that expected negative effects of competition on creativity depended upon whether competitors were visible, since their visibility might increase the salience of the competition's controlling aspect. Results provided some support for this argument by showing that individuals who competed with others present in the same room exhibited lower creativity when these others were visible vs. in conditions in which they were not visible. Zhou (2003) showed that both noncontrolling and supportive behavior on the part of supervisors had stronger, positive effects on creativity when coworkers were present in the work unit who exhibited high creativity. These results may indicate that the informational aspect of supervisory behavior was more salient when creative coworkers were present because such behavior provided individuals a clear roadmap to achieve the creativity they observed in others.

The studies reviewed above suggest that inconsistent context-creativity relations might be explained by considering other contextual conditions. It is also possible that the effects of contextual characteristics shown to have consistent effects on creativity might be further amplified by simultaneously considering other contextual conditions. For example, it may be that the informational properties of a characteristic such as job complexity will become even more salient when a second contextual characteristic is present that reinforces these informational properties. A few studies have examined this possibility and provide results consistent with this argument (Oldham & Cummings, 1996; Shalley & Perry-Smith, 2001). For example, Zhou (1998) examined interactions between feedback style (informational and controlling) and feedback type (positive and negative). Results demonstrated that positive feedback delivered in an informational style produced the highest creativity, and negative feedback provided in a controlling style the lowest. Likewise, Shalley (1995) found that creativity was highest when individuals had a creativity goal, worked alone in a private room, and anticipated receiving a developmental evaluation of their work.

In summary, results suggest that employees' personality and cognitive style do influence the way they respond to contextual factors. Also, different contextual characteristics have been found to interact with one another in influencing employee creativity. However, more research is needed. First, since previous research focused on only a limited number of contextual factors (e.g., supervisory style), work is needed to examine whether other conditions (e.g., judgmental evaluation) interact with personality or cognitive style variables. Second, work is needed to sort out the seemingly conflicting results obtained for the CPS and openness to experience personality measures. Perhaps including direct measures of employee values and assessing the extent to which contextual factors actually provide support and competence information to employees would allow us to better understand these conflicting results. Third, research is needed that examines the effects of personal characteristics not discussed in this article. For example, employees' "growth need strength" has been shown to moderate the effects of complex jobs on employee outcomes such as performance and job satisfaction (Hackman & Oldham, 1980). It may be that it also influences employees' creative responses to complex jobs. Also, further studies are needed that examine interactions among multiple contextual characteristics. For example, do job complexity, supervisory support and spatial configuration measures interact with one another to affect creativity? And do other conditions affect the way individuals respond to contextual characteristics discussed above? For example, it may be that contingent, extrinsic rewards have strong negative effects on creativity only when organizational norms are present that suggest that such rewards are inappropriate (see Staw, Calder, Hess & Sandelands, 1980). Finally, work is needed to examine the joint moderating effects of individual characteristics (e.g., cognitive style and personality) on relations between employee creativity and a variety of contextual conditions.

New Directions in Creativity Research

In this section we discuss a number of new directions for creativity research. Unlike much of the research reviewed, many of these new directions take very different approaches to understanding creativity that are not directly related to the person, context, and interactionist perspective that has served to organize our literature review. All, we believe, hold substantial promise for future research.

Intrinsic Motivation as a Mediator

We argued throughout this article that contextual conditions influence creativity via their effects on employees' intrinsic motivation. Although this perspective has often been discussed in the literature (see Amabile, 1996), few studies have directly tested it. That is, many of the studies reviewed provide results consistent with the argument that contextual factors affect creativity via their effects on individuals' intrinsic motivation, yet few studies actually measured intrinsic motivation and tested whether it empirically mediates the context-creativity relation (Zhou & Shalley, 2003). Moreover, the studies that have examined the mediating role of intrinsic motivation provide results that are rather inconsistent (e.g., Amabile, 1979; Amabile et al., 1990). For example, Shin and Zhou (2003) found that a measure of intrinsic motivation only partially mediated the relation between transformational leadership and creativity. In addition, Shalley and Perry-Smith (2001) found no significant mediation for intrinsic motivation in the relation between expected evaluation and creativity.

One explanation for these relatively weak mediating effects involves the measures of intrinsic motivation used in the previous investigations. It may be that the questionnaire measures that have been used to tap the intrinsic motivation construct are inadequate and that alternative measures should be developed and tested. Another possibility is that contextual characteristics do not affect creativity via intrinsic motivation but rather via alternative mediating conditions. One such mediator, employee positive mood states, is discussed below. Finally, it could be that high intrinsic motivation is important for creativity but that it needs to exist along with other intervening variables to have a significant effect on creativity. Research is now needed to investigate these possibilities by including a variety of measures of intrinsic motivation and other potential mediators, and contrasting the extent to which they explain relations between contextual conditions and creativity.

Mood States

Researchers and theorists have begun to examine the possible effects of employees' mood states on their creativity (see Isen, 1999; Madjar et al., 2002). Moods are pervasive generalized affective states that are relatively transient in nature, are experienced over the short run, fluctuate, and may be affected by contextual factors (George & Brief, 1992). Previous work suggests that mood consists of two separate dimensions: positive (emotions ranging from high to low levels of excitation and elatedness) and negative (feelings of distress and fear) (Burke et al., 1989).

Much of the prior work in this area focused on positive mood. It suggests that when individuals experience positive moods, their cognitive or motivational processes are enhanced and their creative thinking and problem-solving skills are facilitated (Hirt, Levine, McDonald & Melton, 1997). Isen (1999) argued that when individuals experience positive moods, they make more connections between divergent materials, use broader categories, and see more associations among stimuli. As a result, individuals may be more likely to recognize a problem and to integrate a variety of resources, resulting in higher creativity. Moreover, it has been suggested that positive mood mediates the relation between contextual factors and creativity (Madjar & Oldham, 2002; Madjar et al., 2002). For example, a field study showed that positive mood mediated relations between supervisor and coworker support and employees' creativity (Madjar et al., 2002).

A few studies suggest that even negative mood may play a role in employee creativity (e.g., George & Zhou, 2002; Kaufmann & Vosburg, 1997). For example, Zhou and George (2001) theorized that under certain conditions, negative job affect (i.e., job dissatisfaction) might be positively related to employee creativity. They argued that negative job affect or moods do not automatically lead to creativity; rather their impact is context dependent. When negative job affect signals that the status quo is no longer acceptable, under certain conditions (e.g., high continuance commitment and useful feedback from coworkers), it will trigger employees' desire to voice—to come up with new ways of doing things, thereby facilitating creativity. Results of their study supported this perspective. Further, George and Zhou (2002) found that under certain conditions (i.e., high perceived recognition and rewards for creativity and clarity of feelings), negative moods foster creativity and positive ones do not.

More research is now needed to examine the effects of positive and negative mood states on employees' creativity. As noted above, this work should compare and contrast the mediating effects of positive mood with that of intrinsic motivation. Research also should attempt to identify the entire set of conditions that need to be present if negative moods are to boost employee creativity.

Self-Efficacy and Creative Role Identity

Researchers have begun to examine how individuals' views of themselves might translate to creativity. For example, Redmond, Mumford and Teach (1993) demonstrated that individuals' self-efficacy (i.e., the extent that individuals believe they have the ability to accomplish task specific goals and objectives) (Bandura, 1977) was positively related to their creativity. Tierney and Farmer (2002, 2004) extended this work and developed the construct of "creative self-efficacy" (i.e., extent to which employees believe they have the ability to produce creative outcomes). In two field studies, results showed that creative self-efficacy was positively related to creativity, above and beyond contributions of general job self-efficacy. Additionally, Farmer et al. (2003) examined relations between creativity and creative role identity (i.e., whether an individual views him- or herself as a creative person). Results showed that creative role identity was predicted by self-views of creative behaviors, coworker creativity expectations, and high levels of exposure to US culture, with the highest creativity occurring when employees had a strong creative role identity and perceived that their organization valued creative work.

More work is now needed to further examine the effects of employees' self-views on their creativity. This research might include more established measures of personality and cognitive style to determine if creative efficacy contributes to creativity above and beyond these other measures. Finally, work is needed to determine if these two concepts have similar effects across all contextual conditions, or if effects are stronger in some contexts than in others.

Creative Role Models

A few studies have examined the effects of the presence of "creative role models" (e.g., coworkers or supervisors engaged in creative activities) on employee creativity (Shalley & Perry-Smith, 2001; Zhou, 2003). Using social cognitive theory (Bandura, 1986) to develop a social learning perspective, Shalley and Perry-Smith (2001) hypothesized and found that observing creative models allows individuals to acquire relevant strategies and approaches that enable them to exhibit higher creativity in their own work. Possessing creativity-relevant skills and strategies increases the likelihood that one identifies the right problem, generates a variety of ideas, and uses appropriate standards to evaluate and refine the ideas. Observing a creative model's behavior patterns, modes of thought, and standards of work may facilitate the observer's acquisition of creativity-relevant skills and strategies, thus promoting creativity.

Later research supports this perspective. In two field studies, Zhou (2003) showed that the presence of creative coworkers had positive effects on creativity when supervisors engaged in either noncontrolling or supportive behavior, and that this effect was stronger for employees with low CPS. Research is now needed to determine the specific strategies and approaches individuals acquire when they are exposed to creative models, and the extent to which these strategies become a permanent part of their repertoire after exposure.

Creative Process

As described earlier, most of the research has defined creativity as an outcome (i.e., novel, potentially useful ideas). However, several scholars (e.g., Csikszentmihalyi, 1997; Drazin et al., 1999; Mainemelis, 2001; Mumford, 2000) have suggested that there is value in understanding the way in which individuals come to develop creative ideas. For example, they may link ideas from multiple sources, delve into unknown areas to find better or unique approaches to a problem, or seek out novel ways of performing a task. Considerable theoretical work (e.g., Amabile, 1996; Stein, 1967) has suggested that the creative process involves several stages, including (1) identifying a problem/opportunity, (2) gathering information or resources, (3) generating ideas and (4) evaluating, modifying, and communicating ideas. A number of studies have specifically focused on examining various cognitive processes or skills involved in creative problem solving (see Reiter-Palmon & Illies, 2004 for a review). Some of the skills examined in these studies include problem finding, problem construction, combination, generation of alternatives, and idea evaluation, that are part of the creative process (e.g., Mumford, Baughman, Maher, Costanza & Supinski, 1997; Reiter-Palmon, Mumford, Boes & Runco, 1997; Vincent, Decker & Mumford, 2002). Some recent empirical research has focused more on examining employees' overall engagement in creative processes at work (e.g., Gilson, Mathieu, Shalley & Ruddy, in press; Gilson & Shalley, 2004; Kazanjian, Drazin & Glynn, 2000).

Research is now needed that focuses on the different stages of creativity and what personal and contextual characteristics may be most desirable at each stage. For example, it may be that individuals who are high on openness to experience are most likely to generate creative ideas, while those who are extraverted are most likely to communicate these ideas to colleagues. If this were the case, it would suggest the profile of an employee likely to pass through the appropriate stages and produce creative work namely, individuals who were both open and extraverted. Or, it may be that individuals exhibit high levels of creativity when the context facilitates both idea generation (e.g., via a formal program that recognizes new ideas) and idea communication (e.g., via the absence of external evaluation). Thus, understanding the process and stages of creativity may suggest an emphasis on certain personal and contextual characteristics and a de-emphasis on others.

Creativity in International Contexts

The vast majority of the studies that we have reviewed examined the effects of personal and contextual characteristics on the creativity of employees who worked in organizations located in the US or other "Western" nations. Yet, earlier theoretical and empirical work suggests that individuals from non-Western cultures may respond differently to organizational conditions than those from Western nations (Anderson, De Dreu & Nijstad, 2004; England & Harpaz, 1990).

A recent study by Shin and Zhou (2003) suggests that there may be value in considering the international context in which creative work is produced. This study examined whether the cultural value of "conservation" (i.e., one favors propriety and harmony in interpersonal and group relations) (Schwartz, 1992) moderated the relation between transformational leadership and creativity. Using a sample of employees from organizations in Korea, they showed that transformational leadership had a stronger, positive relation to creativity for employees high on conservation (i.e., valuing tradition, conformity, and security) than for those low on conservation, suggesting that employees high on conservation were more willing to accept their leaders' influence and exhibited greater creativity in response to this influence. One interesting implication of their study is that the meaning and function of conservation may be different in Korea than in Western societies. Since Korean employees may focus on acting according to their social roles, conforming to expectations, and on maintaining good relationships with their superiors (Cha, 1994), employees high on conservation may be more willing to accept their leaders' suggestions for using other types of strategies which might enable them to exhibit higher creativity. That is, when their leaders exhibit transformational leadership, employees high on conservation readily accept such influences by becoming more excited and motivated to be creative.

These results highlight the need to conduct cross-cultural creativity studies. For example, research is needed that examines whether conservation values differ by country and whether conservation moderates the effects of contextual conditions for employees from US firms. Also, research that identifies what personal and contextual conditions are most relevant to individuals in different cultures is warranted. For example, different cognitive styles may be preferable for different cultures. Also, the importance of creative role identity across different cultures remains to be examined. The aforementioned Farmer et al. (2003) investigation examined creative role identity in Taiwan, which has a more collectivistic culture. If this concept were examined in an individualistic culture, such as the US, it may have different effects on employees' creativity.

Social Networks

Most of the research reviewed here has examined the effects of contextual characteristics that are associated with the organization or setting in which the employee works. However, early research established that conditions outside of the employees' department or the boundaries of the organization can influence individuals' responses in the workplace (Oldham, 2002). Recently, attention has focused on how formal and informal social interactions with others who are not necessarily directly connected to an employee's job (e.g., in their professional or social network) may have an impact on their creativity (e.g., Madjar et al., 2002; Perry-Smith & Shalley, 2003).

Using concepts from social network theory, Perry-Smith and Shalley (2003) argued that "weaker ties" (i.e., more distant relationships, such as acquaintances or distant colleagues) might be more beneficial for creativity than stronger ties (i.e., good friends or close relationships) because novel, nonredundant information from diverse social circles is more likely to be communicated through weak ties. Such information should help inform the ideas, processes and procedures employees in weak-tie networks develop at work. Perry-Smith and Shalley also argued that individuals' positions in their own network, as well as the connections they have outside their network, could influence their creativity. Specifically, they proposed that employees in peripheral positions with many connections outside their network would be exposed to new ideas and perspectives that contribute to their own creative ideas.

Research is now needed to test these propositions, as well as examining how location in networks may be associated with the personal and contextual conditions described in our review. For example, are certain personalities more likely to have strong or weak ties? Do individuals with different personalities or cognitive styles respond differently to network positions and exhibit different levels of creativity as a function of the network position–person match?

Different Types of Creativity

Throughout this paper, and in the extant literature, the concept of creativity is generally discussed as if it were a unitary construct. However, as stated earlier in our definition of creativity, it is recognized that creative ideas can range from minor adaptations to radical breakthroughs (Mumford & Gustafson, 1988).

In a conceptual piece, Unsworth (2001) argued that the common definition used for creativity implies that creativity is really only one construct without considering the type of idea, why it was generated, or how the process began. She developed a matrix of four creativity types that varied on two dimensions: what was the driver for the engagement (external or internal) and what was the problem type (open or closed). Open ideas are those ideas that are discovered by the individual, while closed ideas are presented to the individual. The four creativity types are: responsive (closed, external), expected (open, external), contributory (closed, internal), and proactive (open, internal). Unsworth argued that there might be differences in processes and predictors for each of these types of creativity. For example, she suggested that internally driven ideas might need to be "sold" more to evaluators in order to make sure they are not dismissed, since they may not be recognized as needed at that time. Research is now needed that empirically tests these ideas. For example, do certain personal or contextual factors have differential effects depending on the type of creativity examined?

The Measurement of Creativity

As discussed earlier, most previous studies have measured creativity using ratings provided by other individuals. In particular, laboratory studies have used the consensual assessment technique (Amabile, 1996) in which two or more expert judges rate the overall creativity of each solution or product generated by a research participant. Such an approach allows for an evaluation of the inter-judge reliability of creativity ratings. If these ratings achieve acceptable levels of reliability, a creativity score is then computed as an average of the creativity ratings for each individual across the generated solutions (e.g., Shalley & Perry-Smith, 2001; Zhou, 1998).

An alternative approach that has been less widely used is to have multiple judges evaluate the two components of creativity originality and usefulness. If the judges' ratings of these two constructs are reliable, separate orginality and usefulness scores are computed for each participant by averaging each of the ratings, respectively. Then, a composite creativity index is formed for each participant by combining the originality and usefulness scores (Zhou & Oldham, 2001). Although both of the above approaches provide creativity measures that are consistent with the definition of creativity, future research needs to examine the relative effectiveness of these two approaches. In addition, research is needed that examines the extent to which expert ratings converge with self-ratings of creativity made by the research participants themselves.

A different approach has been followed in field studies of creativity. In most of these studies, a single supervisor has rated each employee's overall creativity using one of three scales: (a) Oldham and Cummings' (1996) 3-item scale; (b) Tierney and colleagues' (1999) 9-item scale; or (c) George and Zhou's (2001) 13-item scale (e.g., Madjar et al., 2002; Tierney & Farmer, 2004). Systematic research is now needed to evaluate the relative strengths and weaknesses of these different scales in terms of their ability to accurately and reliably assess creativity. Moreover, future field studies should include evaluations of each employee's creativity by multiple judges (e.g., coworkers, other supervisors, and self) in order to assess inter-rater reliability.

In addition, although many field studies have found similar results involving supervisory ratings and objective measures of employee creativity, some studies have found varying results, and still others have found that results vary depending on what particular objective measures are used (e.g., Tierney et al., 1999). For example, in an examination of the relations between several indicators of employee creativity and measures of job complexity and leadership style, Oldham and Cummings (1996) found similar results for patent disclosures and supervisory ratings of creativity. However, a different pattern of results emerged for the number of ideas contributed to the organization's suggestion program. These results suggest that for certain jobs or in certain organizations, different measures of creativity converge, while in other kinds of jobs and in other organizations, different measures tap different types or dimensions of creativity. More research is needed to examine utilities of subjective vs. objective measures of creativity, and among different objective measures.

Finally, as mentioned earlier, the creativity literature has primarily focused on creative outcomes. As researchers turn more attention to studying the creative process itself, valid and reliable process measures need to be developed (Gilson et al., in press).

Team Creativity

As our review highlights, most earlier research has focused on antecedents of individual employee creativity. However, teams are increasingly responsible for work performed in organizations (Sundstrom, 1999). Thus, it is important to address the conditions that contribute to the creativity of teams. To date, little empirical work has been conducted on this topic, although there is a large body of work on group brainstorming, team innovation, and performance on tasks requiring creative solutions that can provide some insights (see Paulus, 2000; Polzer, Milton & Swann, 2002; Sosik, Avolio & Kahai, 1998; Sutton & Hargadon, 1996; West & Farr, 1990).

In general, the few studies that have focused on team creativity (e.g., Gilson & Shalley, 2004; Pirola-Merlo & Mann, 2004; Taggar, 2001, 2002) have followed an input-process-outcome model that is dominant in research on teams (e.g., Cohen & Bailey, 1997). For example, a few studies have focused on how team processes impact team creativity (e.g., Nemiro, 2002). Leenders, van Engelen and Kratzer (2003) found that for new product development teams a moderate frequency of communication was best for creativity. This allowed team members to share their ideas and have a constructive dialogue, while (a) not becoming distracted by the amount of information exchanged and (b) still having the cognitive ability to focus on the value of that information. Furthermore, they found that a low level of communication centralization was best for team creativity because ideas were not being filtered through just one or two of the members. Instead the majority of team members were aware of the different opinions being shared and no one member was dominating the creative process.

Taggar (2002) investigated the interaction between team members' individual disposition to be creative (e.g., cognitive ability, openness to experience, and conscientiousness) and team creativity-relevant processes (e.g., involving others, addressing conflict, and effective communication) on the creativity of products produced by college student teams. He found the highest creativity occurred in teams that had creative members and high levels of creativity-relevant processes. When groups had a low incidence of team creativity-relevant processes, this neutralized the effect of having highly creative members, while having groups with less creative members neutralized the effects of high levels of team creativity-relevant processes.

Gilson and Shalley (2004) studied antecedents to teams engaging in creative processes by examining task design features, attitudes toward team activities, and team characteristics and interactions. They found that more creative teams were those that perceived that they were working on jobs with high task interdependence and that their tasks required high levels of creativity. Also, teams high on shared goals, that valued participative problem solving, and had a climate supportive of creativity were more creative. Finally, members of the more creative teams had moderate amounts of tenure and spent more time socializing with each other, inside and outside of work.

More research is now needed on team creativity. For example, previous studies have demonstrated that team personality composition (e.g., extraversion, openness to experience, conscientiousness) has a significant impact on team performance on creative problem-solving tasks (e.g., Barry & Stewart, 1997; McCrae, 1987). Research is now needed to determine which personality dimensions are particularly relevant to team creativity and what percentage of team members should score high on such dimensions if creativity is to be maximized. For example, is it desirable for all members of a team to score high on openness to experience, or might it be preferable to have a few members of each team score high on each of the FFM personality dimensions?

Previous research also has shown that demographic diversity might contribute to performance on problem-solving tasks by increasing constructive conflict and the number of unique ideas that are brought to bear on the tasks (see Milliken, Bartel & Kurtzberg, 2003). Work is now needed to investigate the effects of diversity on the creativity of products generated by teams. For example, what particular demographic characteristics are most relevant, and is more diversity on each likely to boost team creativity? Work is also needed to understand the processes (e.g., Gilson & Shalley, 2004) that may help convert personality and demographic diversity to creativity in teams. Finally, research is needed that examines the processes that may be appropriate for different stages of a team's life cycle. For example, Ford and Sullivan (2004) argue that the value of novel proposals changes at different stages of a project team's life cycle.

Conclusion

Throughout this article we have discussed creativity as though it were a desirable outcome that had many benefits for organizations (e.g., transferring ideas to other employees for their own use and serving as raw material for later organizational innovations). However, few studies have systematically investigated these potential benefits, and it is not yet clear that boosting creativity at work will necessarily result in more innovative organizations that respond effectively to dynamic market conditions. Research is needed that addresses these issues. For example, research is needed that investigates the nature of creative ideas (e.g., radical vs. incremental) that are most likely to be implemented at the organization level. Also work is needed that examines the organizational conditions and managerial activities that facilitate the conversion of ideas into actual innovations in the organization.

In addition to research on the creativity-innovation connection, work is needed to determine if there are negative, unintended consequences of creativity that offset any possible benefits. Few studies have directly examined this possibility, yet it is reasonable to expect that the production of creative ideas may have unintended effects on other employees or processes in the organization (Janssen, Van der Vliert & West, 2004). For example, it is conceivable that a creative idea developed by one employee may involve changes in work processes that, if implemented, could result in fewer opportunities for other employees in the organization. Or, individuals might expend so much energy developing new ideas that they have little energy remaining for completing their normal, day-to-day assignments. Similarly, when ideas are transferred or made available to other employees, these ideas might distract the attention of the other employees causing them to attend less to their regular duties than to the ideas they are considering. Hopefully, long-term, longitudinal studies will allow us to determine the benefits and costs of creativity for the organization and its employees.

Also, little research has focused on what happens once creative ideas or solutions are generated or under what conditions individuals choose to try to be creative. For example, Ford (1996) suggested that creative and habitual actions are competing behavioral options for an individual. Research is needed to understand more fully under what conditions individuals choose to take creative action rather than sticking to more routine behaviors. In addition, since creativity involves the development of novel and useful ideas, how does being creative at work relate to other aspects of performance that may be more related to reducing variation in behaviors across employees? A recent study has begun to address this issue and found that despite the seemingly contradictory nature of using creative vs. standardized procedures, they actually had complementary effects on performance and customer satisfaction (Gilson et al., in press). In addition, research has not focused on determining under what conditions creative ideas are more likely to be recognized and valued, and when they are overlooked or ignored. For example, creativity's success has been proposed to depend on the capabilities, pressures, resources, and sociotechnical system in which employees work (e.g., Csikszentmihalyi, 1999; Mumford, Scott, Gaddis & Strange, 2002).

Finally, expanding the range of personal and contextual variables examined that might affect the incidence of creativity at work would be beneficial for a better understanding of the antecedents of creativity. As we hope our review highlights, there is now a need for the development of a more comprehensive model of employee creativity that incorporates both what we already know about creativity at work, as well as the new directions discussed. Research of this type should allow us to have a better understanding of employee creativity, the overall value of creativity, and the organizational resources that should be devoted to managing it.

References

Aiello, J. R., De Risi, D. T., Epstein, Y. M., & Karlin, R. A. 1977. Crowding and the role of interpersonal distance preference. *Sociometry*, 40: 271–282.

Amabile, T. M. 1979. Effects of external evaluation on artistic creativity. *Journal of Personality and Social Psychology*, 37: 221–233.

Amabile, T. M. 1996. *Creativity in context*. Boulder, CO: Westview.

Amabile, T. M., & Conti, H. 1999. Changes in the work environment for creativity during downsizing. *Academy of Management Journal*, 42: 630–640.

Amabile, T. M., Conti, R., Coon, H., Lazenby, J., & Herron, M. 1996. Assessing the work environment for creativity. *Academy of Management Journal*, 39: 1154–1184.

Amabile, T. M., Goldfarb, P., & Brackfield, S. C. 1990. Social influences on creativity: Evaluation, coaction, and surveillance. *Creativity Research Journal*, 3: 6–21.

Amabile, T. M., & Gryskiewicz, N. D. 1989. The creative environment scales: Work environment inventory. *Creativity Research Journal*, 2: 231–252.

Amabile, T. M., Hadley, C. N., & Kramer, S. J. 2002. Creativity under the gun. *Harvard Business Review*, 80: 52–61.

Amabile, T. M., Hennessey, B. A., & Grossman, B. S. 1986. Social influences on creativity: The effects of contracted-for reward. *Journal of Personality and Social Psychology*, 50: 14–23.

Amabile, T. M., Schatzel, E. A., Moneta, G. B., & Kramer, S. J. 2004. Leader behaviors and the work environment for creativity: Perceived leader support. *Leadership Quarterly*, 15: 5–32.

Anderson, N., De Dreu, C. K. W., & Nijstad, B. A. 2004. The routinization of innovation research: A constructively critical review of the state-of-the-science. *Journal of Organizational Behavior*, 25: 147–173.

Andrews, F. M., & Farris, F. 1967. Supervisory practices and innovation in scientific teams. *Personnel Psychology*, 20: 497–575.

Andrews, F. M., & Farris, G. F. 1972. Time pressure and performance of scientists and engineers: A five year panel study. *Organizational Behavior and Human Performance*, 8: 185–200.

Andrews, J., & Smith, D. C. 1996. In search of the marketing imagination: Factors affecting the creativity of marketing programs for mature products. *Journal of Marketing Research*, 33: 174–187.

Baer, M., Oldham, G. R., & Cummings, A. 2003. Rewarding creativity: When does it really matter? *Leadership Quarterly*, 14: 569–586.

Bandura, A. 1977. *Social learning theory*. Englewood Cliffs, NJ: Prentice-Hall.

Bandura, A. 1986. *Social foundations of thought and action: A social cognitive theory*. Englewood Cliffs, NJ: Prentice-Hall.

Barron, F., & Harrington, D. M. 1981. Creativity, intelligence, and personality. *Annual Review of Psychology*, 32: 439–476.

Barry, B., & Stewart, G. L. 1997. Composition, process, and performance in self managed groups: The role of personality. *Journal of Applied Psychology*, 82: 62–78.

Bartis, S., Szymanski, K., & Harkins, S. G. 1988. Evaluation and performance: A two edged knife. *Personality and Social Psychology Bulletin*, 14: 242–251.

Burke, M. J., Brief, A., George, J., Roberson, L., & Webster, J. 1989. Measuring affect at work: Confirmatory analyses of competing mood structures with conceptual linkage to cortical regulatory systems. *Journal of Personality and Social Psychology*, 57: 1091–1102.

Carson, P. P., & Carson, K. D. 1993. Managing creativity enhancement through goal setting and feedback. *Journal of Creative Behavior*, 27: 36–45.

Cha, J. H. 1994. Aspects of individualism and collectivism in Korea. In U. Kim & H. Triandis (Eds.), *Individualism and collectivism: Theory, method, and applications:* 157–174. Thousand Oaks, CA: Sage.

Cheek, J. M., & Stahl, S. S. 1986. Shyness and verbal creativity. *Journal of Research in Personality*, 20: 51–61.

Cohen, S. G., & Bailey, D. E. 1997. What makes teams work: Group effectiveness research from the shop floor to the executive suite. *Journal of Management*, 23: 239–290.

Costa, P. T., & McCrae, R. R. 1992. *Revised NEO Personality Inventory (NEO PI-R) and NEO Five-Factor Inventory (NEO-FFI) professional manual*. Odessa, FL: Psychological Assessment Resources.

Csikszentmihalyi, M. 1997. *Creativity: Flow and the psychology of discovery and invention*. New York: Harper Collins.

Csikszentmihalyi, M. 1999. Implications of a system perspective for the study of creativity. In R. Sternberg (Ed.), *Handbook of creativity:* 313–328. New York: Cambridge University Press.

Cummings, A., & Oldham, G. R. 1997. Enhancing creativity: Managing work contexts for the high potential employee. *California Management Review*, 40: 22–38.

Deci, E. L., Connell, J. P., & Ryan, R. M. 1989. Self-determination in a work organization. *Journal of Applied Psychology*, 74: 580–590.

Deci, E. L., & Ryan, R. M. 1985. *Intrinsic motivation and self-determination in human behavior*. New York: Plenum.

Drazin, R., Glynn, M., & Kazanjian, R. 1999. Multilevel theorizing about creativity in organizations: A sense-making perspective. *Academy of Management Review*, 24: 286–307.

Eisenberger, R. 1992. Learned industriousness. *Psychological Review*, 99: 248–267.

Eisenberger, R., & Armeli, S. 1997. Can salient reward increase creative performance without reducing intrinsic creative interest? *Journal of Personality and Social Psychology*, 72: 652–663.

Eisenberger, R., & Rhoades, L. 2001. Incremental effects of rewards on creativity. *Journal of Personality and Social Psychology*, 81: 728–741.

England, G. W., & Harpaz, I. 1990. How working is defined: National contexts and demographic and organizational role influences. *Journal of Organizational Behavior*, 11: 253–266.

Farmer, S. M., Tierney, P., & Kung-McIntyre, K. 2003. Employee creativity in Taiwan: An application of role identity theory. *Academy of Management Journal*, 46: 618–630.

Feist, G. J. 1998. A meta-analysis of personality in scientific and artistic creativity. *Personality and Social Psychology Review*, 4: 290–309.

Feist, G. J. 1999. The influence of personality on artistic and scientific creativity. In R. Sternberg (Ed.), *Handbook of creativity:* 272–296. New York: Cambridge University Press.

Ford, C. M. 1996. A theory of individual creative action in multiple social domains. *Academy of Management Review*, 21: 1112–1142.

Ford, C., & Sullivan, D. M. 2004. A time for everything: How the timing of novel contributions influences project team outcomes. *Journal of Organizational Behavior*, 25: 279–292.

Frese, M., Teng, E., & Wijnen, C. J. 1999. Helping to improve suggestion systems: Predictors of making suggestions in companies. *Journal of Organizational Behavior*, 20: 1139–1155.

George, J. M., & Brief, A. P. 1992. Feeling good–doing good: A conceptual analysis of the mood at work-organizational spontaneity relationship. *Psychological Bulletin*, 112: 310–329.

George, J. M., & Zhou, J. 2001. When openness to experience and conscientiousness are related to creative behavior: An interactional approach. *Journal of Applied Psychology*, 86: 513–524.

George, J. M., & Zhou, J. 2002. Understanding when bad moods foster creativity and good ones don't: The role of context and clarity of feelings. *Journal of Applied Psychology*, 87: 687–697.

Gilson, L. L., Mathieu, J. E., Shalley, C. E., & Ruddy, T. M. (in press). Creativity and standardization: Complementary or conflicting drivers of team effectiveness? *Academy of Management Journal*.

Gilson, L. L., & Shalley, C. E. 2004. A little creativity goes a long way: An examination of teams' engagement in creative processes. *Journal of Management*, 30: 453–470.

Gough, H. G. 1979. A creative personality scale for the Adjective Check List. *Journal of Personality and Social Psychology*, 37: 1398–1405.

Hackman, J. R., & Oldham, G. R. 1980. *Work redesign*. Reading, MA: Addison-Wesley.

Hatcher, L., Ross, T. L., & Collins, D. 1989. Prosocial behavior, job complexity, and suggestion contribution under gainsharing plans. *Journal of Applied Behavioral Science*, 25: 231–248.

Hirt, E. R., Levine, G. M., McDonald, H. E., & Melton, R. J. 1997. The role of mood in quantitative and qualitative aspects of performance: Single or multiple mechanisms? *Journal of Experimental Social Psychology*, 33: 602–629.

Isen, A. M. 1999. On the relationship between affect and creative problem solving. In S. Russ (Ed.), *Affect, creative experience and psychological adjustment*: 3–17. Philadelphia: Brunner/Mazel.

Janssen, O., Van der Vliert, E., & West, M. 2004. The bright and dark sides of individual and group innovation: A special introduction. *Journal of Organizational Behavior*, 25: 129–145.

Kaufmann, G., & Vosburg, S. K. 1997. "Paradoxical" mood effects on creative problem-solving. *Cognition and Emotion*, 11: 151–170.

Kazanjian, R. K., Drazin, R., & Glynn, M. A. 2000. Creativity and technological learning: the roles of organization architecture and crisis in large-scale projects. *Journal of Engineering and Technology Management*, 17: 273–298.

Keller, R. T. 1986. Predictors of the performance of project groups in R&D organizations. *Academy of Management Journal*, 29: 715–726.

Kelly, J. R., & McGrath, J. E. 1985. Effects of time limits and task types on task performance and interaction of four-person groups. *Journal of Personality and Social Psychology*, 49: 395–497.

Kirton, M. J. 1976. Adaptors and innovators: A description and measure. *Journal of Applied Psychology*, 61: 622–629.

Kirton, M. J. 1994. *Adaptors and innovators: Styles of creativity and problem solving* (2nd ed.). New York: Routledge.

Kristof, A. L. 1996. Person-organization fit: An integrative review of its conceptualizations, measurement and implications. *Personnel Psychology*, 49: 1–49.

Kruglanski, A. W., Friedman, I., & Zeevi, G. 1971. The effects of extrinsic incentive on some qualitative aspects of task performance. *Journal of Personality*, 39: 606–617.

Kwang, N. A., & Rodrigues, D. 2002. A big-five personality profile of the adaptor and innovator. *Journal of Creative Behavior*, 36: 254–268.

Leenders, R. Th. A. J., van Engelen, J. M. L., & Kratzer, J. 2003. Virtuality, communication, and new product team creativity: A social network perspective. *Journal of Engineering and Technology Management*, 20: 69–92.

Lowe, E. A., & Taylor, W. G. K. 1986. Creativity in life sciences research. *R&D Management*, 16: 45–61.

Madjar, N., & Oldham, G. R. 2002. Preliminary tasks and creative performance on a subsequent task: Effects of time on preliminary tasks and amount of information about the subsequent task. *Creativity Research Journal*, 14: 239–251.

Madjar, N., Oldham, G. R., & Pratt, M. G. 2002. There's no place like home? The contributions of work and non-work creativity support to employees' creative performance. *Academy of Management Journal*, 45: 757–767.

Mainemelis, C. 2001. When the muse takes it all: A model for the experience of timelessness in organizations. *Academy of Management Review*, 26: 548–565.

Masten, W. G., & Caldwell-Colbert, A. T. 1987. Relationship of originality to Kirton's scale for innovators and adaptors. *Psychological Reports*, 61: 411–416.

McCrae, R. R. 1987. Creativity, divergent thinking, and openness to experience. *Journal of Personality and Social Psychology*, 52: 1258–1265.

McCrae, R. R., & Costa, P. T. 1997. Conceptions and correlates of Openness to Experience. In R. Hogan, J. Johnson, & S. Briggs (Eds.), *Handbook of personality psychology:* 825–847. San Diego, CA: Academic Press.

McGlynn, R. P., Gibbs, M. E., & Roberts, S. J. 1982. Effects of cooperative versus competitive set and coaction on creative responding. *Journal of Social Psychology*, 118: 281–282.

Milliken, F. J., Bartel, C. A., & Kurtzberg, T. 2003. Diversity and creativity in work groups: A dynamic perspective on the affective and cognitive processes that link diversity and performance. In P. Paulus & B. Nijstad (Eds.), *Group creativity:* 32–62. New York: Oxford University Press.

Mumford, M. D. 2000. Managing creative people: Strategies and tactics for innovation. *Human Resources Management Review*, 10: 313–351.

Mumford, M. D., Baughman, W. A., Maher, M. A., Costanza, D. P., & Supinski, E. P. 1997. Process based measures of creative problem solving skills: 4. Category combination. *Creativity Research Journal*, 10: 59–71.

Mumford, M. D., & Gustafson, S. B. 1988. Creativity syndrome: Integration, application, and innovation. *Psychological Bulletin*, 103: 27–43.

Mumford, M. D., Scott, G. M., Gaddis, B., & Strange, J. M. 2002. Leading creative people: Orchestrating expertise and relationships. *Leadership Quarterly*, 13: 705–750.

Nemiro, J. E. 2002. The creative process in virtual teams. *Creativity Research Journal*, 14: 69–83.

Nonaka, I. 1991. The knowledge-creating company. *Harvard Business Review*, 69: 96–104.

Oldham, G. R. 2002. Stimulating and supporting creativity in organizations. In S. Jackson, M. Hitt, & A. DeNisi (Eds.), *Managing knowledge for sustained competitive advantage:* 243–273. San Francisco: Jossey-Bass.

Oldham, G. R., & Cummings, A. 1996. Employee creativity: Personal and contextual factors at work. *Academy of Management Journal*, 39: 607–634.

Oldham, G. R., Cummings, A., & Zhou, J. 1995. The spatial configuration of organizations. In G. Ferris (Ed.), *Research in personnel and human resources management:* vol. 13. 1–37. Greenwich, CT: JAI Press.

Paulus, P. B. 2000. Groups, teams, and creativity: The creative potential of idea-generating groups. *Applied Psychology—An International Review*, 49: 237–262.

Perry-Smith, J. E., & Shalley, C. E. 2003. The social side of creativity: A static and dynamic social network perspective. *Academy of Management Review*, 28: 89–106.

Piedmont, R. L., McCrae, R. R., & Costa, P. T. 1991. Adjective checklist scales and the five-factor model. *Journal of Personality and Social Psychology*, 60: 630–637.

Pirola-Merlo, A., & Mann, L. 2004. The relationship between individual creativity and team creativity: Aggregating across people and time. *Journal of Organizational Behavior*, 25: 235–257.

Polzer, J. T., Milton, L. P., & Swann, W. B. 2002. Capitalizing on diversity: Interpersonal congruence in small work groups. *Administrative Science Quarterly*, 47: 296–325.

Redmond, M. R., Mumford, M. D., & Teach, R. 1993. Putting creativity to work: Effects of leader behavior on subordinate creativity. *Organizational Behavior and Human Decision Processes*, 55: 120–151.

Reiter-Palmon, R., & Illies, J. J. 2004. Leadership and creativity: Understanding leadership from a creative problem-solving perspective. *Leadership Quarterly*, 15: 55–77.

Reiter-Palmon, R., Mumford, M. D., Boes, J. O., & Runco, M. A. 1997. Problem construction and creativity: The role of ability, cue consistency, and active processing. *Creativity Research Journal*, 10:

9–23.

Rodan, S., & Galunic, C. 2004. More than network structure: How knowledge heterogeneity influences managerial performance and innovativeness. *Strategic Management Journal*, 25: 541–562.

Roos, P. A., & Treiman, D. J. 1980. Worker functions and work traits for the 1970 U.S. census classification. In A. Miller (Ed.), *Work, jobs and occupations:* 336–389. Washington, DC: National Academy Press.

Schaefer, C. E. 1969. The prediction of creativity from a biographical inventory. *Educational and Psychological Measurement*, 29: 431–437.

Schneider, B. 1987. The people make the place. *Personnel Psychology*, 40: 437–453.

Schwartz, S. H. 1992. Universals in the content and structure of values: Theory and empirical tests in 20 countries. In M. Zanna (Ed.), *Advances in experimental social psychology:* vol. 25. 1–65. New York: Academic Press.

Scratchley, L. S., & Hakstian, A. R. 2000. The measurement and prediction of managerial creativity. *Creativity Research Journal*, 13: 367–384.

Shalley, C. E. 1991. Effects of productivity goals, creativity goals, and personal discretion on individual creativity. *Journal of Applied Psychology*, 76: 179–185.

Shalley, C. E. 1995. Effects of coaction, expected evaluation, and goal setting on creativity and productivity. *Academy of Management Journal*, 38: 483–503.

Shalley, C. E., & Gilson, L. L. 2004. What leaders need to know: A review of social and contextual factors that can foster or hinder creativity. *Leadership Quarterly*, 15: 33–53.

Shalley, C. E., Gilson, L. L., & Blum, T. C. 2000. Matching creativity requirements and the work environment: Effects on satisfaction and intention to leave. *Academy of Management Journal*, 43: 215–223.

Shalley, C. E., & Oldham, G. R. 1997. Competition and creative performance: Effects of competitor presence and visibility. *Creativity Research Journal*, 10: 337–345.

Shalley, C. E., & Perry-Smith, J. E. 2001. Effects of social-psychological factors on creative performance: The role of informational and controlling expected evaluation and modeling experience. *Organizational Behavior and Human Decision Processes*, 84: 1–22.

Shin, S., & Zhou, J. 2003. Transformational leadership, conservation, and creativity: Evidence from Korea. *Academy of Management Journal*, 46: 703–714.

Soriano de Alencar, E., & Bruno-Faria, M. 1997. Characteristics of an organizational environment which stimulate and inhibit creativity. *Journal of Creative Behavior*, 3: 271–281.

Sosik, J. J., Avolio, B. J., & Kahai, S. S. 1998. Inspiring group creativity: Comparing anonymous and identified electronic brainstorming. *Small Group Research*, 29: 3–31.

Stahl, M. J., & Koser, M. C. 1978. Weighted productivity in R&D: Some associated individual and organizational variables. *IEEE Transactions on Engineering Management*, EM-25: 20–24.

Staw, B. M., Calder, B. J., Hess, R. K., & Sandelands, L. E. 1980. Intrinsic motivation and norms about payment. *Journal of Personality*, 48: 1–14.

Stein, M. I. 1967. Creativity and culture. In R. Mooney & T. Razik (Eds.), *Explorations in creativity:* 109–119. New York: Harper.

Sundstrom, E. 1986. *Work places*. London: Cambridge Press.

Sundstrom, E. 1999. The challenges of supporting work team effectiveness. In *Supporting work team effectiveness:* 3–23. San Francisco, CA: Jossey-Bass.

Sutton, R. I., & Hargadon, A. 1996. Brainstorming groups in context: Effectiveness in a product design firm. *Administrative Science Quarterly*, 41: 685–734.

Szymanski, K., & Harkins, S. G. 1992. Self-evaluation and creativity. *Personality and Social Psychology Bulletin*, 18: 259–265.

Taggar, S. 2001. Group composition, creative synergy, and group performance. *Journal of Creative Behavior*, 35: 261–286.

Taggar, S. 2002. Individual creativity and group ability to utilize individual creative resources: A multilevel model. *Academy of Management Journal*, 45: 315–330.

Tierney, P., & Farmer, S. M. 2002. Creative self-efficacy: Potential antecedents and relationship to creative performance. *Academy of Management Journal*, 45: 1137–1148.

Tierney, P., & Farmer, S. M. 2004. The Pygmalion process and employee creativity. *Journal of Management*, 30: 413–432.

Tierney, P., Farmer, S. M., & Graen, G. B. 1999. An examination of leadership and employee creativity: The relevance of traits and relationships. *Personnel Psychology*, 52: 591–620.

Torrance, E. P. 1965. *Rewarding creative behavior*. Englewood Cliffs, NJ: Prentice-Hall.

Unsworth, K. 2001. Unpacking creativity. *Academy of Management Review*, 26: 289–297.

Utman, C. H. 1997. Performance effects of motivational state: A meta-analysis. *Personality and Social Psychology Review*, 1: 170–182.

Van Dyne, L., Jehn, K. A., & Cummings, A. 2002. Differential effects of strain on two forms of work performance: Individual employee sales and creativity. *Journal of Organizational Behavior*, 23: 57–74.

Vincent, A. S., Decker, B. P., & Mumford, M. D. 2002. Divergent thinking, intelligence & expertise: A test of alternative models. *Creativity Research Journal*, 14: 163–178.

West, M. A., & Farr, J. L. 1990. Innovation at work. In M. West & J. Farr (Eds.), *Innovation and creativity at work: Psychological and organizational strategies:* 3–13. Chichester, England: Wiley.

Woodman, R. W., Sawyer, J. E., & Griffin, R. W. 1993. Toward a theory of organizational creativity. *Academy of Management Review*, 18: 293–321.

Zhou, J. 1998. Feedback valence, feedback style, task autonomy, and achievement orientation: Interactive effects on creative performance. *Journal of Applied Psychology*, 83: 261–276.

Zhou, J. 2003. When the presence of creative coworkers is related to creativity: Role of supervisor close monitoring, developmental feedback, and creative personality. *Journal of Applied Psychology*, 88: 413–422.

Zhou, J., & George, J. M. 2001. When job dissatisfaction leads to creativity: Encouraging the expression of voice. *Academy of Management Journal*, 44: 682–696.

Zhou, J., & George, J. M. 2003. Awakening employee creativity: The role of leader emotional intelligence. *Leadership Quarterly*, 14: 545–568.

Zhou, J., & Oldham, G. R. 2001. Enhancing creative performance: Effects of expected developmental assessment strategies and creative personality. *Journal of Creative Behavior*, 35: 151–167.

Zhou, J., & Shalley, C. E. 2003. Research on employee creativity: A critical review and directions for future research. In J. Martocchio (Ed.), *Research in personnel and human resource management:* 165–217. Oxford, England: Elsevier.

5   Work Motivation and Performance

5.1   RELATIONAL JOB DESIGN AND THE MOTIVATION TO MAKE A PROSOCIAL DIFFERENCE

Adam M. Grant

This chapter illustrates how work contexts motivate employees to care about making a positive difference in other people's lives. I introduce a model of relational job design to describe how jobs spark the motivation to make a prosocial difference, and how this motivation affects employees' actions and identities. Whereas existing research focuses on individual differences and the task structures of jobs, I illuminate how the relational architecture of jobs shapes the motivation to make a prosocial difference.

Why do I risk my life by running into a burning building, knowing that at any moment . . . the floor may give way, the roof may tumble on me, the fire may engulf me? . . . I'm here for my community, a community I grew up in, a community where I know lots of people, a community that knows me (firefighter; International Firefighters' Day, 2004).

On my bad days I feel I have wasted three years working here in the ghetto. . . . You can work four days straight, sixteen hours a day . . . until your eyes start falling out . . . . we charge one-tenth of what a lawyer would normally charge. . . . It's just physically too much—and emotionally. . . . You're aware of the suffering of your client. . . . You know the pressure he's under. It makes you all the more committed. We don't help them only with their legal problems. If they're suffering from a psychological problem we try to hook them up with a psychiatrist. . . . You get to know them intimately. We're very close. . . . The people I work with here are my life (inner-city attorney; Terkel, 1972: 538–539).

Employees often care about making a positive difference in other people's lives. In the popular press, it is widely assumed that employees want to make a difference (Bornstein, 2004; Everett, 1995; May, 2003; Quinn, 2000). In order to motivate employees, many organizations define their missions in terms of making a difference (Collins & Porras, 1996; Margolis & Walsh, 2001, 2003; Thompson & Bunderson, 2003). Qualitative research and quantitative research reveal that many employees describe the purpose of their work in terms of making a positive difference in others' lives (Colby, Sippola, & Phelps, 2001; Ruiz-Quintanilla & England, 1996), and research in diverse bodies of literature suggests that this motivation to make a prosocial difference is prevalent in a variety of work contexts. For example, in business, managers often attempt to improve the experiences of organizational members by persuading top administrators to address important issues (Dutton & Ashford, 1993; Meyerson & Scully, 1995) and by taking proactive steps to help protégés develop skills and advance their careers (Higgins & Kram, 2001). In public service, employees often place their own lives in jeopardy, beyond the call of duty, in order to protect the welfare of others: police officers chase armed suspects in order to safeguard their communities (Marx, 1980), and ambulance drivers speed through red lights at busy intersections in order to rescue victims (Regehr, Goldberg, & Hughes, 2002).

Despite the evidence that employees are motivated to make a positive difference in other people's lives, the organizational literature is relatively silent about the sources of this motivation. Existing research suggests that dispositions may shape employees' motivations to make a prosocial difference. Employees who see their work as a calling want their efforts to make the world a better place, whereas employees with other orientations toward work usually do not (Wrzesniewski, McCauley, Rozin, & Schwartz, 1997). Employees with altruistic values are more concerned with making a positive difference in others' lives than employees with egoistic values (McNeely & Meglino, 1994; Meglino & Korsgaard, 2004; Penner, Midili, & Kegelmeyer, 1997; Rioux & Penner, 2001). Benevolent employees, unlike their less benevolent counterparts, are willing to give more to others than they receive (Huseman, Hatfield, & Miles, 1987). These findings suggest that employees' dispositional orientations and enduring values determine whether they are motivated to make a positive difference in other people's lives.

Aside from selecting employees with calling orientations, altruistic values, or benevolent dispositions, what resources do managers have for fulfilling organizations' missions—and employees' motives—to make a prosocial difference? Surprisingly little research has addressed the role of work contexts in shaping the motivation to make a prosocial difference. Several decades ago, Hackman and Oldham (1976, 1980) proposed that task significance—the degree to which an employee's work affects the health and well-being of other people—is an important characteristic of jobs. Task significance contributes to work motivation by enabling employees to experience their work as meaningful (e.g., Fried & Ferris, 1987; Hackman & Oldham, 1976; Katz, 1978). Although Hackman and Oldham's model focuses primarily on how employees respond to the structural properties of their tasks, the construct of task significance provides clues that jobs may spark the motivation to make a prosocial difference by shaping how employees interact and develop relationships with the people affected by their work. However, the influence of job characteristics and interpersonal relationships on the motivation to make a prosocial difference has been neglected, since the construct of task significance largely has been abandoned in theory and research (Dodd & Ganster, 1996: 331; Ferris & Gilmore, 1985; Gerhart, 1988; Hogan & Martell, 1987; Sims, Szilagyi, & Keller, 1976).

Based on current trends in theory, research, and practice, the time is ripe to examine how the relational design of jobs can support organizations' efforts, and fulfill individuals' motives, to make a prosocial difference. In a recent General Social Survey, Americans reported that important, meaningful work is the job feature they value most—above promotions, income, job security, and hours (Cascio, 2003). A growing body of research suggests that interpersonal relationships play a key role in enabling employees to experience their work as important and meaningful (Barry & Crant, 2000; Bradbury & Lichtenstein, 2000; Gersick, Bartunek, & Dutton, 2000; Kahn, 1990, 1998; Wrzesniewski, Dutton, & Debebe, 2003). Furthermore, research on social networks indicates that interpersonal relationships often enhance employees' motivations, opportunities, and resources at work (Adler & Kwon, 2002; Ibarra, 1993; Leana & Rousseau, 2000; Rangan, 2000). Despite these relational advances in organizational research, a relational perspective has not yet been incorporated into theories of job design and work motivation. Whereas traditional models of job design focus on the task structures of jobs, such as task identity, variety, and feedback (Hackman & Oldham, 1976, 1980), little research on job design examines the relational structures of jobs (Grant et al., in press; Latham & Pinder, 2005). Similarly, most research on work motivation overlooks the relational context of work (Locke & Latham, 2004; Shamir, 1991).

As illustrated later in this article, the motivation to make a prosocial difference is an inherently relational phenomenon; interpersonal relationships both cultivate and result from the motivation to make a prosocial difference. The motivation to make a prosocial difference is a timely topic, given that the importance of relationships increasingly is being emphasized at work. The service sector, a context in which work is defined in terms of relationships, has the highest rate of job growth in the United States, and more than three-quarters of Americans now work in service jobs (Bureau of Labor Statistics, 2001; Cascio, 1995; Johnston, 1993). The service sector is also growing rapidly in Europe (European Commission, 2004; Parker, Wall, & Cordery, 2001). Managers are emphasizing the importance of relationships both externally, with clients and customers (Cascio, 1995), and internally, with a greater focus on teamwork and collaboration (Osterman, 1994, 2000). In these external and internal relationships, employees are encouraged by their organizations to make a positive difference in the lives of coworkers, supervisors, subordinates, clients, customers, students, and patients.

In light of these trends, both researchers and practitioners need a deeper understanding of how work contexts cultivate the motivation to make a prosocial difference. Although the dispositional perspective discussed earlier illuminates the characteristics of particular employees who tend to care about making a prosocial difference, it offers little information about the role of work contexts in motivating employees to care about making a prosocial difference, an issue of considerable interest to scholars and practitioners. Hackman and Oldham's construct of task significance offers valuable but incomplete insights into how jobs cultivate the motivation to make a prosocial difference. In this article I build on these insights to introduce a model of relational job design. My goal is to revitalize research on job design and work motivation by accentuating the relational architecture of jobs and examining its influence on the motivation to make a prosocial difference. This endeavor to recast job design as a relational phenomenon fills a gap in the organizational literature about the role of work contexts in cultivating the motivation to make a prosocial difference, and it unpacks and broadens current understandings of the design and experience of meaningful work.

The first section of this article introduces relational job design and the components of the relational architecture of jobs—job impact on beneficiaries and contact with beneficiaries. The second section introduces the constructs of perceived impact on beneficiaries and affective commitment to beneficiaries—the psychological states that energize the motivation to make a prosocial difference—and illustrates how they are cultivated by relational job design. The third section examines how the broader social, organizational, and occupational contexts in which jobs are embedded moderate these psychological effects of relational job design. The fourth section explores the behavioral and psychological effects of the motivation to make a prosocial difference on employees. The concluding section delineates theoretical and practical implications and directions for future research.

Relational Job Design

Scholars have traditionally defined jobs as collections of tasks designed to be performed by one employee, and tasks as the assigned pieces of work that employees complete (Griffin, 1987; Ilgen & Hollenbeck, 1992; Wong & Campion, 1991). This definition of tasks as the sole building blocks of jobs overlooks the fact that jobs are designed with elaborate relational architectures that affect employees' interpersonal interactions and connections. Although the majority of job design research focuses on task structures and neglects these relational architectures, organizational researchers have offered hints that they not only exist but also shape employees' experiences in important ways. For example, the literature on task and goal interdependence reveals that jobs structure the nature and content of employees' relationships with coworkers by configuring particular patterns of interaction, cooperation, and collaboration (e.g., Kiggundu, 1983; Stewart & Barrick, 2000; Thompson, 1967; Wageman, 1995; Wong & Campion, 1991). Similarly, the literature on emotional labor and that on customer service behavior indicate that jobs structure the quality and quantity of employees' interactions with customers (e.g., Gutek, Bhappu, Liao-Troth, & Cherry, 1999; Hochschild, 1983; Rafaeli & Sutton, 1987). Furthermore, theoretical work on job crafting suggests that jobs are designed with relational boundaries, as well as task boundaries, that provide and curtail opportunities for employees to alter their work environments and experiences (Wrzesniewski & Dutton, 2001). Together, these bodies of literature indicate that the relational architecture of jobs merits further attention.

The emphasis in this article is on the relational architecture of jobs that increases the motivation to make a prosocial difference by connecting employees to the impact they are having on the beneficiaries of their work. Beneficiaries are the people and groups of people whom employees believe their actions at work have the potential to positively affect. I define beneficiaries from the employee's perspective based on past research indicating that relationships with intended beneficiaries (McNeely & Meglino, 1994) and perceived beneficiaries (Maurer, Pierce, & Shore, 2002) are important influences on employees' experiences and behaviors. I explore the sources of employees' attitudes toward beneficiaries later in this article; here, my central point is that the definition of beneficiaries adopts the employee's perspective, which signifies that beneficiaries can include individuals and social collectives internal or external to the organization, such as coworkers, supervisors, subordinates, clients, customers, patients, and communities.

In the following sections I introduce the relational architecture of jobs that structures opportunities for employees to have impact on, and form connections with, beneficiaries. I propose that jobs vary in whether they enable employees to make a lasting difference or an ephemeral difference in beneficiaries' lives, affect many or few beneficiaries, impact beneficiaries daily or occasionally, and prevent harm or promote gains to beneficiaries. Together, these dimensions describe the potential impact of a job on beneficiaries. However, the motivation to make a prosocial difference is not merely shaped by the opportunities for impact that a job offers. I introduce contact with beneficiaries as a second relational characteristic of jobs that enhances the motivation to make a prosocial difference by enabling employees to perceive their impact on, and become attached to, these beneficiaries. Figure 5.1.1 displays the job impact framework—the conceptual model that provides the scaffolding for this effort to explain how work contexts motivate employees to care about making a positive difference in other people's lives.

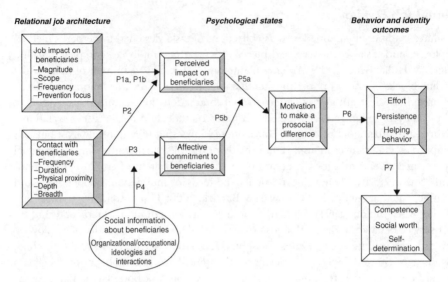

Figure 5.1.1 The Job Impact Framework.

The Relational Architecture of Jobs

The *relational architecture of jobs* refers to the structural properties of work that shape employees' opportunities to connect and interact with other people. Here I focus on the relational architecture of jobs that connects employees to the impact of their actions on other people. For example, firefighting jobs typically involve enriched relational architectures (e.g., Thompson & Bono, 1993). They provide frequent opportunities to make a lasting difference in the lives of many beneficiaries, as well as meaningful contact with these beneficiaries through physically and emotionally close interactions that occur in the performance of fire rescues, delivery of emergency medical services, and instruction of community fire safety courses. Conversely, janitorial jobs typically involve relatively depleted relational architectures (e.g., Wrzesniewski & Dutton, 2001). They provide few opportunities to have an enduring impact on beneficiaries' lives, as well as little contact with these beneficiaries as a result of job specifications, managerial decisions, scheduling discrepancies, and social stigma.

Along with varying between job types, relational architectures can vary within job types. For example, journalism jobs can involve either enriched or depleted relational architectures (e.g., Eide & Knight, 1999; Weaver & Wilhoit, 1996). Journalism jobs with enriched relational architectures provide opportunities to communicate valuable information and advice to broad audiences, sometimes including lifesaving warnings about impending risks such as natural disasters. These jobs also provide opportunities for journalists to have contact with the beneficiaries of their work through focus groups, public presentations, and feedback from and dialogue with readers. Journalism jobs with depleted relational architectures, however, provide opportunities to communicate relatively trivial information to small audiences with little interaction.

Now that I have given these examples to briefly illustrate how relational architectures can vary both between and within job types, in the following sections I introduce the two components of the relational architecture of jobs discussed in this chapter: job impact on beneficiaries and contact with beneficiaries.

Job Impact on Beneficiaries

Job impact on beneficiaries is the degree to which a job provides opportunities for employees to affect the lives of beneficiaries. I assume that opportunities for impact are motivating at the level of the job—how employees experience their collections of tasks—rather than at the level of the single task (Wong & Campion, 1991). The rationale behind this assumption is that, within a job, tasks can vary in their impact on beneficiaries. The global properties of the job appear to be substantially more influential than single tasks in shaping employees' experiences, given that it is psychologically, statistically, and practically difficult to aggregate the large number of single tasks that employees carry out into the experience of a whole job (Taber & Alliger, 1995).

Jobs can impact different aspects of beneficiary well-being. Opportunities to impact the physical well-being (Danna & Griffin, 1999; Edwards, 1992) of beneficiaries are prevalent in jobs that protect and promote the health and safety of others (e.g., nurse, police officer, security guard). Opportunities to impact the hedonic well-being (Kahneman, Diener, & Schwarz, 1999) of beneficiaries are common in jobs that increase the positive emotions and satisfaction experienced by others (e.g., chef, magician, musician). Opportunities to impact the eudaimonic well-being (Ryan & Deci, 2001) of beneficiaries are pervasive in jobs that promote the growth, fulfillment, and development of others (e.g., career counselor, coach, teacher). Opportunities to impact the material well-being (Alwin, 1987; Groenland, 1990) of beneficiaries are widespread in jobs that protect and promote the socioeconomic prosperity and instrumental "affordances" of others (e.g., accountant, attorney, construction worker). In order to gain a deeper understanding of the nature of job impact on beneficiaries, it is useful to examine the dimensions of the construct that capture the extent of opportunities for impact that the job provides.

Four key dimensions are likely to describe the potential impact of a job on beneficiaries. The first dimension is the *magnitude* of impact—the degree and duration of the potential effects of the job on beneficiaries. For example, surgeons have opportunities to save victims' lives, resulting in significant, enduring impact (Edmondson, Bohmer, & Pisano, 2001), whereas cashiers have opportunities for relatively insignificant, fleeting impact on their customers (Stone & Gueutal, 1985). The second dimension is the scope of impact—the number or breadth of people potentially affected by the job. Automotive design engineers have opportunities to carry out work that impacts many drivers; speech therapists generally have opportunities to impact a smaller number of people. The third dimension is the *frequency* of impact—how often the job provides opportunities for affecting others. Restaurant chefs prepare meals that impact patrons many times per day, whereas research chemists typically produce findings that affect others less frequently. The magnitude, scope, and frequency dimensions of job impact can each be characterized in terms of a fourth dimension of job impact, the *focus* of the impact—whether the job primarily provides opportunities to prevent harm or promote gains to other people. For instance, lifeguards prevent harm of high magnitude by protecting swimmers from drowning, whereas gasoline station attendants prevent harm of lower magnitude by protecting owners from theft; special needs teachers promote gains of high magnitude by educating developmentally disabled students, whereas comedians promote gains of lower magnitude by entertaining audiences. In summary, the potential impact of a job on beneficiaries can be captured by examining the magnitude, scope, frequency, and focus of opportunities for impact that the job provides.

Contact with Beneficiaries

Contact with beneficiaries is the degree to which a job is relationally structured to provide opportunities for employees to interact and communicate with the people affected by their work. Contact with beneficiaries can range from having no exposure to beneficiaries, seeing them briefly, or exchanging occasional emails and letters to carrying out intense, daily interactions with them (Gutek et al., 1999). This relational job characteristic is virtually orthogonal to job impact: jobs vary in their degrees of contact with beneficiaries independent of their degrees of impact on these beneficiaries. Support for this notion appears in a multidimensional scaling study conducted by Stone and Gueutal (1985), which suggests that the extent to which a job involves interacting with, entertaining, or providing a service to beneficiaries is an important dimension in an employee's experience and is distinct from the opportunities for impact on beneficiaries provided by the job.

Stone and Gueutal's (1985) findings that contact with beneficiaries appears to be distinct from impact on them indicate that job impact does not capture employees' personal relationships with the beneficiaries of their work. An employee can be carrying out impactful tasks without having a personal, emotional connection to the beneficiaries of these tasks. Employees not only seek meaningful tasks but also seek meaningful relationships (e.g., Baumeister & Leary, 1995; Kahn, 1998; Wrzesniewski et al., 2003). For example, as a police officer explains, "We have lost complete contact with the people. . . . They have taken me away from the people I'm dedicated to serving—and I don't like it" (Terkel, 1972: 134). Although the officer knows that his job impacts citizens, he craves contact with these citizens. When employees have contact with the beneficiaries of their work, their experiences become emotionally charged; they are more affectively engaged in their work as a result of firsthand exposure to their actions affecting living, breathing human beings.

From the literature on customer service behavior and on emotional labor (e.g., Gutek et al., 1999; Rafaeli & Sutton, 1987), I find five dimensions of contact with beneficiaries meriting consideration. The first dimension is the *frequency* of contact—how often the job provides opportunities to interact with beneficiaries. For example, taxi drivers are able to communicate more frequently with their passengers than are commercial pilots. The second dimension is the *duration* of contact—the length of time for interactions with beneficiaries that the job provides. Haristylists and attorneys generally have extended interactions with clients, whereas flight attendants generally have brief interactions with passengers. The third dimension is the *physical proximity* of contact—the degree of geographic and interpersonal space in the interaction that the job provides. Clinical psychologists tend to have physically proximate interactions with clients, whereas manufacturing employees tend to have physically distant interactions with recipients of their products. The fourth dimension is the *depth* of contact—the degree to which the job enables the mutual expression of cognitions, emotions, and identities. Social workers typically have deep, expressive interactions with clients, whereas directory assistance telephone operators typically have more superficial interactions with callers. The fifth dimension is the *breadth* of contact—the range of different groups of beneficiaries the job places in communication with the employee. An orchestra musician may have broad contact with beneficiaries, from fellow musicians and conductors to audience members, whereas a clerical worker who interacts only with a supervisor has narrow contact with beneficiaries.

These five dimensions may be integrated under the general rubric of experienced meaning: the more frequent, extended, physically proximate, expressive, and broad the contact with beneficiaries, the more meaningful the contact is to employees. Now that I have defined the relational job characteristics of job impact on beneficiaries and contact with beneficiaries, I turn to their psychological effects on employees.

The Motivational Impact of Relational Job Design

In this section I examine how relational job design cultivates the psychological underpinnings of the motivation to make a prosocial difference. Motivation is a set of psychological processes that directs, energizes, and sustains action (Mitchell & Daniels, 2003; see also Ambrose & Kulik, 1999; Campbell & Pritchard, 1976; Donovan, 2001; Katzell & Thompson, 1990; Pittman, 1998; Staw, 1977). When employees are motivated, they have "an inner desire to make an effort" (Dowling & Sayles, 1978: 16). Regardless of whether their dispositional orientations are egoistic or altruistic, employees can experience the *motivation to make a prosocial difference*, a psychological state—a fluctuating internal condition that is usually caused externally (Chaplin, John, & Goldberg, 1988)—in which they are focused on having a positive impact on other people. This motivation to make a prosocial difference is an allocentric psychological state—the employee's attention is directed toward the thoughts, feelings, preferences, and welfare of other people in the interest of improving their lives (Staub, 1984).

The motivation to make a prosocial difference emerges through the experience of two psychological states: perceived impact on beneficiaries (an awareness that one's actions affect other people) and affective commitment to beneficiaries (a concern for the welfare of these people). The basic rationale for these two psychological states shaping the motivation to make a prosocial difference is that both behavior-outcome contingencies and valuing of outcomes are critical to directing, energizing, and sustaining motivation (Staw, 1977; Vroom, 1964). Perceived impact signifies that outcomes are contingent on employees' behaviors, and affective commitment signifies that employees value these outcomes. I address this issue in further detail later in this article; in the following sections I examine how relational job design affects these two components of the motivation to make a prosocial difference.

Perceived Impact on Beneficiaries

Perceived impact on beneficiaries is the degree to which employees are aware that their actions affect others. For example, coaches are typically aware that their feedback affects the skills and performances of work teams (Hackman & Wageman, 2005), and members of flight crews are generally attuned to how their work affects coworkers (Weick & Roberts, 1993). Perceived impact is not only a state of awareness or attunement; it is also a state of subjective meaning, a way of experiencing one's work as significant and purposeful through its connection to the welfare of other people. When employees perceive impact, they are cognizant that their actions have consequences for other people, and, accordingly, they experience their actions as meaningfully connected to these people. In the two subsequent sections I examine how the relational architecture of jobs affects perceived impact.

Job impact and perceived impact. Early job design researchers assumed a strong correspondence between the opportunities for impact provided by the objective structures of a job and an employee's subjective awareness of the impact (Hackman & Oldham, 1976). In general, objective opportunities for impact on beneficiaries leave an imprint on the subjective experiences of job incumbents, who are likely to identify their work at a high level in terms of its meaning or purpose, rather than at a low level in terms of the physical and cognitive processes involved in carrying out the work (Hackman & Oldham, 1976; see also Vallacher & Wegner, 1987). However, it is important to examine how the specific structural dimensions of job impact affect an employee's perception of impact.

Research suggests that the greater the magnitude, scope, and frequency of job impact on beneficiaries, the greater an employee's perception of impact on these beneficiaries. First, when jobs provide opportunities for impact of high magnitude, the well-being and potential ill-being of beneficiaries is particularly salient to employees, who become aware that their efforts can have a substantial impact on the beneficiaries. This notion is supported by research indicating that people are more likely to recognize the potential impact of their actions on others when they encounter objective opportunities to significantly benefit others (Batson, 1991; Latané & Darley, 1970). For example, an ambulance driver's impact is salient in the face of an opportunity to save a victim's life, whereas a restaurant cashier may not be able to discern his or her impact on customers paying bills. Second, the broader the scope of job impact, the more attentive employees may become to their impact, since a larger number of beneficiaries provides more sources of information that others are depending on their efforts. This idea is supported by findings that individuals are more willing to help large groups of people than small groups (Burnstein, Crandall, & Kitayama, 1994). Third, the more frequently a job provides opportunities for impact, the more occasions employees have for grasping their impact, and the more likely they are to attribute the impact to their own personal actions, rather than exogenous circumstances or chance, as suggested by attribution research (Heider, 1958; Weiner, 1986).

Proposition 1a: The greater the magnitude, scope, and frequency of job impact on beneficiaries, the stronger the employee's perception of impact on beneficiaries.

The focus of job impact is also likely to affect the employee's perception of impact. Extensive evidence suggests that loss aversion is a robust human tendency; people are more attentive to losses than gains (Baumeister, Bratslavsky, Finkenauer, & Vohs, 2001; Rozin & Royzman, 2001; Tversky & Kahneman, 1992). The awareness that others may be harmed typically leads people to experience empathy and to search for opportunities to prevent or redress the harm (Batson, 1990, 1991, 1998). In loss prevention modes, people tend to be especially attentive to threats and vigilant in their efforts to counteract these threats (e.g., Brockner & Higgins, 2001). Accordingly, when employees work in jobs with a prevention impact focus, they are more likely to become attuned to their impact on beneficiaries. For example, public relations managers whose jobs involve preventing crises and image threats may be more aware of their impact on organizational members than public relations managers whose jobs involve promoting positive images of the organization. As such, I predict that jobs focusing on the prevention of harm are more likely to draw an employee's attention to impact than are jobs focusing on the promotion of gains.

Proposition 1b: The greater the prevention focus (as opposed to promotion focus) of job impact on beneficiaries, the stronger the employee's perception of impact on beneficiaries.

Contact with beneficiaries and perceived impact. Jobs that provide opportunities for impact do not always enable employees to grasp the impact of their actions on others. Without contact with the beneficiaries of their work, employees can find it difficult to know how their work is affecting these beneficiaries. For example, when production teams become isolated from their customers, they lose awareness of customers' expectations and specifications (Hackman, 1990; see also Hackman, Oldham, Janson, & Purdy, 1975) and may be uncertain about how their work is affecting customers.

Conversely, contact with beneficiaries provides employees with access to feedback about their impact. Beneficiaries convey a series of nonverbal and verbal cues about how employees are affecting them. For example, at Microsoft, software developers designed programs to benefit users but were often unaware of how their programs were affecting users. When Microsoft introduced a program enabling developers to observe users testing new programs, the developers were able to receive feedback about the impact of their programs on users (Cusumano & Selby, 1995; Heath, Larrick, & Klayman, 1998). Developers likely received nonverbal feedback about their impact from beneficiaries in the form of smiles and frowns, and verbal feedback in the form of expressions of gratitude (e.g., Bennett, Ross, & Sunderland, 1996; Lawler, 1992; McCullough, Kilpatrick, Emmons, & Larson, 2001) and hostility (e.g., Grandey, Dickter, & Sin, 2004).

Both positive and negative feedback convey information to employees that their work has the potential to affect beneficiaries. The more frequent, extended, physically proximate, and deep the contact with beneficiaries provided by the job, the greater the employee's access to nonverbal and verbal feedback. The broader the contact with different groups of beneficiaries provided by the job, the greater the employee's access to diverse evidence of opportunities to affect others.

Proposition 2: The greater the frequency, duration, physical proximity, depth, and breadth of contact with beneficiaries provided by the job, the stronger the employee's perception of impact.

Affective Commitment to Beneficiaries

Thus far, I have focused on the role of relational job design in promoting perceived impact. However, being motivated to make a positive difference in others' lives consists of more than merely perceiving one's impact; it also involves caring about the people affected. *Affective commitment to beneficiaries* refers to emotional concern for and dedication to the people and groups of people impacted by one's work. For example, many domestic violence counselors care about their clients (Mann, 2002), and many teachers care about their students (Ashton & Webb, 1986). Consistent with past research on commitment (e.g., Meyer & Herscovitch, 2001), affective commitment to beneficiaries describes both the form (affective) and target (beneficiaries) of the employee's commitment. With respect to form, the commitment is affective because the desire to improve the welfare of other people is strongest when it is emotionally charged (Batson, 1991). With respect to target, the construct builds on research on affective commitment to supervisors (e.g., Becker, Billings, Eveleth, & Gilbert, 1996; Meyer, Becker, & Vandenberghe, 2004; Stinglhamber & Vandenberghe, 2003) by extending the target of commitment to any beneficiaries of an employee's efforts.

In addition to increasing an employee's perception of impact on beneficiaries, contact with beneficiaries serves a second function: it increases an employee's affective commitment to these beneficiaries. Employees can be aware of their impact without experiencing an emotional tie to the beneficiaries of the impact. When jobs do not provide contact with beneficiaries, even the most significant impact is impersonal and indirect. Contact with beneficiaries personalizes the experience of impact by embedding jobs in interpersonal relationships that can enable employees to care about beneficiaries. For example, as a fire-fighter explains, "Being in the fire department has changed my life. I'm . . . more committed to helping people" (Smith, 1988: 311). As a second example, the medical technology company Medtronic holds annual parties at which employees meet patients whose lives have been improved by their products. According to the company's former CEO, "All Medtronic employees have a 'defining moment' in which they come face to face with a patient whose story deeply touches them" (George, 2003: 88). This appears to motivate employees to care about patients.

These assertions are supported by evidence that people often come to care about others as a result of having contact with them (e.g., Schoenrade, Batson, Brandt, & Loud, 1986). The general mechanism for explaining how contact enhances affective commitment is a sense of identification with beneficiaries. As Weick explains, "When two people encounter one another, there is some possibility that each can benefit the other. For each, the contact with another person affords the possibility of increased need-satisfaction and self-expression" (1979: 90).

First, frequent contact is likely to increase affective commitment, based on findings that increasing the frequency of exchange between people tends to increase identification and, therefore, cohesion (Lawler & Yoon, 1998). Second, high duration of contact is likely to increase affective commitment, drawing on evidence that extended interactions can enable service providers to identify and build close relationships with customers (Gutek et al., 1999). Third, physically proximate contact is likely to increase affective commitment, based on findings that increasing physical proximity between people tends to increase identification and liking (Bornstein, 1989; Festinger, Schachter, & Back, 1950; Saegert, Swap, & Zajonc, 1973), as well as perspective taking (Parker & Axtell, 2001). Fourth, deep contact is likely to increase affective commitment, drawing on evidence that increasing the expressiveness of interactions can enable people to experience empathy for, and a close sense of identification with, each other (e.g., Batson et al., 1997). Fifth, broad contact with beneficiaries from different social groups is likely to increase affective commitment, provided that the contact occurs under conditions of equal power and task and goal interdependence (e.g., Pettigrew, 1998; Sherif, Harvey, White, Hood, & Sherif, 1961). Because individuals organize their mental representations in terms of groups, contact with one beneficiary can make the entire group that the beneficiary represents more salient to the employee (Sia, Lord, Blessum, Thomas, & Lepper, 1999) and can lead the employee to care about the entire group of beneficiaries that the single beneficiary represents (Batson, Chang, Orr, & Rowland, 2002). For example, when a novice domestic violence counselor meets a battered woman, he or she may come to care about the individual woman but also may learn to empathize with other women who have experienced similar ordeals (Mann, 2002), and he or she may become more affectively committed to this entire group of beneficiaries.

Proposition 3: The greater the frequency, duration, physical proximity, depth, and breadth of contact with beneficiaries provided by the job, the stronger the employee's affective commitment to beneficiaries.

The Moderating Role of Social Information about Beneficiaries

Thus far, I have focused on the psychological impact of relational job design. However, among the important insights to emerge from organizational research in the past three decades is that the broader contexts in which a job is embedded play an important role in influencing an employee's experience of the job. Whereas extant job design research has focused primarily on individual-difference moderators such as growth need strength, knowledge, and skill (Fried & Ferris, 1987; Hackman & Oldham, 1976), contextual moderators have sparsely been integrated into job design theory and research. Research indicates that employees' reactions to the structural characteristics of jobs are affected by the social, organizational, and occupational contexts in which these jobs are situated (e.g., Griffin, 1983, 1987; Salancik & Pfeffer, 1978; Taber & Taylor, 1990; Tetlock, 1985). Specifically, employees' reactions to relational job design are likely influenced by social information that shapes the ways in which the employees evaluate the beliefs, emotions, behaviors, group memberships, and intrinsic worth of beneficiaries.

Social information about beneficiaries is communicated by organizational and occupational ideologies—the normatively espoused values and principles that surround jobs (e.g., Thompson & Bunderson, 2003). Organizational and occupational ideologies can serve as a form of social control (e.g., Hochschild, 1983; O'Reilly & Chatman, 1996; Van Maanen & Kunda, 1989) by focusing on particular individuals as primary beneficiaries (Blau & Scott, 1962) and defining these beneficiaries as important, valuable human beings (Ashforth & Kreiner, 1999). For example, Mary Kay's ideology focuses on enriching women's lives, and Wal-Mart's ideology portrays customers as people who deserve opportunities to buy valuable goods at reasonable prices (Collins & Porras, 1996; Thompson & Bunderson, 2003). Similarly, the occupational ideologies of restaurant chefs define consumers as important beneficiaries of their work (Fine, 1996), and the occupational ideologies of public defenders define defendants as innocent victims who deserve to have their constitutional rights protected (Ashforth & Kreiner, 1999).

As well as esteeming beneficiaries, organizational and occupational ideologies can communicate information that stigmatizes, devalues, and degrades beneficiaries. For example, military ideologies define members of opposing armies as enemies (e.g., Fiske, Harris, & Cuddy, 2004; Gal, 1986), and sales ideologies often define coworkers as competitors (Puffer, 1987). As such, the organizational and occupational ideologies that surround jobs can provide favorable (positive) and unfavorable (negative) social information about beneficiaries.

Of course, social information about beneficiaries is also provided by interactions with the beneficiaries themselves. According to the literature on burnout, emotional labor, and customer service behavior, interactions provide favorable information about beneficiaries when beneficiaries appear amiable, receptive to help, or appreciative (Cohen & Sutton, 1998; Guerrier & Adib, 2003; Lively, 2002; Locke, 1996); even a mere smile from beneficiaries may encourage employees to be cooperative and trusting (Scharlemann, Eckel, Kacelnik, & Wilson, 2001). Interactions provide unfavorable information about beneficiaries when beneficiaries appear disrespectful, difficult to help, aggressive, rude, or hostile (Grandey et al., 2004; Maslach, Schaufeli, & Leiter, 2001; Zapf, 2002). As such, interactions with beneficiaries can provide favorable or unfavorable social information about them.

Social Information about Beneficiaries Moderates the Effect of Contact on Affective Commitment to Beneficiaries

When social information about beneficiaries from ideologies and interactions is favorable, contact with them is likely to promote affective commitment to them. The mechanism underlying this proposition is the activation of a prosocial identity (see Grube & Piliavin, 2000, and Piliavin & Charng, 1990). Prosocial identity is the component of the self-concept concerned with helping and contributing; when it is activated, people experience their identities as oriented toward positively affecting others, and they are more likely to volunteer to help others (Nelson & Norton, 2005).

Exposure to favorable social information about a beneficiary activates employees' prosocial identities, which influence the relational models under which they operate: they are likely to enact their relationships with beneficiaries as communal relationships—connections that involve a concern for the welfare of others (Clark & Mills, 1979, 1993; Fiske, 1992). Accordingly, when employees are exposed to favorable social information about a beneficiary, contact is likely to increase their affective commitments to the beneficiary. Alternatively, when employees encounter unfavorable social information about a beneficiary, contact may actually decrease their affective commitments. Employees may see the beneficiary as incompetent (Fisher, Nadler, & Whitcher-Alagna, 1982; Lee, 1997, 2002), as deserving harm (Lerner & Miller, 1978), or as a stigmatized member of an outgroup (Ashforth & Mael, 1989). Exposure to unfavorable social information about beneficiaries often brings about a fight-or-flight response: employees tend to lash out at beneficiaries or seek emotional distance from them (Sutton, 1991; Van Maanen & Kunda, 1989). Thus, social information about beneficiaries plays an important role in moderating the effect of contact with beneficiaries on affective commitment to beneficiaries.

Proposition 4: Social information about beneficiaries moderates the effect of contact with beneficiaries on affective commitment to them such that the more favorable (unfavorable) the information, the stronger the positive (negative) effect of contact with beneficiaries on affective commitment to them.

The Motivation to Make a Prosocial Difference

The preceding propositions have focused on the contextual antecedents of perceived impact and affective commitment to beneficiaries. I begin this section by describing how these two psychological states increase the motivation to make a prosocial difference—the desire to positively affect the beneficiaries of one's work—and then examine how this motivation affects employees' actions and identities.

Perceived Impact, Affective Commitment, and the Motivation to Make a Prosocial Difference

Perceived impact is likely to increase the motivation to make a prosocial difference. As discussed previously, when employees perceive impact, they recognize a connection between their behavior and outcomes in others' lives. Perceived impact signifies the behavior-outcome contingency that is instrumental to initiating and sustaining motivation. When people perceive behavior-outcome contingencies, they are motivated to set goals and to develop action plans and strategies; when they do not, they often respond with learned helplessness (Bandura, 1977, 1997; Pittman, 1998; Staw, 1977; Vroom, 1964). Thus, when employees perceive that their actions have an impact on beneficiaries, they are likely to engage in the pursuit of making a positive difference in these beneficiaries' lives. This pursuit can provide them with a sense of efficacy (Bandura, 1977, 1997)—they feel capable of making a prosocial difference. Conversely, when employees perceive that their actions do not have impact, they are not likely to pursue the outcome of making a prosocial difference, since they do not feel that they have the opportunity to achieve this outcome.

Proposition 5a: The stronger the employee's perception of impact on beneficiaries, the stronger the employee's motivation to make a prosocial difference.

The awareness that behavior affects outcomes is necessary, but not sufficient, for motivation; in order to be motivated to pursue the outcomes that their behavior brings about, employees must value these outcomes (Ajzen, 1991; Staw, 1977; Vroom, 1964). Cross-cultural evidence suggests that employees generally value the outcome of prosocial impact. Benevolence, the value of protecting and improving the welfare of other people with whom one is in regular contact, is the most important value for the majority of the people in the majority of fifty-six cultures across the world (Schwartz, 1992; Schwartz & Bardi, 2001). However, employees are most likely to value this outcome when they care personally about the beneficiaries.

Indeed, research indicates that individuals are motivated to expend more energy to benefit others who are important to them or emotionally connected to them (Batson et al., 1997; Burnstein et al., 1994; Korchmaros & Kenny, 2001). When employees care about the beneficiaries of their work, they begin to see their identities as overlapping with beneficiaries' identities (Cialdini, Brown, Lewis, Luce, & Neuberg, 1997), and they perceive acting in the interest of these beneficiaries as consistent with their core personal values (Sheldon & Elliot, 1999; Sheldon & Houser-Marko, 2001). Thus, I propose that affective commitment to beneficiaries increases the effect of perceived impact on the motivation to make a prosocial difference. When employees are affectively committed to beneficiaries, perceived impact signifies opportunities to achieve personally valued outcomes and, thus, is more likely to cultivate the motivation to make a prosocial difference.

Proposition 5b: Affective commitment to beneficiaries increases the positive effect of perceived impact on the motivation to make a prosocial difference.

Consequences of the Motivation to Make a Prosocial Difference

The motivation to make a prosocial difference is not merely a psychological state cultivated by relational job design; it is also a driving force behind employees' actions and identity construction efforts. In the following sections I explore the behavioral and psychological consequences of the motivation to make a prosocial difference.

Behavioral consequences: Effort, persistence, and helping behavior. The motivation to make a prosocial difference is likely to increase effort, persistence, and helping behavior. Effort is how hard the employee works, and persistence is how long the employee works (Mitchell & Daniels, 2003); helping behavior encompasses the voluntary, extrarole actions that individuals undertake to benefit other individuals or groups (Anderson & Williams, 1996; Brief & Motowidlo, 1986; George & Brief, 1992; McNeely & Meglino, 1994). When employees are motivated to make a prosocial difference, they are likely to invest considerable time and energy in their assigned work, as predicted by traditional expectancy and planned behavior theories of motivation (e.g., Ajzen, 1991; Staw, 1977; Vroom, 1964): because they are aware of behavior-outcome contingencies and value these outcomes, they are likely to invest high levels of effort in, and to persist in effectively completing, their assigned work.

The added behavioral value of the motivation to make a prosocial difference above traditional motivation theories is that employees are likely to provide help to beneficiaries beyond the prescriptions of their jobs. The rationale for this prediction derives from evidence that when employees care about others, they are more likely to help them (Batson, 1990, 1991, 1998), without contemplating the personal consequences of helping (Korsgaard, Meglino, & Lester, 1997; see also Carlson, Charlin, & Miller, 1988). Accordingly, employees motivated to make a prosocial difference are likely to invest time and energy in voluntary helping behaviors without being deterred by the personal costs of these behaviors. In support of these predictions, research suggests that when members of flight crews are aware of the impact of their actions on coworkers and care about these coworkers, they are often motivated to invest additional time and energy in their assigned tasks and to voluntarily provide help to coworkers (Ginnett, 1990; Weick & Roberts, 1993).

Proposition 6: The stronger the employee's motivation to make a prosocial difference, the greater the employee's effort, persistence, and helping behavior.

Identity consequences: Competence, self-determination, and social worth.
The effort, persistence, and helping behaviors cultivated by the motivation to make a prosocial difference are likely to affect employees' identities. Identity is an umbrella concept that encapsulates people's responses to the question "Who am I?" (Stryker & Burke, 2000). Psychologists have assembled evidence that people have basic motives to experience their identities in terms of competence, or self as capable; self-determination, or self as internally directed; and social worth, or self as valued in interpersonal relationships (Ryan & Deci, 2000, 2001; see also Baumeister & Leary, 1995, and McAdams & de St. Aubin, 1992). These themes of competence, self-determination, and social worth can be traced back to the etymology of the term *impact*. Its Latin root *impactus* refers to "effective action of one thing or person upon another," implying competent, self-determined action, and "to fix or fasten," implying pacts and bonds with others—that is, social worth (*Oxford English Dictionary*, 1989).

When the relational architecture of jobs sparks behavior directed at making a prosocial difference, employees are likely to develop identities as competent, self-determined, and socially valued individuals. With respect to competence, when employees dedicate greater effort and persistence toward reaching an outcome that is important to them, they are more likely to achieve, and feel capable of achieving, the outcome (Bandura, 1977, 1997; Locke & Latham, 2002). Furthermore, even if employees have not objectively succeeded, because they have voluntarily invested greater time and energy in their work in order to benefit others, they are likely to justify their efforts as successful (Bem, 1972; Festinger, 1957). With respect to self-determination, because employees feel that their own actions are affecting others, and because they feel personally responsible for the choice to expend greater effort, persistence, and helping behavior, they are likely to experience their actions as self-determined (Ryan & Deci, 2000). With respect to social worth, helping others appears to increase an employee's social status and worth (Flynn, 2003; Penner, Dovidio, Piliavin, & Schroeder, 2005). When employees engage in behavior directed at making a prosocial difference, they are often able to make important contributions to beneficiaries' lives, which enables them to feel valuable to, and valued by, these beneficiaries (Harkins & Petty, 1982; Rosen, Mickler, & Collins, 1987). Thus, when employees display high levels of effort, persistence, and helping behavior in the interest of making a prosocial difference, they are likely to construct identities as competent, self-determined, socially valued individuals.

Proposition 7: The greater the effort, persistence, and helping behavior cultivated by the motivation to make a prosocial difference, the stronger the employee's identity as competent, self-determined, and socially valued.

Discussion

Although recent trends in theory, research, and practice have designed and depicted jobs and organizations as composed of and shaped by interpersonal relationships, researchers have sparsely incorporated this perspective into theories of work design and motivation. I have proposed that jobs with enriched relational architectures can motivate employees to care about making a positive difference in other people's lives and can affect what they do and who they become. When jobs provide opportunities to affect the lives of beneficiaries, employees become aware of their impact on these beneficiaries. When jobs provide opportunities for contact with beneficiaries, employees become more aware of their impact on beneficiaries, and they also come to care about the welfare of beneficiaries, provided that they are exposed to favorable social information about these beneficiaries. When the relational architecture of jobs enables employees to perceive their impact on and care about beneficiaries, employees are motivated to make a positive difference in the lives of these beneficiaries. As a result, they invest time and energy in prescribed and voluntary activities, which enables them to construct identities as competent, self-determined, socially valued individuals. Relationships thus shape and are shaped by the motivation to make a prosocial difference. With these insights, this article expands existing knowledge about why employees are motivated to make a positive difference in other people's lives and how the relational architecture of jobs affects the actions and identities of employees. As such, this article offers valuable contributions to our understanding of job design, work motivation, self-interest, and cooperation, as well as meaning making and identity construction in organizations.

Job Design

Research on motivational job design has largely stagnated in recent years, and many scholars have assumed that this stagnation is warranted (Ambrose & Kulik, 1999). Declarations of the death of job design research may be premature in light of recent calls for systematic research on issues of practical relevance in organizations (e.g., Aldag, 1997; Dutton, 2003; Ford et al., 2003; Ghoshal, 2005; Heath & Sitkin, 2001; Larwood & Gattiker, 1999; Latham, 2001; Lawrence, 1992; Pearce, 2004; Rynes, Bartunek, & Daft, 2001; Van de Ven & Johnson, 2006). As managers search for new levers of motivation, particularly in a resource-sparse, growing service economy, researchers can make a more significant difference in practice by examining how jobs can be relationally structured to enhance and sustain employee motivation. By introducing a set of relational job characteristics, elaborating their dimensions, and examining their effects on employees, I take a step toward expanding and reorienting job design research and practice to the relational sphere of work. The focus on job impact on beneficiaries and contact with beneficiaries illustrates the larger relational architecture of jobs and articulates one set of links among this architecture, employee motivation, and the desire to make a prosocial difference.

Further, existing organizational research provides relatively little information about how jobs shape opportunities to affect the lives of others and how these opportunities are sources of both motivation and meaning at work. I have unpacked and elaborated the construct of task significance to explore how the multiple dimensions of job impact affect employees. Impactful jobs can be characterized in terms of how often they provide opportunities to make a difference, how enduring the difference is in beneficiaries' lives, how many beneficiaries are affected, and whether the job prevents harm or promotes gains in different aspects of beneficiaries' lives. However, an employee's experience of an impactful job is not only shaped by the opportunities for impact that the job provides. The relational architecture of the job also shapes the nature and forms of relationships that the employee builds with beneficiaries of the impact. As such, the employee's experience of impact depends on jobs providing opportunities to both affect beneficiaries' lives and form connections with these beneficiaries. These insights expand our understanding of impactful jobs as those that spark the motivation to make a prosocial difference by providing meaningful opportunities for impact on and relationships with beneficiaries.

Work Motivation, Self-Interest, and Cooperation

In addition to advancing job design research, this article extends our understanding of work motivation, self-interest, and cooperation. In focusing on the motivation to make a prosocial difference, I move beyond predominantly individualistic, rationalistic theories of work motivation (see Kahn, 1990; Michaelson, 2005; Shamir, 1991) toward an understanding of employees as motivated to experience their actions and identities as meaningfully connected to other people. Organizational scholars have devoted extensive attention to understanding whether employee motivation is self-interested (e.g., Barry & Stephens, 1998; Bolino, 1999; Ferraro, Pfeffer, & Sutton, 2005; Locke & Becker, 1998) and, as discussed previously, have abandoned the assumption that all employees are motivated by self-interest in favor of an individual-differences approach suggesting that some employees are motivated by other-interest (e.g., Chen, Chen, & Meindl, 1998; Huseman et al., 1987; Meglino & Korsgaard, 2004; Rioux & Penner, 2001). Alternatively, I suggest that it is prudent to move beyond these questions of "*Do* employees care about others?" and "*Which employees* are likely to care about others?" to ask, "*When and under what conditions* do employees care about others?"

The framework presented here represents one step toward understanding when and under what conditions employees are motivated to care about others. Rather than concentrating on whether employees are ultimately self-interested, I have suggested that well-designed jobs can motivate employees of all dispositions to care about improving the welfare of other people. Indeed, altruistic and egoistic motives may be complementary in the process of making a prosocial difference, as employees face opportunities to benefit not only others but also themselves through constructing valued relationships and identities.

Accordingly, this article furthers our understanding of how it is possible to build conditions in organizations that motivate employees to care about and thus cooperate with others. This understanding is important not only in organizational research but also in fields across the social and natural sciences. Self-interest and cooperation is an issue hotly contested in economics (e.g., Margolis, 1982; Rabin, 1998), sociology (e.g., Etzioni, 1988; Piliavin & Charng, 1990), psychology (e.g., Batson, 1991; Schroeder, Penner, Dovidio, & Piliavin, 1995), biology (e.g., Dawkins, 1976, 1986; Wilson, 1975), and political science (e.g., Axelrod, 1984). Based on current research suggesting that virtually all people have the capacity to care about others (e.g., Batson, 1990, 1991, 1998; Eisenberg, 2000; Penner et al., 2005; Rabin, 1998; Schroeder et al., 1995; Schwartz & Bardi, 2001), social and natural scientists have become increasingly interested in building groups, communities, and societies characterized by care, compassion, and cooperation (e.g., *American Behavioral Scientist*, 2002; Smith, Carroll, & Ashford, 1995; Van Vugt, Snyder, Tyler, & Biel, 2000). An understanding of the role that work contexts play in motivating employees to care about others can contribute to these interdisciplinary efforts.

Meaning Making and Identity Construction in Organizations

This article also advances existing knowledge about meaning making and identity construction in organizations. People generally are motivated to understand their actions as purposeful and meaningful, as suggested by organizational researchers (e.g., Alderfer, 1972; Brief & Nord, 1990; Hackman & Oldham, 1980; Shamir, 1991; Wrzesniewski et al., 2003), as well as anthropologists (e.g., Becker, 1974) and psychologists (e.g. Frankl, 1959; Ryan & Deci, 2001; Ryff, 1989). In order to experience their work as meaningful, people often aim to construct identities that are simultaneously distinguished from and integrated with others' identities. This presents an "optimal distinctiveness" challenge to strike a balance between fitting in and standing out (Brewer, 1991; see also Lawrence & Nohria, 2002; Lee & Tiedens, 2001; Meyerson & Scully, 1995).

Brewer and colleagues (Brewer, 1991; Roccas & Brewer, 2002) propose that people resolve this tension between differentiation and integration by affiliating with groups that permit them to achieve an ideal balance between the two. Little research has examined how people negotiate the tension between differentiation and integration through means other than group membership. This article provides an alternative pathway to solving this puzzle, suggesting that jobs with enriched relational architectures can enable employees to strike a balance between differentiation and integration. A sense of differentiation is achieved through feelings of competence and self-determination that result from making distinct, volitional contributions to others' lives. A sense of integration is achieved through feeling valued by and connected to the beneficiaries of these contributions.

Directions for Future Research

This article poses a series of important directions for future research, the first set of which pertains to job design. Researchers should develop instruments to measure the relational architecture of jobs and test the propositions presented in this article. Further, although promising steps have been taken in critical reviews (Parker & Wall, 1998), expanded and interdisciplinary models of job design (Campion & McClelland, 1993; Edwards, Scully, & Brtek, 2000; Morgeson & Campion, 2002; Parker et al., 2001), and theory on necessary evils—tasks that require employees to harm others in the interest of a "greater good" (Molinsky & Margolis, 2005)—the job design literature focuses on a rather narrow, limited set of job characteristics defined largely by Hackman and Oldham's model. A deeper understanding of the diverse relational features of jobs, and the mechanisms through which they affect the actions, relationships, experiences, and identities of employees, is needed.

The sources of relational job design also merit exploration. The relational architectures of jobs may in large part be shaped by managers' goals and organizational structures

(Morgeson & Campion, 2002; Oldham & Hackman, 1981; Parker et al., 2001), but employees themselves may also play a role in shaping these architectures. Whereas job design research treats employees as relatively passive recipients of jobs, recent scholarship suggests that employees can be active crafters of jobs (Wrzesniewski & Dutton, 2001). Research that examines how, why, and when employees exercise agency in crafting the relational architectures of their jobs, and that aims to integrate these apparently competing job design and job crafting perspectives, will be fruitful. Toward this end, the framework presented in this article suggests that relational job design may actually spark the job crafting process. Relational job design promotes cognitive job crafting by enabling employees to become aware of their impact and to redefine their work in terms of making a prosocial difference, and it promotes physical job crafting by motivating employees to incorporate new activities into their jobs in order to help beneficiaries. Furthermore, insofar as relational job design enables employees to construct identities as competent, self-determined, socially valued individuals, employees may begin to expand their roles (Morrison, 1994; Parker, Wall, & Jackson, 1997) to recognize, seek, and create more opportunities for impact. Thus, future research should build on this framework to advance toward the theoretical integration of top-down and bottom-up perspectives on work design and motivation.

Future research should also explore additional implications of this framework for research on work motivation. First, although I have focused on the motivation to make a prosocial difference, researchers should explore how work contexts support, sustain, and undermine an employee's perceived and actual ability to make a prosocial difference (e.g., Small & Loewenstein, 2003). Second, although this article has painted a largely rosy picture of the motivation to make a prosocial difference, researchers should explore its dark sides, which may include positive illusions about one's capabilities and achievements (Taylor & Brown, 1994) and a vulnerability to social control (e.g., Lofland, 1977; Lofland & Stark, 1965; O'Reilly & Chatman, 1996; Pratt, 2000). Moreover, trade-offs may exist between meaning and manageability (Little, 1989, 2000; McGregor & Little, 1998) such that individuals find high levels of the motivation to make a prosocial difference depleting and difficult to sustain (e.g., Bolino & Turnley, 2005; Bolino, Turnley, & Niehoff, 2004; Kiviniemi, Snyder, & Omoto, 2002). Third, the relationship between the motivation to make a prosocial difference and intrinsic motivation is not yet clear. On the one hand, the two states may be complementary, given that competence, self-determination, and social worth are important enablers of intrinsic motivation (Amabile, 1993; Gagné & Deci, 2005; Ryan & Deci, 2000). On the other hand, the motivation to make a prosocial difference may undermine intrinsic motivation by overjustifying work so that it is no longer interesting for its own sake (Staw, 1977, 1980). These two perspectives may be reconciled by classifying the motivation to make a prosocial difference not as pure intrinsic motivation but, rather, as a state of integrated regulation (Ryan & Deci, 2000) in which employees are working toward value-congruent, personally meaningful outcomes (see also Clary & Snyder, 1999). Future research will be instrumental in addressing these questions.

Next, in order to identify conditions under which relational job design is more or less likely to cultivate the motivation to make a prosocial difference, researchers may focus on adverse conditions—work circumstances that inflict unusual physical, social, psychological, and/or economic costs on the employee. Researchers have studied dangerous work (Britt, Adler, & Bartone, 2001; Harding, 1959; Jermier, Gaines, & McIntosh, 1989; Suedfeld & Steel, 2000) and dirty work (Ashforth & Kreiner, 1999; Hughes, 1951, 1962) as examples of adverse conditions in which employees are subjected to negative physical, social, psychological, and/or economic outcomes. Adverse conditions are cases of insufficient justification (Salancik & Pfeffer, 1978): the conditions make it difficult for employees to justify carrying out the work. Employees are highly motivated to publicly and privately rationalize and justify working in such conditions (Bem, 1972; Festinger, 1957; Staw, 1980; Weick, 1995; Wong & Weiner, 1981). Accordingly, relational job design may be particularly important in adverse conditions because the costs inherent in the work prevent employees from understanding its purpose in terms of standard physical, social, psychological, and economic benefits for themselves. When these justifications are absent, relational job design can provide employees with a justification for doing the work: it affects, and has the potential to improve, the welfare of others. Thus, researchers should examine whether adverse conditions amplify the effect of relational job design on the motivation to make a prosocial difference.

Similarly, along with examining the moderating role of work contexts, researchers should consider how individual differences moderate the motivational impact of relational job design. For instance, employees with strong communal motives may be more responsive to relational job design than employees with predominantly agentic motives (e.g., Chen, Lee-Chai, & Bargh, 2001). As a second example, employees' deep-seated beliefs and values may play an important role in shaping their affective commitments to beneficiaries. Employees are likely to evaluate beneficiaries who are members of their ingroups more favorably than those who are members of outgroups, being prejudiced and discriminating against beneficiaries who are dissimilar to them (Ashforth & Mael, 1989; cf. Stürmer, Snyder, & Omoto, 2005) and favoring beneficiaries with similar backgrounds and experiences (Bunderson, 2003). Furthermore, employees may differ in their trust of and cynicism toward beneficiaries, openness to emotional cues from beneficiaries, and receptivity to information about beneficiaries (e.g., Kramer, 1999; Swann & Rentfrow, 2001; Tetlock, Peterson, & Berry, 1993). Therefore, researchers should explore how individual differences that affect the processes of filtering, encoding, and interpreting information about others moderate employees' reactions to relational job design.

Practical Impact of the Job Impact Framework

Hackman and Oldham (1976, 1980) developed their model in part because they believed that changing the work itself was more practical than changing organizational cultures or employees. Nevertheless, job redesign interventions can be laborious and can sometimes have weak effects and unintended negative consequences (e.g., Morgeson & Campion, 2003). One limitation of job redesign interventions may be that they focus primarily on enriching tasks with less attention to enriching the relational architectures of jobs. Whereas tasks are largely specified by external requirements of products and services and the expectations of clients and customers, relationships may be more flexible, tractable, and actionable for interventions. Managers need relatively little time and effort to increase an employee's contact with beneficiaries. Introducing a textbook editor to a group of students who benefit from her editing, for example, may enhance her motivation to make a prosocial difference. As such, relational job redesign may give rise to motivation that managers and employees alike can harness to energize action.

Conclusion

John Lubbock wrote, "To make others happier and better is the highest ambition, the most elevating hope, which can inspire a human being" (1923: 202–203). Whereas existing research focuses on individual differences and the task structures of jobs, I have proposed that the relational design of jobs can motivate employees to care about making others happier and better. This perspective fits with recent relational trends in theory, research, and practice and adds conceptual rigor to recurrent discussions in the popular press about "making a difference." It puts a human, social face on the design and experience of jobs, highlighting how the structure of an employee's work plays a critical role in shaping this employee's relationships with other people. It advances both the job design and work motivation literature with the assertion that jobs have important relational architectures that can motivate employees to care about improving the welfare of other people. This article thus enriches our understanding of how making a difference makes a difference for employees and their organizations.

Acknowledgments

The National Science Foundation provided valuable financial support for the preparation of this essay. For generative feedback on previous drafts. I am grateful to former action editor Elizabeth Mannix, Sue Ashford, Art Brief, Jane Dutton, Amy Edmondson, Richard Hackman, LaRue Hosmer, Fiona Lee, Brian Little, Andy Molinsky, Mike Pratt, Rick Price, Ryan Quinn, Barry Schwartz, Wendy Smith, Scott Sonenshein, Kathie Sutcliffe, Allison Sweet, Amy Wrzesniewski, and three anonymous reviewers. For impactful conversations, I am thankful to Peter Anderson, Tal Ben-Shachar, Eric Best, Ruth Blatt, Bill Boroughf, Kim Cameron, Marlys Christianson, Mark Grant, Susan Grant, Traci Grant, Ben Krutzinna, Joshua Margolis, Lou Penner, Todd Pittinsky, Lilach Sagiv, Lance Sandelands, Gretchen Spreitzer, Palmer Truelson, Karl Weick, the Visible College, the May Meaning Meeting, the Michigan Organizational Psychology Brown Bag, the Quality of Life Interdisciplinary Forum, and members of the Impact Lab (especially Beth Campbell, Grace Chen, Keenan Cottone, Christy Flanagan, Melissa Kamin, David Lapedis, and Karen Lee).

References

Adler, P. S., & Kwon, S. 2002. Social capital: Prospects for a new concept. *Academy of Management Review*, 27: 17–40.

Ajzen, I. 1991. The theory of planned behavior. *Organizational Behavior and Human Decision Processes*, 50: 179–211.

Aldag, R. J. 1997. Moving sofas and exhuming woodchucks: On relevance, impact, and the following of fads. *Journal of Management Inquiry*, 6: 8–16.

Alderfer, C. P. 1972. *Existence, relatedness, and growth: Human needs in organizational settings*. New York: Free Press.

Alwin, D. F. 1987. Distributive justice and satisfaction with material well-being. *American Sociological Review*, 52: 83–95.

Amabile, T. M. 1993. Motivational synergy: Toward new conceptualizations of intrinsic and extrinsic motivation in the workplace. *Human Resource Management Review*, 3: 185–201.

Ambrose, M. L., & Kulik, C. T. 1999. Old friends, new faces: Motivation in the 1990s. *Journal of Management*, 25: 231–292.

American Behavioral Scientist. 2002. Special issue: Cooperation in society: Fostering community action and civic participation. 45(5).

Anderson, S. E., & Williams, L. J. 1996. Interpersonal, job, and individual factors related to helping processes at work. *Journal of Applied Psychology*, 81: 282–296.

Ashforth, B. E., & Kreiner, G. E. 1999. "How can you do it?": Dirty work and the challenge of constructing a positive identity. *Academy of Management Review*, 24: 413–434.

Ashforth, B. E., & Mael, F. 1989. Social identity theory and the organization. *Academy of Management Review*, 14: 20–39.

Ashton, P. T., & Webb, R. B. 1986. *Making a difference: Teachers' sense of efficacy and student achievement.* New York: Longman.

Axelrod, R. 1984. *The evolution of cooperation.* New York: Basic Books.

Bandura, A. 1977. Self-efficacy: Toward a unifying theory of behavioral change. *Psychological Review*, 84: 191–215.

Bandura, A. 1997. *Self-efficacy: The exercise of control.* New York: Freeman.

Barry, B., & Crant, J. M. 2000. Dyadic communication relationships in organizations: An attribution/expectancy approach. *Organization Science*, 11: 648–664.

Barry, B., & Stephens, C. U. 1998. Objections to an objectivist approach to integrity. *Academy of Management Review*, 23: 162–169.

Batson, C. D. 1990. How social an animal? The human capacity for caring. *American Psychologist*, 45: 336–346.

Batson, C. D. 1991. *The altruism question: Toward a social-psychological answer.* Hillsdale, NJ: Lawrence Erlbaum Associates.

Batson, C. D. 1998. Altruism and prosocial behavior. In D. T. Gilbert, S. T. Fiske, & G. Lindzey (Eds.), *The handbook of social psychology*, vol. 2 (4th ed.): 282–316. New York: McGraw-Hill.

Batson, C. D., Chang, J., Orr, R., & Rowland, J. 2002. Empathy, attitudes and action: Can feeling for a member of a stigmatized group motivate one to help the group? *Personality and Social Psychology Bulletin*, 28: 1656–1666.

Batson, C. D., Sager, K., Garst, E., Kang, M., Rubchinsky, K., & Dawson, K. 1997. Is empathy-induced helping due to self-other merging? *Journal of Personality and Social Psychology*, 73: 495–509.

Baumeister, R. E., Bratslavsky, E., Finkenauer, C. & Vohs, K. D. 2001. Bad is stronger than good. *Review of General Psychology*, 5: 323–370.

Baumeister, R. F., & Leary, M. R. 1995. The need to belong: Desire for interpersonal attachments as a fundamental human motivation. *Psychological Bulletin*, 117: 497–529.

Becker, E. 1974. *The denial of death.* New York: Free Press.

Becker, T. E., Billings, R. S., Eveleth, D. M., & Gilbert, N. L. 1996. Foci and bases of employee commitment: Implications for job performance. *Academy of Management Journal*, 39: 464–482.

Bem, D. J. 1972. Self-perception theory. *Advances in Experimental Social Psychology*, 6: 1–62.

Bennett, L., Ross, M. W., & Sunderland, R. 1996. The relationship between recognition, rewards and burnout in AIDS caring. *AIDS Care*, 8: 145–153.

Blau, P. M., & Scott, W. R. 1962. *Formal organizations.* San Francisco: Chandler.

Bolino, M. C. 1999. Citizenship and impression management: Good soldiers or good actors? *Academy of Management Review*, 24: 82–98.

Bolino, M. C., & Turnley, W. H. 2005. The personal costs of citizenship behavior: The relationship between individual initiative and role overload, job stress, and work-family conflict. *Journal of Applied Psychology*, 90: 740–748.

Bolino, M. C., Turnley, W. H., & Niehoff, B. P. 2004. The other side of the story: Reexamining prevailing assumptions about organizational citizenship behavior. *Human Resource Management Review*, 14: 229–246.

Bornstein, D. 2004. *How to change the world: Social entrepreneurs and the power of new ideas.* New York: Oxford University Press.

Bornstein, R. 1989. Exposure and affect: Overview and meta-analysis of research, 1968–1987. *Psychological Bulletin*, 106: 265–289.

Bradbury, H., & Lichtenstein, B. M. B. 2000. Relationality in organizational research: Exploring the space between. *Organization Science*, 11: 551–564.

Brewer, M. B. 1991. The social self: On being the same and different at the same time. *Personality and Social Psychology Bulletin*, 17: 475–482.

Brief, A. P., & Motowidlo, S. J. 1986. Prosocial organizational behaviors. *Academy of Management Review*, 11: 710–725.

Brief, A. P., & Nord, W. R. 1990. *Meanings of occupational work: A collection of essays*. Lexington, MA: Lexington Books.

Britt, T. W., Adler, A. B., & Bartone, T. 2001. Deriving benefits from stressful events: The role of engagement in meaningful work and hardiness. *Journal of Occupational Health Psychology*, 6: 53–63.

Brockner, J., & Higgins, E. T. 2001. Regulatory focus theory: Its implications for the study of emotions in the workplace. *Organizational Behavior and Human Decision Processes*, 86: 35–66.

Bunderson, J. S. 2003. Recognizing and utilizing expertise in work groups: A status characteristics perspective. *Administrative Science Quarterly*, 48: 557–591.

Burnstein, E. C., Crandall, C., & Kitayama, S. 1994. Some neo-Darwinian decision rules for altruism: Weighing cues for inclusive fitness as a function of the biological importance of the decision. *Journal of Personality and Social Psychology*, 67: 773–789.

Bureau of Labor Statistics, 2001. *www.bls.gov/*. Washington, DC: U.S. Department of Labor.

Campbell, J. P., & Pritchard, R. D. 1976. Motivation theory in industrial and organizational psychology. In M. D. Dunnette (Ed.), *Handbook of industrial and organizational psychology*: 63–130. Chicago: Rand McNally.

Campion, M. A., & McClelland, C. M. 1993. Follow-up and extension of the interdisciplinary costs and benefits of enlarged jobs. *Journal of Applied Psychology*, 78: 339–351.

Carlson, M., Charlin, V., & Miller, N. 1988. Positive mood and helping behavior: A test of six hypotheses. *Journal of Personality and Social Psychology*, 55: 211–229.

Cascio, W. F. 1995. Whither industrial and organizational psychology in a changing world of work? *American Psychologist*, 50: 928–939.

Cascio, W. F. 2003. Changes in workers, work, and organizations. In W. Borman, R. Klimoski, & D. Ilgen (Eds.), *Handbook of psychology. Volume 12: Industrial and organizational psychology*: 401–422. New York: Wiley.

Chaplin, W. F., John, O. P., & Goldberg, L. R. 1988. Conceptions of states and traits: Dimensional attributes with ideals as prototypes. *Journal of Personality and Social Psychology*, 54: 541–557.

Chen, C. C., Chen, X., & Meindl, J. R. 1998. How can cooperation be fostered? The cultural effects of individualism-collectivism. *Academy of Management Review*, 23: 285–304.

Chen, S., Lee-Chai, A. Y., & Bargh, J. A. 2001. Relationship orientation as a moderator of the effects of social power. *Journal of Personality and Social Psychology*, 80: 173–187.

Cialdini, R. B., Brown, S. L., Lewis, B. P., Luce, C., & Neuberg, S. L. 1997. Reinterpreting the empathy-altruism relationship: When one into one equals oneness. *Journal of Personality and Social Psychology*, 73: 481–494.

Clark, M. S., & Mills, J. 1979. Interpersonal attraction in exchange and communal relationships. *Journal of Personality and Social Psychology*, 37: 12–24.

Clark, M. S., & Mills, J. 1993. The difference between communal and exchange relationships: What it is and is not. *Personality and Social Psychology Bulletin*, 19: 684–691.

Clary, E. G., & Snyder, M. 1999. The motivations to volunteer: Theoretical and practical considerations. *Current Directions in Psychological Science*, 8: 156–159.

Cohen, R. C., & Sutton, R. I. 1998. Clients as a source of enjoyment on the job: How hairstylists shape demeanor and personal disclosures. In J. A. Wagner, III (Ed.), *Advances in qualitative organization research*: 1–32. Greenwich, CT: JAI Press.

Colby, A., Sippola, L., & Phelps, E. 2001. Social responsibility and paid work in contemporary American life. In A. Rossi (Ed.), *Caring and doing for others: Social responsibility in the domains of family, work, and community:* 349–399. Chicago: University of Chicago Press.

Collins, J. C., & Porras, J. I. 1996. Building your company's vision. *Harvard Business Review*, 74(5): 65–77.

Cusumano, M. A., & Selby, R. W. 1995. *Microsoft secrets.* New York: Free Press.

Danna, K., & Griffin, R. W. 1999. Health and well-being in the workplace: A review and synthesis of the literature. *Journal of Management*, 25: 357–384.

Dawkins, R. 1976. *The selfish gene.* Oxford: Oxford University Press.

Dawkins, R. 1986. *The blind watchmaker.* New York: Norton.

Dodd, N. G., & Ganster, D. C. 1996. The interactive effects of task variety, autonomy, and feedback on attitudes and performance. *Journal of Organizational Behavior*, 17: 329–347.

Donovan, J. J. 2001. Work motivation. In N. Anderson, D. S. Ones, H. K. Sinangil, & C. Viswesvaran (Eds.), *Handbook of industrial, work, and organizational psychology*, vol. 2: 53–76. London: Sage.

Dowling, W. F., & Sayles, L. R. 1978. *How managers motivate: The imperatives of supervision.* New York: McGraw-Hill.

Dutton, J. E. 2003. Breathing life into organizational studies. *Journal of Management Inquiry*, 12: 5–19.

Dutton, J. E., & Ashford, S. J. 1993. Selling issues to top management. *Academy of Management Review*, 18: 397–428.

Edmondson, A. C., Bohmer, R. M., & Pisano, G. P. 2001. Disrupted routines: Team learning and new technology implementation in hospitals. *Administrative Science Quarterly*, 46: 685–716.

Edwards, J. R. 1992. A cybernetic theory of stress, coping, and well-being in organizations. *Academy of Management Review*, 17: 238–274.

Edwards, J. R., Scully, J. A., & Brtek, M. D. 2000. The nature and outcomes of work: A replication and extension of interdisciplinary work-design research. *Journal of Applied Psychology*, 85: 860–868.

Eide, M., & Knight, G. 1999. Public/private service: Service journalism and the problems of everyday life. *European Journal of Communication*, 14: 525–547.

Eisenberg, N. 2000. Emotion, regulation, and moral development. *Annual Review of Psychology*, 51: 665–697.

Etzioni, A. 1988. *The moral dimension: Toward a new economics.* New York: Free Press.

European Commission. 2004. *Employment in Europe, 2004.* http://europa.eu.int/comm/employment_social/employment_analysis/employ_2004_en.htm, accessed February 23, 2005.

Everett, M. 1995. *Making a living while making a difference: A guide to creating careers with a conscience.* New York: Bantam Books.

Ferraro, F., Pfeffer, J., & Sutton, R. I. 2005. Economics language and assumptions: How theories can become self-fulfilling. *Academy of Management Review*, 30: 8–24.

Ferris, G. R., & Gilmore, D. C. 1985. A methodological note on job complexity indexes. *Journal of Applied Psychology*, 70: 225–227.

Festinger, L. 1957. *A theory of cognitive dissonance.* Stanford, CA: Stanford University Press.

Festinger, L., Schachter, S., & Back, K. 1950. *Social pressures in informal groups: A study of human factors in housing.* Stanford, CA: Stanford University Press.

Fine, G. A. 1996. Justifying work: Occupational rhetorics as resources in restaurant kitchens. *Administrative Science Quarterly*, 41: 90–115.

Fisher, J. D., Nadler, A., & Whitcher-Alagna, S. 1982. Recipient reactions to aid. *Psychological Bulletin*, 91: 27–54.

Fiske, A. P. 1992. The four elementary forms of sociality: Framework for a unified theory of social relations. *Psychological Review*, 99: 689–723.

Fiske, S. T., Harris, L. T., & Cuddy, A. J. C. 2004. Why ordinary people torture enemy prisoners. *Science*, 306: 482–483.

Flynn, F. J. 2003. How much should I give and how often? The effects of generosity and frequency of favor exchange on social status and productivity. *Academy of Management Journal*, 46: 539–553.

Ford, E. W., Duncan, W. J., Bedeian, A. G., Ginter, P. M., Rousculp, M. D., & Adams, A. M. 2003. Mitigating risks, visible hands, inevitable disasters, and soft variables: Management research that matters to managers. *Academy of Management Executive*, 17(1): 46–60.

Frankl, V. 1959. *Man's search for meaning.* New York: Pocket Books.

Fried, Y., & Ferris, G. R. 1987. The validity of the job characteristics model: A review and meta-analysis. *Personnel Psychology*, 40: 287–322.

Gagné, M., & Deci, E. L. 2005. Self-determination theory and work motivation. *Journal of Organizational Behavior*, 26: 331–362.

Gal, R. 1986. Unit morale: From a theoretical puzzle to an empirical illustration: An Israeli example. *Journal of Applied Social Psychology*, 16: 549–564.

George, B. 2003. *Authentic leadership: Rediscovering the secrets to creating lasting value.* San Francisco: Jossey-Bass.

George, J. M., & Brief, A. P. 1992. Feeling good—doing good: A conceptual analysis of the mood at work—organizational spontaneity relationship. *Psychological Bulletin*, 112: 310–329.

Gerhart, B. 1988. Sources of variance in incumbent perceptions of job complexity. *Journal of Applied Psychology*, 73: 154–162.

Gersick, C. J. G., Bartunek, J. M., & Dutton, J. E. 2000. Learning from academia: The importance of relationships in professional life. *Academy of Management Journal*, 43: 1026–1044.

Ghoshal, S. 2005. Bad management theories are destroying good management practices. *Academy of Management Learning & Education*, 4: 75–91.

Ginnett, R. 1990. Airline cockpit crew. In J. R. Hackman (Ed.), *Groups that work (and those that don't):* 427–448. San Francisco: Jossey-Bass.

Grandey, A. A., Dickter, D. N., & Sin, H. P. 2004. The customer is not always right: Customer aggression and emotion regulation of service employees. *Journal of Organizational Behavior*, 25: 397–418.

Grant, A. M., Campbell, E. M., Chen, G., Cottone, K., Lapedis, D., & Lee, K. In press. Impact and the art of motivation maintenance: The effects of contact with beneficiaries on persistence behavior. *Organizational Behavior and Human Decision Processes.*

Griffin, R. W. 1983. Objective and social sources of information in task redesign: A field experiment. *Administrative Science Quarterly*, 28: 184–200.

Griffin, R. W. 1987. Toward an integrated theory of task design. *Research in Organizational Behavior*, 9: 79–120.

Groenland, E. A. 1990. Structural elements of material well-being: An empirical test among people on social security. *Social Indicators Research*, 22: 367–384.

Grube, J. A., & Piliavin, J. A. 2000. Role identity, organizational experiences, and volunteer performance. *Personality and Social Psychology Bulletin*, 26: 1108–1119.

Guerrier, Y., & Adib, A. 2003. Work at leisure and leisure at work: A study of the emotional labor of tour reps. *Human Relations*, 56: 1399–1417.

Gutek, B. A., Bhappu, A. D., Liao-Troth, M. A., & Cherry, B. 1999. Distinguishing between service relationships and encounters. *Journal of Applied Psychology*, 84: 218–233.

Hackman, J. R. (Ed.). 1990. *Groups that work (and those that don't): Creating conditions for effective teamwork.* San Francisco: Jossey-Bass.

Hackman, J. R., & Oldham, G. R. 1976. Motivation through the design of work: Test of a theory. *Organizational Behavior and Human Performance*, 16: 250–279.

Hackman, J. R., & Oldham, G. R. 1980. *Work redesign.* Reading, MA: Addison-Wesley.

Hackman, J. R., Oldham, G., Janson, R., & Purdy, K. 1975. A new strategy for job enrichment. *California Management Review*, 17(4): 57–71.

Hackman, J. R., & Wageman, R. 2005. A theory of team coaching. *Academy of Management Review*, 30: 269–287.

Harding, F. D. 1959. Incentives for hazardous work: A survey. *Personnel*, 36: 72–79.

Harkins, S. G., & Petty, R. E. 1982. Effects of task difficulty and task uniqueness on social loafing. *Journal of Personality and Social Psychology*, 43: 1214–1229.

Heath, C., Larrick, R. P., & Klayman, J. 1998. Cognitive repairs: How organizations compensate for the shortcoming of individual learners. *Research in Organizational Behavior*, 20: 1–37.

Heath, C., & Sitkin, S. 2001. Big-B versus Big-O: What is organizational about organizational behavior? *Journal of Organizational Behavior*, 22: 43–58.

Heider, F. 1958. *The psychology of interpersonal relations.* New York: Wiley.

Higgins, M. C., & Kram, K. E. 2001. Reconceptualizing mentoring at work: A developmental network perspective. *Academy of Management Review*, 26: 264–288.

Hochschild, A. R. 1983. *The managed heart: Commercialization of human feeling.* Berkeley: University of California Press.

Hogan, E. A., & Martell, D. A. 1987. A confirmatory structural equations analysis of the job characteristics model. *Organizational Behavior and Human Decision Processes*, 39: 242–263.

Hughes, E. C. 1951. Work and the self. In J. H. Rohrer & M. Sherif (Eds.), *Social psychology at the crossroads:* 313–323. New York: Harper & Brothers.

Hughes, E. C. 1962. Good people and dirty work. *Social Problems*, 10: 3–11.

Huseman, R. C., Hatfield, J. D., & Miles, E. W. 1987. A new perspective on equity theory: The equity sensitivity construct. *Academy of Management Review*, 12: 222–234.

Ibarra, H. 1993. Personal networks of women and minorities in management: A conceptual framework. *Academy of Management Review*, 18: 56–87.

Ilgen, D. R., & Hollenbeck, J. R. 1992. The structure of work: Job design and roles. In M. Dunnette & L. Hough (Eds.), *Handbook of industrial and organizational psychology*, vol. 2: 165–207. Palo Alto, CA: Consulting Psychologists Press.

International Firefighters' Day. 2004. *http://www.iffd.net/stories/stories24.html*, accessed February 23, 2005.

Jermier, J. M., Gaines, J., & McIntosh, N. J. 1989. Reactions to physically dangerous work: A conceptual and empirical analysis. *Journal of Organizational Behavior*, 10: 15–33.

Johnston, B. J. 1993. The transformation of work and educational reform policy. *American Educational Research Journal*, 30: 39–65.

Kahn, W. A. 1990. Psychological conditions of personal engagement and disengagement at work. *Academy of Management Journal*, 33: 692–724.

Kahn, W. A. 1998. Relational systems at work. *Research in Organizational Behavior*, 20: 39–76.

Kahneman, D., Diener, E., & Schwarz, N. (Eds.). 1999. *Well-being: Foundations of hedonic psychology.* New York: Russell Sage Foundation.

Katz, R. 1978. Job longevity as a situational factor in job satisfaction. *Administrative Science Quarterly*, 23: 204–223.

Katzell, R. A., & Thompson, D. E. 1990. Work motivation: Theory and practice. *American Psychologist*, 45: 144–153.

Kiggundu, M. N. 1983. Task interdependence and job design: Test of a theory. *Organizational Behavior and Human Performance*, 31: 145–172.

Kiviniemi, M. T., Snyder, M., & Omoto, A. M. 2002. Too many of a good thing? The effects of multiple motivations on stress, cost, fulfillment and satisfaction. *Personality and Social Psychology Bulletin*, 28: 732–743.

Korchmaros, J., & Kenny, D. A. 2001. Emotional closeness as a mediator of the effect of genetic relatedness on altruism. *Psychological Science*, 12: 262–265.

Korsgaard, M. A., Meglino, B. M., & Lester, S. W. 1997. Beyond helping: Do other-oriented values have broader implications in organizations? *Journal of Applied Psychology*, 82: 160–177.

Kramer, R. 1999. Trust and distrust in organizations: Emerging perspectives, enduring questions. *Annual Review of Psychology*, 50: 569–598.

Larwood, L., & Gattiker, U. E. (Eds.). 1999. *Impact analysis: How research can enter application and make a difference.* Mahwah, NJ: Lawrence Erlbaum Associates.

Latané, B., & Darley, J. 1970. *The unresponsive bystander: Why doesn't he help?* New York: Appleton-Century-Crofts.

Latham, G. P. 2001. The reciprocal transfer of learning from journals to practice. *Applied Psychology: An International Review*, 50: 201–211.

Latham, G. P., & Pinder, C. C. 2005. Work motivation theory and research at the dawn of the twenty-first century. *Annual Review of Psychology*, 56: 495–516.

Lawler, E. J. 1992. Affective attachments to nested groups: A choice-process theory. *American Sociological Review*, 57: 327–339.

Lawler, E. J., & Yoon, J. 1998. Network structure and emotion in exchange relations. *American Sociological Review*, 63: 871–894.

Lawrence, P., & Nohria, N. 2002. *Driven: How human nature shapes our choices*. San Francisco: Jossey-Bass.

Lawrence, P. R. 1992. The challenge of problem-oriented research. *Journal of Management Inquiry*, 1: 139–142.

Leana, C. R., & Rousseau, D. (Eds.). 2000. *Relational wealth: The advantages of stability in a changing economy*. New York: Oxford University Press.

Lee, F. 1997. When the going gets tough, do the tough ask for help? Help seeking and power motivation in organizations. *Organizational Behavior and Human Decision Processes*, 72: 336–363.

Lee, F. 2002. The social costs of seeking help. *Journal of Applied Behavioral Science*, 38: 17–35.

Lee, F., & Tiedens, L. 2001. Is it lonely at the top? The independence and interdependence of power holders. *Research in Organizational Behavior*, 23: 43–91.

Lerner, M. J., & Miller, D. T. 1978. Just world research and the attribution process: Looking back and ahead. *Psychological Bulletin*, 85: 1030–1051.

Little, B. R. 1989. Personal projects analysis: Trivial pursuits, magnificent obsessions, and the search for coherence. In D. Buss & N. Cantor (Eds.), *Personality psychology: Recent trends and emerging directions*: 15–31. New York: Springer-Verlag.

Little, B. R. 2000. Free traits and personal contexts: Expanding a social ecological model of well-being. In W. B. Walsh, K. H. Craik, & R. Price (Eds.), *Person-environment psychology* (2nd ed.): 87–116. New York: Guilford Press.

Lively, K. J. 2002. Client contact and emotional labor: Upsetting the balance and evening the field. *Work and Occupations*, 29: 198–225.

Locke, E. A., & Becker, T. E. 1998. Rebuttal to a subjectivist critique of an objectivist approach to integrity in organizations. *Academy of Management Review*, 23: 170–175.

Locke, E. A., & Latham, G. P. 2002. Building a practically useful theory of goal setting and task motivation: A 35-year odyssey. *American Psychologist*, 57: 705–717.

Locke, E. A., & Latham, G. P. 2004. What should we do about motivation theory? Six recommendations for the twenty-first century. *Academy of Management Review*, 29: 388–403.

Locke, K. 1996. A funny thing happened! The management of consumer emotions in service encounters. *Organization Science*, 7: 40–59.

Lofland, J. 1977. Becoming a world-saver revisited. *American Behavioral Scientist*, 20: 805–818.

Lofland, J., & Stark, R. 1965. Becoming a world-saver: A theory of conversion to a deviant perspective. *American Sociological Review*, 30: 862–875.

Lubbock, J. 1923. (First published in 1894.) *The use of life*. New York: Macmillan.

Mann, R. M. 2002. Emotionality and social activism: A case study of a community development effort to establish a shelter for women in Ontario. *Journal of Contemporary Ethnography*, 31: 251–284.

Margolis, H. 1982. *Selfishness, altruism, and rationality*. Cambridge: Cambridge University Press.

Margolis, J. D., & Walsh, J. P. 2001. *People and profits? The search for a link between a company's social and financial performance*. Mahwah, NJ: Lawrence Erlbaum Associates.

Margolis, J. D., & Walsh, J. P. 2003. Misery loves companies: Rethinking social initiatives by business. *Administrative Science Quarterly*, 48: 268–305.

Marx, G. T. 1980. The new police undercover work. *Urban Life*, 8: 399–446.

Maslach, C., Schaufeli, W. B., & Leiter, M. P. 2001. Job burnout. *Annual Review of Psychology*, 52: 397–422.

Maurer, T. J., Pierce, H. R., & Shore, L. M. 2002. Perceived beneficiary of employee development activity: A three-dimensional social exchange model. *Academy of Management Review*, 27: 432–444.

May, M. 2003. *Absolute impact: The drive for personal leadership*. Los Angeles: Peloton.

McAdams, D. P., & de St. Aubin, E. 1992. A theory of generativity and its assessment through self-report, behavioral acts, and narrative themes in autobiography. *Journal of Personality and Social Psychology*, 62: 1003–1015.

McCullough, M. E., Kilpatrick, S. D., Emmons, R. A., & Larson, D. B. 2001. Is gratitude a moral affect? *Psychological Bulletin*, 127: 249–266.

McGregor, I., & Little, B. R. 1998. Personal projects, happiness, and meaning: On doing well and being yourself. *Journal of Personality and Social Psychology*, 74: 494–512.

McNeely, B. L., & Meglino, B. M. 1994. The role of dispositional and situational antecedents in prosocial organizational behavior: An examination of the intended beneficiaries of prosocial behavior. *Journal of Applied Psychology*, 79: 836–844.

Meglino, B. M., & Korsgaard, M. A. 2004. Considering rational self-interest as a disposition: Organizational implications of other orientation. *Journal of Applied Psychology*, 89: 946–959.

Meyer, J. P., Becker, T. E., & Vandenberghe, C. 2004. Employee commitment and motivation: A conceptual analysis and integrative model. *Journal of Applied Psychology*, 89: 991–1007.

Meyer, J. P., & Herscovitch, L. 2001. Commitment in the workplace: Toward a general model. *Human Resource Management Review*, 11: 299–326.

Meyerson, D. E., & Scully, M. A. 1995. Tempered radicalism and the politics of ambivalence and change. *Organization Science*, 6: 585–600.

Michaelson, C. 2005. Meaningful motivation for work motivation theory. *Academy of Management Review*, 30: 235–238.

Mitchell, T. R., & Daniels, D. 2003. Motivation. In W. C. Borman, D. R. Ilgen, & R. J. Klimoski (Eds.), *Handbook of psychology. Volume 12: Industrial and organizational psychology*: 225–254. New York: Wiley.

Molinsky, A., & Margolis, J. 2005. Necessary evils and interpersonal sensitivity in organizations. *Academy of Management Review*, 30: 245–268.

Morgeson, F. P., & Campion, M. A. 2002. Avoiding tradeoffs when redesigning work: Evidence from a longitudinal quasi-experiment. *Personnel Psychology*, 55: 589–612.

Morgeson, F. P., & Campion, M. A. 2003. Work design. In W. Borman, R. Klimoski, & D. Ilgen (Eds.), *Handbook of psychology. Volume 12: Industrial and organizational psychology*: 423–452. New York: Wiley.

Morrison, E. W. 1994. Role definitions and organizational citizenship behavior: The importance of the employee's perspective. *Academy of Management Journal*, 37: 1543–1567.

Nelson, L. D., & Norton, M. I. 2005. From student to superhero: Situational primes shape future helping. *Journal of Experimental Social Psychology*, 41: 423–430.

Oldham, G. R., & Hackman, J. R. 1981. Relationships between organization structure and employee reactions: Comparing alternative frameworks. *Administrative Science Quarterly*, 25: 66–83.

O'Reilly, C. A., & Chatman, J. 1996. Culture as social control: Corporations, cults, and commitment. *Research in Organizational Behavior*, 18: 167–210.

Osterman, P. 1994. How common is workplace transformation and who adopts it? *Industrial and Labor Relations Review*, 47: 173–188.

Osterman, P. 2000. Work reorganization in an era of restructuring: Trends in diffusion and effects on employee welfare. *Industrial and Labor Relations Review*, 53: 179–196.

Parker, S. K., & Axtell, C. M. 2001. Seeing another viewpoint: Antecedents and outcomes of employee perspective taking. *Academy of Management Journal*, 44: 1085–1100.

Parker, S. K., & Wall, T. 1998. *Job and work design: Organizing work to promote well-being and effectiveness*. London: Sage.

Parker, S. K., Wall, T. D., & Cordery, J. L. 2001. Future work design research and practice: Towards an elaborated model of work design. *Journal of Occupational and Organizational Psychology*, 74: 413–440.

Parker, S. K., Wall, T. D., & Jackson, P. R. 1997. "That's not my job": Developing flexible employee work orientations. *Academy of Management Journal*, 40: 899–929.

Pearce, J. L. 2004. What do we know and how do we really know it? *Academy of Management Review*, 29: 175–179.

Penner, L. A., Dovidio, J. F., Piliavin, J. A., & Schroeder, D. A. 2005. Prosocial behavior: Multilevel perspectives. *Annual Review of Psychology*, 56: 365–392.

Penner, L. A., Midili, A. R., & Kegelmeyer, J. 1997. Beyond job attitudes: A personality and social psychology perspective on the causes of organizational citizenship behavior. *Human Performance*, 10: 111–132.

Pettigrew, T. F. 1998. Intergroup contact theory. *Annual Review of Psychology,*, 49: 65–85.

Piliavin, J. A., & Charng, H. 1990. Altruism: A review of recent theory and research. *Annual Review of Sociology*, 16: 27–65.

Pittman, T. S. 1998. Motivation. In D. T. Gilbert, S. T. Fiske, & G. Lindzey (Eds.), *The handbook of social psychology*, vol. 1 (4th ed.): 549–590. Boston: McGraw-Hill.

Pratt, M. G. 2000. The good, the bad, and the ambivalent: Managing identification among Amway distributors. *Administrative Science Quarterly*, 45: 456–493.

Puffer, S. M. 1987. Prosocial behavior, noncompliant behavior, and work performance among commission sales-people. *Journal of Applied Psychology*, 72: 615–621.

Quinn, R. E. 2000. *Change the world: How ordinary people can achieve extraordinary results*. San Francisco: Jossey-Bass.

Rabin, M. 1998. Psychology and economics. *Journal of Economic Literature*, 36: 11–46.

Rafaeli, A., & Sutton, R. I. 1987. The expression of emotion as part of the work role. *Academy of Management Review*, 12: 23–37.

Rangan, S. 2000. The problem of search and deliberation in economic action: When social networks really matter. *Academy of Management Review*, 25: 813–828.

Regehr, C., Goldberg, G., & Hughes, J. 2002. Exposure to human tragedy, empathy, and trauma in ambulance paramedics. *American Journal of Orthopsychiatry*, 72: 505–513.

Rioux, S. M., & Penner, L. A. 2001. The causes of organizational citizenship behavior: A motivational analysis. *Journal of Applied Psychology*, 86: 1306–1314.

Roccas, S., & Brewer, M. 2002. Social identity complexity. *Personality and Social Psychology Review*, 6: 88–106.

Rosen, S., Mickler, S. E., & Collins, J. E. 1987. Reactions of would-be helpers whose offer of help is spurned. *Journal of Personality and Social Psychology*, 53: 288–297.

Rozin, P., & Royzman, E. B. 2001. Negativity bias, negativity dominance, and contagion. *Personality and Social Psychology Review*, 5: 296–320.

Ruiz-Quintanilla, S. A., & England, G. W. 1996. How working is defined: Structure and stability. *Journal of Organizational Behavior*, 17: 515–540.

Ryan, R. M., & Deci, E. L. 2000. Self-determination theory and the facilitation of intrinsic motivation, social development, and well-being. *American Psychologist*, 55: 68–78.

Ryan, R. M., & Deci, E. L. 2001. To be happy or to be self-fulfilled: A review of research on hedonic and eudaimonic well-being. *Annual Review of Psychology*, 52: 141–166.

Ryff, C. D. 1989. Happiness is everything, or is it? Explorations on the meaning of psychological well-being. *Journal of Personality and Social Psychology*, 57: 1069–1081.

Rynes, S. L., Bartunek, J. M., & Daft, R. L. 2001. Across the great divide: Knowledge creation and transfer between practitioners and academics. *Academy of Management Journal*, 44: 340–355.

Saegert, S., Swap, W., & Zajonc, R. B. 1973. Exposure, context, and interpersonal attraction. *Journal of Personality and Social Psychology*, 25: 234–242.

Salancik, G. R., & Pfeffer, J. 1978. A social information processing approach to job attitudes and task design. *Administrative Science Quarterly*, 23: 224–253.

Scharlemann, J. P. W., Eckel, C. C., Kacelnik, A., & Wilson, R. K. 2001. The value of a smile: Game theory with a human face. *Journal of Economic Psychology*, 22: 617–640.

Schoenrade, P. A., Batson, C. D., Brandt, J. R., & Loud, R. E. 1986. Attachment, accountability, and motivation to benefit another not in distress. *Journal of Personality and Social Psychology*, 51: 557–563.

Schroeder, D. A., Penner, L. A., Dovidio, J. F., & Piliavin, J. A. 1995. *The psychology of helping and altruism.* New York: McGraw-Hill.

Schwartz, S. H. 1992. Universals in the content and structure of values: Theoretical advances and empirical tests in 20 countries. *Advances in Experimental Social Psychology*, 25: 1–65.

Schwartz, S. H., & Bardi, A. 2001. Value hierarchies across cultures: Taking a similarities perspective. *Journal of Cross-Cultural Psychology*, 32: 268–290.

Shamir, B. 1991. Meaning, self and motivation in organizations. *Organization Studies,*, 12: 405–424.

Sheldon, K. M., & Elliot, A. J. 1999. Goal striving, need-satisfaction, and longitudinal well-being: The self-concordance model. *Journal of Personality and Social Psychology*, 76: 482–497.

Sheldon, K. M., & Houser-Marko, L. 2001. Self-concordance, goal attainment and the pursuit of happiness: Can there be an upward spiral? *Journal of Personality and Social Psychology*, 80: 152–165.

Sherif, M., Harvey, O. J., White, B. J., Hood, W. R., & Sherif, C. W. 1961. *Intergroup conflict and cooperation: The Robbers' Cave experiment.* Norman: Oklahoma Book Exchange.

Sia, T. L., Lord, C. G., Blessum, K. A., Thomas, J. C., & Lepper, M. R. 1999. Activation of exemplars in the process of accessing social category attitudes. *Journal of Personality and Social Psychology*, 76: 517–532.

Sims, H. P., Szilagyi, A. D., & Keller, R. T. 1976. The measurement of job characteristics. *Academy of Management Journal*, 19: 195–212.

Small, D. A., & Loewenstein, G. 2003. Helping a victim or helping the victim: Altruism and identifiability. *Journal of Risk and Uncertainty*, 26: 5–16.

Smith, D. 1988. *Firefighters: Their lives in their own words.* New York: Doubleday.

Smith, K. G., Carroll, S. J., & Ashford, S. J. 1995. Intra- and interorganizational cooperation: Toward a research agenda. *Academy of Management Journal*, 38: 7–23.

Staub, E. 1984. Steps toward a comprehensive theory of moral conduct: Goal orientation, social behavior, kindness and cruelty. In W. M. Kurtines & J. L. Gewirtz (Eds.), *Morality, moral behavior, and moral development:* 241–260. New York: Wiley.

Staw, B. M. 1977. Motivation in organizations: Toward synthesis and redirection. In B. M. Staw & G. Salancik (Eds.), *New directions in organizational behavior:* 55–95. Chicago: St. Clair Press.

Staw, B. M. 1980. Rationality and justification in organizational life. *Research in Organizational Behavior*, 2: 45–80.

Stewart, G. L., & Barrick, M. R. 2000. Team structure and performance: Assessing the mediating role of intrateam process and the moderating role of task type. *Academy of Management Journal*, 43: 135–148.

Stinglhamber, F., & Vandenberghe, C. 2003. Organizations and supervisors as sources of support and targets of commitment: A longitudinal study. *Journal of Organizational Behavior*, 24: 251–270.

Stone, E. F., & Gueutal, H. G. 1985. An empirical derivation of the dimensions along which characteristics of jobs are perceived. *Academy of Management Journal*, 28: 376–396.

Stryker, S., & Burke, P. J. 2000. The past, present and future of identity theory. *Social Psychology Quarterly*, 63: 284–297.

Stürmer, S., Snyder, M., & Omoto, A. M. 2005. Prosocial emotions and helping: The moderating role of group membership. *Journal of Personality and Social Psychology*, 88: 532–546.

Suedfeld, P., & Steel, G. D. 2000. The environmental psychology of capsule habitats. *Annual Review of Psychology*, 51: 227–253.

Sutton, R. I. 1991. Maintaining norms about expressed emotions: The case of bill collectors. *Administrative Science Quarterly*, 36: 245–268.

Swann, W. B., & Rentfrow, P. J. 2001. Blirtatiousness: Cognitive, behavioral, and physiological consequences of rapid responding. *Journal of Personality and Social Psychology*, 81: 1160–1175.

Taber, T. D., & Alliger, G. M. 1995. A task-level assessment of job satisfaction. *Journal of Organizational Behavior*, 16: 101–121.

Taber, T. D., & Taylor, E. 1990. A review and evaluation of the psychometric properties of the Job Diagnostic Survey. *Personnel Psychology*, 43: 467–500.

Taylor, S. E., & Brown, J. D. 1994. Positive illusions and well-being revisited: Separating fact from fiction. *Psychological Bulletin*, 116: 21–27.

Terkel, S. 1972. *Working.* New York: Pantheon.

Tetlock, P. E. 1985. Accountability: The neglected social context of judgment and choice. *Research in Organizational Behavior*, 7: 297–332.

Tetlock, P. E., Peterson, R. S., & Berry, J. M. 1993. Flattering and unflattering personality portraits of integratively simple and complex managers. *Journal of Personality and Social Psychology*, 64: 500–511.

Thompson, A. M., & Bono, B. A. 1993. Work without wages: The motivation for volunteer firefighters. *American Journal of Economics and Sociology*, 52: 323–343.

Thompson, J. A., & Bunderson, J. S. 2003. Violations of principle: Ideological currency in the psychological contract. *Academy of Management Review*, 28: 571–586.

Thompson, J. D. 1967. *Organizations in action.* New York: McGraw-Hill.

Tversky, A., & Kahneman, D. 1992. Advances in prospect theory: Cumulative representations of uncertainty. *Journal of Risk and Uncertainty*, 5: 297–323.

Vallacher, R. R., & Wegner, D. M. 1987. What do people think they're doing? Action identification and human behavior. *Psychological Review*, 94: 3–15.

Van de Ven, A. H., & Johnson, P. E. 2006. Knowledge for theory and practice. *Academy of Management Review*, 31: 802–821.

Van Maanen, J., & Kunda, G. 1989. Real feelings: Emotional expression and organizational culture. *Research in Organizational Behavior*, 11: 43–104.

Van Vugt, M., Snyder, M., Tyler, T. R., & Biel, A. (Eds.). 2000. *Cooperation in modern society: Promoting the welfare of communities, states and organizations.* New York: Routledge.

Vroom, V. H. 1964. *Work and motivation.* New York: Wiley.

Wageman, R. 1995. Interdependence and group effectiveness. *Administrative Science Quarterly*, 40: 145–181.

Weaver, D. H. G., & Wilhoit, G. C. 1996. *The American journalist in the 1990s: U.S. news people at the end of an era.* Mahwah, NJ: Lawrence Erlbaum Associates.

Weick, K. E. 1979. *The social psychology of organizing* (2nd ed.). Reading, MA: Addison-Wesley.

Weick, K. E. 1995. *Sensemaking in organizations.* Thousand Oaks, CA: Sage.

Weick, K. E., & Roberts, K. 1993. Collective mind in organizations: Heedful interrelating on flight decks. *Administrative Science Quarterly*, 38: 357–381.

Weiner, B. 1986. *An attributional theory of motivation and emotion.* New York: Springer-Verlag.

Wilson, E. O. 1975. *Sociobiology: The new synthesis.* Cambridge, MA: Harvard University Press.

Wong, C., & Campion, M. A. 1991. Development and test of a task level model of motivational job design. *Journal of Applied Psychology*, 76: 825–837.

Wong, P. T. P., & Weiner, B. 1981. When people ask "why" questions, and the heuristics of attributional search. *Journal of Personality and Social Psychology*, 40: 650–663.

Wrzesniewski, A., & Dutton, J. E. 2001. Crafting a job: Revisioning employees as active crafters of their work. *Academy of Management Review*, 26: 179–201.

Wrzesniewski, A., Dutton, J. E., & Debebe, G. 2003. Interpersonal sensemaking and the meaning of work. *Research in Organizational Behavior*, 25: 93–135.

Wrzesniewski, A., McCauley, C. R., Rozin, P., & Schwartz, B. 1997. Jobs, careers, and callings: People's relations to their work. *Journal of Research in Personality*, 31: 21–33.

Zapf, D. 2002. Emotion work and psychological well-being: A review of the literature and some conceptual considerations. *Human Resource Management Review*, 12: 237–268.

5.2   INTEGRATING THEORIES OF MOTIVATION

Piers Steel and Cornelius J. König

Progress toward understanding human behavior has been hindered by discipline-bound theories, dividing our efforts. Fortunately, these separate endeavors are converging and can be effectively integrated. Focusing on the fundamental features of picoeconomics, expectancy theory, cumulative prospect theory, and need theory, we construct a temporal motivational theory (TMT). TMT appears consistent with the major findings from many other investigations, including psychobiology and behaviorism. The potential implications of TMT are numerous, affecting our understanding on a wide range of topics, including group behavior, job design, stock market behavior, and goal setting.

The fields of economics, decision making, sociology, and psychology share a common desire to understand our human nature—that is, our essential character, disposition, or temperament. This extensive, multidisciplinary interest in establishing who we are reflects the enormous ramifications of the endeavor. As Pinker (2002) catalogs, theories of human nature have been used to direct relationships, lifestyles, and governments—with disastrous effects when based on faulty models. On a smaller applied scale, treatments, training, compensation, and selection all depend on our theories of human behavior. Even job design, which is an overtly physical enterprise, requires positing human elements such as "growth need strength" (Hackman & Oldham, 1976). To ensure the efficacy of our interventions, we need to determine what describes, drives, or decides our actions.

Ironically, our understanding of behavior has been hindered by the very extent of our efforts. There is a superabundance of motivational theories. Not only does each field have its particular interpretation, but there are ample subdivisions within each discipline. Psychology, for example, has the traditions of self-regulation, motivation, and personality, each with its own nomenclature, structure, and etiology. These subdivisions necessarily divide our efforts, limiting the extent to which insights can be shared. This problem has recently been recognized and lamented by many prominent researchers (e.g., Barrick & Mount, 1991; Elliot & Thrash, 2002; Judge & Ilies, 2002), but it is by no means a new issue. Consider the words of Irving Fisher, the venerated economist, which are regrettably still far too relevant:

> The fact that there are still two schools, the productivity school and the psychological school, constantly crossing swords on this subject [time preference/implicit interest rates] is a scandal in economic science and a reflection on the inadequate methods employed by these would-be destroyers of each other (1930: 312).

Fortunately, our theories also have several strong commonalities, and their effective integration seems achievable (Klein, 1989; Larrick, 1993; Mischel & Shoda, 1999). If it is possible to do this—to effectively combine these different conceptions of human nature—we will have substantially progressed toward a common theory of basic motivation. To use E. O. Wilson's term, this convergence is an excellent example of *consilience*. Consilience is "a 'jumping together' of knowledge by the linking of facts and fact-based theory across disciplines to create a common groundwork of explanation" (1998: 8). If a theory can be shown to have consilience, its scientific validity is vastly improved, since it represents different avenues of inquiry coming to similar conclusions. We begin by further reviewing the importance and advantages of such integration.

After this, we integrate four closely related motivational theories, using the insights of each to inform the others. We start with picoeconomics (Ainslie, 1992), which we then subsequently extend with expectancy theory (e.g., Vroom, 1964), cumulative prospect theory (Tversky & Kahneman, 1992), and need theory (e.g., Dollard & Miller, 1950). It is important to note that none of these theories is definitive, each containing various limitations. However, we are not attempting a full integration of their every detail; instead, we are focusing on linking together these theories' most enduring and well-accepted basic features. One of the most important of these features is time.

Time is a critical component of choice or motivated behavior. As Drucker notes, "The time dimension is inherent in management because management is concerned with decisions for action" (1954: 15). Similarly, Luce states that "quite clearly any empirical realization of a decision tree has a strong temporal aspect," and the failure to include time "is a clear failing of the modeling" (1990: 228). Also, Kanfer (1990) and Donovan (2001) critique theories that are episodic and, thus, have difficulty accounting for behavior over time and events. Fortunately, time or delay does feature in several motivational formulations, its application is consistent where included, and through integration it can be extended to other theories where it was previously absent. Consequently, we label the outcome of our integrative efforts *temporal motivational theory* (TMT) because of its emphasis on time as a motivational factor.

After constructing TMT, we review its essential elements and when it, rather than its source theories, should be applied. We also use procrastination, a prototypical performance problem, to explicate the workings of TMT. As a general theory of human behavior, the applications of TMT are numerous. We identify four diverse areas that might benefit by employing it in specific ways. Also, we note that this model of human behavior, like all models, must strike a balance between precision and parsimony. Some refinements may add undue complexity while accounting for only minimal incremental variance. We consider whether and when TMT may be too complex or too simple. Finally, we note that in future research on TMT scholars may choose to exploit two powerful but under-used venues: a computerized personal system of instruction and computer simulations.

The Case for Integration

A common theme across the disparate disciplines of decision making and motivation is the desire for more comprehensive and integrated theories (Cooksey, 2001; Eisenhardt & Zbaracki, 1992; Langley, Mintzberg, Pitcher, Posada, & Saint-Macary, 1995; Leonard, Beauvais, & Scholl, 1999; Mellers, Schwartz, & Cooke, 1998). For example, Locke and Latham, writing about the future of motivational research, conclude that "there is now an urgent need to tie these theories and processes together into an overall model" (2004: 389). Also, Donovan recommends in his review of motivation that "future work should move towards the development and validation of an integrated, goal-based model of self-regulation that incorporates *the important components of various theories*" (2001: 69; emphases added). This desire reflects two fundamental challenges in motivational research. First, many traditional paradigms are inadequate for discussing or exploring many realistic and complex situations. Second, the very progress of our field is being hindered by segregation.

Because there has yet to be a broad, integrated theory of motivation, any particular theory necessarily deals with only a subset of motivational factors. Although a theory may deal with these factors very well, it potentially will have trouble in intricate, realistic situations. Owing to a situation's very complexity, a larger variety of forces may be operating.

Consequently, no single theory can adequately explain the observed phenomena. For example, expectancy theory, which represents rationality in economics, is the simplest and consequently has been criticized for its limitations. Considerable research has been summarized that indicates we act less than logically (Lopes, 1994; Thaler, 1992). In fact, irrational behavior is so pervasive that Albanese concludes, "The economic assumption of rationality is violated in the behavior of every person" (1987: 14).

Rather than abandon expectancy theory, which has long been the dominant paradigm and has proven value, we can make it much more flexible by integrating it with other established motivational principles. This approach has already been proposed by George Akerlof (1991), the Nobel Prize-winning economist. Akerlof argues that his field should take *salience* into account, salience referring to individuals' undue sensitivity to the present and consequent undervaluing of the future. He shows that the concept allows expectancy theory to more fully grasp a broad range of areas, such as retirement savings, organizational failures, cults, crime, and politics. Later in this paper, we also discuss several complex topics where a larger variety of motivational factors appear to be operating than typically considered. An integrated perspective is invaluable in better understanding them.

In addition, scholars have observed as well as argued that continued segregation of our motivational theories is detrimental to scientific progress. The problem is *serious*. Steers, Mowday, and Shapiro note that the theoretical development of work motivation has significantly lagged behind other fields, that we still widely rely on obsolete and discredited theories, and that intellectual interest in the topic has "seemed to decline precipitously" (2004: 383). As Zeidner, Boekaerts, and Pintrich conclude, a major reason for this decline is that "the fragmentation and disparate, but overlapping, lines of research within the self-regulation domain have made any attempt at furthering our knowledge an arduous task" (2000: 753). Similarly, Wilson (1998), as well as Staats (1999), argues that the progress for the social sciences is slow specifically because of the lack of consilience—the lack of integration. As Wilson writes:

> Social scientists by and large spurn the idea of the hierarchical ordering of knowledge that unites and drives the natural science. Split into independent cadres, they stress precision in their words within their specialty but seldom speak the same technical language from one specialty to the next (1998: 182).

Wilson notes, however, that the medical sciences advance rapidly primarily because of consilience. Researchers can approach problems at many different but mutually supporting levels of complexity, allowing insights to be passed into adjacent fields and different solutions to be effectively harmonized.

Consider economists and psychologists. As Lopes notes, they have been less than collegial in the past, tending to view each other with considerable "suspicion and distaste" (1994: 198). Similarly, Wärneryd (1988) quotes several eminent economists whose words on psychology border on the vitriolic. In fact, Loewenstein (1992) observes that there has long been an active attempt to erase any psychological content from economics. But, more recently, there has been some integration, in the form of behavioral economics. Traditional economic theory, essentially expectancy theory, is being supplemented with some of the very concepts that we later stress here (e.g., personality traits, temporal discounting, loss aversion). As Camerer, Loewenstein, and Rabin (2004) review, this is fundamentally reshaping the economic field and improving its explanatory power by basing it on more realistic psychological foundations.

Consequently, fostering integration among different motivational disciplines is important and possible. First, it allows the development of a common language among social scientists working in different fields. This should make communication and collaboration across disciplines much easier. Second, it allows more effective responses to complex motivational problems, which can be multifaceted. As a later example of procrastination confirms, self-regulatory failure can occur for many reasons, and effective treatment requires investigating all these possibilities to find the most promising and pliable junctures for intervention. Third, it allows insights to be shared with fields overlapping in terms of features and complexity (i.e., "cross-pollenation"). Psychological treatments for addiction, for example, may inform the economic formulations of retirement saving programs (e.g., Akerlof, 1991; Loewenstein & Elster, 1992). As we show later, an integrative theory facilitates the generation of new and plausible hypotheses in a range of topics, from group behavior to goal setting.

Developing TMT

To develop TMT, we consider four related understandings of human nature: picoeconomics, expectancy theory, cumulative prospect theory (CPT), and need theory. These four postulations are particularly well suited for consolidation, since they reflect common sources in their development and, thus, share many terms. Consequently, areas of overlap are quite definite. Furthermore, they can be expressed formulaically, allowing their integration with minimal translation and in a relatively straightforward manner. The terms in these formulations also provide a ready summary of each theory's primary features, which are also evident in a variety of other formulations. To further underscore that we are integrating motivational fundamentals, we begin each section by noting similarities with other prominent theories. We start with picoeconomics since it, of all the theories considered, has time as its most central feature.

Picoeconomics or Hyperbolic Discounting

Ainslie (1992), under the title of *Picoeconomics*, and Ainslie and Haslam (1992), under the title of *Hyperbolic Discounting*, discuss a theory that helps to account for choice of behavior over time. The theory already demonstrates considerable consilience, with Ainslie drawing support from a variety of research literature, including sociology, social psychology, and psychodynamic psychology, as well as behaviorist psychology and economics in particular. For example, the personality traits of impulsiveness and future orientation all have strong commonalities to the concept of hyperbolic discounting. In addition, recent work in psychobiology underscores the importance of hyperbolic discounting, with the journal of *Psychopharmacology* recently dedicating an entire issue to the construct (e.g., Ho, Mobini, Chiang, Bradshaw, & Szabadi, 1999).

In its basic form, the theory is simple. We must choose from a variety of possible rewarding activities. In choosing among them, we have an innate tendency to inordinately undervalue future events. We tend, then, to put off tasks leading to distant but valuable goals in favor of ones with more immediate though lesser rewards. Inevitably, however, time marches on, and as the once-future events loom ever closer, we see their value more clearly. Eventually, we experience regret if we have irrationally put off pursuing this more valuable goal to the extent that it can no longer be realistically achieved.

Going beyond this qualitative description, the theory of picoeconomics tries to express the effects of temporal discounting mathematically. Summarizing the efforts from behaviorist and economic perspectives, Ainslie (1992) notes several attempts to provide an accurate equation. Of these, the *matching law* is one of the first and simplest (Chung & Herrnstein, 1967).[1] The matching law considers how frequency, magnitude, and delay of reinforcement affect choices, with delay being the critical feature. It is the dominant model describing choice among various concurrently administered, variable-interval schedules (Ainslie, 1992). In other words, when we must choose among several courses of action that all result in a reward, albeit at different times, this model best predicts the aggregate behaviors of adults (see Myerson & Green, 1995). Similarly, a related version of this law used in the economic field also shows extremely strong validity (see Loewenstein & Prelec, 1992).

The simplest version of the matching law contains just four components:

$$\text{Utility} = \frac{\text{Rate} \times \text{Amount}}{\text{Delay}} \tag{1}$$

Utility indicates preference for a course of action. Naturally, the higher the utility, the greater the preference. The next three variables reflect aspects of the reward or payout of the action. Rate indicates the expectancy or frequency that the action will lead to the reward. It ranges from 0 percent to 100 percent, with 100 percent reflecting certainty. Amount indicates the amount of reward that is received on payout. Essentially, it indicates the magnitude of the incentive. Finally, delay indicates how long, on average, one must wait to receive the payout. Since delay is in the denominator of the equation, the longer the delay, the less valuable the course of action is perceived.

There also have been several modifications of the basic matching law. Rate is often dropped, since it can be *partially* expressed in terms of delay alone; over repeated trials, rewards delivered at lower rates necessarily create longer *average* delays. Also, a new parameter is typically included to capture individual differences regarding sensitivity to delay. The greater the sensitivity, the larger the effect delays have on choice. Of all these modifications, Mazur's (1987) equation is likely the simplest and most widespread:

$$\text{Utility} = \frac{\text{Amount}}{Z + \Gamma(T - t)} \tag{2}$$

Aside from dropping rate, there are three changes from the original matching law. $T - t$ refers to the delay of the reward in terms of "time reward" minus "time now." Γ refers to the subject's sensitivity to delay. The larger Γ is, the greater the sensitivity. Finally, Z is a constant derived from when rewards are immediate. It prevents the equation rocketing toward infinity under periods of small delay and, thus, in Shizgal's (1999) terminology, can be considered the determinant of *instantaneous utility*. In addition, the reciprocal of this equation can be used to predict preferences among punishers instead of rewards (Mazur, 1998). Consequently, people prefer distant punishers to more instant ones.

There have been several other attempts to further refine this equation, but without established success. For example, explorations into using other mathematical expressions (e.g., Logue, Rodriguez, Peña-Correal, & Maruo, 1984), particularly exponential functions,[2] tend not to be as accurate (Green, Myerson, & McFadden, 1997; Mazur, 2001), although they are still favored in economic circles because of their close resemblance to a purely rational discount model. In economics, this phenomenon is studied under the designation of *time preference* or *implicit interest rate* (Antonides, 1991).

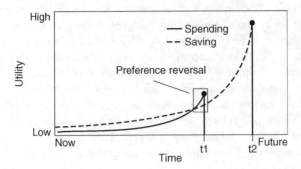

Figure 5.2.1 Preference Reversal Between Spending and Saving as a Function of Time Remaining to Cash Bonus and Hyperbolic Discounting.

Figure 5.2.1 outlines picoeconomics by displaying the utility curves for two courses of action: saving or immediately spending an expected financial bonus. From a distance, both options are effectively discounted, and the benefits of saving appear superior. However, when the bonus is received from the employer, at time t1, the spending benefits are immediate while the saving benefits remain distant. Because of temporal discounting, people likely find themselves changing their original intentions, and this crossing of utility lines reflects the well-established phenomenon of preference reversal (Ainslie, 1992; Loewenstein & Prelec, 1992; Steel, in press). What is planned today does not always turn into tomorrow's actions.

Expectancy Theory

Expectancy theory, or expectancy × value ($E \times V$) theory, represents an extensive family of individual formulations. Vroom (1964) first introduced the notion to industrial-organizational psychology, but it has an earlier history in the cognitive field (e.g., Rotter, 1954) that, in turn, can be predated by economic investigations under the rubric of subjective expected utility (Bernoulli, 1954). Its core elements appear in several theories. To begin with, Bandura (1997) integrates Ajzen's (1991) theory of planned behavior into the traditional $E \times V$ framework. In turn, self-efficacy theory, which has been championed by Bandura, is closely related to expectancy, if not identical in some respects (Bandura & Locke, 2003; Skinner, 1996; Vancouver, Thompson, & Williams, 2001). Also, Gollwitzer, when discussing his model of action phases, states, "Preferences are established by employing the evaluative criteria of feasibility and desirability" (1996: 289). Plainly, feasibility is related to expectancy, while desirability is a form of value.

$E \times V$ theories suggest that a process akin to rational gambling determines choices among courses of action. For each option, two considerations are made: (1) what is the probability that this outcome will be achieved, and (2) how much is the expected outcome valued? Multiplying these components, expectancy and value (i.e., $E \times V$), the action that is then appraised as largest is the one most likely to be pursued. A major limitation to $E \times V$ models is that they are episodic and, as mentioned, have difficulty accounting for behavior over time (Kanfer, 1990). This limitation may partially explain Van Eerde and Thierry's (1996) meta-analytic finding that $E \times V$ often predicts behavior over time rather weakly and significantly less well than one's intention to perform. Fortunately, its incorporation into a hyperbolic discounting model largely rectifies this weakness.

As mentioned, the numerator of the original matching law is composed of two terms:

amount and rate. Respectively, these terms are equivalent to value and expectancy, reflecting a shift from a behavioral to a cognitive standpoint. The behavioral view expresses the equation's variables in terms of what should be objectively observed. The cognitive view recognizes that the impact of all the variables is not uniform but depends on interpretation differences among individuals, although the difficulty in determining these differences may be extreme. Consequently, amount is more accurately described in cognitive terms as the perceived attractiveness or aversiveness of the outcome. It reflects a subjective evaluation, dependent on an individual's perception. Similarly, rate refers to the frequency that actions lead to rewards or, alternatively, the probability of acquiring the expected outcome. By describing amount as value and returning rate to the equation in the form of expectancy, picoeconomics begins to encapsulate expectancy theory. The final equation should be as follows:

$$\text{Utility} = \frac{\text{Expectancy} \times \text{Value}}{Z + \Gamma(T - t)} \tag{3}$$

Of course, other modifications can be argued from expectancy theory. For example, Vroom (1964) breaks expectancy down into two components: expectancy and instrumentality. In this case, expectancy refers to whether the intended course of action can be completed successfully. Instrumentality refers to whether, having been successful, the expected rewards will be forthcoming. Research indicates, however, that this modification may be detrimental to predicting behavior, rather than helpful (Van Eerde & Thierry, 1996). Many other refinements have been proposed, including terms that account for resource allocation (e.g., Kanfer & Ackerman, 1996; Naylor, Pritchard, & Ilgen, 1980) and future orientation (e.g., Raynor & Entin, 1982). Regardless of the individual formulation, $E \times V$ is the core aspect.

CPT

Tversky and Kahneman's (1992) CPT, an update of Kahneman and Tversky's (1979) prospect theory, is a descriptive model closely related to traditional expectancy theory, particularly Atkinson's (1957) formulation. The major revision is the introduction of an "approach/avoidance" dichotomy, which is extremely well supported by other research. Elliot and Thrash (2002), as well as Carver, Sutton, and Scheier (2000), review a confluence of findings from a variety of motivational formulations that supports its existence. Similarly, Ito and Cacioppo (1999), in their psychobiological investigation of motivation, propose a "bivariate model of evaluative space," which they themselves note also provides convergent validity to prospect theory.

Often described as one of the leading theories of decision (e.g., Fennema & Wakker, 1997; Levy, 1992), CPT seeks to describe choice under uncertainty by reconsidering how value is derived, as well as how expectancy should be transformed. Here, we review only the pertinent aspects of CPT: a full discussion of the original and cumulative version of prospect theory requires more attention than can be easily provided, although it is available elsewhere (see Fennema & Wakker, 1997, and Tversky & Kahneman, 1992). Also, for a relevant and recent psychological example, see Hunton, Hall, and Price (1998), who apply original prospect theory to the value of "voice" in participative decision making.

Focusing on its key theoretical elements, CPT is very similar to the original prospect theory. Acknowledging considerable variability across people, both theories codify regularities in how we interpret values and expectancies. First, values are based on outcomes that are defined as losses and gains in reference to some status quo or baseline. These outcomes are transformed following a function that is concave for gains, convex for losses, and steeper for losses than for gains. In other words, losses loom larger than gains. Second, probability (i.e., expectancy) is also transformed following a function that has both convex and concave segments. Lower probabilities tend to be convex (i.e., overweighted), whereas higher probabilities tend to be concave (i.e., underweighted). Similar to the determination of values, the exact parameters for the transformation of probability differ for losses and gains. Consequently, the expected utility of any behavior is based on considering the combined utility of its possible gains and possible losses, with gains and losses each being estimated differently.[3]

By itself, CPT suffers the same limitation that Kanfer (1990) pointed out for expectancy theory—that is, the failure to include time as a variable. Consequently, other researchers have already proposed various integrations of prospect theory with some hyperbolic time-discounting function (Loewenstein & Prelec, 1992; Rachlin, 2000; Schouwenburg & Groenewoud, 1997). Given this foundation and CPT's similarity to expectancy theory, only two terms are needed to incorporate CPT into picoeconomics.

$$\text{Utility} = \sum_{i=1}^{k} \frac{E_{\text{CPT}}^{+} \times V_{\text{CPT}}^{+}}{Z + \Gamma(T-t)} + \sum_{i=k+1}^{n} \frac{E_{\text{CPT}}^{-} \times V_{\text{CPT}}^{-}}{Z + \Gamma(T-t)} \tag{4}$$

For any decision, one considers n possible outcomes. The first term, containing E_{CPT}^{+} and V_{CPT}^{+}, reflects the transformed values for the expectancy associated with k gains and the perceived value of each of these gains. The second term, containing E_{CPT}^{-} and V_{CPT}^{-}, reflects the transformed values for the expectancy associated with $n - k$ losses and the perceived value of each of these losses. Given that losses carry negative value, the second term will always diminish the first and, thus, the overall utility. The summation sign for each term reflects the possibility of multiple outcomes given any act and, thus, multiple possible gains or losses. It is this summation sign that makes CPT cumulative.

Of note, although the ability to model decisions with multiple possible outcomes is a significant improvement, it takes a moment to consider how expectancy is interpreted under this model. With CPT the decision weight or E_{CPT} is not absolute expectancy but the *capacity* of events. The notion of capacity, in Tversky and Kahneman's words, "can be interpreted as the marginal contribution of the respective event" (1992: 301). To combine all possibilities effectively, each outcome is evaluated incrementally—that is, relative to the value of other outcomes. For example, the expectancy weighting for any positive event is the weighted chance it or an even better outcome will occur, minus the weighted chance the next better outcome will occur (e.g., similar to 40 percent − 30 percent = 10 percent, except weighted). It is helpful to keep in mind the simple circumstance where only one positive outcome and/or one negative outcome is considered. In this case, the capacity of each outcome is equal to E_{CPT}, and the equation is more readily interpretable as no summation is necessary. Further discussion of capacity is available in the articles of Fennema and Wakker (1997) and, of course, Tversky and Kahneman (1992).

Need Theory

One of the earlier psychological theories was Murray's (1938) system of needs. As a whole, it is somewhat dated, but key aspects endure in modern personality theory (Tellegen, 1991), as well as in the decision-making paradigm (Loewenstein, 1996). For example, personality traits appear to be the behavioral expression of needs, especially needs as measured by questionnaire (Winter, John, Stewart, Klohnen, & Duncan, 1998). Consequently, we tend to be extraverted partly because of a need for affiliation and conscientious partly because of a need for achievement. We briefly review need theory's fundamental components.

To begin, needs represent an internal energy force that directs behavior toward actions that permit the satisfaction and release of the need itself (i.e., *satiation*). This force is what drives us to do whatever we do. Needs can be primary or *viscerogenic*, directly related to our biological nature (e.g., the need for food), or they can be secondary or *psychogenic*, related to our personality. Of these secondary needs, Murray initially guessed that around twenty might exist, although Winter (1996) suggests that only three are fundamental: the need for achievement, the need for affiliation, and the need for power. The need for achievement is deriving pleasure from overcoming obstacles, the need for affiliation intimacy is deriving pleasure from socializing and sharing with people, and the need for power is deriving pleasure from gaining strength or prestige, particularly by affecting another's well-being. These needs are not stable but tend to fluctuate in intensity, ranging from a slumbering satisfaction to an absolute craving.

Our behaviors are ruled partly by need intensity. At any time, the need that is the most intense is the one we attempt to satisfy or to reduce through our thoughts and behavior. Thus, our actions represent our needs. Of most importance, need intensity can be influenced by external cues, described as *press*. Press occurs when we encounter situations that we *expect* have a good chance of soon satisfying a need, and, consequently, the salience and intensity of that need become acute. Press has strong commonalities with many modern and well-established psychological constructs. In a comprehensive review, Tellegen (1991) connects press to several other theories (e.g., stimulus-response) and theorists (e.g., Allport, 1961).[4]

These aspects of need theory share numerous strong commonalities with our previous formulations. First, need intensity appears analogous to utility. In the same way we pursue actions that most reduce our strongest need, we also pursue actions that provide the most utility. Needs are related to value, helping to determine the actual value that outcomes have. Although needs are often conceptualized at an average or a trait level, they do fluctuate because of satiation. To predict aggregated behavior, the trait level will suffice (Epstein & O'Brien, 1985), but for specific outcomes, we would prefer to know a need's specific strength. Finally, press is essentially a combination of expectancy and time delay. As we discuss later, others have reviewed these connections in great detail.

To some extent, need theory can be further integrated through the works of McClelland (1985) and Dollard and Miller (1950). McClelland reviews the theories of Atkinson (1964), who provides a classic formulation of expectancy theory, as well as Hull (1943), who provides some of the most influential formulations of behavior theory by far (Schwartz, 1989). Of note, behaviorism is, as mentioned, the basis of the original matching law of Chung and Herrnstein (1967). Core aspects of Atkinson's and Hull's theories are virtually identical, both ultimately using expectancy by value frameworks that differ fundamentally only in nomenclature. For example, in place of utility, Hull indicates excitatory potential (sEr), while Atkinson uses tendency to achieve success (Ts). In place of expectancy, Hull refers to habit strength (sHr), while Atkinson uses probability of success (Ps).[5] Finally, in place of value, Hull refers to a combination of drive (D) and incentive (K), while Atkinson uses motive strength (Ms) and incentive value (INs). In McClelland's terms, Ms for success is equivalent to need for achievement. In addition, Atkinson proposes that the utility of any achievement-oriented situation is determined by two individual-difference factors: the need for achievement and the need to avoid failure. The effect each need has on overall utility is calculated separately, as with losses and gains in CPT, with the resulting value indicating the tendency to pursue achievement.

Dollard and Miller (1950) provide even greater connection. They also attempt to describe some of the conflicts observed with psychodynamic drives or needs through behaviorism. Consistent with the concept of press, Dollard and Miller note that drive strength increases as we get closer to the realization of our goals. This, they explain, is due to the combined effect of two more basic principles of behaviorism: the gradients of reinforcement and of stimulus generalization. The gradient of reinforcement reflects the temporal aspect—that is, the more immediately rewards and punishment are expected, the greater their effects. The gradient of stimulus generalization is akin to the element of expectancy. Environmental cues best create approach and avoidance behavior when they reliably predict the occurrence of rewards and punishments.

So far, need theory appears to be largely derived from the same fundamental features as picoeconomics, expectancy theory, and CPT. Behavior is determined by need strength (utility), and long-term considerations (delayed) are only relevant to the extent they affect its present intensity. Need theory also provides two relatively unique contributions. The first has already been mentioned—that need theory explicates the individual determinants of value (e.g., need for achievement). The second regards the discounting constant, Γ, which is presently treated as identical for both losses and gains. However, Dollard and Miller (1950) suggest that this increase in drive occurs at different rates for different needs. In their words, "The strength of avoidance increases more rapidly with nearness than does that of approach. In other words, the gradient of avoidance is steeper than that of approach" (1950: 352). More recent research, as reviewed by Trope and Liberman (2003), suggests the opposite, however—that losses actually are discounted less steeply than gains. Despite these differences, both these results commonly indicate that Γ should not be kept at a constant but should differ for gains and losses. Consequently, our formula is revised in this fashion:

$$\text{Utility} = \sum_{i=1}^{k} \frac{E_{\text{CPT}}^{+} \times V_{\text{CPT}}^{+}}{Z + \Gamma^{+}(T-t)} + \sum_{i=k+1}^{n} \frac{E_{\text{CPT}}^{-} \times V_{\text{CPT}}^{-}}{Z + \Gamma^{-}(T-t)} \tag{5}$$

With this final modification, we have constructed TMT. It is an assimilation of the common and unique fundamental features across our four target theories.

TMT

TMT is derived from the core elements of the above-described four well-established theories of motivation: picoeconomics, expectancy theory, CPT, and need theory. TMT indicates that motivation can be understood by the effects of expectancy and value, weakened by delay, with differences for rewards and losses. The theory is represented by Equation 5, and here we review its fundamental features. We also consider how the use of TMT can be harmonized with its four source theories. Finally, we provide procrastination as an example of TMT—a phenomenon that is uniquely suitable for explanation.

Fundamental Features

TMT has four core features: value, expectancy, time, and different functions for losses versus gains. The first of these, value, appears across all four sources. Drawing on CPT and need theory, value represents how much satisfaction or drive reduction an outcome is believed to realize. The attractiveness of an event depends on both the situation and individual differences. Outcomes can satisfy needs to different degrees. A full meal, for example, can assuage an appetite better than a light snack. Furthermore, the relationship between outcome and value is curvilinear and relative to a reference point, as per Figure 5.2.2. Regarding individual differences, people differ in the degree they typically experience any need (e.g., need for power), and there can be fluctuations around this baseline. Hungry people are more motivated by food than those already sufficiently "suffonsified." To precisely predict value for a specific person and option, we must determine present need strength and how satisfying that option is perceived. If either of these approach zero, then value itself will also become negligible.

Expectancy occurs in each theory except picoeconomics. It represents the perceived probability that an outcome will occur. Like value, this is influenced by both the situation and individual differences. Plainly, different events have higher and lower likelihoods of occurring. However, there are also stable trends regarding how people ultimately perceive these likelihoods. We tend to overestimate low-probability events and underestimate high-probability events, as per Figure 5.2.3. Also, we have generalized expectancies that increase

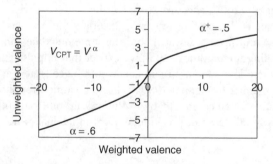

Figure 5.2.2 Weighted Valence (V_{CPT}) as a Function of Unweighted Valence (V), Per Tversky and Kahneman's (1992) CPT.

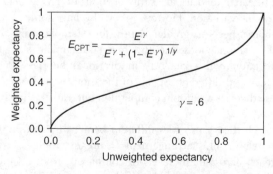

Figure 5.2.3 Weighted Expectancy (E_{CPT}) as a Function of Unweighted Expectancy (E), Per Tversky and Kahneman's (1992) CPT.

and decrease estimation (Carver & Scheier, 1989). A few specific personality traits that affect expectancies are attributional style (Weiner, 1991), self-efficacy (Bandura, 1997), and optimism (Carver & Scheier, 2002).

Temporal discounting appears in picoeconomics and need theory (i.e., press). Being on the bottom of Equation 5, the closer temporally an event becomes, the greater its influence will be. There are three components of TMT that capture the effect of time. The first is Γ, which refers to people's sensitivity to delay. In traditional trait terminology, Monterosso and Ainslie (1999) argue that Γ is largely equivalent to *impulsiveness*, and, indeed, several others have gathered self-report data that empirically support their affinity (Madden, Petry, Badger, & Bickel, 1997; Ostaszewski, 1996, 1997; Petry, 2001; Richards, Zhang, Mitchell, & de Wit, 1999). Impulsiveness should never reach zero and is mostly stable, although there may be environmental influencers such as alcohol (i.e., alcohol myopia; Steele & Josephs, 1990) and drug use (Bretteville-Jensen, 1999; Giordano et al., 2002). The second is the delay itself— that is, $(T - t)$. Simply, it represents the nearness or time required to realize an outcome. The third is ζ. This is a constant that prevents desire or utility from becoming infinite when delay is effectively zero.

Finally, losses and gains are separately calculated in both CPT and need theory. This dichotomy indicates that, for each of TMT's components that are affected by individual differences (value, expectancy, and Γ), there are further differences depending on whether the outcome is perceived negatively or positively. Figures 5.2.2 and 5.2.3, taken from prospect theory, indicate how value and expectancy are likely transformed. Differences between positive and negative impulsiveness have not yet been definitively established, although they do appear to differ. As Camerer et al. (2004) effectively review, there are a variety of methodological confounds that can affect discounting research, including the presence of savoring (i.e., people wishing to delay and savor a reward), and the same outcome can be perceived as a loss or a gain, depending upon context. Still, we expect that impulsiveness follows the same pattern as value, where losses loom larger. This would be consistent with recent psychobiological investigations (Ito & Cacioppo, 1999), reflecting caution for short-term events (e.g., developing "cold feet"), which should be evolutionarily more adaptive (Cosmides & Tooby, 2000). Still, this trend does not preclude atypical individuals who are more impulsive for gains.

Hierarchical Nature of TMT

The relationship between TMT and picoeconomics, expectancy theory, CPT, and need theory is largely that of simplicity. The latter theories are simplifications of TMT, focusing on fewer terms or eliminating idiographic variation. However, they also have some unique features and tend to explore particular aspects in greater depth; for example, only need theory closely examines the role of satiation. Consequently, their commonalities do not make them redundant. As Locke and Latham also conclude, motivational theories "do not so much contradict one another as focus on different aspects of the motivational process" (2004: 389). We argue, then, that these theories are not in competition but, rather, should be viewed hierarchically.

By "hierarchical," we mean that each theory provides different benefits by focusing on specific components and levels of analysis. This arrangement is already implicit in the natural sciences, where "domains reach across many levels of complexity, from chemical physics and physical chemistry to molecular genetics, chemical ecology, and ecological genetics. None of the new specialties is considered more than a focus of research" (Wilson, 1998:

11). For example, a globe, a travel guide, and a housing blue-print are all maps, and although they focus on different features and levels of complexity, they each have their own purpose and do not make the others irrelevant.

In determining which theory to use, we support Albert Einstein's advice on this matter: "Make everything as simple as possible, but not simpler." Choose the theory that emphasizes the features relevant to the issue at hand. The simplest of these is expectancy theory, which comes in two primary forms. Economists typically employ a version called "expected utility theory," which assumes no individual differences regarding the formulation of expectancies. Probabilities reflect the situation entirely, which we perceive without inflection or error. The theory is normative, reflecting how people should behave, *if rational*.

The next level of complexity is subjective expected utility theory, which introduces cognitive limitations and allows rationality to be bounded (Furnham & Lewis, 1986; Simon, 1955). That is, trading accuracy for ease and speed, it can be rational to make adequate although not optimal decisions based on limited input and processing (i.e., we *satisfice* rather than *maximize*). Subjective expected utility theory is *partially* normative, since the assumption is that we take a rational approach when dealing with our cognitive constraints. Consequently, expectancy theory and subjective expected utility theory are most applicable to situations where people do approximate rational decision making, such as in aspects of stock market behavior (e.g., Plott, 1986; Smith, 1991).

CPT, picoeconomics, and need theory can all be considered as operating at the next level of complexity. Each is descriptive in that it is based on empirical findings regarding how people actually behave, but each focuses on different determinants of this behavior. Of these, CPT is most closely related to expectancy theory. Expectancy theory is directly nested under CPT, representing a special case where all the values for the exponential functions are constrained to be to the power of 1 (i.e., exponential functions to the power of 1 straighten the lines in Figures 5.2.2 and 5.2.3). CPT emphasizes how people reconcile pluses and minuses when making decisions. Picoeconomics, however, does not consider expectancy at all, and its treatment of value is less sophisticated. But it is extremely explicit regarding temporal issues. When time is the critical variable, picoeconomics is invaluable. Finally, need theory has elements similar to all those discussed, but they are not always well defined. For example, the theory folds expectancy and time into the single concept of press. The issue this theory best represents is value and how individual differences affect value. When we want to understand how a person's traits affect his or her behavior, need theory is the most useful. Of note, even when we recognize that individual differences are relevant, measurement limitations may still preclude their effective employment.

At the highest level of complexity is TMT, under which all the previous theories are nested. This theory is appropriate for explaining situations where expectancy, value, and time all affect decision making simultaneously and are all influenced by individual differences. Because it has the most number of terms, it is also the most cumbersome to use. However, in the following section we review a common example where all these features are needed for explanation.

An Example of TMT

Procrastination, a prototypical motivational problem, is a phenomenon that occurs in at least 95 percent of the population and *chronically* in approximately 15 to 20 percent of adults and in 33 to 50 percent of students (Steel, in press). It also appears that *only* TMT can account for its empirical findings. As meta-analytic review indicates (Steel, in press), the strongest correlates with procrastination are task characteristics and individual-difference variables related to expectancy (e.g., self-efficacy, task difficulty), value (e.g., need for achievement, task aversiveness), and sensitivity to delay (e.g., impulsiveness, temporal distance). A viable theory must contain variables that address *all* three of these elements at *both* an individual and situational level. Since TMT alone does this, no other theory is feasible. Furthermore, a variety of other results support the TMT model. Procrastinators demonstrate preference reversal, for example, consistent with hyperbolic discounting (see Figure 5.2.1). That is, they plan to work but change their minds and fail to act on their plans.

Consequently, we can use a simplified scenario based on procrastination to demonstrate how TMT relates to behavior. The archetypal setting is the essay paper for the college student. Counter to the student's original intentions, he or she irrationally delays writing the paper and must then complete it close to the final deadline, often incurring great stress and resulting in reduced performance. Although the written assignment is given at the beginning of a semester, the student often ignores it until the last few weeks or even days. From a TMT perspective, this is not surprising.

As TMT predicts, we pursue whatever course of action has the highest level of utility. Writing an essay paper is often an intrinsically aversive activity for many students; there is no delay between engaging in it and experiencing a punishment. The reward of achievement, however, is relatively distant; it may not be felt until the end of the semester, or perhaps even later, when grades are posted. To compound the matter, social activities and other temptations are readily available and intrinsically enjoyable; there is no delay in their pursuit or their rewards. Also, the aversive consequences of socializing are distant. Although indulging in them creates an oppressive backlog of work, we can usually forestall confronting the consequence until much later.

Consider three college students, Anne, Betty, and Colin, who have been assigned an essay at the start of a semester, on September 15. The essay is due on December 15, at the end of the course. All the students like to socialize but hate to be overly stressed, and, conversely, they hate to write but like to get good grades. There are differences in other motivational elements, however. Betty finds good grades somewhat *less* important than Anne and Colin (i.e., she has a *smaller* need for achievement), and she has a lower sense of self-efficacy (i.e., expectancy). Colin, however, desires good grades even more than Anne but is the most impulsive.

Figure 5.2.4 maps the changes in utility for these three over the course of the semester regarding their choices between studying and socializing. In the early days of the semester, socializing's negative component is temporally distant, while its positive component is in the present. This results in a high utility evaluation. These parameters are exactly opposite for writing, giving it a low utility evaluation. By the end of the semester, although socializing's positive component is still temporally unchanged, its negative component is more temporally proximate, diminishing its utility. Similarly, the negative component for writing is still experienced immediately, but now its positive component is also relatively imminent, thus increasing its utility. Writing activity eventually becomes increasingly likely as the deadline approaches, occurring, in this example, on November 29 for Anne, but six days later for Betty and Colin, on December 5. Note that Colin's impulsiveness makes him a mercurial individual, whose motivation during the final moments should overshadow the others' best efforts.

By changing any of the components of TMT, we could generate a multitude of other examples. For instance, if any of the students liked socializing less, they would likely start writing earlier. Importantly, this highlights that self-regulatory failure occurs for a plethora of possibilities. Differences in self-efficacy, task aversiveness, impulsiveness, and the proximity

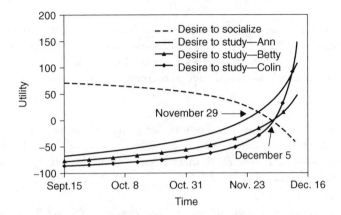

Figure 5.2.4 Graph of Three Students' Utility Estimation for Socializing Versus Writing an Essay over the Course of a Semester that Ends December 15.

of temptations all can create similar observed behavior. Unless we can diagnose these root causes instead of just the symptoms, the effectiveness of any motivational intervention must typically be suboptimal.

Applications and Implications of TMT

When we discussed the advantages of an integrative approach, we highlighted three benefits. First, an integrative theory should provide a common language among social scientists. Second, it should be applicable to complex and realistic situations, improving description and prediction. Finally, it should facilitate the sharing of insights among fields and, consequently, the generation of novel and plausible hypotheses. TMT shows these advantages.

Already, researchers are using the critical components of TMT to investigate topics from an extremely wide variety of complex fields. For example, prospect theory and temporal discounting have been applied to addictive behavior, attention deficit/hyperactivity disorder, consumer behavior, health choices, job search, military deterrence, soil conversation, strategic risk behavior, project management, and workplace violence (e.g., Barkley, Edwards, Laneri, Fletcher, & Metevia, 2001; Baumeister, 2002; Berejikian, 2002; Bleichrodt & Gafni, 1996; Das & Teng, 2001; DellaVigna & Paserman, 2005; Frederick et al., 2002; Glasner, 2003; Glomb, Steel, & Arvey, 2002; Hall & Fong, 2003; Krusell, Kuruşçu, & Smith, 2000; Petry, 2001; Rachlin, 2000; Thaler, 1991; Yesuf, 2003). Also, here we ourselves used TMT to account for all the observed findings regarding procrastination. If the issue involves choice, TMT apparently can be applied.

To further demonstrate the advantages of an integrative approach, we consider four additional areas. For each of these diverse topics, we review evidence that TMT describes fundamental effects and that there are new or rarely considered implications. In increasing levels of complexity, we first begin with group behavior, using it to emphasize both the importance of temporal discounting and that TMT can be applied to more than just individuals. Second, we discuss job design, reviewing research indicating that time and value are factors. Third, we consider stock market behavior, where both prospect theory and temporal discounting appear to be in effect. Finally, we examine goal setting, which potentially exhibits all aspects of TMT.

Group Behavior

Many individual-level decision-making theories, heuristics, and biases are equally appropriate for describing group behavior (Plous, 1993). This also appears to be true of TMT. In an intriguing chapter, Elster (1992) examines *preference reversal* created by temporal discounting (see Figure 5.2.1) and how it is implicitly anticipated and counteracted in many political institutions. He states:

> In the heat of passion or under the influence of some immediate temptation, an individual can deviate from prudent plans formed in advance or do things he will later regret. Groups of individuals, such as voters or members of a political assembly, are no less prone to such irrational behavior (1992: 39–40).

To deal with this inherent weakness, constitutions are often drawn that enact forms of precommitment. Part of this precommitment is limiting rules that we bind ourselves to so as to avoid later regrettable actions. Another precommitment is creating a bicameral system, where decision making must pass through two chambers representing the electorate, such as a congress and a senate (Joint Committee on the Organization of Congress, 1993). Retelling the "saucer anecdote" of George Washington helps to illustrate the wisdom of this built-in delaying mechanism. In a conversation between Thomas Jefferson and Washington, Jefferson asked why a senate should be established. "Why," Washington responded, "do you pour coffee into your saucer?" "To cool it," Jefferson replied. "Even so," Washington said. "We pour legislation into the Senatorial saucer to cool it" (Farrand, 1966: 359). Other countries offer similar explanations. In Canada, the Senate is often referred to as "the house of sober second thought."

Supplementing this political analysis is the issue of the central bank. Central banks are tempted at times to increase the money supply and, thus, cause inflation merely to immediately reduce unemployment (for a review see White, 1999). An unconstrained central bank may excessively exploit this option, to the detriment of the country's long-term economic health. To counteract this trend, Haubrich (2000) discusses the use of policy rules and removing the central bank's discretion. The policy rules are interpreted as a form of precommitment, similar to "Ulysses lashing himself to the mast . . . as both [government and central banks] face temptations to act at a given moment in ways that run counter to their long-range goals" (Haubrich, 2000: 1).

However, in the management arena, most team research has adopted a "punctuated equilibrium" model, championed by Gersick (1991). This model suggests that team performance is not hyperbolic over time but demonstrates a sudden shift or discontinuity around the mid life of a project. Although punctuated equilibrium is a useful evolutionary model and does appear to reflect some forms of organizational and *strategic* development (e.g., Romanelli & Tushman, 1994), hyperbolic discounting appears to better describe group *performance*. Specifically, Waller, Zellmer-Bruhn, and Giambatista note that several studies indicate a "curvilinear increase in the rate of performance of task performance over allotted work time" (2002: 1047).

In addition, we reanalyzed the published data from Gersick's (1989) and Chang, Bordia, and Duck's (2003) work on teams' time statements, which are an indication of work pace. As shown in Figure 5.2.5, the cumulative number of time statements was significantly curvilinear ($p < .0001$) in both cases, reflecting hyperbolic discounting (i.e., work pace increases as the deadline approaches). We expect that future research will find that the average group

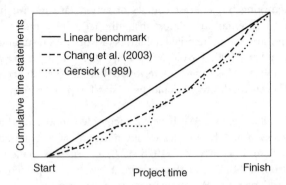

Figure 5.2.5 Graph Demonstrating that Work Pace/Time Statements over the Course of a Group Project Are Not Linear But Curvilinear, Reflecting Hyperbolic Discounting.

levels of impulsiveness will affect the degree of curvilinearity, similar to the results already obtained for time urgency (Waller, Conte, Gibson, & Carpenter, 2001).

Job Design

Job design is intrinsically related to selection. Instead of selecting a person for the job, we redesign the job for the person. Historically, efforts to redesign jobs have focused on simplification, as exemplified by Fredrick Taylor. Unfortunately, Taylorized jobs have a strong tendency to improve performance at the cost of employee satisfaction, causing considerable rebellion when first implemented. Taylor himself was characterized as "a soulless slave driver, out to destroy the workingman's health and rob him of his manhood" (Kanigel, 1997: 1), a vilification that reached such an extent that in 1911 the U.S. House of Representatives authorized a special committee to investigate his and other similar systems of management. Ultimately, job simplification was made palatable by vastly increasing wages, sometimes up to 100 percent when first implemented (Taylor, 1911).

However, job simplification has its limits. Wages cannot always be increased (especially with global competition), work motivation is usually diminished by job simplification, and improving employees' satisfaction is a worthy goal in itself. Consequently, theories focused on improving motivation and satisfaction were developed. Motivation-hygiene theory (Herzberg, 1966) and job characteristic theory (Hackman & Oldman, 1976) are two examples. Parker and Wall's (2001) review demonstrates that, despite several of these theories aspects' *failure to be empirically confirmed*, they were still important developments, emphasizing both that tasks can be better shaped to be rewarding and that individual differences will affect how rewarding these tasks will be.

TMT indicates novel ways we can build on this past work. As the literature summarized here indicates, we are not blank slates. We come with definite tendencies. The challenge then becomes how to design a workplace that is commensurate with our motivational heritage. Ideally, this would result in intrinsically pleasurable tasks—tasks we would choose to do even in the absence of financial compensation. As a step toward this goal, we should attempt to build settings that recognize our tendency to undervalue the future and to develop tasks that satisfy our basic needs. This has yet to be done.

To begin with, hyperbolic discounting indicates we are likely to indulge in frivolous but enjoyable workplace activities if they are easily obtainable. Presently, however, job design studies do not consider whether tempting but inferior courses of actions are too readily available. For example, the internet and email are almost instantly accessible, and, consequently, it is not surprising that they are also influential facilitators of work procrastination (Brackin, Ferguson, Skelly, & Chambliss, 2000; Lavoie & Pychyl, 2001; Steel, in press), reducing productivity by billions of dollars (Mastrangelo, Everton, & Jolton, 2002). If access to these options could be delayed, even modestly, it would be easier for people to make rational use of them.

Needs-based job design shows similar neglect. We have an incomplete understanding regarding *what tasks* typically satisfy *what desires*. Essentially, we still must link what Dunnette calls "the two worlds of human behavioral taxonomies" (1976: 477), a perpetual challenge for our field. Schmitt and Robertson (1990) reflect that this goal has been repeated in virtually every selection review. Even Parker and Wall note, in their more recent chapter on work design, that "knowledge of individual differences as contingencies is scant" (2001: 96).

As TMT indicates, performance is not only the result of having the appropriate motivational drive; it must be stronger than other competing drives. In any given job, its associated tasks may strongly satisfy all the needs of an employee or perhaps only a few. The remaining needs must be met in other ways, perhaps by ineffective socializing, doodling, or daydreaming. Consequently, when we design a job, determining if strong needs are unlikely to be met within the job's confines becomes very important. Previous reviews by Schneider and Green (1977) and Cantor and Blanton (1996) indicate that "rogue" needs can detrimentally affect performance.

Stock Market Behavior

Stock market behavior is largely rational, but not entirely. Schiller (2000) touches on several instances of this, such as the British South Sea bubble of 1720 or the Japanese real estate bubble of the late 1980s. More recently, in 1996, the Dow Jones displayed what Federal Reserve Board Chairperson Alan Greenspan called "irrational exuberance." Economists have, for the most part, concluded that investors do tend to be risk averse, in accordance with prospect theory and, thus, TMT. However, it appears that the stock market is also vulnerable to temporal discounting.

In a series of papers, De Bondt and Thaler (see Thaler, 1991) reviewed research demonstrating that the stock market, as well as stock market analysts, overreact to unexpected and dramatic news events, both favorable and disagreeable in nature. Specifically, "investors seem to attach disproportionate importance to short-run economic developments" (Thaler, 1991: 259). Although De Bondt and Thaler interpret this effect primarily as an instance of Kahneman and Tversky's (1979) representative heuristic, from a TMT perspective it also appears to be an excellent indication of temporal discounting.

Consider the effect of bad news. Unlike anticipated problems, sudden and surprising news of misfortune suggests an impending downturn in the stock price. The company value will diminish and, consequently, so will the value of the stock. Some selling is, of course, then rational, and a dip in price is to be expected. However, stockholders with a high discount function will overvalue this imminent loss and will oversell to minimize it. The stock price will plunge past the optimal point, to where it actually becomes more rational to buy, given its expected long-term performance. This overreaction is formally exploited in the investment technique called "Dogs of the Dow" (O'Higgins, 1991). Also, stock repurchasing programs seem to be an explicit attempt to manage such shareholder shortsightedness (Sanders & Carpenter, 2003).

Goal Setting

One of the most widely used motivational theories within an industrial/organizational context is goal theory (Karoly, 1993), and for good reason. Extensive study unambiguously indicates that goal setting is an extremely powerful technique (see Locke & Latham, 2002, for a recent review). However, it has its limitations, lacking, for example, "the issue of time perspective" (Locke & Latham, 2004: 400). As we will show, TMT can account for goal setting's effects and suggests new hypotheses regarding two of its moderators: goal difficulty and proximity. Importantly, these novel predictions cannot be made on the basis of previous attempts to explain goal setting (e.g., Carver & Scheier, 1998; Fried & Slowik, 2004; Locke & Latham, 2002; Raynor & Entin, 1982).

The effectiveness of goal setting can be largely explained by two aspects of TMT: the principle of diminishing returns (see Figure 5.2.2) and temporal discounting (see Figure 5.2.1). Any division of a project into several smaller and more immediate subgoals appears to take advantage of these two elements. As mentioned, perceived value has a curvilinear relationship to a more objective assessment. Substantial divisions of large goals may result in a series of subgoals, each valued only slightly less than that of the original whole. For example, although completion of an entire project may best satisfy one's need for achievement, each intermediate step also temporarily satiates. Importantly, these smaller subgoals can be completed sequentially, allowing them to be realized more quickly.

This state of affairs presents a potent motivational opportunity. Research has shown that the parsing of situations affects decision making. For example, Rachlin (2000) discusses how gambling behavior is influenced by whether people consider a period of betting as several individual bets or as a single gambling session.[6] By subdividing a large project into smaller goals, *the sum of the parts can be greater than the whole* (to reverse a popular aphorism). Essentially, goal setting increases the duration of motivational dominance, when drive toward a course of action is likely to supercede competing options—an effect exemplified in Figure 5.2.6, where a person has ninety days to finish a project. Actions toward a goal occur only if its drive or utility exceeds that of other pursuits—that is, background temptations as represented by the straight dashed line in Figure 5.2.6. Here, goal setting divides the project into three sub-goals, each valued at 80 percent of the original. With goal setting, a person would

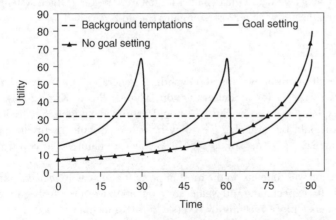

Figure 5.2.6 Graph Demonstrating the Superiority of Goal Setting in Achieving Motivational Dominance over Tempting Alternatives.

find that he or she would be working toward the project for a total of thirty days. Without goal setting, it would be only fifteen.

There are also several moderators that affect the effectiveness of goal setting. TMT makes specific hypotheses regarding the interplay between two of these: goal difficulty and goal proximity. As already understood, increasing goal difficulty tends to increase motivation. In TMT terms, this effect is due to value. Increased self-satisfaction arises from achieving the difficult rather than the easy (Bandura, 1997). Also, the achievement of challenging goals may become associated with rewarding outcomes, thus becoming a secondary reinforcer itself (Eisenberger, 1992). The other moderator is proximity, since increasing the proximity of a goal tends to increase motivation. Although Latham and Seijts argue that proximity affects performance by providing "additional specific information" (1999: 422), TMT suggests a supporting explanation: temporal discounting. Distal goals are substantially delayed, reducing the effectiveness of expectancy and value.

There should be motivational tension between goal difficulty and proximity. By dividing a large goal into variously spaced subgoals, each subgoal may be easier to achieve and, thus, less satisfying. Consequently, there is likely a breakpoint where the further subdivision of a goal decreases its value more than can be offset by the decrease in delay. Since TMT mathematically formalizes the relationship among expectancy, value, and delay, it should indicate where this breakpoint should best occur.

Specifically, impulsive individuals should be more motivated by proximity. It would be best for them to have more frequent but smaller goals. Conversely, those with a higher need for achievement will more likely attend to goal difficulty. Their motivation should be maximized by less frequent but harder goals. By attending to individual differences such as these, TMT should allow us to provide a goal-setting strategy tailored to a specific person, rather than making us rely on general heuristics (e.g., goal difficulty, proximity). Importantly, this should lead to a dramatic improvement in goal-setting power, increasing the duration of any goal's motivational dominance.

Of note, there are still other insights that TMT can provide for goal setting, further demonstrating that it can generate novel and plausible hypotheses. Briefly, the presence of extremely attractive alternatives (e.g., raising temptation's utility in Figure 5.2.6) can indicate when goal setting will be less effective or ineffective. Also, if there are separate motivational systems for losses and gains, then it may be preferable to emphasize *both* the positive outcomes for successfully achieving a goal and the penalties for failure. Assessing which system is dominant in an individual indicates whether losses or gains should be stressed.

Future Research

Aside from improving scientific communication and hypothesis generation, there are several qualitative and quantitative criteria for model evaluation (Myung, Pit, & Kim, 2004). A model should plausibly explain observed findings, it should be understandable (i.e., reflect established constructs), it should be falsifiable (i.e., may be validated), and its predictions should fit the observed data (i.e., "goodness of fit"). TMT, by the very nature of its construction, fulfills these standards.

The strategy for integration was to focus on the most important and heavily *validated* parts of the motivational field. Its expectancy and value components have already been well assessed by many researchers—more recently by Tversky and Kahneman (1992). Its discounting function is the culmination of extensive and varied investigations, as summarized by Ainslie (1992). Needs themselves have been studied for the better part of a century (e.g.,

Murray, 1938; Winter et al., 1998). Consequently, TMT has already been validated piecemeal. Also, adding extra adjustable parameters will *invariably* improve fit to some degree (Forster, 2000). TMT should account for any observed data better than any of its component theories. Still, there are two other standards to consider.

Part of model development is not only to have goodness of fit but to do it parsimoniously. Consequently, most model indices penalize for every extra parameter (e.g., Akaike Information Criterion; AIC). Undue complexity is not desirable, and it remains to be formally shown that the full TMT model accounts for significantly more variance. Furthermore, it is not enough for the full TMT model to be rarely useful. If it is to have value beyond aiding scientific communication and hypothesis generation, it must be *generalizable*, showing repeated merit in a variety of situations. Future research should focus on evaluating when and to what degree the incremental variance that TMT provides is significant. We discuss this further below.

Finally, there are a variety of methodologies with which this future research can be conducted. We suggest that two additional venues should also be strongly considered: a computerized personal system of instruction and computer simulations. Although rarely used, these venues have the advantage of potentially being more realistic and allowing more complexity while retaining research control of key variables. Their nature and advantages are also further reviewed below.

Model Testing: Simplicity Versus Complexity

The details of model testing are extensive and beyond the scope of any paper except a dedicated review (e.g., Myung et al., 2004; Navarro & Myung, 2005). Briefly, it requires the accurate measurement of the observed behavior, as well as the constructs that are thought to give rise to the behavior (i.e., specified by the model). To evaluate TMT, we would then need to measure performance, along with both individual and experimental variables that reflect expectancy, value, and delay for both losses and gains. With this data, we could compare competing models using a choice of indices, ones taking into account both parsimony and completeness (e.g., Akaike or Bayesian information criterion). If superior results are again obtained in related data sets (i.e., cross-validation), the model is generalizable.

We do not expect that the full TMT model will consistently be necessary, as we indicated when discussing its hierarchical nature. However, it is difficult to argue why *only* a subset of the motivational *fundamentals* that compose TMT ever apply. Such a position is radical and unsupported, requiring postulating a new scientific principle that prevents these fundamental components from ever operating in concert. Consequently, for complex situations where there is an assortment of options, considered by a diverse sampling of people, more of TMT's elements should come into play. We already made the case that the full TMT model is necessary to predict procrastination, as well as touched on a wide variety of topics where it should be applicable. The incremental variance potentially provided by TMT will depend on what topic is being investigated and what theory it is being compared against. The more complex the topic (e.g., consumer behavior) and the simpler the competing model (e.g., expected utility theory), the greater TMT's value should be. Naturally, the converse should also be true.

It is possible, however, that TMT occasionally is still not complex enough. One refinement that future research may want to reconsider is the approach and avoidance duality. A trichotomy may be the more appropriate representation. Specifically, the avoidance or negative side of our nature appears to be less than unitary. For expectancy-related research, optimism appears to be better understood as three factors: optimism, pessimism, and "fighting spirit" (Olason & Roger, 2001). For impulsiveness, Cloninger (1987) posits a tridimensional model, with separate systems for gains (i.e., novelty seeking) and for losses (i.e., harm avoidance), and a third system he calls "persistence." This three-factor solution has received recent support (Torrubia, Ávila, Moltó, & Caseras, 2001; Whiteside & Lynam, 2001). Similarly, people's coping styles for uncertainty yield three comparable factors (Greco & Roger, 2001): emotional uncertainty (avoidance), desire for change (approach), and cognitive uncertainty (persistence).

From a broader perspective, Raghunathan and Pham (1999) note substantive differences between the influences of sadness and anxiety on decision making. Similarly, Krueger (1999), in an examination of mental disorders, found that a three-factor model explained comorbidity. Specifically, fear and anxiety-misery were best understood as two subfactors of a high-order internalizing factor. Finally, recent neuropsychological reviews do indicate the presence of other systems (Gray & McNaughton, 1996; Lang, Bradley, & Cuthbert, 1997; Rothbart, Ahadi, & Evans, 2000), such as fight-or-flight. Also, different brain functions, which our motivational theories ultimately model, tend to employ separate as well as common components, making truly orthogonal factors an inevitable fiction (Damasio, 1994).

Regardless of whether the goal is to determine if TMT is too complex or too simple, it is an empirical matter and the same methodology applies. We must accurately measure the relevant variables and use them to compare competing models. As the number of variables increases, there can be technical and administrative obstacles in gathering the requisite data. In the following section we consider two novel venues that can assist testing and applying complex models.

New Research Venues

There are a variety of methodologies that can be used to further study TMT and its implications. Traditional work on related concepts, especially temporal discounting, relied on comparative psychology (i.e., animal research) and "casino" situations, where expectancy and value were expressed explicitly, typically in terms of ratios, dollars, and deaths. Unfortunately, although these situations give a great deal of control, their limited realism and complexity makes their generalizability suspect (Bazerman, 2001). Consequently, we recommend that two other venues also be considered: a computerized personal system of instruction and computer simulations.

Since traditional methodologies have been criticized as potentially unrealistic, there has been a movement toward naturalistic decision-making research (Kühberger, Schulte-Mecklenbeck, & Perner, 2002). Ideally, we would like to test further refinements to TMT on a wide range of people who are striving at their own pace toward an important goal in a standardized but realistic setting where we can precisely but easily measure their behavior. Although this is a long list of specifications, there is at least one venue that presently provides all these features—a computerized personal system of instruction (C-PSI).

A personal system of instructions or programmed learning has been in use for decades, but a computerized version has several desired qualities. As used by Steel, Brothen, and Wambach (2001), hundreds of students simultaneously work toward completing a university course at their own pace, allowing choice and, thus, motivated behavior. Furthermore, progress is assessed at an unparalleled number of points as the course is broken down into numerous assignments (e.g., seventy-eight), all computer administered with completion precisely recorded. Similarly, a host of other observed and self-report measures can be easily inserted into this framework. The only restriction is that students must finish these assignments by the final exam. Consequently, it is a good venue for determining if all aspects of TMT are necessary for prediction. Similarly, the efficacy of self-regulatory interventions based on the TMT model can be clearly evaluated in this setting. We can not only see the outcome but can examine in detail people's progression toward their goals. Future research should consider if other existing realistic research settings could also be adapted to provide similar benefits (e.g., the Kanfer-Ackerman Air Traffic Controller Task; cf. Kanfer & Ackerman, 1989).

Another novel venue for TMT research is the construction of computer simulations. Recent advances in parallel computing are allowing us to effectively model extremely *complex* phenomena, such as global weather patterns (Clauer et al., 2000) and applied nuclear physics (Bigelow, Moloney, Philpott, & Rothberg, 1995). Consequently, this technology is also being applied to recondite areas of human decision making, such as traffic (Pursula, 1999) and market behavior (Janssen & Jager, 2001), as well as several organizational science topics (Hulin, Miner, & Seitz, 2002). Lauded as the "Third Scientific Discipline" (Ilgen & Hulin, 2000), with the first two being experimental and correlational research, it has the potential to open entirely new lines of study.

If consensus indicates that TMT does indeed provide a good approximation of decision making, TMT will provide the foundation for a new generation of simulators that can be used to initially test a wide variety of motivational interventions, such as compensation systems or job design. Already, a rudimentary model incorporating the notion of needs, satiation, and temporal discounting exists. It is *The Sims*, the most popular computer game of all time, based on the principles of consumer and evolutionary psychology (Johnson, 2002; Pearce, 2002).[7]

Conclusion

Although we have benefited by exploring human nature from many different perspectives, we would also gain by considering and consolidating commonalities. Our science would progress more rapidly by sharing the findings from different disciplines. For example, on the one hand, the extremely well-supported time-discounting function evident in behaviorist and economic understanding of human nature is largely overlooked in other areas. In fact, most motivational reviews fail to refer to it (e.g., Franken, 1994; Kanfer, 1990; Kleinbeck, Quast, Thierry, & Häcker, 1990; Mitchell, 1997). On the other hand, economists have maintained, since at least Stigler and Becker (1977), that tastes or preferences—*that is, needs or traits*—provide little or no prediction or explanation of human behavior. During the 1970s, this was a plausible and popular position, even within psychology (e.g., Mischel, 1973). However, as Caplan (2003) outlines, our empirical findings over the last quarter century indicate that it is increasingly outlandish to maintain such a belief.

TMT addresses such dysfunctional separation by unifying insights from several different theories of motivation. Importantly, this is not a definitive model accounting for every aspect of human behavior, but it does provide a common framework of essential features. Using it, the extensive contributions from individual disciplines may be better shared by all, such as cognitive psychology determining how expectancies change with experience or the findings from the self-regulatory disciplines indicating how impulsiveness may be tempered. As Barrick and Mount conclude, "In order for any field of science to advance, it is necessary to have an accepted classification scheme for accumulating and categorizing empirical findings" (1991: 23). This model can provide common ground to enable the necessary dialog.

Notes

1 This matching law can be further decomposed into even more basic behaviorist principles (Hernnstein, 1979)—specifically, *invariance* and *relativity*.
2 For example, Utility = $e^{-\Gamma(T-t)\text{Value}}$ (Frederick, Loewenstein, & O'Donoghue, 2002).
3 Mathematically, both the transformations for value and expectancy create curves reflecting logarithmic functions, notably similar to Fechner's law (1966) describing just noticeable perceptual differences. Fechner's law states that, given x amount, you will notice a change of Δx that allows k to remain a constant, as in $\Delta x/x = k$. To be precise, however, Tversky and Kahneman (1992) actually use a related but exponential form of psychophysical scaling called "Steven's law." Similarly, expectancy is also modeled using an exponential function. Informally, these functions may be described as the principle of diminishing returns.
4 There has been criticism that drive or need reduction is a somewhat simplified view of reinforcement, and in a detailed review Savage (2000) concludes that this is true. However, Savage also notes that, as a general concept, it has proven invaluable for organizing a wide range of motivational states, which is consistent with its use here. Also, see McSweeney and Swindell (1999), who recently revitalized the role that need theory may play in motivation.
5 Highlighting their similarity, Weiner, while reviewing the history of motivational research, notes that "there was some contentment merely in eliminating the term *drive* and replacing the notion of *habit* with that of *expectancy*" (1990: 619).
6 See also Dawes' (1998) summary of sunk costs.
7 For an interesting application, see the political economist Heath (2001), who used *The Sims* to simulate the effects of lifestyle choices on work-family conflict.

Acknowledgments

We are thankful that the editor of our paper was Elizabeth Mannix, who gave us the opportunity to reply to the reviewers' intially critical though insightful comments before passing judgment. With her stewardship, the review process produced a much better paper than what we first submitted. Also, we greatly appreciate the combined contributions from a long chain of prior researchers, who provided the edifice for this present publication. Despite regular academic disagreements, we all appear to be laboring toward a common cause.

References

Ainslie, G. 1992. *Picoeconomics: The strategic interaction of successive motivational states within the person.* New York: Cambridge University Press.

Ainslie, G., & Haslam, N. 1992. Hyperbolic discounting. In G. Loewenstein & J. Elster (Eds.), *Choice over time:* 57–92. New York: Russell Sage Foundation.

Ajzen, I. 1991. A theory of planned behavior. *Organizational Behavior and Human Decision Processes,* 50: 179–211.

Akerlof, G. A. 1991. Procrastination and obedience. *American Economic Review,* 81: 1–19.

Albanese, P. J. 1987. The nature of preferences: An exploration of the relationship between economics and psychology. *Journal of Economic Psychology,* 8: 3–18.

Allport, G. W. 1961. *Pattern and growth in personality.* New York: Holt.

Antonides, G. 1991. *Psychology in economics and business.* Dordrecht, Netherlands: Kluwer Academic.

Atkinson, J. W. 1957. Motivational determinants of risk-taking behavior. *Psychological Review,* 64: 359–372.

Atkinson, J. W. 1964. *An introduction to motivation*. New York: Van Nostrand.

Bandura, A. 1997. *Self-efficacy: The exercise of control*. New York: Freeman.

Bandura, A., & Locke, E. A. 2003. Negative self-efficacy and goal effects revisited. *Journal of Applied Psychology*, 88: 87–99.

Barkley, R. A., Edwards, G., Laneri, M., Fletcher, K., & Metevia, L. 2001. Executive functioning, temporal discounting, and sense of time in adolescents with attention deficit hyperactivity disorder (ADHD) and oppositional defiant disorder (ODD). *Journal of Abnormal Child Psychology*, 29: 541–556.

Barrick, M. R., & Mount, M. K. 1991. The Big Five personality dimensions and job performance: A meta-analysis. *Personnel Psychology*, 44: 1–26.

Baumeister, R. F. 2002. Yielding to temptation: Self-control failure, impulse purchasing, and consumer behavior. *Journal of Consumer Behavior*, 28: 670–676.

Bazerman, M. H. 2001. The study of "real" decision making. *Journal of Behavioral Decision Making*, 14: 353–384.

Berejikian, J. D. 2002. A cognitive theory of deterrence. *Journal of Peace Research*, 39: 165–183.

Bernoulli, D. 1954. (First published in 1738.) Exposition of a new theory of the measurement of risk. *Econometrica*, 22: 23–36.

Bigelow, R., Moloney, M. J., Philpott, J., & Rothberg, J. 1995. *Nuclear and particle physics simulations: The consortium of upper-level physics software*. New York: Wiley.

Bleichrodt, H., & Gafni, A. 1996. Time preference, the discounted utility model and health. *Journal of Health Economics*, 15: 49–67.

Brackin, T., Ferguson, E., Skelly, B., & Chambliss, C. 2000. *College students' use of electronic communication technology: Introverts versus extraverts*. Working paper, Ursinus College, Collegeville, PA.

Bretteville-Jensen, A. L. 1999. Addiction and discounting. *Journal of Health Economics*, 18: 393–407.

Camerer, C. F., Loewenstein, G., & Rabin, M. (Eds.). 2004. *Advances in behavioral economics*. Princeton, NJ: Princeton University Press.

Cantor, N., & Blanton, H. 1996. Effortful pursuit of personal goals in daily life. In P. M. Gollwitzer & J. A. Bargh (Eds.), *The psychology of action: Linking cognition and motivation to behavior*: 338–359. New York: Guilford Press.

Caplan, B. 2003. Stigler-Becker versus Myers-Briggs: Why preference-based explanations are scientifically meaningful and empirically important. *Journal of Economic Behavior and Organization*, 50: 391–405.

Carver, C. S., & Scheier, M. F. 1989. Social intelligence and personality: Some unanswered questions and unresolved issues. In R. S. Wyer, Jr., & T. K. Srull (Eds.), *Social intelligence and cognitive assessments of personality: Advances in social cognition*, vol. 2: 93–109. Mahwah, NJ: Lawrence Erlbaum Associates.

Carver, C. S., & Scheier, M. F. 1998. *On the self-regulation of behavior*. New York: Cambridge University Press.

Carver, C. S., & Scheier, M. F. 2002. Optimism. In C. R. Snyder & S. J. Lopez (Eds.), *Handbook of positive psychology*: 231–243. London: Oxford University Press.

Carver, C. S., Sutton, S. K., & Scheier, M. P. 2000. Action, emotion, and personality: Emerging conceptual integration. *Personality and Social Psychology Bulletin*, 26: 741–751.

Chang, A., Bordia, P., & Duck, J. 2003. Punctuated equilibrium and linear progression: Toward a new understanding of group development. *Academy of Management Journal*, 46: 106–117.

Chung, S., & Herrnstein, R. J. 1967. Choice and delay of reinforcement. *Journal of the Experimental Analysis of Behavior*, 10: 67–74.

Clauer, C. R., Gombosi, T. I., De Zeeuw, D. L., Ridley, R. J., Powell, K. G., van Leer, B., Stout, Q. F., Groth, C. P. T., & Holzer, T. E. 2000. High performance computer methods applied to space weather simulations. *IEEE Transaction on Plasma Science*, 28: 1931–1937.

Cloninger, C. R. 1987. A systematic method for clinical description and classification of personality variants. *Archives of General Psychiatry*, 44: 573–588.

Cooksey, R. W. 2001. Pursuing an integrated decision science: Does "naturalistic decision making" help or hinder? *Journal of Behavioral Decision Making*, 14: 361–362.

Cosmides, L., & Tooby, J. 2000. Evolutionary psychology and the emotions. In M. Lewis & J. M. Haviland-Jones (Eds.), *Handbook of emotions* (2nd ed.): 91–115. New York: Guilford Press.

Damasio, A. R. 1994. *Descartes' error: Emotion, reason, and the human brain.* New York: Putnam.

Das, T. K., & Teng, B.-S. 2001. Strategic risk behavior and its temporalities: Between risk propensity and decision context. *Journal of Management Studies*, 28: 515–534.

Dawes, R. M. 1998. Behavioral decision making and judgment. In D. T. Gilbert & S. T. Fiske (Eds.), *The handbook of social psychology*, vol. 2 (4th ed.): 497–548. Boston: McGraw-Hill.

DellaVigna, S., & Paserman, M. D. 2005. Job search and impatience. *Journal of Labor Economics*, 23: 527–588.

Dollard, J., & Miller, N. E. 1950. *Personality and psychotherapy: An analysis in terms of learning, thinking, and culture.* New York: McGraw-Hill.

Donovan, J. J. 2001. Work motivation. In N. Anderson, D. S. Ones, H. K. Sinangil, & C. Viswesvaran (Eds.), *Handbook of industrial and organizational psychology*, vol. 2: 53–76. Thousand Oaks, CA: Sage.

Drucker, P. F. 1954. *The practice of management.* New York: Harper & Row.

Dunnette, M. D. 1976. Aptitudes, abilities, and skill. In M. D. Dunnette (Ed.), *Handbook of industrial and organizational psychology:* 473–520. Chicago: Rand McNally.

Eisenberger, R. 1992. Learned industriousness. *Psychological Review*, 99: 248–267.

Eisenhardt, K. M., & Zbaracki, M. J. 1992. Strategic decision making. *Strategic Management Journal*, 13: 17–37.

Elliot, A. J., & Thrash, T. M. 2002. Approach-avoidance motivation in personality: Approach and avoidance temperaments and goals. *Journal of Personality and Social Psychology*, 82: 804–818.

Elster, J. 1992. Intertemporal choice and political thought. In G. Loewenstein & J. Elster (Eds.), *Choice over time:* 35–53. New York: Russell Sage Foundation.

Epstein, S., & O'Brien, E. J. 1985. Person-situation debate in historical and current perspective. *Psychological Bulletin*, 98: 513–537.

Farrand, M. (Ed.) 1966. *Records of the federal convention*, vol. 3. New Haven, CT: Yale University Press.

Fechner, G. T. 1966. (First published in 1860.) *Elements of psychophysics.* (Translated by H. E. Adler.) New York: Holt, Rinehart & Winston.

Fennema, H., & Wakker, P. 1997. Original and cumulative prospect theory: A discussion of empirical differences. *Journal of Behavioral Decision Making*, 10: 53–64.

Fisher, I. 1930. *The theory of interest.* New York: Macmillan.

Forster, M. R. 2000. Key concepts in model selection: Performance and generalizability. *Journal of Mathematical Psychology*, 44: 205–231.

Franken, R. E. 1994. *Human motivation* (3rd ed.). Pacific Grove, CA: Brooks/Cole.

Frederick, S., Loewenstein, G., & O'Donoghue, T. 2002. Time discounting and time preference: A critical review. *Journal of Economic Literature*, 40: 351–401.

Fried, Y., & Slowik, L. H. 2004. Enriching goal-setting theory with time: An integrated approach. *Academy of Management Review*, 29: 404–422.

Furnham, A., & Lewis, A. 1986. *The economic mind.* New York: St. Martin's Press.

Gersick, C. J. G. 1989. Marking time: Predictable transitions in task groups. *Academy of Management Journal*, 33: 274–309.

Gersick, C. J. G. 1991. Revolutionary change theories: A multilevel exploration of the punctuated equilibrium paradigm. *Academy of Management Review*, 16: 10–37.

Giordano, L. A., Bickel, W. K., Loewenstein, G., Jacobs, E. A., Marsch, L., & Badger, G. J. 2002. Mild opioid deprivation increases the degree that opioid-dependent outpatients discount delayed heroin and money. *Psychopharmacology*, 163: 174–182.

Glasner, S. V. 2003. Motivation and addiction: The role of incentive processes in understanding and treating addictive disorders. In W. M. Cox & E. Klinger (Eds.), *Handbook of motivational counseling:* 29–47. New York: Wiley.

Glomb, T., Steel, P., & Arvey, R. 2002. Office sneers, snipes, and stab wounds: Antecedents, consequences, and implications of workplace violence and aggression. In R. Lord, R. Klimoski, &

R. Kanfer (Eds.), *Frontiers of industrial and organizational psychology: Emotions and work:* 227–259. San Francisco: Jossey-Bass.

Gollwitzer, P. M. 1996. The volitional benefits from planning. In P. M. Gollwitzer & J. A. Bargh (Eds.), *The psychology of action: Linking cognition and motivation to behavior:* 287–312. New York: Guilford Press.

Gray, J. A., & McNaughton, N. 1996. The neuropsychology of anxiety: Reprise. In D. A. Hope (Ed.), *Perspectives on panic, anxiety, and fear:* 61–134. Lincoln: University of Nebraska Press.

Greco, V., & Roger, D. 2001. Coping with uncertainty: The construction and validation of a new measure. *Personality and Individual Differences,* 31: 519–534.

Green, L., Myerson, J., & McFadden, E. 1997. Rate of temporal discounting decreases with amount of reward. *Memory & Cognition,* 25: 715–723.

Hackman, J. R., & Oldham, G. R. 1976. Motivation through the design of work: Test of a theory. *Organizational Behavior and Human Performance,* 16: 250–279.

Hall, P. A., & Fong, G. T. 2003. The effects of a brief time perspective intervention for increasing physical activity among young adults. *Psychology and Health,* 18: 685–706.

Haubrich, J. G. 2000. *Waiting for policy rules.* Cleveland: Federal Reserve Bank of Cleveland.

Heath, J. 2001. *The efficient society.* Toronto: Penguin Books.

Herrnstein, R. J. 1979. Derivatives of matching. *Psychological Review,* 86: 486–495.

Herzberg, F. 1966. *Work and nature of man.* Cleveland: World.

Ho, M.-Y., Mobini, S., Chiang, T. J., Bradshaw, C. M., & Szabadi, E. 1999. Theory and method in quantitative analysis of "impulsive choice" behavior: Implications for psychopharmacology. *Psychopharmacology,* 146: 362–372.

Hulin, C., Miner, A. G., & Seitz, S. T. 2002. Computational modelling in organizational sciences: Contributions of a third discipline. In F. Drasgow & N. Schmitt (Eds.), *Measuring and analysing behaviour in organizations: Advances in measurement and data analysis:* 498–533. San Francisco: Jossey-Bass.

Hull, C. L. 1943. *Principles of behavior.* New York: Appleton-Century-Crofts.

Hunton, J. E., Hall, T. W., & Price, K. H. 1998. The value of voice in participative decision making. *Journal of Applied Psychology,* 83: 788–797.

Ilgen, D. R., & Hulin, C. L. (Eds.). 2000. *Computational modeling of behavior in organizations: The third scientific discipline.* Washington, DC: American Psychological Association.

Ito, T. A., & Cacioppo, J. T. 1999. The psychophysiology of utility appraisals. In D. Kahneman, E. Diener, & N. Schwartz (Eds.), *Well-being: The foundations of hedonic psychology:* 470–488. New York: Russell Sage Foundation.

Janssen, M. A., & Jager, W. 2001. Fashions, habits and changing preferences: Simulation of psychological factors affecting market dynamics. *Journal of Economic Psychology,* 22: 745–772.

Johnson, S. 2002. Wild things. *Wired Magazine.* http://www.wired.com/wired/archive/10.03/aigames_pr.html, accessed May 26, 2003.

Joint Committee on the Organization of Congress. 1993. Bicameral relations and interchamber cooperation. *Final report of the Joint Committee on the Organization of Congress.* http:// www.house.gov/archives/jcoc2.htm, accessed May 20, 2003.

Judge, T. A., & Ilies, R. 2002. Relationship of personality to performance motivation: A meta-analytic review. *Journal of Applied Psychology,* 87: 797–807.

Kahneman, D., & Tversky, A. 1979. Prospect theory: An analysis of decision under risk. *Econometrica,* 47: 263–291.

Kanfer, R. 1990. Motivation theory. In M. Dunnette & L. Houghs (Eds.), *Handbook of industrial and organizational psychology,* vol. 1 (2nd ed.): 124–151. Palo Alto, CA: Consulting Psychologists Press.

Kanfer, R., & Ackerman, P. L. 1989. Motivation and cognitive abilities: An integrative/aptitude-treatment interaction approach to skill acquisition. *Journal of Applied Psychology,* 74: 657–690.

Kanfer, R., & Ackerman, P. L. 1996. A self-regulatory skills perspective to reducing cognitive interference. In I. G. Sarason, G. R. Pierce, & B. R. Sarason (Eds.), *Cognitive interference: Theories, methods, and findings:* 153–171. Mahwah, NJ: Lawrence Erlbaum Associates.

Kanigel, R. 1997. *The one best way: Frederick Winslow Taylor and the enigma of efficiency.* New York: Viking Press.

Karoly, P. 1993. Mechanisms of self-regulation: A systems view. *Annual Review of Psychology*, 44: 23–52.

Klein, H. J. 1989. An integrated control theory model of work motivation. *Academy of Management Review*, 14: 150–172.

Kleinbeck, U., Quast, H.-H., Thierry, H., & Häcker, H. (Eds.). 1990. *Work motivation*. Hillsdale, NJ: Lawrence Erlbaum Associates.

Krueger, R. F. 1999. The structure of common mental disorders. *Archives of General Psychiatry*, 56: 921–926.

Krusell, P., Kuruşçu, B., & Smith, A. A. 2000. Tax policy with quasi-geometric discounting. *International Economic Journal*, 14(3): 1–40.

Kühberger, A., Schulte-Mecklenbeck, M., & Perner, J. 2002. Framing decisions: Hypothetical and real. *Organizational Behavior and Human Decision Processes*, 89: 1162–1175.

Lang, P. J., Bradley, M. M., & Cuthbert, B. N. 1997. Motivated attention: Affect, activation, and action. In P. J. Lang & R. F. Simons (Eds.), *Attention and orienting: Sensory and motivational processes:* 97–135. Mahwah, NJ: Lawrence Erlbaum Associates.

Langley, A., Mintzberg, H., Pitcher, P., Posada, E., & Saint-Macary, J. 1995. Opening up decision making: The view from the black stool. *Organization Science*, 6: 260–279.

Larrick, R. P. 1993. Motivational factors in decision theories: The role of self-protection. *Psychological Bulletin*, 113: 440–450.

Latham, G. P., & Seijts, G. H. 1999. The effects of proximal and distal goals on performance on a moderately complex task. *Journal of Organizational Behavior*, 20: 421–429.

Lavoie, J. A. A., & Pychyl, T. A. 2001. Cyberslacking and the procrastination superhighway: A web-based survey of online procrastination, attitudes, and emotion. *Social Science Computer Review*, 19: 431–444.

Leonard, N. H., Beauvais, L. L., & Scholl, R. W. 1999. Work motivation: The incorporation of self-concept-based processes. *Human Relations*, 52: 969–998.

Levy, J. S. 1992. An introduction to prospect theory. *Political Psychology*, 13: 171–186.

Locke, E. A., & Latham, G. P. 2002. Building a practically useful theory of goal setting and task motivation: A 35 year odyssey. *American Psychologist*, 57: 705–717.

Locke, E. A., & Latham, G. P. 2004. What should we do about motivation theory? Six recommendations for the twenty-first century. *Academy of Management Review*, 29: 388–403.

Loewenstein, G. 1992. The fall and rise of psychological explanations in the economics of intertemporal choice. In G. Loewenstein & J. Elster (Eds.), *Choice over time:* 3–34. New York: Russell Sage Foundation.

Loewenstein, G. 1996. Out of control: Visceral influences on behavior. *Organizational Behavior and Human Decision Processes*, 65: 272–292.

Loewenstein, G., & Elster, J. 1992. *Choice over time.* New York: Russell Sage Foundation.

Loewenstein, G., & Prelec, D. 1992. Anomalies in intertemporal choice: Evidence and an interpretation. In G. Loewenstein & J. Elster (Eds.), *Choice over time:* 119–145. New York: Russell Sage Foundation.

Logue, A. W., Rodriguez, M. L., Peña-Correal, T. E., & Mauro, B. C. 1984. Choice in a self-control paradigm: Quantification of experience-based differences. *Journal of the Experimental Analysis of Behavior*, 41: 53–67.

Lopes, L. L. 1994. Psychology and economics: Perspectives on risk, cooperation, and the marketplace. *Annual Review of Psychology*, 45: 197–227.

Luce, R. D. 1990. Rational versus plausible accounting equivalences in preference judgments. *Psychological Science*, 1: 225–234.

Madden, G. J., Petry, N. M., Badger, G. J., & Bickel, W. K. 1997. Impulsive and self-control choices in opioid-dependent patients and non-drug-using control patients: Drug and monetary rewards. *Experimental and Clinical Psychopharmacology*, 5: 256–262.

Mastrangelo, P. M., Everton, W., & Jolton, J. A. 2002. *Exploring facets and correlates of counterproductive computer use at work.* Poster session presented at the annual meeting of the Society of Industrial Organizational Psychology, Toronto.

Mazur, J. E. 1987. An adjusting procedure for studying delayed reinforcement. In M. L. Commons & J. E. Mazur (Eds.), *The effect of delay and of intervening events on reinforcement value: Quantitative analyses of behavior*, vol. 5: 55–73. Hillsdale, NJ: Lawrence Erlbaum Associates.

Mazur, J. E. 1998. Procrastination by pigeons with fixed-interval response requirements. *Journal of the Experimental Analysis of Behavior*, 69: 185–197.

Mazur, J. E. 2001. Hyperbolic value addition and general models of animal choice. *Psychological Review*, 108: 96–112.

McClelland, D. C. 1985. How motives, skills, and values determine what people do. *American Psychologist*, 40: 812–825.

McSweeney, F. K., & Swindell, S. 1999. General-process theories of motivation revisited: The role of habituation. *Psychological Bulletin*, 125: 437–457.

Mellers, B. A., Schwartz, A., & Cooke, A. D. J. 1998. Judgment and decision making. *Annual Review of Psychology*, 49: 447–477.

Mischel, W. 1973. Toward a cognitive social learning reconceptualization of personality. *Psychological Review*, 80: 252–283.

Mischel, W., & Shoda, Y. 1999. Integrating dispositions and processing dynamics within a unified theory of personality: The cognitive-affective personality system. In L. A. Pervin & O. P. John (Eds.), *Handbook of personality: Theory and research* (2nd ed.): 197–218. New York: Guilford Press.

Mitchell, T. 1997. Matching motivational strategies with organizational contexts. *Research in Organizational Behavior*, 19: 57–149.

Monterosso, J., & Ainslie, G. 1999. Beyond discounting: Possible experimental models of impulse control. *Psychopharmacology*, 146: 339–347.

Murray, H. A. 1938. *Explorations in personality*. New York: Oxford University Press.

Myerson, J., & Green, L. 1995. Discounting of delayed rewards: Models of individual choice. *Journal of the Experimental Analysis of Behavior*, 64: 263–276.

Myung, I. J., Pitt, M. A., & Kim, W. 2004. Model evaluation, testing and selection. In K. Lambert & R. Goldstone (Eds.), *The handbook of cognition*: 422–436. Thousand Oaks, CA: Sage.

Navarro, D. J., & Myung, I. J. 2005. Model evaluation and selection. In B. Everitt & D. Howel (Eds.), *Encyclopedia of behavioral statistics*, vol. 3: 1239–1242. Chichester, UK: Wiley.

Naylor, J. C., Pritchard, R. D., & Ilgen, D. R. 1980. *A theory of behavior in organizations*. New York: Academic Press.

O'Higgins, M. 1991. *Beating the Dow*. New York: Harper Collins.

Olason, D. T., & Roger, D. 2001. Optimism, pessimism, and "fighting spirit": A new approach to assessing expectancy and adaptation. *Personality and Individual Differences*, 31: 755–768.

Ostaszewski, P. 1996. The relation between temperament and rate of temporal discounting. *European Journal of Personality*, 10: 161–172.

Ostaszewski, P. 1997. Temperament and the discounting of delayed and probabilistic rewards: Conjoining European and American psychological traditions. *European Psychologist*, 2: 35–43.

Parker, S. K., & Wall, T. D. 2001. Work design: Learning from the past and mapping a new terrain. In N. Anderson, D. S. Ones, H. K. Sinangil, & C. Viswesvaran (Eds.), *Handbook of industrial, work and organizational psychology. Volume 1: Personnel psychology*: 90–109. Thousand Oaks, CA: Sage.

Pearce, C. 2002. Sims, battlebots, cellular automata god and go. *Game Studies*, 2. http://www.gamestudies.org/0102/ pearce/, accessed May 27, 2003.

Petry, N. M. 2001. Pathological gamblers, with and without substance abuse disorders, discount delayed rewards at high rates. *Journal of Abnormal Psychology*, 110: 482–487.

Pinker, S. 2002. *The blank slate: The modern denial of human nature*. New York: Penguin.

Plott, C. R. 1986. Rational choice in experimental markets. *Journal of Business*, 59: 301–327.

Plous, S. 1993. *Psychology of judgment and decision making*. Philadelphia: Temple University Press.

Pursula, M. 1999. Simulation of traffic systems: An overview. *Journal of Geographic Information and Decision Analysis*, 3(1): 1–8.

Rachlin, H. 2000. *The science of self-control*. Cambridge, MA: Harvard University Press.

Raghunathan, R., & Pham, M. T. 1999. All negative moods are not equal: Motivational influences of anxiety and sadness on decision making. *Organizational Behavior and Human Decision Processes*, 79: 56–77.

Raynor, J. O., & Entin, E. E. 1982. Achievement motivation as a determinant of persistence in contingent and noncontingent paths. In J. O. Raynor & E. E. Entin (Eds.), *Motivation, career striving, and aging:* 83–92. Washington, DC: Hemisphere.

Richards, J. B., Zhang, L., Mitchell, S. H., & de Wit, H. 1999. Delay or probability discounting in a model of impulsive behavior: Effect of alcohol. *Journal of the Experimental Analysis of Behavior*, 71: 121–143.

Romanelli, E., & Tushman, M. L. 1994. Organizational transformation as punctuated equilibrium: An empirical test. *Academy of Management Journal*, 37: 1141–1166.

Rothbart, M. K., Ahadi, S. A., & Evans, D. E. 2000. Temperament and personality: Origins and outcomes. *Journal of Personality and Social Psychology*, 78: 123–135.

Rotter, J. B. 1954. *Social learning and clinical psychology.* New York: Prentice-Hall.

Sanders, W. G., & Carpenter, M. A. 2003. Strategic satisficing? A behavioral agency perspective on stock repurchasing program announcements. *Academy of Management Journal*, 46: 160–178.

Savage, T. 2000. Artificial motives: A review of motivation in artificial creatures. *Connection Science*, 12: 211–277.

Schiller, R. J. 2000. *Irrational exuberance.* Princeton, NJ: Princeton University Press.

Schmitt, N., & Robertson, I. 1990. Personnel selection. *Annual Review of Psychology*, 41: 289–319.

Schneider, F. W., & Green, J. E. 1977. The need for affiliation and sex as moderators of the relationship between need for achievement and academic performance. *Journal of School Psychology*, 15: 269–277.

Schouwenburg, H. C., & Groenewoud, J. T. 1997. *Studieplanning: Een werkboek voor studenten* [Study planning: A workbook for students]. Groningen, Netherlands: Wolters-Noordhoff.

Schwartz, B. 1989. *Psychology of learning and behavior* (3rd ed.). New York: Norton.

Shizgal, P. 1999. On the neural computation of utility: Implications from studies of brain stimulation reward. In D. Kahneman, E. Diener, & N. Schwartz (Eds.), *Well-being: The foundations of hedonic psychology:* 500–524. New York: Russell Sage Foundation.

Simon, H. A. 1955. A behavioral model of rational choice. *Quarterly Journal of Economics*, 69: 88–118.

Skinner, E. A. 1996. A guide to constructs of control. *Journal of Personality and Social Psychology*, 71: 549–570.

Smith, V. L. 1991. Rational choice: The contrast between economics and psychology. *Journal of Political Economics*, 99: 877–897.

Staats, A. W. 1999. Unifying psychology requires new infrastructure, theory, method, and a research agenda. *Review of General Psychology*, 3: 3–13.

Steel, P. In press. The nature of procrastination: A meta-analytic and theoretical review of quintessential self-regulatory failure. *Psychological Bulletin*.

Steel, P., Brothen, T., & Wambach, C. 2001. Procrastination and personality, performance, and mood. *Personality and Individual Differences*, 30: 95–106.

Steele, C. M., & Josephs, R. A. 1990: Alcoholic myopia: Its prized and dangerous effects. *American Psychologist*, 45: 921–933.

Steers, R. M., Mowday, R. T., & Shapiro, D. L. 2004. The future of work motivation theory. *Academy of Management Review*, 29: 379–387.

Stigler, G., & Becker, G. 1977. De gustibus non est disputandum. *American Economic Review*, 67: 76–90.

Taylor, F. W. 1911. *The principles of scientific management.* New York: Harper & Brothers.

Tellegen, A. 1991. Personality traits: Issues of definition, evidence, and assessment. In W. M. Grove & D. Chicchetti (Eds.), *Thinking clearly about psychology*, vol. 2: 10–35. Minneapolis: University of Minnesota Press.

Thaler, R. H. 1991. *Quasi rational economics.* New York: Russell Sage Foundation.

Thaler, R. H. 1992. *The winner's curse.* Princeton, NJ: Princeton University Press.

Torrubia, R., Ávila, C., Moltó, J., & Caseras, X. 2001. The sensitivity to punishment and sensitivity to reward questionnaire (SPSRQ) as a measure of Gray's anxiety and impulsivity dimensions. *Personality and Individual Differences*, 31: 837–862.

Trope, Y., & Liberman, N. 2003. Temporal construal. *Psychological Review*, 110: 403–421.

Tversky, A., & Kahneman, D. 1992. Advances in prospect theory: Cumulative representation of uncertainty. *Journal of Risk and Uncertainty*, 5: 297–323.

Vancouver, J. B., Thompson, C. M., & Williams, A. A. 2001. The changing signs in the relationships among self-efficacy, personal goals, and performance. *Journal of Applied Psychology*, 86: 605–620.

Van Eerde, W., & Thierry, H. 1996. Vroom's expectancy models and work-related criteria: A meta-analysis. *Journal of Applied Psychology*, 81: 575–586.

Vroom, V. H. 1964. *Work and motivation*. New York: Wiley.

Waller, M. J., Conte, J. M., Gibson, C. B., & Carpenter, M. A. 2001. The effect of individual perceptions of dead-lines on team performance. *Academy of Management Review*, 26: 586–600.

Waller, M. J., Zellmer-Bruhn, M. E., & Giambatista, R. C. 2002. Watching the clock: Group pacing behavior under dynamic deadlines. *Academy of Management Journal*, 45: 1046–1055.

Wärneryd, K. E. 1988. Economic psychology as a field of study. In W. F. Raaij, G. M. van Veldhoven, & K. E. Wärneryd (Eds.), *Handbook of economic psychology:* 3–38. Boston: Kluwer Academic.

Weiner, B. 1990. History of motivational research in education. *Journal of Educational Psychology*, 3: 616–622.

Weiner, B. 1991. Metaphors in motivation and attribution. *American Psychologist*, 46: 921–930.

White, L. H. 1999. *The theory of monetary institutions*. Malden, MA: Blackwell.

Whiteside, S. P., & Lynam, D. R. 2001. The five factor model and impulsivity: Using a structural model of personality to understand impulsivity. *Personality and Individual Differences*, 30: 669–689.

Wilson, E. O. 1998. *Consilience: The unity of knowledge*. New York: Knopf.

Winter, D. G. 1996. *Personality: Analysis and interpretation of lives*. New York: McGraw-Hill.

Winter, D. G., John, O. P., Stewart, A. J., Klohnen, E. C., & Duncan, L. E. 1998. Traits and motives: Towards an integration of two traditions in personality research. *Psychological Review*, 105: 230–250.

Yesuf, M. 2003. *Attitude measures towards risk and rate of time preference: Experimental evidence in Ethiopia*. Paper presented at the First International Conference on the Ethiopian Economy, Addis Ababa, Ethiopia.

Zeidner, M., Boekaerts, M., & Pintrich, P. R. 2000. Self-regulation: Directions and challenges for future research. In M. Boekaerts, P. R. Pintrich, & M. Zeidner (Eds.), *Handbook of self-regulation:* 749–768. New York: Academic Press.

6 Satisfaction and Stress

6.1 WHY DOES AFFECT MATTER IN ORGANIZATIONS?

Sigal G. Barsade and Donald E. Gibson[1]

Executive Overview

Interest in and research about affect in organizations have expanded dramatically in recent years. This article reviews what we know about affect in organizations, focusing on how employees' moods, emotions, and dispositional affect influence critical organizational outcomes such as job performance, decision making, creativity, turnover, prosocial behavior, teamwork, negotiation, and leadership. This review highlights pervasive and consistent effects, showing the importance of affect in shaping a wide variety of organizational behaviors, the knowledge of which is critical for researchers, managers, and employees.

Why Does Affect Matter in Organizations?

An Organizational Vignette . . .

I had just mentioned how small a raise I was going to give to Jerry, my top salesperson this year. I could see a subtle wave of anger and frustration wash over his usually calm features. I had been afraid this was going to happen. But what could I do? I was caught in the middle—the CEO wanted to cut our budget by 6%! Jerry's voice had an edge to it, and I could tell that my explanations about the budget were not going to solve this one. Would he explode? Would he blame me? Worse, would he threaten to quit? I could feel the good mood I had started with this morning rapidly disappearing. The insistent brittleness in his voice made me feel defensive and I was starting to get angry myself. I needed to decide what to do next, but I was having trouble remembering the rationale for the raise. I felt like yelling at him. That, *I told myself*, cannot happen. I need to keep it under control . . . I'm the boss here, remember? He's watching how I act. I need to figure out how I want to deal with his anger—and mine . . .

Affect permeates organizations. It is present in the interdependent relationships we hold with bosses, team members, and subordinates. It is present in deadlines, in group projects, in human resource processes like performance appraisals and selection interviews. Affective processes (more commonly known as emotions) create and sustain work motivation. They lurk behind political behavior; they animate our decisions; they are essential to leadership.

Strong affective feelings are present at any time we confront work issues that matter to us and our organizational performance.

In the last 30 years, an "affective revolution" has taken place, in which academics and managers alike have begun to appreciate how an organizational lens that integrates employee affect provides a perspective missing from earlier views (Barsade, Brief, & Spataro, 2003). While much about affect remains difficult to explain, dramatic progress has been made in understanding individuals' affective lives in organizations. In this article, we examine why affect is important to organizational life. We do so by drawing on a range of studies that help identify critical organizational outcomes driven by affect and show how understanding feelings can help researchers, managers, and employees themselves explain and predict attitudes and behavior in organizations, from turnover to decision making to leadership. We address the question, "How does research seen through the lens of affect cause us to think differently about the assumptions we make about how employees work?"

Defining Affect in Organizations

We begin by defining a range of terms often used in research on affect in organizations (see Table 6.1.1). These terms describe phenomena ranging from discrete emotions (fear, anger, or disgust), to moods (feeling cheerful versus feeling melancholy), to dispositional traits ("He's such a negative person"; "She's always so upbeat!"), to meta-emotional abilities, such as emotional intelligence ("My boss is very good at understanding how the people on our team are feeling"). *Affect* can be thought of as an umbrella term encompassing a broad range of feelings that individuals experience, including *feeling states*, which are in-the-moment, short-term affective experiences, and *feeling traits*, which are more stable tendencies to feel and act in certain ways (Watson & Clark, 1984).[2] Within feeling states there are two established categories: emotions and moods. *Emotions* are elicited by a particular target or cause, often include physiological reactions and action sequences, and are relatively intense and short-lived (Frijda, 1986; Lazarus, 1991). In contrast, *moods* are more diffuse, take the form of a general positive (pleasant) or negative (unpleasant) feeling, and tend not to be focused on a specific cause (Frijda, 1986; Tellegen, 1985). There is only one category of feeling trait: *dispositional affect*. This is a personality *trait* referring to a person's relatively stable, underlying tendency to experience positive and negative moods and emotions (Watson & Clark, 1984).

In terms of research approaches, emotions tend to be assessed and examined differently than moods and dispositional affect. Because emotions are focused on a specific target or cause, they have come to be regarded as *discrete*, and are linked to specific tendencies to act (such as the desire to approach objects in anger and to avoid them in fear; Frijda, 1986). The discrete emotions approach has identified "basic" or primary emotions, including joy, love, anger, fear, sadness, disgust, and surprise, each with a unique set of prototypical antecedents and consequences—though the precise number and identity of discrete emotions are subjects of much debate (see Ekman, 1992; Ortony & Turner, 1990). Moods and dispositional affect, in contrast, tend to be examined through an approach that summarizes the wide variety of possible human affective experiences into a few critical underlying dimensions. Dimensional approaches often arrange affective experience labels (such as "astonished," "enthusiastic," or "grouchy") in a circular graph called an *affective circumplex*, and represent the dimensions as axes on that circumplex (see Figure 6.1.1).

The first factor of the circumplex, on the x axis, is "pleasantness," a dimension ranging from high pleasantness to low pleasantness (or unpleasant). The second dimension, on the y axis, is an "activation/energy" dimension, ranging from high to low energy (Russell, 1980).

Table 6.1.1 Translating Affective Terms

Terms Used in Research	Formal Definition	Colloquial Terms
Affect	Umbrella term encompassing a broad range of feelings that individuals experience, including feeling states, such as moods and discrete emotions, and traits, such as trait positive and negative affectivity (all defined below).	"I feel . . ." "She seems to be feeling . . ." "He is usually unemotional . . ."
Discrete Emotions	Emotions are focused on a specific target or cause—generally realized by the perceiver of the emotion; relatively intense and very short-lived. After initial intensity, can sometimes transform into a mood.	For example, love, anger, hate, fear, jealousy, happiness, sadness, grief, rage, aggravation, ecstasy, affection, joy, envy, fright, etc.
Moods	Generally take the form of a global positive (pleasant) or negative (unpleasant) feeling; tend to be diffuse—not focused on a specific cause—and often not realized by the perceiver of the mood; medium duration (from a few moments to as long as a few weeks or more).	Feeling good, bad, negative, positive, cheerful, down, pleasant, irritable, etc.
Dispositional (Trait) Affect	Overall personality tendency to respond to situations in stable, predictable ways. A person's "affective lens" on the world.	"No matter what, he's always ____." "She tends to be in a ____ mood all the time." "He is always so negative."
a) (Trait) Positive Affectivity	Individuals who tend to be cheerful and energetic, and who experience positive moods, such as pleasure or well-being, across a variety of situations as compared to people who tend to be low energy and sluggish or melancholy.	"She's always so energetic and upbeat!" "He's such a downer all the time!"
b) (Trait) Negative Affectivity	Individuals who tend to be distressed and upset, and have a negative view of self over time and across situations, as compared to people who are more calm, serene and relaxed.	"She is always so hostile in her approach." "Why is he always so anxious/nervous?" "I admire his steady calmness and serenity."
Emotional Intelligence	"The ability to monitor one's own and others' feelings and emotions, to discriminate among them, and to use this information to guide one's thinking and actions" (Salovey & Mayer, 1990: 189).	"My manager is terrible at expressing his emotions." "My teammate is great at knowing how everyone else on the team is feeling." "The CEO is brilliant at dealing with her employees' emotions—a real motivator!"
Emotional Regulation	Individuals' attempts to "influence which emotions they have, when they have them, and how they experience and express these emotions" (Gross, 1998a: 275).	"He handles his emotions really well, even under high pressure situations."
Emotional Labor	Requires an employee to "induce or suppress feeling in order to sustain the outward countenance that produces the proper state of mind in others" (Hochschild, 1983: 7).	She has to put on a smile when dealing with customers, because it's part of the job.

(Continued)

Table 6.1.1 Continued.

Terms Used in Research	Formal Definition	Colloquial Terms
Emotional Contagion	Processes that allow the sharing or transferring of emotions from one individual to other group members; the tendency to mimic the nonverbal behavior of others, to "synchronize facial expressions, vocalizations, postures, and movements" with others, and in turn, to "converge emotionally" (Hatfield, Cacioppo, & Rapson, 1994).	"And when we feel good, it's contagious." (Advertising slogan from Southwest Airlines) "I don't know why, but every time I talk to him I feel really anxious afterwards." "Infectious enthusiasm."
Collective Affect	A "bottom-up" approach to collective affect emphasizes the affective composition of the various affective attributes of the group's members. That is, the degree to which individual level affective characteristics combine, often through emotional contagion, to form group level emotion or mood. A "top-down" approach to collective affect emphasizes the degree to which groups are characterized by emotion norms for feeling and expression.	"Our group has a ____ feel to it." "What a negative group!" "In our group showing positivity is very important."

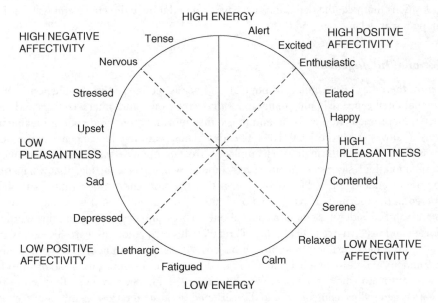

Figure 6.1.1 The Circumplex Model of Affect.

Adapted from Feldman Barrett, L., & Russell, J.A. (1998). Independence and bipolarity in the structure of current affect. *Journal of Personality and Social Psychology*, 74(4), 967–984 and Larsen, R.J., & Diener, E. (1992). Promises and problems with the circumplex model of emotion. In M.S. Clark (Ed.), *Emotion. Review of personality and social psychology* (Vol. 13, pp. 25–59). Thousand Oaks, CA: Sage Publications, Inc.

Moods are usually examined based on their hedonic tone—that is, how pleasant (toward happy) or unpleasant (toward sad) the mood is. Dispositional affect can be examined as trait pleasantness (e.g., Staw & Barsade, 1993) or as the combination of the pleasantness and energy dimensions, creating the two independent constructs of positive affectivity (PA) and negative affectivity (NA) (Watson, Clark, & Tellegen, 1988; see the dotted lines in Figure 6.1.1). For example, individuals characterized by high dispositional NA tend to be distressed, upset, and have a negative view of self over time and across situations, as opposed to the more serene, calm, relaxation shown by people who are low in NA; people high in dispositional PA tend to be cheerful and energetic, and experience positive moods, such as pleasure or well-being, across a variety of situations, as compared to those low in PA who experience more sadness, melancholy, dullness, or lethargy (Watson & Tellegen, 1985). Other affective traits that can influence work behavior include people's propensities to feeling emotions strongly (affective intensity; Larsen & Diener, 1987); being prone to catching other people's emotions (emotional contagion; Hatfield, Cacioppo, & Rapson, 1994; Doherty, 1997); and how emotionally expressive people tend to be (emotional expressivity; Kring, Smith, & Neale, 1994).

New Ways of Approaching Affect in Organizations

The delineation of affective terms outlined above represents significant progress in a field that has traditionally been characterized by little agreement over the meaning and boundaries of basic constructs. This research progress now makes it possible to examine affective influences on organizational outcomes with greater precision and specificity. While this increasing consistency in definitions has helped, the range of approaches to studying affect in organizations remains broad. We identify three emerging trends in conceiving affect in organizations that take the definitions we have outlined in new directions and will continue to shape research language and focus.

Emotional Intelligence

Recently, there has been significant popular and academic interest in the phenomenon of emotional intelligence (EI), an "ability to monitor one's own and others' feelings and emotions, to discriminate among them, and to use this information to guide one's thinking and actions" (Salovey & Mayer, 1990: 189). The idea behind emotional intelligence in the workplace is that it is a skill through which employees treat emotions as valuable data in navigating a situation. Let's say a sales manager has come up with an amazing idea that will increase corporate revenue by up to 200%, but knows that his boss tends to be irritable and short-tempered in the morning. Having emotional intelligence means that this manager will first recognize and consider this emotional fact about his boss, and despite the stunning nature of his idea—and his own excitement—he will regulate his own emotions, curb his enthusiasm, and wait until the afternoon to approach his boss. It also means understanding how one's own emotions and those of others can facilitate thinking. For example, the head of a product development team who is about to embark on a large-scale development effort senses that the team is generally feeling down and disheartened because some key members of the team have left for a different firm. He knows that he must get his team back into a positive, upbeat mood for the team members to be productively creative in the new project. He arranges to take them on a "brain-storming retreat" of white-water river rafting where they can connect as the newly shaped team, and most importantly, raise their positivity as they embark on this new project. In doing so, this project leader is actively managing his own emotions and those of his team to help meet their goals; he is "using emotions to think intelligently."

Mayer and Salovey's (1997) emotional intelligence model elaborates on this premise and is based on the following four factors: (1) *Perceiving Emotions*: the degree to which people are capable of attending to their emotions, expressing those emotions, and reading the emotions of others; (2) *Using Emotions*: the process of knowing which emotions facilitate cognition effectively and using them to do so; (3) *Understanding Emotions*: the understanding of complicated emotional dynamics, including how emotions can change from one to another (e.g., embarrassment can turn into anger rather than apology); and (4) *Managing Emotions*: the knowledge of how to regulate one's own and others' emotions to reach goals (see Salovey & Grewal, 2005 for review).

It is important to note, however, that there is a debate in the emotional intelligence field as to the exact nature of emotional intelligence (see Brackett, Rivers, Shiffman, Lerner, & Salovey, 2006). One group of researchers uses an "abilities" approach based on the four-factor model described above (Mayer & Salovey, 1997), and measures emotional intelligence through performance tests (e.g., the MSCEIT, a computer-based EI test, Mayer, Salovey, Caruso, & Sitarenios, 2003). This approach differs from that of other researchers who take a "mixed model" approach using self-report measures of emotional intelligence.[3] Self-report measures of EI ask respondents for perceptions of their own emotional abilities through ratings on items such as, "I am generally very good at calming someone down when he or she is upset," or "I can tell how people are feeling even if they never tell me." While these self-report measures may indicate respondents' perceptions of emotional self-efficacy (Tett, Fox, & Wang, 2005), there is serious question as to whether respondents can be unbiased about their own emotional skills (Matthews, Roberts, & Zeidner, 2004). One might compare this approach to assessing mathematical skills by asking respondents, "How good are you at solving algebraic equations?" rather than asking the person to actually solve an algebraic equation. There is also serious concern that "mixed model" self-report-based approaches have substantial overlap with other personality measures such as the "Big Five" personality factors leading to issues of construct validity (Brackett, Mayer, & Warner, 2004).[4]

This issue highlights the degree to which emotional intelligence is still a nascent field, both theoretically and methodologically, currently undergoing its own set of growth crises on a variety of dimensions (see Conte, 2005; Daus & Ashkanasy, 2005), including methodological challenges within the current ability-based tests (Matthews et al., 2004). However, overall there is positive support for the validity of the EI construct and its relationship to a variety of life outcomes, including behavior at work (Mayer, Roberts, & Barsade, forthcoming), and we predict that the construct of emotional intelligence, particularly if deconstructed into its component parts (e.g., the four factors), will ultimately have much to offer to our understanding of organizational life.

Emotion Regulation and Emotional Labor

A second focus has been on the degree to which employees manage or regulate their emotional expression through the facial "mask" they present to others. This perspective first notes that an employee's felt emotions can be distinguished from his or her displayed emotions, which are the facial expressions, gestures, tone of voice, and language used to convey feeling (Rafaeli & Sutton, 1989). Displaying emotions that differ from what we are actually feeling involves *emotional regulation*, which is the attempt to influence which emotions we have, when we have them, and how these emotions are experienced or expressed (Gross, 1998a). It thus includes a broad range of regulatory activities, including, as the introductory vignette suggests, controlling anger when a person feels that it will reflect badly on his or her reputation.

When engaging in *emotional labor*, an organization-specific type of regulation, employees manage their public displays of emotions to comply with normative "display rules" (Ekman, 1973; Hochschild, 1983). Such organizational display rules or emotion norms can be used as a mechanism for increasing performance—such as sales-people keeping an upbeat, enthusiastic expression with customers to encourage purchasing behavior (Pugh, 2001; Totterdell & Holman, 2003); lawyers using an aggressive, angry tone to encourage compliance in adversaries (Pierce, 1995); medical professionals adopting norms of intentional affective neutrality (Smith & Kleinman, 1989); and bill collectors attempting to calm or browbeat debtors (Sutton, 1991). This is considered to be labor because part of what these employees are being paid to do is regulating their own emotions to produce the appropriate emotional state in others (Hochschild, 1983). Research in this area has also been advanced by accentuating how the organizational context constrains or encourages emotion norms (e.g., employees showing positive emotions only during less busy times in convenience stores or banks; Pugh, 2001; Rafaeli & Sutton, 1990).

Emotional labor has also been discussed in terms of "surface acting," when employees show emotions without necessarily feeling them (such as when an irked airline customer service agent forces himself to smile and be friendly as a customer becomes increasingly agitated about lost luggage); and "deep acting," when employees display emotions they have actually worked on feeling (such as if the airline customer service agent actually tries to sympathize with the customer and show emotions aligned with feeling empathy). It was initially theorized that a discrepancy between individuals' emotional display and their underlying feelings (characteristic of surface acting) would cause "emotional dissonance" and contribute to work strain (Hochschild, 1983; Morris & Feldman, 1996). That is, when a customer service agent continuously forces himself to smile despite feeling negative affect such as irritation, the dissonance created may be a source of anxiety, depression, and burnout (Grandey, 2003). However, researchers have also found that for many workers surface acting does not cause strain, particularly if workers are "faking in good faith" and believe the act they are putting on is a legitimate part of the work role (Rafaeli & Sutton, 1989: 37; see summary in Côté, 2005). Given these divergent findings, researchers are working to understand the conditions under which emotion regulation in the form of surface acting does result in strain (Côté, 2005), including the role of individual differences and organizational context (Grandey, 2000). One possible clue to this question comes from emotion regulation research suggesting that regulating emotions by anticipating them and engaging in cognitive re-framing (for example, telling oneself in advance to be objective in a potentially emotionally charged situation) causes less strain than regulating emotions through suppression (for example, attempting to "surface act" cheerful when currently feeling angry) (Gross, 1998b).

Emotional Contagion and Collective Affect

The idea that affect not only occurs intrapsychically but has a strong social component which can influence dyadic and group interactions is a third emerging area of research (Barsade & Gibson, 1998; Kelly & Barsade, 2001; Keltner & Haidt, 1999). The process of emotional contagion is a primary mechanism through which emotions are shared and become social, creating collective emotion.

Emotional contagion, characterized as processes that allow the sharing or transferring of emotions from one individual to other group members, often occurs without conscious knowledge (although it can also be consciously induced; Barsade, 2002). This everday, continuous, automatic process has been described as a tendency to mimic the nonverbal behavior of others, to "synchronize facial expressions, vocalizations, postures, and movements" with others, and in turn, to "converge emotionally" (Hatfield, Cacioppo, & Rapson, 1994). Research has suggested this mimicry can be explained by the facial feedback hypothesis, such that individuals who model certain facial displays corresponding to emotions actually begin to experience the same emotions (Larsen & Kasimatis, 1990; Strack, Martin, & Stepper, 1988). The contagion process may be modified by a range of factors, such as the degree to which individuals are good senders and receivers of emotion (Hatfield et al., 1994; Sullins, 1989).

While studies exploring the influence of emotional contagion initially focused primarily on dyadic settings, findings from both lab and field research suggest that contagion also functions at the group level. For example, in one study, contagion occurred and influenced group dynamics both with the deliberate mood induction by the presence of a trained confederate, and within group dynamics without a confederate (Barsade, 2002). Moving to organizational settings, in an in-depth daily tracking of nurse and accountant work groups, collective team mood convergence, a product of contagion, was found to occur, particularly in those with high group cohesion (Totterdell, Kellet, Teuchmann, & Briner, 1998). In a broader study of 70 work teams across 51 different organizational contexts (including product teams, service teams, strategic planning teams, consulting teams, and engineering teams), mood convergence occurred across all dimensions of the affective circumplex (Bartel & Saavedra, 2000). In a recent study of group contagion in a naturalistic team performance setting, not only was contagion shown to occur, but this contagion was stronger for people who had a higher dispositional propensity toward emotional contagion, and also for those who had more collectivistic tendencies toward the team (Ilies, Wagner, & Morgeson, in press).

Why Does Affect Matter in Organizations?

We have laid the groundwork for understanding and answering this question by outlining the parameters of affect as a construct. We now focus on how affect of all sorts influences the thoughts and behaviors of individuals and groups within organizations. We do so by first examining a relationship that has long intrigued researchers: whether employees' feelings influence their work performance. We then examine specific relationships between affect and decision making, creativity, group dynamics, and individual behaviors, such as turnover, helping behavior, negotiation, and leadership. Finally, we draw conclusions from these studies to indicate where we are and what challenges we face in exploring future directions in organizational research.

Affect and Performance

The dominant hypothesis about employee emotions in the 20th century was that happy workers ought to be productive workers (Staw, Bell, & Clausen, 1986). Up until the 1980s, however, "happiness" was often measured using attitudinal measures such as job satisfaction, and the results were decidedly modest.[5] Recently, measures that more directly measure happiness—those focusing on state and trait positive affect—have been used to examine this critical relationship. These studies have produced more compelling results. Indeed, a comprehensive meta-analysis indicated that an individual's tendency to experience positive emotions and moods is associated with increases in a variety of work performance measures, including more positive supervisory evaluations, higher income, enhanced negotiating ability, and performing discretionary acts for the benefit of the organization (Lyubomirsky, King, & Diener, 2005).

Most studies of affect and work-related performance have examined employees' dispositional affect (see Staw & Cohen-Charash, 2005 for a review). For example, an experimental study focusing on managerial performance found that dispositional positive affect was a significant predictor of decision-making effectiveness, interpersonal performance, and ratings of managerial potential (Staw & Barsade, 1993). Longitudinal field research has indicated that employees who tend to meet work obstacles in a positive mood (using both state and trait measures) tend to reap more favorable outcomes—including more favorable supervisor evaluations and higher pay 18 months after the initial measure of positive emotions—than their more negative counterparts (Staw, Sutton, & Pelled, 1994). Within the sales domain, salespeople's general positive affect toward their customers was found to significantly predict sales performance (Sharma & Levy, 2003). Overall, research shows a consistent, strong relationship between trait positive affect measures and various measures of work performance. This relationship has held in experimental, cross-sectional, and longitudinal studies, even after controlling for possible confounding variables and using both objective and subjective ratings (see review in Cropanzano & Wright, 2001).

When examining the influence of mood on performance, researchers have found emotional contagion to be a useful mechanism for understanding performance outcomes. For example, the positive mood of bank tellers was found to lead to positive emotional contagion among their customers, which was then positively associated with customer evaluations of service quality (Pugh, 2001). In a cleverly done coder observation study of emotional contagion within 220 employee-customer encounters in coffee shops, behavioral mimicry, an underlying mechanism of emotional contagion, was shown to occur (the strength of the employees' smiles predicted customers' smiles during the purchase encounter, even above the degree of smiling the customers came into the coffee shop with). This emotional contagion also predicted customers' satisfaction with the encounter (Barger & Grandey, 2006). Similarly, a study involving a short-term affect measure (though not quite a measure of mood) found that in a sample of shoe salespeople, engaging in affectively positive behaviors with customers such as greeting, smiling, and eye contact was found to correlate with customers' in-store positive mood, which was then related to the amount of time the customers spent in the store and their reported willingness to come and shop there again (Tsai & Huang, 2002).

This effect of emotional contagion has also been found at the group level. For example, in a simulated managerial group decision-making task, the degree to which individuals within the group experienced positive contagion predicted how positively other group members rated their performance (Barsade, 2002). In the same study, looking at more collective outcomes, the degree to which groups experienced positive versus negative contagion led to less conflict and greater cooperation in the way money was allocated in the salary decision-making task. Groups in which positive emotional contagion occurred allocated the pot of money more evenly among the group members, as compared to groups in which negative emotional contagion occurred. In a study of the influence of the contagion of mood of a group leader on group members, the positive mood of the leader positively influenced group members at both the individual and collective level with the opposite for leader negative mood. The leader's positive mood also had a subsequent influence on group coordination and effort (Sy, Côté, & Saavedra, 2005).

Relatedly, while we have been focused on emotional contagion as a transient state, one's personality trait propensity toward emotional contagion has also begun to be linked to work outcomes. For example, it has been related to positive salesperson performance, but also to a greater likelihood of burnout (Verbeke, 1997), and greater vulnerability to emotional exhaustion when faced with dealing with death and dying among oncology care providers (LeBlanc, Bakker, Peeters, Van-Heesch, & Schaufeli, 2001).

It is not clear whether dispositional affect or mood has a stronger influence on performance, although there are theories which integrate the two (Weiss & Cropanzano, 1996). There have been more studies examining dispositional affect, but this may be because dispositional affect is more easily measured than mood, and much easier than measuring discrete emotions. In an empirical test of state versus trait affective measures, a study of public sector employees showed that trait measures (using a measure of positive psychological well-being) related to supervisor performance ratings beyond the effects of mood. A replication of the study with social welfare counselors repeated the trait findings, but also found that negative mood was predictive of performance while controlling for trait measures. Thus, both types of affect mattered in accounting for performance (Wright, Cropanzano, & Meyer, 2004). It has been argued that the link between employees' more short-lived feeling states (e.g., moods and emotions) and performance measures such as supervisory ratings are inconsistent because of the time lag problem: employees' moods and emotions may be fleeting and short-term, while performance measures used tend to reflect longer periods of evaluation (usually six months to one year; Wright & Staw, 1999). As we review below, when performance is measured in more time-delimited ways (such as through effective decision making, creativity, or prosocial behaviors), the results for positive mood are quite compelling. We encourage more research examining the influence of mood, and especially discrete emotions, on performance (see Lazarus & Cohen-Charash, 2001).

Last, a more recent line of research examines whether an employee's emotional intelligence leads to increased job performance, with most studies to date finding results with overall emotional intelligence and the sub-factor of emotional recognition/perception (see Mayer et al., forthcoming for a comprehensive review of the influence of emotional intelligence on work outcomes). Emotional intelligence has been found to positively influence performance on problem-solving tasks (Lam & Kirby, 2002; Lyons & Schneider, 2005); and in a variety of managerial simulations, including problem analysis in a managerial in-box exercise, a layoff decision-making task, and a simulated claims adjustment task (Day & Carroll, 2004; Feyerham & Rice, 2002; Matsumoto et al., 2004). There have been some field studies tying emotional intelligence with performance, mainly within the domain of emotion perception skills. A recent meta-analysis reported a positive relationship with greater emotion perception (emotion recognition accuracy) and better work outcomes in occupations as diverse as physicians, medical interns, human service workers, foreign service officers, principals, public service interns, school teachers, business executives, clinicians and business managers (Elfenbein, Foo, White, & Tan, in press). There are significantly fewer field studies looking at emotional intelligence more broadly than emotional perception. One such empirical examination studied 44 analysts and clerical employees from the finance department of a Fortune 500 insurance company and found that the employees with higher emotional intelligence ability scores (which varied by which of the four factors was being examined) received greater merit increases and were employed at a higher rank in the company. Employees with higher emotional intelligence were also rated by both their supervisors and teammates as having better social skills than employees with lower emotional intelligence ability scores (Lopes et al., 2000).

Overall, however, within field settings, the research evidence tying emotional intelligence abilities to work performance is still in its beginning phases and has not yet lived up to the claims of its popular press fame. One possibility may be that the measures for this construct need to be improved, or that outcome variables need to be chosen more carefully. Another likely possibility is that cognitive intelligence or other personality variables (Gohm, Corser, & Dalsky, 2005; Rubin, Munz, & Bommer, 2005) are particularly important in organizational settings and may interact with emotional intelligence in a way that then influences performance. For example, one recent study made exactly this point and found that among staff members in a public university, the influence of high emotional intelligence on performance was more pronounced for employees who had lower cognitive intelligence scores (Côté & Miners, 2006). Finally, it may be that the field has not sufficiently considered the links between the subcomponents of emotional intelligence, taking into account the entire "EI profile," rather than the skills separately. For example, if there are two managers who are both high in ability to read others' emotions, but one is better than the other in regulating her own emotions or those of others, the latter manager may well be more successful at her job.

While many of the preceding studies have used quantitative task output as their measure of performance, the direction of emotions research has been to examine a variety of other outcome variables that may also be considered measures of "performance," depending on the task context. These include effective decision making, creativity, turnover, prosocial behaviors, and leadership. We turn to these variables next.

Affect and Decision Making

The influence of affect on decision making has been an area of active debate focused on whether positive or negative affect leads to better outcomes. Support for the influence of positive emotions on decision making comes from a variety of domains. Alice Isen and her colleagues, in a voluminous research stream, have consistently shown that positive mood inductions lead to better, more efficient decision making, including decision making requiring more careful, systematic, and thorough processing (see Isen, 2001; Isen & Labroo, 2003 for reviews). For example, in one study in a hospital setting, Estrada, Isen, and Young (1997) induced positive affect in practicing physicians by providing a small gift of candy. The physicians then had to read a description of a patient and think aloud (which was recorded and rated by outside coders) as they tried to determine the correct diagnosis. It was found that while the positive affect-induced doctors considered as many diagnoses as doctors who did not undergo the positive mood induction (received no candy), the positive affect-induced doctors came to the correct solution significantly earlier than control participants, and were less likely to incorrectly anchor on an incorrect hypothesis. This study suggests that positive affect can facilitate the thorough, efficient, and flexible use of new information, which increases decision effectiveness.

However, studies have also found that negative affect can lead to more effective decision making. One set of studies shows that negative affect leads to more concentrated, detailed, and analytic processing (see Schwarz, Bless, & Bohner, 1991 for a review) while positive affect can lead to the opposite (Melton, 1995; Mackie & Worth, 1989). A set of studies in the clinical literature shows a "depressive realism effect" in which people who are depressed (trait affect) have more accurate judgments than nondepressed people (Alloy & Abramson, 1988). Finally, the "mood-as-input" model (Martin, Ward, Achee, & Wyer, 1993) predicts that negative affect will lead to more effortful processing. The rationale for this is that people use their moods as indications of the state of their environment. Thus, negative moods serve as a signal to people that something is wrong, so that active cognitive processing will continue as people try to solve the problem, whereas positive mood signals that all is well and people should not continue to analyze.

Addressing this debate within the organizational domain, Staw and Barsade (1993) directly tackled the question of whether positive versus negative affect contributes to effective decision making. In a managerial simulation with MBA students, they offered competing hypotheses as to whether high versus low trait positive affect participants would do better in decision making on a managerial simulation scored by outside raters. They found a salutary influence of positive affect on a gamut of detailed, effortful decision-making tasks, including: greater decision-making accuracy; greater amount of additional information requested before making decisions; greater use of quantitative indices in the decision making, and greater recognition of situational contingencies. They thus concluded that positive affect led to better decision making than negative affect. Positive affect has also been linked to deeper analytic processing and efficiency in decision making. In a study of graduating university students seeking employment, those with higher trait positive affectivity had more clarity about their job search (integrating information more deeply and efficiently), which then led them to look for a job more intensely and ultimately led to more interviews and job offers (while trait negative affectivity was not found to be associated with job search clarity; Côté, Saks, & Zikic, 2006). A recent meta-analysis showed that the preponderance of evidence indicates that positive emotions are better for myriad facets of decision making (see Lyubomirsky, King, & Diener, 2005). Overall, it may be that positive mood allows people to better process at a level most appropriate to the situation at hand. Thus, when more heuristic, quick answers are needed, people in positive moods can respond with an appropriate decision-making strategy; if the task requires deeper, more analytic processing, people who are in a good mood recognize this necessity and can do so as well (Isen, 2004).

There has been less examination of the influence of discrete emotions on decision making. However, a qualitative study of three British professional symphony orchestras offered an interesting model of how multiple negative emotions such as fear, anxiety, shame, embarrassment, humiliation, anger, and pity influenced decision making (Maitlis & Ozcelik, 2004). The authors effectively used qualitative techniques to capture these phenomena. It would be significantly more difficult to capture the same dynamics quantitatively; this is likely one of the reasons there has been less research of discrete emotions conducted in organizations and particularly the interaction of multiple discrete emotions (Maitlis & Ozcelik, 2004).

Affect and Creativity

A very similar set of competing arguments as were presented in the decision-making literature have been made for the influence of positive versus negative affect states and traits on creativity (see James, Brodersen, & Jacob, 2004 for a review). Positive affect has been proposed to positively influence creativity by leading to a state in which more cognitive material—more variety in the elements that are considered—is available for processing. Then, once those elements are available, positive affect leads to a more complex, flexible thinking, allowing a broader choice of elements to come together and an increased chance that people will in fact put together all of the cognitive elements that have become available (see Isen, 1999; Frederickson, 1998). There is strong support for this theory in laboratory studies of induced positive affect and creativity, with myriad studies showing that when people are in more positive moods, they are more creative (see Isen, 1999 for a review of this literature). This support has recently been extended to studies within organizations. In the first longitudinal study of daily work creativity, a study examined self-reports, other-ratings, and daily diary data from 222 employees in seven companies over the length of an entire project, directly addressing the question of whether negative versus positive affect would enhance creativity (Amabile, Barsade, Mueller, & Staw, 2005). This study found a strong linear relationship between greater positive mood and creativity in organizations. Also, the influence of positive affect on creativity lasted up to two days after the positive mood had been felt. Another recent field study, conducted in the knitwear industry, also found facilitative effects for positive mood on creative performance work by showing that positive but not negative moods mediated the relationship between the support employees get for creative work and their actual creative performance (Madjar, Oldham, & Pratt, 2002). Overall, most research support is for a positive relationship between positive affect and creativity.[6]

Affect and Turnover/Absence

Turnover and absence from work are critical organizational variables, since the cost of replacing employees and lost employee time is extremely high (see Cascio, 1991; Shaw, Delery, Jenkins, & Gupta, 1998). Several studies have linked affect to these variables. In general, studies support the idea that positive affectivity (both state and trait) is associated with reduced absence and intention to turnover, and that negative affectivity (both state and trait) is associated with increased absence, intention to turnover, and actual turnover (George & Jones, 1996; Pelled & Xin, 1999; Thoresen, Kaplan, & Barsky, 2003). Paying attention to the differing effects of positive and negative affect is, however, important. For example, in one study, the experience of positive moods (measured as how employees felt "during the past week") caused employees to be absent less, but the experience of negative moods had no effect on their absence behavior (George, 1989: 321).

Another study on the differential influence of positive and negative affect found an answer to a question that has long puzzled researchers: why does job dissatisfaction result in turnover intentions for some workers, but not for others? Studies find that workers who are dispositionally higher in positive affect are *more* likely to leave their jobs if they are dissatisfied than are people who are characterized by low positive affect (Judge, 1993; Shaw, 1999). One reason behind this relationship is that for low positive affect individuals, the impetus to quit is small because they do not expect a new job to be more satisfying. Conversely, high trait positive affect individuals are more likely to be willing to change their situations when they are dissatisfied. Furthermore, the relationship between job satisfaction and the intent to turnover is strongest among people who feel that their values are not being met at work *and* tend to experience high positive moods. This could be because they feel higher self-efficacy in their skills and ability to find a new job that will meet their values (George & Jones, 1996).

Affect and Prosocial Behavior

Prosocial behaviors are those undertaken to benefit or help another individual, group, or organization (Brief & Motowidlo, 1986). It is well established in the social psychological literature that positive mood is associated with helping behavior in general (Isen, Clark, & Schwartz, 1976; Salovey, Mayer, & Rosenhan, 1991).[7] Research has also been directed at the more specific question of whether an employee's positive mood will enhance prosocial organizational behaviors. Researchers have found that employees who experience positive moods at work are more likely to engage in prosocial behavior both in terms of what their job requires (such as superior customer service) and aspects that go beyond their job description (such as helping peers, or engaging in altruism—George, 1991). In these studies, more proximal positive moods have been shown to have an effect, while dispositional affect appears to have less of an effect. In one study, employees' positive mood predicted prosocial behaviors such as altruism and helping, while dispositional affect (measured as PA) had no effect (George, 1991). That is, unlike turnover or absenteeism, these helping behaviors appear to be more affected by aspects of the immediate situation rather than an individual's relatively stable tendency to experience positive affect.

Prosocial behavior has also been linked to moods expressed by group leaders. A study of sales associates in 37 retail stores examined whether a group leader's positive mood contributed to the extent to which the group engaged in prosocial behavior and reduced the group's voluntary turnover rate. The findings were affirmative (George & Bettenhausen, 1990). It was posited that leaders who experience high levels of positive mood at work would tend to feel "active, excited, enthusiastic, peppy, and strong," and this enthusiasm for the work task would "rub off" on group members, producing an increased incidence of prosocial behaviors (George & Bettenhausen, 1990: 701). The logic behind this emotional connection to prosocial behaviors is that positive mood leaders would be more likely to encourage and notice positive behaviors performed by the group and positively reinforce the group. This study suggests the power of the leader's mood in shaping group members' perceptions of the group *and* their behavior toward each other.

Overall, there is strong support for the idea that positive emotions make prosocial behaviors more likely. Some studies also suggest a corollary: that negative emotions make anti-social behaviors more likely. One study argued that discrete negative emotions produced by environments that are perceived as unjust or stressful increase the frequency of anti-social or deviant organizational behaviors (Spector & Fox, 2002). This approach suggests that in organizational environments (or groups) that encourage positive affective states, employees are more likely to engage in prosocial, supportive, and cooperative behaviors. The opposite is predicted in organizational environments that foster employees' negative emotions (see Frost, 2004).

Affect and Negotiation and Conflict Resolution

Conflict is an inherent part of organizational life and frequently causes strong emotional responses in the conflicting groups and individuals. Negotiation is the primary means by which organization members manage their conflict (Allred, Mallozzi, & Matsui, 1997). After many years of either ignoring emotions or emphasizing practical advice to show neutral emotions and use the proverbial "poker face" (Gibson & Schroeder, 2002), negotiation scholars have begun to recognize the importance of emotions and how emotions influence the negotiation process (see Barry, Fulmer, & Van Kleef, 2004; Thompson, Nadler, & Kim, 1999 for reviews). The results of these studies generally show that positive moods help to resolve conflict (Lyubromirsky et al., 2005). Negotiators in a positive mood (usually induced in experimental settings) tend to be more cooperative and less likely to engage in conflict, and in some cases, come to agreements that enhance joint gains more frequently (Baron, 1990; Barsade, 2002). Positive mood induces individuals to adopt more innovative problem-solving strategies, suggesting that these negotiators will be more likely to come to integrative ("win-win") agreements (Carnevale & Isen, 1986). Positive mood in a negotiator is likely to create more positive feelings in his or her counterpart, and liking between negotiators has been linked to added flexibility in the negotiation when opponents know each other (Druckman & Broome, 1991). Positive mood is also related to persistence and increased confidence levels in negotiators, which have been associated with increased outcomes (Kumar, 1997). Last, a face-to-face negotiation study showed that negotiators can be easily and effectively instructed in how to be emotionally strategic in the emotions they display (an interesting result in its own right). It also showed that positive negotiator emotional display (as compared to neutral or negative displays) led to a desire by negotiating partners to want to continue doing business with the positive negotiator. The positive negotiator was also better able to close a deal in a distributive (win-lose) setting, even through increased concessions from the other party (Kopelman, Rosette, & Thompson, 2006).

Currently, the findings for feeling and displaying negative emotions in a negotiation are typically the inverse of the findings regarding the feeling and display of positive moods and emotions. For example, negotiators in a generally negative mood were more competitive and received poorer outcomes (Forgas, 1998). However, research examining negative moods in conflict management and negotiation are also more likely to examine discrete emotions, which can offer more nuanced insights. For example, one study examining the discrete emotions of anger and compassion found that negotiators who felt high anger and low compassion for their counterpart achieved fewer joint gains in their negotiations (Allred et al., 1997). The study also found that those negotiators' discrete emotions of anger and compassion influenced their negotiations more than their generalized positive or negative moods did. There have also been results showing positive effects of anger, finding that a negotiator facing an angry counterpart is more likely to concede than a negotiator facing a happy counterpart. However, these effects occurred under high time pressure and when the negotiator who faced the angry counterpart had lower power, and in a computer-mediated setting (Van Kleef, De Dreu, & Manstead, 2004). Computer-mediated settings are clearly important to organizational life (e.g., in the use of e-mail), but it is critical to see how the effects of anger operate in face-to-face negotiations as well.

Last, looking at emotional intelligence skills, emotional perception has been shown to influence individual negotiator outcomes in a variety of sometimes contradictory ways. More consistently, they have been shown to increase the integrative outcomes of negotiating dyads (Elfenbein et al., in press; Foo, Elfenbein, Tan, & Aik, 2004). Emotion understanding skill was shown to positively influence how one's negotiation partner felt about his/her negotiation outcome, above and beyond the amount of money that negotiation partner received and his/her trait positive affect (Mueller & Curhan, in press).

Collective Affect and Team Behavior

The role of affect has long been an implicit factor in studies of groups, for example, in studies of group cohesiveness (Ashforth & Humphrey, 1995) and the progression of group development (Tuckman, 1965; Wheelan, 1994). However, there are few studies examining how affect operates as an *explicit* factor within team development, behavior, and outcomes. This is surprising given that in the process of getting work accomplished, groups offer a prime place for intense interactions involving individuals with their own emotional histories, emotional agendas, and affective personalities confronting positive and negative group events. Of the studies that have been conducted, however, there is very promising evidence for the influence of emotion on group outcomes.

One way to conceptualize group emotion and its outcomes is a "bottom-up" approach where group emotion is defined by the affective composition of the various affective attributes of the group's members (Barsade & Gibson, 1998). For example, a group's affective tone, the "consistent or homogenous affective reactions within a group" measured by the group's mean level of positive affect, was found in retail sales groups to be positively related to higher levels of customer service and lower absenteeism (George, 1995).

A different way of looking at group emotion is through affective diversity, or the degree of difference in affective traits that exists between group members. Affective diversity has been shown to influence group outcomes. In a sample of 239 top managers in 62 U.S. corporations, the greater the degree of trait affective diversity on the senior management team, the greater the conflict in the team, the less cooperation and the poorer the firm financial performance (Barsade, Ward, Turner, & Sonnenfeld, 2000). There are a few studies that examined the effect of discrete emotions in groups, such as group envy, which was found to be directly associated with decreased group performance. It was also associated with more absenteeism, less group satisfaction, and poorer group performance via the mechanisms of increased social loafing, decreased cohesion, and decreased feelings of group potency (Duffy & Shaw, 2000).

There is also a "top-down" approach in which collectively held norms—implicit or explicit—about appropriate emotions to express or hold in the group and/or organization, shape the type of emotions that are allowed and expressed in the group context (see Barsade & Gibson, 1998; Kelly & Barsade, 2001, for reviews). There has been much research examining emotion norms within an emotional labor perspective (e.g., see reviews by Grandey, 2000; Rafaeli & Sutton, 1989), but significantly less examining the influence of "affective culture." Affective culture can be thought of as normative systems which include display rules about expressed emotions at the collective level, prescribing the appropriateness or inappropriateness of particular emotional expressions in the organization (Barsade, Brief, & Spataro, 2003; Barsade & O'Neill, 2004). Overall, while we would predict that the influence of affective culture on group and individual dynamics would be a powerful one, of the many areas we have examined showing the influence of collective affect on workplace outcomes, this is currently one of the least studied and most open for development.

Affect and Leadership

We conclude with a critical—but complex—process within organizations, the process of leadership. It has become increasingly apparent that emotions permeate the leadership process, both in terms of the emotions leaders feel and express, and the emotions followers feel toward their leaders (see George, 2000). Leaders must substantially regulate their own emotions. For example, they often must express a positive or upbeat mood about the future, while suppressing expressions of anxiety or sadness that might de-motivate followers. They must also manage the emotions of others, for example, by understanding and empathizing with employees' emotions about change so that change efforts will be accepted (Huy, 2002). While the notion of emotions as critical to the leadership process is not new (see, for example, Ashforth & Humphrey, 1995; Wasielewski, 1985), recent advances in emotions research and emotional intelligence in particular have sparked an increase in the study of leadership and emotion.

In terms of positive affectivity and leadership, the work cited above on prosocial behavior, creativity, and decision making suggest that PA should contribute to leader effectiveness. There is some empirical support for this connection. In a simulated managerial setting, high trait positive affect MBA students were rated by their peers and outside observers as being better leaders (Staw & Barsade, 1993). Trait positive affectivity was related to leader-follower liking and perceived similarity in a simulated interview setting (Fox & Spector, 2000), and in a lab study, leaders in positive versus negative moods had groups who performed better in their task, expending less unnecessary effort and more coordination in completing the task (Sy, Côté, & Saavedra, 2005). Testing this within organizations, in a customer service field setting, leaders' positive moods were found to be associated with higher performance of the leader's group (George, 1995).

Transformational leadership is a setting in which the importance of emotions in leadership effectiveness has been specifically emphasized (Ashkanasy & Tse, 2000).[8] For example, a recent study examining the effects of emotional intelligence and personality traits on transformational leadership behavior found that leaders with high trait positive affectivity were more likely to be rated as engaging in transformational leadership behaviors. As might be expected, trait PA was not a significant predictor of transactional or contingent reward behavior (Rubin, Munz, & Bommer, 2005). This study also found an intriguing interaction: the researchers focused on ability to read others' emotions (using the DANVA test) as a particularly important dimension of emotional intelligence that should relate to transformational leadership behavior. But as they predicted—and found—the leadership personality trait of extraversion (being outgoing and deriving energy from other people) moderated this relationship. Specifically, while extraversion alone did not have a direct effect on transformational leadership behavior, extraversion combined with emotion recognition skills did have an effect. Thus, high extraversion provided a clear benefit to leaders who *also* possess the ability to accurately recognize emotion. Conversely, leaders who "possessed low extraversion and high emotion recognition abilities did not seem to reap the benefits of their emotion recognition ability" (Rubin, Munz, & Bommer, 2005: 854). These findings point to an important characteristic of emotional intelligence that we referred to earlier: it does not operate separately, but rather in conjunction with other abilities and personality traits.

While leadership researchers have emphasized the critical place of followers in determining leadership style and shaping leadership behavior, much less work has focused on *followers'* emotions in response to leadership. Several researchers emphasize that leader effectiveness is at least partially defined by the satisfaction and emotional liking of followers (Ashforth & Humphrey, 1995; Conger & Kanungo, 1987; Dasborough & Ashkanasy, 2002). There is also evidence that followers are influenced by leaders' displays of emotions. As noted above, leaders' expressions of positive emotions are thought to arouse positive emotions in others through the mechanism of emotional contagion, where the positive, upbeat emotions of the leader are emulated by followers, resulting in positive outcomes (George & Bettenhausen, 1990; Hatfield et al., 1994).

Laboratory studies have also examined the effects of leader displays of negative emotions and found more complex results. Following a contagion argument, leader displays of negative emotions could cause followers to similarly feel and display negative emotions, potentially hindering morale and motivation. Leader expressions of negative emotions such as sadness and anger, for example, have been shown to influence how employees view the leader, reducing their perceptions of leader effectiveness (Lewis, 2000). However, recent studies also show that a leader expressing anger may increase perceptions of the leader's power, while a leader expressing sadness may decrease those perceptions (Tiedens, 2001). Displays of negative emotion by the leader may also focus followers' attention on situations that require attention. For example, a leader's anger about an issue of discrimination or fairness may direct resources to solving the problem (George, 2000).

Leadership and emotion studies are also just beginning to examine the more detailed processes and interactions involved in a leaders' management of their teams' emotional responses (e.g., Huy, 2002). A recent model examines how leaders can "set the emotional tone" of a group and use emotional skills to focus group members on goals. In order to do this, the emergent leader of a group must first empathize and identify the collective emotional state of a group and also understand the aspects of the situation that are causing this emotional state. The leader must then craft a response to the situation that takes into account the emotional tone, and communicates that response effectively (Pescosolido, 2002).

Overall, work in emotions and leadership is emerging as a very exciting area that will enhance our knowledge of what leadership means and how leaders can be effective, but it is also an area in which work needs to be done to sharpen constructs more effectively so that our understanding of the intersection of these two domains can be better understood.

Conclusions

This article offers a review of "what we know" about emotions in organizations at the present time. The review, albeit not exhaustive, indicates that the study of affect in organizations is a vibrant and growing area. It is characterized by a wide breadth of approaches, developing measures, and refinement of variables and outcomes. Organization researchers are increasingly recognizing that affect is inherent to the human experience, and thus inherent to any situation in which humans interact with each other and their environment, including at work. We draw the following conclusions from this wide range of studies.

Affect Influences Critical Organizational Variables

This article has identified a range of ways that affect is critical to explaining outcomes that concern managers in organizations. We have outlined effects on performance, decision making, turnover, prosocial behavior, negotiation and conflict resolution behavior, group dynamics, and leadership. These are discrete categories that help us to group variables as scientific studies have conceived them, but it is our view that affect permeates virtually every aspect of organizational life, even those areas that have been traditionally thought of as the exclusive province of cognitive behavior, such as decision making and task performance. The evidence is overwhelming that experiencing and expressing positive emotions and moods tends to enhance performance at individual, group, and organizational levels. As a recent meta-analysis has shown, positive affect is fundamentally linked with an individual's "active involvement with goal pursuits and with the environment" (Lyubomirsky et al., 2005: 804). This desire to develop new goals and engage with them is linked with confidence, optimism, self-efficacy, likability, activity, energy, flexibility, and coping with challenges and stress, among other abilities and behaviors. The evidence is compelling that feeling and expressing positive affect is critical to success in organizations and in life.

It is particularly ironic that while positive affect has been found to show greater influence on workplace outcomes, it has been studied significantly less than negative affect (Lyubomirsky et al., 2005; Thoresen et al., 2003). A rationale for why positive affect has been found to have a relatively stronger effect on these outcomes could be that positive affect has been shown to consistently be related more strongly than negative affect to socially related processes (McIntyre, Watson, Clark, & Cross, 1991; Watson, Clark, McIntyre, & Hamaker, 1992), which are particularly critical to effective organizational interactions. Negative affect, on the other hand, is more strongly related to non-social intrapsychic outcomes, such as stress and burnout (Watson et al., 1988). Thus both sets of emotions serve a role in important outcomes, but in different arenas.

The Influence of Negative Affect is Complex

Conclusions about the meaning and influence of negative affect on organizational life are far more complex. The history of reactions to negative employee affect has tended to be simplistic: managers ought to avoid negative affect in their employees and suppress negative affect in themselves (see Stearns & Stearns, 1986). Given the power of positive affect identified above, this approach is understandable. However, current research has helped us to appreciate more of the complexity of negative affective responses, allowing us to be more nuanced in our approach. First, we must acknowledge that the evidence for the deleterious effects of individual negative affect is substantial, particularly since they tend to be strongly felt by employees (Miner, Glomb, & Hulin, 2005). Negative affective expressions can poison organizational cultures (Aquino, Douglas, & Martinko, 2004), negatively influence perceptions of leaders (Lewis, 2000), and potentially lead to aggression or violence (Fox & Spector, 1999). However, negative emotions (especially anger) may also draw our attention to situations of unfairness and injustice (George, 2000), enhance perceptions of power (Tiedens, 2001), and enhance negotiating outcomes (Van Kleef, De Dreu, & Manstead, 2004). Research and practice should be directed to the important questions of, "Under what conditions can negative affective responses lead to positive organizational outcomes?" To do so, it would be helpful for emotion scholars to focus on examining the various discrete negative emotions, as the outcomes that will come from angry versus anxious versus sad employees, for example, are likely going to be very different.

Constructs and Methods are Advancing

No longer is there a "one size fits all" way to measure work-related affect, such as using general attitudinal measures like job satisfaction. Drawing from and contributing to the robust literature of affect in psychology, our understanding of affect has been both expanded and refined via the study of discrete emotions, the affective circumplex, emotional labor, emotional contagion, and emotional intelligence. Methods are becoming more varied and sophisticated to match the variety and complexity of the phenomena, so that in addition to surveys, methods include controlled mood inductions, diary studies, daily experience sampling research, coding of behavior in-situ and video coding.

Future Directions

While much current work is being directed to refining the variables and relationships we have examined above, we also anticipate new approaches to studying affect. First, extant studies of affect assume that most important affective experiences arise through face-to-face interactions, and that most of emotional communication occurs through facial, or at least auditory communication, with very little occurring through text (Mehrabian, 1972). However, the impact of an entirely text-based technology on emotions must be explored. Significant communication in organizations now takes place through synchronous (e.g., instant messaging) or asynchronous (e.g., e-mail) text-based means, which removes critical nonverbal sources of emotion and tone. How can emotions be best conveyed via these media? What is the effect of conveying emotionally charged messages via text, when these messages are more likely to be misconstrued? How must we re-think emotional contagion and other social processes in an organizational world in which many meetings take place online? Indeed, a recent study examining e-mail versus face-to-face communication suggests that individuals tend to be overconfident in their ability to accurately convey the emotions they wish via e-mail, particularly when they are trying to be sarcastic or humorous (Kruger, Epley, Parker, & Ng, 2005). The use of emoticons (:-)) may be somewhat helpful in this regard, but are also open to substantial misinterpretation or may be perceived as unprofessional in the business context. Video conferencing, also increasing in its use, has more cues, but is also not yet the same as interacting face to face, particularly in group situations. Given that these technologies continue to grow as a primary means of communication within the business world, it is crucial that we understand how the interpretation and communication of affect occurs in these contexts.

Second, research on affect has primarily focused on *conscious* feelings and expressions, those moods and emotions we are aware of and can possibly trace to their source and are thus amenable to regulation. However, there is also substantial developing research on affective processes existing at a level *below* consciousness: emotions existing at the subconscious or unconscious level that nonetheless have an impact on our conscious feelings and behavior. Subconscious affective processes include the automatic mimicry of others' emotions characterizing emotional contagion, as we have discussed earlier (Hatfield, Cacioppo, & Rapson, 1994), and automatic emotion regulation (Mauss, Evers, Wilhelm, & Gross, 2006). These processes also include our "emotional unconscious," which can be explained as an individual being consciously aware of his or her current emotional state, but not being aware of the source of that state, which may come from a current or past experience (Kihlstrom, 1999). That is, rather than being consciously driven, individuals' current emotions may be reflections of their "implicit memory" of past events, which may create moods that are out of our awareness (e.g., Singer & Salovey, 1988) and implicit perceptions and emotions (see Kihlstrom, 1999, for a review).

Much of this future work will likely need to consider that people do not walk into organizations as *tabula rasa*, but rather have life and work experiences that may shape current behavior—either consciously or unconsciously. People may not always be aware of this, as is exemplified in the phenomenon of transference, where "representations of significant others, stored in memory, are activated and used in new social encounters on the basis of a new person's resemblance to a given significant other" (Berk & Andersen, 2000: 546; also known as the "You vaguely remind me of that kid in elementary school who I hated, and I don't like you much either" phenomenon—Kelly & Barsade, 2001: 109). Such inquiry may well spark new research on long-ignored constructs such as transference, ego defensive routines, and attachment relationships and their effect on individuals' behaviors in organizations. The benefit now is our ability to conduct rigorous empirical research to better help us understand how these phenomena occur (Glassman & Andersen, 1999; Westen & Gabbard, 2002).

Last, the research findings we cite for negotiation and social influence suggest that affect can be used strategically: individuals can "put on" particular emotional expressions in order to influence others (Gibson & Schroeder, 2002; Kopelman et al., 2006). However, the emotion labor literature has also emphasized that there is a cost to masking authentic emotions— by acting like we're feeling something we actually aren't, we may experience emotional dissonance and lose touch with our authentic selves (see Hochschild, 1983). This research suggests that employees would be better off if they could engage in *less* emotion regulation and that employees need organizations where they can express themselves more authentically (Erickson & Wharton, 1997). There is a paradox, however, in the assumption that authenticity is the desired state for employees. We know that authenticity in our feeling and expression of affect is desirable; however, we also know that regulating emotions is often essential: in order for managers to be encouraging, inspiring, and motivating to their employees (despite having a bad day, for example) they *must* engage in regulation in order to be effective. Part of the job is to be strategic with our emotions; indeed, emotional regulation of self and others is an important part of emotional intelligence construct (Mayer & Salovey, 1997). The question is, at what point do individuals "over-regulate" their emotions? What is the point at which regulated emotion is too far removed from authenticity? Current studies of the differing antecedents of surface and deep acting (e.g., Grandey, 2000) may hold a clue to these questions, but more work remains. Thus, the paradox we need to explore is that authenticity may be desirable, but regulation is essential to meeting personal and organizational goals.

To that end, we would like to see researchers explore to what degree and under what conditions individuals in organizations can and should express their authentic emotions, and how an organization's affective culture and the national culture in which it is embedded may influence these processes. We also urge researchers to explore the ethical implications of being inauthentic as part of the work role. Is emotional labor, which involves regulating and changing emotions to fit work requirements, something that organizations should be able to expect from their employees as a necessary part of the job? We are inclined to think that this is acceptable as long as employees know what they have signed up for, and that this emotional labor has logical performance outcomes favorable to the company (see Rafaeli & Sutton, 1989), but could see opposing views to this and encourage a thorough discussion of this issue within the field.

Why does affect matter in organizations? The state of the literature shows that affect matters because employees are not isolated "emotional islands." Rather, they bring all of themselves to work, including their traits, moods, and emotions, and their affective experiences and expressions influence others. Thus, an understanding of how these affective experiences and expressions operate and influence organizational outcomes is an essential piece in understanding how work is done and how to do it better.

Notes

1 Order of authorship is alphabetical; both authors contributed equally. We would like to thank Peter Cappelli, Yochi Cohen Charash, Chia-Jung Tsay, Marina Milonova, Amanda O'Neill and our anonymous reviewers for their help and insights.
2 These affective states and traits differ from *sentiments* or even *attitudes* (e.g., job satisfaction) in that the latter reflect an evaluation of a particular object, and whether that object is evaluated as something that is liked or disliked (Kelly & Barsade, 2001; Weiss, 2002).
3 This includes researchers who base their self-report assessments on the four-factor EI model, and researchers who expanded the construct to include components outside that model (see Mayer, Salovey, & Caruso, 2000 for a more detailed discussion of these differences).
4 The Big Five model of personality traits measures the dimensions of extraversion, conscientiousness, agreeableness, emotional stability (also known as neuroticism) and openness to experience in individuals (McCrae & Costa, 1987). These factors have emerged in a wide variety of studies of personality dimensions and are widely accepted by personality psychologists (Hogan, Hogan, & Roberts, 1996), and have been found to be relevant to a variety of organizational outcomes (Barrick & Mount, 1991).
5 Recent meta-analyses indicate that job satisfaction and performance are correlated in the range of .17 (Iaffaldano & Muchinsky, 1985) to .30 (Judge et al., 2001). A problem with using an attitudinal measure such as job satisfaction as a proxy for happiness, however, is that much of job satisfaction also involves a cognitive component—how employees think or feel *about* work, whether they like it or not, which is different from the experience of affect *at work* (Brief & Weiss, 2002; George, 1989), which is how an employee actually feels while on the job and their emotional approach to life and work.

6 While most evidence points to a strong positive relationship between positive affect and creativity, it is important to note that there have been some indications that the influence of negative affect on creativity should at least be considered. For example, there is some support for the influence of negative emotions on creativity from studies of affective illness (e.g., depression and manic-depression; Jamison, 1993; see Feist, 1999 for a review). There is also organizational evidence from a field study based on the "mood-as-input" model. In this cross-sectional study in a large manufacturing organization, there was a positive relationship between negative affect and creativity when both recognition and rewards for creativity, and clarity of feelings (ability to recognize one's own feelings) are high (George & Zhou, 2002).

7 However, under the rubric of "motivated cognitive processing theory" which indicates that people want to maintain their positive moods and on average avoid situations which would reduce their positive emotions (Clark & Isen, 1982; Forgas, 1991), there is evidence that people in positive moods are more prone to help if helping does not negatively influence their positive mood (Isen & Simmonds, 1978; Forest et al., 1979). But see Parrott (1993) for an additional perspective.

8 Transformational leadership is characterized by a leader's ability to articulate a shared vision of the future, intellectually stimulate employees, motivate colleagues and followers to look beyond their own interests and towards group interests, and provide individual consideration and support for followers (Bass, 1998; Lowe, Kroeck, & Sivasubramaniam, 1996). Transformational leadership has been contrasted with transactional leadership, which is based on motivating followers by emphasizing reward and exchange relationships.

References

Alloy, L.B., & Abramson, L.Y. (1988). Depressive realism: Four theoretical perspectives. In L.B. Alloy (Ed.), *Cognitive process in depression* (pp. 223–265). New York: Guilford.

Allred, K.G., Mallozzi, J.S., & Matsui, F. (1997). The influence of anger and compassion on negotiation performance. *Organizational Behavior and Human Decision Processes*, 70(3), 175–187.

Amabile, T.M., Barsade, S.G., Mueller, J.S., & Staw, B.M. (2005). Affect and creativity at work. *Administrative Science Quarterly*, 50(3), 367–403.

Aquino, K., Douglas, S., & Martinko, M.J. (2004). Overt anger in response to victimization: Attributional style and organizational norms as moderators. *Journal of Occupational Health Psychology*, 9, 152–164.

Ashforth, B.E., & Humphrey, R.H. (1995). Emotion in the workplace: A reappraisal. *Human Relations*, 48(2), 97–125.

Ashkanasy, N.M., & Tse, B. (2000). Transformational leadership as management of emotion: A conceptual review. In N. Ashkanasy, C. Härtel, & W. Wilfred (Eds.), *Emotions in the workplace: Research, theory, and practice* (pp. 221–235). US: Quorum Books/Greenwood Publishing Group, Inc.

Barger, P., & Grandey, A. (2006). "Service with a smile" and encounter satisfaction: Emotional contagion and appraisal mechanisms. *Academy of Management Journal*, 49(6), 1229–1238.

Baron, R.A. (1990). Environmentally induced positive affect: Its impact on self-efficacy, task performance, negotiation, and conflict. *Journal of Applied Social Psychology*, 20(5, Pt 2), 368–384.

Barrick, M.R., & Mount, M.K. (1991). The Big Five personality dimensions and job performance: A meta-analysis. *Personality Psychology*, 44, 1–26.

Barry, B., Fulmer, I.S., & Van Kleef, G. (2004). I laughed, I cried, I settled: The role of emotion in negotiation. In M.J. Gelfand and J.M. Brett (Eds.), *The handbook of negotiation and culture: Theoretical advances and cross-cultural perspectives* (pp. 71–94). Palo Alto, CA: Stanford University Press.

Barsade, S.G. (2002). The ripple effect: Emotional contagion and its influence on group behavior. *Administrative Science Quarterly*, 47(4), 644–675.

Barsade, S., Brief, A., & Spataro, S. (2003). The affective revolution in organizational behavior: The emergence of a paradigm. In J. Greenberg (Ed.), *Organizational behavior: The state of the science* (pp. 3–52). London: Lawrence Erlbaum Associates, Publishers.

Barsade, S.G., & Gibson, D.E. (1998). Group emotion: A view from top and bottom. In D. Gruenfeld (Ed.), *Composition* (pp. 81–102). US: Elsevier Science/JAI Press.

Barsade, S.G., & O'Neill O.A. (2004). Affective Organizational Culture. Academy of Management Presentation. New Orleans, LA.

Barsade, S.G., Ward, A.J., Turner, J.D.F., & Sonnenfeld, J.A. (2000). To your heart's content: A model of affective diversity in top management teams. *Administrative Science Quarterly*, 45(4), 802–836.

Bartel, C., & Saavedra, R. (2000). The collective construction of work group moods. *Administrative Science Quarterly*, 45(2), 197–231.

Bass, B.M. (1998). *Transformational leadership: Industrial, military, and educational impact.* Mahwah, NJ: Lawrence Erlbaum Associates, Publishers.

Berk, M.S., & Andersen, S.M. (2000). The impact of past relationships on interpersonal behavior: Behavioral confirmation in the social-cognitive process of transference. *Journal of Personality and Social Psychology*, 79, 546–562.

Brackett, M.A., Mayer, J.D., & Warner, R.M. (2004). Emotional intelligence and its relation to every-day behavior. *Personality and Individual Differences*, 36(6), 1387–1402.

Brackett, M.A., Rivers, S.E., Shiffman, S., Lerner, N., & Salovey, P. (2006). Relating emotional abilities to social functioning: A comparison of self-report and performance measures of emotional intelligence. *Journal of Personality and Social Psychology*, 91, 780–795.

Brief, A.P., & Motowidlo, S.J. (1986). Prosocial organizational behaviors. *Academy of Management Review*, 11(4), 710–725.

Brief, A.P., & Weiss, H.M. (2002). Organizational behavior: Affect in the workplace. *Annual Review of Psychology*, 53(1), 279–307.

Carnevale, P.J., & Isen, A.M. (1986). The influence of positive affect and visual access on the discovery of integrative solutions in bilateral negotiation. *Organizational Behavior and Human Decision Processes*, 37(1), 1–13.

Cascio, W.F. (1991). *Applied psychology to human resource management* (5th ed.). Upper Saddle River, NJ: Prentice-Hall.

Clark, M.S., & Isen, A.M. (1982). Towards understanding the relationship between feeling states and social behavior. In Albert H. Hastorf and Alice M. Isen (Eds.), *Cognitive social psychology* (pp. 73–108). New York: Elsevier-North Holland.

Conger, J.A., & Kanungo, R.N. (1987). Toward a behavioral theory of charismatic leadership in organizational settings. *Academy of Management Review*, 12(4), 637–647.

Conte, J.M. (2005). A review and critique of emotional intelligence measures. *Journal of Organizational Behavior*, 26(4), 433–440.

Côté, S. (2005). A social interaction model of the effects of emotion regulation on work strain. *Academy of Management Review*, 30(3), 509–530.

Côté, S., & Miners, C.T.H. (2006). Emotional intelligence, cognitive intelligence, and job performance. *Administrative Science Quarterly*, 51, 1–28.

Côté, S., Saks, A.M., & Zikic, J. (2006). Trait affect and job search outcomes. *Journal of Vocational Behavior*, 68(2), 233–252.

Cropanzano, R., & Wright, T.A. (2001). When a "happy" worker is really a "productive" worker: A review and further refinement of the happy-productive worker thesis. *Consulting Psychology Journal: Practice and Research*, 53(3), 182–199.

Dasborough, M.T., & Ashkanasy, N.M. (2002). Emotion and attribution of intentionality in leader-member relationships. *Leadership Quarterly*, 13(5), 615–634.

Daus, C.S., & Ashkanasy, N.M. (2005). The case for the ability-based model of emotional intelligence in organizational behavior. *Journal of Organizational Behavior*, 26, 453–466.

Day, A.L., & Carroll, S.A. (2004). Using an ability-based measure of emotional intelligence to predict individual performance, group performance, and group citizenship behaviours. *Personality and Individual Differences*, 36, 1443–1458.

Doherty, R.W. (1997). The emotional contagion scale: A measure of individual differences. *Journal of Nonverbal Behavior*, 21, 131–154.

Druckman, D., & Broome, B.J. (1991). Value differences and conflict resolution: Familiarity or liking? *Journal of Conflict Resolution*, 35(4), 571–593.

Duffy, M.K., & Shaw, J.D. (2000). The Salieri syndrome: Consequences of envy in groups. *Small Group Research*, 31(1), 3–23.

Ekman, P. (1973). Cross-culture studies of facial expression. In P. Ekman (Ed.), *Darwin and facial expression: A century of research in review* (pp. 169–222). New York: Academic Press.

Ekman, P. (1992). An argument for basic emotions. *Cognition & Emotion*, 6(3–4), 169–200.

Elfenbein, H.A., Foo, M.D., White J., & Tan, H.H. (in press). Reading your counterpart: The benefit of emotion recognition accuracy for effectiveness in negotiation. *Journal of Nonverbal Behavior*.

Elfenbein, H.A., & Ambady, N. (2002). Predicting workplace outcomes from the ability to eavesdrop on feelings. *Journal of Applied Psychology*, 87(5), 963–971.

Erickson, R.J., & Wharton, A.S. (1997). Inauthenticity and depression: Assessing the consequences of interactive service work. *Work and Occupations*, 24(2), 188–213.

Estrada, C.A., Isen, A.M., & Young, M.J. (1997). Positive affect facilitates integration of information and decreases anchoring in reasoning among physicians. *Organizational Behavior and Human Decision Processes*, 72(1), 117–135.

Feist, G.J. (1999). The influence of personality on artistic and scientific creativity. In R. Sternberg (Ed.), *Handbook of creativity* (pp. 273–296). New York, NY: Cambridge University Press.

Feldman Barrett, L., & Russell, J.A. (1998). Independence and bipolarity in the structure of current affect. *Journal of Personality and Social Psychology*, 74(4), 967–984.

Feyerherm, A.E., & Rice, C.L. (2002). Emotional intelligence and team performance: The good, the bad and the ugly. *International Journal of Organizational Analysis*, 10, 343–362.

Foo, M.D., Elfenbein, H.A., Tan, H.H., & Aik, V.C. (2004). Emotional intelligence and negotiation: The tension between creating and claiming value. *International Journal of Conflict Management*, 15, 411–429.

Forest, D., Clark, M.S., Mills, J., & Isen, A.M. (1979). Helping as a function of feeling state and nature of the helping behavior. *Motivation & Emotion*, 3, 161–169.

Forgas, J.P. (1998). On feeling good and getting your way: Mood effects on negotiator cognition and bargaining strategies. *Journal of Personality and Social Psychology*, 74, 565–577.

Forgas, J.P. (1991). Affect and person perception. In Joseph P. Forgas (Ed.), *Emotion and social judgments* (pp. 263–290). Oxford: Pergamon.

Fox, S., & Spector, P.E. (2000). Relationship of emotional intelligence, practical intelligence, general intelligence, and trait affectivity with interview outcomes: It's not all just "g." *Journal of Organizational Behavior*, 21(2), 203–220.

Fox, S., & Spector, P.E. (1999). A model of work frustration-aggression. *Journal of Organizational Behavior*, 20(6), 915–931.

Frederickson, B.L. (1998). What good are positive emotions? *Review of General Psychology*, 2, 300–319.

Frijda, N.H. (1986). *The emotions*. Cambridge, UK: Cambridge University Press.

Frost, P.J. (2004). Handling toxic emotions: New challenges for leaders and their organization. *Organizational Dynamics*, 33(2), 111–127.

George, J.M. (1989). Mood and absence. *Journal of Applied Psychology*, 74(2), 317–324.

George, J.M. (1991). State or trait: Effects of positive mood on prosocial behaviors at work. *Journal of Applied Psychology*, 76(2), 299–307.

George, J.M. (1995). Leader positive mood and group performance: The case of customer service. *Journal of Applied Social Psychology*, 25(9), 778–794.

George, J.M. (2000). Emotions and leadership: The role of emotional intelligence. *Human Relations*, 53(8), 1027–1055.

George, J.M., & Bettenhausen, K. (1990). Understanding prosocial behavior, sales performance, and turnover: A group-level analysis in a service context. *Journal of Applied Psychology*, 75(6), 698–709.

George, J.M., & Jones, G.R. (1996). The experience of work and turnover intentions: Interactive effects of value attainment, job satisfaction, and positive mood. *Journal of Applied Psychology*, 81(3), 318–325.

George, J.M., & Zhou, J. (2002). Understanding when bad moods foster creativity and good ones don't: The role of context and clarity of feelings. *Journal of Applied Psychology*, 87(4), 687–697.

Gibson, D.E., & Schroeder, S. (2002). Grinning, frowning, and emotionless: Agent perceptions of power and their effect on felt and displayed emotions in influence attempts. In N. Ashkanasy, C. Hartel, and W. Zerbe (Eds.), *Managing emotions in the workplace* (pp. 184–211). Armonk, NY: M.E. Sharpe.

Glassman, N.S., & Andersen, S.M. (1999). Activating transference without consciousness: Using significant-other representations to go beyond what is subliminally given. *Journal of Personality and Social Psychology*, 77, 1146–1162.

Gohm, C.L., Corser, G.C., & Dalsky, D.J. (2005). Emotional intelligence under stress: Useful, unnecessary, or irrelevant? *Personality and Individual Differences*, 39, 1017–1028.

Grandey, A.A. (2000). Emotional regulation in the workplace: A new way to conceptualize emotional labor. *Journal of Occupational Health Psychology*, 5(1), 95–110.

Grandey, A.A. (2003). When "the show must go on": Surface acting and deep acting as determinants of emotional exhaustion and peer-rated service delivery. *Academy of Management Journal*, 46(1), 86–96.

Gross, J.J. (1998a). The emerging field of emotion regulation: An integrative review. *Review of General Psychology*, 2(3), 271–299.

Gross, J.J. (1998b). Antecedent and response-focused emotion regulation: Divergent consequences for experience, expression, and physiology. *Journal of Personality and Social Psychology*, 74(1), 224–237.

Hatfield, E., Cacioppo, J., & Rapson, R. (1994). *Emotional contagion*. New York: Cambridge University Press.

Hochschild, A. (1983). *The managed heart: Commercialization of human feeling*. Berkeley: University of California Press.

Hogan, R., Hogan, J., & Roberts, B.W. (1996). Personality measurement and employment decisions. *American Psychologist*, 51(5), 469–477.

Huy, Q.N. (2002). Emotional balancing of organizational continuity and radical change: The contribution of middle managers. *Administrative Science Quarterly*, 47(1), 31–69.

Iaffaldano, M.T., & Muchinsky, P.M. (1985). Job satisfaction and job performance: A meta-analysis. *Psychological Bulletin*, 97(2), 251–273.

Ilies, R., Wagner, D.T., & Morgeson, F.P. In press. Explaining affective linkages in teams: Individual differences in susceptibility to contagion and individualism/collectivism. *Journal of Applied Psychology*.

Isen, A. (1999). On the relationship between affect and creative problem solving. In S.W. Russ (Ed.), *Affect, creative experience and psychological adjustment* (pp. 3–18). Philadelphia: Brunner/Mazel.

Isen, A.M. (2001). An influence of positive affect on decision making in complex situations: Theoretical issues with practical implications. *Journal of Consumer Psychology*, 11(2), 75–85.

Isen, A.M. (2004). Some perspectives on positive feelings and emotions: Positive affect facilitates thinking and problem solving. In A.S.R. Manstead, N. Frijda, & A. Fischer (Eds.), *Feelings and emotions: The Amsterdam symposium* (pp. 263–281). Cambridge, UK: Cambridge University Press.

Isen, A.M., Clark, M., & Schwartz, M.F. (1976). Duration of the effect of good mood on helping: "Footprints on the sands of time." *Journal of Personality and Social Psychology*, 34, 385–393.

Isen, A.M., & Labroo, A.A. (2003). Some ways in which positive affect facilitates decision making and judgment. In S.L. Schneider, & J. Shanteau (Eds.), *Emerging perspectives on judgment and decision research. Cambridge series on judgment and decision making* (pp. 365–393). New York, NY: Cambridge University Press.

Isen, A.M., & Simmonds, S.F. (1978). The effect of feeling good on a helping task that is incompatible with good mood. *Social Psychology*, 41, 346–349.

James, K., Brodersen, M., & Jacob, E. (2004). Workplace affect and workplace creativity: A review and preliminary model. *Human Performance*, 17(2), 169–194.

Jamison, K.R. (1993). Touched with fire: Manic-depressive illness and the artistic temperament. New York: The Free Press.

Judge, T.A. (1993). Does affective disposition moderate the relationship between job satisfaction and voluntary turnover? *Journal of Applied Psychology*, 78(3), 395–401.

Judge, T.A., Thoresen, C.J., Bono, J.E., & Patton, G.K. (2001). The job satisfaction–job performance relationship: A qualitative and quantitative review. *Psychological Bulletin*, 127(3), 376–407.

Kelly, J., & Barsade, S. (2001). Mood and emotions in small groups and work teams. *Organizational Behavior and Human Decision Processes*, 86(1), 99–130.

Keltner, D., & Haidt, J. (1999). Social functions of emotions at four levels of analysis. *Cognition & Emotion*, 13(5), 505–521.

Kihlstrom, J.F. (1999). The psychological unconscious. In L.A. Pervin & O.P. John (Eds.), *Handbook of personality: Theory and research* (2nd ed., pp. 424–442). New York: Guilford.

Kopelman, S., Rosette, A.S., & Thompson, L. (2006). The three faces of Eve: Strategic displays of positive, negative, and neutral emotions in negotiations. *Organizational Behavior and Human Decision Processes*, 99(1), 81–101.

Kring, A.M., Smith, D.A., & Neale, J.M. (1994). Individual differences in dispositional expressiveness: Development and validation of the Emotional Expressivity Scale. *Journal of Personality and Social Psychology*, 66(5), 934–949.

Kruger, J., Epley, N., Parker, J., & Ng, Z. (2005). Egocentrism over e-mail: Can we communicate as well as we think? *Journal of Personality and Social Psychology*, 89(6), 925–936.

Kumar, R. (1997). The role of affect in negotiations: An integrative overview. *Journal of Applied Behavioral Science*, 33(1), 84–100.

Lam, L.T., & Kirby, S.L. (2002). Is emotional intelligence an advantage? An exploration of the impact of emotional and general intelligence on individual performance. *Journal of Social Psychology*, 142(1), 133–143.

Larsen, R.J., & Diener, E. (1987). Affect intensity as an individual difference characteristic: A review. *Journal of Research in Personality*, 21, 1–39.

Larsen, R., & Kasimatis, M. (1990). Individual differences in entrainment of mood to the weekly calendar. *Journal of Personality and Social Psychology*, 58, 164–171.

Lazarus, R.S. (1991). *Emotion and adaptation*. New York: Oxford University Press.

Lazarus, R.S., & Cohen-Charash, Y. (2001). Discrete emotions in organizational life. In R. Payne & C.L. Cooper (Eds.), *Emotions in organizations* (pp. 45–81). Chichester, UK: Wiley.

LeBlanc, P.M., Bakker, A.B., Peeters, M.C.W., Van Heesch, N.C.A., & Schaufeli, W.B. (2001). Emotional job demands and burnout among oncology care providers. *Anxiety, Stress and Coping*, 14, 243–263.

Lewis, K.M. (2000). When leaders display emotion: How followers respond to negative emotional expression of male and female leaders. *Journal of Organizational Behavior*, 21, 221–234.

Lopes, P.N., Grewal, D., Kadis, J., Gall, M., & Salovey, P. (2006). Evidence that emotional intelligence is related to job performance and affect and attitudes at work. *Psicothema*, 18, 132–138.

Lowe, K.B., Kroeck, K.G., & Sivasubramaniam, N. (1996). Effectiveness correlates of transformation and transactional leadership: A meta-analytic review of the MLQ literature. *Leadership Quarterly*, 7(3), 385–425.

Lyons, J.B., & Schneider, T.R. (2005). The influence of emotional intelligence on performance. *Personality and Individual Differences*, 39(4), 693–703.

Lyubomirsky, S., King, L., & Diener, E. (2005). The benefits of frequent positive affect: Does happiness lead to success? *Psychological Bulletin*, 131(6), 803–855.

Mackie, D.M., & Worth, L.T. (1989). Differential recall of subcategory information about in-group and out-group members. *Personality and Social Psychology Bulletin*, 15(3), 401–413.

Madjar, N., Oldham, G.R., & Pratt, M.G. (2002). There's no place like home? The contributions of work and nonwork creativity support to employees' creative performance. *Academy of Management Journal*, 45(4), 757–767.

Maitlis, S., & Ozcelik, H. (2004). Toxic decision processes: A study of emotion and organizational decision making. *Organization Science*, 15(4), 375–393.

Martin, L.L., Ward, D.W., Achee, J.W., & Wyer, R.S. (1993). Mood as input: People have to interpret the motivational implications of their moods. *Journal of Personality and Social Psychology*, 64(3), 317–326.

Matsumoto, D., LeRoux, J.A., Bernhard, R., & Gray, H. (2004). Unraveling the psychological correlates of intercultural adjustment potential. *International Journal of Intercultural Relations*, 28, 281–309.

Matthews, G., Roberts, R.D., & Zeidner, M. (2004). Seven myths about emotional intelligence. *Psychological Inquiry*, 15(3), 179–196.

Mauss, I.B., Evers, C., Wilhelm, F.H., & Gross, J.J. (2006). How to bite your tongue without blowing your top: Implicit evaluation of emotion regulation predicts affective responding to anger provocation. *Personality and Social Psychology Bulletin*, 32(5), 589–602.

Mayer, J.D., Roberts, R.D., & Barsade, S.G. (forthcoming). Emerging research in emotional intelligence. *Annual Review of Psychology*, 59.

Mayer, J.D. & Salovey, P. (1997). What is emotional intelligence? In P. Salovey & D. Sluyter (Eds.), *Emotional development and emotional intelligence: Educational implication* (pp. 3–31). New York: Basic Books.

Mayer, J.D., Salovey, P., Caruso, D.R., & Sitarenios, G. (2003). Measuring emotional intelligence with the MS-CEIT V2.0. *Emotion*, 3(1), 97–105.

Mayer, J.D., Salovey, P., & Caruso, D.R. (2000). Models of emotional intelligence. In R.J. Sternberg (Ed.), *Handbook of intelligence* (pp. 396–420). Cambridge, UK: Cambridge University Press.

McIntyre, C.W., Watson, D., Clark, L.A., & Cross, S.A. (1991). The effect of induced social interaction on positive and negative affect. *Bulletin of the Psychonomic Society*, 29(1), 67–70.

McCrae, R.R., & Costa, P.T. (1987). Validation of the five-factor model of personality across instrument and observers. *Journal of Personality and Social Psychology*, 52(1), 81–90.

Mehrabian, A. (1972). *Nonverbal communication*. Chicago: Aldine-Atherton.

Melton, R.J. (1995). The role of positive affect in syllogism performance. *Personality and Social Psychology Bulletin*, 21(8), 788–794.

Miner, A.G., Glomb, T.M., & Hulin, C. (2005). Experience sampling mood and its correlates at work. *Journal of Occupational and Organizational Psychology*, 78(2), 171–193.

Morris, J.A., & Feldman, D.C. (1996). The dimensions, antecedents, and consequences of emotional labor. *Academy of Management Review*, 21(4), 986–1010.

Ortony, A., & Turner, T.J. (1990). What's basic about basic emotions? *Psychological Review*, 97(3), 315–331.

Mueller, J., & Curhan, J. (in press). Emotional intelligence and counterpart mood induction in a negotiation. *International Journal of Conflict Management*.

Parrott, W.G. (1993). Beyond hedonism: Motives for inhibiting good moods and for maintaining bad moods. In D.M. Wegner & J.W. Pennebaker (Eds.), *Handbook of mental control*. Englewood Cliffs, NJ: Prentice-Hall.

Pelled, L.H., & Xin, K.R. (1999). Down and out: An investigation of the relationship between mood and employee withdrawal behavior. *Journal of Management*, 25(6), 875–895.

Pescosolido, A.T. (2002). Emergent leaders as managers of group emotion. *The Leadership Quarterly*, 13, 583–599.

Pierce, J.L. (1995). *Gender trials: Emotional lives in contemporary law firms*. Berkeley, CA: University of California Press.

Pugh, S.D. (2001). Service with a smile: Emotional contagion in the service encounter. *Academy of Management Journal*, 44(5), 1018–1027.

Rafaeli, A., & Sutton, R.I. (1989). The expression of emotion in organizational life. In B.M. Staw & L.L. Cummings (Eds.), *Research in organizational behavior* (pp. 1–42). Greenwich, CT: JAI Press.

Rafaeli, A., & Sutton, R.I. (1990). Busy stores and demanding customers: How do they affect the display of positive emotion? *Academy of Management Journal*, 33(3), 623–637.

Rubin, R.S., Munz, D.C., & Bommer, W.H. (2005). Leading from within: The effects of emotion recognition and personality on transformational leadership behavior. *Academy of Management Journal*, 48(5), 845–858.

Russell, J.A. (1980). A circumplex model of affect. *Journal of Personality and Social Psychology*, 39, 1161–1178.

Salovey, P., & Grewal, D. (2005). The science of emotional intelligence. *Current Directions in Psychological Science*, 14(6), 281–285.

Salovey, P., & Mayer, J. (1990). Emotional intelligence. *Imagination, Cognition and Personality*, 9, 185–211.

Salovey, P., Mayer, J.D., & Rosenhan, D.L. (1991). Mood and helping: Mood as a motivator of helping and helping as a regulator of mood. In M.S. Clark (Ed.), *Prosocial behavior* (pp. 215–237). Thousand Oaks, CA: Sage.

Schwarz, N., Bless, H., & Bohner, G. (1991). Response scales as frames of reference: The impact of frequency range on diagnostic judgments. *Applied Cognitive Psychology*, 5(1), 37–49.

Sharma, A., & Levy, M. (2003). Salespeople's affect toward customers: Why should it be important for retailers? *Journal of Business Research*, 56(7), 523–528.

Shaw, J.D. (1999). Job satisfaction and turnover intentions: The moderating role of positive affect. *Journal of Social Psychology*, 139(2), 242–244.

Shaw, J.D., Delery, J.E., Jenkins, Jr., G.D., & Gupta, N. (1998). An organization-level analysis of voluntary and involuntary turnover. *Academy of Management Journal*, 41(3), 511–535.

Singer, J.A., & Salovey, P. (1988). Mood and memory: Evaluating the network theory of affect. *Clinical Psychology Review*, 8, 211–251.

Smith, A.C., & Kleinman, S. (1989). Managing emotions in medical school: Students' contacts with the living and the dead. *Social Psychology Quarterly*, 52(1), 56–69.

Spector, P.E., & Fox, S. (2002). An emotion-centered model of voluntary work behavior: Some parallels between counterproductive work behavior and organizational citizenship behavior. *Human Resource Management Review*, 12, 269–292.

Staw, B.M., & Barsade, S.G. (1993). Affect and managerial performance: A test of the sadder-but-wiser vs. happier-and-smarter hypothesis. *Administrative Science Quarterly*, 38(2), 304–331.

Staw, B.M., Bell, N.E., & Clausen, J.A. (1986). The dispositional approach to job attitudes: A lifetime longitudinal test. *Administrative Science Quarterly*, 31(1), 56–77.

Staw, B.M., & Cohen-Charash, Y. (2005). The dispositional approach to job satisfaction: More than a mirage, but not yet an oasis: Comment. *Journal of Organizational Behavior*, 26(1), 59–78.

Staw, B.M., Sutton, R.I., & Pelled, L.H. (1994). Employee positive emotion and favorable outcomes at the work-place. *Organization Science*, 5(1), 51–71.

Stearns, C.Z., & Stearns, P.N. (1986). *Anger: The struggle for emotional control in America's history*. Chicago: University of Chicago Press.

Strack, F., Martin, L., & Stepper, S. (1988). Inhibiting and facilitating conditions of the human smile: A nonobtrusive test of the facial feedback hypothesis. *Journal of Personality and Social Psychology*, 54, 768–776.

Sullins, E. (1989). Perceptual salience as a function of nonverbal expressiveness. *Personality and Social Psychology Bulletin*, 15, 584–595.

Sutton, R.I. (1991). Maintaining norms about expressed emotions: The case of bill collectors. *Administrative Science Quarterly*, 36, 245–268.

Sy, T., Côté, S., & Saavedra, R. (2005). The contagious leader: Impact of the leader's mood on the mood of group members, group affective tone, and group processes. *Journal of Applied Psychology*, 90(2), 295–305.

Tellegen, A. (1985). Structures of mood and personality and their relevance to assessing anxiety, with an emphasis on self-report. In A.H. Tuma, & J.D. Maser (Eds.), *Anxiety and the anxiety disorders* (pp. 681–706). Hillsdale, NJ: Erlbaum.

Tett, R.P., Fox, K.E., & Wang, A. (2005). Development and validation of a self-report measure of emotional intelligence as a multidimensional trait domain. *Personality and Social Psychology Bulletin*, 31(7), 859–888.

Thompson, L.L., Nadler, J., & Kim, P.H. (1999). Some like it hot: The case for the emotional negotiator. In L.L. Thompson, J.M. Levine, & D.M. Messick (Eds.), *Shared cognition in organizations: The management of knowledge* (pp. 139–161). Mahwah, NJ: Erlbaum.

Thoresen, C.J., Kaplan, S.A., & Barsky, A.P. (2003). The affective underpinnings of job perceptions and attitudes: A meta-analytic review and integration. *Psychological Bulletin*, 129(6), 914–945.

Tiedens, L.Z. (2001). Anger and advancement versus sadness and subjugation: The effect of negative emotion expressions on social status conferral. *Journal of Personality and Social Psychology*, 80(1), 86–94.

Totterdell, P., & Holman, D. (2003). Emotion regulation in customer service roles: Testing a model of emotional labor. *Journal of Occupational Health Psychology*, 8(1), 55–73.

Totterdell, P., Kellet, S., Teuchmann, K., & Briner, R. (1998). Evidence of mood linkage in work groups. *Journal of Personality and Social Psychology*, 74, 1504–1515.

Tsai, W.C., & Huang, Y.M. (2002). Mechanisms linking employee affective delivery and customer behavioral intentions. *Journal of Applied Psychology*, 87(5), 1001–1008.

Tuckman, B.W. (1965). Developmental sequence in small groups. *Psychological Bulletin*, 63(6), 384–399.

Van Kleef, G.A., De Dreu, C.K.W., & Manstead, A.S.R. (2004). The interpersonal effects of emotions in negotiations: A motivated information processing approach. *Journal of Personality and Social Psychology*, 87(4), 510–528.

Verbeke, W. (1997). Individual differences in emotional contagion of salespersons: Its effect on performance and burnout. *Psychology & Marketing*, 14(6), 617–636.

Wasielewski, P.L. (1985). The emotional basis of charisma. *Symbolic Interaction*, 8(2), 207–222.

Watson, D., & Clark, L.A. (1984). Negative affectivity: The disposition to experience negative emotional states. *Psychological Bulletin*, 96, 465–490.

Watson, D., Clark, L.A., McIntyre, C.W., & Hamaker, S. (1992). Affect, personality and social activity. *Journal of Personality and Social Psychology*, 63, 1011–1025.

Watson, D., Clark, L.A., & Tellegen, A. (1988). Development and validation of brief measures of positive and negative affect: The PANAS scales. *Journal of Personality and Social Psychology*, 54, 1063–1070.

Watson, D., & Tellegen, A. (1985). Toward a consensual structure of mood. *Psychological Bulletin*, 98(2), 219–235.

Weiss, H.M. (2002). Deconstructing job satisfaction: Separating evaluations, beliefs and affective experiences. *Human Resources Management Review*, 12, 173–194.

Weiss, H.M., & Cropanzano, R. (1996). Affective events theory: A theoretical discussion of the structure, causes and consequences of affective experiences at work. In B.M. Staw & L.L. Cummings (Eds.), *Research in organizational behavior* (Vol. 18, pp. 1–74). Greenwich, CT: JAI Press.

Westen, D., & Gabbard, G.O. (2002). Developments in cognitive neuroscience: I. Conflict, compromise, and connectionism. *Journal of the American Psychoanalytic Association*, 50(1), 53–98.

Wheelan, S.A. (1994). *Group processes: A developmental perspective*. Needham Heights, MA: Allyn & Bacon.

Wright, T.A., Cropanzano, R., & Meyer, D.G. (2004). State and trait correlates of job performance: A tale of two perspectives. *Journal of Business and Psychology*, 18(3), 365–383.

Wright, T.A., & Staw, B.M. (1999). Affect and favorable outcomes: Two longitudinal tests of the happy-productive worker thesis. *Journal of Organizational Behavior*, 20(1), 1–23.

6.2   ADVANCES IN OCCUPATIONAL HEALTH

From a Stressful Beginning to a Positive Future

Marilyn Macik-Frey, James Campbell Quick, and Debra L. Nelson

The authors briefly review the literature on occupational health, including occupational medicine, occupational health psychology, and occupational safety, framing the current convergence of these from their scientific origins in preventive medicine and its most basic science of epidemiology, in psychology, and in engineering. They give attention to the burden of suffering, which concerns issues of morbidity and mortality within a population group, and consider both the economic and humanitarian perspectives of the burden of suffering, which may occur within a working population as a result of poor occupational health. The authors see reason for optimism for the future and identify two sets of emerging trends: one set that includes four positive advances—positive health, leadership, mood and emotions, and interventions—and one that falls under the authors' rubric of new horizons—technology, virtual work, globalization, and aging. The authors conclude with attention to zest at work, along with cardiovascular health and well-being.

Assessing where a discipline stands and where it needs to go in the future can be an invaluable asset to researchers in that discipline. Our aim is to provide such a resource for occupational health researchers, with some key foundations as our starting points. Ganster and Schaubroeck's (1991) *Journal of Management* (*JOM*) review of work stress and employee health found evidence from occupational studies that differences in health and mortality were not easily explained by factors other than work stress. In addition, they identified several within-subject studies that demonstrated causal effects of work experiences on physiological and emotional responses of employees. At about the same time, Raymond, Wood, and Patrick (1990) conceptualized and defined occupational health psychology (OHP) as an interdisciplinary specialty of overlapping theory and research from psychology, management, public health, preventive medicine, industrial engineering, epidemiology, and occupational medicine and nursing. The interlocking interests and collaborations among the American Psychological Association, the National Institute for Occupational Safety and Health, and the Academy of Management helped to anchor and extend this emerging nexus of concerns for occupational health and employee well-being. Key objectives in this movement included the prevention of occupational injuries, diseases, and disorders, coupled with the enhancement and advancement of occupational health and vitality. One important outcome of these joint forces was the creation of *Journal of Occupational Health Psychology* (*JOHP*).

Several years later, Danna and Griffin (1999) provided a widely cited complementary review examining health and well-being in the workplace. We now stand at the 15-year milestone from Ganster and Schaubroeck's (1991) state-of-the-art review and the emergence of OHP as a recognized, interdisciplinary specialty. Many of the premises of the Danna and Griffin article related to how we define health, and these definitions are being expanded over the course of time. We propose to reframe these complementary forces; provide a comprehensive, updated review of the literature within this 15-year period; and develop future-oriented implications for management scholars based on several cutting-edge trends in the field of management and organization. We will provide an examination of how effectively occupational health and OHP have extended both theory and research, how these disciplines have been applied through organizational interventions, and where occupational health is headed.

Why is such a review important? First, occupational health and OHP are at a timely juncture for providing worthwhile contributions to the behavioral, emotional, and managerial sciences. Second, the early emphasis on stress and stress-related topics has dominated the past 15 years, and a fresh look at ways to broaden and enrich the study of occupational health is needed. There are emergent and cutting-edge trends that can be reinforced and extended in a major review of occupational health, including virtual work, positive health initiatives, new issues in leadership research, and a renewed emphasis on emotion at work.

Third, the editors of the *JOHP*, each of whom is a management scholar, along with other key management and psychology researchers in occupational health, have encouraged research in exciting new areas, such as positive health and intervention studies. As such, management scholars have played central roles in the emergence of this field. We note here that occupational health is a broader concept than OHP, more heavily drawing on preventive medicine and public health contributions. Although OHP is somewhat narrower in scope, it is truly interdisciplinary and draws on medicine, management, and other disciplines in addition to psychology. Through an analysis of the history of occupational health, we present a conceptual model of how the field has evolved over time. This analysis provides a working conceptualization of occupational health for the purposes of this review.

In summary, we encourage a broader scope of study that moves beyond work stress and employee health, beyond a concern for the prevention of distress and negative consequences, to an emphasis on positive employee health and well-being. By reframing, updating, and extending occupational health and OHP, we aim to strengthen theory and research to ensure that the next 15 years builds on the success of the past 15.

History, Emergence, and Scope of Occupational Health

Occupational health lies at the interdisciplinary nexus of medicine, psychology, engineering, and management. Although occupational health spans organizational boundaries and addresses spillover issues from the workplace to venues outside the organization, the primary context is research in, and the practice of, occupational health in organizations. Figure 6.2.1 shows the scientific origins, the current convergence, and the future directions of occupational health. Although the scientific origins date back well more than a century and provide a backdrop to the current focus on the past two decades, the key points of departure for this review date from the reviews by Ganster and Schaubroeck (1991) and Danna and Griffin (1999). Danna and Griffin, in particular, aimed to define and distinguish health and well-being in the workplace. Our goal is to frame a clearer understanding of occupational health and its origins and then continue where the two previous reviews ended and extend into our vision of the future.

The science and practice of preventive medicine emerged from the study of disease epidemics during the 1800s. This might more properly be labeled *epidemiology*, which is the most basic science and fundamental practice of public health and preventive medicine (Wallace & Doebbeling, 1998) and has its origins in Greek (*epi* [upon] + *demos* [people]). Epidemiology has roots in the Bible (Leviticus 11 includes dietary laws for safe food consumption) and in the writings of Hippocrates (1994, a translation of Hippocrates' writings on disease epidemics), as does much of Western medicine. However, when the famous Hungarian physician Ignace Semmelweis discovered in the mid-1800s that the incidence of

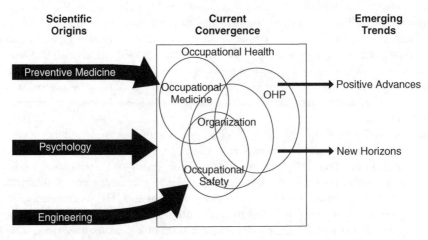

Figure 6.2.1 Occupational Health in Context.

Note: OHP = occupational health psychology.

puerperal fever could be drastically cut by hand-washing standards in obstetrical clinics, the foundations for the germ theory of disease were set. Although public sanitation and personal hygiene were advanced in the United States during the very late 1800s, Milton J. Rosenau (1913) was the first medical doctor to pull together the emerging body of knowledge and practice in what has become the classic handbook and reference manual on public health and preventive medicine (Wallace & Doebbeling, 1998). The many editions of *Preventive Medicine & Hygiene* gave way to the emergence of later editions after 1950 titled *Public Health & Preventive Medicine*. In this process, occupational and environmental health, especially in the context of the organization, were added to the original topics of communicable diseases, noncommunicable diseases, and chronic disabling conditions, such as heart disease and psychiatric disorders.

The science of psychology was not far behind preventive medicine in its concern for human well-being. In the same year Rosenau published his classic work in preventive medicine, Hugo Münsterberg (1913) published his classic volume *Psychology and Industrial Efficiency*. One of Münsterberg's concerns was with industrial accidents that were a relatively common feature of the early years of the industrial revolution, dating into the late 1800s with steel and iron manufacturing in Pittsburgh, along with railroad and locomotive injuries and accidents. The basic science of human behavior was concerned with workers, as in Münsterberg's case, and with executives, as in Laird's (1929) case. Laird's contribution complements Münsterberg's work by applying psychology at the executive level. He may be the first psychologist concerned with executive health, and his theme was "every executive his own psychologist" (Laird, 1929: 13). In particular, his work focused on efficiency, effectiveness, less fatigue, loyal morale, and personal development for executives. We see in Figure 6.2.1 that these early emphases gave way in the 1970s and 1980s to the emergence of what has become known as OHP, a special emphasis within the science.

Engineering, the applied science of physics, matter, and motion, is a third stream contributing to the current framework and practice of occupational health. Frederick Winslow Taylor's (1911) classic work in scientific management initially aimed at translating engineering principles into human work systems through time and motion studies, performance standards, and functional foremanship. These ideas were to be applied on the shop floor. As his thinking matured based on early struggles in the U.S. steel industry, Taylor (1912) saw the heart of scientific management as a transformation of the labor–management relationship from a competitive one to a cooperative one. Subsequent engineers, especially industrial engineers, used engineering principles and concepts to transform work environments into more anthropocentric ones, with humans at the center of the design process (cf. Lucak, 1992, in Nelson & Quick, 2006: 478).

From these scientific origins, organizational health has emerged as an overlapping set of concerns with occupational medicine, engineering safety, and OHP. We now focus on the current convergence in Figure 6.2.1 and the work of the past two decades. In addition to occupational medicine (i.e., public health and preventive medicine at work), environmental safety, and OHP, we consider the subsets of occupational stress and organizational health because of their additional contributions to occupational health.

Occupational Medicine: Public Health and Preventive Medicine at Work

Employee mental health and well-being has a long history (cf. Elkind, 1931—*Preventive Management: Mental Hygiene in Industry*), and *Occupational Medicine* has been published since circa 1950. Public health and preventive medicine have been key foundations for the dramatic rise in human life expectancies, as much as 50% to 100% increases in various population groups around the world (Quick, Cooper, Nelson, Quick, & Gavin, 2003). Life expectancy in the United States rose from about 47 circa 1900 to 77 circa 2000 while more than doubling in the People's Republic of China from about 34 to more than 70. The extension of preventive medicine into occupational medicine, and its subset of environmental medicine, gave rise to an emphasis on toxicology, ergonomics, and occupational safety. In the 14th edition of *Public Health and Preventive Medicine*, Wallace and Doebbeling (1998) expanded the scope to address important occupational and organizational health hazards such as noise, musculoskeletal disorders, and industrial hygiene, along with behavioral factors affecting health, such as social relationships and substance abuse. They placed an emphasis on special working groups such as women, minorities, those with disabilities, and those affected by violence. Sickness absence continues to be a key outcome (Ihlebaek, Brage, & Eriksen, 2007).

There are three key concerns of occupational medicine in public health and preventive medicine (Last & Tyler, 1998). First is a concern with active and passive surveillance mechanisms that lead to early identification of health problems or disorders (Halperin, Monson, & Baker, 2001). This is a key to the early identification of problems and the establishment of warning systems for others who may be at risk. The types of surveillance systems include routine reporting of health incidents, sentinel or gateway systems, special studies within populations, and targeted supervision or structured studies. A second concern is with the identification of health risk factors. In occupational contexts, health risk factors include secondhand smoke, which is the most lethal occupational health risk (M. O'Donnell, personal communication, February 13, 2007); noise and vibrations; toxic exposures; and increasingly recognized psychosocial health risk factors such as role conflicts. Third is the development of intervention and treatment strategies for improving health and averting disorders. Such strategies fall under the rubric of preventive stress management, to include primary, secondary, and tertiary prevention (VandenBos, 2007).

Occupational Safety

Occupational safety emerged from an engineering tradition yet is importantly influenced by psychology and preventive medicine. Safety is in part determined by the characteristics of the physical work environment and in part by the behavior and actions of humans within that physical environment. Health and safety were more recently linked by Geller (1996), with an emphasis on practices aimed at improving safe working practices while reducing accidents and injuries. The concept of "safety climate" is well established, anchored in the theoretical concepts of Zohar (1980). His own subsequent research included supervisory safety practices studied in the context of Israeli infantry units (Zohar & Luria, 2004) and organization-level and group-level climates studied in the manufacturing context of small- and medium-sized firms (Zohar & Luria, 2005).

In a meta-analysis ($N = 35$) investigating the relationship between safety climate and safety performance, Clarke (2006) found that safety climate was significantly related to occupational accidents and injuries. She captured a significant number of industrial sectors in the studies screened into her analysis, including manufacturing, chemical processing, offshore oil and gas production, nuclear energy, construction, service telecommunication, health care, military, food processing, and fishery. Sulzer-Azaroff (1987) has argued for a long time that occupational safety behavior can be modified, suggesting that a safety climate is not invariant. One of Clarke's key conclusions was that a positive safety climate is associated with lower accidents and injury rates. These lower rates translated into better occupational health for working populations.

Occupational Stress

Stress on the job is associated with accidents both on and off the job and job site. Since 1991, work stress, distress, coping, and/or the negative consequences of work stress continue as dominant occupational health themes in organizations. Perrewé and Ganster's (2002–2006) *Research in Occupational Stress and Well Being* series brings important managerial and organizational connections to the concerns with occupational health. Initially concerned with exploring theoretical mechanisms and perspectives, Perrewé and Ganster go on to examine various aspects of the stress–health connection in their series, before turning to emotional and physiological processes and then to positive intervention strategies.

Stress has emerged as a key issue within occupational medicine and among physician and surgeon leaders. For example, Wadsworth, Dhillon, Shaw, Bhui, Stansfeld, and Smith (2007) found that perceived work stress may be underpinned by exposure to racial discrimination at work among Black African–Caribbean women, and this may affect their psychological well-being (PWB). Even positive racial stereotypes can have negative effects on people at work (Cocchiara & Quick, 2004). The American Orthopaedic Association is concerned with the adverse effects of stress and burnout on the profession's leaders (Quick et al., 2006).

Thus, although the "stress" theme continues to dominate within the broader domain of occupational health, despite journal editors and others within the field calling for the broadening, it is still a powerful rubric that cannot be ignored. A review of PsychArticles and PsychInfo databases conducted March 13, 2007, resulted in 127,108 citations when using the keywords *work stress* and *job stress*.

Organizational Health

Adkins (1999) pioneered the concept of organizational health as an extension of OHP, with a clear organizational focus and context. She did this in the Air Force Materiel Command, a *Fortune* 100 sided industrial organization with five air logistics and maintenance depots and more than 100,000 employees, the vast majority of whom were federal civil servants and a small minority of whom were military personnel. Her concept was formalized within an organizational health center that directly reported to the commanding general officer of the depot, thus making it a key staff function. Although an interdisciplinary center for linking medical personnel, chaplains, psychologists, public health officers, human resource personnel, and safety experts, the organizational health center was not directly under either the medical or the psychology department.

Adkins (1998) developed the concept for use in major industrial restructuring and downsizing initiative in the early to mid-1990s. However, the concept can be equally applied well in growing, dynamic, and world-class organizational contexts (Adkins, Quick, & Moe, 2000). One evaluation in the former context found savings in terms of the prevention of suicides and workplace violence and cost avoidance, in one depot amounting to $33 million in costs avoided (Quick, Tetrick, Adkins, & Klunder, 2003).

Organizational health addresses both occupational health and its impact on managerial and employee well-being and organizational effectiveness and functioning. Although occupational health and organizational health are distinct, they have some common variance. Ryff and Singer's (1998) attempt at a more positive definition of human health was one element of Cooper and Quick's (2007) *Journal of Management Studies* special issue titled "Managerial Dimensions of Organizational Health." They define organizational health in terms of purpose, relationships, positive self-regard, and mastery.

OHP

The origins of OHP date to 1990 within the National Institute for Occupational Safety and Health (Sauter, Murphy, & Hurrell, 1990), and the history has previously been recapped (cf. Barling & Griffith, 2003). Although psychological disorders were the central concern within OHP, this interdisciplinary specialty within psychology also addresses behavioral disorders and safety issues in the workplace. OHP takes some core notions from preventive medicine and public health, from the occupational stress research dating to the classic organizational stress studies of Robert Kahn and his associates (Kahn, Wolfe, Quinn, Snoek, & Rosenthal, 1964), and from organizational health, then translates them into an organizational context for purposes of the preventive management of individual and organizational health (Quick, 1999a, 1999b; Quick, Camara, et al., 1997; Sauter, Hurrell, Fox, Tetrick, & Barling, 1999).

One dominant source of peer-reviewed research in occupational health is *JOHP*. A review of articles in this journal since 2000 displays a concentration of published articles in seven categories: stress, to include physical and emotional; burnout; work–family; aggression, violence, and harassment; safety; employment issues; and health issues. A search using the PsychArticles, PsychInfo, and Psychology and Behavioral Sciences Collection databases from 1988 to the present resulted in only 328 citations matching the search for *occupational health psychology*, of which 322 were *JOHP* articles. A more organizational behavior-oriented search using Academic Search Premier and Business Source Complete databases resulted in 135 matches for *occupational health psychology* during the same period; again, the vast majority of these articles were published in *JOHP*.

Prior to the emergence of OHP, the field of occupational health was well prepared to deal with the physical, biological, and chemical hazards of the workplace yet less able to deal with psychological, behavioral, and social sciences issues (Sauter & Hurrell, 1999). Today, these are accepted components of managerial and employee health, as is the realization that the mind and body are intricately linked. The idea that work stress can and does lead to physical illness or injury is well supported.

The Burden of Suffering

Ganster and Schaubroeck (1991) discussed the risks of mental and physical ill health associated with job stress, whereas Danna and Griffin (1999) focused on the consequences of low levels of health and well-being in their examination of health in the workplace. We take a slightly different perspective in considering the burden of suffering within an occupational context, a concept originally used within the public health community. Our reference to the burden of suffering captures both morbidity and mortality. Morbidity rates refer to either the incidence rate (number of new cases) or the prevalence rate (total number of cases) of a particular health problem, disease, or disorder within a population group. Mortality refers to the number of deaths in a population group. Epidemiology is important in this context as a way of studying the burden of suffering, which Doll, Bonzo, Sleet, and Mercy (2007) use, for example, in estimating the costs of unintentional and violent injuries.

The burden of suffering concept includes both the economic costs and the humanitarian concerns in the workplace. Each of these two aspects of the burden of suffering is of importance, the former because economic costs have an impact on the financial bottom line for companies and the latter because of the emotional pain and suffering that are associated with either illness or death. There are comparatively different difficulties in calculating the costs and effects in each case. The difficulty in developing an accurate set of cost data or cost estimates for morbidity and mortality in working populations is that there are not accepted, standardized measures, nor is there a consolidated set of databases. The U.S. Bureau of Labor Statistics, the International Labor Organization in Geneva, Switzerland; the U.S. Center for Disease Control and Prevention; the American Institute of Stress; and the National Safety Council are among the organizations that track parts of the data.

The difficulty in developing or measuring the costs and effects of pain and suffering relate to the complications in quantifying, for example, emotions. How do we monetize emotion? Can we monetize emotion? What is the value of a human life? These are among the complicated humanitarian questions related to the timeless human problem of suffering. As a complement to this humanitarian perspective, Murray, Nicholson, Pauly, and Berger (2006) take the employer's perspective in considering investing in health to boost employee productivity. Theirs is an investment approach to health-related expenditures in health-promotion services and health care coverage for employees, considering issues of prevention, quality, benefit design, disease management, and case management.

In examining the organizational consequences of stress, Quick, Quick, Nelson, and Hurrell (1997) broadly categorized the costs of organizational distress into direct costs and indirect costs. The direct costs included participation and membership, such as absenteeism and turnover; performance on the job, such as accidents and poor-quality productivity; health care costs, such as insurance rates; and compensation awards, such as court awards for sexual harassment. The indirect costs included loss of vitality, communication break-downs, faulty decision making, and quality of work relations. In his presidential remarks to the American College of Occupational and Environmental Medicine, Bernacki (2002) focused on the employer's perspective in the valuation of morbidity and mortality, suggesting such valuation includes

- Direct costs of diagnosis and treatment of occupational and nonoccupational conditions
- Disability costs
- Higher wage costs
- Lost production
- Idle assets
- Employee turnover
- Planned overstaffing
- And indirect business taxes and nontax liabilities

He estimated that the direct cost to U.S. business of worker ill health adds up to approximately 7% of labor costs. Depending on the industry, about half of that cost is related to nonoccupational medical costs and the other half to the medical and indemnity cost of occupationally related conditions. Between 1990 and 2001, the cost estimates of worker stress for American businesses have widely varied, from $50 billion to $300 billion annually in health care and lost job productivity (Rosch, 2001; Sauter et al., 1990). This variance reflects the challenge of getting good and accurate estimates for the broader concept of occupational health.

Occupational Fatal Injury Costs

Biddle, Hartley, Starkey, Fabrega, and Richardson (2005) conducted a pilot study to test an accurate, timely, and readily available state-based estimate of the costs associated with fatal occupational injuries. A key challenge in developing a cost calculator for fatal injuries is that there are two fundamental economic approaches to assessing costs, one a willingness-to-pay method and the other a cost-of-illness method. They derive an approach using both direct costs, in their case considering only medical expenditures, and indirect costs, using an algebraic cost calculator. Our point is that the development of cost data for occupational fatalities is complicated and can, depending on the assumptions made, lead to widely differing estimates.

The International Labour Office (ILO) estimated that 2.2 million people die of work-related accidents and diseases each year. This they reported at the 17th World Congress on Safety and Health at Work in September 2005. Furthermore, ILO estimated that this number may be vastly underestimated because of poor reporting and coverage systems in many countries.

Work Loss and Productivity

Mortality is only one component for Berger, Murray, Xu, and Pauly (2001) in examining the indirect costs (i.e., work loss and productivity costs) from an employer's perspective. The other two components are morbidity and reduced productivity. Here, we again encounter differing perspectives and alternative valuations. In addition to the employer's perspective, there are the individual's perspective on these matters and society's perspective on the same matters. They point out that the American Heart Association in 1999 used the traditional societal perspective to estimate the indirect costs of CHD (the leading cause of death in the United States) to be $46.7 billion, $6.9 billion of which related to morbidity and the remaining $39.8 billion (81%) to mortality. The authors suggest that the estimates may be quite different if one uses the employer's perspective for CHD.

Presenteeism. The lost productivity costs of occupational health may exceed the direct medical costs. Although most evaluations of occupational health outcomes examine only the medical costs of poor health, a broader view should consider absences and presenteeism (diminished productivity resulting from health issues while at work) as well. Does presenteeism really exist? Collins et al. (2005) pay particular attention to the impact of chronic health conditions, such as allergies, arthritis, asthma, back and neck disorders, breathing disorders, depression and anxiety, and the leading disabling issue of cardiovascular problems. These chronic conditions can diminish employee productivity even when they are physically present and on the job. In addition, Ricci, Chee, Lorandeau, and Berger (2007) estimated the prevalence of fatigue in the American workplace and concluded that workers with fatigue cost employers $136.4 billion annually in health-related lost productive time, an excess of $101.0 billion compared to workers without fatigue. With regard to absences, Nicholson, Pauly, Polsky, Sharda, Szrek, and Berger (2006) found in a survey of 800 managers across 12 industries that the cost associated with missed work varied across jobs according to the ease with which a manager could find a perfect replacement for the absent worker.

Workplace bullying. Rayner, Hoel, and Cooper (2001) and Einarsen, Hoel, Cooper, and Zapf (2003) have brought attention to the negative effects of workplace bullying and emotional abuse on the health of the workplace. Workplace bullying is a form of emotional abuse and harassment that has a huge impact on a company's bottom line. Urbanski (2002) estimated that workplace bullying cost about $180 million in lost time and productivity. Some of these costs are related to health care costs resulting from the bully's target becoming affected by stress-related illnesses. In essence, bullying is the repeated, health-endangering, illegitimate mistreatment of a person by a cruel perpetrator driven by some unconscious psychological need. Increasingly, human resource managers recognize that there are real productivity costs resulting from workplace bullying and with emotional abuse of employees, peers, and others at work.

Health Insurance Trends and Costs

Health insurance costs are an increasingly important concern in America for employers and employees alike. From a consumer or employee perspective, Langer (2004) found 78% of respondents are dissatisfied with the cost of the nation's health care system, including 54% who were very dissatisfied. The National Women's Business Council (2003) found that access to capital was the number one concern and that a close second was affordability of health care coverage, with less than 50% being able to provide health care coverage to their employees. Many of these women business owners reported having to pass on an increasing amount of the cost of insurance coverage to the employee or to consider changing coverage because of increasing costs.

When the costs of health coverage for employees are not borne in the organizational context, that throws some of the occupational health care costs into the larger public health system to be borne by society. Because the United States funds its health care system significantly differently from virtually every other industrialized nation, this is a matter of consequence. Although the United States has the best medical system in the world that can treat the sick, it does not have the best health system in the world with an emphasis on prevention (J. D. Quick, personal communication, May 30, 2007). Two alternative models are a national health insurance model, as used in Switzerland, where private providers are reimbursed 100% by the government for services, and a national health service model, as used in the United Kingdom, where health care providers are effectively government employees. The United States follows neither model and has more than 40 million uninsured Americans.

Shen and Long (2006) examined what is driving the downward trend in employer-sponsored health insurance. Chernew, Cutler, and Keenan (2005) examined the impact of rising health insurance premiums on coverage rates. They concluded that any efforts to expand coverage and reduce the number of uninsured Americans will meet resistance because of this rising cost of health insurance premiums. In this same domain, Glied, Lambrew, and Little (2003) found a growing share of the uninsured workforce employed by large firms. In this rapidly changing health insurance environment, we question how meaningful overall occupational health insurance cost data are. Employers continue to be concerned with tracking and understanding their companies' insurance health care costs.

Intrinsic Value: A Matter of Virtue

All of the issues we have discussed so far are somehow related to the utilitarian value of a man or woman. That is, they are concerned with their role as a means of production, achievement, and output. However, we began this section by pointing out that the burden of suffering bridges both economic costs and humanitarian concerns. For us to consider the latter, we must bring focus to the intrinsic value of a man or a woman. A person's intrinsic value stands apart from his or her utilitarian value. Kant's (1958) metaphysic of morals may be one of the best pathways for helping us understand human intrinsic value. We suggest that it is a matter of virtue, and maybe of character too.

Kant's (1958) first categorical imperative is this: Act only on that maxim through which you can at the same time will that it should become a universal principle. Thus, he takes a subjective maxim and moves it to a universal law in human action and behavior. It is important to note here that men and women are subjects, not objects, even within a business or corporate context. So we move to Kant's practical imperative, which is this: Act in such a way that you always treat humanity, whether in your own person or in the person of any other, never simply as a means but *always* at the same time as an end. Men and women may have utilitarian value as means of production at one level, but they also and always are ends in and of themselves according to Kant. It is for that reason that we should be concerned as employers, fellow employees, and followers for the health and well-being, and the pain and suffering, of those with whom we labor. To do otherwise, in Lee Iacocca's words, turns the company into a sweat shop or, worse, a labor camp in which people are treated as slave labor.

The Academy of Management, originally founded to help meet society's social and economic objectives to serve the public interest, has produced scholarship primarily focused on society's economic objectives much more than the latter during the period of 1958 to 2000 (Walsh, Weber, & Margolis, 2003). It is in the social domain that intrinsic value falls, yet this does not have to be inherently in conflict with utilitarian and economic value. For example, in one case study of a major industrial restructuring and closure process, the chief executive placed the care and well-being of all employees as a top priority, a very close second to the mission of the organization (Quick, Tetrick, et al., 2003). During the 6-year process affecting 13,000 employees, there was not a single fatality (neither suicide nor homicide), not a single substantive incidence of workplace violence, and more than $33 million in cost avoidance because of low conflict levels in the workplace.

The Past 15 Years of Occupational Health Research

The past 15 years have seen a merging of multiple disciplinary approaches to occupational health as the community of researchers better understands the interconnectedness of physical health, PWB, safety, and the outcomes of organizations. Each can have significant impacts on the others, and all operate interdependently for the health of the individual worker and the organization. Appreciating how the field of occupational health has evolved over time requires more than reviewing the historical and theoretical foundations outlined by those who have been devoted to its study. A comprehensive overview of what has been published in the area provides unique insight into how well the research stream has matched the vision of those who founded and continue to promote study in this area.

We reviewed three major journals to get an impression of how the research in occupational health has progressed and what topics have merited publication. These are *JOHP*,

JOM, and *Journal of Organizational Behavior (JOB)*. *JOHP* began publication in 1996. It is a key source of peer-reviewed research in the area of occupational health, with strong links to psychology, management, and organizational behavior disciplines and a strong international contingent, all of which makes it an excellent baseline resource to use to gain an overview of the published research topics. We reviewed the articles in *JOHP* from its inception and categorized them into major topic areas. We then searched *JOM* and *JOB* for all articles within the same period using *occupational health, health, well-being,* and each of the 20 major topic areas identified in the *JOHP* overview. This overview resulted in quantity counts by topic for each publication for a variety of topics. It held true that those topics identified in the *JOHP* review were also prevalent in the *JOM* and *JOB* reviews, but there were also some additional topics identified as well.

Table 6.2.1 provides the results of this overview. It is important to understand that the purpose of this overview is not to comprehensively review the content of these articles but rather to gain an understanding of the major topic areas that merited publication during the period in question. We also acknowledge that search engines and our own synthesis of topics are likely to contain some errors and/or omissions of works in each topic area. However, we feel it is a fairly accurate general representation of the status of the published literature. The analysis provides interesting insights not only into topics that have remained strong throughout the 10- to 15-year range but also into how well these match the topics proposed by key researchers as new and most relevant to the changing work environment.

Table 6.2.1 Incidence of Occupational Health Topics by Journal and Time Segments: Past 15 Years

Topics	Journal of Occupational Health Psychology			Journal of Management			Journal of Organizational Behavior		
	1996	1997 to 2001	2002 to 2006	1992 to 1996	1997 to 2001	2002 to 2006	1992 to 1996	1997 to 2001	2002 to 2006
Stress (coping, social support, demand, control)	11	24	30	2	5	4	37	35	13
Burnout	0	7	8	0	0	1	12	11	4
Work–family	2	14	14	1	4	1	3	7	8
Violence, aggression, discrimination	2	11	18	0	3	1	1	3	5
Safety	1	12	7	0	0	0	8	1	10
Health and well-being	1	0	8	1	1	0	1	0	1
Employment, unemployment	0	2	14	0	0	1	1	5	5
Job insecurity	0	5	4	0	1	0	2	3	1
Substance abuse	0	1	4	0	1	0	3	1	1
Work design and environment	3	1	5	0	0	0	0	0	0
Gender	2	3	3	0	1	0	3	4	2
Conflict	0	4	2	0	0	3	1	2	2
Recovery	0	1	1	0	0	0	0	0	0
Leadership	1	2	3	0	0	0	0	2	2
Aging	1	0	2	1	2	0	1	0	1
Justice	0	4	0	0	1	0	1	0	3
Workaholism	0	0	1	1	1	0	0	0	1
Psychological contract	0	0	0	0	0	0	3	6	7
Positive organizational behavior	0	1	2	0	0	0	0	1	2

The overview shows that the stress theme continues to dominate the field, despite calls from journal editors and others within the field to move toward a more comprehensive view of health. However, there are areas particularly related to positive health that have been understudied despite long-standing calls to expand occupational health research into those areas. Editorials by the three editors of *JOHP* (Barling, 2005; Quick, 1999b; Tetrick, 2006) suggested that occupational health or OHP as a subset of this field is more than the study of stress, and they proposed new areas for study. Barling (2005) proposed two main areas to focus on (a) positive organizational behavior (POB) and positive psychology and (b) well-controlled intervention studies. Tetrick (2006) encouraged more research on the antecedents of occupational illness and injuries, positive health, intervention, underrepresented populations, and work–life issues and increased international studies.

Positive health and positive psychology are new areas that are in need of future validation, and study has not been heavily explored in the literature. Only two articles in *JOHP*, three in *JOB*, and none in *JOM* dealt with positive health or positive psychology as they relate to health and well-being. We also found limited coverage of intervention or promotion programs, despite repeated calls for more work in these areas. An explanation of the lack of positive articles is the relative newness of the concepts and the drastically different way that both positive movements tend to define health. The lack of promotion and intervention program studies is most likely related to the difficulty in getting the needed data over the periods required to assess the effectiveness of such programs.

In summary, an overview of the published peer-reviewed literature in three major publications shows that occupational health during the past 15 years has continued to be dominated by stress and stress-related topics such as burnout, job control and demands, social support, and coping. There are emerging topics that show fertile areas to expand occupational health. This review will now address the *positive* agenda, leadership, emotion, aging, technology, globalization, and intervention or promotion.

Occupational Health: Toward a More Positive Future

The preceding review of research within the domain of OHP revealed that some themes are clearly the cornerstones of the discipline. In addition, the review identified some themes that might best be categorized as "emerging." Research along these themes has been called for from several quarters, and some studies have emerged. Although there are smatterings of several research areas that are fairly new to occupational health, we believe that four hold potential to significantly add to occupational health's scope and, in particular, add balance in terms of emphasizing the positive in addition to repairing the negative at work.

Positive Health

The philosophical roots of positive health might be traced to Aristotle (2000), who described eudaimonia as the realization of one's true potential. Ryff and Singer (1998, 2002) noted that researchers and health practitioners alike tended to define health as the absence of negative states as opposed to the presence of positive states. They called for a holistic perspective of health, one that would include both mind–body interactions and wellness. In their integrative scheme, PWB encompasses six components: autonomy, personal growth, mastery of the environment, positive relationships with others, purpose in life, and self-acceptance (Ryff & Singer, 2001; Ryff, Singer, & Love, 2004).

Psychology has experienced a shift toward the positive as spurred by calls for positive psychology, the science of positive subjective experience (Seligman & Csikszentmihalyi, 2000). Included in positive psychology's mission is the need to focus on both human strengths and positive institutions. Extending the ideas of positive health and positive psychology, Luthans (2002a, 2002b) called for POB, building human strengths at work rather than altering weaknesses. He contended that POB researchers should investigate states that are positive psychological strengths, can be validly measured, and are malleable in terms of interventions in organizations to improve work performance. More recently, Nelson and Cooper (2007) called for a broader and more inclusive view of POB, to include states, traits, and processes.

Research in occupational health has followed a similar evolution and has been informed by positive psychology and POB. Wright and Cropanzano (2000b) noted that earlier occupational health research was conducted within a perspective of the disease model, that is, a focus on fixing what is wrong, including worker ill health and dissatisfaction. The more contemporary focus is on the health model, which focuses on what is right with people, including well-being and job satisfaction. The shift in emphasis is from preventing and/or resolving the negative at work to promoting the positive, and it has important implications in the workplace. Two studies indicated, for example, the contribution of PWB in predicting job performance (Wright & Cropanzano, 2000a).

The shift in occupational health toward studying positive outcomes is being accompanied by the study in the antecedents of positive outcomes at work. Borrowing from POB and positive organizational scholarship, the relationship between human strengths and positive health outcomes at work is receiving attention. Hardiness (Maddi, 2006), engagement (Britt, Adler, & Bartone, 2001), interpersonal trust (R. C. Mayer & Gavin, 2005), and vigor (Shirom, 2004) are among the strengths that have been studied. Eustress, the positive response to stress, is also being studied in terms of its potential influence on health and work performance (Nelson & Simmons, 2004). The task remains for researchers to connect these strengths and experiences to positive health outcomes at work in well-designed studies.

Leadership

Leadership is one of the more widely studied areas of psychology and management, and it has been linked with follower outcomes such as performance, satisfaction, and commitment. Some researchers have suggested that it is the most important issue in human sciences (cf. Hogan & Kaiser, 2005). Within occupational health, conceptual and theoretical articles have centered on the basic proposition that in addition to the more traditionally studied outcomes such as productivity, leaders can also influence outcomes such as health and happiness at work (Quick & Quick, 2004). Part of the leader's role, in essence, is encouraging employee well-being, in addition to creating and sustaining healthy organizations.

The form of leadership mentioned most often in such writings as applicable to occupational health outcomes is authentic leadership, a process that results in self-awareness and self-regulated positive behaviors that are demonstrated by both leaders and followers (Luthans and Avolio, 2003). Authentic leaders express their true selves and display hope, optimism, and confidence. It has been suggested that authentic leaders influence follower well-being through multiple channels. Some of these pathways include unconditional trust on the part of the follower, positive emotions engendered by the leader, and self-determination as fostered by the leader, who places a premium on follower development (Ilies, Morgeson, & Nahrgang, 2005).

Studies are emerging that link leadership with occupational health outcomes such as follower well-being and safety. Charismatic leadership was negatively related to workplace aggression in a study of employees from a wide variety of organizations (Hepworth & Towler, 2004). In a study of health care teams, leader inclusiveness, the extent to which leaders invited others' contributions, predicted psychological safety, which in turn was related to quality improvement work (Nembhard & Edmondson, 2006). Safety-specific transformational leadership has been shown to have a direct, positive effect on safety consciousness and safety climate and an indirect effect on reduced safety-related injuries (Barling, Loughlin, & Kelloway, 2002). In addition, passive leadership (laissez-faire and management by exception) has been shown to have the opposite effect: It had negative effects on safety consciousness and safety climate and was related to increased safety-related injuries (Kelloway, Mullen, & Francis, 2006). Studies of leadership in military settings have shown that supportive leader behavior was associated with increased job engagement and buffered soldiers from the adverse health effects of extremely stressful environments (Britt, Davison, & Bliese, 2004). In addition, hardy leaders increased hardy cognitions and behaviors among their followers, thereby increasing resilient responses under stressful circumstances (Bartone, 2006).

There has been little study of the processes whereby leadership affects follower well-being in terms of specifying precise mechanisms. A study conducted among employees of Community Trusts (health care organizations in Britain) demonstrated that leader behavior and subordinate well-being are linked via a complex reciprocal process. The same study indicated that the influence of leader behavior on follower well-being is likely to occur within a short period (van Dierendonck, Haynes, Borrill, & Stride, 2004).

Mood and Emotions

Within occupational health, positive and negative affect have a long history of research in terms of their effects on the stressor–strain relationship (Burke, Brief, & George, 1993). This emphasis accompanied the affective movement in the broader field of organizational behavior. Mood, or state affect, is of fairly long duration and often without a salient cause. Emotions, in contrast, tend to be of shorter duration and often are linked with identifiable causes. Both mood and emotions are playing a more focal role in occupational health research.

Positive mood, for example, has been linked with better immune system functioning (Stone, Cox, Vladimarsdottier, & Jandorf, 1987; Stone, Neale, Cox, & Napoli, 1994) and higher performance at work (Erez & Isen, 2002). Negative mood has been related to self-reported ill health, whereas positive mood was related to better subjective health (Benyamini, Idler, Leventhal, & Leventhal, 2000). Perceived organizational politics were positively related to depressed mood at work among workers from a wide array of occupations (Byrne, Kacmar, Stoner, & Hockwarter, 2005). A daily diary study of human resource employees demonstrated that individuals who believe that work demands thwart their work performance or that work demands lead to bad moods were more likely to experience unpleasant moods on the same day (Harris & Daniels, 2005).

Discrete emotions have been studied less frequently but have become part of conceptual models of well-being at work. Frederickson's (1998) broaden-and-build theory, for example, contends that positive emotions such as joy and contentment broaden the individual's scope of attention, cognition, and action. This leads to resource building, which in turn increases well-being. Negative emotions, in contrast, narrow the thought–action pathway and lead individuals to excessively focus on problems. Wright, Cropanzano, and Bonett (2007) adapted their work on PWB to the broaden-and-build framework, finding that PWB moderated the job satisfaction–job performance relationship. Consistent with broaden-and-build theory, performance was highest when employees reported higher scores on both PWB and job satisfaction. The authors extended the moderating effect of PWB to the job satisfaction–employee retention relationship, finding that the relationship between job satisfaction and retention was stronger for those employees with high levels of PWB (Wright & Bonett, 2007). Thus, the more positive the employee's PWB, the more likely the employee will remain on the job, regardless of the level of job satisfaction.

Emotional labor, or emotion work, is managing emotions for a wage (Hochschild, 1983). Grandey (2000) presented a model in which emotional regulation, including deep acting and surface acting, was linked with individual well-being (burnout and job satisfaction) and organizational well-being (performance and withdrawal behavior). When employees engage in deep acting, in attempts to seem authentic, they modify their feelings by changing their perceptions of the situation. When employees surface act, they regulate their expressions of emotions, including suppressing or faking emotions, to execute their job duties. Grandey's model was tested among customer service employees in a call center (Totterdell & Holman, 2003). Deep and surface acting had different consequences for employees. Surface acting was related to emotional exhaustion, but deep acting was not. Deep acting was related to the display of positive emotions and to job performance, but surface acting was not.

Emotional intelligence, or emotional competence, has been introduced as an integrated set of affect-related skills at work (cf. J. D. Mayer, Caruso, & Salovey, 2000). In a study of German retail workers, emotional competence was found to be an important work-related resource that helped service employees cope with the demands of their jobs and the emotional dissonance that often results from emotion work (Giardini and Frese, 2006). Emotional competence served as a buffer in the relationship between emotional labor and employee well-being.

In summary, the affective revolution has made its mark on occupational health research, spurring a move toward studying discrete emotions and emotional processes at work such as emotional labor. In addition, emotional competence is emerging as a set of resources that may buffer employees from negative health outcomes at work.

Interventions

Lest we paint an overly positive picture of occupational health's future, a caveat is in order. Despite calls for well-designed intervention studies, few have emerged. Although considerable knowledge has accumulated concerning risk factors in organizations, along with their connections to occupational illnesses and injuries, comparably less is known about effective interventions for reducing the risk factors. Reviews of the intervention literature have produced disappointing results. Health-promotion programs, along with other occupational health and safety interventions as a whole, have not demonstrated sustained changes in employee behaviors (Heaney, 2003). It should be recognized that researchers face challenges in studying interventions and that control group designs and randomization are not often possible. And interventions are often guided by practical considerations rather than being informed by theory.

Interventions also evolve and change once they are implemented. Consider, for example, the history of health circles used in Germany (Aust & Ducki, 2004). Adapted from quality circles and other employee participation approaches, health circles operate on the assumption that employees are in the best position to improve their own job conditions (Brandenburg & Slesina, 1994). Health circles evolved from simple research projects focused on changing work conditions (risk factors) to comprehensive programs that are now commonly used to enhance employees' health. A typical health circle process takes 15 months to complete, including a health report and survey, multiple health circle meetings, and evaluation. Originally, health circles included only employees, but some companies now use separate health circles for managers (Brandenburg & Marshall, 1999). A review of research evidence indicated that reliable indications of the success of health circles were absent, in large part because of the weaknesses of the methods used in the studies (Aust & Ducki, 2004).

The good news is that as occupational health evolves, so can the foci of interventions. Many early interventions focused on stress prevention (Cigrang, Todd, & Carbone, 2000; de Jong & Emmelkamp, 2000; Giga, Cooper, & Faragher, 2003; Kompier, Aust, van den Berg, & Siegrist, 2000), along with preventing depression (Vuori, Silvonen, Vinokur, & Price, 2002) and burnout (Halbesleben, Osburn, & Mumford, 2006; Hätinen, Kinnunen, Pekkonen, & Aro, 2004). As the definition of health becomes more holistic and positive, interventions should target the enhancement of individual strengths that promote overall well-being and individual states that promote health. As we accumulate research evidence that such strengths as resilience, vigor, engagement, and hope are linked with health outcomes, we must, as a natural next step, design and examine ways to enhance these strengths in the workplace and evaluate the interventions in well-designed, scientific studies. Care must also be taken to address the level of change intended (individual and/or organizational). Many studies have focused on the individual as the target of change and have shown that individual-level interventions alone may not enhance health if the organization does not change as well (Heaney, 2003). The concept of healthy organizations means that along with profits and productivity, the collective well-being of employees is an important outcome.

New Horizons: Expanding the Realm and Vision of Occupational Health Research

As occupational health continues to evolve as a field of study, we believe that along with the prevailing topics of the past, there are several new or minimally addressed topics that hold high potential. These new horizons in occupational health deal with the need to address the changing nature of organizations and workers and how these changes relate to health. We include advances in technology, virtual work, globalization, and the aging of the workforce as four significant areas for exploration. We propose that these areas provide the most potential for moving occupational health into the next 15 years and beyond.

Technology

Technological advances are usually considered as positive resources to assist with improved performance, increased productivity, and economic growth. Yet the rapid pace in which technological change has progressed has resulted in many unexpected and potentially problematic outcomes. The impact of a world where technology is increasing our work capacity, eliminating space and time boundaries, and challenging individuals to keep up with constant and rapid change is an increasingly important area for occupational health scientists. We need to further investigate how the rapidly changing technology affects worker health and how to best promote health within this technologically dependent society.

The growing dependence on information technology, with long hours spent behind computer terminals and with decreasing amounts of human interaction, is a key factor to investigate (Sparks, Faragher, & Cooper, 2001). Negative physical and psychological health consequences of working with technology have been shown (e.g., Aaras, Horgen, & Ro, 2000; Dillon & Emurian, 1996; Ekberg et al., 1995; Sparks et al., 2001). The ever-increasing rate and quantity of information that workers must manage and the elimination of time and space barriers present high potential for stress and its negative outcomes. With technology, we have a loss of a specific "workday" and "workplace," leaving workers with a 24-hr workday that can be accomplished in any location. Demands for worker accessibility anytime and anywhere result in e-mails being sent from home at 3:00 a.m. and addictions to devices such as the Blackberry (aka "Crackberry"). Incredible changes in the way people work and how it affects health is a key area of study for the future.

Virtual Work

Within the technology area, virtual work is of increasing importance to organizational health. *Virtual work* has been used to describe a variety of work situations, from part-time telecommuting to entire job settings in which the worker is separated by time, space, or both from his coworkers and clients. Lipnack and Stamps (2000) define virtual work as work in which people interact in an interdependent relationship using various electronic or technology-based means of communication with little or no face-to-face contact. Telecommuting or telework also has the worker separated by time or distance from other workers and uses computer-based technologies, but the work is usually more independent and requires less collaboration (Townsend & DeMarie, 1998). Regardless of the level of "virtuality," these new job structures are common options (Kirkman, Rosen, Gibson, Tesluk, & McPherson, 2002; Townsend & DeMarie, 1998).

Although the benefits of virtual work are well documented both from the employer's and from the employee's perspectives (Harpaz, 2002), virtual work may also present its own unique set of challenges from an occupational health perspective. Some studies show that predicted productivity and job satisfaction benefits are not being realized (Bailey & Kurland, 2002; Crandall & Wallace, 1997). One of the most prevalent predictions related to virtual work is the threat of social isolation (Baruch & Nicholson, 1997; Cascio, 2000; Connaughton & Daly, 2004; Crossan & Burton, 1993; DeSanctis, 1984; Kirkman et al., 2002; McQuillen, 2003).

Harpaz (2002) suggested that major disadvantages included impaired feelings of belonging, feelings of isolation, lack of professional support, and personality unsuitability. Lynch (2000) suggested that the manner of communication inherent in virtual work lacks the interpersonal connectedness that humans require for health and well-being. Virtual work thus increases the risks of social isolation and loneliness, which are important risk factors for cardiovascular health that are as detrimental as risks more readily accepted such as smoking, obesity, and family history. Other researchers agree that social isolation and loneliness are associated with negative psychological and physical outcomes (Anderson & Anderson, 2003; Hawkley, Berntson, Burleson, & Cacioppo, 2003; Pennebaker, 1990).

Although the research on the impact of isolation on health is fairly consistent and compelling, the research on the prevalence and impact of isolation on virtual workers is less so. The expectation that the "isolated" nature of virtual work will lead to perceptions of isolation is not uniformly supported. Virtual work may enhance rather than hinder effective social support and relationship development (Walther, 1995), and adaptation to alternate forms of communication that allow for similar relational capacity as traditional communication forms may be possible (Townsend & DeMarie, 1998). Potential moderators of the relationship between virtual work and the perceptions of social isolation might include individual differences in coping, comfort, and competency with communication technologies, type and patterns of communication interactions, early trust development, and presence of other social networks (Macik-Frey, 2006). Thus, from the occupational health perspective, virtual work appears to be an area ripe for discovery. Why do some individuals thrive in this environment whereas others suffer? How can organizations address the potential risks, select appropriate employees, and monitor the success of their virtual workers?

Globalization

As the workplace becomes increasingly global, there are interesting areas to explore related to globalization and occupational health. As discussed in Spielberger and Reheiser (2005), the issue of the health and well-being of the worker is not simply a U.S. issue. There is a growing interest in the need to protect the health, safety, and general welfare of the global workforce (World Health Organization, 2000). This globalization of occupational health issues leads to interesting topics for study. What impact do cultural differences have on the perception of health, the impact of stressors, and the ability to overcome health and safety issues? Are there universal principles related to the safety and occupational health of workers? Can these principles be implemented across cultures? Spector et al. (2002), for example, found that the positive relationship of work locus of control and physical well-being that is characteristic of the United States was not consistent across the 24 cultures they studied. What other differences related to occupational health and culture will be found?

Other globalization topics include the implications of cultural differences related to work values, dress code, language, religion, training needs, and leadership attitudes toward diversity (Sparks et al., 2001). Issues of discrimination, cultural awareness, and racism and their relationships to the health and well-being of employees are also important to explore. Likewise, research on selecting appropriate employees across cultures has been limited (Ployhart, 2006) and has suggested significant impact on the ultimate success of workers in the global workplace.

The International Commission on Occupational Health (ICOH) is a 90-country, multi-disciplinary organization that has as its mission the promotion of occupational health at an international level. ICOH has expressed the need to reorient its activities to address new technologies and the globalization of the economy. Members advocate a transcultural approach to the problems of occupational health (Caillard, 1999). Organizations such as ICOH are likely to continue to be vehicles for research in multinational issues related to the health and well-being of workers.

Aging

The aging of the population in the United States and throughout the world is a challenge for many organizations (Bovbjerg, 2001; Holtz-Eakin, Lovely, & Tosun, 2004; P. G. Peterson, 2002; Rice & Fineman, 2004; Spiezia, 2002; U.S. Census Bureau, 1995; World Bank, 1999). P. G. Peterson (2002) described this worldwide phenomenon as "a transformation—even a revolution—with few parallels in humanity's past. Indeed, this revolution has already begun. Perhaps two-thirds of all people who have ever reached the age of 65 are alive today" (p. 189). The baby boomer generation of 78 million, born between the years of 1946 and 1964, is the largest birth cohort in our history and is rapidly moving into the older age groups (Bovbjerg, 2001; Gutheil, 1996). The proportion of the U.S. population in the 65 and older age group has grown from 4.0% at the turn of the century to 8.1% in the 1950s and to

12.4% in 2000. And predictions suggest that by 2030 it could reach as high as 20.0% (Social Security Administration, 2000; U.S. Census Bureau, 2000). From 2000 to 2010, the number of persons aged 25 to 54 is expected to increase by 1.2%, whereas the number of persons 55 to 64 is expected to increase by more than 47.0% (Purcell, 2000). According to a U.S. Census Bureau (1995) report, since 1900, the number of persons in the United States 65 and younger has tripled, whereas the number of persons older than 65 has increased 11 times. From 1960 to 1994, the U.S. population grew 45%, with the 65 and older group growing 100% and the 85 and older group growing at an astounding 274%!

This "age wave," also referred to as the "demographic transition" (Holtz-Eakin et al., 2004), describes the rapid aging of the developed and, increasingly, the less developed of the world's population. Along with aging, people are living healthier lives, and the expectation is that the workforce average age will continue to increase. These changes have significant implications for the field of occupational health, ranging from the physical health to the PWB of this older workforce. Despite these projections, Bovbjerg (2001), in a report to House of Representatives committee members from the Employer–Employee Relations and the Education of the Workforce committees, concludes that few organizations are implementing changes to address the aging workforce. Bovbjerg, based on interviews of human capital representatives from the private and public sectors, union officials, pension and human capital experts from consulting firms, economists, academics, and various advocacy group representatives and on data from the Current Population Survey (CPS), the Displaced Workers Supplement to CPS, and the Health and Retirement Study, concluded that very little is being done by organizations to address the age wave. Some exceptions exist, such as CVS pharmacies, Wal-Mart, and Home Depot, which specifically target the older workforce as sales associates and cashiers; however, these positions are lower paid, less skilled options (Ruiz, 2006). At this point, little empirical research is available to identify what, if anything, is being done at the organizational level to verify any age wave impact or to address contingency plans related to the older worker, especially related to retaining knowledge workers. This research, and its implications for occupational health, is an important future area for the field.

Two disturbing trends worthy of exploration from an occupational health perspective are early retirement and ageism. First, older workers, although living longer and healthier lives, are exiting the workforce earlier, although this is not always in their best economic or psychosocial interests (Spiezia, 2002). An American Association of Retired Persons (1999) study showed that 80% of older workers expect to work in their retirement years. Forteza and Prieto (1994) report that as many as two thirds of those contemplating retirement perceive it as unpleasant, an end to future opportunities, and the beginning of a generally dull existence. There appears to be a discontinuity in the trend for older workers to leave the workforce earlier, either by choice or force, and their expressed desires to remain actively engaged. How this paradoxical situation affects occupational health and well-being is a key area for study.

Creative strategies to retain older workers are emerging. Morrison, Erickson, and Dychtwald (2006) discuss six such strategies: (a) provide fresh assignments and challenges, such as different geographic locations where new skills can be gained and old skills can be renewed, usually done through lateral moves; (b) offer internal career changes within the organization; (c) put experienced employees into mentoring and knowledge-sharing roles; (d) provide fresh training and development throughout the range of workers, not assuming that older, more experienced workers no longer need training; (e) offer sabbaticals for regeneration; and (f) expand leadership-development programs. This article provides numerous examples of organizations that are beginning to implement these strategies.

Unique options for employment to address the need of workers to continue to work and of employers to retain them are also emerging. Bridge employment, employment that takes place after a person's retirement from a full-time position but before the person's permanent withdrawal from the workforce, includes creative options to retain workers, as does changing attitudes about "appropriate" retirement ages and changing pension and tax laws that discourage bridge employment (Garten, 2005).

The second trend is that older workers disproportionately suffer from downsizing and layoffs (Bovbjerg, 2001), receive less training and development (Ranzijn, 2004; Simpson, Greller, & Stroh, 2002; Spiezia, 2002), and receive less on-the-job training (Booth, 1993; Frazis, Gitterman, & Joyce, 1998). Based on the Displaced Workers Survey for 2000, 9% of older workers versus 11% of younger workers lost their jobs, and 57% of older workers retired following a job loss. Once these older workers retired, they rarely reentered the workforce. Thus, a job loss with this older segment often results in premature exiting from the workforce (Bovbjerg, 2001). Late-career workers are only half as likely to participate in training as younger workers (Simpson et al., 2002), and there is a negative correlation between increases in age and levels of reported on-the-job training (Frazis et al., 1998).

At a time when the average age of workers in the United States and other developed countries is increasing along with their healthy life expectancy, we are not seeing comparable levels of change in attitudes, biases, and stereotypes about aging. Ageism seems to be pervasive in the workforce and in society at large (Cardinali & Gordon, 2002; Finkelstein, Burke, & Raju, 1995; Greller & Stroh, 2004; Grossman, 2005; Hassell & Perrewé, 1995; Maurer & Rafuse, 2001; Paul & Townsend, 1993; Tougas, Lagace, De La Sablonniere, & Kocum, 2004). A general belief exists by workers, even older workers, that aging results in declines in performance, flexibility, creativity, safety, and ability to continue in the workforce, which significantly affects selection, promotion, and training decisions (Greller & Stroh, 2004). A meta-analytic study found that discrimination against older workers was higher when participants were younger, when participants had no job-relevant information about the older worker, and when participants simultaneously rated older and younger workers (Finkelstein et al., 1995). The issue of ageism and how it affects occupational health is another rich area for study.

Finally, long-standing stereotypes regarding aging include the perception that older workers have decreased performance, have decreased stamina, are difficult to train, are inflexible, are greater safety risks, and have less capacity to work. Along with these beliefs is the assumption that these are "natural" outcomes of getting older. Research has systematically shown that these assumptions for the most part are false, but they are responsible for ongoing discrimination that can significantly affect older workers (Johnson & Neumark, 1997). First, a large number of individuals remain healthy and free of significant decline well into their 70s. Exercise, diet, and healthy lifestyles significantly affect the presence of cognitive, perceptual, and behavioral declines. Second, performance is not significantly different for younger and older workers, except when the work requires heavy physical labor (Avolio, Waldman, & McDaniel, 1990; Greller & Simpson, 1999; McEvoy & Cascio, 1989; Warr, 1994). One possibility to explore in future research is whether job performance changes considered a result of the "normal" declines of aging may be confused with the effects of limiting the human capital investment in older workers and thus reducing the ongoing skill retention and development. Additional study is needed to determine what changes are related to growing older and what are resulting from the treatment older workers receive, the attitudes of others, and the resultant decreased motivation in that segment of the workforce. We also need to address what changes or interventions will best support the aging workforce.

Conclusion

Since Ganster and Schaubroeck's (1991) and Danna and Griffin's (1999) earlier reviews, much has transpired in the realm of occupational health. We have seen a slow shift from a field dominated by stress research to one experiencing a growing positive paradigmatic shift. We have seen the merging of various disciplinary approaches and cultural perspectives to occupational health as representative of our growing understanding of the interconnectedness of the mind, the body, the environment, and the social networks in which we live. No longer will it suffice to think of safety, ergonomics, stress, and physical and psychological health or any number of other occupational health factors in isolation. With the growing understanding that the mind and body are not separate and that both are constantly influenced by the physical and social world, we see exciting changes coming.

This review falls in line with those that preceded and helps chronicle the progress of the field. We foresee the next version 15 years from now, and we are intrigued by what we imagine will be seen. First, the general notion of health in the traditional, medical sense will be obsolete. Issues such as absenteeism, burnout, strain, depression, cardiovascular disease, despair, and withdrawal will be replaced with engagement, purpose, thriving, hope, vigor, and optimism. Much less of health will involve overcoming deficiencies and illness, and much more will be learning the secrets of the self-actualized person. Organizations will address the health of their workers from this more holistic paradigm, providing increased respite, opportunities for autonomy, challenging and meaningful goals, and social support. It will be commonplace for organizations to work to create mutual purpose with their employees, not just because it is the right thing to do for the individual but because the benefits to the organization are becoming realized. These premises will no longer be practiced as only a benefit to the individual but because research and time demonstrate that the healthy worker is the best worker and the business that promotes this new sense of health is good business.

Along this line, zest, which is characterized by anticipation, energy, and excitement, will emerge as a positive trait among people at work (C. Peterson, Park, Hall, & Seligman, in press). In their large-scale study of more than 9,800 working adults, C. Peterson et al. (in press) found that zest predicted an orientation to work as a calling, to the experience of work satisfaction, and to the experience of general life satisfaction. All these are positive outcomes. However, the health risk of cardiovascular disease as the leading cause of death for men and women cannot be ignored. In this vein, Wright, Cropanzano, Bonett, and Diamond (in press) found that PWB was predictive of composite cardiovascular health as measured by pulse product, a new way of looking at cardiovascular health.

The occupational health research field continues to deal with stress, and stress is both directly and indirectly related to cardiovascular health and well-being. However, occupational health is no longer preoccupied with just the negative aspects; it seeks instead how to harness the positive benefits of eustress. The focus shifts from topics such as how to avoid burnout to how to increase engagement. Research is also likely to span multiple disciplines. The physical, psychological, environmental, organizational, and social aspects of a particular work situation as approached by teams from medicine, psychology, engineering, management, and sociology bring broader conceptualizations more in line with the reality and the complexity of work life. We see a growing segment of research that draws on this knowledge and applies the principles in organizational systems through interventions that incorporate ongoing evaluation so that real progress is possible toward improved health of the global worker. We see new, innovative ways to harness technology to lighten the burden of the worker rather than add to it. Finally, we see a growing line of research that helps us understand and apply what we know about occupational health throughout the world.

Acknowledgments

The authors wish to thank Cary L. Cooper, Lennart Levi, Ronald C. Kessler, Larry Murphy, Jonathan D. Quick, Paul Rosch, and Lois Tetrick for their comments and suggestions in the development of this chapter. They thank Joel A. Quintans for his graphic expertise, Carol Byrne for her information technology expertise, and Deeti Chudgar for his research assistance.

References

Aaras, A., Horgen, G., & Ro, O. 2000. Work with the visual display unit: Health consequences. *International Journal of Human-Computer Interaction*, 12: 107–134.

Adkins, J. A. 1998. Base closure: A case study in occupational stress and organizational decline. In M. K. Gowing, J. D. Kraft, & J. C. Quick (Eds.), *The new organizational reality: Downsizing, restructuring, and revitalization:* 111–142. Washington, DC: American Psychological Association.

Adkins, J. A. 1999. Promoting organizational health: The evolving practice of occupational health psychology. *Professional Psychology: Research and Practice*, 30: 129–137.

Adkins, J. A., Quick, J. C., & Moe, K. O. 2000. Building world class performance in changing times. In L. R. Murphy & C. L. Cooper (Eds.), *Healthy and productive work: An international perspective:* 107–132. Philadelphia: Taylor & Francis.

American Association of Retired Persons. 1999. *"Stealing time" study: A summary of findings.* http://research.aarp.org/health/pbs_1.html.

Anderson, N. B., & Anderson, P. E. 2003. *Emotional longevity: What really determines how long you live.* New York: Viking Penguin.

Aristotle. 2000. *The Nicomachean ethics* (R. Crisp, trans.). Cambridge, UK: Cambridge University Press.

Aust, B., & Ducki, A. 2004. Comprehensive health promotion interventions at the workplace: Experiences with health circles in Germany. *Journal of Occupational Health Psychology*, 9: 258–270.

Avolio, B. J., Waldman, D. A., & McDaniel, M. A. 1990. Age and work performance in nonmanagerial jobs: The effects of experience and occupational type. *Academy of Management Journal*, 33: 407–423.

Bailey, D. E., & Kurland, N. B. 2002. A review of telework research: Findings, new directions, and lessons for the study of modern work. *Journal of Organizational Behavior*, 23: 383–400.

Barling, J. 2005. Editorial: "And now, the time has come." *Journal of Occupational Health Psychology*, 10: 307–309.

Barling, J., & Griffith, A. 2003. A history of occupational health psychology. In J. C. Quick & L. E. Tetrick (Eds.), *Handbook of occupational health psychology:* 9–33. Washington, DC: American Psychological Association.

Barling, J., Loughlin, C., & Kelloway, E. K. 2002. Development and test of a model linking safety-specific transformational leadership and occupational safety. *Journal of Applied Psychology*, 87: 488–496.

Bartone, P. T. 2006. Resilience under military operational stress: Can leaders influence hardiness? *Military Psychology*, 18: S131–S178.

Baruch, Y., & Nicholson, N. 1997. Home, sweet work: Requirements for effective home working. *Journal of General Management*, 23: 15–30.

Benyamini, Y., Idler, E. L., Leventhal, H., & Leventhal, E. A. 2000. Positive affect and function as influences on self-assessment of health: Expanding our view beyond illness and disability. *Journals of Gerontology*, 55B: 107–116.

Berger, M. L., Murray, J. F., Xu, J., & Pauly, M. 2001. Alternative valuations of work loss and productivity. *Journal of Occupational and Environmental Medicine*, 43: 18–24.

Bernacki, E. J. 2002. *Presidential remarks*. Presented at the annual meeting of the American College of Occupational and Environmental Medicine, Chicago.

Biddle, E., Hartley, D., Starkey, S., Fabrega, V., & Richardson, S. 2005. *Deriving occupational fatal injury costs: A state pilot study*. Washington, DC: Bureau of Labor Statistics.

Booth, A. L. 1993. Private sector training and graduate earnings. *Review of Economics and Statistics*, 75: 164–170.

Bovbjerg, B. D. 2001. *Older workers—Demographic trends pose challenges for employers and workers*. Washington, DC: Government Printing Office.

Brandenburg, U., & Marshall, B. 1999. "Healthcoming" for supervisors. In B. Badura, M. Litsch, & C. Vetter, (Eds.), *Absence report 1999: Psychological strain at the workplace. Figures, data, facts from all business branches:* 254–268. Berlin, Germany: Springer.

Brandenburg, U., & Slesina, W. 1994. Health promotion circles: A new approach to health promotion at worksite. *Homeostasis in Health and Disease*, 35: 43–48.

Britt, T. W., Adler, A. B., & Bartone, P. T. 2001. Deriving benefits from stressful events: The role of engagement in meaningful work and handiness. *Journal of Occupational Health Psychology*, 6: 53–63.

Britt, T. W., Davison, J., & Bliese, P. D. 2004. How leaders can influence the impact that stressors have on soldiers. *Military Medicine*, 169: 541–545.

Burke, M. J., Brief, A. P., & George, J. M. 1993. The role of negative affectivity in understanding relations between self-reports of stressors and strains: A comment on the applied psychology literature. *Journal of Applied Psychology*, 78: 402–412.

Byrne, Z. S., Kacmar, C., Stoner, J., & Hochwarter, W. A. 2005. The relationship between perceptions of politics and depressed mood at work: Unique moderators across three levels. *Journal of Occupational Health Psychology*, 10: 330–343.

Caillard, J.-F. 1999. Introduction to the special section on psychological and behavior approaches to occupational health. *Journal of Occupational Health Psychology*, 4: 84–86.

Cardinali, R., & Gordon, Z. 2002. Ageism: No longer the equal opportunity stepchild. *Equal Opportunities International*, 21: 58–68.

Cascio, W. F. 2000. Managing a virtual workplace. *Academy of Management Executive*, 14: 81–90.

Chernew, M., Cutler, D., & Keenan, P. 2005. Increasing health insurance costs and the decline of insurance coverage. *Health Services Research*, 40: 1021–1039.

Cigrang, J., Todd, S., & Carbone, E. 2000. Stress management training for military trainees returned to duty after a mental health evaluation: Effect on graduation rates. *Journal of Occupational Health Psychology*, 5: 48–55.

Clarke, S. 2006. The relationship between safety climate and safety performance: A meta-analytic review. *Journal of Occupational Health Psychology*, 11: 315–327.

Cocchiara, F. K., & Quick, J. C. 2004. The negative effects of positive stereotypes: Ethnicity-related stressors and implications on organizational health. *Journal of Organizational Behavior*, 25: 781–785.

Collins, J. J., Baase, C. M., Sharda, C. E., Ozminkowski, R. J., Nicholson, S., Billotti, G. M., Gurpin, R. S., Olson, M., Turpin, O., & Berger, M. L. 2005. The assessment of chronic health conditional on work performance, absence and total economic impact for employers. *Journal of Occupational and Environmental Medicine*, 47: 547–557.

Connaughton, S. L., & Daly, J. A. 2004. Long distance leadership: Communicative strategies for leading virtual teams. In D. J. Pauleen (Ed.), *Virtual teams: Projects, protocols and processes:* 116–142. Hershey, PA: Idea Group.

Cooper, C. L., & Quick, J. C. (Eds.). 2007. Managerial dimensions of organizational health. *Journal of Management Studies*, 44: 189–350.

Crandall, N. F., & Wallace, M. J. 1997. Inside the virtual workplace: Forging a new deal for work and rewards. *Compensation and Benefits Review*, 29: 22–36.

Crossan, G., & Burton, P. F. 1993. Teleworking stereotypes: A case study. *Journal of Information Science*, 19(5): 349–362.

Danna, K., & Griffin, R. W. 1999. Health and well-being in the workplace: A review and synthesis of the literature. *Journal of Management*, 25: 357–384.

de Jong, G., & Emmelkamp, P. 2000. Implementing a stress management training: Comparative trainer effectiveness. *Journal of Occupational Health Psychology*, 5: 309–320.

DeSanctis, G. 1984. Attitudes toward telecommuting: Implications for work-at-home programmes. *Information & Management*, 7: 133–139.

Dillon, T. W., & Emurian, H. H. 1996. Some factors affecting reports of visual fatigue resulting from use of a VDU. *Computers in Human Behavior*, 12: 49–59.

Doll, L. S., Bonzo, S. E., Sleet, D. A., & Mercy, J. A. 2007. *Handbook of injury and violence prevention*. New York: Springer.

Einarsen, S., Hoel, H., Cooper, C. L., & Zapf, D. 2003. *Bullying and emotional abuse in the workplace*. London: Taylor & Francis.

Ekberg, K., Eklund, J., Tuvesson, M., Oetengren, R., Odenrick, P., & Ericson, M. 1995. Psychological stress and muscle activity during data entry at visual display units. *Work and Stress*, 9: 475–490.

Elkind, H. B. (Ed.). 1931. *Preventive management: Mental hygiene in industry*. New York: B. C. Forbes.

Erez, A., & Isen, A. 2002. The influence of positive affect on the components of expectancy motivation. *Journal of Applied Psychology*, 87: 1055–1067.

Finkelstein, L. M., Burke, M. J., & Raju, N. S. 1995. Age discrimination in simulated employment contexts: An integrative analysis. *Journal of Applied Psychology*, 80: 652–663.

Forteza, J. A., & Prieto, J. M. 1994. Aging and work behavior. In H. C. Triandis, D. Marvin, & L. M. Hough (Eds.), *Handbook of industrial and organizational psychology* (2nd ed.), vol. 4: 485–550. Palo Alto, CA: Consulting Psychologists Press.

Frazis, H., Gitterman, M., & Joyce, M. 1998. *Determinants of training: An analysis using both employer and employee characteristics*. http://www.bls.gov/ore/pdf/ec980010.pdf.

Frederickson, B. L. 1998. What good are positive emotions? *Review of General Psychology*, 2: 300–319.

Ganster, D. C., & Schaubroeck, J. 1991. Work stress and employee health. *Journal of Management*, 17: 235–271.

Garten, J. 2005. Keep boomers on the job. *Business Week*, 3959: 162.

Geller, E. S. 1996. *Working safe: How to help people actively care for health and safety*. Boca Raton, FL: CRC Press.

Giardini, A., & Frese, M. 2006. Reducing the negative effects of emotion work in service occupations: Emotional competence as a psychological resource. *Journal of Occupational Health Psychology*, 11: 63–75.

Giga, S. I., Cooper, C. L., & Faragher, B. 2003. The development of a framework for a comprehensive approach to stress management interventions at work. *International Journal of Stress Management*, 10: 280–296.

Glied, S., Lambrew, J., & Little, S. 2003. *The growing share of uninsured workers employed by large firms*. New York: Commonwealth Fund.

Grandey, A. (2000). Emotional regulation in the workplace: A new way to conceptualize emotional labor. *Journal of Occupational Health Psychology*, 5: 95–110.

Greller, M. M., & Simpson, P. 1999. In search of late career: A review of contemporary social science research applicable to understanding late career. *Human Resource Management Review*, 9: 309–347.

Greller, M. M., & Stroh, L. K. 2004. Making the most of "late career" for employers and workers themselves: Becoming elders not relics. *Organizational Dynamics*, 33: 204–214.

Grossman, R. J. 2005. The under-reported impact of age discrimination and its threat to business vitality. *Business Horizons*, 48: 71–78.

Gutheil, I. A. 1996. Introduction. The many faces of aging: Challenges for the future. *Gerontologist*, 36: 13–14.

Halbesleben, J. R. B., Osburn, H. K., & Mumford, M. D. 2006. Action research as a burnout intervention: Reducing burnout in the federal fire service. *Journal of Applied Behavioral Studies*, 42: 244–266.

Halperin, W., Monson, R. R., & Baker, E. L. 2001. *Public health surveillance*. New York: John Wiley.

Harpaz, I. 2002. Advantages and disadvantages of telecommuting for the individual, organization and society. *Work Study*, 51: 74–80.

Harris, C., & Daniels, K. 2005. Daily affect and daily beliefs. *Journal of Occupational Health Psychology*, 10: 415–428.

Hassell, B. L., & Perrewé, P. L. 1995. An examination of beliefs about older workers: Do stereotypes still exist? *Journal of Organizational Behavior,* 16: 457–468.

Hätinen, M., Kinnunen, U., Pekkonen, M., & Aro, A. 2004. Burnout patterns in rehabilitation: Short-term changes in job conditions, personal resources, and health. *Journal of Occupational Health Psychology,* 9: 220–237.

Hawkley, L. C., Berntson, G. G., Burleson, M. H., & Cacioppo, J. T. 2003. Loneliness in everyday life: Cardiovascular activity, psychosocial context, and health behaviors. *Journal of Personality and Social Psychology,* 85: 105–120.

Heaney, C. A. 2003. Worksite health interventions: Targets for change and strategies for attaining them. In J. C. Quick & L. E. Tetrick (Eds.), *Handbook of occupational health psychology:* 305–323. Washington, DC: American Psychological Association.

Hepworth, W., & Towler, A. 2004. The effects of individual differences and charismatic leadership on workplace aggression. *Journal of Occupational Health Psychology,* 9: 176–185.

Hippocrates. 1994. *Hippocrates, volume VII—Epidemics 2, 4–7.* (W. D. Smith, Ed. & Trans.). Cambridge, MA: Harvard University Press.

Hochschild, A. R. 1983. *The managed heart.* Berkeley: University of California Press.

Hogan, R., & Kaiser, R. B. 2005. What we know about leadership. *Review of General Psychology,* 9: 169–180.

Holtz-Eakin, K. D., Lovely, M. E., & Tosun, M. S. 2004. Generational conflict, fiscal policy, and economic growth. *Journal of Macroeconomics,* 26: 1–23.

Ihlebaek, C., Brage, S., & Eriksen, H. R. 2007. Health complaints and sickness absence in Norway, 1996–2003. *Occupational Medicine,* 57: 43–49.

Ilies, R., Morgeson, F. P., & Nahrgang, J. D. 2005. Authentic leadership and eudaemonic well-being: Understanding leader-follower outcomes. *Leadership Quarterly,* 16: 373–394.

Johnson, R. W., & Neumark, D. 1997. Age discrimination, job separations, and employment status of older workers: Evidence from self reports. *Journal of Human Resources,* 32: 779–811.

Kahn, R. L., Wolfe, D. M., Quinn, R. P., Snoek, J. D., & Rosenthal, R. A. 1964. *Organizational stress: Studies in role conflict and ambiguity.* New York: John Wiley.

Kant, I. 1958. *Groundwork of the metaphysic of morals* (H. J. Paton, Trans.). New York: Harper & Row.

Kelloway, E. K., Mullen, J., & Francis, L. 2006. Divergent effects of transformational and passive leadership on employee safety. *Journal of Occupational Health Psychology,* 11: 76–86.

Kirkman, B. L., Rosen, B., Gibson, C. B., Tesluk, P. E., & McPherson, S. O. 2002. Five challenges to virtual team success: Lessons from Sabre, Inc. *Academy of Management Executive,* 16: 67–80.

Kompier, M. A. J., Aust, B., van den Berg, A.-M., & Siegrist, J. 2000. Stress prevention in bus drivers: Evaluation of 13 natural experiments. *Journal of Occupational Health Psychology,* 5: 11–31.

Laird, D. 1929. *Psychology and profits.* New York: B. C. Forbes.

Langer, G. 2004. *Health care pains: Growing health care concerns fuel cautious support for change.* http//abc-news.go.com/sections/living/US/healthcare031020_poll.html.

Last, J. M., & Tyler, C. W., Jr. 1998. Public health methods. In R. B. Wallace & B. N. Doebbeling (Eds.), *Maxcy-Rosenau-Last public health & preventive medicine* (14th ed.): 1–66. Stamford, CT: Appleton & Lange.

Lipnack, J., & Stamps, J. 2000. *Virtual teams: People working across boundaries with technology* (2nd ed.). New York: John Wiley.

Luthans, F. 2002a. The need for and meaning of positive organizational behavior. *Journal of Organizational Behavior,* 23: 695–706.

Luthans, F. 2002b. Positive organizational behavior: Developing and managing psychological strengths. *Academy of Management Executive,* 16: 57–72.

Luthans, F., & Avolio, B. 2003. Authentic leadership: A positive development approach. In K. S. Cameron, J. E. Dutton, & R. E. Quinn (Eds.), *Positive organizational scholarship: Foundations of a new discipline:* 241–261. San Francisco: Berrett-Koehler.

Lynch, J. J. 2000. *A cry unheard: The medical consequences of loneliness.* Baltimore: Bancroft.

Macik-Frey, M. 2006. *Virtual work: Loneliness, isolation, and health outcomes.* Paper presented at the Academy of Management Meeting, Atlanta, GA.

Maddi, S. 2006. Hardiness: The courage to grow from stresses. *Journal of Positive Psychology*, 1: 160–168.

Maurer, T. J., & Rafuse, N. E. 2001. Learning, not litigating: Managing employee development and avoiding claims of age discrimination. *Academy of Management Executive*, 15: 110–122.

Mayer, J. D., Caruso, D. R., & Salovey, P. 2000. Emotional intelligence meets traditional standards for intelligence. *Intelligence*, 27: 267–298.

Mayer, R. C., & Gavin, M. B. 2005. Trust in management and performance: Who minds the shop while the employees watch the boss? *Academy of Management Journal*, 48: 874–888.

McEvoy, G. M., & Cascio, W. F. 1989. Cumulative evidence of the relationship between age and job performance. *Journal of Applied Psychology*, 74: 11–17.

McQuillen, J. S. 2003. The influence of technology on the initiation of interpersonal relationships. *Education*, 123: 616–622.

Morrison, R., Erickson, T., & Dychtwald, K. 2006. Managing middlescence. *Harvard Business Review*, March: 79–86.

Münsterberg, H. 1913. *Psychology and industrial efficiency*. Boston: Houghton Mifflin.

Murray, J. F., Nicholson, S., Pauly, M., & Berger, M. L. 2006. Investing in health to boost employee productivity: The employer's perspective. In R. C. Kessler & P. E. Stang (Eds.), *Health and work productivity: Making the business case for quality health care:* 185–206. Chicago: University of Chicago Press.

National Women's Business Council. 2003. *Access to capital, health insurance costs remain key concerns for women business owners.* http://www.nwbc.gov.

Nelson, D. L., & Cooper, C. L. 2007. Positive organizational behavior: An inclusive view. In D. L. Nelson & C. L. Cooper (Eds.), *Positive organizational behavior:* 3–8. London: Sage.

Nelson, D. L., & Quick, J. C. 2006. *Organizational behavior: Foundations, realities & challenges* (5th ed.). Mason, OH: Southwestern/Thomson.

Nelson, D. L., & Simmons, B. 2004. Eustress: An elusive construct, an engaging pursuit. In P. L. Perrewé & D. C. Ganster (Eds.), *Research in occupational stress and well being, vol. 3: Emotional and physiological processes and positive intervention strategies:* 265–322. Oxford, UK: JAI/Elsevier.

Nembhard, I. M., & Edmondson, A. C. 2006. Making it safe: The effects of leader inclusiveness and professional status on psychological safety and improvement efforts in health care teams. *Journal of Organizational Behavior*, 27: 941–966.

Nicholson, S., Pauly, M. V., Polsky, D., Sharda, C., Szrek, H., & Berger, M. L. 2006. Measuring the effects of workloss on productivity with team production. *Health Economics*, 15: 111–123.

Paul, R. J., & Townsend, J. B. 1993. Managing the older worker: Don't just rinse away the gray. *Academy of Management Executive*, 7: 67–74.

Pennebaker, J. W. 1990. *Opening up: The healing power of confiding in others.* New York: William Morrow.

Perrewé, P. L., & Ganster, D. C. 2002–2006. *Research in occupational stress and well being.* Amsterdam: Elsevier/JAI.

Peterson, C., Park, N., Hall, N., & Seligman, M. E. P. In press. Zest and work. *Journal of Organizational Behavior*.

Peterson, P. G. 2002. The shape of things to come: Global aging in the twenty-first century. *Journal of International Affairs*, 56: 189–199.

Ployhart, R. E. 2006. Staffing in the 21st century: New challenges and strategic opportunities. *Journal of Management*, 32: 868–897.

Purcell, P. J. 2000. Older workers: Employment and retirement trends. *Monthly Labor Review*, 123: 19–30.

Quick, J. C. 1999a. Occupational health psychology: The convergence of health and clinical psychology with public health and preventive medicine in organizational contexts. *Professional Psychology: Research and Practice*, 30(2): 123–128.

Quick, J. C. 1999b. Occupational health psychology: Historical roots and future directions. *Health Psychology*, 18(1): 82–88.

Quick, J. C., Camara, W. J., Hurrell, J. J., Johnson, J. V., Piotrkowski, C. S., Sauter, S. L., & Spielberger, C. D. 1997. Introduction and historical overview. *Journal of Occupational Health Psychology*, 2(1): 3–6.

Quick, J. C., Cooper, C. L., Nelson, D. L., Quick, J. D., & Gavin, J. H. 2003. Stress, health, and well-being at work. In J. Greenberg (Ed.), *Organizational behavior: The state of the science* (2nd ed.): 53–89. Mahwah, NJ: Lawrence Erlbaum.

Quick, J. C., & Quick, J. D. 2004. Healthy, happy, productive work: A leadership challenge. *Organizational Dynamics*, 33: 329–337.

Quick, J. C., Quick, J. D., Nelson, D. L., & Hurrell, J. J. 1997. *Preventive stress management in organizations*. Washington, DC: American Psychological Association.

Quick, J. C., Saleh, K. J., Sime, W. E., Martin, W., Cooper, C. L., Quick, J. D., & Mont, M. A. 2006. Stress management skills for strong leadership: Is it worth dying for? *Journal of Bone & Joint Surgery*, 88–A(1): 217–225.

Quick, J. C., Tetrick, L. E., Adkins, J. A., & Klunder, C. 2003. Occupational health psychology. In I. Weiner (Ed.), *Comprehensive handbook of psychology*: 569–589. New York: John Wiley.

Ranzijn, R. 2004. Role ambiguity: Older workers in the demographic transition. *Aging International*, 29: 281–308.

Raymond, J. S., Wood, D. W., Patrick, W. D. 1990. Psychology training in work and health. *American Psychologist*, 45: 1159–1161.

Rayner, C., Hoel, H., & Cooper, C. L. 2001. *Workplace bullying*. London: Taylor & Francis.

Ricci, J. A., Chee, E., Lorandeau, A. L., & Berger, J. 2007. Fatigue in the U. S. workforce: Prevalence and implications for lost productive work time. *Journal of Occupational and Environmental Medicine*, 49(1): 1–10.

Rice, D. P., & Fineman, N. 2004. Economic implications of increased longevity in the United States. *Annual Review of Public Health*, 25: 457–473.

Rosch, P. J. 2001. The quandary of job stress compensation. *Health and Stress*, 3: 1–4.

Rosenau, M. J. 1913. *Preventive medicine and hygiene*. New York: Appleton.

Ruiz, G. 2006. Gray eminence. *Workforce Management*, 6: 32–36.

Ryff, C. D., & Singer, B. 1998. The contours of positive human health. *Psychological Inquiry*, 9: 1–28.

Ryff, C. D., & Singer, B. H. 2001. *Emotion, social relationships, and health*. New York: Oxford University Press.

Ryff, C. D., & Singer, B. 2002. From social structures to biology: Integrative science in pursuit of human health and well-being. In C. R. Snyder & S. J. Lopez (Eds.), *Handbook of positive psychology*: 541–555. New York: Oxford University Press.

Ryff, C. D., Singer, B. H., & Love, G. D. 2004. Positive health: Connecting well-being with biology. *Philosophical Transactions of the Royal Society of London*, 359: 1383–1394.

Sauter, S. L., & Hurrell, J. J. 1999. Occupational health psychology: Origins, content and direction. *Professional Psychology: Research and Practice*, 30: 117–122.

Sauter, S. L., & Hurrell, J. J., Fox, H. R., Tetrick, L. E., & Barling, J. 1999. Occupational health psychology: An emerging discipline. *Industrial Health*, 37: 199–211.

Sauter, S. L., Murphy, L. R., & Hurrell, J. J. 1990. Prevention of work-related psychological distress: A national strategy proposed by the National Institute of Occupational Safety and Health. *American Psychologist*, 45: 1146–1158.

Seligman, M. E. P., & Csikszentmihalyi, M. 2000. Positive psychology. *American Psychologist*, 55: 5–14.

Shen, Y.-C., & Long, S. K. 2006. What's driving the downward trend in employer-sponsored health insurance? *Health Services Research*, 20(6): 2074–2096.

Shirom, A. 2004. Feeling vigorous at work? The construct of vigor and the study of positive affect in organizations. In P. L. Perrewé & D. C. Ganster (Eds.), *Research in occupational stress and well being, vol. 3: Emotional and physiological processes and positive intervention strategies*: 135–164. Oxford, UK: JAI/Elsevier.

Simpson, P. A., Greller, M. M., & Stroh, L. K. 2002. Variations in human capital investment activity by age. *Journal of Vocational Behavior*, 61: 109–138.

Social Security Administration. 2000. *Actuarial publications*. http://www.ssa.gov/OACT/TR.

Sparks, K., Faragher, B., & Cooper, C. L. 2001. Well-being and occupational health in the 21st century workplace. *Journal of Occupational and Organizational Psychology*, 74: 489–509.

Spector, P. E., Cooper, C. L., Sanchez, J. I., O'Driscoll, M., Sparks, K., Bernin, P., Bussing, A., Dewe, P., Hart, P., Luo, L., Miller, K., deMoraes, L. R., Ostrognay, G., Pagon, M., Pitariu, H., Poelmans,

S., Radhakrishnan, P., Russinova, V., Salamatov, V., & Salgado, J. 2002. Locus of control and well-being at work: How generalizable are Western findings? *Academy of Management Journal*, 45: 453–466.

Spielberger, C. D., & Reheiser, E. 2005. Occupational stress and health. In A.-S. G. Antoniou & C. L. Cooper (Eds.), *Research companion to organizational health psychology:* 441–454. Northampton, MA: Edward Elgar.

Spiezia, V. 2002. The graying population: A wasted human capital or just a social liability? *International Labour Review*, 141: 1–2, 70–113.

Stone, A. A., Cox, D. S., Vladimarsdottier, H., & Jandorf, L. 1987. Evidence that secretory IgA antibody is associated with daily mood. *Journal of Personality and Social Psychology*, 52: 988–993.

Stone, A. A., Neale, J. M., Cox, D. S., & Napoli, A. 1994. Daily events are associated with a secretory immune response to an oral antigen in men. *Health Psychology*, 13: 400–418.

Sulzer-Azaroff, B. 1987. The modification of occupational safety behavior. *Journal of Occupational Accidents*, 9: 177–197.

Taylor, F. W. 1911. *The principles of scientific management.* New York: Norton.

Taylor, F. W. 1912. *Testimony before Special Committee of the House of Representatives to Investigate the Taylor and Other Systems of Shop Management Under Authority of House Resolution 90*, vol. 3: 1377–1508. Washington, DC: Government Printing Office.

Tetrick, L. 2006. Editorial. *Journal of Occupational Health Psychology*, 11: 1–2.

Totterdell, P., & Holman, D. 2003. Emotion regulation in customer service roles: Testing a model of emotional labor. *Journal of Occupational Health Psychology*, 8: 55–73.

Tougas, F., Lagace, M., De La Sablonniere, R., & Kocum, L. 2004. A new approach to the link between identity and relative deprivation in the perspective of ageism and retirement. *International Journal of Aging and Human Development*, 59: 1–23.

Townsend, A. M., & DeMarie, S. M. 1998. Virtual teams: Technology and the workplace of the future. *Academy of Management Executive*, 12: 17–30.

Urbanski, L. 2002. Workplace bullying's high cost: $180M in lost time, productivity. *Orlando Business Journal*, March 18.

U.S. Census Bureau. 1995. *Bureau of Census statistical brief: Sixty-five plus in the United States.* http://www.census.gov/socdemo/www/agebrief.html.

U.S. Census Bureau. 2000. *Projections of the total resident population by 5-year age groups, race, Hispanic origin with special age categories: Middle series, 2025 to 2045.* http://www.census.gov/population/projections/nation/summary/np-t4-f.txt.

VandenBos, G. (Ed.). 2007. *APA dictionary of psychology.* Washington, DC: American Psychological Association.

van Dierendonck, D., Haynes, C., Borrill, C., & Stride, C. 2004. Leadership behavior and subordinate well-being. *Journal of Occupational Health Psychology*, 9: 165–175.

Vuori, J., Silvonen, J., Vinokur, A., & Price, R. 2002. The Työhön job search program in Finland: Benefits for the unemployed with risk of depression or discouragement. *Journal of Occupational Health Psychology*, 7: 5–19.

Wadsworth, E., Dhillon, K., Shaw, C., Bhui, K., Stansfeld, S., & Smith, A. 2007. Racial discrimination, ethnicity and work stress. *Occupational Medicine*, 57: 18–24.

Wallace, R. B., & Doebbeling, B. N. 1998. *Maxcy-Rosenau-Last public health and preventive medicine* (14th ed.). Stamford, CT: Appleton & Lange.

Walsh, J. P., Weber, K., & Margolis, J. D. 2003. Social issues and management: Our lost cause found. *Journal of Management*, 29: 859–881.

Walther, J. B. 1995. Relational aspects of computer-mediated communication: Experimental observation over time. *Organizational Science*, 6(2): 186–203.

Warr, P. 1994. Age and job performance. In J. Snel & R. Cremer (Eds.), *Work and aging: A European perspective*: 309–322. London: Taylor & Francis.

World Bank. 1999. *World development indicators.* Washington, DC: Author.

World Health Organization. 2000. *Occupational health.* http://www.who.int/oeh/OCHweb/OCHweb/OSHpages/OSHdocuments/Global/Strategy/GlobalStrategyonOccupationalHealth.htm.

Wright, T. A., & Bonett, D. G. 2007. Job satisfaction and psychological well-being as nonadditive predictors of workplace turnover. *Journal of Management*, 33: 141–160.

Wright, T. A., & Cropanzano, R. 2000a. Psychological well-being and job satisfaction as predictors of job performance. *Journal of Occupational Health Psychology*, 5: 84–94.

Wright, T. A., & Cropanzano, R. 2000b. The role of organizational behavior in occupational health psychology: A view as we approach the millennium. *Journal of Occupational Health Psychology*, 5: 5–10.

Wright, T. A., Cropanzano, R., & Bonett, D. G. 2007. The moderating role of employee positive well-being on the relation between job satisfaction and job performance. *Journal of Occupational Health Psychology*, 12: 93–104.

Wright, T. A., Cropanzano, R., Bonett, D. G., & Diamond, W. J. In press. The role of employee well-being in cardiovascular health: When the twain shall meet. *Journal of Organizational Behavior*.

Zohar, D. 1980. Safety climate in industrial organizations: Theoretical and applied implications. *Journal of Applied Psychology*, 65: 96–101.

Zohar, D., & Luria, G. 2004. Climate as a social-cognitive construction of supervisory safety practices: Scripts as proxy of behavior patterns. *Journal of Applied Psychology*, 89: 322–333.

Zohar, D., & Luria, G. 2005. A multilevel model of safety climate: Cross-level relationships between organization and group-level climates. *Journal of Applied Psychology*, 65: 96–101.

7 Efficiency, Motivation, and Quality in Work Design

7.1 WORK REDESIGN AND PERFORMANCE MANAGEMENT IN TIMES OF DOWNSIZING

A.S. Evangelista and Lisa A. Burke

Reductions in force can have a serious impact on employee workloads, as well as a troubling ripple effect on the integrity of performance management systems. Organizations and managers who are operating "in extremis"—doing as much or more as before but with fewer people—need help with reconceptualizing tasks and managing performance during downscalings. Coupled with specific illustrations, this proposed operational framework can help them reconfigure work duties and establish a fair performance management process for those employees who remain.

The decade of the 1990s yielded a false sense of security among management and employees that the economy was boundless. However, the topic in many copy rooms, cubicles, and break areas today is downsizing, or the inevitability of more corporate bloodletting. Executives are rallying back to the lines to reengage, where they sense little time for streamlining, reevaluating, or reallocating business processes, tasks, and activities. The reality of the present corporate situation is that many downsizing firms face the immediate challenge of keeping operations going with a minimum number of staff, at least for a short term until the outlook becomes more stable. With layoffs occurring across many industries—the tech sector, retailing, entertainment, manufacturing, and air travel, to name a few—the situation presents an opportunity to address associated issues of downsizing for sensible recovery.

Although management literature has focused on certain aspects of downsizing, such as communication strategies, employee cynicism, stress, potential litigation, morale, retention, and survivor support, one area remains essentially untouched: the effect of reductions in force on employee workloads and the troubling ripple effect on the integrity of performance management systems. Even though the topics of downsizing and performance management each boast an established practitioner literature base, research at the intersection of these topics remains scant.

Thus, it is our purpose here to help organizations and managers who are operating "in extremis"—doing as much or more but with fewer people—reconfigure work duties and establish a fair performance management process for surviving employees. The framework proposed here is targeted for solution-hungry managers caught in the throes of downsizing organizations who need a solid recipe for work redesign.

Productivity in Downsizing

A recent article in *HR Focus* that summarized data gathered by the Families and Work Institute ("Focus resources now . . ." 2001) reported that corporate downsizings often mean extended hours and a heavier workload for surviving employees. The effects of the resulting stress vary from making more errors to feeling bitter toward coworkers to simply leaving the job altogether. Assuming that companies keep their best employees and managers during downsizing, organizations should theoretically be in a position to perform better. But case studies have shown that productivity often declines. In *The People Side*, by Richard Koonce (1991), Dr. Jackie Greaner refers to the productivity paradox as a source of regression:

> Let's say a corporation decides, for financial reasons, to undertake a downsizing or restructuring to improve its bottom-line profitability and productivity. If it doesn't deal with the "people factors" associated with change—that is, effectively manage the human resources issues that are part of any corporate reorganization—its productivity and profitability will suffer anyway. This is the so-called "productivity paradox." It's quite common in organizations going through transition today.

Such an observation highlights the inadequate attention paid to the "people aspects" of previous organizational restructurings. Clearly, one goal of these types of corporate change must be to provide indubitable improvement in productivity and profitability so that surviving employees remain viable stakeholders in corporate progress. But as Slavin (1994) suggests, "If you eliminate people, the ones who remain will make choices about how to react. The best often leave the company—the brain drain. The rest either work longer or harder, or they just don't do certain tasks."

Many more authors also point out that in corporate downsizings the survivors end up working longer and are heavily taxed with a bigger workload. As a result, morale often goes into the proverbial dumpster. Place the performance management process against this backdrop and it is easy to discern potential problems.

Downsizing and Performance Management Dilemmas

Consider the following: Caroline has escaped a recent volley of layoffs at her manufacturing firm. The company's dreary situation will likely continue into the foreseeable future and she is concerned about her job security. She has been a superior performer who takes pride in being able to complete all assigned duties well and on time. When the latest cuts trimmed several people from her department and management divided up the work among those who were left, Caroline took over much of the workload of one of the terminated employees. The stress of the current work environment is taking a toll on her and her peers and is beginning to affect her work. Caroline knows that her annual performance appraisal is around the corner and that she has not performed up to her usual potential, although she has tried. There is just too much to do and too little time to get it all done; some tasks never get touched and others are only half-heartedly completed. This once exemplary employee now actually feels she is average, and she is distressed about it. She fears not only that she will be appraised unfairly because she has been asked to do so much more and has done all that she could, but that others might actually get away with task avoidance, something she does not feel comfortable doing.

Michael, Caroline's supervisor, is also under a great deal of stress. Not only is he responsible for his own performance but that of the Quality Assurance Department as well. The department has consistently produced above average performance. But lately Michael has noticed that several of his key employees—employees that he urged be saved from the corporate chopping block—are performing marginally. Several work assignments that absolutely must be done are either late or inadequate. Even employees he relies on the most, such as Caroline, are turning in weaker performances. He also senses they are on the verge of a morale slump as a result of the burgeoning workloads. Performance appraisals are due in six months and Michael prides himself on being fair and accurate. Given that the departmental workload has increased, however, he feels there will be several challenges to confront.

This scenario illustrates some of the complexities surrounding the fallout from corporate downsizing, especially concerning employee workloads and performance management. Before the company cut heads, Caroline was working at or near her effective capacity—she had the time, opportunity, ability, and energy to be a superior performer. She completed all of her duties and did so in an outstanding manner; plus, she enjoyed her work. Michael regards Caroline as one of his best employees. But left with additional duties to distribute among his remaining employees after the layoffs, he effectively gave her the work of at least two people. He sees her performance faltering, sees her turning in relatively lackluster work and even failing to complete a couple of tasks.

Michael realizes he must now get his group focused appropriately (and quickly) on their new work reality if he is to maintain the unit's performance. He also wants to deliver fair and accurate performance appraisals in the post-downsizing environment. Stepping back, he realizes he needs to first review departmental tasks in this environment to maximize his unit's productivity; then he will be in a better position to evaluate employee performance fairly. Our framework can help him do just that.

Work Redesign

In downsizing situations, it is vital for managers to assess business unit obligations and internal tasks to effectively and fairly manage and balance workloads among remaining employees. Typical problems they may face during employee reductions are: (1) the failure or inability to identify and categorize duties and assignments, (2) the failure to identify when they have over-tasked an employee, and (3) the failure to see when a business unit's demands exceed its capacity.

When a firm enters the downsizing mode, the top managers need to redefine their goals for the restructured company in order to meet the demands of their business environment. According to Slavin, this process also involves examining and identifying the more essential operational tasks. Maintaining that certain tasks are more strategically important than others is consistent with Wright, McMahan, McCormick, and Sherman (1998), who demonstrated that a focus on the most strategically important tasks in a performance management system will enhance company performance. As such, we propose a process for this important task categorization duty, as shown in Figure 7.1.1.

To proceed in this new corporate direction, managers need to identify and categorize all projects and tasks to determine which activities are to be retained and which are to be eliminated. *Critical tasks* are those that enable a company to accomplish its primary organizational objectives; they are essential to maintaining the firm's strategic intent, and must be performed to completion at the highest quality standard. One example from Michael's department is the task of quality control, a vital function that is performed on incoming parts to the department and that requires certain sample inspections to ensure that those

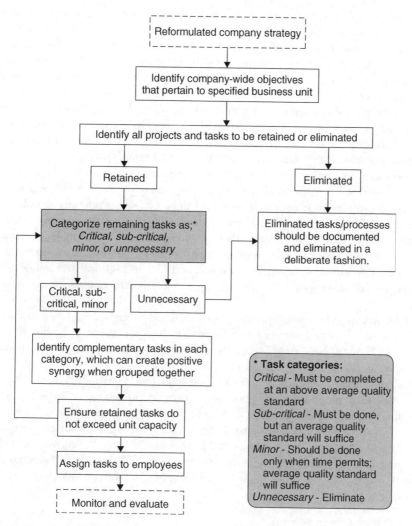

Figure 7.1.1 Work Redesign Process.

parts meet or exceed standards. There is no wiggle room in this function—failure to identify problems could lead to catastrophic results.

A *sub-critical task* is one that needs to be performed, but an average standard of quality will suffice. An example might be a job that is perceived as critical in the near future once the company restabilizes, thus requiring that it be maintained to ensure proficiency when reinstated. All sub-critical duties contribute to the achievement of organizational goals but are just as effective when a bare-bones approach to completion is taken. One example in Michael's department that fits this category is a specific quality monthly report. Prior to the downsizing the report was a work of art. The responsible team member had the opportunity to produce a visually stimulating presentation reporting certain quality assurance data. The data could have been presented just as accurately in a straightforward, "no-frills" report and still would have met the needs of the recipients while taking less than half the time. Another sub-critical example could be maintenance on a piece of test equipment that is not used at current production levels but is likely to become critical when production rebounds.

A *minor task* is one that adds value to the firm but will not hinder operations or organizational goals if left undone. An example would be maintaining workplace tidiness. And an *unnecessary task* is one that can be discarded because it most likely drains needed resources away from the critical or sub-critical tasks—for example, quality inspections of products that have been temporarily ceased until demand picks up again. Denoting such tasks is particularly relevant in a restructured firm, as business goals may have changed. Taking the time to document discarded tasks and the lessons learned may prevent future mistakes and yield valuable information if the company decides to resurrect similar projects.

In most cases, an employee does not need to stop performing critical or sub-critical tasks to advance workplace aesthetics. Because the opportunity to do each task will vary daily, regardless of category, time management skills will be ever-important. Some tasks complement each other and may be more effective when assigned together. This may seem intuitive, but synergy can lead to greater efficiency and productivity. Examples are tasks that require close coordination with another department or specific areas within another department. If Michael's unit has a critical task and some sub-critical and minor ones that all require coordination with the marketing department, then these tasks should be assigned together.

After formulating the work redesign process outlined in Figure 7.1.1, we modified our model in response to an interview with Steven Finch, a supervisor at Philips Broadband Networks of Manlius, New York. Mr. Finch said that when his company began to downsize, he knew his department would need to do a task assessment in order to pare down the workload into "necessary" and "unnecessary" components. He requested that each member of his department brainstorm and produce a task list, including all steps necessary to accomplish assigned duties. Then he compared their lists with departmental functions, as conceived in the company's new focus. If certain functions were no longer necessary, he removed them and their corresponding tasks. Finally, he allocated the downsized employees' duties to remaining members to ensure that necessary functions were completed. This approach to task categorization is consistent with Figure 7.1.1 and provides some semblance of face validity verification.

Reconceptualizing Performance Management

As Figure 7.1.1 shows, then, redesigning work around critical, sub-critical, and minor tasks while eliminating unnecessary ones forms the foundation for performance appraisal content. Using this framework, managers can assess the completion of each type of task, as well as the specified level of quality for each. The output from the work categorization process must be shared with all employees so they have a list of the critical, sub-critical, and minor tasks they are accountable for. These same tasks are then used to drive the performance management process. Employee communication and understanding will be vital to the success of this effort because the manager will formally evaluate the three types of duties as performed by that group of employees.

The manager must evaluate the level of work that was assigned to employees and then assess whether they are performing those duties at the appropriate levels. Because each task has been categorized, the manager can ensure that critical tasks are all being performed to the highest standards, sub-critical tasks to adequate levels for functional requirements to be met, and minor tasks only when possible or as needed. Each employee is then in a much better position to receive a fair and accurate performance appraisal, further removed from problems that occur due to ineffective task assignment after downsizing.

Figure 7.1.2 outlines a proposed method for effectively and fairly dealing with employee overload in the performance management process. A generic example of translating re-engineered workloads for performance management purposes is illustrated, with the goal of assigning each newly sorted task a proper weight. It is essentially a weighted evaluation system, in which managers translate each member's workload into numerical values so that they can evaluate each task and obtain an overall percentage for each employee. More specifically, the manager creates a task assessment, including both normal workload and overload tasks. Various tasks of all types exist, both above and below the "overload limit line," each with a different rating scale because of varying importance. For example, while critical tasks are rated on a scale of 5 (excellent) to −3 (unacceptable), sub-critical tasks are on

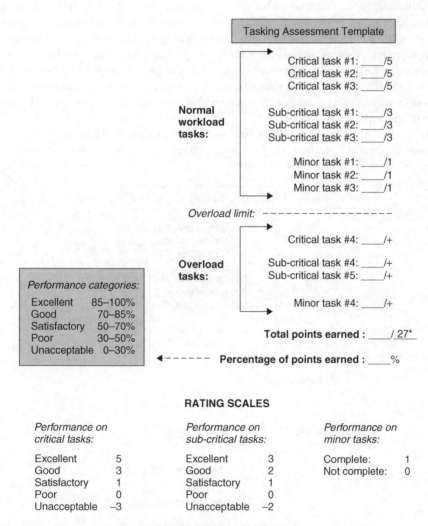

Figure 7.1.2 Performance Management in Task Overload Situations.

* Note: The workload denominator will likely vary across employees because it is task- and job-specific.

a 3 to −2 scale, and minor tasks are either complete (1) or incomplete (0). These varying endpoints communicate to employees the relative importance across the task types in the thrust of their daily efforts.

The "total points earned" ratio comprises a numerator (the employee's total earned points across all tasks) and a denominator (the manager's determination of a fair workload). Note that this workload denominator, being task- and job-specific, will likely vary across employees and organizations. Regardless, an employee's total earned points divided by his workload denominator gives a percentage of points earned and places his performance in a category of excellent, good, satisfactory, poor, or unacceptable. Of course, firms can tailor these ratings and categories for their particular needs.

Our suggested process requires managers to acknowledge when employees are overloaded, while subordinates must acknowledge that the manager values the completion of various tasks differently. Examining employee overload based on the *importance* of tasks, and then explaining to the employees what *level* of performance is expected on the various tasks and how the appraisal process will work, allows a manager to more fairly administer periodic formal evaluations. For example, it may be tempting to give a high performance rating when an employee is overloaded; however, based on our approach, the rating would depend on the employee's performance and not simply on emotional appeal. In addition, downsizing firms can more closely tie any merit bonuses to deserving performances in order to keep a "pay for performance" mentality foremost in employees' minds and ensure corporate dollars are wisely distributed.

To illustrate our point, we apply our task assessment framework to Caroline's situation. As shown in Figure 7.1.3, Caroline has made a concerted attempt over the last four or five

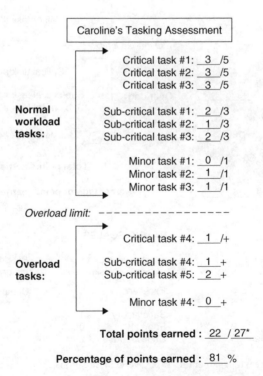

Figure 7.1.3 Example of Performance Management in Task Overload Situation.

months to complete work assigned in Michael's task categorization system. Even though she is only producing mostly "good" results, she is performing consistently across assigned tasks, both old and new. Adding up her task scores, we see that she has produced a value of 22, resulting in an 81 percent of points earned and a good rating. As such, her performance appraisal reflects her results across the various tasks.

Caroline's normal workload was broken down by task type to encourage appropriate focus—all complete with clear performance standards. Michael assigned what he determined to be a fair workload in the employees' restructured work reality and a fair division of departmental work responsibilities. But performance appraisal results are based on the types of tasks that were assigned and, more important, on the level at which those tasks were performed. Caroline is not an average performer, as she has lately felt; instead, she has exhibited quite good performance over the last several months. Michael gives her clear direction on which tasks are valued the most, and with continued coaching and experience, Caroline will likely make it to the excellent category soon. Ultimately, Michael is confident that his department's task load has been fairly and accurately distributed and that employees will become more comfortable and proficient with the new system over time.

Perhaps organizations other than downsized firms could benefit from considering our outlined approach as well. When a firm becomes mature and duties become routine, this method could be useful in revitalizing it—to do some housecleaning by identifying critical, sub-critical, and minor tasks and eliminating unnecessary ones. Nevertheless, it is crucial in a downsized environment for managers and supervisors to reexamine workloads, prioritize duties, and communicate how the task hierarchy will be reflected during the performance appraisal process. The effort must be made to ensure that employees who are retained are being used effectively, treated fairly, and rewarded appropriately for their contribution to the organization.

References and Selected Bibliography

Appelbaum, Steven H. 1991. How to slim successfully and ethically: Two case studies of "downsizing." *Leadership & Organization Development Journal* 12: 11–17.

Beam, Henry H. 1997. Survivors: How to keep your best people on board after downsizing. *Academy of Management Executive* 11: 92–94.

Feldman, Daniel C., and Carrie R. Leana. 1994. Better practices in managing layoffs. *Human Resource Management* 33 (Summer): 239–261.

Finch, Steven. 2001. Supervisor, Philips Broadband Networks, Manlius, New York, phone interview (17 November).

Focus resources now on retained employees. 2001. *HR Focus* 78/10: 11–16.

Gutknecht, John E., and J. Bernard Keys. 1993. Mergers, acquisitions and takeovers: Maintaining morale of survivors and protecting employees. *Academy of Management Executive* 7/3: 26–37.

Koonce, Richard. 1991. The "people side" of organizational change. *Credit Magazine* 17/6: 22–25.

The negative effects of overwork and related stress. 2001. *HR Focus* 78/11 (November): 9+.

Siriginidi, Subba Rao. 2000. Enterprise resource planning in reengineering business. *Business Process Management Journal* 6: 376.

Slavin, Roy H. 1994. Re-engineering: A productivity paradox. *Quality* 33/6 (June): 18.

Wright, Patrick M., Gary C. McMahan, B. McCormick, and W.S. Sherman. 1998. Strategy, core competence, and HR involvement as determinants of HR effectiveness and refinery performance. *Human Resource Management* 37/1 (Spring): 17–29.

7.2   WORK DESIGN THEORY

A Review and Critique with Implications for Human
Resource Development

Richard J. Torraco

Six theoretical perspectives on work design are examined for their contributions to our understanding of how work is organized and designed in organizations: sociotechnical systems theory, process improvement, adaptive structuration theory, the job characteristics model, technostructural change models, and activity theory. A critique of these theories raises concerns about their ability to explain the design of work in new work environments. The critique highlights the need to eliminate the discontinuity in how theory explains the structure and articulation of work among system levels. The implications of this study for further research on work design theory and for human resource development practice are discussed.

Work design is tightly woven into the structure and function of organizations. The nature of work and how it is structured and related to human activity affects every aspect of the organization. Work design is the basis for how work is conceived in broad terms, translated across organizational levels, and structured for the units and the individuals who perform the work. The structure, technology, and resources available in one's work environment are fundamental to the meaning and value one places in work. As such, the organization and design of one's work environment significantly shape the contribution one makes to the organization.

The nature of work continues to change (Howard, 1995; Cappelli, Bassi, Katz, Knoke, Osterman, & Useem, 1997), and the rate of change in work design and technology continues to accelerate (Adler, 1992; Tenner, 1996). With the instant availability of information and reduced geographical distances (Schick, Gordon, & Haka, 1990), today's work processes are fundamentally different from those routinely used just a decade ago (Barley & Orr, 1997; Luff, Hindmarsh, & Heath, 2000; Norman, 1998). New work requirements have brought about major changes in how work is designed (Parker & Wall, 1998) and accomplished (Osterman, 1994). This raises important questions about the adequacy of our understanding of work and work design. Has work design theory kept up with the reality of practice? Do the theories we rely on to explain how work is organized accurately reflect today's fluid work environments? An important development in work design is the increasing opportunity for virtual work and the emergence of alternative locations for work (Apgar, 1998). How well do existing theories explain work design in virtual and other nontraditional work environments? Have the realities of practice outstripped the capacity of theory to provide an adequate understanding of these issues? The problem addressed by this article is that many features of emerging work designs are not adequately explained by existing work design theories, which means that managers, human resource development (HRD) professionals, and others may be relying on outdated models for making decisions about work design, job require-ments, and the employee skills needed to meet these requirements.

This article reviews and critiques existing work design theories and then uses this critique to stimulate new ways of thinking about work design that explain more effectively the challenges and opportunities for employees in today's workplace. HRD professionals are concerned about work design because those who are responsible for employee development cannot afford to lose sight of these recent developments in work design since many new skills in need of development emerge from changes in work requirements and work design. John P. Campbell and colleagues reminded us of the importance of linking training design with work design: "Training contents do not just fall out of some big training bin in the sky" (Campbell, McCloy, Oppler, & Sager, 1993, p. 38). The nature and design of the work itself will always be an important determinant of the composition of employee skills needed to perform the work.

As the basis for a critique of how well existing work design theories explain the realities of today's workplace, this article reviews six theoretical perspectives on work design: sociotechnical systems theory, the job characteristics model, process improvement, technostructural change models, activity theory, and adaptive structuration theory. Each theory is examined for its ability to explain work design in new work environments and is shown to offer a different perspective on the design of work. Finally, the implications for further research on work design theory and for the practice of HRD are discussed.

Work design shapes the context of work through traditional structural means and through the reciprocal relationship of structure and human agency (Miller & Droge, 1986). New work environments are characterized by complex, nonlinear dynamics (Weick, 1990) in which the mutual dependence on structure and action means that structure is both a medium and outcome of practice (Giddens, 1979). Action triggers change, intended and unintended, that influences interdependent actors and creates structure. Work activity unfolds within a context that reflects the residuals of prior work activities. In other words, actions are embedded in the structures they generate. In this sense, the term *structure* is used synonymously in this article with *context* as they apply to the work environment. Work design is a primary catalyst of context, and, conversely, the context of work reflects structural dimensions. The role of structure in creating context is similar to adaptive structuration (DeSanctis & Poole, 1994), in which rules and resources from technology and other structures are incorporated into action. Within this broader meaning of structure, *work design* is defined as the systemic organization, design, and articulation of work activities at one or more levels of the organization: systemwide, process, group, job, and task. Work design can occur at any point along the continuum between systemwide work structures and the design of individual tasks. The environment or context within which work design occurs is the work environment.

Theories Selected for the Review

Six theoretical perspectives on work design were selected for review and critique in this study. Three criteria were used to select theories for the study:

* The theory's main purpose includes explaining the organization and design of work.
* The theory applies to one or more of the following domains of work: systemwide, process, group, job, or task.
* The theory includes both human and technical concepts to explain work design.

Theories were selected that address work design ranging in scope from task design to organization-wide work design and that range in age from ten to more than fifty years old. The theories reviewed are sociotechnical systems theory, the job characteristics model, process improvement, technostructural change models, activity theory, and adaptive structuration theory.

Work design is central to the purpose of these six theories and provides the basis for the interaction of key conceptual elements of them. Sociotechnical systems theory, the job characteristics model, process improvement, and technostructural change models are work design frameworks that have been discussed frequently in HRD and related literatures. Activity theory has only recently been considered as a potentially valuable theory for HRD and related disciplines (Ardichvili, 2003; Engestrom, 2000). Adaptive structuration theory has received little or no attention in the HRD literature despite its power to explain adaptations to technology as key factors in organizational change (DeSanctis & Poole, 1994). Other theories were eliminated from consideration for this study because their primary theoretical domains did not include work design. Among them were human capital theory (Becker, 1993), institutional theory (Zucker, 1987), agency theory (Eisenhardt, 1989), and transaction cost theory (Jones & Hill, 1988). The domains over which these theories apply would have to be artificially stretched to include work design. Conversely, the theories supporting organizational transformation (Miller & Friesen, 1984; Tushman & Romanelli, 1985) and contingency theory (Schoonhoven, 1981) embrace all dimensions of the organization and its environment (philosophy, culture, strategy, environmental contingencies, and structure) and exceed the scope of work design theory. Each of the six theories chosen for this study is reviewed next.

Sociotechnical Systems Theory. As first conceptualized by Eric Trist during his work at the Tavistock Institute for Human Relations in London, sociotechnical systems (STS) theory was clearly influenced by an early publication of von Bertalanffy's open systems theories (Trist & Bamforth, 1951). STS theory seeks to enhance job satisfaction and improve productivity through a design process that focuses on the interdependencies between and among people, technology, and the work environment (Emery & Trist, 1969). The recognition that production processes were systems fundamentally composed of human and technological elements led to work designs based on STS theory that were responsive to both the task requirements of the technology and the social and psychological needs of employees (Trist, 1981; Trist, Higgin, Murray & Pollock, 1963). The overarching goal of this approach is the joint optimization of the social and technical aspects of work design.

Early implementations of the STS approach to work design demonstrated its value for enriching jobs and improving productivity in coal mining (Trist & Bamforth, 1951; Mills, 1976), automotive plants (Junsson & Lank, 1985), an Indian weaving mill (Rice, 1953), the shipping industry (Thorsrud, 1968), and other industrial environments (Rice, 1958; Macy, 1980). Also relevant to HRD are subsequent applications of STS that served as the basis for conceptualizing self-managed teams, (Pasmore, Francis, Haldeman, & Shani, 1982), the redesign of work for productivity improvements (Cummings & Molloy, 1977), and as a framework for understanding the dependencies among ideal work design features and the relative impact of choosing not to implement one ideal feature on the effectiveness of other ideal features (Majchrzak, 1997). Recent applications of STS theory underlie innovative work designs and team-based structures that are now prevalent in organizations (Cherns, 1987; Lawler, Mohrman, & Ledford, 1998; Reese, 1995).

Sociotechnical systems thinking has also been applied at the macrolevel to community and environmental issues. According to Heller (1997), Eric Trist first conceptualized STS theory in extraorganizational terms as a model for integrating human and technological elements for environmental and ecological purposes. However, the macrolevel application of STS research was hindered by the exigent priorities imposed by the opportunities and demands of fieldwork in three British coalmines. Nonetheless, extraorganizational applications are evident in early STS theory research (Emery & Trist, 1969) and in Emery and Trist's book, *Toward a Social Ecology* (1973).

Despite the persistence of STS theory, it has been criticized for offering little in the way of prescriptions for how to design work, relying instead on general principles for achieving sociotechnical work environments (Kelly, 1992). In addition, new organizational paradigms suggest that the application of sociotechnical principles alone is insufficient, since design innovations at the subunit level are unlikely to survive if the organization as a whole is not aligned systemically in the same way (Frei, Hugentobler, Schurman, Duell, & Alioth, 1993). According to critics of the theory, more explicit attention to organizational culture and values is needed (Parker & Wall, 1998).

Job Characteristics Model. Among the models of work design derived from STS theory, perhaps the most influential is the job characteristics model (Hackman & Oldham, 1980). The job characteristics model (JCM) is among the most well-known and complete theories for explaining job design characteristics and their relationships to work motivation. According to this theory, any job can be described in terms of the following five core job dimensions: skill variety, task identity, task significance, autonomy, and feedback. Seen as being more motivating and satisfying to workers who perform jobs with these characteristics, the five core job dimensions influence psychological states of workers that are more likely to lead to favorable work outcomes: high work productivity and low absenteeism and turnover. The theory further asserts that people with high growth needs are more likely to experience the psychological states with motivating jobs than are people with weaker growth needs. In addition to the JCM itself, Hackman and Oldham (1980) developed the Job Diagnostics Survey, an instrument for measuring the motivation potential of jobs and for guiding work redesign projects.

Since its development more than twenty-five years ago, the JCM has spawned an impressive body of related research on work design. Campion and Thayer (1985) extended Hackman and Oldham's work by developing the Multimethod Job Design Questionnaire (MJDQ), a job design instrument with scales to assess the motivational, biomechanistic, and perceptual-motor aspects of jobs. Other extensions and refinements of the JCM include modifications of the original job diagnostics survey to produce more reliable data (Fried, 1991; Johns, Xie, & Fang, 1992), studies of the relative effects of job redesign on attitudinal versus behavioral outcomes (Kelly, 1992; Parker & Wall, 1998), the addition of achievement motivation and job longevity as moderators to the JCM (Arnold & House, 1980), cross-cultural applications of the JCM (Welsh, Luthans, & Sommer, 1993), revisions to the critical psychological states component of the model (Renn & Vandenburg, 1995), studies of the effects of work context (for example, lack of privacy, high worker densities) on job satisfaction (Parker & Wall, 1998), a framework for job design in which employees actively craft their jobs (Wrzesniewski & Dutton, 2001), and meta-analyses of the effects of the JCM on motivation, satisfaction, and performance (Fried & Ferris, 1987; Loher, Noe, Moeller, & Fitzpatrick, 1985). As these studies demonstrate, the JCM has had a persistent influence on work design thinking and has catalyzed an impressive array of related research.

Process Improvement. An organization's work, whether product or service related, is accomplished through a series of phases, or processes, during which value is added. As a value chain for accomplishing work, the work process is a major component of the organization's structure and function and a key element in work design. Davenport (1993) defined a work process as "a structured, measured set of activities designed to produce a specified output for a particular customer or market. . . . A process is a specific ordering of work activities *across time and place*, with a beginning, an end, and clearly identified inputs and outputs: a structure for action" (p. 5). Davenport's notion that work activities can span across time and space is an important observation because it expands the scope of a work process beyond a single functional area. Indeed, major work processes such as customer order processing and new product development require activities that draw on multiple functional areas. Those that span the boundaries between organizational units are called cross-functional processes.

Process improvement, a major tenet of quality improvement theory, derives from the notion that understanding how work is accomplished during various phases of the process is the key to successful efforts to improve or redesign work. Quality improvement theory is based on the work of Walter Shewhart (1931), W. Edwards Deming (1986), and Joseph Juran (1974). Quality improvement theory espouses a management philosophy that orients all of an organization's activities around the concept of quality. Quality improvement is based on a diverse body of knowledge composed of theory and methods for continuous quality improvement, statistical measurement, process improvement, employee involvement, and education and training. According to quality improvement theory, in order for process improvement to occur, there must be agreement as to what constitutes a work process, that is, the work activities that are specifically included in the process. Work processes that have an identifiable flow or structure, whether they are small, discrete processes or more elaborate, cross-functional processes, can be analyzed and improved using methods such as statistical process control. Process improvement based in quality improvement theory provides employees with the information and decision-making power to make process changes, it is a continuous process (improvement efforts never end), and it increases both employee well-being and organizational productivity (Shetty, 1986). Indeed, continuous process improvement is the primary vehicle for work redesign in organizations that follow the quality improvement philosophy (Garvin, 1988).

Technostructural Change Models. Technostructural change models affect change by reconfiguring the organization's technology and structure. Technostructural change models evolved from consideration of the factors thought to be key determinants of organizational structure. Early theories explained that organizational structure was largely a function of contextual factors such as organization size, environment, technology, or scale of operation (Galbraith, 1970). These theories offered the simplest theoretical explanation of how organization design was related to structural variables, which were assumed to be influenced by particular, primarily economic, constraints (Pugh, Hickson, Hinings, & Turner, 1969). Structural models then were developed based on research showing that organizations that faced dynamic markets and technological environments were more economically successful with flexible, organic organizational structures, while organizations in relatively stable environments were more successful with highly structured organizations (Lawrence & Lorsch, 1967). Early studies of the introduction of technology and its effects on organization design showed that computer-based automation promoted the specialization of expertise, facilitated the movement toward process technologies, increased ratios of supervisory and staff personnel, and decentralized authority away from headquarters to individual plant locations (Blau, Falbe, McKinley, & Tracy, 1976; Adler, 1992). Subsequent theories have emphasized the importance of strategic decision making as a necessary precursor to organizational structure and work design (Child, 1972; Miles & Snow, 1978; Mintzberg, 1994).

Technostructural change is receiving increased attention with the current emphasis on organizational effectiveness and sustained competitive advantage. Technostructural change is large-scale change brought about through deliberate attempts to change an organization or subunit toward a different and more effective state by altering its structure and technology (Cummings & Worley, 2001; Galbraith, 1977). Since they focus on structure and technology as major determinants of the environment within which people work, technostructural change models are frequently used to complement other interventions that affect change primarily through social processes and HRD. Technostructural change models are used to design or redesign major processes or work units or to restructure entire organizations; they are of broader scope than the work design models discussed previously. They embrace a set of interventions that include models for functional design, downsizing and work reengineering, and recent structural designs including self-contained units, matrix organizations, and network-based structures (Cummings & Worley, 2001).

Functional design continues to be the most widely used organizational structure in the world today. This is the pyramidal structure with senior management at the top, middle and supervisory management spread out below, and the rest of the nonmanagement workforce at the bottom. As seen in specialized functional units such as marketing and sales, engineering, and accounting and finance, functional design promotes the specialization of skills and resources, allows specialists to share their expertise, and enhances career development within one's functional specialty. Care must be taken with functional designs that departmental outputs are integrated with the contributions of other units to enhance the performance of the organization as a whole. Downsizing is a model for organizational restructuring intended to reduce the size of the organization and cut costs primarily through reductions in the workforce. Reduction in organizational size can occur through any one or a combination of layoffs, attrition, redeployment, reduction in management levels, early retirement, outsourcing, reorganization, divestiture, or delayering (Cascio, 1993; McKinley, Sanchez, & Schick, 1995). In most cases downsizing is associated with greater use of the contingent workforce. Temporary or permanent part-time employees are needed since the reduction in the workforce is not matched by a corresponding reduction in workload; fewer employees must accomplish the same amount of work.

Work reengineering is a radical approach to organizational restructuring that replaces the existing work structure with a completely new design, and since jobs are eliminated through work reengineering, it also results in fewer employees (Hammer & Champy, 1993). Work is reengineered by literally starting over and redesigning it from scratch. It requires the redesign of work processes and the integration of tasks to eliminate the errors, delays, and rework that are associated with having different people do different parts of the same process. In order for work reengineering to result in fewer jobs, called the horizontal reorganization of work, vertical reorganization of work is also needed. Those who remain after jobs are eliminated are expected to handle broader tasks and make more decisions.

Recent structural designs include self-contained units, matrix organizations, and network-based structures. Self-contained units group organizational activities on the basis of products, services, customers, or geography. They are typically set up with all or most of the resources needed to accomplish their specific objectives and are often created, either temporarily or permanently, to handle a specific product, service, customer, or region. The matrix organization is an attempt to maximize the strengths and minimize the weaknesses of both the functional and self-contained unit structures. It superimposes the lateral structure of a product or project coordinator on a vertical functional structure. The matrix organization evolved to deal with environments in which changing customer demands and technological conditions caused managers to focus on lateral relationships between functions to develop a flexible and adaptable system of resources and procedures and to achieve multiple project objectives (Kolodny, 1981). Network-based structures redraw organizational boundaries and link separate organizations to facilitate task interaction. In network-based structures, functions that are traditionally performed within a single organization are performed by different network members. The essence of networks is the arrangement of relationships between organizations so that each organization handles what it does best (Powell, 1990). Often used as the basis for joint ventures and other collaborative relationships between organizations, networks are considered to be uniquely suited to deal with complex, dynamic interorganizational exchanges since they allow for vertical disaggregration and flexible coordination across participating organizations (Achrol, 1997).

Activity Theory. Activity theory explains purposeful behavior by focusing on the structure of the activity itself (Leont'ev, 1978, 1981). Rather than viewing the mind or behavior as the primary object of analysis, activity theory focuses on the actual processes of interaction in which humans engage with the world and each other. It is rooted in the work of preeminent Soviet psychologist Lev Vygotsky and the concept of *deyatel'nost*, a term with meaning similar to that associated with the Western notion of activity. In a significant departure from Western views at the time, Vygotsky believed that mental functioning could be understood only by going outside the individual to examine the sociocultural processes from which it derives—a conception of cognition that removed the distinction between internal mental processes and the external world (Vygotsky, 1978). Leont'ev, one of Vygotsky's first students, developed a coherent and integrated framework for activity theory. Activity theory has recently been applied to work and can serve as a flexible framework for the conceptualization of work activity.

At the core of activity theory is the concept of activity as a unit of analysis that includes both the individual and his or her culturally defined environment. From Leont'ev's perspective, "the psychological experiment can no longer be set up entirely to model philosophical speculation: it must model the phenomena of everyday, practical activity" (Cole, 1981, p. ix). Leont'ev conceived of activity as systems of organized units for performing mental functions involving the individual and others engaged in the same activity within a culturally defined environment (Leont'ev, 1978, 1981). The environment is not seen simply as a means of getting access to the individual, but as an integral element of the activity itself. This multidimensional conception of activity, which takes the environment into account, is the basis of activity theory and is considered to be the appropriate unit of analysis for human behavior.

According to the theory, an activity can be analyzed at three levels. First, at the highest level of organization is the motivation of the activity itself, a broader concept than in Western thinking, closer in meaning to that of strategy than task. Activities are distinguished on the basis of their motive and the object toward which they are oriented. At the next level are goal-directed actions, a flexible system of actions for accomplishing the activity that can incorporate various methods and patterns. At the third level are operations, or the specific conditions under which goal-directed actions are carried out. For example, if our action is traveling from one place to another in the service of some activity (for example, pursuing leisure and recreation), whether we walk, drive, or use some other means of transportation is an operation that depends on distance and other conditions related to the action.

The dynamic relationships among these three elements of activity theory provide a flexible framework for better understanding the design of work environments. Activities, actions, and operations may change positions in the hierarchy relative to one another according to changing situations, new knowledge, and the intention of human agents. Since activities, actions, and operations are defined according to their functions rather than properties inherent in the elements themselves, an activity can lose its motivating force and become an action in the service of another activity (for example, losing interest in the intrinsic value of one's job and performing it primarily for income). Hence, the theory allows work activity to be studied at different levels of analysis: the activity, the action, and the operation. Since activity is conceptualized as a dynamic system, methods of studying activity can change as the activity changes and as new questions about it emerge. Conceptualizing work activity using activity theory allows designers to use the work design process to bridge from the present to the desired work environment and to move easily across levels of activity as dictated by the design process. The malleability of activity theory provides a flexible framework for the study of work activity.

Although limited in number, applications of activity theory to the study of work design and HRD include Scribner's study (1984) of the practical thinking strategies used by workers to economize on mental and physical effort, Engestrom's examination (2000) of work redesign in a Finnish pediatric health care facility, and Ardichvili's proposal (2003) that activity theory be used as a basis for developing socially situated learning experiences considered to be especially useful for work-related education and training.

Adaptive Structuration Theory. Adaptive structuration theory is a framework for studying the variations in organizational change that occur as advanced technologies are implemented and used (DeSanctis & Poole, 1994). According to adaptive structuration theory, adaptation of technology by organizational actors is a key factor in organizational change that can be examined from two vantage points: the types of structures that are provided by advanced technologies and the structures that actually emerge in human action as people interact with these technologies. The term *structures* refers to the general rules and resources that guide human activity in organizations such as reporting hierarchies, organizational knowledge, and standard operating procedures. The act of bringing the rules and resources from an advanced technology or other structural sources into action is termed *structuration*. Since actual behavior when using advanced technologies frequently differs from intended use, adaptive structuration theory is embraced by researchers who believe that the effects of advanced technologies are as much a function of the properties inherent in the technologies as of how they are used by people. The theory focuses on the interplay between two types of structures, intended and actual, to gain a deeper understanding of the processes through which advanced technologies are implemented and the impacts of advanced technologies on organizations.

The structuration process can be captured by isolating a group's application of a specific technology-based rule or resource within a specific context and at a specific point in time. The immediate, visible actions that indicate deeper structuration processes are called *appropriations* of the technology. By examining appropriations, we can uncover exactly how a given rule or resource within a specific technology is brought into action. Technology structures become stabilized in the interactions of a work group if the group appropriates them in a consistent way, reproducing them in similar form over time. Once emergent structures are used and accepted, they may become institutions in their own right and the change is fixed in the organization (DeSanctis & Poole, 1994).

Adaptive structuration theory posits that four major sources of structure—technology, task, environment, and the work group's internal system—affect social interaction. Work design features are present in these sources of structure. Work design is represented in technology structures that enable innovations or improvements to existing work methods (for example, technical innovations in electronic messaging or group decision support). It is reflected in a given work task, since existing work practices must be altered to allow for the use of new or modified resources. Resources and constraints afforded by the organizational environment (such as budgets, political pressures, history of task accomplishment, and cultural beliefs) also reflect the overall design of work. Since adaptive structuration theory identifies structures that emerge in human action as people adapt to technology, it can offer new insights into the relationship between work design as intended by designers and how a new design structure influences the work practices that emerge over time. Workers naturally discern the valuable features of new designs while bypassing other features made available by designers. Work practices evolve as users modify their activities to technical innovations.

Empirical studies using adaptive structuration theory include Orlikowski, Yates, Okamura, and Fujimoto's study (1995) of the implementation of a computer conferencing system in a Japanese research and development project; Chin, Gopal, and Salisbury's development and validation (1997) of a measurement scale to assess the appropriations of advanced technology structures by users; and Griffith's use (1999) of adaptive structuration theory as the basis of a model of sense making of new technologies. Adaptive structuration theory and subsequent empirical studies based on the theory have advanced our knowledge of organization development and change and the role of technology implementation in change processes.

Discussion

Each of these six theories—STS theory, the job characteristics model, process improvement, technostructural change models, activity theory, and adaptive structuration theory—serves a particular purpose for explaining the organization and design of work. Each emerged during a different time period to address needs related to particular concerns about the organization and design of work at that time:

Responding to mid-twentieth-century concerns about the effects of advancements in manufacturing technologies on people and productivity, STS theory offered a fundamentally new perspective on the organization of work—work design for joint optimization of its social and technical dimensions.

The job characteristics model established specific task design characteristics and the conditions under which they enhance work motivation and work-related outcomes.

Grounded in quality improvement theory, process improvement derives from the notion that understanding how work is accomplished and flows through the organization is the key to successful efforts to improving or redesigning work processes.

Several technostructural change models have emerged to address the need for different types of work structures, including traditional structural and functional designs. Recent designs such as matrix organizations and network-based structures address complex organizational and environmental dynamics.

Adaptive structural theory attempts to explain variations in organizational change that occur as new technologies are introduced and adapted for use.

Recently applied to work activity, activity theory and its conceptual levels—activities, actions, and operations—allow a flexible framework for the conceptualization of work activity.

In short, each theory arose within a particular sociohistorical context to meet a specific purpose related to concerns about the organization and performance of work at that time. These theories continue to guide our thinking about work design. Some do so by aiding our understanding of work design issues present in today's work environments (adaptive structuration theory, process improvement, technostructural change models), some earlier theories have shaped current thinking on work design (STS theory, the JCM), and some hold promise as future explanations of the design of work (activity theory).

Each theory varies in the scope of its application to work design in organizations. Work design theories can be construed broadly into categories according to their scope of application (Frei et al., 1993). Three levels of application that apply to all organizations are systemwide, intermediate, and individual (Rashford & Coghlan, 1994). The intermediate range of the scale lies between systemwide and job- or task-specific and encompasses teams, functional groups, departments, divisions, and other subunits of the system. A continuum using these levels to show the scope of application of work design theories appears in Figure 7.2.1.

Each work design theory was formulated to cover a domain of knowledge broad enough to support the theory's distinctive contributions to knowledge of work design. Consistent with its purpose, each theory varies in the scope of its application to work design from systemwide (technostructural change) to job- or task design-specific (job characteristics model). Technostructural change theory applies to entire systems (such as organizations) and major subsystems. The job characteristics model applies to the design of jobs and tasks. Thus, technostructural change and the job characteristics model have different scopes of application to work design and are shown at opposite ends of the continuum in Figure 7.2.1.

Adaptive structuration theory is potentially relevant to any work setting affected by technology-triggered change. Similarly, STS theory supports work design intended to jointly optimize social and technical design issues in a broad range of workplaces. Each of these theories can be applied at the job or task, intermediate, or systemwide levels. Although they potentially apply across the organization, STS theory and adaptive structuration theory most often explain the design of organizational subsystems (intermediate range). Process improvement also applies to the intermediate range of the scale between systemwide and job- or task-specific since it is an approach to improving or redesigning work processes, a construct at the intermediate range. Since these three theories can explain both intermediate-range work designs and job or systemwide work designs concurrently (for example, explaining how

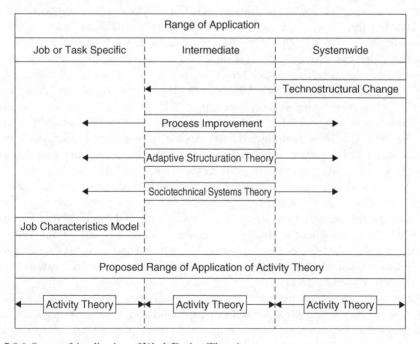

Figure 7.2.1 Scope of Application of Work Design Theories.

a job fits with a cross-functional process to which the job contributes), arrows appear in Figure 7.2.1 pointing to the left and right indicating these scopes of application for the three intermediate-range theories.

The scope of application of activity theory to work design has not been addressed explicitly in the literature. It is proposed that this theory applies to the full range of the continuum shown in Figure 7.2.1. Since the domain of activity theory embraces activities, actions, and operations and can include one or more levels of work activity, the theory can potentially apply to work issues at the job or task, intermediate, or systemwide levels. Since activity theory can be used at any level or combination of adjacent levels in Figure 7.2.1, it can facilitate the integration of work design across levels. Conceptualizing work activity using activity theory allows designers to move easily across levels of activity as dictated by the design process.

Critique and Implications for Further Research

Two concerns emerge from this discussion about the explanations of work design offered by these theories. First, these theories do not provide an adequate conceptual foundation for work design in new work environments, including virtual and alternative work environments, that are increasingly common (Bailey & Kurland, 2002; Liker, Haddad, & Karlin, 1999). They explain work designs of the past better than they explain how to design work for some present and future settings. Second, since these theories were developed for particular purposes and applications (such as job design or restructuring), they explain work design in ways that allow discontinuities in how work is structured and articulated between and among organizational levels. These concerns and their implications for further research on work design theory are discussed next.

The Changing Nature of Work. The notion of work discussed in this article does not assume a separation of work from other aspects of life. Work-life integration brings one's work activities and life activities (nonwork) into a mutually reinforcing balance (Friedman, Christensen, & DeGroot, 1998). The distinction between work and nonwork has been blurred since the structure and location of work has been altered by the increasing prevalence of flexible work situations that are not time and place specific (Bridges, 1994; Smith, 1997). These new work situations include virtual work (Hill, Miller, & Weiner, 1998) and the emergence of the alternative workplace (Apgar, 1998). Flexible structures are appealing to organizations that are responding to hypercompetitive business environments (Volberda, 1998). Reflecting the movement toward more flexible employment relationships sought by both employees and employers, the alternative workplace represents a multitude of locations where work can be accomplished other than the traditional office or shop floor (Apgar, 1998). Virtual work is associated with the terms *telework* and *telecommuting*, although each of these has a different meaning. *Telework* is a broad term for doing one's job away from the office through the use of telecommunications equipment (Hill et al., 1998). *Telecommuting* (Potter, 2003) was introduced to emphasize that telework could eventually replace the daily commute. Unlike most telecommuters who have a fixed alternative worksite at home, virtual work and the virtual office refer to situations in which workers have the flexibility to work from a variety of locations.

Recent research has compared virtual with traditional work environments on a variety of perceptual and business measures. Studies have found that resistance to telecommuting can originate from managers who rely on traditional line-of-sight management styles (Potter, 2003), that telecommuting can reduce costs but also may result in the need to alter management practices (Watad & DiSanzo, 2000), and that virtual reality systems can improve certain dimensions of the telecommuting experience (Venkatesh & Johnson, 2002). Hill et al. (1998) found that use of the virtual office was significantly related to higher productivity and greater flexibility, but not to work-life balance, morale, and other perceptions of employee well-being.

Studies of the consequences of organizational restructuring show that managers and subordinates should not be expected to have the same reactions to a new organizational structure (Luthans & Sommer, 1999) and that the sense of purpose felt by managers as a result of restructuring may not be shared by subordinates (McKinley & Scherer, 2000). Thus, although alternative work designs can reduce operating costs, this may occur at the expense of creativity (Amabile & Conti, 1999), innovation (Dougherty & Bowman, 1995), employee morale (Hill et al., 1998), organizational connectedness (Raghuram, Garud, Wiesenfeld, & Gupta (2001), and other indicators of employee well-being (Fisher & White, 2000).

Recent work design developments go beyond the notion of the alternative workplace. For an increasing number of workers, the work environment is characterized not only by alternative work settings but also by frequent change in setting and geographical location. Enabled by ever more sophisticated technology, many workers now migrate between several work settings depending on what setting is most advantageous for conducting the task at hand. One can work from home, from multiple office locations, and on the road virtually unbounded by geographical location. This represents a new polymorphic work environment in which continuous change is possible; the work setting can change frequently and continuously depending on business-related needs. This fluidity of work settings represents a fundamental departure from traditional work environments and from fixed alternative worksites, such as at home.

Organizations continue to respond to the appeal of these new, alternative work designs to get work done more efficiently. The time and cost savings from instituting alternative work designs are readily apparent to managers and have a significant influence on work design decisions. However, beyond their short-term effects, much remains unknown about these work environments, a situation exacerbated by the continually changing nature of these environments. Postimplementation studies to assess the merits of instituting new work designs often show that the trade-offs and consequences of alternative work environments, both beneficial and detrimental, become apparent only after investing in these changes (Cascio, Young, & Morris, 1997; Fisher & White, 2000; Hill et al., 1998; McKinley & Scherer, 2000; Parker, Wall, & Jackson, 1997). This occurs in part because relevant theories and models for decision making are not yet available to inform work design considerations when they are initially conceived.

Indeed, the social reality of work design and technology implementation is quite complex (Liker et al., 1999). The efficacy of work redesign is influenced by many factors, including economics, management philosophy, labor-management relations, the degree of shared agreement about how the work is reorganized, and the process through which new work designs and technology are implemented (Salvendy & Karwowski, 1994). On what basis do we separate employees physically and temporally from the organization when considering the use of virtual and alternative work environments? How are those who work in environments that are not time and place specific expected to relate to their work, each other, and the organization? How should the design of work for these environments be conceived and implemented? How well does existing work design theory address these questions?

Although existing theory provides some insight into this area, it seems insufficient for providing a full understanding of these new work environments. The theories reviewed here do not adequately explain how to organize, design, and articulate work activities for flexible work situations that are not time and place specific:

STS theory emphasizes the design of work to optimize the match between the task requirements of the technology and the social and psychological needs of employees. But how are such work designs conceived in virtual environments where workers may experience physical and psychological separation from others?

Although the JCM shows how worker productivity and motivation can be enhanced by emphasizing five core job dimensions, this theory was never intended to explain how to design these job dimensions (skill variety, task identity, task significance, autonomy, and feedback) in work environments characterized by the geographical and temporal separation of the worker from supervisors and others.

The principles of process improvement were developed for service and manufacturing processes deeply rooted in the technology and infrastructure of specific commercial applications. Workers are now less reliant on the support and resources afforded by a fixed work environment.

Activity theory has been applied only recently to work settings, and although it may prove useful for explaining how to design work activities in the future, no known studies have applied activity theory to virtual or alternative work environments.

Traditional work design models were not developed for what, at the time of their development, would have been considered futuristic work environments. How should designers respond to the unpredictability and changing nature of these work settings? Would better work designs emerge from theory influenced by constructivist thinking (Gergen, 1999)? Could social constructionist theory offer a richer explanation of how work experience is created and given meaning by those who perform it (Turnbull, 2002)? What explanations can be offered for the effects these new work environments have on the worker, relevant others, and the performance of the work itself? Better theory is needed to support work design for these new environments.

The Need for Multilevel Work Design Theory. As defined in this article, work design can occur at any point along the continuum from systemwide work structures to the design of work at the job and task levels. Organizing and aligning work activities across organizational levels is a challenging endeavor due to the many considerations involved in the integration of these work activities. Translating strategic initiatives into operational terms involves accommodating contingencies and optimizing multiple, often competing requirements at several operational levels (Mintzberg, 1994). The mission and goals of the organization must be conceptually and operationally related to work design, even though the linkage of strategic goals to supporting work structures may not be immediate or complete (Holton, 1999; Miles & Snow, 1978). Nonetheless, when discontinuity occurs in work design across levels, it is readily apparent to employees. Staw and Boettger (1990) studied the problem of task revision and illustrated the relationship of work design to employee performance. They manipulated actual tasks to contain erroneous information and showed that participants had little natural tendency toward task revision and a high level of conformity to established procedures, especially those reinforced by organizational hierarchy and control systems, even when tasks contained obviously erroneous content. They demonstrated that inconsistencies across levels in work structures and requirements can impede employee performance.

Unfortunately, existing theory explains work design in ways that allow inconsistency and discontinuity across system levels. This occurs when multidimensional phenomena are conceptualized in ways that ignore their systemic implications. Existing work design models were not developed for the systemwide organization and design of work. As shown in Figure 7.2.1, each of the six theories has a different scope of application. Technostructural change models address the systemwide organization of work, the job characteristics model addresses work design at the job and task levels, and the remaining theories in Figure 7.2.1 address intermediate levels of the system. Designs that are work unit-specific ignore systemwide interdependencies (Galbraith & Lawler, 1993), and fail to address the systemic alignment of reward systems with performance (Rummler & Brache, 1995). Other models of work design apply to jobs (Ilgen & Hollenbeck, 1992) and groups (Hackman, 1990; Guzzo & Dickson, 1996). None of the theories provides the conceptual basis for work design frameworks that are integrated across system-level strategy, operations, and, ultimately, job and task requirements.

These concerns about the design and articulation of work across levels can be addressed by developing multilevel work design theory. Such theory provides a framework for the design of work that relates to multiple levels of the organization. Developing multilevel theory requires the consideration of both the structure and function of constructs as they apply to work design.

Joint Consideration of Construct Structure and Function. The development of multilevel work design theory requires consideration of both the structure and function of work design constructs since each dimension of the construct provides a different perspective on the construct's utility for multilevel theory (Morgeson & Hofmann, 1999). A focus on the structure of work design constructs tends to highlight the differences across levels. For example, job design, which reflects the task specification and resource needs of the individual, is structurally dissimilar from cross-functional process design, which must account for multiple, functional transactions and contingencies. The structure of the construct alone does not allow for the cross-level comparison of work design features since it emphasizes the differences between levels. Explicit consideration of the construct's function allows integration of functionally similar (but structurally dissimilar) constructs into broader networks of constructs. Since organizational structures can be purposefully designed to yield outputs (information, programs, products, services, and so on) that are compatible across levels regardless of the level at which the work occurs, work designs can be structurally dissimilar yet yield outputs that are consistent from level to level. Theoretical emphasis is placed on the joint consideration of construct structure and function when developing multilevel theory. Multilevel work design theory requires the analysis of both the structure and function of work design constructs.

Measurement is another important consideration in the development of multilevel work design theory since theorists must consider both conceptual and measurement issues when operationalizing constructs (Klein, Dansereau, & Hall, 1994). Since a multilevel theory of work design is expected to explain the organization of work across levels of the system, measures of work design are needed that can be applied to two or more system levels simultaneously. However, most measures of work outcomes and processes apply to specific levels of the system only (measures of job output, departmental performance, plant productivity, and so on). Existing instruments and measures of work design include Hackman and Oldham's job diagnostic survey (1980); Campion and Thayer's MJDQ (1985); the measures of job control, cognitive demand, and production responsibility developed by Jackson, Wall, Martin, and Davids (1993); measures of work design dependencies (Majchrzak, 1997); statistical measures to assess variance in process quality (Gitlow & Hertz, 1983); measures of work redesign for information technology in advanced manufacturing (Parker & Wall, 1998); and assessments of the psychometric properties of the MJDQ (Edwards, Scully, & Brtek,

1999). Each of these measures has been developed to assess work-related phenomena at a specific level of the system only (Jackson et al., 1993). Measures of work design constructs that apply to two or more system levels simultaneously are needed to test and refine a multilevel work design framework. They may be based on the resources and materials needed for work, process requirements, cross-functional transactions, temporal consider-ations for work, information characteristics, structural requirements, work outputs, and other dimensions of the work. They will help to measure work design interrelationships across levels for a better understanding of this phenomenon.

Theorists need not start from scratch when developing multilevel work design theory. Activity theory provides a framework for work design that can potentially apply to any systems level or combination of levels. This theory embraces activities, actions, and oper-ations and can be applied to work issues at the job or task, intermediate, or systemwide level. Conceptualizing work activity using activity theory allows designers to move easily across levels of activity as dictated by the design process. Thus, activity theory is proposed as a basis for the further development of multilevel work design theory.

Implications for Human Resource Development Practice. Those who are responsible for employee development cannot afford to lose sight of recent developments in work design since many new skills in need of development emerge from changes in work design. Ample evidence exists in the literature cited here of the discontinuity in theories that address multilevel phenomena. HRD scholars have also acknowledged the need for theory that reflects the multilevel integration of systemic phenomena in areas such as performance domains (Holton, 1999), organizational structure and strategy (Semler, 1997), individual and organizational learning (Confessore & Kops, 1998), learning and performance improvement (Torraco, 2000), and the vertical integration of HRD in organizations (Wognum, 2000). These studies demonstrate the importance of theory that enables the multilevel integration of systemic phenomena in HRD.

Multilevel work design theory can generate models for decision making that improve HRD practice. Coordination among work units for shared resources means that work design changes at one level affect the design of work in other areas. Organizational goals shape work processes requirements, which in turn influence the knowledge and capabilities needed by employees who contribute to these processes. Opportunities for HRD exist at all levels— individual, group, process, and systemwide. Since work design changes have multiple effects and important needs for HRD emerge from these changes, HRD practice can be more effective when framed as a systemic intervention informed by multilevel theory. Multilevel work design theory is needed that reflects the conceptual, analytical, and measurement issues discussed here.

Better theories of work design are also needed because of the negative implications for employee development of poorly articulated work designs. Engagement in learning by the most committed employees can be wasted when the application of what is learned to the workplace is hindered by poorly designed work environments (Tracey, Tannenbaum, & Kavanaugh, 1995). HRD scholars are cognizant of the social, psychological, and organiza-tional influences on employee learning and performance and are well positioned to use this expertise to develop theory that supports effective work design. Since they study the development of managers and employees at all levels of the organization, HRD scholars recognize the need for work systems that enable seamless performance across levels of the organization so that employee development has beneficial results.

Implications for HRD also arise from changes in work reflected in virtual and alternative work environments. The preparation of those who work in these environments should now include consideration of the opportunities and challenges of employment both in and outside organizations (Hall, 2002). Work environments that are not time and place specific require different skills from those needed in traditional work settings (Apgar, 1998; Kanter, 2001). Although communities of practice can develop in virtual environments, they face unique barriers and prerequisites for success (Ardichvili, Page, & Wentling, 2002). Physical and temporal separation from the major locus of work activity also requires the capability for visualizing situations that are developing elsewhere without sentient cues and information on the events themselves (Torraco, 2002). Today's information-rich work environments require work designs that draw attention to the most important information and place more emphasis on the development of higher-level evaluation and problem-solving skills (Norman, 1993). Finally, the HRD implications of new work environments again underscore the importance of developing a workforce with the capabilities for continuous learning. Learning and sense making are more important than ever before for adapting resourcefully to new environments and unforeseen circumstances.

References

Achrol, R. (1997). Changes in the theory of interorganizational relations in marketing: Toward a network paradigm. *Journal of the Academy of Marketing Science, 25,* 56–71.

Adler, P. S. (1992). Introduction. In P. S. Adler (Ed.), *Technology and the future of work.* New York: Oxford University Press.

Amabile, T. M., & Conti, R. 1999. Changes in the work environment for creativity during down sizing. *Academy of Management Journal, 42,* 630–640.

Apgar, M. (1998). The alternative workplace: Changing where and how people work. *Harvard Business Review, 62,* 121–136.

Ardichvili, A. (2003). Constructing socially situated learning experiences in human resource development: An activity theory perspective. *Human Resource Development International, 5* (3), 301–325.

Ardichvili, A., Page, V., & Wentling, T. (2002). Virtual knowledge-sharing communities of practice at Caterpillar: Success factor and barriers. *Performance Improvement Quarterly, 15* (3), 94–113.

Arnold, H. J., & House, R. J. (1980). Methodological and substantive extensions of the job characteristics model of motivation. *Organizational Behavior and Human Performance, 25,* 161–183.

Bailey, D. E., & Kurland, N. B. (2002). A review of telework research: Findings, new directions, and lessons for the study of modern work. *Journal of Organizational Behavior, 23,* 383–400.

Barley, S. R., & Orr, J. E. (1997). *Between craft and science: Technical work in U.S. settings.* Ithaca, NY: ILR Press.

Becker, G. S. (1993). *Human capital: A theoretical and empirical analysis with special reference to education* (3rd ed.). Chicago: University of Chicago Press.

Blau, P. M., Falbe, C. M., McKinley, W., & Tracy, P. K. (1976). Technology and organization in manufacturing. *Administrative Science Quarterly, 21,* 20–40.

Bridges, W. (1994, September 19). The end of the job. *Fortune,* 62–74.

Campbell, J. P., McCloy, R. A., Oppler, S. H., & Sager, C. E. (1993). A theory of performance. In N. Schmitt & W. C. Borman (Eds.), *Personnel selection in organizations* (pp. 35–70). San Francisco: Jossey-Bass.

Campion, M. A., & Thayer, P. W. (1985). Development and field evaluation of an interdisciplinary measure of job design. *Journal of Applied Psychology, 70,* 29–43.

Cappelli, P., Bassi, L., Katz, H., Knoke, D., Osterman, P., & Useem, M. (1997). *Change at work.* New York: Oxford University Press.

Cascio, W. F. (1993). Downsizing: What do we know? What have we learned? *Academy of Management Executive, 7,* 95–104.

Cascio, W. F., Young, C. E., & Morris, J. R. (1997). Financial consequences of employment change decisions in major U.S. corporations. *Academy of Management Journal, 40,* 1175–1189.

Cherns, A. (1987). Principles of sociotechnical design revisited. *Human Relations, 40,* 153–162.

Child, J. (1972). Organizational structure, environment and performance: The role of strategic choice. *Sociology, 6,* 1–22.

Chin, W. W., Gopal, A., & Salisbury, W. D. (1997). Advancing the theory of adaptive structuration: The development of a scale to measure faithfulness of appropriation. *Information Systems Research, 8,* 342–367.

Cole, M. (1981). Preface. In J. V. Wertsch (Ed.), *The concept of activity in Soviet psychology.* Armonk, NY: M. E. Sharpe.

Confessore, S., & Kops, W. (1998). Self-directed learning and the learning organization. Examining the connection between the individual and the learning environment. *Human Resource Development Quarterly, 9* (4), 365–375.

Cummings, T. G., & Molloy, E. (1977). *Improving productivity and the quality of work life.* New York: Praeger.

Cummings, T. G., & Worley, C. G. (2001). *Organization development and change* (8th ed.). Cincinnati, OH: South-Western College Publishing.

Davenport, T. H. (1993). *Process innovation: Reengineering work through information technology.* Boston: Harvard Business School Press.

Deming, W. E. (1986). *Out of the crisis.* Cambridge, MA: Center for Advanced Engineering Study.

DeSanctis, G., & Poole, M. S. (1994). Capturing the complexity in advanced technology use: Adaptive structuration theory. *Organization Science, 5* (2), 121–147.

Dougherty, D., & Bowman, E. H. (1995). The effects of organizational downsizing on product innovation. *California Management Review, 37* (4), 28–44.

Edwards, J. R., Scully, J. A., & Brtek, M. D. (1999). The measurement of work: Hierarchical representation of the multimethod job design questionnaire. *Personnel Psychology, 52* (2), 305–334.

Eisenhardt, K. M. (1989). Agency theory: An assessment and review. *Academy of Management Review, 14* (2), 488–511.

Emery, F. E., & Trist, E. L. (1969). Sociotechnical systems. In F. E. Emery (Ed.), *Systems thinking* (pp. 281–296). London: Penguin Books.

Emery, F. E., & Trist, E. L. (1973). *Toward a social ecology.* London: Plenum Press.

Engestrom, Y. (2000). Activity theory as a framework for analyzing and redesigning work. *Ergonomics, 43* (7), 960–975.

Fisher, S. R., & White, M. A. (2000). Downsizing in a learning organization: Are there hidden costs? *Academy of Management Review, 25* (1), 244–251.

Frei, F., Hugentobler, M., Schurman, S., Duell, W., & Alioth, A. (1993). *Work design for the competent organization.* Westport, CT: Quorum.

Fried, Y. (1991). Meta-analytic comparison of the job diagnostic survey and job characteristics inventory as correlates of work satisfaction and performance. *Journal of Applied Psychology, 76* (5), 690–697.

Fried, Y., & Ferris, G. (1987). The validity of the job characteristics model: A review and meta-analysis. *Personnel Psychology, 40,* 287–322.

Friedman, S. D., Christensen, P., & DeGroot, J. (1998). Work and life: The end of the zero-sum game. *Harvard Business Review, 76* (6), 119–129.

Galbraith, J. R. (1970). Environmental and technological determinants of organizational design. In J. W. Lorsch & P. R. Lawrence (Eds.), *Studies in organizational design.* Homewood, IL: Irwin.

Galbraith, J. R. (1977). *Organization design.* Reading, MA: Addison-Wesley.

Galbraith, J. R., & Lawler, E. F. (1993). *Organizing for the future: The new logic for managing complex organizations.* San Francisco: Jossey-Bass.

Garvin, D. (1988). *Managing quality: The strategic and competitive edge.* New York: Free Press.

Gergen, K. J. (1999). *An invitation to social construction.* Thousand Oaks, CA: Sage.

Giddens, A. (1979). *Central problems in social theory.* Los Angeles: University of California Press.

Gitlow, H. S., & Hertz, P. T. (1983, September–October). Product defects and productivity. *Harvard Business Review,* 131–141.

Griffith, T. L. (1999). Technology features as triggers for sensemaking. *Academy of Management Review, 24* (3), 472–488.

Guzzo, R. A., & Dickson, M. W. (1996). Teams in organizations: Recent research on performance and effectiveness. *Annual Review of Psychology, 47*, 307–338.

Hackman, J. R. (Ed.). (1990). *Teams that work (and those that don't)*. San Francisco: Jossey-Bass.

Hackman, J. R., & Oldham, G. R. (1980). *Work redesign*. Reading, MA: Addison-Wesley.

Hall, D. T. (2002). *Careers in and out of organizations*. Thousand Oaks, CA: Sage.

Hammer, M., & Champy, J. (1993). *Reengineering the corporation: A manifesto for business revolution*. New York: HarperCollins.

Heller, F. (1997). Sociotechnology and the environment. *Human Relations, 50* (5), 605–624.

Hill, E. J., Miller, B. C., & Weiner, S. P. (1998). Influences of the virtual office on aspects of work and work/life balance. *Personnel Psychology, 51* (3), 667–683.

Holton, E. F. III (1999). Performance domains and their boundaries. *Advances in Developing Human Resource, 1*, 26–46.

Howard, A. (Ed.). (1995). *The changing nature of work*. San Francisco: Jossey-Bass.

Ilgen, D. R., & Hollenbeck, J. R. (1992). The structure of work: Job design and roles. In M. D. Dunnette & L. M. Hough (Eds.), *Handbook of industrial and organizational psychology* (2nd ed., pp. 165–207). Palo Alto, CA: CPP.

Jackson, P. R., Wall, T. D., Martin, R., & Davids, K. (1993). New measures of job control, cognitive demand, and production responsibility. *Journal of Applied Psychology, 78*, 753–762.

Johns, G., Xie, J. L., & Fang, Y. (1992). Mediating and moderating effects on job design. *Journal of Management, 18*, 657–676.

Jones, G., & Hill, C. (1988). Transaction cost analysis of strategy-structure choice. *Strategic Management Journal, 9*, 159–172.

Junsson, B., & Lank, A. G. (1985, Winter). Volvo: A report on the workshop on production technology and quality of working life. *Human Resources Management*, 459–468.

Juran, J. M. (1974). *Quality control handbook* (3rd ed.). New York: McGraw-Hill.

Kanter, R. M. (2001). *E-volve! Succeeding in the digital culture of tomorrow*. Boston: Harvard Business School Press.

Kelly, J. E. (1992). Does job re-design theory explain job re-design outcomes? *Human Relations, 45*, 753–774.

Klein, K. J., Dansereau, F., & Hall, R. J. (1994). Levels issues in theory development, data collection, and analysis. *Academy of Management Review, 19*, 105–229.

Kolodny, H. (1981). Managing in a matrix. *Business Horizons, 24*, 17–35.

Lawler, E., Mohrman, S., & Ledford, G. (1998). *Strategies of high-performance organizations*. San Francisco: Jossey-Bass.

Lawrence, P. R., & Lorsch, J. W. (1967). *Organization and environment: Managing differentiation and integration*. Cambridge, MA: Harvard Graduate School of Business.

Leont'ev, A. N. (1978). *Activity, consciousness, and personality*. Upper Saddle River, NJ: Prentice Hall.

Leont'ev, A. N. (1981). *Problems of the development of mind*. Moscow: Progress Publishers.

Liker, J. K., Haddad, C. J., & Karlin, J. (1999). Perspectives on technology and work organization. *Annual Review of Sociology, 25*, 575–596.

Loher, B. T., Noe, R. A., Moeller, N. L., & Fitzpatrick, M. P. (1985). A meta-analysis of the relation of job characteristics to job satisfaction. *Journal of Applied Psychology, 70* (2), 280–289.

Luff, P., Hindmarsh, J., & Heath, C. (2000). *Workplace studies: Recovering work practice and informing system design*. Cambridge: Cambridge University Press.

Luthans, F., & Sommer, S. M. (1999). The impact of downsizing on work attitudes: Differing reactions of managers and staff in a health care organization. *Group and Organization Management, 24*, 46–70.

Macy, B. A. (1980, July). The quality of work life project at Bolivar. *Monthly Labor Review*, 42–51.

Majchrzak, A. (1997). What to do when you can't have it all: Toward a theory of sociotechnical dependencies. *Human Relations, 50* (5), 535–565.

McKinley, W., Sanchez, C. M., & Schick, A. G. (1995). Organizational downsizing: Constraining, cloning, learning. *Academy of Management Executive, 9* (3), 32–44.

McKinley, W., & Scherer, A. G. (2000). Some unanticipated consequences of organizational restructuring. *Academy of Management Review, 25* (4), 735–752.

Miles, R., & Snow, C. (1978). *Organization strategy, structure, and process.* New York: McGraw-Hill.

Miller, D., & Droge, C. (1986). Psychological and traditional determinants of structure. *Administrative Science Quarterly, 31,* 539–560.

Miller, D., & Friesen, P. (1984). *Organizations: A quantum view.* Upper Saddle River, NJ: Prentice Hall.

Mills, T. (1976, October). Altering the social structure in coal mining: A case study. *Monthly Labor Review,* 3–10.

Mintzberg, H. (1994). *The rise and fall of strategic planning.* New York: Free Press.

Morgeson, F. P., & Hofmann, D. A. (1999). The structure and function of collective constructs: Implications for multilevel research and theory development. *Academy of Management Review, 24* (2), 249–265.

Norman, D. A. (1993). *Things that make us smart: Defending human attributes in the age of the machine.* Reading, MA: Addison-Wesley.

Norman, D. A. (1998). *The invisible computer: Why good products can fail, the personal computer is so complex, and information appliances are the solution.* Cambridge, MA: MIT Press.

Orlikowski, W. J. (1992). The duality of technology: Rethinking the concept of technology in organizations. *Organization Science, 3* (3), 398–427.

Orlikowski, W. J., Yates, J., Okamura, K., & Fujimoto, M. (1995). Shaping electronic communication: The metastructuring of technology in the context of use. *Organization Science, 6* (4), 423–444.

Osterman, P. (1994). How common is workplace transformation and who adopts it? *Industrial and Labor Relations Review, 47* (2), 173–188.

Parker, S., & Wall, T. (1998). *Job and work design: Organizing work to promote well-being and effectiveness.* Thousand Oaks, CA: Sage.

Parker, S., Wall, T., & Jackson, P. R. (1997). "That's not my job": Developing flexible employee work orientations. *Academy of Management Journal, 40* (4), 899–929.

Pasmore, W., Francis, C., Haldeman, J., & Shani, A. (1982). Sociotechnical systems: A North American reflection on empirical studies of the seventies. *Human Relations, 35,* 1179–1204.

Potter, E. E. (2003). Telecommuting: The future of work, corporate culture, and American society. *Journal of Labor Research, 24* (1), 73–84.

Powell, W. (1990). Neither market nor hierarchy: Network forms of organization. In B. Staw & L. Cummings (Eds.), *Research in organizational behavior,* 12 (pp. 295–3346). Greenwich, CT: JAI Press.

Pugh, D. S., Hickson, D. J., Hinings, C. R., & Turner, C. (1969). The context of organization structures. *Administrative Science Quarterly, 14,* 91–114.

Raghuram, S., Garud, R., Wiesenfeld, B., & Gupta, V. (2001). Factors contributing to virtual work adjustment. *Journal of Management, 27* (3), 383–405.

Rashford, N. S., & Coghlan, D. (1994). *The dynamics of organizational levels.* Reading, MA: Addison-Wesley.

Reese, R. (1995). Redesigning for dial tone: A sociotechnical systems case study. *Organizational Dynamics, 24,* 80–90.

Renn, R. W., & Vandenburg, R. J. (1995). The critical psychological states: An underrepresented component in job characteristics model research. *Journal of Management, 21* (2), 279–303.

Rice, A. K. (1953). Productivity and social organization in an Indian weaving shed: An examination of some aspects of the sociotechnical system of an experimental automatic loom shed. *Human Relations, 6,* 297–329.

Rice, A. K. (1958). *Productivity and social organization: The Ahmedabad experiments.* London: Tavistock.

Rummler, G. A., & Brache, A. P. (1995). *Improving performance: How to manage the white space on the organization chart* (2nd ed.). San Francisco: Jossey-Bass.

Salvendy, G., & Karwowski, W. (1994). *Design of work and development of personnel in advanced manufacturing.* New York: Wiley-Interscience.

Schick, A. G., Gordon, L. A., & Haka, S. (1990). Information overload: A temporal approach. *Accounting, Organization and Society, 15,* 199–220.

Schoonhoven, C. B. (1981). Problems with contingency theory: Testing assumptions hidden within the language of contingency "theory." *Administrative Science Quarterly, 26,* 349–377.

Scribner, S. (1984). Studying working intelligence. In B. Rogoff & J. Lave (Eds.), *Everyday cognition: Its development in social context.* Cambridge, MA: Harvard University Press.

Semler, S. (1997). Systematic agreement: A theory of organizational alignment. *Human Resource Development Quarterly, 8* (1), 23–40.

Shetty, Y. K. (1986). Quality, productivity, and profit performance: Learning from research and practice. *National Productivity Review, 5* (2), 166–173.

Shewhart, W. A. (1931). *The economic control of manufactured products.* New York: Van Nostrand.

Smith, V. (1997). New forms of work organization. *Annual Review of Sociology, 23,* 315–339.

Staw, B. M., & Boettger, R. D. (1990). Task revision: A neglected form of work performance. *Academy of Management Journal, 33* (3), 534–559.

Tenner, E. (1996). *Why things bite back: Technology and the revenge of unintended consequences.* New York: Knopf.

Thorsrud, D. E. (1968). Sociotechnical approach to job design and organization development. *Management International Review, 8* (4–5), 120–131.

Torraco, R. J. (2000). The relationship of learning and performance improvement at different system levels. *Performance Improvement Quarterly, 13* (1), 60–83.

Torraco, R. J. (2002). Cognitive demands of new technologies and the implications for learning theory. *Human Resource Development Review, 1,* 439–467.

Tracey, J. B., Tannenbaum, S. I., & Kavanaugh, M. J. (1995). Applying trained skills of the job: The importance of the work environment. *Journal of Applied Psychology, 80,* 239–252.

Trist, E. L. (1981). *The evolution of sociotechnical systems.* Toronto: Ontario Quality of Work Life Centre.

Trist, E. L., & Bamforth, K. W. (1951). Some social and psychological consequences of long-wall methods of coal getting. *Human Relations, 4,* 3–38.

Trist, E. L., Higgin, G. W., Murray, H., & Pollock, A. B. (1963). *Organizational choice.* London: Tavistock.

Turnbull, S. (2002). Social construction research and theory building. *Advances in Developing Human Resources, 4,* 317–334.

Tushman, M., & Romanelli, E. (1985). Organizational evolution: A metamorphosis model of convergence and reorientation. In L. L. Cummings & B. M. Staw (Eds.), *Research in organization behavior* (Vol. 7, pp. 171–222). Greenwich, CT: JAI Press.

Venkatesh, V., & Johnson, P. (2002). Telecommuting technology implementations: A within- and between-subjects longitudinal field study. *Personnel Psychology, 55* (3), 661–687.

Volberda, H. W. (1998). Toward the flexible form: How to remain vital in hypercompetitive environments. In A. Y. Ilinitch, A. Lewin, & R. D'Aveni (Eds.), *Managing in times of disorder: Hypercompetitive organizational responses* (pp. 267–296). Thousand Oaks, CA: Sage.

Vygotsky, L. S. (1978). *Mind and society: The development of higher psychological processes.* Cambridge, MA: Harvard University Press.

Watad, M. M., & DiSanzo, F. J. (2000). The synergism of telecommuting and office automation. *Sloan Management Review, 41* (2), 85–96.

Weick, K. A. (1990). Technology as equivoque: Sensemaking in new technologies. In P. S. Goodman, L. S. Sproull, & Associates (Eds.), *Technology and organizations.* San Francisco: Jossey-Bass.

Welsh, D. H. B., Luthans, F., & Sommer, S. M. (1993, February). Managing Russian factory workers: The impact of U.S.-based behavioral and participative techniques. *Academy of Management Journal,* 58–79.

Wognum, I. A. M. (2000). Vertical integration of HRD within companies. In K. P. Kuchinke (Ed.), *Academy of Human Resource Development Conference Proceedings* (pp. 1083–1090). Baton Rouge, LA: AHRD.

Wrzesniewski, A., & Dutton, J. E. (2001). Crafting a job: Revisioning employees as active crafters of their work. *Academy of Management Review, 26* (2), 179–201.

Zucker, L. G. (1987). Institutional theories of organizations. In W. R. Scott (Ed.), *Annual review of sociology* (pp. 443–464). Palo Alto, CA: Annual Reviews.

8 Interdependence and Role Relationships

8.1 TEAM IMPLICIT COORDINATION PROCESSES

A Team Knowledge-Based Approach

Ramón Rico, Miriam Sánchez-Manzanares, Francisco Gil, and Cristina Gibson

We present an integrated theoretical framework that models the development of team situation models and implicit coordination behaviors. We first define these concepts and then examine the role of several team and context variables in facilitating the emergence of implicit coordination patterns, as well as in moderating their effects on team performance. Finally, we discuss the implications of the model for team coordination theory, team cognition research, and effective management of work teams.

Coordination in work teams is an emergent phenomenon involving the use of strategies and behavior patterns aimed at integrating and aligning the actions, knowledge, and objectives of interdependent members, with a view to attaining common goals (e.g., Arrow, McGrath, & Berdahl, 2000; Brannick, Prince, Prince, & Salas, 1995; Malone & Crowston, 1994; Zalesny, Salas, & Prince, 1995). Most models based on input-process-output relationships treat coordination as a key process for team effectiveness (e.g., Cohen & Bailey, 1997; Gladstein, 1984; McGrath & Argote, 2001; Tannenbaum, Beard, & Salas, 1992). Coordination ensures that a team functions as a unified whole (Brannick & Prince, 1997; Van de Ven, Delbecq, & Koening, 1976). When a team attains a high level of coordination, the work of all its members contributes to results, but when coordination is poor, the ensuing process losses have a negative impact on outcomes (Steiner, 1972; Wilke & Meertens, 1994).

Several different concepts have been developed to explain how work teams coordinate. Traditionally, research has focused on planning and communication as the basic mechanisms of team coordination, both of which constitute examples of *explicit coordination*, because team members use them intentionally to manage their multiple interdependencies (Espinosa, Lerch, & Kraut, 2004; Malone & Crowston, 1994). Coordination via planning, also known as programming (March & Simon, 1958), impersonal coordination (Van de Ven et al., 1976), and administrative coordination (Faraj & Sproull, 2000), refers to the set of practices and devices used by a team to manage the more stable and predictable aspects of its work, such as deadlines, plans, schedules, and programs. Coordination via communication includes feedback processes (March & Simon, 1958) and personal coordination (Van de Ven et al., 1976), and it encompasses the exchange of information between two or more team members through formal or informal and oral or written transactions in order to integrate their respective contributions (Kraut & Streeter, 1995).

We argue that the focus on explicit coordination so prevalent in past research offers a relatively static picture of team functioning. Despite their undoubted importance, explicit coordination mechanisms reveal only one aspect of team coordination. Drawing on team cognition research, we contend that the concept of *implicit coordination* broadens our understanding of the way team members coordinate their contributions in the midst of interaction. Implicit coordination takes place when team members *anticipate* the actions and needs of their colleagues and task demands and *dynamically adjust* their own behavior accordingly, without having to communicate directly with each other or plan the activity (Cannon-Bowers, Salas, & Converse, 1993; Espinosa et al., 2004; Wittembaum, Stasser, & Merry, 1996). For instance, when making decisions in a top management team, members must process a large body of information about different aspects of their business. Complete examination of all information by all members is infeasible. So, given knowledge of others' expertise, past behavior, and interests, members often make assumptions about the kinds of information other members will attend to (e.g., Peter always examines accounting information in detail, Susan thinks logistical information is important, Michael predicts success by sales results). Thus, by anticipating what others in the team are likely to do, members can adapt their own behavior to facilitate the team's task completion without explicit discussion of who should do what.

Various research streams provide general support for the phenomenon of implicit coordination. These include findings regarding the propensity of teams to use habitual routines (Gersick & Hackman, 1990), the swift development and permanence of work distribution and interrelation patterns among team members (Gersick, 1988; Weick & Roberts, 1993), and the low frequency of group discussions concerning the strategies required to resolve a joint task (Hackman & Morris, 1975). Further, research into team cognition has underscored the need to examine the cognitive structures and processes employed by teams if we are fully to understand team coordination (e.g., Fiore & Salas, 2004; Gibson, 2001; Marks, Sabella, Burke, & Zaccaro, 2002; Marks, Zaccaro, & Mathieu, 2000; Mathieu, Heffner, Goodwin, Salas, & Cannon-Bowers, 2000). Addressing this gap, we argue that the underlying mechanism that enables implicit coordination is the existence of emergent team-level knowledge structures—team situation models (TSMs)—that are shared and accurate. TSMs are dynamic, context-driven mental models concerning key areas of the team's work, such as the objectives or roles of colleagues (Cooke, Kiekel, Salas, Stout, Bowers, & Cannon-Bowers, 2003; Cooke, Salas, Cannon-Bowers, & Stout, 2000).

Our paper consists of three sections. We begin by defining the theoretical construct of implicit team coordination as contrasted with explicit team coordination and other related constructs. We then develop an integrated, empirically verifiable model of team implicit coordination that captures the relationships among TSMs, implicit coordination, and team performance. We examine the role of several critical characteristics of work teams within three major categories, including team composition (longevity, knowledge diversity), team-specific attributes (trust, group efficacy), and team performance environment (task routineness, task interdependence, virtuality), in developing TSMs and in moderating the impact of implicit coordination on team performance. Finally, we discuss the implications of the propositions derived from the model for team coordination theory, team cognition research, and effective management of work teams.

By considering the system of variables pertaining to team coordination and how they interrelate to impact team performance, our model contributes to theory and research on team cognition and team effectiveness areas in three ways. First, we focus on the analysis of implicit coordination, facilitating a more nuanced approach to theorizing about team coordination and performance processes that helps us broaden our treatment of teams as dynamic action systems. Second, we define the concepts of implicit coordination and TSMs and the specific links between them and team performance, reinforcing the team effectiveness literature with a team knowledge-based perspective of team coordination and providing propositions that can be investigated empirically. Third, we identify a set of variables that promote the development of TSMs, as well as a set of contextual conditions under which implicit coordination is more or less important to effective team performance. In doing so, we explicate the specific features of teams and their task context that must be addressed in order to fully understand implicit coordination.

Overall, our model is aimed at improving comprehension of the coordinated functioning of work teams by developing the construct of implicit coordination. Implicit coordination addresses the most dynamic, subtle, and ongoing aspects of coordination taking place among team members during team performance through anticipation and dynamic adjustment behaviors. Our explanation of team coordination in terms of implicit coordination complements traditional explanations mainly focused on explicit coordination mechanisms. Thus, our model is not intended to be a substitute for prior theory but to extend and refine it. Here we provide a research agenda to examine some of the most challenging and theoretically significant issues around the phenomenon of implicit coordination: How does implicit coordination manifest in the behavior of work teams? How is it related to team knowledge? How does it affect team performance? When is it more or less useful to team performance? In examining these issues, we develop a more complete, nuanced, and comprehensive view of team coordination.

Theoretical Foundations

The concept of implicit coordination was originally applied to explain the capacity of decision-making and action teams to maintain optimum levels of performance under conditions of intense workload by notably reducing intrateam communication (e.g., Cannon-Bowers & Salas, 2001; Kleinman & Serfaty, 1989; Orasanu, 1990; Serfaty, Entin, & Volpe, 1993). Implicit coordination is distinct from explicit coordination, which requires that team members communicate in order to articulate plans, define responsibilities, negotiate deadlines, and seek information to undertake common tasks. Implicit coordination captures the ability of a team to act in concert by predicting the needs of the task and the team members and adjusting behavior accordingly, without the need for overt communication (Espinosa et al., 2004; Fiore, Salas, & Cannon-Bowers, 2001; MacMillan, Entin, & Serfaty, 2004; Wittembaum et al., 1996).

Implicit and explicit coordination patterns play similar roles in work teams—that is, allowing members to manage their multiple interdependencies. However, there are important differences in their underlying mechanisms. Implicit team coordination processes have been characterized by the following behaviors: (1) providing task-relevant information, knowledge, or feedback to other team members without a previous request; (2) proactively sharing a workload or helping a colleague; (3) monitoring the progress of the activity and the performance of teammates; and (4) adapting behavior to the expected actions of others (e.g., Entin & Serfaty, 1999; MacMillan, Paley, Entin, & Entin, 2004; Serfaty et al., 1993; Wittembaum et al., 1996).

The above manifestations suggest that implicit coordination comprises two basic components: (1) *anticipation*, which is revealed in the expectations and predictions team members formulate regarding the demands of the task and the actions and needs of others, without being directly notified of these actions or needs; (2) *dynamic adjustment*, which appears in those actions taken by team members on an ongoing basis in order to mutually adapt their behavior. Consider a team of firefighters coping with a fire in an apartment building. When the firefighters unroll the hose along the stairs of the building, the hose fittings linking the hose can become caught in the corners or railings of the stairs, preventing full extension of the hose to the firefighters nearest the fire. Anticipating this potential problem, team members estimate the hose length their frontline teammates will need, and they place the hose fittings in safe places along the stairs in order to avoid the problem. Although firefighters do not discuss or explicitly require such behavior during a collective undertaking, in doing so, the frontline firefighters are able to control the fire without risking their lives.

Our focus on anticipation and dynamic adjustment, which constitute implicit coordination, can be compared and contrasted with other concepts that have appeared in the literature. Among these are collective mind (Weick & Roberts, 1993) and habitual routines (Gersick & Hackman, 1990). Collective mind has been defined as a pattern of heedful interrelations among the actions of organizational members (Weick & Roberts, 1993). The concepts of implicit coordination and collective mind share a common focus on interrelating patterns as a central feature of collective action, an emphasis on the dynamic aspects of such patterns, and the use of collective-level, cognition-related notions to explicate them. However, implicit coordination differs from the concept of collective mind in two important ways.

First, the constructs differ in the assumptions made about cognition. Collective mind captures the tendency of members in a social system to act in a certain manner. Accordingly, the analysis of collective mind is focused on how it is revealed in collective action (i.e., patterns of heedful interrelating). Typically, in such analyses, no clear distinctions are made between cognition and action. In contrast, our model of implicit coordination overtly addresses the structure and content of knowledge (as reflected in TSMs) and distinguishes these from the actions and process behaviors influenced by this knowledge (as evidenced by implicit coordination).

Second, a central idea in Weick and Roberts' (1993) work is that the patterns of interrelation among individuals' actions that constitute collective mind can range from *heedful* to *heedless*. Heedfulness is thoughtful attentiveness and awareness. Weick and Roberts (1993) argue that the extent to which such patterns are heedful is critical for organizational effectiveness. As heedful interrelating increases, then, organizational members' understanding of unfolding events improves and errors decrease. Although the concept of implicit coordination also denotes a type of interrelating pattern among individual actions, it does not address the heedful nature of such a pattern. A team can coordinate implicitly and yet not be heedful (i.e., members may not be fully aware of the implicit coordination). In fact, since it occurs without explicit discussion or evaluation among team members, implicit coordination may sometimes appear to be automatic and unconscious. Thus, like other types of coordination, implicit coordination can range from heedless to heedful. When members develop anticipation and dynamic adjustment in a more attentive, careful, or vigilant manner, it becomes more heedful. Hence, implicit–explicit and heedful–heedless refer to different facets of the way members of a social system (e.g., a work team) integrate their actions to attain collective goals.

Implicit coordination can also be contrasted with habitual team routines. Habitual routines are patterned ways of responding to predictable situations (Gersick & Hackman, 1990). Although implicit coordination may be involved in habitual routines, there are several important differences between the concepts. First, implicit coordination and habitual routines refer to different team-level phenomena. Implicit coordination addresses how team members dynamically change, adjust, and adapt their contributions to attain common goals, whereas habitual routines capture repetitious patterns of responses under particular work situations. Further, habitual routines involve responses that are not necessarily related to team coordination. For example, routines might be developed regarding the expression of socioemotional behaviors, such as how to respond emotionally in a conflict. Implicit coordination concerns only those behaviors that affect the integration of team members' task inputs.

Second, implicit coordination is a broad team-level process that is not restricted to particular stimuli or situations. That is, implicit coordination describes a general way in which team members coordinate their multiple contributions across different situations. In contrast, a team-level habitual routine describes a pattern of response used by a team to deal with a specific and frequent situation, task, or problem present in its work setting.

Finally, researchers examining team routines have argued that routines operate automatically, without team members' conscious evaluation of or selection between different alternatives of behavior (e.g., Gersick & Hackman, 1990; Langer, 1989; Louis & Sutton, 1991; Zellmer-Bruhn, 2003). In contrast, as discussed previously, implicit coordination involves cognitive activity that can be more or less automatic, depending on the way team members integrate their work in a given situation.

By way of summary, although implicit coordination shares several features with the concepts of collective mind and habitual routines, it is a distinct process that captures a unique aspect of team functioning. Having contrasted implicit coordination with related constructs in the team literature, we next examine the team knowledge structures that produce implicit coordination.

Team Knowledge and Implicit Coordination

The team cognition literature suggests that the two basic components that form the nucleus of implicit coordination—anticipation and dynamic adjustment—are rooted in team knowledge structures (e.g., Cannon-Bowers et al., 1993; Klimoski & Mohammed, 1994; Kraiger & Wenzel, 1997). Accordingly, modeling implicit team coordination requires understanding the nature and role of team knowledge.

Most conceptualizations of team knowledge draw on the construct of team mental models, or TMMs (e.g., Langan-Fox, Code, & Langfield-Smith, 2000; Marks et al., 2002; Mohammed & Dumville, 2001; Stout, Cannon-Bowers, Salas, & Milanovich, 1999). TMMs are team-level stable mental representations, including key knowledge about undertaking team tasks related to both teamwork (e.g., team member roles) and taskwork (e.g., typical task strategies). Researchers examining TMMs maintain that they are critical for effective coordination (Fiore et al., 2001; Klimoski & Mohammed, 1994). We argue that in order to understand team knowledge involved in implicit coordination, our focus needs to shift from the stable knowledge representations TMMs comprise to the dynamic knowledge structures that teams develop when engaging in a task.

The concept of TSMs has been proposed to address this distinction (Cooke et al., 2000, 2003; MacMillan et al., 2004). A TSM is the mental representation associated with a dynamic understanding of the current situation (i.e., environment, task, team) that is developed by team members moment by moment (e.g., understanding by a consulting team of the particular financial problem facing a client company). A TMM comprises the longer-term knowledge base brought to bear on this dynamic understanding (e.g., knowledge of finance held by a consulting team; Cooke, Salas, Kiekel, & Bell, 2004; Endsley & Jones, 2001). To explain implicit coordination, we focus here on TSMs (rather than TMMs), based on the logic that implicit coordination is itself more dynamic, impromptu, and situationally driven. Knowledge in situ is more closely linked to processes that are context dependent. Unlike explicit coordination, which can be developed prior to any execution, implicit coordination by definition is much more fluid. As a result, it is likely that TSMs play a much stronger role than TMMs in implicit coordination.

Importantly, note that a TSM is an emergent group property characterizing a team as a whole (e.g., Cooke et al., 2004; Marks et al., 2002; Mathieu et al., 2005). A TSM derives from the situation models provided by individual team members to form an aggregate phenomenon at the team level (Kozlowski & Klein, 2000). Since the *team* forms the *context* where members operate, it is a powerful force driving individual cognition. Team members' situation models are combined and amplified through interaction processes and dynamics to manifest as a team-level phenomenon. People in teams exchange information, affect, and valued resources; share ideas; communicate feelings and moods; performs acts; and exchange work products. Communication and exchanges may be direct (e.g., face-to-face interaction) or indirect (e.g., technology-mediated information exchange). The nature of the interaction process, in combination with team members' situation models, shapes the emergent TSM.

Implicit coordination and TSMs are not one and the same. Implicit coordination is a process—it is the team interaction behavior that is coordinated in the absence of overt communication—whereas TSMs refer to the team-level knowledge structures facilitating those behaviors. That is, team members develop a TSM of the situation at hand, and they use it to generate predictions of others' actions and task demands, thereby adapting their behavior. For example, members of a soccer team develop a TSM of the strategy being used by the opposing team during a match ("our opponent is displaying an attack strategy"). This TSM leads the team to select a counterattack strategy to overcome its opponent. Accordingly, midfield and defender players anticipate the need for providing forward players with well-centered passes to shoot at the opponent's goal, thereby advancing lines to increase opportunities for such passes.

Although a particular TSM could affect different team process behaviors (e.g., communication, leadership, decision making), in this paper we are specifically interested in analyzing its role in implicit coordination. Further, we highlight two features of TSMs that we believe are critical for understanding implicit coordination: sharedness and accuracy. *Sharedness* of a TSM is the degree to which team members' situation models are consistent with one another (Cannon-Bowers & Salas, 2001; Cooke et al., 2003). Researchers often argue that team processes and performance improve to the extent that members share their knowledge structures (Langan-Fox et al., 2000; Rentsch & Woehr, 2004). Although there is some empirical support for this approach (Mathieu et al., 2000; Stout et al., 1999), the available evidence remains fragmented and ambiguous. These equivocal results may be attributed to lack of agreement around what it means for knowledge to be "shared," as well as to the often simplistic analyses of team knowledge (Cooke et al., 2000, 2004).

We contend that individuals in smoothly functioning teams hold a compatible understanding of what is happening for those elements that are overlapping, shared, or needed across different positions in the team (e.g., in a software development team, understanding the stage of development of the new software being created). Not all information needs to be shared by all team members. Since team members usually have specific functions and roles, sharing every detail of each other's job would impede optimal team performance. Only that information relevant to the coordination among team members needs to be shared.

Although content will largely depend on the team's function and domain, TSMs enabling effective implicit coordination generally comprise content relevant to the system (the environment in which the team is operating), the task (task strategies), and the team (members' abilities). For instance, in an operating room, doctors, nurses, and technicians have their own specific tasks for which they develop specific situation models (e.g., a doctor holds a complete model of the medical state and evolution of the particular patient; a technician holds a model of the functioning of the systems and devices being used). In this scenario, a shared TSM might develop for behavior required by each team member in the management of the patient. This TSM would allow the team to generate compatible performance expectations, thereby implicitly coordinating successfully. If such a TSM does not emerge, team members will have different expectations as to who should do what in operating on the patient, and the team is likely to behave in a very uncoordinated fashion (e.g., time-lagged responses, lack of assistance to each other, no backup in an emergency). Thus, throughout this paper, a shared TSM refers to the compatible understanding among team members regarding key overlapping requirements for team coordination.

Accuracy of a TSM is defined as the similarity between the team's TSM and a comparison set of referent or high-quality knowledge structures established by experts or researchers (Anand, Clark, & Zellmer-Bruhn, 2003; Carley, 1997; Lim & Klein, 2006; Mathieu, Heffner, Goodwin, Cannon-Bowers, & Salas, 2005; Smith-Jentsch, Campbell, Milanovich, & Reynolds, 2001). A shared TSM may not necessarily be accurate. The fact that team members share an understanding of a given situation does not ensure it will be accurate and beneficial for team performance (e.g., team members can hold similar situation models, yet all can be wrong). Recent studies exploring the role of accuracy in shared knowledge representations suggest that sharedness and accuracy have both unique and interactive effects on team processes and outputs, such as coordination, team learning, and task performance (Lim & Klein, 2006; Marks et al., 2000; Mathieu et al., 2005; Wong, 2003).

Sharedness and accuracy of TSMs jointly facilitate implicit coordination behaviors. To the extent that shared situation models are also accurate, team members will be able to correctly predict others' actions and task demands and adjust their own behaviors effectively. Consider, for example, members of an air traffic control team sharing an accurate model of each other's mental workload status. They can anticipate and provide the kind of assistance required by a teammate who is experiencing intense fatigue in order to help him/her complete the task. In contrast, if members share an inaccurate model of the current situation (e.g., none of them recognize the fatigue), the team will neglect the need for assistance by the fatigued member, thereby increasing the likelihood of technical errors and accidents.

Overall, we argue that effective implicit coordination requires team members to develop situation models providing a shared and accurate understanding of key overlapping aspects of their work. Much research remains to be done to understand how sharedness and accuracy of TSMs develop in teams and what their implications are for team coordination and performance. We attempt to address this gap in our model, as elaborated below.

Relationships with Team Performance

Our integrated framework is presented in Figure 8.1.1. We first describe relationships among TSMs, implicit coordination, and performance in work teams. We then examine how certain team and context parameters facilitate the development of implicit coordination patterns

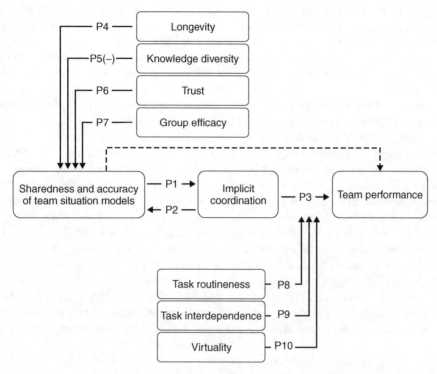

Figure 8.1.1 An Integrated Framework for Team Implicit Coordination Processes.

and moderate their impact on team performance. Note that we seek to provide a conceptual model that explicates main links in the TSMs–implicit coordination–team performance sequence, taking into account teams' features and task contexts.

The central part of Figure 8.1.1 illustrates the reciprocal relationships between TSMs and implicit coordination processes. Both components emerge dynamically in the course of specific performance episodes through interactions among team members. TSMs comprise the mental representations of knowledge generated and effectively used by teams to perform their work in a given situation, whereas implicit coordination represents the team process behaviors that link individual contributions of team members (Cooke et al., 2000), in the absence of overt communication among them. Within the limits of a performance episode, a TSM *influences* and *is influenced by* implicit coordination behaviors. When members of a team hold a shared and accurate TSM (e.g., regarding clients' needs, each other's performance, or a joint technology being used), they are able to formulate compatible and precise performance expectations and adjust their behaviors accordingly to meet the demands of the collective activity, without explicit discussion of how to perform it. When a team lacks such a TSM, its members will no longer be able to implicitly coordinate.

Likewise, implicit coordination behaviors may affect the nature of the current TSM that emerges in a team. Since the formation of a TSM is an iterative and ongoing process (Cooke et al., 2004), information unfolding in the situation as a team performs its task serves as a basis to update team members' situation models. Coordination actions of teammates and outcomes of these actions represent relevant sources of information for interdependent members of a work team that can potentially modify their current understanding of the situation. Thus, both implicit coordination behaviors of team members during collective undertaking (e.g., providing others with information about a client without previous request) and situational changes, as well as the results derived from these behaviors (e.g., properly meeting a client's need), generate a new set of information cues. This information, in turn, will contribute to modification, expansion, or refinement of the situation models held by team members.

Therefore, as team behavior unfolds and individual inputs are integrated, feedback from implicit coordination processes is expected to update the content, structure, or both aspects of the current TSM (Endsley & Jones, 2001; MacMillan et al., 2004; Stout et al., 1999) by producing either qualitative changes (e.g., integration of new information into the TSM) or quantitative changes (e.g., increase in the similarity between situation models of two team members). For example, members of a service team share an accurate understanding of the current high demand for work in the restaurant at lunch time ("the restaurant is crowded"). By anticipating the need for more sets of silverware and the little time the waiters will have to prepare the sets, the bar staff can proactively clean and place silverware on the counter. This implicit coordinating behavior accelerates the performance of the waiters, who are able to properly serve all the customers. In turn, these changes in the task setting will update the dynamic understanding of the situation among team members ("all the tables in the restaurant are served; no more sets of silverware are required"). Accordingly, we expect that shared and accurate situation models among team members will enable implicit coordination behaviors, and these behaviors, in turn, will modify the situation models currently held.

Proposition 1: In a given performance episode, the presence of shared and accurate TSMs will increase the likelihood of implicit coordination behaviors.

Proposition 2: In a given performance episode, implicit coordination processes will result in alterations to current TSMs.

Recent empirical evidence indicates that shared TMMs improve team processes, which, in turn, enhance team performance (Marks et al., 2000, 2002; Mathieu et al., 2000, 2005). However, researchers have yet to examine the effects of TSMs and implicit coordination on team performance. TSMs and implicit coordination likely play key roles in effective team performance because they reflect the active information processing at a team level under particular circumstances (Klimoski & Mohammed, 1994; Kraiger & Wenzel, 1997; Levine & Choi, 2004). We argue that implicit coordination partially mediates the positive relationship between sharedness and accuracy of TSMs and team performance outcomes. To the extent that a TSM enables the anticipation and dynamic adaptation of members' behaviors to achieve common goals, performance gains will be realized by the team. The ability to predict others' actions and needs during collective undertaking promotes effective helping, monitoring, and workload sharing behaviors among team members (Fiore et al., 2001). In addition, compatible and accurate expectations of task demands can help the team avoid process losses from coordination, such as responses that are technically correct but poorly timed and unnecessary duplications of effort (Larson & Schaumman, 1993). Also, the ability of team members to dynamically adjust their behaviors based on those expectations enables team self-regulation and adaptability under changing situations (Entin & Serfaty, 1999; Hutchins, 1995). Finally, since it reduces the need for overt communication between team members, implicit coordination facilitates fluid team interaction and increases time available for other task-relevant activities (MacMillan et al., 2004).

Adopting a broad brush approach to team performance, we expect that implicit coordination processes contribute to team performance effectiveness indicators, such as timeliness, productivity, security, product/service quality, and accurate decisions (Gibson, Zellmer-Bruhn, & Schwab, 2003; Smith-Jentsch, Mathieu, & Kraiger, 2005). At the same time, we acknowledge that TSMs may have effects on team performance independent of their effects on implicit coordination. For example, TSMs may affect decision making or learning behaviors, which, in turn, influence team performance, regardless of the level of implicit coordination (e.g., Cannon-Bowers et al., 1993; Cooke et al., 2004; Mathieu et al., 2000; Orasanu, 1990). Hence, we propose only partial, rather than full, mediation by implicit coordination.

Proposition 3: In a given performance episode, team implicit coordination processes will partially mediate the relationship between the sharedness and accuracy of TSMs and team performance.

Having identified the basic relationships among TSMs, implicit coordination, and team performance, we next propose key characteristics of work teams that give rise to implicit coordination dynamics, as well as features of their task environment that affect when they operate to drive performance.

Team Composition

Team composition features that vary dramatically in teams in organizational contexts have seldom been examined empirically in the team cognition literature. Conceptually, scholars have suggested that team composition variables, such as longevity and knowledge diversity, might impact the nature of team knowledge—that is, stable TMMs (e.g., Klimoski & Mohammed, 1994; Marks et al., 2000; Rentsch & Klimoski, 2001). Extending this thinking, we propose that team composition factors can, importantly, affect the capacity of team members to develop a shared and accurate in situ TSM, thus implicitly coordinating their behaviors to attain common goals. We then specifically examine the effects of longevity and knowledge diversity on dynamic TSMs enabling implicit coordination.

Longevity. One of the common presumptions in the literature is that the existence and nature of team knowledge structures depend on team longevity—the length of time team members have been working together as a team. Extensive social relationships, socialization processes, mutual learning, and repeated practice operate to increase the convergence and accuracy of team members' mental models over time (e.g., Langan-Fox, Anglim, & Wilson, 2004; Levesque, Wilson, & Wholey, 2001; Mathieu et al., 2000; Rentsch & Woehr, 2004). Some scholars have pointed out that a TMM effectively influences the functioning of a team when it has attained a certain degree of conceptual development (Levine & Choi, 2004; McClure, 1990). Similarly, although newly formed teams may fairly quickly generate shared TSMs of their task, each other, and their work context, these are likely to be more abstract and general in nature. Researchers examining team cognition have remarked that the creation of accurate, specific team knowledge requires experience in team activities (Klimoski & Mohammed, 1994; Kraiger & Wenzel, 1997).

In this regard, Langan-Fox (2003) has argued that the mental representations of immature teams are less refined and relevant for team performance than those of mature teams because they are in a premature phase of declarative knowledge (i.e., the facts, rules, relations, and concepts about the task). In addition, recent studies indicate that members of long-standing teams hold shared and accurate knowledge of each other's expertise (i.e., a component of a transactive memory system) that enables them to successfully integrate their behaviors during collective undertaking (e.g., Austin, 2003; Faraj & Sproull, 2000; Lewis, 2003; Rau, 2005). Further, research on group decision making suggests that familiarity among team members promotes their willingness to express and reconcile conflicting views and perspectives on the common task and to pool unique information relevant to team performance, when necessary (Gruenfeld, Mannix, Williams, & Neale, 1996). In turn, this increased group information processing by teams with high familiarity can lead them to achieve a better understanding of their task setting. In contrast, members of immature teams will be unfamiliar with each other and may not properly understand the knowledge currently held by each person for the task at hand. Accordingly, we propose that members of long-standing teams will have greater ability to properly integrate their mental representations into a compatible and accurate TSM than will members of newly formed teams, who are only just beginning to collaborate.

Proposition 4: Team longevity will be positively related to sharedness and accuracy of TSMs.

Knowledge diversity. This refers to the distribution of knowledge relevant to the purpose or task of a team among its members (Jackson, Joshi, & Erhardt, 2003; West, Borrill, & Unsworth, 1998). Differences in this knowledge may decisively affect the capacity of team members to develop a TSM. When team members share common prior educational, organizational, or team experiences, they will also hold similar mental models regarding taskwork and teamwork, and this will predispose them to select, codify, and retrieve information in a like manner (e.g., Klimoski & Mohammed, 1994; Kraiger & Wenzel, 1997; Rentsch & Klimoski, 2001; Rentsch & Zelno, 2003). This facilitates the creation of shared situation models among team members under particular working conditions. For example, Bettenhausen and Murnigham (1985) noted that groups with homogeneous knowledge tended to generate similar definitions of their mission and appropriate actions based on prior common assumptions about their tasks.

In contrast, members of diverse teams (e.g., a multifunctional product development team) possess knowledge in different domains or business specialities, and this creates differences in their world views, languages, and symbols (Dougherty, 1992). Unique perspectives may result in ethnocentrism, unwillingness to exchange critical task-focused or team-focused information, and low motivation to accept new ideas or interact with other relevant colleagues in the team (Anand et al., 2003). Existing research suggests that diverse teams take longer and encounter frequent difficulties in integrating their different knowledge stores to reach a consensus and solve problems because of misperceptions, poor mutual understanding, and inhibited information sharing (e.g., Argote & McGrath, 1993; Gruenfeld et al., 1996; Jackson et al., 2003). However, the impact of these diverse knowledge stores on in situ TSMs has yet to be systematically investigated. We propose that all these factors together will make the formation of shared and accurate TSMs more complicated and time consuming for knowledge-diverse teams.

Proposition 5: Knowledge diversity in teams will be negatively related to sharedness and accuracy of TSMs.

Team-Specific Attributes

Researchers examining team cognition have remarked on the need to analyze the interplay between team-specific attributes and the creation and utilization of team knowledge (e.g., Fiore et al., 2001; Kraiger & Wenzel, 1997; Smith-Jentsch, Kraiger, Cannon-Bowers, & Salas, 2000), but little research to date has examined these relationships. Recent studies indicate that team-specific attributes, such as trust and perceived group efficacy, may affect intrateam communication, learning, and knowledge exchange patterns among team members, therefore influencing the formation of team knowledge (Edmondson, 2003; Gibson, 2001; Gibson & Manuel, 2003; Rau, 2005). However, these scholars have most often assumed explicit incorporation of that knowledge, rather than implicit coordination processes. Here we extend previous work on team cognition by addressing specific links between trust and group efficacy and dynamic TSMs underlying implicit coordination.

Trust. Trust has been defined as the willingness to be vulnerable to the actions of another party (Mayer, Davis, & Schoorman, 1995). Thus, trust is critical for collective tasks that require high levels of interpersonal risk, mutual dependence, and continuous adaptation of team members' actions and knowledge (De Vries, 1999). The formation of shared and accurate TSMs requires intrateam trust (Fiore et al., 2001). When the members of a team trust each other, they perceive that interaction with other teammates is safe, easy, and feasible, and this, in turn, increases their motivation to actively participate in team processes (Edmondson, 2003). Teams with high levels of trust exhibit an open exchange of information and engage in conversations about relevant work and personal issues (Alper, Tjosvold, & Law, 1998; Jones & George, 1998; Pistole, 1993). This increased communication helps members acquire a wide base of common information regarding key aspects of each other, the team, and its task setting; refine their perceptions; and cultivate shared mutual understandings (Klimoski & Mohammed, 1994; Rau, 2005; Wong, 2003).

In addition, trust plays a critical role in the exhibition of effective team learning behaviors that make the creation of shared, high-quality knowledge possible, such as talking about errors, experimenting, asking for help, and sharing concerns (e.g., Alper et al., 1998; Edmondson, 2003; Gibson & Manuel, 2003; Mohammed & Dumville, 2001; Rentsch & Zelno, 2003). Trust is also related to perspective-taking behaviors, which may enhance the understanding of colleagues' messages, intentions, and interpretations. Burnett, Rentsch, and Zelno (2002) have found that teams with high levels of trust are more likely to adopt the outlook of teammates and to report others' mental models more precisely than teams with low levels of trust. Further, recent work on team decision making suggests that trust promotes the information exchange between team members necessary to integrate their different perspectives on the situation into a common understanding (van Ginkel & van Knippenberg, 2005).

In contrast, members of low-trust teams may be hesitant to express and discuss their personal views on issues relevant to team performance and to let others know about their intended actions, for fear this information will be used to their detriment. Hence, low intrateam trust may result in too little or too poor interaction among team members, inhibiting their ability to learn from one another and thereby to develop effective team knowledge representations. Accordingly, we propose that trust may play a critical role in the development of dynamic TSMs that are both shared and accurate. Such development requires impromptu and improvised knowledge exchange that is more likely when members feel safe to speak openly and share sensitive information. This relationship has not been examined in previous research.

Proposition 6: Intrateam trust will be positively related to sharedness and accuracy of TSMs.

Group efficacy. Group efficacy is a team's shared belief in its capacity to successfully undertake a given task (Gibson & Earley, 2007). This belief captures team members' perceptions regarding their joint ability to coordinate and communicate (Gibson, 1999, 2003; Paskevich, Brawley, Dorsch, & Widmeyer, 1999). Group efficacy may positively predict sharedness and accuracy of a TSM, since it influences what team members choose to do in a team and how much effort they put into tasks. As members feel more confident in their team ability level, they are willing to devote extra cognitive and behavioral efforts in collaborative activities aimed at achieving team goals (Gibson, 2003; Quinn & Dutton, 2005; Smith-Jentsch et al., 2000). These activities may include exchanging key task- or team-related information, defining task requirements and strategies, negotiating members' roles, interpreting performance feedback, and so forth. Such activities provide team members with the opportunity to articulate and refine their mental models on the current situation (Cooke et al., 2004), which, in turn, facilitates the creation of a shared and accurate TSM about key overlapping aspects of team coordination (e.g., customers' needs, contributions of each member).

Additionally, group efficacy may influence TSMs through increased members' attachment to their team. In highly efficacious teams, members are likely to develop a strong feeling of collective responsibility for performance (Fiore et al., 2001; Kraiger & Wenzel, 1997). This may focus members' attention on team processes, which may provide a common and deeper understanding of the task setting and each other's status. In contrast, members of nonefficacious teams are more likely to focus their efforts on attaining individual goals, and this may lead to different and inaccurate understandings of team performance. Marks (1999) has suggested that teams with high levels of group efficacy are able to use their shared knowledge (TMMs) in order to adapt their behavior patterns to novel task settings. However, the impact of group efficacy on the dynamic TSMs teams employ to implicitly coordinate under particular circumstances has not been examined. Based on our prior discussion, we expect the following.

Proposition 7: Group efficacy is positively related to sharedness and accuracy of TSMs.

Performance Environment

Scholars have argued that the features of the task and the context within which work teams usually operate (i.e., the performance environment) play a critical role as moderators of the effects of team cognition (Hutchins, 1995; Kraiger & Wenzel, 1997; Mathieu et al., 2005; Smith-Jentsch et al., 2005). Theoretical work and empirical evidence indicate that the appropriateness of team coordination mechanisms depends on contextual contingencies, such as task interdependence and uncertainty (e.g., Argote, 1982; Kraut & Streeter, 1995; Malone & Crowston, 1994). Extending this contingent view of team cognition and coordination, we contend that the impact of implicit coordination on team performance effectiveness will be greater under particular conditions. Specifically, we examine the potential moderating roles of task routineness, task interdependence, and virtuality in the relationship between implicit coordination and team performance. Prior research has consistently shown that these variables influence patterns of task work, coordination needs, and cognition in work teams (e.g., Gibson & Cohen, 2003; Tesluk, Zaccaro, Marks, & Mathieu, 1997; Wageman, 1995; Weingart, 1992). Researchers have yet to explore relationships with implicit coordination.

Task routineness. Integrating various approaches (Anand et al., 2003; Weingart, 1992; Wood, 1986; Xiao, Hunter, Mackenzie, Jeffries, & Horst, 1996), we conceptualize task routineness as a continuum, with highly routine tasks being well-defined, highly structured, and encompassing predictable situations that can be resolved using standardized procedures (e.g., a production line task) and nonroutine tasks being ill-defined, uncertain, and characterized by frequently changing requirements that involve more unique acts, many sources of information, and often shifting process or output criteria (e.g., a managerial decision-making task).

The value of implicit coordination for team performance may vary, depending on the levels of routineness involved in the specific task a team faces. Uncertain, nonroutine conditions impose increased demands on team members and challenge coordination patterns, increasing the probability that performance problems will occur. Studies of action teams (e.g., medical emergency units, military teams, flight crews) indicate that implicit coordination facilitates smooth performance most of the time, except when highly unusual situations arise (Hutchins, 1995; Smith-Jentsch et al., 2005; Xiao et al., 2001). Under these circumstances, teams encounter a number of difficulties in adapting their habitual functioning to changing task requirements (e.g., doubts regarding who should do what, less helping and cooperating behaviors), which prevent them from attaining optimum performance (Foushee, 1982; Weick, 1990).

As Xiao and collaborators' findings demonstrate (1996, 2001; Xiao, Seagull, Mackenzie, Ziegart, & Klein, 2003), teams that increase explicit communication levels when unusual task demands emerge are more effective at adapting their work structures than those teams that continue integrating work by programmed operation procedures or shared knowledge. Similarly, Edmondson (2003) has argued that important changes in the team task setting increase the need for real-time communication to coordinate team members' actions that previously were sufficiently well-known to enable effective performance without overtly speaking. Yet none of these researchers has examined routineness specifically as an important task moderator of implicit coordination processes. We argue that relying only on implicit coordination may actually detract from team performance when dealing with very unusual situations (that are different from everyday scenarios) because team members need to communicate in order to modify or create new mental models. The explicit communication can then help the team to regain smooth coordination (Argote, 1982; Larson & Schaumman, 1993; Smith-Jentsch et al., 2005).

Proposition 8: Task routineness will moderate the relationship between implicit coordination and team performance. In particular, implicit coordination facilitates team performance when task routineness is high, whereas the exclusive use of implicit coordination will have a detrimental effect on team performance when task routineness is low.

Task interdependence. Task interdependence refers to the interconnections among the tasks of team members (Saavedra, Earley, & Van Dyne, 1993). When tasks are highly interdependent members have to share and coordinate their task inputs (e.g., information, knowledge, resources) in order to complete work successfully. In contrast, tasks that are not significantly interdependent may be divided easily, and, thus, members will work alone most of the time (Van der Vegt, Emans, & Van de Vliert, 2000; Wageman, 1995).

Task interdependence may affect the extent to which implicit coordination benefits team performance. Implicit coordination processes are expected to be synergistic for teams undertaking highly interdependent tasks. When team members must rely on each other to carry out a joint task, coordinating activities, whether implicit or explicit, are key for effective team performance (Kraut & Streeter, 1995; Wageman, 1995). Individuals in highly interdependent teams need to know not only what is going on in their particular worlds but what others in the team are likely to do or need (e.g., a team in charge of monitoring the security of a nuclear power plant). The use of a shared and accurate understanding of the situation at hand by members of these teams may facilitate the anticipation and dynamic adjustment of one another's task inputs and, therefore, team performance (Edmondson, 2003; Espinosa et al., 2004; Larson & Schauman, 1993).

For instance, Minionis, Zaccaro, and Perez (1995) have reported that the existence of a shared mental model results in improved effectiveness only in teams completing highly interdependent tasks. When few task dependencies among team members exist, members are able to accomplish their particular tasks independently, with little need for coordination (Saavedra et al., 1993; Van der Vegt et al., 2000). Similarly, based on the work of Thompson (1967) and Tesluk et al. (1997), Mathieu et al. (2005) argued that task settings requiring more intensive forms of interdependence among team members (e.g., reciprocal interdependence) place a premium on teamwork and may heighten the effects of team processes rooted in shared knowledge structures, compared to settings that impose less intense interdependence (e.g., pooled or sequential interdependence). These researchers focused on stable TMMs, but the same effect is likely true in TSMs that develop dynamically. Hence, we propose that the greater the degree of task interdependence, the greater the importance of implicit coordination.

Proposition 9: Task interdependence will moderate the relationship between implicit coordination and team performance. In particular, the effect of implicit coordination on team performance will be greater when teams perform highly interdependent tasks.

Virtuality. Following Kirkman and Mathieu's (2005) work, we define team virtuality using three dimensions: (1) the extent to which team members rely on virtual tools to coordinate and execute team processes, (2) the amount of informational value provided by such tools, and (3) the synchronicity of team member interaction. All teams, then, can be described in terms of their virtuality. Teams with high levels of virtuality rely on a range of asynchronous technology of low informational value (e.g., email) to accomplish their tasks, whereas teams with low levels of virtuality meet or work face to face on a regular basis, working in a synchronous manner.

We argue that implicit coordination may be particularly useful for the effective performance of teams working under conditions of high virtuality. Virtuality notably alters interactions among team members (e.g., Gibson & Cohen, 2003; Gibson & Gibbs, in press; Kirkman, Tesluk, Rosen, & Gibson, 2004), making team coordination especially difficult. Coordination based on direct interpersonal communication between team members is infrequent (at times impossible) in teams with high virtuality, because most interactions are electronically mediated and asynchronous. Thus, these teams do not enjoy the opportunities for ongoing, informal, and interpersonal communications open to teams with low virtuality (Kirkman et al., 2004; Rasker, Post, & Schraagen, 2000). In addition, the lack of a shared physical working space in teams with high virtuality may reduce the necessary common ground for appropriate and accurate electronically mediated communication among team members (Clark & Brennan, 1991; Olson & Olson, 2000), because they can be unaware of the task setting constraints within which other colleagues operate at different places. This, in turn, increases the likelihood that misunderstandings and misinterpretations will occur within the team.

Given the greater difficulties encountered by highly virtual teams in achieving coordination based on communication (i.e., restricted interpersonal communication, risk of inaccurate electronically mediated communication), we propose that implicit coordination affects the performance of these teams more than teams with low virtuality. Since it occurs with minimal overt communication, implicit coordination allows team members to integrate their task inputs under the restricted communication and interaction conditions they face, thereby maintaining optimal team performance (Espinosa et al., 2004; Gutwin & Greenberg, 2004).

Consider, for instance, an environmental conservation team undertaking a week-long mission that consists of measuring the water temperature of all the rivers and lakes of a vast forest reserve. Team members are dispersed across many miles, do not see each other face to face, and can only communicate with one another through a specific system based on asynchronous text messages. During their collective mission, they can integrate their work by using such a mail system, but they can also implicitly coordinate based on their shared situation models. As a result, despite diminished communication facilities, team members can adapt their behaviors to those of the others and to the task demands, facilitating completion of the team mission. For example, a team member may double up on the duty of measuring the water temperature of streams because he or she anticipates that the member in charge will have difficulties doing so, having little experience in the task. Regardless of the difficulties, the team has the data it needs on water temperatures. If the team had been less virtual, this implicit coordination might not have been as critical to the mission. Accordingly, we propose that the importance of implicit coordination will be more significant for the performance of teams with high virtuality, in contrast to teams with low virtuality, whose members have access to a wider range of mechanisms to achieve work coordination.

Proposition 10: Virtuality will moderate the relationship between implicit coordination and team performance. In particular, the effect of implicit coordination on team performance will be greater for teams working under conditions of high virtuality.

Implications and Conclusions

In this paper we have distinguished between the traditional focus on explicit and implicit coordination and between stable TMMs and dynamic TSMs. We placed anticipation and dynamic adjustment at the center of explanations of the coordinated behavior of work teams. The foundation of our framework is the idea that TSMs and implicit coordination influence each other reciprocally in the course of emergent interaction among team members. Implicit coordination, in turn, contributes, through anticipation and dynamic adjustment behaviors, to team performance outcomes.

We have extended prior research on team coordination by addressing the challenging question of how members of work teams dynamically integrate their multiple task inputs during collective undertaking without the need for overt communication. Implicit coordination helps us answer this question, revealing the dynamic and self-organized nature of team coordination (Arrow et al., 2000). The concept of implicit coordination helps illuminate the impression that many of us have, when analyzing teams in action, that there must be *something else* driving the coordinated performance of these teams, beyond members' explicit efforts to communicate or plan the activity. Implicit coordination behaviors can be that something else. Although these behaviors easily go unnoticed because of their tacit nature, they can make the difference for team performance when coming into play to help teams execute their work.

Our framework also considers the role of several team characteristics in the formation of TSMs enabling implicit coordination patterns. We proposed that team longevity, intrateam trust, and group efficacy perceptions actively foster shared and accurate situation models among team members, whereas team knowledge diversity hinders these situation models. As illustrated throughout our paper, these elements may impact the levels of sharedness and accuracy of TSMs through their decisive roles in the core processes of team knowledge building (e.g., Anand et al., 2003; Gersick & Hackman, 1990; Mathieu et al., 2000; Wong, 2003). Team knowledge (1) evolves over time, as reflected in team longevity; (2) is partially imported from the prior experience of team members, as reflected in knowledge diversity; and (3) develops via confident and open social interaction between team members, which depends to a great extent on trust and group efficacy.

Further, we have proposed a set of contextual moderators that can shape the effects of implicit coordination on team performance. Situations that make team tasks more predictable (routineness), increase the need for team coordination (task interdependence), and restrict the opportunities and resources available to team members to communicate (virtuality) will especially benefit from the utilization of implicit coordination mechanisms.

Our model departs from existing theory in that we seek to provide an explanation of the cognitive factors underlying the phenomenon of implicit coordination. The model illustrates the value of team cognition-related constructs in broadening our comprehension of key team processes, such as coordination. In addition, our model contributes to the team cognition literature by providing an explanation of how team knowledge (TSMs) can influence team performance outcomes through implicit coordination, taking into account team and task features in this relationship. Here we join other scholars in highlighting the importance of adopting a contingent and integrated approach to exploring the formation and effects of team knowledge on team processes and outcomes (e.g., Espinosa et al., 2004; Hutchins, 1995; Kraiger & Wenzel, 1997; Mathieu et al., 2005). Bounding team cognition research by team and performance environment factors will help us refine current explanations and increase the validity of empirical findings in the area.

Finally, from a managerial perspective, our model suggests that managers need to recognize and address the dynamics of shared cognition and implicit coordination operating in the work teams they manage. In doing so, cognitive-focused interventions aimed at facilitating key team knowledge may be a valuable approach, beyond traditional behavior-focused interventions aimed at modifying specific coordinating actions. Thus, the paper invites both scholars and practitioners to reshape their thinking about the coordinated behavior of work teams.

Research Implications

Defining the theoretical foundations of team coordination from a team knowledge perspective and deriving propositions is only a starting point. We encourage progress on methodological and empirical fronts in order to fully exploit the utility of our model. Below we identify measurement and research strategies to test the model empirically, highlighting issues of particular importance for future research.

Methodological issues. The conceptualizations we have offered in this paper serve as a basis for developing appropriate measures of implicit coordination and TSMs. The reliable and valid measurement of these concepts is essential not only to test the propositions we have developed but also to advance our understanding of team cognition (Cannon-Bowers & Salas, 2001; Salas & Fiore, 2004). Measures based on team behaviors can be employed to assess implicit coordination patterns. Recent studies have proposed various indexes based on anticipation ratios, which capture the degree to which the members of a team are able to anticipate the needs of colleagues (e.g., information, help; Levine & Choi, 2004; Stout et al., 1999). Another alternative is to design scales with behavioral markers that include descriptions of specific actions involved in implicit coordination (e.g., providing task-relevant information to another teammate without previous request). These scales can be completed by both team members and external raters (Entin & Entin, 2001; MacMillan et al., 2004).

Regarding the assessment of team knowledge, our framework underscores the need to consider two key issues. First, team knowledge elicitation methods should address the TMM/TSM distinction. This requires the use of cognitive measurement techniques that capture not only long-term, stable knowledge but also the actual use of knowledge by teams to interpret and resolve particular issues in situ. Team cognition researchers have begun to develop some promising measures of dynamic TSMs, such as the display of situation aware-ness queries during team performance or the content analysis of team communication protocols (Cooke et al., 2000, 2004; Langan-Fox et al., 2000).

Second, team knowledge evaluation should target a range of dimensions, including sharedness and accuracy. This would allow researchers to explore the individual and joint effects of various forms of team knowledge on team coordination and performance. In this regard, recent research approaching team knowledge from a multidimensional stand-point provides some useful guidelines to develop measures of sharedness and accuracy (see Austin, 2003; Cooke et al., 2003; Lim & Klein, 2006; Marks et al., 2000; Mathieu et al., 2005; Wong, 2003).

To this point, we would also like to emphasize that a TSM can (at least conceptually) emerge through either compilation or composition processes and that these different forms by which a TSM emerges constitute an empirical issue in need of future research. That is, we agree with Kozlowski and Klein (2000) that a given group phenomenon does not necessarily exhibit a universal form of emergence in all circumstances. TSMs can result from compilation processes such that certain pairs of members hold a common situation model and other pairs of members hold different (yet compatible) situation models. In this case (e.g., variant form of emergence, patterned emergence), simply computing the aver-age of the situation models would not adequately reflect the TSM. Instead, nonlinear combination rules, such as indexes of variance or proportions, should be used to represent the TSM. Alternatively, the TSM could be formed through composition processes such that all members hold essentially identical situation models. In this case (e.g., convergent emergence, pooled constrained emergence), additive linear rules or average-based rules (e.g., sum, means) would be appropriate to represent the team-level property. We suggest that researchers should select the most appropriate method of capturing TSMs based on the emergence processes they assume. These assumptions should then be tested empirically.

Finally, to date, the majority of empirical studies examining the role of team knowledge in team processes and outcomes have used experimental, ad hoc teams that perform contrived tasks. Although laboratory research is capable of making significant contributions to the study of teams, the external validity of the research findings must be tested in applied settings (Mathieu et al., 2005). Future research should examine past findings using different types of intact work teams. In this respect, descriptive field studies and experimental simulations in organizational settings (e.g., health care, industrial manufacturing, high technology, military) may be valuable approaches (Arrow et al., 2000) for research into implicit coordination dynamics. These studies can also provide a foundation for additional theoretical and research development in the area of team cognition.

Research themes. The propositions we have advanced here suggest new avenues for empirical research into team coordination and team cognition. We note two areas of great theoretical and applied interest. One has to do with the potential moderating role of virtuality in the implicit coordination–team performance link. Virtual teams are growing in number and importance; a study by the Gartner Group indicates that more than 60 percent of professional employees work in teams characterized by virtuality (Kanawattanachai & Yoo, 2002). Such teams bring great potential for facilitating acquisition and application of knowledge to critical tasks in global firms (e.g., Gibson & Gibbs, in press; Sole & Edmondson, 2002). Implicit coordination based on shared knowledge may be especially useful for teams with high virtuality, since they are faced with the challenge of successfully integrating their work under restricted communication conditions. Future research should examine how implicit coordination behaviors manifest in these teams and the implications of these behaviors for team performance. This would contribute to the scarce existing theory and empirical support for the role of team knowledge in virtual teamwork configurations.

Another major issue refers to the effect of time on team knowledge and team coordination. Our approach reflects the role of time in two ways. First, time is revealed in the inherent evolving nature of TSMs. As mentioned previously, shared knowledge develops over time through repeated practice and social interaction, and we proposed that long-standing teams are better able to create shared and accurate TSMs than immature teams. In addition, teams are often designed to stimulate mutual learning among members, which accelerates changes in team knowledge. Team cognition researchers, however, have conducted primarily cross-sectional or longitudinal studies over very short time periods and using ad hoc teams. These temporary teams may be representative of team processes in the early stages of performance, but they are unlikely to reflect the evolving knowledge dynamics of teams that have a history (Levine & Choi, 2004).

Second, time appears in the transitions between explicit and implicit coordination. In practice, teams likely use a mix of implicit and explicit coordination activities to complete work. Accordingly, our understanding of coordinated team functioning would be better served not by investigating whether a team X coordinates in a manner Y at a moment Z but by modeling fluctuations in coordination patterns—analyzing why they occur and what they reveal about team knowledge. In future studies team researchers should consider the interplay between implicit and explicit coordination mechanisms and how it may give rise to complementary and interaction effects on team performance over time. For instance, as indicated by previous research, explicit coordination activities, such as team planning prior to performance episodes and team member communications (e.g., Cooke et al., 2004; Orasanu, 1990; Rasker et al., 2000; Stout et al., 1999), may enable the formation of shared and accurate TSMs. This, in turn, can lead team members to implicitly coordinate their behaviors. When implicit coordination is established, explicit coordination is likely to decrease. From this perspective, explicit and implicit coordination mechanisms would be linked by team-level knowledge structures (i.e., TSMs).

Empirical research is needed to test these ideas. The importance of time-related issues emphasizes the need to extend our research approach to include temporal dynamics. In this respect, a complex systems perspective of teams may help us transcend limitations of past research in dealing with time (McGrath & Tschan, 2004).

Practical Implications

At this early stage, our approach contributes primarily to theory and research, yet it also has some practical implications. Knowledge-based explanations of team coordination and performance afford knowledge-based interventions by which team effectiveness can be improved. The general question is "How can we foster the development of TSMs capable of optimizing implicit team coordination?" Team-based organization design models suggest that one way of doing this is identifying and designing the appropriate team structures (Harris & Beyerlein, 2003). Our model indicates basic guidelines in this regard. For example, forming teams with high levels of knowledge diversity may result in serious coordination problems, given members difficulties in aligning their different situational models on common tasks. A plan for gradually building shared TSMs among members of those teams regarding key overlapping requirements for team performance can help to prevent the potential pitfalls associated with knowledge diversity. This would better serve organizations requiring teams with highly specialized, diverse, task-relevant knowledge, such as global, high-technology, and professional services firms.

In addition, intervention strategies, such as cross-training (i.e., team members are pro-vided with exposure to and practice with the roles of the other team members), regular leader debriefings (i.e., a team receives briefings on important up-to-the-minute elements in the task setting from its leader), and the use of certain forms of advanced communication technologies and collaborative teamware as part of an organizational routine, could be used to facilitate development of targeted team knowledge structures (e.g., Cooke et al., 2003; Day, Gronn, & Salas, 2004; Marks et al., 2002). Ensuring a certain degree of stability in team composition or members' experience working together may also stimulate the early forma-tion of shared knowledge, which fosters the growth of team implicit coordination mechan-isms (Levine & Choi, 2004).

This study also has implications for the adaptability and flexibility of work teams. Our model suggests that implicit coordination benefits team performance primarily under certain conditions (i.e., under high levels of task routineness, interdependence, and virtuality). Another way of thinking about this relationship is that when team members face these conditions, they will benefit most from implicit coordination. If teams can be trained to identify these conditions, they will be best positioned to take advantage of implicit coordination. Hence, teams will likely gain from greater awareness of, and attention to, their own processes.

Direct interventions aimed at helping teams actively monitor the shared knowledge they use in coordinating and executing their work may increase the likelihood that members will catch an inappropriate TSM and develop a new TSM that is uniquely suited to the situation at hand. In this regard, team adaptation training (i.e., aimed at helping the team to detect particular characteristics in a situation that make it necessary to change members' coping strategies, allowing for dynamic adjustment of these strategies), team metacognitive training (i.e., to increase team members' awareness and understanding of their thoughts and cognitive processes, as well as their ability to regulate these processes), and performance feedback can be useful strategies to reinforce team cognitive flexibility (e.g., Day et al., 2004; Entin & Serfaty, 1999; Gersick & Hackman, 1990; Zellmer-Bruhn, 2003). For example, structured discussions among team members focused on team strategies, visualization and analysis of recorded performance episodes focused on strengths and weaknesses in team performance, and self-questioning activities are useful components of team metacognitive training programs.

Conclusion

This paper adds to a growing body of research on team cognition that has revealed the role of team knowledge structures in coordination processes and performance of work teams. We illustrate how the analysis of implicit team coordination from a team knowledge perspective provides a more comprehensive picture of team coordination. The propositions we advance here raise intriguing questions concerning how and when teams implicitly integrate their work based on dynamic team knowledge representations. In doing so, we hope to stimulate theoretical discussion and empirical research in the future. Understanding the cognitive mechanisms underlying team performance is of paramount importance if we want to improve the effectiveness of work teams.

Acknowledgments

This article is dedicated to the memory of Susan G. Cohen. We thank associate editor Elizabeth Mannix and three anonymous reviewers for their outstanding feedback on previous drafts.

References

Alper, S., Tjosvold, D., & Law, K. S. 1998. Interdependence and controversy in group decision making: Antecedents to effective self-managing teams. *Organizational Behavior and Human Decision Processes*, 74: 33–52.

Anand, V., Clark, M. A., & Zellmer-Bruhn, M. 2003. Team knowledge structures: Matching task to information environment. *Journal of Managerial Issues*, 15: 15–31.

Argote, L. 1982. Input uncertainty and organizational coordination in hospital emergency units. *Administrative Science Quarterly*, 27: 420–434.

Argote, L., & McGrath, J. 1993. Group processes in organizations: Continuity and change. *International Review of Psychology*, 8: 333–389.

Arrow, H., McGrath, J. E., & Berdahl, J. L. 2000. *Small groups as complex systems.* Thousand Oaks, CA: Sage.

Austin, J. R. 2003. Transactive memory in organizational groups: The effects of content, consensus, specialization and accuracy on group performance. *Journal of Applied Psychology*, 88: 866–878.

Bettenhausen, K. L., & Murnighan, J. K. 1985. The emergence of norms in competitive decision-making groups. *Administrative Science Quarterly*, 30: 350–372.

Brannick, M. T., & Prince, T. 1997. An overview of team performance measurement. In E. Salas & C. Prince (Eds.), *Team performance assessment and measurement:* 3–16. Mahwah, NJ: Lawrence Erlbaum Associates.

Brannick, M. T., Prince, A., Prince, C., & Salas, E. 1995. The measurement of team process. *Human Factors*, 37: 641–651.

Burnett, D. D., Rentsch, J. R., & Zelno, J. A. 2002. *Composing great teams: The role of person perception in building team member schema similarity.* Symposium presented at the annual conference of the Society for Industrial and Organizational Psychology, Toronto.

Cannon-Bowers, J. A., & Salas, E. 2001. Reflections on shared cognition. *Journal of Organizational Behavior,* 22: 195–202.

Cannon-Bowers, J. A., Salas, E., & Converse, S. A. 1993. Shared mental models in expert decision-making teams. In N. J. Castellan, Jr. (Ed.), *Current issues in individual and group decision making:* 221–246. Hillsdale, NJ: Lawrence Erlbaum Associates.

Carley, K. M. 1997. Extracting team mental models through textual analysis. *Journal of Organizational Behavior,* 18: 533–558.

Clark, H. H., & Brennan, S. A. 1991. Grounding in communication. In L. B. Resnick, J. M. Levine, & S. D. Teasley (Eds.), *Perspectives on socially shared cognition:* 127–149. Washington, DC: APA Books.

Cohen, S. G., & Bailey, D. E. 1997. What makes teams work: Group effectiveness research from the shop floor to the executive suite. *Journal of Management,* 23: 239–290.

Cooke, N. J., Kiekel, P. A., Salas, E., Stout, R., Bowers, C., & Cannon-Bowers, J. 2003. Measuring team knowledge: A window to the cognitive underpinnings of team performance. *Group Dynamics: Theory, Research, and Practice,* 7(3): 179–199.

Cooke, N. J., Salas, E., Cannon-Bowers, J. A., & Stout, R. J. 2000. Measuring team knowledge. *Human Factors,* 42(1): 151–173.

Cooke, N. J., Salas, E., Kiekel, P. A., & Bell, B. 2004. Advances in measuring team cognition. In E. Salas & S. Fiore (Eds.), *Team cognition: Understanding the factors that drive process and performance:* 83–107. Washington, DC: APA Books.

Day, D. V., Gronn, P., & Salas, E. 2004. Leadership capacity in teams. *Leadership Quarterly,* 15: 857–880.

De Vries, M. F. 1999. High-performance teams: Lessons from the pygmies. *Organizational Dynamics,* 27(3): 66–77.

Dougherty, D. 1992. Interpretive barriers to successful product innovation in large firms. *Organization Science,* 3: 179–202.

Edmondson, A. C. 2003. Speaking up in the operating room: How team leaders promote learning in interdisciplinary action teams. *Journal of Management Studies,* 40: 1419–1452.

Endsley, M. R., & Jones, W. M. 2001. A model of inter- and intrateam situational awareness: Implications for design, training, and measurement. In M. McNeese, E. Salas, & M. Endsley (Eds.), *New trends in cooperative activities:* 46–68. Santa Monica, CA: Human Factors and Ergonomics Society.

Entin, E. E., & Entin, E. B. 2001. Measures for evaluation of team processes and performance in experiments and exercises. *Proceedings of the 6th International Command and Control Research and Technology Symposium:* 1–14.

Entin, E. E., & Serfaty, D. 1999. Adaptive team coordination. *Human Factors,* 41: 312–325.

Espinosa, J. A., Lerch, J., & Kraut, R. 2004. Explicit vs. implicit coordination mechanisms and task dependencies: One size does not fit all. In E. Salas & S. M. Fiore (Eds.), *Team cognition: Understanding the factors that drive process and performance:* 107–129. Washington, DC: APA Books.

Faraj, S., & Sproull, L. 2000. Coordinating expertise in software development teams. *Management Science,,* 46: 1554–1568.

Fiore, S. M., & Salas, E. 2004. Why we need team cognition. In E. Salas & S. M. Fiore (Eds.), *Team cognition: Understanding the factors that drive process and performance:* 235–248. Washington, DC: APA Books.

Fiore, S. M., Salas, E., & Cannon-Bowers, J. A. 2001. Group dynamics and shared mental models development. In M. London (Ed.), *How people evaluate others in organizations:* 309–336. Mahwah, NJ: Lawrence Erlbaum Associates.

Foushee, H. C. 1982. The role of communications, sociopsychological, and personality factors in the maintenance of crew coordination. *Aviation, Space, and Environmental Medicine,* 53: 1062–1066.

Gersick, C. J. G. 1988. Time and transition in work teams: Toward a new model of group development. *Academy of Management Journal,* 41: 9–41.

Gersick, C. J. G., & Hackman, J. R. 1990. Habitual routines in task-performing groups. *Organizational Behavior and Human Decision Processes*, 47: 65–97.

Gibson, C. B. 1999. Do they do what they believe they can? Group efficacy and group effectiveness across tasks and cultures. *Academy of Management Journal*, 42: 138–152.

Gibson, C. B. 2001. From accumulation to accommodation: The chemistry of collective cognition in work groups. *Journal of Organizational Behavior*, 22: 121–134.

Gibson, C. B. 2003. Factors related to the formation of group efficacy. *Journal of Applied Social Psychology*, 33: 2153–2186.

Gibson, C. B., & Cohen, S. G. 2003. The last word: Conclusions and implications. In C. B. Gibson & S. G. Cohen (Eds.), *Virtual teams that work: Creating conditions for virtual team effectiveness:* 403–421. San Francisco: Jossey-Bass.

Gibson, C. B., & Earley, P. C. 2007. Collective cognition in action: Accumulation, interaction, examination, and accommodation in the development and operation of group efficacy beliefs in the workplace. *Academy of Management Review*, 32: 438–458.

Gibson, C. B., & Gibbs, J. In press. Unpacking the effects of virtuality on team innovation. *Administrative Science Quarterly.*

Gibson, C. B., & Manuel, J. A. 2003. Building trust: Effective multi-cultural communication processes in virtual teams. In C. B. Gibson & S. G. Cohen (Eds.), *Virtual teams that work: Creating conditions for virtual team effectiveness:* 59–86. San Francisco: Jossey-Bass.

Gibson, C. B., Zellmer-Bruhn, M. E., & Schwab, D. P. 2003. Team effectiveness in multinational organizations: Evaluation across contexts. *Group and Organization Management*, 28: 444–474.

Gladstein, D. 1984. Groups in context: A model of task group effectiveness. *Administrative Science Quarterly*, 29: 499–517.

Gruenfeld, D., Mannix, E., Williams, K., & Neale, M. 1996. Group composition and decision making: How member familiarity and information distribution affect process and performance. *Organizational Behavior and Human Decision Processes*, 67: 1–15.

Gutwin, C., & Greenberg, S. 2004. The importance of awareness for team cognition in distributed collaboration. In E. Salas & S. M. Fiore (Eds.), *Team cognition: Understanding the factors that drive process and performance:* 177–203. Washington, DC: APA Books.

Hackman, J. R., & Morris, C. G. 1975. Group tasks, group interaction processes, and group performance effectiveness: A review and proposed integration. *Advances in Experimental Psychology*, 8: 45–99.

Harris, C. L., & Beyerlein, M. M. 2003. Navigating the team-based organizing journey. In M. M. Beyerlein, D. A. Johnson, & S. T. Beyerlein (Eds.), *Advances in interdisciplinary studies of work teams:* 1–29. Oxford: Elsevier.

Hutchins, E. 1995. *Cognition in the wild.* Cambridge, MA: MIT Press.

Jackson, S. E., Joshi, A., & Erhardt, N. L. 2003. Recent research on teams and organizational diversity: SWOT analysis and implications. *Journal of Management*, 29: 801–830.

Jones, G. R., & George, J. M. 1998. The experience and evolution of trust: Implications for cooperation and teamwork. *Academy of Management Review*, 23: 531–546.

Kanawattanachai, P., & Yoo, Y. 2002. Dynamic nature of trust in virtual teams. *Journal of Strategic Information Systems*, 11: 187–213.

Kirkman, B. L., & Mathieu, J. E. 2005. The dimensions and antecedents of team virtuality. *Journal of Management*, 31: 700–718.

Kirkman, B. L., Tesluk, P. E., Rosen, B., & Gibson, C. B. 2004. The impact of team empowerment on virtual team performance: The moderating role of face-to-face interaction. *Academy of Management Journal*, 47: 175–192.

Kleinman, D. L., & Serfaty, D. 1989. Team performance assessment in distributed decision-making. *Proceedings of the Interactive Networked Simulation for Training Conference:* 22–27.

Klimoski, R. J., & Mohammed, S. 1994. Team mental model: Construct or metaphor? *Journal of Management*, 20: 403–437.

Kozlowski, S. W. J., & Klein, K. J. 2000. A multilevel approach to theory and research in organizations: Contextual, temporal, and emergent processes. In K. J. Klein & S. J. W. Kozlowski (Eds.),

Multilevel theory, research, and methods in organizations: Foundations, extensions, and new directions: 3–90. San Francisco: Jossey-Bass.

Kraiger, K., & Wenzel, L. C. 1997. Conceptual development and empirical evaluation of measures of shared mental models as indicators of team effectiveness. In M. T. Brannick, E. Salas, & C. Prince (Eds.), *Team performance assessment and measurement: Theory, methods, and applications:* 45–84. Mahwah, NJ: Lawrence Erlbaum Associates.

Kraut, R., & Streeter, L. 1995. Coordination in large scale software development. *Communications of the ACM*, 38(3): 69–81.

Langan-Fox, J. 2003. Team mental models and group processes. In M. A. West, D. Tjosvold, & K. G. Smith (Eds.), *International handbook of organizational teamwork and cooperative working:* 321–360. London: Wiley.

Langan-Fox, J., Anglim, J., & Wilson, J. R. 2004. *Mental models, team mental models and performance: Process, development and future directions.* Special Feature: Distinguished Paper Series, Human Factors & Ergonomics in Manufacturing. Hoboken, NJ: Wiley InterScience.

Langan-Fox, J., Code, S., & Langfield-Smith, K. 2000. Team mental models: Techniques, methods, and analytic approaches. *Human Factors*, 42: 242–271.

Langer, E. J. 1989. Minding matters: The mindlessness/mindfulness theory of cognitive activity. In L. Berkowitz (Ed.), *Advances in experimental social psychology:* 86–104. New York: Academic Press.

Larson, J. R., & Schaumann, L. 1993. Group goals, group coordination, and group member motivation. *Human Performance*, 6: 49–69.

Levesque, L. L., Wilson, J. M., & Wholey, D. R. 2001. Cognitive divergence and shared mental models in software development project teams. *Journal of Organizational Behavior*, 22: 135–144.

Levine, J. M., & Choi, H. S. 2004. Impact of personnel turnover on team performance and cognition. In E. Salas & S. M. Fiore (Eds.), *Team cognition: Understanding the factors that drive process and performance:* 153–177. Washington, DC: APA Books.

Lewis, K. 2003. Measuring transactive memory systems in the field: Scale development and validation. *Journal of Applied Psychology*, 88: 587–604.

Lim, B., & Klein, K. J. 2006. Team mental models and team performance: A field study of the effects of team mental model similarity and accuracy. *Journal of Organizational Behavior*, 27: 403–418.

Louis, M. R., & Sutton, R. I. 1991. Switching cognitive gears: From habits of mind to active thinking. *Human Relations*, 44: 55–76.

MacMillan, J., Entin, E. E., & Serfaty, D. 2004. Communication overhead: The hidden cost of team cognition. In E. Salas & S. Fiore (Eds.), *Team cognition: Understanding the factors that drive process and performance:* 61–83. Washington, DC: APA Books.

MacMillan, J., Paley, M., Entin, E. B., & Entin, E. E. 2004. Questionnaires for distributed assessment of team mutual awareness. In N. A. Stanton, A. Hedge, K. Brookhuis, E. Salas, & H. Hendrick (Eds.), *Handbook of human factors and ergonomics methods:* 51-1–51-9. London: Taylor and Francis.

Malone, T. W., & Crowston, K. 1994. The interdisciplinary study of coordination. *ACM Computing Surveys*, 26(1): 87–119.

March, J., & Simon, H. A. 1958. *Organizations.* New York: Wiley.

Marks, M. A. 1999. A test of the impact of collective efficacy in routine and novel performance environments. *Human Performance*, 12: 295–309.

Marks, M. A., Sabella, M. J., Burke, C. S., & Zaccaro, S. J. 2002. The impact of cross-training on team effectiveness. *Journal of Applied Psychology*, 87: 3–13.

Marks, M. A., Zaccaro, S. J., & Mathieu, J. E. 2000. Performance implications of leader briefings and team-interaction training for team adaptation to novel environments. *Journal of Applied Psychology*, 85: 971–986.

Mathieu, J. E. Heffner, T. S., Goodwin, G. E., Cannon-Bowers, J. A., & Salas, E. 2005. Scaling the quality of teammates' mental models: Equifinality and normative comparisons. *Journal of Organizational Behavior*, 26: 37–56.

Mathieu, J. E., Heffner, T. S., Goodwin, G. F., Salas, E., & Cannon-Bowers, J. 2000. The influence of shared mental models on team process and performance. *Journal of Applied Psychology*, 85: 273–283.

Mayer, R. C., Davis, J. H., & Schoorman, F. D. 1995. An integrative model of organizational trust. *Academy of Management Review*, 20: 709–715.

McClure, B. A. 1990. The group mind: Generative and regressive groups. *Journal for Specialists in Group Work*, 15: 159–170.

McGrath, J. E., & Argote, L. 2001. Group processes in organizational contexts. In M. A. Hogg & R. S. Tindale (Eds.), *Blackwell handbook of social psychology: Group processes*, vol. 3: 603–627. Oxford: Blackwell.

McGrath, J. E., & Tschan, F. 2004. *Temporal matters in social psychology: Examining the role of time in the lives of groups and individuals.* Washington, DC: APA Books.

Minionis, D. P., Zaccaro, S. J., & Perez, R. 1995. *Shared mental models, team coordination, and team performance.* Paper presented at the 10th annual conference of the Society for Industrial/Organizational Psychology, Orlando.

Mohammed, S., & Dumville, B. C. 2001. Team mental models in a team knowledge framework: Expanding theory and measurement across disciplinary boundaries. *Journal of Organizational Behavior*, 22: 89–106.

Olson, G. M., & Olson, J. S. 2000. Distance matters. *Human-Computer Interaction*, 15: 139–178.

Orasanu, J. M. 1990. *Shared mental models and crew decision making.* CSL report No. 46. Princeton, NJ: Princeton University, Cognitive Science Laboratory.

Paskevich, D. M., Brawley, L. R., Dorsch, K. D., & Widmeyer, W. N. 1999. Relationship between collective efficacy and team cohesion: Conceptual and measurement issues. *Group Dynamics*, 3(3): 210–222.

Pistole, M. C. 1993. Attachment relationships: Self-disclosure and trust. *Journal of Mental Health Counseling*, 15: 94–106.

Quinn, R. W., & Dutton, J. E. 2005. Coordination as energy-in-conversation. *Academy of Management Review*, 30: 36–57.

Rasker, P. C., Post, W. M., & Schraagen, J. M. 2000. Effects of two types of intra-team feedback on developing a shared mental model in command and control teams. *Ergonomics*, 43: 1167–1189.

Rau, D. 2005. The influence of relationship conflict and trust on the transactive memory: Performance relation in top management teams. *Small Group Research*, 36: 746–771.

Rentsch, J. R., & Klimoski, R. J. 2001. Why do great minds think alike? Antecedents of team member schema agreement. *Journal of Organizational Behavior*, 22: 107–120.

Rentsch, J. R., & Woehr, D. J. 2004. Quantifying congruence in cognition: Social relations modeling and team member schema similarity. In E. Salas & S. Fiore (Eds.), *Team cognition: Understanding the factors that drive process and performance:* 11–33. Washington, DC: APA Books.

Rentsch, J. R., & Zelno, J. 2003. The role of cognition in managing conflict to maximize team effectiveness. In M. A. West, D. Tjosvold, & K. G. Smith (Eds.), *International handbook of organizational teamwork and cooperative working:* 131–150. London: Wiley.

Saavedra, R., Earley, P. C., & Van Dyne, L. 1993. Complex interdependence in task performing groups. *Journal of Applied Psychology*, 78: 61–72.

Salas, E., & Fiore, S. M. 2004. Why team cognition? An overview. In E. Salas & S. Fiore (Eds.), *Team cognition: Understanding the factors that drive process and performance:* 3–9. Washington, DC: APA Books.

Serfaty, D., Entin, E. E., & Volpe, C. 1993. Adaptation to stress in team decision-making and coordination. *Proceedings of the Human Factors and Ergonomics Society:* 1228–1232.

Smith-Jentsch, K. A., Campbell, G. E., Milanovich, D. M., & Reynolds, A. M. 2001. Measuring teamwork mental models to support training needs assessment, development, and evaluation: Two empirical studies. *Journal of Organizational Behavior*, 22: 179–194.

Smith-Jentsch, K. A., Kraiger, K., Cannon-Bowers, J. A., & Salas, E. 2000. *Familiarity breeds teamwork: A case for training teammate-specific competencies.* Unpublished manuscript, University of Central Florida, Orlando.

Smith-Jentsch, K. A., Mathieu, J. E., & Kraiger, K. 2005. Investigating linear and interactive effects of shared mental models on safety and efficiency in a field setting. *Journal of Applied Psychology*, 90: 523–535.

Sole, D., & Edmondson, A. 2002. Situated knowledge and learning in dispersed teams. *British Journal of Management*, 13: 17–34.

Steiner, I. D. 1972. *Group processes and productivity.* New York: Academic Press.

Stout, R. J., Cannon-Bowers, J. A., Salas, E., & Milanovich, D. M. 1999. Planning, shared mental models, and coordinated performance: An empirical link is established. *Human Factors*, 41: 61–71.

Tannenbaum, S. I., Beard, R. L., & Salas, E. 1992. Team building and its influence on team effectiveness: An examination of conceptual and empirical developments. *Issues, Theory, and Research in Industrial/Organizational Psychology*, 82: 117–153.

Tesluk, P., Zaccaro, S. J., Marks, M. A., & Mathieu, J. E. 1997. Task and aggregation issues in analysis and assessment of team performance. In M. T. Brannick, E. Salas, & C. Prince (Eds.), *Team performance assessment and measurement: Theory, methods, and applications*: 197–226. Mahwah, NJ: Lawrence Erlbaum Associates.

Thompson, J. D. 1967. *Organizations in action.* New York: McGraw-Hill.

Van der Vegt, G., Emans, B., & Van de Vliert, E. 2000. Team members' affective responses to patterns of intragroup interdependence and job complexity. *Journal of Management*, 26: 633–655.

Van de Ven, A. H., Delbecq, L. A., & Koening, R. J. 1976. Determinants of coordination modes within organizations. *American Sociological Review*, 41: 322–338.

van Ginkel, W. P., & van Knippenberg, D. 2005. *Group-level information processing and group decision making: The role of shared task representations.* Paper presented at the 12th biannual meeting of the European Association of Work and Organizational Psychology, Istanbul.

Wageman, R. 1995. Interdependence and group effectiveness. *Administrative Science Quarterly*, 40: 145–180.

Weick, K. E. 1990. The vulnerable system: An analysis of the Tenerife air disaster. *Journal of Management*, 16: 571–593.

Weick, K. E., & Roberts, K. H. 1993. Collective mind in organizations: Heedful interrelating on flight decks. *Administrative Science Quarterly*, 38: 357–381.

Weingart, L. R. 1992. Impact of group goals, task component complexity, effort, and planning on group performance. *Journal of Applied Psychology*, 77: 682–693.

West, M. A., Borrill, C. S., & Unsworth, K. L. 1998. Team effectiveness in organizations. *International Review of Industrial and Organizational Psychology*, 13: 1–48.

Wilke, H. A. M., & Meertens, R. W. 1994. *Group performance.* London: Routledge.

Wittembaum, G. M., Stasser, G., & Merry, C. J. 1996. Tacit coordination in anticipation of small group task completion. *Journal of Experimental Social Psychology*, 32: 129–152.

Wong, S. 2003. *Collective cognition in teams: The role of interactive learning and effects on team performance.* Paper presented at the annual meeting of the Academy of Management, Seattle.

Wood, R. E. 1986. Task complexity: Definition of the construct. *Organizational Behavior and Human Decision Processes*, 37: 60–82.

Xiao, Y., Hunter, W. A., Mackenzie, C. F., Jeffries, N. J., & Horst, R. L. T. 1996. Task complexity in emergency medical care and its implications for team coordination. *Human Factors*, 38: 636–645.

Xiao, Y., Hunter, W. A., Mackenzie, C. F., Jeffries, N. J., & Horst, R. L. T. 2001. Understanding coordination in a dynamic medical environment: Methods and results. In M. McNeese, E. Salas, & M. Endsley (Eds.), *New trends in co-operative activities*: 242–258. Santa Monica, CA: Human Factors Society.

Xiao, Y., Seagull, F. J., Mackenzie, C., Ziegart, J., & Klein, K. J. 2003. Team communication patterns as measures of team processes: Exploring the effects of task urgency and shared team experience. *Proceedings of the Human Factors and Ergonomics Society*: 1502–1506.

Zalesny, M. D., Salas, E., & Prince, C. 1995. Conceptual and measurement issues in coordination: Implications for team behavior and performance. *Research in Personnel and Human Resources Management*, 13: 81–115.

Zellmer-Bruhn, M. E. 2003. Interruptive events and team knowledge acquisition. *Management Science*, 49: 514–528.

8.2   THE MANAGEMENT OF ORGANIZATIONAL JUSTICE

Russell Cropanzano, David E. Bowen, and Stephen W. Gilliland

Executive Overview

Organizational justice has the potential to create powerful benefits for organizations and employees alike. These include greater trust and commitment, improved job performance, more helpful citizenship behaviors, improved customer satisfaction, and diminished conflict. We demonstrate the management of organizational justice with some suggestions for building fairness into widely used managerial activities. These include hiring, performance appraisal, reward systems, conflict management, and downsizing.

Justice, Sir, is the greatest interest of man on earth

—Daniel Webster

Business organizations are generally understood to be economic institutions. Sometimes implicitly, other times explicitly, this "rational" perspective has shaped the relationship that many employers have with their workforce (Ashforth & Humphrey, 1995). Many organizations, for example, emphasize the quid pro quo exchange of monetary payment for the performance of concrete tasks (Barley & Kunda, 1992). These tasks are often rationally described via job analysis and formally appraised by a supervisor. Hierarchical authority of this type is legitimized based upon the manager's special knowledge or expertise (Miller & O'Leary, 1989). Employee motivation is viewed as a quest for personal economic gain, so individual merit pay is presumed to be effective. Using the rational model, one can make a case for downsizing workers who are not contributing adequately to the "bottom line." And the rational model is found at the heart of the short-term uptick in the stock price of firms that carry out aggressive cost-cutting measures (Pfeffer, 1998).

Businesses certainly are economic institutions, but they are not *only* economic institutions. Indeed, adherence to this paradigm without consideration of other possibilities can have problematic side effects. Merit pay is sometimes ineffective (Pfeffer & Sutton, 2006), downsizing often has pernicious long-term effects (Pfeffer, 1998), and bureaucratic management can straitjacket workers and reduce innovation. We should attend to economic matters, but also to the sense of duty that goes beyond narrowly defined quid pro quo exchanges. It includes the ethical obligations that one party has to the other. Members may want a lot of benefits, but they also want something more. Organizational justice—members' sense of the moral propriety of how they are treated—is the "glue" that allows people to work together effectively. Justice defines the very essence of individuals' relationship to employers. In contrast, *in*justice is like a corrosive solvent that can dissolve bonds within the community. Injustice is hurtful to individuals and harmful to organizations.

In this paper we will discuss organizational justice, with an emphasis on how it can be brought to the workplace. We first define justice, paying careful attention to its three core dimensions: distributive, procedural, and interactional. We then examine why justice is important; we will consider various criterion variables that justice favorably influences. Once we understand the nature of justice we will be in a better position to describe how it can be brought about. The lesson here is that organizational justice actually has to be managed. This paper will provide specific techniques and recommendations for doing so.

What Is Organizational Justice?

Prescription vs. Description

Philosophers and social commentators were writing about justice long before management scientists were. Among the ancient Greeks, for example, Herodotus' *History* and Plutarch's *Lives* described the achievements of the lawgiver Solon, who reformed Athenian government. These are the *prescriptive* approaches, since they seek to logically determine what sorts of actions *truly are just*. As such, they reside comfortably within the domain of business ethics.

While organizational justice borrows from these older traditions, it has its own distinctions. Unlike the work of philosophers and attorneys, managerial scientists are less concerned with what *is* just and more concerned with what people *believe* to be just. In other words, these researchers are pursuing a *descriptive* agenda. They seek to understand why people view certain events as just, as well as the consequences that follow from these evaluations. In this regard, justice is a subjective and descriptive concept in that it captures what individuals believe to be right, rather than an objective reality or a prescriptive moral code. As defined here, organizational justice is a personal evaluation about the ethical and moral standing of managerial conduct. It follows from this approach that producing justice requires management to take the perspective of an employee. That is, they need to understand what sorts of events engender this subjective feeling of organizational justice. On this important competency, many fall short.

Why Employees Care About Justice

Managers too often assume that justice, in the minds of employees, means only that they receive desirable outcomes. These managers are confusing outcome *favorability* with outcome *justice*. The former is a judgment of personal worth or value; the latter is a judgment of moral propriety. Evidence shows that outcome justice and outcome favorability are distinct (Skitka, Winquist, & Hutchinson, 2003) and correlated between .19 and .49, depending on where and how the variables are measured (Cohen-Charash & Spector, 2001). In so many words, it's important to get what you want, but other things matter as well. For this reason it is useful to consider three reasons justice matters to people (for details, see Cropanzano, Rupp, Mohler, & Schminke, 2001).

Long-range benefits. People often "sign on" for the long haul. Consequently, they need to estimate *now* how they are likely to be treated *over time*. A just organization makes this prediction easy. According to the "control model," employees prefer justice because it allows them to predict and control the outcomes they are likely to receive from organizations. According to the control model of justice, appropriate personnel policies signal that things are likely to work out eventually. Most of us understand that every personnel decision cannot go our way, but justice provides us with more certainty regarding our future benefits.

For this reason the control model proposes that people are often motivated by economic and quasi-economic interests (cf. Tyler & Smith, 1998). People want fairness because fairness provides things they like. There is more than a little truth to this idea. For instance, when individuals are rewarded for successfully completing a task they report being happy (Weiss, Suckow, & Cropanzano, 1999) and having pride in their performance (Krehbiel & Cropanzano, 2000). This is so even when their success resulted from cheating.

At the same time, these individuals also report feeling guilty for their unfair behavior, suggesting that individuals can recognize and react to injustice, even when it is personally beneficial.

There is sometimes a certain tension between getting what we want and playing by the rules. The two tend to go together, but less so than many believe. For example, pay satisfaction is only modestly correlated with perceptions of pay justice (Williams, McDaniel, & Nguyen, 2006). If "justice" were based exclusively on obtaining benefits, then one would expect a higher association. Later we shall discuss evidence suggesting that individuals can accept an unfortunate outcome as long as the process is fair and they are treated with interpersonal dignity (e.g., Goldman, 2003; Skarlicki & Folger, 1997).

Social considerations. People are social animals. We wish to be accepted and valued by important others while not being exploited or harmed by powerful decision-makers. In the "group-value model," just treatment tells us that we are respected and esteemed by the larger group. We are also at less risk for mistreatment. This sense of belonging is important to us even apart from the economic benefits it can bring (Tyler & Blader, 2000; Tyler & Smith, 1998). As you might expect, this can pose a potential problem for organizations. To the extent that justice signals our value to an employer, the more we care about the organization the more distressed we become when we are treated unfairly. Brockner, Tyler, and Cooper-Schneider (1992) assessed the commitment of a group of employees before a layoff occurred. After the downsizing those people who were initially the *most* committed responded the *most* negatively to the downsizing. When we treat workers unfairly, we may end up doing the most harm to those who are most loyal.

Ethical considerations. People also care about justice because they believe it is the morally appropriate way others should be treated (Folger, 2001). When individuals witness an event they believe is ethically inappropriate, they are likely to take considerable risks in the hopes of extracting retribution (Bies & Tripp, 2001, 2002). Such unfortunate (from the organization's point of view) reactions may occur even when an employee simply witnesses the harm and is not personally wronged (Ellard & Skarlicki, 2002; Spencer & Rupp, 2006). Consider, for example, a day-to-day problem faced by many service workers. When these employees see a customer treating one of their coworkers unfairly, the observing worker is apt to experience stress symptoms. Through this mechanism, injustice may spread ill will throughout a workgroup.

Three Components of Justice

Research has shown that employees appraise three families of workplace events. They examine the justice of outcomes (distributive justice), the justice of the formal allocation processes (procedural justice), and the justice of interpersonal transactions they encounter with others (interactional justice). These are shown in Table 8.2.1.

Distributive, procedural, and interactional justice tend to be correlated. They can be meaningfully treated as three components of overall fairness (Ambrose & Arnaud, 2005; Ambrose & Schminke, 2007), and the three components can work together. However, if one's goal is to promote workplace justice, it is useful to consider them separately and in detail. This is because each component is engendered in distinct ways, arising from different managerial actions.

Table 8.2.1 Components of Organizational Justice

1. Distributive Justice: Appropriateness of outcomes.
   - Equity: Rewarding employees based on their contributions.
   - Equality: Providing each employee roughly the same compensation.
   - Need: Providing a benefit based on one's personal requirements.

2. Procedural Justice: Appropriateness of the allocation process.
   - Consistency: All employees are treated the same.
   - Lack of Bias: No person or group is singled out for discrimination or ill-treatment.
   - Accuracy: Decisions are based on accurate information.
   - Representation of All Concerned: Appropriate stakeholders have input into a decision.
   - Correction: There is an appeals process or other mechanism for fixing mistakes.
   - Ethics: Norms of professional conduct are not violated.

3. Interactional Justice: Appropriateness of the treatment one receives from authority figures.
   - Interpersonal Justice: Treating an employee with dignity, courtesy, and respect.
   - Informational Justice: Sharing relevant information with employees.

Distributive Justice

Researchers call the first component of justice *distributive justice* because it has to do with the allocations or outcomes that some get and others do not. Distributive justice is concerned with the reality that not all workers are treated alike; the allocation of outcomes is differentiated in the workplace. Individuals are concerned with whether or not they received their "just share." Sometimes things are distributively just, as when the most qualified person gets promoted. Other times they are not, as when advancement goes to corporate "insiders" with a political relationship to upper management.

Equity theory. Perhaps the earliest theory of distributive justice can be attributed to Aristotle. In his *Nicomachean Ethics*, the philosopher maintained that just distribution involved "something proportionate," which he defined as "equality of ratios." Specification, and a bit of rearrangement, led Adams (1965) to represent his influential equity theory of distributive justice with the following equation:

$$\frac{O_1}{I_1} = \frac{O_2}{I_2}$$

According to equity theory, we are interested in how much we get (outcomes or O_1) relative to how much we contribute (inputs or I_1). Such a ratio is meaningless, however, unless anchored against some standard. To accomplish this, we examine the outcomes (O_2) and inputs (I_2) of some referent. Usually, though not necessarily, this is another person who is similar to us. Things are "equitable" when the ratios, not the individual terms, are in agreement. When the ratios are out of alignment, employees may feel uneasy. They are motivated to "balance" the equation by modifying the terms. For example, one who is underpaid might reduce inputs by a corresponding amount.

This simple equation leads to a number of predictions, some of which are not obvious. For example, an individual who earns less than another may still be satisfied, as long as he or she also contributes less. Likewise, a person who is paid equally to another may feel unjustly treated if he or she also contributes substantially more to the organization. These consequences often do not occur to managers, but they make good sense in light of equity theory. But by far the most famous prediction from equity theory is the "over-reward effect"—that is, what happens when the equation is unbalanced in one's own favor.

According to equity theory, when one is *overpaid* the two sides of the ratios are misaligned. Consequently, one must work harder (i.e., increase inputs) in order to be equitable. These effects seem to occur. Greenberg (1988) studied managers who were temporarily moved to higher- or lower-status offices than their position actually warranted. Those moved to higher-status offices boosted performance, whereas those moved to lower-status offices showed decrements. These gains and losses later disappeared when individuals were returned to status-appropriate office spaces. Apart from its impact on performance, inequity can also cause workplace sabotage (Ambrose, Seabright, & Schminke, 2002) and employee theft (Greenberg, 1993). It is personally painful for employees, as distributive injustice is associated with stress symptoms (Cropanzano, Goldman, & Benson, 2005).

Recent advances in distributive justice. As Table 8.2.1 makes clear, there is more to distributive justice than simple equity. These different standards can be in conflict with one another. Generally speaking, we can distinguish three allocation rules that can lead to distributive justice if they are applied appropriately: equality (to each the same), equity (to each in accordance with contributions), and need (to each in accordance with the most urgency). These rules map onto Aristotle's famous dictum that all men wish to be treated like all other people (equality), like some other people (equity), and like no other person (need). While it is no mean task to find the correct alchemistic combination among these three allocation rules, there are three basic suggestions that can be helpful.

First, it is useful to consider one's strategic goals (Colquitt, Greenberg, & Zapata-Phelan, 2005). Equity tends to provide individual rewards for high performance, whereas equality tends to build esprit de corps among teammates. If one desires to stimulate individual motivation, err toward equity. If one desires to build group cohesion, err toward equality. We shall return to this issue later when we discuss reward systems.

Second, organizations can balance these considerations by mixing equality and equity together. It need not be either-or. Experiments with work groups suggest that it is often best to provide team members with a basic minimum of benefit. This is analogous to equality. Above that minimum, however, it can be useful to reward based on performance. This is analogous to equity. This sort of hybrid approach has been adopted by many organizations. Their compensation systems contain a "fixed" base; everyone in a particular job class and with a particular tenure receives this base. Employees are also encouraged to go beyond this minimum, earning additional pay through the allocation of merit bonuses (Milkovich & Newman, 2005, see especially Chapters 9 and 10).

Third, different rewards should be provided in accordance with different rules. Equity works well for some things, such as money, but less well for others, such as status symbols. Among American managers, it is often seen as fair to allocate economic benefits in accordance with equity (i.e., those who perform better might earn more). On the other hand, social-emotional benefits, such as reserved parking places, are best allocated equally (Martin & Harder, 1994). Employees often see themselves and their peers as belonging to a group or, in the most beneficial case, a community. Allocating social-emotional rewards equally signals that everyone in the organization matters and is worthy of respect.

Procedural Justice

Procedural justice refers to the means by which outcomes are allocated, but not specifically to the outcomes themselves. Procedural justice establishes certain principles specifying and governing the roles of participants within the decision-making processes. In three papers, Leventhal and his colleagues (Leventhal, 1976, 1980; Leventhal, Karuza, & Fry, 1980) established some core attributes that make procedures just; these are displayed in Table 8.2.1. A just process is one that is applied consistently to all, free of bias, accurate, representative of relevant stakeholders, correctable, and consistent with ethical norms. Though surprising to some, research has shown that just procedures can mitigate the ill effects of unfavorable outcomes. Researchers have named this the "fair process effect."

To illustrate let us consider the case of strategic planning. Kim and Mauborgne (1991, 1993) reported that when managers believed that their headquarters used a fair planning process, they were more supportive of the plan, trusted their leaders more, and were more committed to their employers. In their well-known book, *Blue Ocean Strategy*, Kim and Mauborgne (2005) explain why. Fair processes lead to intellectual and emotional recognition. This, in turn, creates the trust and commitment that build voluntary cooperation in strategy execution. Procedural injustice, on the other hand, produces "intellectual and emotional indignation," resulting in "distrust and resentment" (p. 183). Ultimately, this reduces cooperation in strategy execution.

We can go further. Procedural justice seems to be essential to maintaining institutional legitimacy. When personnel decisions are made, individuals are likely to receive certain outcomes. For instance, one may or may not be promoted. According to Tyler and Blader (2000), outcome favorability tends to affect satisfaction with the particular decision. This is not surprising. What is more interesting is that procedural justice affects what workers believe about the organization as a whole. If the process is perceived as just, employees show greater loyalty and more willingness to behave in an organization's best interests. They are also less likely to betray the institution and its leaders.

Interactional Justice

In a sense, *interactional justice* may be the simplest of the three components. It refers to how one person treats another. A person is interactionally just if he or she appropriately shares information and avoids rude or cruel remarks. In other words, there are two aspects of interactional justice (Colquitt, Conlon, Wesson, Porter, & Ng, 2001). The first part, sometimes called *informational justice* refers to whether one is truthful and provides adequate justifications when things go badly. The second part, sometimes called *interpersonal justice*, refers to the respect and dignity with which one treats another. As shown in Table 8.2.1, both are important.

Because interactional justice emphasizes one-on-one transactions, employees often seek it from their supervisors. This presents an opportunity for organizations. In a quasi-experimental study, Skarlicki and Latham (1996) trained union leaders to behave more justly. Among other things, these leaders were taught to provide explanations and apologies (informational justice) and to treat their reports with courtesy and respect (interpersonal justice). When work groups were examined three months later, individuals who reported to trained leaders exhibited more helpful citizenship behaviors than individuals who reported to untrained leaders.

Working Together: The Three Components of Justice Interact

Maintaining the three components of justice simultaneously is a worthwhile task, but it may also seem daunting. Fortunately, there is good news. Evidence suggests that the three components of justice interact (Cropanzano, Slaughter, & Bachiochi, 2005; Skarlicki & Folger, 1997). Though this interaction can be described in different ways, the key point is this: The ill effects of injustice can be at least partially mitigated if at least one component of justice is maintained. For example, a distributive and a procedural injustice will have fewer negative effects if interactional justice is high.

To understand this phenomenon one can look at a study by Goldman (2003). Goldman studied the relationship between justice and filing legal claims for alleged workplace discrimination. He found that claimants were most likely to pursue litigation when distributive, procedural, and interactional justice were all low. If just one component of justice was judged to be high, the likelihood of a legal claim dropped. This is good news, because it suggests that organizations have three bites at the apple. If they can get at least one component of justice right, some important benefits should result. We will consider the beneficial consequences of justice in our next section.

The Impact of Organizational Justice

Over the past few decades a considerable body of research has investigated the consequences of just and unjust treatment by work organizations. This literature has been summarized in three different meta-analytic reviews (Cohen-Charash & Spector, 2001; Colquitt et al., 2001; Viswesvaran & Ones, 2002). While these quantitative reviews differ in some specifics, they all underscore the propitious effects of workplace justice. We will look at each of the findings individually.

Justice Builds Trust and Commitment

Trust is a willingness to become vulnerable with respect to another party. As one might expect given our comments so far, Colquitt and his colleagues (2001) found that all three components of justice (distributive, procedural, and interactional) predict trust. These relationships can be quite strong. For example, the association between perceptions of just procedures and trust can be as high as .60. In a like fashion, justly treated employees are also more committed to their employers. Findings again vary somewhat with how justice is measured, but the correlation of perceived justice and affective commitment can range between .37 and .43 (Cohen-Charash & Spector, 2001).

Justice Improves Job Performance

As is true for other scholars, we use the term "job performance" to refer to formal job duties, assigned by organizational authorities and evaluated during performance appraisals (for a similar discussion, see Organ, 1988). Workplace justice predicts the effectiveness with which workers discharge their job duties (Colquitt et al., 2001), though more so in field settings and less so in the undergraduate laboratory (Cohen-Charash & Spector, 2001). As Lerner (2003) observed, justice effects are often strongest in real life. In part, this is because, over time, fairness leads to strong interpersonal relationships. In two studies, Cropanzano, Prehar, and Chen (2002) and Rupp and Cropanzano (2002) examined whether supervisors treated their reports with interactional justice. When they did, the leader and the subordinate had a higher-quality relationship. This strong relationship, in turn, motivated employees to higher job performance. Supervisors worried that just pay and process are expensive and time-consuming might take heart. These costs may be partially defrayed by higher productivity.

Justice Fosters Employee Organizational Citizenship Behaviors

Organizational citizenship behaviors (OCBs) are employee behaviors that go beyond the call of duty (Organ, 1988). Several studies have found that justly treated employees are more likely to comply with workplace policies, show extra conscientiousness, and behave altruistically toward others (Cohen-Charash & Spector, 2001). Indeed, workers tend to tailor their citizenship behaviors carefully, doling them out to those groups or individuals who have treated them justly and withholding them from those who have not.

To illustrate this point, consider the case of temporary employees. A contingent worker is likely to be associated with two different organizations—the temporary agency and the organization that contracts with it. In an interesting study, Liden, Wayne, Kraimer, and Sparrowe (2003) surveyed contingent workers who were assigned to a Fortune 500 manufacturing firm. Liden and his colleagues discovered that citizenship behaviors toward this manufacturing organization were influenced by the procedural fairness with which the manufacturing company treated the workers. Contingent employees who received just processes from the contracting organization (the manufacturing firm) performed more OCBs. However, the procedural justice these workers received from the employment agency did nothing to boost citizenship behaviors toward the manufacturing firm. In other words, individuals repaid procedural justice with hard work, but they reciprocated only to the organization that treated them justly in the first place. The manufacturing firm did not benefit from the temporary agency's efforts at procedural justice. If you want justice to work to your benefit, you have to do it yourself.

Justice Builds Customer Satisfaction and Loyalty

Justice-inspired employee OCBs, such as behaving altruistically toward others, sound much like employee customer service-oriented behaviors, such as helping others and listening carefully to their needs. Building on this, Bowen, Gilliland and Folger (1999) suggested that just treatment of employees would lead to OCBs that "spill over" to customers. This "just play" results in customers feeling appropriately treated, thereby yielding customer satisfaction and loyalty. These types of internal-external relationships have been empirically validated by such scholars as Masterson (2001) and Maxham and Netemyer (2003). For example, Masterson (2001) asked a large group of university instructors how they were being treated. When teachers felt that they received distributive and procedural justice they tended to report higher organizational commitment. This commitment, in turn, improved student responses toward the instructor. Since small gains in customer loyalty can translate into much larger gains in profitability (e.g., Heskett, Sasser, & Schlesinger, 1997; Smith, Bolton, & Wagner, 1999), these are very potent effects.

Thoughts Before Moving On

More broadly, we suggest that justice can be a core value that defines an organization's identity with its stakeholders, both internally and externally. When justice is espoused as a core value of an organization's management philosophy and enacted through a set of internally consistent management practices, it can build a "culture of justice," a system-wide commitment that is valuable and unique in the eyes of employees and customers, and tough to copy in the minds of competitors. And that can translate into the makings of sustainable competitive advantage. In our next section, we will look at management practices that can help develop a culture of justice.

How to Create Perceptions of Justice

We will now turn to common and important workplace situations, discussing a variety of managerial and personnel functions. These are displayed in Table 8.2.2. In each case, we will provide a lesson for promoting justice, including some normative recommendations regarding how individuals should be treated. And in each case we will return to one or more of our conceptual observations, such as the fair process effect and the two-factor model, illustrating how these phenomena affect real-life organizations.

Selection Procedures: Positive Job Candidates

For most job candidates, the recruiting and selection process is their first introduction to an organization. How they are treated at this time can have ramifications later. Applicants who feel justly treated are more likely to form positive impressions of the organization (Bauer et al., 2001) and recommend it to their friends (Smither, Reilly, Millsap, Pearlman, & Stoffey, 1993). And the flip side is also true. When applicants feel unjustly treated they are more likely to consider litigation as a potential remedy (Bauer et al., 2001). This research suggests that it pays for organizations to put their best foot forward. By treating applicants justly in the hiring process, organizations are setting the foundation for a relationship of justice and trust when those applicants become employees.

The research on job candidates' reactions to recruiting and hiring processes suggests that it is about much more than whether or not someone gets the job. Further, because applicants don't often know why they didn't get the job or the qualifications of the person who did, distributive justice is less of a concern in selection. However, managers do need to be mindful of procedural and interactional justice. It is also important to realize that the selection process begins with recruiting and initial communication, and encompasses all contact with job candidates up to and including extending an offer and rejecting an individual for a job (Gilliland & Hale, 2005). In terms of procedural justice, research has identified two broad sets of concerns:

- *Appropriate questions and criteria* are critical for procedural justice. Job candidates expect interview questions and screening tests to be related to the job, or at least to appear to be related to the job (Gilliland, 1994; Ryan & Chan, 1999). Overly personal interview

Table 8.2.2 Building Justice Into Management Systems

1. Positive Job Candidates: The Justice Paradox in Selection Procedures.
2. Justly Balancing Multiple Goals: The Two-Factor Model in Just Reward Systems
3. You Don't Have to Win: How the Process by Outcome Interaction Helps Us Resolve Conflicts
4. Softening Hardship: The Fair Process Effect in Layoffs
5. Keeping Score Fairly: A Due Process Approach to Performance Appraisal.

questions and some screening tests, such as honesty tests, are often seen as inappropriate and an invasion of candidates' privacy (Bies & Moag, 1986; Kravitz, Stinson, & Chavez, 1996).

- *Adequate opportunity to perform* during the selection process means giving job candidates the chances to make a case for themselves and allowing sufficient time in interviews (Truxillo, Bauer, & Sanchez, 2001). If standardized tests are used to screen applicants, justice can be enhanced by allowing candidates to retest if they feel they did not perform their best (Truxillo et al., 2001).

On the face, these two criteria seem reasonable and pretty straightforward. However, when compared with recommended hiring practices, managers are often faced with a "justice paradox" (Folger & Cropanzano, 1998). That is, many of the selection procedures with the highest predictive validity—those that are the best screening tools—are unfortunately those that fail to satisfy these justice concerns. Consider cognitive ability and personality tests. These screening methods have high demonstrated validity (Schmidt & Hunter, 1998), but both are seen by job applicants as not particularly fair (Steiner & Gilliland, 1996). Questions on these tests are often not related to the job, and applicants don't feel they have an opportunity to present their true abilities. The converse is also observed with the justice paradox. Traditional unstructured interviews have long demonstrated weak predictive validity, not much better than chance (Huffcutt & Arthur, 1994). However, job applicants perceive these interviews as having high procedural justice because they are able to demonstrate their qualifications (Latham & Finnegan, 1993). Adding structured situations and questions to the interview increases predictive validity, but decreases perceptions of procedural justice.

So how can this justice paradox be managed effectively? We have three suggestions. First, there are some screening tools that have both predictive validity and procedural justice. Work sample tests and performance-based simulations demonstrate reasonable predictive validity (Roth, Bobko, & McFarland, 2005) and are also seen as procedurally just (Steiner & Gilliland, 1996). A second solution is to modify existing screening tools to increase job applicants' perceived procedural justice. Smither and colleagues (1993) found that cognitive ability tests with concrete, rather than abstract, items tended to be viewed more positively by job applicants. Based on the observation that applicants perceive greater justice in unstructured interviews, Gilliland and Steiner (1999) suggest a combined interview that has both structured behavioral questions to maximize predictive validity and unstructured questions to allow applicants the "opportunity to perform."

The third suggestion is based on our earlier discussion of interactional justice. Recall that interactional justice can attenuate the negative effects of procedural injustice. Research has demonstrated that interactional justice is very important for job candidates (Bies & Moag, 1986; Gilliland, 1995). With attention to considerate interpersonal treatment, honest information, and timely feedback, organizations can create hiring processes that embody interactional justice. Research has demonstrated that the informational components are particularly important if there are unanticipated delays or unusual screening procedures involved in the process (Rynes, Bretz, & Gerhart, 1991).

Reward Systems: Justly Balancing Multiple Goals

At the most basic level, rewards systems need to accomplish two goals: They need to motivate individual performance, and they need to maintain group cohesion. While both goals are worthwhile, distributive justice research tells us that it is difficult to accomplish them simultaneously. Equity allocations, which reward for performance, can spur individual effort. But the resulting inequality that is likely to occur can be disruptive. In a study of academic faculty, Pfeffer and Langton (1993) examined wage dispersion in their home departments. When wage dispersion was high, faculty reported less satisfaction and less collaboration with colleagues. Overall research productivity dropped as well. This is not what merit pay is supposed to do.

Paying everyone the same thing, though, is not the answer either. Indeed, equality distributions can boost group harmony, but they bring troubles of their own. A key problem is one of external equity. High-performing employees, or those with rare skills, may be worth more in the external marketplace. If their salaries are "capped" to maintain internal equality, these workers may seek employment elsewhere. This is just another way of saying that no matter how people are paid, not everyone will be satisfied.

How then to position rewards? The research discussed earlier underscores an opportunity. To be sure, individuals who do not receive the compensation they desire will want more. However, they often remain loyal to their employer if the pay administration procedures are viewed as fair. Consequently, if an organization needs to maintain external equity, it can do so and risk internal inequality, but only as long as the allocation process is just. To illustrate, McFarlin and Sweeney (1992) surveyed more than 600 banking employees. As expected, when distributive justice was low, workers reported less pay satisfaction and less job satisfaction. This is bad news, but it is partially compensated for by the procedural justice results. When procedural justice was high, workers experienced higher organizational commitment and a positive reaction to their supervisors. This is the two-factor model in action. Individuals who were not necessarily satisfied with their pay were still unlikely to derogate the organization when the procedures were just.

In addition to procedural justice, interactional justice can be helpful in administering pay fairly. To illustrate this point, let us consider a situation that everyone dislikes: pay cuts. Greenberg (1993) found that differences in how pay cuts were managed at two manufacturing plants produced dramatically different outcomes. The key is interpersonal treatment. In one, an executive politely, but quickly in about 15 minutes, announced a 15% pay cut. In the other, an executive spent about an hour and a half speaking, taking questions, and expressing regrets about making an identical pay cut. During a subsequent 10-week period, employee theft was about 80% lower in the second case, and employees in that plant were 15 times less likely to resign. No one wanted to have his or her pay cut. But workers understood why it happened, appreciated the supportive interpersonal treatment, and did not vent their ire on the organization.

Conflict Management: You Don't Have to Win

Thomas and Schmidt (1976) tell us that managers may spend about 20% of their time settling disputes among employees, and they are not always successful (Schoorman & Champagne, 1994). Conflict resolution is likely to be most difficult when one or both parties is intransigent. At this point the manager may listen to both disputants, but will need to impose a settlement on them. This is called arbitration, and it is ultimately autocratic. As a result, arbitration may sound risky because it hazards a distributive injustice; the settlement is imposed and not approved in advance by other parties.

There is good news, however. If *any* component of justice is present during arbitration (distributive or procedural or interactional), the overall appraisal of the situation will be improved (Goldman, 2003). Because arbitration preserves procedural justice, an unfortunate outcome is less destructive than one might imagine. Or, we might say, managers can make hard choices, but they have to make them justly (for details see Folger & Cropanzano, 1998). This illustrates a simple yet powerful lesson from research on conflict resolution: If you can't give people the outcome they want, at least give them a fair process.

Layoffs: Softening Hardship

So far we have reviewed evidence pertaining to justice in the context of hiring, reward systems, and conflict resolution. These are everyday events in a large organization, and each will function more effectively if justice is taken into account. Even a reader willing to indulge our arguments so far might be wondering whether justice helps when something really bad happens.

Among common management situations that affect employees, downsizing is among the worst (Richman, 1993). Layoffs have pernicious effects, harming the victims while under-mining the morale of survivors who remain employed. Though downsizing is a widely used cost-cutting strategy, it is highly risky. The costs of workforce reductions often outweigh the benefits (Kammeyer-Mueller, Liao, & Arvey, 2001). In these circumstances people not only lose, they lose big. The event can be so negative that a sense of distributive injustice is virtually a given. Can the guidelines suggested in this paper do any good at all?

As a matter of fact, they can. When a layoff is handled with procedural and interactional justice, victims are less likely to derogate their former employers (Brockner et al., 1994, Study 1). Indeed, justice can have direct bottom-line effects. Lind, Greenberg, Scott, and Welchans (2000) interviewed a large number of layoff victims. Many of these individuals considered legal action following their downsizing, and almost a quarter of the victims went so far as to speak to an attorney. The single best predictor of willingness to take legal action was the justice of the treatment they received at the time of their discharge. Among those who felt unjustly treated, Lind and his colleagues found that a full 66% contemplated litigation. Among those who felt justly treated, this dropped to just 16%. These are impressive findings. Although managers are often coached by attorneys or HR representatives to avoid apologiz-ing—an apology can be seen as an admission of guilt—these results suggest that an apology may help promote the feelings of interactional justice that actually reduce the risk of litigation. Justice, it would seem, provides a useful way to survive a crisis with one's business reputation intact.

While we have so far discussed the victims of layoffs, workforce reductions also affect survivors. Those left behind, though retaining their jobs, tend to suffer from "survivor guilt" (Brockner & Greenberg, 1990). However, if organizations provide a good explan-ation as to why the downsizing is necessary—an aspect of interactional justice—the remaining employees respond much less negatively (Brockner, DeWitt, Grover, & Reed, 1990). Providing unemployment benefits is also advantageous, as one might expect. How-ever, if these benefits are lacking, an advance warning that a layoff is about to occur will blunt the negative reactions that might otherwise transpire (Brockner et al., 1994, Studies 2 and 3).

Performance Appraisals: Keeping Score Fairly

In order to assign rewards, identify candidates for promotion, and develop human capital, most large organizations conduct performance evaluations. While these appraisals are use-ful, concerns remain, and their implementation is often troubled. For example, scholars have observed a phenomenon called the "vanishing performance appraisal" (for a review, see Folger & Cropanzano, 1998). When surveyed, most managers reported having provided performance reviews, while many of their subordinates reported never receiving one. Other research suggests that evaluations are affected by political considerations (Longenecker, Gioia, & Sims, 1987), cognitive processing limitations of the rater (DeNisi & Williams, 1988), and the social context in which they are conducted (Levy & Williams, 2004). These concerns tell us that the performance appraisal process often contains a good deal of ambiguity as well as room for reasonable people to disagree.

For this reason, it is helpful to approach performance evaluations with an eye to their subjectivity. Historically, much of the advice academics provided to practitioners encouraged them to think of the performance review as a sort of test, whereby the central task is to assign a valid rating to a more-or-less objective quantity. For example, raters have been advised to "become expert at applying principles of test development" (Banks & Roberson, 1985, p. 129) and that "psychometric issues surrounding performance measurement [are] more relevant than ever" (DeVries, Morrison, Shullman, & Gerlach, 1981). This venerable, measurement-oriented understanding of performance appraisal has been termed the "test metaphor" (Folger, Konovsky, & Cropanzano, 1992).

More recent performance appraisal work has taken a broader perspective, emphasizing the social setting (Levy & Williams, 2004) and input from multiple sources (Smither, London, & Reilly, 2005). In this vein, Cawley, Keeping, and Levy (1998) meta-analyzed 27 field studies, each of which examined employee participation in performance appraisal. They found that when employees had a voice they were more satisfied, saw the process as more fair, and were more motivated to do better. This is interesting, but probably not terribly surprising. The really impressive finding was that these effects occurred even when participation could not affect the rating. Simply being able to speak one's mind (what Cawley and coauthors termed "value-expressive" participation) caused employees to be more favorable toward the performance appraisal system. Notice how these findings are consistent with the fair process effect mentioned earlier.

Research on organizational justice is providing a new paradigm for understanding performance review. Consistent with Folger, Konovsky, and Cropanzano (1992), we call this the due process approach to performance appraisal. Adopting a due process metaphor sensitizes one to the distinct interpretations, potential conflicts of interest, and legitimate disagreement about facts. The due process approach to performance review has three core elements: adequate notice, just hearing, and judgment based on evidence.

- *Adequate notice*, as one might expect, involves letting people know in advance when they will be appraised and on what criteria they will be appraised. However, from a justice point of view, it goes beyond this. It is also useful to have workers involved in devising performance standards and making these widely available. Of course, it follows that feedback should be provided regularly.
- *Just hearing* means limiting the feedback review to "admissible" evidence, such as worker performance rather than personal attacks. It also means providing workers with a chance to provide their own interpretation of events, including disagreeing with the supervisor where this is appropriate.
- *Judgment based on evidence* means that the standards should be accurate, data should be gathered, and decisions should be based on this formal process. Steps should be taken to provide rater training, so as to improve accuracy and to keep the process free of political influence.

Taylor, Tracy, Renard, Harrison, and Carroll (1995) redesigned the performance appraisal system of a large state agency so that it included these principles of due process. They discovered that workers preferred the new system, finding it fairer and more effective. Managers liked it as well, believing that it allowed them to be honest and feeling that it was more effective for solving work problems. This occurred even though workers in the due process system received *lower* ratings than did workers under the older approach.

This is all to the good, but there are risks involved. Adequate notice, just hearing, and judgment based on evidence are complicated to administer. A key problem is that they may raise expectations while simultaneously providing employees with a set of tools for making their discontent felt. Consider the case of two companies studied over six years by Mesch and Dalton (1992). Each firm was in the same region, and workers in each were represented by the same union. In fact, grievances at both organizations were assigned to the same union local. After 36 months, one of the firms decided to improve its grievance process by adding a fact-finding intervention. Before the grievance process began, both the union and management provided a "fact finder" to determine the merits of the case, prevent concealment of information, and encourage negotiated settlements. This provided an additional stage of process protection. The result? The number of grievances filed skyrocketed at the firm with the new procedural safeguard, but stayed roughly constant at the other organization. After about two years, the fact-finding intervention was abandoned, and the grievance rate returned to normal. The new intervention seems to have raised expectations and thereby encouraged workers to complain about real and imagined ill-treatment. In the long run this was counterproductive. The implications of Mesch and Dalton's (1992) study need to be appreciated. If procedures are not designed appropriately, they could create more problems than they solve.

Concluding Thoughts

There are two sides to the justice coin. On the negative side, the absence of justice is likely to provide problems for organizations. There is strong evidence that injustice can provoke retaliation, lower performance, and harm morale (Cohen-Charash & Spector, 2001; Colquitt et al., 2001; Viswesvaran & Ones, 2002). On the positive side, justice can do more than forestall these unfortunate outcomes. Justice acts as a sort of buffer, allowing employees to maintain respect and trust for an organization even when things do not go as they would have liked (Brockner & Wiesenfeld, 1996). It is inevitable in life that things will not always go our way. However, the negative effects of an unfortunate event are less severe if an organization is able to maintain procedural and interactional justice (Goldman, 2003; Skarlicki & Folger, 1997).

Justice provides an excellent business opportunity, from reaping specific returns such as stronger employee commitment to gaining an overall tough-to-copy competitive edge that resides in a "culture of justice." In this paper we have examined justice from the perspective of five managerial tasks: hiring, reward systems, conflict management, layoffs, and performance appraisals. These tasks are diverse, but they all involve a degree of risk. Each has the potential to designate some as "winners" and others as "losers." After all, there will always be people who fail to get the job, receive a lower than expected performance appraisal, or are downsized in the face of business exigencies. As a result, organizations hazard the ill will of employees simply because they are making the sorts of decisions necessary to run their businesses. Organizational justice allows managers to make these tough decisions more smoothly. Just play certainly does not guarantee all parties what they want. However, it does hold out the possibility that power will be used in accordance with normative principles that respect the dignity of all involved. This is sound business advice. *It is also the right thing to do.*

References

Adams, J. S. (1965). Inequity in social exchange. In L. Berkowitz (Ed.), *Advances in experimental social psychology* (Vol. 2, pp. 267–299). New York: Academic Press.

Ambrose, M. L., & Arnaud, A. (2005). Are procedural justice and distributive justice conceptually distinct? In J. A. Colquitt & J. Greenberg (Eds.), *Handbook of organizational justice* (pp. 85–112). Mahwah, NJ: Lawrence Erlbaum Associates.

Ambrose, M. L., & Schminke, M. (2007). Examining justice climate: Issues of fit, simplicity, and content. In F. Dansereau & F. J. Yammarino (Eds.), *Research in multilevel issues* (Vol. 6, pp. 397–413). Oxford, England: Elsevier.

Ambrose, M. L., Seabright, M. A., & Schminke, M. (2002). Sabotage in the workplace: The role of organizational injustice. *Organizational Behavior and Human Decision Processes, 89*, 947–965.

Ashforth, B. E., & Humphrey, R. H. (1995). Emotion in the workplace: A reappraisal. *Human Relations, 48*, 97–125.

Banks, C. G., & Roberson, L. (1985). Performance appraisers as test developers. *Academy of Management Review, 10*, 128–142.

Barley, S. R., & Kunda, G. (1992). Design and devotion: Surges of rational and normative ideologies of control in managerial discourse. *Administrative Science Quarterly, 37*, 363–399.

Bauer, T. N., Truxillo, D. M., Sanchez, R. J., Craig, J., Ferrara, P., & Campion, M. A. (2001). Applicant reactions to selection: Development of the selection procedural justice scale (SPJS). *Personnel Psychology, 54*, 387–419.

Bies, R. J., & Moag, J. S. (1986). Interactional justice: Communication criteria for justice. In B. Sheppard (Ed.), *Research on negotiation in organizations* (Vol. 1, pp. 43–55). Greenwich, CT: JAI Press.

Bies, R. J., & Tripp, T. M. (2001). A passion for justice: The rationality and morality of revenge. In R. Cropanzano (Ed.), *Justice in the workplace* (pp. 197–208). Mahwah, NJ: Lawrence Erlbaum Associates.

Bies, R. J., & Tripp, T. M. (2002). "Hot flashes, open wounds": Injustice and the tyranny of its emotions. In S. W. Gilliland, D. D. Steiner, & D. P. Skarlicki (Eds.), *Emerging perspectives on managing organizational justice* (pp. 203–221). Greenwich, CT: Information Age Publishing.

Bowen, D. E., Gilliland, S. W., & Folger, R. (1999). HRM and service justice: How being just with employees spills over to customers. *Organizational Dynamics, 27*, 7–23.

Brockner, J., DeWitt, R. L., Grover, S., & Reed, T. (1990). When it is especially important to explain why: Factors affecting the relationship between managers' explanations of a layoff and survivors' reactions to the layoff. *Journal of Experimental Social Psychology, 26*, 389–407.

Brockner, J., & Greenberg, J. (1990). The impact of layoffs on survivors: An organizational justice perspective. In J. S. Carroll (Ed.), *Applied social psychology and organizational settings* (pp. 45–75). Hillsdale, NJ: Erlbaum.

Brockner, J., Konovsky, M., Cooper-Schneider, R., Folger, R., Martin, C., & Bies, R. J. (1994). Interactive effects of procedural justice and outcome negativity on victims and survivors of job loss. *Academy of Management Journal, 37*, 397–409.

Brockner, J., Tyler, T. R., & Cooper-Schneider, R. (1992). The influence of prior commitment to an institution on reactions to perceived unfairness: The higher they are, the harder they fall. *Administrative Science Quarterly, 37*, 241–261.

Brockner, J., & Wiesenfeld, B. M. (1996). An integrative framework for explaining attractiveness of decisions: The interactive effects of outcomes and processes. *Psychological Bulletin, 120*, 189–208.

Cawley, B. D., Keeping, L. M., & Levy, P. E. (1998). Participation in the performance appraisal process and employee reactions: A meta-analytic review of field investigations. *Journal of Applied Psychology, 83*, 615–633.

Cohen-Charash, Y., & Spector, P. E. (2001). The role of justice in organizations: A meta-analysis. *Organizational Behavior and Human Decision Processes, 86,* 278–321.

Colquitt, J. A., Conlon, D. E., Wesson, M. J., Porter, C. O. L. H., & Ng, K. Y. (2001). Justice at the millennium: A meta-analytic review of 25 years of organizational justice research. *Journal of Applied Psychology, 86,* 425–445.

Colquitt, J. A., Greenberg, J., & Zapata-Phelan, C. P. (2005). What is organizational justice? A historical overview. In J. Greenberg & J. A. Colquitt (Eds.), *Handbook of organizational justice* (pp. 3–56). Mahwah, NJ: Lawrence Erlbaum Associates.

Cropanzano, R., Goldman, B., & Benson, L., III. (2005). Organizational justice. In J. Barling, K. Kelloway, & M. Frone (Eds.), *Handbook of work stress* (pp. 63–87). Beverly Hills, CA: Sage.

Cropanzano, R., Prehar, C. A., & Chen, P. Y. (2002). Using social exchange theory to distinguish procedural from interactional justice. *Group and Organizational Management, 27,* 324–351.

Cropanzano, R., Rupp, D. E., Mohler, C. J., & Schminke, M. (2001). Three roads to organizational justice. In J. Ferris (Ed.), *Research in personnel and human resources management* (Vol. 20, pp. 1–113). Greenwich, CT: JAI Press.

Cropanzano, R., Slaughter, J. E., & Bachiochi, P. D. (2005). Organizational justice and black applicants' reactions to affirmative action. *Journal of Applied Psychology, 90,* 1168–1184.

DeNisi, A. S., & Williams, K. J. (1988). Cognitive research in performance appraisal. In K. Rowland & G. S. Ferris (Eds.), *Research in personnel and human resources management* (Vol. 6, pp. 109–156). Greenwich, CT: JAI Press.

DeVries, D. L., Morrison, A. M., Shullman, S. L., & Gerlach, M. L. (1981). *Performance appraisal on the line.* New York: Wiley.

Ellard, J. H., & Skarlicki, D. P. (2002). A third-party observer's reactions to employee mistreatment: Motivational and cognitive processes in deservingness assessments. In S. W. Gilliland, D. D. Steiner, & D. P. Skarlicki (Eds.), *Emerging perspectives on managing organizational justice* (pp. 133–158). Greenwich, CT: Information Age Publishing.

Folger, R. (2001). Justice as deonance. In S. W. Gilliland, D. D. Steiner, & D. P. Skarlicki (Eds.), *Research in social issues in management* (Vol. 1, pp. 3–33). New York: Information Age Publishing.

Folger, R., & Cropanzano, R. (1998). *Organizational justice and human resource management.* Beverly Hills, CA: Sage.

Folger, R., Konovsky, M. A., & Cropanzano, R. (1992). A due process metaphor for performance appraisal. In B. M. Staw & L. L. Cummings (Eds.), *Research in organizational behavior* (Vol. 14, pp. 129–177). Greenwich, CT: JAI Press.

Gilliland, S. W. (1994). Effects of procedural and distributive justice on reactions to a selection system. *Journal of Applied Psychology, 79,* 691–701.

Gilliland, S. W. (1995). Justice from the applicant's perspective: Reactions to employee selection procedures. *International Journal of Selection and Assessment, 3,* 11–19.

Gilliland, S. W., & Hale, J. (2005). How do theories of organizational justice inform just employee selection practices? In J. Greenberg & J. A. Colquitt (Eds.), *Handbook of organizational justice: Fundamental questions about justice in the workplace* (pp. 411–438). Mahwah, NJ: Erlbaum.

Gilliland, S. W., & Steiner, D. D. (1999). Applicant reactions to interviews: Procedural and interactional justice of recent interview technology. In R. W. Eder & M. M. Harris (Eds.), *The employment interview: Theory, research, and practice* (pp. 69–82). Thousand Oaks, CA: Sage.

Goldman, B. M. (2003). The application of reference cognitions theory to legal-claiming by terminated workers: The role of organizational justice and anger. *Journal of Management, 29,* 705–728.

Greenberg, J. (1988). Equity and workplace status: A field experiment. *Journal of Applied Psychology, 73,* 606–613.

Greenberg, J. (1993). Stealing in the name of justice: Informational and interpersonal moderators of theft reactions to underpayment inequity. *Organizational Behavior and Human Decision Processes, 54,* 81–103.

Heskett, J. L., Sasser, W. E., Jr., & Schlesinger, L. A. (1997). *The service profit chain: How leading companies link profit and growth to loyalty, satisfaction, and value.* New York: The Free Press.

Huffcutt, A. I., & Arthur, W. Jr. (1994). Hunter and Hunter (1984) revisited: Interview validity for entry-level jobs. *Journal of Applied Psychology, 79*, 184–190.

Kammeyer-Mueller, J., Liao, H., & Arvey, R. D. (2001). Downsizing and organizational performance: A review of the literature from a stakeholder perspective. In G. R. Ferris (Ed.), *Research in personnel and human resource management* (Vol. 20, pp. 269–329). Amsterdam: JAI Press.

Kim, W. C., & Mauborgne, R. A. (1991). Implementing global strategies: The role of procedural justice. *Strategic Management Journal, 12*, 125–143.

Kim, W. C., & Mauborgne, R. A. (1993). Procedural justice, attitudes, and subsidiary top management compliance with multinationals' corporate strategic decisions. *Academy of Management Journal, 36*, 502–526.

Kim, W. C., & Mauborgne, R. A. (2005). *Blue ocean strategy: How to create uncontested market space and make competition irrelevant*. Cambridge, MA: Harvard Business School Press.

Kravitz, D. A., Stinson, V., & Chavez, T. L. (1996). Evaluations of tests used for making selection and promotion decisions. *International Journal of Selection and Assessment, 4*, 24–34.

Krehbiel, P. J., & Cropanzano, R. (2000). Procedural justice, outcome favorability, and emotion. *Social Justice Research, 13*, 337–358.

Latham, G. P., & Finnegan, B. J. (1993). Perceived practicality of unstructured, patterned, and situational interviews. In H. Schuler, J. L. Farr, & M. Smith (Eds.), *Personnel selection and assessment: Individual and organizational perspectives* (pp. 41–55). Hillsdale, NJ: Erlbaum.

Lerner, M. J. (2003). The justice motive: Where social psychologists found it, how they lost it, and why they may not find it again. *Personality and Social Psychology Review, 7*, 388–389.

Leventhal, G. S. (1976). Justice in social relationships. In J. W. Thibaut, J. T. Spence, & R. C. Carson (Eds.), *Contemporary topics in social psychology* (pp. 211–240). Morristown, NJ: General Learning Press.

Leventhal, G. S. (1980). What should be done with equity theory? New approaches to the study of justice in social relationships. In K. Gergen, M. Greenberg, and R. Willis (Eds.), *Social exchange: Advances in experimental and social psychology* (Vol. 9, pp. 91–131). New York: Plenum.

Leventhal, G. S., Karuza, J., & Fry, W. R. (1980). Beyond justice: A theory of allocation preferences. In G. Mikula (Ed.), *Justice and social interaction* (pp. 167–218). New York: Springer-Verlag.

Levy, P. E., & Williams, J. R. (2004). The social context of performance appraisal. *Journal of Management, 30*, 881–905.

Liden, R. C., Wayne, S. J., Kraimer, M. L., & Sparrowe, R. T. (2003). The dual commitments of contingent workers: An examination of contingents' commitment to the agency and the organization. *Journal of Organizational Behavior, 24*, 609–625.

Lind, E. A., Greenberg, J., Scott, K. S., & Welchans, T. D. (2000). The winding road from employee to complainant: Situational and psychological determinants of wrongful termination claims. *Administrative Science Quarterly, 45*, 557–590.

Longenecker, C. O., Gioia, D. A., & Sims, H. P. (1987). Behind the mask: The politics of employee appraisal. *Academy of Management Executive, 1*, 183–193.

Martin, J., & Harder, J. W. (1994). Bread and roses: Justice and the distribution of financial and socioemotional rewards in organizations. *Social Justice Research, 7*, 241–264.

Masterson, S. (2001). A trickle-down model of organizational justice: Relating employees' and customers' perceptions of and reactions to justice. *Journal of Applied Psychology, 86*, 594–604.

Maxham, J. G., & Netemyer, R. G. (2003). Firms reap what they sow: The effects of shared values and perceived organizational justice on customers' evaluations of complaint handling. *Journal of Marketing, 67*, 46–62.

McFarlin, D. B., & Sweeney, P. D. (1992). Distributive and procedural justice as predictors of satisfaction with personal and organizational outcomes. *Academy of Management Journal, 35*, 626–637.

Mesch, D. J., & Dalton, D. R. (1992). Unexpected consequences of improving workplace justice: A six-year time series assessment. *Academy of Management Journal, 5*, 1099–1114.

Milkovich, G. T., & Newman, J. M. (2005). *Compensation* (8th Ed.). Boston: McGraw-Hill.

Miller, P., & O'Leary, T. (1989). Hierarchies and American ideals: 1900–1940. *Administrative Science Quarterly, 14*, 250–265.

Organ, D. W. (1988). *Organizational citizenship behavior: The good soldier syndrome.* Lexington, MA: Lexington Books.

Pfeffer, P. (1998). *The human equation: Building profits by putting people first.* Cambridge, MA: Harvard Business School Press.

Pfeffer, J., & Langton, N. (1993). The effect of wage dispersion on satisfaction, productivity, and working collaboratively: Evidence from college and university faculty. *Administrative Science Quarterly, 38,* 382–407.

Pfeffer, J., & Sutton, R. I. (2006). *Hard facts, dangerous half-truths, and total nonsense: Profiting from evidence-based management.* Cambridge, MA: Harvard Business School Press.

Richman, L. S. (1993, September 20). When will the layoffs end? *Fortune,* pp. 54–56.

Roth, P. L., Bobko, P., & McFarland, L. A. (2005). A meta-analysis of work sample test validity: Updating and integrating some classic literature. *Personnel Psychology, 58,* 1009–1037.

Rupp, D. E., & Cropanzano, R. (2002). The mediating effects of social exchange relationships in predicting workplace outcomes from multifoci organizational justice. *Organizational Behavior and Human Decision Processes, 89,* 925–946.

Ryan, A. M., & Chan, D. (1999). Perceptions of the EPPP: How do licensure candidates view the process? *Professional Psychology, 30,* 519–530.

Rynes, S. L., Bretz, R. D., & Gerhart, B. (1991). The importance of recruitment on job choice: A different way of looking. *Personnel Psychology, 33,* 529–542.

Schmidt, F. L., & Hunter, J. E. (1998). The validity and utility of selection methods in personnel psychology: Practical and theoretical implications of 85 years of research findings. *Psychological Bulletin, 124,* 262–274.

Schoorman, F. D., & Champagne, M. V. (1994). Managers as informal third parties: The impact of supervisor-subordinate relationships on interventions. *Employee Responsibilities and Rights Journal, 7,* 73–84.

Skarlicki, D. P., & Folger, R. (1997). Retaliation in the workplace: The roles of distributive, procedural, and interactional justice. *Journal of Applied Psychology, 82,* 434–443.

Skarlicki, D. P., & Latham, G. P. (1996). Increasing citizenship behavior within a labor union: A test of organizational justice theory. *Journal of Applied Psychology, 81,* 161–169.

Skitka, L. J., Winquist, J., & Hutchinson, S. (2003). Are outcome justice and outcome favorability distinguishable psychological constructs? A meta-analytic review. *Social Justice Research, 16,* 309–341.

Smith, A. K., Bolton, R. N., & Wagner, J. (1999). A model of customer satisfaction with service encounters involving failure and recovery. *Journal of Marketing Research, 36,* 356–372.

Smither, J. W., London, M., & Reilly, R. R. (2005). Does performance improve following multisource feedback? A theoretical model, meta-analysis, and review of empirical findings. *Personnel Psychology, 58,* 33–66.

Smither, J. W., Reilly, R. R., Millsap, R. E., Pearlman, K., & Stoffey, R. W. (1993). Applicant reactions to selection procedures. *Personnel Psychology, 46,* 49–77.

Spencer, S., & Rupp, D. E. (2006, May). *Angry, guilty, and conflicted: Injustice toward coworkers heightens emotional labor.* Paper presented at the Annual Meeting of the Society for Industrial and Organizational Psychology, Dallas, TX.

Steiner, D., & Gilliland, S. W. (1996). Justice reactions to personnel selection techniques in France and the United States. *Journal of Applied Psychology, 81,* 134–141.

Taylor, M. S., Tracy, K. B., Renard, M. K., Harrison, J. K., & Carroll, S. J. (1995). Due process in performance appraisal: A quasi-experiment in procedural justice. *Administrative Science Quarterly, 40,* 495–523.

Thomas, K. W., & Schmidt, W. H. (1976). A survey of managerial interests with respect to conflict. *Academy of Management Journal, 19,* 315–318.

Truxillo, D. M., Bauer, T. N., & Sanchez, R. J. (2001). Multiple dimensions of procedural justice: Longitudinal effects on selection system justice and test-taking self-efficacy. *International Journal of Selection and Assessment, 9,* 330–349.

Tyler, T. R., & Blader, S. L. (2000). *Cooperation in groups: Procedural justice, social identity, and behavioral engagement.* Philadelphia: Psychology Press.

Tyler, T. R., & Smith, H. J. (1998). Social justice and social movements. In D. Gilbert, S. T. Fiske, & G. Lindzey (Eds.), *Handbook of social psychology* (Vol. 4, pp. 595–629). Boston: McGraw-Hill.

Viswesvaran, C., & Ones, D. S. (2002). Examining the construct of organizational justice: A meta-analytic evaluation of relations with work attitudes and behaviors. *Journal of Business Ethics, 38,* 193–203.

Weiss, H. M., Suckow, K., & Cropanzano, R. (1999). Effects of justice conditions on discrete emotions. *Journal of Applied Psychology, 84,* 786–794.

Williams, M. L., McDaniel, M. A., & Nguyen, N. T. (2006). A meta-analysis of the antecedents and consequences of pay level satisfaction. *Journal of Applied Psychology, 91,* 392–413.

9 Group Dynamics and Team Effectiveness

9.1 GROUP LEARNING

Jeanne M. Wilson, Paul S. Goodman, and Matthew A. Cronin

We clarify the construct of group learning, encouraging new directions for research. Definitions of group learning vary considerably across studies, making it difficult to systematically accumulate evidence. To reconcile disparate approaches, we first present a set of features for distinguishing group learning from other concepts. We then develop a framework for understanding group learning that focuses on learning's basic processes at the group level of analysis: sharing, storage, and retrieval. By doing so, we define the construct space, identify gaps in current treatments of group learning, and illuminate new possibilities for measurement.

- In an eight-person product development team, one member from Engineering learns a new method for three-dimensional graphing and starts using it in her rough product designs. As a result, the team's development costs decrease.
- Based on its experience with the Love Me cybervirus, a national internet security team agrees that, in the future, the team should wait to send out alerts until it has a tested fix to recommend. Seven weeks later, when the Me Too bug strikes, the team delays sending out an alert for an extra four hours while it develops a patch. This response is roundly criticized in the internet security community.

Does either of these examples represent group learning? The answer is difficult to determine because the literature is so inconsistent about what constitutes group learning. Each of the above examples would be endorsed by some researchers but discounted by others. Because agreement on the definition of a construct is a prerequisite to effectively testing ideas about it (Rosenthal & Rosnow, 1991), a unifying view of group learning would help advance our understanding of this important phenomenon. In this paper we clarify the construct of group learning, focusing on four objectives. First, we present a set of features differentiating group learning from other concepts. Second, we identify gaps in the research literature on group learning. Third, we present an illustrative set of new propositions from our conceptualization of group learning. Fourth, we outline some implications for research and methods.

Several factors make the need for clarity about group learning increasingly important. First, because groups have become an important building block of organizational effectiveness over the past twenty years, understanding whether and how groups learn is important for predicting organizational performance. Second, group research has shifted from primarily focusing on group effectiveness models to understanding critical group processes, one of which is group learning (Argote & McGrath, 1993). Third, there has been a growing body of theory and empirical research on group learning, but, as in most early stages of research, definitions of the construct have varied considerably across studies, and there are gaps and ambiguities in those conceptualizations (cf. Snyder & Gangestad, 1986). These discrepancies have led others to note that "the group learning literature suffers from the problem of insufficient cohesion. Greater consensus in the development of a theoretical framework would be helpful in generating more empirical research" (Mohammed & Dumville, 2001: 97).

Current State of Research on Group Learning

A review of the current literature on group learning brings this lack of agreement into focus. We examined the existing literature on group learning, including studies that either purported to be about group learning or actually measured group learning, even if done under a different label (cf. Argote, 1996; Argote, Beckman, & Epple, 1990; Blickensdorfer, Cannon-Bowers, & Salas, 1997; Carley, 1992; Edmondson, Bohmer, & Pisano, 2001; Ellis, Hollenbeck, Ilgen, & Porter, 2003; Hollingshead, 2001; Lant, 1992; Moreland, Argote, & Krishnan, 1998; Van der Vegt & Bunderson, 2005; Wong, 2004; Zellmer-Bruhn, 2003). Group learning has been defined as "the activities through which individuals acquire, share and combine knowledge through experience with one another" (Argote, Gruenfeld, & Naquin, 2001: 370). Edmondson has defined group learning as "an ongoing process of reflection and action, characterized by asking questions, seeking feedback, experimenting, reflecting on results and discussing errors" (1999: 353). Others have suggested that learning is primarily a process of error detection and correction (Argyris & Schön, 1995) or that group-level learning is primarily about the processes of interpretation and integration (Crossan, Lane, & White, 1999). Additional definitions and related constructs are displayed in Table 9.1.1.

A review of these definitions reveals little consensus. Some focus on individuals learning in a group, while others focus on a team's level of collective knowledge. Some focus on processes, while others examine outcomes. All of these definitions raise questions about (1) the appropriate level of analysis, (2) critical learning processes, (3) distinguishing learning outcomes from other constructs such as performance, and (4) changes in group learning over time.

Many scholars have made the case that a theory or research model must contain an explicit description of the levels to which generalization is appropriate (Rousseau, 1985) and that critical problems result when the level of the theory is inconsistent with the prevailing level of measurement or statistical analysis (Klein, Dansereau, & Hall, 1994). Some treatments of group learning confuse levels of analysis by not distinguishing "individual learning in the context of groups" from "group-level learning." What we mean by this is that individuals can learn within the context of a group, and their learning may improve the group's performance, but it still is individual learning unless shared by members of the group. If an individual leaves the group and the group cannot access his or her learning, the group has failed to learn. As with other group-level constructs, group learning should be an emergent property of the group exerting influence beyond the individual members involved in the original learning process (Morgeson & Hofmann, 1999).

It was apparent from our review that most current conceptualizations of group learning are not explicit about basic learning processes. Existing definitions of group learning contain process verbs, such as "share," "reflect," "feedback," and "interpret," all of which can facilitate learning at the group level. Groups that seek feedback and reflect on errors are more likely to learn (Edmondson, 1999). Nonetheless, research on group-level learning has

Table 9.1.1 Definitions of Group Learning

Paper	Definition
Edmondson (1999: 129)	An ongoing process of reflection and action, characterized by asking questions, seeking feedback, experimenting, reflecting on results, and discussing errors or unexpected outcomes of actions
Argote, Gruenfeld, & Naquin (2001: 370)	The activities through which individuals acquire, share, and combine knowledge through experience with one another
Edmondson (2002: 129)	A process in which a team takes action, obtains and reflects on feedback, and makes changes to adapt or improve
Sole & Edmondson (2002: S18)	The acquisition and application of knowledge that enables a team to address team tasks and issues for which solutions were not previously obvious
Ellis, Hollenbeck, Ilgen, Porter, & West (2003: 822)	A relatively permanent change in the team's collective level of knowledge and skill produced by the shared experience of team members
Gibson & Vermeulen (2003: 203–204)	The exploration of knowledge through experimentation, the combination of insights through reflective communication, and the explication and specification of what has been learned through codification
Gruenfeld, Martorana, & Fan (2003: 46–47)	The acquisition, persistence, diffusion, and depreciation of group knowledge
London, Polzer, & Omoregie (2005: 114)	The extent to which members seek opportunities to develop new skills and knowledge, welcome challenging assignments, are willing to take risks on new ideas, and work on tasks that require considerable skill and knowledge

paid little or no attention to basic learning processes, such as how information is encoded, stored, or retrieved. This is a fundamental problem. The individual learning literature (Anderson, 2000) and recent work on organizational learning (Argote, 1999) show that the basic processes of storing and retrieving new routines are central to learning. We analyzed papers on learning cited in one of the most recent reviews of group research (Ilgen, Hollenbeck, Johnson, & Jundt, 2005). Only 10 percent of the papers in the group learning section of this most recent review were explicit about these processes.

A third problem with current conceptualizations of group learning is a failure to distinguish learning as an outcome from other constructs. Only 20 percent of the empirical papers in the group learning section of the Ilgen et al. review (2005) actually examined group learning rather than other constructs. One of the constructs most commonly confused with group learning is performance, despite a long-standing conceptual distinction in the literature (Tolman, 1932). Still, authors equate learning with performance (Fiol & Lyles, 1985), assuming that no change in performance means that learning did not take place (Cook & Yanow, 1993). We argue that learning may have occurred, even when there was no change in a group's overall performance. For example, the group may have learned something but may not have had an opportunity to apply the learning in a way that would change its performance. Conversely, performance can change without any learning actually taking place—for example, when the environment changes (e.g., when a product development team is able to reduce time to market because a supplier delivers a key component early). Finally, learning does not always result in positive outcomes. Research on group learning needs to account for the possibility of dysfunctional learning, as in the case of superstitious learning, where a group learns a false connection between its actions and some outcome (Levitt & March, 1988).

Finally, many treatments of group learning do not examine changes over time, even though many fundamental aspects of learning, such as practice or forgetting, occur over time. Learning is a necessarily dynamic construct. Without a change in the repertoire of potential behavior, there is no learning, and in order to assess change, one must consider the role of time. Our coding of the research cited in the Ilgen et al. review (2005) showed that fewer than 30 percent of the studies cited in the section on team learning actually measured or conceptualized the construct of group learning over time. Time is a critical aspect of the definition of group learning, and it helps to distinguish group learning from other constructs, such as group decision making.

Our Approach

Given the current limitations in the literature, we propose four criteria to be considered in a theory of group learning:

1. Level of analysis: Learning must be at the group level of analysis. Hence, we propose as a *definition* that group learning represents a change in the group's repertoire of potential behavior. We are explicitly stating that the theory, measurement, and analysis of group learning should focus on changes in the group's repertoire (cf. Klein et al., 1994). An aggregation of what individual members learn does not constitute group-level learning.
2. Fundamental processes: We propose that the processes inherent in the construct of group learning include *sharing, storage,* and *retrieval* of group knowledge, routines, or behavior. The processes of sharing, storage, and retrieval are the basic elements or mechanisms of the learning process (Hinsz, Tindale, & Vollrath, 1997). In general, current research on group learning does not explicitly deal with the processes of sharing, storage, and retrieval or their interrelationships. Attention to processes is important because it helps us understand not only why constructs come about (Whetten, 1989) but also the systematic reasons for a particular occurrence or nonoccurrence of a phenomenon (Sutton & Staw, 1995)—in this case, of group learning.
3. Learning as an outcome: Our conceptualization treats learning as an outcome—specifically, a change in the range of a group's potential behavior, following Huber (1991). Any change in the group's *range of potential behavior*, whether or not it is manifested in externally observable behavior, constitutes evidence of group learning. Learning as an outcome should be distinguished from other criterion variables, such as performance or decision making.
4. Time: Our definition explicitly incorporates time by requiring a *change* in the group's repertoire of potential behavior over some interval. This feature of our definition allows us to distinguish group learning from other group-level phenomena, such as decision making, shared mental models, and problem solving.

In advancing "a change in the group's repertoire of potential behavior" as a definition of group learning, we implicitly adopt a cognitive approach to this construct. This is not only consistent with general trends in the field of organizational behavior (Ilgen & Klein, 1989) and groups research in particular (Moreland, Hogg, & Hanes, 1994) but is appropriate because group learning is essentially about the internal and external manifestations of information processing.

Applying our criteria to the examples offered at the beginning of the paper clarifies the meaning of group learning. The case of the engineer who learns a new procedure does not meet the criteria for group learning, even though the new procedure she starts using makes the group perform better. When one person in a group learns something that is not shared with other members of the group, as in this example, this constitutes individual learning, not group learning. In the case of the incident response team, however, learning does occur, because the range of the group's behavior changes (i.e., delaying alerts until a fix is available becomes part of the group's repertoire). As this example reveals, however, not all learning results in positive changes in performance. This example helps to illustrate that, taken alone, changes in performance are not accurate indicators of group learning.

To highlight specific points about group learning, we rely on a group situation that we observed over a period of three years at a national computer emergency response center. The purpose of the center is to respond to threats or attacks on the internet infrastructure (such as a widespread worm or virus). Whenever such attacks occur, an incident response team is formed to deal with the attack. This team works with external experts to identify a fix or patch, keeps the broader community informed about the incident, and generally serves as an unbiased source of information (not affiliated with any software providers). At the time of our observation, the core members of this team included Kyle (the team leader), Aaron, Seth, Alex, Chris, Mitch, and Sam. Depending on the nature of the attack, the team can expand to include members of other incident response teams, experts at vendor sites (when vulnerabilities in their software are being exploited), and government officials. In a serious attack, the team may field hundreds of emails about the incident, work around the clock for several days, and deal with dozens of national media inquiries about the incident.

Building on this case and previous research on group learning, we outline an approach to group learning that specifies the necessary and sufficient conditions for group learning to occur. Our approach to group learning clarifies theoretical issues about level of analysis while disentangling group learning from other related constructs, such as group performance or decision making. We also focus attention on critical but understudied topics, such as negative learning, and neglected processes, such as storage and retrieval. Previous definitions of group learning (Argote et al., 2001; Crossan et al., 1999; Edmondson, 1999) have focused primarily on the process of sharing in group learning; as a result, most of the empirical research to date samples only part of the total construct space. Finally, our approach highlights opportunities for new methods in studying group learning.

Basic Features of Group Learning

Sharing

We define sharing as the process by which new knowledge, routines, or behavior becomes distributed among group members and members understand that others in the group possess that learning. Group learning must be shared, taking on structural properties and exerting influence beyond the individuals who constitute the collective, before it becomes a legitimate group construct (Morgeson & Hofmann, 1999). An example of sharing can be found in Devadas and Argote (1995), who showed that when a group embedded knowledge in its roles and procedures, this learning managed to persist, even in the face of extensive turnover within the group.

There are at least three stages in the development of shared knowledge. In the first stage an individual member's repertoire changes to incorporate some new knowledge, routine, or behavior, *x*. For example, in the incident response teams we studied, a major responsibility is disseminating accurate information about an attack. And, in this case, an example of a change in knowledge (*x*) was Alex's realization that "we need to use a set of Frequently Asked Questions (FAQs) because 95 percent of the questions from the media are the same." This does not change the group's repertoire, since only one person possesses the learning. If that person leaves the group, the knowledge is lost.

At the second stage in the acquisition of shared knowledge, imagine that several of the other group members have the same understanding about *x*, in this case the need for FAQs to reduce redundancy when responding to media inquiries. However, the other members each acquired the same knowledge of how to handle redundant media questions independently, and each person thinks that he or she is the only group member who knows about the redundancy. In such a situation, although each member possesses the learning, there still is no shared understanding at the group level about *x*, the need for a set of FAQs—no group-level learning has occurred. The learning would not be enacted in a situation that required the other members to share the knowledge, because each person thinks he or she is the only group member who knows about the redundancy.

In the third stage a shared understanding of *x* allows knowledge to be transferred to new group members and decreases the probability that the learning will be lost over time. We stipulate that group learning occurs when the members possess both the knowledge (in this case, that using FAQs will help them deal with redundant media questions) and an understanding (either explicit or tacit) that others have the same knowledge and it is a property of the group. This means that a new group repertoire now exists, and it is independent of any particular individual. The process of sharing also serves to legitimate the knowledge for the group. When this happens, the learning becomes a group-level construct that can survive the turnover of any members. More important, people in the group are able to anticipate how other members will respond in certain situations and to act accordingly, a crucial capability when tasks are interdependent.

Shared information is also mutually enhancing for group members—validating members' knowledge and helping group members relate to each other (Wittenbaum, Hubbell, & Zuckerman, 1999). When sharing is complete, these factors are present and, consequently, learning occurs at the level of the group. From this conceptualization of sharing, we propose that the depth and breadth of sharing about any given learning are directly related to the probability of group retrieval of that learning. "Depth of group learning" refers to the level of detail about any particular knowledge, routine, or behavior that is shared by members of the group (such as under what circumstances it is appropriate to apply the new learning). For instance, by focusing on when to use the new knowledge or routine, the retrieval cues become clearer. "Breadth of group learning" refers to the distribution of the learning within the group—how many members share understanding about the new knowledge or routine. The more group members share the learning, the greater the probability it will be retrieved in the future. Greater depth and breadth of shared understanding should be associated with stronger encoding of that learning. Accordingly, we predict the following.

Proposition 1: The depth and breadth of sharing among group members about any given knowledge, routine, or behavior improve storage and retrieval of that information.

Some current research on group learning does address the concept of sharing. Edmondson (2002) theoretically develops the specific processes by which sharing can happen—that is, by having the group take time to raise questions and to reflect on what happens as members work. She also discusses how a lack of sharing disrupts learning, as well as situations that inhibit sharing, such as when the group becomes too absorbed in what it is doing to take time for reflection and, thus, loses an opportunity for sharing. Laughlin and Shupe (1996) provide a good example of empirically validating whether sharing occurred when assigning groups the task of learning the correct rule for partitioning a deck of cards. By observing and modeling the processes each group used to reach a decision (e.g., voting), they could track exactly when and how individual learning became shared within the group.

For sharing to be effective, several subprocesses must take place. The group must (1) focus its attention on the information that is to be learned, (2) develop a shared understanding of the specific learning, and (3) marshal some shared understanding about using this new knowledge in the future. Most research has focused on how groups develop a shared understanding of some event (typically through discussion or observation; cf. Gruenfeld, Martorana, & Fan, 2000; Moreland & Myaskovsky, 2000). Measures of the constructs of reflexivity (Schippers, Den Hartog, & Koopman, 2007) and team learning behavior (Van der Vegt & Bunderson, 2005) are also closely related to this aspect of sharing. We know much less about the first and third subprocesses—that is, why groups focus on a particular item and how they develop a collective understanding of how and when to use the knowledge in the future. Below we show how concentrating on these neglected aspects of sharing leads to interesting research possibilities.

We start by considering how a group's focus of attention affects what it learns. Why do groups learn some things easily but repeatedly fail to learn other—often important—items? As an example, the computer emergency response teams we observed seemed quite capable of learning how to do technical processes differently but repeatedly failed to learn how to improve their internal team processes. For instance, they frequently adjusted their automated email system to send more timely alerts to the internet community but continually failed to change their staffing patterns in order to respond more effectively to serious attacks.

Biases in a group's focus of attention may provide one overlooked explanation for the observation that organizational groups often seem incapable of learning how to improve their own functioning (Argyris, 2003; Tjosvold, Yu, & Hui, 2004). One of the contributing factors may be the phenomenon of "team halo"—the observation that both groups and individuals are more likely to attribute failures to individuals and successes to the group (Naquin & Tynan, 2003). In other words, both groups and individuals have difficulty thinking of "the group" as the source of problems. So when members of a group are faced with a problem and are inclined to think about how to change in the future, they are predisposed to think of *individual-level*—not group-level—actions. We observed this phenomenon in our own study of the computer emergency response teams. In group discussions regarding their performance on recent incidents, team members would be more likely to focus on individual-level changes ("Next time *I* will notify the Australians first") than on group-level changes ("*We* should hold press conferences whenever the incident spreads beyond 500 users"). This is one reason that group learning can be especially difficult.

Proposition 2: Groups are more likely to focus their attention on changes to individual-level rather than group-level routines, decreasing the probability that group learning will occur.

Even if the group effectively focuses its attention and develops a shared understanding of what it needs to learn, it still may not achieve a shared intention to behave differently in the future (the third component of sharing). Psychological safety, characterized by a willingness to confront one another and an openness to experimentation, is one predictor of group members sharing an intention to change their repertoire of behaviors. In her study of learning patterns in an office products company, Edmondson (2002) describes two teams, the Strategy team and the Radar team, both of which failed to change their repertoires because they avoided conflicts associated with committing to a specific future direction. In comparison, teams that were characterized by higher levels of psychological safety were able to commit to using their knowledge in the future. We propose that, in addition to psychological safety, there are also other variables at the group level of analysis that affect the extent to which groups will share a commitment to change their own routines. Factors such as collective efficacy and the presence of group goals may increase the probability that groups will focus on future applications of new knowledge or routines.

Proposition 3: Groups with higher levels of collective efficacy will be more likely to share a commitment to changing their own routines.

Proposition 4: Group discussion about performance discrepancies that reflects past, present, and future scenarios increases the probability of group learning.

We recognize that the notion of how shared an understanding needs to be within a group is a complex question and has been the subject of debates in the literature on shared mental models (Cannon-Bowers, Salas, & Converse, 1993; Klimoski & Mohammed, 1994; Levine, Resnick, & Higgins, 1993). One issue is how many members have to share knowledge before group learning occurs. Shared learning in groups is not an all-or-nothing phenomenon. It is analogous to partial learning in individuals—when a person learns some, but not all, of what he or she needs to know about a particular issue. Another question is whether members may possess slightly different variations on the same knowledge yet still call it shared (in our computer emergency response teams, think of a set of FAQs versus a set of automated responses versus a set of talking points for the hotline staff). For example, in Edmondson et al. (2001), one member claimed that the group had learned to be less hierarchical because team members were referring to each other by their first names. Without asking other members if they shared this perception, however, we do not know whether they had different interpretations of what it means to address people by their first names.

Sharing is a key feature for defining group-level learning that also shapes two other important learning processes: knowledge storage and retrieval. Future research on group learning needs to be more explicit about why groups focus on certain objects in their environment but not others, and how groups develop a shared understanding about using their knowledge in the future.

Storage

Another feature of group learning is that the change in the group's repertoire needs to be stored in memory. Storage is necessary for learning to persist over time, so much so that others have defined learning as the exploitation of stored knowledge (Moorman & Miner, 1998). In our discussion of storage, we focus on how knowledge that has been learned by the group comes to be stored and retained in memory repositories or storage bins used in group-level learning.

A review of the group learning literature reveals little attention to storage processes or memory systems. The notable exception is work on transactive memory. That research focuses on who knows what within the group, how that information is acquired, and the consequences of levels of transactive memory for group functioning (Moreland et al., 1998). A growing body of work suggests that as group members gain experience with one another and gather knowledge of their fellow members' competencies, a variety of group outcomes improve (e.g., quality, satisfaction).

Unfortunately, the research literature on group-level storage is otherwise limited. Researchers primarily have focused on a single repository (human memory) and only considered the types of knowledge that are largely explicit and concrete, rather than implicit or tacit. The interaction between type of knowledge and repository remains unexplored. A variety of repositories (e.g., human memory, computer databases) and different types of knowledge (i.e., tacit or explicit) must be taken into account in order to fully understand how groups store knowledge. One unexplored area is the fit between different types of repositories and different types of knowledge and the implications of fit (or lack thereof) for group-level learning.

Under the heading of storage, there is little group research about retention—the persistence, decay, or distortion of stored knowledge, routines, or behavior over time. Because most experimental studies of group learning have taken place within a single session (e.g., Mathieu, Heffner, Goodwin, Salas, & Cannon-Bowers, 2000) or over the relatively short span of a week (e.g., Moreland et al., 1998), they provide little opportunity to test the persistence or accuracy of group knowledge over time. Since most organizational actions and decisions rely on knowledge that has been stored for more than a few hours or a week, it seems imperative to understand the effect that time has on a group's stored knowledge, as well as the decay rates of different types of repositories.

How can we expand our theoretical understanding of group storage or memory processes? In this section we consider the common features of storage repositories that are available to groups and then the differences in these storage repositories. We also examine how the type of storage repository interacts with characteristics of the learning itself, and how different features of groups affect their storage practices. Finally, we consider how time and the group's external environment affect group storage through practice.

Because groups have access to a greater range of storage repositories than individuals, research is needed about the advantages and liabilities of each type of repository. Memories of group members constitute the most obvious group repository. This has been the focus of the research on transactive memory. In this case, creating a division of labor among the members in terms of who knows what illustrates one power of storage at the group versus individual level. Another type of repository includes formal group memory systems that emerge from groups' information technology structure. Shared databases, bulletin boards, and expert systems are examples of this type of repository (Olivera, 2000). Finally, structural storage repositories such as standard rules, procedures, and cultural artifacts can store group knowledge (Argote, 1999). Acknowledging these multiple repositories is important, because they represent different systems for storage and different functionalities for acquisition, retention, and retrieval.

Group storage repositories have a number of common features that impact group-level learning. Indexing, filtering, and maintenance functions are important components of any storage system (Olivera, 2000). Good indexing systems facilitate both where information is stored and how it is retrieved. Filtering is a process that screens out irrelevancies before information is stored. Maintaining a memory system refers to updating information, deleting obsolete data, and so forth. We expect that these features of storage systems will affect both the use and the utility of the storage process. We propose that group storage systems with indexing, filtering, and maintenance capabilities will be used more often than systems without those features. Similarly, groups that use storage systems with strong indexing, filtering, and maintenance capabilities will ultimately exhibit higher rates of learning.

Indexing, filtering, and maintenance of stored group memories can be much more complex, and therefore potentially more interesting, than corresponding processes at the individual level of analysis. For instance, we expect that the network structure of the group will affect the indexing and updating of stored memories. We predict that members with higher centrality in the group will play a stronger role in indexing than other members of the group. A member with high centrality is more likely to know where knowledge is stored in the group and to serve as a pointer to that knowledge. This also means that the loss of group members with high centrality is likely to sever the "connective tissue" that enables many group storage systems to work. For all of these reasons we need to know much more about how groups use different storage systems.

Proposition 5: Group storage systems with strong indexing, filtering, and maintenance capabilities will be used more often than systems without those features. Groups that use storage systems with indexing, filtering, and maintenance capabilities will ultimately exhibit higher rates of learning than groups that do not.

Proposition 6: Group members with high centrality in the group will be more involved in indexing stored memories than other members of the group.

There are also important differences among the types of storage repositories available to groups. In the case of group members' memories, this repository can manage relatively complex material and handle both tacit and explicit knowledge. Of course, there are limits to the information any individual can process (Simon, 1947), but a formal division of labor can enhance the total memory capacity of the group. In comparison, formal memory systems (such as databases) can store large amounts of data, if they have good indexing, filtering, and maintenance processes. But these systems are better for concrete and less complex knowledge (Goodman & Darr, 1996). In structural repositories one can embed both explicit and tacit understandings and complex ideas in rules and procedures. However, future generations will have difficulty accessing the meta-ideas that lead to these new production procedures, and may therefore find it difficult to modify the rules and procedures for new contextual situations. That is, there may be a lot of know-how (both explicit and implicit) behind the creation of a new rule or learning, but typically the production rule is stored in structural repositories on its own, without any of the knowledge that led to its creation. We propose that there is an interaction between the type of knowledge and the type of group storage repository that influences the effectiveness of storage and retrieval.

Proposition 7: Knowledge or routines that are primarily explicit can be stored in any of the three types of group storage repositories. Knowledge or routines that are more tacit can be more easily stored and retrieved in human memory systems.

In addition to having access to a range of storage repositories, groups provide unique (and largely unexplored) opportunities for practice and storage. With individual-level learning we know that elaborative processing improves memory or storage through the enhancement of retrieval cues (Anderson, 2000). "Elaboration" refers to a process by which subjects create additional ways of recalling information. For instance, nonelaborative processing at the individual level, on the one hand, might involve simply reading an assigned passage about chemistry. Elaborative processing, on the other hand, might include generating questions before reading the text and drawing a concept map of the key points.

In the context of group learning, group discussion can serve as a form of elaboration or practice. In our example of the computer emergency response teams, elaboration would include a group discussion in which members would review how best to respond to an attack and consider—as a group—the circumstances under which they might or might not use a press conference to disseminate information to the outside world. The more elaborated the discussion of when to use a press conference and the greater the consensus, the more likely the group is to retrieve their shared learning regarding a press conference in the future. Through elaboration, the learning becomes stronger, and it is stored with multiple group members. Indicators of elaboration could include differentiated discussions of (1) situations in which particular learning should or should not be retrieved or (2) alternative storage and retrieval mechanisms.

Proposition 8: Elaboration by the group about when and where to use learning strengthens the memory record.

Time and a group's external environment also affect group storage—through practice (reinforcement of the learning through rehearsal). The effectiveness of storage depends on how the practice schedules are distributed over time. When practice schedules are distributed over time, it may take groups longer to acquire the knowledge or routine, but the rate of forgetting may be slower than in a more massed practice schedule (Donovan & Radosevich, 1999). Also, the better the match between the distributed practice schedule and the timing of the event evoking the learning, the better the retention of the learning. In the case of the computer emergency response teams, for instance, major incidents occurred several times a year. In this situation, if the group reviewed its routines for responding to attacks on a periodic basis, it would be more likely to successfully retrieve group learning when the next attack occurred. Matching the practice schedule to the rhythm of events in their environment improves storage for two reasons. First, group members learn that there are lags (i.e., months rather than days) in evoking these new routines; second, rehearsing or practicing periodically creates additional contextual cues that can enhance retrieval processes.

Proposition 9: The more closely a group's practice schedule matches the rhythm of events in its environment, the greater the probability of retrieving the group learning.

Retrieval

The final requirement for group learning is retrieval. Retrieval means that group members can find and access the knowledge for subsequent inspection or use. It is not unusual for members of a group to think that they have stored new learning, only to discover that the group does not access it when the next opportunity to apply the learning presents itself. We observed this multiple times with the response teams, when, for instance, members shared learning about the importance of establishing a protocol for real-time updating of all team members' technical understanding of an incident as it unfolded. Even though this learning was repeatedly shared among team members and was stored in at least one formal After Action Review document and in the memories of at least four team members, core team members failed to even mention the learning, much less enact it, during subsequent incidents. Despite the importance of retrieval for group learning and the fact that retrieval has been identified as the most critical part of the learning process at the individual level (Anderson, 2000; Loewenstein, Thompson, & Gentner, 2003), this process has been largely ignored in the literature on group learning.

Few studies of group learning even discuss the process of retrieval, and even fewer actually measure whether and how retrieval occurs. One exception is Hollingshead's (1998) study of the effects of communication during learning and recall in dyads of strangers and dyads of couples. She found that when partners could communicate during the learning task, strangers actually recalled *more* words than dating couples. She suggested that communication can impede the coordination of learning new material in groups when the members try to develop new strategies for storage and retrieval that depart from their implicit knowledge about each other's relative expertise. In another study Cohen and Bacdayan (1994) focused on how retrieval in groups can be reliable but not valid. These authors described how a feature in the task environment should cue the retrieval of particular learning, arguing that when the rules change, the same feature will cause the retrieval mechanism to misfire. Their experimental manipulation demonstrated exactly this process: they changed the rules of their task and showed that groups still retrieved the old (and now outmoded) learning.

Unfortunately, what we know about the retrieval of group learning is not only limited by the fact that there are very few studies but also by the context of the laboratory tasks. In many laboratory studies of learning, learning is not examined over time, and the researchers control the stimuli. Consequently, we know very little about whether groups will undertake a search for stored memories over time, what their search strategies will entail, and how they will respond if their search fails. We need a framework that accounts for the complexities of group learning in an organizational setting.

For a group to effectively retrieve stored knowledge, several subprocesses must take place: (1) the group or one of its members, faced with some stimulus object, must recognize the need to access stored knowledge; (2) the group, or at least one member, must identify where the knowledge is stored; and, finally, (3) the group must actually retrieve the knowledge. Eventually, we must also consider whether the group can apply the retrieved knowledge in the new situation. Although these subprocesses also occur in individual-level learning, several unique aspects of these subprocesses are critical to understanding how learning occurs at the group level. As we will explain, there are a number of reasons why individual recall may not translate into group retrieval.

In complex organizational settings, group retrieval is difficult for a number of reasons. First, time plays an important role. The longer the time period, the greater the probability of forgetting the original learning event, the more difficult it will be to reconstruct the meaning of the earlier event for the present stimulus, and the more the contexts between the earlier and present events are likely to differ. Second, in groups, the social distance between members may also interfere with retrieval. In the case of the incident response teams we studied, it may be especially difficult for Chris to help the group retrieve what Sam has stored, because Sam's knowledge is less familiar or salient to Chris. Because Sam and Chris are not close in the social network, the group learning stored in their respective memories is less accessible to each other.

A third factor is that the group may have learned subsequent knowledge, behavior, or routines that make it difficult to access the original learning. Groups present unique opportunities for interference (the negative relationship between learning two sets of material—when learning x interferes with the learning of y). The interesting dimensions of this problem at the group level are apparent in the case of a product development team. Effective group learning of a new quality improvement process was diminished by retrieval problems. A critical mass of group members (primarily the designers) had mental models of quality that were focused more on aesthetics than on precise measurement. Even though the knowledge of the quality improvement process was shared through training and stored in manuals on everyone's desk, the principles of the new process were not retrieved or applied. Prior learning and existing group mental models about quality interfered with the retrieval of the new learning.

Proactive interference (when previous learning interferes with the retrieval of new learning) may make group learning or adaptation to new circumstances particularly difficult. To understand why this may be so, we extend well-understood principles of group information sharing to propose new ways of thinking about group learning. Group retrieval can be thought of as a sampling problem (Stasser & Titus, 1985). To change the range of potential behavior in the group, the understandings and memories of multiple team members must be updated in the same time frame. If this is not accomplished, a group attempting to retrieve learning will be more likely to retrieve old (and possibly outmoded) learning.

Extending this reasoning to our understanding of group learning has interesting implications. It suggests that the longer groups are in existence (and the stronger their established practice effects), the lower the probability the groups will retrieve new (and updated) learning. This group tenure effect may account for differences in perceptions of group learning between laboratory studies (where new groups are formed and group learning is treated as routine; Gruenfeld et al., 2000; Moreland et al., 1998) and field studies (where groups have been in existence for some time and group learning is treated as difficult and rare; Argyris & Schön, 1995; Edmondson, 1999; Gersick & Hackman, 1990).

Proposition 10: The longer group members have worked together, the stronger the established practice effects and the lower the probability of retrieving new learning.

Social processes in groups may also interfere with effective retrieval (Finlay, Hitch, & Meudell, 2000). We know that on free recall tasks, collaborating groups retrieve fewer items than the same number of individuals working in nominal groups (Basden, Basden, Bryner, & Thomas, 1997). Although there is some preliminary evidence that cognitive social loafing does *not* account for collaborative retrieval problems (Weldon, Blair, & Huebsch, 2000), there may be other phenomena in groups that make retrieval in social situations more difficult. The combination of status differences and evaluation apprehension (Diehl & Stroebe, 1987) may combine to cause low-status group members to withhold knowledge or cues for retrieving collective learning. It is clear that more research is needed to understand how group members retrieve and collectively evaluate memory evidence when social issues such as status, familiarity, and group faultlines can affect the outcomes.

It is interesting to consider what features of groups or group-level learning would offset some of the difficulties of retrieval and would differentiate this literature from individual-level retrieval. First, groups represent collections of individuals and are subject to division of labor, where members divide the responsibility for storing different learning. Second and less well-recognized, group members serve not only as potential repositories for group learning but also as cues for the retrieval of particular information. We know that people serve as particularly strong cues for recall (Smith & Vela, 2001). So, when the computer emergency response teams were learning to use press conferences early in the trajectory of an incident, the team leader, Kyle, spent the most time advocating the use of press conferences originally (sharing) and was implicitly designated as the repository for this learning (storage). Traditionally, researchers would have focused on Kyle's role in personally retrieving the use of press conferences as an instance of group learning during the next incident. In our observation, however, even though Kyle was present in the early deliberations during the next incident, he did not personally retrieve the group's agreement that they would call an early press conference in major incidents. Kyle's physical presence seemed to prime another team member (Aaron) to recall the particular group learning regarding early press conferences. This example of retrieval highlights important but neglected aspects of the group learning process, beyond the explicit division of labor for the recall of group learning. Individual team members serve two roles in group retrieval: (1) as repositories for group learning and (2) as cues to search for particular knowledge or routines. Group members have been explored as *repositories* of group knowledge in the transactive memory literature, but the larger literature has ignored their function as cues for retrieval.

From this expanded view of the group member as both a repository of learning and as a cue for recall, we would expect that for groups operating in complex and dynamic environments, cognitive division of labor with respect to individual members explicitly responsible for storage and recall should enhance the probability of recall. At the same time, we would expect more rapid decay of learning among group members who are not explicitly responsible for either storage or retrieval of certain information that has been learned by the group. Therefore, groups with more stable membership will have more reliable retrieval processes. In groups with explicit role assignments for storage and recall, the retrieval will be affected by the presence or absence of members, something particularly important in geographically distributed groups whose members do not necessarily "see" one another while working together. These unexplored effects of group member presence on group retrieval are highlighted below.

Proposition 11: The presence of a member with stored knowledge can cue retrieval of that knowledge without any additional priming, improving the group's chances for successful retrieval.

Proposition 12: The reduced "presence" of group members in geographically distributed groups will be associated with less reliable retrieval of group learning.

Overlap of Sharing, Storage, and Retrieval

Although we have dealt with sharing, storage, and retrieval separately for the sake of clarity, in practice, the three processes are intertwined. All three processes must take place for group learning to occur (represented as an equation: GL = Sharing * Storage * Retrieval). Without sharing there can only be individual learning in a group context. Without storage and retrieval of shared learning, the group's repertoire cannot change over time. The relationships among the three processes are illustrated in Figure 9.1.1. One advantage of our framework is that it highlights the interactions among these processes of group learning. For instance, one of the interesting possibilities we have discussed is the interaction between sharing and a group's ability to store and retrieve particular learning. One general principle about group learning is that sharing affects the robustness of the group learning through storage and retrieval. We have suggested that, in groups, increasing the breadth of sharing provides a buffer against the decay of learning because the learning is stored in multiple team members' memories (path 1 in Figure 9.1) and sharing creates a wider net of people able to respond to retrieval cues (path 4).

Although it may be clear that sharing affects storage (path 1) and storage affects retrieval

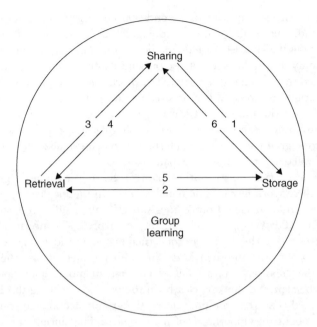

Figure 9.1.1 Interaction of Sharing, Storage, and Retrieval in Group Learning.

(path 2), there are also reverse feedback loops such that retrieval affects storage and sharing. A general principle about the relationship between retrieval and the other group learning processes is that nothing can be retrieved without at least subtly changing the content of group learning or the path to that group learning. For example, in the process of retrieving knowledge, behavior, or routines that have been learned, a group's paths to some storage mechanisms are strengthened while others decay (i.e., retrieval affects storage; path 5). As the computer emergency response team attempted to retrieve its learning about automated email updates, the group relied on Kyle to retrieve this learning, completely forgetting that the learning was stored in an After Action Review document on its intranet. The path to Kyle started out stronger for the team than its path to the intranet storage bin, and the team's continued reliance on Kyle as a retrieval mechanism further weakened its path to the intranet storage repository. This preference for retrieval paths not only affects the current instance of group learning but reinforces a general norm that the team will look to individual members to remind them of agreed-upon changes to their routines. In other words, the preference not only affects the group's current learning but also affects group norms about which storage bins it consults in the future. Thus, one of the uniquely "group" aspects of learning is that the processes of sharing, storage, and retrieval change not only the group's knowledge but the group's norms as well.

One of the other uniquely "group" aspects of learning is that the retrieval process can also serve as a sharing mechanism (path 3). In individual learning, retrieval is a largely nonverbal, cognitive process. In groups, however, retrieval often requires verbal interaction. One group member, Alex, may recognize the need to retrieve learning ("Didn't we agree on a different way to handle this?"). Another group member, Mitch, may direct the group to a particular storage bin ("Yes, I think it is in our notes from 7/18"). A third group member, Sam, may shortcut the search by saying that the group agreed to post a press release on its web site whenever an incident spreads beyond 500 end users. A fourth group member, Seth, may "second" this recall. As the group engages in sensemaking, it recreates shared understanding about the knowledge. This additional round of sharing can often strengthen the original memory record. However, it also presents an opportunity for the original learning to be distorted so that what gets retrieved (a short, one-page press release) is different from what was originally stored (a live press conference). The now-distorted retrieval can then replace or overwrite the original learning in the group's memory. So while verbal interaction upon retrieval can serve as a form of sharing, it also provides an opportunity for distortion as the group attempts to reinterpret or recontextualize the recalled learning. In this way, retrieval develops into sharing (path 3).

Group storage can also lead to sharing (path 6). Storing learning in group-accessible spaces provides the opportunity for additional sharing. In the incident response teams we studied, having clearly understood procedures was critical for effective responding during crises. During the TCP Wrappers incident, the team became concerned about what it termed *distraction protection*. Members were concerned that an intruder might launch a second attack while the group was absorbed in dealing with the first attack. The group shared learning about the importance of sending some team members home for sleep so that someone would be alert and thinking clearly. In the process of storing this learning in the group's documented crisis response procedures, the group encountered seemingly contradictory learning about the importance of increasing staffing during crises so that some team members could monitor the normal traffic of incoming emails. This prompted additional discussion about priorities and resulted in the modification of both the old and new learning.

Identifying the processes that constitute group learning not only clarifies the necessary and sufficient conditions for group learning but also focuses attention on the relationships among these processes. While it is possible to examine each of these processes independently, we think the interactions among the processes have the greatest potential for study and practice. These relationships also provide a roadmap for diagnosing group learning failures. When groups fail to retrieve knowledge, the cause is not necessarily with group retrieval mechanisms; it may be traced to problems in sharing or storage, or the interaction of the processes.

Discussion and Implications

The framework we have outlined in this paper is designed to change how people study group learning. Our goals were to identify (1) the features of group learning, (2) gaps in the literature, (3) new propositions for research, and (4) new ways of thinking about group learning. We have argued that change is needed because there currently is no integrated view of group-level learning. The varied definitions we highlighted earlier point to the disjointed treatment of this fundamental construct. Papers purporting to cover group learning measure everything from individual learning in the context of groups to changes in group performance (confusing other variables with group learning). We have advanced a conceptualization that reconciles different views of group learning with an emphasis on the processes that define learning at the group level. Without a shared understanding of group learning, it will be impossible to accumulate evidence in any coherent way.

To advance the study of group learning, it is especially important to be clear about the level of analysis (in both the conceptualization of group learning and its measurement). In particular, group learning should not be confused with individual learning in the context of groups. Individual-level learning in social situations is already amply covered by such concepts as social learning (Bandura, 1977) and situated learning (Lave & Wenger, 1991). Nor should learning by top management teams be confused with organizational learning. Failure to be clear about issues related to the level of analysis leads to imprecision in models, confusion in data collection and analysis, and controversy regarding conclusions (Klein et al., 1994).

We also have argued for an increased focus on the processes inherent in group learning: sharing, storage, and retrieval. There are two important reasons for this. First, when we talk about learning, our expectation is that a group confronting a new but similar situation can retrieve what it learned at an earlier time. Retrieval is intimately tied to the storage and sharing processes. We are not interested in whether a group was trained or it stored some information but, rather, whether it can enact these basic processes in an integrated way. Second, without a focus on the basic mechanisms of group learning, it can be difficult to distinguish learning from other exogenously induced group performance changes. For instance, if a group's level of customer satisfaction improves, is this due to changes in the group's routines or changes in the group's mix of customers? Without understanding the group's processes of sharing, storage, and retrieval, it is hard to attribute the change to learning. A focus on the processes of group learning opens up new and exciting avenues for research regarding practice, decay, priming, and other processes reviewed in the propositions we have outlined.

In addition, defining the construct space brings critical gaps in the literature into focus. First, there is a gap in understanding basic concepts such as group-level storage and retrieval. For example, little work has been done on alternative storage systems and their impact on retrieval. Second, researchers have focused on a very limited set of learning outcomes. Research to date has examined the learning of fairly simple concrete knowledge, as opposed to more complex, abstract, or tacit knowledge or routines. We encourage researchers to explore the full range of group learning outcomes, including cognitive outcomes (we think differently about responding to media requests), behavioral outcomes (we act differently in situations involving media requests), and emotional outcomes (we feel differently when confronted with media requests). Third, the majority of group learning research has a positive bias. The prevailing assumption is that learning generally leads to beneficial effects. Little attention is given to how groups learn dysfunctional routines or how groups learn about incorrect relationships.

In addition to responding to gaps and testing new propositions, there are other new opportunities for research. One interesting opportunity deals with the form of groups to study. One can contrast traditional face-to-face groups, composed of members from the same organization that persist over time, with groups operating in a distributed environment, composed of members from different organizations, which by their nature have a very short life (Goodman & Wilson, 2000). Most of the larger computer emergency groups we studied functioned together for several hours or a few days, but then never met again. The question is how do the processes of sharing, storage, and retrieval occur in these very different kinds of groups? Can we talk about group-level learning for a group that lasts for three hours, disbands, and never meets again? Thinking about groups that vary along these multiple dimensions challenges our thinking about how groups learn.

Another opportunity deals with the impact of the external environment on learning. In contrast to individual learning research conducted in the laboratory, groups in organizations typically operate in more dynamic environments; the groups' composition often is in flux; and the knowledge, routines, and behavior they must learn are more complex. For groups embedded in organizations, the environment can change—meaning that learning valid at one time can easily become counterproductive at another time. This suggests that how groups interact with their external environments may significantly affect their ability to adapt. To date, most of the research on group learning has focused on the internal workings of groups. However, we expect that a group's orientation to its external environment (e.g., Ancona & Caldwell, 1992) also will affect the quality and extent of its learning.

Our conceptualization also highlights the possibilities for *implicit* learning at the group level—that is, learning that does not depend on a group's conscious awareness of the learning (Reber, 1989). Our observations indicate that there often are instances in which groups gradually adopt new habits or procedures over time, without being consciously aware that they are changing. Just as individuals often pick up mannerisms unconsciously from their contact with others, we expect that groups will change their repertoires through observation or contact with others. However, we know very little about this form of learning in groups. Thus, key questions for future research include "Under what circumstances is implicit learning most likely to occur?" and "Are there certain group characteristics that make it more likely?"

The final important implication of our framework concerns the methods for studying group learning, which must not only account for learning over time but must also measure the construct at the appropriate level of analysis. As we have illustrated, time is a critical feature of learning. We need to move to research designs that permit different types of practice schedules. We need to examine learning over time to understand such processes as retrieval and transfer of learning. Also, we need to operationalize the concept of group learning and separate learning from performance or other outcomes (Druskat & Kayes, 2000). In terms of data collection, understanding storage or retrieval processes will require detailed, real-time observation. For instance, identifying and analyzing implicit learning requires multiple observations of the same group over time. Because the learning is not necessarily consciously accessible, asking the group members about what they have learned will not uncover any changes. Edmondson (2002) provides a good example of the kind of observation that can identify implicit learnings. By repeatedly observing a senior team over time, she was able to identify learned patterns of behavior (e.g., using metaphors to score philosophical points) that members were not consciously aware of.

A more comprehensive approach for measuring group learning and its component processes can be illustrated using an example from the computer emergency response teams we studied. One learning repeatedly shared in the teams' After Action Reviews was the idea that they should schedule interactive press conferences, rather than simply issuing press releases, in response to major attacks on the internet. This idea was widely discussed after the Love Letters incident, and the incident response team leader was implicitly designated as the storage repository for this knowledge (although it was also stored in the After Action Review notes from both the Love Letters and the TCP Wrappers attacks). A complete measure of group learning in this situation would be spread across at least two time periods. At Time 1 it would be possible to measure sharing and preliminary storage. The *process of sharing* could be studied by observing the group's discussion of the learning at Time 1. For example, we observed the incident response team discuss interactive press conferences as group learning in April following the Love Letters virus. At that time, five group members were present; two (Seth and Alex) explicitly shared the learning during the discussion. The depth of the group's sharing about the interactive press conference learning could be coded on the following scale: 1 = discussed the learning; 3 = discussed the learning and where it should be stored; 5 = discussed the learning, where it should be stored, and the conditions under which it should be evoked in the future. The *outcome of sharing* could be measured by administering a survey with an open-ended item (What did the group learn as a result of this incident?) at the end of time period one (April). The percentage of group members who reported the learning about interactive press conferences would be an indicator of the breadth of sharing. The Time 1 *storage* of learning could be measured on the same survey, by asking group members to indicate where each item the group learned was stored.

Measurement of longer-term storage and retrieval would require an assessment of whether the group could produce the learned response when the appropriate stimuli presented themselves (i.e., at Time 2). One practical problem with this requirement is that it is not always possible to predict when the stimuli to elicit the group learning will next occur in organizations. To deal with the problem of waiting for the next trigger event, we propose an adaptation of the scenario method. Researchers can present groups with scenarios that call for previously learned responses and observe what learning individual members retrieve, as well as the ultimate response produced by the group. So, in our example of response teams, in order to measure longer-term *storage and decay* of this learning, we would recommend waiting for the average interval between incidents (in the case of major attacks on the internet, approximately one month) and then giving each member of the group a scenario describing another major attack and asking how each thinks the group should respond to the incident. In this case, it may be that only two members of the group (Kyle and Aaron) individually recall the idea of using interactive press conferences. This Time 2 result can be compared with the Time 1 storage results to determine the decay of the learning in the group members' memories (e.g., five members stored the learning at Time 1, but it persisted in only two members' memories a month later). To measure actual group *retrieval*, we would also ask the group to agree on a collective approach to the situation in the scenario (to observe patterns in the retrieval process). By observing the group's discussion of how to respond in the situation, we would observe what storage repositories the group uses (e.g., Does anyone mention the After Action Review agreements?) and what is, or is not, ultimately retrieved. It may be that neither of the members who individually recalled the press conference learning would bring it up in the group retrieval period. In that case, even though the learning is still stored in the memories of two group members, it is not effectively retrieved by the group as a whole. The scenario method provides the condition for identifying the persistence of the learning, as well as any anomalies in group retrieval.

The conceptualization of group learning that we have presented also has implications for practice. The fundamental processes that we have defined in this paper could be leveraged in the design and diagnosis of groups to improve their adaptability. Groups could be designed with more explicit storage repositories and procedures. Group practice schedules could be developed that more closely mirror changes in the group's environment. And assessments of group functioning could specifically include attention to how the group shares, stores, and retrieves key information. Although group learning has long been recognized as an important indicator of group functioning (Gladstein, 1984), most practical assessments of groups do not yet cover depth and breadth of sharing, the types of storage repositories groups use, or the reliability of their retrieval mechanisms (Fitz-Enz, 1997; Jones & Schilling, 2000).

Groups have been identified as the principal vehicle for learning in organizations

(Edmondson, 2002; Senge, 1990). If groups are so central to the adaptive process in organizations, we need a clearer understanding of group learning. In this paper we have outlined a comprehensive conceptualization of group learning. We have specified the necessary and sufficient conditions for group learning to occur and have used the conceptualization to highlight new areas for inquiry. Our hope is to ultimately advance our ability to explain and predict group learning.

Acknowledgments

We thank Ed Conlon, Amy Edmondson, Carrie Leana, Michelle Marks, Don Moore, Dick Moreland, John Levine, Brandi Pearce, Denise Rousseau, and Susan Straus for their comments on earlier versions of this paper.

References

Ancona, D. G., & Caldwell, D. F. 1992. Bridging the boundary: External activity and performance in organizational teams. *Administrative Science Quarterly*, 37: 634–666.

Anderson, J. R. 2000. *Learning & memory: An integrated approach*. New York: Wiley.

Argote, L. 1996. Organizational learning curves: Persistence, transfer, and turnover. *International Journal of Technology Management*, 11: 759–770.

Argote, L. 1999. *Organizational learning: Creating, retaining and transferring knowledge*. Norwell, MA: Kluwer.

Argote, L., Beckman, S. L., & Epple, D. 1990. The persistence and transfer of learning in industrial settings. *Management Science*, 36: 140–155.

Argote, L., Gruenfeld, D. H., & Naquin, C. 2001. Group learning in organizations. In M. E. Turner (Ed.), *Groups at work: Advances in theory and research*: 369–411. Mahwah, NJ: Lawrence Erlbaum Associates.

Argote, L., & McGrath, J. E. 1993. Group processes in organizations: Continuity and change. *International Review of Industrial and Organizational Psychology*, 8: 333–389.

Argyris, C. 2003. A life full of learning. *Organization Studies*, 24: 11–78.

Argyris, C., & Schön, D. 1995. *Organizational learning: Theory, method and practice*. New York: Addison-Wesley.

Bandura, A. 1977. *Social learning theory*. Englewood Cliffs, NJ: Prentice-Hall.

Basden, B. H., Basden, D. R., Bryner, S., & Thomas, R. L. 1997. A comparison of group and individual remembering: Does collaboration disrupt retrieval strategies? *Journal of Experimental Psychology: Learning, Memory and Cognition*, 23: 1176–1189.

Blickensdorfer, E., Cannon-Bowers, J. A., & Salas, E. 1997. *Training teams to self-correct: An empirical investigation*. Paper presented at the 12th annual meeting of the Society for Industrial and Organizational Psychology, St. Louis.

Cannon-Bowers, J. E., Salas, E., & Converse, S. 1993. Shared mental models in expert team decision-making. In J. Castellan (Ed.), *Individual and group decision making: Current issues*: 221–247. Hillsdale, NJ: Lawrence Erlbaum Associates.

Carley, K. 1992. Organizational learning and personnel turnover. *Organization Science*, 3: 20–46.

Cohen, M. D., & Bacdayan, P. 1994. Organizational routines are stored as procedural memory: Evidence from a laboratory study. *Organization Science*, 5: 554–568.

Cook, S. D., & Yanow, D. 1993. Culture and organizational learning. *Journal of Management Inquiry*, 2: 373–390.

Crossan, M. M., Lane, H. W., & White, R. E. 1999. An organizational learning framework: From learning to institution. *Academy of Management Review*, 24: 522–537.

Devadas, R., & Argote, L. 1995. *Collective learning and forgetting: The effects of turnover and group structure*. Paper presented at the Midwestern Academy of Management, Chicago.

Diehl, M., & Stroebe, W. 1987. Productivity loss in brainstorming groups: Toward the solution of a riddle. *Journal of Personality and Social Psychology*, 53: 497–509.

Donovan, J. J., & Radosevich, D. J. 1999. A meta-analytic review of the distribution of practice effect: Now you see it, now you don't. *Journal of Applied Psychology*, 84: 795–805.

Druskat, V. U. & Kayes, D. C. 2000. Learning versus performance in short-term project teams. *Small Group Research*, 31: 328–353.

Edmondson, A. 1999. Psychological safety and learning behavior in work teams. *Administrative Science Quarterly*, 44: 350–383.

Edmondson, A. 2002. The local and variegated nature of learning in organizations: A group level perspective. *Organization Science*, 13: 128–146.

Edmondson, A. C., Bohmer, R. M., & Pisano, G. P. 2001. Disrupted routines: Team learning and new technology implementation in hospitals. *Administrative Science Quarterly*, 46: 685–716.

Ellis, A. P., Hollenbeck, J. R., Ilgen, D. R., Porter, C. O., & West, B. J. 2003. Team learning: Collectively connecting the dots. *Journal of Applied Psychology*, 88: 821–832.

Finlay, F., Hitch, G. J., & Meudell, P. R. 2000. Mutual inhibition in collaborative recall: Evidence for a retrieval-based account. *Journal of Experimental Psychology: Learning, Memory and Cognition*, 26: 1556–1567.

Fiol, C. M., & Lyles, M. A. 1985. Organizational learning. *Academy of Management Review*, 10: 803–813.

Fitz-Enz, J. 1997. Measuring team effectiveness. *HR Focus*, 74(8): 3–7.

Gersick, C. J. G., & Hackman, J. R. 1990. Habitual routines in task-performing groups. *Organizational Behavior and Human Decision Processes*, 47: 65–97.

Gibson, C., & Vermeulen, F. 2003. A healthy divide: Subgroups as a stimulus for team learning behavior. *Administrative Science Quarterly*, 48: 202–224.

Gladstein, D. 1984. Groups in context: A model of task group effectiveness. *Administrative Science Quarterly*, 29: 499–517.

Goodman, P. S., & Darr, E. D. 1996. Computer-aided systems for organizational learning. *Trends in Organizational Behavior*, 3: 81–97.

Goodman, P. S., & Wilson, J. M. 2000. Substitutes for socialization in exocentric teams. *Research in Groups and Teams*, 3: 53–77.

Gruenfeld, D. H., Martorana, P. V., & Fan, E. T. 2000. What do groups learn from their worldliest members? Direct and indirect influence in dynamic teams. *Organizational Behavior and Human Decision Processes*, 82: 45–59.

Hinsz, V. B., Tindale, R. S., & Vollrath, D. A. 1997. The emerging conceptualization of groups as information processors. *Psychological Bulletin*, 121: 43–65.

Hollingshead, A. B. 1998. Communication, learning and retrieval in transactive memory systems. *Journal of Experimental Social Psychology*, 34: 423–442.

Hollingshead, A. B. 2001. Cognitive interdependence and convergent expectations in transactive memory. *Journal of Personality and Social Psychology*, 81: 1–10.

Huber, G. P. 1991. Organizational learning: The contributing processes and literatures. *Organization Science*, 2: 88–115.

Ilgen, D. R., Hollenbeck, J. R., Johnson, M., & Jundt, D. 2005. Teams in organizations: From I-P-O models to IMOI models. *Annual Review of Psychology*, 56: 517–543.

Ilgen, D. R., & Klein, H. J. 1989. Organizational behavior. *Annual Review of Psychology*, 40: 327–351.

Jones, S. D., & Schilling, D. J. 2000. *Measuring team performance*. New York: Wiley.

Klein, K. J., Dansereau, F., & Hall, R. J. 1994. Levels issues in theory development, data collection, and analysis. *Academy of Management Review*, 19: 195–229.

Klimoski, R., & Mohammed, S. 1994. Team mental model: Construct or metaphor? *Journal of Management*, 20: 403–437.

Lant, T. K. 1992. Aspiration level adaptation: An empirical exploration. *Management Science*, 38: 623–645.

Laughlin, P. R., & Shupe, E. I. 1996. Intergroup collective induction. *Organizational Behavior and Human Decision Processes*, 68: 44–57.

Lave, J., & Wenger, E. 1991. *Situated learning: Legitimate peripheral participation.* Cambridge: Cambridge University Press.

Levine, J. M., Resnick, L. B., & Higgins, E. T. 1993. Social foundations of cognition. *Annual Review of Psychology,* 44: 585–612.

Levitt, B., & March, J. G. 1988. Organizational learning. *Annual Review of Sociology,* 14: 319–340.

Loewenstein, J., Thompson, L., & Gentner, D. 2003. Analogical learning in negotiation teams: Comparing cases promotes learning and transfer. *Academy of Management Learning & Education,* 2: 119–127.

London, M., Polzer, J. T., & Omoregie, H. 2005. Interpersonal congruence, transactive memory, and feedback processes. *Human Resource Development Review,* 4(2): 114–135.

Mathieu, J. E., Heffner, T. S., Goodwin, G. F., Salas, E., & Cannon-Bowers, J. A. 2000. The influence of team mental models on team process and performance. *Journal of Applied Psychology,* 85: 273–283.

Mohammed, S., & Dumville, B. C. 2001. Team mental models in a team knowledge framework: Expanding theory and measurement across disciplinary boundaries. *Journal of Organizational Behavior,* 22: 89–106.

Moorman, C., & Miner, A. S. 1998. Organizational improvisation and organizational memory. *Academy of Management Review,* 23: 698–723.

Moreland, R., Hogg, M. A., & Hanes, S. C. 1994. Back to the future: Social psychological research on groups. *Journal of Experimental Social Psychology,* 30: 527–555.

Moreland, R. L., Argote, L., & Krishnan, R. 1998. Training people to work in groups. In R. S. Tindale (Ed.), *Theory and research in small groups:* 37–60. New York: Plenum Press.

Moreland, R. L., & Myaskovsky, L. 2000. Exploring the performance benefits of group training: Transactive memory or improved communication? *Organization Behavior and Human Decision Processes,* 82: 117–133.

Morgeson, F. P., & Hofmann, D. A. 1999. The structure and function of collective constructs: Implication for multi-level research and theory development. *Academy of Management Review,* 24: 249–265.

Naquin, C. E., & Tynan, R. O. 2003. The team halo effect: Why teams are not blamed for their failures. *Journal of Applied Psychology,* 88: 332–340.

Olivera, F. 2000. Memory systems in organizations: An empirical investigation of mechanisms for knowledge collection, storage and access. *Journal of Management Studies,* 37: 811–832.

Reber, A. S. 1989. Implicit learning and tacit knowledge. *Journal of Experimental Psychology: General,* 118: 219–235.

Rosenthal, R., & Rosnow, R. L. 1991. *Essentials of behavioral research: Methods and data analysis.* New York: McGraw-Hill.

Rousseau, D. M. 1985. Issues of level in organizational research: Multi-level and cross-level perspectives. *Research in Organizational Behavior,* 7: 1–37.

Schippers, M. C., Den Hartog, D. N., & Koopman, P. L. 2007. Reflexivity in teams: A measure and correlates. *Applied Psychology: An International Review,* 56: 189–211.

Senge, P. M. 1990. *The fifth discipline: The art and practice of the learning organization.* New York: Doubleday.

Simon, H. A. 1947. *Administrative behavior.* New York: Macmillan.

Smith, S. M., & Vela, E. 2001. Environmental context-dependent memory: A review and meta-analysis. *Psychonomic Bulletin and Review,* 8: 203–220.

Snyder, M., & Gangestad, S. 1986. On the nature of self-monitoring: Matters of assessment, matters of validity. *Journal of Personality and Social Psychology,* 51: 125–139.

Sole, D., & Edmondson, A. 2002. Situated knowledge and learning in dispersed teams. *British Journal of Management,* 13: 17–34.

Stasser, G., & Titus, W. 1985. Pooling of unshared information in group decision-making: Biased information sampling during discussion. *Journal of Personality and Social Psychology,* 48: 1467–1478.

Sutton, R. I., & Staw, B. M. 1995. What theory is not. *Administrative Science Quarterly,* 40: 371–384.

Tjosvold, D., Yu, Z., & Hui, C. 2004. Team learning from mistakes: The contribution of cooperative goals and problem-solving. *Journal of Management Studies,* 41: 1223–1245.

Tolman, E. C. 1932. *Purposive behavior in animals and man.* New York: Appleton-Century-Crofts.

Van der Vegt, G. S., & Bunderson, J. S. 2005. Learning and performance in multi-disciplinary teams: The importance of collective identification. *Academy of Management Journal*, 48: 532–547.

Weldon, M. S., Blair, C., & Huebsch, P. D. 2000. Group remembering: Does social loafing underlie collaborative inhibition? *Journal of Experimental Psychology: Learning, Memory and Cognition*, 26: 1568–1577.

Whetten, D. A. 1989. What constitutes a theoretical contribution? *Academy of Management Review*, 14: 490–495.

Wittenbaum, G. M., Hubbell, A. P., & Zuckerman, C. 1999. Mutual enhancement: Toward an understanding of the collective preference for shared information. *Journal of Personality and Social Psychology*, 77: 967–978.

Wong, S. S. 2004. Distal and local group learning: Performance tradeoffs and tensions. *Organization Science*, 15: 645–656.

Zellmer-Bruhn, M. E. 2003. Interruptive events and team knowledge acquisition. *Management Science*, 49: 514–528.

9.2   TEAM EFFECTIVENESS 1997–2007

A Review of Recent Advancements and a Glimpse into the Future

John Mathieu, M. Travis Maynard, Tammy Rapp, and Lucy Gilson

The authors review team research that has been conducted over the past 10 years. They discuss the nature of work teams in context and note the substantive differences underlying different types of teams. They then review representative studies that have appeared in the past decade in the context of an enhanced input-process-outcome framework that has evolved into an inputs-mediators-outcome time-sensitive approach. They note what has been learned along the way and identify fruitful directions for future research. They close with a reconsideration of the typical team research investigation and call for scholars to embrace the complexity that surrounds modern team-based organizational designs as we move forward.

Cohen and Bailey's (1997) review of the work teams literature has proven to be one of the most influential *Journal of Management* articles, with more than 545 citations as of 2007 (Harzing, 2007). Although they concluded at the time that substantial knowledge about teams had accumulated, they predicted that much would be learned in the future. As they anticipated, there has been an explosion of work in the decade since their review. Literally hundreds of primary studies have been conducted, several meta-analyses have been performed, and numerous reviews of the literature have been published (e.g., Ilgen, Hollenbeck, Johnson, & Jundt, 2005; Kozlowski & Bell, 2003; Kozlowski & Ilgen, 2006; McGrath, Arrow, & Berdahl, 2001; Salas, Stagl, & Burke, 2004; Sundstrom, McIntyre, Halfhill, & Richards, 2000). Given the enormity of the body of literature on work teams, and the fact that several high-quality reviews exist, we have taken a somewhat different approach for this article. Rather than attempting to provide a comprehensive review of work that has been done over the past 10 years, we have opted to highlight particular examples of themes or trends in the teams research arena. In so doing, we identify what is known, and what remains unknown, in each area. Notably, rather than focusing attention on what has been done, our orientation is more in terms of looking ahead and outlining a future agenda for the next 10 years.

We begin by defining teams and discussing the evolution of the input-process-outcome (IPO) framework for studying team effectiveness. Using this as our foundation, we feature selected works from the past decade that have focused on different aspects of the team effectiveness model. We have chosen these studies because they are either representative of the work that has been done or because they provide a vehicle for highlighting a novel finding or approach. In many cases, meta-analyses have been conducted during this period that serve to summarize trends in the research. Afterwards, we revisit the five substantive areas that Cohen and Bailey (1997) advocated that research should consider and summarize the progress that has been made to date. Finally, we conclude with our own recommendations for future teams research.

Teams Defined

Numerous definitions of groups, teams, and other forms of collectives have been proffered over the years. Such definitions share many attributes and have subtle differences. Given that our focus is on work teams, we adopt a definition advanced by Kozlowski and Bell (2003: 334):

> collectives who exist to perform organizationally relevant tasks, share one or more common goals, interact socially, exhibit task interdependencies, maintain and manage boundaries, and are embedded in an organizational context that sets boundaries, constrains the team, and influences exchanges with other units in the broader entity.

Notably, some of the key elements of this definition are that work teams have some level of interdependence and operate in an organizational context that influences their functioning. Whereas we include research that has been conducted in laboratory or simulated work environments, the target of generalizations for us are *teams in organizations* rather than social groups, sports teams, or collectives that operate in other contexts.

Teams come in many different configurations and are tasked with performing different types of functions. Accordingly, several taxonomies of team types have been advanced in the literature (e.g., Cohen & Bailey, 1997; Devine, 2002; Hackman, 1990; Sundstrom, 1999). Whereas taxonomies draw attention to the fact that not all teams are alike, it is important to appreciate that the categories themselves are simply proxies for more substantive issues. For example, some teams contain fairly functionally homogeneous members, whereas others are usually more functionally heterogeneous. Furthermore, whereas certain teams operate in intense and complex environments, others' environments are more stable. Finally, teams can be distinguished based upon how long they are together as a unit and the fluidity of the team's membership. A theme that we will continually revisit throughout this review is that it is critically important to remember that different types of teams face different demands and as a result function quite differently; it is also true that often there is as much heterogeneity within team types as there is across types. Accordingly, we focus our attention on what we consider to be underlying substantive themes rather than types of teams.

Team Effectiveness Framework

More than 40 years ago, McGrath (1964) advanced an input-process-outcome (IPO) framework for studying team effectiveness. Figure 9.2.1 contains an adapted version of this framework. *Inputs* describe antecedent factors that enable and constrain members'

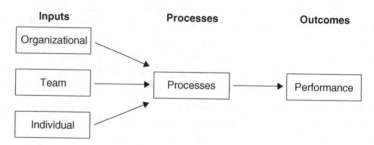

Figure 9.2.1 Input-Process-Outcome (IPO) Team Effectiveness Framework.

interactions. These include *individual team member characteristics* (e.g., competencies, person-alities), *team-level factors* (e.g., task structure, external leader influences), and *organizational and contextual factors* (e.g., organizational design features, environmental complexity). These vari-ous antecedents combine to drive team *processes*, which describe members' interactions dir-ected toward task accomplishment. Processes are important because they describe how team inputs are transformed into outcomes. *Outcomes* are results and by-products of team activity that are valued by one or more constituencies (Mathieu, Heffner, Goodwin, Salas, & Cannon-Bowers, 2000). Broadly speaking, these may include *performance* (e.g., quality and quantity) and members' *affective reactions* (e.g., satisfaction, commitment, viability).

The IPO model has served as a valuable guide for researchers over the years, but it has also been modified and extended in several ways (Cohen & Bailey, 1997; Hackman & Morris, 1975; Ilgen et al., 2005; McGrath et al., 2001; Salas, Dickinson, Converse, & Tannenbaum, 1992). Most of the adaptations to the IPO model have either placed it in a larger context, emphasized a temporal element, or rediscovered more subtle aspects of the model that have gone overlooked. For example, Cohen and Bailey (1997) addressed the contextual issue by depicting environmental factors as drivers of team and compositional inputs. In effect, this approach embraces the inherent multilevel nature of teams, in that individuals are nested in teams, which in turn are nested in organizations, which exist in

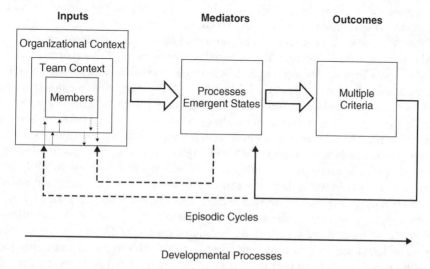

Figure 9.2.2 Input-Mediator-Outcome (IMO) Team Effectiveness Framework.

environments. Whereas more complex work arrangements exist as well (a point we will return to later), this nesting arrangement of entities is a hallmark of multilevel models (Klein & Kozlowski, 2000). As shown in Figure 9.2.2, the nesting arrangement suggests that environmental and organizational contextual factors affect the nature of leadership practices, task design, and other features that teams will likely enact. In turn, the team context and demands place premiums on certain competencies of members and the distributions of such competencies throughout the team. Generally speaking, outer layers (i.e., higher level factors) influence inner layers (shown by solid lines in the left-hand side of Figure 9.2.2) more so than the reverse, although upward influences can be evident as well (shown by the dotted lines in the left-hand side of Figure 9.2.2).

IPO models have been criticized for failing to distinguish multiple types of "processes" and outcomes. Ilgen et al. (2005: 520) noted that "many of the mediational factors that intervene and transmit the influence of [team] inputs to outcomes are not processes." For example, Cohen and Bailey (1997) differentiated internal processes from group psychological traits. Marks, Mathieu, and Zaccaro (2001) advanced a similar distinction in the context of an episodic model of team effectiveness. They noted that team processes involved members' actions, whereas other mediating mechanisms are better conceived of as cognitive, motivational, or affective states. They referred to these latter mediators as *emergent states* (e.g., potency, psychological safety, and collective affect). Given this development, Ilgen et al. (2005) coined the phrase input-mediator-outcome (IMO) model to differentiate this approach from the standard IPO framework.

Numerous authors have also emphasized that time plays a critical role in team functioning that is not adequately depicted in typical unidirectional I→P→O frameworks (Ancona & Chong, 1999; Marks et al., 2001; McGrath, 1991). The past decade, however, has seen a much greater appreciation of temporal dynamics in teamwork. Although time can be depicted in a number of ways (Ancona, Goodman, Lawrence, & Tushman, 2001; Ancona, Okhuysen, & Perlow, 2001), two of the more prominent approaches are (a) developmental models and (b) episodic approaches. The *developmental models* illustrate how teams qualitatively change and are differentially influenced by various factors as they mature over time (Kozlowski, Gully, Nason, & Smith, 1999). In contrast, the *episodic approaches* argue that teams must execute different processes at different times, depending on task demands that recur in a cyclical fashion (cf. Marks et al., 2001; McGrath, 1984).

As shown by the solid line running at the bottom of Figure 9.2.2, developmental processes unfold over time as teams mature. Also depicted are feedback loops that represent the more cyclical or episodic processes. Ilgen et al. (2005) recognized this feature as well and referred to their framework as IMOI (input-mediator-output-input) to represent the inherent cyclical nature of team functioning. We should note that such feedback actually occurs as teams transition from *one episode to another*, not within episodes as such depictions are sometimes thought to imply. The solid line from outcomes to subsequent mediators, within Figure 9.2.2, suggests that feedback of this type is likely to be quite influential, whereas the dashed line suggests that outcome and process influences on subsequent inputs would likely be less potent. This follows from the fact that team states are likely to be readily influenced by their progress over time, and teams may readily adopt different processes as a function of outcomes. Alternatively, the influence of team outcomes or mediators on subsequent member composition, team structure, organizational contextual factors, or other inputs, is likely to be less immediate or malleable. Finally, we should note that team effectiveness criteria have evolved over the past decade to include many different forms (e.g., creativity, customer service) and combinations. In this sense, what constitutes "effectiveness" has become far more complex in recent years. We delve into this point more extensively in the next section.

The remainder of this article is organized as follows. First, moving from right to left across Figure 9.2.2, we feature work that has been done over the past decade that informs each of the linkages depicted. Along the way, we note directions for future research in each area. Second, we revisit the challenges for future research outlined by Cohen and Bailey (1997) and highlight where progress has been made, as well as areas where progress is still needed. Finally, we pose a challenge for future scholars to move beyond our current paradigm and to pursue more complex approaches to the study of team effectiveness.

Team Outcomes

When considering the outcomes of interest in teams research, Cohen and Bailey (1997) categorized effectiveness into three categories: performance, attitudes, and behaviors. Other reviews also have more fully delineated the construct of team effectiveness. For example, Sundstrom et al. (2000) listed more than 20 outcomes that were studied in the 1980s and 1990s. However, the range of outcomes considered in the extant literature and the subtle nuances used to differentiate them makes neat categorizations difficult.

Teams exist to perform tasks and "performance is the most widely studied criterion variable in the organizational behavior and human resource management literatures" (Bommer, Johnson, Rich, Podsakoff, & MacKenzie, 1995: 587). Interestingly, in teams research the focus is predominantly on *who* is a member of the team, *how* they work together, and *what* they do to perform their work—hence, the construct of performance has been "less systematically addressed" (Ilgen, 1999: 131). This has resulted in a literature where there is a great deal of consistency and construct clarity on the left-hand side of the equation (i.e., antecedents and mediating influences) and much less so when it comes to the criterion, or right-hand side. In part, this can be attributed to measurement issues. Whereas there are many established and valid measures of inputs, processes, and emergent states, criterion measures, and in particular performance indices, are often idiosyncratic and organizationally specific. That said, the notion of spending a great deal of time delineating and describing predictor variables as opposed to outcomes is not new to the applied social science literature (Beal, Cohen, Burke, & McLendon, 2003; Smith, 1976). Accordingly, we discuss outcomes in terms of traditional broad classifications, yet also identify fruitful areas for future research concerning work team effectiveness criteria.

Team Performance

There is an extensive literature that has incorporated team performance as the criterion variable of interest because it has long been argued that the definition of a team is that they produce something useful to an organization (Argote & McGrath, 1993; Goodman, 1986). We organize our review of the team performance literature along three subcategories: (a) organizational-level performance, (b) team performance behaviors and outcomes, and (c) role-based performance.

Organizational-level performance. Team research has recently started to incorporate organizational-level outcomes. Organizational performance is particularly relevant for top management teams (TMTs) where there is a one-to-one alignment between team characteristics and organizational outcomes. For example, Barrick, Bradley, Kristof-Brown, and Colbert (2007) found that communication and cohesion among credit union TMTs positively affected their firms' financial ratios. Similarly, Srivastava, Bartol, and Locke (2006) reported organizational-level performance data for hotel management teams, while Bunderson and Sutcliffe (2002) measured profitability as it related to unit outcomes adjusted for team history and market conditions. Whereas it is relatively easy to align TMT functioning and organizational outcomes, this is not the case when teams operate at a lower level of analysis. In these instances, a compilation model needs to be advanced to associate collective lower level team outcomes with higher level indices of effectiveness. This might be relatively easy to do in cases such as sales teams—where their outcomes align well with organizational profits. However, it will be much harder to derive a direct linkage, for example, between teams of maintenance workers and organizational outcomes. Accordingly, as organizations continue to adopt team-based designs, particularly ones that have high interteam interdependence (cf. Mathieu, Marks, & Zaccaro, 2001), there will be a need to articulate models of how team outcomes combine to yield organizational benefits.

Team performance behaviors and outcomes. In a meta-analysis of the relationship between cohesion and team performance, Beal and his colleagues (2003) differentiated between *performance behaviors* and *performance outcomes.* Behaviors are actions that are relevant to achieving goals, whereas outcomes are the consequences or results of performance behaviors. Examples of performance behaviors include team process improvement, learning behaviors, and cognitive task performance. Kirkman, Rosen, Tesluk, and Gibson (2004) assessed team process improvements by measuring feedback seeking, error discussion, and experimentation, which they argued should lead to the ability to adapt and improve. Similarly, Edmondson (1999) examined team learning behaviors whereas Jehn and Shah (1997) assessed team cognitive task performance, or the degree to which a team's decision matches those of an expert committee. Finally, Kirkman and Rosen (1999) had team leaders rate teams' levels of proactivity, which encompassed behaviors such as whether the team could fix things and whether they were always looking for better ways to do something.

In terms of team outcomes, Tesluk and Mathieu (1999) examined both work crew problem management (behavior) along with supervisor-rated performance (outcome) for construction and maintenance road crews. As another example of performance outcomes, Langfred (2000) used supervisors' ratings of the accuracy and quality of the work performed by social services and military teams. Mathieu, Gilson, and Ruddy (2006) used a composite measure of archival indices (e.g., parts expenditure and machine breakdown times) that was sensitive to differences across teams. Elsewhere, Lester, Meglino, and Korsgaard (2002) used both the dollar sales of student-run companies and instructor-rated performance scores as criteria.

Other types of team-level outcomes have gained prominence in the past decade. For example, Kirkman, Tesluk, and Rosen (2004) used evaluations of satisfaction with team service. Tjosvold, Tang, and West (2004) had managers rate team innovativeness, whereas Perretti and Negro (2007) used archival measures to understand the role of team membership changes on innovation in the film industry. Mathieu et al. (2006) employed measures of external customer satisfaction, whereas Kirkman and Rosen (1999) employed supervisor ratings of customer service.

Role-based performance. Some research has focused on indices of *role-based performance* believed to be generalizable across teams. Role-based outcomes capture the extent to which members exhibit the requisite competencies necessary to perform their jobs (Welbourne, Johnson, & Erez, 1998). In several recent publications, Chen and his colleagues (Chen, 2005; Chen, Kirkman, Kanfer, Allen, & Rosen, 2007; Chen & Klimoski, 2003) have used this approach to examine whether teams are competent with regard to their task, team, and organizational roles. This body of work yields measures that are comparable across teams. However, this issue of time has not been fully exploited. Specifically, how long does it take teams to internalize their roles, and does the amount of time differ by role? For some roles, immediate behaviors may be apparent, whereas for others it may take time for members to be "on board" with what is expected of them.

Performance composites. In contrast to the above works where performance behaviors and outcomes can be differentiated, many studies have used blended or a *composite* measure of team outcomes. For instance, Lester and colleagues (2002) defined performance as meeting constituent needs, achieving objectives, and recognizing key survival factors. Likewise, Hiller, Day, and Vance (2006) used a measure of effectiveness composed of planning, problem solving, support and consideration, mentoring and development, and overall effectiveness. Similarly, Van der Vegt and Bunderson (2005) had supervisors rate efficiency, quality, overall achievement, productivity, and mission fulfillment. Elsewhere, Barrick, Stewart, Neubert, and Mount (1998) included knowledge, quality, quantity, initiative, interpersonal skills, planning, and overall commitment in their measure of performance.

Given that teams perform multiple functions, these blended composite measures may well be excellent indicators of overall team effectiveness as compared to those that only assess one aspect of performance. In effect, they more closely map onto work that utilized a balanced scorecard approach (e.g., Kirkman, Rosen, et al., 2004). Interestingly, whereas the balanced scorecard remains a popular practitioner tool, it is not used all that frequently in the academic literature. Work by Pritchard (Pritchard, 1995; Pritchard, Jones, Roth, Stuebing, & Ekeberg, 1988) offered an outcome productivity measure (ProMES) that asked teams to identify their key outcomes, estimate how each outcome contributed to their unit's effectiveness, and then use these weighted scales to assess their overall productivity. This measure addresses both the organizational relevance concern raised earlier and the multiple functions performed by teams. Unfortunately, because the ProMES scale development is both cumbersome and time-consuming, it has not been used that often. Moreover, the multiple dimensions do not always evidence discriminant validity. For example, although research sought to capture quality and planning, all items loaded onto a single dimension. Hence, measures that are composed of multiple dimensions rated by different constituencies may be hard to interpret and understand.

Members' Affect and Viability

A review of team outcomes would be remiss not to mention members' *affective reactions* and *viability* outcomes, which continue to receive attention and guide research—although it should be noted that they are considerably less prevalent than they were 10 years ago. Team, job, and organizational satisfaction (e.g., Janz, Colquitt, & Noe, 1997; Kirkman & Rosen, 1999; Tesluk & Mathieu, 1999) along with team and organizational commitment (e.g., Janz, Colquitt, & Noe, 1997; Kirkman & Rosen, 1999; Tesluk & Mathieu, 1999) continue to receive the most attention. An interesting perspective on affective outcomes was adopted by Janssen, Van de Vliert, and Veenstra (1999), who asked members to evaluate whether their team had a good atmosphere and if they were treated with respect.

Team viability remains a popular criterion measure yet suffers from much construct confusion. Sometimes viability is conceived of as team-level criterion whereby members have a collective sense of belonging (similar to the notion of social cohesion). Elsewhere, viability is likened to team membership stability over time. Yet further, viability is often considered in terms of the extent to which individuals wish to remain as members of the team. Thus, team viability has become a generic term for a variety of different constructs. Moreover, team viability (i.e., Barrick et al., 2007) is often combined with affect or attitudinal measures. For example, in their meta-analyses, Balkundi and Harrison (2006) included measures of group member satisfaction, team climate or atmosphere, team commitment, and group cohesion as indicators of viability. Although conceptually important, viability and affective outcomes are often not used as primary criteria because of their self-report nature. However, several studies have tried to use supervisor ratings (e.g., Barrick et al., 2007; Hiller et al., 2006; Lester et al., 2002; Stewart & Barrick, 2000) of both viability and affective outcomes and found that they lack discriminant validity from team performance. This finding is likely due to some sort of a "halo effect" or measurement artifact leading researchers to employ composite approaches as discussed previously.

Summary Impressions and Future Directions

The criteria side of the team effectiveness framework continues to be the least well specified. With the exception of TMT studies, few investigations offer any sort of compilation model to link team performance with organizational outcomes. Development in this arena would be beneficial. Additionally, although research should continue to use performance measures that are organizationally relevant, investigators also should consider using measures that offer greater generalizability across organizational settings, such as role-based performance.

One of the difficulties with generalizing performance is that it is context specific and, thus, often varies between studies by virtue of teams' being nested within organizations. For example, the much cited and often used performance measure developed by Kirkman and Rosen (1999) captures components of meeting or exceeding goals and completing tasks on time, which they reported were relevant performance metrics in the four organizations they studied. However, for some teams exceeding goals may be a relevant performance metric, whereas for others it may not. Therefore, are these dimensions all relevant to the subsequent organizations in which this measure has been applied? To this end, research needs to start to more clearly define performance to ensure that the outcomes measured are relevant, not only to the teams in question but also to the entire organization. For instance, for production teams quantity and quality of outputs are appropriate metrics, whereas customer satisfaction would be a more accurate gauge of team performance for service teams. Accordingly, team performance criteria should be (a) carefully tied to the function and tasks of the teams being studied, (b) differentiated into constituent parts (e.g., quality, quantity, or customer satisfaction) rather than a general all-encompassing composite, and (c) combined using a formally articulated combination algorithm such as that employed in balanced scorecard techniques.

In our introduction, we discussed the importance of understanding temporal dynamics in team research. Time is particularly relevant to the collection of outcome data, and time lags have not been sufficiently considered. For example, does performance data cumulated for three months after a survey (e.g., Mathieu et al., 2006) represent the same thing as data cumulated for six months (e.g., Kirkman & Rosen, 1999) or one year (e.g., Barrick et al., 2007)? Similarly, several lab studies measure performance at multiple points in time (e.g., Johnson, Hollenbeck, Humphrey, Ilgen, Jundt, & Meyer, 2006) but devote relatively little attention to how many episodes are meaningful to the task being performed by the team. We urge future researchers to link their outcomes to either the developmental stage (Kozlowski et al., 1999) or episodic (Marks et al., 2001) models of group development. This approach makes the issues of what to use as criteria measures, and when to measure them, more substantive decisions. In effect, decisions concerning the outcome measure(s) employed, when to collect them, and for how long should be guided by the team task and performance environment.

Related to time is the relationship between performance behaviors and outcomes. Recent work has started to consider several performance behaviors as outcomes (e.g., learning [Edmondson, 1999] or creativity [Gilson & Shalley, 2004]) as well as mediators in subsequent work (e.g., Gilson, Mathieu, Shalley, & Ruddy, 2005). This suggests that at some stage during a team's life cycle such behaviors are outcomes of interest, yet at other stages they are antecedents or mediators driving performance outcomes. What does this cycle look like? The answer to this question, again, needs to be tied directly to the episodic nature of the performance environment within which teams work. For instance, for some teams a sales cycle may be two months, whereas others may work on a two-year sales cycle (e.g., in the aero-space industry). Therefore, the effects of trying new things (creativity) on outcomes may be manifest quite differently across settings. A similar relationship may exist between affect, viability, and performance outcomes. Teams that have more satisfied and committed members may, at some later point in time, exhibit higher performance. In short, we need to think not only in terms of what should be measured to understand team effectiveness, but when should different variables be assessed. Decisions of this type are particularly important when studying, for example, project-based teams whereby different activities are being performed at different stages of project completion. In contrast, such issues would become relatively less salient for production or sales teams who might perform the same types of activities for long periods of time. Regardless, we do need to emphasize that researchers should establish reasonable discriminant validity between measures of team mediators and outcomes. All too often, we would submit, close inspection of mediator–outcome relationships reported in team research reveals that the criterion measures were at least partially contaminated with measures of team states or processes. Such shortcomings can be overcome if researchers begin with a clear articulation of the team criterion space.

Finally, related to the above concerns are issues of aggregation. Historically, team researchers were concerned with aggregation of data from the individual- to the team-level. However, we have, to some extent, moved beyond this concern with the development of a number of good team-level measures. Whereas we now have several methods to test multilevel effects (Kozlowski & Klein, 2000), models of how team process and outcomes compile to yield organizational benefits are still lacking. With the advent of more complex teams-of-teams style organizational designs (cf. Mathieu et al., 2001), the combination of team-level variables becomes a more challenging task. Nevertheless, the challenge needs to be met for research to be relevant for modern-day organizational arrangements.

Mediator–Team Outcome Relationships

During the past decade, researchers have begun to give more attention to "mediating processes that explain why certain inputs affect team effectiveness and viability" (Ilgen et al., 2005: 519). Accordingly, in this section we consider a number of mediators and their relationship with team outcomes. As detailed previously, mediators fall into two major categories: processes and emergent states, in addition to those that represent a blending of these two categories.

Team Processes

Team processes have played a central role in most, if not all, team effectiveness models (Gist, Locke, & Taylor, 1987; Guzzo & Shea, 1992; Hackman, 1983). Historically, team processes were categorized as either "taskwork" or "teamwork" (McIntyre & Salas, 1995; Oser, McCallum, Salas, & Morgan, 1989; Stout, Cannon-Bowers, Salas, & Milanovich, 1999). At its essence, *taskwork* describes functions that individuals must perform to accomplish the team's task, whereas *teamwork* describes the interaction between team members (McIntyre & Salas, 1995). Building upon this foundation, Marks et al. (2001) developed a taxonomy of processes that included three superordinate categories: transition, action, and interpersonal. During *transition* phases, team members focus on activities such as mission analysis, planning, goal specification, and formulating strategies. Later, during *action* phases, members concentrate on task accomplishments, monitoring progress and systems, coordinating team members, as well as monitoring and backing up their fellow team members. Last, the *interpersonal* category includes conflict management, motivation and confidence building, and affect management and may be salient across episodic phases. Table 9.2.1 presents examples of studies that have featured team processes as important mediator variables.

Transition processes. Marks and colleagues (2001) conceptualized team processes as unfolding episodically with transition processes setting the stage for later actions. Transition processes, however, have received the least amount of empirical attention. As an example of such research, Janicik and Bartel (2003) found that planning contributed to the development of norms concerning how teams would manage time (e.g., deadlines). In turn, those temporal norms were found to relate significantly to performance.

Hiller et al. (2006) found that collective leadership enactment, which included variables such as planning and organizing, positively predicted supervisor-rated team performance. Mathieu and Schulze (2006) employed an episodic model of team processes and found that dynamic planning (i.e., contingency and reactive planning) was positively related to performance. Elsewhere, Mathieu and Rapp (in press) illustrated how initial team activities, such as the quality of deliberate performance plans and team charters, related significantly to the patterns of team performance exhibited over time.

Action processes. Whereas transition processes have received limited attention, action processes are frequently included in team studies. As a result, there is a wealth of research that demonstrates the critical role that processes such as communication and coordination play in team performance (see LePine, Piccolo, Jackson, Mathieu, & Saul, in press, for a review). For example, Tesluk and Mathieu (1999) evidenced that team coordination affected problem management actions. De Dreu and West (2001) demonstrated the importance of team member participation. Specifically, within two separate samples, it was found that participation interacts with minority dissent to increase team innovation. Similarly, Johnson and colleagues (2006) showed that a team's reward system can influence their level of information sharing and consequently the shape, speed, and accuracy of their decision making. Elsewhere, Porter (2005) demonstrated that backup behaviors had a positive relationship with decision-making performance.

Interpersonal processes. The interpersonal process dimension includes conflict, motivation, confidence building, and affect. Whereas research has been conducted on all of these topics, work on conflict is the most prevalent. In a meta-analysis De Dreu and Weingart (2003) found that both relationship and task conflict have strong, negative correlations with team performance and member satisfaction. Jehn, Northcraft, and Neale (1999) focused on task conflict and provided evidence that it was the means by which informational diversity

Table 9.2.1 Exemplar Team Process Mediator Studies

Study	Sample	Process Variable	Additional Variable(s)	Outcomes	Key Findings
Jehn, Northcraft, and Neale (1999)	92 teams from the household goods moving industry	Relationship and task conflict	Informational and value diversity, interdependence, task complexity	Team performance,[4] satisfaction,[5] intent to remain,[5] group commitment[5]	Informational diversity—performance relationship was mediated by task conflict. Value diversity—affective outcomes effect was mediated by relationship conflict.
Johnson et al. (2006)	80 undergraduate student teams working on a simulation	Cooperation	Reward structures, information sharing	Decision accuracy,[1] decision speed[3]	Teams that switched from competitive to cooperative reward systems demonstrated less cooperation and performance.
LePine, Piccolo, Jackson, Mathieu, and Saul (in press)	Meta-analytic review of 138 studies	Transition, action, and interpersonal	Cohesion, potency	Team performance,[4] member satisfaction[5]	All processes related to performance and member satisfaction, and strongly related to cohesion and potency.
Mathieu, Gilson, and Ruddy (2006)	121 service technician teams	Team processes	Team empowerment	Team performance,[4] customer satisfaction[2]	Team processes mediated the relationship between empowerment and performance.
Mathieu and Schulze (2006)	29 student teams working on a simulation	Transition and interpersonal team processes	Team knowledge, use of formal plans	Team performance[4]	Formal planning and interpersonal process was directly related to performance.

Note: Performance: 1 = quantity, 2 = quality, 3 = timeliness, 4 = mixed, 5 = affective outcomes, 6 = individual-level outcomes.

positively influenced performance. Raver and Gelfand (2005) assessed relationship conflict and found that it mediated the association between ambient sexual hostility and team financial performance.

Research has considered interpersonal processes besides conflict. For instance, research has illustrated that feedback has a positive impact on motivation, interpersonal trust, and ultimately performance in virtual teams (Geister, Konradt, and Hertel, 2006). Additionally, Mathieu and Schulze (2006) considered a composite measure of interpersonal processes and found a significant, positive relationship with performance. Likewise, Maynard, Mathieu, Marsh, and Ruddy (2007) noted that such a composite measure of interpersonal processes provided the cross-level mechanism by which team-level resistance to empowerment climate related to individual-level satisfaction. Finally, Bradley, White, and Mennecke (2003: 361) argued that "the temporal dimensions of team and task are critical to the impact of interpersonal interventions on team performance." They noted that most previous studies were conducted with teams that briefly performed contrived tasks and were then disbanded. On the basis of their meta-analysis, Bradley et al. (2003) concluded that there is abundant support for the contention that interpersonal processes relate positively to team performance when teams engage in longer term tasks.

Other processes. Although the work of Marks et al. (2001) provides a convenient taxonomy, not all team processes fall neatly into one of the three higher order dimensions. For example, team creative processes have been defined as "members working together in such a manner that they link ideas from multiple sources, delve into unknown areas to find better or unique approaches to a problem, or seek out novel ways of performing a task" (Gilson & Shalley, 2004: 454). It has long been argued that creativity is a vital driver of team effectiveness (Hackman & Morris, 1975; Stein, 1974; Taggar, 2002; Tesluk, Farr, & Klein, 1997), and recent research has found that team creative processes have a significant positive effect on performance (Gilson et al., 2005). Furthermore, whereas Gilson et al. (2005) found no direct relationship between creativity and customer satisfaction, they did find that creativity inter-acted with standardization such that high standardization and creativity resulted in high levels of customer satisfaction. No research that we are aware of has examined team creative processes and affective outcomes. However, it is interesting to note that the brainstorming literature has consistently found that groups who brainstorm are *more* satisfied and pleased with the ideas they generate (Paulus, 2000). These findings open the door for future research on creative processes and affective outcomes.

Summary impressions and future directions. A recent meta-analysis by LePine and colleagues (in press) found support for the implicit hierarchical arrangement of team processes advanced by Marks et al. (2001). Moreover, this work found substantial support for positive effect sizes between each of the lower order and higher order dimensions, as related to team outcomes. That said, most of the team process research to date is fragmented. To this point we found only three articles that have considered more than one of the higher order process dimensions (i.e., transition, action, and interpersonal) within a single study.

DeShon, Kozlowski, Schmidt, Milner, and Wiechmann (2004) found that team perform-ance was positively affected by both strategy planning (i.e., transition processes) and team-focused effort (i.e., action process). Mathieu et al. (2006) considered the role that a compos-ite measure of team processes played within the team empowerment–team performance nomological network and found that processes provided the link by which empowerment had an indirect effect on both customer satisfaction and objective performance. However, in further analyses separating the three team process dimensions, they found that only transi-tion processes had a marginally significant relationship with customer satisfaction, whereas only action processes were significantly related to quantitative performance. Similar to these results, Maynard et al.'s (2007) cross-level study found that transition processes were posi-tively related to customer satisfaction, whereas action processes appeared more salient for quantitative performance. However, this study also provided evidence that interpersonal processes had a significant, cross-level relationship with individual employees' level of satisfaction.

In summary, whereas it is clear that processes play a key role within team effectiveness models, many questions remain. Namely, while work has been done to provide a framework of team processes (e.g., Marks et al., 2001) researchers have yet to fully investigate *when* the respective team processes are most critical in explaining performance. Therefore, we call on researchers to devote more attention to the specific types of processes, assessing multiple types within a single study, and to more fully understand their individual and collective relationships with team outcomes.

Emergent States

Marks and colleagues (2001: 357) described emergent states as "cognitive, motivational, and affective states of teams [that are] . . . dynamic in nature and vary as function of team context, inputs, processes, and outcomes." Examples of emergent states that have received significant attention during the past decade include team confidence, empowerment, team climate, cohesion, trust, and collective cognition (e.g., shared mental models, strategic consensus). Table 9.2.2 presents examples of studies that have featured emergent states.

Team confidence. The team confidence category of emergent states includes two related, but distinct, constructs—team efficacy and potency. *Team efficacy* has been defined as "a shared belief in a group's collective capability to organize and execute courses of action required to produce given levels of goal attainment" (Kozlowski & Ilgen, 2006: 90). *Potency*, on the other hand, is generally defined as a collective belief regarding the team's ability to be successful (Shea & Guzzo, 1987). The primary distinction between the two is that *efficacy* relates to the team's belief that it can be successful on a *specific* task whereas *potency* refers to a team's more *general* sense of its capabilities in relation to various tasks and different contexts. It should be noted that both constructs assume that these underlying beliefs are shared by all team members (e.g., Gully, Incalcaterra, Joshi, & Beaubien, 2002). Accordingly, these constructs do not represent the simple aggregation of team members' self-efficacy or their individual beliefs in themselves across various tasks (e.g., Kozlowski & Ilgen, 2006).

Team efficacy and potency are theorized to have a positive impact on performance through their respective effects on the actions teams take (i.e., which goals are set), their level of effort, and resilience when task performance does not attain the aspired level. There is a large body of empirical research that has supported the positive relationship between team efficacy and potency with performance (e.g., Jung & Sosik, 1999). For example, Lester et al. (2002) provided evidence that potency was positively related to satisfaction, effort, and overall performance, whereas Knight, Durham, and Locke (2001) provided support for efficacy having a positive relationship with a team's level of strategic risk.

Gully and colleagues (2002) conducted a meta-analytic review of this literature and concluded that team efficacy and potency exhibit mean corrected correlations with performance of .41 and .37, respectively. Moreover, they found that the relationship between efficacy and performance was higher when teams had greater, as compared to less, interdependence. This finding is consistent with the results of Gibson (1999), who found that the relationship between team efficacy and performance was moderated by task uncertainty and collectivism. Whereas work subsequent to Gully et al.'s meta-analyses has generally provided further support for the positive relationship that team efficacy and potency have on performance (e.g., Srivastava et al., 2006), de Jong, de Ruyter, and Wetzels (2005) provided a unique perspective indicating that potency can have negative implications on performance—in this case, service quality.

Team empowerment. To date, there have been two primary conceptions of team empowerment: structural and psychological (Mathieu et al., 2006). Structural empowerment considers the impact that the actual practice of delegating authority and responsibility can have on performance (e.g., Arnold, Arad, Rhoades, & Drasgow, 2000). Psychological empowerment is a team's "collective belief that they have the authority to control their proximal work environment and are responsible for their team's functioning" (Mathieu et al., 2006: 98). Within this section, we are concerned with emergent state constructs and, accordingly, we

Table 9.2.2 Exemplar Emergent States Mediator Studies

Study	Sample	Emergent States	Additional Variable(s)	Outcomes	Key Findings
Austin (2003)	27 continuing groups within sporting goods company	Transactive memory systems	N/A	Goal performance, group evaluations[4]	Transactive memory systems were positively related to goal performance, external and internal group evaluations.
Beal, Cohen, Burke, and McLendon (2003)	Meta-analytic review of 64 studies	Cohesion	N/A	Team performance[4]	Cohesion was more highly correlated with performance than other outcomes, and more highly with efficiency than effectiveness.
Edmondson (1999)	51 work teams in a manufacturing company	Team learning	Psychological safety; team efficacy; team safety	Team performance[2]	Team learning behavior mediates the relationship between psychological safety and team performance.
Gibson and Gibbs (2006)	56 aerospace design teams	Psychological safety	Team virtuality	Innovation[4]	Each of the four dimensions of team virtuality were negatively associated with innovation.
Gully, Incalcaterra, Joshi, and Beaubien (2002)	Meta-analytic review of 67 studies	Team efficacy; team potency	Level of analysis, interdependence	Team performance[4]	Both efficacy and potency had positive relationships with performance.
Kilduff, Angelmar, and Mehra (2000)	35 simulated management teams	Strategic consensus	Demographic and cognitive diversity	Firm performance[4]	High-performance teams did not exhibit consensus at the beginning but converged as the team interacted.
Langfred (2005)	89 manufacturing teams	Individual- and team-level autonomy	Task interdependence	Team performance[4]	Individual- and team-level autonomy interacted with task interdependence to explain team performance.
Lubatkin, Simsek, Ling, and Veiga (2006)	139 top management teams	Behavioral integration	Ambidextrous orientation	Firm performance[4]	TMT behavioral integration was indirectly associated with firm performance.
Mathieu, Heffner, Goodwin, Cannon-Bowers, and Salas (2005)	70 undergraduate teams working on a combat simulation	Task- and team-shared mental models	Team processes	Team performance[4]	The relationship between task SMMs and performance was mediated by team processes. Team SMMs interacted with the quality of SMMs in shaping team processes and performance.
Schneider, Ehrhart, Mayer, Saltz, and Niles-Jolly (2005)	56 supermarket departments	Service climate	Leader behavior, citizenship behavior	Customer satisfaction[2] and unit sales[1]	Service climate was significantly, positively related to customer-focused citizenship behavior.
Stewart (2006)	Meta-analytic review of 93 studies	Team design-related psychological states	Group composition, leadership	Performance[4]	Meaningfulness exhibited a relationship with performance. Autonomy and intrateam coordination corresponded with higher performance.

Note: Performance: 1 = quantity, 2 = quality, 3 = timeliness, 4 = mixed, 5 = affective outcomes, 6 = individual-level outcomes. TMT = top management team; BI = behavioral integration; SMM = shared mental model.

focus on psychological rather than structural empowerment. Initially, research focused on the relationship between psychological empowerment and overall team performance with Hyatt and Ruddy (1997) finding a positive relationship. Kirkman and Rosen (1999) broadened the scope of psychological empowerment by considering a variety of performance and affective outcomes. Specifically, in a study of teams from four different organizations, they evidenced that empowerment had a positive impact on customer service, job satisfaction, and organizational and team commitment. Mathieu et al. (2006) found that psychological empowerment had a positive indirect effect on both performance and customer satisfaction, as transmitted through team processes.

Team empowerment has also been examined from a multilevel perspective. Empirical support has demonstrated that psychological empowerment is distinct from individual-level psychological empowerment (e.g., Seibert, Silver, & Randolph, 2004). Specifically, Seibert and colleagues (2004) found that team empowerment can influence individuals' performance and job satisfaction through its relationship with individual-level empowerment. More recently, Chen et al. (2007) examined how individual- and team-level empowerment interacted in shaping individual performance. Namely, they demonstrated a positive relationship between team empowerment and team-level performance and found that team-level empowerment moderated the relationship between individual-level empowerment and individual-level performance.

Climate. Climate refers to "the set of norms, attitudes, and expectations that individuals perceive to operate in a specific social context" (Pirola-Merlo, Hartel, Mann, & Hirst, 2002: 564) and was originally conceptualized as an organizational-level construct (e.g., Dickson, Resick, & Hanges, 2006). With the trend toward establishing teams with greater discretion in terms of policy setting and procedure implementation, it has been suggested that climate is more salient at the team-level of analysis (e.g., Tesluk, Vance, & Mathieu, 1999). The impetus for considering the role of climate at the team-level is that members' understanding of a situation has been shown to affect their attitudes and behaviors (e.g., Naumann & Bennett, 2002).

Whereas most research has examined the relationship between a general team climate and performance (e.g., Pirola-Merlo et al., 2002), there has been a noticeable trend for researchers to follow Schneider's (1975) recommendation and focus on specific dimensions of team climate. Climate research now includes such concepts as creativity climate (Gilson & Shalley, 2004) and learning transfer climate (e.g., Smith-Jentsch, Salas, & Brannick, 2001). In addition to considerations of such climate dimensions, there is a sizeable body of research on safety, service, and justice climates—as discussed below.

Safety climate. Zohar (2000) was one of the first researchers to measure safety climate at the team-level. His work developed a measure that demonstrated both within-group homogeneity and between-groups variation within a manufacturing company and also demonstrated that safety climate significantly predicted time-lagged team accident rates. Building upon this work, Katz-Navon, Naveh, and Stern (2005) examined four dimensions of safety climate and their respective, and interactive, effects on the number of treatment errors within hospital units. Their results revealed that perceived detailing of safety procedures exhibited a curvilinear relationship with treatment errors and that perceived priority of safety moderated the relationship between perceived detailing of safety procedures and the number of treatment errors. Safety climate research also has evidenced cross-level effects, with Neal and Griffin (2006) finding that team-level safety climate predicted subsequent changes in individual-level safety motivation.

Service climate. Service climate has been conceptualized as employees' assessment of the organization's concern for customer well-being (Borucki & Burke, 1999). Accordingly, de Jong, de Ruyter, and Lemmink (2005) found that service climate was positively related to customer-rated perceptions of service quality. Additionally, in a study of units in a supermarket chain, Schneider, Ehrhart, Mayer, Saltz, and Niles-Jolly (2005) found that service climate has an indirect effect on customer satisfaction as mediated by unit customer-focused citizenship behavior. Finally, Hui, Chiu, Yu, Cheng, and Tse (2007) assessed the interactive effect of service climate and leadership behaviors on individual-level service. Their findings suggested that leadership was most critical to individual-level service quality within unfavorable service climates. In contrast, leadership was not as critical for individual-level service quality within favorable service climates. In fact, for internal customers, the results implied that leadership may actually be detrimental for service quality.

Justice climate. Naumann and Bennett (2002: 882) provided one of the first examinations of the group-level justice climate construct—"distinct group-level cognition about how a work group as a whole is treated." Colquitt, Noe, and Jackson (2002) assessed the relationship between procedural justice climate and team-level outcomes, finding that team-level procedural justice climate was significantly related to both performance and absenteeism. In addition, this study illustrated that the linear effect of justice climate was accentuated by the strength of the climate perceptions. Finally, Yang, Mossholder, and Peng (2007) considered the cross-level effects of procedural justice climate on individual-level organization commitment. Their study of Taiwanese work groups suggested that team-level procedural justice climate had a positive incremental impact on individual-level organizational commitment. Additionally, their work provided evidence that the climate construct interacted with team-level power distance as related to individual-level organizational commitment.

Cohesion. Cohesion, or the commitment of team members to the team's overall task or to each other (Goodman, Ravlin, & Schminke, 1987), has been one of the more thoroughly researched emergent states (Kozlowski & Ilgen, 2006). For example, Bass, Avolio, Jung, and Berson (2003) found support for cohesion as a mediator of the transformational leadership–performance relationship. Elsewhere, Raver and Gelfand (2005) found support for cohesion as a mediator of team-level ambient sexual hostility's negative influence on team financial performance. Michalisin, Karau, and Tangpong (2004) found a positive relationship between TMT cohesion and overall returns within their simulation study.

Given the amount of research pertaining to team cohesion, there are several meta-analytic reviews (e.g., Gully et al., 2002; Webber & Donahue, 2001). Most recently, Beal et al. (2003) examined studies conducted between 1951 and 2002 and found that cohesion had a mean corrected correlation with performance behaviors and performance outcomes of .30 and .17, respectively. Furthermore, Beal and colleagues illustrated that three dimensions of cohesion (*interpersonal*, *task*, and *group pride*) were each significantly related to team performance and that "as team workflow increased, the cohesion-performance relationship became stronger" (p. 998).

Trust. Another prominent emergent state construct is trust. Most researchers have adopted the definition of trust advanced by Mayer, Davis, and Schoorman (1995):

> the willingness of a party to be vulnerable to the actions of another party based on the expectation that the other will perform a particular action important to the trustor, irrespective of the ability to monitor or control the other party. (p. 712)

Langfred (2004) provided evidence that team-level trust exhibits a downward concave curve relationship with the level of monitoring within the team. His results showed that monitoring and the level of individual autonomy within the team interact, such that when individual autonomy is high and monitoring is low, team performance is negatively affected. Elsewhere, Kirkman, Rosen, Tesluk, and Gibson (2006) found trust served as a positive moderator of a team training proficiency–performance relationship. Finally, trust also appears to be a moderator within TMT performance models with Simons and Peterson (2000) finding that intragroup trust moderated the relationship between task and relationship conflict.

Collective cognition. Answering a call made by Klimoski and Mohammed (1994), extensive work has been done in the area of collective cognition during the past decade. For example, researchers have pointed toward shared mental models (e.g., Levesque, Wilson, & Wholey, 2001; Mathieu, Heffner, Goodwin, Cannon-Bowers, & Salas, 2005) and strategic consensus (e.g., Ensley & Pearce, 2001; Kellermanns, Walter, Lechner, & Floyd, 2005) as important antecedents to team effectiveness.

Shared mental models (SMMs). SMMs, or "an organized understanding or mental representation of knowledge that is shared by team members" (Mathieu et al., 2005: 38), is one of the more developed collective cognition literature streams. Early theoretical work within the SMM literature suggested that teams hold multiple mental models simultaneously (e.g., Klimoski & Mohammed, 1994; Wilson & Rutherford, 1989). Based upon such arguments, Cannon-Bowers, Salas, and Converse (1993) developed a typology, and their dimensions included (a) technology, (b) task, (c) team interaction, and (d) team. Whereas this SMM typology is widely accepted, research has predominantly only focused on a single dimension within a given study or collapsed the SMM dimensions into a composite measure. For example, Marks, Sabella, Burke, and Zaccaro (2002) investigated the role of cross-training on the development of team interaction SMMs. As an example of the later approach, Marks, Zaccaro, and Mathieu (2000) assessed the role that team interaction training and leader briefings had on the development of an omnibus SMM construct and found positive relationships.

When researchers have sought to measure more than one type of SMM, more often than not, they have collapsed the dimensions into two (task and team). *Task SMMs* suggest that team members hold a common schema regarding their task and the potential role that the broader environment may play. In contrast, *team SMMs* represent a shared understanding among team members about how they will interact with one another. For example, Mathieu et al. (2000) provided evidence that team SMMs have a direct impact on performance, in contrast to task SMMs, which evidenced an indirect effect through their effect on processes.

Research has begun to consider the interaction between the dimensions of SMMs. In a study of safety and efficiency in air traffic control towers, Smith-Jentsch, Mathieu, and Kraiger (2005) reported that neither category of SMMs evidenced a direct effect, but the interaction of the two SMMs exhibited a positive relationship with both tower safety and efficiency. Another recent development within the SMM literature is the consideration of whether it is the "sharedness" of mental models that is most critical to team performance, as compared to the accuracy or quality of the underlying mental models (e.g., Lim & Klein, 2006). Work by Edwards, Day, Arthur, and Bell (2006) suggests that accuracy is a stronger predictor of team performance as compared to SMM similarity. Moreover, Marks et al. (2000) and Mathieu et al. (2005) found that SMM sharedness and quality interacted to positively influence both team processes and performance.

Strategic consensus. Kellermanns et al. (2005: 721) defined strategic consensus as "the shared understanding of strategic priorities among managers at the top, middle, and/or operating levels of the organization." In contrast to SMMs, which consider overlapping mental representations on various factors, strategic consensus represents the agreement on strategic priorities. Although we should note that early strategic consensus work focused exclusively on TMTs (e.g., Amason, 1996; Bourgeois, 1985), more recent work has broadened the application to management teams across the organizational hierarchy (e.g., Floyd & Lane, 2000).

Given the focus on high-level management teams, Kellermanns and colleagues (2005) noted that the criteria for strategic consensus is typically in terms of organizational or major unit outcomes. For example, Iaguinto and Fredrickson (1997) showed that strategic consensus within TMTs was positively related to organizational performance. Additionally, research indicates that the positive impact of strategic consensus on organizational performance may be mediated by consensus on decision commitment (Dooley, Fryxell, & Judge, 2000). Finally, Kilduff, Angelmar, and Mehra (2000) illustrated that successful TMTs did not possess strategic consensus at the beginning of their life cycle but gradually moved toward consensus near the end of their life cycle. Additionally, this work suggested that strategic consensus and firm performance have a reciprocal relationship, whereby firm performance is affected by and likewise affects strategic consensus.

Blended Mediators

Whereas the constructs discussed above are easily categorized as either processes or emergent states, there are several other mediators of the team input-outcome relationship that are a blend of processes and emergent states. We consider three: (a) team learning, (b) behavioral integration, and (c) transactive memory.

Team learning. Edmondson (1999: 350) was one of the first to acknowledge that the teams and learning literatures had developed with little "cross-fertilization." The construct of team learning is said to represent an ongoing process of reflection and action, through which teams acquire, share, combine, and apply knowledge (Argote, Gruenfeld, & Naquin, 1999; Edmondson, 1999). In this sense, it reflects an active set of team processes, and yet team learning is also referred to as knowledge being embedded within the team (Argote & Olivera, 1999). Embedding knowledge requires that teams codify what they have learned by documenting their work processes and thus converting tacit knowledge into explicit knowledge (Gibson & Vermeulen, 2003). Knowledge codification, however, represents a state that characterizes what a team has learned at any given time (Cohendet & Steinmueller, 2000).

Zellmer-Bruhn and Gibson (2006) found a positive relationship between team learning and both task performance and the quality of intrateam relations. Wong (2004) assessed the relationship between learning that occurs from within (i.e., local learning), as well as from outside the team (i.e., distal learning) and found both to be positively related to efficiency and innovativeness. Moreover, the two forms of team learning interacted, such that distal learning negatively affected the relationship between local learning and team efficiency. Edmondson (1999) provided insight into other variables that are included in the team learning nomological network. Specifically, in assessing the relationship between team learning and performance, Edmondson provided evidence that team learning served as a mediator for the relationship between psychological safety ("a shared belief held by members of a team that the team is safe for interpersonal risk taking" [p. 350]) and performance.

Behavioral integration. In the context of his work on TMTs, Hambrick (1994: 189) introduced the concept of behavioral integration proposing that it "has three major elements: (a) quantity and quality (richness, timeliness, accuracy) of information exchange, (b) collaborative behavior, and (c) joint decision making." In other words, a state of behavioral integration (BI) exists when teams engage in the above three types of processes. Thus, BI is a blended construct that describes how three related processes yield a resulting state.

Simsek, Veiga, Lubatkin, and Dino (2005) found evidence that TMT goal preference diversity, educational diversity, and size were negatively related to BI. Elsewhere, Lubatkin, Simsek, Ling, and Veiga (2006) found that BI exhibited a positive relationship with firm performance, as mediated by TMT ambidextrous orientation. Finally, Carmeli and Schaubroeck (2006) found that BI was positively associated with decision quality and negatively with organizational decline.

Transactive memory systems (TMSs). TMSs have been defined as the collection of knowledge possessed by each team member and a collective awareness of who knows what (e.g., Austin, 2003; Rulke & Rau, 2000). Accordingly, TMSs should benefit teams through enhanced communication and coordination as a result of the groups' awareness of the collective knowledge that is available and where it resides within the team (e.g., Wegner, 1986). For example, Rulke and Rau (2000: 373) found that individuals within teams that possess higher levels of TMSs "declared domains of expertise during earlier rather than later periods of group interaction, and the frequency with which members evaluated others' expertise and competence increased with time." Lewis (2004) reported a positive relationship between the presence of TMSs and both team performance and viability.

As with SMMs, Austin (2003) considered whether teams could have multiple TMSs. Specifically, he examined the relationship between task and external relationship TMSs and team performance and provided evidence that both types of TMSs had a positive impact on various measures of team performance (i.e., goal performance, as well as both internal and external group evaluations). Lewis, Lange, and Gillis (2005) further developed the TMS construct when they suggested that the positive benefits of TMSs go beyond the specific task for which the TMS was developed. In fact, these researchers provided evidence that TMSs affect a team's ability to apply prior learning to new tasks—a concept referred to as learning transfer. Finally, research has begun to consider various types of team cognitive constructs within a single study. As an example, Ellis (2006) investigated the role of acute stress on the performance of teams working on a command-and-control simulation. The results of this study indicate that the negative effect of stress on performance is attributable to the negative impact that stress had on both SMMs and TMSs.

Summary Impressions and Future Directions

The distinction between process and emergent states appears to be gaining acceptance in the literature and helping to sort out the mediator portion of many team effectiveness models. Moreover, as discussed previously, there is growing empirical evidence to support the various team process dimensions. Nevertheless, empirical analyses have demonstrated that different processes are highly correlated. Moreover, conceptually distinguishable types of emergent processes are typically highly correlated with one another. And to make matters worse, measures of processes and emergent states are typically highly correlated with each other—particularly when assessed at the same time and from the same source of measurement.

What are the implications of this collinearity? First, if processes, emergent states, and other variables are highly correlated, then any study that features only one type of variable is susceptible to problems associated with what is commonly referred to as omitted- or 3rd-variable issues. For example, if empowerment is found to be a significant mediator, one might wonder if the effect is really attributable to cohesion, planning processes, or other mediators, unless they too were measured and incorporated into the analyses. Second, if these various mediators are highly correlated, one might question their discriminant validity. Whereas powerful statistical techniques such as confirmatory factor analyses may support their empirical differentiation, researchers are still left to wonder whether members can really make such fine distinctions as compared to developing more general impressions about how well their team functions.

Finally, the high correlations found among different mediators are no doubt somewhat attributable to the modal study design employed by most researchers. LePine et al. (in press) argued that high correlations likely result from researchers measuring all processes and states at the same point in time and often from the same source. They called for more research that uses time-based designs that align the different measurements of constructs with when they are thought to be activated (e.g., transition processes prior to action processes). Furthermore, they suggested that researchers consider using multiple forms of measurement so as to minimize same-source concerns. We echo those sentiments, as well as Tesluk et al.'s (1997) recommendations that different sources of measurement are likely to be better suited for assessing different constructs. For example, emergent states such as cohesion are perhaps best assessed by team members, as they refer to individuals' collective social psychological feelings. In contrast, backup behaviors are visible and thus can be assessed by others who are not actively engaged in team activities. Deliberate plans typically yield physical traces and other by-products that can be assessed by other techniques. In short, more elaborate research designs and measurement systems can better inform us about the empirical differentiation (or not) of various mediating mechanisms and their interrelationships.

In a related temporal theme, emergent states are believed to do just that—*emerge* over time. Therefore, numerous intriguing questions about such constructs have yet to be addressed. For example, once a team is formed, how long does it take for shared perceptions of collective efficacy to form and solidify? How vulnerable to transgressions are shared perceptions of trust? Does it matter when such transgressions occur? These questions and others like them home in on the issues of when emergent states develop and how impervious they are over time. Morgeson and Hofmann (1999) referred to this issue as the emergence of the collective structure of constructs over time. Here again, adopting a developmental perspective has much to offer our understanding of team mediators. Moreover, such development may not be a simple linear progression over time. Salient questions in this regard include whether there are critical moments or stages in development or whether discontinuous changes such as "tipping points" might increase our understanding of the function of team mediators over time.

Team Composition Inputs

Team composition research focuses on the attributes of team members and the impact of the combination of such attributes on processes, emergent states, and ultimately outcomes. Composition has been incorporated into studies of team effectiveness for nearly 50 years (e.g., Mann, 1959) and has been conceptualized as including job-related (Webber & Donahue, 2001) as well as surface and deep-level attributes (Harrison, Price, & Bell, 1998). Individual inputs to team mediators implicitly evoke *composition* or *compilation* processes. Kozlowski and Klein (2000) described *composition processes* as relatively simple combination rules, such as averaging lower level units to represent a higher level construct. Diversity indices are also compositional in nature, as they represent the higher level construct as a variance of lower level entity characteristics. An important point to note about compositional models is that all lower level entities are presumed to be comparable and weighted equally in the construction of the higher level construct. In contrast, "in *compilation models*, the higher-level phenomenon is a complex combination of diverse lower-level contributions" (Kozlowski & Klein, 2000: 17). In other words, compilation describes a situation where the higher level construct is something different than a mere descriptive statistic of lower level entities. For example, team performance may be unduly influenced by the least (or most) competent individual member. Over the past 10 years, researchers have emphasized the operationalization of members' attributes in team effectiveness models, because different methods of indexing can yield different results (Barrick et al., 1998). Below we review three general approaches to indexing team composition. Two approaches, *mean values* and *diversity indices* are compositional models, whereas the last, which we refer to as *complex combinations*, is a compilational approach. Table 9.2.3 presents examples of studies that have used team composition variables as drivers of mediators and outcomes.

Mean Values

The form of emergence that underlies the average of member attributes is referred to as a summary index (Chen, Mathieu, & Bliese, 2004) and relies on some measure of central tendency of members' attributes. Using this methodology, the pooled value of a characteristic is presumed to affect a team, regardless of how that characteristic is distributed among members (Barrick et al., 1998; Stewart, 2006).

Personality. Several trends are evident in the team personality research. First, the range of personality factors being considered has been extended beyond the Big Five to include achievement orientation, dependability (LePine, 2003), assertiveness (Pearsall & Ellis, 2006), and locus of control (Boone, Van Olffen, Van Witteloostuijn, & De Brabander, 2004). Second, there has been increasing recognition that complex dynamics accompany personality factors. For instance, Halfhill, Sundstrom, Lahner, Caldrone, and Nielsen (2005) found that teams composed of members with high levels of both conscientiousness and agreeableness exhibited the highest levels of performance. Others suggest that the effects of personality on team performance may vary according to the nature of the task (e.g., English, Griffith, & Steelman, 2004; LePine, Colquitt, & Erez, 2000; Neuman & Wright, 1999).

Recently, Bell (2007) conducted a meta-analysis on the relationship between personality and performance. Her results indicate that average team conscientiousness, agreeableness, extraversion, emotional stability, and openness to experience related positively to performance in field settings. In addition to the direct effects, research has also begun to examine the mediators through which compositional variables relate to outcomes, such as by facilitating cooperation, conflict resolution, communication, and teamwork (e.g., Barrick et al., 1998). Ellis, Hollenbeck, Ilgen, Porter, West, and Moon (2003) revealed that teams with high average levels of cognitive ability learned more when the team's workload was evenly distributed. In comparison, teams composed of people with high average agreeableness were not as adept in terms of team learning.

Competencies. Because of the unique demands of working in a team, the knowledge, skills, and abilities (KSAs) needed for effective performance differ from those needed by individuals working alone (Morgeson, Reider, & Campion, 2005). The interaction required in team settings introduces a unique set of teamwork KSAs (see Stevens & Campion, 1994, for a full discussion) that have been shown to facilitate performance (e.g., Cooke, Kiekel, Salas, & Stout, 2003; Hirschfeld, Jordan, Feild, Giles, & Armenakis, 2005; McClough & Rogelberg, 2003; Stevens & Campion, 1999).

Table 9.2.3 Exemplar Team Composition Input Influence Studies

Study	Sample	Composition Factor	Team Mediators	Outcomes	Findings
Barrick, Stewart, Neubert, and Mount (1998)	41 assembly and maintenance teams	Personality; ability	Cohesion	Performance;[4] team viability[5]	General mental ability (GMA), conscientiousness, agreeableness, extraversion, and emotional stability related positively to team performance. GMA, extraversion, and emotional stability related positively to team viability. Cohesion partially mediated some relationships.
Bell (2007)	Meta-analysis of 89 studies	Personality; ability		Performance[4]	The strength of team composition and performance was moderated by the study setting (lab or field) and the operationalization of the team composition variable. Minimum agreeableness and mean conscientiousness, openness to experience, collectivism, and preference for teamwork were strong predictors of performance in field studies.
Bunderson and Sutcliffe (2002)	45 business unit management teams	Functional diversity	Information sharing	Performance[1]	Dominant function diversity (extent to which team members differ in the functional areas within which they have spent the greater part of their careers) had a negative, and intrapersonal functional diversity, a positive effect on information sharing and team performance.
Ellis, Bell, Ployhart, Hollenbeck, and Ilgen (2005)	65 command and control simulation teams[3]	Teamwork; knowledge	Communication	Competencies[2]	Teamwork training related positively to cognitive and skill-based outcomes. Also, the effects of declarative knowledge differed across team members depending on their roles and responsibilities. The team benefited the most from the knowledge held by the team member who occupied the most critical position in the workflow.
Harrison, Price, and Bell (1998)	71 hospital and grocery store teams[2]	Demographic, personality, ability, and attitude diversity		Cohesion[5]	The length of time team members worked together weakened the effect of surface-level diversity and strengthened the effects of deep-level diversity.

Note: Performance: 1 = quantity; 2 = quality; 3 = timeliness, 4 = mixed, 5 = affective outcomes, 6 = individual-level outcomes.

In a meta-analysis of 19 studies, Devine and Philips (2001: 523) concluded "that the functional amount of cognitive ability in teams does indeed predict team performance across a broad variety of team contexts." They submitted that the effects would likely be most pronounced for teams who performed intellectual or decision-making tasks as compared to more physical ones. Whereas member cognitive ability may be valuable for teams in general, task-related knowledge levels are likely to be even more important to teams that perform a task over time. For example, Mathieu and Schulze (2006) found that teams with high levels of task-related knowledge not only performed better but were better able to execute transition processes.

Other attributes. Numerous other characteristics have been used to index team composition. For example, in contrast to stable traits that predispose one to adopt a particular response pattern across situations, orientations refer to transient dispositions that prompt situationally determined responses (Button, Mathieu, & Zajac, 1996). Goal orientations (i.e., an individual's approach to achievement situations: Dweck, 1986) and teamwork orientation (i.e., propensity for accomplishing work as part of a team as opposed to individually: Driskell & Salas, 1992) have been used as composition variables. Researchers have conceptualized goal orientation as the average of members' orientations (LePine, 2005; Porter, 2005) as well as a referent-shift-type construct (Chen, Mathieu, & Bliese, 2004) that considers the effects associated with a team's goal orientation (e.g., Bunderson, 2003; DeShon et al., 2004). Results indicate that goal orientation is predictive of team mediators (e.g., commitment, efficacy, processes) as well as performance. Bunderson and Sutcliffe (2003) suggested that team learning orientation can have both positive and negative consequences. Specifically, team learning orientation can enhance team adaptive behaviors and overall team performance in the long run, although in the short term, an extreme focus on learning and competence development can impair performance. Finally, LePine (2005) found that members' goal orientation interacted with goal difficulty to predict adaptability in a dynamic environment, and that goal orientation predicted team processes and ultimately performance. LePine's study demonstrates that orientations may combine with other factors in complex ways, and provides insight into some of the mechanisms by which orientations influence performance.

Other research has suggested that average member teamwork orientation enhances effectiveness (e.g., Bell, 2007; Harris & Barnes-Farrell, 1997; Jung & Sosick, 1999; Watson, Johnson, & Merritt, 1998), teamwork (Eby & Dobbins, 1997; Harris & Barnes-Farrell, 1997), and ultimately viability (Harris & Barnes-Farrell, 1997). With regard to member attitudes, Harrison et al. (1998) found that the average levels of job, supervisor, and work satisfaction related positively to cohesion. Similarly, Jehn and Mannix (2001) found that group value consensus related positively to beneficial patterns of conflict via higher levels of trust, respect, cohesiveness, and liking. Hobman, Bordia, and Gallois (2004) found that a team's openness to diversity exhibited a positive relationship with team involvement.

Diversity

Diversity factors consider the influence of the heterogeneity of team member characteristics on team mediators and outcomes (Chen et al., 2004). Findings indicate that diversity is a complex input factor in team effectiveness models, with studies reporting diversity as being beneficial, detrimental, and having no impact on processes, states, and performance (see Webber & Donahue, 2001). Additionally, research has shown diversity effects interact with time (Harrison et al., 1998), task type (Joshi & Jackson, 2003; Pelled, Eisenhardt, &

Xin, 1999), and organizational culture (Brickson, 2000; Ely & Thomas, 2001). Although there is a large literature dealing with team diversity and several comprehensive reviews (Jackson, Joshi, & Erhardt, 2003; Jackson, May, & Whitney, 1995; Milliken & Martins, 1996; Williams & O'Reilly, 1998), we focus on the diversity among team members in terms of demographic, functional background, personality, and attitudes/values, as well as complex combinations.

Demographic. A meta-analysis by Webber and Donahue (2001) sought to distill the influence of demographic diversity, and found no support for a relationship with either cohesion or performance. However, a number of studies have found diversity in age (Kilduff et al., 2000) and tenure (Jehn & Bezrukova, 2004) to be beneficial to performance. In contrast, race/ ethnicity, gender, age, tenure, and education (e.g., Jackson, Joshi, & Erhardt, 2003; Kirkman, Tesluk, & Rosen, 2001; Leonard, Levine, & Joshi, 2004; Li & Hambrick, 2005; Mohammad & Angell, 2003, 2004; Pelled et al., 1999; Simons, Pelled, & Smith, 1999; Timmerman, 2000; Townsend & Scott, 2001; Watson et al., 1998) have all been shown to be detrimental to processes (e.g., relationship conflict), emergent states (e.g., empowerment; organizational commitment), and performance. Interestingly, when time is added into the equation, the results vary. For instance, Harrison et al. (1998) found that surface-level diversity (e.g., age) interacted with time such that its influence was neutralized as members spent more time working together. Also notable in this area are the studies that consider complex interactions among diversity attributes. Jackson and Joshi (2004) found evidence of a three-way diversity interaction, with sales team performance being lowest for teams with a combination of relatively high tenure, gender, and ethnic diversities. In summary, it appears that the effect of diversity may vary as a function of a team's task and embedding context, such as culture and climate, as well as time (see Jackson et al., 2003).

Functional. Functional diversity has been examined primarily within the context of management teams, and it is thought to provide them with a breadth of perspectives, skills, and expertise (Hoffman & Maier, 1961). However, functional diversity has not always been associated with higher performance (e.g., Carpenter, 2002; Jehn & Bezrukova, 2004; Pelled et al., 1999; Pitcher & Smith, 2001) and has, in fact, been shown to inhibit processes and effectiveness through increased conflict (Knight et al., 1999; Pelled et al., 1999), reduced information sharing (Ancona & Caldwell, 1992), and slower competitive response (Hambrick, Cho, & Chen, 1996). Despite this, there have been some recent theoretical and operational developments related to functional diversity. Specifically, Bunderson and Sutcliffe (2002) demonstrated that the various conceptualizations of functional diversity may differentially affect processes and performance. They also introduced the notion of intrapersonal functional diversity (i.e., the extent to which team members are functional specialists or broad generalists with work experiences spanning a range of functional areas) and found that interpersonal functional diversity (i.e., between-person heterogeneity) exhibited a negative effect, whereas average intrapersonal (i.e., within-person heterogeneity) exhibited a positive effect, on team information processing and thereby performance.

Personality. Much like the findings associated with the diversity of other attributes, heterogeneity in personality traits has yielded a vast array of mixed results. Researchers have found diversity of team extraversion (Mohammad & Angell, 2003; Neuman, Wagner, & Christiansen, 1999) and emotional stability (Neuman et al., 1999) to relate positively to performance. Diversity in extraversion, however, has been shown to be detrimental to processes (Mohammad & Angell, 2004), whereas member diversity in terms of agreeableness and neuroticism have been shown to negatively affect performance (Halfhill et al., 1999; Mohammad & Angell, 2003). Moving beyond the Big Five, Mohammad and

Angell (2004) found that diversity in members' time urgency (i.e., a trait variable relating to perceptions of deadlines, time awareness, and the rate at which tasks must be performed; Landy, Rastegary, Thayer, & Colvin, 1991) was positively related to relationship conflict in teams.

Attitudes/values. While sparse team composition research has examined the diversity of team member attitudes, work by Harrison and his colleagues (Harrison et al., 1998; Harrison, Price, Gavin, & Florey, 2002) represents an exception. In their earlier (1998) study, they differentiated between surface (i.e., easily identifiable attributes such as race, age, and gender) and deep-level attributes (i.e., underlying attributes such as attitudes, values, etc.). More recently, Harrison et al. (2002) examined the diversity of members' attitudes regarding terminal values, task meaningfulness, and outcome importance. They employed a four-wave longitudinal design that highlighted the interaction between time and diversity and delved deeper into the dynamics associated with attitudinal diversity including the interplay of perceived and actual diversities.

Complex Combinations

Although means and variances of individuals' characteristics represent popular compositional approaches for indexing member influences, more complex compilational approaches have also been advanced in the past decade.

Faultlines. The concept of faultlines was introduced by Lau and Murnighan (1998) and refers to hypothetical dividing lines that split a group into subgroups based on one or more attributes (e.g., demographic, functional and educational background, geographical location, etc.). Faultline strength has been shown to exhibit a negative relationship with processes (Li & Hambrick, 2005; Polzer, Crisp, Jarvenpaa, & Kim, 2006; Thatcher, Jehn, & Zanutto, 2003) and emergent states such as cohesion (Molleman, 2005) and behavioral/social integration (Li & Hambrick, 2005; Rico, Molleman, Sanchez-Manzanares, & Van der Vegt, 2007). However, Lau and Murnighan (2005) unexpectedly found that faultline strength was associated with less conflict and more group learning, psychological safety, and team satisfaction. Their counterintuitive findings suggest that faultlines are not yet fully understood. More complex relationships have also been investigated, and results indicate that the influence of faultlines depends on autonomy (e.g., Molleman, 2005; Rico et al., 2007) and that the effectiveness of communications depends on faultline strength (Lau & Murnighan, 2005). Thatcher et al. (2003) simultaneously examined faultlines composed of multiple team member characteristics and found evidence of a curvilinear relationship, with groups having no or strong faultlines exhibiting higher levels of conflict and lower levels of morale and satisfaction than teams with moderate faultlines. In sum, the literature on faultlines is somewhat limited compared to other composition issues. It offers promise, however, in terms of unraveling the dynamics given rise to by composition differences among team members and can certainly be expanded to consider the mechanisms by which faultlines influence performance, as well as how the effect of faultlines may change over time.

Position and status issues. Team composition research that focused on relative position or status often attends only to the highest or lowest individual composition score in a team. The underlying assumption is that a single individual, such as the most intelligent team member, can have a significant and disproportional influence on a team. Researchers often rely on Steiner's (1972) task classification to justify operationalizing a composition factor in this way. For instance, Steiner argued that in disjunctive tasks (e.g., problem solving), team performance is influenced by the smartest member, whereas in conjunctive tasks (e.g., assembly line), the capabilities of the weakest member tend to limit overall performance. Similarly, Barrick et al. (1998) argued that a single disagreeable member could hamper a team's ability to work together cooperatively and that a single emotionally unstable member can impair a team's functioning. This approach has been used by other researchers (e.g., Beersma, Hollenbeck, Humphrey, Moon, Conlon, & Ilgen, 2003; Halfhill et al., 1999; Neuman & Wright, 1999; Pearsall & Ellis, 2006; Day, Arthur, Miyashiro, Edwards, Tubre, & Tubre, 2004; Ellis, Bell, Ployhart, Hollenbeck, & Ilgen, 2005). Recently, Bell (2007) conducted a meta-analysis on deep-level composition factors and found that in lab settings, both minimum and maximum general cognitive ability predicted performance, whereas in field settings, minimum agreeableness was a strong predictor of performance. There also appear to be opportunities for integration between this and the network conceptualization of composition, as research on the "critical member" (cf. Ellis et al., 2005) also points to issues of position and status. While less prevalent among team composition research, considerations of the circumstances under which, and the mechanisms by which, a single member or subset can substantively influence processes and performance is an area that would benefit from future research.

Network features. The network perspective is increasingly prevalent in teams research (Borgatti & Foster, 2003). Research that examines network features associated with teams focuses on the social connections (i.e., ties) that link members between and within teams. One research stream considers the dynamics associated with network connections among members of a single team and suggests that factors relating to individuals in specific network positions within a team can influence outcomes at the team-level (e.g., Ellis et al., 2005; Mehra, Kilduff, & Brass, 2001; Pearsall & Ellis, 2006). Ellis and colleagues (2005), for instance, focused on criticality (i.e., the extent to which removing a particular task position might break down the team's workflow) and found that the knowledge held by critical team members was especially important for effectiveness. Their research suggests that criticality can play an important role in team settings, because critical team members may serve as a conduit for effective team functioning. Klein, Lim, Saltz, and Mayer (2004) considered how composition factors function as antecedents and found that member personality and demographic factors can predict member centrality. Specifically, they found that members with high levels of education and low levels of neuroticism were highly central.

A second vein of this research considers the network position of a team within its larger embedding context. Balkundi and Harrison (2006) conducted a meta-analysis of 37 studies and found that social networks have important implications for team performance and viability. Specifically, teams with dense configurations of ties (i.e., the level of interrelatedness among all possible social ties) exhibited higher levels of goal attainment and were more likely to remain together as compared to teams with sparse network ties. Their study also found that teams with leaders who were high, rather than low, in centrality tended to be more productive and that a team's centrality in an interteam network was conducive to performance. Centrality appeared to provide teams with advantages in terms of acquiring and applying resources. Finally, Balkundi and Harrison illustrated a moderating effect of time (i.e., in terms of both familiarity and temporal precedence) and tie content. This dual approach of examining networks within and between teams offers a comprehensive perspective of social networks in team context. It also provides a realistic perspective in terms of inherently recognizing that teams do not work in a vacuum, but instead they function within larger organizational networks and are in themselves social networks of team members.

Summary Impressions and Future Directions

Over the past decade, the team composition research has continued to flourish and to answer important questions about assembling individuals to work together as a team. Yet as many questions remain as have been answered. Below we outline six areas that we believe warrant further attention.

First, we believe that greater scrutiny should be devoted to the construct validity of compositional (mean and variance approaches) variables. In other words, *what does the average level or variance of individual characteristics represented within a team really mean?* Is average cognitive ability a resource that can be deployed by the team if it has effective transactive memory systems in place? Does a high variance in conscientiousness imply that there will be disagreements about how and when things should be done (i.e., a sign of a weakness), or does it imply that the team is "balanced" in terms of who will monitor work and keep the team on pace (i.e., a sign of strength)? In short, we believe that many team compositional studies may be ones of convenience where researchers had measures of individual differences available and sought to "make something interesting out of them." While we encourage creative thinking in research, we worry about Type I errors that may result from scholars looking at myriad combination strategies and featuring the ones that "work out best." In contrast to such approaches, Hofmann and Jones (2005) advocated an isomorphic referent-shift theory of team personality that likened Big 5 constructs at the team-level of analysis to emergent climate variables. This is one example of construct development that goes beyond a simple aggregation of individuals' attributes.

A second issue concerns *how compositional indices operate over time.* Recall that Harrison and colleagues (1998, 2002) demonstrated that the influence of surface-level differences diminished over time, whereas the influence of deeper differences strengthened. Their studies, however, are more the exception than the norm, and our understanding is far from complete. Teams do not operate in static environments, yet more often than not, team composition research is cross-sectional and provides little insight into temporal dynamics.

Third, we believe that future advances are likely to come from viewing *team composition as a complex combination of member attributes.* Mean and diversity indices implicitly assume that all members contribute equally to a team composition, we believe that it is far more often the case that members exert disproportionate influences on team functioning by virtue of the positions that they occupy, their relative status, and so forth.

Fourth, there has been very little in the way of research on *dynamic team composition.* The modal composition study indexes team composition at one point in time and associates it with mediators and outcomes measured at later times. However, members move on and off teams for a variety of reasons ranging from promotions and turnover to changing task demands that necessitate compositional changes. For example, the second author conducted a study of accounting audit teams that worked with several different organizations. Few team members were present throughout the entire project, as some members worked the initial stages and left while others came in and wrapped up the latter portions of each project. Very few studies that we are aware of mentioned such dynamics, let alone accounted for them empirically.

Fifth, there are interesting questions regarding *how to best balance team composition needs with the desire to develop individual members.* In real organizational settings, managers often face decisions about staffing a team with an individual that is most qualified for the task, or a less qualified individual for whom the assignment would provide an important developmental opportunity. While managers appear to rely on some internal cognitive algorithm to make such decisions, the research on teams has not yet begun to address this issue. Thus, there are opportunities for researchers to investigate when, and under which circumstances, team leaders may consider incorporating developmental considerations into team staffing decisions.

Finally, although scholars have acknowledged *that individuals often belong to multiple teams simultaneously* (e.g., Espinosa, Cummings, Wilson, & Pearce, 2003), there is scant research devoted to how this influences either teams or individuals. For instance, in project-based settings, individuals are often part of a resource pool that is drawn from according to some combination of their KSAs and the needs of the project or team task. Individuals may simultaneously be members of four or five teams. How do such work arrangements influence their contributions, identity, and so forth to each team? What impact does this have on the members themselves? Does it matter if they occupy similar or widely different roles across those various team memberships? Although this type of work arrangement is quite prominent these days, very little is known about its implications for teams and individuals alike.

Team-Level Inputs

There are numerous team-level input variables discussed within the literature that influence mediators and outcomes. In the following section, we focus on a select group of such constructs that have received substantial attention within the past decade: interdependence, virtuality, training, leadership, and team structure. Table 9.2.4 presents examples of studies that employed team-level variables as antecedents of mediators and outcomes.

Interdependence

Researchers have long sought to distinguish between different types of teams based on the contexts within which they work, their type of task, and the length of time the team is together (e.g., Chen, 2005). Using such variables as evaluative characteristics, various typologies of teams have been suggested (e.g., Cohen & Bailey, 1997; Katzenbach & Smith, 1993; Mohrman, Cohen, & Mohrman, 1995; Sundstrom, De Meuse, & Futrell, 1990). However, a potentially more informative way in which to characterize teams is according to their underlying substantive nature, such as in terms of their degree and type of interdependence.

At its core, interdependence describes the "extent to which team members cooperate and work interactively to complete tasks" (Stewart & Barrick, 2000: 137). Although prominent in many definitions of organizational teams (e.g., Guzzo & Dickson, 1996; Kozlowski & Bell, 2003), researchers have continued to call for empirical work to include considerations of interdependence. In fact, Kozlowski and Bell (2003) stated that research that fails to consider interdependence has little value in developing knowledge about organizational teams. In an attempt to include greater depth to discussions of team interdependence, many researchers have attempted to highlight different types of interdependence and assess their respective impacts on processes and effectiveness (e.g., Guzzo & Shea, 1992). The primary types of interdependence discussed include input, process, and outcome interdependence.

Wageman (1995) was one of the first to differentiate *input* and *process* interdependence. Specifically, she suggested that team members' level of interaction (or interdependence) is shaped by their individual skill sets and the extent to which they must share resources and technologies (i.e., input interdependence). Likewise, the way in which the work is structured (i.e., process interdependence) can also affect the level of interdependence within the team. For example, Wageman described the job of salespeople and how their work can be designed to either make sales calls individually or as a team. Campion, Medsker, and Higgs (1993) described a third type of interdependence—reward and feedback interdependence (or what

Table 9.2.4 Exemplar Team-Level Input Influence Studies

Study	Sample	Input Factor	Emergent States	Processes	Outcomes	Findings
Balkundi and Harrison (2006)	Meta-analysis of 37 studies	Network density, team leaders; centrality; familiarity			Performance,[4] team viability[5]	Network density related positively to team performance and viability, and time (i.e., familiarity and precedence) moderated structure–performance relationships. Team and team leader centrality also related positively to performance.
Burke et al. (2006)	Meta-analysis (50 studies, 113 effect sizes)	Leadership	Internal team environment	Team learning	Performance[4]	Task-focused leader behaviors moderately related to team effectiveness (.33, .20); person-focused behaviors related positively to team effectiveness (.36, .28) and to team learning (.56).
Carson, Tesluk, and Marrone (2007)	59 consulting teams	Shared leadership	Psychological safety	Shared leadership emergence	Performance[2]	The internal team environment and external coaching related positively to shared leadership, which predicted team performance.
Gibson and Gibbs (2006)	56 aerospace design teams	Team virtuality			Innovation[4]	Each of the four dimensions of team virtuality was negatively associated with innovation.
Kirkman and Rosen (1999)	111 teams from 4 organizations	Leader behaviors, team responsibility			Productivity,[1] customer service,[2] job satisfaction,[5] organizational commitment,[5] team commitment[5]	External leaders' actions enhanced team empowerment experiences. Empowered teams exhibited higher levels of productivity, customer service, job satisfaction, organizational and team commitment.
Kirkman, Rosen, Tesluk, and Gibson (2004)	40 geographically distributed service teams	Training proficiency	Trust		Performance[2]	Training proficiency related positively to performance when teams had high levels of trust and technology support, and when team leaders had longer tenures.

(Continued)

Table 9.2.4 Continued

Study	Sample	Input Factor	Emergent States	Processes	Outcomes	Findings
Langfred (2005)	89 manufacturing teams	Task interdependence	Individual- and team-level autonomy		Team performance[4]	Individual- and team-level autonomy interacted with task interdependence to explain team performance.
Moreland, Argote, and Krishnan (1998)	186 student assembly (lab) teams	Training condition (individuals vs. intact teams)	Transactive memory		Performance[4]	Teams trained as intact groups exhibited higher levels of transactive memory and performance.
Stewart (2006)	Meta-analytic review of 93 studies	Team design (meaningfulness, autonomy, intrateam coordination)			Performance[4]	Meaningfulness exhibited a model relationship with performance. Additionally, autonomy and intrateam coordination corresponded with higher performance.

Note: Performance: 1 = quantity, 2 = quality, 3 = timeliness, 4 = mixed, 5 = affective outcomes, 6 = individual-level outcomes.

Guzzo & Shea [1992] referred to as outcome interdependence). The importance of *outcome* interdependence is based on the statement that "individual feedback and rewards should be linked to the group's performance in order to motivate group-oriented behavior" (Campion et al., 1993: 827). Equally important to considerations of the various types of interdependence is the manner in which interdependence is conceptualized. Specifically, researchers have considered it as both an input variable and as a moderating variable.

Stewart and Barrick (2000) assessed the level of process interdependence and found that task type greatly affected the relationship between interdependence and manager-rated team performance. Specifically, they found that for conceptual tasks, teams with both low and high levels of interdependence exhibited strong performance results (i.e., interdependence exhibited a u-shaped relationship with performance). Conversely, for behavioral tasks—that is, execution of manual tasks (McGrath, 1984), interdependence exhibited an inverted u-shaped relationship with performance. While such findings in terms of the relationship between interdependence and performance are consistent with earlier interdependence research (e.g., Saavedra, Earley, & Van Dyne, 1993; Wageman, 1995), Stewart and Barrick extended this work by demonstrating that intrateam processes (e.g., communication, conflict, flexibility, and shirking) served as a mediator of the relationship.

De Dreu (2007: 634) focused on outcome interdependence and found that "cooperative outcome interdependence related to more information sharing, to learning, and to higher levels of team effectiveness when task reflexivity was high." In contrast, Langfred (2005) found that interdependence interacted with team-level autonomy in shaping overall performance. Specifically, he provided evidence of "a positive relationship between team autonomy and team performance under conditions of high task independence and a negative relationship between team autonomy and team performance under conditions of low task interdependence" (p. 520). Similarly, Barrick et al. (2007) illustrated that interdependence positively moderated the relationship between a blended cohesion and communication team mediator and organizational performance. Finally, Van Der Vegt, Emans, and Van De Vliert (2000) featured team interdependence as a cross-level moderator variable of individual-level task interdependence—individual-level affective outcomes (e.g., job satisfaction, team satisfaction, job commitment, and team commitment) and found that the lower level relationships were stronger when teams had higher levels of interdependence.

Technology / Virtuality

Technological advancements have allowed organizations to make greater use of virtual teams. In fact, estimates suggest that 60% of professional workers work within virtual teams (VT; Kanawattanachai & Yoo, 2002). Martins, Gilson, and Maynard's (2004) review of the VT literature noted that early research typically contrasted VT functioning to that of traditional face-to-face teams. Rather than replicate Martins et al.'s work, herein we focus on two topics that they highlighted as needing more research attention and that have subsequently been considered—leadership and the extent of virtuality.

VT leadership has received some attention (e.g., Hedlund, Ilgen, & Hollenbeck, 1998; Johnson, Suriya, Yoon, Berrett, & La Fleur, 2002), but is still an area that is not all that well understood. For example, Carte, Chidambaram, and Becker (2006) studied semester-long virtual student project teams and found that higher performing VTs displayed significantly more leadership behaviors. However, they extended prior work by providing evidence that specific leadership behaviors, namely, behaviors focused on *performance* and *keeping track of group work*, were the primary drivers of such an effect. In contrast, Hambley, O'Neill, and Kline (2007) investigated the role of leadership style (i.e., transformational, transactional) and failed to find any significant relationships with either style and the quality of team interactions.

Martins et al. (2004) also highlighted that not all VTs are created equal, and therefore researchers should consider the effect that a team's *extent of virtuality* has on mediators and outcomes. Researchers appear to have taken this recommendation to heart, as work has evolved to consider virtuality as an enabling mechanism for many if not all types of teams. For instance, Kirkman and Mathieu (2005) defined team virtuality in terms of three dimensions: (a) the degree of reliance on virtual tools, (b) the informational value of the mediums used, and (c) the synchronicity of interactions. Empirically, Kirkman et al. (2004) demonstrated that the extent to which teams met face to face moderated the relationship between team empowerment and performance (i.e., process improvement). Elsewhere, Gibson and Gibbs (2006) found evidence that four dimensions of virtuality (geographic dispersion, electronic dependence, structural dynamism, and national diversity) were distinct and had differential negative effects on team innovation.

Team Training

Training refers to a systematic, planned intervention aimed at facilitating the development of job-related KSAs (Goldstein, 1992). There has been much research on the basic principles of team training and a number of comprehensive reviews on the training literature (e.g., Kozlowski & Bell, 2003; Kozlowski & Ilgen, 2006; Salas & Cannon-Bowers, 2001; Salas, Rozell, Mullen, & Driskell, 1999; Salas, Wilson, Burke, & Wrightman, 2006). Still, key questions remain about what to train, how to train, and when to train (Kozlowski & Bell, 2003). A recent team training meta-analysis conducted by Salas, Nichols, and Driskell (2007) confirmed a small to moderate correlation of .29 for the overall influence of team training on improvements in both objective and supervisor ratings of team performance. Furthermore, their analysis found training interventions focused on adaptive team mechanisms exerted the strongest influence on team performance, relative to guided team self-correction and cross-training interventions.

There are numerous aspects of team training that can be discussed including training needs analyses, training motivation, specific training/learning approaches, transfer, and evaluation. Because a full review of the training literature is beyond the scope of this article, we focus on three areas that we believe are particularly in need of attention: individual versus intact-team training, delivery systems, and embedded training.

Individual versus intact-team training. Given the limited empirical evidence concerning the benefits of training individuals versus intact teams, Kozlowski and Bell (2003: 357) asserted that "research on this issue is virtually nonexistent." Most researchers agree that training designed to develop task-relevant skills should be directed at individual team members (Dyer, 1984). Alternatively, training teamwork skills, or those focused on the behaviors and attitudes necessary for effective team functioning, are believed to be best delivered to intact teams rather than to individual members (e.g., Cannon-Bowers, Tannenbaum, Salas, & Volpe, 1995; Moreland, Argote, & Krishman, 1998). The logic underlying this position is that training intact teams provides opportunities for members to integrate their teamwork skills and to jointly practice complex coordinated actions (Kozlowski, 1998; Kozlowski, Brown, Weisbein, Cannon-Bowers, & Salas, 2000). Cannon-Bowers and colleagues' (1995) framework continues to guide researchers' decisions about this training design issue. They depicted competencies as either task-related or team-related, and specific (i.e., contextually related to the team or its task) or generic (i.e., applicable and transportable across team and task contexts). Their work provides the foundation for an emerging literature that demonstrates that generic teamwork competencies can be improved through training interventions (e.g., Chen, Donohue, & Klimoski, 2004; Ellis et al., 2005; Rapp & Mathieu, 2007).

Delivery system. While most team training research has focused on traditional, face-to-face training (Goldstein & Ford, 2002), there are alternative training delivery methods, such as self-administered CD, multimedia instruction, and Web-based training, which have received less attention (Kirkman, Rosen, Tesluk, & Gibson, 2006; Rapp & Mathieu, 2007). Because these new methods offer superior flexibility and exploit the increased computing power, low cost, and enhanced connectivity that characterizes today's environment (Kozlowski & Bell, 2003), organizations are increasingly leveraging technology in their delivery of training (Salas & Cannon-Bowers, 2001). These technologies stand to make "going-to" training obsolete (Salas & Cannon-Bowers, 2001: 483) yet raise concerns about whether the implementation of technologically based delivered team training technologies is occurring without the benefit of rigorous scientific theory and evaluation (Kirkman, Lowe, & Gibson, 2006; Salas & Cannon-Bowers, 2001). There is emerging evidence that teamwork skills training delivered via computer-assisted means (e.g., CD-based) is indeed effective (e.g., Kirkman, Lowe, & Gibson, 2006; Rapp & Mathieu, 2007), but more research is needed to determine how best to deliver training content via technology, the conditions under which the various delivery mechanisms are most effective, and how to provide trainees with feedback.

Embedded. Research that considers the notion of embeddedness stresses that training is inextricably linked to the larger organizational context and cannot be isolated from the larger system that it supports (Salas & Cannon-Bowers, 2001). Kozlowski and Salas (1997) presented a conceptual, multilevel model for training implementation and transfer that was fully built upon the notion of embeddedness. They emphasized alignment between embedding contextual features that support training transfer systems (i.e., downward congruence processes) as well as processes that allow the aggregation of training-induced changes to affect the intended, higher level targets (i.e., upward composition processes). Some training research has taken a step toward addressing such concerns by incorporating the role that the larger embedding context plays in training transfer processes. In fact, Tracey and Tews (2005) noted that

> although the nature and relevance of such constructs as "perceived organizational support" have been established and linked to a variety of work-related attitudes and outcomes . . . focused attention should be given to the conceptual meaning and operationalization of constructs associated with the work environment that are specific to training. (p. 354)

Accordingly, opportunities exist for researchers to adopt a more complex, conceptually grounded view of training embeddedness. Whereas sparse training research has adopted an embeddedness perspective, we believe such a perspective offers great promise for future research because it inherently recognizes the linkages among factors crossing the individual, team/unit, and organizational levels of analysis that allow training provided to individuals and teams to "bubble up" and yield the anticipated changes at higher levels of analysis (see Mathieu & Tesluk, in press).

Team Leadership

Zaccaro, Rittman, and Marks (2001: 452) observed that despite the abundance of literature on leadership and team dynamics, "we know surprisingly little about how leaders create and manage effective teams." There is a vast literature on leadership in teams that has been the subject of several thorough literature reviews (e.g., Kozlowski & Bell, 2003; Kozlowski & Ilgen, 2006; Zaccaro et al., 2001) as well as a recent meta-analysis (Burke, Stagl, Klein, Goodwin, Salas, & Halpin, 2006). In light of these works, we direct our review toward three aspects of leadership in teams that we believe hold particular promise for future research efforts: external team leaders, team coaching, and shared leadership.

External leadership. External team-oriented leadership represents the traditional paradigm and focuses on the influence of a leader who is responsible for, and has authority for, the team's performance. In effect, this work generally adopts an average leadership style presuming that the external leader's behavior influences the team as a whole. Although there are dyadic leadership models, they are not typically directed at influencing team mediators or outcomes.

The influence of external leader behaviors on team mediators and outcomes has been widely documented (see Burke et al., 2006), and it has been argued that the actions of an external team leader can make or break their success (Druskat & Kayes, 2000). Overall, the research indicates that team leadership is an important ingredient in realizing team affective (e.g., Foels, Driskell, Mullen, & Salas, 2000) and behavior-based (Burke et al., 2006) outcomes. Leadership is viewed primarily as an input factor that influences processes (e.g., coordination, creativity processes, knowledge sharing, problem management/action strategies, team learning), emergent states (e.g., affective tone, efficacy, empowerment, potency, organizational and team commitment, task, leader, and team satisfaction), and performance (Ahearn, Ferris, Hockwarter, Douglas, & Ammeter, 2006; Chen et al. 2007; Kirkman & Rosen, 1999; Lim & Ployhart, 2004; Srivastava et al., 2006; Sy, Cote, & Saavedra, 2005; Tesluk & Mathieu, 1999). The pervasive assumption is that external team leaders are valuable because they serve as coordinators of operations, as liaisons to external teams or management, and as guides for setting the team's vision (Zaccaro et al., 2001; Morgeson, 2005).

The functional approach to understanding the roles of external leaders dates back many years (e.g., Fleishman et al. 1991; McGrath, 1962). Although many labels have been assigned to the various leader functions, they distill down to two general categories that concern facilitating teamwork and taskwork dimensions. The recent meta-analysis by Burke and colleagues (2006) echoed this notion by classifying leader behaviors as either person-focused (i.e., behaviors focused on developing team members or maintaining socioemotional aspects of the team) or task-focused (i.e., those dealing with task accomplishment). Their analysis revealed that with respect to person-focused behaviors, transformational and consideration behaviors were positively related to perceived team effectiveness ($r = .34$ and $.25$, respectively). Task-focused behaviors including initiating structure and boundary spanning related positively to perceived team performance ($r = .31$ and $.49$, respectively). They also found team interdependence to be a moderating influence with regard to perceived team effectiveness. Druskat and Wheeler (2003: 455) observed that despite this recognition, "external leaders appear to be a forgotten group" and that "scholars have provided little theory to clarify their role." More recently, Burke et al. (2006) lamented that there is a lack of integration concerning the relationship between external leader behaviors and team performance. Consequently, there remains much to be learned about the nature of the external leader's influence on teams.

Coaching. Team coaching refers to "direct interaction with a team intended to help members make coordinated and task-appropriate use of their collective resources in accomplishing the team's work" (Hackman & Wageman, 2005: 269). Examples of coaching behaviors include identifying team problems, process consultation, cueing and rewarding self-management, and problem-solving consultation (Wageman, 2001). Teams researchers have acknowledged the coaching-type leadership behaviors for more than 50 years (see Wageman, 2001, for a review). After a hiatus of sorts, however, the concept has reemerged and taken hold in the literature on work teams. With regard to the relationship between coaching and team performance, the results are equivocal with some showing a positive influence (e.g., Edmondson, 1999) and others showing no influence (e.g., Wageman, 2001). Delving deeper than performance, however, studies have shown that coaching positively influences self-management, team member relationship quality, member satisfaction (Wageman, 2001), team empowerment (Kirkman & Rosen, 1999), and psychological safety (Edmondson, 1999).

Other research has suggested that the effects of coaching behaviors are dependent on other conditions, such as team design factors (e.g., Wageman, 2001) and the stability of the task environment (e.g., Morgeson, 2005). Most recently, Hackman and Wageman (2005) introduced a theory of team coaching that emphasizes functional and developmental perspectives. They delineated several functions that coaches fill in teams, including motivational (i.e., encouraging process gains), consultative (i.e., encouraging effective task performance strategies), and educational (i.e., addresses members' knowledge and skills). Hackman and Wageman adopted a temporal perspective and emphasized that coaching behaviors may be more or less important to a team's functioning at different stages of development. The coaching aspect of leadership offers a promising avenue of research, and we hope to see future research that examines the conditions (e.g., task, team, contextual, developmental) under which team coaching can meaningfully influence team performance.

Shared leadership. In recent years, there has been an increasing acceptance of the idea that leadership does not only stem from an external individual in a top-down process, but can also emerge from within the team itself (for a review, see Bennett, Harvey, Wise, & Woods, 2003). Despite nuanced differences in definitions, this latter perspective of leadership has been discussed in terms of shared, emergent, distributed, and lateral leadership (see Day, Gronn, & Salas, 2004). Shared leadership refers to an emergent team property resulting from leadership functions being distributed across multiple team members rather than arising from a single, formal leader (Carson, Tesluk, & Marrone, 2007). In effect, team-level leadership emerges from members' collective knowledge, skills, and abilities.

Relatively little research has been done in this area, although researchers have identified several antecedents to shared leadership, including a team's internal environment, external leader coaching (Carson et al., 2007), and a collectivist orientation among team members (Hiller et al., 2006). Researchers have also demonstrated that shared leadership relates positively to team performance (e.g., Carson et al., 2007; Ensley, Hmieleski, & Pearce, 2006; Hiller et al., 2006; Pearce & Simms, 2002; Pearce, Yoo, & Alavi, 2004; Sivasubramaniam, Murry, Avolio, & Jung, 2002; Taggar, Hackett, & Saha, 1999). Yet others (e.g., Mehra, Smith, Dixon, & Robertson, 2006) have found that distributed, or shared, leadership did not necessarily benefit performance. They found that only certain structures (i.e., distributed–coordinated) of shared leadership do and emphasized that to better understand the phenomenon, researchers must consider the structure of leadership within teams. Other research has highlighted conditions under which shared leadership may be effective. Carson et al. (2007), for instance, found that external leader coaching was important for developing shared leadership in teams that lacked a strong internal environment, whereas Taggar et al.

(1999) found that the effect of emergent leadership was greatest when other team members also demonstrated high levels of leadership influence. Hiller et al. (2006) sought to differentiate which aspects of shared leadership drive performance benefits, and concluded that developing and mentoring functions were most important.

Recent shared leadership work has made strides in terms of advancing more complete conceptualizations of the construct that take into account the relational dynamics inherent to it by leveraging a network lens (e.g., Carson et al., 2007; Mehra et al., 2006), which should provide a foundation for more rigorous research in the area. However, there are clear opportunities for future research to enrich the theory by taking into account the dynamic, interactive, and temporal elements that underlie Day et al.'s (2004) shared leadership model, which suggests that team leadership resources serve as input in the ongoing cycle and episodic nature of teams (Marks et al., 2001), as well as an output that is used in subsequent team performance cycles.

Team Structure

There are numerous ways in which an organization can structure its teams. Although not considered extensively, the way in which teams are structured can be important as it "serves as a bridge between organization-level strategy decisions and staffing decisions" (Hollenbeck et al., 2002: 600). Two of the more widely considered team structural options are functional and divisional team departmentalization. In essence, *functional* departmentalization occurs when individuals within a team are organized according to the similarity of the tasks they will perform. *Divisional* team departmentalization, on the other hand, organizes individuals within the team based on the geographic area served and/or the specific type of product for which they are responsible. Most of the research that considered team structure has been conducted in laboratory settings using undergraduate students working on computer simulations. For example, Hollenbeck et al. (2002) argued that managers need to consider the composition of their teams when deciding upon which specific type of structure to employ. Specifically, they illustrated that a divisional team structure was most effective for teams that possess high levels of cognitive ability. Hollenbeck et al. (2002) also demonstrated that a divisional structure combined with high levels of member cognitive ability is not beneficial if there is a poor fit between the team's structure and the external environment.

Ellis et al. (2003) broadened the team structure literature when they considered its influence on members sharing the same versus having unique pieces of information. Specifically, they articulated that a *divisional* team structure allows all individuals to share the same information which could have potential efficiency benefits for the team. However, they also highlighted research that has demonstrated that teams composed of members holding unique information often make better, more creative decisions (e.g., Hinsz, Tindale, & Vollrath, 1997). However, Ellis et al. (2003: 824) argued that whereas the *functional* and *divisional* structures predispose teams to having either unique or shared information, respectively, neither type of team structure offers "the optimal balance between commonly and uniquely distributed information within the team." As such, the researchers advocated a compromise type of structure which they labeled *pair-based* team structures. At their core, pair-based team structures motivate members to share expertise and responsibilities, and thereby "may allow for the best mix of common and unique information within the team" (Ellis et al., 2003: 824). In fact, findings from their research suggested that teams that were pair-based experienced significantly more learning than teams that were either functionally or divisionally structured. In an innovative consideration of team structure that included temporal factors, Moon et al. (2004) assessed how changing team structures influences performance. Their findings suggested that teams were likely to perform better when transitioning from a functional to divisional structure rather than the reverse.

Whereas research on functional, divisional, and pair-based team structures is one of the more fully developed literature streams pertaining to team structure, scholars have also considered other structural or team design dimensions. Specifically, Cohen and Bailey (1997: 243) discussed design factors in their review of the team literature defining factors as "those features of the task, group, and organization that can be directly manipulated by managers to create the conditions for effective performance." These would include variables within our discussion of individual- and team-level inputs. That said, researchers have considered the role that team-level self-management (e.g., Wageman, 2001) and self-leadership (e.g., Stewart & Barrick, 2000) play within an IPO or IMO team effectiveness framework.

Summary Impressions and Future Directions

Research focused on team-level inputs has made great strides in recent years, yet there remains a wealth of opportunities for further development. For example, while researchers have considered the impact that different types of interdependence have on team mediators and outcomes, scholars have yet to test whether the different types have interactive effects. Beyond the many directions for future VT research outlined by Martins et al. (2004), the team virtuality area is ripe for further development. For example, most of the work has focused on the nuances associated with interacting through different mediums. Yet virtuality enables different combinations of members to be part of a team. In other words, "going virtual" means that the composition of teams may differ markedly from who would be on the team if they had to be colocated. Rather than asking whether the same people can interact effectively through different media versus what they could do face to face, perhaps the more important question is whether comprising a virtual team of certain members is advantageous as compared to comprising a team of different members who are colocated.

As for the question of leading teams effectively, we believe that research needs to move beyond whether external leaders are superior to member-based leadership. If we adopt a perspective that team leadership is a set of functions that need to be somehow fulfilled (see Day et al., 2004), it changes the basic research questions. In other words, the question becomes, Who is best positioned to fulfill which types of leadership tasks? If leadership is distributed, how should the allocation of functions be determined? Should the allocation of functions remain fixed or be rotated among members and their leader? If they are rotated, on what basis should they change (e.g., randomly, temporally sequenced, etc.)? If leadership is a distributed function, what are the mechanisms for integrating different aspects of it? In short, we encourage researchers to take the next step beyond comparing external versus member-based leadership and explore the complexities of distributed leadership.

The topic of team coaching is becoming quite popular. Implicit in the approach outlined by Hackman and Wageman (2005) is that the same people can effectively operate as external leaders and coaches. This assumption, however, warrants closer examination. For example, do we know if people can easily transform from the leader role to a coaching role? Are those two skill sets likely to reside in the same people, and are they willing and able to transform their behaviors as necessary? Are formal leaders the best source of coaching, or might some third party better fulfill that role? Finally, do team members readily accept their external leader as a coach? Would they prefer that such encouragement come from a third party or perhaps from their teammates? The topic of team coaching is gaining attention in the practitioner and academic literatures, and we encourage researchers to explore these and other variations on the theme.

Finally, we wish to raise an important issue that relates to research about all team-level inputs. There is an implicit assumption that team-level inputs are uniform within teams and over time. Yet such an assumption is not likely to be true, and perhaps unpacking the variance that resides within teams might offer great insights. For example, it may well be that some members of a team need to work fairly closely with one another, share resources, coordinate their actions, and so forth, whereas others might work fairly independently. How would the overall interdependence of such a team be described? The VTs literature refers to "hybrid" arrangements where some members are colocated and work primarily face to face, whereas others might be at a distance and only linked to the rest of the team through virtual means. Some team leadership functions may be completed by the external team leader whereas others might be widely distributed across members. In short, a single descriptive index may not adequately capture the nature of a team-level input if it might take on different forms. There are probably lessons to be learned from the network literature and thinking about team functioning as a series of dyadic exchanges generating network properties. In sum, future research would benefit from considering more complex and differentiated team-level input factors.

Organizational/Contextual Inputs

Gully (2000: 27) submitted that "to conduct research on work teams in the organizational context, the team has to be treated as the primary level of analysis." His comment illustrates the notion that teams operate in contexts that facilitate or hinder their functioning. Moreover, contexts can be distinguished in terms of features of the embedding organizational system, as well as features of the larger environment outside of the organization. Accordingly, we define organizational contextual variables as sources of influence that are external to the team, yet emanate from the larger organizational system within which they are nested. In contrast, we define environmental contextual variables as sources of influence that emanate from outside of the organization yet influence team functioning.

Whereas the influence of context on team effectiveness has long been recognized (Gladstein, 1984; Hackman & Morris, 1975; McGrath, 1964), there is surprisingly little research devoted to it even in the past decade. Furthermore, many of the studies that purportedly test contextual influences do so at the team-level of analysis (e.g., Gladstein, 1984). In effect, these studies liken contextual influences to those that covary at the team-level of analysis rather than sources of influence that emanate from a higher level of analysis. Zellmer-Bruhn and Gibson (2006) referred to this approach as the "micro-context" and argued that it describes aspects of the setting that are often tailored to specific team needs. In contrast, they referred to "macro-[organizational] contexts" as including subsidiary and corporation characteristics that vary little among teams in an organization (or larger context) and are not likely to vary substantially across teams within a given setting. In other words, micro-contexts really describe team-level inputs, whereas macro-contexts refer to sources of influence that stem from a higher level of analysis. With this distinction in mind, below we consider work that has featured either organizational or environmental influences on team effectiveness. Table 9.2.5 presents examples of studies that have indexed different types of contextual variables as predictors of team mediators and outcomes.

Table 9.2.5 Exemplar Contextual-Level Influence Studies

Study	Sample	Contextual Variable	Team Mediators	Outcomes	Findings
Atuahene-Gima and Li (2004)[a]	256 TMTs of Chinese new technology ventures	Technology uncertainty		New product performance[1]	Technology uncertainty negatively moderated a relationship between team decision comprehensiveness and product performance.
Carpenter (2002)[a]	247 Industrial TMTs	Internationalization (complexity)		Return on assets[1]	Internationalization positively interacted with TMT heterogeneity as related to return on assets.
Gibson (2003)[b]	71 U.S. and Indonesian nursing teams	Culture	Quality improvement focus	Quality of service provided[2]	Indonesian teams exhibited higher quality of service as mediated by a quality improvement focus.
Keck (1997)[a]	74 TMTs in cement and minicomputer industries	Environmental stability		Financial performance[1]	Environmental stability positively interacted with TMT composition variables as related to performance.
Kirkman and Rosen (1999)[a]	111 mixed team types	Team-based HR policies, and social support	Empowerment	Performance;[4] customer service[2]	Team-based HR policies and social support related positively to performance and customer service, as mediated by empowerment.
Marks, DeChurch, Mathieu, Panzer, and Alonso (2005)[b]	92 lab action teams	MTS action transition	MTS and team action processes	MTS performance[1]	MTS transition processes related positively with MTS performance as partially mediated by MTS action processes.
Mathieu, Gilson, and Ruddy (2006)[a]	120 service teams	Team-based HR policies and supportive climate	Empowerment overall processes	Performance;[1] customer satisfaction[2]	Team-based HR policies and social support related positively to performance and customer satisfaction, as mediated by empowerment and processes.
Mathieu, Maynard, Taylor, Gilson, and Ruddy (2007)[b]	90 service teams	MTS coordination, and openness climate	Overall processes	Performance[1]	MTS coordination related positively to team performance, whereas openness climate related positively to team processes.
Sosik and Jung (2002)[b]	83 Korean and U.S. student teams	Individualism–collectivism	Potency	Performance[1]	Individualistic teams reported greater potency and performance that grew larger over time.
Zellmer-Bruhn and Gibson (2006)[b]	115 pharmaceutical teams	Global integration, and local responsiveness	Team learning, interpersonal relations	Task performance[1]	Global integration related negatively, whereas local responsiveness related positively to interpersonal relations and performance as mediated by learning.

Notes: Performance: 1 = quantity; 2 = quality; 3 = timeliness, 4 = mixed; 5 = affective outcomes, 6 = individual-level outcomes. TMT = top management team; MTS = multiteam systems; HR = human resources.
a. Team/organizational single-level design.
b. Cross-level design.

Organizational Contexts

Human resource systems. Gladstein (1984) and Campion and colleagues (Campion et al., 1993; Campion, Papper, & Medsker, 1996) were among the first to consider the influence of organizational contextual features on team mediators and outcomes. In the decade since Cohen and Bailey's (1997) review, Hyatt and Ruddy (1997) provided evidence that organizational factors such as recognitions and rewards and training systems had both direct and indirect effects on group effectiveness. Kirkman and Rosen (1999) found that team-based human resource policies related positively to team empowerment. Notably, however, both of these investigations employed a micro-context approach and operationalized contextual influences at the team-level of analysis. In other words, researchers have employed team members' perceptions of organizational features as indices of context without taking into consideration the hierarchical nesting of teams in contexts. In contrast, Zellmer-Bruhn and Gibson (2006) employed a cross-level design and found that multinational corporations (MNCs) that emphasized global integration related negatively to team learning, whereas MNCs that emphasized local responsiveness related positively to team learning. In turn, team learning was related positively to externally rated team performance and interpersonal relations. Thus, Zellmer-Bruhn and Gibson illustrated what Mathieu and Taylor (2007) described as a meso-mediational design, whereby the effects of higher level macro-organizational contextual variables on lower level team outcomes were transmitted through a lower level blended team mediator (i.e., team learning).

Openness climate. Lawler (1993) has long advocated a systems perspective that emphasizes employee involvement as the key ingredient of successful organizational designs. He argued that the role of top management is to sculpt a vision, implement various structures and rewards, and create a general climate that is supportive of employee involvement and teamwork. Kirkman and Rosen (1999) found that an organizational climate of openness in terms of a well-developed social structure and sociopolitical support was related positively with team empowerment and outcomes. Similarly, Mathieu et al. (2006) found support for positive correlations between openness climate with team empowerment and processes. Spreitzer, Cohen, and Ledford (1999) found a significant correlation between employee involvement context and manager-rated productivity among self-managed teams. Again, however, all three of these studies were conducted at the team-level of analysis and therefore operationalized the micro-context.

However, based on our review, we noted two studies that used cross-level designs to test the influence of macro organizational district-level influences on team mediators and outcomes. Tesluk et al. (1999) found that district-level management's attitudes toward employee involvement related significantly to unit-level climates for participation in decision making. They concluded "that the extent to which the climate within a work unit [team] encourages participation is, in part, a function of the practices and policies that support employee involvement in the broader organizational context" (Tesluk et al., 1999: 293). Additionally, Mathieu, Maynard, Taylor, Gilson, and Ruddy (2007) obtained a significant and positive cross-level relationship between organizational district-level openness climate and subsequent lower level team processes.

Multiteam systems coordination. Gully (2000: 32) argued that "organizational teams are coupled to one another and to the organization as a whole, but their boundaries are distinct enough to give them a separate identity. This is similar to the notion of loose coupling, or partial inclusion. In this sense, boundaries of teams both separate and link the work done by teams." Mathieu et al. (2001) advanced the notion of multiteam systems (MTSs), a particular organizational arrangement whereby teams of teams work collaboratively to achieve collective goals. Hyatt and Ruddy (1997) suggested that teams function more effectively as self-contained units when they have strong information networks along with communication and cooperation channels both within and between teams. Kirkman and Rosen (1999); de Jong et al. (2005); and Mathieu et al. (2006) all found that teams benefit from working in (micro-) contexts that have effective MTS coordination. Mathieu et al.'s (2007) cross-level study found that macro-organizational district MTS coordination related significantly to lower level team performance, but not to team processes. They also found a cross-level interaction whereby MTS coordination moderated lower level team process–performance relations. In a cross-level laboratory flight simulation, Marks, DeChurch, Mathieu, Panzer, and Alonso (2005) found that *intra*team processes were enhanced by effective MTS coordination (i.e., transition processes) only when teams worked in interdependent settings.

Environmental Context

While research on the influence of organizational contexts has been relatively sparse, that which has incorporated environmental factors from outside of the embedding organizations is even rarer. There have, however, been two exceptions to this trend. One area involves the interface between TMT features and organizational environments, whereas the other concerns the influence of cultural factors on team-level phenomena.

TMT–environment interface. TMT-context studies represent a unique situation when viewed from a "levels perspective." Normally teams are nested in larger entities such as organizations, which in turn are nested in strategic groups, industries, and so forth. However, given that there is only one TMT per organization, they reside at the same level of analysis as organizational properties and their environments. Nevertheless, team-contextual relationships are still salient.

Carpenter (2002) found positive relationships between TMT educational, functional, and tenure heterogeneity and performance in relatively complex versus relatively simple environments. Goll and Rasheed (1997) found that environmental munificence and dynamism moderated the relationship between TMT rational decision making and performance. Keck (1997) examined the relationship between various indices of TMT composition and organizational performance. She hypothesized and found support for positive relationships between team tenure heterogeneity, member replacements, less stratification, and shorter team tenure with organizational performance in relatively turbulent versus stable environmental periods. Hough and White (2003) tested whether pervasiveness of knowledge within teams is related to the quality of the decisions they make. Their results showed that pervasiveness of knowledge was positively related to decision quality in moderate to stable environments, but not in dynamic environments. Finally, Atuahene-Gima and Li (2004) found that team decision comprehensiveness related positively to new product performance when there was relatively low technology uncertainty, but not when there was relatively high technology uncertainty.

In summary, the research evidence is fairly consistent in terms of the role of the external environmental and TMT functioning. Complex environments place a premium on heterogeneous TMT compositions and flexible processes. In this sense, although the nature of the performance environments certainly differ between TMTs and other types of teams, the underlying nature of the team IMOI relationships appear to be fairly generalizable across team types (cf. Barrick et al., 2007).

Cultural influence on teams. Several studies have sought to examine the nature of team-related relationships in the context of cultures presumed to be supportive, or not, of such work arrangements. For example, Sosik and Jung (2002) examined the relationships between functional heterogeneity, potency, and performance of student teams from the United States and Korea. They found that U.S. student teams reported greater functional heterogeneity, potency, and performance as compared to Korean student teams, and these differences grew larger over time. Gibson (2003) studied the relationship between team quality improvement focus and the quality of service delivered by Indonesian and U.S. nursing teams. She found that Indonesian teams reported significantly greater social quality improvement, as compared to U.S. teams. In turn, social quality improvement was related positively with service quality suggesting a mediated relationship. Notably, numerous other studies examined the influence of culture on team-level mediators and outcomes but did so indexing culture as a team composition variable (i.e., as an average of members' individual cultural orientations; e.g., Gibson, 1999; Kirkman & Shapiro, 2001). Therefore, we consider those studies as indicative of team composition effects rather than micro- or macro-contextual influences.

In summary, work on the role of the larger cultural context on team functioning is beginning to emerge. That literature, however, has indexed culture in terms of (a) average individual orientations, (b) a team climate variable, or (c) a description of some larger context such as a region or country. Whereas all approaches represent viable ways to study cultural influences, they are not the same or interchangeable (Kirkman et al., 2006). When viewed in terms of an embedding context, however, cultures that are consistent with cooperation, collective activities, and so forth, appear to facilitate team effectiveness.

Summary Impressions and Future Directions

Although the extant literature has long theorized that both micro- and macro-contexts influence team functioning, relatively little research has examined such relationships. The vast majority of the work that has been done along these lines has featured micro-contextual variables with noticeably few true cross-level investigations. No doubt this pattern is somewhat attributable to the difficulties associated with sampling teams across contexts. Traditional team-focused studies are difficult to conduct, as teams constitute the focal level of analysis and securing a sufficient number of comparable ones for statistical analyses is challenging. Moreover, sampling a large number of teams from contexts that differ along substantive variables of interest is indeed a daunting task. Nevertheless, true progress along these lines will require such investments. Alternatively, this is clearly a domain where in-depth case studies offer a powerful alternative research design. If such cases are sampled selectively to represent varying levels of some substantive input (e.g., individual vs. team-based organizational reward systems, placid vs. turbulent performance environments), then qualitative investigations may prove to be particularly enlightening. Alternatively, large-scale collaborative efforts such as the *Globe Project* (House, Javidan, Hanges, & Dorfman, 2002) represent rare opportunities to test contextual hypotheses with adequate statistical power.

The alignment of micro- and macro-contextual features represents a fruitful avenue for future research (cf. Tesluk et al., 1999; Zellmer-Bruhn & Gibson, 2006). On one hand, one might expect that the more proximal micro-contexts would exert the most immediate influence on team mediators and outcomes given their immediate salience to team members. On the other hand, given the more pervasive influence of macro-contextual variables, in the long run perhaps they would influence team mediators and processes more so than micro-factors. And perhaps such factors may interact (cf. Mathieu et al., 2007; Tesluk et al., 1999). Additional research is clearly warranted in this area.

Given the proliferation of MNCs and the globalization of business, cultural influences are likely to play a larger and larger role on team functioning. The diversity literature to date has predominantly examined the compositional mixes of teams sampled from a given organization. Yet what is the role of culture on the functioning of, say, sales teams promoting the same product in different regions of the world? How does culture influence the functioning of cross-organizational teams? Would such effects be accentuated or mitigated if the teams interacted primarily through virtual rather than face-to-face means? In short, the open frontier for future researchers is to "look up" and consider downward influences on team functioning, as well as to explore further how members work to shape such contexts.

Conclusion

Looking Back

About a decade ago Cohen and Bailey (1997) provided a comprehensive review of the team literature. They identified five key areas that future research should explore: (a) group cognition, affect, and mood, (b) group potency and collective self-efficacy, (c) virtual and global teams, (d) environmental (institutional) factors, and (e) time. Using their recommendations as a framework, we have summarized our impressions of progress along these lines as detailed in Table 9.2.6. As shown, we conclude that there has been substantial work and great progress in the areas of group cognition, group potency and collective efficacy, and virtual and global teams. The topics of team affect and mood have garnered far less attention, although they continue to offer interesting avenues for future research. Most notably, although we see important theoretical advancements in the areas of environmental (institutional) factors and time, empirical research has not developed at the same pace. We believe that these two areas represent prime territories for future advancements.

Looking beyond Cohen and Bailey's (1997) recommendations, summing up the research that has been done over the past decade, we are quite impressed with both the quality and quantity of work conducted. As this and other reviews have documented, researchers are dealing with multifaceted questions, advancing and testing more complex models, and enhancing our overall understanding of team effectiveness. Moreover, the field has become more differentiated. Laboratory research continues to be done, but now often using highly complex and informative simulations. These have enabled researchers to test far more realistic team dynamics than were possible before the advent of today's technology. That said, field studies are now far more prevalent than they have been in the past and represent a particular strength that organizational scholars have brought to the study of groups. In short, the field is alive, well, and thriving. Yet we believe there is still something lacking.

The IPO model and its latter-day derivatives (e.g., IMOI) have served the field well. They have articulated the nature of the components that drive team effectiveness (i.e., inputs), the nature of the "black box" linking such drivers with outcomes (i.e., mediators), and the complex nature of the criteria space (i.e., outcomes). However, the IPO/IMOI frameworks were most suitable for situations where a given set of members operate within a clearly defined boundary for a set period of time and produce some quantifiable output or service. Modern-day organizational designs call into question such arrangements and, therefore, the applicability of the predominant research frameworks.

Table 9.2.6 Progress Regarding Cohen and Bailey's (1997) Agenda

Agenda Items	Summary Impressions
Group cognition	Substantial progress in the areas of shared mental models (e.g., Marks, Sabella, Burke, & Zaccaro, 2002), strategic consensus (e.g., Iaquinto & Fredrickson, 1997), and transactive memory systems. Numerous laboratory and field investigations, and recent moves toward more complex combinations. Future research would benefit from a synthesis of different forms of team cognition.
Affect	Relatively little work in the past decade, although there has been work on the construct validity of collective affect (e.g., Mason & Griffin, 2005) and evidence of a negative relationship between positive affective tone and group absenteeism (Mason & Griffin, 2003).
Mood	Some work in this area including how a leader's mood can influence the affective tone of the team (Sy, Cote, & Saavedra, 2005) and how teammates' moods can influence other members (Totterdell, 2000). Other work has examined the role that environmental factors play in the development of group-level mood (e.g., Kelly & Barsade, 2001).
Group potency and collective efficacy	Substantial work in this area as chronicled by numerous meta-analyses (e.g., Gully, Incalcaterra, Joshi, & Beaubien, 2002). Group potency and collective efficacy have both evidenced fairly consistent and moderate correlations with outcomes, particularly for highly interdependent teams. Future work should consider the evolution of such effects over time, as well as the antecedents of these emergent states.
Virtual and global teams	Work in this area has exploded in the past decade. The construct of virtuality has been elaborated (cf. Kirkman & Mathieu, 2005; Martins, Gilson, & Maynard, 2004) and field investigations are becoming more prominent. Future research should consider the role of virtual team compositions more deeply and investigate emergent state variables that have not received sufficient attention to date (e.g., shared cognition).
Environmental (institutional) factors	Whereas the theoretical distinction between "micro-context" and "macro-context" has been advanced, relatively little research has been done—with especially few cross-level studies of macro influences.
Time	While theoretical advancements concerning team maturation (e.g., Kozlowski, Gully, Nason, & Smith, 1999) and episodic approaches (e.g., Marks, Mathieu, & Zaccaro, 2001) have been made over the past decade, relatively little empirical work has featured time as a substantive variable. There are encouraging signs that this issue is attracting greater attention in recent years (e.g., Harrison, Price, & Bell, 1998; Harrison, Price, Gavin, & Florey, 2002; Mathieu & Rapp, in press)—a pattern that we hope accelerates in the future.

A Look Forward—Embrace the Complexity

Let us revisit the typical modern-day organizational team research design where members are sampled from a number of teams at some point in time (e.g., Mathieu et al., 2007). Initially, usually using either archival information or members' ratings, variables such as team composition, leadership, and other predictors are typically indexed. Then, perhaps at some later point in time, measures of team processes or emergent states, often along with perceptions of contextual factors, are gathered, again usually from team members. These inputs and mediators are then associated with outcome indices, ideally gathered at some later time either from team members, supervisors, or organizational records. Appreciate that such an approach represents more of an ideal than common design, as researchers often gather inputs, mediators, and even outcomes during one or two measurement occasions. This is not necessarily bad or sloppy research, as it is difficult to gain access and to measure relevant variables repeatedly in real-world teams. The current authors have faced a number of such challenges, invested a great deal of time, and know how difficult it is to move beyond the typical design. But we must begin to ask ourselves whether such an approach truly reveals the important dynamics of modern-day teamwork. For instance, is the initial assessment conducted at a uniformly meaningful point in time to use as a base point going forward for all teams in the sample? Probably not. We may well be sampling teams that vary widely in terms of their history of working together, stage of development, and so forth. Whereas some of these factors may be adequately indexed using measures such as team tenure, clearly many important nuances are not captured. In short, there are no doubt a slew of maturation differences, historical influences, and a wide variety of other threats to validity that go as simply unrecognized in our typical research designs.

Modern-day organizational designs are far more complex than ones from the past. As an example, consider a project team assigned with the design of a new product. Some of the members of this team may have a long history of working together (both good and bad), whereas others may be complete strangers assigned to the group solely for this task. They might meet face to face initially to determine the project scope, constituencies, resources, and so forth. An external leader may play a prominent role in this early stage, but then "hand off" control to the team members once they get rolling. The team may then break into individual or subgroup work and coordinate their subsequent actions, in part, through virtual means. Some individuals or subgroups are likely to work closely with one another, whereas others might work largely on their own for a while. They may well come together at various times for gateway reviews or checkpoints (i.e., episode transitions), and they may reconfigure into different working arrangements as the project develops. Sometimes feedback may be encouraging and generate positive affect and momentum; at other times the feedback could reveal performance problems and heighten anxieties.

As the project progresses from one stage to another, members may leave or join the team in different capacities. Some of these replacements may be planned, and some may arise because of a specific challenge being faced by the team or because a team member was unexpectedly needed elsewhere. In such a scenario, the team's developmental stage, progress toward their ultimate goal, episodic processes, interpersonal relationships, degree of virtuality, interdependence, structure, and leadership are all likely *dynamic inputs* to their later processes, emergent states, and outcomes. All the while team members are each working on other teams, sometimes with the same people, and sometimes not. These multiple team memberships are not likely to be all that well coordinated, meaning that at any given moment some members may be underutilized while others may be subject to undue pressures. Moreover, organizational and larger contexts are not static and often vary wildly over time. Time lines are slashed, budgets are cut, and some teams are even disbanded in midstream because their product was not progressing sufficiently or is no longer needed. Customer requirements change, projects creep into areas never anticipated, or some regulation may change project parameters or operating constraints. The clear message here is that investigating the function of such a team on two or three occasions is likely to miss far more of the important dynamics than it is to capture them, thereby rendering the traditional research design as lacking. The simple fact is that team arrangements suitable for IPO-style investigations may be more of the exception than the rule in modern-day organizations.

So, our challenge for future researchers is to embrace the complexity of current team arrangements. Rather than viewing these complex features of organizational teams as confounds or design problems to overcome, we submit that they are important variances to assess, model, and understand. They may, in fact, be the most important sources of influence to understand. This may well necessitate a new research paradigm, one that incorporates both quantitative and qualitative methodologies and one that is time sensitive and able to capture the inherent multifaceted nature of teamwork. Strategies in this regard may include qualitative research, time-sampling or diary-style investigations, and clever archival approaches. For example, teams who interact through virtual means leave traces of their interactions (e.g., threaded discussion lists, e-mails, video conferences), which, with the proper ethical consideration, can be used to index member interaction in a far more detailed way than would be available for traditional face-to-face teams.

In summary, we believe that great progress has been made in team research over the past decade. Additionally, there is every reason to feel confident that such progress will continue into the future. But, we also believe that we are at a turning point in that we have a solid theoretical foundation and empirical base from which to ground our future work. However, as we move forward, we need to not only build on what we have, but be willing to take great strides and in some cases leaps to ensure that we are capturing and embracing the complexities of current team arrangements and seeking to better understand them rather than to fit them into our current frameworks. We encourage researchers to "go there" in the next decade.

References

Ahearn, K., Ferris, G. R., Hockwarter, W. A., Douglas, C., & Ammeter, P. P. 2006. Leader political skill and team performance. *Journal of Management*, 30: 309–327.

Amason, A. C. 1996. Distinguishing the effects of functional and dysfunctional conflict on strategic decision making: Resolving a paradox for top management teams. *Academy of Management Journal*, 39: 123–148.

Ancona, D. G., & Caldwell, D. F. 1992. Demography and design: Predictors of new product team performance. *Organization Science*, 3: 321–341.

Ancona, D. G., & Chong, C. 1999. Cycles and synchrony: The temporal role of context in team behavior. *Research on Managing Groups and Teams*, 2: 33–48.

Ancona, D. G., Goodman, P. S., Lawrence, B. S., & Tushman, M. L. 2001. Time: A new research lens. *Academy of Management Review*, 26(4): 645–663.

Ancona, D. G., Okhuysen, G. A., & Perlow, L. A. 2001. Taking time to integrate temporal research. *Academy of Management Review*, 26: 512–529.

Argote, L., Gruenfeld, D., & Naquin, C. 1999. Group learning in organizations. In M. E. Turner (Ed.), *Groups at work: Advances in theory and research*, New York: Lawrence Erlbaum.

Argote, L., & McGrath, J. E. 1993. Group process in organizations: Continuity and change. In C. I. Cooper & I. T. Robertson (Eds.), *International Review of Industrial and Organizational Psychology*, Vol. 8: 333–389. London: Wiley.

Argote, L., & Olivera, F. 1999. Organizational learning and new product development: CORE processes. In L. L. Thompson, J. M. Levine, & D. M. Messick (Eds.), *Shared cognition in organizations: The management of knowledge*: 297–325. Mahwah, NJ: Lawrence Erlbaum.

Arnold, J. A., Arad, S., Rhoades, J. A., & Drasgow, F. 2000. The Empowering Leadership Questionnaire: The construction and validation of a new scale for measuring leader behaviors. *Journal of Organizational Behavior*, 21: 249–269.

Atuahene-Gima, K., & Li, H. Y. 2004. Strategic decision comprehensiveness and new product development outcomes in new technology ventures. *Academy of Management Journal*, 47(4): 583–597.

Austin, J. R. 2003. Transactive memory in organizational groups: The effects of content, consensus, specialization, and accuracy on group performance. *Journal of Applied Psychology*, 88: 866–878.

Balkundi, P., & Harrison, D. A. 2006. Ties, leaders, and time in teams: Strong inference about network structure's effects on team viability and performance. *Academy of Management Journal*, 49(1): 49–68.

Barrick, M. B., Bradley, B. H., Kristof-Brown, A. L., & Colbert, A. E. 2007. The moderating role of top management team interdependence: Implications for real teams and working groups. *Academy of Management Journal*, 50: 544–557.

Barrick, M. R., Stewart, G. L., Neubert, J. M., & Mount, M. K. 1998. Relating member ability and personality to work team processes and team effectiveness. *Journal of Applied Psychology*, 83: 377–391.

Bass, B. M., Avolio, B. J., Jung, D. I., & Berson, Y. 2003. Predicting unit performance by assessing transformational and transactional leadership. *Journal of Applied Psychology*, 88: 207–218.

Beal, D. J., Cohen, R. R., Burke, M. J., & McLendon, C. L. 2003. Cohesion and performance in groups: A meta-analytic clarification of construct relations. *Journal of Applied Psychology*, 88: 989–1004.

Beersma, B., Hollenbeck, J. R., Humphrey, S. E., Moon, H., Conlon, D. E., & Ilgen, D. R. 2003. Cooperation, competition, and team performance: Toward a contingency approach. *Academy of Management Journal*, 46: 572–590.

Bell, S. T. 2007. Deep-level composition variables as predictors of team performance: A meta-analysis. *Journal of Applied Psychology*, 92: 595–615.

Bennett, N., Harvey, J. A., Wise, C., & Woods, P. A. 2003. *Desk study review of distributed leadership*. Nottingham, UK: National College for School Leadership.

Bommer, W. H., Johnson, J. L., Rich, G. A., Podsakoff, P. M., & MacKenzie, S. B. 1995. On the interchangeability of objective and subjective measures of employee performance: A meta-analysis. *Personnel Psychology*, 48: 587–605.

Boone, C., Van Olffen, W., Van Witteloostuijn, A., & De Brabander, B. 2004. The genesis of top management team diversity: Selective turnover among top management teams in Dutch newspaper publishing, 1970–1994. *Academy of Management Journal*, 47: 633–656.

Borgatti, S. P., & Foster, P. 2003. The network paradigm in organizational research: A review and typology. *Journal of Management*, 29: 991–1013.

Borucki, C. C., & Burke, M. J. 1999. An examination of service-related antecedents to retail store performance. *Journal of Organizational Behavior*, 20: 943–962.

Bourgeois, L. J. 1985. Strategic goals, perceived uncertainty, and economic performance in volatile environments. *Academy of Management Journal*, 28: 548–573.

Bradley, J., White, B. J., & Mennecke, B. E. 2003. Teams and tasks—A temporal framework for the effects of interpersonal interventions on team performance. *Small Group Research*, 34(3): 353–387.

Brickson, S. 2000. The impact of identity orientation on individual and organizational outcomes in demographically diverse settings. *Academy of Management Review*, 25: 82–101.

Bunderson, J. S. 2003. Team member functional background and involvement in management teams: Direct effects and the moderating role of power centralization. *Academy of Management Journal*, 46: 458–474.

Bunderson, J. S., & Sutcliffe, K. M. 2002. Comparing alternate conceptualizations of functional diversity in management teams: Process and performance. *Academy of Management Journal*, 45: 875–893.

Bunderson, J. S., & Sutcliffe, K. M. 2003. Management team learning orientation and business unit performance. *Journal of Applied Psychology*, 88: 552–560.

Burke, C. S., Stagl, K. C., Klein, C., Goodwin, G. F., Salas, E., & Halpin, S. M. 2006. What type of leadership behaviors are functional in teams? A meta-analysis. *Leadership Quarterly*, 17: 288–307.

Button, S. B., Mathieu, J. E., & Zajac, D. 1996. Goal orientation in organizational research: A conceptual and empirical foundation. *Organizational Behavior and Human Decision Processes*, 67: 26–48.

Campion, M. A., Medsker, G. J., & Higgs, A. C. 1993. Relations between work group characteristics and effectiveness: Implications for designing effective work groups. *Personnel Psychology*, 46: 823–850.

Campion, M. A., Papper, E. M., & Medsker, G. J. 1996. Relations between work team characteristics and effectiveness: A replication and extension. *Personnel Psychology*, 49: 429–452.

Cannon-Bowers, J. A., Salas, E., & Converse, S. A. 1993. Shared mental models in expert team decision making. In J. N. J. Castellan (Ed.), *Current issues in individual and group decision making*: 221–246. Hillsdale, NJ: Lawerence Erlbaum.

Cannon-Bowers, J. A., Tannenbaum, S. I., Salas, E., & Volpe, C. E. 1995. Defining team competencies and establishing team training requirements. In E. Salas (Ed.), *Team effectiveness and decision making in organizations*: 333–380. San Francisco: Jossey-Bass.

Carmeli, A., & Schaubroeck, J. 2006. Top management team behavioral integration, decision quality, and organizational decline. *The Leadership Quarterly*, 17: 441–453.

Carpenter, M. A. 2002. The implications of strategy and social context for the relationship between TMT heterogeneity and firm performance. *Strategic Management Journal*, 23: 275–284.

Carpenter, M. A., & Sanders, W. G. 2002. Top management team compensation: The missing link between CEO pay and firm performance? *Strategic Management Journal*, 23(4): 367–375.

Carson, J. B., Tesluk, P. E., & Marrone, J. A. 2007. Shared leadership in teams: An investigation of antecedent conditions and performance. *Academy of Management Journal*, 50: 1217–1234.

Carte, T. A., Chidambaram, L., & Becker, A. 2006. Emergent leadership in self-managed virtual teams. *Group Decision and Negotiation*, 15: 323–343.

Chen, G. 2005. Newcomer adaptation in teams: Multilevel antecedents and outcomes. *Academy of Management Journal*, 48: 101–116.

Chen, G., Donahue, L. M., & Klimoski, R. J. 2004. Training undergraduates to work in organizational teams. *Academy of Management Learning & Education*, 3: 27–40.

Chen, G., Kirkman, B. L., Kanfer, R., Allen, D., & Rosen, B. 2007. A multilevel study of leadership, empowerment, and performance in teams. *Journal of Applied Psychology*, 92: 331–346.

Chen, G., & Klimoski, R. J. 2003. The impact of expectations on newcomer performance in teams as mediated by work characteristics, social exchanges, and empowerment. *Academy of Management Journal*, 46(5): 591–607.

Chen, G., Mathieu, J. E., & Bliese, P. D. 2004. A framework for conducting multilevel construct validation. In F. J. Yammarino & F. Dansereau (Eds.), *Research in multilevel issues: Multilevel issues in organizational behavior and processes*, Vol. 3: 273–303. Oxford, UK: Elsevier.

Cohen, S. G., & Bailey, D. E. 1997. What makes teams work: Group effectiveness research from the shop floor to the executive suite. *Journal of Management*, 23: 239–290.

Cohendet, P., & Steinmueller, W. E. 2000. The codification of knowledge: A conceptual and empirical exploration. *Industrial and Corporate Change*, 9: 195–209.

Colquitt, J. A., Noe, R. A., & Jackson, C. L. 2002. Justice in teams: Antecedents and consequences of procedural justice climate. *Personnel Psychology*, 55: 83–109.

Cooke, N. J., Kiekel, P. A., Salas, E., & Stout, R. 2003. Measuring team knowledge: A window to the cognitive underpinnings of team performance. *Journal of Applied Psychology*, 7: 179–199.

Day, D. V., Gronn, P., & Salas, E. 2004. Leadership capacity in teams. *Leadership Quarterly*, 15: 857–880.

Day, E. A., Arthur, W. J., Miyashiro, B., Edwards, B. D., Tubre, T. C., & Tubre, A. H. 2004. Criterion-related validity of statistical operationalizations of group general cognitive ability as a function of task type: Comparing the mean, maximum, and minimum. *Journal of Applied Social Psychology*, 34: 1521–1549.

De Dreu, C. K. W. 2007. Cooperative outcome interdependence, task reflexivity, and team effectiveness: A motivated information processing perspective. *Journal of Applied Psychology*, 92: 628–638.

De Dreu, C. K. W., & Weingart, L. R. 2003. Task versus relationship conflict: Team performance, and team member satisfaction: A meta-analysis. *Journal of Applied Psychology*, 88: 741–749.

De Dreu, C. K. W., & West, M. A. 2001. Minority dissent and team innovation: The importance of participation in decision making. *Journal of Applied Psychology*, 86: 1191–1201.

de Jong, A., de Ruyter, K., & Lemmink, J. 2005. Service climate in self-managing teams: Mapping the linkage of team member perceptions and service performance outcomes in a business-to-business setting. *Journal of Management Studies*, 42(8): 1593–1620.

de Jong, A., de Ruyter, K., & Wetzels, M. 2005. Antecedents and consequences of group potency: A study of self-managing service teams. *Management Science*, 51: 1610–1625.

DeShon, R. P., Kozlowski, S. W. J., Schmidt, A. M., Milner, K. R., & Wiechmann, D. 2004. A multiple-goal, multilevel model of feedback effects on the regulation of individual and team performance. *Journal of Applied Psychology*, 89: 1035–1056.

Devine, D. J. 2002. A review and integration of classification systems relevant to teams in organizations. *Group Dynamics-Theory Research and Practice*, 6(4): 291–310.

Devine, D. J., & Philips, J. L. 2001. Do smarter teams do better?—A meta-analysis of cognitive ability and team performance. *Small Group Research*, 32(5): 507–532.

Dickson, M. W., Resick, C. J., & Hanges, P. J. 2006. When organizational climate is unambiguous, it is also strong. *Journal of Applied Psychology*, 91: 351–364.

Dooley, R. S., Fryxell, G. E., & Judge, W. Q. 2000. Belaboring the not-so-obvious: Consensus, commitment, and strategy implementation speed and success. *Journal of Management*, 26: 1237–1257.

Driskell, J. E., & Salas, E. 1992. Collective behavior and team performance. *Human Factors*, 34: 277–288.

Druskat, V. U., & Kayes, D. C. 2000. Learning versus performance in short-term project teams. *Small Group Research*, 31(3): 328–353.

Druskat, V. U., & Wheeler, J. V. 2003. Managing from the boundary: The effective leadership of self-managing work teams. *Academy of Management Journal*, 46: 435–457.

Dweck, C. S. 1986. Motivational processes affecting learning. *American Psychologist*, 41: 1040–1048.

Dyer, J. L. 1984. Team research and training: A state of the art review. In F. A. Muckler (Ed.), *Human Factors Review*: 285–323. Santa Monica, CA: Human Factors and Ergonomics Society.

Eby, L. T., & Dobbins, G. H. 1997. Collectivistic orientation in teams and individual and group-level analysis. *Journal of Organizational Behavior*, 18: 275–295.

Edmondson, A. 1999. Psychological safety and learning behavior in work teams. *Administrative Science Quarterly*, 44: 350–383.

Edwards, B. D., Day, E. A., Arthur, W., & Bell, S. T. 2006. Relationships among team ability composition, team mental models, and team performance. *Journal of Applied Psychology*, 91: 727–736.

Ellis, A. P. J. 2006. System breakdown: The role of mental models and transactive memory in the relationship between acute stress and team performance. *Academy of Management Journal*, 49: 576–589.

Ellis, A. P. J., Bell, B. S., Ployhart, R. E., Hollenbeck, J. R., & Ilgen, D. R. 2005. An evaluation of generic teamwork skills training with action teams: Effects on cognitive and skill-based outcomes. *Personnel Psychology*, 58: 641–672.

Ellis, A. P. J., Hollenbeck, J. R., Ilgen, D. R., Porter, C., West, B. J., & Moon, H. 2003. Team learning: Collectively connecting the dots. *Journal of Applied Psychology*, 88: 821–835.

Ely, R. J., & Thomas, D. A. 2001. Cultural diversity at work: The effects of diversity perspectives on work group processes and outcomes. *Administrative Science Quarterly*, 46: 229–273.

English, A., Griffith, R. L., & Steelman, L. A. 2004. Team performance: The effect of team conscientiousness and task type. *Small Group Research*, 35: 643–665.

Ensley, M. D., Hmieleski, K. M., & Pearce, C. L. 2006. The importance of vertical and shared leadership within new venture top management teams: Implications for the performance of start-ups. *Leadership Quarterly*, 17: 217–231.

Ensley, M. D., & Pearce, C. L. 2001. Shared cognition in top management teams: Implications for new venture performance. *Journal of Organizational Behavior*, 22: 145–160.

Espinosa, J. A., Cummings, J. N., Wilson, J. M., & Pearce, B. M. 2003. Team boundary issues across global firms. *Journal of Management Information Systems*, 19: 157–190.

Fleishman, E. A., Mumford, M. D., Zaccaro, S. J., Levin, K. Y., Korotkin, A. L., & Hein, M. B. 1991. Taxonomic efforts in the description of leader behavior: A synthesis and functional interpretation. *Leadership Quarterly*, 2: 245–287.

Floyd, S. W., & Lane, P. J. 2000. Strategizing throughout the organization: Managing role conflict in strategic renewal. *Academy of Management Review*, 25: 154–177.

Foels, R., Driskell, J. E., Mullen, B., & Salas, E. 2000. The effects of democratic leadership on group member satisfaction: An integration. *Small Group Research*, 31: 676–701.

Geister, S., Konradt, U., & Hertel, G. 2006. Effects of process feedback on motivation, satisfaction, and performance in virtual teams. *Small Group Research*, 37: 459–489.

Gibson, C., & Vermeulen, F. 2003. A healthy divide: Subgroups as a stimulus for team learning behavior. *Administrative Science Quarterly*, 48(2): 202–239.

Gibson, C. B. 1999. Do they do what they believe they can do? Group efficacy and group effectiveness across task and cultures. *Academy of Management Journal*, 42(2): 138–152.

Gibson, C. B. 2003. Quality of team service—The role of field independent culture, quality orientation, and quality improvement focus. *Small Group Research*, 34(5): 619–646.

Gibson, C. B., & Gibbs, J. L. 2006. Unpacking the concept of virtuality: The effects of geographic dispersion, electronic dependence, dynamic structure, and national diversity on team innovation. *Administrative Science Quarterly*, 51(3): 451–495.

Gilson, L. L., Mathieu, J. E., Shalley, C. E., & Ruddy, T. M. 2005. Creativity and standardization: Complementary or conflicting drivers of team effectiveness. *Academy of Management Journal*, 48: 521–531.

Gilson, L. L., & Shalley, C. E. 2004. A little creativity goes a long way: An examination of teams' engagement in creative processes. *Journal of Management*, 30: 453–470.

Gist, M. E., Locke, E. A., & Taylor, M. S. 1987. Organizational behavior: Group structure, process, and effectiveness. *Journal of Management*, 13: 237–257.

Gladstein, D. 1984. Groups in context: A model of task group effectiveness. *Administrative Science Quarterly*, 29: 499–517.

Goldstein, I., & Ford, J. K. 2002. *Training in organizations* (4th ed.). Belmont, CA: Wadsworth.

Goldstein, I. L. 1992. *Training in organizations*. Pacific Grove, CA: Brooks/Cole.

Goll, I., & Rasheed, A. M. A. 1997. Rational decision-making and firm performance: The moderating role of environment. *Strategic Management Journal*, 18(7): 583–591.

Goodman, P. S. 1986. The impact of task and technology on group performance. In P. Goodman & Associates (Eds.), *Designing effective work groups*: 120–167. San Francisco: Jossey-Bass.

Goodman, P. S., Ravlin, E., & Schminke, M. 1987. Understanding groups in organizations. *Research in Organizational Behavior*, 9: 121–173.

Grawitch, M. J., Munz, D. C., & Kramer, T. J. 2003. Effects of member mood states on creative performance in temporary workgroups. *Group Dynamics-Theory Research and Practice*, 7(1): 41–54.

Gross, N., & Martin, W. E. 1952. On group cohesiveness. *American Journal of Sociology*, 57: 546–564.

Gully, S. M. 2000. Work teams research: Recent findings and future trends. In M. M. Beyerlein (Ed.), *Work teams: Past, present and future*: 25–44. The Netherlands: Kluwer Academic.

Gully, S. M., Incalcaterra, K. A., Joshi, A., & Beaubien, J. M. 2002. A meta-analysis of team-efficacy, potency, and performance: Interdependence and level of analysis as moderators of observed relationships. *Journal of Applied Psychology*, 87: 819–832.

Guzzo, R. A., & Dickson, M. W. 1996. Teams in organizations: Recent research on performance and effectiveness. *Annual Review of Psychology*, 47: 307–338.

Guzzo, R. A., & Shea, G. P. 1992. Group performance and intergroup relations in organizations. In M. D. Dunnette & L. M. Hough (Eds.), *Handbook of industrial and organizational psychology*, Vol. 3: 269–313. Palo Alto, CA: Consulting Psychologists Press.

Hackman, J. R., & Morris, C. G. 1975. Group tasks, group interaction processes, and group performance effectiveness: A review and proposed integration. *Advances in experimental social psychology*, Vol. 8: 45–99. New York: Academic Press.

Hackman, J. R., & Wageman, R. 2005. A theory of team coaching. *Academy of Management Review*, 30: 269–287.

Hackman, J. R. 1983. *A normative model of work team effectiveness* (Technical Report No. 2). New Haven, CT: Yale School of Organization and Management.

Hackman, R. 1990. *Groups that work and those that don't*. San Francisco: Jossey-Bass.

Halfhill, T., Sundstrom, E., Lahner, J., Calderone, W., & Nielsen, T. M. 2005. Group personality composition and group effectiveness—An integrative review of empirical research. *Small Group Research*, 36(1): 83–105.

Hambley, L. A., O'Neill, T. A., & Kline, T. J. B. 2007. Virtual team leadership: The effects of leadership style and communication medium on team interaction styles and outcomes. *Organizational Behavior and Human Decision Processes*, 103: 1–20.

Hambrick, D., Cho, T., & Chen, M. 1996. The influence of top management team heterogeneity on firms' competitive moves. *Administrative Science Quarterly*, 41: 659–684.

Hambrick, D. C. 1994. Top management groups: A conceptual integration and reconsideration of the team label. In B. M. Staw & L. L. Cummings (Eds.), *Research in organizational behavior*, Vol. 16: 171–214. Greenwich, CT: JAI.

Harris, T. C., & Barnes-Farrell, J. L. 1997. Components of teamwork: Impact on evaluations of contributions to work team effectiveness. *Journal of Applied Social Psychology*, 27: 1694–1715.

Harrison, D. A., Price, K. H., & Bell, M. P. 1998. Beyond relational demography: Time and the effects of surface-and deep-level diversity on work group decisions. *Academy of Management Journal*, 41: 96–107.

Harrison, D. A., Price, K. H., Gavin, J. H., & Florey, A. T. 2002. Time, teams and task performance: Changing effects of surface- and deep-level diversity on group functioning. *Academy of Management Journal*, 45: 1029–1045.

Harzing, A. W. 2007. *Publish or perish*. Melbourne, Australia: Tarma Software Research, LTD.

Hedlund, J., Ilgen, D. R., & Hollenbeck, J. R. 1998. Decision accuracy in computer-mediated versus face-to-face decision-making teams. *Organizational Behavior and Human Decision Processes*, 76: 30–47.

Hiller, N. J., Day, D. V., & Vance, R. J. 2006. Collective enactment of leadership roles and team effectiveness: A field study. *Leadership Quarterly*, 17: 387–397.

Hinsz, V. B., Tindale, R. S., & Vollrath, D. A. 1997. The emerging conceptualization of groups as information processors. *Psychological Bulletin*, 121: 43–64.

Hirschfeld, R. R., Jordan, M. H., Feild, H. S., Giles, W. F., & Armenakis, A. A. 2005. Teams' female representation and perceived potency as inputs to team outcomes in a predominantly male field setting. *Personnel Psychology*, 58: 893–924.

Hobman, E. V., Bordia, P., & Gallois, C. 2004. Perceived dissimilarity and work group involvement: The moderating effects of group openness to diversity. *Group & Organization Management*, 29: 560–587.

Hoffman, L. R., & Maier, N. R. F. 1961. Sex differences, sex composition, and group problem solving. *Journal of Abnormal & Social Psychology*, 63: 453–456.

Hofmann, D. A., & Jones, L. M. 2005. Leadership, collective personality, and performance. *Journal of Applied Psychology*, 90: 509–522.

Hollenbeck, J. R., Moon, H., Ellis, A. P. J., West, B. J., Ilgen, D. R., Sheppard, L., et al. 2002. Structural contingency theory and individual differences: Examination of external and internal person-team fit. *Journal of Applied Psychology*, 87: 599–606.

Hough, J. R., & White, M. A. 2003. Environmental dynamism and strategic decision-making rationality: An examination at the decision-level. *Strategic Management Journal*, 24(5): 481–489.

House, R., Javidan, M., Hanges, P., & Dorfman, P. 2002. Understanding cultures and implicit leadership theories across the globe: An introduction to project GLOBE. *Journal of World Business*, 37: 3–10.

Hui, C. H., Chiu, W. C. K., Yu, P. L. H., Cheng, K., & Tse, H. H. M. 2007. The effects of service climate and the effective leadership behavior of supervisors on frontline employee service quality: A multi-level analysis. *Journal of Occupational and Organizational Psychology*, 80: 151–172.

Hyatt, D. E., & Ruddy, T. M. 1997. An examination of the relationship between work group characteristics and performance: Once more into the breech. *Personnel Psychology*, 50: 553–585.

Iaquinto, A. L., & Fredrickson, J. W. 1997. Top management team agreement about the strategic decision process: A test of some of its determinants and consequences. *Strategic Management Journal*, 18: 63–75.

Ilgen, D. R. 1999. Teams embedded in organizations—Some implications. *American Psychologist*, 54(2): 129–139.

Ilgen, D. R., Hollenbeck, J. R., Johnson, M., & Jundt, D. 2005. Teams in organizations: From input-process-output models to IMOI models. *Annual Review of Psychology*, 56: 517–543.

Jackson, S. E., & Joshi, A. 2004. Diversity in a social context: A multi-attribute, multilevel analysis of team diversity and sales performance. *Journal of Organizational Behavior*, 25: 675–702.

Jackson, S. E., Joshi, A., & Erhardt, N. L. 2003. Recent research on team and organizational diversity: SWOT analysis and implications. *Journal of Management*, 29: 801–830.

Jackson, S. E., May, K. E., & Whitney, K. 1995. Understanding the dynamics of diversity in decision-making teams. In R. A. Guzzo, E. Salas, & Associates (Eds.), *Team effectiveness and decision making in organizations*: 204–261. San Francisco: Jossey-Bass.

Janicik, G. A., & Bartel, C. A. 2003. Talking about time: Effects of temporal planning and time awareness norms on group coordination and performance. *Group Dynamics: Theory, Research, and Practice*, 7: 122–134.

Janssen, O., Van de Vliert, E., & Veenstra, C. 1999. How task and person conflict shape the role of positive interdependence in management teams. *Journal of Management*, 25: 117–141.

Janz, B. D., Colquitt, J. A., & Noe, R. A. 1997. Knowledge worker team effectiveness: The role of autonomy, interdependence, team development, and contextual support variables. *Personnel Psychology*, 50: 877–904.

Jehn, K., & Mannix, E. 2001. The dynamic nature of conflict: A longitudinal study of intragroup conflict and group performance. *Academy of Management Journal*, 44: 238–251.

Jehn, K. A., & Bezrukova, K. 2004. A field study of group diversity, group context, and performance. *Journal of Organizational Behavior*, 25: 1–27.

Jehn, K. A., Northcraft, G. B., & Neale, M. A. 1999. Why differences make a difference: A field study of diversity, conflict, and performance in workgroups. *Administrative Science Quarterly*, 44: 741–763.

Jehn, K. A., & Shah, P. P. 1997. Interpersonal relationships and task performance. An examination of mediation processes in friendship and acquaintance groups. *Journal of Personality and Social Psychology*, 72: 775–790.

Johnson, M. D., Hollenbeck, J. R., Humphrey, S. E., Ilgen, D. R., Jundt, D., & Meyer, C. J. 2006. Cutthroat cooperation: Asymmetrical adaptation to changes in team reward structures. *Academy of Management Journal*, 49: 103–119.

Johnson, S. D., Suriya, C., Yoon, S. W., Berrett, J. V., & La Fleur, J. 2002. Team development and group processes of virtual learning teams. *Computers and Education*, 39: 379–393.

Joshi, A., & Jackson, S. E. 2003. Understanding work team diversity: Challenges and opportunities. In M. West, D. Tjosvold, & K. Smith (Eds.), *The international handbook of organizational teamwork and cooperative working*: 277–296. West Sussex, UK: Wiley.

Jung, D. I., & Sosik, J. J. 1999. Effects of group characteristics on work group performance: A longitudinal investigation. *Group Dynamics: Theory, Research, and Practice*, 3: 279–290.

Kahai, S. S., Sosik, J. J., & Avolio, B. J. 2003. Effects of leadership style, anonymity, and rewards on creativity—relevant processes and outcomes in an electronic meeting system context. *Leadership Quarterly*, 14: 499–524.

Kanawattanachai, P., & Yoo, Y. 2002. Dynamic nature of trust in virtual teams. *Journal of Strategic Information Systems*, 11: 187–213.

Katzenbach, J. R., & Smith, D. K. 1993. *The wisdom of teams: Creating the high performance organization.* Boston: Harvard Business School Press.

Katz-Navon, T., Naveh, E., & Stern, Z. 2005. Safety climate in health care organizations: A multi-dimensional approach. *Academy of Management Journal*, 48: 1075–1089.

Keck, S. L. 1997. Top management team structure: Differential effects by environmental context. *Organization Science*, 8(2): 143–156.

Kellermanns, F. W., Walter, J., Lechner, C., & Floyd, S. W. 2005. The lack of consensus about strategic consensus: Advancing theory and research. *Journal of Management*, 31: 719–737.

Kelly, J. R., & Barsade, S. G. 2001. Mood and emotions in small groups and work teams. *Organizational Behavior and Human Decision Processes*, 86: 99–130.

Kilduff, M., Angelmar, R., & Mehra, A. 2000. Top management-team diversity and firm performance: Examining the role of cognitions. *Organization Science*, 11: 21–34.

Kirkman, B. L., Lowe, K. B., & Gibson, C. B. 2006. A quarter century of culture's consequences: A review of empirical research incorporating Hofstede's cultural values framework. *Journal of International Business Studies*, 37(3): 285–320.

Kirkman, B. L., & Mathieu, J. E. 2005. The dimensions and antecedents of team virtuality. *Journal of Management*, 31: 700–718.

Kirkman, B. L., & Rosen, B. 1999. Beyond self-management: Antecedents and consequences of team empowerment. *Academy of Management Journal*, 42: 58–74.

Kirkman, B. L., Rosen, B., Tesluk, P. E., & Gibson, C. B. 2004. The impact of team empowerment on virtual team performance: The moderating role of face-to-face interaction. *Academy of Management Journal*, 47: 175–192.

Kirkman, B. L., Rosen, B., Tesluk, P. E., & Gibson, C. B. 2006. Enhancing the transfer of computer-assisted training proficiency in geographically distributed teams. *Journal of Applied Psychology*, 91(3): 706–716.

Kirkman, B. L., & Shapiro, D. L. 2001. The impact of team members' cultural values on productivity, cooperation, and empowerment in self-managing work teams. *Journal of Cross-Cultural Psychology*, 32(5): 597–617.

Kirkman, B. L., Tesluk, P. E., & Rosen, B. 2001. Alternative methods of assessing team-level variables: Comparing the predictive power of aggregation and consensus methods. *Personnel Psychology*, 54: 645–667.

Kirkman, B. L., Tesluk, P. E., & Rosen, B. 2004. The impact of demographic heterogeneity and team leader-team member demographic fit on team empowerment and effectiveness. *Group & Organization Management*, 29(3): 334–368.

Klein, K., & Kozlowski, S. W. J. 2000. *Multilevel theory, research and methods in organization*. San Francisco: Jossey-Bass.

Klein, K. J., Lim, B., Saltz, J. L., & Mayer, D. M. 2004. How do they get there? An examination of the antecedents of centrality in team networks. *Academy of Management Journal*, 47: 952–963.

Klimoski, R., & Mohammed, S. 1994. Team mental model: Construct or metaphor? *Journal of Management*, 20: 403–437.

Knight, D., Durham, C. C., & Locke, E. A. 2001. The relationship of team goals, incentives, and efficacy to strategic risk, tactical implementation, and performance. *Academy of Management Journal*, 44: 326–338.

Knight, D., Pearce, C. L., Smith, K. G., Olian, J. D., Sims, H. P., Smith, K. A., et al. 1999. Top management team diversity, group process, and strategic consensus. *Strategic Management Journal*, 20: 445–465.

Kozlowski, S. W. J. 1998. Training and development in adaptive teams: Theory, principles, and research. In J. A. Cannon-Bowers & E. Salas (Eds.), *Making decisions under stress: Implications for individual and team training*: 247–270. Washington, DC: American Psychological Association.

Kozlowski, S. W. J., & Bell, B. S. 2003. Work groups and teams in organizations. In W. C. Borman, D. R. Ilgen, & R. J. Klimoski (Eds.), *Handbook of psychology: Industrial and organizational psychology*, Vol. 12: 333–375. London: Wiley.

Kozlowski, S. W. J., Brown, K., Weisbein, D., Cannon-Bowers, J., & Salas, E. 2000. A multi-level approach to training effectiveness: Enhancing horizontal and vertical transfer. In K. Klein & S. W. J. Kozlowski (Eds.), *Multilevel theory, research, and methods in organizations*. San Francisco: Jossey-Bass.

Kozlowski, S. W. J., Gully, S. M., Nason, E. R., & Smith, E. M. 1999. Developing adaptive teams: A theory of compilation and performance across levels and time. In D. R. Ilgen & E. D. Pulakos (Eds.), *The changing nature of work performance: Implications for staffing, personnel actions, and development*: 240–292. San Francisco: Jossey-Bass.

Kozlowski, S. W. J., & Ilgen, D. R. 2006. Enhancing the effectiveness of work groups and teams. *Psychological Science in the Public Interest*, 7: 77–124.

Kozlowski, S. W. J., & Klein, K. J. 2000. A multilevel approach to theory and research in organizations: Contextual, temporal, and emergent processes. In K. J. Klein & S. W. J. Kozlowski (Eds.), *Multilevel theory, research, and methods in organizations*: 3–90. San Francisco: Jossey-Bass.

Kozlowski, S. W. J., & Salas, E. 1997. A multilevel organizational systems approach for the implementation and transfer of training. In J. K. Ford (Ed.), *Improving training effectiveness in work organizations*: 247–287. Mahwah, NJ: Lawrence Erlbaum.

Landy, F. J., Rastegary, H., Thayer, J., & Colvin, C. 1991. Time urgency: The construct and its measurement. *Journal of Applied Psychology*, 76: 644–657.

Langfred, C. W. 2000. Work-group design and autonomy—A field study of the interaction between task interdependence and group autonomy. *Small Group Research*, 31(1): 54–70.

Langfred, C. W. 2004. Too much of a good thing? Negative effects of high trust and individual autonomy in self-managing teams. *Academy of Management Journal*, 47: 385–399.

Langfred, C. W. 2005. Autonomy and performance in teams: The multilevel moderating effect of task interdependence. *Journal of Management*, 31: 513–529.

Lau, D., & Murnighan, J. K. 2005. Interactions within groups and subgroups: The effects of demographic faultlines. *Academy of Management Journal*, 48: 645–659.

Lau, D. C., & Murnighan, J. K. 1998. Demographic diversity and faultlines: The compositional dynamics of organizational groups. *Academy of Management Review*, 23: 325–340.

Lawler, E. E. 1993. Managing employee involvement. In C. G. Thor (Ed.), *Handbook for productivity measurement and improvement*. Cambridge, MA: Productivity Press.

Leonard, J., Levine, D., & Joshi, A. 2004. Do birds of a feather shop together? The effects on performance of employees' similarity with one another and with customers *Journal of Organizational Behavior*, 25: 731–754.

LePine, J. A. 2003. Team adaptation and post-change performance: Effects of team composition in terms of members' cognitive ability and personality. *Journal of Applied Psychology*, 88: 27–39.

LePine, J. A. 2005. Adaptation of teams in response to unforeseen change: Effects of goal difficulty and team composition in terms of cognitive ability and goal orientation. *Journal of Applied Psychology*, 90: 1153–1167.

LePine, J. A., Colquitt, J. A., & Erez, A. 2000. Adaptability to changing task contexts: Effects of general cognitive ability, conscientiousness, and openness to experience. *Personnel Psychology*, 53: 563–593.

LePine, J. A., Piccolo, R. F., Jackson, C. L., Mathieu, J. E., & Saul, J. R. In press. A meta-analysis of teamwork processes: Tests of a multidimensional model and relationships with team effectiveness criteria. *Personnel Psychology*.

Lester, S. W., Meglino, B. M., & Korsgaard, M. A. 2002. The antecedents and consequences of group potency: A longitudinal investigation of newly formed work groups. *Academy of Management Journal*, 45: 352–368.

Levesque, L. L., Wilson, J. M., & Wholey, D. R. 2001. Cognitive divergence and shared mental models in software development project teams. *Journal of Organizational Behavior*, 22: 135–144.

Lewis, K. 2004. Knowledge and performance in knowledge-worker teams: A longitudinal study of transactive memory systems. *Management Science*, 50: 1519–1533.

Lewis, K., Lange, D., & Gillis, L. 2005. Transactive memory systems, learning, and learning transfer. *Organization Science*, 16: 581–598.

Li, J. T., & Hambrick, D. C. 2005. Factional groups: A new vantage on demographic faultlines, conflict, and disintegration in work teams. *Academy of Management Journal*, 48: 794–813.

Lim, B. C., & Klein, K. J. 2006. Team mental models and team performance: A field study of the effects of team mental model similarity and accuracy. *Journal of Organizational Behavior*, 27(4): 403–418.

Lim, B. C., & Ployhart, R. E. 2004. Transformational leadership: Relations to the five-factor model and team performance in typical and maximum contexts. *Journal of Applied Psychology*, 89(4): 610–621.

Lubatkin, M. H., Simsek, Z., Ling, Y., & Veiga, J. F. 2006. Ambidexterity and performance in small- to medium-sized firms: The pivotal role of top management team behavioral integration. *Journal of Management*, 32: 646–672.

Mann, R. D. 1959. A review of the relationships between personality and performance in small groups. *Psychological Bulletin*, 56: 242–270.

Marks, M. A., DeChurch, L. A., Mathieu, J. E., Panzer, F. J., & Alonso, A. 2005. Teamwork in multiteam systems. *Journal of Applied Psychology*, 90(5): 964–971.

Marks, M. A., Mathieu, J. E., & Zaccaro, S. J. 2001. A temporally based framework and taxonomy of team processes. *Academy of Management Review*, 26(3): 356–376.

Marks, M. A., Sabella, M. J., Burke, C. S., & Zaccaro, S. J. 2002. The impact of cross-training on team effectiveness. *Journal of Applied Psychology*, 87: 3–13.

Marks, M. A., Zaccaro, S. J., & Mathieu, J. E. 2000. Performance implications of leader briefings and team-interaction training for team adaptation to novel environments. *Journal of Applied Psychology*, 85: 971–986.

Martins, L. L., Gilson, L. L., & Maynard, M. T. 2004. Virtual teams: What do we know and where do we go from here? *Journal of Management*, 30: 805–835.

Mason, C. M., & Griffin, M. A. 2003. Group absenteeism and positive affective tone: A longitudinal study. *Journal of Organizational Behavior*, 24: 667–687.

Mason, C. M., & Griffin, M. A. 2005. Group task satisfaction: The group's shared attitude to its task and work environment. *Group & Organization Management*, 30: 625–652.

Mathieu, J. E., Gilson, L. L., & Ruddy, T. M. 2006. Empowerment and team effectiveness: An empirical test of an integrated model. *Journal of Applied Psychology*, 91: 97–108.

Mathieu, J. E., Heffner, T. S., Goodwin, G. F., Cannon-Bowers, J. A., & Salas, E. 2005. Scaling the quality of teammates' mental models: Equifinality and normative comparisons. *Journal of Organizational Behavior*, 26: 37–56.

Mathieu, J. E., Heffner, T. S., Goodwin, G. F., Salas, E., & Cannon-Bowers, J. A. 2000. The influence of shared mental models on team process and performance. *Journal of Applied Psychology*, 85: 273–283.

Mathieu, J. E., Marks, M. A., & Zaccaro, S. J. 2001. Multi-team systems. In N. Anderson, D. Ones, H. K. Sinangil, & C. Viswesvaran (Eds.), *International handbook of work and organizational psychology*: 289–313. London: Sage.

Mathieu, J. E., Maynard, M. T., Taylor, S. R., Gilson, L. L., & Ruddy, T. M. 2007. An examination of the effects of organizational district and team contexts on team processes and performance: A meso-mediational model. *Journal of Organizational Behavior*, 28: 891–910.

Mathieu, J. E., & Rapp, T. L. In press. Laying the foundation for successful team performance trajectories: The role of team charters and deliberate plans. *Journal of Applied Psychology*.

Mathieu, J. E., & Schulze, W. 2006. The influence of team knowledge and formal plans on episodic team process-performance relationships. *Academy of Management Journal*, 49: 605–619.

Mathieu, J. E., & Taylor, S. 2007. A framework for testing meso-mediational relationships in organizational behavior. *Journal of Organizational Behavior*, 28: 141–172.

Mathieu, J. E., & Tesluk, P. E. In press. A multi-level perspective on training & development effectiveness. In S. W. J. Kozlowski & E. Salas (Eds.), *Learning, training, and development in organizations* (SIOP Frontiers Book Series). Mahwah, NJ: Lawrence Erlbaum.

Mayer, R. C., Davis, J. H., & Schoorman, F. D. 1995. An integrative model of organizational trust. *Academy of Management Review*, 20: 709–734.

Maynard, M. T., Mathieu, J. E., Marsh, W. M., & Ruddy, T. M. 2007. A multilevel investigation of the influences of employees' resistance to empowerment. *Human Performance*, 20: 147–171.

McClough, A. C., & Rogelberg, S. G. 2003. Selection in teams: An exploration of the teamwork knowledge, skills, and ability test. *International Journal of Selection and Assessment*, 11: 56–66.

McGrath, J. E. 1962. *Leadership behavior: Some requirements for leadership training*. Washington, DC: U.S. Civil Service Commission, Office of Career Development.

McGrath, J. E. 1964. *Social psychology: A brief introduction*. New York: Holt, Rinehart & Winston.

McGrath, J. E. 1984. *Groups: Interaction and performance*. Englewood Cliffs, NJ: Prentice Hall.

McGrath, J. E. 1991. Time, interaction, and performance (TIP): A theory of groups. *Small Group Research*, 22: 147–174.

McGrath, J. E., Arrow, H., & Berdahl, J. L. 2001. The study of groups: Past, present, and future. *Personality & Social Psychology Review*, 4(1): 95–105.

McIntyre, R. M., & Salas, E. 1995. Measuring and managing for team performance: Emerging principles from complex environments. In R. A. Guzzo & E. Salas (Eds.), *Team effectiveness and decision making in organizations*. San Francisco: Jossey-Bass.

Mehra, A., Kilduff, M., & Brass, D. J. 2001. The social networks of high and low self-monitors: Implications for workplace performance. *Administrative Science Quarterly*, 46: 121–146.

Mehra, A., Smith, B., Dixon, A., & Robertson, B. 2006. Distributed leadership in teams: The network of leadership perceptions and team performance. *Leadership Quarterly*, 17: 232–245.

Michalisin, M. D., Karau, S. J., & Tangpong, C. 2004. Top management team cohesion and superior industry returns: An empirical study of the resource-based view. *Group & Organization Management*, 29: 125–140.

Milliken, F. J., & Martins, L. L. 1996. Searching for common threads: Understanding the multiple effects of diversity in organizational groups. *Academy of Management Review*, 21: 402–433.

Mohammed, S., & Angell, L. C. 2003. Personality heterogeneity in teams: What differences make a difference in team performance? *Small Group Research*, 34: 651–677.

Mohammed, S., & Angell, L. C. 2004. Surface and deep-level diversity in workgroups: Examining the moderating effects of team orientation and team process on relationship conflict. *Journal of Organizational Behavior*, 25: 1015–1039.

Mohrman, S. A., Cohen, S. G., & Mohrman, A. M., Jr. 1995. *Designing team-based organizations: New forms for knowledge work*. San Francisco: Jossey-Bass.

Molleman, E. 2005. Diversity in demographic characteristics, abilities and personality traits: Do faultlines affect team functioning? *Group Decision and Negotiation*, 14: 173–193.

Moon, H., Conlon, D. E., Humphrey, S. E., Quigley, N., Devers, C. E., & Nowakowski, J. M. 2003. Group decision process and incrementalism in organizational decision making. *Organizational Behavior and Human Decision Processes*, 92(1/2): 67–79.

Moon, H., Hollenbeck, J. R., Humphrey, S. E., Ilgen, D. R., West, B. J., Ellis, A. P. J., et al. 2004. Asymmetric adaptability: Dynamic team structures as one-way streets. *Academy of Management Journal*, 47: 681–695.

Moreland, R. L., Argote, L., & Krishnan, R. 1998. Training people to work in groups. In G. M. Wittenbaum, S. I. Vaughan, G. Stasser, & R. S. Tindale (Eds.), *Theory and research on small groups*: 37–61. New York: Plenum.

Morgeson, F. P. 2005. The external leadership of self-managing teams: Intervening in the context of novel and disruptive events. *Journal of Applied Psychology*, 90: 497–508.

Morgeson, F. P., & Hofmann, D. A. 1999. The structure and function of collective constructs: Implications for multilevel research and theory development. *Academy of Management Review*, 24: 249–265.

Morgeson, F. P., Reider, M. H., & Campion, M. A. 2005. Selecting individuals in team settings: The importance of social skills, personality characteristic, and teamwork knowledge. *Personnel Psychology*, 58: 583–611.

Naumann, S. E., & Bennett, N. 2002. The effects of procedural justice climate on work group performance. *Small Group Research*, 33: 361–377.

Neal, A., & Griffin, M. A. 2006. A study of the lagged relationships among safety climate, safety motivation, safety behavior, and accidents at the individual and group levels. *Journal of Applied Psychology*, 91: 946–953.

Neuman, G. A., Wagner, S., & Christiansen, N. 1999. The relationship between workteam personality composition and the job performance of teams. *Group & Organizational Management*, 24: 28–45.

Neuman, G. A., & Wright, J. 1999. Team effectiveness: Beyond skills and cognitive ability. *Journal of Applied Psychology*, 84: 376–389.

Oser, R., McCallum, G. A., Salas, E., & Morgan, B. B. 1989. *Toward a definition of teamwork: An analysis of critical team behavior* (Technical Report: TR-89–004). Orlando, FL: Naval Training Systems Center.

Paulus, P. B. 2000. Groups, teams, and creativity: The creative potential of idea-generating groups. *Applied Psychology—An International Review—Psychologie Appliquee—Revue Internationale*, 49(2): 237–262.

Pearce, C. L., & Simms, H. P. J. 2002. The relative influence of vertical vs. shared leadership on the longitudinal effectiveness of change management teams. *Group Dynamics, Theory, Research, and Practice*, 6: 172–197.

Pearce, C. L., Yoo, Y., & Alavi, M. 2004. Leadership, social work and virtual teams: The relative influence of vertical vs. shared leadership in the nonprofit sector. In R. E. Riggio & S. Smith-Orr (Eds.), *Improving leadership in nonprofit organizations*: 180–203. San Francisco: Jossey-Bass.

Pearsall, M. J., & Ellis, A. P. J. 2006. The effects of critical team member assertiveness on team performance and satisfaction. *Journal of Management*, 32(4): 575–594.

Pelled, L. H., Eisenhardt, K. M., & Xin, K. R. 1999. Exploring the black box: An analysis of work group diversity, conflict, and performance. *Administrative Science Quarterly*, 44: 1–28.

Perretti, F., & Negro, G. 2007. Mixing genres and matching people: A study of innovation and team composition in Hollywood. *Journal of Organizational Behavior*, 28: 563–586.

Pinto, M. B., Pinto, J. K., & Prescott, J. E. 1993. Antecedents and consequences of project team cross-functional cooperation. *Management Science*, 39: 1281–1297.

Pirola-Merlo, A., Hartel, C., Mann, L., & Hirst, G. 2002. How leaders influence the impact of affective events on team climate and performance in R&D teams. *The Leadership Quarterly*, 13: 561–581.

Pitcher, P., & Smith, A. D. 2001. Top management team heterogeneity: Personality, power, and proxies. *Organization Science*, 12: 1–18.

Polzer, J. T., Crisp, C. B., Jarvenpaa, S. L., & Kim, J. W. 2006. Extending the faultline model to geographically dispersed teams: How collocated subgroups can impair group functioning. *Academy of Management Journal*, 49: 679–692.

Porter, C. O. L. H. 2005. Goal orientation: Effects on backing up behavior, performance, efficacy, and commitment in teams. *Journal of Applied Psychology*, 90: 811–818.

Priem, R. L., Lyon, D. W., & Dess, G. D. 1999. Inherent limitations of demographic proxies in top management team heterogeneity research. *Journal of Management*, 25: 935–953.

Pritchard, R. D. 1995. Lessons learned about ProMES. In R. D. Pritchard (Ed.), *Productivity measurement and improvement: Organizational case studies*: 325–365. New York: Praeger.

Pritchard, R. D., Jones, S., Roth, P., Stuebing, K., & Ekeberg, S. 1988. Effects of group feedback, goal setting, and incentives on organizational productivity. *Journal of Applied Psychology*, 73: 337–358.

Rapp, T. L., & Mathieu, J. E. 2007. Evaluating an individually self-administered generic teamwork skills training program across time and levels. *Small Group Research*, 38: 532–555.

Raver, J. L., & Gelfand, M. J. 2005. Beyond the individual victim: Linking sexual harassment, team processes, and team performance. *Academy of Management Journal*, 48: 387–400.

Rico, R., Molleman, E., Sanchez-Manzanares, M., & Van der Vegt, G. S. 2007. The effects of diversity faultlines and team task autonomy on decision quality and social integration. *Journal of Management*, 33: 111–132.

Rulke, D. L., & Rau, D. 2000. Investigating the encoding process of transactive memory development in group training. *Group & Organization Management*, 25: 373–396.

Saavedra, R., Earley, P. C., & Van Dyne, L. 1993. Complex interdependence in task-performing groups. *Journal of Applied Psychology*, 78: 61–72.

Salas, E., & Cannon-Bowers, J. A. 2001. The science of training: A decade of progress. *Annual Review of Psychology*, 52: 471–499.

Salas, E., Dickinson, T. L., Converse, S. A., & Tannenbaum, S. I. 1992. Toward an understanding of team performance and training. In R. W. Swezey & E. Salas (Eds.), *Teams: Their training and performance*. Norwood, NJ: Ablex.

Salas, E., Nichols, D. R., & Driskell, J. E. 2007. Testing three team training strategies in intact teams. *Small Group Research*, 38: 471–488.

Salas, E., Rozell, D., Mullen, B., & Driskell, J. E. 1999. The effect of team building on performance. *Small Group Research*, 30(3): 309–330.

Salas, E., Stagl, K. C., & Burke, C. S. 2004. 25 years of team effectiveness in organizations: Research themes and emerging needs. In C. L. Robertson (Ed.), *International review of industrial organizational psychology*, Vol. 19: 47–92. New York: John Wiley.

Salas, E., Wilson, K. A., Burke, C. S., & Wrightman, D. C. 2006. Does crew resource management training work? An update, an extension, and some critical needs. *Human Factors*, 48: 392–412.

Schneider, B. 1975. Organizational climates: An essay. *Personnel Psychology*, 28: 447–479.

Schneider, B., Ehrhart, M. G., Mayer, D. M., Saltz, J. L., & Niles-Jolly, K. 2005. Understanding organization-customer links in service settings. *Academy of Management Journal*, 48: 1017–1032.

Seibert, S. E., Silver, S. R., & Randolph, W. A. 2004. Taking empowerment to the next level: A multiple-level model of empowerment, performance, and satisfaction. *Academy of Management Journal*, 47: 332–349.

Shea, G. P., & Guzzo, R. A. 1987. Groups as human resources. In K. M. Rowland & G. R. Ferris (Eds.), *Research in personnel and human resources management*, Vol. 5: 323–356. Greenwich, CT: JAI.

Simons, T., Pelled, L. H., & Smith, K. G. 1999. Making use of difference: Diversity, debate, and decision comprehensiveness in top management teams. *Academy of Management Journal*, 42: 662–673.

Simons, T. L., & Peterson, R. S. 2000. Task conflict and relationship conflict in top management teams: The pivotal role of intragroup trust. *Journal of Applied Psychology*, 85: 102–111.

Simsek, Z., Veiga, J. F., Lubatkin, M. H., & Dino, R. N. 2005. Modeling the multilevel determinants of top management team behavioral integration. *Academy of Management Journal*, 48: 69–84.

Sivasubramaniam, N., Murry, W. D., Avolio, B. J., & Jung, D. I. 2002. A longitudinal model of the effects of team leadership and group potency on group performance. *Group & Organization Management*, 27(1): 66–96.

Smith, P. C. 1976. Behavior, results, and organizational effectiveness: The problem of criteria. In M. D. Dunnette (Ed.), *Handbook of industrial and organizational psychology*: 745–775. Chicago: Rand McNally.

Smith-Jentsch, K. A., Mathieu, J. E., & Kraiger, K. 2005. Investigating linear and interactive effects of shared mental models on safety and efficiency in a field setting. *Journal of Applied Psychology*, 90: 523–535.

Smith-Jentsch, K. A., Salas, E., & Brannick, M. T. 2001. To transfer or not to transfer? Investigating the combined effects of trainee characteristics, team leader support, and team climate. *Journal of Applied Psychology*, 86: 279–292.

Sosik, J. J., & Jung, D. I. 2002. Work-group characteristics and performance in collectivistic and individualistic cultures. *Journal of Social Psychology*, 142(1): 5–23.

Sparrowe, R. T., Liden, R. C., Wayne, S. J., & Kraimer, M. L. 2001. Social networks and the performance of individuals and groups. *Academy of Management Journal*, 44: 316–325.

Spreitzer, G. M., Cohen, S. G., & Ledford, G. E., Jr. 1999. Developing effective self-managing work teams in service organizations. *Group & Organization Management*, 24(3): 340–366.

Srivastava, A., Bartol, K. M., & Locke, E. A. 2006. Empowering leadership in management teams: Effects on knowledge sharing, efficacy, and performance. *Academy of Management Journal*, 49: 1239–1251.

Stein, M. I. 1974. *Stimulating creativity*, Vol. 1. New York: Academic Press.

Steiner, I. D. 1972. *Group process and productivity*. New York: Academic Press.

Stevens, M. J., & Campion, M. A. 1994. The knowledge, skill, and ability requirements for teamwork: Implications from human resource management. *Journal of Management*, 20: 503–530.

Stevens, M. J., & Campion, M. A. 1999. Staffing work teams: Development and validation of a selection test for teamwork settings. *Journal of Management*, 25: 207–227.

Stewart, G. L. 2006. A meta-analytic review of relationships between team design features and team performance. *Journal of Management*, 32: 29–54.

Stewart, G. L., & Barrick, M. R. 2000. Team structure and performance: Assessing the mediating role of intrateam process and the moderating role of task type. *Academy of Management Journal*, 43: 135–148.

Stout, R. J., Cannon-Bowers, J. A., Salas, E., & Milanovich, D. M. 1999. Planning, shared mental models, and coordinated performance: An empirical link is established. *Human Factors*, 41: 61–71.

Sundstrom, E. 1999. The challenges of supporting work team effectiveness. In E. Sundstrom & Associates (Eds.), *Supporting work team effectiveness*: 3–23. San Francisco: Jossey-Bass.

Sundstrom, E., De Meuse, K. P., & Futrell, D. 1990. Work teams: Applications and effectiveness. *American Psychologist*, 45: 120–133.

Sundstrom, E., McIntyre, M., Halfhill, T., & Richards, H. 2000. Work groups: From Hawthorne studies to work teams of the 1990s and beyond. *Group Dynamics: Theory, Research, and Practice*, 4(1): 44–67.

Sy, T., Cote, S., & Saavedra, R. 2005. The contagious leader: Impact of the leader's mood on the mood of group members, group affective tone, and group processes. *Journal of Applied Psychology*, 90: 295–305.

Taggar, S. 2002. Individual creativity and group ability to utilize individual creative resources: A multilevel model. *Academy of Management Journal*, 45: 315–330.

Taggar, S., Hackett, R., & Saha, S. 1999. Leadership emergence in autonomous work teams: Antecedents and outcomes. *Personnel Psychology*, 52: 899–926.

Tesluk, P. E., Farr, J. L., & Klein, S. R. 1997. Influences of organizational culture and climate on individual creativity. *Journal of Creative Behavior*, 31: 27–41.

Tesluk, P. E., & Mathieu, J. E. 1999. Overcoming roadblocks to effectiveness: Incorporating management of performance barriers into models of work group effectiveness. *Journal of Applied Psychology*, 84: 200–217.

Tesluk, P. E., Vance, R. J., & Mathieu, J. E. 1999. Examining employee involvement in the context of participative work environments. *Group & Organization Management*, 24: 271–299.

Thatcher, S. M., Jehn, K. A., & Zanutto, E. 2003. Cracks in diversity research: The effects of faultlines on conflict and performance. *Group Decision and Negotiation*, 12: 217–241.

Thibaut, J., & Walker, L. 1975. *Procedural justice: A psychological analysis*. Hillsdale, NJ: Lawrence Erlbaum.

Timmerman, T. A. 2000. Racial diversity, age, diversity, interdependence, and team performance. *Small Group Research*, 31: 592–606.

Tjosvold, D., Tang, M. M., & West, M. 2004. Reflexivity for team innovation in China: The contribution of goal interdependence. *Group & Organization Management*, 29: 540–559.

Totterdell, P. 2000. Catching moods and hitting runs: Mood linkage and subjective performance in professional sport teams. *Journal of Applied Psychology*, 85: 848–859.

Townsend, A. M., & Scott, K. D. 2001. Team racial composition, member attitudes, and performance: A field study. *Industrial Relations*, 40: 313–337.

Tracey, J. B., & Tews, M. J. 2005. Construct validity of a general training climate scale. *Organizational Research Methods*, 8: 353–374.

Van der Vegt, G. S., & Bunderson, J. S. 2005. Learning and performance in multidisciplinary teams: The importance of collective team identification. *Academy of Management Journal*, 48: 532–547.

Van der Vegt, G., Emans, B., & Van De Vliert, E. 2000. Team members' affective responses to patterns of intragroup interdependence and job complexity. *Journal of Management*, 26: 633–655.

Van Mierlo, H., Rutte, C. G., Kompier, M. A. J., & Doorewaard, H. 2005. Self-managing teamwork and psychological well-being: Review of a multilevel research domain. *Group & Organization Management*, 30(2): 211–235.

Wageman, R. 1995. Interdependence and group effectiveness. *Administrative Science Quarterly*, 40: 145–180.

Wageman, R. 2001. How leaders foster self-managing team effectiveness: Design choices versus hands-on coaching. *Organization Science*, 12: 559–577.

Watson, W. E., Johnson, L., & Merritt, D. 1998. Team orientation, self-orientation, and diversity in task groups. *Group & Organization Management*, 23: 161–188.

Webber, S. S., & Donahue, L. M. 2001. Impact of highly and less job-related diversity on work group cohesion and performance: a meta-analysis. *Journal of Management*, 27: 141–162.

Wegner, D. 1986. Transactive memory: A contemporary analysis of the group mind. In G. Mullen & G. Goethals (Eds.), *Theories of group behavior*: 185–208. New York: Springer-Verlag.

Welbourne, T. M., Johnson, D. E., & Erez, A. 1998. The role-based performance scale: Validity analysis of a theory-based measure. *Academy of Management Journal*, 41: 540–555.

Williams, K. Y., & O'Reilly, C. A. 1998. Demography and diversity in organizations. *Research in Organizational Behavior*, 20: 77–140.

Wilson, J. R., & Rutherford, A. 1989. Mental models: Theory and application in human factors. *Human Factors*, 31: 617–634.

Wong, S. S. 2004. Distal and local group learning: Performance trade-offs and tensions. *Organization Science*, 15: 645–656.

Yang, J., Mossholder, K. W., & Peng, T. K. 2007. Procedural justice climate and group power distance: An examination of cross-level interaction effects. *Journal of Applied Psychology*, 92: 681–692.

Zaccaro, S. J., Rittman, A. L., & Marks, M. A. 2001. Team leadership. *Leadership Quarterly*, 12: 451–483.

Zellmer-Bruhn, M., & Gibson, C. 2006. Multinational organization context: Implications for team learning and performance. *Academy of Management Journal*, 49(3): 501–518.

Zohar, D. 2000. A group-level model of safety climate: Testing the effect of group climate on microaccidents in manufacturing jobs. *Journal of Applied Psychology*, 85: 587–596.

10 Leadership of Groups and Organizations

10.1 LEADERSHIP AND ADVOCACY

Dual Roles for Corporate Social Responsibility and Social Entrepreneurship

Manuel London

When we think about corporate leadership, we generally don't think about the role of social advocate. Yet advocacy has become increasingly important as organizations recognize their social obligations to stockholders and the communities in which they operate. In for-profit organizations, corporate social responsibility has become a competitive advantage and, sometimes, a way to generate new revenue streams. Corporate leaders become advocates for social causes such as environmental sustainability, education, health, and economic conditions that generate employment opportunities, pay fair wages, and reduce poverty. Corporate social action takes place locally and globally. In addition, corporate advocacy addresses issues that affect employees and the organization's bottom line, such as policies for health benefits, work-family balance, and working conditions. Corporate officers spearhead solutions to these issues within their own organization and in the corporate community at large. In not-for-profit organizations that have social advocacy as their principal aim, the founder/advocate is an entrepreneur, generating organization structures that respond to situational conditions, including beneficiaries' needs, availability of financial and non-financial support, and existence of adversaries and those who stand to lose if the organization's goals are met. These advocates must become effective leaders.

The roles of leader and advocate are complementary. Leaders need to understand and develop their role as advocate and recognize how it fits with other roles and requirements of organizational leadership. Advocates need to understand and develop their role as leader as they garner support and create organizations to accomplish their advocacy goals. This article describes advocacy processes, examines conditions that encourage and discourage advocacy, and recommends ways for corporate leaders to be more effective advocates and for social entrepreneurs to be more effective leaders.

Defining Advocacy

Advocacy is the act of supporting an idea, need, person, or group. Social advocates take public action to engender fair treatment or further the cause of people in need who can't speak for themselves (or do so effectively). The goal may be to promote social welfare in general (e.g., protect the environment) and/or improve the conditions of individuals or groups (e.g., bring aid to a village in Africa that is desperate for food, clothing, health care, and education). The benefits may be direct, visible, and immediate, such as sheltering the homeless, or they may be indirect and long-term, such as raising money for medical research that will cure cancer someday. Advocates speak out and take action to effect change, often overcoming resistance. They increase awareness of an issue and generate positive attitudes. They recruit and retain volunteers who become advocates themselves. They influence government policies. They deliver services, raise money, and build organizations to sustain their advocacy goals.

Advocacy as a general process happens all the time within corporations. Leaders advocate for ideas and issues that promote organizational profitability, quality, and performance. They advocate for corporate social responsibility in a variety of ways linked to the organization's contribution to the community, for instance, donating to the arts or other charities, promoting ethical decisions, or being sensitive to the environment. These initiatives may affect the bottom line directly through product improvement or increased sales or indirectly through good publicity and recruitment of talented employees.

Corporate social responsibility is more than demonstrating concern for the environment, fair business practices, and socially responsible business decisions. It can entail making extra efforts to improve social welfare. Fortunately, we have many examples of corporate leaders who extended themselves and their organizations to donate efforts and profits.

Some Examples

Jonathan Schwartz, President and Chief Executive Officer, Sun Microsystems, wrote in the Sun's 2007 CSR Report that the company is "100% committed to developing and adhering to principles that guide our actions in business and social conduct . . . to enable the sharing of knowledge and technologies for positive social and environmental impact." Raytheon's chairman, William H. Swanson, stated in the company's 2006 annual report that Raytheon is ". . . committed to creating dramatic and lasting change through strategic charitable giving." He cited the company's focus on supporting math and science education with MathMoves U, an online system designed to inspire middle school students to study math. Businesses mesh charity with profit-making missions. Ben and Jerry's and Newman's Own come to mind. John Sage established a Fair Trade coffee business, Pura Vida, to fund programs for the poor. Lee Zimmerman's Evergreen Lodge outside of Yosemite National Park hires promising young people from low-income areas.

There are numerous examples of advocates becoming social entrepreneurs, founding and leading organizations to promote their advocacy goals. Some are common household names, such as Al Gore, whose Nobel Prize winning initiatives focused attention on global environmental issues, Bill Gates, whose foundation is working to eradicate illness and poverty, and Jimmy Carter, whose support of Habitat for Humanity helped the organization gain worldwide attention. Others are unsung, local heroes. For instance, Pattye Pece and her associates, Jonathan and Vanessa Langer, founded a totally volunteer-operated, not-for-profit Fair Trade store in Hampton Bays, New York, to provide funds for AIDS-orphaned children in Kenya and Zambia. Mary Ann Bell founded a soup kitchen for the homeless in Port Jefferson, New York. David Krause, a paleontologist, started a school and health clinic in a remote area of Madagascar, the location of his discovery of predatory dinosaur remains. Patricia Wright, another anthropologist working in Madagascar, founded the national Ranomafana rain forest to protect the environment and rare species of the area.

Now consider two role models who demonstrate leadership for social advocacy: an executive who spearheads corporate social responsibility initiatives and an emerging successful social entrepreneur. They are father and son.

Stanley M. Bergman has been Chairman and CEO of Henry Schein, Inc. since 1989. A CPA educated in South Africa, he is responsible for the firm's substantial growth and financial success and the continuation of a cutting edge social mission that has been a hallmark of the firm since its founding in 1932. The company distributes health care products and services to office-based clinicians (dentists, dental labs, physicians, veterinarians, and government and other institutions) throughout North America, Europe, Australia and New Zealand. Stanley Bergman started with the firm in the early 1980s and worked closely with its founder, Henry Schein, to grow the business, and with it, the company's tradition of social action. They forged a commitment to understand community problems and ways their resources could be used effectively to respond to current needs and prepare for emergencies. The company structures its social mission into categories that allow tracking and reporting contributions and results. Bergman communicates his personal and corporate values through a history of action and social justice that is a legacy for the firm's future. The company has a global social responsibility program to support health care advocacy and education, increase access to care for underserved populations, prepare and respond to disasters, and generally strengthen community wellness programs. The company has donated millions of dollars in products, services, and cash. The firm's philosophy is to help people and groups at the grassroots level through a variety of local programs that often involve company personnel raising money and delivering services.

Edward J. Bergman co-founded Miracle Corners of the World, Inc. (MCW), a non-profit organization, which serves young people worldwide, primarily through programs of leadership training, community center and housing development, and health care outreach. The organization's motto is "Local Change Through Global Exchange." MCW focuses on Africa but has projects in the U.S. and China as well. Eddie traveled to Africa on missions when he was a high school student in the late 1990s. He continued his volunteer work as an undergraduate student in hotel and tourism management at New York University and a graduate student at NYU, where he created an individualized study program in social entrepreneurship. Now in his mid 20s, Eddie is director of the Africa Travel Association in addition to his leadership of MCW. He has a passion for service and creating initiatives that do good. Influenced by his father, Stan Bergman and Team Schein as role models and sources of encouragement, Eddie is a passionate social entrepreneur with innovative ideas and a can-do attitude. MCW has helped develop community centers in Arusha and Songea, Tanzania, and Kissey, Sierra Leone. In Addis Ababa, Ethiopia, the MCW-built community center supports orphans and teaches community members about organic gardening, environmentalism, and health. MCW's annual Youth Leadership Retreat brings teens and young adults from underdeveloped countries to Burlington, Vermont, to learn about advocacy and social entrepreneurship. Eddie understands networking and fund raising. MCW's third annual gala in New York City in 2007 honored tennis legend Billie Jean King, World Team Tennis CEO and Commissioner Ilana Kloss, Cal Ramsey of the New York Knicks, and Baltimore Ravens linebacker and Super Bowl MVP Ray Lewis.

As advocates, both Stanley and Eddie Bergman create a compelling vision of problems and how to address them. Their strategy is to act locally by garnering support globally. They travel extensively, identify local needs, spearhead partnerships with local groups, and find supporters in the U.S. and elsewhere. They recognize political realities locally, and have an active network of board members, educators, health care professionals, and philanthropists who participate in many ways, including fund raising and volunteering. They listen closely and provide a voice and avenues for action. They report results as they grow their respective initiatives for corporate social responsibility and social entrepreneurship.

Individual Characteristics Affecting Advocacy

Individual dispositions affect a person's motivation to get involved in social advocacy, whether the individual is a corporate leader or independent social entrepreneur. Think of advocacy motivation as a combination of three categories of individual characteristics:

1. *Conviction about caring for others*: Advocates want to help. They don't ignore or avoid issues. When they see a homeless person in the street, they take action. They seek solutions and implement them.
2. *Self-confidence to overcome barriers*: Successful advocates and leaders are high in self-efficacy; they have a sense that they can make a difference.
3. *Transformational skills*: Advocates and leaders convey a compelling vision and inspire others through their values.

Overall, advocates are altruistic, committed to social justice and fairness, extroverted, not hesitant to express a strong opinion on a controversial subject, open to new ideas, creators of change, conscientious, empathic, and the type to go out of their way to do more than is expected of them (pro-social behavior). They create a vision of what could be and identify paths for accomplishing their goals. Advocates need to be strong communicators, insightful and influential politicians, entrepreneurs, and change agents. They need to have resilient personality characteristics such as self-confidence, internal control, self-efficacy, insight into their own and others' strengths and weaknesses, and flexibility to adapt as conditions change.

Conditions That Stimulate Action

Leaders are more likely to get involved in advocacy efforts the more the need is local and personal. Examples are social or health problems that involve employees, their families, and/or community members, such as a child suffering from a disease. Of course, people feel empathy and are stimulated to help distant groups or individuals who are anonymous and not related to the organization or its community when information demonstrates the need. Videos, site visits, and/or testimonials from those who were first hand witnesses make the need personal. (Think about corporate and community responses to Hurricane Katrina and the Thailand Tsunami.) Another condition that promotes advocacy is an initiative that allows participants to have direct, visible impact—for instance, building (or raising money to build) a community center or homeless shelter. The physical structure itself is evidence of success. Other success measures may be the number of programs started, the amount of dollars raised, and the number of people served.

So, for instance, Mary Ann Bell's local food pantry was the direct response of one individual who saw the need of the poor and homeless, recruited volunteers, and developed an on-going program for soliciting donations and providing food. Pattye Pece worked with other local Long Islanders to found a small Fair Trade gift store operated and staffed entirely by volunteers. The product sales benefit craftsmen and coffee and tea growers around the world. The profits are sent to orphanages in Africa. David Krause's Madagaskar Ankizy (meaning children) Fund built a school in the remote village close to his anthropological digs. He and his colleagues were so touched by the welcome and acceptance they felt during several years of their research that they wanted to help by building a two room school house and raising money to hire a teacher and purchase books.

Generally, people are likely to become advocates when they believe they can be effective. Stanley Bergman's corporate initiatives at Henry Schein Inc. and Eddie Bergman's initiatives with Miracle Corners of the World are focused on local communities. They and their teams identify needs, get to know the people involved, establish local initiatives that put a personal face on the recipients and volunteers, and communicate the need to others who have resources to help. Social advocacy efforts tend to have high costs to get underway and sustain, at least relative to available resources. Moreover, they often have a low, or at least uncertain, probability of success. The larger the effort, the more challenging it is to tackle and achieve.

Advocacy and Leadership

Advocates become leaders as they communicate a vision, garner support, set strategies, and organize tasks to accomplish their goals. Similarly, leaders of organizations become advocates when they identify issues and promulgate solutions for the benefit of their stockholders, employees, customers, suppliers, and community members. This raises several questions: What makes an advocate a good leader, and what makes a leader a good advocate? Does advocacy require special leadership skills in addition to skills needed by all leaders? Do leaders who become advocates need to do something different than other advocates?

Table 10.1.1 (left column) lists advocacy behaviors. Advocates identify one or more problems that need to be addressed. They recognize situational conditions that are likely to support or thwart their efforts. Their behaviors demonstrate their personal characteristics that underlie and motivate their social concern. They set goals, formulate strategies, take actions, and then evaluate their progress and learn from their successes and failures. In the process, they develop leadership and advocacy skills.

Leaders as Advocates

Table 10.1.1 (middle column) describes advocating for corporate social responsibility. Leaders articulate problems and recognize their company's role to help solve them. The issue or situation may stimulate their involvement, particularly if they have direct exposure to the issue. For instance, a corporate executive may establish a manufacturing plant in an impoverished area and recognize how the company can train unskilled young people in the community to give them employable skills. In taking social action, corporate leaders demonstrate their integrity, honesty, altruism, and willingness to take risks with organizational resources. These leaders attempt to mesh corporate and social goals. These goals may conflict. Also, social goals may not have an immediate benefit to the corporation of the people they intend to help. Of course, they may increase the company's good will with its customers and employees. CEOs' motives are complex with uncertain relationships between social welfare and stakeholder perceptions, cost control, and profit maximization. A classic example is the case of P. Roy Vagelos, the Merck CEO, who, in the 1980s, gave away the drug that cured river blindness, recognizing that it would benefit only poor people who could not afford to pay for the drug and finding that governments and private nonprofits were unwilling to pay. The decision demonstrated the company's underlying value that medicine is for people, and profits will follow . . . sometimes.

Table 10.1.1 Examples of Leadership and Social Advocacy Roles

Advocacy Behaviors	The Leader as Advocate for Corporate Social Responsibility	The Advocate as Leader for Social Entrepreneurship
Identify the problem(s)	Step up to the plate to address problems, recognize organization's role in corporate social responsibility, be ready to use leadership skills to address the issue	Focus on ways to create a compelling vision of the problem and potential solutions to attract others' attention and commitment
Recognize situational conditions	Having direct experience with the problem, seeing an issue close-up and personal	Generating sources of support, recognizing stakeholders
Demonstrate personal characteristics that motivate advocacy	Integrity, honesty, altruism, willingness to take risks and speak up, knowledge of organizational change	Ability to communicate, understanding others' situation and vested interests, political skills
Set goals	Meet organization's and personal goals while also addressing advocacy issues	Focus on meeting the needs of beneficiaries
Formulate strategies	Use power of position and own leadership skills, draw on idiosyncrasy credits and call in favors	Develop and coordinate support structures, recognize adversaries
Take action	Make decisions, allocate resources, form coalitions, constrain others' behaviors	Use commitment building and influence tactics, such as listening closely and giving others public voice to confirm their support.
Evaluate and learn from outcomes	Collect bottom-line measures, show that this is a win-win situation (positive outcomes for beneficiaries, supporters, and the organization)	Report and celebrate results, acknowledge losses, learn and improve
Develop advocacy and leadership skills	Take risks, identify and communicate values, link corporate social responsibility to organizational goals, don't tolerate—and certainly don't contribute to—social injustice, indeed redress social injustices and promote fair treatment	Develop skills (communications, transformational and transactional leadership, openness to new ideas, teambuilding, continuous learning)

Being a leader in social responsibility is not necessarily enough to ensure social welfare. Mattel recalled millions of toys with lead paint in the summer of 2007 despite having spent $10 million for ten years to monitor its 13 Asian factories and many more contract suppliers for employee safety and product quality. CEO Robert A. Eckert, apologized to Congress and to Chinese officials for the lead-paint failures. Some companies appear to act responsibly in some respects, but not in others. Wal-Mart, for example, has been called to task for its treatment of employees. Lee Scott, CEO of Wal-Mart went to its Battle Creek, Michigan store in December, 2007, to announce a $1 million national donation to the Salvation Army.

Leaders as advocates have an advantage over social entrepreneurs. Corporate leaders have resources, position power, control, idiosyncrasy credits (freedom to do what they like up to a point), and time before they are held accountable. Corporate leaders are likely to have an infrastructure at their disposal including the technology for data collection, storage, retrieval, evaluation of outcomes, and communication about need and accomplishments. Their social advocacy is evident in their business decisions, allocation of resources, coalitions they form, and constraints they impose of employees' and contractors' behaviors. Corporate leaders use the power of their positions as well as their leadership skills to demonstrate the value of social advocacy for beneficiaries, supporters, and the organization.

Leaders as advocates seek social justice, accept social responsibility, and link doing good with doing well. The organization gains value by producing socially beneficial outcomes and learning in the process. For instance, employees and customers who contribute to environmental sustainability through recycling (e.g., Toshiba's and Best Buy's jointly-sponsored electronics recycling events around the U.S.) learn how to establish and track the success of a program across functional and geographic areas. They celebrate their success together, enhancing their sense of belonging, teamwork, and loyalty to the organization. The leader and the organization gain credibility, which may have spin-off benefits in increasing revenue and reducing costs. Small successes in one area can lead to new initiatives (e.g., first recycling paper, later saving energy in a host of ways). Leaders and their companies teach others, including their competitors. Mattel acted affirmatively when lead paint was discovered. Companies such as Evergreen Lodge and Pura Vida are role models for win-win situations for beneficiaries and investors.

CEOs may not be natural advocates. They reach beyond traditional corporate goals to attack problems that may be unpopular and do not have immediate benefit. The corporate leader as advocate learns to take risks, identify and communicate personal and corporate values, and relate corporate social responsibility to organizational goals. Corporate leaders are likely to become successful advocates when they identify and understand different stakeholders, recognize intended and unintended costs (who benefits and who loses), and have realistic expectations and accurate perceptions of others' behavior and attitudes.

Community Advocates as Leaders

Table 10.1.1 (right column) describes how social entrepreneurs use leadership. The social entrepreneur creates a compelling vision of the problem and potential solutions in order to attract and sustain others' attention and support. Garnering resources and building a set of committed stakeholders are critical early steps in the advocacy process. The advocate must communicate clearly and forcefully, take into account competition for tight recourses, and possibly face adversaries—those who stand to lose if the advocacy initiative is successful. The advocate must be skillful at commitment building and influence tactics, such as listening closely and giving others public voice to confirm their support.

Advocacy has leadership challenges. Advocates elicit the support of people who don't have a clear stake in contributing to the advocacy effort. The effort may depend on people committing to a set of distinct values or beliefs that may not be held by others or that are not usually what motivates behavior—for instance, an initiative that is not well known and beneficiaries who are anonymous. Advocates often start with limited or no resources. They may be rebuffed frequently as people turn down their requests for action, given the competition among other good causes. The goal may seem insurmountable or only making a small dent in a large problem. Within organizations, advocacy for an issue may seem risky, especially if the effort is unpopular, unusual, or complex, even if the organization stands to benefit. People in the organization may not see the value or be willing to commit resources to social responsibility goals that do not have an immediate positive impact on the bottom line.

Advocates need tact (political skills), resilience, and an understanding of human behavior that goes beyond the usual demands of a leader.

Social entrepreneurs as leaders are passionate and focused on the needs of their bene-ficiaries as their primary goals. They engage in transactional management. They organize, plan, delegate, monitor, and reward. They also engage in transformational leadership, showing passion, inspiring others, and building relationships. Social entrepreneurs have advantages over corporate leaders. Although corporate leaders have resources and a power base, community advocates have flexibility. They are not constrained by corporate responsi-bilities. They are not locked in by stockholders and potentially conflicting goals. They don't have a fixed base of operation. If one potential source of support doesn't materialize, they can turn elsewhere. They seek resources from like-minded individuals and groups, develop-ing and coordinating support structures when necessary. They are not accountable, at least, not until they form an organization with a board of directors and other structures. They take less risk because they don't face competing goals. Still, they may face adversaries. For example, Ralph Nader promoted automobile safety in the face of massive industry lobbying. Sometimes advocates need to acknowledge losses as they encounter barriers that are not easily overcome. In the process, they develop skills that are vital for successful advocacy, such as communications, transformational and transactional leadership, teambuilding and openness to new ideas and continuous learning.

The Advocacy Process

Advocacy begins with the kernel of an idea prompted by evidence of a need. Advocates as entrepreneurs test the waters by talking with others about their idea and how to respond. Does the idea make sense to others? Are people interested and concerned? Will they help? In this early stage, advocates conceptualize and define the problem. They discuss and agree to general goals and methods of accomplishing them. They determine needed resources and possible sources. They identify the decision makers who need to be influenced and other stakeholders whose opinions need to be shaped. They also identify groups and individuals who are likely to be antagonistic, and they consider ways to react, for example, by focusing on common interests, convincing them of the need, demonstrating threats or benefits, etc. The advocacy initiative evolves as it gains public awareness, vocal support, financial resources, and partners or allies. Eventually, it begins to affect attitudes, behaviors, and/or policy decisions, and ultimately affects the intended beneficiaries without harming others. This is an evolutionary process. The effort may progress in fits and starts. It may falter and dissolve altogether. It may take new directions that were initially unanticipated, perhaps because the problem was resolved and the resources and organizational structures could be devoted to other challenging problems (e.g., the Jimmy Fund shifting from raising money to eradicate polio to raising funds for muscular dystrophy). Advocates who are open to continu-ous feedback throughout the process are likely to adapt to situational conditions and changes, sometimes altering methods and other times altering goals.

Stages of Advocacy

Generally speaking, there are four stages of advocacy that are repeated as the effort develops.

1. *Defining the goal*: This includes conceptualizing the problem (e.g., the need to change

awareness, attitudes, behaviors, and/or decisions), its scope (whether local and/or global), and time line.

2. *Mapping the territory*: This includes recognizing stakeholders; forming partnerships, alliances, and networks; setting targets; identifying resources; and distinguishing roles. Also, it may entail competing for resources and attention and is influenced by advocates' values, drive/passion, and underlying beliefs about people (e.g., that indeed they are generous or that they can change their attitudes).

3. *Call to action*: This is selecting and implementing strategies to accomplish advocacy goals while maintaining control. It includes developing strategies and actions focused on specific, realistic, time-bound goals (e.g., specifying how much money needs to be raised during the next six months)

4. *Evaluation*: This is determining the effectiveness of the advocacy effort and making adjustments in strategy and tactics to improve outcomes.

Advocacy Strategies

Advocacy uses political and social influence to alter attitudes, behaviors, and/or decisions. *Cognitive advocacy strategies* are giving information to generate awareness for an issue and encourage action. *Emotional strategies* include warnings or threats, inducements of guilt or fear, or promises of satisfaction or delight. *Behavioral strategies* include modeling the desired behavior (as when the advocate contributes financially and volunteers) and rewarding desired behaviors (the ubiquitous recognition award dinners, for instance).

Advocates' beliefs about others are likely to affect their advocacy behaviors. For instance, if advocates believe that people don't change their attitudes and behaviors, or at least don't change them easily, the advocates may be likely to take forceful action or not get involved altogether. If advocates believe people do change, they may focus on cognitive strategies that simply provide people with information or data, assuming that once they are informed, they will see the light and do what is needed. If advocates believe that people are more sensitive to losses than gains, they are likely to use threats, highlighting the bad things that will occur if the decision or behaviors do not change. If advocates believe that people will act affirmatively when they understand how their behavior can help, advocates will highlight behavior-outcome relationships and the value of the outcomes.

Conditions That Facilitate and Discourage Advocacy

Table 10.1.2 (left column) lists situational conditions that influence advocacy. The situation includes contact with the beneficiary, time frame for action, the clarity of goals and actions, the degree of difficulty of goals and actions, and the cost of action relative to the gain. Advocacy goals differ in the extent to which trying to do something positive has a direct, visible, and immediate impact. Another condition is the extent of support available, including alliances, social support, and, conversely, the extent to which there are adversaries, nay-sayers, and doubters, and extent of support.

Conditions That Facilitate Advocacy

Conditions that facilitate advocacy are described in Table 10.1.2 (middle column). These include being personally acquainted with one or more people who have a visible need and having a short time frame to deliver services or make a decision. Having clear goals and high

Table 10.1.2 Conditions That Facilitate and Discourage Social Advocacy

Situational Conditions	Conditions that Facilitate Advocacy	Conditions that Discourage Advocacy
Contact with the beneficiary	Personal beneficiary (the advocate or someone close: identifiable by name), visible need	Impersonal (e.g., a village in Africa) or general common good (e.g., global warming)
Time frame for action	Short-term, immediate outcomes; help needed now—e.g., to assist flood victims	Long-term outcomes, outcomes will occur sometime in the future—e.g., save energy, promote green construction
Clarity of goals and action	Clear goals and high agreement about what to do	Ambiguous goals and low agreement about what to do
Goal and action difficulty	Low—desired outcomes require minimal effort and resources	High—desired outcomes require considerable effort and resources
Cost and value	Action is low cost, high value	Action is high cost and low immediate value (but presumably high long-term value)
Relationship between effort and effect	High—direct impact; high relationship between effort, action, and goal accomplishment (e.g., seeking volunteers to drive cancer patients to chemotherapy appointments)	Low–low impact; low relationship between effort, action, and goal accomplishment (e.g., raising money for cancer research, which eventually affects medical treatment and outcomes)
Support	Clear alliances and coalitions with shared goals, volunteers readily available	Few shared interests
Social encouragement (peer pressure and reinforcement)	High	Low
Adversaries, nay-sayers, and doubters (controversy and potential polarization)	Low	High

agreement about what to do helps. So does having a sense that the outcomes can, indeed, be produced. Support is also important, of course. Support may be from alliances and volunteers who are readily available and happy to participate. Pattye Pece's Fair Trade initiative was a partnership with a small group of other religiously-committed people with similar beliefs, values, and goals. David Krause was able to elicit the imagination of contributors, never tiring of the chance to generate excitement with his emotionally moving slide presentation and dynamic talk. The relationship between effort and outcomes needs to be strong. That is, there is a high relationship between effort, action, and goal accomplishment. David Krause showed that small amounts of money went a long way in Madagascar. Naturally it helps to be encouraged by others and have few if any adversaries to block the way.

Conditions That Discourage Advocacy

Conditions that discourage advocacy (Table 10.1.2, right column) include having an impersonal and/or ambiguous goal, long-term outcomes, low agreement about what to do, the need for considerable effort and resources to accomplish the goal, little support from other organizations (low shared interests), low social support, many adversaries, low impact objectives, and a high cost of action with low immediate value. There may be too many competing interests for the same resources. Potential volunteers and donors may be put off by warnings. The costs may be viewed as too high relative to the benefits. For instance, people are reluctant to give up energy-consuming luxuries for small, long-term, or imperceptible gains. Another factor that weakens advocacy is not bothering to evaluate the outcomes and communicate change as success.

We don't hear much about failed advocacy initiatives. Many individuals would like to make a difference but don't even try. Others make an attempt and then burn out. They work too hard with little result and the effort fizzles. This could happen when the problem and sources of support are not clear. Outcomes take ages to achieve if anything positive happens at all. Goals are unclear, the problem seems too big, and there is little agreement about what to do to help. Efforts that seem easy at first may become difficult, for instance, when bureaucratic red tape intervenes. Most advocacy efforts impose some barriers. These may be rules and regulations that have to be overcome or just convincing people who control the resources that this is something that is important to do. Alliances may be present one day, and gone the next. People may not share the interest, and the advocate may not help them visualize the problem or what they can do to make a difference. Nay-sayers may abound— people who doubt the value of the effort, fail to see its relationship to the mission of a company, or are not ready to stick out their necks until others are on board.

Recommendations for Action

Corporate leaders as advocates can go wrong, for instance, by acting without a clear purpose or following others' ideas without linking the effort to organizational goals. They can be criticized for taking time and resources away from bottom-line business objectives. Social entrepreneurs can go wrong in many ways, too, for instance, by assuming others will share their goals, taking up the gauntlet for an issue few people are willing to support, not learning from failed attempts, ignoring feedback, not delegating for fear of losing control, or not changing course when strategies have failed and other methods should be tried. Here are some recommendations to promote effective leadership and advocacy within organizations:

- *Get the word out*: Educate employees about corporate social responsibility, how the organization is contributing, and how they can help. Provide education and opportunities for participation about specific issues and initiatives, whether they are corporate-wide donation campaigns and team efforts (the United Way, Habitat for Humanity), individual employees volunteering in the community (one employee starting a soup kitchen for the homeless in a local community), or corporate investments in environmental sustainability in the community (a recycling initiative).
- *Link to bottom-line objectives*: Clarify the tie between social advocacy and the corporation's success. Don't assume that stakeholders will see the relationship. Explain how the effort helps to attract more customers or talented employees, for instance.
- *Recognize accomplishments*: Celebrate (reinforce) achievements to build organizational commitment and loyalty and honor those who contributed most.
- *Highlight spin-off benefits*: Show how corporate social responsibility can increase employee pride and loyalty, enhance teambuilding, improve communication between departments, and generate good will that benefits sales and attracts and retains valued employees.

- *Invest corporate resources*: Provide support for individuals who want to be involved in corporate advocacy efforts or start their own. Consider starting a community service support center that would offer materials, advice from fellow employees who are social entrepreneurs, and money (for instance, small grants, micro-loans, or contributions from company-wide fund raising efforts with employees determining how to distribute the proceeds).
- *Encourage employee participation*: Identify people who have a proclivity to work on and lead advocacy efforts. Ask for volunteers. Assess their skills and development needs (e.g., design an assessment center or on-line, self-administered assessment tools) to evaluate advocacy skills such as communication ability, political sensitivity, and knowledge of change management. Involve executives in corporate social responsibility projects to increase the projects' visibility and importance. These can become developmental assignments for high potential managers. Don't make these assignments for soon-to-be downsized executives or people who are being forced to retire.

Here are some ways to overcome these barriers and respond to nay-sayers and doubters:

- *Provide convincing data or other information*: This may be information about the numbers of people affected; the costs to the individual, the company, or society; testimonies from those affected or helped; or other demonstrations of the seriousness of the problem or issue and the positive impact that is possible.
- *Join forces with others who have like minds or shared interests*: There is power in numbers, especially if others are opinion leaders, people who are respected and have resources.
- *Negotiate with opposing forces*: People who object strongly may be amenable to small trial efforts, or experiments to demonstrate the value of the initiative. If the goal is seeking volunteers for a community initiative, the advocate may start in one department or business unit to see how people react. In general, small, local efforts may be more palatable to the organization than grandiose ambitions. Small efforts can get employees involved and demonstrate impact. Note that Henry Schein Inc.'s social programs are targeted initiatives. Over the years, specific efforts have become part of a corporate strategy for social advocacy in relation to the health care mission of the business.
- *Use behavioral tactics (e.g., demonstrations, ad campaigns, petitions)*: Today, there are many methods to gain attention including on-line blogs, YouTube, and television sound bites. Corporate leaders can use such technology within their organizations to build momentum and enthusiasm for a social issue.
- *Learn advocacy skills*: Leaders can learn and practice advocacy skills. One step in that direction is understanding the advocacy process. Here are some steps that can be taken to educate leaders in advocacy. Leaders can observe successful advocates, such as Stanley and Eddie Bergman and the others I described here. Consider examples of advocates for local and global initiatives. Also, look for examples of advocates who have a personal objective (i.e., to help specific individuals) and those who benefit others in general or in communities far removed. Examples might reflect a variety of topics and goals, such areas as social welfare (poverty, education, wellness, health care), the environment, politics, and religion. Include goals such as raising money, delivering services, building awareness, preventing negative outcomes, and influencing others' votes and resource allocation decisions. Understand how these advocates carried out the basic elements of advocacy including issue identification, solution formulation, taking action, and evaluating and refining the effort. Think about the problems these advocates

faced; how what could have been done (or still could be done) differently. Consider the skills and knowledge that advocates need to be effective. These include communication skills (e.g., ways to formulate a clear message and how to use media effectively), how to elicit support (e.g., recruiting volunteers and raising money), political and cultural sensitivity, knowledge of change management (unfreezing seemingly intransigent attitudes), forming alliances and coalitions and seeking compromise, and resolving conflicts and negotiating agreements.

- *Practice advocacy*: Leaders can practice and fine tune their advocacy efforts. Try the following: Write a mission statement. Are your goals clear? Collect to determine the nature and scope of the problem(s). Set short-term goals that target specific outcomes, (e.g., increase recycling in the organization by 5% within the next year). What actions will you take? Determine who controls policies and brainstorm ways to approach policy makers (e.g., a letter writing campaign, forums for speaking, anticipating questions and practicing answers). What transformational and transactional leadership steps will you take to recruit, motivate, and direct volunteers? Consider how you can evaluate and report outcomes, celebrate your successes, and learn from failures.

Conclusion

Advocacy and leadership skills are important for corporate social responsibility and social entrepreneurship initiatives. Corporate leaders need to be effective advocates, and advocates need to be effective leaders. Advocates lead by communicating their vision, securing support and resources, and organizing goal-centered tasks. Corporate leaders seek ways to benefit the organization in a socially responsible manner. Corporate and independent advocacy requires transactional and transformational leadership, showing passion and conveying inspiration. Leaders are motivated by strength of conviction for doing good, self-confidence in the face of difficult goals, and their transformational abilities. They are more likely to initiate social action when there is a local and personal need, volunteers can work directly with the people who benefit, and the value of the initiative is clear; in short, they believe they can make a difference.

Successful advocates define their goals clearly, recognize the scope of their goals and efforts including the range of stakeholders involved, and initiate a clear call to action—that is, indicate just what needs to be done by whom and by when. In addition, they incorporate evaluation in the process, tracking, reporting, and celebrating their accomplishments. Advocacy strategies depend on the leader's beliefs about how people will react to their initiatives. For instance, advocates inform people, warn them, and/or constrain or reward their behaviors. Also, they recognize conditions that discourage and encourage advocacy. Advocacy is more difficult when goals are impersonal, positive outcomes are years away, and there is little agreement about what to do.

Generally, leaders know that corporate social responsibility is not an easy sell. Critics abound and resource expenditures must be justified. Effective leadership and advocacy requires education about corporate responsibility and advocacy processes, tying social action to the company's bottom line when possible, celebrating and reinforcing achievements, and encouraging employee participation. Barriers to advocacy can be overcome by providing convincing information, joining forces with allies, negotiating with opponents, and actions that demonstrate beliefs (e.g., "putting your money where your mouth is").

10.2   INDIVIDUAL REACTIONS TO LEADERSHIP SUCCESSION IN WORKGROUPS

Gary A. Ballinger and F. David Schoorman

We integrate theories of cognitive appraisal, relational leadership, and trust to develop a model of how individual affective reactions to leadership succession influence work attitudes and behaviors. We predict that the quality of the relationship with the prior leader will influence an affective reaction to that leader's departure. This affective reaction will influence the group member's initial trust in the new leader, task communication with the new leader, organizational citizenship behaviors, motivation to perform, job satisfaction, and turnover.

Research on leadership has shown that workgroup members have different relationships with the formal leader of the workgroup (Dansereau, Graen, & Haga, 1975; Graen & Scandura, 1987). This suggests that changes in the formal leadership of workgroups should result in changes not only in workgroup processes and performance (Finkelstein & Hambrick, 1996; Grusky, 1960; Vancil, 1987) but also in the affect and work attitudes of members of the group who remain after the change (Gordon & Rosen, 1981). Leadership succession research at the workgroup and top management team level has focused primarily on attempting to explain group- or organization-level responses to the succession event and its context (Kesner & Sebora, 1994); rarely have researchers engaged in empirical investigation of processes that occur within individuals and their workgroups during these episodes. We propose a stage-based model of individual reactions to leader succession that relates individuals' affective reactions to the departure of the old leader to subsequent judgments about the new leader, as well as to judgments about their job and behaviors on the job.

We believe this model will facilitate greater understanding of how succession has the potential to disrupt group performance and the steps leaders and firms can take to minimize such disruption. Our process model of individual reactions to leadership succession draws from cognitive appraisal theories of emotion (Ortony, Clore, & Collins, 1988; Smith & Ellsworth, 1985) and its relationship with subsequent judgments and behaviors (Forgas, 2000; Forgas & George, 2001), as well as relational leadership theories (Graen & Scandura, 1987; Mayer, Davis, & Schoorman, 1995), to explain the timing and intensity of affective reactions to the departure of the outgoing leader and to link these reactions to subsequent changes in attitudes and behaviors of group members.

Research on Leadership Succession and Level of Analysis

In prior research on leadership succession, scholars have focused primarily on the relationship between a succession episode and organizational performance (see Kesner & Sebora, 1994). Over four decades have passed since debate emerged over the existence of a "succession effect" that explained (or didn't explain) performance changes following leadership succession in organizations (Gamson & Scotch, 1964; Grusky, 1960, 1963). Subsequent research efforts disclosed multiple intervening situational or contextual variables that might better predict the outcomes, including the timing of the succession in relation to the workgroup's schedule (Allen, Panian, & Lotz, 1979; Brown, 1982), the incoming leader's expertise (Pfeffer & Davis-Blake, 1986), the political activity surrounding the succession (Welsh & Dehler, 1988), whether the new leader was selected from inside or outside the group

(Helmich & Brown, 1972), and the combination of insider/outsider status and the extent of changes in the composition of the workgroup or management team following the succession (Shen & Cannella, 2002). We believe that the existence of so many moderators of succession's impact on group performance stems in part from the fact that the effect of the succession episode on individual workgroup members is not uniform.

A relatively smaller number of case studies (with interview data) of leader succession (e.g., Fauske & Ogawa, 1987; Gouldner, 1954; Guest, 1962; Heller, 1989; Pitcher, Chreim, & Kisfalvi, 2000) give us some insights into the outcomes at the individual level of analysis. But a lack of empirical research at the individual level has required researchers looking for the succession effect in groups to make assumptions regarding the processes underlying these effects. As an example, Rowe, Cannella, Rankin, and Gorman assume that "the immediate disruptiveness of the event leads to a lowering of morale and a lack of cohesiveness" (2005: 203) within the workgroup following the prior leader's departure (see also Cannella & Rowe, 1995). We argue that the impact of a succession episode on group members is a more complex function of the form and content of the relationships between the prior leader and the individual members of the group prior to the episode. We hope this theoretical model stimulates longitudinal empirical research into the effects of succession on the individual members of workgroups.

The Leadership Succession Episode and Its Consequences

We follow Gordon and Rosen's definition of leadership succession as "the planned or unplanned change of the formal leader of a group or organization" (1981: 227). By distinguishing between the formal leader of the organization or group and other potential leaders, this definition allows us to focus on the individual who has legitimate power (French & Raven, 1959) within the workgroup and, thus, is held responsible by the organization (and its stakeholders) for the performance outcomes of the group. Our focus on the formal leader eliminates doubt about the occurrence of the event; different group members may not share a perception of who an "informal" leader of a workgroup is. Our level of analysis is the individual member of the workgroup. Our time frame of interest in measurement begins from the time a leadership departure is announced until a period after the official vesting of legitimate power in the successor that is long enough to permit the formation of new exchange relationships.

Measuring individual reactions to succession requires the researcher to pay careful attention to when such measurements are taken. Detailed investigations of succession in organizations (e.g., Gephart, 1978; Gouldner, 1954; Heller, 1989; Pitcher et al., 2000) all show that the phenomenon is made up of a series of events, and measurement at each point in time will allow for a more complete understanding of the process (Mitchell & James, 2001). At each event, different reactions can be expected to occur based on the individual's interpretation of the event or the actions of the departing or incoming group leader. Leadership succession in organizations may also take place in a multitude of contexts: it may be planned or unplanned, and it may occur under such circumstances as retirement, voluntary resignation, firing, demotion, promotion within the organization, or death (Friedman & Singh, 1989; Gephart, 1978). Group members' reactions can be expected to vary in form and intensity as a function of the context surrounding the event (see discovery stage in Figure 10.2.1).

We define a *succession episode* as that series of events that occur from the moment a single workgroup member discovers that there will be a change in formal leadership through the

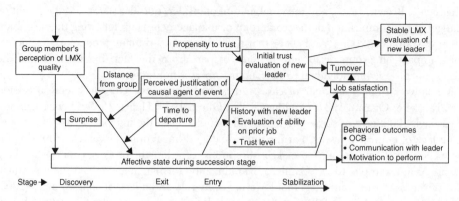

Figure 10.2.1 The Relationships Between Affective Reactions to Leadership Succession Events and Individual Outcomes.

actual change in formal group leadership, and it continues until work roles stabilize following the event. The first of these events is that time when the old leader's intention to depart becomes known to group members (discovery). The next event in the sequence is when the old leader actually departs the group (exit). The third event involves the entry of or appointment of an individual to a new position of formal group leadership (entry). The fourth is when work roles and relationships within the workgroup stabilize (role stabilization). An individual's affective, attitudinal, and behavioral reaction to an event at one stage should be expected to influence his or her reaction to an event later in the episode.

The consequences of succession at the group level have been well documented in the literature (Kesner & Sebora, 1994; Rowe et al., 2005). Ocasio (1994) noted that CEOs in his sample were at an increased risk of failure and replacement in the first few years after appointment, a finding consistent with earlier research (Vancil, 1987). We believe that judgments about the trustworthiness of the new leader are critical to this early success. Researchers have found that early evaluations are critical in the development of relationships with group leaders and that these relationships facilitate the communication of critical information, the execution of the leader's changes, and perceptions of transformational leadership (Dirks & Ferrin, 2002; Gabarro, 1987; Pillai, Schriesheim, & Williams, 1999).

Communication of task information between workgroup members and new team leadership plays a critical role in new leaders' ability to increase group effectiveness (Gabarro, 1987; Porter, Lorsch, & Nohria, 2004). High levels of team member turnover or low levels of accurate communication between group members and the new leader have been shown to precipitate a downward spiral in performance (Hambrick & D'Aveni, 1992). We also consider early willingness of group members to engage in organizational citizenship behaviors (OCBs), which have been shown to be related to group and organizational performance (Borman & Motowidlo, 1993; Dunlop & Lee, 2004; Podsakoff, Ahearne, & MacKenzie, 1997). Affect also has been proposed as a driver of job-related effort (Seo, Barrett, & Bartunek, 2004), and we believe these affective reactions to succession can lead to changes in individual motivation to perform. Finally, job satisfaction levels are included as relevant outcomes because judgments about the job are relevant outcomes at the individual level, with the potential to impact group processes through their impact on group membership (via turnover) or other relevant behaviors (including OCBs).

Individual Reactions During Leadership Succession Episodes

The notion that the development of leader-member relations, trust, and group socialization occur in stages is not new to the literature in psychology and organizational behavior. Moreland and Levine (1989) proposed that group members go through stages of selection, commitment, and role transition as they enter and become full members of groups. Graen and Scandura (1987) suggested that leaders and group members form relationships in stages encompassing role making, role taking, and role routinization. Trust formation takes place in a process involving an initial evaluation of trustworthiness, which leads to actions that either reinforce this impression or change it and result in a more stable level of trust between the two parties (Mayer et al., 1995).

The stage model that we propose (discovery → exit → entry → role stabilization) is consistent with each of these stage models as they apply to relational leadership and role development. The integration of knowledge from cognitive appraisal theories of emotion allows us to model more specifically the affective reactions to each event as individuals move through the succession episode. In the following sections we examine the process as it unfolds in each stage in turn. We introduce each of the theoretical perspectives in the discovery stage and develop the implications of these perspectives through the subsequent stages.

Discovery

For a group member, the experience of the succession process begins when he or she discovers that the group leader is leaving that role within the group. In an organizational setting, this may precede the actual event by weeks, or even months, depending on the circumstances of the departure. The succession may be called for by the rules or norms of the organization, as in the case of regular managerial rotations or fixed terms of office for public officials. Notification may be secret or public; it may come from the leader personally (e.g., by way of a confidential aside), from the organization (e.g., a memorandum), or through "the grapevine." If the group member trusts the source and believes that the leader will be departing the group, the succession episode has begun.

Group members' initial reactions to the discovery will be affective. These affective reactions are driven by an individual's primary and secondary appraisal of what the event means to him/her and his/her goals (Frijda, 1993). Because emotions have long been held to be critical in determining how individuals deal with uncertain and changing conditions (Simon, 1967), we believe that these reactions play a major role in relevant outcomes during and after the episode. Individuals' reactions include the initial evaluation of the new leader's trustworthiness and a reevaluation of their own job satisfaction (Breckler, 1993; Weiss & Cropanzano, 1996). These reactions can lead to behavioral responses, such as quitting one's job (Lee & Mitchell, 1994; Maertz & Campion, 2004), changes in levels of OCBs (Brief & Motowidlo, 1986; George, 1991; McNeely & Meglino, 1994), and changes in the form and content of communications with the new formal group leader (Forgas, 1998, 1999), as well as changes in the level of effort expended on the job (Seo et al., 2004).

Affective Reactions to Succession

The term *affect* is frequently used to cover both moods and emotions, especially in relation to studying the relationship between moods and emotions and organizational behavior phenomena (e.g., Forgas & George, 2001). For the purposes of this model, affect does not refer to an individual's disposition to experience particular emotional states, often referred to as *trait affect* (Tellegen, 1985; Watson & Clark, 1984; Watson, Clark, & Tellegen, 1988). We are concerned instead with the change in a person's affective state that occurs when that person discovers that his or her leader is leaving the workgroup.

Watson and colleagues (e.g., Watson, 2000; Watson & Tellegen, 1985; Watson, Wiese, Vaidya, & Tellegen, 1999) describe affect along two dimensions of experience: positive affect (PA) and negative affect (NA). PA "reflects the extent to which a person feels enthusiastic, active, and alert. High PA is a state of high energy, full concentration, and pleasurable engagement, whereas low PA is characterized by sadness and lethargy" (Watson et al., 1988: 1063). NA "is a general dimension of subjective distress and unpleasurable engagement that subsumes a variety of aversive mood states, including anger, contempt, disgust, fear and nervousness, with low NA being a state of calmness and serenity" (Watson et al., 1988: 1063). Previous research on PA and NA (see Watson et al., 1999, for a review) has shown these dimensions to be independent using factor analytic methods on responses to verbal scales. For example, individuals can report that they experience low PA (e.g., calm, relaxed) and low NA (e.g., apathetic) independently.

Cognitive Appraisal of Succession Events

Researchers have shown that anxiety and anticipation accompany succession events (e.g., Fauske & Ogawa, 1987; Gilmore & Ronchi, 1995; Kotin & Sharaf, 1967; Ogawa, 1991; Pitcher et al., 2000). These reported sensations involve changes in affective states—changes in the feelings or mood of an individual that occur as a result of an event. The changes in affect levels occur as a result of the group member's appraisal of what the event means to him or her in terms of his or her ability to reach critical goals (Frijda, 1993). The impact of the prior relationship is most likely to be noticed in the immediate emotional reactions of the group members to the discovery of the change in leadership.

Cognitive theories of emotional reactions generally hold that appraisals take place in two stages (Ortony et al., 1988; Smith & Ellsworth, 1985). First, an event is perceived by an individual and a primary appraisal takes place where the affective reaction is based on the extent to which the event impacts the individual's ability to reach his or her goals (Frijda, 1993). Ortony and colleagues (1988) have separated these individual goals into active-pursuit (achievement) goals and interest goals. Active-pursuit goals are those individuals want to accomplish, whereas interest goals are "things one wants to see happen" (Ortony et al., 1988: 41). Whether or not individuals believe that the event impedes their ability to reach the goal determines the direction (positive or negative) of the affective reaction. The extent to which an individual believes the goal impacted by the event is important determines (in part) the intensity of the reaction. This intensity is also affected by the surprise of the event and individual differences in the intensity of the affective reactions (Ortony et al., 1988).

Following the primary, goal-oriented appraisal of the focal event, individuals engage in a secondary appraisal of events. In this secondary appraisal, individuals evaluate the impact of events on goals across multiple dimensions and build more complex affective responses based on these evaluations. Smith and Ellsworth (1985) have demonstrated that individuals' affective reactions to events are conditioned on five dimensions: pleasantness of the event, the individuals' anticipated effort required in response to the event, the certainty of the event, whether the event requires greater or less future attention to the matter at hand, and whether the event is in the control of the individual. Understanding the link between cognitive appraisals of events at work and affective responses is important in determining how events at work impact workers' affective states. Brief and Weiss (2002) have identified several factors in the workplace that have been shown to produce affective reactions, including stressful events, work conditions, groups, the distribution of rewards and punishments, and leaders and their behaviors. A change in leadership in a workgroup would certainly be considered an event producing a cognitive appraisal that should change an individual's current affective state.

Relational Leadership

There is evidence of within-group variance in the content of the relationships that group members have with their leaders. Relational approaches to leadership (Dansereau et al., 1975; Liden & Graen, 1980) provide support for the proposition that leaders develop relationships with workgroup members that differ markedly from member to member in the terms and amount of goods and emotional support exchanged. Some individuals in groups enjoy relationships with the leader marked by high levels of affect, loyalty, respect, and trust (Dienesch & Liden, 1986; Graen & Scandura, 1987), whereas others experience relationships that are more formal in quality and never exceed the basic terms of economic exchange between leader and subordinate.

The dimensions of the relationship that matter in terms of protection for the individual member include *exchange* and *trust*. Graen and Cashman (1975) hold that managers exchange five different types of resources for members' collaboration on unstructured tasks: information, influence, tasks, latitude, and support. Dienesch and Liden (1986) have proposed that LMX is made up of three distinct dimensions, including loyalty, perceived contribution, and affect. The emotional impact of a sudden change in the amount and quality of an exchange relationship can be expected to be large, since the relationship is characterized by affection and access to future benefits (Graen & Scandura, 1987; Sparrowe & Liden, 1997).

The other important aspect of the relationship is trust in the leader. Trust is linked with LMX, and the two are correlated but separable constructs (Brower, Schoorman, & Tan, 2000). It is possible to develop trust in a new leader before an exchange relationship stabilizes. Individuals can have high initial levels of trust in a new leader (McKnight, Cummings, & Chervany, 1998; Rotter, 1967, 1971) that can be established even prior to the process of role establishment described by Graen and Scandura (1987). Indeed, such a high initial trust relationship may facilitate the delegation of tasks, leading to increased quality of LMX (Bauer & Green, 1996). For those with both high- and low-quality relationships, the impending change in group leadership initiates a cognitive appraisal of how this change is likely to affect their goals. On the discovery of an impending change in leadership, we can expect lower levels of PA for those with high-quality relations, because we can expect them to lose enthusiasm for work during the period when they face uncertainty over the loss of their outgoing leader, who perhaps served as a mentor or trusted friend and coach. For those with low-quality relationships with the outgoing leader, higher levels of PA can be expected at discovery of succession, because these individuals should be expected to be motivated to form better relationships and to gain more from a new relationship with the incoming leader (Levine & Moreland, 1985).

Proposition 1a: The quality of the relationship with the predecessor will predict the change in PA at the discovery of the intended departure of the old leader. Individuals with high-quality relationships will experience decreased levels of PA; those with low-quality relationships will experience increased levels of PA.

Proposition 1b: The quality of the relationship with the predecessor will predict the change in NA at the discovery of the intended departure of the old leader. Individuals with high-quality relationships will experience increased levels of NA; those with low-quality relationships will experience decreased levels of NA.

Expectation of the Succession

Researchers studying the intensity of affective reactions to events believe that the unexpectedness of the event is related to the intensity of the reaction: the more unexpected the event, the more intense the affective reaction (Ortony et al., 1988). The unexpected nature of the event results in greater cognitive efforts aimed at attributing the event to some cause (Clary & Tesser, 1983; Weiner, 1985). This is relevant because certain leadership succession events are expected by members of the workgroup and can be anticipated, whereas others are completely unexpected. Friedman and Saul (1991) have proposed that the amount of disruption surrounding a CEO succession determines, in part, the impact of the event on company morale. They posit that "whether a succession is planned influences the extent of successor-induced change" (1991: 626), and this signals a disruption for company employees. One example where the departure is a surprise is when the leader is fired and removed from the premises that day. Another example is when the leader gets a job in another organization after secretly interviewing outside the job. Other departures are planned in advance. Leaders can retire at predetermined time periods, or give notice of their departure some time in advance. They can be a part of a scheduled job rotation or have a specified term in office.

Vancil (1987) describes a model for CEO succession known as "relay succession," in which the new leader is identified ahead of time as the heir apparent to the departing leader. The principal logic of relay succession is to reduce the surprise and turbulence associated with leader succession (Zhang & Rajagopalan, 2004). The advance knowledge of departure allows group members to prepare emotionally for the departure. For expected changes in leadership, followers can plan in advance for the day when that leader is not around, and they can brace for the disruption that is likely to follow such an event. If, however, the leader departs immediately, as in the case of a firing or where the leader abruptly quits for a better job, individuals have no preparation for the event, and this should heighten the intensity of those affective reactions more closely tied to NA (e.g., fear, anxiety).

Proposition 2a: Whether a departure is expected or unexpected moderates the relationship between the quality of the relationship and the level of PA after the discovery of the succession event. Expected events result in smaller changes in levels of PA that occur after the event compared to unexpected events.

Proposition 2b: Whether a departure is expected or unexpected moderates the relationship between the quality of the relationship and the level of NA after the discovery of the succession event. Expected events result in smaller changes in levels of NA that occur after the event compared to unexpected events.

Exit

While the direction of the affective reaction is determined by the primary appraisal of the discovery of the event, workgroup members subsequently discover more facts about the context of the succession that will impact the intensity of their affective reaction. Several factors that individuals learn, usually during the period following the discovery of the impeding change and the actual departure of the old leader, will impact the secondary appraisal of the event. This is the exit stage of the succession episode. These factors will moderate the connection between the quality of the relationship with the departing leader and the intensity of affective reactions to the departure. The intensity of the reaction will be moderated by the psychological distance between the old leader's destination and the workgroup, the length of time between discovery and the actual departure of the individual, and the perceived justification of the causal event. The exit stage ends when the new leader is introduced to the group, an event that may truncate this stage before some of the moderating variables are processed. We believe that the exit stage is truncated because what matters in terms of determining the outcomes of interest from this model is the affective state of the group member at the time the new leader enters the workgroup.

Destination of the Outgoing Leader

The exit stage involves the revelation of the final destination of the leader, and the workgroup members should be able to evaluate how the leader's new workgroup relates to their group. After discovery, there is a process of variable length during which the leader prepares to depart. It is during this stage that individual group members have time to evaluate and confirm the information received during the "discovery" stage and to evaluate the implications of the destination of the departing leader. Exleaders can remain in the group, as in the case of the kibbutz (Leviatan, 1978), or they can be promoted to a group one level up the organizational hierarchy from their old group, as was the case in five of the fourteen successions examined by Gabarro (1987).

   In organizational settings, former leaders can exercise considerable influence over their prior workgroup; they can direct resources to the group or provide advice or help recruit members for the group. These contributions are directly related to the favorability of the circumstances under which that member leaves the group (Levine & Moreland, 1985). Group members engage in remembrance of those who have left the group, and this can also lead to a sensitivity to their subsequent actions that affect the success (or failure) of the workgroup (Moreland & McMinn, 1999). Ziller (1965) proposed that the old leader's power over the group at the time of departure is based, in part, on the power of their new group in relation to the old group. If the leader leaves the organization altogether, we would expect that he or she will have no legitimate power and the affective reaction to his or her departure will be the same as that expressed in Proposition 1. A leader's promotion to a level above the current workgroup may not elicit the same intensity of affective reaction within group members, because the outgoing leader can still provide resources and other network benefits to the favored members of his or her prior workgroup (Sparrowe & Liden, 1997). But if the old leader is moving to a closely related group inside the organization with power over the old group (e.g., a direct promotion), then followers having high-quality relationships should experience a suppression of the affective reaction proposed earlier.

The critical issue in measuring the power of the exleader is the distance between his or her destination group and the old group. This is defined as the extent to which (1) the old leader's destination group has control over strategic contingencies required for the success of the workgroup and (2) the extent of communication between the old leader's destination group and the old group. Those members of the old group having high-quality relationships with the outgoing leader should be expected to experience less anxiety and fear if the leader remains close (in a strategic and communicative sense) to the group. The inverse should also be expected to hold. What this results in is a cancellation of the affective reaction to discovery, since a group member who becomes anxious when finding out the leader is leaving should become less anxious when he or she finds out the individual will remain close.

Proposition 3a: The distance between the outgoing leader's destination and his or her prior workgroup moderates the relationship between the quality of the relationship and the level of PA during the exit stage of the succession event. Greater distance should result in greater increases in levels of PA as the quality of the relationship with the predecessor decreases.

Proposition 3b: The distance between the outgoing leader's destination and his or her prior workgroup moderates the relationship between the quality of the relationship and the level of NA during the exit stage of the succession event. Greater distance should result in greater increases in levels of NA as the quality of the relationship with the predecessor increases.

Time to Departure

In succession episodes there is frequently a variable length of time between group members' discovery of the impending leadership change and the actual physical departure of the leader from the group. In case examples from the literature, we have seen a range of events studied, from immediate changes in leadership (Gephart, 1978) to changes occurring at regular intervals, such as a principal change occurring between school years (Fauske & Ogawa, 1987). A retiring manager or CEO may set a retirement date far off into the future, or in some cases a fired manager may be escorted out of the building immediately. The length of this period should have an impact on the intensity of an individual's affective reaction.

Following Smith and Ellsworth's (1985) rationale, a short time between discovery and departure should intensify a member's affective reaction, because the group member will feel that the event is more certain to occur and is out of his or her control. The longer the time frame, the more likely it is that the event could possibly be reversed, such as through a counteroffer or "change of heart"; group members' affective reactions should be less intense because they have more time to prepare for the departure of the old leader and the new work environment that will result.

Proposition 4: The length of time between members' discovery of the outgoing leader's departure and the actual departure will moderate the relationship between quality of the relationship and the levels of PA and NA after the discovery of the succession event. A longer time period will result in less intense reactions.

Justification of the Causal Agent

The perceived justification of the causal agent can intensify or negate an affective reaction. Ortony and colleagues (1988) have proposed that we react affectively to the actions of agents; actions that we consider to be against our values (blameworthy) invoke reactions of scorn that can intensify existing negative affective reactions to the departure of the leader. When others' behavior violates our standards, we react negatively. This approach is supported in theories of attribution (Weiner, 1985, 2004). In cases where a person has a high-quality relationship with the prior leader and believes that the person was fired unjustly, this should be expected to have an impact on his or her affective reaction. Weiner (2004) argues that the individual should experience anger in this case. However, feeling that the departure of the outgoing leader is justified can reduce the sting of the event.

This effect is most likely in cases where a leader is removed from a team (either through firing or forced resignation) by others in control of that group. Members with low-quality relationships should be expected to have an increase in PA and decrease in NA as a reaction to the discovery. We believe that these members' efforts to attribute motives for the old leader's departure will have an extremely limited impact on their primary affective reaction. They benefit from the event in that the leader they believed blocked their achievement of important goals is now soon to be gone. However, those individuals who were close to the departing leader will search for greater information on the causes of the departure and will make attributions based on their perceptions. These attributions may intensify their affective reaction if they believe that the agents responsible for the old leader's departure behaved unjustly. But their affective reactions may be muted by their subsequent judgment that the reasons for removing the old leader were just.

Proposition 5: The perceived justification of the causal agent of the succession episode will moderate the relationship between the quality of the relationship and the affective reaction for those with high-quality relationships with the prior leader only. An unjustified action leading to the event will intensify negative affective reactions, and a justified action leading to the event will suppress negative affective reactions.

In discussing the transition between stages, we note that the changes in core affect levels and job attitudes that occur as a result of the discovery of the departure and the exit of the old leader are likely to persist over the course of the entire series of succession events (see Figure 10.2.1). This is meaningful because the affective reaction to the exit of the old leader has a large impact on the judgments about the new leader, judgments about the job, and subsequent behaviors on the job. Understanding the processes by which the affective reaction to the end of the prior relationship impacts the quality of the relationship in the new leader-member dyad is the focus of the next section.

It is important to note that even though we have modeled the discovery and exit stages as being sequential and separated in time, these two stages can occur simultaneously. Indeed, it is conceivable that a group member can discover that a leader has been removed after the event has occurred, as in the case of an employee returning from vacation to find that his or her leader has been fired. Similarly, it is possible that the entry of the new leader occurs prior to the departure of the old leader so as to ensure a period of orientation and training. In these cases, the processes that go into the evaluation of the event are the same as proposed in the model; what changes is the quantity of information that goes into the evaluation of the event as it relates to the individual's goals (Ortony et al., 1988). Despite these exceptions, we believe it is useful to model the leadership succession episode in terms of the proposed stages.

Entry

When a new leader ascends to the position of workgroup leader, there will necessarily be a process of dyadic relationship formation between this individual and each other member of the workgroup. Consistent with approaches to dyadic exchange relationship formation proposed by Graen and Scandura (1987) and supported by Bauer and Green (1996), we believe that the entry of the new leader into the group is followed by processes of role definition in the dyad that are preceded by trust evaluations. Williams (2001) argues that perceived social group membership has an impact on initial trust through positive or negative affect. Graen and Scandura (1987) have proposed a three-phase process where dyad members go through a process of role taking, role making, and role routinization. The initial process of role taking is supported by cognitive evaluations of the trustworthiness of the other party in the dyad (Bauer & Green, 1996). Although meaningful LMX relationships take a while to develop, early in the relationship it is possible to measure the initial development of trust. For new relationships, an individual's initial willingness to trust is based on a combination of the individual's propensity to trust and his or her initial evaluation of the ability, benevolence, and integrity of the other person (Mayer et al., 1995).

Affective Reactions and Initial Trust of the New Leader

The development of new relationships between leaders and workgroup members is, in part, a trust-building process (Bauer & Green, 1996; Lewicki & Bunker, 1996; McKnight et al., 1998; Williams, 2001). Research suggests that individual and environmental factors jointly determine the level and nature of the subordinate's trust in the leader. These are the workgroup member's propensity to trust and any history with the successor. We believe that the affective reaction of an individual to the departure of his or her old leader has an impact on that individual's initial willingness to trust his or her new leader.

The affective reaction serves as the central mediating process because of the timing of events and the role emotion has been shown to play in cognitive processes. The primary affective appraisal that occurs after discovery precedes the subsequent relevant cognitions, judgments, and decisions in relation to trust formation and future exchange quality. The form and content of these judgments are influenced, in part, by the form and content of the affective appraisal (Forgas & George, 2001). Therefore, we agree with affective events theory in proposing that a model of individual reactions to critical events at work (such as leadership succession) should flow through the affective reactions to the event, because such reactions can drive subsequent behaviors and attitude changes (Weiss & Cropanzano, 1996).

Proponents of the affect infusion model (Forgas, 1995; Forgas & George, 2001) argue that affect changes the way individuals select and process information about a target when making complex judgments. Negative affective states are associated with a detail-focused collection of evidence regarding the target that relies on information and cues that generally lead to unfavorable evaluations of the target (Forgas, 2000). Positive affective states, however, lead to a more big-picture, less detail-oriented style of evidence collection that generally leads to favorable evaluations of the target, because individuals may then be more likely to overlook information about the target that is negative (Bower, 1981; Forgas, 2000; Forgas &

Bower, 1987). This means that an affective reaction to a recent relevant event, which leads to a change in the valence of one's moods or emotions, should be a factor in the initial judgment to trust a new workgroup leader one has not met before.

McKnight and colleagues (1998) have proposed a model of trust, arguing that initial trust formation is based on dispositional, institutional, and cognitive factors. Rotter (1967, 1971) believed that a dispositional factor results in trust. Mayer and colleagues (1995) have recast this dispositional factor, "propensity to trust," as an initial trusting *intention* within an individual that has an impact on the formation of the initial trust relationship. The existence of a stable difference in individuals in their willingness to enter into trusting relationships is supported by the literature on interpersonal relationships. Individuals have "interpersonal orientations" (Kelley & Thibaut, 1978; Rusbult & Arriaga, 2000) that come from serially achieving good outcomes from relationships from their early development.

The change in a workgroup member's affective state during discovery and exit provides a key link between the presuccession factors and postsuccession factors discussed by Gordon and Rosen (1981). Like other cognitive evaluations made in organizational contexts (Forgas & George, 2001; Isen & Baron, 1991), the initial trustworthiness evaluations that are critical to the initial stages of LMX development can be impacted by the affective state of either member of the dyad at the time of the evaluation.

Proposition 6a: Increases in PA levels resulting from leader exit will be positively related to group members' initial trustworthiness evaluation of the new leader.

Proposition 6b: Increases in NA levels resulting from leader exit will be negatively related to group members' initial trustworthiness evaluation of the new leader.

History with the New Leader

Within organizations it is common for new leaders and workgroup members to have a prior relationship or an acquaintance before the succession episode. In cases where an individual has already encountered the person chosen to be the new workgroup leader, the process of forming initial trust levels has already taken place. Shen and Cannella (2002) propose three types of CEO successors, and we believe this typology can be extended to investigations of workgroup leadership changes as well. In their model, *follower* successors are appointed after a normal, preplanned departure of a workgroup leader. *Contender* successors are appointed from inside the organization following competition for the role among multiple individuals; the losers of that competition are dismissed from the organization following selection of the winner. Finally, *outside* successors are appointed to leadership from positions outside the group. In cases of follower or contender succession, it is likely that the members of the group will have a history with the new leader; they should have formed an assessment of the leader's ability based on either a prior track record or personal interaction with that individual.

This prior history can be acquired either through a prior working relationship or awareness of the characteristics, track record, or abilities of the incoming group leader. Research on leadership succession in sports teams has shown that the record of the incoming coach does impact the subsequent performance of the workgroup (Cannella & Rowe, 1995; Pfeffer & Davis-Blake, 1986); one way we propose this occurs is that group members can use public information (e.g., the previous win-loss record of the new coach) to assess the ability of the incoming leader and can use this information in their initial evaluation of the trustworthiness of the new leader. The resulting increase in trust then facilitates group performance (Dirks, 2000). Another case may arise where the new leader and group member share a social network contact and that contact may be relied on to provide commentary on the record and history of the new leader (Sparrowe & Liden, 1997).

Researchers testing the role of affect in interpersonal judgments point out that affect is unlikely to impact routine decision making and judgments of familiar objects (Forgas, 2000). The components of the history a group member has with the new leader that matter for the judgment of initial trustworthiness should be information about that leader's ability, benevolence, and integrity. Thus, individuals who have direct access to information about the new leader's performance on a prior job or who know that person well enough to have previously formed judgments about that person's trustworthiness will not be prone to affective influences on their initial willingness to trust that new leader.

Proposition 7: An individual's prior evaluation of the trustworthiness of the new leader based on personal interaction or awareness of that individual's behavior will negate the impact of affective state at entry on initial trust evaluations.

Attitudinal and Behavioral Outcomes of Succession Episodes

What takes place during the primary and secondary appraisal process during the discovery and exit stages should be expected to have a direct link to judgments about the job and behaviors on the job. Research and theoretical explorations of the important role of affect on job attitudes (Weiss & Cropanzano, 1996) lead us to explore the role that the affective reaction to the departure of the old leader has on an individual's job satisfaction. There is also a significant body of theory and empirical research relating the role of affect in critical behaviors that should be related to future group performance. These include proactivity in communication of critical task information with the new leader (Borgatti & Cross, 2003; Forgas, 1999), OCBs directed toward the organization (Lee & Allen, 2002; McNeely & Meglino, 1994), motivation to perform the job (Seo et al., 2004), and the decision to leave the job (Lee & Mitchell, 1994; Maertz & Campion, 2004).

Succession and Communication with the New Leader

Communication of task information within top management teams is a critical ingredient in organizational performance. Hambrick and D'Aveni (1992) have proposed that one reason failing firms experience the "vicious cycle" of poor performance leading to top management team changes that lead to further poor performance is scapegoating behavior within the team, which leads to poor information processing within the team. This problem is even more critical than in workgroups at lower levels of the organization, because stakeholders are unwilling or unable to provide group leaders with substantial periods of time to evaluate a situation and develop strategies for performance improvement. In top management teams, new CEOs have been counseled to spend up to six months reading the situation and gathering information about work processes and performance (Gabarro, 1987; Porter et al., 2004). New project managers, however, are expected to begin making a difference by changing team processes almost immediately (Heller, 1989).

Research on the impact of affect and mood states on communication behaviors (Forgas,

1999) lends support to the proposition that increases in NA should lead to changes in the content of communication of requests. The motivations of withdrawal found to be associated with increased levels of NA and approach associated with PA (Carver & White, 1994) lend support to the view that affective state should impact group members' willingness to engage a new leader by approaching the leader with critical task information. There is also a strong relational component to the desire to gain information from another person in a communication network (Borgatti & Cross, 2003). The affective reaction to events during succession episodes should be expected to color these judgments.

Proposition 8a: The positive affective reaction to the old leader's departure will be associated with group members' willingness to communicate task information to the new leader. Increases in PA will be associated with greater willingness to communicate task information to the new leader.

Proposition 8b: The negative affective reaction to the old leader's departure will be associated with group members' willingness to communicate task information to the new leader. Increases in NA will be associated with less willingness to communicate task information to the new leader.

Succession and OCBs

The willingness of group members to engage in helping behaviors directed toward the organization is critical to the performance of workgroups (Dunlop & Lee, 2004; Podsakoff et al., 1997). OCBs are generally defined as discretionary actions that are not compensated or required by the organization but are important to the performance of the organization (McNeely & Meglino, 1994; Organ, 1988). Individuals' willingness to engage in these behaviors on the job can be impacted by their current affective state (George, 1991; Isen & Baron, 1991; Lee & Allen, 2002). OCBs are preceded by complex cognitive processes (Organ & Konovsky, 1989), and their relationship to a group member's current affective state is consistent with the affect infusion model of Forgas and George (2001). What we argue here is that *state* affect at the time of new leader entry impacts the cognitions that precede the willingness to engage in OCBs directed toward the organization that might be perceived to help the incoming leader.

Individuals who have increased levels of NA and decreased levels of PA at the departure of the old leader of the workgroup will likely be less willing to help the organization through engaging in helping behavior or other acts of altruism (Lee & Allen, 2002; McNeely & Meglino, 1994). They may be distracted by their anxiety about future job prospects or engaged in behaviors aimed at preserving their achievement goals. During this critical time of the succession episode, the new leader entering the group might find that many group members who were closely connected to the old leader will be engaged in self-interested behavior (perhaps looking for work internally or externally or hoarding personal resources to increase their leverage against the firm) or anxious about the consequences of risking their reputation by attempting to go the extra mile on the job. Those group members who have an increase in PA and decrease in NA at the old leader's departure, however, should be expected to engage in greater levels of these behaviors, since their affective commitment to the organization may grow (Williams & Anderson, 1991) and they may feel motivated to engage in actions that help ensure the new leader's success.

Proposition 9a: The positive affective reaction to the old leader's departure will be associated with levels of an individual's OCBs directed toward the organization (OCB-O). Increases in PA will be associated with increased levels of OCB-O.

Proposition 9b: The negative affective reaction to the old leader's departure will be associated with levels of an individual's OCBs directed toward the organization (OCB-O). Increases in NA will be associated with decreased levels of OCB-O.

Motivation to Perform the Job

Just as leadership succession might affect the willingness of group members to engage in OCBs, it might also impact inrole behaviors and influence individual job performance. The likely mechanism through which job performance would be affected is the motivation of the individual to continue to perform at the previous level. Seo and colleagues (2004) have reviewed the literature on the relationship between affective reactions and motivation to perform and make the argument that affective reactions to events will influence the motivation of the individual, defined as the direction, intensity, and persistence of behavior.

Two possible mechanisms have been proposed for how affective experiences at work drive motivation. Weiss and Cropanzano (1996) have proposed that positive reactions at work are related to increases in arousal levels, whereas negative reactions drive coping strategies that reduce work-related effort. Another mechanism by which affective reactions may influence work motivation is through their impact on the way individuals interpret task-related feedback information and their progress toward reaching benchmarks (George & Brief, 1996). Positive affective states drive increases in work motivation by increasing the likelihood of positive interpretation of feedback information, whereas negative states drive more detailed, aversive evaluations of such data.

Proposition 10a: The positive affective reaction to the old leader's departure will be associated with an individual's motivation to perform. Increases in PA will be associated with increased motivation.

Proposition 10b: The negative affective reaction to the old leader's departure will be associated with an individual's motivation to perform. Increases in NA will be associated with decreased motivation.

Succession and Job Satisfaction

Affective experiences combine with judgment factors to result in changes in attitudes (Edwards, 1990). Research has shown that events at work are related to changes in mood (Alliger & Williams, 1993). Moods can result from "the impact of emotionally significant events" (Frijda, 1993: 388) and generally flow in a similar direction. Negative events produce symptoms such as depression, irritability, and anger; positive events are activating and increase enthusiasm. Changes in job satisfaction may occur because "mood may color the interpretation of events. . . . as such, being in a negative mood may result in a neutral event being interpreted as negative" (Weiss & Cropanzano, 1996: 48).

Weiss, Nicholas, and Daus (1999) found that average pleasantness levels collected over a three-week period were associated with job satisfaction levels. They concluded that "global job satisfaction judgments are a function of both episodic affective experiences and beliefs about the job" (1999: 18). In a subsequent study, Ilies and Judge (2002) found that both PA and NA were related to job satisfaction. As proposed above, the discovery of the old leader's departure is a work event that should result in changes in attitudes among members of workgroups. There is ample evidence that trust in the leader impacts job attitudes as well (Dirks & Ferrin, 2002; Driscoll, 1978). We believe that the initial trustworthiness evaluation of the new leader will have a significant main effect on job satisfaction measured after the entry of the new leader.

Proposition 11a: The positive affective reaction to the old leader's departure will be associated with subsequent levels of job satisfaction. Increases in PA will be associated with increases in job satisfaction.

Proposition 11b: The negative affective reaction to the old leader's departure will be associated with subsequent levels of job satisfaction. Increases in NA will be associated with decreases in job satisfaction.

Succession and Turnover

There exists substantial evidence that an increased rate of turnover in top management teams following succession occurs at the initiation of the incoming leader (e.g., Gouldner, 1954; Helmich & Brown, 1972; Wiersema & Bantel, 1993). There is also evidence that executives leave firms willingly after succession episodes to go to better jobs (Cannella, Fraser, & Lee, 1995) or because they interpret the new leader's behavior as a signal of their being unwelcome in the group (Pitcher et al., 2000). Employee turnover can be an automatic process that stems from a shock that triggers an impulsive decision to quit, or it may result from more elaborate processes involving job attitudes and evaluations of prospects for better employment (Lee & Mitchell, 1994). Lee and Mitchell propose that turnover decisions can start with a "shock to the system" that is "a very distinguishable event that *jars* employees toward making judgments about their jobs, and perhaps to voluntarily quit their job" (1994: 60). One can imagine an employee becoming sufficiently distraught over a traumatic end to a high-quality exchange relationship with his or her supervisor that he or she decides to leave as well.

Using Lee and Mitchell's (1994) model, Maertz and Campion (2004) found a strong relationship between negative affective evaluations of the organization or current situation and turnover. The affective reaction to events occurring during succession episodes impacts those more elaborate decision processes called for in the Lee and Mitchell model. Forgas and George (2001) propose that when substantive processing of information cues is required, affect can prime decisions. Affect infuses these "should I stay or should I go" decisions by limiting the number of alternatives considered or by framing the selection and evaluation of alternatives. Individuals who have a higher level of NA following a succession event will not process information cues in the same way that individuals will under circumstances when that affective reaction has not been primed. Given that, they are more likely to view leaving as a viable alternative when it was not considered viable prior to the knowledge of the succession event.

Proposition 12a: The positive affective reaction to the old leader's departure will be associated with the rate of turnover from the workgroup. Increases in PA will be associated with a decreased rate of turnover.

Proposition 12b: The negative affective reaction to the old leader's departure will be associated with the rate of turnover from the workgroup. Increases in NA will be associated with an increased rate of turnover.

An example of this may be seen in the veterinary medicine business, where the administration of several small local hospitals may be handled from a central office located in another geographic region. Often, strong relationships are developed between the medical director of the hospital and the staff who work closely with the doctor. If the corporation fires the medical director for violating company policies (e.g., medical protocols, billing practices), the model would predict that a number of the staff will quit. Firing an abusive medical director (we presume with a number of poor relationships with the staff), however, can stem the tide of a high rate of employee turnover.

Role Stabilization

The final stage of interest in the succession episode involves the process of finding a new equilibrium in the leader-member dyad, in terms of the quality of the relationship. This stage has been addressed quite extensively in the LMX literature, and our model is consistent with the propositions of LMX theory. In this paper we focus on the unique impact the succession has on role stabilization.

As formulated by Graen and Scandura, leader-member relationships begin in a "sampling phase" (1987: 180), which they term *role taking*, where the leader delegates tasks to group members to communicate his or her role expectations to them and evaluates the behavioral responses of the group members. LMX researchers traditionally have proposed that the leader is the initiator and that most of the variance in the quality of exchange between the leader and group members can be described in terms of the leader's evaluations and perceptions of the members' behaviors (Liden, Sparrowe, & Wayne, 1997). In the Graen and Scandura model, the definition of roles continues through a phase of *role making*, whereby "working together on unstructured tasks they test various dyadic interdependencies" (1987: 181) and thereby begin to determine the terms of the exchange between leader and member.

Leadership succession complicates our study of exchange relationship formation in that the initiation and sending of role information does not start when a member goes through the process of being socialized into the group; instead, it starts when the leader is socialized into a group where members have already formed their initial evaluations of whether they can enter into trust relationships with this newcomer. In leadership succession episodes, the process of exchange relationship formation is likely to proceed in the same steps as those proposed by Graen and Scandura (1987), but the outcome is likely to be affected by characteristics of both the leader and the member.

As noted earlier, when the new leader arrives, the group member already has (or had) a role within the group as it was previously run by the old group leader. There has been an affective reaction to the departure of the old leader, and this has an impact on the group member's evaluation of whether to trust this new group leader. It may be the case that there is no combination of leader actions or tasks that can be delegated that can overcome the low initial evaluation of trustworthiness held by the member, and this will predict the formation of a low-quality exchange relationship. The link between the relationship the group member held with the old leader and the quality of the relationship with the new leader is defined by how the affective reaction to the departure impacts the willingness of the member to enter into the type of trust relationship that is necessary for the formation of higher-quality exchange relations in the dyad.

Proposition 13: Evaluations of initial trustworthiness on leader entry will be related to the quality of subsequent LMX relationships formed during role stabilization.

Summary

The search for a "leadership succession effect" that can be generalized across groups has covered forty years of research in organizational behavior (cf. Kesner & Sebora, 1994; Rowe et al., 2005). The focus of this research primarily has been at the executive level, where changes in organizational performance have been examined following publicly announced leadership successions. In this paper we have developed a model of individual reactions to succession episodes by integrating research in cognitive appraisal theory, LMX theory, and theories of trust.

Implications for Research

A theory of individual reactions to leadership succession in workgroups offers several benefits over previous approaches. It allows us to study succession episodes at all levels of the organization, as opposed to executive succession episodes only, which dramatically increases the number of samples available for study and increases the generalizability of the theory in the management of organizations. An individual approach to leadership succession allows us to consider the episode's impact on individual affect as a factor in the formation of initial trust relationships with leaders of workgroups. Examining succession effects at the individual level brings leadership succession in line with relational approaches to leadership, which show that considerable variance exists in the quality of relationships with workgroup leaders. Finally, such an approach also provides us with additional tools (e.g., measurement of process) for examining group-level outcomes to succession events, such as turnover rates and group performance.

The theory proposed considers the affective, attitudinal, and behavioral reactions of the outgoing leaders' direct reports at the workgroup level. It does not necessarily generalize to the effects of top management or executive succession on individual employees several levels below the team in question. Our primary interest is in how leadership succession affects members of standing workgroups, such as project groups, "standing crews," or "task forces" (McGrath, 1986) within organizations. The model would be useful in understanding outcomes of CEO succession in terms of the reactions of members of the top management team, but would not apply to analyzing the impact of CEO turnover on a cohort of middle managers three levels down in the corporate hierarchy. This is an important distinction, given that much of the literature on leadership succession and its performance effects has been conducted using CEOs as the leader of reference (Kesner & Sebora, 1994). This model focuses instead on individuals within the immediate workgroup of the departing leader as the unit of analysis.

Testing of this theory is also likely to shed light on the process of new relationship formation in leader-member dyads. Theory and research in this area (e.g., Graen & Scandura's leadership making model, 1987) generally have treated the leader-member relationship as being driven primarily by leader actions (Liden et al., 1997). Theories of trust formation in new relationships (e.g., McKnight et al., 1998) have focused on the aspects of trustor and trustee, but neither of these approaches has taken a step back in time to consider the impact of the group member's prior supervisory relationship on the formation of a new relationship. In addition, these models of trust formation in organization settings generally do not consider the affective state of the trustor as playing a role in the initial trust evaluation. In this model we integrate existing knowledge bases in experimental social psychology (Forgas, 2000; Forgas & George, 2001) with strictly cognitive models of trust formation to explicitly incorporate the trustor's affective state into trust evaluations. Tests of relationship formation that take into account the affective reaction to the end of prior relationships also offer us the ability to test whether individuals serially form good relationships with supervisors, as would be predicted by interdependence theory (Rusbult & Arriaga, 2000), or whether the NA created by the loss of a close friend and mentor inhibits the formation of a new trust relationship.

Implications for Practice

Research from cognitive appraisal theories helps us understand the impact of succession on the early stages of leader-subordinate relationships and shows that each relationship will get off to a unique start that is predicted by our model. An understanding of this phenomenon will also be of considerable importance to organizations in their succession planning and leadership training initiatives. Executives within organizations who hire and place new leaders in ongoing workgroups need to consider the affective reaction of group members to the departure of the prior leader when making decisions regarding how to introduce and train replacement leaders. The new leader should be apprised of the circumstances of the prior leader's departure and given some understanding of what the relationships were between group members and their prior leader. Knowledge of the relationships in the prior group will help new leaders understand how their actions and changes to group processes and work rules will be interpreted by group members. Several of the variables in our model can easily be manipulated by the organization as it goes through a leadership succession episode. Particularly when the departing leader is well liked by the group, providing more notice of the departure, explanations for the departure, and transition time between discovery and exit will ease the negative consequences for the new leader.

Bringing research on leadership succession to the individual level is a new frame of reference for this research and opens up a new perspective for measuring the outcomes of these commonplace organizational events. For researchers, this opens up the possibility of finding a generalized succession effect, albeit one that takes place at the individual level. The relevance of this theory for the practice of management clearly lies in its ability to predict the reactions of workers to events occurring during succession episodes within their context and can offer organizations the chance to minimize the swings in individual and group performance that might be caused by the increased tumult created by succession episodes. It also holds promise for organizations in understanding how events within workgroups can change the composition and dynamics of those groups.

Acknowledgments

We thank Bradley J. Alge, Steve Green, Cynthia G. Emrich, and three anonymous reviewers for their comments on earlier drafts of this manuscript. The work was supported in part by a grant from the Purdue Research Foundation.

References

Allen, M. P., Panian, S. K., & Lotz, R. E. 1979. Managerial succession and organizational performance. *Administrative Science Quarterly*, 27: 538–547.

Alliger, G. M., & Williams, K. J. 1993. Using signal-contingent experience sampling methodology to study work in the field: A discussion and illustration examining task perceptions and mood. *Personnel Psychology*, 46: 525–549.

Bauer, T. N., & Green, S. G. 1996. The development of leader-member exchange: A longitudinal test. *Academy of Management Journal*, 39: 1538–1567.

Borgatti, S. P., & Cross, R. 2003. A relational view of information seeking and learning in social networks. *Management Science*, 49: 432–445.

Borman, W. C., & Motowidlo, S. J. 1993. Expanding the criterion domain to include elements of contextual performance. In N. Schmitt & W. C. Borman (Eds.), *Personnel selection in organizations*: 71–98. San Francisco: Jossey-Bass.

Bower, G. H. 1981. Mood and memory. *American Psychologist*, 36: 129–148.

Breckler, S. J. 1993. Emotion and attitude change. In M. Lewis & J. M. Havilland (Eds.), *Handbook of emotions*: 461–473. New York: Guilford Press.

Brief, A. P., & Motowidlo, S. J. 1986. Prosocial organizational behaviors. *Academy of Management Review*, 11: 710–725.

Brief, A. P., & Weiss, H. M. 2002. Organizational behavior: Affect in the workplace. *Annual Review of Psychology*, 53: 279–307.

Brower, H. H., Schoorman, F. D., & Tan, H. H. 2000. A model of relational leadership: The integration of trust and leader-member exchange. *Leadership Quarterly*, 11: 227–250.

Brown, M. C. 1982. Administrative succession and organizational performance: The succession effect. *Administrative Science Quarterly*, 27: 1–16.

Cannella, A. A., Jr., Fraser, D. R., & Lee, D. S. 1995. Firm failure and managerial labor markets: Evidence from Texas banking. *Journal of Financial Economics*, 38: 185–211.

Cannella, A. A., Jr., & Rowe, W. G. 1995. Leader capabilities, succession and competitive context: A study of professional baseball teams. *Leadership Quarterly*, 6: 69–88.

Carver, C. S., & White, T. L. 1994. Behavioral inhibition, behavioral activation and affective responses to impending reward and punishment: The BIS/BAS scales. *Journal of Personality and Social Psychology*, 67: 319–333.

Clary, E. G., & Tesser, A. 1983. Reactions to unexpected events: The naive scientist and interpretive activity. *Personality and Social Psychology Bulletin*, 9: 609–620.

Dansereau, F., Graen, G. B., & Haga, W. J. 1975. A vertical dyad linkage approach to leadership within formal organizations: A longitudinal investigation of the role making process. *Organizational Behavior and Human Performance*, 13: 46–78.

Dienesch, R. M., & Liden, R. C. 1986. Leader-member exchange model of leadership: A critique and further development. *Academy of Management Review*, 11: 618–634.

Dirks, K. T. 2000. Trust in leadership and team performance: Evidence from NCAA basketball. *Journal of Applied Psychology*, 85: 1004–1012.

Dirks, K. T., & Ferrin, D. L. 2002. Trust in leadership: Meta-analytic findings and implications for research and practice. *Journal of Applied Psychology*, 87: 611–628.

Driscoll, J. W. 1978. Trust and participation in organizational decision making as predictors of satisfaction. *Academy of Management Journal*, 21: 44–56.

Dunlop, P. D., & Lee, K. 2004. Workplace deviance, organizational citizenship behavior, and business unit performance: The bad apples do spoil the whole barrel. *Journal of Organizational Behavior*, 25: 67–80.

Edwards, K. 1990. The role of affect and cognition in attitude formation and change. *Journal of Personality and Social Psychology*, 59: 202–216.

Fauske, J. R., & Ogawa, R. T. 1987. Detachment, fear, and expectation—A faculty's response to the impending succession of its principal. *Educational Administration Quarterly*, 23(2): 23–44.

Finkelstein, S., & Hambrick, D. C. 1996. *Strategic leadership: Top executives and their effect on organizations.* St. Paul: West Educational Publishing.

Forgas, J. P. 1995. Mood and judgment: The Affect Infusion Model (AIM). *Psychological Bulletin*, 117: 39–66.

Forgas, J. P. 1998. On feeling good and getting your way: Mood effects on negotiator cognitions and bargaining strategies. *Journal of Personality and Social Psychology*, 74: 565–577.

Forgas, J. P. 1999. On feeling good and being rude: Affective influences on language use and request formulation. *Journal of Personality and Social Psychology*, 76: 928–939.

Forgas, J. P. 2000. Affect and information processing strategies: An interactive relationship. In J. P. Forgas (Ed.), *Feeling and thinking: The role of affect in social cognition:* 253–280. Cambridge: Cambridge University Press.

Forgas, J. P., & Bower, G. H. 1987. Mood effects on person perception judgments. *Journal of Personality and Social Psychology*, 53: 53–60.

Forgas, J. P., & George, J. M. 2001. Affective influences on judgments and behavior in organizations: An information processing perspective. *Organizational Behavior and Human Decision Processes,*, 86: 3–34.

French, J. R. P., & Raven, B. 1959. The bases of social power. In D. Cartwright & A. Zander (Eds.), *Group dynamics:* 150–167. New York: Harper & Row.

Friedman, S. D., & Saul, K. 1991. A leader's wake: Organization member reactions to CEO succession. *Journal of Management*, 12: 619–642.

Friedman, S. D., & Singh, H. 1989. CEO succession and stockholder reaction: The influence of organizational context and event context. *Academy of Management Journal*, 32: 718–744.

Frijda, N. H. 1993. Moods, emotion episodes, and emotions. In M. Lewis & J. M. Havilland (Eds.), *Handbook of emotions:* 381–403. New York: Guilford Press.

Gabarro, J. 1987. *The dynamics of taking charge.* Cambridge, MA: Harvard Business School Press.

Gamson, W., & Scotch, N. 1964. Scapegoating in baseball. *American Journal of Sociology*, 70: 69–76.

George, J. M. 1991. State or trait: Effect of positive mood on prosocial behaviors at work. *Journal of Applied Psychology*, 76: 299–307.

George, J. M., & Brief, A. P. 1996. Motivational agendas in the workplace: The effects of feelings on focus of attention and work motivation. *Research in Organizational Behavior*, 18: 75–109.

Gephart, R. P. 1978. Status degradation and organizational succession: An ethnomethodological approach. *Administrative Science Quarterly*, 23: 553–581.

Gilmore, T. N., & Ronchi, D. 1995. Managing predecessors' shadows in executive transitions. *Human Resource Management*, 34: 11–26.

Gordon, G. W., & Rosen, N. A. 1981. Critical factors in leadership succession. *Organizational Behavior and Human Performance*, 27: 227–254.

Gouldner, A. W. 1954. *Patterns of industrial bureaucracy.* New York: Free Press.

Graen, G. B., & Cashman, J. F. 1975. A role making model in formal organizations: A developmental approach. In J. Hunt & L. Larson (Eds.), *Leadership frontiers:* 143–165. Kent, OH: Kent State Press.

Graen, G. B., & Scandura, T. A. 1987. Toward a psychology of dyadic organizing. *Research in Organizational Behavior*, 9: 175–208.

Grusky, O. 1960. Administrative succession in formal organizations. *Social Forces*, 39: 105–115.

Grusky, O. 1963. Managerial succession and organizational effectiveness. *American Journal of Sociology*, 69: 21–31.

Guest, R. H. 1962. Managerial succession in complex organizations. *American Journal of Sociology*, 68: 47–54.

Hambrick, D. C., & D'Aveni, R. A. 1992. Top team deterioration as part of the downward spiral of large corporate bankruptcies. *Management Science*, 38: 1445–1466.

Heller, T. 1989. Conversion processes in leadership succession: A case study. *Journal of Applied Behavioral Science*, 25: 65–77.

Helmich, D. L., & Brown, W. B. 1972. Successor type and organizational change in the corporate enterprise. *Administrative Science Quarterly*, 17: 371–381.

Ilies, R., & Judge, T. A. 2002. Understanding the dynamic relationships among personality, mood and job satisfaction: A field experience sampling study. *Organizational Behavior and Human Decision Processes*, 89: 1119–1139.

Isen, A. M., & Baron, R. A. 1991. Positive affect as a factor in organizational behavior. *Research in Organizational Behavior*, 13: 1–53.

Kelley, H. H., & Thibaut, J. W. 1978. *Interpersonal relations: A theory of interdependence.* New York: Wiley.

Kesner, I. F., & Sebora, T. C. 1994. Executive succession—Past, present and future. *Journal of Management*, 20: 327–372.

Kotin, J., & Sharaf, M. R. 1967. Management succession and administrative style. *Psychiatry*, 30: 237–248.

Lee, K., & Allen, N. J. 2002. Organizational citizenship and workplace deviance: The role of affect and cognitions. *Journal of Applied Psychology*, 87: 131–142.

Lee, T. W., & Mitchell, T. R. 1994. An alternative approach: The unfolding model of employee turnover. *Academy of Management Review*, 19: 51–89.

Leviatan, U. 1978. Organizational effects of managerial turnover in kibbutz production branches. *Human Relations*, 31: 1001–1018.

Levine, J. M., & Moreland, R. L. 1985. Innovation and socialization in small groups. In S. Moscovici, G. Mugny, & E. Van Avermaert (Eds.), *Perspectives on minority influence:* 143–169. Cambridge: Cambridge University Press.

Lewicki, R. J., & Bunker, B. B. 1996. Developing and maintaining trust in work relationships. In R. Kramer & T. Tyler (Eds.), *Trust in organizations: Frontiers of theory and research:* 114–139. Thousand Oaks, CA: Sage.

Liden, R. C., & Graen, G. B. 1980. Generalizability of the vertical dyad linkage model of leadership. *Academy of Management Journal*, 23: 451–465.

Liden, R. C., Sparrowe, R. T., & Wayne, S. J. 1997. Leader-member exchange theory: The past and potential for the future. *Research in Personnel and Human Resources Management*, 15: 47–119.

Maertz, C. P., & Campion, M. A. 2004. Profiles in quitting: Integrating process and content turnover theory. *Academy of Management Journal*, 47: 566–582.

Mayer, R. C., Davis, J. H., & Schoorman, F. D. 1995. An integrative model of organizational trust. *Academy of Management Review*, 20: 709–734.

McGrath, J. E. 1986. Studying groups at work: Ten critical needs for theory and practice. In P. Goodman (Ed.), *Designing effective work groups:* 362–391. San Francisco: Jossey-Bass.

McKnight, D. H., Cummings, L. L., & Chervany, N. L. 1998. Initial trust formation in new organizational relationships. *Academy of Management Review*, 23: 473–490.

McNeely, B. L., & Meglino, B. M. 1994. The role of dispositional and situational antecedents in prosocial organizational behavior: An examination of the intended beneficiaries of prosocial behavior. *Journal of Applied Psychology*, 79: 836–844.

Mitchell, T. R., & James, L. R. 2001. Building better theory: Time and the specification of when things happen. *Academy of Management Review*, 26: 530–547.

Moreland, R. L., & Levine, J. M. 1989. Newcomers and oldtimers in small groups. In P. Paulus (Ed.), *Psychology of group influence:* 143–186. Hillsdale, NJ: Lawrence Erlbaum Associates.

Moreland, R. L., & McMinn, J. G. 1999. Gone, but not forgotten: Loyalty and betrayal amongst ex-members of small groups. *Personality and Social Psychology Bulletin*, 25: 1476–1486.

Ocasio, W. 1994. Political dynamics and the circulation of power: CEO succession in U.S. industrial corporations. *Administrative Science Quarterly*, 39: 285–312.

Ogawa, R. T. 1991. Enchantment, disenchantment, and accommodation: How a faculty made sense of the succession of its principal. *Educational Administration Quarterly*, 27(1): 30–60.

Organ, D. W. 1988. *Organizational citizenship behavior: The good soldier syndrome.* Lexington, MA. Lexington Books.

Organ, D. W., & Konovsky, M. 1989. Cognitive versus affective determinants of organizational citizenship behavior. *Journal of Applied Psychology*, 74: 157–164.

Ortony, A., Clore, G. L., & Collins, A. 1988. *The cognitive structure of emotions.* Cambridge: Cambridge University Press.

Pfeffer, J., & Davis-Blake, A. 1986. Administrative succession and organizational performance: How administrator experience mediates the succession effect. *Academy of Management Journal*, 29: 72–83.

Pillai, R., Schriesheim, C. A., & Williams, E. S. 1999. Fairness perceptions and trust as mediators for transformational and transactional leadership: A two-sample study. *Journal of Management*, 25: 897–933.

Pitcher, P., Chreim, S., & Kisfalvi, V. 2000. CEO succession research: Methodological bridges over troubled waters. *Strategic Management Journal*, 21: 625–648.

Podsakoff, P. M., Ahearne, M., & MacKenzie, S. B. 1997. Organizational citizenship behavior and the quality and quantity of work group performance. *Journal of Applied Psychology*, 82: 974–983.

Porter, M. E., Lorsch, J. W., & Nohria, N. 2004. Seven surprises for new CEOs. *Harvard Business Review*, 82(10): 62–72.

Rotter, J. B. 1967. A new scale for the measurement of interpersonal trust. *Journal of Personality*, 35: 651–665.

Rotter, J. B. 1971. Generalized expectancies for interpersonal trust. *American Psychologist*, 35: 1–7.

Rowe, W. G., Cannella, A. A., Jr., Rankin, D., & Gorman, D. 2005. Leader succession and organizational performance: Integrating the common-sense, ritual scapegoating and vicious-circle succession theories. *Leadership Quarterly*, 16: 197–219.

Rusbult, C. E., & Arriaga, X. B. 2000. Interdependence in personal relationships. In W. Ickes & S. Duck (Eds.), *The social psychology of personal relationships:* 79–108. New York: Wiley.

Seo, M.-G., Barrett, L. F., & Bartunek, J. M. 2004. The role of affective experience in work motivation. *Academy of Management Review*, 29: 423–439.

Shen, W., & Cannella, A. A., Jr. 2002. Revisiting the performance consequences of CEO succession: The impacts of successor type, postsuccession senior executive turnover, and departing CEO tenure. *Academy of Management Journal*, 45: 717–733.

Simon, H. A. 1967. Motivational and emotional controls of cognition. *Psychological Review*, 74: 29–39.

Smith, C. A., & Ellsworth, P. C. 1985. Patterns of cognitive appraisal in emotion. *Journal of Personality and Social Psychology*, 48: 813–838.

Sparrowe, R. T., & Liden, R. C. 1997. Process and structure in leader-member exchange. *Academy of Management Review*, 22: 522–552.

Tellegen, A. 1985. Structures of mood and personality and their relevance to assessing anxiety, with an emphasis on self-report. In A. H. Tuma & J. D. Maser (Eds.), *Anxiety and the anxiety disorders:* 681–706. Hillsdale, NJ: Lawrence Erlbaum Associates.

Vancil, R. F. 1987. *Passing the baton: Managing the process of CEO succession.* Boston: Harvard Business School Press.

Watson, D. 2000. *Mood and temperament.* New York: Guilford Press.

Watson, D., & Clark, L. A. 1984. Negative affectivity: The disposition to experience aversive emotional states. *Psychological Bulletin*, 96: 465–490.

Watson, D., Clark, L. A., & Tellegen, A. 1988. Development and validation of brief measures of positive and negative affect: The PANAS scales. *Journal of Personality and Social Psychology*, 54: 1063–1070.

Watson, D., & Tellegen, A. 1985. Toward a consensual structure of mood. *Psychological Bulletin*, 98: 219–235.

Watson, D., Wiese D., Vaidya, J., & Tellegen, A. 1999. The two general activation systems of affect: Structural findings, evolutionary considerations and psychobiological evidence. *Journal of Personality and Social Psychology*, 76: 820–838.

Weiner, B. 2004. Social motivation and moral emotions: An attribution perspective. In M. J. Martinko (Ed.), *Attribution theory in the organizational sciences:* 1–24. Greenwich, CT: Information Age Publishing.

Weiner, B. 1985. "Spontaneous" causal thinking. *Psychological Bulletin*, 97: 74–84.

Weiss, H. M., & Cropanzano, R. 1996. Affective events theory: A theoretical discussion of the structure, causes and consequences of affective experiences at work. *Research in Organizational Behavior*, 18: 1–74.

Weiss, H. M., Nicholas, J. P., & Daus, C. S. 1999. An examination of the joint effects of affective experiences and job beliefs on job satisfaction and variations in affective experiences over time. *Organizational Behavior and Human Decision Processes*, 78: 1–24.

Welsh, M. A., & Dehler, G. E. 1988. Political legacy of administrative succession. *Academy of Management Journal*, 31: 948–961.

Wiersema, M. F., & Bantel, K. A. 1993. Top management team turnover as an adaptation mechanism: The role of the environment. *Strategic Management Journal*, 14: 485–504.

Williams, L. J., & Anderson, S. E. 1991. Job satisfaction and organizational commitment as predictors of organizational citizenship and in-role behaviors. *Journal of Management*, 17: 601–617.

Williams, M. 2001. In whom we trust: Group membership as an affective context for trust development. *Academy of Management Review*, 26: 377–396.

Zhang, Y., & Rajagopalan, N. 2004. When the known devil is better than an unknown god: An empirical study of the antecedents and consequences of relay CEO succession. *Academy of Management Journal*, 47: 483–500.

Ziller, R. C. 1965. Toward a theory of open and closed groups. *Psychological Bulletin*, 64: 164–182.

11 Power, Politics, and Conflict

11.1 WANT COLLABORATION?

Accept—and Actively Manage—Conflict

Jeff Weiss and Jonathan Hughes

The quest for harmony and common goals can actually obstruct teamwork. Managers get truly effective collaboration only when they realize that conflict is natural and necessary.

The challenge is a long-standing one for senior managers. How do you get people in your organization to work together across internal boundaries? But the question has taken on urgency in today's global and fast-changing business environment. To service multinational accounts, you increasingly need seamless collaboration across geographic boundaries. To improve customer satisfaction, you increasingly need collaboration among functions ranging from R&D to distribution. To offer solutions tailored to customers needs, you increasingly need collaboration between product and service groups.

Meanwhile, as competitive pressures continually force companies to find ways to do more with less, few managers have the luxury of relying on their own dedicated staffs to accomplish their objectives. Instead, most must work with and through people across the organization, many of whom have different priorities, incentives, and ways of doing things.

Getting collaboration right promises tremendous benefits: a unified face to customers, faster internal decision making, reduced costs through shared resources, and the development of more innovative products. But despite the billions of dollars spent on initiatives to improve collaboration, few companies are happy with the results. Time and again we have seen management teams employ the same few strategies to boost internal cooperation. They restructure their organizations and reengineer their business processes. They create cross-unit incentives. They offer teamwork training. While such initiatives yield the occasional success story, most of them have only limited impact in dismantling organizational silos and fostering collaboration—and many are total failures.

(See Box 11.1.1. "The Three Myths of Collaboration.")

So what's the problem? Most companies respond to the challenge of improving collaboration in entirely the wrong way. They focus on the symptoms ("Sales and delivery do not work together as closely as they should") rather than on the root cause of failures in cooperation: conflict. The fact is you can't improve collaboration until you've addressed the issue of conflict.

This can come as a surprise to even the most experienced executives, who generally don't fully appreciate the inevitability of conflict in complex organizations. And even if they do

Box 11.1.1 THE THREE MYTHS OF COLLABORATION

Companies attempt to foster collaboration among different parts of their organizations through a variety of methods, many based on a number of seemingly sensible but ultimately misguided assumptions:

1. Effective collaboration means "teaming"

Many companies think that teamwork training is the way to promote collaboration across an organization. So they'll get the HR department to run hundreds of managers and their subordinates through intensive two- or three-day training programs. Workshops will offer techniques for getting groups aligned around common goals, for clarifying roles and responsibilities, for operating according to a shared set of behavioral norms, and so on.

Unfortunately, such workshops are usually the right solution to the wrong problems. First, the most critical breakdowns in collaboration typically occur not on actual teams but in the rapid and unstructured interactions between different groups within the organization. For example, someone from R&D will spend weeks unsuccessfully trying to get help from manufacturing to run a few tests on a new prototype. Meanwhile, people in manufacturing begin to complain about arrogant engineers from R&D expecting them to drop everything to help with another one of R&D's pet projects. Clearly, the need for collaboration extends to areas other than a formal team.

The second problem is that breakdowns in collaboration almost always result from fundamental differences among business functions and divisions. Teamwork training offers little guidance on how to work together in the context of competing objectives and limited resources. Indeed, the frequent emphasis on common goals further stigmatizes the idea of conflict in organizations where an emphasis on "polite" behavior regularly prevents effective problem solving. People who need to collaborate more effectively usually don't need to align around and work toward a common goal. They need to quickly and creatively solve problems by managing the inevitable conflict so that it works in their favor.

2. An effective incentive system will ensure collaboration

It's a tantalizing proposition: You can hardwire collaboration into your organization by rewarding collaborative behavior. Salespeople receive bonuses not only for hitting targets for their own division's products but also for hitting cross-selling targets. Staff in corporate support functions like IT and procurement have part of their bonuses determined by positive feedback from their internal clients.

Unfortunately, the results of such programs are usually disappointing. Despite greater financial incentives, for example, salespeople continue to focus on the sales of their own products to the detriment of selling integrated solutions. Employees continue to perceive the IT and procurement departments as difficult to work with, too focused on their own priorities. Why such poor results? To some extent, it's because individuals think—for the most part correctly—that if they perform well in their own operation they will be "taken care of" by their bosses. In addition, many people find that the costs of working with individuals in other parts of the organization—the extra time required, the aggravation—greatly outweigh the rewards for doing so.

Certainly, misaligned incentives can be a tremendous obstacle to cross-boundary collaboration. But even the most carefully constructed incentives won't eliminate tensions between people with competing business objectives. An incentive is too blunt an instrument to enable optimal resolution of the hundreds of different trade-offs that need to be made in a complex organization. What's more, overemphasis on incentives can create a culture in which people say, "If the company wanted me to do that, they would build it into my comp plan." Ironically, focusing on incentives as a means to encourage collaboration can end up undermining it.

3. Organizations can be structured for collaboration

Many managers look for structural and procedural solutions—cross-functional task forces, collaborative "groupware," complex webs of dotted reporting lines on the organization chart—to create greater internal collaboration. But bringing people together is very different from getting them to collaborate.

Consider the following scenario. Individual information technology departments have been stripped out of a company's business units and moved to a corporatewide, shared-services IT organization. Senior managers rightly recognize that this kind of change is a recipe for conflict because various groups will now essentially compete with one another for scarce IT resources. So managers try mightily to design conflict out of, and collaboration into, the new organization. For example, to enable collaborative decision making within IT and between IT and the business units, business units are required to enter requests for IT support into a computerized tracking system. The system is designed to enable managers within the IT organization to prioritize projects and optimally deploy resources to meet the various requests.

Despite painstaking process design, results are disappointing. To avoid the inevitable conflicts between business units and IT over project prioritization, managers in the business units quickly learn to bring their requests to those they know in the IT organization rather than entering the requests into the new system. Consequently, IT professionals assume that any project in the system is a lower priority—further discouraging use of the system. People's inability to deal effectively with conflict has undermined a new process specifically designed to foster organizational collaboration.

recognize this, many mistakenly assume that efforts to increase collaboration will significantly reduce that conflict, when in fact some of these efforts—for example, restructuring initiatives—actually produce more of it.

Executives underestimate not only the inevitability of conflict but also—and this is key—its importance to the organization. The disagreements sparked by differences in perspective, competencies, access to information, and strategic focus within a company actually generate much of the value that can come from collaboration across organizational boundaries. Clashes between parties are the crucibles in which creative solutions are developed and wise trade-offs among competing objectives are made. So instead of trying simply to reduce disagreements, senior executives need to embrace conflict and, just as important, institutionalize mechanisms for managing it.

Even though most people lack an innate understanding of how to deal with conflict effectively, there are a number of straightforward ways that executives can help their people—and their organizations—constructively manage it. These can be divided into two main areas: strategies for managing disagreements at the point of conflict and strategies for managing conflict upon escalation up the management chain. These methods can help a company move through the conflict that is a necessary precursor to truly effective collaboration and, more important, extract the value that often lies latent in intra-organizational differences. When companies are able to do both, conflict is transformed from a major liability into a significant asset.

Strategies for Managing Disagreements at the Point of Conflict

Conflict management works best when the parties involved in a disagreement are equipped to manage it themselves. The aim is to get people to resolve issues on their own through a process that improves—or at least does not damage—their relationships. The following strategies help produce decisions that are better informed and more likely to be implemented.

Devise and implement a common method for resolving conflict. Consider for a moment the hypothetical Matrix Corporation, a composite of many organizations we've worked with whose challenges will likely be familiar to managers. Over the past few years, salespeople from nearly a dozen of Matrix's product and service groups have been called on to design and sell integrated solutions to their customers. For any given sale, five or more lead salespeople and their teams have to agree on issues of resource allocation, solution design, pricing, and sales strategy. Not surprisingly, the teams are finding this difficult. Who should contribute the most resources to a particular customer's offering? Who should reduce the scope of their participation or discount their pricing to meet a customer's budget? Who should defer when disagreements arise about account strategy? Who should manage key relationships within the customer account? Indeed, given these thorny questions, Matrix is finding that a single large sale typically generates far more conflict inside the company than it does with the customer. The resulting wasted time and damaged relationships among sales teams are making it increasingly difficult to close sales.

Most companies face similar sorts of problems. And, like Matrix, they leave employees to find their own ways of resolving them. But without a structured method for dealing with these issues, people get bogged down not only in what the right result should be but also in how to arrive at it. Often, they will avoid or work around conflict, thereby forgoing important opportunities to collaborate. And when people do decide to confront their differences, they usually default to the approach they know best: debating about who's right and who's wrong or haggling over small concessions. Among the negative consequences of such approaches are suboptimal, "split-the-difference" resolutions—if not outright deadlock.

Establishing a companywide process for resolving disagreements can alter this familiar scenario. At the very least, a well-defined, well-designed conflict resolution method will reduce transaction costs, such as wasted time and the accumulation of ill will, that often come with the struggle to work though differences. At best, it will yield the innovative outcomes that are likely to emerge from discussions that draw on a multitude of objectives and perspectives. There is an array of conflict resolution methods a company can use. But to be effective, they should offer a clear, step-by-step process for parties to follow. They should also be made an integral part of existing business activities—account planning, sourcing, R&D budgeting, and the like. If conflict resolution is set up as a separate, exception-based process—a kind of organizational appeals court—it will likely wither away once initial managerial enthusiasm wanes.

At Intel, new employees learn a common method and language for decision making and conflict resolution. The company puts them through training in which they learn to use a variety of tools for handling discord. Not only does the training show that top management sees disagreements as an inevitable aspect of doing business, it also provides a common framework that expedites conflict resolution. Little time is wasted in figuring out the best way to handle a disagreement or trading accusations about "not being a team player"; guided by this clearly defined process, people can devote their time and energy to exploring and constructively evaluating a variety of options for how to move forward. Intel's systematic method for working through differences has helped sustain some of the company's hallmark qualities: innovation, operational efficiency, and the ability to make and implement hard decisions in the face of complex strategic choices.

Provide people with criteria for making trade-offs. At our hypothetical Matrix Corporation, senior managers overseeing cross-unit sales teams often admonish those teams to "do what's right for the customer." Unfortunately, this exhortation isn't much help when conflict arises. Given Matrix's ability to offer numerous combinations of products and services, company managers—each with different training and experience and access to different information, not to mention different unit priorities—have, not surprisingly, different opinions about how best to meet customers' needs. Similar clashes in perspective result when exasperated senior managers tell squabbling team members to set aside their differences and "put Matrix's interests first." That's because it isn't always clear what's best for the company given the complex interplay among Matrix's objectives for revenue, profitability, market share, and long-term growth.

Even when companies equip people with a common method for resolving conflict, employees often will still need to make zero-sum trade-offs between competing priorities. That task is made much easier and less contentious when top management can clearly articulate the criteria for making such choices. Obviously, it's not easy to reduce a company's strategy to clearly defined trade-offs, but it's worth trying. For example, salespeople who know that five points of market share are more important than a ten point increase on a customer satisfaction scale are much better equipped to make strategic concessions when the needs and priorities of different parts of the business conflict. And even when the criteria do not lead to a straightforward answer, the guidelines can at least foster productive conversations by providing an objective focus. Establishing such criteria also sends a clear signal from management that it views conflict as an inevitable result of managing a complex business.

At Blue Cross and Blue Shield of Florida, the strategic decision to rely more and more on alliances with other organizations has significantly increased the potential for disagreement in an organization long accustomed to developing capabilities in-house. Decisions about whether to build new capabilities, buy them outright, or gain access to them through alliances are natural flashpoints for conflict among internal groups. The health insurer might have tried to minimize such conflict through a structural solution, giving a particular group the authority to make decisions concerning whether, for instance, to develop a new claims-processing system in-house, to do so jointly with an alliance partner, or to license or acquire an existing system from a third party. Instead, the company established a set of criteria designed to help various groups within the organization—for example, the enterprise alliance group, IT, and marketing—to collectively make such decisions.

The criteria are embodied in a spreadsheet-type tool that guides people in assessing the trade-offs involved—say, between speed in getting a new process up and running versus ensuring its seamless integration with existing ones—when deciding whether to build, buy, or ally. People no longer debate back and forth across a table, advocating their preferred outcomes. Instead, they sit around the table and together apply a common set of trade-off criteria to the decision at hand. The resulting insights into the pros and cons of each approach enable more effective execution, no matter which path is chosen. (For a simplified version of the trade-off tool, see Box 11.1.2 "Blue Cross and Blue Shield: Build, Buy, or Ally?")

Use the escalation of conflict as an opportunity for coaching. Managers at Matrix spend much of their time playing the organizational equivalent of hot potato. Even people who are new to the company learn within weeks that the best thing to do with cross-unit conflict is to toss it up the management chain. Immediate supervisors take a quick

---

Box 11.1.2 BLUE CROSS AND BLUE SHIELD: BUILD, BUY, OR ALLY?

One of the most effective ways senior managers can help resolve cross-unit conflict is by giving people the criteria for making trade-offs when the needs of different parts of the business are at odds with one another. At Blue Cross and Blue Shield of Florida, there are often conflicting perspectives over whether to build new capabilities (for example, a new claims-processing system, as in the hypothetical example below), acquire them, or gain access to them through an alliance. The company uses a grid-like poster (a simplified version of which is shown here) that helps multiple parties analyze the trade-offs associated with these three options. By checking various boxes in the grid using personalized markers, participants indicate how they assess a particular option against a variety of criteria: for example, the date by which the new capability needs to be implemented; the availability of internal resources such as capital and staff needed to develop the capability; and the degree of integration required with existing products and processes. The table format makes criteria and trade-offs easy to compare. The visual depiction of people's "votes" and the ensuing discussion help individuals see how their differences often arise from such factors as access to different data or different prioritizing of objectives. As debate unfolds—and as people move their markers in response to new information—they can see where they are aligned and where and why they separate into significant factions of disagreement. Eventually, the criteria-based dialogue tends to produce a preponderance of markers in one of the three rows, thus yielding operational consensus around a decision.

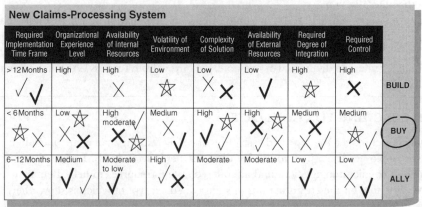

Participant 1 = ✓ Participant 2 = ✔ Participant 3 = ☆ Participant 4 = ✕ Participant 5 = ✗

Source: Blue Cross and Blue Shield of Florida

pass at resolving the dispute but, being busy themselves, usually pass it up to *their* supervisors. Those supervisors do the same, and before long the problem lands in the lap of a senior-level manager, who then spends much of his time resolving disagreements. Because the senior managers are a number of steps removed from the source of the controversy, they rarely have a good understanding of the situation. Furthermore, the more time they spend resolving internal clashes, the less time they spend engaged in the business, and the more isolated they are from the very information they need to resolve the disputes dumped in their laps. Meanwhile, Matrix employees get so little opportunity to learn about how to deal with conflict that it becomes not only expedient but almost necessary for them to quickly bump conflict up the management chain.

While Matrix's story may sound extreme, we can hardly count the number of companies we've seen that operate this way. And even in the best of situations—for example, where a companywide conflict-management process is in place and where trade-off criteria are well understood—there is still a natural tendency for people to let their bosses sort out disputes. Senior managers contribute to this tendency by quickly resolving the problems presented to them. While this may be the fastest and easiest way to fix the problems, it encourages people to punt issues upstairs at the first sign of difficulty. Instead, managers should treat escalations as opportunities to help employees become better at resolving conflict. (For an example of how managers can help their employees improve their conflict resolution skills, see Box 11.1.3 "IBM: Coaching for Conflict.")

At KLA-Tencor, a major manufacturer of semiconductor production equipment, a materials executive in each division oversees a number of buyers who procure the materials and component parts for machines that the division makes. When negotiating a company-wide contract with a supplier, a buyer often must work with the company commodity manager, as well as with buyers from other divisions who deal with the same supplier. There is often conflict, for example, over the delivery terms for components supplied to two or more divisions under the contract. In such cases, the commodity manager and the division materials executive will push the division buyer to consider the needs of the other divisions, alternatives that might best address the collective needs of the different divisions, and the standards to be applied in assessing the trade-offs between alternatives. The aim is to help the buyer see solutions that haven't yet been considered and to resolve the conflict with the buyer in the other division.

Initially, this approach required more time from managers than if they had simply made the decisions themselves. But it has paid off in fewer disputes that senior managers need to resolve, speedier contract negotiation, and improved contract terms both for the company as a whole and for multiple divisions. For example, the buyers from three KLA-Tencor product

---

IBM: COACHING FOR CONFLICT

Managers can reduce the repeated escalation of conflict up the management chain by helping employees learn how to resolve disputes themselves. At IBM, executives get training in conflict management and are offered online resources to help them coach others. One tool on the corporate intranet (an edited excerpt of which is shown here) walks managers through a variety of conversations they might have with a direct report who is struggling to resolve a dispute with people from one or more groups in the company—some of whom, by design, will be consulted to get their views but won't be involved in negotiating the final decision.

If you hear from someone reporting to you that . . .	*The problem could be that . . .*	*And you could help your report by saying something like . . .*
"Everyone still insists on being a decision maker."	The people your report is dealing with remain concerned that unless they have a formal voice in making the decision—or a key piece of the decision—their needs and interests won't be taken into account.	"You might want to explain why people are being consulted and how this information will be used." "Are there ways to break this decision apart into a series of subissues and assign decision-making roles around those subissues?" "Consider talking to the group about the costs of having everyone involved in the final decision."
"If I consult with this person up front, he might try to force an answer on me or create roadblocks to my efforts to move forward."	The person you are coaching may be overlooking the risks of not asking for input— mainly, that any decision arrived at without input could be sabotaged later on.	"How would you ask someone for input? What would you tell her about your purpose in seeking it? What questions would you ask? What would you say if she put forth a solution and resisted discussing other options?" "Is there a way to manage the risk that she will try to block your efforts other than by not consulting her at all? If you consult with her now, might that in fact lower the risk that she will try to derail your efforts later?"
"I have consulted with all the right parties and have crafted, by all accounts, a good plan. But the decision makers cannot settle on a final decision."	The right people were included in the negotiating group, but the process for negotiating a final decision was not determined.	"What are the ground rules for how decisions will be made? Do all those in the group need to agree? Must the majority agree? Or just those with the greatest competence?" "What interests underlie the objective of having everyone agree? Is there another decision-making process that would meet those interests?"

divisions recently locked horns over a global contract with a key supplier. At issue was the trade-off between two variables: one, the supplier's level of liability for materials it needs to purchase in order to fulfill orders and, two, the flexibility granted the KLA-Tencor divisions in modifying the size of the orders and their required lead times. Each division demanded a different balance between these two factors, and the buyers took the conflict to their managers, wondering if they should try to negotiate each of the different trade-offs into the contract or pick among them. After being coached to consider how each division's business model shaped its preference—and using this understanding to jointly brainstorm alternatives—the buyers and commodity manager arrived at a creative solution that worked for everyone: They would request a clause in the contract that allowed them to increase and decrease flexibility in order volume and lead time, with corresponding changes in supplier liability, as required by changing market conditions.

Strategies for Managing Conflict upon Escalation

Equipped with common conflict resolution methods and trade-off criteria, and supported by systematic coaching, people are better able to resolve conflict on their own. But certain complex disputes will inevitably need to be decided by superiors. Consequently, managers must ensure that, upon escalation, conflict is resolved constructively and efficiently—and in ways that model desired behaviors.

Establish and enforce a requirement of joint escalation. Let's again consider the situation at Matrix. In a typical conflict, three salespeople from different divisions become involved in a dispute over pricing. Frustrated, one of them decides to hand the problem up to his boss, explaining the situation in a short voice-mail message. The message offers little more than bare acknowledgment of the other salespeoples' viewpoints. The manager then determines, on the basis of what he knows about the situation, the solution to the problem. The salesperson, armed with his boss's decision, returns to his counterparts and shares with them the verdict—which, given the process, is simply a stronger version of the solution the salesperson had put forward in the first place. But wait! The other two salespeople have also gone to *their* managers and carried back stronger versions of *their* solutions. At this point, each salesperson is locked into what is now "my manager's view" of the right pricing scheme. The problem, already thorny, has become even more intractable.

The best way to avoid this kind of debilitating deadlock is for people to present a disagreement jointly to their boss or bosses. This will reduce or even eliminate the suspicion, surprises, and damaged personal relationships ordinarily associated with unilateral escalation. It will also guarantee that the ultimate decision maker has access to a wide array of perspectives on the conflict, its causes, and the various ways it might be resolved. Furthermore, companies that require people to share responsibility for the escalation of a conflict often see a decrease in the number of problems that are pushed up the management chain. Joint escalation helps create the kind of accountability that is lacking when people know they can provide their side of an issue to their own manager and blame others when things don't work out.

A few years ago, after a merger that resulted in a much larger and more complex organization, senior managers at the Canadian telecommunications company Telus found themselves virtually paralyzed by a daily barrage of unilateral escalations. Just determining who was dealing with what and who should be talking to whom took up huge amounts of senior management's time. So the company made joint escalation a central tenet of its new organizationwide protocols for conflict resolution—a requirement given teeth by managers' refusal to respond to unilateral escalation. When a conflict occurred among managers in different departments concerning, say, the allocation of resources among the departments, the managers were required to jointly describe the problem, what had been done so far to resolve it, and its possible solutions. Then they had to send a joint write-up of the situation to each of their bosses and stand ready to appear together and answer questions when those bosses met to work through a solution. In many cases, the requirement of systematically documenting the conflict and efforts to resolve it—because it forced people to make such efforts—led to a problem being resolved on the spot, without having to be kicked upstairs. Within weeks, this process resulted in the resolution of hundreds of issues that had been stalled for months in the newly merged organization.

Ensure that managers resolve escalated conflicts directly with *their* counterparts. Let's return to the three salespeople at Matrix who took their dispute over pricing to their respective bosses and then met again, only to find themselves further from agreement than before. So what did they do at that point? They sent the problem *back* to their bosses. These three bosses, each of whom thought he'd already resolved the issue, decided the easiest thing to do would be to escalate it themselves. This would save them time and put the conflict before senior managers with the broad view seemingly needed to make a decision. Unfortunately, by doing this, the three bosses simply perpetuated the situation their salespeople had created, putting forward a biased viewpoint and leaving it to their own managers to come up with an answer. In the end, the decision was made unilaterally by the senior manager with the most organizational clout. This result bred resentment back down the management chain. A sense of "we'll win next time" took hold, ensuring that future conflict would be even more difficult to resolve.

It's not unusual to see managers react to escalations from their employees by simply passing conflicts up their own functional or divisional chains until they reach a senior executive involved with all the affected functions or divisions. Besides providing a poor example for others in the organization, this can be disastrous for a company that needs to move quickly. To avoid wasting time, a manager somewhere along the chain might try to resolve the problem swiftly and decisively by herself. But this, too, has its costs. In a complex organization, where many issues have significant implications for numerous parts of the business, unilateral responses to unilateral escalations are a recipe for inefficiency, bad decisions, and ill feelings.

The solution to these problems is a commitment by managers—a commitment codified in a formal policy—to deal with escalated conflict directly with their counterparts. Of course, doing this can feel cumbersome, especially when an issue is time-sensitive. But resolving the problem early on is ultimately more efficient than trying to sort it out later, after a decision becomes known because it has negatively affected some part of the business.

In the 1990s, IBM's sales and delivery organization became increasingly complex as the company reintegrated previously independent divisions and reorganized itself to provide customers with full solutions of bundled products and services. Senior executives soon recognized that managers were not dealing with escalated conflicts and that relationships among them were strained because they failed to consult and coordinate around cross-unit issues. This led to the creation of a forum called the Market Growth Workshop (a name carefully chosen to send a message throughout the company that getting cross-unit conflict resolved was critical to meeting customer needs and, in turn, growing market share). These monthly conference calls brought together managers, salespeople, and frontline product specialists from across the company to discuss and resolve cross-unit conflicts that were hindering important sales—for example, the difficulty salespeople faced in getting needed technical resources from over-stretched product groups.

The Market Growth Workshops weren't successful right away. In the beginning, busy senior managers, reluctant to spend time on issues that often hadn't been carefully thought through, began sending their subordinates to the meetings—which made it even more difficult to resolve the problems discussed. So the company developed a simple preparation template that forced people to document and analyze disputes before the conference calls. Senior managers, realizing the problems created by their absence, recommitted themselves to attending the meetings. Over time, as complex conflicts were resolved during these sessions and significant sales were closed, attendees began to see these meetings as an opportunity to be involved in the resolution of high-stakes, high-visibility issues.

Make the process for escalated conflict resolution transparent. When a sales conflict is resolved by a Matrix senior manager, the word comes down the management chain in the form of an action item: Put together an offering with this particular mix of products and services at these prices. The only elaboration may be an admonishment to "get the sales team together, work up a proposal, and get back to the customer as quickly as possible." The problem is solved, at least for the time being. But the salespeople—unless they have been able to divine themes from the patterns of decisions made over time—are left with little guidance on how to resolve similar issues in the future. They may justifiably wonder: How was the decision made? Based on what kinds of assumptions? With what kinds of trade-offs? How might the reasoning change if the situation were different?

In most companies, once managers have resolved a conflict, they announce the decision and move on. The resolution process and rationale behind the decision are left inside a managerial black box. While it's rarely helpful for managers to share all the gory details of their deliberations around contentious issues, failing to take the time to explain how a decision was reached and the factors that went into it squanders a major opportunity. A frank discussion of the trade-offs involved in decisions would provide guidance to people trying to resolve conflicts in the future and would help nip in the bud the kind of speculation—who won and who lost, which managers or units have the most power—that breeds mistrust, sparks turf battles, and otherwise impedes cross-organizational collaboration. In general, clear communication about the resolution of the conflict can increase people's willingness and ability to implement decisions.

During the past two years, IBM's Market Growth Workshops have evolved into a more structured approach to managing escalated conflict, known as Cross-Team Workouts. Designed to make conflict resolution more transparent, the workouts are weekly meetings of people across the organization who work together on sales and delivery issues for specific accounts. The meetings provide a public forum for resolving conflicts over account strategy, solution configuration, pricing, and delivery. Those issues that cannot be resolved at the local level are escalated to regional workout sessions attended by managers from product groups, services, sales, and finance. Attendees then communicate and explain meeting resolutions to their reports. Issues that cannot be resolved at the regional level are escalated to an even higher-level workout meeting attended by cross-unit executives from a larger geographic region—like the Americas or Asia Pacific—and chaired by the general manager of the region presenting the issue. The most complex and strategic issues reach this global forum. The overlapping attendance at these sessions—in which the managers who chair one level of meeting attend sessions at the next level up, thereby observing the decision-making process at that stage—further enhances the transparency of the system among different levels of the company. IBM has further formalized the process for the direct resolution of conflicts between services and product sales on large accounts by designating a managing director in sales and a global relationship partner in IBM global services as the ultimate point of resolution for escalated conflicts. By explicitly making the resolution of complex conflicts part of the job descriptions for both managing director and global relationship partner—and by making that clear to others in the organization—IBM has reduced ambiguity, increased transparency, and increased the efficiency with which conflicts are resolved.

Tapping the Learning Latent in Conflict

The six strategies we have discussed constitute a framework for effectively managing organizational discord, one that integrates conflict resolution into day-to-day decision-making processes, thereby removing a critical barrier to cross-organizational collaboration. But the strategies also hint at something else: that conflict can be more than a necessary antecedent to collaboration.

Let's return briefly to Matrix. More than three-quarters of all cross-unit sales at the company trigger disputes about pricing. Roughly half of the sales lead to clashes over account control. A substantial number of sales also produce disagreements over the design of customer solutions, with the conflict often rooted in divisions' incompatible measurement systems and the concerns of some people about the quality of the solutions being assembled. But managers are so busy trying to resolve these almost daily disputes that they don't see the patterns or sources of conflict. Interestingly, if they ever wanted to identify patterns like these, Matrix managers might find few signs of them. That's because salespeople, who regularly hear their bosses complain about all the disagreements in the organization, have concluded that they'd better start shielding their superiors from discord.

The situation at Matrix is not unusual—most companies view conflict as an unnecessary nuisance—but that view is unfortunate. When a company begins to see conflict as a valuable resource that should be managed and exploited, it is likely to gain insight into problems that senior managers may not have known existed. Because internal friction is often caused by unaddressed strains within an organization or between an organization and its environment, setting up methods to track conflict and examine its causes can provide an interesting new perspective on a variety of issues. In the case of Matrix, taking the time to aggregate the experiences of individual salespeople involved in recurring disputes would likely lead to better approaches to setting prices, establishing incentives for salespeople, and monitoring the company's quality control process.

At Johnson & Johnson, an organization that has a highly decentralized structure, conflict is recognized as a positive aspect of cross-company collaboration. For example, a small internal group charged with facilitating sourcing collaboration among J&J's independent operating companies—particularly their outsourcing of clinical research services—actively works to extract lessons from conflicts. The group tracks and analyzes disagreements about issues such as what to outsource, whether and how to shift spending among suppliers, and what supplier capabilities to invest in. It hosts a council, comprising representatives from the various operating companies, that meets regularly to discuss these differences and explore their strategic implications. As a result, trends in clinical research outsourcing are spotted and information about them is disseminated throughout J&J more quickly. The operating companies benefit from insights about new off-shoring opportunities, technologies, and ways of structuring collaboration with suppliers. And J&J, which can now piece together an accurate and global view of its suppliers, is better able to partner with them.

Furthermore, the company realizes more value from its relationship with suppliers—yet another example of how the effective management of conflict can ultimately lead to fruitful collaboration.

J&J's approach is unusual but not unique. The benefits it offers provide further evidence that conflict—so often viewed as a liability to be avoided whenever possible—can be valuable to a company that knows how to manage it.

11.2 BUILDING ORGANIZATION THEORY FROM FIRST PRINCIPLES

The Self-Enhancement Motive and Understanding Power and Influence

Jeffrey Pfeffer and Christina T. Fong

In developing and advancing organization theory, it is useful if we can uncover fundamental constructs that can then be used to integrate larger areas of inquiry, even as we continue to accumulate more knowledge, evidence, and concepts. However, accomplishing this will require a somewhat different approach to theory building and testing. We illustrate the process of building an integrated model from fundamental constructs by using the idea of self-enhancement to explore phenomena of power and influence. We argue that many psychological processes related to power and social influence (such as escalation of commitment, similarity attraction and in-group favoritism, the disinhibiting effects of power, and the persistence of hierarchical structures) can all be logically derived from the self-enhancement idea, the desire to see oneself and one's actions in a positive light. The conceptual model can help us understand apparently anomalous behavior (such as individuals being willing to tolerate poor treatment at the hands of leaders), bringing together a number of ideas and constructs frequently treated as distinct in the literature and providing some hypotheses for future research.

As the study of organizations has grown, size has led to differentiation (Blau 1970) with a consequent specialization and fractionation. Researchers are encouraged to discuss how their ideas or empirical observations are different or novel (e.g., Mone and McKinley 1993), and the effort to differentiate one's research and invent new terms for the same phenomena has sometimes occurred at the expense of integration and an emphasis on the interrelated nature of organizational science.

We argue that this current state of affairs is neither desirable nor inevitable. After briefly reviewing some of the negative consequences of failing to build integrated theoretical structures, and noting some other efforts in the literature to do just that, we provide a "demonstration project" by showing how the idea of self-enhancement can help in building an integrated model of many aspects of power and influence, and in the process illuminating fruitful areas for further inquiry.

Does Theoretical Integration Matter?

As Davis and Marquis (2005) have argued and empirically illustrated, organization theory has, with the exception of population ecology, "largely abandoned the idea of cumulative work within a particular paradigm in favor of problem-driven work that is theoretically agnostic" (p. 334). They noted that of 89 articles examined in *Administrative Science Quarterly*, only 11% had the form where "the research question flowed directly from the logic of a particular theory" (p. 334). The rest focused on topic problems and were theoretically eclectic. Note that their observation does not mean that organization theory has failed to achieve paradigmatic consensus (Pfeffer 1993), although that is also certainly true. Paradigmatic consensus implies not only that research is cumulative and theory driven, but also that there is general agreement on what the dominant theoretical paradigm should be. Davis and Marquis (2005) show that research in organization studies is no longer much about developing and testing specific theories, regardless of whether or not there is consensus on what the most promising theoretical approaches are. Instead, they argue that organizational research is increasingly oriented toward explaining events in the world and mustering whatever ideas, theories, or data seem to be appropriate for the task at hand. A logical, natural, and indeed inevitable consequence of this trend is building the field of organization studies based on a set of ad hoc theoretical approaches and lists of concepts that seem to be useful for explaining whatever the specific focus of attention is at the time.

Building a theoretically integrated, logically consistent structure of ideas or, alternatively, pursuing a problem or phenomenon-oriented approach to organizational analysis is a choice that affects the process of research and also that of reviewing and evaluating articles. To wit, if the goal is explaining a phenomenon in the world, an evaluation of the extent to which some research has achieved that goal would appropriately focus on the amount of variation explained and, even more importantly, whether the explanations mustered are comprehensive and take into account alternative ways of understanding the phenomenon being examined. On the other hand, if the goal is evaluating whether or not a particular integrated theoretical approach is useful, the question is not whether every alternative explanation has been considered, but rather the extent to which the particular approach being used helps in understanding a broad range of organizational processes and outcomes. The implication is that building integrated organization theory really requires a somewhat different orientation to the research process than is currently the norm in organization studies, except in a few subfields.

If one accepts, as we do, the Davis and Marquis (2005) story of how organizational research has changed (not just for macro-organizational behavior but for the field as a whole), the next question is: so what? We believe there are many consequences, and most of them are negative. One consequence is that reviews of the field of organization studies (e.g., Pfeffer 1997, Scott 1998) are increasingly difficult to create, read, and remember because they inevitably are comprised of multiple, somewhat unconnected lists of theories, variables, concepts, and perspectives. Even in subsets of organizational behavior, such as the study of influence, Cialdini's (2001) overview of principles of influence is presented in list-like form. As a second consequence, this fractionated, list-like character of concepts and theories makes it more difficult to teach organization science to undergraduates and graduate students, who often complain that they have trouble studying for exams because it is hard for them to see the connection among diverse, apparently unrelated, topics. The absence of integrated theories also makes it more difficult for graduate students to master the literature of the field (Zammuto and Connolly 1984), and also means that it is less likely that researchers will see possible connections among topics and theories as well as uncover gaps in our understanding.

There are enormous benefits for memory and understanding from coherent, integrated theoretical structures of thought. Chase and Simon (1973) demonstrated long ago that experienced chess players are able to recall with much greater accuracy the placement of more pieces on a chess board, even though their short-term memory is no better than novices (e.g., de Groot 1965). This is because master players see in "larger perceptual chunks" that are "held together by more abstract relations" (Chase and Simon 1973, p. 80). In other words, a more developed theory of the game of chess—in this case acquired through experience—permits better recall and also more effective action. In a similar fashion, more developed theories, based on integrated conceptual frameworks, should permit more recall and more effective action in either the domains of organizational practice or in research.

There are some other consequences of our form of theorizing as well, although empirical research would be useful to make the case more strongly in each instance. Organization studies as a field does not seem to garner a lot of respect or status from students, particularly in MBA programs (e.g., Rynes et al. 2003). Although the hiring practices of employers, who claim to want leadership and "soft" skills but screen mostly on quantitative analytic abilities, are certainly part of the problem, it is also likely that organization studies suffers in comparison to accounting, operations, and economics because it appears to be less "scientific" and rigorous. One reason for this perception is not only that organization studies is not as quantitative as these other fields, but also that there seems to be less of an integrated and coherent set of ideas compared to some other business disciplines.

Yet another possible consequence of the absence of integrated theoretical structures is the growing dominance of economics as the foundation for policy and practice (e.g., Bazerman 2005; Bernstein 2001, p. 3; Ghoshal 2005). This prominence comes not only from paradigmatic consensus, but also from the fact that economic theories appear to be more rigorous and scientific. Ghoshal (2005) used the example of agency theory to pose a conundrum: How and why can a theory that is "bad for practice" (Ghoshal and Moran 1996) and frequently incorrect in its predictions have such staying power? His answer was that agency theory "wins" because the organization theory alternatives to explain the same phenomena do not have the same deductive logic, and therefore appear less internally consistent and tightly argued.

The problems just enumerated have actually stimulated several efforts to build a reasonably unified conceptualization of organizational and human behavior using a relatively small set of concepts as fundamental building blocks. For example, Haslam (2000) has used social identity theory as a way of attempting to draw a number of phenomena such as leadership, motivation, power, and group decision making into a more coherent, integrated portrayal of organizational life. Lawrence and Nohria (2002, p. 5) argued that a unified understanding of human behavior in all its diversity could be built by considering "four innate drives—the drive to acquire, the drive to bond, the drive to learn, and the drive to defend." Fiske (2004, p. 24) has written a social psychology textbook oriented around "five core social motives—belonging, understanding, controlling, self-enhancing, and trusting." And as Davis and Marquis (2005) noted, population ecology proceeds from a small set of concepts and first principles and is increasingly engaged in the enterprise of building formal, deductive models (e.g., Peli et al. 2000). Miller has noted that one of the best ways for organizational behavior and social psychology to compete more effectively in the marketplace of ideas is to find some core concepts that can be used to build connected logical structures of related ideas that help in understanding a range of behaviors.

Our paper represents yet another effort at building an integrated conceptual structure. However, our goals are more modest than some—to use one particular theoretical idea, self-enhancement, to explore one particular set of phenomena, those associated with power and influence, to see to what extent we can organize a set of unrelated ideas under a single conceptual rubric and to see what hypotheses and insights such an effort produces. If we are successful in linking a number of ideas together and showing how such an effort leads to new insights and hypotheses, we hope to encourage others to make similar efforts using self-enhancement or other fundamental ideas to build integrated theoretical structures for other organizational processes.

Self-Enhancement and Related Phenomena

We chose the concept of self-enhancement as our primitive construct because it is one of Fiske's (2004) core motives and because we believe it can provide a great deal of leverage in understanding interpersonal relations in power and influence behavior. In this paper, we define *self-enhancement* as the desire or observed reality of seeing oneself and by extension one's actions, traits, and attitudes in the most positive light.

The idea that people seek to maintain a positive self-evaluation is an old one in both social psychology (e.g., Heider 1958) and more generally in the social science literature (James 1907). The existence of a tendency to self-enhance has been extensively documented in a variety of domains. For instance, research has demonstrated that people are more likely to perceive themselves as superior to other individuals along a variety of positive dimensions (Brown 1986, Goethals et al. 1991, John and Robins 1994), to define traits in idiosyncratic ways that will be favorable to the self (Dunning et al. 1989), to see themselves more positively than others see them (e.g., Lewinsohn et al. 1980), to believe that they are above average (Kruger and Dunning 1999), to take credit for success but avoid blame for their failures (Bradley 1978, Campbell and Sedikides 1999, Miller and Ross 1975), and to affirm themselves in domains that will lead to greater self-esteem (e.g., Steele and Liu 1981). Furthermore, individuals will often derogate the accomplishments of other individuals, especially those with whom they might be compared in competitive situations (Wills 1981, Wood and Taylor 1991), view their own groups as superior to other groups (Tajfel and Turner 1986), and engage in self-serving attributions when explaining in-group performance while derogating the performance of out-groups (Brewer 1979, Brewer and Kramer 1985).

The tendency for individuals to self-enhance results in important consequences, such as attributions about life outcomes (e.g., Hastorf et al. 1970), differences in intergroup behavior (e.g., Polzer et al. 1997), sources of identity investment (e.g., Eccles and Wigfield 1995), and behavior in interpersonal relationships (e.g., Tesser 1998). Self-enhancement tendencies also influence the judgment and recall of information (e.g., Sedikides and Green 2000a), with more positive information about oneself being more likely to be remembered.

Research has demonstrated that self-enhancement tendencies can influence perception and behavior in two ways. First, individuals can selectively perceive or construe ambiguous information in a manner that makes the individual appear more accomplished, successful, and capable (e.g., Kunda and Sanitoso 1989). Another mechanism for self-enhancement is to ignore or avoid situations that might expose one to unflattering information in the first place (e.g., Sedikides and Green 2000b), for instance, by selectively choosing social comparisons to make oneself look better and to choose situations that are more likely to result in self-enhancing outcomes. Until now, there has not been much research ascertaining which of these mechanisms is used and under what conditions, which means that some fundamental questions in self-enhancement research remain to be examined.

As we have seen, there are many empirical manifestations of self-enhancement phenomena, and our intent is not to list all of them, which is well beyond the scope of this paper. We simply want to note the pervasiveness of the self-enhancement idea in the literature of social psychology and the numerous ways in which self-enhancement becomes manifested in social and organizational life.

Beyond Conceptual Controversies About Self-Enhancement

There are some conceptual issues surrounding the self-enhancement concept that are important as we develop implications of self-enhancement for the dynamics of power and influence. The first issue is that there is evidence that self-enhancement is primarily found in Western cultures (Heine et al. 1999, Heine and Lehman 1997a). For example, compared to Canadians, Japanese were less likely to enhance either themselves or their group (Heine and Lehman 1997b), suggesting that the motivations for enhancing one's self and one's group are similar to each other and that both are culturally based. Of course, the cultural specificity of social psychological processes is true for many psychological and organizational principles, such as the fundamental attribution error (e.g., Morris and Peng 1994) and the extrinsic incentives bias (Heath 1999), and does not limit the importance of those theoretical ideas. In what follows, the reader should recognize that the arguments and predictions that we make may be culturally bound, and testing the ideas and arguments in different cultures that vary in their likelihood of self-enhancing is an important and worthwhile task. Furthermore, on occasion we illustrate how different assumptions about both the strength of the tendency to self-enhance and its manifestations can lead to hypotheses about the different ways power and influence processes might operate in different cultural contexts.

A second issue is the ongoing controversy as to whether the observed tendency toward self-enhancement and the related phenomenon of in-group favoritism is the consequence of motivation or the consequence of information processing and cognitive processes. Miller and Ross (1975), for instance, argued that much of the research used to demonstrate a motivation to self-enhance could be explained in terms of cognitive, non-motivational explanations, such as the results being produced by the cognitive operation of prior beliefs and expectancies. Kunda (1990, p. 480) attempted to resolve this apparent conflict between motivation and cognitive processes by noting that "people rely on cognitive processes and representations to arrive at their desired conclusions, but motivation plays a role in determining which of these will be used on a given occasion." In other words, as Heider (1958) suggested, people want to develop self-enhancing cognitions but are compelled to do so in ways that plausibly take account of the existing data. In the arguments that we develop, we assume the existence of a self-enhancing bias but do not particularly need to rely on whether such bias comes from motivation, from cognition or, more plausibly, from both sources as we develop our arguments and predictions.

The third issue is that researchers have debated the benefits or disadvantages of self-enhancement for individuals. On one side, some researchers have argued that self-enhancers are in poor mental health, disliked by others around them, fail to take advantage of opportunities to learn from experience, and can be narcissistic or insensitive to social feedback (Blaine and Crocker 1993, Carver and Scheier 1998, Crocker 2002). There is also evidence that people with high self-esteem, when confronted with a threat to the self, set overly risky goals, which lead to a higher incidence of failure (Baumeister et al. 1993). Others, however, have argued that self-enhancement is an adaptive trait, and self-enhancing thoughts and behaviors have been linked to higher self-esteem (e.g., Taylor and Armor 1996, Taylor and Brown 1988), as well as other indicators of good mental health (Taylor et al. 2003). We acknowledge that there are probably times when self-enhancement is beneficial for individuals and even for the organizations and groups to which they belong and times when self-enhancement can lead to detrimental attitudes and behaviors because individuals do not hold veridical views of the world. In the model of self-enhancement, power, and political processes that we will outline, it will be evident that self-enhancement ideas can be useful for understanding tactics that help individuals advance, and that behaviors that come from self-enhancement can also, on occasion, lead to problematic personal and organizational outcomes.

The Relationship of Self-Enhancement to Power and Influence Processes

We organize our discussion of self-enhancement and power around the stages of acquiring, maintaining, and losing power and influence. At the start of a person's career, the individual has little influence and works in a subordinate relationship with others. Two interesting issues at this stage are how to find a place, a location in organizational space where one is likely to be more successful, and also how to understand the relationship with those in authority who, on occasion, may treat the individual in a very demeaning way. As one progresses through one's career and begins to acquire more influence, an important part of this process is attracting allies and supporters, and here again self-enhancement ideas can help make sense of some commonly observed tactics to accomplish this. Once one has power and is making decisions and taking action, self-enhancement helps the individual understand the commonly observed and discussed commitment to chosen courses of action and also helps him/her comprehend the less-commonly discussed aspect of decisions seldom being evaluated or questioned, a phenomenon that frequently surprises people who expect to see more assiduous evaluation of outcomes. Self-enhancement ideas can also illuminate the processes through which people develop illusions of their own influence, overestimate their own personal efficacy, and therefore how and why hierarchical relationships persist in organizations. This overestimation of power produces disinhibition in behavior, something that occasionally leads to behaviors that result in the loss of power. Drawing the theoretical connections among a number of distinct social psychological theories and examining the role of self-enhancement at each of the steps in the path to power can help us understand some occasionally counterintuitive observations about power and political behavior in organizations and create a more integrated framework for the field. We summarize the hypotheses and arguments developed throughout the text in Table 11.2.1.

Starting on the Path to Power: Relationships with High-Status Others

The path to power usually begins for individuals when they are in relatively powerless situations. People in relationship with others apparently more powerful than they are sometimes exhibit seemingly anomalous behavior, particularly if one assumes that individuals prefer to be in situations in which they can feel more positively about themselves and their attributes. Specifically, there are numerous examples of people who apparently voluntarily remain in demeaning and unpleasant situations in which they subordinate themselves to another (e.g., Lipman-Blumen 2004). Robert Caro's (1982) description of Lyndon Johnson (as a legislative aide to Congressman Richard Kleberg) giving a young, talented, and quite proper L. E. Jones dictation from the toilet is perhaps the most vivid. However, few descriptions of Oracle and Larry Ellison or Apple Computer, particularly in the early days, and

Table 11.2.1 The Role of Self-Enhancement in "Paradoxical" Organizational Occurrences

Organizational anomaly	Role of self-enhancement / Contributing psychological mechanisms	Individual-level implications / Hypotheses	Organizational-level implications / Hypotheses
Voluntary subjugation to powerful others	Basking in reflected glory for low-power person Disinhibition for high-power person	Proposition 1: People who are successful AND who symbolically include others in their successes will be able to abuse their subordinates more than unsuccessful OR noninclusive supervisors, (i.e., you need an interaction effect).	Successful organizations may want to build in checks and balances to protect low-power people and discourage abuse.
Homosocial reproduction	Similarity/Attraction and in-group favoritism predict that powerful people give similar others advantages.	Proposition 5: Individuals who can build perceived similarity with powerful others will succeed. Proposition 4: Individuals who are more similar to those in power will advance higher than those who are dissimilar. Proposition 2: Moderated mediation of similarity self-enhancement, and postchoice emotion for choosing partners: One's propensity for self-enhancement will predict the amount of positive affect that results from associating with a similar other. However, when one associates with a dissimilar other, there will be no effect of self-enhancement on the resulting affective experiences.	Organizations that emphasize diversity will attract people lower in self-enhancement than organizations that do not. Organizations that create opportunities for fluidity of social identity and networking will encourage success of individuals who are skilled in building perceived similarity.
Ostracization of unsuccessful others/The black sheep effect	Similarity/Attraction and out-group derogation would predict that the failure of similar others would be more self-implicating (and therefore more harshly judged) than the failure of dissimilar others.	Proposition 3: As perceived similarity of a target to the self increases so does punitive behavior toward that target in response to failure or demonstration of incompetence.	
The absence of evaluation of decisions	Escalation of commitment	Proposition 8: Evaluation of decisions is less likely in domains that are self-implicating than domains that are not implicating (or important for self-image). Proposition 7: Commitment processes will be weaker when changing one's mind or admitting fallibility is itself associated with a favorable or positive view of the self	Proposition 6: Organizations that deemphasize individual accountability will see increased evaluation of decisions.
Persistence of hierarchy	Illusion of control	Individuals will rate their contribution to a project as higher when that project is seen as successful than when it is not. Proposition 9: Feelings of self-worth mediate the illusions of control and influence effects.	
Fall from power	Disinhibition	Proposition 10: Individuals who are more likely to self-enhance should show increased disinhibition in response to power.	

Steve Jobs fail to mention the mercurial and often demeaning behavior of these two executives toward their subordinates (e.g., Rose 1989).

The fundamental question is why do people, at least some people for some time (note that strong, seasoned executives such as Ray Lane eventually left Oracle) appear to willingly subject themselves to psychological harassment and verbal abuse, or continue in situations in which they are badly treated? There are a number of possible explanations, and these explanations are not mutually exclusive (Lipman-Blumen 2004). Perhaps it is because they have no alternative, given the conditions of the job market. In other words, for L. E. Jones in the height of the Great Depression, a bad job as Johnson's assistant with difficult working conditions and long hours was better than no job at all.

Another possible explanation for why people remain in difficult and demeaning positions relies on the phenomenon of the consequences of escalation of commitment—having once chosen to be where they are, individuals reconstruct or rationalize their situations as being not so bad (e.g., Salancik 1977). Indeed, it is just this explanation that is offered for the results of a classic study that showed that participants who expected to undergo a noxious task—in this case, eating an earthworm—actually wanted to eat the worm even when they no longer had to (Comer and Laird 1975). The idea was that once one had chosen to be in the situation and had come to terms with it, perhaps by rationalizing that one's participation in the study helped advance science, people wanted to persist in their chosen course of action, even when it was unpleasant and they no longer had to (also see Festinger 1957).

Without denying the plausibility of commitment effects or the effects of external labor market conditions on rational choice, self-enhancement ideas offer another perspective on the situations in which people appear to voluntarily put up with abusive behavior in their work life. We argue that one reason they may do so is that because of our interest in feeling positively about ourselves and enhancing our self-image, we want to be associated with "winners" so we can bask in their reflected glory (Cialdini et al. 1976), and we are sometimes willing to put up with quite a bit to attain these high-status associations (Lipman-Blumen 2004).

There is little doubt that people do prefer to associate with winners. Consider the classic study that demonstrated a "basking in reflected glory" effect (Cialdini et al. 1976). In that study, the authors found that when the university's football team won on the weekend, the proportion of students wearing university-insignia apparel (such as T-shirts or sweatshirts) was higher the following Monday than on the Mondays following a loss. In fact, because of this presumed association between wearing insignia-decorated apparel and having positive feelings about the organization, presumably because one believes it is a good and effective organization, when Gordon Bethune (1998), was CEO of Continental Airlines during its turnaround he tracked employee purchases of items with Continental Airlines insignia on them as a way of measuring the extent to which the employees were feeling better about and more proud of the company. The desire to associate with winners means that public opinion polls asking who people voted for after election results become known are unreliable because more people claim to have voted for the winning candidate than actually did.

If we desire to associate and be identified with winners and with success, as a way of basking in reflected glory and thereby enhancing the self, then there is a plausible explanation for why people might be willing to put up with abusive bosses, toxic work environments, and sports coaches—such as basketball coach Bobby Knight and the late football coach Woody Hayes—who throw chairs and hit players. People want to associate with winners and with success and are willing to subjugate their own interests and emotions, at least for some time and to some degree, to do so. This explanation is consistent with the accounts provided in corporate and personal biographies, where people explain that, for example, they could tell that Lyndon Johnson was going to be a big success, so they wanted to be part of his circle; that they believed that Apple Computer was changing the world of personal computing, and they wanted to be a part of that quest; that the Ohio State football team under Woody Hayes and the Indiana basketball team under Bobby Knight were successful sports programs, and that putting up with the coach's behavior was a price one paid for being on a winning team and part of a successful, nationally ranked, and prominent program.

This line of reasoning suggests that at least the appearance or illusion of current or future success is crucial for attracting allies and supporters, particularly if current rewards for these individuals are small and they are possibly subjected to difficult or degrading working conditions. Moreover, it suggests that less-successful or less-powerful teams, leaders, and organizations will have much less discretion or slack when it comes to how they treat those around them than those with more success or perceived potential. Therefore, if associating with winners helps in maintaining a positive self-evaluation, then we would expect to observe that behavior such as basking in reflected glory should be more evident when there have been threats to one's self-concept. That is precisely what Cialdini and Richardson (1980) found. After giving participants either a success or failure experience and then an opportunity to rate their own and a rival university, "the tendency to compliment one's own university and blast the rival . . . increased with prior threat to self-evaluation" (Tesser 1988, p. 208).

Another important element in the process of identifying with a leader or organization is the perceived willingness to symbolically share the spotlight. We expect that basking in reflected glory and voluntary subjugation should be more likely when leaders are more willing to symbolically include others, at least to some degree, in their success. Thus, this focus on self-enhancement tendencies as an underlying cause for voluntary subjugation yields an interesting empirical prediction. We predict that the amount of ill treatment that subordinates are willing to tolerate should be a function of the interaction between their leader's success and their leader's willingness to symbolically include subordinates in the collective success (see Table 11.2.1, Proposition 1).

The interaction of these two separate factors plays an important part in disentangling self-enhancement explanations from other potential alternative ways of understanding voluntary subjugation. First, voluntary subjugation could be perceived as a product of a damaged self-image on the part of the powerless. For example, a subordinate with a low self-image may tolerate abuse because they are simply not empowered enough to leave or because of self-verification motives (e.g., Swann 1997). If these types of motives were solely responsible for voluntary subjugation, then individuals would not attend to the success of their abusers; namely, individuals interested solely in self-verification would not care if they were being abused by a successful or nonsuccessful supervisor or in a more- or less-successful organization. On the other hand, one might argue that voluntary subjugation is the result of an individual's calculation of long-term gains, in which individuals have decided to tolerate short-term abuse in exchange for potential long-term benefits. However, if this is the sole explanation for voluntary subjugation, then subordinates would not be concerned with whether they were able to bask in reflected glory or not because the potential long-term gains would be what were important (as long as symbolic inclusiveness is not seen as a signal of future benefits). Thus, if evidence of our predicted interaction were found to predict willingness to put up with difficult bosses and less desirable working environments and conditions, we could be more confident that self-enhancement does play some role in understanding how and why people make the choices to associate with particular leaders and organizations.

Similarity Attraction, In-Group Favoritism, and Career Dynamics

While self-enhancement ideas can help us understand why individuals in positions of less power might choose to voluntarily put themselves in difficult situations, self-enhancement concepts also provide insight into some ways that individuals can begin to obtain power as well. In the power acquisition stage, individuals are often concerned with issues regarding their relationships with others: who you know and what groups you belong to are extremely important in getting the desired jobs and being seen as part of the inner circle. Being part of a successful organization is therefore one aspect of the process of beginning to acquire influence through association with a prestigious place. Moreover, as many social scientists have noted, the idea of similarity attraction plays a crucial role in interpersonal interactions as people seek sponsorship and career advancement.

Self-enhancement ideas lead quite logically and directly to the observed relationship between similarity, or at least perceived similarity, and interpersonal attraction (e.g., Berscheid and Walster 1969, Byrne 1971, Clore and Byrne 1974, McGuire 1985). One of the seldom-asked questions about the similarity attraction paradigm and the various studies that showed people preferred those with similar attributes is *why* people prefer those who are similar, particularly if one takes an evolutionary or natural selection perspective on decision making and human psychology. After all, there are many functional reasons in both group and organizational contexts to actively seek out and associate with people who are different. For instance, the literature on group decision making suggests that better-quality solutions and more-innovative ideas often come from assembling different people with different perspectives who, therefore, can bring different insights, perspectives, and abilities to the task (e.g., Nemeth 1994, Nemeth and Kwan 1987). In the social networks literature, the idea of the strength of weak ties (Granovetter 1973) relies on the insight that a person accesses more diverse information and resources if that individual's social ties are themselves not so closely tied and homophilous, providing another reason to associate with less-similar people. There is also literature on diversity, including demographic diversity, which speaks to the potential advantages of differences in various dimensions of task performance (see Williams and O'Reilly 1998).

One answer to the question of why we do not observe more accessing of dissimilar others is that these advantages of associating, interacting, and valuing others who are different, and to whom one is less closely tied, come at a price. For instance, researchers have demonstrated that homogeneous groups are characterized by more trust, better communication, and better rapport (e.g., O'Reilly et al. 1989, Zenger and Lawrence 1989, Tsui et al. 1995), and that groups where members are similar perform better than groups where members are diverse (Barsade et al. 2000). However, attention to the self-enhancement idea also illuminates another price of diversity: the valuing of difference and dissimilarity can logically imply a diminished valuation of oneself and one's attributes, skills, and traits. Conversely, choosing to associate with and value others who are more similar is self-validating because in effect a person is choosing him- or herself. Therefore, we often prefer those who are similar to ourselves because we validate the desirability and attractiveness of our own attitudes and traits.

Therefore, self-enhancement theories would predict a moderated mediation effect for our affective reactions to associating with others (Proposition 2): when we choose a similar other to associate with, the extent to which we are prone to self-enhancement should mediate the extent of the positive feeling that results from choosing that similar other. On the other hand, when we associate with a dissimilar other, there should be no mediating effect of tendency to self-enhance on the resulting feelings that we experience after association. To the extent that self-enhancement is less-strongly observed in other cultures, we would expect to see less of the similarity attraction effect in those settings.

For similar self-enhancement reasons, we often favor groups of which we are members, and derogate groups that are seemingly more different from ourselves and our friends. Because we are identified and associated with groups in which we hold membership, favoring those groups and denigrating competing groups acts to enhance our feelings of self-worth. In-group favoritism has been demonstrated in many contexts for many different decisions (e.g., Brewer 1979, Ng 1981, Lewis and Sherman 2003). Furthermore, the research literature suggests that in-group favoritism is particularly likely to be exhibited when there is a situation of intergroup conflict or competition, a result demonstrated by Sherif et al. (1961) decades ago. Competition and conflict with outsiders increase threats to the self; therefore, it is not surprising that we observe more favoritism toward those similar to us when we confront such circumstances.

It is particularly noteworthy how simple it is to induce a sense of shared social identity by reminding people of what they have in common (Billig and Tajfel 1973). Thus, for instance, in one study by Kramer et al. (1993), simply reminding participants that they were all MBAs caused them to orient toward the task in terms of their MBA identity. Burger et al. (2004) found that telling people they shared a birthday, first name, or similarities in fingerprints was sufficient to induce enough shared social identity to increase compliance with requests. These experimental inductions that produce a feeling of group solidarity remind us that each person is potentially a member of many groups and is at once both similar to and different from others on numerous dimensions. The experimental literature induces shared identity by making certain associations and affiliations relatively more salient.

It is interesting to point out, however, that self-enhancement ideas can also help us understand the circumstances under which people will be *less* likely to choose or favor others similar to themselves or from their group. A great deal of empirical literature has demonstrated that individuals will report that they possess a trait that they believe is positive (Krueger 1998). In a similar fashion, an extension of that argument would suggest that individuals will follow the same pattern when claiming or advertising their group memberships. In other words, individuals will take advantage of the fluid nature of group membership to claim membership in groups that they believe are positive and to disavow membership in groups that are not perceived as positive.

For example, people will not identify with a similar other when that person is perceived as not competent or in some other way confirms a negative stereotype (Lewis and Sherman 2003) about a shared social identity. Much of the research on this "black sheep" effect, where in-group members are more derogatory toward in-group than out-group members, has developed from the perspective of establishing group norms and identifying and punishing deviants (Marques et al. 2001). However, our model suggests a more intraindividual process at work. Rather than derogating in-group members in an effort to maintain group integrity, individuals might also derogate unsuccessful in-group members in an effort to maintain a positive self-image. In other words, people will distance themselves more from similar others who are having problems, doing badly, or appear to be incompetent than they will from dissimilar others in identical circumstances because of the possibility of negative associations to the self from the more-close association with similar others who are failing. This phenomenon suggests that someone having difficulty demonstrating competence is more likely to get help or assistance from dissimilar others, who are not as threatened by their association with the individual, than from in-group members. Thus, we would predict a positive relationship between the extent of perceived similarity to oneself and an unsuccessful similar other, and the punitive or disassociating behaviors directed toward that person (Proposition 3). That is, if an individual is not succeeding, the more similar to me that he or she is perceived, the less likely I will be to help him or her.

To obtain power, then, one strategy is for individuals to show they are similar to individuals and groups with more power, thereby building a relationship and identity with these more-powerful others. There are many case examples of individuals who leveraged the similarity-attraction principle and strategically both "joined" groups and distanced themselves from other groups to build a pathway to career success. For instance, Reggie Lewis, as a young black man trying to be successful at Harvard Law School, did not associate himself with protests against the Vietnam War or overt demonstrations in favor of civil rights (Lewis et al. 1994). He sought to fit in with and be successful in a power structure that was largely white: therefore, he did nothing in terms of expressing political or social views to disassociate himself and his identity from that white world.

In a similar fashion, Henry Kissinger, while a student at Harvard just after World War II, was voluble on most subjects of politics except on issues pertaining to Israel and the Holocaust (Isaacson 1992), even though Kissinger's family had fled Germany and many of his relatives had perished in German concentration camps. Again, according to Isaacson, Kissinger's efforts to fit in to a world—Harvard—that had just begun accepting Jews in any number seemed to require him to do things that would not remind others of his difference from them along this salient social dimension.

Both the Kissinger and Lewis cases illustrate something else: The disassociation from direct competitors that we have described as well as a distancing from a social identity (in one case African-Americans and in the other case Jewish people) that might not be, at the time of their actions, perceived as helpful to their advancement. Kissinger was quite different from the other students in the Harvard government department, was not particularly well-liked, and was not really close to many of his colleagues. In a similar fashion, Lewis kept apart from many of his classmates at Harvard Law School. In both instances, these individuals were interested in being seen as similar to those in power while building relationships with them (professors, mentors, and potential employers). However, in circumstances of competition with their fellow students, each strategically differentiated himself.

Building a shared social identity, the connection between perceived similarity and interpersonal attraction, and in-group favoritism all have consequences for understanding career dynamics in organizations. First of all, career success is very likely to be related to the similarity of the individual to those in power in the organization who make career decisions, where such similarity is measured by departmental affiliation, educational background (both degree and school) and possibly race, gender, and ethnicity as well. It is important to note that similarity is a relational construct, like relational demography (Tsui et al. 1992). There have been numerous studies showing, for instance, that people from elite colleges/universities do better in their careers (e.g., Useem and Karabel 1986) than graduates from less-prestigious colleges/universities. We would argue that such studies would be even more predictive if they considered not just the educational background of the subject, but also the background of others in elite positions in the organizations where the subjects are working. More consistent with our argument are case studies such as Halberstam's (1986) analysis of the rise of finance in Ford Motor Company. People in finance favored others from finance and those with MBAs in the performance-evaluation process and in promotions. At Ford during the 1950s and 1960s, career attainment was clearly related to one's departmental affiliation and even to how people dressed and comported themselves in ways that created similarity to those in power.

There are a number of implications concerning this line of reasoning in understanding power and influence processes in organizations. First, the model points to one particular path to power and interpersonal influence for individuals operating in power hierarchies. Self-enhancement leads us to favor others who are similar to us and to favor in-groups and situations where we feel membership and a shared social identity. At the same time, perceptions of similarity and group membership are fluid and depend on what dimensions and aspects are salient at any one point in time. Together, these arguments imply that attempts to "construct" similarity and create feelings of "we-ness," or shared social identity, can lead to successful influence based on (perceived) similarity. The importance of accomplishing this building a sense of "we-ness" is evident from the data that show that people's willingness to help others, ranging from activities such as donating blood to providing loans or charity, varies significantly depending on whether those others are deemed to share a social identity or familial attachment with the person (e.g., Kenrick et al. 2002, pp. 301–305). Thus, self-enhancement theories would predict that individuals who are perceived as similar to those in power will advance more quickly and achieve higher positions within an organization than those who are seen as dissimilar (Proposition 4).

Because people intuitively know that their chances of success in requesting help or favors from others depends on whether the target of their influence attempts sees them as similar, sharing social affiliations, and being "one of us," people often use conversational gambits that attempt to build a sense of shared identity early in interpersonal interactions. Thus, when someone meets another who is important in terms of building a social relationship or getting a job or some other resource, often the first thing that happens is a search for something in common—a common educational background, hobbies and interests, previous employers—to build a sense of connection and social similarity. We would expect that those who employ such conversational gambits will, other things being equal, create perceptions of similarity that will reinforce their interpersonal influence attempts. In other words, we predict that individuals who are skilled in building perceptions of perceived similarity with those in power will be more likely to receive help and resources (such as favors, mentoring, and social inclusion, in addition to promotions, advances, and higher salaries) than individuals who are not as skilled in building perceived similarity (Proposition 5).

The importance of shared social identification for career advancement is consistent with studies showing the importance of network ties for advancement (e.g., Podolny and Baron 1997, Ibarra 1992) and also with studies showing the effect of departmental affiliation on salary (e.g., Moore and Pfeffer 1980, Pfeffer and Konrad 1991), where those from higher-power departments earn more, other things being equal. However, our argument is somewhat different from what was explored in these studies. We hypothesize that it is the shared social identity that mediates the observed effects, for instance, of social ties and shared departmental affiliation on career advancement. In other words, consistent with the arguments offered by Ibarra et al. (2005), it is not just one's position and connections in network terms that matter, but the extent to which those network connections actually result in a sense of shared identity and perceived social similarity. Therefore, tests for mediation should show smaller effects for departmental affiliation and network position on career outcomes when perceptions of similarity and shared social identity are included in the model. In a similar fashion, powerful departments can advance the careers of people in those departments, but they will do so only to the extent that the departmental members are seen as loyal and representative of those departments and similar to others in the powerful departments.

As we have shown, the theoretical integration of relational effects with a self-enhancement logic can add refinement to existing models and approaches to understanding careers, such as the prediction that the effect of network ties and departmental power on career success is mediated, at least partly, by perceptions of shared social identity.

Escalating Commitment and the Absence of Evaluation of Consequences

Once individuals have achieved positions providing more power and influence, their behavior can still be analyzed through recourse to self-enhancement ideas. The desire to see oneself in the most favorable light can often affect decision-making processes as well as the ability to learn from experience and mistakes. One example is the reluctance to revisit, reevaluate, and therefore learn from decisions or even to assess decision outcomes.

People, particularly students, sometimes believe that the use of power in decision making inside organizations, especially business organizations that seek to achieve profit in a competitive world, is constrained by some market-like efficiency logic. If people make decisions that benefit themselves, their friends, or their department at the expense of the total organization, there will presumably be consequences from those decisions, and if those consequences are not good for the organization, the people who have made the decisions will suffer. Thus, there is an implicit presumption of a feedback process in which actual business or economic results constrain the ability of people to act on their or their department's own parochial interests and advance agendas unrelated to organizational performance. This logic requires the assumption that decisions have consequences for the decision maker, which therefore also implies that there is at least occasionally some effort to review what has occurred and to ascribe blame or glory to those who were seemingly responsible.

Given these presumptions, it is surprising to encounter on a regular basis the real-world case examples where there seems to be little effort expended in evaluating what went right or wrong with decisions and even less attempt to punish the people who seemingly made bad decisions. For instance, even though the research literature shows that most mergers actually destroy economic value (e.g., Heracleous and Murray 2001), there are seldom consequences for the CEOs who drive the value-destroying merger decisions. In fact, companies often become "serial acquirers," not only failing to learn from previous problems, but going on to repeat the same decisions. Byron's (1986) description of Time, Inc.'s unsuccessful launch of a printed cable TV listings magazine that in the process wasted $50 million, nicely describes the surprise of the junior analysts involved in the decision when they saw that senior executives who championed what was clearly a poor choice apparently suffered no ill effects and, in fact, in one case obtained a promotion.

The seemingly anomalous behavior of the absence of evaluation of decisions and their consequences is quite understandable when we recognize that there is often commitment to a decision once it has been made, and when we further understand that this commitment comes, in part, from a desire to not appear to be "wrong," a phenomenon quite consistent with self-enhancement logic. Making mistakes is, under most conditions, not a self-enhancing thing to do and neither, unfortunately, is admitting to one's mistakes. After all, admitting that one has made a mistake is inconsistent with our desire to believe that we are competent, effective, and better than most others. There are several ways to maintain a positive sense of self (including seeing bad outcomes as good, which can lead to further investment in the chosen course of action) or selectively choosing to emphasize the more positive aspects of the multiple-dimensioned outcomes that typically accompany decisions.

There is some literature consistent with this association of commitment effects with the process of self-enhancement. Bobocel and Meyer (1994) found that public justification of decisions was not required to observe escalating commitment; even asking subjects to justify their decisions to themselves was sufficient. This result is completely consistent with the interpretation that commitment comes from a desire to enhance the self, not just from a need to manage the impressions of others. Brockner et al. (1986) also found commitment results consistent with a self-enhancement explanation. When subjects believed that performance was due more to skill than to luck, they tended to exhibit more escalation of commitment because decisions and their outcomes had more implications for their self-perception under the skill condition.

Another way of maintaining a positive sense of self would be not going back and reviewing past choices. In other words, the best way not to find a mistake or error is not to look in the first place. This avoidance of reviewing past actions makes maintaining a positive view of the self easier than finding past problems and having to come up with rationalizations that excuse the self, although this latter course is also possible.

Reviewing the enormous literature documenting commitment and escalating commitment studies is well beyond what we need to do here—suffice it to say that commitment and escalating commitment to apparently failing courses of action are quite common (e.g., Staw 1976, Cialdini 2001), indeed, so common that we should be able to stipulate that this a quite general social psychological process. However, the fact that commitment derives from self-enhancement helps us understand some circumstances in which the commitment effect would *not* be observed. First, we would expect to see less commitment to the extent that mistakes, errors, or any decision is framed not so much as being associated with one individual or a small group of individuals but rather as being a consequence of the organizational system and, furthermore, when instead of assigning individual accountability and blame, reviews are conducted for the purposes of learning, with few or no individual consequences (Proposition 6).

Gittell's (2000) study contrasting Southwest with American Airlines is quite consistent with this view of the consequences of associating performance and its consequences with individuals or subunits. She noted that at American Airlines under Robert Crandall, there was an intense emphasis on both individual and departmental accountability. The result was that when a problem arose, people spent a lot of time trying to pin the blame elsewhere and dodge responsibility for themselves and their department. By contrast, at Southwest Airlines the company moved to the idea of a team delay with less attempt to assign specific blame to either individuals or departments for the problem. This was done with the explicit goal of increasing learning and, at the same time, diminishing commitment to strategies and practices that were ineffective and needed to be changed.

Deming (Gabor 1990) and other writers on the quality movement were particularly critical of the idea of assigning individual blame, or credit for that matter, to results that were more likely the result of the system in which individuals were working. To Deming, this seemed unfair and focused attention on the wrong thing: fixing (or replacing) people rather than understanding and intervening in the system that was actually responsible for the results. However the quality movement's focus on systems rather than people would have another effect: It would tend to make individuals feel less personally identified with specific actions or decisions, thereby leaving them more willing and able to admit problems and produce change and improvement. Paradoxically, the demand for accountability heard so frequently in contemporary management circles may have the unintended and undesirable effect of causing people to resist uncovering, admitting, or learning from their mistakes because of the implications of individual or subgroup accountability for feelings of self-worth and self-enhancement when things go badly. Again, to the extent that self-enhancement operates less strongly in some other cultures, those cultures might be characterized by less escalation of commitment and a diminished tendency to avoid revisiting and assessing the quality of decision making. Perhaps that is one reason that the quality movement has found a more comfortable home in Japan than in the United States, where Deming and others first developed the ideas.

Second, commitment processes would be weaker when changing one's mind or admitting fallibility is itself associated with a favorable or positive view of the self, such as when the ability to make mistakes is seen or perceived as a positive trait, which may even increase status (Proposition 7). Just such a situation exists at IDEO Product Development, where the CEO at the time, David Kelley, introduced a new organizational structure with the statement that he was sure that although the structure was the best they could think of at that time, it was temporary and wrong. IDEO simply had to do the best it could and keep working to get better.

Salancik's (1977) insightful look at commitment processes represents an illustration of the importance of understanding self-enhancement for changing behavior. Because commitment was, in his words, too easy (people are almost inevitably going to identify themselves with their actions and decisions and hence be reluctant to change because of the implications for their self-concept) his strategies for changing behavior entailed separating people psychologically from the self-evaluating implications of their actions. This separation could be done by telling them (a) that the decision they had made seemed right at the time but because of changed circumstances that no one could have foreseen, the decision might no longer be optimal, or (b) telling them that even though they may have felt that they made the decision without constraint and were therefore identified with it because it was their choice, in fact, given various external circumstances, they actually had no choice.

This strategy of separating people from the self-defining implications of their choices is nicely illustrated in the film *12 Angry Men* in which the protagonist, an architect originally played by Henry Fonda, has the task of changing the minds of 11 fellow jurors who have already publicly declared that they believe the defendant is guilty. His way of separating people from their public commitment to the defendant's guilt largely relies on permitting people to change their minds without having to admit they made an error in judgment that would reflect badly on themselves. Fonda's character argues that, given the evidence they saw and the skill and interest (low) of the public defender, it was reasonable for them to think the defendant was guilty, but that the jurors did not see all the evidence because the defense attorney, a public defender taking on an unpopular case for little reward, might not have done a good job. The tactic of separating people from issues is one that is also advocated in the influential text on negotiations *Getting to Yes* (Fisher and Ury 1983). Consistent with self-enhancement theories, they argue that one common reason why negotiations are so often unsuccessful is because people tend to become personally involved with the negotiation issues and perceive negotiation attempts as personal attacks. By separating people from their positions, effective negotiators can deemphasize self-enhancing tendencies that may prevent all parties from recognizing integrative and efficient solutions.

Finally, this line of argument would suggest that evaluation of decisions will be less likely in domains that are self-implicating or central to one's self-image (Proposition 8). Note that this type of behavior seems particularly maladaptive. Our tendency to self-enhance might lead us to be most vulnerable to not learning or seeing mistakes in the most important domains. Another implication of this type of escalation of commitment is that we are not as likely to learn from our mistakes as our successes. A great deal of social psychological literature has demonstrated that, in part because of self-enhancement motives, individuals are more likely to attribute positive outcomes to internal, personal causes and to attribute negative outcomes to external causes (e.g., Bernstein et al. 1979, Miller 1977, Miller and Ross 1975). And, as self-enhancement tendencies would predict, people are even more likely to assume personal responsibility for success, but disavow personal responsibility for failure in domains that are seen as important to them (Campbell and Sedikides 1999, Miller 1977).

It should be noted that some research has empirically demonstrated that increased accountability can also lead to decreased self-enhancement effects. Sedikides et al. (2002) demonstrated that when they made participants accountable by asking them to justify and defend their own self-evaluations, participants were less likely to self-enhance. However, in their research, participants were already engaged in self-evaluation processes because they were being asked to grade themselves. We are arguing that self-enhancement will generally lead to a decreased desire to evaluate oneself, and lowering accountability might lead to more willingness for evaluation, therefore decreasing the tendency to escalate commitment.

The Illusion of Influence, Overestimation of Individual Efficacy, the Persistence of Hierarchy, and Disinhibition

Once having achieved a position of influence, self-enhancement can contribute to the processes that maintain individuals in powerful positions. It also contributes to those behaviors that result in an ultimate fall from power. One of the ways in which power becomes institutionalized is through formal positions and titles, part and parcel of the organizational hierarchy. People defer to others because of their role and formal authority, and that authority derives from the organizational structure. The interesting question is why, in spite of many claims that hierarchical arrangements are disappearing in a world in which knowledge rather than position is increasingly important, hierarchy is so persistent (Tiedens and Fragale 2003).

There are some interesting implications of self-enhancement ideas that can help us understand (a) why organizations persist in using hierarchical arrangements even though there is extensive evidence for the positive effects of more participative, decentralized arrangements (e.g., Levine and Tyson 1990), and (b) some aspects of leader behavior such as the acceptance of large compensation packages by CEOs and the tendency of leaders and others in high-status positions to more actively intervene in situations, even when they do not necessarily have the knowledge or experience to actually make things better. Some research has already demonstrated a self-serving bias in causal attributions. For example, Ross and Sicoly (1979) demonstrated that group members, such as married couples and basketball team players, overestimate the amount that they contributed to a group outcome. We argue that not only is the quantity of contribution overestimated, but the quality of our contributions is also judged to be higher. The critical dynamic is this: To feel positively about oneself and one's actions, it is likely that not only will a person overestimate his or her possession of positive traits and overvalue traits that they believe they hold, but in a similar fashion come to overvalue and overestimate the efficacy of their interventions in situations.

This phenomenon is nicely illustrated in a study demonstrating faith in one's own supervision of work (Pfeffer et al. 1998). In the experimental study, participants in all three conditions believed that they were supervising the work of a colleague (who had come to the experiment at the same time) working on developing an advertisement. In one condition, participants were told that they would be too busy to oversee the work of their subordinate and would, therefore, only see the final draft of an advertisement for the Swatch Watch case. In a second condition, participants were told they would see an intermediate draft of the advertisement but would not be able to provide feedback to their colleague. In the final condition, participants saw the same intermediate draft and ostensibly provided feedback for improving the advertisement on a standardized form. In each of the three conditions, participants saw and rated the identical final advertisement. In the third condition, participants rated the advertisement significantly more positively and also rated both their effectiveness as a manager and the quality of their subordinate as better than in the other conditions. The relationship between perceived involvement in the managerial process and the rating of the work product was linear, with the advertisement being most highly rated in the third condition, less highly rated in the second, and least highly rated in the first condition. Interestingly, when the advertisement was shown to a control group not involved in the experiment at all, they rated it even less favorably, providing some evidence that the mere participation in the study was enough to cause participants to respond to their involvement in the situation by rating the work product more favorably.

The results of this study are consistent with the large literature on the illusion of control (Langer 1983) that shows that people are willing to bet more on random events when they have the opportunity to actually roll the dice or draw the card from the deck. The illusion of control is an effect completely compatible with the self-enhancement concept: one way of maintaining a favorable view of the self is to see that self as efficacious and competent. Therefore, to the extent one is actively involved in overseeing or actually doing some task, there is a motive to believe that this activity is going to be effective, in order to maintain a positive self image. Therefore, individuals will believe that their intervention in supervisory situations makes things better and that, even in random events, their intervention will produce a better outcome, on which they are actually willing to wager more money. This illusion of control effect may also help account for why people invest more in more actively managed mutual funds, again believing that intervention, including their intervention to find the "best" fund and the actions of fund managers, contributes to success. The argument suggests that feelings of self-worth mediate illusion of control and illusion of influence effects, a possibility that is worth empirical examination (Proposition 9).

Given this illusion of influence (Pfeffer and Cialdini 1998) in which people believe that their interventions have effects and make things better, it is not at all surprising to see the persistence of hierarchical arrangements in organizations. To give up supervision or control is to, following the logic of self-enhancement, run the substantial risk of having worse decisions made and worse outcomes occur because things are better when we intervene and provide direction. Moreover, intervention makes us feel more positively about ourselves and our abilities and even feel more positively about those we are directing. Consequently, decentralization and the devolution of control must fight these compelling social psychological forces to be implemented.

The overestimation of one's personal effectiveness in intervening in situations would logically lead to overvaluing one's contributions to organizational success. One of the perplexing questions raised in light of escalating CEO salaries is, "How could they be so greedy?" One possible answer is that senior executives do not see themselves as greedy at all, but rather as the causal force responsible for the success of their organizations and key to the future of those companies. As described above, self-enhancement tendencies can lead individuals to attribute blame to external causes when negative events occur, but when positive events (such as company success) occur, self-enhancement will lead CEOs to attribute this success to their own internal causes (Bradley 1978, Campbell and Sedikides 1999, Miller and Ross 1975). Thus, the desire to self-enhancement will drive CEOs to attribute company success to their own leadership abilities, and may also drive them to pay themselves accordingly. Moreover, the same dynamic would affect the board members who set their salaries. We have already noted that people prefer to associate with winners and with success. To set a CEO's salary at a high level helps to signify and signal the success of that individual and, by association, the members of the board. To set the CEO's salary at a comparatively low level means that the CEO and, by association and extension, the board doing that salary setting are not above average.

The overestimation of personal effectiveness and the illusion of control can also lead to negative consequences for powerful people, including behaviors that ultimately cause them to lose power. Keltner et al. (2003) have argued that the experience of power leads to certain consequences, including disinhibited behavior. They argue that because power is associated with rewards, it activates the approach system, which influences behaviors such as eating, aggression, and sexual behaviors. Their comprehensive review of the power literature demonstrates that individuals experiencing elevated power are more likely to invade others' personal space, display disinhibited sexual behavior, and act on their desires in socially inappropriate ways. For example, Ward and Keltner (1998) randomly assigned one individual in a group of three to a high power position by giving them the task of assigning experimental points to the other two. These experimenters then had the group of three engage in a 30 minute discussion, at which time the group was given a plate of five cookies. They found that high-power individuals were more likely to take a second cookie, and furthermore they were more likely to eat in disinhibited ways, chewing with their mouths open and getting crumbs on the table.

This study, in conjunction with several others, provides compelling evidence of some pernicious effects of power. First, these types of experiments demonstrate the apparent ease in priming a feeling of power, a phenomenon that is quite consistent with the tendency to self-enhance. Second, the studies underscore a potential path to the loss of power, by demonstrating that high-power people are less likely to attend to social norms and social context. In other words, Keltner et al. (2003) argue that high-power individuals attend more to themselves and less to the interests of others. The paradox is that people often reach positions of power precisely by knowing what others want and need and being able to provide those behaviors and resources that cause others to rely on them. Why would people, once in power, "forget" the behaviors and strategies they used to acquire power in the first place? Of course, not all do. However to self-enhance, individuals will not necessarily want to remember earlier times when they had less power and will, instead, prefer to see themselves as more powerful than others because of their inherent traits and abilities, not because they worked harder or were more attentive to the needs of others. This leads to the prediction that individuals who are more prone to self-enhancement will also be more vulnerable to the disinhibiting effects of power (Proposition 10). Consequently, self-enhancement and the effects of power on the power holder will, if unchecked, tend to produce behaviors that will cause people to lose power, with this problem being attenuated by the fact that others, preferring to associate with successful people, will not necessarily be inclined to question or challenge those in power.

Discussion

By emphasizing one fundamental and frequently empirically demonstrated phenomenon, that individuals tend to see themselves and their actions in a positive light, we have drawn a number of connections between literatures that are often treated as distinct and unrelated. In particular, we have argued that the phenomena of escalating commitment, similarity attraction, disinhibition by the powerful, illusion of control, persistence of hierarchical arrangements, reluctance to delegate discretion to others, and occasional voluntary subjugation of the self are all conceptually related to self-enhancement ideas. We have also suggested potential empirical studies of both mediation and main effects that can elucidate the operation of self-enhancement in organizational situations of power and influence. By starting investigations of power and influence processes and related phenomena by asking what the implications and connections are to ideas of self-enhancement, it is possible to more parsimoniously account for various behaviors and derive a logical and coherent account for many observations of organizational life.

We are certainly not asserting either that self-enhancement accounts for everything, nor that it even accounts for all of the causes of homosocial reproduction (Kanter 1977), submission of the self to degrading conditions, the perseverance of hierarchical relationships, the resistance of hierarchy to being eliminated, and the avoidance of evaluation of decisions and their consequences accompanied by perseverance and commitment. There are obviously other fundamental social motives and social processes at work, and behavior is complex enough that no single explanation could be expected to be complete and all inclusive.

We have tried to illustrate, at least in one domain of interest, that it is possible to build a conceptual structure that ties a number of ideas and phenomena together in a way that provides both coherence and some interesting insights and observations. We do this to encourage other efforts of the same sort, both in this topic domain and in others, using self-enhancement and other foundational theoretical constructs that can provide similar conceptual leverage. Conceptual model building of this sort seems to be an important task for building an organization science that can be remembered, transmitted, and can compete successfully with other conceptually integrated, parsimonious approaches to understanding social behavior.

Acknowledgments

The authors appreciate the comments of Dale Miller and Charles O'Reilly on an earlier draft of this paper.

References

Barsade, Sigal G., Andrew J. Ward, Jean D. F. Turner, Jeffrey A. Sonnenfeld. 2000. To your heart's content: A model of affective diversity in top management teams. *Admin. Sci. Quart.* **45** 802–805.

Baumeister, Roy E., Todd F. Heatherton, Dianne M. Tice. 1993. When ego threats lead to self-regulation failure: Negative consequences of high self-esteem. *J. Personality Soc. Psych.* **64** 141–156.

Bazerman, Max H. 2005. Conducting influential research: The need for prescriptive implications. *Acad. Management Rev.* **30** 25–31.

Bernstein, Michael. 2001. *A Perilous Progress: Economists and Public Purpose in Twentieth-Century America.* Princeton University Press, Princeton, NJ.

Bernstein, William M., Walter G. Stephan, Mark H. Davis. 1979. Explaining attributions for achievement: A path analytic approach. *J. Personality Soc. Psych.* **65** 198–204.

Berscheid, Ellen, Elaine H. Walster. 1969. *Interpersonal Attraction.* Addison-Wesley, Reading, MA.

Bethune, Gordon. 1998. *From Worst to First.* Wiley, New York.

Billig, Michael, Henri Tajfel. 1973. Social categorization and similarity in intergroup behavior. *Eur. J. Soc. Psych.* **3** 27–52.

Blaine, Bruce, Jennifer Crocker. 1993. Self-esteem and self-serving biases in reaction to positive and negative events: An integrative review. R. F. Baumeister, ed. *Self-Esteem: The Puzzle of Low Self-Regard.* Erlbaum, Hillsdale, NJ, 55–85.

Blau, Peter M. 1970. A formal theory of differentiation in organizations. *Amer. Sociological Rev.* **35** 201–218.

Bobocel, D. Ramona, John P. Meyer. 1994. Escalating commitment to a failing course of action: Separating the role of choice and justification. *J. Appl. Psych.* **79** 360–363.

Bradley, Gifford W. 1978. Self serving biases in the attribution process: A reexamination of the fact or fiction question. *J. Personality Soc. Psych.* **36** 56–71.

Brewer, Marilyn B. 1979. In-group bias in the minimal intergroup situation: A cognitive-motivational analysis. *Psych. Bull.* **86** 307–324.

Brewer, Marilyn B., Roderick M. Kramer. 1985. The psychology of intergroup attitudes and behavior. *Ann. Rev. Psych.* **36** 219–243.

Brockner, Joel, Robert Houser, Gregg Birnbaum. 1986. Escalation of commitment to an ineffective course of action: The effect of feedback having negative implications for self-identity. *Admin. Sci. Quart.* **31** 109–126.

Brown, Jonathan D. 1986. Evaluations of self and others: Self-enhancement biases in social judgments. *Soc. Cognition* **4** 353–376.

Burger, Jerry M., Nicole Messian, Shebani Patel, Alicia del Prado, Carmen Anderson. 2004. What a coincidence! The effects of incidental similarity on compliance. *Personality Soc. Psych. Bull.* **30** 35–43.

Byrne, David. 1971. *The Attraction Paradigm.* Academic Press, New York.

Byron, Christopher M. 1986. *The Fanciest Dive.* W. W. Norton, New York.

Campbell, Keith W., Constantine Sedikides. 1999. Self-threat magnifies the self-serving bias: A meta-analytic integration. *Rev. General Psych.* **3** 23–43.

Caro, Richard A. 1982. *The Path to Power: The Years of Lyndon Johnson.* Knopf, New York.

Carver, Charles S., Michael F. Scheier. 1998. *On the Self-Regulation of Behavior.* Cambridge University Press, New York.

Chase, William G., Herbert A. Simon. 1973. Perception in chess. *Cognitive Psych.* **4** 55–81.

Cialdini, Robert B. 2001. *Influence: Science and Practice,* 4th ed. Allyn & Bacon, Boston, MA.

Cialdini, Robert B., K. D. Richardson. 1980. Two indirect tactics of image management: Basking and blasting. *J. Personality Soc. Psych.* **39** 406–415.

Cialdini, Robert B., Richard J. Borden, Avril Thorne, Marcus R. Walker, Steven Freeman, Lloyd R. Sloan. 1976. Basking in reflected glory: Three (football) field studies. *J. Personality Soc. Psych.* **34** 366–375.

Clore, Gerald L., Donn A. Byrne. 1974. A reinforcement-affect model of attraction. T. L. Huston, ed. *Foundations of Interpersonal Attraction.* Academic Press, New York, 143–170.

Comer, Ronald, James D. Laird. 1975. Choosing to suffer as a consequence of expecting to suffer: Why do people do it? *J. Personality Soc. Psych.* **32** 92–101.

Crocker, Jennifer. 2002. The costs of seeking self-esteem. *J. Soc. Issues* **3** 597–615.

Davis, Gerald F., Christopher Marquis. 2005. Prospects for organization theory in the early 21st century: Institutional fields and mechanisms. *Organ. Sci.* **16**(4) 332–343.

de Groot, A. D. 1965. *Thought and Choice in Chess.* The Hague, Mouton, The Netherlands.

Dunning, David, Judith A. Meyerowitz, Amy D. Holzberg. 1989. Ambiguity and self-evaluation: The role of idiosyncratic trait definitions in self-serving assessments of ability. *J. Personality Soc. Psych.* **57** 1082–1090.

Eccles, Jacquelynne S., Allan Wigfield. 1995. In the mind of the actor: The structure of adolescents' achievement task values and expectancy related beliefs. *Personality Soc. Psych. Bull.* **21** 215–225.

Festinger, Leon. 1957. *A Theory of Cognitive Dissonance*. Stanford University Press, Stanford, CA.

Fisher, Roger, William Ury. 1983. *Getting to Yes: Negotiating Agreement Without Giving In*. Penguin Books, New York.

Fiske, Susan T. 2004. *Social Beings: Core Motives in Social Psychology*. Wiley, New York.

Gabor, Andrea. 1990. *The Man Who Discovered Quality*. Times Books, New York.

Ghoshal, Sumantra. 2005. Bad management theories are destroying good management practice. *Acad. Management Learn. Ed.* **4** 75–91.

Ghoshal, Sumantra, Peter Moran. 1996. Bad for practice: A critique of the transaction cost theory. *Acad. Management Rev.* **21** 13–47.

Gittell, Jody H. 2000. Paradox of coordination and control. *California Management Rev.* **42** 1–17.

Goethals, George R., David M. Messick, Scott T. Allison. 1991. The uniqueness bias: Studies of constructive social comparison. Jerry Suls, Thomas Ashby, eds. *Social Comparison: Contemporary Theory and Research*. Lawrence Erlbaum, Hillsdale, NJ, 149–176.

Granovetter, Mark. 1973. The strength of weak ties. *Amer. J. Sociology* **78** 1360–1380.

Halberstam, David. 1986. *The Reckoning*. William Morrow, New York.

Haslam, S. Alexander. 2000. *Psychology in Organizations: The Social Identity Approach*. Sage, London, UK.

Hastorf, Albert, David Schneider, Judith Polefka. 1970. *Person Perception*. Addison-Wesley, Reading, MA.

Heath, Chip. 1999. On the social psychology of agency relationships: Lay theories of motivation overemphasize extrinsic incentives. *Organ. Behavior Human Decision Process* **78** 25–62.

Heider, Fritz. 1958. *The Psychology of Interpersonal Relations*. Wiley, New York.

Heine, Steven J., Darrin R. Lehman. 1997a. Culture, dissonance, and self-affirmation. *Personality Soc. Psych. Bull.* **23** 389–400.

Heine, Steven J., Darrin R. Lehman. 1997b. The cultural construction of self-enhancement: An examination of group-serving biases. *J. Personality Soc. Psych.* **72** 1268–1283.

Heine, Steven J., Darrin R. Lehman, Hazel R. Markus, Shinobu Kitayama. 1999. Is there a universal need for positive self-regard? *Psych. Rev.* **106** 766–794.

Heracleous, Loizos, John Murray. 2001. The urge to merge in the pharmaceutical industry. *Eur. Management J.* **19** 430.

Ibarra, Herminia. 1992. Homophily and differential returns: Sex differences in network structures and access in an advertising firm. *Admin. Sci. Quart.* **37** 422–447.

Ibarra, Herminia, Martin Kilduff, Wenpin Tsai. 2005. Zooming in and out: Connecting individuals and collectivities at the frontiers of organizational network research. *Organ. Sci.* **16**(4) 359–371.

Isaacson, Walter. 1992. *Kissinger: A Biography*. Simon and Schuster, New York.

James, William. 1907. *The Principles of Psychology*, Vol. 1. Holt, New York.

John, Oliver P., Richard W. Robins. 1994. Accuracy and bias in self-perception: Individual differences in self-enhancement and the role of narcissism. *J. Personality Soc. Psych.* **66** 206–219.

Kanter, Rosabeth M. 1977. *Men and Women of the Corporation*. Basic, New York.

Keltner, Dacher, Deborah H. Gruenfeld, Cameron Anderson. 2003. Power, approach, and inhibition. *Psych. Rev.* **110** 265–284.

Kenrick, Douglas T., Steven L. Neuberg, Robert B. Cialdini. 2002. *Social Psychology: Unraveling the Mystery*. Allyn and Bacon, Boston, MA.

Kramer, Roderick M., Elizabeth Newton, Pamela L. Pommerenke. 1993. Self-enhancement biases and negotiator judgment: Effects of self-esteem and mood. *Organ. Behavior Human Decision Process* **56** 110–133.

Krueger, Jennifer. 1998. Enhancement bias in descriptions of self and others. *Personality Soc. Psych. Bull.* **24** 505–516.

Kruger, Justin, David Dunning. 1999. Unskilled and unaware of it: How difficulties in recognizing one's own incompetence lead to inflated self-assessments. *J. Personality Soc. Psych.* **77** 1121–1134.

Kunda, Ziva. 1990. The case for motivated reasoning. *Psych. Bull.* **108** 480–498.

Kunda, Ziva, Rasyid Santioso. 1989. Motivated changes in the self-concept. *J. Experiment. Soc. Psych.* **25** 272–285.

Langer, Ellen J. 1983. *The Psychology of Control.* Sage, Beverly Hills, CA.

Lawrence, Paul R., Nitin Nohria. 2002. *Driven: How Human Nature Shapes Our Choices.* Jossey-Bass, San Francisco, CA.

Levine, David I., Laura D. Tyson. 1990. Participation, productivity, and the firm's environment. A. S. Blinder, ed. *Paying for Productivity: A Look at the Evidence.* Brookings Institution, Washington, D.C., 183–237.

Lewis, Amy C., Steven J. Sherman. 2003. Hiring you makes me look bad: Social-identity based reversals of the ingroup favoritism effect. *Organ. Behavior Human Decision Process* **90** 262–276.

Lewis, Reginald F., Blair S. Walker, Hugh B. Price. 1994. *Why Should White Guys Have All the Fun? How Reginald Lewis Created a Billion-Dollar Business Empire.* John Wiley, New York.

Lewisohn, Peter M., Walter Mischel, William Chaplin, Russell Baron. 1980. Social competence and depression: The role of illusory self-perceptions. *J. Abnormal Psych.* **89** 203–212.

Lipman-Blumen, Jean. 2004. *The Allure of Toxic Leaders: Why We Follow Destructive Bosses and Corrupt Politicians—And How We Can Survive Them.* Oxford University Press, New York.

Marques, Jose M., Dominic Abrams, Rui G. Serodio. 2001. Being better by being right: Subjective group dynamics and derogation of in-group deviants when generic norms are undermined. *J. Personality Soc. Psych.* **81** 436–447.

McGuire, William J. 1985. Attitudes and attitude change. G. Lindzey, E. Aronson, eds. *The Handbook of Social Psychology,* 3rd ed. Random House, New York, 233–346.

Miller, Dale T. 1977. Ego involvement and attributions for success and failure. *J. Personality Soc. Psych.* **34** 901–906.

Miller, Dale T., Michael Ross. 1975. Self-serving biases in the attribution of causality: Fact or fiction? *Psych. Bull.* **82** 213–225.

Mone, Mark A., William McKinley. 1993. The uniqueness value and its consequences for organization studies. *J. Management Inquiry* **2** 284–296.

Moore, William L., Jeffrey Pfeffer. 1980. The relationship between departmental power and faculty careers on two campuses: The case for structural effects on faculty salaries. *Res. Higher Ed.* **13** 291–306.

Morris, Michael W., Kaipeng Peng. 1994. Culture and cause: American and Chinese attributions for social and physical events. *J. Personality Soc. Psych.* **67** 949–971.

Nemeth, Charlan J. 1994. The value of minority dissent. S. Moscovici, A. Mucchi-Faina, eds. *Minority Influence.* Nelson-Hall Publishers, Chicago, IL, 3–15.

Nemeth, Charlan J., Julianne L. Kwan. 1987. Minority influence, divergent thinking and detection of correct solutions. *J. Appl. Soc. Psych.* **17** 788–799.

Ng, Sik H. 1981. Equity theory and the allocation of rewards between groups. *Eur. J. Soc. Psych.* **11** 439–443.

O'Reilly, Charles A., Diane F. Caldwell, William P. Barnett. 1989. Work group demography, social integration and turnover. *Admin. Sci. Quart.* **34** 21–37.

Peli, Gabor L., Lazlos Polos, Michael Hannan. 2000. Back to inertia: Theoretical implications of alternative styles of logical formalization. *Soc. Theory* **18** 195–215.

Pfeffer, Jeffrey. 1993. Barriers to the advance of organizational science: Paradigm development as a dependent variable. *Acad. Management Rev.* **18** 599–620.

Pfeffer, Jeffrey. 1997. *New Directions for Organization Theory.* Oxford, New York.

Pfeffer, Jeffrey, Robert B. Cialdini. 1998. Illusions of influence. Roderick M. Kramer, Margaret A. Neale, eds. *Power and Influence in Organizations.* Sage, Thousand Oaks, CA, 1–20.

Pfeffer, Jeffrey, Alison M. Konrad. 1991. The effects of individual power on earnings. *Work Occupations* **18** 385–414.

Pfeffer, Jeffrey, Robert B. Cialdini, Benjamin Hanna, Kathleen Knopoff. 1998. Faith in supervision and the self-enhancement bias: Two psychological reasons why managers don't empower workers. *Basic Appl. Soc. Psych.* **20** 313–321.

Podolny, Joel M., James N. Baron. 1997. Resources and relationships: Social networks, mobility, and satisfaction in the workplace. *Amer. Sociological Rev.* **62** 673–693.

Polzer, Jeffrey T., Roderick M. Kramer, Margaret A. Neale. 1997. Positive illusions about oneself and one's group: Antecedents and consequences. *Small Group Res.* **28** 243–266.

Rose, Frank. 1989. *West of Eden: The End of Innocence at Apple Computer.* Penguin, New York.

Ross, Michael, Fiore Sicoly. 1980. Egocentric biases in availability and attribution. *J. Personality Soc. Psych.* **37** 322–336.

Rynes, Sara L., Christine Q. Trank, Anne M. Lawson, Remus Ilies. 2003. Behavioral coursework in business education: Growing evidence of a legitimacy crisis. *Acad. Management Learn. Ed.* **2** 269–283.

Salancik, Gerald R. 1977. Commitment and the control of organizational behavior and belief. Barry M. Staw, Gerald R. Salancik, eds. *New Directions in Organizational Behavior.* St. Clair Press, Chicago, IL, 1–54.

Scott, W. Richard. 1998. *Organizations: Rational, Natural, and Open Systems,* 4th ed. Prentice Hall, Upper Saddle River, NJ.

Sedikides, Constantine, Jeffrey D. Green. 2000a. On the self-protective nature of inconsistency negativity management: Using the person memory paradigm to examine self-referent memory. *J. Personality Soc. Psych.* **79** 906–922.

Sedikides, Constantine, Jeffrey D. Green. 2000b. The rocky road from affect to attentional focus. Herbert Bless, Joseph P. Forgas, eds. *The Message Within: The Role of Subjective Experience in Social Cognition and Behavior.* Psychology Press, Philadelphia, PA, 203–215.

Sedikides, Constantine, Kenneth C. Herbst, Deletha P. Hardin, Gregory J. Dardis. 2002. Accountability as a deterrent to self-enhancement: The search for mechanisms. *J. Personality Soc. Psych.* **83** 592–605.

Sherif, Muzafer, O. J. Harvey, B. Jack White, William R. Hood, Carolyn W. Sherif. 1961. *Intergroup Conflict and Cooperation: The Robber's Cave Experiment.* University of Oklahoma Press, Norman, OK.

Staw, Barry M. 1976. Knee deep in the big muddy: A study of escalating commitment to a chosen course of action. *Organ. Behavior Human Performance* **16** 27–44.

Steele, Claude M., Thomas J. Liu. 1981. Making the dissonance act unreflective of the self: Dissonance avoidance and the expectancy of a value affirming response. *Personality Soc. Psych. Bull.* **45** 5–19.

Swann, William B. Jr. 1997. The trouble with change: Self-verification and allegiance to the self. *Psych. Sci.* **8** 177–180.

Tajfel, Henri, John C. Turner. 1986. The social identity theory of intergroup behavior. Stephen Worchel, William G. Austin, eds. *Psychology of Intergroup Behavior.* Nelson-Hall, Chicago, IL, 7–24.

Taylor, Shelley E., David A. Armor. 1996. Positive illusions and coping with adversity. *J. Personality* **64** 873–899.

Taylor, Shelley E., Jonathan D. Brown. 1988. Illusion and well-being: A psychological perspective on mental health. *Psych. Bull.* **103** 193–210.

Taylor, Shelley E., Jennifer S. Lerner, David K. Sherman, Rebecca M. Sage, Nina K. McDowell. 2003. Portrait of the self-enhancer: Well adjusted and well liked or maladjusted and friendless? *J. Personality Soc. Psych.* **84** 165–176.

Tesser, Abraham. 1988. Toward a self-evaluation maintenance model of social behavior. L. Berkowitz, ed. *Advances in Experimental Social Psychology,* Vol. 21. Academic Press, New York, 181–227.

Tiedens, Larissa Z., Alison R. Fragale. 2003. Power moves: Complimentarity in dominant and submissive nonverbal behavior. *J. Personality Soc. Psych.* **84** 558–568.

Tsui, Anne S., Terri D. Egan, Charles A. O'Reilly. 1992. Being different: Relational demography and organizational attachment. *Admin. Sci. Quart.* **37** 549–579.

Tsui, Anne S., Terri D. Egan, Katherine R. Xin. 1995. Diversity in organizations: Lessons from demography research. Martin Chemers, Mark Costanzo, Stuart Oskamp, eds. *Diversity in Organizations.* Sage, Newbury Park, CA, 191–219.

Useem, Michael, Jerome Karabel. 1986. Pathways to top corporate management. *Amer. Sociological Rev.* **51** 184–200.

Ward, G., Dacher Keltner. 1998. Power and the consumption of resources. Unpublished manuscript.

Williams, Katherine Y., Charles A. O'Reilly. 1998. Demography and diversity in organizations: A review of 40 years of research. Barry M. Staw, Robert I. Sutton, eds. *Research in Organizational Behavior*. Vol. 20. JAI Press, Greenwich, CT, 77–140.

Wills, Thomas A. 1981. Downward comparison principles in social psychology. *Psych. Bull.* **90** 245–271.

Wood, Joanne V., Katherine L. Taylor. 1991. Serving self-relevant goals through social comparison. Jerry Suls, Thomas A. Wills, eds. *Social Comparison: Contemporary Theory and Research*. Lawrence Erlbaum Associates, Hillsdale, NJ, 23–41.

Zammuto, Ray F., Terry Connolly. 1984. Coping with disciplinary fragmentation. *Organ. Behavior Teaching Rev.* **9** 30–37.

Zenger, Todd R., Barbara S. Lawrence. 1989. Organizational demography: The differential effects of age and tenure distributions on technical communication. *Acad. Management J.* **32** 353–376.

12 Structuring the Organization

12.1 WHAT IS THE RIGHT ORGANIZATION DESIGN?

N. Anand and Richard L. Daft

Introduction

A start-up company in Florida, called World Response Group (WRG), developed an unusual woven mat for the horticulture industry that was made from all-natural fibers. Horticulture growers in the U.S. produce hundreds of millions of potted plants each year. The product, called SmartGrow, dramatically reduced weed growth in potted plants and simultaneously provided important nutrients—all with no chemicals. SmartGrow raw materials and manufacturing expertise were available in China and India. As the company grew, the managers and board members talked frequently about organization structure. Two schools of thought emerged. One group wanted to import raw materials into the U.S. for manufacturing by WRG and thereby have direct control over manufacturing, marketing, and sales. These functions would be departments within WRG. The second group wanted to import already manufactured and packaged products from overseas, outsource marketing to an agency, and hire a horticulture distribution company to handle sales. The second group pushed the concept that no one within the company would ever touch the product. Nor would there be functional departments for manufacturing, marketing, and sales.

That discussion of structure within WRG would not have occurred 30 years ago when Robert Duncan published his seminal article, "What is the Right Organization Structure?" in *Organization Dynamics* in 1979. At that time, organizations were thought to be self-contained, and structure defined the reporting relationships among internal functional departments. Duncan's article provided important insights about the conditions under which different internal arrangements would achieve a company's mission. His insights are still referenced in management textbooks today.

The purpose of this article is to present key developments in organization structure and design that have occurred since Duncan's article and describe when each can be used for greatest effect. We will briefly review the important structural designs from 30 years ago and then describe key developments since that time. The concepts are organized into three eras, which reflect substantive changes in management thinking from vertical organization to horizontal organizing to open boundaries via outsourcing and partnering.

Era 1: Self-Contained Organization Designs

The first era of organizational design probably took hold in the mid-1800s, and was dominant until the late 1970s. In Era 1, the ideal organization was self-contained. It had clear
boundaries between it and suppliers, customers or competitors. Inputs arrived at the organization's gate, and after a transformation process, left as a completed product or service. Almost everything that was required during the transformation process was supplied
internally. Design philosophies from this era emphasized the need to adapt to different
environmental and internal contingencies and the ability to control the different parts of the
organization through reporting relationships in a vertical chain of command.

The structure of self-contained organizations can be thought of as: (1) the grouping of
people into functions or departments; (2) the reporting relationships among people and
departments; and (3) the systems to ensure coordination and integration of activities both
horizontally and vertically. The structures of this era, including functional, division, and
matrix designs, rely largely on the vertical hierarchy and chain of command to define
departmental groupings and reporting relationships.

Functional

In a functional structure, activities are grouped together by common function from the
bottom to the top of the organization. Each functional activity—accounting, engineering,
human resources, manufacturing, etc.—is grouped into a specific department. Most small
companies use this structure, as do many large government organizations and divisions of
large companies.

Divisional

The divisional structure occurs when departments are grouped together based on organizational outputs. The divisional structure is sometimes called a product structure or profit
center. Most large companies have separate divisions that use different technologies or serve
different customers. People within each division have more product focus, accountability,
and flexibility than would be the case if they were part of a huge functional structure. For
example, United Technologies Corporation (UTC), which is among the 50 largest U.S.
industrial firms, has product divisions for air-conditioning and heating (Carrier), elevators
and escalators (Otis), aircraft engines (Pratt & Whitney), helicopters (Sikorsky), and aero-
space (Hamilton Sundstrand), among others. Each division acts like a stand-alone company,
doing its own product development, marketing, and finance.

Horizontal Overlays and Matrix

Few organizations can be successful today with a pure functional structure, because the
resulting functional or divisional silos inhibit the amount of coordination needed in a changing competitive environment. Organizations break down silos by using a variety of horizontal linkage mechanisms to improve communication among departments and divisions.
These coordination relationships are often drawn on organization charts as dotted lines.
Many organizations use full-time product managers, project managers, or brand managers,
to coordinate the work of several departments. The brand manager for Planters Peanuts, for
example, serves as an integrator by coordinating the sales, advertising, and distribution for

that product. General Motors Corp. has brand managers who are integrators responsible for marketing and sales strategies for each of GM's new models.

Organizations that need even stronger horizontal coordination may evolve to a matrix structure. The matrix combines a vertical structure with an equally strong horizontal overlay. While the vertical structure provides traditional control within functional departments, the horizontal overlay provides coordination across departments to achieve profit goals. This structure has lines of formal authority along two dimensions, such as functional and product or product and region. Some employees report to two bosses simultaneously. For example, after a regional marketing promotion went $10 million over budget, Nike Inc. managers engineered a matrix structure that assigned dual responsibility by product and region to manage the introduction of new products each year. Headquarters establishes which product to push. Then product managers determine how to do it, but regional managers have authority to modify plans for their regions. Nike's matrix provides a counterbalance between product manager and regional manager ambitions.

Era 2: Horizontal Organization Design with Team- and Process-Based Emphasis

The second era of organizational design started in the 1980s. As the world grew increasingly complex, organizations of Era 2 experienced the limits of traditional designs. Coordination between departmental silos within the organization became more difficult, and vertical authority-based reporting systems often were not effective in creating value for customers. At the same time, information processing capacity of organizations improved greatly, due to the availability of personal computers and networks. Design philosophies of this era emphasize the need to reshape the internal boundaries of the organization in order to improve coordination and communication.

The horizontal organization emphasizes reengineering along workflow processes that link organizational capabilities to customers and suppliers. While traditional self-contained organizations of Era 1 embodied the need for hierarchical control and separate functional specializations, the horizontal organization advocated the dispensing of internal boundaries that are an impediment to effective business performance. If the traditional structure can be likened to a pyramid, the metaphor that best applies to the horizontal organization is a pizza—flat, but packed with all the necessary ingredients.

Examples

New product development is one context in which the horizontal organization design is most appropriate. Take the example of Ford Motor Co.'s Escape gas-electric hybrid sport utility vehicle (SUV), conceived in response to consumer demand and competition from rivals such as Toyota Motor Corp. and Nissan Motor Co. Ford adopted the horizontal organization design, which involved creation of a cross-functional team to handle the entire workflow for developing and launching a new automobile model. The team included highly accomplished individuals from research and product engineering—two groups that are traditionally in separate silos in Ford. There were two team leaders, one with experience in product development and another with expertise in launching vehicles in the market on time. In the development phase, the team invested a considerable amount of time learning about customer requirements firsthand, by talking to potential owners in addition to relying on market research reports. The research scientists and engineers shared a common office space, discussed emerging issues over group lunches, and improved product design through hallway chats. The team was sheltered from the rest of the organization and provided with resources rapidly as and when required. For example, when discussions with the Japanese battery supplier were stalling because of language difficulty, the Ford corporate office dispatched an engineer fluent in Japanese to help the team out. Once the prototype vehicle was developed, the team shifted into launch mode in order to get it ready for production. The team started working more intensively with outside suppliers that provided critical parts for the new vehicle and were always around to solve manufacturing problems. The Escape Hybrid SUV was launched on time and is regarded by industry experts as a successful product for Ford.

Other firms that have used the horizontal organization for new product development include Xerox Corp., Lexmark Printers, and Eastman Kodak Co. Another domain in which this design works effectively is in back-office tasks of financial services firms that involve handoffs to multiple departments. Barclays Bank in the U.K. uses the horizontal design for its mortgage services, incorporating legal and relocation services in addition to traditional tasks such as loan sanctioning and credit assessment.

The design features of the horizontal organization are summarized in Table 12.1.1.

Design Principles

Five principles govern the design of a horizontal organization. First, organize around complete workflow processes rather than departments. The key is to move away from a traditional department-centered mindset of breaking things down by functions. Instead, think about how different pieces of work are holistically accomplished in the organization. For example, at Progressive Casualty Insurance Company, adjusters and claims personnel are organized into teams that handle the entire claims process from beginning to end. Departmental boundaries are eliminated, and the claims response takes a few hours rather than a week. Second, diminish hierarchical differences and use teams to carry out the work, which is what Progressive does. The use of team structure empowers employees, decentralizes decision-making, and allows for greater learning across the organization. Third, appoint team leaders to manage the internal process in addition to coordinating the work. It is important to realize that monitoring the team's processes is as important as taking care of expected outputs. In the Escape Hybrid team, one individual took the lead role during development and adopted a relaxed and exploratory mindset, while another individual took on a more task-oriented and deadline-driven role during the launch phase. Fourth, allow team members to interact with customers and suppliers directly, so as to adapt and respond quickly if required. Direct contact allows members to keep abreast of changes in the environment more quickly. Finally, provide required expertise from the outside as and when requested by the team. A good team realizes that it does not have all the answers, and therefore it should not be shy about asking for help when needed.

Advantages

There is rapid communication among team members with different functional backgrounds, resulting in reduction in the time for getting workflows completed. Members of a team develop a broader perspective and become adept at solving problems that have the potential to hinder the effectiveness of the entire organization. Employees become more flexible in terms of skill and competence by being aware of the roles of others, and thus feel more

Table 12.1.1 Design Features of the Horizontal Organization

Features	Horizontal Organization
Figure	Core processes in the firm are organized cross-functionally.
What is it?	Breaking down internal boundaries and vertical silos to make subunits work together *horizontally*
Design principles	(1) Organize around complete workflow processes rather than tasks. (2) Flatten hierarchy and use teams to manage everything. (3) Appoint process team leaders to manage internal team processes. (4) Let supplier and customer contact drive performance. (5) Provide required expertise from outside the team as required.
Advantages	(1) Rapid communication and reduction in cycle time of work done. (2) Individuals working together on teams develop broader perspective, more flexible and empowered roles. (3) Rapid organizational learning is facilitated. (4) Improved customer responsiveness.
Disadvantages	(1) Separation of business activities into processes and non-process functions may be problematic. (2) Cinderella problem: non-process bits of the organization could feel neglected. (3) Teamwork could get in the way of functional specialization. (4) Traditional departments may instigate turf battles.
When to use	When the organization can create better value by improving internal coordination to enable greater flexibility and tailored responses to fit customer needs.

empowered to make decisions. Being part of the team also guarantees some recognition and social support. Overall, the level of learning within the horizontal organization increases tremendously compared with the traditional pyramid structure, because of close contact with both customers and suppliers at either end of the workflow. For example, Ford executives used the horizontal approach to customer service for the Escape SUV. Several horizontally aligned groups were responsible for core processes such as parts supply and logistics, vehicle service programs, and technical support. As the processes took hold, learning and responsiveness increased sharply.

Disadvantages

As with any design option, the horizontal organization has its fair share of drawbacks. First, the identification of complete and self-contained work processes within an organization can be problematic. It may be difficult to separate workflows from departmental tasks in a straightforward manner. Strong departments within a firm might fight hard because they might perceive a loss of "turf." Even where the identification is done well and in a politically astute manner, there can be a short-run increase in costs while transitional arrangements are perfected and as employees adjust to the lack of traditional and direction. Second, there is the Cinderella problem: employees belonging to parts of the organization that have not been earmarked as horizontal might feel relatively neglected. The emphasis on cross-disciplinary team-work and immediate customer gratification could stand in the way of deeper technical specialization that can result in innovative products. Finally, managers in entrenched departments may feel a loss of turf and may act politically to stymie attempts at effective horizontal collaboration.

When to Use

The horizontal design is best when the organization can create better customer value by improving internal coordination so as to be flexible and responsive to customers' needs. By creating key workflow processes and defining support tasks, there is a better line of sight to customers. This design should be used when the organization is able to move to the mindset of a team-based structure without great difficulty, and also when it is able to trade off the short-term losses incurred in making the new structure work against the gains that eventually accrue from it.

Era 3: Organizational Boundaries Open Up

The third era of organizational design came into its own in the mid-1990s, with rapid improvements in communication technology in the form of the Internet and mobile phones. Era 3 also coincides with the rise of emerging economies such as China and India, where there is a great pool of skilled expertise in performing very specific tasks such as low-cost manufacturing and software development. The external and internal boundaries of the organization opened up as never before. Managers became increasingly comfortable with the idea that their organization could not efficiently perform all of the tasks required to make a product or service. In the early years of the era, large and bloated organizations shed a lot of tasks that were completed internally, and this led to a difficult period of adjustment. Later on, start-up organizations were designed at the outset to be more lightweight by having a number of tasks performed externally.

Hollow Organization

The biggest trend in the design of organizations in Era 3 has been, without doubt, the outsourcing of various pieces of work done internally to outside partners. The phenomenon became most noticeable in the shifting of the manufacturing function from the U.S. to cheaper areas of production in Asia. In 1986, a *Business Week* article noted that a number of industries—including auto, steel, machine tools, consumer electronics, and semiconductor chips—were shifting their production elsewhere, and hence could be characterized, in contrast to traditional manufacturers, as "hollow corporations." More than 20 years later, business commentators recognize that adopting the hollow organization design form has led to more value creation, because U.S. firms now focus on honing profit-making functions such as design and marketing.

Examples

There are now few industries that remain untouched by the hollow organization design option. Take the case of the U.S. military. Faced with contradictory demands—for greater troop deployment to fight terrorism around the world and pressure to cap the number of active personnel and reservists who are called up—the military has turned towards ever increasing use of private military company (PMC) contractors to provide all services except the core one of fighting battles and securing defensive positions. For instance, Kellog Brown & Root, a subsidiary of the Haliburton Corporation, builds and maintains military bases that have been deployed in Iraq and also provides for all catering and cleaning requirements and its employees (comprising engineers, architects, logistics experts, cooks, and cleaners) live and work alongside servicemen and women in many active theatres around the world. Much of the sophisticated weaponry used by the military—such as the F-117 fighters, the Patriot missile, and the Global Hawk drone—is maintained on site by PMCs. A study of the use of PMCs by the military in Bosnia showed that outsourcing had reduced troop numbers by 24% and cut operational costs by 27%. As this illustration shows, the hollow design form allows for more flexibility, better use of specialist external technology, and greater efficiency.

More conventional examples of the hollow design abound. Sneaker companies Nike and Reebok Ltd. pioneered outsourcing of manufacturing to Southeast Asian contractors more than 20 years ago, and showed how profitability could be improved by adopting a hollow design. More recently, much of the mundane work of the financial services industry—such as processing insurance claims, approving mortgage loans, and analyzing financial statements of companies—has been accomplished by outsourcing partners located more than halfway across the globe. Another area is customer service work, from simple tasks such as confirming bank or credit card balances to sophisticated ones such as providing technical support for computer users. Rapid developments in communication technologies have allowed work that would have previously been kept in-house to migrate abroad. This trend has affected large and small companies alike. For example, Fluor Corp., a medium-sized California-based architectural services company, outsourced much of the work of generating blueprints and specifications for a multi-billion dollar Saudi Arabian petrochemical complex to a team of 200 Filipino architects employed by a partner firm in Manila. Likewise, solo architects working in the U.S. can make use of freelance architectural contractors based in Hungary (where there is an abundance of trained architects) to render plans into three-dimensional specifications.

The design features of the horizontal organization are summarized in Table 12.1.2.

Design Principles

There are three principles governing the design of the hollow organization. First, determine core and non-core business processes in the organization. Typically, core processes share these characteristics: they are critical to business performance, they create current or potential business advantage, and they are likely to drive future growth and rejuvenation. All other processes can be deemed non-core and are likely candidates for being outsourced. For example, in building the Cayenne SUV, Porsche retained critical processes such as engine production, transmission manufacturing, and final assembly—contributing to just about 10% of the finished automobile as core—and outsourced everything else. Second, harness market forces to outsource non-core processes. With increasing globalization and installation

Table 12.1.2 Design Features of the Hollow Organization

Features	Hollow Organization
Figure	

Firms B and C supply internal organizational processes to Firm A.

Features	Hollow Organization
What is it?	Outsourcing internal organization *processes* that support an organization's mission
Design principles	(1) Determine non-core processes—those that are *not* (a) critical to business performance, (b) creating current or potential business advantage, (c) likely to drive growth or rejuvenation. (2) Harness market forces to get non-core processes done efficiently. (3) Create an effective and flexible interface through a contract that aligns incentives.
Advantages	(1) Cost savings due to less capital expenditure and overhead. (2) Tapping into best sources of specialization and technology. (3) Market discipline that leads to supplier competition and innovation. (4) Flexibility in using lower cost and higher quality inputs.
Disadvantages	(1) Loss of in-house skills. (2) Possible decrease in internal innovation capacity. (3) Costs of transitioning to hollow state. (4) Higher monitoring to align incentives. (5) Reduced control over supply. (6) Competitive threat of being supplanted by suppliers.
When to use	When there is heavy price competition with pressure to cut costs and there is enough of a market outside the organization to perform required processes.

of high-touch informational technology systems, it is possible to offshore work to places that are not only cheaper, but also of higher quality. Big tax and audit firms, for example, routinely outsource the filing of individual and corporate tax returns to India-based firms such as MphasiS where highly qualified local accountants complete the task at a fraction of the price that an equivalent U.S. employee would cost. Third, write an effective and flexible contract to align incentives between the firm and the outsourcing provider. One sensitivity issue in using PMCs in war zones is that such firms are ultimately accountable to shareholders rather than the U.S. military, and therefore incentives have to be put in place to ensure continued cooperation.

Advantages

The main advantage of the hollow organization is in the cost savings that come from utilizing a lesser amount of capital expenditure and in carrying a less administrative over-head. This design also provides greater organizational flexibility by allowing the use of higher quality inputs at less cost. Firms can focus on what they do best, while tapping into the best sources of specialization and technology that outsourcers can bring with them. The growing market for outsourced services, in turn, makes providers more competitive and innovative, thereby adding more to the bottom line of the hollow organization.

Disadvantages

There are several downsides to using the hollow design option. There is a loss of in-house skills, and with that possibly the reduced capacity to innovate. The costs of transitioning to a hollow state are high, and include intangibles such as reduced employee morale. Also, if the supplier is distant both geographically and culturally, then there may be additional costs in terms of increased monitoring or switching to another supplier. Hollow organizations have less control over the supply of their products because of dependence on outsourcing partners, and there is even a threat of being supplanted by suppliers. To illustrate, Motorola Inc. hired BenQ, a Taiwanese manufacturer, to design and develop handsets for its American markets; BenQ then used the expertise gained to create a market for itself in mainland China.

When to Use

The hollow design is usually considered when an organization faces heavy price competition, and consequently, pressure to cut costs. This prompts managers to see what processes can be done cheaper outside the organization. In order to avoid being held hostage to a single supplier, there has to be enough of a market to stimulate efficiency in the performance of outsourced processes.

Modular Organization

The modular organization was another design that was popularized in the early 1990s. The image that it presents of the organization is one of a collection of Lego bricks that can snap together or be hived off as necessary. The design is similar to the hollow organization in its use of outsourcing. Crucially, however, what is different and distinctive about this form is that outsourcing conforms to pieces of the product rather than outsourcing organizational *processes* (e.g., human resources, warehousing, and logistics) in the hollow form. The assembly of decomposable product chunks provided by internal and external subcontractors is the defining feature of modular organization design.

Examples

The making of Bombardier's Continental business jet shows how flexible modular organizations can be. The jet can fly eight passengers comfortably from coast to coast in the U.S. without stopping to refuel. Bombardier has broken up the design of the aircraft into 12 large chunks provided by internal divisions and external contractors. The cockpit, center, and forward fuselage are produced in-house, but other major parts are supplied by manufacturers spread around the globe: tailcone (Hawker de Havilland, Australia), stabilizers and rear fuselage (Aerospace Industrial Development, Taiwan), engines (General Electric Co., U.S.A.), wing (Mitsubishi, Japan), fairings to improve aerodynamics (Fischer, Austria), landing gear (Messier-Dowty, Canada), and avionics (Rockwell Collins, U.S.A.). It takes just four days for employees in Bombardier's factory in Wichita, Kansas to snap the parts together. There were a number of upsides for Bombardier in using the modular design. The firm was able to share development costs with its partners, slash the cycle time required to launch a new product, and enter the market at a price point that was about $3 million less than its nearest competitor.

Other industries in which modular organizations tend to be prevalent include automobile manufacture, bicycle production, consumer electronics, household appliances, power tools, computing products, and software.

The design features of the horizontal organization are summarized in Table 12.1.3.

Table 12.1.3 Design Features of the Modular Organization

Features	Modular Organization
Figure	 Firm A assembles product modules produced by Firms A, B, and C
What is it?	Assembling decomposable *product chunks (modules)* provided by internal and external subcontractors
Design principles	(1) Break products into manageable modules. (2) Design interfaces that allow different chunks to work together. (3) Outsource product chunks that are produced more efficiently by others. (4) Design the organization to focus on assembling and distributing chunks created in-house and outside.
Advantages	(1) Cost savings and speed of responsiveness. (2) Take advantage of competence beyond one's boundary. (3) Scope to experiment with different suppliers that focus on improving their own part. (4) Increased ability to innovate through recombination of modules in different ways.
Disadvantages	(1) Not all products may be amenable to chunking into modules. (2) Poorly specified interfaces that hinder modules from work can hamper assembly. (3) Laggards can hold up innovation that occurs concurrently across a chain of collaborators.
When to use	When it is possible to specify the nature of product modules and to design interfaces that allow them to join up and function.

Design Principles

Four principles govern the design of modular organization. First, break products up into separable modules that can be made on a stand-alone basis. Second, design interfaces that allow different modules to work with each other. If this aspect is poorly done, then it can cause tremendous headaches down the line. Bombardier learned this principle from tough experience while outsourcing modules for aircraft that it developed before the Continental jet. Third, outsource product chunks that can be made more efficiently by external contractors. PalmOne Inc., the manufacturer of personal digital assistants, uses modularity in the product to focus on developing the software while outsourcing various hardware modules to subcontractors such as HTC of Taiwan. Finally, enable the organization to focus on assembling the different chunks of the product created in-house and outside.

Advantages

The prime advantage of the modular structure is its efficiency and speed of response. Nissan operates the most efficient automobile plants in the U.S., thanks to its modular organizational design. Parts such as the frame, dashboard, and seats are built by contractors and shipped to the assembly line. Modular design also allows firms to take advantage of competence beyond their own boundaries. By partnering with HTC, PalmOne was able to reduce defects by 50%. Firms can experiment with the use of different suppliers that focus on being the best in their class. Another advantage for modular firms is the increased ability to innovate through the recombination of modules in different ways. Nissan, for example, can use its assembly line to build many more different models of autos than rivals, thanks to its greater modularity.

Disadvantages

One key issue that limits applicability of the modular organization design is the fact that not all products or production processes are amenable to chunking into modules. Second, poorly designed interfaces can hinder modules from working with each other and lead to costly rework. DaimlerChrysler adopted a highly modular design for its two-seater Smart Car, but the launch was beset with a number of problems because various parts of the car would not snap into place as planned and required extensive debugging. Finally, firms have to manage partner firms as if they were part of one large coalition—and this is where the modular design differs significantly from hollow. Innovation has to occur concurrently across a chain of partner firms in order to create a new generation of products, and laggards can hold up the entire development cycle.

When to Use

The modular design is used when it is possible to break up the organization's product into self-contained modules, and where interfaces can be specified such that the modules work when they are joined together.

Virtual Organization

Few of today's companies can go it alone under a constant onslaught of international competitors, changing technology, and new regulations. Organizations around the world are embedded in complex networks of relationships: competing fiercely in some markets while collaborating in others. Collaboration or joint ventures with competitors usually takes the form of a virtual organization—a company outside a company created specifically to respond to an exceptional market opportunity that is often temporary. The metaphor for this design comes from virtual memory in a computer, which makes it act as if there were more storage capacity than actually present.

Examples

When Marks & Spencer (M&S), the venerable British retail chain, suffered dramatically declining sales in its core product of women's clothing, it turned to a one-time rival for help. George Davies is a serial entrepreneur who has previously set up two companies that have competed successfully with M&S. Together they created a virtual organization called Per Una, with the objective of getting younger women interested in a range of fashionable but reasonably priced clothing. The arrangement was unusual for M&S, which is famously insular and likes to keep all its branding and merchandising in-house. In launching Per Una, M&S provided only retail shelf space and marketing support. Davies contributed everything else, including apparel and accessories, logistics, and sales training. M&S benefited from increased traffic into its stores, while Davies retained a major share of the profits. Per Una proved to be a big hit and helped revive M&S's business fortunes, and was later absorbed completely into M&S. This example illustrates the key features of the virtual organization—willingness to collaborate with unlikely partners, capitalizing on market opportunity, and dissolving the virtual entity when it has served its purpose.

Virtual organization design is very prevalent in the high-technology industry where concurrent competition and cooperation is rife. For example, Symbian Ltd., a software developer for mobile phones, is a virtual organization set up by a consortium of competitors for handsets, including Nokia AB oyj, Sony Ericsson, Samsung Electronics Co., Panasonic, and Siemens AG. Large and mature companies also use virtual organization design to respond swiftly to a commercial opportunity. For example, rivals P&G and Clorox have recently collaborated with each other to create a new generation of plastic wrap, Glad Press 'n Seal, to compete with market leader Saran.

The design features of the horizontal organization are summarized in Table 12.1.4.

Design Principles

There are four principles governing the design of the virtual organization. First, create boundaries around a temporary organization with external partners. The organization may look like a separate entity as in a joint venture. Second, use technology to link people, assets, and ideas. Often the virtual organization is not tangible in terms of separate offices, facilities, and other types of infrastructure. It exists in people's minds. What makes it coherent is the sense of purpose and resources that are dedicated to achieving goals. For example, Billable Hour, a small business specialty wristwatch and greeting card retailer, relies on a far-flung network of partnerships, linked by technology, to produce its goods. Third, each partner brings its domain of excellence to bear. Fourth, disband or absorb once the opportunity evaporates. For example, at the height of the dot-com boom, Procter & Gamble Co. used technology partners to create a virtual organization called Reflect.com, with the aim of selling cosmetics online. After the boom faded away, P&G disbanded the organization and absorbed the learning from the experience into a more traditional cosmetics division.

Table 12.1.4 Design Features of the Virtual Organization

Features	Virtual Organization
Figure	Firms A and B collaborate (ab) to supply Firm A and/or other firms.
What is it?	Creating a *company-outside-a-company* to respond to an exceptional (often temporary) opportunity
Design principles	(1) Create boundaries around a temporary organization with external partners. (2) Use technology to link people, assets, and ideas. (3) Each partner brings its domain of excellence. (4) Disband or absorb once the opportunity evaporates.
Advantages	(1) Ability to move nimbly to respond to market opportunity. (2) Allows a firm to provide product extension or one-stop-shop service. (3) Leverage organizational assets distributed across partners forming the virtual firm. (4) No commitment to keeping the organization going after initial opportunity vanishes.
Disadvantages	(1) Increase in the load of communication to ensure there is no duplication or redundancy. (2) Lack of trust could break down communication and coordination. (3) Employees in the virtual entity may have partisan or weak organizational identification.
When to use	When it is possible to explore a fleeting market opportunity by partnering with other organizations.

Advantages

The virtual organization provides firms with the ability to move nimbly to exploit a favorable market opportunity. Virtual design also allows a firm to provide a product extension that would have been impossible otherwise, and also to jointly leverage organizational assets that are distributed across partnering firms. In the Glad joint venture, for example, the wrap was invented in P&G labs but marketed under Clorox's well-established Glad brand name. Since then, the two companies have continued the collaboration with the introduction of Glad Force Flex trash bags, which make use of a stretchable plastic also invented in P&G labs. Finally, another advantage of the virtual form is that it can be easily disbanded or absorbed once the opportunity for collaboration goes away, or it can be made into a stand-alone entity if the opportunity becomes larger.

Disadvantages

The major downside of virtual organization design is that it requires a tremendous amount of communication and understanding to keep it going. Partners need to talk to each other to avoid duplication and redundancy. One recurring problem with the Per Una organization was that some of its apparel was strikingly similar to what M&S had designed. Another problem is that lack of trust or misalignment of incentives could break down communication and coordination. In the Per Una case this problem manifested itself in terms of M&S's indefinite return policy—customers can bring in goods that they are dissatisfied with any time; George Davies, on the other hand, wanted a time limit on when customers could come back in to claim a refund or exchange, so as to protect the profitability of the operation and also its reputation for fair commercial exchange. A final drawback is that employees in the virtual entity may have partisan or weak organizational identification, and this, in turn, may reduce their commitment.

When to Use

The virtual design is used when it is possible to explore a fleeting market opportunity by partnering with complementary organizations. In such situations, typically one organization does not have the necessary capability to respond, and it is necessary to look around to see what other organizations (including competitors) can offer. The design works best when there is clear understanding among partnering organizations as to their rights and obligations.

New Demands on Managers and Organizations

The shifting emphasis from vertical designs to horizontal designs to partnership designs has reshaped the roles of managers. The biggest change has been from having direct control over resources required for performance toward dependence on others over whom there is no direct control. Even with more dependence and less control under newer structural designs, managers are still responsible for performance outcomes. For a manager who is used to a traditional top-down approach, it is hard to let go of control. The late business guru Peter Drucker once noted that the problem with large company managers is that they are used to giving orders and not to working with a partner—a totally different proposition.

A nice example is provided by the transition of Strida, a U.K.-based company that sells lightweight foldable bicycles, from a functional design, vertically integrated manufacturer to a completely hollow form. In 2001, Strida received a large order from an Italian customer, willing to buy at a price that was below the cost of producing the bicycles in the U.K. The CEO of the company, Steedman Bass, immediately began investigating ways of making the organization more efficient. First, he decided to shut down the in-house production plant and identified a manufacturing partner in the Far East who could make the bike at lower cost. He used expert contractors to continue developing new bicycle models, to design the owner's manual, to design the company's Web site. He used various Web-based software services to ensure smooth communication between the designers and the manufacturer, to manage accounts, materials and documents. He then turned to a long-time vendor to take over the back-end operation of the company—including warehouse management, order fulfillment, inventory control, customer service, inbound container management, and accounts generation. The company has low overhead and is now structured to ramp up and down quickly in response to market fluctuations. Bass focuses almost exclusively on managing the various relationships that make up the business. Bass had loved making his own bikes, and therefore the biggest barrier in making the transition was in his willingness to find, trust, and hand over that responsibility to someone else that could do it more efficiently.

A study of the fit between executive style and executive roles by the Hay Group distinguished between *operations roles* and *collaborative roles*. Operations roles have traditional line authority and are accountable for business results, typically through direct control over people and resources. Successful operations managers set goals, establish analyses, take risks, and are intensely focused on results. Collaborative roles, however, lack direct authority over horizontal colleagues or partners, and are nonetheless accountable for key business results. Successful managers in collaborative roles are extremely flexible and proactive, achieve outcomes through personal communication and influence tailored to people and situations, and assertively seek out needed information.

The old way of managing was to defend the unit's boundaries and oversee its performance by emphasizing operations roles. However, collaborative roles are more common in new organizational structures. The key manager demands for succeeding with newer structural designs are as follows.

Get the Right Partner on the Bus

In a hollow or modular design this means spending time to get to know a potential partner's strengths, weaknesses, and goals. For routine, commodity-type sourcing, due diligence is less important. But for a significant partnership, trust in the partner is essential. Check for gaps in skills and competency to assess whether the partner can deliver what your business needs. It is good to investigate prospective partners by talking to other companies they've partnered with and to develop a sense of how well suited their culture and priorities are to your own. For hollow and modular designs, it is good to understand the process being outsourced and what to expect from the partner. When the partner takes it over, your control will be gone. The partner will get most of the benefit from improvements, innovation, and efficiencies.

Select People With Lateral Organizing Skills

Lateral organizing skills refers to the ability to work with people across organizations, including those with whom lines of responsibility and accountability are a little fuzzy. People who are part of a horizontal team or who work with outside partners must have excellent coordination, personal influence, and negotiation skills. Soft skills dominate hard skills in the newer organization designs. A process owner or a partner cannot simply order a change. It's about influence, influence, and influence to adjust the relationship to serve new demands. Managers with lateral organizing skills may also act as evangelists, convincing people to give up their own needs for the greater good of collaboration for customer satisfaction.

Seek Clarity, Not Control

As relationships move from vertical to horizontal and from work that can be observed to work performed elsewhere, much time has to be devoted to the front end of the relationship—setting expectations and creating structure. Every conceivable issue must be discussed and probably written down in contracts with outside partners. Memos of understanding are effective for process teams. The respective goals, incentives, and desired outcomes should be defined in advance. During the relationship, problems surely will arise and changes will be made, but clarity in the beginning is essential. Steedman Bass of Strida says that careful negotiation beforehand is critical. "Good contracts are important. They may be time-consuming, but taking the time to write and negotiate good contracts that work for both parties is essential. You're placing a lot of reliance on people, and it has to work. We did our homework up front, thinking of how we wanted the relationships to work, and that has probably eliminated 98% of the potential misunderstandings on either our part or theirs." Bass also emphasized, "I had never used contracts to sue or punish partners; I used them to mutually establish the playing field and rules of the game."

Design Coordination Mechanisms

Some amount of mutual control with partners can be asserted through explicit collaboration mechanisms. For an outside partner, example mechanisms might include a Leadership Governance Board of senior executives that meets quarterly, or monthly meetings of team leaders, or periodic visits to each others' sites to see the work, build relationships, and discuss results. Scheduled periodic discussions of metrics, performance results, and written reports should also be part of the coordination process with internal or external partners.

Conclusion

After much debate, the managers at WRG, the start-up horticulture supply company referred to at the beginning of this article, decided to adopt a hollow rather than a functional organization design. It was a learning process for managers and board members because the team's experience had been in traditional structures. A manager and board member made trips to India and China to meet and build personal relationships with suppliers. The product had to be supplied in bulk for horticulture nurseries, and in appealing individual packages for retail sales. The time and travel overseas was only a fraction of the cost of buying machines and building a small manufacturing plant. Building strong relationships with sales distributors and a marketing agency was more challenging. These businesses were focused on their own needs more than on a partnership. Moreover, the board member who worked with distributors had something of an autocratic temperament, which made it hard to connect with the prospective partners. The CEO, however, had a knack for building horizontal relationships with growers and university researchers for testing product efficacy. The science supporting the superior efficiency of SmartGrow was thereby accomplished at minimal cost. After some trial and error, the hollow organization form proved a boon to WRG.

The movement from Era 1 to Era 3 has vastly expanded the array of organization design choices available to managers. The new designs—particularly variations of the horizontal and hollow forms—that have evolved in the past three decades offer a number of advantages, but as we have noted, each has particular challenges as well. The shift from vertical to horizontal thinking and behavior can be difficult. The implementation of a horizontal or sourcing design has its own challenges. Realigning a large company along horizontal processes can require a wrenching change in people and culture. Adopting a hollow form may require less change in culture, but a new manager paradigm will be needed, with special focus on finding suitable external partners and building relationships that serve both partners. Maintaining external collaboration requires its own expertise. With increasing global competition, managers have to be astute and realistic about the organization design that provides them with competitive advantage and their customers with greatest value.

Selected Bibliography

Robert Duncan's original article titled "What Is the Right Organization Structure? Decision Tree Analysis Provides the Answer," *Organizational Dynamics*, 1979 (winter), 59–80, provides a brief overview of functional, divisional, and matrix structures. Stewart A. Clegg's book *Modern Organizations* (Sage, 1990) traces the evolution from traditional to contemporary organization designs. The classic reference on divisional structures is *Strategy and Structure* (MIT Press, 1962) by Alfred Chandler. *Matrix* (Addison-Wesley, 1979) by Stanley Lawrence and Paul Davis is the definitive introduction to the topic. Jay Galbraith's *Designing Complex Organizations* (Addison-Wesley, 1973) provides a brief yet comprehensive description of Era 1 designs.

In their book *Reengineering the Corporation* (HarperBusiness, 1993) Michael Hammer and James Champy discuss how reengineering horizontal processes can cut costs and improve customer value. John A. Bryne's "The Horizontal Corporation," *Business Week*, 20 December 1993, 76–81, provides a number of original illustrations of companies that have adopted the horizontal design. The principles of team-oriented organization design are succinctly articulated by Albert Cherns in "The Principles of Sociotechnical Designs," *Human Relations*, 1976, 29, 783–792. The Ford Escape SUV example used in the article is adapted from Chuck Salter's article "Ford's Escape Route," *FastCompany*, October 2004, 106–110. Frank Ostroff's book *The Horizontal Organization* (Oxford University Press, 1999) is a comprehensive exposition of that design option. A wonderful firsthand report of an organization moving from predominantly Era 1 vertical lines of command to Era 2 horizontal processes can be found in Mary Walton's *Car* (W.W. Norton, 1999).

Norman Jonas's 1986 article "The Hollow Corporation," *Business Week*, 3 March, 57–59, attracted widespread attention to the growing trend in outsourcing. The key principles of the hollow form are summarized by Simon Domberger in *The Contracting Organization* (Oxford University Press, 1998). Examples of the hollow form can be found in the following articles: Anthony Bianco and Stephanie Anderson Forest, "Outsourcing War," *Business Week*, 15 September 2003, 42–49; Pete Engardio, Aaron Berstein, and Manjeet Kripalani, "The New Global Job Shift," *Business Week*, 3 February 2003, 36–48; and Pete Engardio and Bruce Einhorn, "Outsourcing Innovation," *Business Week*, 21 March 2005, 86–94. More generally, John Hagel III and Marc Singer discuss the Era 3 philosophy of design in their aptly titled article "Unbundling the Corporation," *Harvard Business Review*, March–April 1999, 133–141.

The article titled "The Modular Corporation" by Shawn Tully and Tricia Welsh, *Fortune*, 8 February 1993, 106–115, helped spread awareness of this Era 3 option to a wide business audience. A comprehensive discussion of the modular form can be found in Carliss Y. Baldwin and Kim B. Clark, *Design Rules: The Power of Modularity v.1* (MIT Press, 2000). Academic articles discussing the key features of the modular form include the following: Ron Sanchez and Joseph T. Mahoney, "Modularity, Flexibility, and Knowledge Management in Product and Organizational Design," *Strategic Management Journal*, 1996, 17, 63–76; and Melissa A. Schilling and Kevin T. Steensma, "The Use of Modular Organizational Forms: An Industry Level Analysis," *Academy of Management Journal*, 2001, 44, 1149–1168. Examples of the modular form can be found in Philip Siekman's "The Snap-Together Business Jet," *Fortune*, 21 January 2002, 104A–104H; and David Welch's "How Nissan Laps Detroit," *Business Week*, 22 December 2003, 60–62.

William Davidow and Michael Malone's book *The Virtual Corporation* (HarperCollins, 2003) provides a good introduction to the opportunities and challenges of the virtual form. A framework that considers when the virtual form should be favored is provided by Henry

Chesbrough and David Teece in their article "When is Virtual Virtuous? Organizing for Innovation," *Harvard Business Review*, January–February 1996, 65–73. Shona Brown and Kathleen Eisenhardt theorize the virtues of temporary organizations in their book *Competing on the Edge* (Harvard Business School Press, 1998). The P&G-Clorox virtual organization example was drawn from Patrica Seller's article "Teaching an Old Dog New Tricks," *Fortune*, 31 May 2004, 166–180.

Transitioning from a traditional organization design to a more contemporary option can be challenging. A number of books provide guidance on how the redesign challenge can be met, including Bruce Pasternack and Albert Viscio's *The Centreless Corporation* (Simon & Schuster, 1998); David Nadler and Michael Tushman's *Competing by Design* (Oxford, 1997); Henk Volbreda's *Building the Flexible Firm* (Oxford, 1998); Jay Galbraith's *Designing Organizations* (Jossey-Bass, 2002); and Michael Goold and Andrew Campbell's *Designing Effective Organizations* (Jossey-Bass, 2002).

12.2 DOES DECENTRALIZATION MAKE A DIFFERENCE FOR THE ORGANIZATION?

An Examination of the Boundary Conditions Circumscribing Decentralized Decision-Making and Organizational Financial Performance*

Hettie A. Richardson, Robert J. Vandenberg, Terry C. Blum, and Paul M. Roman

Recently, there has been increased interest in the organizational gains that can be achieved by decentralizing decision-making authority to lower level employees. Yet, literature examining the relationship of decentralization to organizational performance is both scarce and equivocal. The current study examines decentralization's influence on financial performance in a sample of behavioral healthcare treatment centers. As expected, the decentralization–financial performance relationship is moderated by key organizational characteristics. Implications of the findings are presented.

Contemporary practitioners and researchers are increasingly interested in the competitive advantages that can be achieved by leveraging the value of human resources (Becker & Huselid, 1998; Lawler, Mohrman & Ledford, 1995; Vandenberg, Richardson & Eastman, 1999). This interest is largely due to increasing evidence that human capital can have a major impact on firm performance. For instance, Arthur (1994) found that between 42 and 65% of the variability in organizational performance (i.e., labor hours and scrap rate) is due to the use of "high commitment" human resource practices. Over the years, a number of approaches to managing human capital have developed, all of which are predicated on the value of human resources. Examples of these approaches include high involvement work processes (Lawler, 1996), participative decision-making (Locke & Schweiger, 1979), empowerment (Spreitzer, 1995), delegation (Leana, 1986), and self-managed teams (Cohen, Ledford & Spreitzer, 1996).

While each approach differs with respect to the processes and practices for leveraging value from an organization's human capital, a common element among them is the expectation that organizational gains can be achieved by providing employees with greater access to decision-making authority (Aiken & Hage, 1966; Knoke, 1981; Pugh, Hickson, Hinings, MacDonald, Turner & Lupton, 1963). That is, each of these approaches shares the theoretical premise that, contrary to authoritarian and bureaucratic methods of organizational control, methods and structures which promote social control through employee autonomy and authority link workers' self-interests with those of the organization in order to facilitate higher quality decisions and the achievement of organizational goals (Ashmos, McDaniel & Duchon, 1990; Wooldridge & Floyd, 1990). At the organizational level, social control is represented by structural characteristics such as an overall decentralization of decision-making authority to lower organizational levels (Aiken & Hage, 1966; Pugh, Hickson, Hinings & Turner, 1968).

While decentralization may reside at the core of many contemporary practices and research, the extent to which organizational-level performance gains are actually achieved *via* decentralized decision-making authority remains unclear. As early as 1965, Porter and Lawler concluded that research on organizational decentralization has provided little unequivocal support for the positive influence of decentralization on performance outcomes, such as financial gain and improvements in organizational output. Though some researchers have empirically related decentralization to positive attitudinal and employee morale outcomes (i.e., subjective outcomes; Hodson, 1985; Knoke, 1981), evidence of positive influences on more objective indices (e.g., financial performance) has been much harder to obtain (Wagner, 1994; Wagner, Leana, Locke & Schweiger, 1997).

Because of the equivocal results regarding its influence on organizational outcomes, some have argued that the primary benefit of decentralization and its related practices is not organizational but attitudinal and, as such, have come to question its practical benefits (Knoke, 1981; Wagner, 1994). In other words, decentralization may primarily serve to make employees feel good about their jobs, selves, and organizations, but do little to enhance the financial position of an organization. It is possible, though, that the relationship of decentralization to organizational outcomes is more complex than has typically been portrayed in the literature.

Much research has treated decentralization—in any of its forms—as a "best practice," uniformly expected to result in positive effects (e.g., Aiken & Hage, 1966; Cohen et al., 1996; Morse & Reimer, 1956; Ouchi, 1977). Though the notion of "best practices" is appealing in its parsimony, it is yet to receive blanket support in any domain of the organizational sciences. That is, the value of most approaches to managerial control is circumscribed by various boundary conditions that either enhance or limit their effectiveness. Perhaps more importantly, the theoretical literature also suggests that decentralized decision-making authority, especially at the organizational level, is not likely to be a panacea for improved performance.

Drawing on the Pfeffer and Salancik (1978, p. 1) argument that "organizations are inescapably bound up with the conditions of their environments," Ranson, Hinings and Greenwood (1980) use contingency theory rationale to assert that the design of an effective organization must be adapted to deal with the circumstances of its internal and external environment. More recently, Wagner et al. (1997, pp. 57–59) suggested that the findings casting doubt upon the practical efficacy of certain forms of decentralized decision-making perhaps stemmed from past researchers' failure to consider the favorableness of the context in which decentralization was implemented. Also using a contingency rationale, Wagner et al. (1997) challenged future researchers to seek out conditions in which decentralized decision-making may be embedded and which act to support or undermine decentralization's influence upon outcomes, particularly objective ones such as those describing organizational performance.

We interpret this challenge as positing that direct effects upon objective indices of organizational performance may be too simplistic—masking the reality that decentralization may only exert influences under certain conditions and may actually have a negative impact under other circumstances. Thus, we examine whether the relationship between decentralization and organizational outcomes is contingent on contextual organizational characteristics.

We begin with an overview of the conceptual premises underlying decentralization. We then examine financial performance and develop hypotheses regarding the impact of decentralization on this outcome. The goal is to show that only examining the direct effects of decentralization may result in misleading conclusions and that sound reasons exist to postulate a moderated influence of decentralization upon objective indices of short-term financial performance. We examine these expectations in a sample of behavioral health treatment centers. Treatment centers as the units of analysis are particularly apt in this role. In response to turbulent and uncertain environmental conditions and the increasingly scarce resources associated with them (D'Aunno & Sutton, 1992), many treatment centers face growing pressures to more effectively use their human capital (Blum, 1998), and healthcare researchers have begun advocating that centers do so by moving toward decentralized decision-making (Ashmos et al., 1990). Continued public concern about the quality of healthcare also requires these organizations to perform more effectively overall (Scheid & Greenley, 1997).

Decentralization and Effectiveness

Over the years, many related methods have been proposed for providing employees with greater decision-making authority. While distinctions between these methods can be made, their common foundation (i.e., the belief that greater employee decision-making authority is associated with performance outcomes) has resulted in confusion about how they differ (Glew, O'Leary-Kelly, Griffin & Van Fleet, 1995; Leana, 1986). As Leana points out, each of these methods can be located on a continuum of processes by which employees can be involved in decision-making. This continuum ranges from completely autocratic decision-making to processes that provide employees with maximum authority, such as the complete delegation of decisions to employees. Falling between these two extremes are processes such as participation and decentralization. Whereas participation is commonly defined as joint decision-making between supervisors and subordinates (Locke & Schweiger, 1979), decentralization can be broadly defined as "a dynamic participative philosophy of organizational management that involves selective delegation of authority to the operational level" (Przestrzelski, 1987).

Our focus is on the general notion of employees' access to decision-making at the organizational level, which we broadly refer to and measure as internal structural decentralization. We specifically examine Aiken and Hage's (1966) hierarchy of authority dimension of decentralization. According to these authors, this dimension of decentralization is the "extent to which members are assigned tasks and then provided with the freedom to implement them without interruption from supervisors" (Aiken & Hage, 1966, p. 498). Because of the existing confusion in the literature, similar concepts have been referred to as both participation and delegation in other work (Glew et al., 1995; Locke & Schweiger, 1979). As such, we draw on the participation, delegation, and decentralization literatures.

For decades, the primary expectation has been that decentralization will positively influence organizational functioning as indicated through both subjective (e.g., collective satisfaction) and objective (e.g., organizational financial) indices (Aiken & Hage, 1966; Morse

& Reimer, 1956; Ouchi, 1977). The reasoning behind this expectation is the premise that, "The properties of structural frameworks have important consequences for the organization's effectiveness: the extent of . . . centralization . . . will influence the effectiveness of control (cf. Ouchi, 1977), adaptability, and member motivation . . ." (Ranson et al., 1980). In terms of objective outcomes, decentralization is treated as "a means for realizing the larger goals of the organization and its management" (Leana & Florkowski, 1992, p. 245) and assumes that employees have information managers lack (Miller & Monge, 1986). In complex, dynamic environments—such as the healthcare environment—upper-level managers may be faced with more information than they are capable of processing on their own (Ashmos et al., 1990; Wooldridge & Floyd, 1990). Thus, decentralization allows organizations to reap benefits by taking advantage of the capabilities of lower-level employees whose contributions are often overlooked in more autocratic, centralized decision environments (Ashmos et al., 1990; Locke & Schweiger, 1979; Miller & Monge, 1986).

Despite expectations for relationships with objective outcomes, most existing decentralization research has focused on only two issues: (a) the factors resulting in decentralization or the relationship of decentralization to other structural characteristics (e.g., Aiken & Hage, 1968; Pugh et al., 1968; Pugh, Hickson & Hinings, 1969), and (b) the influence of decentralization on subjective outcomes (e.g., employee attitudes; Hodson, 1985; Knoke, 1981). The small cadre of empirical work that does consider objective outcomes generally has examined (a) related practices (e.g., participative decision-making, PDM) and their influence on individual-level outcomes or (b) how involving middle-level managers in strategic decision-making influences organizational-level performance. Research in the former category has not been very encouraging. Meta-analytic reviews of the studies linking PDM to performance outcomes have shown that such links tend to be small or non-existent (Wagner, 1994; Wagner et al., 1997), leading researchers to call for future work examining the conditions that may support or undermine decentralization's influence on performance.

Research considering the decentralization of strategic decision-making to middle managers has been much more encouraging. Floyd and Wooldridge (1992, 1997) and Wooldridge & Floyd (1990) conducted a series of studies examining the influence of middle managers on organizational performance, and their findings indicate that this form of decentralization can impact the quality of decisions made and, thus, organizational outcomes such as overall financial performance, return on assets, and growth rate. Wooldridge and Floyd (1990) also point out, though, that decentralization may not be desirable in all situations. For instance, when rapid response is required, the time and energy associated with decentralization to middle managers may outweigh potential benefits. As such, these authors encourage future researchers to seek out the internal and external environmental conditions that intensify the need for involvement.

We interpret the results of these two streams of research (PDM and the work of Floyd and Wooldridge) as indicating that decentralization can positively influence organizational performance outcomes, but that the relationship between decentralization and objective performance might be dependent upon contextual contingencies that determine the variability of organizational outcomes (Ranson et al., 1980). Interestingly, much of the initial writing on decentralization is based on the idea that organizational characteristics interact with one another to influence the organization (Hickson et al., 1971; Perrow, 1967). Perrow (1967), for example, suggests that decentralization represents choices among many means, and the consequences of such choices should not directly influence organizational goals but rather should indirectly influence goals dependent upon other organizational and environmental characteristics.

What, then, are the contextual constraints that might circumscribe the decentralization–performance relationship? Most possible contingencies fall into two broad categories: organizational characteristics and environmental characteristics. The problem is that researchers can and have suggested almost an infinite variety of organizational and environmental factors that may serve as moderators or contingency factors, and there is no one overarching theory from which a clear set of contingencies or boundary conditions can be derived. For example, the initial writings of Pugh, Hickson, Hinings and colleagues discuss how organizational characteristics such as decentralization should fit with other structural characteristics such as formalization, and research has been done in this area. Yet these authors and others (e.g., work by Aiken and Hage, also Floyd and Wooldridge) also suggest that there may be many other factors that could be taken into consideration when examining fit and the influence of fit on outcomes.

The boundary conditions we consider are derived from multiple theoretical literatures. Specifically, the conditions we examine are (1) the degree of decentralization between a center and its parent organization; (2) the condition of the center in terms of growth, stability, or shrinkage; (3) the percentage of professionals employed by the center; (4) the amount of competition the center faces; and (5) the performance aspirations of the center. Each of these is associated with key conditions to which modern healthcare organizations must respond. For example, healthcare organizations must learn to operate in complex environments due to increased vertical and horizontal integration and competition (Conrad & Shortell, 1996). Many healthcare centers are entering and leaving the field or changing their own services in reaction to these changes (Blum, 1998). Likewise, pressure to perform at lower costs is often forcing these organizations to become more financially oriented and operate effectively with reduced resources (D'Aunno & Sutton, 1992). The following paragraphs introduce the five conditions, the rationale underlying their inclusion as constraints, and related hypotheses.

Parent–Center Decentralization

The boundary condition of parent–center decentralization parallels the contingency factor that Pugh et al. (1969) refer to as dependence on a parent organization. Aiken and Hage (1966, 1968) distinguish this factor from an organization's internal decentralization (i.e., decentralized decision-making authority within a given treatment center) in terms of the autonomy the organization has from other organizations. Modern healthcare organizations face increased complexity due to horizontal integration among hospitals and independent centers, vertical integration of treatment providers with HMOs, and strategic interorganizational alliances among a variety of healthcare providers (Conrad & Shortell, 1996). These conditions suggest that many treatment centers may find themselves in relationships with larger parent organizations that constrain the centers' ability to pursue various management styles or develop certain organizational structures. Thus, it is reasonable to consider the authority given to a center as a whole by the parent organization, or parent–center decentralization, as distinct from the authority the center gives to its own internal employees (i.e., the primary decentralization construct of this study, internal decentralization).

The concept of coupling (Weick, 1976) suggests that some degree of simultaneous centralization–decentralization among organizations and their parents may be desirable. Centralization between a center and its larger parent organization can serve to buffer the center from environmental turbulence, enabling the center to achieve dependability and avoid excessive internal disorder. At the same time, the turbulent environment in which centers operate necessitates some degree of decentralization in order to achieve flexibility and adaptability. Research (Jansen & Chandler, 1994) supporting this notion suggests that tightly coupling centers with their parent organizations (e.g., centralization; providing a center with little general autonomy in terms of making decisions about how it is run) may serve to buffer the centers from the environment, creating reliable administrative and structural order. Concurrently providing the employees throughout a center with the authority to take independent action within the order created by parent–center centralization may result in responsiveness and flexibility at the point of service delivery without unnecessary irregularity (Jansen & Chandler, 1994; Lawler, 1996).

Work by Brown and Eisenhardt (1998) also supports the concept of simultaneous decentralization and centralization at different levels of an organization. According to these authors, the most successful organizations should be those that are neither so *structured* and rigid as to encourage little to no action, nor so *unstructured* as to prevent purposive action. The reason behind this logic is that, without any structure, there are too many possible actions and inaction is likely. Yet, with too much structure, action becomes less effective and organizations lose their ability to be flexible and to adapt to the changing demands of competition. Thus, the optimal situation would be one in which there is more structure in at least one level of the organization, but less structure at other levels. Therefore, our first hypothesis is:

Hypothesis 1: Parent–center decentralization will moderate the relationship between internal decentralization and center financial performance such that for centralized parent–center relationships the internal decentralization–financial performance relationship will be positive and for decentralized parent–center relationships the internal decentralization–financial performance relationship will be negative.

Organizational Condition

Pugh et al. (1969) point out that an organization's historical condition, which may manifest itself in terms of changes in the range of products and services offered, is an important contextual characteristic to consider when also considering aspects of an organization's structure. As such, we suggest that the success of internal decentralization may also depend on whether the treatment center is in a period of growth, shrinkage, or stability (Lawler, 1996). Researchers (e.g., Ashmos, Duchon, Hauge & McDaniel, 1996; D'Aunno & Sutton, 1992) suggest that organizational reductions in staff and services lead to increased disorder—making it increasingly important for remaining staff to broaden their roles and to innovatively provide competitive services with reduced resources. Supporting the need for decentralized decision-making during difficult organizational times, Ashmos, Duchon and McDaniel (1998) found hospitals with poorer past performance tended to bring more people into decision situations and use them in more decision situations.

Additionally, D'Aunno and Sutton (1992) described leaders facing shrinkage as experiencing high levels of personal anxiety, with greater anxiety limiting the leaders' abilities to process the vast amounts of ambiguous information on which key organizational decisions and activities are often based. As mentioned, the expectation for decentralization's influence on organizational outcomes is based on the assumption that, in turbulent environments, better decisions will be made when decisions are made by those most capable of making them rather than only by top managers (Ashmos et al., 1990; Floyd & Wooldridge, 1992, 1997). Work by Floyd and Wooldridge (1992, 1997) and Wooldridge & Floyd (1990) provides some support for this assumption. For example, their 1990 study shows that performance improves when lower-level managers are involved in strategic decision-making and that the benefits of decentralized decision-making stem from the complexity of current business environments.

By implication, these findings and existing theory suggest that, in less complex or dynamic environments, decentralized decision-making may be less crucial. It follows, then, that decentralization might actually have proportionally greater positive impact on organizational outcomes in shrinking firms than in firms where organizational effectiveness is inherently augmented by other key factors (e.g., robust growth or a strong, stable market position) and where the time and effort associated with decentralized decision-making might outweigh the additional benefits that decentralization can bring to an organization already performing well. For these reasons, the following is hypothesized:

Hypothesis 2: Organizational condition will moderate the relationship between internal decentralization and financial performance such that for shrinking organizations the internal decentralization–financial performance relationship will be positive and strong, while for growing organizations the internal decentralization–financial performance relationship will be positive and weak.

Workforce Characteristics

A basic premise of decentralized authority is that benefits can be gained from providing employees with greater opportunities to make quality decisions on behalf of their organizations (Floyd & Wooldridge, 1997; Locke & Schweiger, 1979; Miller & Monge, 1986). For instance, decentralization is intended to increase decision-making authority among employees who would typically not be given such authority under more bureaucratic structures, but who may have a great deal to contribute to certain decisions.

Historically, organizations such as treatment centers have been considered what Pugh et al. (1969) referred to as "personnel bureaucracies." They were organizations staffed by large numbers of professional employees that were characterized by high concentration of authority, but low structuring of work centers. Professional employees in these organizations were generally hired because their knowledge and training allowed them to effectively work with relative autonomy at the operational level. This was particularly true in the treatment industry, where skilled professionals such as nurses and licensed counselors were largely responsible for service delivery. The importance of providing these professionals with authority over work tasks is often considered a necessity because they are the employees with treatment expertise. Research by Ashmos et al. (1998) also indicates that involving professionals in strategic, as opposed to only bureaucratic, decisions can positively influence hospital performance.

Recently, however, pressures to reduce costs have led many centers to increasingly rely on non-professional employees (e.g., unlicensed counselors, clinical technicians) for service delivery. Logically, though still knowledgeable, these employees should not have the need for autonomy or expertise that professionals do. While decentralization may still be useful in organizations employing a low percentage of professionals, it may be less necessary and valuable to those organizations. Based on the arguments, our third hypothesis is as follows:

Hypothesis 3: The proportion of professional workers (i.e., nurses and licensed counselors) employed by a center will moderate the relationship between decentralization and financial performance such that for organizations with a low proportion of professionals the internal decentralization–financial performance relationship will be positive and weak, while for organizations with a high proportion of professionals the internal decentralization–financial performance relationship will be positive and strong.

Competitive Environment

Individual centers experience varying degrees of competition from other centers or treatment providers. A common argument found in some decentralization literature is that the highly competitive nature of the modern marketplace requires successful organizations to develop human resources who are proactively involved in the organization and who are capable of moving beyond the boundaries and tasks of traditionally defined jobs (Koch & McGrath, 1996; Lawler, 1996). Theory also suggests that decisions in predictable, stable (e.g., less competitive) environments should also be predictable and stable (Mintzberg & Waters, 1985). This proposition led Wooldridge and Floyd (1990) to suggest that decentralization should be deliberately pre-empted in such conditions in order to avoid potentially negative consequences. It follows that, in highly competitive environments, centers adopting decentralization should perform more successfully than those that do not. Under conditions of low competition, the greater workforce utilization associated with decentralization would be unnecessary and provide no discernable advantages for a center. The cost and effort of establishing decentralization under conditions of low competition may negatively impact a center's performance. Therefore, the fourth hypothesis is as follows:

Hypothesis 4: The nature of the competitive environment in which a center operates will moderate the relationship between internal decentralization and financial performance such that for centers in highly competitive environments the internal decentralization–performance relationship will be positive, while for centers in relatively non-competitive environments the internal decentralization–performance relationship will be negative.

Performance Aspirations

It has been argued that organizational performance and initiatives intended to improve performance can only be realistically considered in the context of organizational objectives (Rogers & Wright, 1998). The focal point of the present study is the relationship between decentralization and organizational *financial* effectiveness, and it is believed that decentralization can positively influence organizational effectiveness when used within certain boundary conditions. Thus, this study relies heavily on the assumption that improved financial effectiveness is an important goal or objective for treatment centers.

Strong financial performance aspirations, however, are not necessarily characteristic of all treatment centers. For instance, the primary performance aspiration for some centers might be outstanding customer service or mere survival. Among centers that do not emphasize financial effectiveness as an organizational objective, there may be little value in extensively pursuing an initiative like decentralization that is intended to improve financial performance. Similar to the argument for competitive environment, the effort and expense of decentralization in an organization that is not pursuing financial performance may not be worthwhile and may even be detrimental. Accordingly, our final hypothesis is as follows:

Hypothesis 5: A treatment center's performance aspirations will moderate the relationship between internal decentralization and financial performance such that for centers with strong financial performance aspirations, the decentralization–financial performance relationship will be positive, while for centers with low financial aspirations the decentralization–financial performance relationship will be negative.

Method

Sample

Data for this study were collected at two time periods. Time 1 data were gathered in 1995 and 1996 as the first phase of the "National Treatment Center Study." Time 2 data, from which the follow-up financial performance measure was derived, were collected in 1997 (for those centers where Time 1 data were collected in 1995) and 1998 (for those centers where Time 1 data were collected in 1996). The centers represented a national sample of private-sector behavioral healthcare treatment programs. Centers were drawn from a stratified random sample of geographic areas throughout the United States, and the data constituted a random sample of for- and not-for-profit behavioral healthcare and substance abuse treatment centers. Overall, 450 centers participated in the study, resulting in an 89% response rate for Time 1.

For each participating center at Time 1, the program administrator (i.e., the top position in the center) was identified as the primary respondent and on-site interviews were conducted with him/her by one of a team of full-time interviewers. The average administrator respondent was white (87.9%), was male (57%), was between the ages of 40 and 49 (45%), and held at least a master's degree (64%). Fifty-five percent had been educated either in social work, medicine (including nursing), psychology, or counseling, while 14% had been educated in business and 8% held degrees in multiple fields. Fifty-nine percent of the administrators were clinically licensed. Average center tenure was about 7 years and average position tenure was 5 years.

In addition to the on-site interviews, questionnaires were left with the administrators to be completed and returned *via* mail. The response rate for the questionnaires was 89% ($n = 401$) of the respondents at the 450 participating centers. Of these centers, 383 agreed to participate at Time 2, resulting in an 85% response rate. Time 2 data were also collected *via* on-site interviews with the administrators. Listwise deletion of cases with missing data on the variables included in the analyses resulted in a maximum usable sample of 280 centers at Time 1. At Time 2, listwise deletion of data resulted in a maximum usable sample size of 211.

Because the usable samples represented little more than half of the original sample, we conducted mean difference tests between the included centers and the excluded centers on both the dependent and independent variables. There was no significant mean difference on the financial performance index at Time 1 ($F[1, 314] = .05$; n.s.) or at Time 2 ($F[1, 236] = .93$; n.s.). The only significant differences among the independent variables excluded for missing financial performance data at Time 1 were for centers located in hospitals or on hospital campuses and for parent–center decentralization. The usable centers were slightly less likely to be located in a hospital ($F[1, \text{vari } 449] = 15.28$; $p < .001$; μ for included centers $= .67$; μ for excluded centers $= .80$) and reported slightly higher levels of parent–center decentralization ($F[1, 361] = .01$; $p < .05$; μ for included centers $= 4.71$; μ for excluded centers $= 4.50$). For centers excluded for missing financial performance data at Time 2, there were also two significant differences. Excluded centers were slightly more likely to be non-profit ($F[1, 449] = 8.53$; $p < .01$; μ for included centers $= .30$; μ for excluded centers $= .42$) and reported slightly higher levels of competition ($F[1, 435] = 5.53$; $p < .05$; μ for included centers $= 6.01$; μ for excluded centers $= 6.63$). In order to maximize our usable sample, we used mean replacement with the regression imputation technique recommended by Mac-Donald, Thurston and Nelson (2000) on those independent variables for which there were greater than 50 cases missing. Replacement was used on internal decentralization (85 cases), parent–center decentralization (87 cases), and performance aspirations (86 cases).

Measures

The constructs operationalized in the current study were internal decentralization, parent–center decentralization, organizational condition, percentage of professionals, competition, performance aspirations, financial performance, and a number of control variables. All measures except financial performance were administered either during the Time 1 on-site interviews with administrators or in the Time 1 administrator questionnaires. Financial performance data were derived from organizational records at both Times 1 and 2.

Internal Decentralization

Internal decentralization was measured using a 5-item subset of Aiken and Hage's (1966) centralization scale completed as part of the administrator questionnaire. Originally developed and used in a sample of social welfare and healthcare organizations (see Aiken & Hage, 1966, 1968), this measure has been found to be reliable and valid at the organizational level (Dewar, Whetten & Boje, 1980). Items had an organizational frame of reference and asked center administrators to assess *what it is generally like for employees to work at their centers* by rating five statements according to how reflective each was of working at their centers. The five statements were: (1) there can be little action taken until a supervisor approves a decision; (2) people who want to make their own decisions would be quickly discouraged; (3) even small matters must be referred to someone higher up for approval; (4) employees must ask their supervisors before doing almost anything; and (5) any decisions employees make must have their bosses' approval. Responses were on a 7-point Likert scale ranging from "not at all true" to "definitely true" and were coded such that higher scores represented greater decentralization. The average across items was used in the analyses. The internal reliability coefficient was .87.

Boundary Conditions

It was necessary to operationalize five boundary conditions or moderators of the decentralization–effectiveness relationship. The first condition was *parent–center decentralization*. One way of conceptualizing parent–center decentralization is as the amount of authority given to center leadership by the parent organization or, as Aiken and Hage (1968) refer to it, organizational autonomy. Parent–center decentralization was measured using a scale derived from Khandwalla (1977). Each administrator was asked *how much autonomy his/her center's on-site administration is given by the parent organization to make decisions* regarding raising capital for new investments; determining the center's operating budget; developing, marketing, and pricing treatment services; hiring, firing, and disciplining senior personnel; allocating excess revenue; opening/closing satellite facilities; and setting compensation policies. Thus, while the internal decentralization items emphasized decentralization as it is applied to employees throughout a center, this measure emphasized decentralization as it is applied to a center's top management by a larger parent organization. All responses were on a 7-point Likert scale anchored on one end with "no authority" and the other with "complete authority." The mean of these items was used to create the decentralization construct. Higher scores represented greater parent–center decentralization, while lower scores represented greater parent–center centralization. The internal reliability coefficient for the measure was .92.

The second boundary condition, *organizational condition*, was operationalized through two interview items asking administrators if there were imminent or in-progress plans for their centers to either expand or decrease staff, services, or the number of clients treated. Responses to these questions were coded to create a variable where growth (1); stability (0); shrinkage (−1). Growth indicated those centers planning expansion but not planning any decreases. Shrinking centers were those centers planning reductions but no expansion. Stable centers were those planning (a) neither expansion nor reduction ($n = 161$) and (b) those planning expansions in some areas but reductions in others ($n = 19$).

The third boundary condition, *proportion of professional workers*, was operationalized as the total number of nurses and licensed counselors divided by the total number of center employees. This proportion ranged from .00 to 1.00 with an average proportion of .47. The fourth condition, *competitive environment*, was operationalized with a single question asking respondents how much overall competition their centers faced at that time of the interview. Responses for this item ranged from 1 (no competition) to 10 (intense competition), with a mean response of 6.35. The final boundary condition, *performance aspirations*, was measured as the mean of five items taken from the administrator questionnaire and adapted from Khandwalla (1977). These items asked respondents the degree to which their organizations focused on generating average revenues, maintaining below average operating costs, maintaining high rates of growth, and securing high, above average financial strength as primary goals for their organizations. Again, items were on a 7-point agree–disagree format. Items were averaged to create the scale and coded such that higher responses represented greater financial performance aspirations. Internal reliability for this scale was .74.

Financial Performance

Organizational effectiveness refers to an absolute level of performance assessed by the degree to which an organization achieves certain goals (Ostroff & Schmitt, 1993). It is difficult to obtain financial performance data standardized for an entire sample of behavioral healthcare treatment centers. The primary reason is that smaller centers often feel vulnerable and are reluctant to provide hard financial data (Kamalesh, Subramanian & Yauger, 1997). To initiate control and standardization on our measure of financial performance, we asked administrators during the Times 1 and 2 on-site interviews to provide total center revenues and total center expenses from the most recent fiscal year. We used the information to create a measure of *gross total margin* at both time periods by subtracting expenses from revenues, then dividing the resulting number (net income$_{Ti}$) by revenues, i.e. (revenues$_{Ti}$—expenses$_{Ti}$)/revenues$_{Ti}$) (Tennyson & Fottler, 1997).[1] Clement, D'Aunno and Poyzer (1993) have argued that margin is an excellent indicator of short-term financial performance in healthcare organizations. While the length of time between Time 1 and 2 is probably too long to be considered purely "short-term," looking at Time 2 margin allows us to add a longitudinal dimension to the study that would be missed if we focused only on Time 1. Because neither the Time 1 nor 2 margin was normally distributed, both were transformed by taking their natural logs. This transformation reduced margin skewness from −3.22 to −.95 for Time 1 and from −2.58 to −.68 for Time 2. In both cases, greater logged margin represented greater performance.

Control Variables

It is to be expected that variations in financial performance may be due in part to differences in centers' sizes, ages in years, profit status, and whether they are located in or on hospital campuses. Thus, measures of the latter conditions were included as control variables. Organizational size and age have both been hypothesized to influence various organizational outcomes. Size is often associated with increased standardization and formalization (Scott, 1987), making organizational initiatives more standardized, as well, and less likely to have a large impact on organizations. Large organizations are also more likely to report stronger financial results in terms of raw numbers than are smaller organizations. Similarly, older organizations are also likely to be standardized and routinized (Scott, 1987), again making their performance generally stable and less susceptible to a liability of newness. For this study, *size* was measured as the total number of FTE employees working for a center in the year immediately prior to the on-site interview. *Age* was measured as the year of the interview minus the year of a center's founding. Analyses indicated that size and age were not normally distributed, so these variables were transformed by taking their natural logs. The log transformation reduced skewness from 3.83 to −.07 for size and from 3.24 to −.94 for age.

Profit status and whether the center was hospital-based were also used as controls. Though for-profit and non-profit organizations both face the need to perform well (Dees, 1998), for-profit organizations might face greater pressures for achieving higher profit margins than non-profit organizations. While some argue that a shared interest in the bottom-line and increased competition have narrowed the differences between profit and non-profit healthcare providers (Flower, 1997; Dees, 1998), we felt it would be safest to control for status. *Profit status* was measured with a single question asking administrators whether their centers were organized as for- or not-for-profit under the guidelines provided by the U.S. Department of Treasury, Internal Revenue Service. For-profit centers were coded 1, while not-for-profit centers were coded 0. Research has also shown that when larger corporations form subsidiaries there is a positive effect on financial performance (e.g., Clement et al., 1993). Further, profit margin may benefit from resource exchanges (e.g., client referrals) in units that are on larger organizational campuses. Thus, a single item assessing *center setting* was included as a control. Centers located on a hospital campus or located in a hospital setting were coded 1, while centers neither owned by hospitals nor located in hospitals were coded 0.

Analytical Procedures

Hierarchical moderated regression was used to test the hypotheses. Testing each hypothesis required forming the interaction between internal decentralization and a given boundary condition. In all cases, the multiplicative term was used to represent the interaction in the analyses. Two regression equations were tested: one with Time 1 margin as the dependent variable and one with Time 2 margin as the dependent variable. In both, the independent variables were entered in three steps. The control variables were entered first, followed by the main effects for decentralization and all of the boundary conditions. The final step entered all of the two-way interaction terms. Decentralization and all of the boundary condition variables were centered about their respective means (Cohen & Cohen, 1983). Moderation existed if an interaction term was significant and if the block of interaction terms accounted for significant residual variance in the dependent variable after the inclusion of the control variables and main effects. Observed significant interactions were plotted graphically (Cohen & Cohen, 1983).

Results

Correlations, means, and standard deviations are presented in Table 12.2.1. Results from the regression analyses are presented in Tables 12.2.2 and 12.2.3, and the plots of observed interactions are presented in Figures 12.2.1 and 12.2.2. Time 1 analyses demonstrated support for most of our hypotheses. As shown in Table 12.2.2, the controls (5%), main effects (8%), and interaction effects (5%) explained 18% of the total variance in performance ($p < .001$). The main effect of internal decentralization by itself was not significantly associated with Time 1 performance ($\beta = -.03$; n.s.). There were, however, statistically significant main effects for condition ($\beta = .11$; $p < .05$), percentage of professionals ($\beta = .21$; $p < .001$), competition ($\beta = -.12$; $p < .05$), and performance aspirations ($\beta = .16$; $p < .01$). Most important, though, the adjusted R^2 increased from 13 to 18% when the set of interaction terms was entered into the equation. Thus, as expected, boundary conditions play a major role in explaining the relationship of decentralization to Time 1 performance.

Specifically, expectations from Hypothesis 1 were that internal decentralization would interact with parent–center decentralization to influence the internal decentralization–performance relationship. As indicated in Table 12.2.2 and seen in Figure 12.2.1, this hypothesis was supported. Centers experiencing more centralized relationships with their parent organizations exhibited stronger margins when they also had high internal decentralization. Centers with high internal decentralization and low parent–center decentralization exhibited much stronger margins than internally decentralized centers with high parent–center decentralization.

Hypothesis 2, which stated that the effects of decentralization on organizational financial performance would be greatest in shrinking centers, was partially supported. Looking at Time 1 margin in Table 12.2.2, the interaction was statistically significant ($\beta = -.12$; $p < .01$). However, as seen in Figure 12.2.1, while organizations that were shrinking exhibited slightly higher margins when they also reported high levels of decentralization, growing organizations with high levels of decentralization reported lower levels of performance than did growing centers with low levels of decentralization. In fact, high decentralization in growing organizations was associated with about the same level of performance as shrinking organizations with high decentralization. Thus, decentralization appeared to be an enhancer for shrinking organizations, yet detrimental in growing organizations at Time 1.

Hypothesis 3 stated that the decentralization–financial performance relationship would be strongest for centers with many professional employees. This expectation was not supported in that the interaction between decentralization and percentage of professionals was not significantly associated with Time 1 margin ($\beta = -.08$; n.s.). Hypothesis 4 was not supported either. The interaction between decentralization and competition was not statistically significant ($\beta = -.05$; n.s.). Thus, neither percentage of professionals nor competitive environment served as boundary conditions for decentralization's relationship with Time 1 financial performance in the current sample.

Finally, Hypothesis 5 stated that the impact of high competition on the decentralization–performance relationship would be positive and the impact of low competition would be negative. As expected, the interaction between decentralization and aspirations was significantly associated with performance ($\beta = .13$; $p < .05$). The plot of the interaction (Figure 12.2.1) indicated that centers with high financial performance aspirations exhibited

Table 12.2.1 Descriptive Statistics

Variables	Mean	S.D.	N	1	2	3	4	5	6	7	8	9	10	11
Margin at Time 1	.17	.38	316											
Margin at Time 2	.19	.35	238	.30***										
Size	47.74	59.51	450	-.01	-.02									
Age	14.46	11.17	450	-.05	-.16*	.26***								
Profit status	.37	.48	450	.02	.15*	.06	-.14**							
Hospital based	.72	.45	450	.23***	.18**	-.16***	-.12**	-.35***						
Internal decentralization	5.23	1.12	450	.03	-.07	.01	.08	-.04	-.04					
Parent–center decentralization	4.69	1.22	450	-.01	-.08	.17***	.01	.24***	-.33***	.17***				
Condition	.51	.57	429	.09	-.05	.08	-.12*	.05	.05	.01	.11*			
Professionals (%)	.47	.22	425	.26***	.01	-.30***	-.11*	-.19***	.35***	.08	-.12**	-.01		
Competition	6.35	2.58	437	-.13*	.01	.09	.10*	.04	-.02	-.01	.00	.04	-.03	
Performance aspirations	4.80	1.09	450	.12*	.14*	.14**	-.03	.21***	.00	-.15**	-.01	.6	-.06	.02

*$p < .05$.
**$p < .01$.
***$p < .001$.

Table 12.2.2 Regression Results with Time 1 Margin as the Dependent Variable

	Step 1	Step 2	Step 3
Size	.07	.10	.06
Age	.00	.05	.04
Profit status	.13	.13*	.07
Hospital based	.28***	.22**	.16*
Internal decentralization		.04	−.03
Parent–center decentralization		.02	.00
Condition		.10⁺	.11*
Percentage professionals		.22***	.21***
Competition		−.16**	−.12*
Performance aspirations		.13*	.16**
Internal decentralization × parent–center decentralization			−.16*
Internal decentralization × condition			−.12**
Internal decentralization × professionals			−.08
Internal decentralization × competition			−.05
Internal decentralization × performance aspirations			.13*
Adjusted R^2	.05	.13	.18
F	4.83***	4.98***	5.00***
F-change, $N = 280$		4.81***	4.41***

$^+p < .10.$
$p < .05.$
$^{**}p < .01.$
$^{***}p < .001.$

Table 12.2.3 Regression Results with Time 2 Margin as the Dependent Variable

	Step 1	Step 2	Step 3
Size	.07	.05	.07
Age	−.06	−.06	−.03
Profit status	.29***	.25***	.30***
Hospital based	.28***	.28***	.31***
Internal decentralization		.02	.04
Parent–center decentralization		−.05	−.06
Condition		−.06	−.06
Percentage professionals		−.07	−.09
Competition		.01	−.02
Performance aspirations		.13⁺	.13⁺
Internal decentralization × parent–center decentralization			.07
Internal decentralization × condition			.19*
Internal decentralization × professionals			.14*
Internal decentralization × competition			.07
Internal decentralization × performance aspirations			.08
Adjusted R^2	.10	.10	.13
F	6.72***	3.23***	3.15***
F-change, $N = 211$		.91	2.71*

$^+p < .10.$
$^*p < .05.$
$^{***}p < .001.$

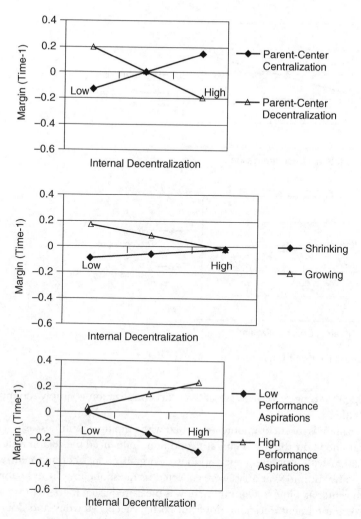

Figure 12.2.1 Plots of Significant Interactions with Margin at Time 1.

much higher Time 1 margins when they also reported high levels of decentralization, while low aspiration centers with high decentralization performed relatively worse.

Results for Time 2 margin were not as strong as those for Time 1, but nonetheless are interesting—especially given that Time 2 margin information was collected 2 years after that of Time 1 margin. Among the interaction terms, those with condition and percentage of professionals were both significant. This time, results for condition ($\beta = .19$; $p < .05$) were contrary to those with Time 1 margin as the dependent variable and Hypothesis 1. As shown in Figure 12.2.2, growing centers performed better at Time 2 when they had high rather than low decentralization. Likewise, shrinking centers performed better at Time 2 when they had low rather than high decentralization. Though the results for percentage of professionals were not significant at Time 1, they were significant at Time 2 ($\beta = .14$; $p < .05$). These results were also contrary to Hypothesis 2. Over time, organizations with a high percentage of professionals performed slightly worse with high internal decentralization than with low internal decentralization. Much as was argued for parent–center decentralization,

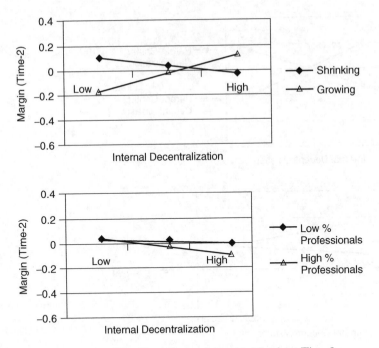

Figure 12.2.2 Plots of Significant Interactions with Margin at Time 2.

it is possible that a high percentage of professionals *and* decentralization is simply too much freedom without a buffer.

Because decentralization is most commonly associated with employee attitudes, as *post hoc* analyses, we also examined how the five boundary conditions influenced the relationship of internal decentralization with employees' perceptions of organizational commitment and job satisfaction. These two attitude variables were collected *via* questionnaires from a sample of counselors at each center at Time 2. Commitment was measured using the 7-item version of the organizational commitment questionnaire from Porter, Steers, Mowday and Boulian (1974). Job satisfaction was measured with three items from Hackman and Oldham's measure of general job satisfaction. Responses for both constructs were on a 7-point Likert scale ranging from "strongly agree" to "strongly disagree," and items for both were averaged so that higher scores represented greater organizational commitment and job satisfaction, respectively.[2] Internal reliability for organizational commitment was .80. For job satisfaction it was .92. Commitment and satisfaction were regressed onto the controls, main effects, and interaction terms using the same procedures used for margin.

Results for the two regression equations with the attitudes are presented in Table 12.2.4 and Figure 12.2.3. Beginning with the results for organizational commitment, Table 12.2.4 shows that, unlike the results for margin, the main effect for internal decentralization was positively associated with employees' organizational commitment ($\beta = .15$; $p < .05$). Three of the interaction terms were worth discussing. The strongest of the interactions was between internal decentralization and percentage of professionals ($\beta = .15$; $p < .05$). The interactions with condition ($\beta = -.13$; $p < .10$) and performance aspirations ($\beta = -.13$; $p < .10$) were both marginally significant. As shown in the plots in Figure 12.2.3, high decentralization was associated with better organizational commitment for all three boundary conditions.

Table 12.2.4 Regression Results with Time 2 Attitudes as the Dependent Variables

	Organizational commitment			Job satisfaction		
	Step 1	Step 2	Step 3	Step 1	Step 2	Step 3
Size	−.18**	−.18*	−.17*	−.10	−.09	−.12
Age	.00	.01	.04	−.02	−.02	.02
Profit status	−.17*	−.15⁺	−.16*	−.09	−.06	−.08
Hospital based	−.23**	−.21**	−.21**	−.18*	−.16*	−.16*
Internal decentralization		.09	.15*		.05	.10
Parent–center decentralization		.00	−.03		.03	.01
Condition		−.04	−.04		−.08	−.08
Percentage professionals		.03	.01		.06	.02
Competition		−.14*	−.14*		−.05	−.06
Performance aspirations		−.01	.06		−.05	.00
Internal decentralization × parent–center decentralization			−.02			−.03
Internal decentralization × condition			−.13⁺			−.10
Internal decentralization × professionals			.15*		.17*	
Internal decentralization × competition			.01			.13⁺
Internal decentralization × performance aspirations			−.13⁺			−.08
Adjusted-R^2	.05	.06	.09	.01	.00	.04
F	4.13**	2.32**	2.39**	1.70	1.06	1.58⁺
F-change, N = 221		1.10	2.38*		.65	2.54*

⁺$p < .10$.
*$p < .05$.
**$p < .01$.

However, the relationship of decentralization to commitment was enhanced under conditions of shrinkage, high percentage of professionals, and low performance aspirations.

Results for job satisfaction were somewhat different. The main effect of decentralization on satisfaction was not significant ($\beta = .10$; n.s.); however, the interaction between decentralization and professionals was significant ($\beta = .17$; $p < .05$). Satisfaction was strongest for high, as opposed to low, decentralization for both low and high percentages of professionals, but the benefit of high decentralization was slightly greater for organizations with a high percentage of professionals. The interaction between decentralization and competition was marginally significant ($\beta = .13$; $p < .10$). Figure 12.2.3 indicates that, in terms of satisfaction, high decentralization was particularly beneficial in organizations with strong competition. The overall equation was only marginally significant ($F = 1.58$; $p < .10$).

Discussion

This study examined the boundary conditions that circumscribe decentralization's relationship with financial performance. Consistent with expectations, the relationship of decentralization with both Time 1 and Time 2 financial performance was moderated by multiple key organizational and environmental variables, indicating that the relationship between decentralization and outcomes is not the same in all situations. In the present sample, the high performing organizations at Time 1 included those with simultaneous decentralization and centralization at two levels of the organization. Findings indicated that high internal

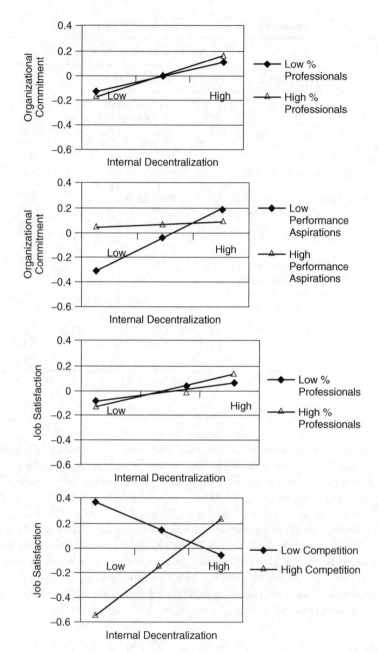

Figure 12.2.3 Plots of Significant Interactions with Organizational Commitment and Job Satisfaction at Time 2.

decentralization was associated with lower concurrent financial performance for treatment centers that were decentralized from their parent organizations. As such, the findings were congruent with the loose–tight coupling notion that there is no single appropriate approach for organizations in turbulent environments, and such organizations can benefit from simultaneous centralization and decentralization across different levels of the organization (Brown & Eisenhardt, 1998; Jansen & Chandler, 1994; Weick, 1976). That is, decentralizing decisions can be important in achieving immediate gains, but organizations also need buffering from the environment to achieve some level of order (Jansen & Chandler, 1994).

It is important to point out, though, that because Time 1 data were cross-sectional, an alternative explanation for the moderating effect of parent–center decentralization is *post hoc* rationalization by respondents. Financial performance could have caused decentralization or how respondents perceived decentralization. When current financial performance was high, administrators may have taken credit by claiming more parent–center decentralization and less internal decentralization (i.e., performance was due to my great decisions). Similarly, when current financial performance was low, administrators may have shifted blame elsewhere by claiming high parent–center centralization or high decentralization to subordinates (i.e., performance was due to the poor decisions of others). Because the interaction between internal decentralization and parent–center decentralization was not significant at Time 2, it was impossible to determine whether the buffering explanation or the rationalization explanation was correct.

In terms of organizational condition, the highest level of concurrent financial performance was achieved for growing centers with *low* decentralization, whereas *high* decentralization in growing organizations was associated with lower concurrent financial performance. For shrinking centers, concurrent performance was worst for those with low decentralization, but high decentralization was associated with only slightly better Time 1 performance. Again, the causal relationship between decentralization and performance, as moderated by center condition, could be interpreted two ways. It could be, for example, that low decentralization resulted in greater financial performance for growing centers. Alternately, it could be that administrators in high-performing, growing organizations were more likely to attribute performance to themselves (low decentralization) than to others (high decentralization).

Interestingly, Time 2 financial performance results for organizational condition countered the *post hoc* rationalization explanation and suggested that decentralization may have caused financial performance. In this case, decentralization had a slight detrimental effect for shrinking centers, while growing, high-decentralization centers exhibited much stronger margins at Time 2 than did growing, low-decentralization centers. As shown in Figure 12.2.2, though, the direction of this significant moderation was opposite from both Time 1 and the hypothesized direction. So why was high decentralization associated with lower, rather than higher, margin for shrinking centers at Time 2? One explanation is that decentralized decision-making requires a great deal of both resources and effort (Floyd & Wooldridge, 1997), simply making it too costly for shrinking organizations to pursue. Similarly, while decentralization may be appealing to leaders who need to alleviate immediate anxiety and decision-making overload (Ashmos et al., 1998), it may also add additional turbulence and too much complexity to the internal environment, making the effects of decentralization across time negative in shrinking centers. For these centers, it may be better to expend more effort on immediate, pressing issues (e.g., fiscal concerns) rather than devoting resources to managerial issues such as decentralized decision-making.

While the percentage of professionals did not moderate the relationship between decentralization and Time 1 financial performance, it did for the relationship between decentralization and margin at Time 2. However, much like the results with condition, the effect of the percentage of professionals employed was somewhat different than we anticipated. While centers with a high percentage of professionals reported slightly worse financial performance with high decentralization than with low decentralization, centers with a low percentage of professionals performed similarly at Time 2 regardless of their decentralization. It seems decentralization did little to offset the possible negative performance effects associated with hiring small numbers of professional clinical staff in a healthcare setting.

Finally, decentralization interacted positively with performance aspirations to influence the decentralization–financial performance relationship. Once again, though, because the moderator was only significant at Time 1, little can be inferred about the causal direction of this relationship. Whether organizations with high decentralization and low performance aspirations tend to perform more poorly or whether poorly performing organizations with high decentralization are more likely to claim low performance aspirations remains unclear.

Overall, what do the different findings at Time 1 and Time 2 tell us about the relationship between decentralization and financial performance? At the very least, the results from Time 1 give an idea of what types of organizations may use or claim to use decentralization. In particular, organizations with high internal decentralization were those with high financial performance, with high parent–center centralization, that were shrinking, and that reported high performance aspirations. Organizations with high internal decentralization were also those that exhibited poorer financial performance, reported high parent–center decentralization, were growing, and had low financial performance aspirations.

The results from Time 2, on the other hand, indicated that the equivocal impact of decentralization often reported in the decentralization literature (e.g., Porter & Lawler, 1965; Wagner, 1994; Wagner et al., 1997) may have been a function of previous research approaching decentralization's relationship to outcomes from too simplistic and narrow a perspective. The Time 2 results clearly indicated that decentralization could improve organizational financial performance but only under certain conditions. That is, depending on the boundary conditions in place, high levels of performance could be achieved under both low and high decentralization conditions. Decentralization specifically was associated with relatively stronger Time 2 performance when organizations were growing and when they employed a low proportion of professionals. Time 2 results also indicated that the relationship between decentralization and employee attitudes varied according to an organization's boundary conditions. In this case, percentage of professionals, performance aspirations, and competitive environment had the effect of enhancing or detracting from decentralization's relationship to satisfaction and commitment.

It is clear that the relationship of decentralization to a variety of outcomes is much more complex than typically hypothesized, and this study raises many additional questions. The present results, however, must be considered in light of the study's limitations. First, we only had one measure of performance and were only able to obtain data for this measure at one point in time *after* we collected the data regarding decentralization. It will be very important for researchers to explore the bounded relationship of decentralization with multiple indices of organizational performance (Rogers & Wright, 1998) over time and also to consider changes in decentralization and boundary conditions over time.

Another limitation was that our measure of decentralization reflected the perceptions of each center's highest employee—the center administrator. We chose this measure because we were surveying top managers and attempting to capture an overall measure of decentralization throughout each organization. Though the instructions asked administrators to consider their centers as a whole (rather than their own jobs), it is possible the administrators' perceptions of decentralization were not representative of the perceptions of lower-level employees. We believe several factors mitigate this limitation, however. First, the average size of the centers in our sample was relatively small (48 full-time equivalent employees). As such, administrators in these organizations may have had better perceptions of their employees' beliefs than top managers in larger organizations. Additionally, the majority of the adminis-trators ($n = 308$) in our sample had education and continued experience in behavioral healthcare provision (e.g., as social workers, psychologists, counselors), also suggesting they may have been more in-touch with their employees' perceptions than the average top manager.[3]

While it is true that administrators may perceive their centers partly as a function of their roles and, thus, be more likely to perceive decentralization when in fact little or none exists in the minds of employees, a recent study found that the various subgroups within healthcare organizations tend to agree about *who* participates in the decision-making process in their organizations (Ashmos et al., 1990). Likewise, the self-fulfilling prophecy (SFP) literature argues that managers' perceptions influence how they treat their subordinates and, ultim-ately, the performance of those subordinates (Eden, 1990). While most of the support for this argument has occurred at the individual level, Eden (1990) proposes that the processes by which manager perceptions influence performance can occur at the organizational-level. It will be extremely valuable for future research to simultaneously consider decentralization from the perspectives of top managers, middle managers, and operational-level employees (Ashmos et al., 1990; Floyd & Wooldridge, 1997). Finally, because our sample was limited to organizations in a single industry our results may not generalize to organizations in all industries. While they may be inappropriate for more traditional manufacturing organiza-tions, however, the results should generalize to the larger healthcare industry and to other service organizations.

To conclude, the results indicate a pattern in which decentralization is not universally beneficial and in which it tends to be most positively related to financial performance when used in organizations with certain attributes. At the same time, the results suggest that decentralization can be very detrimental to organizations with other characteristics. Given that high levels of performance are also associated with low decentralization under certain conditions, organizations wanting to improve their performance have many options. Because of the notorious difficulty of achieving large-scale cultural change (Schein, 1992), some alternatives to decentralization may be easier to achieve than successful decentralization.

Does this mean it would be best and easiest for all managers to avoid decentralized decision-making? We argue the answer to this question is "No." Managers and researchers alike must recognize that decentralization (and likely its related practices), is a very complex phenomenon (Ashmos et al., 1990). When used in conjunction with organizational charac-teristics that enhance its effects, decentralization can be quite beneficial to an organization. However, these benefits may not immediately materialize and the effects of decentralization can be negative as well. Thus, simply not pursuing decentralization does not guarantee acceptable performance either, for the benefits of low decentralization are also dependent upon organizational and environmental conditions.

Further, for almost all organizations, decentralization can be a positive influence on employee attitudes. This influence is most pronounced for shrinking organizations, those with a high percentage of professionals, those with low performance aspirations, and those experiencing high competition. Using these results as our guide, we suggest that, before attempting to implement a decentralized organizational structure and related management practices, an organization should carefully consider its most important long- and short-term goals, its other characteristics, and how these goals and characteristics are likely to change in the future.

Our results indicate that there was a strong need in the literature to examine decentralization at both the organization level and in terms of the boundary conditions in which it may be embedded. Prior research, which addressed decentralization more narrowly, presented only a partial picture of the decentralization–outcome relationship and may have led some researchers and practitioners to prematurely "close the book" on decentralization as a means of achieving performance gains as well as to overlook the conditions under which decentralization can be both beneficial *and* detrimental. The research presented here, however, indicates that the impact of decentralization on organizational outcomes can be fairly strong—in both a positive and a negative sense. Indeed, the relationship of decentralization to financial performance appears to be much more complex than has been traditionally conceived. The present study contributes to our understanding of decentralization by beginning to define the general context for which confident conclusions regarding the effects of decentralization can be made.

Notes

* A version of this paper was presented in the Health Care Management Division of the 1998 Academy of Management meetings in San Diego, CA.
1 Where net income$_{Ti}$ represents net income at Time i; revenues$_{Ti}$ represents revenues at Time i, and expenses$_{Ti}$ represents expenses at Time i.
2 In order to bring these individual attitudes to the organizational-level, it was necessary to aggregate organizational commitment and job satisfaction across counselors within each center. ICC(2) was calculated as the reliability of means at the aggregate level (Ostroff & Schmitt, 1993), ICC(2) scores for organizational commitment ranged from 0.90 to 0.92, and for job satisfaction they ranged from 0.57 to 0.82.
3 As a further test of the possibility that our results were a function of *who* our respondents were (as opposed to actual decentralization), we examined the influences of administrators' individual differences on our results. All regression equations were rerun controlling for administrators' level and field of education, position tenure, center tenure, previous administration experience, age, and gender. No significant results were found for any of these variables, and including them did not change the pattern of findings.

Acknowledgments

Support for this research was provided in part by grants from the National Institute on Alcohol Abuse and Alcoholism to Drs. Blum and Roman (R01 AA 10130 and T32 AA 07473). We thank Ann Buchholtz, Allen Amason, Soumen Ghosh, and three anonymous reviewers for their assistance with this manuscript.

References

Aiken, M., & Hage, J. 1966. Organizational alienation. A comparative analysis. *American Sociological Review*, 31: 497–507.
Aiken, M., & Hage, J. 1968. Organizational interdependence and intra-organizational structure. *American Sociological Review*, 33: 912–930.
Arthur, J. B. 1994. Effects of human resource systems on manufacturing performance and turnover. *Academy of Management Journal*, 37: 670–687.
Ashmos, D. P., Duchon, D., Hauge, F. E., & McDaniel, R. R., Jr. 1996. Internal complexity and environmental sensitivity in hospitals. *Hospital & Health Services Administration*, 41: 535–555.

Ashmos, D. P., Duchon, D., & McDaniel, R. R., Jr. 1998. Participation in strategic decision making: The role of organizational predisposition and issue interpretation. *Decision Sciences*, 29: 25–51.

Ashmos, D. P., McDaniel, R. R., Jr., & Duchon, D. 1990. Differences in perception of strategic decision-making processes: The case of physicians and administrators. *Journal of Applied Behavioral Science*, 26: 201–218.

Becker, B. E., & Huselid, M. A. 1998. High performance work systems and firm performance: A synthesis of research and managerial implications. *Research in Personnel and Human Resources Management*, 16: 53–101.

Blum, T. C. 1998. Optimal staffing for drug abuse treatment services. *Issue Paper*. Washington, DC: NIDA Resource Center for Health Services Research.

Brown, S. L., & Eisenhardt, K. M. 1998. *Competing on the edge*. Boston, MA: Harvard Business School Press.

Clement, J. P., D'Aunno, T., & Poyzer, L. M. 1993. The financial performance of diversified hospital subsidiaries. *Health Services Research*, 27: 741–763.

Cohen, J., & Cohen, P. 1983. *Applied multiple regression/correlation analysis for the behavioral sciences* (2nd ed.). Hillside, NJ: Lawrence Erlbaum Associates.

Cohen, S. G., Ledford, G. E., Jr., & Spreitzer, G. M. 1996. A predictive model of self-managing work team effectiveness. *Human Relations*, 49: 643–676.

Conrad, D. A., & Shortell, S. M. 1996. Integrated health systems: Promise and performance. *Frontiers of Health Services Management*, 13: 3–40.

D'Aunno, T., & Sutton, R. I. 1992. The responses of drug abuse treatment organizations to financial adversity: A partial test of the threat-rigidity thesis. *Journal of Management*, 18: 117–131.

Dees, G. J. 1998. Enterprising nonprofits. *Harvard Business Review*, 76(1): 55–67.

Dewar, R. D., Whetten, D. A., & Boje, D. 1980. Examination of the reliability and validity of the Aiken and Hage scales of centralization. *Administrative Science Quarterly*, 25: 120–128.

Eden, D. 1990. *Pygmalion in management: Productivity as a self-fulfilling prophecy*. Lexington, MA: Lexington Books.

Flower, J. 1997. Is the war between investor-owned institutions and not-for-profits over? *Healthcare Forum Journal*, 40(5): 59–64.

Floyd, S. W., & Wooldridge, B. 1992. Middle management involvement in strategy and its association with strategic type. *Strategic Management Journal*, 13: 153–167.

Floyd, S. W., & Wooldridge, B. 1997. Middle management's strategic influence and organizational performance. *Journal of Management Studies*, 34: 465–483.

Glew, D. J., O'Leary-Kelly, A. M., Griffin, R. W., & Van Fleet, D. D. 1995. Participation in organizations: A preview of the issues and proposed framework for future analysis. *Journal of Management*, 23: 395–421.

Hickson, D. J., Hinings, C. R., Lee, C. A., Schneck, R. E., & Pennings, J. M. 1971. Strategic contingencies theory of intraorganizational power. *Administrative Science Quarterly*, 16: 216–229.

Hodson, R. 1985. Corporate structure and job-satisfaction. A focus on employer characteristics. *Sociology and Social Research*, 69: 22–49.

Jansen, E., & Chandler, G. N. 1994. Innovation and restrictive conformity among hospital employees: Individual outcomes and organizational considerations. *Hospital & Health Services Administration*, 39: 63–80.

Kamalesh, K., Subramanian, R., & Yauger, C. 1997. Performance-oriented: Toward a successful strategy. *Marketing Health Services*, 17: 10–20.

Khandwalla, P. N. 1977. *The design of organizations*. New York: Harcourt Brace Jovanovich.

Knoke, D. 1981. Commitment and detachment in voluntary associations. *American Sociological Review*, 46: 141–158.

Koch, M. J., & McGrath, R. G. 1996. Improving labor productivity: Human resource management policies do matter. *Strategic Management Journal*, 17: 335–354.

Lawler, E. E., III 1996. *From the ground up: Six principles for building the new logic corporation*. San Francisco: Jossey-Bass.

Lawler, E. E., III, Mohrman, S. A., & Ledford, G. E. 1995. *Creating high performance organizations*. San Francisco: Jossey-Bass.

Leana, C. R. 1986. Predictors and consequences of delegation. *Academy of Management Journal*, 29: 754–774.

Leana, C. R., & Florkowski, G. W. 1992. Employee involvement programs: Integrating psychological theory and management practice. *Research in Personnel and Human Resources Management*, 10: 233–270.

Locke, E. A., & Schweiger, D. M. 1979. Participation in decision-making: One more look. In B. Staw & L. L. Cummings (Eds.), *The innovative organization: Productivity programs in practice*: 265–339. Greenwich, CT: JAI Press.

MacDonald, R. A., Thurston, P. W., & Nelson, M. R. 2000. A Monte Carlo study of missing item methods. *Organizational Research Methods*, 3: 70–91.

Miller, K. I., & Monge, P. R. 1986. Participation, satisfaction, and productivity: A meta-analytic review. *Academy of Management Journal*, 29: 727–753.

Mintzberg, H., & Waters, J. 1985. Of strategies deliberate and emergent. *Strategic Management Journal*, 6: 257–272.

Morse, N. C., & Reimer, E. 1956. The experimental change of a major organization variable. *Journal of Abnormal Psychology*, 52: 120–129.

Ostroff, C., & Schmitt, N. 1993. Configurations of organizational effectiveness and efficiency. *Academy of Management Journal*, 36: 1345–1361.

Ouchi, W. G. 1977. The relationship between organizational structure and organizational control. *Administrative Science Quarterly*, 22: 95–113.

Perrow, C. 1967. A framework for the comparative analysis of organizations. *American Sociological Review*, 32: 194–208.

Pfeffer, J., & Salancik, G. 1978. *The external control of organizations*. New York: Harper & Row.

Porter, L. W., & Lawler, E. E., III. 1965. Properties of organizational structure in relation to job attitudes and job behavior. *Psychological Bulletin*, 64: 23–51.

Porter, L. W., Steers, R. M., Mowday, R. T., & Boulian, P. V. 1974. Organizational commitment, job satisfaction, and turnover among psychiatric technicians. *Journal of Applied Psychology*, 59: 603–609.

Przestrzelski, D. 1987. Decentralization: Are nurses satisfied? *Journal of Nursing Administration*, 19: 23–28.

Pugh, D. S., Hickson, D. J., & Hinings, C. R. 1969. An empirical taxonomy of work organization structures. *Administrative Science Quarterly*, 14: 115–126.

Pugh, D. S., Hickson, D. J., Hinings, C. R., & Turner, C. 1968. Dimensions of organization structure. *Administrative Science Quarterly*, 13: 65–105.

Pugh, D. S., Hickson, D. J., Hinings, C. R., Turner, C., & Lupton, T. 1963. A conceptual scheme for organizational analysis. *Administrative Science Quarterly*, 8: 289–315.

Ranson, S., Hinings, B., & Greenwood, R. 1980. The structuring of organizational structures. *Administrative Science Quarterly*, 25: 1–17.

Rogers, E. W., & Wright, P. M. 1998. Measuring organizational performance in strategic human resource management: Problems, prospects, and performance information markets. *Human Resource Management Review*, 8: 311–331.

Scheid, T. L., & Greenley, J. R. 1997. Evaluations of organizational effectiveness in mental health programs. *Journal of Health and Social Behavior*, 38: 403–426.

Schein, E. H. 1992. *Organizational culture and leadership*. San Francisco: Jossey-Bass.

Scott, W. R. 1987. *Organizations: Rational, natural, and open systems*. Englewood Cliffs, NJ: Prentice-Hall.

Spreitzer, G. M. 1995. Psychological empowerment in the workplace: Dimensions, measurement, and validation. *Academy of Management Journal*, 38: 1442–1465.

Tennyson, D. H., & Fottler, M. D. 1997. Does system membership enhance financial performance in hospitals? In L. N. Dosier & J. B. Keys (Eds.), *Academy of management best paper proceedings*: 123–127. Georgia: Office of Publications and Faculty Research Services, College of Business Administration, Georgia Southern University.

Vandenberg, R. J., Richardson, H. A., & Eastman, L. J. 1999. The impact of high involvement work processes upon organizational effectiveness: A 2nd-order latent variable approach. *Group and Organization Management*, 24: 300–339.

Wagner, J. A., III. 1994. Participation's effects on performance and satisfaction: A reconsideration of research evidence. *Academy of Management Journal*, 19: 312–330.

Wagner, J. A., III, Leana, C. R., Locke, E. A., & Schweiger, D. M. 1997. Cognitive and motivational frameworks in U.S. research on participation: A meta-analysis of primary effects. *Journal of Organizational Behavior*, 18: 49–65.

Weick, K. E. 1976. Educational organizations as loosely coupled systems. *Administrative Science Quarterly*, 21: 1–19.

Wooldridge, B., & Floyd, S. W. 1990. The strategy process, middle management involvement, and organizational performance. *Strategic Management Journal*, 11: 231–241.

13 Technology, the Environment, and Organization Design

13.1 ORGANIZATION DESIGNS TO RENEW COMPETITIVE ADVANTAGE

David Lei and John W. Slocum Jr.

The industrial graveyard is full of names of companies that once dominated their industries. Enron Corp., RCA, Sperry, and Zenith are just a few names of well-known firms that were synonymous with American innovation in the recent past. Today, companies like Cisco Systems Inc., Oracle Corp., Qualcomm Inc., AOL Time Warner Inc., and Intel Corp. define competition and innovation in their respective industries. Will these firms' enormous success and profitability be the same forces that ultimately drive them into oblivion?

It is our contention that the rise of new technologies, new forms of competition, and new avenues to add customer value have already begun to redefine the basis of strategic thinking and competitive advantage in many industries. Building and sustaining competitive advantage requires the firm to learn and adapt at an ever faster rate in order to distinguish itself from competitors. In many industries, first-mover advantage at best lasts a few months, if not weeks—even in such staid industries as automotive, medical equipment, electronic instruments, and financial services. Product life cycles have been compressed to the point that today's cutting-edge products and services are becoming commodities in ever-shorter time spans. Astonishingly, even intellectual capital and proprietary technologies, once protected by layers of patents and enshrouded in corporate secrecy, have themselves become widely available. For example, the latest software (Linux), microprocessor designs (Transmeta), financial instruments (Quicken), music offerings (MP3), and even medical advice (Healtheon/WebMD) have become established fixtures on the Internet. Today's cutting-edge products and services raise the competitive bar as they become the basis for customers' expectations tomorrow. And yet, there is no shortage of companies (both existing and new) attempting to capitalize on the latest technologies and customer demand trends to become the behemoths of their respective industries.

This article highlights some of the most important organizational issues confronting firms as they deal with their competitive landscape. The first part of this article analyzes the nature of some of the most salient environmental developments that firms must address. Second, we examine how some firms across a variety of different industries are successfully utilizing the forces of change to create new sources of competitive advantage, while simultaneously limiting the effects of inertia that ordinarily would have impeded their adaptation. Several distinct strategic patterns of behavior emerge that may help explain how some firms are better able to survive and compete successfully in this complex, ever-changing environment. Third, we examine some of the internal challenges that all firms face when attempting to reshape their organization designs to accommodate these new strategic patterns, behaviors, and initiatives.

The New Competitive Environment: Epicenters of Sudden Change

In his popular management book *Only the Paranoid Survive*, Andy Grove, chairman of Intel, wrote that all industries will eventually face significant changes in their competitive environments that result from dramatic breakthroughs in new technologies, changes in customer demand, or the rise of new competitors. Grove used the term "inflection point" to characterize the nature of these profound, sudden changes in the environment that often spell a major crisis for firms. Inflection points are important because they signify the potential for a radical transformation of an industry's structure. Inflection points within an industry open up opportunities to new entrants and competitors that can exploit breakthrough technologies or develop new products and services which ultimately redefine the basis of value creation.

Over time, each industry will face its own unique set of inflection points, depending on the specific nature of the technology used, the type of customer served, and the likelihood of new competitor entry. Nevertheless, the nature of these profound changes shares several common trends, including (1) the rising importance of knowledge work, (2) the growth of substitute products and services, and (3) the growing information-intensive nature of many industries' value-adding activities. Any one of these trends can redefine the basis of competition in an industry. However, the presence of two or even all three of these trends that surface within an industry contributes to change of an even greater magnitude. Firms competing in an industry where knowledge work, substitute offerings, and information-intensity (e.g., software, semiconductors, digital media) are critical to sustaining a competitive advantage are more likely to confront epicenters of change that redefine the competitive landscape than those firms in industries where only one of these trends occurs (e.g., ship-building, petroleum refining, construction). Table 13.1.1 highlights how these industry change drivers, or inflection points, impact the design of organizations.

Table 13.1.1 Everything Changes: Organizational Redefinition

Organizational Design Characteristic	Traditional Competitive Advantage	Innovation Drivers
Customer/supplier linkages	Industry-centered supply/buyer chains	Industry-spanning Web-driven hubs
Role of CEO	Craft and execute corporate and business strategies	Foster entrepreneurial activities at every level
Nature of value-added	Physical value chains dominate	Information drives value creation
Strategic focus	Control and protect scarce resources	Identify and capture new capabilities
Role of corporate capabilities	Defend existing sources of advantage	Internalize activities to grow
Role of outsourcing	Attain low-cost efficiency	Assemble virtual corporations
Role of employees	Careers within an organization	Knowledge workers flow across organizations

Knowledge Work

In many industries, knowledge work has become the primary that defines how well firms innovate and compete with one another. In the pharmaceutical, biotechnology, semi-conductor, software, and publishing industries, knowledge work in the form of advanced research and development (R&D), continuous experimentation, and the creation of new technological standards defines how well a firm can create products and services in advance of its competitors. More importantly, the shift toward knowledge work places a greater emphasis on how well managers can attract and retain talent—a key competitive advantage for firms in those industries.

In places such as Silicon Valley, Research Triangle, and other hotbeds of innovation, the recruitment, training, and development of knowledge workers shape a firm's basis for future technologies and product ideas. Often, firms will attempt to recruit technical talent from their competitors, and from companies in other industries as well. This growing flow of people between firms within and across different industries promotes the rapid flow of ideas, insights, and innovation that give rise to the kind of innovative ferment from which new technologies and businesses are spawned.

Substitute Products and Services

The competitive landscape can shift rapidly in those industries where existing products and services face competitive threats from substitutes. Firms in related or neighboring industries often produce substitutes. In effect, the innovation of substitute products creates opportunities for new entrants and innovators to change the way firms must compete. For example, the rise of Internet-based telephony, threatens traditional phone companies, such as AT&T Corp. and Verizon Communications. The growth of the Internet serves as a substitute technology that displaces the traditional circuit switches used by existing telecommunications firms. In another case, the growth of video-on-demand threatens the established broadcasting infrastructure of many entertainment and network-based firms, as well as the production of standard television sets and VCRs. Video-on-demand, which enables consumers to watch any movie or any show at any time, means that people no longer need to use their existing televisions and VCRs in the way they have become accustomed. Instead, they are able to bypass traditional networks (with their rigid time schedules) and access the show or film they want to see (through digital coding). This development, in turn, makes it more difficult for the established network firms to compete using their traditional methods and sources of revenue (through the capture of advertising dollars).

Rising Information Intensity

The growing information-intensive nature of many industries means that the costs of creating, transmitting and disseminating information are steadily declining over time. We are witnessing emerging developments where products are actually dropping in price with each new generation, and in some cases, services are almost entirely free to the consumer. Information-intensive industries, in particular, are subject to this phenomenon. The costs of creating and transmitting information on a wider scale appear to be declining as the information content becomes richer. For example, e-mail is a service whose value to the user grows as it becomes more pervasive and easier to use. On the other hand, the costs of transmitting and delivering e-mail to this wider population are declining as new networking technologies substantially lower the cost of each message. The same compelling economics of information also partially explain the rapid rise of Internet portal companies, such as Yahoo! and Terra Lycos. It also explains why AOL Time Warner and Microsoft Corp. are racing one another to create ever more friendly Internet browsers and a huge subscription-based network that links customers with e-commerce firms and other providers of digital-based services. These companies bring together a growing base of users with advertisers and other e-commerce sites that facilitate faster and more efficient business and information-intensive transactions.

What impact do these factors—knowledge work, substitute offerings, and information-intensity—have on the competitive environment? Firms can expect that their strategies and sources of competitive advantage will come under renewed assault from new forms of competition. As a result, industry structures are becoming less stable over time. The cumulative effect of these changes will likely give rise to significant changes in the way organizations formulate and implement their strategies. Table 13.1.2 highlights some of the features of this new competitive environment.

Impact of the Shifting Landscape

The massive growth and availability of the Internet has spawned the rise of new substitute products and services that are now challenging the strategies and management practices implemented by long established firms in the brokerage industry, such as Merrill Lynch & Co., UBS Paine Webber, and Morgan Stanley Dean Witter & Co. In addition, the brokerage industry is becoming more information-intensive, as new products and services are created and offered to investors through a variety of media—including computers, digital cell phones, and interactive trading software. Investors can place trades directly through the phone or via the Internet and confirm their executions through instantaneous e-mail messages. Traditional brokerages now confront a new force that threatens to rapidly erode their existing customer bases and sources of competitive advantage. These firms can no longer count on investors to place their trades through full-service, commissioned brokers that are the heart of their business. Instead, high commission fees are encouraging many investors to establish accounts with Ameri-trade and E-trade as these new entrants offer a significantly less costly and more convenient alternative. The combination of new technology and the rise of new competitors now promise to transform the underlying economics of the brokerage industry.

In general, we should expect to see the impact of frequent and massive change on an industry in three ways. The broader impacts of these changes are three-fold.

Table 13.1.2 Impact of New Competitive Environment on Industry Competitiveness

Redefinition of Industry Structure	*Impact on Firm Strategy*
Marked reduction in prices; trend toward commoditization	Inability to sustain product differentiation
Rapid product obsolescence	New product proliferation and breakthrough technologies
Widespread knowledge	Sophisticated and demanding users
Rapid erosion of traditional entry barriers	Competitors enter from new and unforeseen industries
Competitors change	Need to think across traditional industry boundaries
Rise of different customer bases	Creation of new markets

Commoditization of new technologies. One major trend that is already well on its way to reshaping a variety of industries is the growing availability of state-of-the-art technology to anyone who wants it. Today's innovations are rapidly becoming commodity-like products. Shifts in operating platforms and technical standards have created dinosaurs overnight (e.g., dedicated word-processing programs) and opportunities for next-generation providers (e.g., Linux). In addition, new technology products, such as virus-scanning software, programmable logic devices (PLDs), flash memory chips, and fast modems to connect with the Internet, are rapidly becoming standard features in many of today's computer and electronics products. Browsers and search engines to harness the Internet are routinely pre-packaged into new versions of computer operating systems. This type of economic behavior has long defined innovation and product development in the semiconductor industry. Today's personal computers, for example, are likely to come with an Intel microprocessor that is twice as fast as one initially offered just 18 months before.

Rapidly declining unit costs. Even some of the most sophisticated forms of knowledge are becoming widely available on the Internet for a very low cost, and in several cases, for free. Healtheon/WebMD, for example, offers access to state-of-the-art medical research and evaluation methods for patients interested in learning more about different kinds of ailments and preventive care. Even computer software, ranging from sophisticated operating systems to video plug-ins, is free to users. Linux, now considered an important competitive alternative to Microsoft's 2000 NT system, can be downloaded free to any customer.

The growing spread of "freeware" over the Internet, however, creates both opportunities as well as threats. For record and music companies, the rise of new software that enables consumers to record, digitize, and store music on their personal computers could be ominous. Using a format known as MP3, consumers can now easily download a wide range of music selections from the Internet and store them in their hard drives at little or no cost. The rise of these formats clearly demonstrates some of the dilemmas facing music and media firms such as Warner Music, Sony, Bertelsmann AG, and Vivendi Universal. If these firms cling too long to retail stores as their established channel of distribution, they will begin to lose sales under the pressure of Internet-driven technologies. On the other hand, if these firms embrace the Internet, new forms of digital storage and playback technologies in order to preempt and co-opt the rise of new digital upstarts, they risk alienating not only their traditional wholesaler channels, but also some of their recording artists—who are under contract and are paid through the royalties garnered from the physical sale of CDs.

Burden of strategic commitment. The ability of an established firm to learn and create new sources of competitive advantage over time becomes steadily more difficult. Change often requires new managerial mindsets and a willingness to challenge assumptions about how to add value to emerging customer needs. Often, established firms become wedded to ingrained patterns of behavior that slow senior managers' ability to scan for emerging developments, or more important, to ask the right questions on how best to learn. Core competencies built and refined from an earlier time become shackles and blinders that constrain learning.

Firms tend to focus on rivals within a narrow definition of their own industry, or on competition within a small strategic group. Intel's long obsession with arch rival Advanced Micro Devices Corp. (AMD) has potentially given upstart Transmeta an unforeseen opportunity to begin selling its novel power-saving Crusoe microprocessors to manufacturers of laptop computers, where users need to conserve battery life for extended periods of time. On the other hand, many sources of change often begin or emanate from other industries that initially appear distant, but may actually incubate new competitors in the future. For example, GE Capital has recently designed products that substitute for many commercial banks' offerings. Yet, most banks do not consider GE Capital a competitor in their immediate business domain. Thus, it is important for firms to continue monitoring how their products and services are likely to evolve over time, especially if their offerings begin to assimilate or absorb the characteristics of technologies or product offerings from other industries. This means that potential competitors from very different and previously unforeseen industries could arise suddenly.

Sustaining Competitive Advantage: Change Faster than the Industry

Our central contention is that firms can only survive and prosper to the extent that they are able to change as fast or faster than the rate at which their industry is changing. Firms need to change on a series of critical dimensions. First, they need to recognize that when their customers are able to dictate prices and offerings, their products and services have already become commodities. Second, firms are able to generate high profitability to the extent that they are able to differentiate themselves in a significant way from their competitors. Long-term profitability is a direct function of distinctiveness; the lack of distinctiveness translates into an unsustainable business position. Third, firms must balance their organization designs to promote the kind of innovation, experimentation, and thinking that will encourage self-renewal and reinvention. One of the biggest conundrums facing established firms is that as they become larger and more successful over time, they tend to implement practices and organizational structures that promote stability at the cost of bold innovation. At the same time however, this quest for greater internal stability and control sharply delimits a manager's ability to learn and bring in the kinds of new insights, skills, and the "out-of-the-box" ways of thinking that promote change.

In a nutshell, the kernel of corporate survival means learning how to innovate as quickly as the new entrant, while assimilating new technologies within the established firm's infrastructure, brand(s), or existing economies of scale. Oftentimes, it may be necessary to foster a process of "self-cannibalization," in which the firm deliberately aims to seek out and absorb innovations from competing firms or other industries to transform itself in a very short time. Likewise, it could mean acquiring a whole new technology or idea by completing a buyout of the entrant before it has time to encroach upon an incumbent firm's competitive advantage. The recent spate of mergers occurring in the Internet, communications, and entertainment industries points to the high degree of flux occurring among all three arenas. America Online's recent merger with Time Warner hopes to mesh together two complementary sources of strength (Internet savvy and technology with traditional content, publishing, music, and film production) to become a full-fledged digital media giant.

Although the evidence is still preliminary, several strategic patterns of firm behavior have been emerging that may point to new sources of sustainable competitive advantage. Table 13.1.3 presents some new strategies that firms from a variety of industries have implemented to embrace change in order to learn and craft new sources of competitive advantage.

Pursue Self-Cannibalization Opportunities

One of the most potent ways an incumbent firm can deal with a rapidly shifting industry landscape is to embrace the change as part of its future core vision. The faster an incumbent

Table 13.1.3 Strategic Imperatives to Manage Change

Imperative	Do's	Don'ts
Pursue opportunities for self-cannibalization	Fund new technologies internally and externally Create special units to pursue new ideas/breakthroughs	Keep special units reporting to older businesses Protect older technologies from new types of innovations
Buy out the entrant	Keep acquisitions small and autonomous Search for distant technologies to create new product ideas	Buy a similar size firm to protect existing core businesses Buy a firm in same state of technological development
Learn from potential new entrants	Align with a firm that has similar ambitions/complementary skills Utilize alliances to bring in new skills/chart industry standards	Hesitate and be forced to choose from also-rans Rely on partner for developing core skills entirely
Manage parallel development teams	Foster internal competition to search for best ideas Look for new partners to accelerate innovation	Over centralize R&D or idea development Use vertical integration to compensate for creativity

firm embraces the change, the less time a new entrant or competitor has to establish a beachhead in the industry.

Case of Intel. Intel Corporation, the world's largest semiconductor firm, has aggressively pursued self-cannibalization opportunities each time it designs a next-generation micro-processor for personal computers and other electronics. Intel realizes that the pace of semiconductor manufacturing and other scientific advances is accelerating with each new product generation. As the microchip becomes smaller, the technical challenges of getting the design to market faster become greater. Intel is well aware that any misstep will open up numerous opportunities for established rivals (e.g., Advanced Micro Devices) and new entrants (Via Technologies of Taiwan, Transmeta and Tensellica of the U.S.) to enter its core market. Thus, Intel deliberately creates an entirely separate product team within the firm whose sole purpose is to come up with new challenges and ways to defeat its own product designs. By forcing a high degree of internal competition among different chip design teams, Intel is harnessing internal "paranoia" to deal with competitors.

Over the past 2 years, Intel has realized that the core of semiconductor growth and advances is steadily moving away from the personal computer (PC) market and toward electronic devices that allow for fast and seamless connectivity with the Internet. In response to this major challenge, Intel has invested aggressively in learning and innovating new forms of chip architectures that have already enabled the firm to secure major contracts with digital cell phone (Ericsson, Nokia) and other companies. It has also acquired a host of different companies, such as Dialogic, Level One Communications, with emerging tech-nologies that will accelerate Intel's internal innovation efforts. Intel believes that by acquiring these firms in their infancy, it can preempt the rise of new competitors from penetrating its existing core business. Whether all of these acquisitions will prove successful is unknown. If successful, Intel can transform itself by commercializing these new developments faster than the new entrants can do by themselves, since Intel is able to combine new technologies with its own state-of-the-art manufacturing prowess, brand equity, and investment capital.

Case of Eastman Kodak. Companies that attempt to harness new technologies or ideas within the organizational hierarchy of existing business units often face a much more difficult task, as was the case with Eastman Kodak Company. Technical advances, such as charge-coupled devices (CCDs), flash memories, and interpolation technologies, have their scientific roots based on semiconductor and software competencies. Traditional photographic imaging is based entirely on a chemical-based competence. By fostering the development of new CCDs within their traditional imaging businesses, Kodak faced significant difficulties in trying to innovate leading-edge products for a demanding market. On the one hand, managers and technical staff who have been long involved with developing conventional photographic technologies experienced great difficulties in attempting to learn entirely new competencies, while simultaneously "unlearning" their traditional sets of routines for product development that were based on silver halide-based processes. The skills required for faster commercialization of digital technologies required technical and marketing staffs to learn new ways of approaching the consumer electronics marketplace. Even after 11 restructurings over the past 10 years, Kodak is still struggling with this core change. Ironically, many of the latest advances in digital imaging borrow on Kodak's original discoveries and patents in the field.

In order to successfully exploit self-cannibalization opportunities, firms will need to form special units that have reporting relationships outside of "normal" channels. These special units must be encouraged to develop their own set of product development routines, insights, and innovative cultures away from the confines, reporting relationships, and preexisting norms of other parts of the firm. Toys "R" Us implemented this approach when it established an e-business unit in San Francisco, far away from its headquarters in New Jersey. Senior management at the toy giant gave the newly formed unit a clear mandate to grow its business. By bypassing the normal chain of command, e-business managers gained access to senior managers for resources, information, and knowledge workers that might have been lost in the labyrinth of the traditional hierarchy. In general, we believe that if senior management tries to assimilate these special units too quickly into the fabric of the existing organization, it runs the risk of stifling the unique, maverick product development approach that is often needed for successful transformation. More often than not, these units will need to develop their own pace of innovation faster and bolder than those pursued by the firm's other lines of business.

Buy Out the Threat or Entrant

Large established companies, such as Cisco Systems and Microsoft, have appeared to capture the recent lessons of history. In the fast-moving high technology world, new entrants with promising new technologies are rising everyday, threatening to challenge the industry leader's market position. However, these companies have boldly acquired new entrants that possess cutting-edge technologies that could have markedly threatened their sources of competitive advantage. These companies have established internal venture capital units that are designed to finance promising ideas and technologies that were created by competitors. These firms realize there is no possible way that they can manage the pace of industry evolution within the confines of their own operations. Yet, they know that the fundamental scientific advances leading to new products and technologies could emanate from anywhere around the world. Both companies will screen and potentially fund any idea related to computer networks or software, respectively, in order to remain vigilant leaders in their industries.

Case of Cisco Systems. The growth of Cisco Systems is especially noteworthy, given the fact that this company went public just 10 years ago. Up to 80% of the Internet's traffic flow is along Cisco's routers, bridges, switches, and hubs. These are the "plumbing" of modern communications and networking systems. Cisco has earned a market capitalization of $194 billion and a dominant market share for networking equipment by staying ahead of its competitors through aggressively acquiring other smaller firms that offered opportunities for growth and acquisition. CEO John Chambers readily admits that many of the best ideas and technologies come from outside Cisco. Over the past 5 years, the pace of Cisco's acquisition strategy has picked up markedly as new developments in software, photonics, optical networking, and network security systems become part of a technology solution set to customers. Chambers knows that the routers it pioneered as recently as 2 years ago have already become mature goods and face ever-tougher commodity-like pricing. Even with the most recent severe downturn in the market for optical networking equipment, Cisco's aggressive learning and assimilation of new technologies will likely help strengthen the company's position once customer demand returns.

What is the secret to Cisco's success in managing and integrating all of these acquisitions? As long as the size of the acquisition is kept small, there is growth potential, and the firm can be acquired at the right price. Cisco's top leadership believes the acquired firm should be given considerable autonomy to do what it does best: innovate without worrying about financing and corporate politics.

Case of 3Com. 3Com's experiences over the past 3 years point to some of the difficulties that an established firm faces when it is slow to embrace change and to adopt the latest technologies. 3Com was a competitor to Cisco Systems in the networking equipment industry throughout the early 1990s. At the time, senior management believed that its market position in chassis hubs, remote access devices and network interface cards (all of which are devices that route data in computer networks) gave 3Com a defensible position that would allow it to confront Cisco head on. 3Com thought that corporate buyers would not want to purchase all of their networking equipment needs from a single buyer. However, Cisco's relentless pace of acquiring other firms and investing in new technologies made it difficult for 3Com to sustain its market share. New developments in router and optical technologies accelerated the pace of innovation and technological commoditization of existing product lines.

In March 1997, hoping to bolster its plateauing market position in networking cards and computer modems, 3Com purchased U.S. Robotics, a firm that was comparable in both size and technological skill. Unfortunately, the acquisition of U.S. Robotics greatly complicated 3Com's learning and development of even newer technologies since senior management now faced the complex task of integrating such a large acquisition in a short period of time. To complicate matters even further for 3Com, Intel in May 1997 developed its own set of network interface cards that were significantly faster and cheaper than that of 3Com's offerings. Moreover, Intel could leverage its strong vendor position with PC makers to sell both microprocessors and network cards at a lower price than 3Com could. Today, 3Com is still struggling to chart a new corporate direction, and Cisco Systems' lead is so overwhelming that it appears unlikely that 3Com would ever be as strong a contender as it was just a few years ago.

Learn From the New Entrant

Even for those firms willing to take on the risks of acquiring firms for their technological prowess, some of the newest and most interesting opportunities may arise in industries that are very distant from the firm's current lines of business. Frequently, the best ideas for improving a firm's core business may actually have roots in other industries. Thus, it is important to identify a likely potential competitor early on, before it has sufficient time and resources to challenge the incumbent firm(s) on its own. As Borders Books & Music, Barnes & Noble, Blockbuster Inc. and Toys "R" Us Inc. discovered, Amazon.com was able to seize the initiative in redefining the book, music and toy retailing business by establishing direct distribution channels with consumers. As traditional retailers, none of them realized the enormous power that Amazon.com could deploy in three short years to change the competitive forces in their industries.

In the field of music recording and entertainment, a similar series of events is now occurring. Sony, Vivendi Universal, EMI Group, and Bertelsmann are discovering that with the advent of new digital formats (e.g., MP3) that could challenge these firms' lucrative royalty-based business models (e.g., sales of physical compact disks), new strategic choices are needed. Vivendi Universal's music unit, in particular, has become particularly sensitive to this development and has begun establishing alliances with software and digital security firms in order to establish an industry-wide basis for containing and managing the new threats.

Case of Ford Motor Company. Many of the challenges that have confronted consumer-oriented firms are now reshaping the industrial product environment as well. Ford is aggressively building new industry-spanning supply chains that will link every part and component supplier with its own factories, using real-time ordering part-fulfillment systems. Ford's new direction requires competencies and technical breakthroughs that go well beyond its core automotive manufacturing operations. By working with such firms as i2 Technologies, Cisco Systems, Commerce One and Oracle, Ford hopes to use its e-commerce relationships to set the standard for future business transactions in the highly competitive auto and component businesses. In fact, Ford has even begun working with arch rivals General Motors Corp. and Daimler-Chrysler to develop new formats to standardize the technologies and platforms used to promote new forms of electronic commerce. By working with its traditional rivals, Ford hopes to harmonize the ordering of parts from suppliers and thus save billions of dollars a year by moving to faster, more responsive and less paper-intensive supply chain configurations.

Case of Wal-Mart Stores. Firms from all industries are utilizing a broad array of alliances and other cross-firm relationships to forestall potential competitors and even to learn how a future competitor does business. Consider what is perhaps the most telling example of how even a giant retailer with tremendous marketing clout is beginning to feel the competitive pressures of new entrants encroaching upon its market base. Wal-Mart Stores Inc., the largest retail establishment in the world, continues to ponder the formation of a broad strategic alliance with AOL Time Warner and other firms in order to set up a large e-commerce presence on the Internet in a very short time. Wal-Mart realizes that the longer it waits, the more likely that it will face the same kinds of competitive dilemmas and delays that have long plagued Sears, Roebuck & Co., J. C. Penney Company Inc. and other large department stores in the mid-1990s. If Wal-Mart waits too long to embrace the Internet, it would likely lose significant market share in different product categories to much more focused new entrants in the future.

Manage Parallel Product Development Teams

When developing new technologies or product offerings, it is important that firms manage the level of internal competition in the shortest time period. Developing new products and processes are often complicated tasks. Sometimes several initiatives need to be tried simultaneously to determine which approach is better. Running multiple projects reduces the likelihood that a superior approach or design is overlooked. As teams work on a solution to a given problem, people will develop skills and insights that can prove useful in thinking about future products. Thus, carefully managed product development teams that work "in parallel" across functions and departments will enable a firm to engage in much higher levels of organizational learning. The need to manage parallel product development teams to capture the best ideas is especially salient when firms are competing in such fast-changing industries as entertainment, publishing, and music recording. In these markets, it is difficult to accurately decipher what forces influence trends, tastes, and preferences without establishing a close degree of empathy and understanding of the consumer's needs. Oftentimes, it is necessary for firms to "cast a wide net" in order to search for the next blockbuster idea or hit. This learning is essential in order to help the firm understand which technologies, product standards, and marketing approaches work best. Ideally, this approach to managing product development cultivates a healthy degree of internal competition for critical resources with a dual focus on continuous improvement and breakthrough innovations.

Case of Sony. Sony's legendary success with its portable Walkman radio/cassette player reveals the enormous power of managing product development teams in parallel to generate and commercialize breakthrough ideas quickly. Several project teams worked on this initiative, helping to determine which format would be most satisfactory for customers and the most easily manufactured. Sony was able to quickly create an entirely new consumer electronics product segment that gave the entire company an aura of innovation and creativity that has been difficult for its competitors to imitate. Even today, Sony still actively cultivates a high level of internal competition to produce music and electronic gadgets that are directly tied to the Internet. Sony Music Entertainment has begun to sell digital versions of its songs directly online to consumers over the Web.

At the same time, it is rapidly developing an entirely new series of MP3-based products that will enable customers to order, copy, store and play back music on portable players. These products will completely bypass the traditional compact-disc route. Recently, Sony has unveiled two new products that offer both easy-to-access music, as well as copyright protection to prevent piracy. Known as the Memory Stick Walkman and the Vaio Music Clip, both products use advanced flash memory technology to substitute for CDs. To sustain its leadership in this new electronics arena, Sony has also begun working with a host of different digital media and technology companies (e.g., Microsoft, Liquid Audio, AOL Time Warner, RealNetworks) to further learn how music recording and playback is likely to evolve. In addition, Sony will also learn how to improve and develop newer forms of digital copyright protection formats from its partners.

Case of Hewlett-Packard. Hewlett-Packard Co. has traditionally fostered a high degree of internal competition among product development teams to create a steady stream of advanced laser and ink-jet printers, scanners and other equipment. In particular, throughout the company's long history, H-P has thrived in promoting strong inter-unit competition that has germinated numerous key innovations in the imaging, electronic instruments, testing equipment, communications equipment, and other industries. H-P has long been known for its scorn of corporate bureaucracy, committees, and other impediments to speed. Its newest initiative is to create state-of-the-art software and other products that will make the Internet much more user-friendly to consumers. In May 2002, Hewlett-Packard completed its merger agreement with Compaq Computer that will create a high-tech colossus. Given the enormous size of this merger, however, it remains to be seen whether the new Hewlett-Packard will be able to sustain its distinctive approach to promoting fast innovation through its traditional product development approach.

Capture the Full Potential of Value-Creating Networks

In this new competitive environment, very few firms are able to innovate and commercialize new technologies, products or services entirely on their own. As the confluence of knowledge workers, substitute offerings and information intensity become present in a growing number of industries, the pace of change will accelerate. The proliferation of new ideas, insights, and product standards from anywhere around the world means that firms must be able to network with and learn from different suppliers, customers, and competitors—all on a real-time basis. The massive investment in supply chain management, enterprise resource planning (ERP) software, knowledge management, Internet-based ordering systems, and virtual corporations point to the growing realization that the value creation process is now increasingly knowledge-based. To a large extent, the massive growth in these new technologies reveals how many firms have realized that they must be able to respond and compete on an Internet time frame. Developments in new technologies and the rise of new entrants mean that firms must be able to engage in all of the above strategic initiatives simultaneously in order to create new sources of competitive advantage.

Fast Learning

Many of the alliances, mergers, and acquisitions that have taken place over the past few years are an outgrowth of corporate searches and responses to this new fast-changing competitive environment. Within the firm, each stage of the traditionally-defined value-adding process—including R&D, operations, marketing, finance, call centers, and even human resource management—now involves a high level of coordination and interaction with partners outside the firm. Often, suppliers can provide the same value-adding activity at significantly lower cost or with a faster turnaround time. Vertical integration to build economies of scale may no longer be a viable competitive strategy, particularly in those industries exposed to frequent and radical change.

The Eastman Kodak and 3Com cases reveal that vertical integration is no substitute for fast learning and innovation. It is becoming increasingly difficult for any given firm to master every value-adding activity in-house. With technology itself rapidly becoming a commodity that can be readily imitated, many firms are beginning to focus and concentrate their innovation efforts. At the same time, however, they are forming closer relationships among a vast array of partners to capture brand equity and consumer awareness in the "market space" and the conventional "marketplace." Building relationships to foster innovation has become more important than maintaining control through vertical integration, particularly when fast-changing customer needs are driving product development.

From Physical to Virtual Value Chains

The revolutions shaking the music recording and distribution industry in just the last 18 months illustrate our perspective. Traditionally, this industry has been dominated by AOL Time Warner, Sony, Bertelsmann AG, EMI Group, and Vivendi Universal. These firms signed long-term royalty contracts with artists and entertainers, managed their own studios, mass-produced their own CDs in factories, and controlled significant marketing programs (e.g., wholesalers and radio stations) to ensure the steady sales of music through wholesalers and retailers. With the advent of digital media formats and new technical standards for recording and disseminating music, however, this traditional, vertically-integrated and linear value-creating structure is increasingly becoming a liability. It limits each firm's degree of freedom to maneuver, to co-opt new digital media entrants, and to learn new digital-based technologies. Instead, as music (like other forms of information) becomes widely available over the Internet, the traditional value of the CD to the consumer wanes. The consumer can access music (and other forms of content) anytime, anywhere from anything.

Music firms, such as Vivendi Universal and Sony, must now reconfigure their value-chain approaches to a more distributed, network-platform to create and add value for the customer. This means forming an array of alliances with Internet service providers (e.g., Earth-Link, Microsoft), Internet portals to reach preferred customers (e.g., Yahoo!, Terra Lycos, Infoseek), digital retailers (e.g., Amazon.com, Barnes & Noble.com, MP3.com), and even software firms to create new standards for digital encryption (RealNetworks, IBM Corp., Verisign). As consumers move away from the CD as their sole source of music, recording companies must create virtual organizations with Internet service providers to create new technical standards and products to capture new customers (e.g., Sony, RealNetworks, Microsoft, Intel). In time, even the virtual value chain will give way to a highly dispersed set of value-creating networks and "market spaces," where any company or recording artist will be able to plug in to the system and directly link to consumers anywhere around the world.

The Evolution of New Value-Creating Technologies

The rise of new value-creating activities in both the market place and the market space is occurring at a rapid rate for both manufacturing and service industries. The health-care industry is now in the midst of a massive revolution in which different organizations are embracing both new medical technologies and novel ways of sharing information to deliver better patient care. Hospitals, health maintenance organizations (HMOs), insurance firms, outpatient service firms, and physicians are rapidly specializing in a particular area of medicine while outsourcing to partners to provide the patient with a full range of care options. Hospitals are no longer the vertically-integrated behemoths that provide all services ranging from any type of surgery to radiation services to community outreach. Instead, many hospitals themselves have been forming their own medical practice networks in which physicians, radiologists, dietitians and other skilled staff work through a sophisticated information network that integrates many activities into one advanced, software-driven system. This system provides instantaneous updates on what patients will likely need. Physicians themselves have become much like the "knowledge brokers" who work with a specific client to provide him/her with a full range of services. This knowledge broker (or physician) also serves as the primary contact point that helps the customer (or patient) migrate through multiple providers to seek what he/she needs most.

Emergence of Shared Networks

As new breakthroughs make themselves felt across traditional industry boundaries, emerging organizational designs will increasingly be based on new configurations where information, knowledge, innovation, manufacturing, and marketing all converge together along a shared network. This shared network brings together not only different parts of the firm, but also different firms that may be from different industries as well. It is no accident that many industry structures are steadily evolving towards this increasingly distributed, yet agile flexible network approach to define new sources of competitive advantage. These networks evolve and compete on the basis of fast innovation, the sharing of ideas, and rapid product development. Many firms competing within this larger knowledge Web are building highly specialized sources of skills and knowledge that give them considerable bargaining power and influence in shaping the development and delivery of future products and services. The rise of the so-called "virtual organization," whereby each company specializes, but interacts with a host of different firms, is just one manifestation of this broader trend.

At the same time that each firm is attempting to specialize, it must also foster the capability to reconfigure itself in a way so that it can work with a number of different partners, suppliers, and customers. The entertainment, managed health care, telecommunications, financial services, and software industries are rife with firms who are attempting to make themselves more virtual so they can enter into new sets of relationships. Even though there is considerable collaboration to share resources to develop new technologies and products, these competing organizations are dueling among themselves to capture market share, future sources of innovation, and growth. This form of organization also serves to accelerate the diffusion of future innovations and breakthroughs as well. As information, knowledge, and value flow across many firms, any firm operating within the "virtual organization" is a potential source for future innovation, learning, and inflection points that can dramatically change the skills and competencies needed to compete effectively. Likewise, managers need to enhance their capability to detect and sense emerging opportunities and threats that may emanate from anywhere within the network's scope of innovation and growth.

As traditional firms learn how to form strategic alliances with future competitors, it is likely that we will begin to see the rise of more complicated and intricate alliance relationships among competitors, suppliers, newly emerging firms, and customers. Many of these relationships will have a dual offensive/defensive rationale. On the one hand, these relationships enable traditional firms to learn new technologies and to capture them before a similar rival can do so (e.g., Wal-Mart in retailing). On the other hand, these arrangements have a defensive flavor that enables a firm to buy time and to learn new skills as it reinvents itself (e.g., AOL Time Warner and Vivendi Universal as related to digital content). More important, as relationships among suppliers and competitors grow through complicated e-commerce-driven alliances, the firm that is able to embrace change the fastest is likely to have the most influence over the entire network.

As firms become more networked, that part of the network that is the most innovative and technologically advanced will have significant power over other alliance members. Far-reaching alliances among firms from many different industries will likely accelerate the spread and transformation of industry-changing practices from one sector to another. Thus, any firm that collaborates together with a host of other firms needs to ensure that it can, at a very minimum, learn as quickly as its partners within the network. To the extent that a firm can enhance and even accelerate its learning, it will be able to exert a greater influence on how the overall network will evolve. Conversely, if a firm within the network is unable to sustain the high rate of learning needed to acquire new skills and insights, then it is likely to become a peripheral player over time. It will then lose the ability to participate in shaping future industry or technological trends.

Steering Through Shifting Landscapes

The advent of new forms of competition, customer needs, and technologies has given rise to a competitive environment in which organizations in many industries are questioning their traditional sources of competitive advantages and means for creating value. The growing importance of knowledge-based work, the innovation of substitute products, and rising information intensity have spawned ever more frequent change that challenges many established firms' existing strategies and organization designs. In particular, we have noted that established firms in many industries might find that their earlier sources of competitive advantage have become potentially difficult obstacles to learning and creating new products and technologies to compete in the future. As firms deal with the numerous changes and challenges posed by epicenters of massive change, it is important that managers broaden the scope of their skills to accommodate and learn new insights and perspectives that will help them become more effective. As each firm's economic and technological sources of competitive advantage shift over time, managers need to develop new competencies to steer their firm through these shifting landscapes. We note five of these.

Look for New Skills and Insights Across Industries

Often, new developments in what appear to be a "distant" or unrelated industry may exert a considerable impact on a firm's strategy, approach to product development, and existing sources of competitive advantage. Managers need to become more comfortable with monitoring and understanding how new ideas and innovations developed in another industry could affect their own firm's future. This is especially important for established firms whose underlying value-creating activities are becoming more information-intensive over time. Environmental scanning activities should encompass not only existing competitors, but also future entrants from other industries. As industry structures become boundaryless, the scope of environmental scanning should broaden to include a much greater range of nontraditional competitive arenas.

Legitimize and Encourage Multiple Perspectives

As established firms face a growing number of challenges from new entrants, senior managers need to expand the strategic "lenses" by which they examine and understand future developments. In many cases, this means that established firms must actively cultivate and encourage managers from all levels of the firm to contribute a multitude of perspectives and ideas about what skills, technologies, and competencies will be needed to thrive in the future. In particular, senior managers should encourage employees to work on a host of different ideas and technologies, with the hope that the firm can be the first to capitalize upon potential new breakthroughs and ideas. However, the cultivation of diverse perspectives means that managers must be willing to listen and embrace those ideas and viewpoints that are very different—and even contrary—to what they traditionally believe and what has driven them to their current status. In particular, the growth of knowledge work in an expanding number of industries means that when firms do not listen to employees with new ideas, then they will often take root and prosper in a more willing competitor as employees shift employers.

Reward Innovative Thinking and Practices

Employees need to know that new ideas, which may challenge an existing set of practices, will not be stifled or suppressed. In fact, it is essential that firms design and implement reward systems that support new practices. This is particularly important for those firms that nurture new business units whose mission is to explore and exploit breakthrough ideas that may cannibalize the firm's existing products and competencies. Managers in these units should report directly to the CEO, and not through the hierarchical channels and planning practices of existing business units. Each manager should be evaluated not only in the context of performing his/her current job requirements, but also on the basis of his/her contribution of new ideas and ways to renew the firm's existing business.

Understand That Knowledge Work Cuts Across Industries

Senior managers need to broaden their scope of recruiting new talent. This talent should come from not only their existing sources, but also from more "distant" or unrelated sources that may actually be the repository of fresh ideas and practices. Knowledge work that is applicable in one industry setting is likely to be relevant in another. Best practices on how to select, develop, and promote people in one industry will often become the benchmark for human resources practices in another. Frequently, this means that managers in one industry should understand how trends and developments affecting the growth of another industry shape and redefine the skill sets that will be needed in the future. These same trends will likely have a major impact on how knowledge workers are trained, developed, and managed over time.

Learn and Jointly Develop Key Skills From Your Partners

As firms continue to cooperate with one another, it is important that each member of an expanding alliance relationship contributes and learns from another. Skills and insights developed from one set of products/services may be directly applicable to others. Thus, alliance partners need to ensure that they are capable of continuous learning, not only from one another, but also from their own internal efforts. A constant balance of mutual learning and contribution helps to keep the alliance relationships stable, and to promote risk sharing when working together to develop future innovations.

The issue of learning is especially salient for firms in those industries where knowledge work, substitute products, and rising information intensity are simultaneously interacting to redefine industry structure and the underlying bases of value creation. In industries characterized by accelerating rates of change, (especially with greater force and frequency), firms must remain vigilant for new types of competitors and customer needs. Moreover, these are likely to be the same industries whereby firms' traditional organizational structures and approaches to value creation will undergo the most significant metamorphosis. As each firm develops its own unique approach to renew its competitive advantage, a key task facing senior management will be to foster a willingness by managers at all levels in the organization to call into question their firm's strategies and practices as new developments occur in the environment.

Acknowledgments

The authors would like to thank Warren Boeker, Don Hellriegel, Michael A. Hitt, William Joyce, Richard Mason, Gary Moskowitz, and Charles Snow for their time and comments on an earlier version of this paper. Portions of this paper were presented at the Pan Pacific conference, Gold Coast, Australia, June 2000. This research was sponsored by the OxyChem Corporation.

Selected Bibliography

There is a growing literature examining the relationships between organization designs, learning, and strategic renewal. See, for example, M. Beer and N. Nohria, *Breaking the Code of Change* (Boston, MA: Harvard Business School Press, 2000); D. Bovet and J. Martha, *Value Nets: Breaking the Supply Chain to Unlock Hidden Profits* (New York: John Wiley & Sons, 2000); M. J. Cronin, *Unchained Value: The New Logic of Digital Business* (Boston, MA: Harvard Business School Press, 2000); M. H. Boisot, *Knowledge Assets: Securing Competitive Advantage in the Information Economy* (New York: Oxford University Press, 1999); L. Argote, *Organizational Learning: Creating, Retaining and Transferring Knowledge* (Boston, MA: Kluwer Academic Press, 1999); R. H. Miles, *Leading Corporate Transformation: A Blueprint for Business Renewal* (San Francisco: Jossey-Bass, 1997); M. E. McGill and J. W. Slocum, Jr., *The Smarter Organization. How to Build a Company That Learns, Unlearns, and Capitalizes on Marketplace Needs* (New York: John Wiley & Sons, 1994); J. B. Quinn, *The Intelligent Enterprise* (New York: Free Press, 1992).

For an examination of some key strategic and organizational issues related to fostering innovation and new forms of competitive advantage, see, for example, D. C. Galunic and K. M. Eisenhardt, "Architectural Innovation and Modular Corporate Forms," *Academy of Management Journal*, 2001, 44(6), 1229–1249; J. Child and R. G. McGrath, "Organizations Unfettered: Organizational Form in an Information-Intensive Economy," *Academy of Management Journal*, 2001, 44(6), 1135–1148; W. J. Ferrier, "Navigating the Competitive Landscape: The Drivers and Consequences of Competitive Aggressiveness," *Academy of Management Journal*, 2001, 4(4), 858–877; D. C. Hambrick and J. W. Fredrickson, "Are You Sure You Have a Strategy?" *Academy of Management Executive*, 2001, 15(4), 48–59; M. Schulz, "The Uncertain Relevance of Newness: Organizational Learning and Knowledge Flows," *Academy of Management Journal*, 2001, 44(4), 661–681; G. J. Young, M. P. Charns, and S. Shortell, "Top Manager and Network Effects of the Adoption of Innovative Management Practices: A Study of TQM in a Public Hospital," *Strategic Management Journal*, 2001, 22, 935–952; A. Takeishi, "Bridging Inter- and Intra-Firm Boundaries: Management of Supplier Involvement in Automobile Product Development," *Strategic Management Journal*, 2001, 22, 403–434; A. N. Afuah, "How Much Do Your Co-opetitor's Capabilities Matter in the Face of a Technological Change?" *Strategic Management Journal*, 2000, 21, 387–404; D. J. Teece, G. Pisano, A. Shuen, and D. N. Sull, "Why Good Companies Go Bad," *Harvard Business Review*, 1999, 77(4), 42–52; D. Lei, J. W. Slocum, and R. A. Pitts, "Designing Organizations for Competitive Advantage: The Power of Unlearning and Learning," *Organizational Dynamics*, 1999, 27, 24–38; D. B. Yoffie and M. A. Cusumano, "Judo Strategy: The Competitive Dynamics of internet Time," *Harvard Business Review*, 1999, 77(1), 70–83; "Dynamic Capabilities and Strategic Management," *Strategic Management Journal*, 1997, 18, 509–533; P. B. Evans and T. S. Wurster, "Strategy and the New Economics of Information," *Harvard Business Review*, 1997, 75(6), 70–82; A. Y. Illinitch, R. A. D'Aveni, and A. Y. Lewin, "New Organizational Forms and Strategies for Managing in Hypercompetitive Environments,"

Organization Science, 1996, 7, 211–220; D. Lei, M. A. Hitt, and J. D. Goldhar, "Advanced Manufacturing Technology: Organizational Design and Strategic Flexibility," *Organization Studies*, 1996, 17, 501–523; M. J. Kiernen, "The New Strategic Architecture: Learning to Compete in the Twenty-First Century," *Academy of Management Executive*, 1993, 7(1), 7–21.

13.2 ADAPTIVE FIT VERSUS ROBUST TRANSFORMATION

How Organizations Respond to Environmental Change*

Cynthia A. Lengnick-Hall and Tammy E. Beck

Previous research has examined a variety of ways by which firms adapt to environmental change and surprise. Most recommendations emphasize ways to achieve an adaptive fit between a firm and its environment. The authors propose that an alternate response to the uncertainty caused by a dynamic environment—robust transformation—should be examined as well. Organizational routines for dealing with complexity are seen as shaping the institutional response to environmental uncertainty. Resilience capacity is introduced as an internal factor that influences the repertoire of available routines and helps a firm decide whether routines directed toward adaptive fit or robust transformation are more appropriate to implement.

Keywords: *adaptation, robust transformation, adaptive fit, resilience capacity*

Most mainstream perspectives suggest that organizations adapt to uncertainty and environmental change by taking deliberate, intentional, and rational steps to regain equilibrium (Chakravarthy, 1982; Ginsberg, 1988; Zajac & Kraatz, 1993). However, an alternate approach, which argues that a more effective response may be for organizations to promote "creative, innovative, continually changeable behavior" and develop the capacity for "spontaneous changeability" (Stacey, 1995: 478), has also been proposed. Each of these views follows a similar sequence of activities, including (a) the experience of environmental change and uncertainty, (b) the execution of organizational routines to deal with or avoid heightened uncertainty and complexity, and (c) the realization of organizational outcomes and performance consequences.

The driving premise of this article is that prevailing perspectives do not capture the full range of environmental conditions that organizations must face. We contrast the ideas supporting adaptive fit with an alternate set of assumptions. This allows a reexamination of organizational responses and yields different prescriptions from those found in prior research. We also introduce the concept of resilience capacity and explain how this attribute influences both the routines a firm is able to develop and its choice of which routines to implement. We conclude, with a discussion of implications and an agenda for further research.

Rethinking Uncertainty and Adaptive Fit

Uncertainty has been defined in a variety of ways in the literature, but most researchers emphasize the difficulty of accurate prediction or probability assessment (Duncan, 1972; Milliken, 1987; Pfeffer & Salancik, 1978) or insufficient knowledge of cause-and-effect relationships (Duncan, 1972; Lawrence & Lorsch, 1967). Milliken (1987) argued that three distinct types of uncertainty (state, effect, and response) are generated by events that surprise an organization and call into question its foundation premises about what to do. Environmental shifts (Ginsberg, 1988), environmental turbulence (D'Aveni, 1994; Eisenhardt & Tabrizi, 1995), and environmental jolts (Meyer, 1982) can produce all three types of uncertainty.

Adaptive Fit and the Underlying Assumptions

Organizational adaptation research has examined a variety of ways in which firms respond to environmental uncertainity, change, and surprise (Chakravarthy, 1982; Dutton & Dukerich, 1991; Ginsberg, 1988; Jennings & Seaman, 1994; Tripsas & Gavetti, 2000). Empirical evidence generally supports an integrative view of the relationship between environmental change and subsequent organizational activities (e.g., Ginsberg & Buchholtz, 1990). From an integrative view, both environmental conditions and organizational capabilities shape a firm's response and the ultimate consequences of disruptive events.

In his seminal article, Chakravarthy (1982) proposed a framework of *adaptive fit* that included three states: unstable fit, stable fit, and neutral fit. Each of these states can lead to organization survival. He uses the term *adaptive fit* to mean that a firm is able to accommodate the level of complexity presented by its environment. Each of the three states of adaptive fit is well suited for a different environmental condition.

A defensive strategic posture (i.e., a strategy based on reducing a firm's interactions with its environment) coupled with a mechanistic organizational design promotes *unstable fit*. Firms with unstable fit remain very vulnerable to external events and rely on buffers to protect themselves from any adverse consequences of environmental change. Unstable fit relies on passive insulation for survival and is best suited for an environment that changes slowly and predictably (Simon 1969).

A reactive strategy (i.e., trying to meet every environmental change with a corresponding organization action) and a bureaucratic organizational structure can foster *stable fit* (Chakravarthy, 1982). When a firm achieves stable fit, it has adequate resources to respond to environmental shifts but is constrained by its administrative arrangements. These organizations attempt to sense and respond to environmental changes in ways that conserve resources but also effectively realign the firm with new environmental conditions. Survival requires effective reactions to negative feedback (Simon, 1969). This form of adaptive fit is appropriate for firms facing moderate levels of environmental complexity and clear mandates for what is expected.

A proactive strategy (i.e., forecasting and preemptive adjustment) and an organic organizational architecture can yield *neutral fit*. This is the highest level of fit proposed in the prior literature and reflects an effective match between a firm's material resources and its ability to exploit those resources through innovative action. Highly complex environments require neutral fit so that firms are able to reduce their vulnerability to change by anticipating and capitalizing on external shifts.

Several assumptions underpin the concept of adaptive fit. First, the presumption is the environment shifts from one state of equilibrium to another. Therefore, the focus of adaptive activity is to adjust the firm's internal activities to accommodate the new equilibrium conditions in the external environment. Second, effectiveness and efficiency are assumed to require an optimal balance between creative activities (exploring new opportunities) and productive activities (exploiting current capabilities). Each of the three adaptive states demonstrates a different blend of these two activities and thereby responds to a different level of environmental complexity. Third, a firm's particular mix of strategic posture (defensive, reactive, proactive) and organizational arrangements (mechanistic, bureaucratic, organic) yields a specific type of adaptive fit. Fourth, once a given level of adaptive fit is achieved and a firm is able to compete effectively, it generates slack resources. The notion of adaptive fit presumes that a firm should invest these slack resources in developing the resources and organization structure needed to move to a higher fitness level. At each successive level from unstable to stable to neutral fit, a firm achieves greater immunity from environmental fluctuations.

Limitations of Assumptions Leading to Adaptive Fit

Recent research on dynamic environments suggests the need for a reexamination of these underlying assumptions. Sutcliffe and Vogus (2003) and others argued that environmental complexity has reached a new threshold and as a consequence, the potential for surprise; uncertainty; and abrupt, crisis-level shocks to equilibrium has increased. Of greater import-ance, the objective of seeking "immunity" from environmental change is not an effective orientation for organizations operating in hypercompetitive environments or in markets that depend on a firm's ability to promote fluid, relentlessly shifting conditions (Ferrier, Smith, & Grimm, 1999). Effective strategies in high-velocity, hypercompetitive markets require firms to maintain an intimate connection with the environment. Moreover, if change is relentless, success depends on a firm's ability to establish momentum and persistently destabilize the marketplace (D'Aveni, 1994). Meyer (1982) introduced an additional situation, which he defines as jolts, in which the environment undergoes an abrupt, unexpected, significant, but temporary shock. When a jolt occurs, the environment is changed dramatically but temporarily. Taken together, these conditions highlight four limitations of prior views of organizational adaptation.

One, if an environmental change is not a shift from one equilibrium condition to another, then an effective response should recognize the inherent instability of the situation. Eccles and Nohria (1998) argued transitory conditions call for a robust response that achieves short-term goals but maintains long-term flexibility. Therefore, strategies such as those leading to stable fit (i.e., imitation and compliance) are inappropriate because they tend to undermine the potential for long-term competitiveness.

Two, although an overall pattern of persistent uncertainty might be anticipated, the particular conditions to be faced cannot always be forecast. As a result, a key requirement for Chakravarthy's (1982) state of neutral fit (i.e., anticipation of changes) is eliminated. In addition, hypercompetition and high-velocity environments call for actions that promote, rather than dampen, environmental uncertainty and complexity.

Three, continuously morphing conditions require ongoing reassessment of expectations and reevaluation of theories-in-use to reflect the immediate situation (Meyer, 1982). This requires direct, unfiltered information and observations. The buffers that enable unstable fit may screen out the very information needed for effective reinterpretation. Therefore, efforts to achieve unstable fit contradict effective reassessment activities.

Four, dynamic shifts, hypercompetition, and jolts are often linked with crisis. Crisis situ-ations may require organizations to respond in ways that are unorthodox and unprecedented (Starbuck, Greve, & Hedberg, 1978). An emphasis on achieving "fit" makes both the recognition and the implementation of unconventional actions more difficult.

In summary, these limitations demonstrate that some situations present a set of conditions that contradict the premises of adaptive fit. The environment is not always headed toward a new equilibrium state that an organization can attempt to match. The environment may be inherently unpredictable and unsettled, so that it is not possible to prevent events or restructure the firm in anticipation of their occurrence. Erecting barriers to protect a firm from environmental fluctuation may simultaneously prevent the firm from obtaining the information it needs to respond effectively. Finally, unfamiliar actions that contradict prior organizational choices may be the most effective options for responding to some environmental conditions.

Alternate Assumptions and Robust Transformation

Most adaptation research looks at organizational responses to conditions in which the environment changes from one set of conditions to a new and different equilibrium (Chakravarthy, 1982). For example, when Wal-Mart enters a community, the retailers in the area must adjust to a new competitive reality. However, this is not the only accurate portrait of environmental change. Dynamic shifts, hypercompetition, and jolts create a very different context. D'Aveni (1994) and Eisenhardt and Tabrizi (1995) described hypercompetitive or high-velocity environments as being in perpetual flux. Levy (1994) and Stacey (1995) described environments that shift in nonlinear, dynamic patterns that never establish equilibrium. Meyer examined environmental jolts, which he defined as "transient perturbations whose occurrences are difficult to foresee and whose impact on organizations are disruptive and potentially inimical" (1982: 515). These conditions call for a very different set of assumptions from the ones underpinning adaptive fit. We propose an alternative to adaptive fit, which we term *robust transformation*, and then examine the contrasting assumptions that explain how this construct addresses the limitations of an adaptive-fit approach.

Robust transformation is an organizational condition useful in situations that are either very temporary or undergoing continuous change. Like adaptive fit, robust transformation enables a firm to accommodate the level of complexity in its environment. Unlike adaptive fit, robust transformation does not presume that specific environmental conditions will move to a new equilibrium.

Robust transformation is defined as a deliberately transient, episodic response to a new, yet fluid, environmental condition. Robust transformation enables a firm to capitalize on environmental change in ways that create new options and capabilities. It does not trigger the firm's immune system response. Although robust transformation responds to emerging environmental situations, actions also may challenge prevailing environmental conditions and promote even greater instability. Robust transformation does not attempt to reestablish equilibrium. In contrast, most actions to achieve adaptive fit tend to promote equilibrium by reinforcing the current status in the environment. Robust transformation is grounded in the following four assumptions that are quite different from the assumptions underpinning adaptive fit.

First, organizational attention is on the transition condition rather than on a new equilibrium to which the organization must adjust. Robust transformation uses dynamic interactions and spontaneous turbulence to fuel the development of new capabilities. A state of robust transformation is intentionally temporary and allows a firm to respond in a provisional way to, an episodic condition. For example, when a fire crippled Philips Electronics' mobile-phone chip factory in spring 2000, leaving Nokia without its key supplier, a substantial, but impermanent, solution was needed. Nokia sent its employees to help Philips recover, temporarily increased orders from other Philips facilities, used its network to secure other suppliers, and capitalized on its rival's stagnation by introducing new phones.

Second, robust transformation assumes a dynamic tension, rather than an optimal balance, between creativity and productivity. There is a fluid emphasis on trying something new versus capitalizing on existing expertise. For example, in Meyer's (1982) study of hospitals responding to the sudden and unprecedented jolt of striking physicians, he found that the effective hospitals temporarily chose paths that were counterintuitive given their normal operating habits.

Third, robust transformation is often a process of moving beyond immediate strategic effectiveness to reconfigure a firm's strategy and organizational arrangements rapidly and radically to respond to uncertainty in a way that enhances future viability (Sutcliffe & Vogus, 2003). Contrary to adaptive fit, this may require a discordant blend of strategic postures and organizational arrangements. For example, Southwest Airlines was known for cultivating a reputation for fun, informality, and quick turnaround. Following September 11, 2001, fears and drastic new regulations made informality impossible, quick turnarounds more cumbersome, and fun temporarily inappropriate. Although maintaining its concern with customer satisfaction, Southwest replaced frivolity with assurance and substituted clear, well-explained, decisive action for informality. Over time, they reintroduced their signature style as conditions evolved.

Fourth, robust transformation redirects the use of slack resources toward developing responsiveness, flexibility, and an expanded action repertoire rather than toward achieving higher levels of adaptive fit. Morgan Stanley, an investment bank, was the largest tenant in the World Trade Center prior to September 11, 2001. After the 1993 attack on the World Trade Center, Morgan Stanley drilled its employees on what to do in the event of a catastrophe, designated three different recovery sites where employees could congregate and conduct business following a disaster, and created numerous backup systems. These investments did not improve Morgan Stanley's fit with its existing environment nor did they alter core business operations, but they did promote responsiveness and flexibility when the unexpected occurred.

A comparison of the two different sets of assumptions suggests the following conclusion: *Adaptive fit does not adequately accommodate the full range of environmental conditions that organizations encounter. Moreover, the robust transformation perspective addresses the environmental conditions that adaptive fit neglects.*

Environmental change affects what organizations do. Regardless of the content and duration of environmental change, three responses are visible.

First, organizations implement routines that have evolved over time in reaction to the change that has taken place. These routines (i.e., action patterns that summarize knowledge and experience) capture the firm's assumptions about what should be done and set in motion certain organizational activities (Pentland & Reuter, 1994). Three different patterns of routines are particularly likely to be implemented in response to environmental change. These will be discussed in the next section.

Second, the routines that are implemented yield one of three organizational conditions. Depending on which set of routines is implemented, an organization achieves a state of adaptive fit, or it accomplishes robust transformation, or it reinforces established organization practices.

Third, each of these organization conditions has predictable performance consequences given the nature and duration of the environmental change. These performance consequences will be examined following our discussion of organization routines.

Implementing Organization Routines

Nelson and Winter (1982) described routines as complicated patterns of social action that capture organizational experiences. As Pentland and Reuter (1994) pointed out, not all organizational routines are fixed and automatic. Instead, routines reflect organizational memory and present a set of possible action patterns that a firm could use when responding to a given situation. In this way, routines define sets of possibilities. As the range and diversity of an organization's routines expand, its repertoire of potential responses grows. By implication, then, the variety of environmental conditions for which it is prepared also grows.

Routines develop through an evolutionary process and reflect the accumulated knowledge and experience of organization members for dealing with particular situations (Nelson & Winter, 1982). The interaction of external conditions and organizational behavior is a dynamic process. This mirrors the integrated perspective of adaptation introduced by Ginsberg and Buchholtz (1990) and considers both environmental conditions and organization assets.

Over time, patterns of effective responses become embedded in organizational memory. If most of a firm's experiences with environmental uncertainty require similar responses, a narrow set of routines can become habituated. The broader the range of uncertain conditions that are encountered, the wider the assortment of different routines a firm is likely to develop. Boisot and Child (1999) argued that organizational routines for dealing with complexity are particularly crucial for responding to environmental shifts.

Routines and Complexity

To thrive, organizations should deliberately reflect the nature of complexity in their environment with sufficient organizational complexity (Ashby, 1954). In general, complexity arises from the number of different elements that comprise a system, the nature of the interactions among the elements, and how tightly they are coupled (Weick, 1995). Different environmental conditions give rise to different levels of external and internal complexity.

Boisot and Child (1999) argued that organizations have a fundamental choice of either achieving an appropriate level of fit with their environment (i.e., complexity reduction) or creating sufficient autonomy that environmental conditions do not directly constrain organizational decisions and actions (i.e., complexity absorption). They indicate that most firms develop characteristic routines following one or the other of these approaches. Other research suggests that a third alternative is to abdicate choice and disregard an explicit concern with complexity and respond based on other prevailing habits and pressures (Weick, 1995). An organization's tendency to disregard complexity, reduce complexity, or absorb complexity is shaped by the routines that have evolved from the interaction of past experience and current organizational resources, capabilities, and perspectives. Not only do organization routines prompt organization actions, but they also are pivotal in shaping the way in which uncertain situations are framed and labeled (Boisot & Child, 1999).

Routines that disregard complexity. In some organizations, habitual reactionary patterns of behavior override an intentional interest in actively managing complexity through either reduction or absorption. Two particularly strong routines associated with this pattern of behavior are *threat rigidity* and *escalation of commitment*.

Threats are defined within the strategic decision-making literature as negative situations where loss is likely and lack of control is apparent (Dutton & Jackson, 1987; Staw, Sandelands, & Dutton, 1981). Managers are more likely to perceive threats when incoming information is ambiguous and prone to diverse interpretations (Jackson & Dutton, 1988). When threat rigidity prevails, organization routines promote situational withdrawal and avoidance, focus on easily accessible internal activities, and encourage taking greater risks to avoid potential losses (Dutton & Jackson, 1987).

Escalation of commitment, the tendency for decision makers to persist with failing courses of action (Brockner, 1992: 39), is a second habituated response to uncertainty and change. Escalation of commitment overrides concerns with complexity because of a need for self-justification (Staw et al., 1981) or because feedback is framed in a negative (as opposed to neutral or problem-solving) manner (Tversky & Kahneman, 1981). Routines that reinforce consistency and previously established choices initiate escalation of commitment. Both threat rigidity and escalation of commitment are emergent strategies (i.e., patterns that develop from circumstances) rather than the result of deliberate decisions (Mintzberg & Waters, 1985). Both are implemented through routines that respond to uncertainty and complexity in terms of the perceived threat rather than the potential opportunity.

Routines that reduce complexity. Complexity reduction means that an organization "elicits the most appropriate single representation" of the state of the environment and develops "an adapted response to match it" (Boisot & Child, 1999: 238). This is consistent with adaptive fit. A synthesis of the literature suggests that when organizations tend toward adaptive fit, they develop three types of routines. One, they develop routines that emphasize the importance of order and stability. Two, they develop routines that act to reduce or regulate interactions and relationships. Three, they develop routines designed to limit differentiation across organizational elements and constrain the number of different factors that must be coordinated. These routines evolve in organizations that demonstrate their aptitude for diagnosing environmental changes and articulating the new equilibrium (Boisot & Child, 1999). Complexity reduction routines are deliberate choices to achieve adaptive fit, not emergent strategies (Mintzberg & Waters, 1985). They often develop in firms with a history of successfully matching environmental conditions with designated organizational processes and structures.

Routines that absorb complexity. Complexity absorption means that an organization maintains a broad repertoire of options and enough action flexibility to create an effective response for emerging contingencies (Boisot & Child, 1999). As indicated, routines that absorb complexity are needed for robust transformation. A review of prior literature suggests that firms develop three types of routines in order to absorb complexity. One, they develop routines to create plans that are malleable and sufficiently general that they can be used in a variety of situations. Two, they develop routines to notice exceptions and unexpected events. Three, they develop routines that prevent imposition of a ready-made structure on decisions. Complexity absorption routines are not designed to achieve a tight match between organizational structures or processes and environmental conditions. Instead, complexity absorption routines accommodate high levels of complexity by maintaining a broad array of potential actions.

Routines for complexity absorption are likely to evolve in firms with a history of unstable governance because of the high levels of uncertainty this creates (Boisot & Child, 1999). It is often hard to determine the source of order these routines produce. This is because the routines focus on shaping organizational features such as culture or knowledge management practices rather than on driving policies and rules that are easier to observe. Routines that absorb complexity tend to increase the number of differentiated parts in a firm that are mixed and matched as new needs arise. Routines for complexity absorption develop from a comfort with emerging orderliness rather than control.

The following conclusion summarizes the relationship between environmental change and organization routines regarding complexity: *Three distinct patterns of organization routines (disregarding complexity, reducing complexity, absorbing complexity) can emerge from a firm's experience with environmental change.*

Organizational Outcomes and Performance Consequences

A synthesis of prior research demonstrates that organizations are likely to implement one of three sets of routines when they encounter environmental shifts (Boisot & Child, 1999; Chakravarthy, 1982; Staw et al., 1981). Some organizations disregard complexity and fall back on routines of threat rigidity and escalation of commitment. Some firms implement routines intending to achieve complexity reduction. Other firms implement routines designed to accomplish complexity absorption. Each of the three sets of routines can lead to an effective response pattern if it is appropriate for the environmental conditions triggering the cycle of events. We now examine the contingent relationship between specific sets of routines and performance consequences.

There are two possible performance outcomes: organizations can either prosper in the face of environmental change, uncertainty, and complexity or they can be unsuccessful. If firms implement routines that are consistent with the conditions they face, they are likely to do well. If they implement routines that are incompatible with environmental reality, they will do poorly. Prior research has shown that several combinations of routines and conditions can lead to favorable outcomes and that several other combinations can lead to poor performance.

Combinations Leading to Strong Performance

The most well-documented route to favorable performance outcomes is the sequence of an equilibrium-to-equilibrium shift in the environment to which an organization responds with complexity reduction routines. These routines enable the firm to achieve adaptive fit and effectively meet the new environmental conditions (Chakravarthy, 1982). For example, when AT&T agreed to divest its local exchange services (i.e., the "Baby Bells") in 1984, the telecommunications giant faced a new competitive reality and devised ways to adapt to competition in its remaining markets with substantially fewer human and financial resources. Actions resulting from complexity reduction routines create a solid fit with environmental conditions and maintain a balance between efficiency and productivity. As Chakravarthy (1982) noted, specific organizational forms correspond to specific strategic intents. Routines that reduce complexity enable firms to efficiently blend material and organizational capacity.

The types of adaptive fit that Chakravarthy (1982) described are equilibrium conditions that become increasingly organic and proactive as a firm moves from unstable to neutral fit. At the highest level, firms succeed despite environmental shifts because they are able to anticipate changes and develop organizational practices that meet the new equilibrium conditions. Routines that reduce complexity enable firms to use their resources and internal capabilities in an optimal way because decision makers are able to understand complexity and act on it directly (Boisot & Child, 1999). The competing pressures of efficiency and innovation respond well to routines that limit the number of differentiated elements, actively manage the interactions among them, and strategies and structures designed to achieve specified outcomes. Decision makers can follow a rational, clearly articulated process for using organizational capabilities to accommodate environmental conditions in a planned way.

A second route to favorable performance also has empirical support. Sometimes, equilibrium-to-equilibrium shifts followed by routines leading to threat rigidity and escalation of commitment can also lead to adaptive fit. The typical threat-induced routines that restrict information processing, increase control, and conserve resources may be appropriate under certain conditions. Staw et al. (1981) argued that consistent responses may actually reduce threats when causal relationships remain stable and the dominant response is appropriate for performance. For example, some university departments weathered budget cuts and university politics well by standardizing procedures and increasing centralization (Rubin, 1977). If the new equilibrium reflects conditions that are consistent with the prior environmental state, threat rigidity and/or escalation of commitment can lead to an effective response. As such, persistence in established activities may result in balance between efficiency and productivity, acceptable organizational configurations, and adaptive fit.

A third route to success is the alternative to adaptive fit introduced in this article. When environmental change is either very temporary or never ending, routines for complexity absorption are the most effective response. These routines acknowledge that there may be little fit between a specific response and a particular state of the environment (Boisot & Child, 1999). Rather than planning to achieve equilibrium, routines for complexity absorption yield an emergent flow of activities that draw iteratively from a broad repertoire of possible actions. No single, stable portrait of the environment is established. Rather, decision makers may hold multiple and conflicting representations of environmental variations and act on these representations simultaneously and differentially.

Robust transformation realizes that there is no new equilibrium toward which the firm can adapt. It relies on intricate, emergent organizational resources and relationships to thrive in fluid situations. Routines for complexity absorption promote robust transformation because they preserve flexibility while they respond effectively to current demands. Nokia's emphasis on helping its key supplier recover by loaning employees and temporarily increasing orders from other Philips facilities illustrates this approach. Robust transformation means a firm uses unfamiliar experiences to initiate new organizational capabilities. For example, Johnson & Johnson needed to develop new packaging skills to make Tylenol tamper-proof. Routines for complexity absorption enable firms to maintain a fluid, emergent, transformational stance rather than trying to anticipate a new equilibrium condition that should be matched.

A comparison of these three routes to success yields several important observations. First, the effectiveness of any of the routines for dealing with environmental uncertainty and complexity is contingent on the duration as well as the content of environmental change. Second, although threat rigidity and escalation of commitment are often viewed as dysfunctional, they can promote adaptive fit under certain circumstances. Third, although robust transformation enables a firm to accommodate high levels of environmental complexity, it should not be seen as just another level of adaptive fit because it is appropriate under a very different set of environmental conditions. Chakravarthy's (1982) three states of adaptive fit all apply to equilibrium-to-equilibrium shifts. Neutral fit also accommodates high levels of complexity.

Environmental Conditions

Fourth, although robust transformation is an important alternative to consider, it is not the "right answer" for all conditions. As Figure 13.2.1 illustrates, the key issue is the stability of the environmental conditions.

Combinations Leading to Poor Performance

If a firm does not meet the needs of its environment, competitive performance suffers. If an environmental change is temporary, an ineffective response, at best, creates a temporary disadvantage. If the environmental condition is more enduring, poor choices have long-lasting consequences. Both the nature of the environmental shift and the duration of the change should be considered.

If the triggering event is a radical disturbance to the existing equilibrium, effective responses call for actions that depart from prevailing organization practices. Appropriate responses are characterized as resourceful, inventive, situation-specific, and often counter-intuitive (Meyer, 1982). Radical change often requires a firm to interpret its circumstances in light of a new, unprecedented, and fluid reality.

Threat rigidity and escalation of commitment lead to outcomes that are the antithesis of these characteristics. The adverse consequences of such choices are well documented (Staw et al., 1981). Rigidity does not help resolve uncertainty when the underlying relationships are radically altered. Likewise, unyielding pursuit of the current course of action does not enable a firm to either rethink the situation or redirect its efforts toward unconventional solutions (Kelly & Amburgey, 1991). Forces of organizational inertia are energized by threat rigidity and escalation of commitment and make any inventive or unfamiliar action difficult to implement (Miller & Chen, 1994; Tushman & Romanelli, 1985). Persistence along an established path makes it more difficult to recognize, absorb, or use new insights. Clearly, threat rigidity and escalation can lead to poor performance if more inventive responses are required.

However, it is equally important to recognize that adaptive fit and robust transformation also can lead to undesirable performance outcomes. If environmental conditions present either a temporary change or a relentlessly shifting condition, adaptive fit is not an effective choice. Large-scale realignment of structure and resources to accommodate temporary conditions is inefficient at best. When the environment is in perpetual flux, efforts to identify a stable environmental condition before acting can prevent a firm from responding at all. On the other hand, if the environment changes from one equilibrium state to another, robust transformation is certainly inefficient and potentially ineffective as well. D'Aveni (1994) suggested that such a pattern might nudge both the firm and its environment toward hypercompetition with its accompanying challenges. Implications from prior research suggest that robust transformation in response to a new equilibrium would misallocate organizational efforts and resources, creating unnecessary inefficiencies and long-term problems. Robust transformation would not position a firm to capitalize on enduring environmental conditions.

Consideration of the performance outcomes associated with adaptive fit and robust transformation as shown in Figure 13.2.1 suggests the following conclusions: *When environmental change is equilibrium to equilibrium, organizations should strive for adaptive fit. Moreover, when environmental change is either very temporary or continuous, organizations should strive for robust transformation.*

Impact of Resilience Capacity

Resilience capacity is a multidimensional construct at the organizational level that describes collective behaviors and attitudes. We argue that resilience capacity influences an organization's response to environmental change in two important ways. First, resilience capacity encourages a firm to develop a broad and varied repertoire of routines for responding to

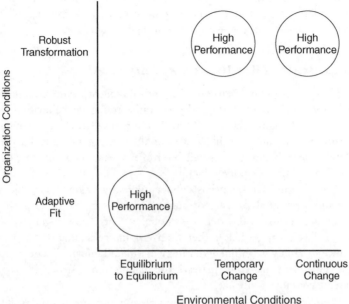

Figure 13.2.1 The High Performance Map.

uncertainty and complexity. Resilience capacity encourages a firm to pay attention to certain types of experiences and hone particular capabilities that expand the action options that are available. In this way, resilience capacity helps a firm develop routines that ensure complexity reduction and complexity absorption are both viable alternatives. Second, resilience capacity encourages a firm to think about its environment in ways that improve its ability to determine both the content and the duration of change. Resilience capacity provides a foundation for gathering information and insights from varied sources. In this way, resilience capacity helps firm decide whether adaptive fit or robust transformation is the most effective option to pursue. As indicated previously, routines evolve from environmental conditions, internal organization experiences, and other factors. We propose that resilience capacity is an important internal factor that shapes both the routines that evolve and the routines that are used.

Resilience capacity is defined as a unique blend of cognitive, behavioral, and contextual properties that increase a firm's ability to understand its current situation and to develop customized responses that reflect that understanding. Discussions of organizational resilience have become more salient as terrorist attacks, economic downturns, and other substantial disruptions associated with an unpredictable environment create a climate of uncertainty and crisis (Balu, 2001; Coutu, 2002; Horne & Orr, 1998; Mallak, 1998).

The concept of resilience capacity presented in this article synthesizes and builds on psychological literature examining individual resilience and practitioner literature describing resilient firms. Resilience capacity combines six organization subroutines and characteristics into three organizational properties: cognitive resilience, behavioral resilience, and contextual resilience. We propose that as an organization develops its resilience capacity, it interprets uncertain situations more creatively (cognitive resilience) and therefore is better able to conceive of both familiar and unconventional activities (behavioral resilience) that take advantage of relationships and resources (contextual resilience). Resilience capacity provides the foundation for a firm to respond to uncertainty by increasing information flow, initiating double-loop learning, and elaborating its action repertoire.

Three Components of Resilience Capacity

Resilience capacity is a multidimensional, organizational attribute that results from the interaction of three organizational properties: cognitive resilience, behavioral resilience, and contextual resilience (Lengnick-Hall & Beck, 2003). Overall resilience capacity is highest when an organization has achieved high levels of all three components. Further research is needed to determine whether a threshold level of resilience capacity can be reached by achieving only some of the component factors.

Cognitive resilience. Cognitive resilience is a conceptual orientation that enables an organization to notice, interpret, analyze, and formulate responses in ways that go beyond simply surviving an ordeal. Firms with cognitive resilience encourage ingenuity and look for opportunities to develop new skills rather than emphasize standardization and need for control. Southwest's ability to rethink its strategy of fun and informality demonstrates cognitive resilience. Two elements, constructive sensemaking and a strong ideological identity, combine to create cognitive resilience.

Constructive sensemaking is "the reciprocal interaction of information seeking, meaning ascription, and action" (Thomas, Clark, & Gioia, 1993: 240). It has roots in both individual and social activity (Weick, 1995). Sensemaking focuses on situation-specific interpretations and judgments rather than programmed explanations. This is essential when events are unprecedented and require responses that go beyond an organization's normal repertoire.

Individual cognitive capabilities such as an empowering interpretation of the world (Aitken & Morgan, 1999), a positive perception of experiences (Mallak, 1998), realism (Coutu, 2002), and a tolerance for uncertainty (Mallak, 1998) contribute to organizational sensemaking. The process of integrating individual traits into organizational capabilities is similar to the spirals of reciprocal interaction that Lindsley, Brass, and Thomas (1995) described in moving from individual to collective organizational efficacy. Following their reasoning, as sensemaking leads to effective actions at each level of activity, the positive feedback that results encourages future sensemaking activities at the next level of analysis.

A *strong ideological identity* is the second ingredient in cognitive resilience. The role of a strong, value-driven, core identity that offers a prime directive for organizational choices is a prevailing theme in reports on resilient organizations (Collins & Porras, 1994). For example, a dominant explanation offered for Sandler, O'Neill & Partners' resilient response to the 9/11 attack is their highly visible moral purpose that enabled the firm to motivate employees, to perceive opportunities despite disaster, to gain help from outsiders, and to unleash extraordinary physical and psychological resources (Freeman, Hirschhorn, & Maltz, 2004).

Behavioral resilience. Behavioral resilience is the engine that moves an organization forward. This property enables a firm to learn more about the situation and to fully use its own resources and capabilities through collaborative actions (Argyris, 1980). 3M's resource allocation practices, its policies that encourage risk taking and trying new ideas, and its behaviors that enable employees to learn from both success and failure are examples of behavioral resilience. Two elements, a complex and varied action inventory and functional habits, combine to create behavioral resilience.

A *complex and varied action inventory* enables organizations to follow a dramatically different course of action from that which is their norm (Sutcliffe & Vogus, 2003: 107). Firms with a broad repertoire of action alternatives are more motivated and able to take inventive action upon learning that familiar past actions are no longer effective. Ferrier and colleagues (1999) found that the number and diversity of competitive actions available in a firm were strongly related to its ability to adopt unexpected and timely responses to market shifts. A toolkit of multiple actions increases the odds of success simply because there are more options available for consideration (Eisenhardt & Tabrizi, 1995).

An important juxtaposition to counterintuitive behaviors is the development of *functional habits*. As discussed, many firms metaphorically "circle the wagons" to erect barriers and defend a position when faced with uncertainty. Functional habits, in contrast, are rehearsed routines that automatically open communication channels, create interpersonal ties, and seek multiple sources of information when uncertainty increases. For example, Odwalla implemented functional habits when a little girl died from drinking its contaminated apple juice. The firm's immediate response was to change the pace of communication so that the core management team was meeting every 15 minutes. It also altered the range of communication to forge new links with employees (via mass conference calls), with the press (providing frequent updates), with trade partners (through in-house distributors), and with customers (by purchasing advertisements announcing the recall and introducing a new quality-control process). Because an organization cannot predict in advance what information will be most useful for dealing with unexpected situations, habits of continuous dialogue provide the raw material for constructing meaning and direction in ambiguous circumstances (Eisenhardt, 1993).

Contextual resilience. Contextual resilience provides the setting for integrating and using cognitive resilience and behavioral resilience. Contextual resilience is composed of connections and resources. Two organizational characteristics create contextual resilience: deep social capital and a broad resource network.

Social capital is the goodwill available to individuals, groups, and organizations that lies in the structure and content of their interpersonal relationships (Adler & Kwon, 2002). Just as deep pockets help firms to weather financial turbulence and capitalize on unexpected opportunities, *deep social capital* provides the interpersonal foundation for thriving despite uncertainty and for developing rapid responses to emerging conditions.

Deep social capital evolves from repeated, personal interactions between people and between organizations and is most effective when based on trust (Ireland, Hitt, & Vaidyanath, 2002). Benefits of deep social capital include access to broader information sources (Adler & Kwon, 2002) and expanded knowledge and resource pools (Inkpen & Tsang, 2005). In addition, as groups recognize their interdependence, resource exchange becomes easier (Tsai & Ghoshal, 1998). Deep social capital builds commitment and a sense of purpose that enables people to find meaning in uncertain situations (Coutu, 2002; Mallak, 1998).

Broad resource networks encompass both tangible and intangible resources. Studies (e.g., Coutu, 2002; Werner & Smith, 2001) suggest that resilient people have an unusual ability to get others to help them out, which is often rooted in some visible talent (i.e., athletic ability) or interpersonal skill (i.e., networking ability). There are parallels at the organizational level. Firms that make highly visible contributions (i.e., Centers for Disease Control); that occupy crucial economic positions (i.e., Boeing); or that are seen as essential factors of production (i.e., agriculture); are able to obtain resources, concessions, and assistance that other organizations are denied.

Empirical analysis of social network exchanges supports the organizational benefits of broad resource networks (Liebeskind, Oliver, Zucker, & Brewer, 1996). An ability to obtain resources externally promotes organizational slack. Beyond this, external resources are likely to introduce variety and diversity into an organization. Slack and variety stimulate the action inventory and encourage challenges to prevailing assumptions. Overall, improved access to resources coupled with interdependent bonds with various environmental agents creates a setting that facilitates cognitive and behavioral resilience repertoires.

Resilience Capacity and Organizational Routines Regarding Complexity

In summary, resilience capacity is achieved through cognitive, behavioral, and contextual factors. It is a measure of an organization's ability to interpret unfamiliar situations; to devise news ways of confronting these events; and to mobilize people, resources, and processes to transform these choices into reality (Kobasa, Maddi, Puccetti, & Zola, 1985). Moreover, resilience capacity is learned. It is composed of organizational subroutines and characteristics that are developed and honed over time as a firm encounters unexpected challenges. One consequence of resilience capacity is a firm's ability to thrive and become better in part *because* it was faced with difficulties that were overcome. Resilience capacity enables firms to move beyond survival and actually prosper in complicated, uncertain, and threatening environments.

As indicated, resilience capacity influences the routines that a firm implements in response to environmental change for two reasons. First, resilience capacity increases the feasibility of evolving routines that absorb complexity by providing the perspective, behavior patterns, and setting in which these routines are encouraged to develop. Success reinforces these routines. Thus, in firms with high resilience capacity, both routines for complexity reduction and routines for complexity absorption are viable options. Second, cognitive resilience and contextual resilience make it more likely that a firm will be able to accurately distinguish between temporary, permanent, and continuous changes in external conditions. Consequently, resilience capacity enhances a firm's ability to decide which routines are most appropriate to implement in response to environmental conditions.

In this way, resilience capacity increases the likelihood that a firm will select complexity absorption routines for either temporary or perpetual change and complexity reduction routines for equilibrium-to-equilibrium changes. These ideas lead to the following conclusions: *High levels of resilience capacity increase the range of different routines that a firm is likely to develop for dealing with uncertainty and complexity. Moreover, high levels of resilience capacity increase the likelihood that a firm will accurately distinguish between equilibrium and nonequilibrium environmental changes.*

Discussion

Methodological Considerations

As Schwab (1980) contended, construct measurement must precede theory testing. We introduce two new constructs in this article. Prior research offers several potential measures for elements in both robust transformation and resilience capacity. For example, organizations can assess degrees of responsiveness and flexibility, key attributes of robust transformation, with indicators such as the number of available contingency plans (Coutu, 2002) and alterations in control systems (Volberda, 1996). Systematic problem solving and learning from others can be assessed through various total quality management and benchmarking tools (Garvin, 1993). In addition, dynamic capabilities have been quantified by measuring resource configurations and allocations (Eisenhardt & Martin, 2000).

Prior research also suggests ways in which the components of resilience capacity might be measured. Sensemaking routines and mindfulness have been captured with case scenarios and multi-item scales (Thomas et al., 1993; Weick & Sutcliffe, 2001). Content analysis techniques can be used to infer sensemaking activities from the vocabulary in organizational documents. Surveys and observations of discussion patterns have been used to measure many of the elements building collective organization identity (Aitken & Morgan, 1999; Coutu, 2002; Dutton & Dukerich, 1991; Mallak, 1998; Weick, 1995).

Measures drawn from competitive dynamics (e.g., Ferrier et al., 1999) can be used to measure the extent and complexity of the action inventory directly, and observations and measures used in research on learning organizations (Garvin, 1993; Senge, 1990) can be used to measure the behaviors that build these inventories. Tools such as the balanced scorecard measure many of the behaviors and investment strategies considered functional habits (Kaplan & Norton, 2001).

Social capital research and social exchange theory provide an array of measures for social capital and resource networks. Relevant indicators could be the number, strength, and directionality of interpersonal connections; investments in collaborative technologies; and the overlap of strong and weak ties across key networks (Ireland et al., 2002).

Directions for Future Research

The components of resilience capacity need to be better understood. We propose that all three components are necessary for resilience capacity to be achieved. However, the threshold levels for the component properties (cognitive, behavioral, and contextual) and for each of the six contributory factors leading to these properties need to be determined.

A related agenda is to compare the new constructs and relationships introduced here with similar factors in related domains. For example, although many activities that contribute to robust transformation are similar to actions that promote learning organizations, there is one important difference. Learning organizations are measured in terms of durable patterns of behavior that persist regardless of specific environmental conditions (Garvin, 1993). We argue that robust transformation is not an effective approach under all circumstances. Robust transformation should be a situation-specific choice and a distinct, deliberate, episodic set of responses to an environmental condition rather than an underlying organization design paradigm.

Similarly, much of the research on complexity reduction and complexity absorption argues that these patterns are relatively stable organization phenomena that are consistent across time (Ashmos, Duchon, & McDaniel, 2000; Boisot & Child, 1999). We argue that a firm is better prepared to respond effectively to a wide range of different environmental conditions if these routines are implemented selectively and deliberately in response to the expected duration of environmental turbulence. Empirical examination of these relationships could lead to better understanding and improved organization performance.

Conclusion

The ideas presented in this article contribute to our understanding of the relationship between an organization and its environment in several ways. One, these ideas begin to establish useful boundary conditions for the concept of adaptive fit. The limitations of even the highest level of adaptive fit become clear. As a consequence, it is apparent that the duration, as well as the nature, of environmental change should be considered in determining whether to pursue adaptive fit. Two, the role of organization routines in shaping the interaction between organizations and their environments is examined from a more diverse perspective than in prior research. Literature from research streams as diverse as threat rigidity and escalation of commitment, complexity views of organizations, adaptation research, and competitive dynamics is integrated to provide a new look at routines a firm may implement when faced with environmental change. Finally, these ideas elaborate on the integrative perspective of organizational adaptation by introducing resilience capacity as an important organizational characteristic that influences both the routines a firm has available to respond to environmental changes and the choice it makes regarding the type of response it wants to implement.

Acknowledgments

* We thank Mark Lengnick-Hall, Ari Ginsberg, Robert Beck, Donde Plowman, Stephanie Thomas, and three anonymous reviewers for their helpful comments and critique during this process.

References

Adler, P. S., & Kwon, S. 2002. Social capital: Prospects for a new concept. *Academy of Management Review*, 27: 17–40.

Aitken, S., & Morgan, J. 1999. How Motorola promotes good health. *Journal for Quality and Participation*, 22(1): 54–57.

Argyris, C. 1980. Some limitations of the case method: Experiences in a management development program. *Academy of Management Review*, 5: 291–298.

Ashby, W. R. 1954. *An introduction to cybernetics*. London: Methuen.

Ashmos, D. P., Duchon, D., & McDaniel, R. R., Jr. 2000. Organizational responses to complexity: The effect on organizational performance. *Journal of Organizational Change Management*, 13: 577–594.

Balu, R. 2001. How to bounce back from setbacks. *Fast Company*, 45: 148–156.

Boisot, M., & Child, J. 1999. Organizations as adaptive systems in complex environments: The case of China. *Organization Science*, 10: 237–252.

Brockner, J. 1992. The escalation of commitment to a failing course of action: Toward theoretical progress. *Academy of Management Review*, 17: 39–61.

Chakravarthy, B. S. 1982. Adaptation: A promising metaphor for strategic management. *Academy of Management Review*, 7: 35–44.

Collins, J. C., & Porras, J. I. 1994. *Built to last: Successful habits of visionary companies*. New York: Harper Business.

Coutu, D. L. 2002. How resilience works. *Harvard Business Review*, 80(5): 46–55.

D'Aveni, R. A. 1994. *Hypercompetition: Managing the dynamics of strategic maneuvering*. New York: Free Press.

Duncan, R. B. 1972. Characteristics of organizational environments and perceived environmental uncertainty. *Administrative Science Quarterly*, 17: 313–327.

Dutton, J. E., & Dukerich, J. M. 1991. Keeping an eye on the mirror: Image and identity in organizational adaptation. *Academy of Management Journal*, 34: 517–554.

Dutton, J. E., & Jackson, S. E. 1987. Categorizing strategic issues: Links to organizational action. *Academy of Management Review*, 12: 76–90.

Eccles, R., & Nohria, N. 1998. Strategy as a language game. In S. Segal-Horn (Ed.), *The strategy reader* (pp. 50–72). Oxford, UK: Basis Blackwell.

Eisenhardt, K. M. 1993. High reliability organizations meet high velocity environments: Common dilemmas in nuclear power plants, aircraft carriers, and microcomputer firms. In K. H. Roberts (Ed.), *New challenges to understanding organizations* (pp. 117–135). New York: Macmillan.

Eisenhardt, K. M., & Martin, J. 2000. Dynamic capabilities: What are they? *Strategic Management Journal*, 21: 1105–1121.

Eisenhardt, K. M., & Tabrizi, B. N. 1995. Accelerating adaptive processes: Product innovation in the global computer industry. *Administrative Science Quarterly*, 40: 84–111.

Ferrier, W. J., Smith, K. G., & Grimm, C. M. 1999. The role of competitive action in market share erosion and industry dethronement: A study of industry leaders and challengers. *Academy of Management Journal*, 42: 372–388.

Freeman, S. F., Hirschhorn, L., & Maltz, M. 2004. *Organization resilience and moral purpose: Sandler O'Neill and partners in the aftermath of 9/11/01.* Paper presented at the National Academy of Management meetings, New Orleans, LA.

Garvin, D. A. 1993. Building a learning organization. *Harvard Business Review*, 71(4): 78–91.

Ginsberg, A. 1988. Measuring and modeling changes in strategy: Theoretical foundations and empirical directions. *Strategic Management Journal*, 9: 559–575.

Ginsberg, A., & Buchholtz, A. 1990. Converting to for-profit status: Corporate responsiveness to radical change. *Academy of Management Journal*, 33: 445–477.

Horne, J. F. I., & Orr, J. E. 1998. Assessing behaviors that create resilient organizations. *Employment Relations Today*, 24(4): 29–39.

Inkpen, A. C., & Tsang, E. W. K. 2005. Social capital, networks, and knowledge transfer. *Academy of Management Review*, 30: 146–165.

Ireland, R. D., Hitt, M. A., & Vaidyanath, D. 2002. Alliance management as a source of competitive advantage. *Journal of Management*, 28(3): 413–446.

Jackson, S. E., & Dutton, J. E. 1988. Discerning threats and opportunities. *Administrative Science Quarterly*, 33: 370–387.

Jennings, D. F., & Seaman, S. L. 1994. High and low levels of organizational adaptation: An empirical examination of strategy, structure, and performance. *Strategic Management Journal*, 15: 459–475.

Kaplan, R. S., & Norton, D. P. 2001. *The strategy-focused organization: How balanced scorecard companies thrive in the new business environment.* Boston: Harvard Business School Press.

Kelly, D., & Amburgey, T. L. 1991. Organizational inertia and momentum: A dynamic model of strategic change. *Academy of Management Journal*, 34: 591–612.

Kobasa, S. C., Maddi, S. R., Puccetti, M. C., & Zola, M. A. 1985. Effectiveness of hardiness, exercise, and social support as resources against illness. *Journal of Psychosomatic Resources*, 29: 525–533.

Lawrence, P. R., & Lorsch, J. W. 1967. *Organization and environment.* Boston: Harvard University Graduate School of Business Administration.

Lengnick-Hall, C. A., & Beck, T. E. 2003. *Beyond bouncing back: The concept of organizational resilience.* Paper presented at the National Academy of Management meetings, Seattle, WA.

Levy, D. 1994. Chaos theory and strategy: Theory, application, and managerial implications. *Strategic Management Journal*, 15(Special Issue: Strategy): 167–178.

Liebeskind, J. P., Oliver, A. L., Zucker, L., & Brewer, M. 1996. Social networks, learning, and flexibility: Sourcing scientific knowledge in new biotechnology firms. *Organization Science*, 7: 428–443.

Lindsley, D. H., Brass, D. J., & Thomas, J. B. 1995. Efficacy-performance spirals: A multilevel perspective. *Academy of Management Review*, 20: 645–678.

Mallak, L. A. 1998. Putting organizational resilience to work. *Industrial Management*, 40(6): 8–13.

Meyer, A. D. 1982. Adapting to environmental jolts. *Administrative Science Quarterly*, 27: 515–537.

Miller, D., & Chen, M. J. 1994. Sources and consequences of competitive inertia: A study of the U.S. airline industry. *Administrative Science Quarterly*, 39: 1–23.

Milliken, F. J. 1987. Three types of perceived uncertainty about environments: State, effect, and response uncertainty. *Academy of Management Review*, 12: 133–143.

Mintzberg, H., & Waters, J. A. 1985. Of strategies, deliberate and emergent. *Strategic Management Journal*, 6: 257–272.

Nelson, R. R., & Winter, S. G. 1982. *An evolutionary theory of economic change.* Cambridge, MA: Belknap.

Pentland, B. T., & Reuter, H. H. 1994. Organizational routines as grammars for action. *Administrative Science Quarterly*, 39: 484–510.

Pfeffer, J., & Salancik, G. R. 1978. *The external control of organizations: A resource dependence perspective.* New York: Harper & Row.

Rubin, I. 1977. Universities in stress: Decision making under conditions of reduced resources. *Social Science Quarterly*, 58(2): 242–254.

Schwab, D. P. 1980. Construct validity in organizational behavior. In B. M. Staw & L. L. Cummings (Eds.), *Research in organizational behavior* (Vol. 2, pp. 3–43). Greenwich, CT: JAI.

Senge, P. M., 1990. *The fifth discipline: The art and practice of the learning organization.* New York: Doubleday.

Simon, H. A. 1969. *The sciences of the artificial.* Cambridge, MA: MIT Press.

Stacey, R. D. 1995. The science of complexity: An alternative perspective for strategic change processes. *Strategic Management Journal*, 16: 477–495.

Starbuck, W. H., Greve, A., & Hedberg, B. L. T. 1978. Responding to crises. *Journal of Business Administration*, 9: 111–137.

Staw, B. M., Sandelands, L. E., & Dutton, J. E. 1981. Threat-rigidity effects in organizational behavior: A multilevel analysis. *Administrative Science Quarterly*, 26: 501–524.

Sutcliffe, K. M., & Vogus, T. J. 2003. Organizing for resilience. In K. S. Cameron, J. E. Dutton, & R. E. Quinn (Eds.), *Positive organizational scholarship: Foundations of a new discipline* (pp. 94–110). San Francisco: Berrett-Koehler.

Thomas, J. B., Clark, S. M., & Gioia, D. A. 1993. Strategic sensemaking and organizational performance: Linkages among scanning, interpretation, action, and outcomes. *Academy of Management Journal*, 36: 239–271.

Tripsas, M., & Gavetti, G. 2000. Capabilities, cognition, and inertia: Evidence from digital imaging. *Strategic Management Journal*, 21: 1147–1161.

Tsai, W., & Ghoshal, S. 1998. Social capital and value creation: The role of intrafirm networks. *Academy of Management Journal*, 41: 464–476.

Tushman, M. L., & Romanelli, E. 1985. Organizational evolution: A metamorphosis model of convergence and reorientation. In L. Cummings & B. Staw (Eds.), *Research in organizational behavior* (Vol. 7, pp. 171–222). Greenwich, CT: JAI.

Tversky, A., & Kahneman, D. 1981. The framing of decisions and the psychology of choices. *Science*, 211: 453–458.

Volberda, H. W. 1996. Toward the flexible form: How to remain vital in hypercompetitive environments. *Organization Science*, 7: 359–374.

Weick, K. E. 1995. *Sensemaking in organizations.* Thousand Oaks, CA: Sage.

Weick, K. E., & Sutcliffe, K. M. 2001. *Managing the unexpected: Assuring high performance in an age of complexity.* San Francisco: Jossey-Bass.

Werner, E. E., & Smith, R. S. 2001. *Journeys from childhood to midlife: Risk, resilience, and recovery.* Ithaca, NY: Cornell University Press.

Zajac, E. J., & Kraatz, M. S. 1993. A diametric forces model of strategic change: Assessing the antecedents and consequences of restructuring in the higher education industry. *Strategic Management Journal*, 14(Summer special issue): 83–103.

Biographical Notes

Cynthia A. Lengnick-Hall (Ph.D., University of Texas at Austin) is a professor of management at the University of Texas at San Antonio. Her current research interests include knowledge management as a source of competitive advantage, strategic human resource management, organizational resilience, and action-based strategies for dynamic competition.

Tammy E. Beck is a Ph.D. candidate in Organization and Management Studies at the University of Texas at San Antonio. Her research interests include cooperative relationships among organizations, especially those based on trust; organizational resilience; organizational interpretation; and various management and change issues in nonprofit organizations.

14 Culture, Change, and Organization Development

14.1 THE SIX LEVERS FOR MANAGING ORGANIZATIONAL CULTURE

David W. Young

Over the past decade, a great deal has been written about organizational culture and the important role it plays in successful performance. Edgar Schein (1992), one of the leading authorities on culture, defines it as

> . . . a pattern of shared basic assumptions that the [organization] learned as it solved its problems of external adaptation and internal integration, that has worked well enough to be considered valid and, therefore, to be taught to new members as the correct way to perceive, think, and feel in relation to those problems.

Schein describes three levels of culture: *artifacts; shared values;* and *shared basic assumptions.*

- **Artifacts** are visible, audible, tactile manifestations of underlying cultural assumptions, such as behavior patterns, rituals, physical environment, dress codes, stories, and myths. They are relatively easy to understand. For example, many firms have dress codes, such as uniforms or proper business attire, that are indicative of some underlying culture. When IBM and Lotus merged some years ago, the prediction of a cultural clash was due, in part, to this outward manifestation of their cultures—IBM's dress code that stipulated proper business attire, and Lotus employees wearing T-shirts and sandals. More recently, a merger between Beth Israel and Deaconess Hospitals in Boston encountered a clash in cultures, one outward manifestation of which was arrival time for meetings. At Beth Israel, meetings started in "BI time," which meant they began about 15 to 20 minutes after their scheduled start time. There was no such "artifact" at Deaconess, and shortly after the merger, individuals from Deaconess would become irate while waiting for BI people to arrive so that a meeting could begin.
- **Shared values**, also quite easily understood, are the espoused reasons why things should be as they are, such as norms, codes of ethics, company value statements, and so on. For example, many firms have goal or mission statements boldly emblazoned in their reception areas for all to see, informing both their customers and their employees what the firm stands for, and saying something about the espoused culture as well. Similarly, some firms have codes of ethics, which are often related to the professional

norms of their employees. Doctor-patient and lawyer-client relationships are examples. Other firms have rather rigid rules of behavior, some of which constitute grounds for dismissal when broken. A company might forbid its employees to discuss their salaries, with termination as the consequence of breaching the rule.

- **Basic assumptions** are somewhat more difficult to define and examine. They comprise the invisible but identifiable reasons why group members perceive, think, and feel the way they do about external survival and internal operational issues, such as a mission, means of problem solving, relationships, time, and space. They can be viewed most easily in terms of behavior that one would find totally unacceptable, as well as, of course, its counterpart: highly desirable behavior. The importance of "saving face" (especially in Asia), the relevance of financial rewards as performance motivators, and a subordinate's ability to question a supervisor's decisions are all examples of these basic assumptions.

Of considerable importance, in Schein's view, is the need for senior management to focus on this third level of culture. Artifacts can be replaced; new values can be articulated by, say, introducing or modifying a mission statement or code of ethics. But unless the basic assumptions are addressed, the firm's culture will likely remain the same or change only slightly.

The precise dividing line between shared values and basic assumptions is not always clear. Consider the experience of Price Waterhouse-Coopers culled from a *Business Week* story (Moore 2000) that discussed breaches of auditor independence:

> Half of PWC's 2,700 U.S. partners owned stock in companies the firm audits, according to the report done by law firm Lankler Siffert & Wohl at the behest of the SEC. The report also revealed that 1,885 people at the firm—1 in every 20 employees—committed violations, prompting Lankler Siffert to conclude that PWC has serious structural and cultural problems. . . . Five partners were forced to resign, a sixth [was] on the way out, and five other managers and staffers were dismissed.

On the one hand, these "cultural problems" were at the shared values level, representing a broken code of ethics that constituted grounds for dismissal. On the other hand, the shared basic assumptions—behavior patterns that one would find totally unacceptable—were also violated. Or more likely in Stein's view of culture, PWC had not adequately instilled the requisite shared basic assumptions in its employees, such that many did not consider owning client stock to be totally unacceptable.

There is no one "right" set of basic assumptions for all organizations. One could not imagine the U.S. Army being successful with a collegial set of basic assumptions like that of an academic institution, or vice versa. A basic research laboratory, such as a biotech firm, would not function well if its leaders tried to institute the rule-centered set of basic assumptions one finds in, say, a welfare office. The issue for senior management, then, is not choosing the "correct" basic assumptions but identifying those that will promote the most successful organizational performance, and either maintaining them if they already exist or moving the firm toward adopting them if they do not.

To maintain or transform a culture at the level of basic assumptions requires addressing some of the fundamental ways the firm operates—the "cultural levers." Not only are these levers important tools for senior management to employ, but all six must be used consistently to mutually reinforce each other.

Cultural Levers

The six organizational processes senior management can use to either maintain or modify an existing culture are (1) strategy formulation, (2) authority and influence, (3) motivation, (4) management control, (5) conflict management, and (6) customer management. They are shown in Figure 14.1.1. In some instances, the use of one of these processes as a cultural lever is relatively easy; in others, it is quite complex and difficult. It is important to note again, however, that as the lines indicate, all six levers must fit together in such a way that they are mutually reinforcing.

These levers may seem similar to the McKinsey 7-S Model described in Peters and Waterman (1982). But there are important differences, which are highlighted in Table 14.1.1. One primary difference is that there are several specific levers within the category that the McKinsey model calls "systems." In addition, as will be discussed below, the cultural levers are more process-oriented than the McKinsey elements.

Lever #1. The Strategy Formulation Process

Strategy formulation relates to the way a firm defines itself and its overall direction. There are two broad schools of thought on how the process works: the *coalitionists* and the *top-down*

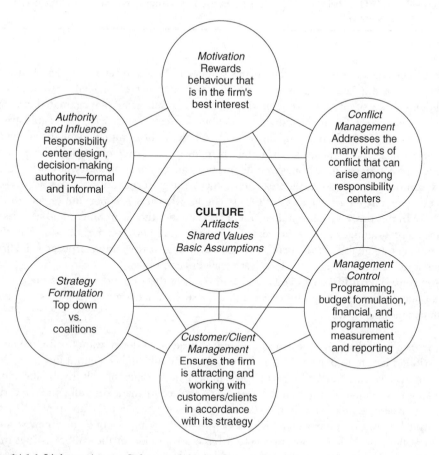

Figure 14.1.1 Linkages Among Culture and the Six Organizational Levers.

Table 14.1.1 Relationship of the Cultural Levers to the McKinsey 7-S Framework

7-S Model Element	Cultural Lever Element
Strategy	Focuses on the *process* by which strategy is *formulated*, rather than on the strategy itself.
Structure	Goes beyond organizational structure per se to how responsibility centers are designed and how authority and influence *flow* in the organization.
Systems	Unbundles "systems" into several key processes that constitute cultural levers, such as motivation, conflict management, customer management, and management control (programming, budgeting, measuring, and reporting).
Staff	Considers staff not from the perspective of personnel categories, but from the cultural perspective. Focuses on how to imbue staff with the necessary shared basic assumptions that are consistent with the desired culture.
Style	Does not consider managerial style explicitly, but rather recognizes that different managers will desire different cultures and will use the cultural levers differently to attain them.
Skills	Does not consider skills. Assumes that these will be attained via the recruitment aspect of the authority and influence process.
Shared Values	Goes below shared values to shared basic assumptions, and hence to a deeper view of culture.

theorists. The coalitionists argue that a firm's strategy is the end result of a series of struggles among competing interest groups, or coalitions. If a firm has sufficient resources, each coalition can pursue its own strategic direction. The result is an "amalgamated strategy," which is the sum total of all the individual coalition strategies. Such a situation could arise in a large, multidivisional conglomerate whose strategy is the summation of the individual division strategies. Or it could exist in a single firm, such as an academic medical center, where different physician groups emphasize different programs, such as oncology or cardiology.

By contrast, the top-down theorists argue that strategy formulation follows a three-step process, generally referred to as a SWOT (strengths, weaknesses, opportunities, and threats) analysis. In this process, senior management (1) examines the environment and assesses the financial, programmatic, and other signals—both positive and negative, (2) compares these environmental signals with the firm's strengths and weaknesses and incorporates the firm's values into the analysis, and (3) selects a strategic direction.

Strategy Formulation Levers. The end result of these considerations is the need for senior management to answer two key cultural questions as it designs or redesigns its strategy formulation process:

* Does it want the firm to have a single, unified strategy, or does it want to allow coalitions within the firm to pursue their own strategies with only limited central direction? Both approaches can work, but each will exhibit a quite different culture. In the unified approach, a basic assumption is that strategic choices are made centrally, and the various organizational units contribute to the chosen strategic direction. Unacceptable behavior would consist of a particular division or program "going it alone" in a new strategic direction. In the coalition approach, a basic assumption of the culture is that many strategic decisions are made by the coalitions without significant input from corporate

headquarters. Unacceptable behavior in this scenario might consist of tying up corporate headquarters with unnecessary requests for approval of new strategic directions.

- If senior management prefers a unified strategy, does it wish to solicit input from middle managers and others to gain as much knowledge as possible about opportunities, threats, strengths, and weaknesses? Some companies solicit relatively little input from middle managers; some invite considerable involvement from them. Again, the two approaches will exhibit contrasting cultures. In firms that solicit input, a basic assumption is that the middle managers' views have value. In firms that do not solicit such input, unacceptable behavior would consist of attempts by middle managers to become involved in formulating the strategy.

Lever #2. The Flow of Authority and Influence

Authority and influence can flow in a variety of ways in an organization, ranging from hierarchical to collegial. The former is exemplified by the military; the latter by many universities. Although an organization chart can identify the formal authority arrangements, it frequently excludes many key decision makers. In some hospitals, physicians who admit a large number of patients have a great deal of influence on organizational decision making, even though they may be independent practitioners and not even appear on the organization chart. And in some consumer product companies, the R&D department has considerably more power than the chart might indicate. In his classic 1964 study of bureaucracy, Michel Crozier identified maintenance workers as having a great deal of influence in an industrial monopoly due to their ability to reduce machine down-time.

For a unified culture, the flow of authority and influence (A&I) must reinforce senior management's decisions concerning the strategy formulation process. A decision to allow coalitions cannot be accompanied easily, if at all, by a hierarchical flow of A&I. If senior management decides to formulate strategy without the involvement of middle managers and others, it will have a difficult time espousing a collegial flow of A&I.

Defining Responsibility Centers. One of the most important decisions management faces in designing (or redesigning) the flow of A&I lies with the firm's network of responsibility centers. In particular, management must decide whether it wishes to have investment or profit centers and, if so, whether there will be cross-subsidization among them. Investment or profit centers without cross-subsidization, and with rewards linked to bottom line performance, constitute a powerful motivating device, essentially creating a series of small business units sometimes referred to as "every tub on its own bottom," or "ETOB."

An ETOB structure can create a "fortress-like" mentality among the affected responsibility center managers, leading to a quite different culture than would exist in a firm with cross-subsidization among its responsibility centers. The ETOB culture would be consistent with the coalition approach to strategy formulation and a collegial flow of A&I, but would present difficulties if management attempted to implement a more unified strategy formulation process—one that entailed coordination and subsidization and used a more hierarchical flow of A&I. In short, senior management must align the firm's responsibility center structure with both the strategy formulation process and the desired flow of A&I.

Regardless of the type of responsibility centers it uses, senior management must consider whether and how it will give the firm's responsibility center managers the ability to control their revenues and expenses. If senior management asks a manager to head a profit center and then allows the accounting staff to allocate corporate overhead into that center, it has created a largely unworkable arrangement. By asking the manager to be responsible for some expenses he or she cannot control, it has violated Vancil's (1973) "fairness criterion." Such a situation can create considerable conflict between responsibility center managers and senior management, leading to both a less-than-optimal management of resources and a quite different culture from one in which managers control their centers' expenses.

A&I Levers. Although no cultural change happens quickly, a relatively rapid change can result from shifting the firm's responsibility center structure from, say, an ETOB approach to one involving cross-subsidization, or vice versa. Dramatic change can also result from centralizing revenue and establishing a series of expense centers. As a result, the responsibility center network constitutes a powerful but often neglected cultural lever for senior management—one that can have a relatively quick impact on the culture.

In addition to the responsibility center design, senior managers have four other levers they can use to maintain or modify a firm's A&I process: recruitment, training, promotion, and severance. In the absence of an organizational "blood bath," however, using these levers to affect a change in culture can take considerably longer than altering the responsibility centers. Nevertheless, all four levers need to be included in the repertoire of senior managers attempting to introduce cultural change or wishing to preserve an existing culture. Doing so means, for example, ensuring that the recruiting process emphasizes people who not only possess the skills needed for the job openings but are also prepared to support the kind of culture senior management desires. If a manager with an ETOB mentality is hired by a firm with cross-subsidization among its profit centers, there will no doubt be some significant cultural clashes. Similarly, if an existing manager is not comfortable in a newly created ETOB environment, it may be necessary to arrange for an early severance. Finally, training sessions can be designed not only to impart the requisite skills, but also to imbue the participants with the fundamental elements of the firm's culture. In an ETOB structure, for example, unacceptable behavior would consist of operating a responsibility center at a loss.

The external environment may constrain A&I choices. In a welfare office, legislative and regulatory requirements may make it impossible for the director to shift from a hierarchical, rule-oriented culture to a more collegial one. Similarly, military combat conditions dictate that an army have a hierarchical culture. As such, an important task for senior management is to determine where it has "A&I latitude," and to consider its approach accordingly. In this regard, senior management must be careful not to interpret its constraints too literally. Anthony and Young (1999) report on a repair garage manager in the New York City Sanitation Department who was able to use the prices charged by private garages to create "pseudo" profit centers, even though his department had no earned revenue.

Regardless of the approach taken, changing a firm's A&I process can be extremely difficult, and senior management can expect considerable resistance. In academic institutions, most university faculties have a profoundly embedded collegial culture that, coupled with the presence of tenure, limits a dean's ability to affect the A&I process. In general, only the recruitment and promotion levers are available to a dean, and even those usually require faculty consensus. Other organizations have a somewhat easier time employing the A&I levers, although employment contracts and various forms of managerial resistance can slow the pace of change. Still, once some of these changes have been introduced, they will fundamentally alter the basic assumptions that are the essence of culture.

Lever #3. The Motivation Process

In considering the motivation process, senior managers must focus on a fit among (1) employee personalities, (2) the five other cultural levers, and (3) the firm's external environment, including customers, competitors, regulators, lenders, and shareholders. According to Lorsch and Morse (1974), a hierarchical A&I process—with many controls on decision making and highly structured ways of organizing employee behavior—is appropriate when the external environment is relatively certain, and when members of the organization prefer dependent authority relationships and have a relatively low tolerance for ambiguity. By contrast, a more collegial A&I process—with few controls on decisions and relatively unstructured ways of organizing employee behavior—is appropriate for an uncertain external environment, in which employees prefer considerable autonomy and can tolerate ambiguity well.

The motivation process can reinforce this A&I process. Motivation for workers on an assembly line might be tied to work standards, with supplemental compensation linked to increased productivity. By contrast, motivation for scientists engaged in exploratory research might be related to collaboration and the sharing of ideas, with recognition and peer approval seen as more important than financial rewards. In either case, the motivation process constitutes an important lever for affecting the culture.

There is an important link between the motivation process, the firm's responsibility center structure, and its management control process (discussed below). Some firms clarify this link by paying bonuses to key operating managers for achieving budgetary targets. Nevertheless, many organizations, especially nonprofit ones, often have difficulty finding a link between job performance and rewards. Some encourage entrepreneurial behavior and provide extra budgetary resources to successful managers. Others provide nonfinancial bonuses, such as sabbatical leaves. In some instances, the creation of a "game-playing" culture can have an important impact on motivation, as when the above-mentioned repair garage manager created teams and began using shadow pricing to compare each team's productivity to the cost of a similar repair job in a private garage.

Motivation Levers. For the above reasons, the design of the motivation process depends to a great extent on the kind of culture senior management seeks. As with other levers, it will affect employees' understanding of what is desirable and undesirable behavior. Entrepreneurial behavior by profit center managers will be difficult to achieve with a hierarchical A&I process, or if the strategy formulation process seeks to create a unified strategy rather than allowing individual coalitions some latitude to determine their own strategies. At the same time, entrepreneurial behavior will be difficult to put into place unless the motivation process provides appropriate rewards for the kinds of risks being taken, or if there is an absence of fairness in the way expenses are assigned to profit centers.

In effect, one approach to developing a unified culture and linking the strategy formulation, A&I, and motivation processes is to (a) establish profit centers, (b) give profit center managers some latitude to do as they wish, and (c) develop a motivation process with a large, risk-sharing, incentive-compensation component. However, unless these levers are consistent and mutually reinforcing, considerable frustration will result, with a concomitant undermining of senior management's desired culture. In particular, there will be a lack of clarity around the basic assumptions of the culture and what constitutes desirable and undesirable behavior.

Lever #4. The Management Control Process

The management control process consists of four activities: programming, budgeting, measuring, and reporting. These activities are linked to several other cultural levers.

Programming. In many firms, decision making about new programs and large capital expenditures tries to ensure that programs (or product lines) are consistent with—and flow from—strategy. For this to happen, program or product line managers must understand the linkages between their activities and the firm's overall strategic direction. According to the top-down theorists, this can be difficult for senior management. If a strategy is to evolve over time because of shifting environmental demands and changing organizational strengths and weaknesses, senior management must find ways to monitor and manage the programs and product lines so they remain consistent with and supportive of the strategy.

By contrast, in a culture with a coalition approach to strategy formulation, senior management may not review programming decisions at all. Or it might review only those above a certain financial threshold. A large, multidivisional corporation might require that a division receive corporate approval before deciding to construct a new plant, reasoning that although individual coalitions may make some programming decisions on their own, big-ticket decisions have a major impact on the overall strategic direction of the firm.

In short, the way management establishes the constraints on and the approaches to programming can have a profound impact on the firm's culture. Indeed, in most firms programming is an especially important cultural lever that senior management can wield quickly and significantly. Stated bluntly, the "power of the purse" is a major lever for affecting the autonomy of the line managers and hence the firm's culture.

Budgeting. The budgeting activity, also reflecting the power of the purse, must fit well with both the strategy formulation process and the programming activity of the management control process. Indeed, by budgeting for both nonfinancial and financial goals and objectives, senior management can relate each program or product line to the firm's overall strategic direction.

This idea is not new. It has always been an issue for nonprofit organizations. One of the first for-profit companies to introduce the idea was Texas Instruments. More recently, Kaplan and Norton (1992, 1993) have described it in terms of a "balanced scorecard."

If senior management has established profit centers as part of the A&I lever, it must address several important issues in formulating annual budgets: (a) setting the profitability goal of each center; (b) deciding whether there should be cross-subsidization among the centers; and (c) if there is cross-subsidization, determining the subsidy amounts. Because reaching acceptable answers to these questions and related ones is quite difficult, some firms have designated their operating entities as standard or discretionary expense centers, and have either centralized all revenue or created separate revenue centers.

These sorts of decisions can have an important impact on a culture. Centralizing revenue and establishing expense centers, for example, is consistent with a hierarchical culture, whereas the use of ETOB profit centers is more consistent with a collegial, coalition-based culture. Profit centers with cross-subsidization—sometimes called the "portfolio approach"—lie somewhere between these two.

Transfer Prices. The issue of transfer prices arises in conjunction with the above types of decisions and, more generally, whenever responsibility centers use each other's services. Intra-organizational transactions can exist between two profit centers in a relatively small company or between two divisions in a large multidivisional corporation. A transfer price is equally appropriate in, say, a hospital when a pediatric department orders a test from the hospital's lab, or at General Motors, when the Chevrolet Division uses batteries produced by the Delco Division.

The way senior management establishes transfer prices, whether it allows buying entities to purchase from outside the firm if they wish to do so, and how it fashions a variety of other "transfer pricing rules" not only can influence the budgeting activity significantly but will also have a deep impact on the firm's culture. A "hands-off" approach by senior management is consistent with a more decentralized, coalition-based culture, whereas an interventionist approach is consistent with a hierarchical culture.

Measuring and Reporting. Firms typically provide their responsibility center managers with information about how their programs (or product lines) perform compared to budgeted objectives. As a result, there is a need for activities that measure and report both financial and nonfinancial information. These measuring and reporting activities can be designed in a wide variety of ways, depending on considerations such as each person's responsibilities, the kinds of action senior management expects line managers to take, and, more generally, the culture that senior management wishes to establish.

Measuring and reporting activities can also be related to budget formulation and the firm's motivation process. Some firms identify their "cost drivers," link the budget to them, measure and report variances by cost driver in each responsibility center, and reward the center managers in light of their performance with respect to the cost drivers under their control. Other firms do not have this sort of rigor in their management control process. Instead, they formulate budgets more generally (perhaps using line items and trend analysis), measure and report financial and nonfinancial information in an equally general way, and reward responsibility center managers on the basis of something other than performance against the budget. Clearly these two types of firms will have quite contrasting cultures.

Management Control Levers. The management control process constitutes an important cultural lever. It includes the approach used to establish, retain, or eliminate programs; the nature of budgeting; the information that is measured; the kinds of reports responsibility center managers receive; and the actions senior management expects them to take on the basis of those reports. Moreover, like responsibility center design, it is a lever that management can influence relatively quickly. Indeed, the three levers of A&I (including responsibility center design), management control, and motivation can be effective in creating an internally consistent culture, but only if they are used in concert, both with each other and with other processes, such as strategy formulation.

Lever #5. The Conflict Management Process

Conflict can be either beneficial or detrimental to a firm. The tension that exists between line managers and the controller's staff during budget formulation is an example of potentially beneficial conflict. Each party brings a different but important perspective to the table, the resolution of which can lead to improved organizational performance. For a good decision to emerge, however, the conflict must be managed well. In the above example, well-managed conflict might lead to a tight but attainable budget that directly supports a firm's strategy, helps ensure that customers receive high-quality products or services, and motivates line managers to stretch themselves to attain the agreed-upon goals.

Similar conflict can exist in a wide variety of situations. Examples include: (a) new product design, where engineers would prefer a lengthy design and testing period but marketing personnel want an early launch; (b) production scheduling, where manufacturing personnel prefer long lead times and sales personnel want to respond to customers' requests for immediate delivery; and (c) R&D, where basic research personnel wish to do "good science" and applied research personnel wish to develop new materials or products quickly.

There are two related aspects to the conflict management process: the *type*, which must fit with the level of conflict, and the *mode*, which must fit with the firm's A&I process. Both aspects can influence the firm's culture.

Types of Conflict Management. The various types of conflict management mechanisms are shown in Table 14.1.2, along with an example of where each might be appropriate. Each type works best when it is aligned with the degree of conflict that exists in a particular situation.

As Table 2 indicates, the types of conflict management can range from information flows (such as the exchange of interoffice memos or e-mails) to permanent committees. A manager might use the former to schedule a meeting (where there is usually a relatively low level of one-time conflict) and the latter to make resource allocation or operational decisions (where there tends to be a relatively high level of continuing conflict). Many hospitals have a permanent committee that is charged with scheduling the operating room—a matter of continual, and frequently intense, conflict.

Occasionally, there is a need for an individual or department outside the official organizational hierarchy to help manage conflict—what Lawrence and Lorsch (1967) call an "integrator." This person's (or department's) job is to understand thoroughly the two or more perspectives that create the conflict, and to work with the involved parties to resolve their differences.

Modes of Conflict Management. At one end of the spectrum of conflict management modes is *forcing*, which has a heavy, top-down emphasis. The conflicting parties appeal their differences to a supervisor (or other authority), who then makes a decision. At the other end is *direct confrontation*, in which the parties resolve their differences together without intervention by supervisors or others. Between the two is *smoothing*, in which the conflict is resolved by having a third person find a solution that is acceptable to both parties.

To be successful, the mode of conflict management must fit with the flow of A&I as well as with the type of conflict being addressed. To attempt a forcing mode in a collegial culture would be difficult and perhaps counterproductive, as would direct confrontation in a firm where the decision ultimately would be made by the supervisor of the conflicting parties. In this latter instance, the mode would not only be a poor fit with the flow of A&I but would likely be a poor use of time for the involved parties.

Direct confrontation is often used in situations where two professionals of equal status need to make a decision or reach an agreement. Examples include researchers seeking an appropriate study design, engineers agreeing on an effective product design, physicians finding a suitable test or procedure for a patient, and professors preparing a fair exam policy for students.

Table 14.1.2 Types of Conflict Management Mechanisms

Type of Conflict	Example	Mechanism
Low level, one-time, with multiple perspectives	Scheduling a meeting	Information flows (paper, e-mail, telephone)
Moderate, one-time, with two perspectives	Determining who will attend a conference or a training program	Hierarchy
Moderate, one-time, with multiple perspectives	Designing and launching a new product	Ad hoc cross-disciplinary teams
High, continuing, with two perspectives	Obtaining fiscal approval for additional staff in a laboratory	Integrator
High, continuing, with multiple perspectives	Capital investment decisions; production scheduling for a plant used by several product managers	Permanent cross-disciplinary teams

Conflict Management Levers. Senior management can use several conflict management levers to influence culture. Its response to a situation of ongoing conflict could be to (a) take part in resolving it, (b) appoint a committee to deal with it, or (c) assign an integrator. All three approaches can be effective, but each suggests a different culture and a different sense of what is acceptable and unacceptable behavior. Similarly, the membership of both permanent committees and ad hoc task forces sends important cultural signals. If senior management were to combine an equal number of middle managers and assembly line workers on a reengineering task force, it would send a signal to the company about both the importance of line workers' opinions and the value it attached to middle managers' time. More generally, the approaches taken by senior management to deal with the several kinds of conflict shown in Table 2 constitute highly visible intra-organizational signals of the kind of culture it desires.

Lever #6. The Customer Management Process

Most firms have a process that identifies customers and "manages" them. It includes activities that take place *within* the firm as well as those designed to attract customers *to* the firm. These activities combine both operations management and marketing, and include product design and manufacturing, service provision and scheduling, price setting, facility siting, and the delivery of after-sale services. All these activities have a heavy cultural overlay. Indeed, the way a company manages its customers is perhaps the most visible external indicator of its culture.

Of all the cultural levers, the customer management process is the one undergoing the closest thing to a revolution. How firms interact with their customers, both during and after the sale, is coming under intense scrutiny from many quarters, especially as the distinction between products and services becomes increasingly blurred. Moreover, changes such as increased information flows to consumers from the Internet, new forms of competition, and shortening product life cycles are all having an impact on customer loyalty.

From a somewhat more conceptual perspective, with any product or service there are five steps in customer decision making: awareness, interest, trial, repetition, and commitment. At each stage, a firm needs to engage in different activities. Promotion, for example, is relatively important for the first three activities but relatively unimportant for the latter two. That is, creating awareness of a product or service, generating customers' interest in it, and convincing them to make an initial trial or purchase is not enough to ensure success. Repetition and commitment depend mainly on the quality of the product or service provided and the customer's satisfaction with value. Specifically, customers must be pleased with what they receive, both initially and over time, and they must be charged a price that they perceive as fair. Some years ago, now-defunct Eastern Airlines mounted an extensive promotional campaign that convinced thousands of people to fly Eastern for the first time. But because of Eastern's poor on-time performance and cabin service during the flight, most of those people chose another airline for their next flight.

At the same time companies are redefining their customers and exploring new services and new ways of providing them, they are also experiencing an upheaval in their production efforts. Reengineering, total quality management, continuous quality improvement, and the like have affected the cost, quality, and delivery cycles of many companies' products and services. One of the acknowledged leaders in this effort is Toyota, with its well-known Toyota Production System (TPS). To understand that, explain Spear and Bowen (1999), one must first recognize that Toyota's definition of the ideal plant is one in which "a Toyota customer could drive up to a shipping dock, ask for a customized product or service, and get it at once at the lowest possible price and with no defects." Until this ideal is achieved, Toyota is committed to making constant, albeit usually small, improvements in its plants.

What makes Toyota's plant definition most unusual, however, is its focus on the customer. Few companies would define an ideal plant with such a heavy customer emphasis. It is this link that perhaps most vividly demonstrates Toyota's focus, not on marketing or production per se, but on *customer management*—a process that contains elements of both marketing and production but without the usual walls between the two.

Many companies in a variety of industries have tried, usually unsuccessfully, to imitate the TPS. Their lack of success is in no small way the result of a failure to attain what Toyota calls a "learning culture." Based on the scientific method, this is a key aspect of the TPS, and is linked directly to Toyota's customer management process. Developing and then maintaining this *basic assumption* is one of the key reasons for the success of the TPS. So is the company's A&I process, which gives low-level line workers the power to initiate change, "teach" their superiors about problems in the production effort, and propose ways to improve that effort.

Finally, Toyota's management control process must fit all these elements so as to support the learning culture. The company must be prepared to accept new programmatic efforts based on changes initiated at the floor level. Budgets must be developed with a recognition that time will be spent on process improvements, conflict management, and data collection, as well as on actual production activities. A basic assumption of the culture must be the constant development of new measures to address the experiments taking place, and the management control reports that are prepared for both line managers and senior management must be in a constant state of flux. Clearly, the TPS represents a radically different culture from a traditional manufacturing plant. Perhaps most important, however, this culture is maintained with several levers, all of which fit with the customer management process.

Customer Management Levers. As with other processes, the customer management process can be influenced by senior management in a variety of ways. Market segmentation decisions can be decentralized to responsibility center managers or other coalitions, or they can be determined more hierarchically, as can product design, facility siting, and a variety of other similar decisions concerning customers. Moreover, there will frequently be conflicting views about the best way to approach these decisions, and senior management's approach to addressing the resulting conflict will play an important role in maintaining or modifying the firm's culture. Once again, in making these sorts of decisions management is sending important signals about what is desirable and undesirable behavior in the firm—the basic assumptions of its desired culture.

As Figure 1 suggests, the six processes discussed above all constitute levers management can use to either maintain or transform a firm's culture. The lines connecting the six processes indicate that no process operates in isolation from the others. Indeed, there are important links among all six, and a key goal for senior management it to design each process in such a way that it operates in concert with the other five in moving the firm toward the desired culture.

Perhaps most important, senior management must recognize that there is no single correct culture. Rather, the one that is most suitable for a given organization will depend partly on the environmental constraints the firm faces and partly on senior management's wishes. It is the latter category in which the six processes can be used as levers to help preserve a culture or to modify it in accordance with senior management's preferences.

References

Kenneth R. Andrews, *The Concept of Corporate Strategy* (Homewood, IL: Dow Jones-Irwin, 1980).

• Robert N. Anthony and V.J. Govindarajan, *Management Control Systems*, 10th ed. (Burr Ridge, IL: Irwin-McGraw-Hill, 1999).

Robert N. Anthony and David W. Young, *Management Control in Nonprofit Organizations*, 6th ed. (Burr Ridge, IL: Irwin-McGraw-Hill, 1999).

Joseph Bower, *Managing the Resource Allocation Process* (Boston: Division of Research, Graduate School of Business Administration, Harvard University, 1970).

Robin Cooper, "The Rise of Activity-Based Costing—Part Three: How Many Cost Drivers Do You Need, and How Do You Select Them?" *Journal of Cost Management*, Winter 1989, pp. 34–46.

Robin Cooper and Robert S. Kaplan, "Measure Costs Right: Make the Right Decisions," *Harvard Business Review*, September-October 1988, pp. 96–103.

Michel Crozier, *The Bureaucratic Phenomenon* (Chicago: University of Chicago Press, 1964).

Richard M. Cyert and James G. March, *A Behavioral Theory of the Firm* (Englewood Cliffs, NJ: Prentice-Hall, 1963).

Stan Davis and Christopher Meyer, *Blur: The Speed of Change in the Connected Economy* (Reading, MA: Addison-Wesley, 1998).

W. Edwards Deming, *Out of the Crisis* (Cambridge, MA: The MIT Press, 1982, 1986).

Michael Hammer and Steven A. Stanton, *The Reengineering Revolution* (New York: Harper Business, 1995).

C.W.L. Hart, J.L. Heskett, and W.E. Sasser, Jr., "The Profitable Art of Service Recovery," *Harvard Business Review*, July-August 1990, pp. 148–156.

James L. Heskett, *Managing in the Service Economy* (Boston: Harvard Business School Press, 1986).

K. Ishikawa, ed., *Guide to Quality Control*, 2nd rev. ed. (Tokyo: Asian Productivity Organization, 1986).

J.M. Juran, *Juran on Planning for Quality* (New York: The Free Press, 1988).

Robert S. Kaplan and David P. Norton, "The Balanced Scorecard—Measures that Drive Performance, *Harvard Business Review*, January-February 1992, pp. 71–79.

Robert S. Kaplan and David P. Norton, "Putting the Balanced Scorecard to Work, *Harvard Business Review*, September-October 1993, pp. 134–147.

John P. Kotter, "Leading Change: Why Transformation Efforts Fail," *Harvard Business Review*, March-April 1995, pp. 59–67.

John P. Kotter, "Power, Success, and Organizational Effectiveness," *Organizational Dynamics*, Winter 1978, pp. 26–40.

Paul R. Lawrence and Jay W. Lorsch, *Organization and Environment* (Boston: Division of Research, Graduate School of Business Administration, Harvard University, 1967).

Theodore Levitt, "Production-Line Approach to Service," *Harvard Business Review*, September-October 1972, pp. 41–52.

Jay W. Lorsch and J.J. Morse, *Organizations and Their Members* (New York: Harper and Row, 1974).

Pamela L. Moore, "This Scandal Changes Everything," *Business Week*, February 28, 2000, pp. 140–143.

Thomas J. Peters and Robert H. Waterman, Jr., *In Search of Excellence: Lessons from America's Best-Run Companies* (New York: Harper and Row, 1982).

Edgar H. Schein, *Organizational Culture and Leadership*, 2nd ed. (San Francisco: Jossey-Bass, 1992).

Philip Selznick, *Leadership in Administration* (Evanston, IL: Row, Peterson, 1957).

Alfred E. Sloan, *My Years with General Motors* (New York: Macfadden-Bartell, 1965, 1963).

David Solomons, *Divisional Performance: Measurement and Control* (Homewood, IL: R.D. Irwin, Inc., 1965).

Steven Spear and H. Kent Bowen, "Decoding the DNA of the Toyota Production System," *Harvard Business Review*, September-October 1999, pp. 96–106.

Richard F. Vancil, "What Kind of Management Control Do You Need?" *Harvard Business Review*, March-April 1973, pp. 75–86.

Robert H. Waterman, Jr., Thomas J. Peters, and Julien Phillips, "Structure is Not Organization," *Business Horizons*, June 1980, pp. 14–26.

David W. Young and Diana Barrett, "Managing Clinical Integration in Integrated Delivery Systems: A Framework for Action," *Hospital & Health Services Administration*, Summer 1997, pp. 255–279.

David W. Young and Richard B. Saltman, *The Hospital Power Equilibrium* (Baltimore and London: The Johns Hopkins Press, 1985).

14.2   ASSESSING THE FIELD OF ORGANIZATION DEVELOPMENT

Jeana Wirtenberg, Lilian Abrams, and Carolyn Ott

This article describes Phase I of a larger organization development (OD) initiative. A survey was sent to more than 6,000 members of the Organization Development Network, Organization Development Institute, and International Organization Development Association to assess present weaknesses and potential strengths of the field. Respondents to this survey indicated that the field of OD (a) lacks a clear, distinct definition; (b) needs greater quality control/effectiveness and business acumen among OD practitioners; and (c) lacks clarity around its return on investment and perceived value of the work performed. At the same time, OD has significant strengths that can be leveraged. These include a systemic orientation in organizations, an ability to assist in change management, teamwork and leadership development, and the values OD brings to its practice. Building on these results, a literature review, and interviews with business leaders, six key integrated themes that have implications for the OD profession are described.

The Global Committee on the Future of Organization Development (OD)—Background and Introduction

The field of organization development is at a crossroads. In *Organization Development at Work: Conversations on the Values, Applications, and Future of OD*, Billie Alban (2003) describes the present as follows:

> We are going through some difficult times right now. Many external consultants are finding it hard to get work. Internal consultants are fearful of being laid off. With business working at the survival level in terms of the Maslow hierarchy, many things that we offer are put on the back burner. We are a superfluous service to organizations unless we can help them see the value we bring. (pp. 125–126)

Over the past several years, there has been a sharp increase in the number of OD practitioners "in transition" (i.e., whose jobs have been restructured or eliminated). Trends point to downward spirals for both internal and external practitioners, who find themselves constantly challenged to justify the value of OD. A number of internal practitioners have lost their jobs as organizations continue to "right size" their staffs, ostensibly to "enhance their productivity." Furthermore, as these transitions occur, the OD work is not always outsourced to OD practitioners. Instead, some of the work is transferred to human resources (HR) generalists or HR business partners; sometimes it goes to traditional management consultant firms whose approaches are very different from traditional OD, whereas in other cases, it is eliminated altogether. At the same time, a number of external practitioners are finding it increasingly challenging to win new contracts as demand for traditional OD work appears to be decreasing.

The study reported here is a part of a larger initiative jointly sponsored by the Organization Development Institute (ODI), Organization Development Network (ODN), and International Organization Development Association (IODA) called the Global Committee on the Future of Organization Development. Comprised of more than 200 OD practitioners, the Global Committee initiative is guided by a coalition of advisory boards from business (consisting of heads of OD from 34 highly successful global corporations and nonprofit organizations), academia, and a government advisory board representing federal, state, and local governments in the United States.[1]

Methodology

In Phase I of the initiative, research was conducted along the following four parallel tracks:

a. Literature review: An extensive analysis was conducted synthesizing business challenges and opportunities from more than 80 recent research documents.
b. Strengths, weaknesses, opportunities, and threats (SWOT): A survey was sent to more than 6,000 OD practitioners with more than 900 responses.
c. Business leader interviews: Business leaders from the companies represented by the advisory board members were interviewed one on one.
d. Business and academic advisory board interviews: Business OD leaders represented on the business advisory board and academic advisory board members were interviewed one on one.

The next section focuses in detail on the findings and results specifically from the SWOT analysis. This is followed in the discussion section by the six key integrated themes that incorporate the synthesis of the inputs from all four of these sources.[2]

SWOT Survey

Procedures

The SWOT was developed by a survey subteam[3] as part of the Global Committee's Phase I exploratory research process. The survey team prepared a questionnaire with six open-ended questions (the questionnaire is available on the portal) asking about the OD profession's strengths, weaknesses, opportunities, threats, value/impact, and other comments. The questionnaire was distributed by the Global Committee's leadership committee to more than 6,000 people, including the membership e-mail addresses from the rosters of ODN (4,000), ODI (300), IODA (300), the New Jersey Organization Development Network (NJODN: 1,200), and National Training Labs (NTL: 300) (some repetition may be expected). Recipients of the survey were encouraged to forward it to their personal networks. The survey was completed by 907 respondents.

The survey demographics measured self-reports of respondents' age, gender, education, and years practicing OD as well as primary geographic regions and industries of OD practice.

The survey results were gathered and reviewed by the four-person team for initial classifications. Based on this review, an extensive coding list was created to enter and track specific issues identified by respondents in the following major categories: profession (what we do, the areas we focus on, the types and categories of work we do, our orientation), practitioners (who we are; our personal qualities, characteristics, and capabilities; how we feel, act, and behave to ourselves and our clients), techniques/processes (how we work, the specific processes and tools we might use to assist our clients), customers (where we work, the environment in which we perform our work, types of clients, types of industries), and results (why we work, the measured and unmeasured outcomes of our work, qualitative and quantitative). Within these major categories, 100 subcategories were created based on the initial review. Team members read and coded each response on the 907 respondents' questionnaires and then reviewed the sorted data to extract the key learnings and themes. Initial findings were presented to the Global Committee in April 2004.

Respondent Demographics and Key Characteristics

There were 907 survey respondents (with more than 6,000 people receiving the survey worldwide), for a 15% response rate (see Table 14.2.1). Because the survey targeted ODI, ODN, and IODA membership lists, the organizations' respondents are most often members of ODN (73%), Regional ODN/ODI (41%), American Society for Training and Development (ASTD; 34%), and Society for Human Resource Management (SHRM; 23%).

Results

Strengths of OD

The SWOT survey questions were open ended, and respondents often provided more than one response to each question. These responses were often represented by more than one code and coding category, as appropriate, which allowed the total response percentages for the overall coding categories (profession, practitioners, techniques/processes, etc.) to exceed 100%.

As summarized in Table 14.2.2, the clear majority of the 907 survey respondents described the strengths of the OD profession as arising from within the profession (74%). Within the profession category, the two most frequent responses given by respondents were an "overall systemic orientation in organizations" (22%) and an "ability to assist in change management" (20%).

To a significantly lesser degree, responses that fell into the techniques and processes category were described as strengths by 21% of respondents. Within this category, support in building teamwork (5%) and leadership development (5%) were equally the most frequent responses. Finally, 15% of survey respondents indicated that strengths lie within OD practitioners themselves. The most frequently mentioned strength that practitioners were said to possess were the "values OD brings to practice" (4%).

Strength 1: Systemic orientation. Many respondents said that a distinct OD contribution was the systemic, or holistic, orientation to the organization. It is looking at the "big picture," including an organization's various stakeholders, constituents, organizational subentities, internal functions, and processes. All of these important elements are on behalf of the "human element" in organizations and directly or indirectly coach clients to hold this perspective as well. Many comments mentioned the advantages of combining the systemic approach with change management, although these two strengths were coded separately. Some representative quotes follow:

Table 14.2.1 Respondent Demographics and Key Characteristics

Survey sample

Survey sent to approximately 6,000 potential respondents, including rosters from Organization Development Institute (300), Organization Development Network (4,000), International Organization Development Association (300), New Jersey Organization Development Network (1,200), and National Training Labs (300)

Survey response rate

Total respondents: 907 (response rate is approximately 15%; survey respondents may or may not be representative of the entire organization development profession)

Survey time frame

The survey was conducted from mid-December 2003 to early January 2004

Respondent demographic characteristics

Survey responses were received from North and South America, Europe, Asia, Africa, and Australia, with more than 80% of responses from the United States and almost half of the U.S. responses from Northeastern United States

Respondents' ages

48% of respondents were age 50 or older; 80% were age 40 or older

Respondents' areas of practice

Respondents could provide more than one answer to the question regarding primary focus of practice; the most often listed areas of primary practice focus were corporate (69%), not for profit (35%), government (31%), education (25%), manufacturing (24%), health (24%), high tech (22%), financial (21%), and pharmaceutical (18%)

Respondents' years of practice

40% of respondents have been OD practitioners for 16 years or longer and 80% for 6 years or longer

Respondents' educational background

9% of respondents have a bachelor's degree, 62% have a master's degree, and 25% have a Ph.D.

Respondents' gender

56% of respondents were women and 43% were men

Respondents' primary work role

Respondent primary work role includes internal practitioner (52%), external practitioner (43%), and academic (3.7%)

Respondents' location of practice

Primary location of practice is virtually identical to where the responses were received from, with more than 80% of responses from the United States and almost half of the U.S. responses from Northeastern United States

---

Table 14.2.2 Top Three Sources of Strengths of Organization Development (OD)

Strength	Percentage
1. Arising within profession	74
Overall systemic orientation in organizations	22
Ability to assist in change management	20
2. Techniques and processes	21
Support in building teamwork	5
Leadership development	5
3. Practitioners themselves	15
Values OD brings to practice	4

- "Ability to look at the system as a whole."
- "The ability to stand back and see the whole system and within that context provide feedback to the client on change, teaming, whatever the organization[al] issue or situation is about."
- "OD approaches the organization from a systemic/whole systems perspective. This approach [is] then used to influence the most senior level leaders in solving systemic business problems."
- "[A] current strength is the courage to facilitate change using the entire system."
- "OD's strength is its system-wide perspective of the organization, and the impact of interventions on a variety of facets of the operation."

Strength 2: Change management. Change management refers both to change in the overall organization in its entirety and to processes of change in smaller subsections of the organization or with the people and groups within it (e.g., divisions, specific work teams, key leaders, etc.). Respondents referred to OD practitioners' expertise in specific change methodologies and techniques as well as a general orientation toward facilitating and managing effective organizational change. They also commented on OD practitioners' ability to partner with managers and leaders to effect change in organizations.

Some representative quotes follow:

- "Provides the opportunity to implement constructive change interventions within organizations. If done well, these interventions can make a significant impact on the lives of individuals and the success of the organizations for which they work."
- "OD stimulates knowledgeable practitioners to grasp the need for change, the process for change, the implications of the change, and the methodology for effective implementation. Practitioners understand and guide clients to understand the far reaches of change and that entry in itself is a change."
- "Information about working with and applying change technologies."
- "The OD perspective causes leaders to think more holistically and longer term about their approaches to change."
- "OD incorporates a wide range of tools and techniques to involve people in change processes."
- "OD partners well with line leaders to assess change needs and develop comprehensive, integrated change management plans. Once developed, OD adds value by actively facilitating and co-managing change implementation."

Strength 3: Teamwork. The importance of teams and teamwork was one of the two most frequently mentioned responses under the OD techniques and processes category. Many respondents referred to teams as a particular area of focus in organizations, in particular when designing and guiding large change efforts. Other comments referred to teams simply as one element in the organization to which OD practitioners do and should pay attention. On its own, team building was said to be an activity where OD practitioners' expertise is valuable. Some representative quotes follow:

- "Does well: Helps organizations, teams, and individuals work together to continuously increase their capabilities to innovate, improve, and perform in the service of their stakeholders."
- "[OD] assist[s] teams with change management strategies."

- "[OD] allows teams to develop and grow."
- "Many of the tools of OD, when properly applied, also . . . add value: i.e. . . . survey feedback, team development interventions, etc."
- "Value is most often seen in change efforts, team building, and M & A transitions."

Strength 4: Leadership development. Leadership development was mentioned by most respondents as a standalone topic, needing no further explication. It was most often mentioned as part of a list of the primary activities that OD practitioners facilitate successfully in organizations and that represents a distinct contribution of OD as a field. A few representative quotes follow:

- "Leadership Development, Facilitation, Large Group Interventions, Change Management."
- "Strategic Planning; Visioning; Change Management; Conflict Management; Leadership Development."

Strength 5: Values. In the category of responses that focused on qualities of OD practitioners themselves, the most frequently mentioned response was about OD practitioners' values as a defining aspect of OD work. Although these values were generally not specifically delineated by respondents, one distinct value that OD practitioners were said to contribute was a "humanistic" value, that OD brings a focus on the "human element" to organizations. Values were said both to be a core tool and a platform from which both OD practitioners and the organizations they work with achieve results and effective change. Some representative quotes follow:

- "We honor a values-based approach to change which strengthens the organization's culture in terms of trust and collaboration."
- "OD still holds values as core to any change process, which can be critical to achieving real results."
- "[One strength of OD is] . . . a clear set of professional values."
- "Providing the voice for the human being part of the system within the organization."
- "Treating people in organizations as human beings instead of as machines."

Weaknesses of OD

As noted earlier, because the SWOT survey questions were open ended, respondents often provided more than one response to each question. These responses were often represented by more than one code and coding category, as appropriate, which allowed the total response percentages for the overall coding categories (profession, practitioners, results, etc.) to exceed 100%.

As summarized in Table 14.2.3, the clear majority of the 907 survey respondents described the weaknesses of the OD profession as arising from within the profession (58%). Within the profession category, the two most frequent responses given by respondents were "lack of definition of the field" (14%) and "lack of distinction of the field" (8%).

The most frequent responses that noted weaknesses of practitioners themselves (49%) focused on the following three areas: lack of quality control (20%), lack of business acumen (12%), and lack of attention to customer needs (5%).

Within the category results of our work, 35% of respondents noted weaknesses, the most frequent being insufficiently clear return on investment (ROI: 20%) and insufficiently clear value of the work (18%).

Weakness 1: Lack of definition and distinctiveness of OD. Many respondents noted the broad set of tools, techniques, and solutions the field of OD encompasses and listed this breadth of knowledge as contributing to a key weakness: the lack of definition of the field. Presenting an unclear brand to our public, being seen as fragmented, lacking in focus, and without international standards were frequent concerns. Another key area of concern was the lack of rigor in defining the field and the specializations within OD as well as the qualifications and criteria for becoming a practitioner (the lack of qualifications and criteria for becoming a practitioner was also noted as a threat). Respondents noted that they are frequently defined by the specialization they work in (change management, leadership development, coaching) rather than by a broader mission for an industry.

In terms of the lack of distinctiveness of OD, concern was noted regarding the "merging" or "blending" of fields, particularly that of HR and OD. The general confusion over the definition of OD combined with the inability to present OD's uniqueness and value proposition were noted as particular weaknesses in marketing the profession to the customer base. Some representative quotes follow:

- "We lack a shared vision, binding us together as a profession."
- "We have a hard time defining OD to our clients because every practitioner has a different definition."
- "There is a general lack of identity as a field of practice and increasingly as a field of academic study."
- "The field needs clearer boundaries, differentiators from related fields such as training, and quality improvement, performance consulting and general management consulting. This blurred distinction makes it hard to attribute specific results to OD interventions."
- "We lack a differentiation of OD practitioners and HR generalists and the clarity about how to best support the business from an OD and HR perspective."

Weakness 2: Lack of quality control of practitioners. The lack of quality control of practitioners focused on the following key themes: the lack of an industry-wide program certifying or credentialing practitioners, protecting the reputation of the field by differentiating credentialed OD practitioners from all others, and the belief that practitioners who enter this field

Table 14.2.3 Top Three Weaknesses of Organization Development (OD)

Weakness	Percentage
1. Arising within profession	58
Lack of definition of the field of OD	14
Lack of distinction of the field of OD	8
2. Practitioners themselves	49
Lack of quality control of practitioners	20
Insufficient business acumen of practitioners	12
Insufficient emphasis on customer needs	5
3. Results of our work	35
Insufficiently clear return on investment	20
Insufficiently clear value of the work	18

without the necessary content knowledge and experience do work that ultimately diminishes the value of OD.

- "The field has virtually no qualifying credentials in order to practice. Virtually anyone can go into the OD consulting business—this lack of regulation hurts the image of the profession with our clients."
- "The lack of a common, industry-wide program certifying high professional, moral, and ethical standards appears to be our biggest weakness—the absence of a certifying board is our greatest vulnerability."
- "There is no international OD standard, no international unified course of study for licensing, no international code of ethics, extreme variances in the capability of practitioners, no international continuing education requirements to ensure customers are getting value."
- "We are too unfocused as a body of knowledge, values and ethics, lacking a core structure as a profession."
- "There are no certifications, qualifying degrees or formal requirements like those that legitimize other professions."
- "Continued development of our field is dependent on quality OD services that are delivered consistently and effectively. Addressing the consistency of services is important to create a stable face and level of quality associated with OD."

Weakness 3: Insufficient business acumen of practitioners/insufficient emphasis on customer needs. Many respondents to the survey noted that the reputation of OD practitioners is more in the "soft" or "touchy-feely" realm than that of a true business partner. A failure to learn the operational aspects of businesses they support and the lack of fluency with business language were often cited as weaknesses. Respondents noted that capable practitioners with content knowledge of a business or business expertise in finance, sales, or operations are better equipped to translate OD services into meaningful business results. Concern was expressed over the dual challenge to stay at the cutting edge of the OD field and be on the leading edge of business to maintain credibility as businesspeople. Understanding how the business runs and the business issues that are on the minds of executives needs to be a core capability for OD practitioners. Particular mention was made of the OD practitioners' lack of economic or financial acumen. Some representative quotes follow:

- "People who do OD are not business focused, they cannot speak the same language as their clients."
- "Many business executives see OD as ancillary to the core business strategy—OD practitioners need to be steeped in the business and be able to speak in business terms. If not executives will see OD as soft and academic."
- "The OD community is typically very weak in understanding business and not good when the business issues are complex."
- "We need to understand the needs of CEOs and provide immediate solutions."
- "OD is still somewhat disconnected from the fundamental concerns of senior management, issues related to profitability, productivity, cost, quality, speed, etc. OD tends to limit its focus strictly to the human side of organizational life and thereby limits both its attractiveness to senior management and its effectiveness. OD should expand its sphere of contribution by integrating the concerns of senior management into its domain."

- "OD practitioners need to have a clear understanding of how businesses operate and then support the core mission of the business they serve—otherwise they will become irrelevant."

Weakness 4: Insufficiently clear ROI/value of the work. Many respondents noted that OD projects are not strongly connected to the business strategies of the clients they serve. They indicated concern that practitioners are not capable of asserting their value and impact on an organization's success. Many expressed the fear that organizations are focusing only on activities with a clear ROI and measurable business results, and the "soft" area of OD is not seen as delivering tangible business results, or worse yet, OD practitioners are not partnering well enough with executives to place the business issues in context with people issues. Without the ability to speak our client's language and indicate a cause and effect relationship between OD and the bottom line, concern was expressed that efforts and initiatives may be dropped due to perceived lack of impact. Some representative quotes follow:

- "Some OD practitioners are not practical and real world. They appear confused between asserting their own value structure and meeting/finding/accepting and assisting the value structure of the client organization. This has led to the demise of many OD functions—at least in U.S. businesses. They did not appear to add value and to be capable of responding appropriately to the business urgencies. They at times do not take the needs of the business seriously."
- "We have difficulty in explaining the ROI of OD. We need to show clear business reasons why OD works and saves companies money in order to survive as a field."
- "We have not sufficiently engaged the executive leaders in understanding the relevance, importance and value of OD in helping organizations achieve business goals and success—this is a critically important stakeholder group."
- "Not well understood by corporate leadership as value added. Usually brought in to fix problems rather than as a strategic business partner. OD practitioners do not position their value well—we're good at the work but not necessarily good at the sell."
- "Unable to understand the business, lack of ability to credibly articulate ROI. More of reacting to business events than behaving like a partner that can help drive change."

Discussion and Implications

In light of the strengths and weaknesses identified by the respondents, there are significant implications for the field of organization development and its future. Many OD practitioners thought that there could be a positive future for OD if acting in our role as change agents, we proactively seize key opportunities presented by current and future business challenges *and* if OD's weaknesses are addressed.

In terms of opportunities, more than half of respondents (58%) mentioned areas of opportunity for OD practitioners. This means that OD practitioners themselves may already hold some of the keys to how to cope with the necessary changes to expand OD's contribution.

As mentioned earlier, all of the research, including the literature review, SWOT findings and results, and executive interviews, was synthesized by the leadership team into six key integrated themes (KITs). Each of these key integrated themes is discussed here along with the implications of that theme for the future of the OD profession, OD practitioners, and value to business leaders and businesses (see Table 14.2.4).

Table 14.2.4 Key Integrated Themes

---

1. Globalization and multicultural and whole system perspective
2. Building great workplace, productivity, and performance culture
3. Leveraging technology and worldwide integration
4. Corporate social responsibility is increasing
5. Building leadership and organizational capabilities for the future
6. Regulatory environment and new organizational forms

Key Integrated Themes

KIT 1: Globalization, multicultural and whole system perspective. In industry after industry, whether it is media, pharmaceuticals, energy, banking, or technology, we are seeing strong trends toward industry consolidation and more and more mergers and acquisitions, with a few giant companies spanning the world. When combined with simultaneous trends toward globalization of work and the workforce, businesses are challenged to meet the demands of the global economy, the marketplace, customers, employees, and shareholders.

Because a clear strength of OD is its whole system perspective, there are numerous possibilities for OD professionals to contribute and add value. OD professionals can leverage this strength in supporting business leaders in becoming "whole system thinkers;" in helping them identify best practices for industry consolidations, mergers, and acquisitions; in supporting businesses in achieving strategic alignment; and in addressing different phases of the business life cycle most appropriately from a people and systems perspective. Furthermore, OD practitioners can help to build skills and competencies of the workforce in multicultural sensitivity, fostering collaborative relationships across traditional organizational boundaries.

What is the value OD can add to business leaders and businesses in the context of this key integrated theme? We posit that

- OD can help businesses align strategies and execute them in a way that meets the firms' financial goals and core values.
- If OD steps up to the challenge, we can ensure more positive results from organizational realignments, industry consolidations, and mergers and acquisitions by understanding and addressing the cultural dimensions that are so often overlooked and the cause of most M&A failures.
- We can contribute to increasing market share and shareholder value due to effective application of change management principles to business and product life cycles.

KIT 2: Building great workplace, productivity, and performance culture. Competitive pressures on margins, aggressive competition, and price wars are leading to demands for greater innovation, flexibility, and speed to market. Ever-shortening R&D cycles mean that those who are first to market dominate the competition, and ever-shortening product life cycles produce fleeting fame and then obsolescence. The consequence is intense scrutiny of core businesses, outsourcing of extraneous businesses, and ever-increasing demands on workers for higher levels of productivity—both quality and quantity of output.

The opportunities for OD professionals to demonstrate their contributions here are profoundly significant given our ability to facilitate organizational alignment and workforce engagement. The OD professional can help to foster employee engagement, enhance skills around innovation and flexibility, and help to build a performance culture in organizations (e.g., training in productivity and quality methods). OD practitioners can partner with business leaders to build workplaces that enhance productivity and ensure work is linked to business imperatives around speed, customers, and innovation.

What is the value to business leaders and businesses? If we meet these challenges, we can

- enhance productivity and profitability through organizational alignment,
- enhance commitment of the workforce for better overall performance,
- increase clarity of purpose and mission to inspire and engage the workforce,
- improve the ability to attract and retain top talent.

KIT 3: Leveraging technology and worldwide integration. We are witnessing simultaneously an explosion of technology (nanotechnology, biotech, life sciences, genetics, robotics, and other emerging technologies) combined with an inextricable dependence on technology. The need to leverage and align technology with business strategies to gain a competitive edge has never been greater. Pressures to balance technology costs and return on investment are intense. Globally, demands are ever increasing for worldwide integration and optimization of technology for increased global access and communications. Security threats to data security and to ensure business continuity in the event of a disaster further place technology front and center among the business imperatives.

In this context, OD professionals may be uniquely qualified to marry the capabilities of technology with individual and organizational needs, recognizing and addressing the challenges of technology from a people perspective. OD practitioners support business leaders in implementing new technologies and fostering continuous learning and knowledge sharing in organizations. At the same time, we need to stay current with technology advances and incorporate them into our own practice.

What is the value to business leaders and businesses? We posit that the value is

- leveraging and alignment of technology with business and people strategies,
- exploiting technology and readily adapting to the latest technological advances for competitive advantage,
- using technology to support learning and innovation for better results.

KIT 4: Corporate social responsibility is increasing. The public has witnessed disturbing trends around the world and in every sector of society. The spate of scandals rocking corporations requires greater accountability for business ethics and governance, especially among its leaders—the senior executives and board of directors. This includes a demand for transparency and ethics in conducting business at every level. At the same time, the continuously widening economic gap between the have and have-not groups both within and between nations as well as increasing expectations for positively influencing human rights issues in countries where the company does business have resulted in a clamor for adopting socially responsible business practices. Moreover, concerns about the sustainability of our way of life and our natural resources are leading to demands for greater accountability for natural resources, including water, the environment, bioengineered products, and so forth.

What does this have to do with the OD profession and OD practitioners? OD can play a key role in identifying best practices in socially responsible business behavior, including ethics and governance, and developing skills and competencies that support these best practices, socially responsible values, and associated results in corporate drivers and key metrics (e.g., balanced scorecards, triple bottom line, etc.). Fundamentally, we can use our values-based practice to create a paradigm shift in the way business is perceived and conducted.

The OD practitioner can coach and support business leaders in shifting/enhancing their socially responsible orientation and actions (e.g., show them what's in it for them) and build expertise in skills, competencies, and understandings regarding ethics, governance, and socially responsible practices.

What is the value to business and business leaders? We posit that if OD steps up to these challenges, we support businesses in

- improving their reputation among citizenries, consumers, and investors;
- enhancing the commitment of employees as they find increased meaning in work through focus on corporate citizenship and contributions;
- mitigating/reducing costs and negatives associated with litigation;
- enhancing sustainability of enterprises through responsible use of natural resources.

KIT 5: Building leadership and organizational capabilities for the future. Building leadership depth and capability is a top priority for business leaders. Leadership talent identification, development, and retention are absolutely critical to an organization's ability to be successful. Leaders are challenged as never before given the increasing complexity of businesses with almost unimaginable global challenges, ever-changing marketplace challenges, an ever-changing workplace and workforce, and an increasingly diverse, multicultural, and multi-generational workforce. In this context, leaders are being asked to exhibit new levels of courage, decision-making abilities, and problem-solving capabilities.

OD professionals can be enormously helpful to business leaders as they try to step up to these formidable challenges. For example, OD professionals can ensure business leaders have a basic understanding of OD theory and practice and build competencies in leveraging diversity for business advantage. The OD profession can apply its conflict mediation and appreciative inquiry skills and competencies among OD professionals around the world. At the same time, OD practitioners can coach leaders to find meaning and purpose in their business endeavors, providing environments that support the whole person. OD practitioners themselves must walk the talk by modeling leadership courage, decision making, and problem solving.

What is the value to business leaders and businesses? If successful in this arena, OD can contribute to

- greater leadership bench strength to build long-term business success,
- enhanced ability to make difficult decisions and address paradoxes,
- access to wide array of choices around models for building organizations, careers, and learning.

KIT 6: Regulatory environment and new organizational forms. In a widening array of industries, businesses are navigating an increasingly difficult regulatory landscape. In the United States, increasing government regulations are posing significant competitive challenges. Regulations concerning products, ingredients, and safety as well as employment and employees are increasing; there are also more restrictions on materials being developed or shipped around the globe. Ultimately, global competition is significantly affected by government regulations.

At the same time, new organizational forms are emerging across traditional sectors, spanning the public-private domains, that pose both challenges and opportunities. In particular, business and government increasingly will find themselves working in partnership and collaborative relationships to successfully navigate the global economy.

In this context, OD professionals can contribute to the development of such partnerships by researching best practices and new models in public-private partnerships, stimulating interest and awareness about emergent organizational forms, and doing action research/action learning with pioneers in collaborative cross-sector emergent organizational forms.

To address these needs, OD practitioners can be open and opportunistic in identifying emerging organizational forms, explore new organizational forms through experimentation (e.g., high potential experiences on special projects), and use OD's win-win values to shift the paradigm from adversarial to partnerships across traditional boundaries (organizations, sectors, industries).

What is the value to business leaders and businesses? If OD makes the contributions we are proposing, some of the results we hypothesize would be

- ameliorating "intractable problems" that can only be addressed at the "systems level;"
- producing better results through enhanced win-win collaborative relationships and partnerships among public, private, and nonprofit sectors;
- reducing costs and faster speed to market for critical products (e.g., drugs) as shared commitments and values become a priority.

Summary and Conclusions

The six key integrated themes point to critical areas for the OD profession to address along with important skills and competencies for OD professionals to demonstrate. Although many OD practitioners currently exhibit some of these skills and competencies, they need to be more clearly demonstrated in terms of what business leaders recognize and value (e.g., ROI). Furthermore, there still is no clear definition that distinguishes the OD profession (e.g., from HR). Clearly, there is a higher need to focus on productivity, profitability, and ROI; expand business acumen to a greater extent than what OD practitioners currently demonstrate; and establish credible partnerships between OD professionals and business leaders. We have seen the need for practical applications of OD, new models, research, and theory for OD practitioners to succeed in all sectors. Academic and business partnerships are a potential solution to be developed and explored in this regard.

The work described throughout this chapter is a call to action for greater demonstration by OD practitioners of the ways in which we already use our values and tools to create positive work environments. The need in organizations to manifest socially responsible values and create win-win business results has never been greater. OD is in an excellent position to seize the opportunity to build bridges, find common ground, and address organizational and cultural divides.

Notes

1. The members of the Leadership Team for the Global Committee on the Future of OD as well as advisory board members; research summaries; bibliographies; complete strengths, weaknesses, opportunities, and threats (SWOT) results; and other information can be found on the Global Committee on the Future of OD Knowledge Management Portal at http://orgdev.programshop. com/public/.

2. Results for each of the other three sources as well as the overall synthesis are available on the Global Committee on the Future of OD Knowledge Management Portal (http://orgdev.programshop. com/public/).

3. The SWOT research team members include Howard Deutsch, CEO, Quantisoft, LLC, and Carolyn Tal, Ph.D., team leader, SWOT research team. Based on requirements by the Leadership Team, Quantisoft, LLC provided Web survey services and created survey reports. Special acknowledgment goes to Elliott Greene, CTO, Quantisoft, LLC, for creating and running the SWOT survey reports.

Acknowledgments

Significant contributions to this article and overall initiative were made by Ted Nguyen, leader, Global Committee on the Future of OD; Elena Feliz, leader, Community Outreach, Global Committee on the Future of OD; and Howard Deutsch, CEO, Quantisoft, LLC.

Reference

Alban, B. (2003). The future. In M. Wheatley, R. Tannenbaum, P. Y. Griffin, & K. Quade, (Eds.), *Organization development at work: Conversations on the values, applications and future of OD* (pp. 113–136). San Francisco, CA: Pfeiffer.

15 International Organizational Behavior

15.1 THE NEW GLOBAL MANAGER

Learning Cultures on the Fly

Luciara Nardon and Richard M. Steers

Many years ago, a popular film making the rounds of the local movie theatres was *If It's Tuesday, It Must Be Belgium*. The film used humor to highlight the plight of a typical American tourist who was overcome by the cultural differences across the countries included in her whirlwind tour of Europe. The film's underlying message was that tourists—at least American tourists—seldom allow sufficient time in their travels to learn about cultural differences, preferring instead to race from one popular tourist site to another in search of good food, unique experiences, and photographs to show to their friends and family back home. The issue is one of having *been* there, not having *learned* anything. Today, despite a widespread recognition that we live and work in an increasingly interconnected global economy, it is curious that the dilemma posed in this old film is still salient for many contemporary managers and entrepreneurs alike. How serious are we about learning about other cultures? And if we are serious, how do we accomplish this in meaningful ways as part of our busy work schedules?

Working with Global Partners

Today, a major challenge facing managers and entrepreneurs is how to deal with both partners and competitors abroad whom we simply don't understand. More often than not, the problem is not just language differences; it is *cultural* differences. Consider: How can we trust or do business with prospective foreign business partners who won't:

- "Put their cards on the table" and say what they actually mean.
- Work "24/7" and "stay on target" until the job is completed.
- "Step up to the plate," make concrete commitments, and accept responsibility for their side of the partnership.
- "Let their hair down" and open up to us, so we can get to know each other.

In other words, how can we trust or do business with prospective foreign business partners when we know so little about them, their backgrounds, their approaches to business, or their future intents? The obvious question here is what to do. Unfortunately, the answer to this question is not as simple as perhaps it once was. Gone are the days when prospective managers could learn French or German or Spanish in college to prepare themselves for their careers. Learning a foreign language and foreign culture is obviously helpful, but it is often impractical in view of the rapidity with which business opportunities appear and disappear around the world.

This challenge of understanding people from other cultures is made more difficult by the increasing speed with which business often occurs. A key factor here is the way in which recent technological advancements have pushed both the pace and complexity of globalization to new heights. Communication and information technology makes it possible to collaborate—or compete—globally from anywhere in the world, regardless of one's country of origin or cultural background. As a growing number of organizations have established increased operations around the world, managers' exposure to both partners and competitors from significantly different cultural backgrounds has increased at a rate that has surprised both economists and social scientists. The implication for managers of all types is clear: Managers with a capability to think and understand business relationships from a *global* perspective will more often than not succeed over those with more limited nation-based mindsets.

In this regard, consider a day in the life of Adhira Iyengar, an entrepreneur from Bangalore, India. Adhira woke up early one recent morning, prepared a cup of tea, and logged onto her computer. As expected, Debra Brown, her business partner in California, was already logged on. "Good morning! I have a few questions about your last report and would like to discuss them with you before I leave for the day." As they finished their online meeting, Adhira stared at her calendar and realized that, again, it was going to be a long day. At 10:00 that morning she had a conference call with Mr. Wu, a client from Hong Kong, about some changes in their service contract. At 1:30 p.m. she had a face-to-face meeting with a group of prospective Australian clients in her office in Bangalore. Before the end of the day, she had to complete a report and e-mail it to Mrs. Sanchez, a partner in Mexico City, and she still needed to prepare for her trip to Berlin coming up in the following week.

Developing successful relationships with people from different cultures, as Adhira has done, is challenging by definition. Several reasons account for this, including people's tendencies to have preconceived notions about how the world works (or should work), how individuals behave (or should behave), and which behaviors are acceptable (or unacceptable). These ideas are largely influenced by our personal experiences and the cultures in which we grew up. We tend to approach intercultural interactions based on our own perceptions, beliefs, values, biases, and misconceptions about what is likely to happen. As a result, when we engage in exchanges with people from different cultures, we frequently discover that the consequences of our actions are quite different than the ones we anticipated. The results can range from embarrassment to insult to lost business opportunities. Such consequences can also be career-limiting, to say the least.

Preparing for Global Assignments

How can people like Adhira prepare to succeed in today's highly competitive global economy? More to the point, what can relatively inexperienced managers from any country do when they are assigned to go abroad—for short or long periods—to represent their company's critical business interests? And what can they do when they are required to work with people from other countries before they even have a chance to see what it is like to live abroad? At least three strategies can be identified to help such inexperienced managers: cultural fluency, developing a global mindset, and learning cultures on the fly.

Cultural Fluency

Traditionally, managers have been advised to prepare themselves for an international assignment through *cultural fluency*—that is, by mastering the culture and language of the country to which they were being assigned. Management training programs, both in the home country and host country, have long been used to achieve such goals. Through such programs, managers develop capabilities to interact more effectively with people from another country through learning the local language and culture in depth and behaving in ways that are appropriate to that culture. Thus, a manager who is assigned to work in France for several years may be advised to study French language and culture, make local friends upon arrival in the new location, and be tolerant of experiences that are new or unique.

A key part of such programs is to develop a clear recognition in the minds of the managers that new expatriates frequently experience stress and anxiety as a result of being immersed in an unfamiliar culture—generally referred to as culture shock. Over time, such managers typically learn new ways of coping and eventually become more comfortable living in the culture of the host country. This learning strategy has considerable merit when a manager is being assigned to a specific country for a long period of time. It works less well, however, when the manager in question will be spending the coming years doing business across multiple cultures.

Developing a Global Mindset

With this new multicultural reality, managers are being increasingly advised to develop what has been called a *global mindset*. That is, managers are told to expand their knowledge and understanding of multiple cultures in ways that will help them successfully interact with people from highly diverse backgrounds. Reaching a critical mass of understanding here enables the informed traveler to venture forth and conduct business in multiple locations with competence. As noted by Mansour Javidan and his colleagues, "It is insufficient for a manager who is likely to assume, mistakenly, that being open minded in Atlanta, Helsinki, and Beijing will be perceived identically, or that walking in someone else's shoes will feel the same in Houston, Jakarta, or Madrid. Because of the lack of scientifically compiled information, businesspeople have not had sufficient detailed and context-specific suggestions about how to handle these cross-cultural challenges" (see selected bibliography). Developing a global mindset is advocated as one way to resolve this deficiency.

While some variations exist, most definitions of global mindset suggest that it is an ability to develop and interpret criteria for personal and business performance that are independent of the assumptions of a single country, culture, or context, and to implement those criteria appropriately in different countries, cultures, and contexts. In other words, a global mindset is a cognitive structure or knowledge structure that contains information about several cultures and realities. This knowledge allows managers to interpret situations using multiple cultural frameworks and then select the most appropriate action for each particular situation.

Learning Cultures on the Fly

While both of these approaches—cultural fluency and developing a global mindset—can be very useful, we suggest that the increasing intensity, time sensitivity, and diversity that characterize today's global business environment may require a third approach. Developing broad-based knowledge about one or several cultures, and using such knowledge in appropriate ways, is ideal. In reality, however, achieving this level of understanding is difficult, if not impossible, for at least two reasons. First, learning about another culture from a distance is difficult at best. Second, most managers do not have the time to learn about other cultures and develop a global mindset well before they are asked to be effective in the field. In such cases, we offer an alternative—not a better alternative, but perhaps a more practical one when time is of the essence. We call it *learning cultures on the fly*.

Learning Cultures on the Fly: From Individual to Interdependent Learning

As the international business environment has shifted from a collection of principally bi-cultural business relationships to a more genuinely integrated intercultural one, managers are faced with three principal challenges in attempting to adapt quickly to the new realities on the ground:

1. *Many intercultural encounters happen on short notice, leaving little time to learn about the other culture.* Imagine that you just returned from a week's stay in India where you were negotiating an outsourcing agreement. As you arrive in your home office you learn that an incredible acquisition opportunity just turned up in South Africa and that you are supposed to leave in a week to explore the matter further. You have never been to South Africa, nor do you know anybody from there. What do you do? While there are many books covering the "do's and don'ts" of cultures, they are typically helpful guides on how to eat or behave politely and say little about how local managers behave.

2. *It is often unclear to which culture we should adapt.* Suppose your company has asked you to join a global project team to work in a six-month research and development (R&D) project. The team includes people from Mexico, Germany, China, and Russia. Every member of the team has a permanent appointment in his or her home country, but is temporarily assigned to work on this project at company headquarters in Switzerland. Which culture should team members adapt to? In this case, there is no dominant cultural group to dictate the rules. Considering the multiple cultures involved, and the little exposure each manager has likely had with the other cultures, the traditional approach of adaptation is unlikely to be successful. Nevertheless, the group must be able to work together quickly and effectively to produce results—and protect their careers—despite their differences. What would you do?

3. *Intercultural meetings increasingly occur virtually, not face-to-face.* Suppose you were asked to build a partnership with a Korean partner whom you have never met, and that you know little about Korean culture. Suppose further that this task is to be completed online, without any face-to-face communication or interactions. Your boss is in a hurry for results. What would you do?

Taken together, these three challenges demonstrate how difficult it can be to work across cultures in today's rapidly changing technology-based business environment. The old ways of communicating and doing business are simply less effective than in the past. The question before us, then, is how to facilitate management success in such situations. To accomplish this, we suggest that managers need to *learn how to learn* to deal with other cultures and make sense of varied environments. To this end, consider how individuals learn from experience and how models of learning can be applied to help managers succeed in intercultural contexts.

Individual Learning: Experiential Learning Theory

Following experiential learning theory, individual learning occurs through a combination of grasping and transforming experiences. The learning process is composed of four stages that include the two modes of constructing knowledge: knowledge is grasped through *concrete experience* and *abstract conceptualization* and then transformed through *reflective observation* and *active experimentation*. While it may begin in any of the four stages, learning is a process of experience, observation, and reflection, abstract conceptualization, and active experimentation, as illustrated in Fig. 15.1.1.

Concrete Experience

To understand how experiential learning theory works in practice, imagine that you come from a culture that values direct, straightforward communication. As you engage in a conversation with another individual, you are likely to think that direct questioning is appropriate and will result in a straightforward answer. Now imagine that the individual with whom you are communicating comes from a culture that values indirect communication and the avoidance of public embarrassment. For this person direct questions are inappropriate, and information is exchanged indirectly through subtle suggestions and hints. Now, consider that neither of you is sufficiently knowledgeable to adapt your communication style to suit the other's culture. The most likely result of this scenario is that you will ask a direct question and will get what you perceive as an unsatisfactory response. At this point, you are likely to experience an emotional reaction—discomfort, perplexity, offense, or surprise. The feelings you experience as a result of your actions are referred to as *concrete experience*. In other words, it is your emotional reaction to the results of your actions.

Observation and Reflection

Your experience or feelings may then prompt you to try to understand what is happening. You may engage in *observation and reflection*. That is, once you realize that there is a disconnect between what is happening and what you thought would happen, you observe the other person and try to guess why he or she responded as they did. You may mentally run through a list of possible problems: maybe she did not hear you, maybe she did not understand the

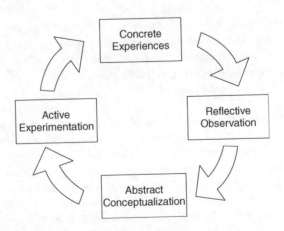

Figure 15.1.1 The Experiential Learning Process.

question, maybe she does not speak English very well, maybe she is shy, maybe she is not comfortable with the question, and so forth. You then search for other clues to her behavior in the context of the situation that can help understand her behavior. Simply put, you look for additional information that will help you make sense of the situation.

Abstract Concepts and Generalizations

This observation and reflection forms the basis of *abstract concepts and generalizations*. As you think about it, you develop a theory of what is happening. You identify a plausible explanation for her behavior and begin searching for alternative solutions to your problem. Let's suppose that you concluded that your partner is uncomfortable with your question. Her body language suggests that she feels embarrassed to answer. Therefore, you theorize that you should pose the question in a different way.

Testing Implications of Concepts

Your newly developed theory will guide any future actions you take to deal with this individual and others from the same culture. As you practice these new actions, you are *testing implications of concepts*. You decide, for example, to formulate your question in a different way, you observe the results, and start a new learning cycle. The cycle continues until you are able to identify successful behaviors. Learning through experience is a process of trial and error in which we perceive a mismatch, reflect on it, identify solutions, and initiate new behaviors. When we identify successful behaviors, we incorporate them into our theories of how to behave. The next time we engage in a similar situation, we draw upon our latest theory for guidance.

We may initiate our learning process at different points of the circular cycle, depending on the situation and our learning preferences. For instance, some people have a preference for abstract concepts and generalizations, preferring to go to the library and read about the other culture prior to engaging with its members. These individuals will strive to develop a theory beforehand, and will improve their theory in the course of the interaction. Others have a preference for observation and may choose to watch foreigners interacting prior to engaging with them. In other words, they will fine-tune their theories based on their observations. Still others may prefer to jump to the situation without prior exposure, and draw on their feelings to decide how to behave. As the circular model suggests, individuals that are able to utilize all four types of abilities are better equipped to learn in the complex environment of intercultural interactions.

Interdependent Learning: the Intercultural Interaction Learning Model

While experiential learning theory has remained one of the most influential theories of management development, it has been criticized for its failure to account for the *social* aspects of learning; that is, it ignores the role of learning from and with others. In an effort to fill this void, the *intercultural interaction learning model* focuses on two or more individuals who are simultaneously experiencing problems, reflecting on them, theorizing about them, and engaging in new corrective actions. In other words, the learning process is seen as interdependent and interactive, not independent or linear. The learning of one party to an intercultural exchange leads to learning by the other party and so forth.

In principle, as people's learning processes interact, new and hopefully better ways of communicating emerge. However, if learning is short-circuited, the relationship suffers, and the interaction fails. For instance, if after asking a question and receiving an unsatisfactory answer the person does not stop to observe the other party and reflect on her behavior, he or she may engage in actions that are detrimental to the relationship. In sum, an effective intercultural interaction is the result of a successful interdependent learning process, in which all parties to an exchange learn to work together more effectively.

In our view, an *intercultural interaction* is an opportunity for interdependent learning in which individuals *both* learn about the other's culture *and* negotiate effective ways of relating to one another. Building on previous communications research, we suggest four main areas that need to be negotiated in intercultural exchanges: identities, meaning, rules, and behaviors. Each of these negotiating activities is based on a specific learning ability: 1) the ability to *negotiate identity* draws on the ability to engage in concrete experiences; 2) the ability to *negotiate meaning* builds on the ability to reflect and observe; 3) the ability to *negotiate new rules* is based on the ability to develop new theories; and 4) the ability to *negotiate new behaviors* is based on the ability to take actions.

Step #1: Negotiating Identity

An individual's self-identity consists of those attributes that are central, enduring, and distinctive about the individual. In other words, identity is the answer to the question, "Who am I?" Identity is constructed through social interactions, whereby individuals create categories and define themselves in relation to others. This process of categorization influences not only how individuals position themselves in relation to others, but also how people act and feel about the interaction. Our own identity or self-image is closely linked to our interpretations of reality. In other words, we make sense of the world based on how we see ourselves. Or as noted in the *Talmud*, "We do not see things as they are, we see them as we are." Social identification theory suggests that one's actions will be congruent with one's self-identity. Individuals tend to engage in activities that are harmonious with their self-concept and to support institutions that embody their identities.

It is for this reason that intercultural interactions are potentially challenging. When we engage with others from a different cultural background, our assumptions, values, and beliefs are often questioned. Our perceptions about who we are, our competence, status, and self-worth may be challenged. An intercultural interaction is likely to produce strong feelings associated with our own identity and how we expect to be treated. For these feelings to be positive, individuals must engage in a process of managing or *negotiating identity*.

Intercultural relations scholars have recognized the importance of negotiating identity in cross-cultural conflicts. According to them, conflicts of interests among different groups or individuals are projected on the basis of identity, and differences in international conflicts must involve a resolution of the parties' identities. Dealing with international conflicts requires first dealing with oneself through reflexive dialogue. In other words, it requires addressing how the issue is reflected "inside" one's mind and how one's identity is challenged or threatened by it.

Negotiating identity is particularly important in situations in which one culture is perceived to be in a more powerful position than the other. For instance, in global business acquisitions, managers from an acquiring company are generally more powerful, have greater status, and may try to impose the "right" way of doing things on the people from the acquired company. Individuals from the less powerful group may find that their cultural-based assumptions and values are criticized, considered inappropriate, and may feel that their own sense of self is being challenged. In other words, their position in the social environment is decreased.

For instance, a Spanish manager may consider that arriving 30 minutes late to a meeting is normal and acceptable. However, the manager of the recently acquired Polish company may see this as a sign of disrespect, and a sign that she is no longer important to the organization. Having one's identity threatened may close off communication, impede learning, and eventually compromise the success of the interaction. Unless both parties can negotiate an acceptable identity for themselves, the interaction is likely to fail.

The process of identity negotiation involves two identities—our own and the other's identity. For an intercultural interaction to be successful, we need to be able to preserve a satisfactory identity for ourselves, while at the same time respecting and preserving the other's identity.

- To preserve our own identity, we need to develop self-awareness. Self-awareness refers to understanding who we are, what our values are, and what our place in the social interaction is. In other words, we need to understand that we are complex cultural beings and that our values, beliefs, and assumptions are a product of our cultural heritage. When we understand that who we are is heavily influenced by our own cultural experiences, we are better equipped to separate our sense of worth from the situation. For example, the Polish manager above may think "As a Polish manager, I do not like to wait," rather than "only people who are not important are kept waiting." The first statement preserves her identity, the second challenges it.
- To preserve the other's identity, it is important to develop empathy towards the other. Empathy refers to the ability to identify and understand the other's feelings and motives. In other words, empathy suggests an understanding that the other is also a complex cultural being and that their actions—like ours—are a product of deep-seated cultural values and beliefs. In other words, when there is a misunderstanding, successful global managers tend to search for a cultural explanation for the other's behavior, before judging the other party's behavior.

For example, suppose you had asked your Egyptian counterpart if an important report would be ready today, and he had answered "yes," but did not deliver it. Instead of judging him based on your own culture (perhaps suggesting that he is not dependable, trustworthy, or competent), you empathize with him on the grounds that his behavior is also a product of culture. Maybe he indirectly told you that he could not finish the report, but you did not understand. Maybe your request was not appropriate or time expectations were not clear. Therefore, you assume that he is acting consistently with his own cultural rules even though you do not understand it. You then proceed to understand what happened, trying to identify a possible miscommunication.

Managers that are open-minded and willing to suspend judgment are more likely to be successful. Skilled managers empathize with others not based on shared values and assumptions, but based on the common fact that we are complex cultural beings and behave in accordance to a complex web of cultural values and beliefs.

In other words, in order to negotiate identities effectively we need to understand that we are cultural beings. We need to know our own values and assumptions, and their relationship with our own culture. We also need to empathize with the other, knowing that he or she is also influenced by culture, even if we do not know what it means. With this in mind, we can negotiate acceptable identities in which our own and the other's sense of self are preserved. When our sense of self is preserved, our feelings in the interaction are more likely to be positive and it becomes easier to continue with the learning experience.

Step #2: Negotiating Meaning

Meaning refers to the interpretation we give to things. For example, what does signing a contract really mean? For some cultures a contract means the end of a negotiation, for others it means the beginning of a relationship. New assignments of meaning are based on current and past experience. Jointly understood meaning is constructed through interaction, as individuals exchange information. Therefore, when two individuals from different cultures interact, they are likely to start with different understandings about the meaning of the concrete topic that they are discussing (for example a contract). However, to be effective, they will need to arrive at a common understanding of the issue; that is, they need to *negotiate meaning*.

In interpersonal interactions, the meanings of messages cannot be transmitted from one person to another, only the message itself can be. When we send a message to another we attach certain meaning to it, based on our interpretation of the issue, ourselves, and the other. When others receive our message, they attach meaning to it based on their interpretation of the issue, the message, themselves, and us.

For example, when you say, "I am glad we were able to sign a contract," you may mean "I am glad the negotiations are over and I can go back to business." However, your Asian counterpart may hear "I am glad we agreed to start a relationship and will continue the negotiations for a long time to come." A common meaning must be constructed for this interaction to be effective.

Most frequently, meaning is constructed through interaction as individuals exchange information. Negotiating meaning involves uncovering hidden cultural assumptions, becoming aware of how culture is shaping perceptions, expectations, and behaviors for all parties involved. To negotiate meaning effectively, individuals must engage in two behaviors: inquiry and advocacy.

- *Inquiry* refers to exploring and questioning one's own reasoning and the reasoning of others. In other words, individuals strive to create and accept a new, common meaning, by asking the following questions: How do I/you perceive the situation? What do I/you wish to achieve in this situation? Which actions am I/are you taking to achieve this goal? Inquiry requires suspending judgment, letting go of a previous understanding, and tolerating uncertainty until a new understanding may be created.
- *Advocacy* refers to expressing and standing for what one thinks and desires. Advocacy suggests stating clearly what you think and want, and explaining the reasoning behind your view. When individuals combine inquiry with advocacy they share information about their cultural assumptions, the meanings they associate with the issue, and the reasoning for their thinking. This sharing of assumptions and interpretations creates the basis for a new, mutually acceptable meaning to emerge.

Engaging in inquiry and advocacy is challenging because it requires uncovering our own perceptions, exposing ourselves, being open to listen to the other's perception, and being willing to give up the safety of our own previous interpretations in order for a new culture-free interpretation to emerge. To make matters worse, cultural-based preferences can also influence how individuals may go about doing this.

For example, in some cultures, individuals prefer to express themselves using open and direct communication, whereas in other cultures individuals are likely to share their assumptions indirectly, making it difficult for direct communicators to fully understand. Some indirect communicators may even feel uncomfortable with direct questioning of their assumptions, which could potentially close communication even further.

Additionally, cultural-based preferences may suggest circumstances in which inquiry and advocacy are more likely to be successful. For instance, in some cultures it may be during formal meetings, in other cultures it may be late at night over drinks, and in still others it may be through informal one-on-one conversations.

As a result, in order to negotiate meaning, individuals must gather information in several different ways, relying on the context, body language, subtle cues, and messages. These abilities typically rely heavily on learning skills associated with observation and reflection: information gathering and analysis.

- *Information gathering* refers to the ability to collect information through various means in order to understand the point of view of others. Competent managers gather information by observing context, body language, face expression, and other behavioral cues, listening to what is being communicated, and asking questions when appropriate, and in a way that is appropriate.
- *Information analysis* refers to the ability to interpret this information in light of what is being discussed, the people involved, and the context in which the interaction is happening.

Step #3: Negotiating New Rules

In a typical intercultural interaction, once the parties agree on acceptable identities and meanings, they turn their attention on developing or *negotiating new rules* that will inform and guide their relationship in the future. These rules are akin to theories of action and over time will ideally create a common context for behavior and interaction.

For example, parties to an interaction need to establish rules about acceptable behaviors regarding time. How late is too late? Managers may agree that, for instance, fifteen minutes is not considered late, but that further delays should be avoided—or at a minimum deserve an apology. Alternatively, they may agree on a more clear specification of time when making appointments: 8:00 Mexican time typically means that delays are expected, while 8:00 American time typically means that punctuality is expected. These rules should cover the most important cultural obstacles to the success of the relationship, whether they are about time, use of titles, style of communication, or any other thing.

In time, these rules will evolve into a new shared culture for the individuals involved. This culture may be a combination of the several cultures involved, or it may be a culture that is unlike any other but is acceptable to all. Sometimes one of the parties will embrace the other's cultural rules in their entirety and adopt them as their own. This last scenario is more common when one of the parties has been exposed to the other's culture for a long time and can adapt. In any case, to develop new rules managers must develop the learning skills associated with integration and transformation of information.

- *Integration of information* refers to the ability to assimilate all the information gathered in the negotiating meaning stage into a coherent theory of action. For example, you noticed that your counterpart looked annoyed when you answered the phone during a meeting, you noticed that he turned his cell phone off, and you noticed that he signaled to the secretary that he should not be interrupted. You integrate all these disparate pieces of information into one theory: your counterpart does not appreciate interruptions.

- *Transformation of information* refers to creating a theory of action based on the information you have. Continuing with the interruption example, you may transform your theory about the other into a theory about what you should do: you should avoid interruptions if at all possible. As these behaviors take place, rules are adjusted and fine-tuned.

Step #4: Negotiating New Behaviors

To complete the cycle after individuals develop new theories of action and agree on a common set of cultural rules to guide the interaction, they will likely move to complete the learning loop by *negotiating new behaviors*.

For example, if the negotiated rule is that delays of more than fifteen minutes should be avoided, you must learn to engage in a new set of behaviors that will allow you to control time, prioritize things differently, and arrive on time. Or, perhaps the new rule suggests that direct communication should be avoided, in which case you will need to learn to engage in a communication style that is more indirect, subtle, and diplomatic.

Clearly, engaging in new behaviors requires high levels of behavioral flexibility, including an ability to engage in different behaviors—being able to switch styles and accomplish things in more than one way. For some individuals it is easy to engage in some behaviors but not others. Successful managers are able to recognize which behaviors are challenging for them, and compensate with other behaviors. For instance, for some individuals it is very difficult to communicate indirectly. They recognize this limitation, and to compensate for it search for opportunities to discuss issues privately so any public embarrassments can be avoided.

Finally, managers need to be mindful of themselves, the other, and the interaction between the two. That is, they must constantly pay attention to what they are feeling and doing, what the other is doing, and how the other reacts to what they say and do. In the process of learning about the other and testing ways to interact, individuals are aware of their own behavior and the effects of their behavior on others involved.

Conclusion

As most successful managers realize, working with foreign partners and competitors is increasingly unavoidable. As the examples throughout this paper suggest, the realities of today's global environment imply that managers often need to do business in several countries and deal with several cultures simultaneously or, at the very least, sequentially. While the examples provided here may suggest easy solutions—e.g., when dealing with Spaniards, know they will be late—the reality of intercultural encounters is considerably more complex for several reasons:

- Individuals are often influenced by multiple cultures—national, regional, organizational, functional, and professional.
- In no country are people monolithic in their beliefs, values, and behaviors. People are different, despite having the same country of origin.
- Our business counterparts are also learning how to deal with foreigners and may deal with us in ways that are not typical of their own culture.

- Culture itself is very complex and may seem paradoxical to an outsider. For this reason, simplistic categorizations of cultures may be helpful explanations of behavior, or good first guesses, but they are not good predictors.

In order to succeed in this business environment, managers are encouraged to develop skills that will allow them to learn how to succeed in each interaction by uncovering cultural assumptions and learning how to deal with them. The Indian manager in our earlier example has to deal with four or five different cultures in one day. It would be difficult for her to acquire fluency in these cultures, while seating in her office in Bangalore. Instead, she needs to develop learning skills that will compensate for cultural knowledge gaps, helping her to negotiate her interactions as they evolve.

In summary, we have suggested that intercultural interactions involve four types of negotiation relating to identities, meaning, rules, and behaviors.

- The negotiation of identities relies on strong self-awareness and empathy, so the emotional experience is managed and the learning experience can proceed.
- The negotiation of meaning relies on information gathering and analysis, which uncovers a new basis of information from which new meanings can be created.
- The negotiation of rules relies on an individual's ability to integrate and transform information into new theories of action.
- Finally, the negotiation of behaviors relies on behavioral flexibility and mindfulness, where managers are able to engage in alternative behaviors accordingly as each situation demands.

The prospects of dealing with people from different cultural backgrounds can be very challenging, but at the same time very rewarding. Interacting with others brings the possibility of learning more about ourselves, discovering new ways of doing things, and finding creative solutions to both new problems and old. It also contributes in no small way to business success. In this endeavor, intercultural learning processes play a significant—and often underappreciated—role.

Selected Bibliography

For interested readers, there is a wealth of information available both on the topic of learning in general and learning across cultures in particular. For a good discussion of learning processes in general, we recommend A. Y. Kolb and D. A. Kolb, "Learning Styles and Learning Spaces: Enhancing Experiential Learning in Higher Education," published in the *Academy of Management Learning and Education*, 2005, 4, 193–212.

For information specifically focused on interdependent learning and intercultural learning we recommend: M. J. Bennet (Ed.), *Basic Concepts of Intercultural Communication. Selected Readings* (Yarmouth, ME: Intercultural Press, 1998) 31–51; D. C. Kayes, "Experiential Learning and its Critics: Preserving the Role of Experience in Management Learning and Education," *Academy of Management Learning and Education*, 2002, 1(2), 137–149; Y. Yamazaki and D. C. Kayes, "An Experiential Approach to Cross-Cultural Learning: A Review and Integration of Competencies for Successful Expatriate Adaptation," *Academy of Management Learning and Education*, 2004, 3(4), 362–379; and T. Imahori and W. R. Cupach, "Identity Management Theory: Face-work in Intercultural Relationships," in William Gudykunst (Ed.), *Theorizing about Intercultural Communication* (Thousand Oaks, CA: Sage Publications, 2005), 195–210.

To learn more about cultural intelligence, we recommend D. C. Thomas and K. Inkson, *Cultural Intelligence: People Skills for Global Business* (San Francisco: Berret-Koehler, 2004); P. C. Earley and S. Ang, *Cultural Intelligence: An Analysis of Individual Interactions Across Cultures* (Palo Alto, CA: Stanford University Press); and P. C. Earley and E. Mosakowski, "Cultural Intelligence," *Harvard Business Review*, 2004, 82(10), 139–146.

For recent research on the concept of the global mindset, readers are referred to Mansour Javidan, Peter Dorfman, Marie S. de Luque, and Robert J. House, "In the Eye of the Beholder: Cross-Cultural Lessons in Leadership from GLOBE Project," *Academy of Management Perspectives*, 2006, 67–90; and Luciara Nardon and Richard M. Steers, "Learning Cultures on the Fly," in Mansour Javidan, Richard M. Steers, and Michael Hitt (Eds.), *Advances in International Management: The Global Mindset* (Amsterdam: Elsevier, 2007), 179–198.

Finally, for more on negotiation of meaning within a cross-cultural setting, we recommend V. J. Friedman and A. Berthoin Antal, "Negotiating Reality: A Theory of Action Approach to Intercultural Competence," *Management Learning*, 2005, 36, 69–86; and Alan Bird and Joyce S. Osland, "Teaching Cultural Sense-Making," in N. Boyacigiller, R. A. Goodman, and M. E. Phillips (Eds.), *Crossing Cultures: Insights from Master Teachers* (London: Routledge, 2003), 89–100.

16 Critical Thinking and Continuous Learning

16.1 IS THERE SUCH A THING AS "EVIDENCE-BASED MANAGEMENT"?

Denise M. Rousseau

I explore the promise organization research offers for improved management practice and how, at present, it falls short. Using evidence-based medicine as an exemplar, I identify ways of closing the prevailing "research-practice gap"—the failure of organizations and managers to base practices on best available evidence. I close with guidance for researchers, educators, and managers for translating the principles governing human behavior and organizational processes into more effective management practice.

Evidence-based management means translating principles based on best evidence into organizational practices. Through evidence-based management, practicing managers develop into experts who make organizational decisions informed by social science and organizational research—part of the zeitgeist moving professional decisions away from personal preference and unsystematic experience toward those based on the best available scientific evidence (e.g., Barlow, 2004; DeAngelis, 2005; Lemieux-Charles & Champagne, 2004; Rousseau, 2005; Walshe & Rundall, 2001). This links how managers make decisions to the continually expanding research base on cause-effect principles underlying human behavior and organizational actions.

Here is what evidence-based management looks like. Let's call this example, and true story, "Making Feedback People-Friendly." The executive director of a health care system with twenty rural clinics notes that their performance differs tremendously across the array of metrics used. This variability has nothing to do with patient mix or employee characteristics. After interviewing clinic members who complain about the sheer number of metrics for which they are accountable (200+ indicators sent monthly, comparing each clinic to the 19 others), the director recalls a principle from a long-ago course in psychology: human decision makers can only process a limited amount of information at any one time. With input from clinic staff, a redesigned feedback system takes shape. The new system uses three performance categories—care quality, cost, and employee satisfaction—and provides a summary measure for each of the three. Over the next year, through provision of feedback in a more interpretable form, the health system's performance improves across the board, with low-performing units showing the greatest improvement. In this example a *principle* (human beings can process only a limited amount of information) is translated into *practice* (provide feedback on a small set of critical performance indicators using terms people readily understand).

Evidence-based management, as in the example above, derives principles from research evidence and translates them into practices that solve organizational problems. This isn't always easy. Principles are credible only where the evidence is clear, and research findings can be tough for both researchers and practitioners to interpret. Moreover, practices that capitalize on a principle's insights must suit the setting (e.g., who is to say that the particular performance indicators the executive director uses are pertinent to all units?). Evidence-based management, despite these challenges, promises more consistent attainment of organizational goals, including those affecting employees, stockholders, and the public in general. This is the promise that attracted me to organizational research at the beginning of my career—but it remains unfulfilled.

The Great Hope and the Great Disappointment

It is ironic that I came to write this article in my role as the sixtieth Academy of Management president. "Management" was a nasty word in my blue collar childhood, where everyone in the family was affected by how the company my father worked for managed its employees. When the supervisor frequently called my father to ask him to put in more overtime in an already long work week, all of us kids got used to covering for him. If the phone rang when my father was home, he'd have us answer it. We all knew what to say if it was the company calling: "Dad's not here." The idea of just telling the supervisor that he didn't want to work never occurred to my father, or anyone else in the family. The threat of disciplinary action or job loss loomed large, reinforced by dinnertime stories about a boss's abusive behavior or some inexplicable company action. From this vantage point, the term *management* connotes harsh and arbitrary behavior, with undertones of otherness. It is a far cry from the dictionary definition of management as "a judicious use of means to accomplish an end" (*Merriam-Webster*, 2005).

I acquired a wholly new perspective on management and managers when I became a business school professor. First, many business students, even at the MBA level, have never experienced what it is like to work for a good manager. In the first business course I taught, in organizational behavior, I gave the students two assignments: (1) write about the worst boss you ever had, describing what made that person the worst and how it impacted you, and (2) write about the best boss you ever had, describing what made that person the best and how it impacted you.

My MBA students with an average of five years of full-time work experience had no problem with assignment 1. For many of them, the assignment was cathartic, and they frequently exceeded its assigned page limit in writing vituperative portrayals of managers variously presented as self-centered, capricious, or otherwise lacking in capability or character. Assignment 2 was another matter. Many students had great difficulty thinking of anyone who qualified as "the best manager." Over a third couldn't think of any boss they could even describe as good.

To the extent that people manage others the way they themselves have been managed, I came to worry about what the future held for these managers-in-the-making. Nonetheless, while these business students may never have had a great boss, they themselves still hoped to become one. (By the way, I have since abandoned this assignment in favor of more self-reflection on the manager students want to become and ways they can develop themselves to move closer to that ideal.)

Second, most business students have never worked for a great company either. (There is the possibility that only dissatisfied people quit their jobs to study full time for an MBA, but in this regard I suspect availability bias.) I never have had any difficulty getting students to share their experiences of dysfunctional organizational practices. However, when it comes to identifying a more functional way to motivate workers or restructure firms, they are often at a loss. Still, in-class discussions and students' own future plans suggest that they do hope to join a company (or to start one) that is better managed than those they have worked for so far.

In class and out, I have spent a lot of time helping students learn how to make a business case, with their future employers in mind, for creating financially successful firms that are good for people too. I have come to feel tremendous respect and affection for those students who have the personal aspiration to be a great manager in a great company. Out of these personal and professional experiences, I have nurtured my great hope—that, through research and education, we can promote effective organizations where managers make well-informed, less arbitrary, and more reflective decisions.

My great disappointment, however, has been that research findings don't appear to have transferred well to the workplace. Instead of a scientific understanding of human behavior and organizations, managers, including those with MBAs, continue to rely largely on personal experience, to the exclusion of more systematic knowledge. Alternatively, managers follow bad advice from business books or consultants based on weak evidence. because Jack Welch or McKinsey says it, that doesn't make it true. (Several decades of research on attribution bias indicate that people have a difficult time drawing unbiased conclusions regarding why they are successful, often giving more credit to themselves than the facts warrant. Management gurus are in no way immune.)

Sadly, there is poor uptake of management practices of known effectiveness (e.g., goal setting and performance feedback [Locke & Latham, 1984]). Even in businesses populated by MBAs from top-ranked universities, there is unexplained wide variation in managerial practice patterns (e.g., how [or if] goals are set, selection decisions made, rewards allocated, or training investments determined) and, worse, persistent use of practices known to be largely ineffective (e.g., downsizing [Cascio, Young, & Morris, 1997; high ratios of executive to rank-and-file employee compensation [Cowherd & Levine, 1992]). The result is a research-practice gap, indicating that the answer to this article's title question is no—at least not yet. What it means to close this gap and how evidence-based management might become a reality are the matters I turn to next.

The "Evidence-Based" Zeitgeist

The phrase "evidence-based" is a buzzword in contemporary public policy, with all the risk of triteness and superficiality that buzzword status conveys. Let's not be misled by its current popularity. Evidence-based practice has tremendous substance and discipline behind it. We can observe its impact in two fields highly influenced by legislative decisions: policing and secondary education. In evidence-based policing, community police officers are trained to treat criminal suspects politely, because doing so has been found to reduce repeat offenses (Sherman, 2002; Tyler, 1990). In evidence-based education, many secondary schools have restored the practice of social promotion, where students who have difficulty passing their courses, even after several tries, are advanced to the next grade level. Research indicates that social promotion's benefits outweigh its costs, because a high school diploma increases the likelihood of subsequent employment and lowers the incidence of drug use, even among students who wouldn't otherwise have qualified for that diploma (Jimerson, Anderson, & Whipple, 2002; National Association of School Psychologists, 2005).

Evidence-based practice is a paradigm for making decisions that integrate the best available research evidence with decision maker expertise and client/customer preferences to guide practice toward more desirable results (e.g., Sackett, Straus, Richardson, Rosenberg, & Haynes, 2000). Proponents are skeptical about experience, wisdom, or personal credentials as a basis for asserting what works. The question is "What is the evidence?"— not "Who says so?" (Sherman, 2002: 221). The answer, as the criminologist Lawrence W. Sherman indicates, can be graded from weak to strong, based on rules of scientific inference, where before-and-after comparisons are stronger than simultaneous correlations—randomized, controlled tests stronger than longitudinal cohort analyses. Strong evidence trumps weak, irrespective of how charismatic the evidence's presenter is. Sherman sums it up: "We are all entitled to our own opinions, but not to our own facts" (2002: 223).

Medicine is a success story as the first domain to institutionalize evidence-based practice. Evidence-based medicine is the integration of individual clinical expertise and the best external evidence. Its origins date back to 1847, when Ignaz Semmelweis discovered the role that infection played in childbirth fever. Semmelweis was vilified by physicians of the time for his assertion that it was doctors themselves who were infecting women by carrying germs between dead bodies and patients. Nonetheless, his work influenced the formulation of germ theory, which gained acceptance with the work of Lister and Pasteur forty years later (*Wikipedia*, 2005). Extensive infrastructures promote evidence-based health care (e.g., the U.S. National Institutes of Health and Institute of Medicine, the Canadian Health Services Research Foundation, and the Cochrane Collaboration).

Evidence-based-clinical care as a way of life in health care organizations is of relatively recent vintage, enjoying its greatest growth after 1990. (If you are wondering what physicians did before, the answer is what managers are doing now, but without medicine's added advantages from common professional training and malpractice sanctions.) The attributes of evidenced-based medicine provide a useful reference point for exploring what its counterpart in management might look like.

By way of example, germ theory is widely understood by clinical care givers. It has led to broad application of infection control systems (gowns, sterile needles, and sterile instruments), medicines to avoid or cure infections, and supporting practices (handwashing). Its application has led to radical but important interpretations of seemingly distant events. Incidence of heart attack, for example, increases immediately after having one's teeth cleaned. Reflecting on this correlation in light of germ theory led to recognition that teeth cleaning disperses mouth bacteria into the heart's arteries. Certain bacteria in these arteries create conditions that give rise to heart attacks. Recognizing this causal link led to a risk-reducing solution: giving heart patients antibiotics to take before dental treatments as a preventive. This application of medical evidence involved *cause-and-effect connections*—how dental practice can disperse mouth bacteria into the heart's arteries. It also required *isolation of variations that affect desired outcomes*, requiring knowledge of the mechanisms triggering heart attacks (and, in this case, knowledge that gum disease may itself trigger heart attacks [see, for instance, Desvarieux et al., 2005]).

Yet more than scientific insight is needed to create evidence-based practice. In fact, only some physicians recommend this preventive action for their heart patients. Others may not see the risk as that great, are unaware of the finding, or merely have forgotten to make this preventive action part of their standard orders for cardiac patients. The involvement of other practitioners further complicates matters: dentists are not necessarily educated to inquire about heart conditions.

Organizational factors affect whether evidence-based practice occurs. In health care settings certain features increase the likelihood that an at-risk patient will get the preventive medication. *Social networks and organizational culture matter.* It helps if the patient's physician is part of a practice or a hospital where others recommend such preventive care. Similarly, impeding this evidence-based practice is the fact that dentists are unlikely to be in the same professional networks as physicians. In a hospital where medical leadership promotes evidence-based medicine, more physicians are likely to be aware of the finding. Such settings are also likely to have staff in-services to update physician knowledge where this practice might be discussed.

Relatedly, *participation in research increases the salience of the evidence base.* It helps if physicians in the immediate environment have participated in clinical research and are engaged in one of the several online communities that review clinical evidence and then create and disseminate recommendations, which raises the next point: *access to information on those practices the evidence supports.* Physicians have online services that provide ready access to clinical practice best supported by research, based on the review and recommendation of health care experts (e.g., Cochrane Collaboration). Such services capitalize on the information explosion and internet connections to build communities of practice enabling experts to communicate their knowledge, identify the best-quality evidence, and disseminate it broadly to care givers (Jadad, Haynes, Hunt, & Browman, 2000).

Decision supports can be designed to make it easier to implement evidence-based practices. A patient care protocol might be written specifying that each heart patient and all post-op cardiac cases be advised of the need to premedicate before teeth cleaning, along with a prescription written for and given to the patient at discharge. This protocol might be formalized to the extent that a premedication instruction is written in each cardiac patient's discharge orders.

Last, *a web of factors—individual (knowledge), organizational (access to knowledgeable others, support for evidence use), and institutional (dissemination of evidence-based practice)—promotes, sustains, and institutionalizes evidence-based medicine.* Britain's national health system, for example, promotes evidence-based practice using the Cochrane Collaboration's recommendations as the standard. Medicare in the United States publishes information on whether hospitals use proven remedies in patient care (Kolata, 2004).

In sum, features characterizing evidence-based practice include

- learning about *cause-effect* connections in professional practices;
- isolating the variations that measurably affect desired outcomes;
- creating a culture of evidence-based decision making and research participation;
- using information-sharing communities to reduce overuse, underuse, and misuse of specific practices;
- building decision supports to promote practices the evidence validates, along with techniques and artifacts that make the decision easier to execute or perform (e.g., checklists, protocols, or standing orders); and
- having individual, organizational, and institutional factors promote access to knowledge and its use.

Now let's consider what such practice might mean for management and organizations.

Why Evidence-Based Management Is Important and Timely

Evidence-based management is not a new idea. Chester Barnard (1938) promoted the development of a natural science of organization to better understand the unanticipated problems associated with authority and consent. Since Barnard's time, however, we have struggled to connect science and practice without a vision or model to do so. Evidence-based management, in my opinion, provides the needed model to guide the closing of the research-practice gap. In this section I address why evidence-based management is timely and practical.

Calling Attention to Facts: "Big E Evidence" and "Little E Evidence"

An evidence orientation shows that decision quality is a direct function of available facts, creating a demand for reliable and valid information when making managerial and organizational decisions. Improving information continues a trend begun in the quality movement over thirty years ago, giving systematic attention to discrete facts, indicative of quality (e.g., machine performance, customer interactions, employee attitudes and behavior [Evans & Dean, 2000]). This trend continues in recent developments regarding open-book management (Case, 1995; Ferrante & Rousseau, 2001) and the use of organizational fact finding and experimentation to improve decision quality (Pfeffer & Sutton, in press).

In all the attention we now give to evidence, it helps to differentiate what might be called "Big E Evidence" from "little e evidence." Big E Evidence refers to generalizable knowledge regarding cause-effect connections (e.g., specific goals promote higher attainment than general or vague goals) derived from scientific methods—the focus of this article. Little e evidence is local or organization specific, as exemplified by root cause analysis and other fact-based approaches the total quality movement introduced for organizational decision making (Deming, 1993; Evans & Dean, 2000). It refers to data systematically gathered in a particular setting to inform local decisions. As the saying goes, "facts are our friends," when local efforts to accumulate information relevant to a particular problem lead to more effective solutions.

Although decision makers who rely on scientific principles are more likely to gather facts systematically in order to choose an appropriate course of action (e.g., Sackett et al., 2000), fact gathering ("evidence") doesn't necessarily lead decision makers to use social science knowledge ("Evidence") in interpretating these facts. In my introductory example of the health care system, the executive director might have concluded that the performance differences across the twenty clinics were due to something about the clinics or their managers. It was his knowledge of a basic principle in psychology that gave him an alternative and, ultimately, more effective interpretation. However, systematic attention to local facts can prompt managers to look for principles that account for their observations. The opening example illustrates how scientific principles and local facts go together to solve problems and make decisions.

Opportunity to Better Implement Managerial Decisions

In highly competitive environments, good execution may be as important as the strategic choices managers make. Implementation is a strong suit of evidence-based management through the wealth of research available to guide effective execution (e.g., goal setting and feedback [Locke & Latham, 1984]; feedback and redesign [Goodman, 2001]). Indeed, with greater orientation toward scientific evidence, health care management's guidelines frequently reference social and organizational research on implementation (e.g., Lemieux-Charles & Champagne, 2004; Lomas, Culyer, McCutcheon, McAuley, & Law, 2005). The continued wide variation we observe in how organizations execute decisions (e.g., in goal clarity, stakeholder participation, feedback processes, and allowance for redesign) is remarkable, given the advanced knowledge we possess about effective implementation and what is at stake should implementation fail.

Better Managers, Better Learning

Given the powerful impact managers' decisions have on the fate of their firms, managerial competence is a critical and often scarce resource. Improved managerial competence is a direct outgrowth of a greater focus on evidence-based management. Managers need real learning, not fads or false conclusions. When managers acquire a systematic understanding of the principles governing organizations and human behavior, what they learn is *valid*—that is to say, it is repeatable over time and generalizable across situations. It is less likely that what managers learn will be wrong.

Today, the poor information commonly available to managers regarding the organizational consequences of their decisions means that experiences are likely to be misinterpreted —subject to perceptual gaps and misunderstandings. Consider the case of a supervisor who overuses threats and punishment as behavioral tools. A punisher who keys on the fact that punishing suppresses behavior can completely miss its other consequence—its inability to encourage positive behavior. Status differences and organizational politics make it unlikely that the punisher will learn the true consequences of that style, by limiting and distorting feedback.

The reality is that managers tend to work in settings that make valid learning difficult. This difficulty is compounded by the widespread uptake of organizational fads and fashions, "adopted overenthusiastically, implemented inadequately, then discarded prematurely in favor of the latest trend" (Walshe & Rundall, 2001: 437; see also Staw & Epstein, 2000). In such settings managers cannot even learn why their decisions were wrong, let alone what alternatives would have been right. Evidence-based management leads to valid learning and continuous improvement, rather than a checkered career based on false assumptions.

Organizational legitimacy is another product of evidence-based management. Where decisions are based on systematic causal knowledge, conditioned by expertise leading to successful implementation, firms find it easier to deliver on promises made to stockholders, employees, customers, and others (e.g., Goodman & Rousseau, 2004; Rucci, Kirn, & Quinn, 1998). Legitimacy is a result of making decisions in a systematic and informed fashion, thus making a firm's actions more readily justifiable in the eyes of stakeholders. Yet, given evidence-based management's numerous advantages, why then is the research-practice gap so large? I next turn to the array of factors that align to perpetuate this evidence-deprived status quo.

Why Managers Don't Practice Evidence-Based Management

The research-practice gap among managers results from several factors. First and foremost, managers typically do not know the evidence. Less than 1 percent of HR managers read the academic literature regularly (Rynes, Brown, & Colbert, 2002), and the consultants who advise them are unlikely to do so either. Despite the explosion of research on decision making, individual and group performance, business strategy, and other domains directly tied to organizational practices, few practicing managers access this work. (I note, however, that of the four periodicals the Academy publishes, it is the empirical *Academy of Management Journal* to which company libraries most widely subscribe. So there is some recognition that this research exists!)

Evidence-based management can threaten managers' personal freedom to run their organizations as they see fit. A similar resistance characterized supervisory responses to scientific management nearly 100 years ago, when Frederick Taylor's structured methods for improving efficiency were discarded because they were believed to interfere with management's prerogatives in supervising employees. Part of this pushback stems from the belief that good management is an art—the "romance of leadership" school of thought (e.g., Meindl, Erlich, & Dukerich, 1985), where a shift to evidence and analysis connotes loss of creativity and autonomy. Such concerns are not unique: physicians have wrestled with similar dilemmas, expressed in the aptly titled article "False Dichotomies: EBM, Clinical Freedom and the Art of Medicine" (Parker, 2005).

Managerial work itself differs from clinical work and other fields engaged in evidence-based practice in important ways. First, managerial decisions often involve long time lags and little feedback, as in the case of a recruiter hiring someone to eventually take over a senior position in the firm. Years may pass before the true quality of that decision can be discerned, and, by then, the recruiter and others involved are likely to have moved on (Jaques, 1976). Managerial decisions often are influenced by other stakeholders who impose constraints (Miller, 1992). Obtaining stakeholder support can involve politicking and compromise, altering the decision made, or even whether it is made at all. Incentives tied to managerial decisions are subject to contradictory pressures from senior executives, stockholders, customers, and employees. Last, it's not always obvious that a decision is being made, given the array of interactions that compose managerial work (Walshe & Randall, 2001). A manager who declines to train a subordinate, for example, may not realize that particular act ultimately may lead the employee to quit.

Evidence-based management can be a tough sell to many managers, because management, in contrast to medicine or nursing, is not a profession. Given the diverse backgrounds and education of managers, there is limited understanding of scientific method. With no formally mandated education or credentials (and even an MBA is no guarantee), practicing managers have no body of shared knowledge. Lacking shared scientific knowledge to add weight to an evidence-based decision, managers commonly rely on other bases (e.g., experience, formal power, incentives, and threats) when making decisions acceptable to their superiors and constituents.

Firms themselves—particularly those in the private sector—contribute to the limited value placed on science-based management practice. Although pharmaceutical firms advertise their investment in biotechnology and basic research, the typical business does not have the advancement of managerial knowledge in its mission.

Historically leading corporations such as Cadbury, IBM, and General Motors were actively engaged in research on company selection and training practices, employee motivation, and supervisory behavior. Their efforts contributed substantially to the early managerial practice evidence base. But few organizations today do their own managerial research or regularly collaborate with those who do, despite the considerable benefits from industry-university collaborations (Cyert & Goodman, 1997); the globally experienced time crunch in managerial work and the press for short-term results have reduced such collaborations to dispensable frills. Nonetheless, hospitals participate in clinical research and school systems evaluate policy interventions.

In contrast to more evidence-oriented domains, such as policing and education, management is most often a private sector activity. It is less influenced by public policy pressures promoting similar practices while creating comparative advantage via distinctiveness. Businesses are characterized by the belief that the particulars of the organization, its practices, and its problems are special and unique—a widespread phenomenon termed the *uniqueness paradox* (Martin, Feldman, Hatch, & Sitkin, 1983). Observed among clinical care givers and law enforcement practitioners too, the uniqueness paradox can interfere with transfer of research findings across settings—unless dispelled by better education and experience with evidence-based practice (e.g., Sackett et al., 2000).

Yet, despite all these factors, the most important reason evidence-based management is still a hope and not a reality is not due to managers themselves or their organizations. Rather, professors like me and the programs in which we teach must accept a large measure of blame. *We typically do not educate managers to know or use scientific evidence.* Research evidence is not the central focus of study for undergraduate business students, MBAs, or executives in continuing education programs (Trank & Rynes, 2003), where case examples and popular concepts from nonresearch-oriented magazines such as the *Harvard Business Review* take center stage. Consistent with the diminution of research in behavioral course work, business students and practicing managers have no ready access to research. No communities of experts vet research regarding effective management practice (in contrast to the collaboratives that vet health care, criminal justice, and educational research [e.g., Campbell Collaboration, 2005; Cochrane Collaboration, 2005]). Few MBAs encounter a peer-reviewed journal during their student days, let alone later. Consequently, it's time to look critically at the role we educators play in limiting managers' knowledge and use of research evidence.

Evidence-Based Management and Our Role as Educators

My biggest surprise as the Academy president turned out to be the most frequent topic of emails sent to me by Academy members: complaints about our journals from self-identified teaching-oriented members. A typical email goes like this: "I want to let you know what a waste the Academy journals are. There's nothing in them at all pertinent to my teaching. The Academy should be for everybody, not just researchers."

My first response was to feel guilty (why hadn't I seen this?). But then I started to think more deeply about what this message implies. It says that educators aren't finding ideas in journals that cause them to *change* what they teach. This might mean that current research is irrelevant to what's being taught if educators focus on other topics. It could mean that the kind of information research articles provide about principles or practices is insufficient to determine what settings or circumstances their findings apply to. Or it could even mean that professors aren't updating their course material when research findings differ from what they teach.

These emails prompted me to wonder *what exactly we are teaching*. If we are teaching what research findings support, the content of a class has to change from time to time, with new evidence or better-specified theory. The concern that prompted this address stemmed from these emails: the role we educators play in the research-practice gap.

How Professors Contribute to the Research-Practice Gap

Management education is itself often not evidence based, something Trank and Rynes implicitly recognize (2003) as the "dumbing down" of management education. They also persuasively demonstrated that, in place of evidence, behavioral courses in business schools focus on general skills (e.g., team building, conflict management) and current case examples. Through these stimulating, ostensibly relevant activities, we capture student interest, helping to deflect the criticism "How is this going to help me get my first job?" Business schools reinforce this by relying heavily on student ratings instead of assessing real learning (Rynes, Trank, Lawson, & Ilies, 2003).

Stimulating courses and active learning must be core features of training in evidence-based management, because these educational features are good pedagogy. The manner and content of our approaches to behavioral courses perpetuate the research-practice gap.

Weak Research-Education Connection

Pick up any popular management textbook and you will find that Frederick Herzberg's work lives, but not Max Weber's. Herzberg's long-discredited two-factor theory is typically included in the motivation section of management textbooks, despite the fact that it was discredited as an artifact of method bias over thirty years ago (House & Wigdor, 1967). I asked a famous author of many best-selling textbooks why this was so. "Because professors like to teach Herzberg!" he answered. "Students want updated business examples but can't really tell if the research claims are valid."

This conversation suggests that professors are likely to teach what they learned in graduate school and not necessarily what current research supports. (Since many management professors are adjuncts valued for their practical experience but are from diverse backgrounds, even educators of comparable professional age may not share scientific knowledge.) I suspect that the persistence of Herzberg will continue until all the professors who learned the two-factor theory in graduate school (*c.* 1960–1970) retire.

However, business schools may discourage inclusion of some well-substantiated topics because they don't "sound" managerial. Paul Hirsch, the well-known sociologist, tells the story that when he flies business class, his seatmates ask what he does for a living. When he identifies himself as a business school professor, the next customary question is "What do you teach?" As a sociologist steeped in Weber and the century of research he spawned, Paul used to say, "Bureaucracy." His seatmates frequently moved to the opposite wing at that point, until Paul wised up and found a more appealing response: "Management" (personal communication).

Paul notes that managers still need to understand bureaucratic processes, so he hasn't changed what he teaches—only what he calls it. I do this too: I no longer call socialization, training, and rules "substitutes for leadership" (Kerr & Jermier, 1978), having found that the last thing a would-be manager wants to hear is how he or she can be replaced. The implications are clear. We frame, and perhaps even slant, what we teach to make it more palatable. Can it be we are on that slippery slope of avoiding teaching the most current social science findings relevant to managers and organizations, from downsizing to ethical decision making, because we fear our audience won't like the implications?

Failure to Manage Student Expectations

Student expectations do drive course content, and current evidence indicates that there is a strong preference for turnkey, ready-to-use solutions to problems these students will face in their first jobs (Trank & Rynes, 2003). What efforts do we make to manage these expectations? Unless students are persuaded to value science-based principles and their own role in turning these principles into sound organizational practice, it will be nigh impossible for faculty to resist the pressure to teach only today's solutions.

We might start by asking students who they think updates more effectively—practitioners trained in solutions or in principles. Effective practices in 2006 need not be the same as those in 2016, let alone 2036, when the majority of today's business students will still be working. If we teach solutions to problems, such as how to obtain accurate information on a worker's performance, students will acquire a tool—perhaps, for example, 360-degree feedback. Yet they won't understand the underlying cognitive processes (whether feedback is task related or self-focused), social factors (the relationships between ratees and raters), and organizational mechanisms (used for developmental purposes or compensation decisions), which explain how, when, and why 360-degree feedback might work (or not). Imagine a doctor who knows to prescribe antibiotics to patients with bronchitis (a common recommendation in the 1980s before recognition of antibiotic overuse [Franklin, 2005]) but doesn't understand the basic physiology that can lead other therapies to be comparable, more effective, or have fewer downsides. In the case of feedback, basic social science research is quite robust regarding how feedback impacts behavior (Kinicki & Kreitner, 2003). Such knowledge is likely to generate broader utility and more durable solutions over time than training in any particular feedback tool.

Lack of Models for Evidence-Based Management

Case methods are de rigueur in business schools, helping to develop students' analytic skills and familiarity with conditions they will face as practicing managers. The cases that I find most effective are those that have an individual manager as a protagonist (as opposed to those that describe an organization without developing one or two central personalities). A central character creates tension and evokes student identification with the events taking place. That character is typically a manager, who can be the change agent responsible for solving the problem or a catalyst for the dysfunctional behavior on which the case focuses.

Either way, students have a model—a positive or negative referent—from which they can learn how to behave (or not) in the future. As with most complex behaviors, from parenting to managing, people learn better when they have competent models (Bandura, 1971). Nonetheless, in twenty-five years of using cases in class, I cannot recall a single time in which a protagonist reflected on research evidence in the course of his or her decision making.

No Expectation for Updating Evidence-Based Knowledge Throughout the Manager's Career

Upon graduation, few business students recognize that the knowledge they may have acquired can be surpassed over time by new findings. Although social science knowledge continues to expand, business school training does not prepare graduates to tap into it. Neither students nor managers have clear ideas of how to update their knowledge as new evidence emerges.

There are few models of what an "expert" manager knows that a novice does not (see Hill, 1992, for an exception). In contrast, expert nurses are known to behave in very different ways from novices or less-than-expert midcareer nurses (Benner, 2001). They more rapidly size up a situation accurately and deal simultaneously with more co-occurring factors. In the professions, extensive postgraduate development exists to deepen expertise to produce a higher quality of practice. In contrast, business schools often imply that MBAs know all they need to know when they graduate.

What we can do to Close the Research-Practice Gap

There is a lot we can do to close the research-practice gap, both as individual educators and through working collectively.

Manage Student Expectations

We can manage student expectations with regard to the role of behavioral course work in the student's broader career. I often introduce myself to full-time students by telling them that the easiest teaching I do has always been to executives, because these experienced managers come to the program convinced that human behavior and group processes are the most critical things they need to learn. At this point in their careers, our full-time students can only be novices whose expertise will grow with time and active effort on their part to understand the dynamics of behavior in organizations. Try asking students what the difference is between ten years of experience and one year of experience repeated ten times. Then let them imagine what ten years of experience in becoming more expert on behavior and group processes in organizations would look like (the types of job, people, settings, etc.). Let them also imagine this for one year repeated ten times. Reflecting on these contrasting visions of their careers gives students an opportunity to raise their expectations of themselves as professional managers.

There are various related means for managing expectations, including the creation of learning contracts based on the learner's anticipated future roles, the behavioral knowledge and skills these roles will necessitate, and how that knowledge and skill will be acquired in the course (Goodman, 2005). It is easier to do this as part of a larger curriculum framed by anticipated future roles—the would-be-manager's story (Schank, 2003). Important also is the next feature: providing models of evidence-based practice and evidence-based managers.

Provide Models of Evidence-Based Practice

We need to model evidence-based practice in our teaching and in the curriculum. Psychological research on learning offers a useful guide for course/curriculum practices (e.g., Kersting, 2005). These include exposing the learner to models of competent evidence-based managers. I have been fortunate to encounter such a person. John Zanardelli is the CEO of Asbury Heights, the Methodist Home for the Aged, Mt. Lebanon, Pennsylvania. I first met John in an executive course on change management at Carnegie Mellon. He peppered me with questions about skills, information, and management tactics and wanted to know the research support behind my answers. Trained as an epidemiologist, John understands the scientific method and regularly looks for scientific corroboration of ideas he comes across in popular management books and from self-proclaimed experts. (Not surprisingly, the calls for evidence-based management largely have come from health care professionals and scholars [e.g., DeAngelis, 2005; Kovner, Elton, & Billings, 2005].) I knew that I was seeing an unusual manager, to say the least, when John, faced with the need to redesign his organization's compensation practices, went off to the Carnegie Mellon library to read J. Stacy Adams' equity theory! His organization's vision statement is built around the concept "Where Loving Care and Science Come Together."

Managers such as John Zanardelli provide exemplars of the complex set of proficiencies required to become a master management practitioner. Using them as examples reinforces the notion that the typical twenty-something student is a novice taking first steps along the path to becoming an expert (e.g., Benner, 2001; Hill, 1992). Active practice, self-reflection, and feedback are core learning principles (Schön, 1983). Developing student competence through active practice entails project work supported by ongoing reflection and debriefing regarding what constitutes valid learning and effective behavior. Similarly, our educational practices, courses, and curricula need that same reflection and evolution to effectively model evidence-based teaching.

Promote Active Use of Evidence

Students need to know that evidence is available, and they need to learn how to apply it. This necessitates a balance between teaching principles—that is, cause-effect knowledge—and practices—that is, solutions to organizational problems—though the mix is subject to dispute (Bennis & O'Toole, 2005). In the spirit of making the course tell a story students can understand and participate in, a course conveying how a novice becomes an expert manager, like any good story, involves a succession of experiences, trials, failures, and successes (Schank, 2003). That story line is marked by the acquisition of distinctly different kinds of knowledge. There is declarative knowledge regarding principles or cause-effect relationships. Students can acquire principles in a variety of ways. They might address the appropriateness of group incentives versus individual incentives by locating evidence in a textbook, in journals, or online. Informing students of the "evidence" through lectures and books has its place, but there is value in identifying and deriving the principles themselves from the sources that will remain available to them throughout their careers.

Students can learn a good deal from actively accessing evidence, using it to solve problems, reflecting—and trying again. Indeed, one of the most powerful forms of learning may be deriving principles from experience and reflection, as when students review cases and then derive the principles governing the underlying outcomes (Thompson, Gentner, & Loewenstein, 2003). Thompson and her colleagues found that students learned better when they developed principles from cases than when they derived solutions, a finding consistent with basic psychological research on learning (Anderson, Fincham, & Douglass, 1997).

Actually using evidence takes a metaskill—the ability to turn evidence-based principles into solutions. A form of procedural knowledge, a solution-oriented approach to evidence use is comparable to product design, where end users and knowledgeable others familiar with the situation in which the product will be used jointly participate in specifying its features and functionality.

Perhaps one of the first products of behavioral research in organizations was the revolving spindle restaurants use to convey customer orders to the kitchen. William Foote Whyte (1948) discovered that status differences between restaurant wait staff (typically female) and the (male) chef led to conflicts, because chefs disliked taking orders from women. The revolving order spindle to which waitresses could attach an order and spin it in the direction of the kitchen allowed customer orders to be conveyed impersonally, reducing workplace conflict and improving communication. Other research-based products include decision supports such as checklists to guide a performance review or action plans to conduct meetings in ways that build consensus (e.g., Mohrman & Mohrman, 1997), effectively translating the evidence into guides for action.

Build Collaborations Among Managers, Researchers, and Educators

As the saying goes, it takes a village to educate people. Changing how we educate managers in professional schools necessitates a collective attitude and behavior shift among educators, researchers, current managers, and recruiters. Pfeffer and Sutton's (in press) book calls attention to managerial heroes—people who use evidence to turn troubled companies around and/or to create sustained successes. As in the case of any change in collective attitudes (Gladwell, 2002), turning evidence-based management from a practice of a prophetic few into the mainstream requires *champions*—credible people like Pfeffer and Sutton's managerial heroes—to advertise its value. *Networks* of individuals, excited by what evidence-based management makes possible, need to exist to disseminate it to others.

One such collaborative network might parallel the Cochrane Collaboration in medicine and the Campbell Collaboration in criminal justice and education. (Such a community has been advocated to promote evidenced-based management of health care organizations [Kovner et al., 2005], suggesting that communities of experts might effectively be built around the management of specific kinds of organizations.) Each represents a worldwide community of experts created to provide ready access to a particular body of evidence and the practices it supports. Community members, practitioners as well as researchers, collaborate in summarizing state-of-the-art knowledge on practices known to be important. Information is presented in sufficient detail regarding evidence and sources of outcome variation to reduce underuse, overuse, and misuse. While these communities are geographically distributed, they also sponsor face-to-face meetings to promote community building, commitment, and learning. Their major product is online access to information, designed for easy use.

Evidence-Based Practice Can Be Misunderstood

On a cautionary note, the label *evidence-based practice* can be misapplied. It can be used to characterize superficial practices (another company's so-called best practice or the latest tool consultants are selling). Alternatively, it can be used as a club (the kind with a nail in it) to force compliance with a standard that may not be universally applicable. One downside of poor implementation of evidence-based medicine is the challenge the British health care system has faced owing to the use of the Cochrane Collaboration's recommendations to regulate clinical care decisions, with enforcement of the recommendations regardless of their suitability for particular patients (Eysenbach & Kummervold, 2005). Evidence-based practice is not one-size-fits-all; it's the best current evidence coupled with informed expert judgment.

Our Own Zeitgeist Promoting Evidence-Based Practice of Management

Forty years elapsed between Semmelweis's discoveries and the formulation of germ theory. One hundred years later, even basic infection-reducing practices such as hand washing still are not consistently performed in hospitals (Johns Hopkins Medicine, 2004). Considering the personal growth and social and organizational changes evidence-based practice requires, our own evidence-based management zeitgeist still has plenty of time to run.

The first challenge is consciousness raising regarding the rich array of evidence that can improve effectiveness of managerial decisions. Educating opinion leaders, including prominent executives and educators, in the nature and value of evidence-based approaches builds champions who can get the word out. Updating management education with the latest research must be ongoing, demanding that educators and textbook writers apprise themselves of new research findings. The onus is on researchers to make generalizability clearer by providing better information in their reports regarding the context in which their findings were observed. All parties need to put greater emphasis on learning how to translate research findings into solutions. In the case of researchers, too much information that might affect the translations of findings to practice remains tacit, in the apparent minutiae research reports omit, known only to the researcher. Educators need to help students acquire the metaskills for designing solutions around the research principles they teach. Managers must learn how to experiment with possible evidence-based solutions and to adapt them to particular settings. We need knowledge-sharing networks composed of educators, researchers, and manager/practitioners to help create and disseminate management-oriented research summaries and practices that best evidence supports.

Building a culture in which managers learn to learn from evidence is a critical aspect of effective evidence use (Pfeffer & Sutton, in press). Developing managerial competence historically has been viewed as a training issue, underestimating the investment in collective capabilities that is needed (Mohrman, Gibson, & Mohrman, 2001).

The promises of evidence-based management are manifold. It affords higher-quality managerial decisions that are better implemented, and it yields outcomes more in line with organizational goals. Those who use evidence (E and e) and learn to use it well have comparative advantage over their less competent counterparts. Managers, educators, and researchers can learn more systematically throughout their careers regarding principles that govern human behavior and organizational actions and the solutions that enhance contemporary organizational performance and member experience. A focus on evidence use may also ultimately help to blur the boundaries between researchers, educators, and managers, creating a lively community with many feedback loops where information is systematically gathered, evaluated, disseminated, implemented, reevaluated, and shared.

The promise of evidence-based management contrasts with the staying power or stickiness of the status quo. Like the QWERTY keyboard created for manual typewriters, but inefficient in the age of word processing, management-as-usual survives, despite being out of step with contemporary needs. Failure to evolve toward evidence-based management, however, is costlier than mere inefficiency. It deprives organizations, their members, our students, and the general public of greater success and better managers. Please join with me in working to make evidence-based management a reality.

Acknowledgments

This article is based on the address I gave at the annual meeting of the Academy of Management in Honolulu, Hawaii. Chuck Bantz, Andy Garman, Paul S. Goodman, Ricky Griffin, Bob Hinings, Paul Hirsch, Sharon McCarthy, Sara Rynes, Laurie Weingart, and John Zanardelli contributed ideas toward its development.

References

Anderson, J. R., Fincham, J. M., & Douglass, S. 1997. The role of examples and rules in the acquisition of a cognitive skill. *Journal of Experimental Psychology: Learning, Memory, and Cognition*, 23: 932–945.

Bandura, A. 1971. *Social learning theory.* New York: General Learning Press.

Barlow, D. H. 2004. Psychological treatments. *American Psychologist*, 59: 869–878.

Barnard, C. I. 1938. *Functions of the executive.* Cambridge, MA: Harvard University Press.

Benner, P. 2001. *From novice to expert: Excellence and power in clinical nursing practice* (commemorative ed.). Menlo Park, CA: Addison-Wesley.

Bennis, W. G., & O'Toole, J. 2004. How business schools lost their way. *Harvard Business Review*, 82(3): 96–104.

Campbell Collaboration. 2005. *http://www.campbellcollaboration.org/*, accessed December 5.

Cascio, W. F., Young, C. E., & Morris, J. K. 1997. Financial consequences of employment-change decisions in major U.S. corporations. *Academy of Management Journal*, 40: 1175–1189.

Case, J. 1995. *Open-book management: The coming business revolution.* New York: Harper Business.

Cochrane Collaboration. 2005. *http://www.cochrane.org/ index0.htm*, accessed December 5.

Cowherd, D., & Levine, D. I. 1992. Product quality and pay equity between lower-level employees and top management: An investigation of distributive justice theory. *Administrative Science Quarterly*, 37: 302–320.

Cyert, R. M., & Goodman, P. S. 1997. Creating effective university-industry alliances: An organizational learning perspective. *Organizational Dynamics*, 25(4): 45–57.

DeAngelis, T. 2005. Shaping evidence-based practice. *APA Monitor*, 35(3): 26–31.

Deming, W. E. 1993. *The new economics for industry, government, and education.* Cambridge, MA: Massachusetts Institute of Technology.

Desvarieux, M., Demmer, R. T., Rundek, T., Boden-Abala, B., Jacobs, D. R., Jr., Sacco, R. L., & Papapanou, P. N. 2005. Periodontal microbiota and carotid intima-media thickness: The oral infections and vascular disease epidemiology study (INVEST). *Circulation*, 111: 576–582.

Evans, J. R., & Dean, J. W., Jr. 2000. *Total quality: Management, organization, and strategy* (2nd ed.). Cincinnati: South-Western Publishing.

Eysenbach, G., & Kummervold, P. E. 2005. Is cybermedicine killing you? The story of a Cochrane disaster. *Journal of Medical Internet Research*, 7(2): article e21.

Ferrante, C. J., & Rousseau, D. M. 2001. Bringing open book management into the academic line of sight. In C. L. Cooper & D. M. Rousseau (Eds.), *Employee versus owner issues* (Trends in Organizational Behavior Series), vol. 8: 97–116. Chichester, UK: Wiley.

Franklin, D. 2005. Antibiotics aren't always the answer. *New York Times*, August 30: D5.

Frieze, I. H. 1976. Causal attributions and information seeking to explain success and failure. *Journal of Research in Personality*, 10: 293–305.

Gladwell, M. 2002. *The tipping point: How little things can make a big difference.* New York: Back Bay Books.

Goodman, P. S. 2001. *Missing organizational linkages.* Newbury Park, CA: Sage.

Goodman, P. S. 2005. *The organizational learning contract.* Working paper, Tepper School of Business, Carnegie Mellon University, Pittsburgh.

Goodman, P. S., & Rousseau, D. M. 2004. Organizational change that produces results. *Academy of Management Executive*, 18(3): 7–19.

Hill, L. A. 1992. *Becoming a manager: How new managers master the challenges of leadership.* Boston: Harvard Business School Press.

House, R. J., & Wigdor, L. A., 1967. Herzberg's dual-factor theory of job satisfaction and motivation. *Personnel Psychology*, 23: 369–389.

Jadad, A. R., Haynes, R. B., Hunt, D., & Browman, G. P. 2000. The internet and evidence-based decision-making: A needed synergy for efficient knowledge management in health care. *Canadian Medical Association Journal*, 162: 362–365.

Jaques, E. 1976. (Reprinted in 1993.) *A general theory of bureaucracy.* London: Gregg Revivals.

Jimerson, S. R., Anderson, G., & Whipple, A. 2002. Winning the battle and losing the war: Examining the relation between grade retention and dropping out of high school. *Psychology in the Schools*, 39: 441–457.

Johns Hopkins Medicine. 2004. Expert on hospital infections talks about hand washing. *http:// www.hopkinsmedicine. org/Press_releases/2004/10_28_04.html*, October 28.

Kerr, S., & Jermier, J. M. 1978. Substitutes for leadership: Their meaning and measurement. *Organizational Behavior and Human Performance*, 22: 375–403.

Kersting, K. 2005. Integrating research into teaching. *APA Monitor*, 35(1): 19.

Kinicki, A., & Kreitner, R. 2003. *Organizational behavior: Key concepts, skills and best practices.* New York: McGraw-Hill.

Kolata, G. 2004. Program coaxes hospitals to see treatments under their noses. *New York Times*, December 2: A1, C8.

Kovner, A. R., Elton, J. J., & Billings, J. D. 2005. Evidence-based management. *Frontiers of Health Services Management*, 16(4): 3–24.

Lemieux-Charles, L., & Champagne, F. 2004. *Using knowledge and evidence in healthcare: Multidisciplinary perspectives.* Toronto: University of Toronto Press.

Locke, E. A., & Latham, G. P. 1984. *Goal setting: A motivational technique that works.* Englewood Cliffs, NJ: Prentice-Hall.

Lomas, J., Culyer, T., McCutcheon, C., McAuley, L., & Law, S. 2005. *Conceptualizing evidence for health system guidance.* Final report to Canadian Health Services Research Foundation, Ottawa, Ontario.

Martin, J., Feldman, M., Hatch, M., & Sitkin, S. B. 1983. The uniqueness paradox in organizational stories. *Administrative Science Quarterly*, 28: 438–453.

Meindl, J. R., Erlich, S. B., & Dukerich, J. M. 1985. The romance of leadership. *Administrative Science Quarterly*, 30: 78–101.

Miller, G. J. 1992. *Managerial dilemmas: The political economy of hierarchy.* Cambridge: Cambridge University Press.

Mohrman, S. A., Gibson, C. B., & Mohrman, A. M. 2001. Doing research that is useful to practice: A model and empirical exploration. *Academy of Management Journal*, 44: 357–375.

Mohrman, S. A., & Mohrman, A. M., Jr. 1997. *Designing and leading team-based organizations: A workbook for organizational self-design.* San Francisco: Jossey-Bass.

National Association of School Psychologists (NASP). 2005. Position statement on grade retention and social promotion. *www.nasponline.org/information/pospaper_graderetent.html*, accessed November 24.

Parker, M. 2005. False dichotomies, EBM, clinical freedom and the art of medicine. *Medical Humanities*, 31: 23–30.

Pfeffer, J., & Sutton, R. I. In press. *Hard facts, dangerous half-truths, and total nonsense: Profiting from evidence-based management.* Boston: Harvard Business School Press.

Rousseau, D. M. 2005. Evidence-based management in health care. In C. Korunka & P. Hoffmann (Eds.), *Change and quality in human service work:* 33–46. Munich: Hampp.

Rucci, A. J., Kirn, S. P., & Quinn, R. T. 1998. The employee-customer-profit chain at Sears. *Harvard Business Review*, 76(1): 82–97.

Rynes, S. L., Brown, K. G., Colbert, A. E. 2002. Seven common misconceptions about human resource practices: Research findings versus practitioner beliefs. *Academy of Management Executive*, 18(3): 92–103.

Rynes, S. L., Trank, C. Q., Lawson, A. M., & Ilies, R. 2003. Behavioral coursework in business education: Growing evidence of a legitimacy crisis. *Academy of Management Learning & Education*, 2: 269–283.

Sackett, D. L., Straus, S. E., Richardson, W. S., Rosenberg, W., & Haynes, R. B. 2000. *Evidence-based medicine: How to practice and teach EBM.* New York: Churchill Livingstone.

Schank, R. C. 2003. *Every curriculum tells a story.* Unpublished manuscript, Carnegie Mellon University, Pittsburgh.

Schön, D. 1983. *The reflective practitioner: How professionals think in action.* London: Temple Smith.

Sherman, L. W. 2002. Evidence-based policing: Social organization of information for social control. In E. Waring & D. Weisburd (Eds.), *Crime and social organization:* 217–248. New Brunswick, NJ: Transaction.

Staw, B., & Epstein, L. 2000. What bandwagons bring: Effects of popular management techniques on corporate performance, reputation, and CEO pay. *Administrative Science Quarterly,* 43: 523–556.

Thompson, L., Gentner, D., & Lowenstein, J. 2003. Avoiding missed opportunities in managerial life: Analogical training more powerful than individual case training. In L. L. Thompson (Ed.), *The social psychology of organizational life:* 163–173. New York: Psychology Press.

Trank, C. Q., & Rynes, S. L. 2003. Who moved our cheese? Reclaiming professionalism in business education. *Academy of Management Learning & Education,* 2: 189–205.

Tyler, T. 1990. *Why people obey the law.* New Haven, CT: Yale University Press.

Walshe, K., & Rundall, T. G. 2001. Evidence-based management: From theory to practice in health care. *Milbank Quarterly,* 79: 429–457.

Whyte, W. F. 1948. *Human relations in the restaurant industry.* New York: McGraw-Hill.

Index